Guide to
ACA-Accredited Camps

2003 Edition

Over 2,400 Day, Resident, Trip and Travel Camps

American Camping Association®

Camps in this edition of the *Guide to ACA-Accredited Camps* were accredited as of October 31, 2002, as verified by on-site accreditation visits to determine compliance with the ACA standards at the time of the visit. Descriptive information in this *Guide* has been provided by the camp. ACA is not in a position to independently verify the marketing descriptions provided to us. ACA is not in a position to choose a camp experience for you. It is the responsibility of the parent/guardian(s) to make their own independent inquiry and evaluation to determine if that camp is appropriate to meet parental expectations and the needs and desires of their camper(s).

Front cover photo credits: Cheley Colorado Camps, Colorado.

First published in 1957 as Directory of Camps
Previous titles include:
Guide to Accredited Camps – 1989
Parents Guide to Accredited Camps – 1977
National Directory of Accredited Camps – 1972
Directory of Accredited Camps – 1962

Printed in the United States of America

© 1957, American Camping Association, Inc. Revised 2002

American Camping Association, Inc.
5000 State Road 67 North
Martinsville, IN 46151-7902
765-342-8456 · fax 765-342-2065 · e-mail bookstore@ACAcamps.org

ISSN 1094-1681
ISBN 0-87603-179-3

**You can also search
ACA's Interactive Camp Database
on the Internet at
www.ACAcamps.org**

For more information on:

Retail and Wholesale Book Sales
Director of Bookstore and Distribution
800-428-CAMP (2267) · e-mail msnider@ACAcamps.org

Media Inquiries and General Questions
765-342-8456, ext. 339 · e-mail pr@ACAcamps.org

Advertising
765-342-8456, ext. 306 · e-mail sholloway@ACAcamps.org

Contents

Chesapeake
(MD, DC)
www.ACAcamps.org/ck
800-653-1409
acachesapeake@yahoo.com

Coronado
(E. NV, UT, AZ, NM)
www.ACAcamps.org/co
480-557-1142
ACACoronado@ACAcamps.org

Evergreen
(MT, N. ID, WA, AK)
www.ACAcamps.org/eg
877-888-2267
evergreen@ACAcamps.org

Great Rivers
(IA, NE, W. MO, KS)
www.ACAcamps.org/gr
888-RIVER83 (748-3783)
641-927-4429
ACAGreatRiversExec@ACAcamps.org

Heart of the South
(AL, AR, KY, LA, MS, TN)
www.ACAcamps.org/hs
888-829-2267
865-379-5187
ACAHeartoftheSouth@ACAcamps.org

Illinois
(N. IL)
www.ACAcamps.org/il
312-332-0833
acail@imaxx.net

Indiana
www.ACAcamps.org/in
888-620-2267
ACAIndiana@ACAcamps.org

Keystone Regional
(DE, PA)
www.ACAcamps.org/kr
888-917-CAMP (PA/DE only)
215-886-5385
acakeystone@i-bob.com

Michigan
www.aca-michigan.org
800-852-8368 (MI only)
734-944-2289
info@aca-michigan.org

New England
(CT, MA, ME, NH, RI, VT)
www.acane-camps.org
800-446-4494
508-647-CAMP(2267)
camp@acane-camps.org

New Jersey
www.ACAcampsnj.org
908-362-8333
ACANewJersey@ACAcamps.org

New York
(New York City and selected surrounding counties)
www.ACA-ny.org
800-777-CAMP(2267)
212-391-5208
camp@aca-ny.org

Northern California
(W. NV, N. CA)
www.ACAnorcal.org
800-362-2236
415-453-1832
aca@vkam.com

Northland
(MN, ND, SD)
www.ACAcamps.org/nl
800-842-0308
763-784-5400
acanorthland@qwest.net

Ohio
www.ACAohio.org
800-837-2269 (OH only)
330-468-1476
ACAOhio@ACAcamps.org

Oregon Trail
(OR, S. ID)
www.ACAcamps.org/ot
503-452-7416
genemhkc@hevanet.com

Rocky Mountain
(CO, WY)
www.ACAcamps.org/rm
888-926-CAMP(2267)
ACARockyMountain@ACAcamps.org

Southeastern
(FL, GA, NC, SC)
www.southeastcamps.org
828-263-0934
woodaca@bellsouth.net

Southern California
(HI, S. CA)
www.ACAcamps.org/sc
818-223-9232
ACASoCal@ACAcamps.org

St. Louis
(E. MO, S. IL)
www.ACAcamps.org/sl
618-695-2489
888-464-7553
Patxdir@midwest.net

Texoma
(TX, OK)
www.acatexoma.org
512-292-9240
888-559-2267 (TX/OK only)
danishaw@acatexoma.org

Upstate New York
(New York counties of: Albany, Allegany, Broome, Cattaraugus, Cayuga, Chautauqua, Chemung, Chenango, Clinton, Columbia, Cortland, Delaware, Erie, Essex, Franklin, Fulton, Genesee, Greene, Hamilton, Herkimer, Jefferson, Lewis, Livingston, Madison, Monroe, Montgomery, Niagara, Oneida, Onondaga, Ontario, Orleans, Oswego, Otsego, Rensselaer, Saratoga, Schenectady, Schoharie, Schuyler, Seneca, Steuben, St. Lawrence, Tioga, Tompkins, Warren, Washington, Wayne, Wyoming, Yates)
www.ACAcamps.org/un
315-675-9838
usnyaca@aol.com

Virginias
(VA, WV)
www.ACAvirginiascamps.org
800-347-7523 (VA,WV,NC,DC,MD)
919-603-0445
ACAVirginias@ACAcamps.org

Wisconsin
www.ACAwisconsin.org
608-663-0051
acawisconsin@charter.net

What Is the American Camping Association?

The American Camping Association (ACA) is a community of camp professionals and is dedicated to enriching the lives of children and adults through the camp experience. For more than 100 years, ACA members have joined together to share knowledge and experience and to ensure the quality of camp programs. As a leading authority in child development, ACA works to preserve, promote, and improve the camp experience. Our association is committed to helping our members and all camps provide:

- safe camp communities
- caring, competent adult role models
- healthy, developmentally-appropriate experiences
- service to the community and the natural world
- opportunities for leadership and personal growth
- discovery, experiential education, and learning opportunities
- excellence and continuous self-improvement

Through our association's efforts, the unique benefits of the camp experience are understood, enjoyed, and open to all.

Where to Find Local Information

ACA has satellite offices located across the country and many provide local directories, referral services and/or camp information fairs. If you desire more information about camps in specific sections of the country, please contact the appropriate office.

Find ACA-accredited camps on the Internet:

www.ACAcamps.org

Academics

Aerobics/Exercise

Aquatic Activities

Specialized Activities Index

ACCREDITED CAMP
American Camping Association

The following pages will help you find a camp that offers the activities that match your child's particular interests. Each ACA-accredited camp is given the opportunity to identify the three specialized activities for which it wants to be known. Therefore, a camp could be listed under three different activities.

To see a list of the top ten activities that each camp offers, go to its listing in the ACA-Accredited Camp Directory beginning on page 89.

Camp Lou Henry Hoover, Middleville, New Jersey

Summer Camp
An American Tradition

It didn't take long for early Americans to display their characteristic fascination with the outdoors. Clustered in cities along the Eastern seaboard, they longed for opportunity and the great open spaces that stretched beyond. In the mid-1800s, Americans began turning in great numbers to the outdoors for inspiration and recreation.

It was at this time that American education took a new turn. Headmaster Frederick W. Gunn of the Gunnery School, a private boarding school in Connecticut, conceived the idea of taking pupils on a summer outing. In 1861, Gunn and his wife Abigail led a two-week expedition, or "gypsy trip," as it was called, to the beach at Long Island Sound. Hiking, boating, sailing, and fishing were the order of the day.

The experience proved so effective that it was repeated in 1863 and 1865. A more permanent Gunnery camp was established on an inland lake where camp was conducted two weeks each August for 12 years.

The camp idea, begun by the Gunnery experience, inspired others to establish private camps and church camps, "fresh-air" camps sponsored by social service agencies, and camps supported by youth groups, including the Boy Scouts, the YMCA, the Girl Scouts, and Camp Fire. Harvard University president Charles W. Eliot said in 1922, "The organized summer camp is the most important step in education that America has given the world."

Today, more than 12,000 day and resident camps of varying types, lengths, and sponsorships flourish in all parts of the country. Whichever one you choose, there's a camp for you and your family.

Camp Young Judaea, Amherst, New Hampshire

Look for This Logo

ACCREDITED CAMP
American Camping Association

When camps display the ACA-accredited camp logo, they are showing that they have earned a true mark of distinction within the camp community. Each camp in the *Guide* has demonstrated compliance with nationally recognized health and safety standards while in operation. What's behind this hard-earned sign? Take a look at the following facts:

■ Accreditation is an educational process of voluntary self-examination and peer-review.

■ ACA's standards program is continuously evaluated and updated.

■ At least once every three years, teams of two or more trained camp professionals observe a camp's operation while in session and compare its practices with the standards of the industry.

■ Although many state and federal laws and regulations may address basic sanitation and food service concerns, ACA's standards go a step further in addressing the specific areas of programming, personnel, and management practices that relate specifically to summer camp. Separate standards are applied to activities such as aquatics, horseback riding, and travel and trip programs.

■ The ACA-accredited camp logo indicates that a camp is owned and operated by camp management committed to the highest standards for the camp industry. These camp owners/operators care enough to put themselves to the toughest tests in the camp profession.

Camp Young Judaea, Amherst, New Hampshire

Start with Your Child

When beginning the camp selection process, consider your child's interests. It's important to know a child's personality and identify what camp programs will benefit him or her most. With a variety of programs and activities, summer camp offers fun and meaningful adventures to match a child's interests and maturity level.

Also, include your child in the decision-making process. Together with your child, explore the array of camp options offered in this guide and then visit the Web sites of camps that interest your child or request more information. Many camps have Web sites that include photos, maps or virtual tours of the camp facility, sample daily schedules and menus, and information about the directors and key staff, all designed to help families become more familiar with the camp. As children become better acquainted with the camp experience and more involved in the decision-making process, they will have less anxiety about going away to camp.

Canoeing

Caving

Ceramics/Pottery

Challenge/Rope Courses

American Camping Association file photo

Life Away From Home
How to Best Adjust

"Summer camp is more than a vacation for children," says Bruce Muchnick, Ed.D., a licensed psychologist who works extensively with day and resident camps. "As a parent, there are a few things to consider to increase the opportunity for a rewarding camp experience for your child." Some helpful suggestions provided by Dr. Muchnick and the American Camping Association include:

■ **Consider camp as a learning experience.**
This is an opportunity for your child to explore a world bigger than his/her neighborhood and a chance for you and your child to practice "letting go." Letting go allows children to develop autonomy and a stronger sense of self, make new friends, develop new social skills, learn about teamwork, be creative, and more. This time also allows parents an opportunity to take care of themselves so that they will feel refreshed when their child returns home.

■ **Prepare for camp together.**
Decisions about camp – like where to go and what to pack – should be a joint venture, keeping in mind your child's maturity. If your child feels a part of the decision-making process, his/her chances of having a positive experience will improve.

■ **Talk about concerns.**
As the first day of camp nears, some children experience uneasiness about going away. Encourage your child to talk about these feelings rather than acting on what you think his/her feelings may be. Communicate confidence in your child's ability to handle being away from home.

■ **Have realistic expectations.**
Camp, like the rest of life, has high and low points. Not every moment will be filled with wonder and excitement. Encourage your child to have a reasonable and realistic view of camp. Discuss both the ups and downs your child may experience. Your child should not feel pressured to succeed at camp, either. The main purposes of camp are to relax and have fun.

Cheley Colorado Camps, Estes Park, Colorado

Climbing/Rappelling

Cure for Homesickness Begins at Home

Parents don't have to wait until a child at camp suffers homesickness – prevention begins at home. As millions of parents prepare to send their children to summer camp, the American Camping Association and clinical child psychologist Christopher Thurber offer suggestions to help reduce – if not eliminate – homesickness among kids.

Among Dr. Thurber's tips for reducing homesickness:

Five questions all parents should ask their child's camp director:
- What is the camp's crisis response plan?
- What is done at camp to keep children safe?
- What contact am I allowed with my son or daughter?
- How will I know my child is having a good time at camp?
- How is your staff trained to meet children's emotional needs?

Ways parents can help prevent intense homesickness:
- Don't make "pick-up deals," such as, "If you feel homesick or don't like camp, I'll come pick you up."
- Avoid ambivalent messages, such as, "Have a great time at camp, I hope I survive without you."
- Arrange practice time away from home, such as an overnight at a friend's or a weekend at grandparents'.
- Review how you will keep in touch, whether through letter writing and postcards, "shared prayer," one-way e-mails, etc.

"Homesickness is a normal, developmental phenomenon," says Thurber. "Those cell phones aren't necessary. The goal should not be to make homesickness feelings go away, but to minimize them so they don't interfere with a child's enjoyment of camp."

Girl Scouts of Limberlost Council/CJ Solis ©2000

Keeping in Touch

Many directors encourage their campers to write home regularly to their parents, brothers, and sisters.

Do's

Give your child pre-addressed, stamped envelopes or postcards so that they can keep you informed of camp activities.

Ask the camp director if electronic communications are available for campers' use. If so, remind your child that you can stay connected with him or her through home e-mail, fax, or the camp's Web site.

Send a note or postcard in advance to the camp so there will be a personalized touch of home when your child arrives. This lets young campers know that the family has not forgotten them. In your correspondence, assure the camper that you know he or she is having a good time and express enthusiasm for the camp's activities.

Don'ts

Although there are benefits in parents keeping their children informed of what's going on, don't go into great detail since the young adventurers might feel they're missing something back home. Directors advise parents not to mention how much they miss their children or "that the dog and cat miss them."

Don't worry. Your natural reaction is to call on the first day just about bedtime to see how your camper is doing. Remember, counselors are trained to recognize and deal with symptoms of homesickness.

As one experienced camp director noted, "We have few homesick children, but we have homesick parents by the dozens."

Nicolet for Girls, Eagle River, Wisconsin

Tips for Parents

Coping with First-time Camp Experiences

The following are helpful tips to consider as you ask yourself, "Who's going through separation anxiety, me or my child?"

- Find opportunities to give your child independence in safe, structured surroundings with caring adults such as the camp environment.

- Understand that separation is natural and necessary; remember your baby's first crawl, the first time your child stepped onto a school bus, and the first overnight at a friend's or relative's — these memories are all important developmental phases you and your child successfully encountered. Each successful separation gives your child confidence for the next challenge.

- Ask the right questions about the camp you are choosing for your child and be sure to match your child's interests and age to the appropriate camp atmosphere. Gathering information about the camp will make you feel better about your decisions.

- Recognize that separating from your child may be just as difficult for you as for your child, maybe even more so.

Books for Parents

For more information about choosing the right camp/preparing your child for the camp experience, visit www.ACAcamps.org/bookstore. Choose "Participant Development and Behavior" and "Working with Parents."

Horseback — Western

International Culture

Kayaking

Language Studies

Leadership Development

CYO Camp Rancho Framasa, Nashville, IN

Top Packing Tips for Resident Camps

Bedding

Sleeping bag, sheets, blanket, and pillow

Towels and Toiletries

Towels should not be the family's best, since they'll be used for swimming and other waterfront activities as well as for showers.

A small duffel bag will help campers carry and keep track of essentials such as soap, shampoo, toothpaste, deodorant, comb, and brush. At some camps, campers walk to separate facilities to shower.

Clothes and Laundry

- If and when clothes are laundered at camp affects how much clothing to pack. Generally, sessions under two weeks in length do not include laundry services.
- Always send along an extra pillowcase or laundry bag for dirty clothing.
- Most camps supply lists of recommended wear and some furnish required uniforms.
- Shorts, T-shirts, and jeans are staples of a camper's wardrobe.
- Long pants for leg protection on hikes and horseback rides are necessary.
- Comfortable, durable shoes — break in new shoes.
- A hat serves as a tick repellent and as sun screen.
- A raincoat or rain poncho is a must.
- Check with camp staff for advice on changing weather and pack accordingly.
- Use a permanent marker to write your camper's name on every item.

Equipment

- Flashlight with extra batteries
- Camera and film
- Canteen or water bottle
- Insect repellent, sunscreen, and lip balm
- Pre-addressed, pre-stamped postcards or envelopes (make sure to put them into a zip-top plastic bag)

Medication

Send medication in original bottles, along with dosage instructions, to the camp nurse or health care facility. Your medical release form should list all medications.

Don't Pack

- Radios, CD players, stereos
- Televisions or portable video games
- Cellular phones or pagers
- Food
- Hunting knives
- Fireworks of any kind
- Expensive clothing or jewelry

Use common sense and think about the activities that will take place. Check with your local airport to ensure you are complying with security regulations regarding what to pack for air travel. And, don't hesitate to call the camp.

Martial Arts

Model Rocketry

Music

Nature/Environment Studies

CCUSA, New York Orientation, Columbia University, New York, New York

What About . . .

Camps usually provide items such as paddles, life jackets, and arts and crafts materials. Check with the camp to see what is supplied and what your camper needs to bring.

Insurance

Camper health and accident insurance may be provided by the camp. Sometimes parents are asked to provide information on family health and accident coverage. It's always a good idea to ask if there are additional charges for insurance.

Spending Money

Many camps have a canteen service and may recommend your child have a certain amount of spending money for these popular items. Because children might lose track of the money, camps sometimes collect it from each child at the beginning of camp and put it in an account. As items are purchased, the costs are deducted from the account. At the end of the session, money remaining in the account is returned to the camper.

Additional Costs

Camp T-shirts, group photos, or special outings may be available. The camp will advise you about any extra money your camper should bring to pay for these items.

Transportation

Bus transportation — especially at day camps — may be included in fees. At some camps, it is an added expense. Some resident camps may offer bus service from centralized locations or provide pick-up service at airports or train stations.

Physical Examinations

All ACA-accredited camps require either a health history or physical examination of campers prior to camp. It's helpful to know this in advance so the exam might be scheduled at the time of another doctor's appointment.

Camp Wekeela for Boys and Girls, Canton, Maine

Head 'em up!
Move 'em out!

Many camps offer trip and travel programs. Trip camps transport themselves to sites by hiking, riding, canoeing, or other means. They usually stay in group campsites in state or national parks, carrying tents and sleeping bags with them on their excursions.

At travel camps, groups are transported by car, van, or bus to places of interest.

Often these two types of camps blend together. For example, a group of travel campers may take a bus from New York to the Rocky Mountains, spending evenings in national parks along the way. When they reach their destination, they may set out for a five-day hiking and camping trip through the back-country into a primitive-type environment.

Swimming — Instructional

American Camping Association file photo

Check These Resources for More Information

Most parents find the *Guide* to be their best resource for selecting a camp. Below are some suggestions for finding additional information about camps in your community.

Camp Fairs

■ During camp fairs, campers and their parents can speak with representatives from different camps.

■ Camp fairs are typically held in gymnasiums, hotels, or malls.

■ These single-day events are open to the public and are scheduled on weekends from January through March.

■ Camp representatives provide promotional materials explaining the camp's activities and philosophies.

To find out about camp fairs in your area, contact your nearest American Camping Association office (see page 4).

Talk with Your Friends

Friends and family may have previous experience in choosing a camp. Many times children want to go to a camp that their friends are attending. Several families may want to review this book together to select the right camp.

Referral Services

Some regional offices of the American Camping Association provide free referral services for parents. Experienced staff take basic information from each caller and then match the person with camps offering those programs.

In some parts of the country, there are also private referral agencies. Most referral firms charge the camp a percentage based on the tuition fee for campers that are actually placed. Other companies charge a flat fee. It is very important to understand the financial arrangement in advance.

Some questions to ask a private referral agency:

■ Are the camps referred by the agency accredited by ACA?

■ How many camps do they represent? Why did they affiliate with these particular camps?

■ Has someone from the agency visited each of the camps and observed the programs in progress?

■ Are references available from campers and their families?

■ Can the agency describe the camp's programs and goals?

Swimming — Recreational

Team Building

Camps for Children and Adults with

Physical and Mental Challenges Index

ACCREDITED CAMP

RCA ®

American Camping Association

All camps on the following pages specialize in the group identified. For example, a camp may offer a three-week resident camp where campers of all sorts are mainstreamed and a one-week session specifically for children with asthma. This camp would be listed here under "Asthma/Respiratory Ailments."

Camp Easter Seal — East, Milford, Virginia

Deaf (See Hearing Impairments)

Diabetes

Down's Syndrome

Drug Abuse (See Substance Abuse)

Epilepsy

HIV (See Human Immunodeficiency Virus)

Hearing Impairment

Heart Defect

Hemophilia (See Blood Disorders)

Human Immunodeficiency Virus

Mental Retardation

Camp Easter Seal — East, Milford, Virginia

The Good Camps Do

- Many ACA-accredited camps offer campers financial assistance, amounts range from small contributions to $1,000,000.

- ACA-accredited camps often incorporate community-service or good deed programs into their camp programming.

- Research on the impact of camp on children with disabilities reported that campers made positive gains during camp in self-reliance, independence, communication, and self-esteem.

- Accredited camps participating in ACA's Camper Scholarship Program, each year give scholarships to campers who are unable to afford the entire camp fee and whose presence at camp will broaden the composition of the camp experience.

Behavioral Problems

Campers from outside the US

Camps for

Special Groups Index

ACCREDITED CAMP

American Camping Association

The camps listed in this index work exclusively with the special group mentioned or offer a special program for them. This index will help in your search for a special camp experience.

Camp Tall Turf, Walkerville, Michigan

Camp Isn't Just a Summer Experience

The nation's largest school district has been putting year-round learning to the test. In July 1998, the New York City Board of Education inaugurated "Break-Aways: Partnership for Year-Round Learning." This unprecedented public school system reform adds up to twenty-eight extra days of nontraditional programming to the regular school year by working with organized camps to implement and expand learning. Children move from school into camp with teachers and counselors who work and learn together.

Camp can complement a child's formal education by providing experiential learning opportunities that in total result in a holistic, developmental learning calendar. Parents are acknowledging the benefits of camp for their children. In a national survey of ACA-accredited camps, camp directors reported that parents rate the most important benefits of camp to be:

- increasing self-confidence and self-esteem
- providing a safe place
- making new friends
- offering fun activities

Camp is a vital element in a child's total development, and it complements the academic skills that are learned in school with experiential based life skills.

Gifted and Talented

Mystic Lake YMCA Camp, Lake, Michigan

What Is ACA Accreditation?

ACA accreditation is the best evidence parents have of a camp's commitment to a safe and nurturing environment for children. Accreditation assures parents that camp practices have been measured against up to 300 national standards and go a step beyond a state's basic licensing requirements. These standards establish criteria for living areas, food service, emergency preparedness, program practices, health care, personnel, transportation, and administrative procedures.

Because accreditation is voluntary, parents know the camp is committed to best practices. Currently, only 25 to 30 percent of the more than 12,000 day and resident camps seek ACA accreditation. Accreditation is an educational process — providing training, guidelines, programs, and publications for camp directors and staff.

No environment is risk free. However, ACA-accredited camps voluntarily go through a rigorous risk-management process to prevent illness or injury to campers — and to have solid crisis management plans in place if an emergency does occur. These steps help camps provide a supervised, positive environment with controlled boundaries where children can grow.

Grief/Bereavement Camps

Inclusion/Main Streaming

Seniors

Weight Loss Camps

Youth-at-Risk

African-American Culture

Christianity

Camps with
Specific Philosophies Index

ACCREDITED CAMP

American Camping Association

The camps listed in this index have identified an underlying philosophy that shapes their camp programs. The following pages will help you locate camps offering these special programs.

B'nai B'rith Camp, Otis, Oregon

Points to Consider

How much does camp cost?
Camp fees vary but generally range from $75 to $350 per week which covers expenses such as professional staffing, accommodations, food, supplies, and insurance. Many camps — nonprofit and profit — offer scholarships and financial assistance. Look for the ♣ icon in the main camp index.

What is the camp's philosophy?
Does it complement your own parenting philosophy? Is it competitive or cooperative? Knowing your child's personality and style of learning is valuable in selecting the right camp.

What is the background of the camp director?
The camp director should possess at least a bachelor's degree and have camp administration experience.

What is the ratio of counselors to campers?
ACA standards require different ratios for varying ages. Depending on the age and ability of the campers, the medium range is one staff member for every seven to eight campers.

What are the ages of counselors?
ACA standards recommend that 80 percent or more of the counseling/program staff be at least eighteen years old. In addition, at least 20 percent of the program/administrative staff must have a bachelor's degree.

How are the camp's staff screened and trained to be sure they are suited to work with children?
Staff screening steps should include defined application process, background checks, references, work-history checks, and personal interviews. All staff must receive training in appropriate methods for relating to campers.

What percentage of the counselors returned from last year?
Most camps have from 40 to 60 percent returning staff. If the rate is lower, find out why.

How does the camp handle special needs?
If your child has special requirements, ask the camp director about needed provisions and facilities. Is there a nurse? Is there a designated place to store insulin or allergy medication? Are special foods available for restricted diets?

How are behavioral and disciplinary problems handled?
Positive reinforcement, assertive role-modeling, and a sense of fair play are generally regarded as key components of camp counseling and leadership.

Other considerations:
■ What about references?
■ How does the camp handle camper homesickness and other adjustment issues?
■ Ask if you can visit the camp before enrolling your child.

Native American Culture

What happens at camp . . .

Brush Ranch Camps for Girls and Boys, Santa Fe, N.M.

they'll hike a trail . . . climb a mountain . . . pitch a tent . . . cook a meal . . . solve problems . . . learn to swim . . . learn to windsurf . . . learn to row . . . learn to sail . . . master a craft . . . resolve a conflict . . . build a fire . . . build a rocket . . . build a log cabin . . . paddle across a lake . . . swing a racquet . . . swing a baseball bat . . . fly to the moon . . . plant a tree . . . save a tree . . . make new friends . . . help others . . . discover buried treasure . . . gain independence . . . gain self-confidence . . . overcome homesickness . . . respect their country . . . respect all walks of life . . . appreciate the earth . . . belong to a community . . . write a story . . . tell a story . . . set goals

Camp Easter Seal – East, Milford, Va.

. . . kick, catch, and throw a ball . . . be a leader . . . be creative . . . be healthy . . . shoot an arrow . . . shoot a camera . . . surf the 'net . . . learn to fly . . . play games . . . play guitar . . . sing songs . . . perform skits . . . perform plays . . . renew spirit . . . ride a horse . . . trust others . . . meet positive role models . . . learn responsibility . . . discover they are a treasure . . . learn about the little things . . . encounter fire flies, frogs, fish . . . navigate by sunlight, moonlight, flashlight . . . create models, key chains, clay pots . . . survive without CDs,

Cheley Colorado Camps, Estes Park, Colo.

TVs, and Sega . . . have the time of their lives!

Day Camps Index

The following pages will help you find day camps accredited by the American Camping Association. At day camps, campers are usually transported to camp in the morning by bus or van or dropped off by parents and then return home each afternoon. The number of day camps in the United States continues to grow as parents recognize the valuable growth and experience opportunities of camp, not available in many other daily care options. Day camps offer an active, community-based program with trained, caring counselors helping each camper develop self-esteem and confidence in a cooperative, child-centered environment.

Look for the ☀ icon in the main camp index for day camps.

Camps are organized by county within the state listing. Camps that do not identify their county are placed at the beginning of the state listing.

American Camping Association file photo

Specific Considerations for Day Camps

Day camps offer experiences that are unique from resident camps. Because of this, there are specific points to consider when choosing a day camp.

■ What training does the staff receive on safety, supervision, counseling, problem solving, and other issues unique to working with young children?

■ Is the price all-inclusive or are there extra charges for:

transportation	overnights
swimming lessons	food service
horseback riding	group pictures
before and after	T-shirts
camp extended care	field trips

■ If transportation is offered, where is the closest pick-up spot?

■ Do they have an "express bus" before or after camp?

■ If before- and after-camp extended care is offered, who is with the children and what activities take place?

■ Is lunch served or do campers bring their own sack lunch? Are snacks and drinks provided?

■ If the camp offers swimming, are there swimming lessons or is it simply recreational swimming?

■ Are campers in a group with a counselor all day? Or, are campers free to go from one activity to another with appropriate supervision? In this case, who would you talk to if you had a question or concern about your child?

■ Is an open house offered before camp starts where you can meet your child's counselor and van/bus driver?

■ Are parents allowed to drop by for visits?

American Camping Association file photo

Partnership of Caring

More than one in ten teens aged twelve to seventeen were users of illicit drugs in 1999, according to the U.S. Department of Justice. Many youth experiment with and use alcohol. Gun violence has jumped in our schools. Newspapers highlight allegations of sexual abuse or experimentation. This alarming news leaves parents wondering where their children will be safe.

No institution of society — churches, schools, youth programs, camps, families — has an impenetrable safety net from the ills of society. However, there are steps parents can take to assure themselves that all reasonable precautions have been taken to provide an environment that make safety for children the top priority.

Parents and camps can form a Partnership of Caring that will help camps stay vigilant and will help parents feel comfortable that their children are participating in programs whose sponsors keep child protection at the forefront.

Here are key questions the American Camping Association urges every parent to ask of the day or resident camp directors to whom they entrust their children:

- How do you screen staff?
- What type of training does your staff receive in the prevention of child abuse?
- How are staff supervised?
- What methods do you use to make your staff sensitive to the needs and concerns of children?
- What experience and background do the staff have who supervise children?
- What are your policies on parent-camper communication while in camp?
- Do you have a reference list of camper parents that I could call?

Parents should not assume that just because a camp is sponsored by an organization with which you are familiar or just because your child's friend went to this camp and had fun that everything will be fine. Ask these questions of the director and choose a director and camp whose answers make sense to you . . . a director and camp who convince you that they are partnering with you for the positive development of your child!

Camp experiences have been magical, productive, positive, and growing experiences for millions of children. We want that to be true for your child, too! For more information, visit ACA's Web site, www.ACAcamps.org.

Rental Facilities Index

Camps who rent their facilities to others

In addition to their traditional summer camp program (day or resident), many camps often rent or lease their facilities to groups for programs year-round. These camps have demonstrated compliance with standards specific to the administration and facilities of the camp and to the services, such as food service and specialized program leadership, provided by the site owner/operator. Groups using camp in this way typically retain primary responsibility for their group members.

Facilities are available for:

- seminars
- conferences
- business meetings
- planning retreats
- religious retreats
- outdoor training courses
- school programs
- environmental education
- company picnics
- family reunions
- special camp sessions

The symbol 🏠 clearly identifies all such rental facilities within the ACA-Accredited Camp Directory.

Rental facilities are organized by county within the state listing. Camps that do not identify their county are placed at the beginning of the state listing.

Cheley Colorado Camps, Estes Park, Colorado

What Is an ACA-Accredited Camp?

The 2,400+ camps accredited by the American Camping Association have met or exceeded the highest nationally recognized standards for health, safety, staff training, and program quality in camps. You can be assured that up to 300 questions have already been asked and appropriately answered. ACA demonstrates a commitment to excellence that makes your job of choosing the right camp much easier.

In addition to their traditional summer camp program (day or resident), camps often rent or lease their facilities to groups for summer or "off-season" programs. These camps have demonstrated compliance with standards specific to the administration and facilities of the camp and to the limited services, such as food service and maintenance, provided by the site owner/operator. Groups using camp facilities in this way typically retain primary responsibility and control of their program and staffing. The symbol 🏠 clearly identifies all such rental facilities within the ACA-Accredited Camp Directory.

Camp Ondessonk, Ozark, Illinois

Camp's Growing Influence

- More than 10 million children and adults annually benefit from summer camp.

- In the past 10 years, the number of ACA-accredited camps reporting family camp programs has increased 154 percent.

- The number of camp personnel in the U.S. camp industry is estimated at over 1,200,000.

- Since 1992, summer camp enrollment continues to rise 8 percent to 10 percent every year.

Wyoming

Alabama 4H Center (est 1980) ⚊

Columbiana, AL (Shelby Co.); (205) 669-4241
Sandra Spencer, Director

Camp comments: Beautiful modern facility, specializes in environmental & summer camp programs, outstanding, knowledgeable staff.
Activities: Archery, Arts/Crafts, Canoeing, Challenge/Rope Courses, Computer, Hiking, Leadership Development, Nature/Environment Studies, Riflery, Swimming — Recreational
Session lengths & capacity: 1/2 & 1 week sessions; 180 campers
Clientele & fees: boys 9-19; girls 9-19; coed 9-19; Fees: B ⚊ 🐷
Contact: Sandra Spencer, 4-H Center Manager at (205) 669-4241; fax: (205) 669-1364
Web site: www.alabama4hcenter.com
Operated by: Alabama 4H Center, 892 4H Rd, Columbiana, AL 35051 at (205) 669-4241 (#6207)

Alpine Camp For Boys

(est 1959) ⚊ 🏠

Mentone, AL (DeKalb Co.); (256) 634-4404
Dick O'Ferrall, Director

Camp comments: Beautiful Lookout Mtn. Traditional private camp. Christian influence. Outstanding staff. Fun summer in a boy's world.
Activities: Aquatic Activities, Archery, Arts/Crafts, Basketball, Canoeing, Challenge/Rope Courses, Climbing/Rappelling, Horseback — Western, Riflery, Tennis
Session lengths & capacity: 2 & 4 week sessions; 240 campers
Clientele & fees: boys 7-15; Fees: E ⚊
Contact: Dick O'Ferrall, Director at (256) 634-4404; fax: (256) 634-4405
e-mail: summer@alpinecamp.com
Web site: www.alpinecamp.com
Operated by: Alpine Camp for Boys, PO Box 297, Mentone, AL 35984 at (256) 634-4404
Group Rental Information

Seasons & Capacity: Spring 50, Summer 325, Fall 50, Winter 50
Facilities: Cabins, Food Service, Hiking Trails, Playing Fields, River
Programs: Boating, Challenge/Ropes Course, Swimming (#863)

ICON LEGEND

☀ Day Camp

⚊ Resident Camp

🏠 Facilities Available To Rent

🚐 Transportation Available

🐷 Financial Aid Available

FEE RANGES PER WEEK

A $0-75

B $75-200

C $201-350

D $351-500

E $501-650

F over $650

ACA-Accredited Camp Directory

ACCREDITED CAMP

® American Camping Association

This section lists all ACA-accredited camps as of October 31, 2002. For the most current listings of ACA-accredited camps, check out ACA's Web site at **www.ACAcamps.org**.

Camps including those with facilities available to rent are listed together alphabetically by state. Icons are used within the listings to identify specific information about each camp. An icon and fee range legend appears on each page spread.

ASCCA (est 1976)

Jacksons Gap, AL (Tallapoosa Co.); (256) 825-9226
Jerry Bynum, Director

Camp comments: World's largest camp for the disabled. Campers experience confidence building skills in fun & accessible environment.
Activities: Aquatic Activities, Arts/Crafts, Canoeing, Challenge/Rope Courses, Fishing, Horseback — Western, Nature/Environment Studies, Riflery, Swimming — Recreational
Session lengths & capacity: June-August; 1 week sessions; 100 campers
Clientele & fees: coed 6-99; Fees: D ▲ 🐷
Contact: Jerry Bynum, Administrator at (256) 825-9226; fax: (256) 825-8332
e-mail: ascca@webshoppe.net
Operated by: Camp Seale Harris, PO Box 1179, Killen, AL 35645 at (256) 765-2431

Group Rental Information
Seasons & Capacity: Spring 286, Fall 286, Winter 286
Facilities: A/V Equipment, Cabins, Dorm-Style, Double Occupancy, Food Service, Hiking Trails, Kitchen Facilities, Lake, Linens, Lodges, Meeting Rooms, Playing Fields, Pool
Programs: Boating, Challenge/Ropes Course, Environmental Education, Swimming (#3204)

Camp Alamisco (est 1966)

Dadeville, AL (Talapoosa Co.); (256) 825-9482
Ken Micheff, Director

Camp comments: Beautiful Lake Martin is open to all denominations. Summer camp available & open to church & youth group retreats.
Activities: Aquatic Activities, Arts/Crafts, Bicycling/Biking, Canoeing, Challenge/Rope Courses, Climbing/Rappelling, Horseback — Western, Sailing, Swimming — Instructional, Waterskiing
Session lengths & capacity: June-July; 8 week sessions; 120 campers
Clientele & fees: coed 6-17; families; seniors; single adults; Fees: **B, C** ▲
Contact: Ken Micheff or Eric Bray, Director or Ranger at (334) 272-7493; fax: (337) 272-7987
e-mail: kmicheff@earthlink.net
Operated by: Gulf States Conf Seventh Day, 6450 Atlanta Highway, Montgomery, AL 36124-0249 at (334) 272-7493

Group Rental Information
Seasons & Capacity: Spring 200, Fall 200, Winter 200
Facilities: Cabins, Dorm-Style, Food Service, Kitchen Facilities, Lake, Lodges, Meeting Rooms
Programs: Boating, Challenge/Ropes Course, Environmental Education, Horseback Riding, Swimming (#11805)

Camp Coleman (est 1925)

Trussville, AL (Jefferson Co.); (205) 655-3782
Laura Elliott, Director

Camp comments: Adventure-based, noncompetitive program instills a sense of accomplishment through progressively challenging activities
Activities: Aquatic Activities, Archery, Challenge/Rope Courses, Climbing/Rappelling, Horseback — English, Horseback — Western, Leadership Development, Riflery, Team Building, Travel/Tour
Session lengths & capacity: June-August; 1/2, 1 & 2 week sessions; 120 campers
Clientele & fees: girls 6-17; families; Fees: **B** ▲ 🐷
Contact: Laura Elliott, Director of Outdoor Program at (205) 980-4750 ext. 117; fax: (205) 980-4753
e-mail: lelliott@cahabagirlscoutcouncil.org
Web site: www.cahabagirlscoutcouncil.org
Operated by: Cahaba GSC, 105 Heatherbrooke Park Dr, Birmingham, AL 35242 at (205) 655-3782

Group Rental Information
Facilities: A/V Equipment, Cabins, Food Service, Hiking Trails, Lodges, Meeting Rooms, Pool
Programs: Boating, Challenge/Ropes Course, Environmental Education, Horseback Riding, Swimming (#846)

Camp Cosby YMCA (est 1922)

Alpine, AL (Talladega Co.); (205) 268-2007
Wheaton Griffin, Director

Camp comments: Large variety of programs on beautiful lakeside setting. Top quality staff focused on YMCA core values. Air conditioned cabins. Life-long friends, skills, fun.
Activities: Backpacking, Bicycling/Biking, Challenge/Rope Courses, Climbing/Rappelling, Counselor Training (CIT), Horseback — Western, Leadership Development, Sailing, Travel/Tour, Waterskiing
Session lengths & capacity: June-August; 1/2, 1 & 2 week sessions; 265 campers
Clientele & fees: coed 6-17; Fees: **C, D** ▲
Contact: Wheaton Crissin, Executive Director at (800) 852-6729; fax: (256) 268-2003
e-mail: campcosby@ymcabham.org
Web site: www.ymcabham.org
Operated by: Birmingham YMCA, 2290 Paul Bear Bryant Rd, Alpine, AL 35014 at (205) 801-9622

Group Rental Information
Site comments: 2 hrs west of Atlanta, central air and heat. Family style meals, recreation, Alpine Towers.
Seasons & Capacity: Spring 250, Summer 250, Fall 250, Winter 250
Facilities: A/V Equipment, Cabins, Dorm-Style, Double Occupancy, Food Service, Hiking Trails, Kitchen Facilities, Lake, Meeting Rooms, Playing Fields, Pool, River
Programs: Boating, Challenge/Ropes Course, Environmental Education, Horseback Riding, Swimming, Winter Sports (#7225)

Camp DeSoto (est 1916)

Mentone, AL (Dekalb Co.); (256) 634-4394
Phil Hurt, Director

Camp comments: A month of growth for girls with a Christian staff and traditional camp program that is peaceful and tons of fun.
Activities: Archery, Arts/Crafts, Backpacking, Bicycling/Biking, Canoeing, Challenge/Rope Courses, Climbing/Rappelling, Horseback — English, Swimming — Recreational, Tennis
Session lengths & capacity: June-August; 4 week sessions; 220 campers
Clientele & fees: girls 8-16; Fees: **E** ▲
Contact: Phil Hurt, Director at (256) 634-4394; fax: (256) 634-4059
e-mail: cdesoto@tds.net
Web site: www.campdesoto.com
Operated by: Camp DeSoto, 264 Hwy Above the Clouds Bx432, Mentone, AL 35984 at (256) 634-4394 (#1322)

Camp Fire Camp Fletcher
(est 1926)

Bessemer, AL; (205) 428-1059

Camp comments: Progressive encounters based on age, interest & skill levels. Campers hike woods & trails. Learn about nature. Make arts.
Activities: Archery, Arts/Crafts, Camping Skills/Outdoor Living, Canoeing, Challenge/Rope Courses, Hiking, Horseback — Western, Nature/Environment Studies, Swimming — Recreational
Session lengths & capacity: June-August; 1/2, 6 & 7 week sessions; 70 campers
Clientele & fees: coed 6-15; Fees: **B** ▲
Contact: Mrs Cledith Fisher, Camp Administrator at (205) 324-2434; fax: (205) 322-7988
Web site: www.campfire-al.org

Operated by: Central Alabama Cncl Camp Fire, 3600 8th Avenue S Suite 502, Birmingham, AL 35222 at (205) 324-2434

Group Rental Information
Facilities: Cabins, Dorm-Style, Food Service, Hiking Trails, Pool, Tents
Programs: Challenge/Ropes Course, Environmental Education, Swimming (#3781)

Camp Lee (est 1965)

Anniston, AL (Calhoun Co.); (256) 238-8941
Contact: Kevin Mc Dade, Director at (256) 238-8941; fax: (256) 238-1711
e-mail: camplee@nti.net
Session lengths: January-December
Operated by: Camp Lee, 70 Camp Lee Main Rd, Anniston, AL 36207 at (256) 238-8941

Group Rental Information
Site comments: Christian emphasis in rustic, mountain setting.
Seasons & Capacity: Spring 250, Winter 250
Facilities: Cabins, Dorm-Style, Double Occupancy, Food Service, Hiking Trails, Kitchen Facilities, Lake, Lodges, Meeting Rooms, Pool
Programs: Boating, Challenge/Ropes Course, Swimming (#13820)

Camp Rap-A-Hope (est 1986)

Citronelle, AL; (334) 866-7946
Judy Park, Director

Camp comments: Specialty camp for children with cancer. Outstanding staff, beautiful setting and medical support. No charge to campers.
Activities: Aquatic Activities, Arts/Crafts, Canoeing, Challenge/Rope Courses, Horseback — Western, Music, Swimming — Recreational
Session lengths & capacity: 1 week sessions; 50 campers
Clientele & fees: coed 7-17
Contact: Sheree LaCoste, Exec Dir Medical Soc Mobile Co at (334) 343-3000; fax: (334) 343-3004
e-mail: msmc@ddyne.com
Operated by: Camp Rap-A-Hope, PO Box 161413, Mobile, AL 36616-1413 at (251) 343-3042 (#2525)

Camp Seale Harris (est 1947)

Jackson Gap, AL; (256) 825-9226
Terry Ackley, Director

Camp comments: A wide variety of recreational activities offered during weekly sessions. Diabetes education / car provided by a comprehensive medical staff.
Activities: Aquatic Activities, Boating, Camping Skills/Outdoor Living, Climbing/Rappelling, Horseback — Western, Leadership Development, Swimming — Recreational
Session lengths & capacity: 1 week sessions; 144 campers
Clientele & fees: boys 1-17; girls 1-17; coed 1-17; Fees: **A, B, C, D** ▲
Contact: Terry Ackley, Executive Director at (256) 765-2431; fax: (256) 765-2432
e-mail: campsealeharris@aol.com
Operated by: Camp Seale Harris, PO Box 1179, Killen, AL 35645 at (256) 765-2431 (#9085)

Camp Skyline Ranch
(est 1947)

Mentone, AL (DeKalb Co.); (800) 448-9279
Sally Cash Johnson, Director

Camp comments: On top of Lookout Mtn. on the banks of Little River. Find adventure, inspiration and fun with Christian emphasis.
Activities: Archery, Arts/Crafts, Canoeing, Challenge/Rope Courses, Gymnastics, Horseback — English, Horseback — Western, Riflery, Swimming — Recreational, Tennis
Session lengths & capacity: June-August; 1 & 2 week sessions; 300 campers

Clientele & fees: girls 6-16; Fees: **F ▲**
Contact: Office Staff at (256) 634-4001; fax: (256) 634-3018
e-mail: info@campskyline.com
Web site: www.campskyline.com
Operated by: Camp Skyline Ranch, PO Box 287, Mentone, AL 35984 at (256) 634-4001
Group Rental Information
Site comments: A camp setting on top of lookout mtn. on the banks of little river. The "Perfect Place" for corporate, business, church or school retreats
Seasons & Capacity: Spring 195, Winter 195
Facilities: Cabins, Food Service, Hiking Trails, Kitchen Facilities, Lodges, Meeting Rooms, Playing Fields, River
Programs: Challenge/Ropes Course, Horseback Riding (#10046)

Kamp Kiwanis (est 1959) ▲

Eclectic, AL (Elmore Co.); (334) 857-2404
Cathy M Whigham, Director

Camp comments: Beautiful Lake Martin Girl Scout Camp with emphasis on fun, swimming, canoeing, arts and crafts, nature discoveries in a caring environment. Summer fun for all.
Activities: Aquatic Activities, Archery, Arts/Crafts, Camping Skills/Outdoor Living, Canoeing, Counselor Training (CIT), Hiking, Nature/Environment Studies, Swimming — Instructional, Team Building
Session lengths & capacity: June-July; 1/2, 1 & 2 week sessions; 90 campers
Clientele & fees: girls 7-17; Fees: **B ▲**
Contact: Cathy M Whigham, Resident Camp Director at (334) 272-9164; fax: (334) 272-6574
e-mail: cwhigham@gssca.org
Operated by: Girl Scouts South Central AL, 145 Coliseum Blvd, Montgomery, AL 36109 at (334) 272-9164 (#855)

Laney For Boys (est 1959) ▲ ⌂

Mentone, AL (DeKalb Co.); (256) 634-4066
Rob Hammond, Director

Camp comments: Traditional boys camp on Lookout Mountain
Activities: Archery, Bicycling/Biking, Canoeing, Challenge/Rope Courses, Golf, Horseback — Western, Riflery, Sports — Field & Team, Swimming — Recreational, Tennis
Session lengths & capacity: June-August; 2 week sessions; 195 campers
Clientele & fees: boys 8-14; Fees: **E ▲**
Contact: Rob Hammond, Director at (256) 634-4066; fax: (256) 634-4098
e-mail: info@camplaney.com
Web site: www.camplaney.com

ICON LEGEND

☀ Day Camp
▲ Resident Camp
⌂ Facilities Available To Rent
🚐 Transportation Available
🐷 Financial Aid Available

FEE RANGES PER WEEK

A $0-75
B $75-200
C $201-350
D $351-500
E $501-650
F over $650

Operated by: Camp Laney for Boys, PO Box 289, Mentone, AL 35984 at (256) 634-4066 (#12497)

Lyman Ward Adventure Camp
(est 1984) ▲ 🚐

Camp Hill, AL (Tallapoosa Co.); (256) 896-4127

Camp comments: Structured, outdoor challenges developing self-discipline/teamwork/leadership/self-esteem.
Activities: Aquatic Activities, Archery, Backpacking, Camping Skills/Outdoor Living, Climbing/Rappelling, Hiking, Leadership Development, Riflery, Team Building, Wilderness Trips
Session lengths & capacity: June-August; 2 week sessions; 60 campers
Clientele & fees: boys 8-11; girls 12-15; Fees: **F ▲**
Contact: CSM Robert W Frayer, Camp Director at (256) 896-2901; fax: (256) 896-4661
e-mail: info@lwma.org
Operated by: Lyman Ward Military Academy, PO Box 550 Hwy 50, Camp Hill, AL 36850 at (256) 896-2901 (#6580)

Pine Hill Day Camp (est 1976) ☀ 🚐

Somerville, AL (Morgan Co.); (256) 778-8433
Carolyn Price, Director

Camp comments: Cooperative small groups. Horseback riding, Certified riding instructors. Challenging program for middle schoolers.
Activities: Aquatic Activities, Archery, Camping Skills/Outdoor Living, Canoeing, Caving, Horseback — English, Swimming — Instructional, Swimming — Recreational, Team Building, Windsurfing
Session lengths & capacity: June-August; 2, 4 & 8 week sessions; 250 campers
Clientele & fees: coed 4-15; Fees: **C ☀**
Contact: Caroyln P Price, Director at (256) 778-8433; fax: (256) 778-7082
e-mail: pinehill@pinehilldaycamp.com
Web site: www.pinehilldaycamp.com
Operated by: Pine Hill Adventures Inc, 113 Pine Hill Dr, Somerville, AL 35670 at (256) 778-8433 (#3637)

Riverview Camp for Girls
(est 1983) ▲ ⌂ 🚐

Mentone, AL (DeKalb Co.); (800) 882-0722
Susan Hooks, Director

Camp comments: Lookout Mtn. Traditional prog. Nondenominational Christian adventure, inspiration, character & confidence. 15+ choices.
Activities: Archery, Canoeing, Challenge/Rope Courses, Dance, Golf, Gymnastics, Horseback — English, Horseback — Western, Swimming — Instructional, Tennis
Session lengths & capacity: June-August; 1 & 2 week sessions; 205 campers
Clientele & fees: girls 6-16; Fees: **E, F ▲**
Contact: (800) 882-0722; fax: (205) 634-3601
Operated by: Riverview Camp for Girls, PO Box 299, Mentone, AL 35984 at (205) 634-4043
Group Rental Information
Facilities: Kitchen Facilities, Lodges, Meeting Rooms, Pool, River
Programs: Boating, Environmental Education (#11876)

Sumatanga (est 1950) ⌂

Gallant, AL (St Clair Co.); (256) 538-9860
Anne Horton, Director
Contact: Anne Horton, Interim Director at (256) 538-9860; fax: (256) 538-3714
e-mail: ahwildlife@cybrtyme.com
Web site: www.sumatanga.org
Operated by: United Methodist Church, 3616 Sumatanga Road, Gallant, AL 35972-3105 at (256) 538-9860

Group Rental Information
Site comments: 40 miles to Birmingham airport. 75 motel type rooms.
Seasons & Capacity: Spring 800, Summer 800, Fall 800, Winter 800
Facilities: A/V Equipment, Cabins, Dorm-Style, Double Occupancy, Food Service, Hiking Trails, Lake, Linens, Lodges, Meeting Rooms, Playing Fields, Pool
Programs: Boating, Challenge/Ropes Course, Environmental Education, Swimming (#3644)

The Childrens Fresh Air Farm
(est 1923) ▲

Birmingham, AL (Jefferson Co.); (205) 822-0150
Alicia Jo Yarboro, Director
Activities: Archery, Arts/Crafts, Basketball, Climbing/Rappelling, Music, Nature/Environment Studies, Sports — Field & Team, Swimming — Instructional, Swimming — Recreational
Session lengths & capacity: June-August; 1 & 2 week sessions; 84 campers
Clientele & fees: coed 7-10; Fees: **A ▲ 🐷**
Contact: Alicia J Yarboro, Camp Program Director at (205) 822-0150; fax: (205) 822-0132
e-mail: cfaf@zebra.net
Operated by: Independent Presbyterian, 3100 Highland Ave, Birmingham, AL 35256 at (205) 933-1830 (#857)

Winnataska (est 1918) ▲ ⌂

Pell City, AL (St Clair Co.); (205) 970-0251
Leslie Ethridge, Director

Camp comments: Christian camping since 1918.Yr round retreat & conference facility with excellent ropes course & horseback riding prog
Activities: Arts/Crafts, Camping Skills/Outdoor Living, Canoeing, Challenge/Rope Courses, Climbing/Rappelling, Hiking, Horseback — Western, Leadership Development, Nature/Environment Studies, Swimming — Recreational
Session lengths & capacity: 1 & 6 week sessions; 190 campers
Clientele & fees: coed 6-16; Fees: **C ▲**
Contact: Alan Jones, Director of Camping Services at (205) 970-0251; fax: (205) 970-0349
Web site: www.lbsa.org
Operated by: Greater Alabama Council BSA, PO Box 43307, Birmingham, AL 35244 at (205) 969-4260
Group Rental Information
Facilities: Kitchen Facilities, Pool
Programs: Boating, Horseback Riding (#845)

WOW Camp River Springs
(est 1994) ▲ ⌂

McKenzie, AL; (334) 374-8080
Charles Windham, Director

Camp comments: Building self-esteem through individual and group activities in a camp setting.
Activities: Aquatic Activities, Archery, Arts/Crafts, Canoeing, Counselor Training (CIT), Riflery, Swimming — Recreational
Session lengths & capacity: June-August; 1 week sessions; 120 campers
Clientele & fees: coed 8-15; seniors; Fees: **A ▲**
Contact: Charles Windham, Coordinator/Director at (334) 244-9695; fax: (334) 244-6685
Web site: www.woodmen.com
Operated by: WOW Life Insurance (HS), 1700 Farnam, Omaha, NE 68120 at (402) 271-7258
Group Rental Information
Seasons & Capacity: Spring 180, Summer 180, Fall 180, Winter 180
Facilities: A/V Equipment, Dorm-Style, Food Service, Hiking Trails, Kitchen Facilities, Meeting Rooms, Pool, River, Tents
Programs: Boating, Swimming (#2529)

WOW North Alabama Youth/Senior (est 1959)

Blountsville, AL (Blount Co.); (205) 466-3180
Norm Love, Director

Camp comments: A fraternal benefit for North Alabama Woodmen of the World members only.
Activities: Aquatic Activities, Archery, Arts/Crafts, Basketball, Canoeing, Challenge/Rope Courses, Climbing/Rappelling, Hiking, Nature/Environment Studies, Riflery
Session lengths & capacity: 1 week sessions; 120 campers
Clientele & fees: boys 8-15; girls 8-15; families; seniors
Contact: Philip D Robertson, Fraternal Coordinator at (256) 351-2022; fax: (256) 350-3495
e-mail: probertson@woodmen.com
Web site: www.woodmen.com
Operated by: WOW Life Insurance (HS), 1700 Farnam, Omaha, NE 68120 at (402) 271-7258

Group Rental Information

Seasons & Capacity: Spring 160, Summer 160, Fall 160
Facilities: Cabins, Food Service, Hiking Trails, Kitchen Facilities, Lake, Meeting Rooms, Playing Fields, Pool, River
Programs: Challenge/Ropes Course, Swimming (#6248)

YMCA Camp Chandler

(est 1929)

Wetumpka, AL (Elmore Co.); (334) 567-4933
Amy Burrows, Director

Camp comments: Covering 475 acres on beautiful lake offers countless activities for youth 5 to 15. Christian emphasis.
Activities: Archery, Canoeing, Challenge/Rope Courses, Climbing/Rappelling, Counselor Training (CIT), Horseback — Western, Riflery, Sailing, Swimming — Recreational, Waterskiing
Session lengths & capacity: 1, 2 & 4 week sessions; 180 campers
Clientele & fees: coed 5-15; Fees: C ⚠ 🚌
Contact: Jeff Reynolds, Executive Director at (334) 269-4362; fax: (334) 269-2387
e-mail: ymcacampchandler@mindspring.com
Web site: www.campchandler.org
Operated by: Montgomery YMCA, PO Box 2336, Montgomery, AL 36102 at (334) 269-4362

Group Rental Information

Facilities: A/V Equipment, Cabins, Dorm-Style, Food Service, Hiking Trails, Lake, Lodges, Meeting Rooms, Playing Fields
Programs: Boating, Challenge/Ropes Course, Environmental Education, Swimming (#848)

Alaska

Birchwood Camp (est 1959)

Chugiak, AK
David Kobersmith, Director

Camp comments: We provide campers with an experience of Christian love in a community which recognizes dependence on God.
Activities: Arts/Crafts, Boating, Camping Skills/Outdoor Living, Counselor Training (CIT), Music, Nature/Environment Studies, Performing Arts, Religious Study, Swimming — Recreational, Wilderness Trips
Session lengths & capacity: 1/2 & 1 week sessions
Clientele & fees: coed 7-18; families; Fees: B ⚠
Contact: Dave Kobersmith, Director-Manager at (907) 688-2734; fax: (907) 688-2734
e-mail: birchwd@alaska.net
Web site: www.alaska.net/~birchwd
Operated by: Birchwood Camp, PO Box 670049, Chugiak, AK 99567-0049 at (907) 688-2734

Group Rental Information

Site comments: Our mission is to be in the ministry of hospitality. We're glad to have you staying with us.
Facilities: Cabins, Hiking Trails, Kitchen Facilities, Lake, Lodges
Programs: Boating (#4264)

Camp Li-Wa (est 1959)

Fairbanks, AK; (907) 457-6059
Ted Franke, Director

Camp comments: Christian emphasis. Building lives worth living.
Activities: Archery, Arts/Crafts, Canoeing, Climbing/Rappelling, Horseback — Western, Leadership Development, Riflery, Swimming — Recreational, Wilderness Trips
Session lengths & capacity: June-August; 1 week sessions; 500 campers
Clientele & fees: coed 5-16; families; Fees: B ⚠ 🚌
Contact: Ted Franke, Director at (907) 457-6059; fax: (907) 457-1325
e-mail: campliwa@polarnet.com
Web site: www.victorymin.com
Operated by: Victory Ministries Inc, HC03 Box 8392, Palmer, AK 99645 at (907) 745-4203

Group Rental Information

Seasons & Capacity: Spring 50, Fall 50, Winter 50
Facilities: Cabins, Food Service, Hiking Trails, Kitchen Facilities, Lodges
Programs: Boating, Horseback Riding (#2106)

Kushtaka (est 1966)

Cooper Landing, AK; (907) 279-3551
Tara Markley, Director

Camp comments: Caring staff with small camper groups. Planned activities in program rich setting. Focus on outdoor living and environmental skills.
Activities: Aquatic Activities, Arts/Crafts, Backpacking, Camping Skills/Outdoor Living, Canoeing, Hiking, Horseback — Western, Leadership Development, Nature/Environment Studies, Team Building
Session lengths & capacity: June-August; 1 & 2 week sessions; 64 campers
Clientele & fees: coed 6-18; families; Fees: C ⚠ 🚌
Contact: Tara Markley, Camp Director at (907) 279-3551; fax: (907) 278-9829
e-mail: kushtaka@campfireak.org
Operated by: Camp Fire USA Alaska Council, 3745 Community Park Drive 104, Anchorage, AK 99508 at (907) 279-3551

Group Rental Information

Site comments: Small, program-rich site. Ideal for outdoor education.
Seasons & Capacity: Spring 60, Summer 60, Fall 60
Facilities: Cabins, Dorm-Style, Food Service, Hiking Trails, Kitchen Facilities, Lake, Lodges, Meeting Rooms, River
Programs: Boating, Environmental Education, Winter Sports (#453)

Si-La-Meo (est 1966)

Anchorage, AK; (907) 279-3551
Theresa Seer-Burek, Director

Camp comments: Caring staff, small camper group plans activities in prog rich setting. Focus on outdoor living, environmental skills.
Activities: Aquatic Activities, Archery, Arts/Crafts, Camping Skills/Outdoor Living, Canoeing, Climbing/Rappelling, Hiking, Horseback — Western, Nature/Environment Studies, Team Building
Session lengths & capacity: June-August; 1 week sessions; 120 campers
Clientele & fees: coed 6-13; Fees: B ☀ 🐷

Contact: Theresa Serr-Burek, Camp Director at (907) 279-3551; fax: (907) 278-9829
e-mail: tburek@campfireak.org
Operated by: Camp Fire USA Alaska Council, 3745 Community Park Drive 104, Anchorage, AK 99508 at (907) 279-3551 (#3258)

Togowoods (est 1958)

Wasilla, AK; (907) 376-1308
Kelly Feder, Director

Camp comments: Togowoods' small community inspires girls to succeed in the arts, aquatics and outdoor skills. Girls build confidence & friendships that last a lifetime.
Activities: Arts/Crafts, Backpacking, Camping Skills/Outdoor Living, Canoeing, Ceramics/Pottery, Counselor Training (CIT), Hiking, Kayaking, Nature/Environment Studies, Wilderness Trips
Session lengths & capacity: June-August; 1/2, 1 & 2 week sessions; 95 campers
Clientele & fees: girls 6-17; families; Fees: C, D ⚠ 🚌
Contact: Laura Pettersen, Resident Camp Director at (907) 376-1310; fax: (907) 376-1358
e-mail: camptogo@alaska.net
Web site: www.girlscouts.ak.org
Operated by: Girl Scouts Susitna Council, 3911 Turnagain Blvd E, Anchorage, AK 99517 at (907) 248-2250

Group Rental Information

Seasons & Capacity: Fall 48, Winter 48
Facilities: Cabins, Hiking Trails, Lake
Programs: Boating, Environmental Education, Winter Sports (#4269)

Trailside Discovery (est 1982)

Anchorage, AK; (907) 274-5437
Thomas Burek, Director

Camp comments: Environmental adventure programs/emphasize interactive enjoyable hands on outdoor experiences
Activities: Backpacking, Bicycling/Biking, Camping Skills/Outdoor Living, Canoeing, Field Trips, Kayaking, Leadership Development, Nature/Environment Studies, Team Building, Wilderness Trips
Session lengths & capacity: June-August; 1 week sessions; 120 campers
Clientele & fees: coed 4-17; Fees: B ☀ 🚌
Contact: Thomas Burek, Environmental Education Director at (907) 274-5437; fax: (907) 274-8733
e-mail: trailside@akcenter.org
Web site: akcenter.org
Operated by: Alaska Center Environment, 807 G St Ste 100, Anchorage, AK 99501 at (907) 274-3621 (#5552)

Victory Bible Camps & Conf Ctr

(est 1947)

Palmer, AK; (907) 745-4203
Stan Gillespie, Director

Camp comments: Christian emphasis. Building lives worth living.
Activities: Archery, Boating, Horseback — English, Horseback — Western, International Culture, Leadership Development, Religious Study, Riflery, Swimming — Recreational, Waterskiing
Session lengths & capacity: 1 week sessions; 300 campers
Clientele & fees: coed 6-99; families; Fees: B, C ⚠ 🚌
Contact: Tim Watt, Program Administrator at (907) 745-4203; fax: (907) 745-4206
e-mail: victory@victorymin.com
Web site: www.victorymin.com
Operated by: Victory Ministries Inc, HC03 Box 8392, Palmer, AK 99645 at (907) 745-4203

Group Rental Information

Seasons & Capacity: Spring 260, Summer 300, Fall 260, Winter 260

Facilities: Cabins, Dorm-Style, Hiking Trails, Lake, Lodges, Meeting Rooms
Programs: Boating, Environmental Education, Horseback Riding (#1451)

Winding Trails (est 1952)

Anchorage, AK; (907) 248-2250
Melinda Dillon, Director

Camp comments: Traditional Girl Scout program plus a different theme each week, wilderness setting complete with Moose. Join us for Fun!
Activities: Archery, Arts/Crafts, Baseball/Softball, Camping Skills/Outdoor Living, Farming/Ranching/Gardening, Nature/Environment Studies, Tennis
Session lengths & capacity: 7 week sessions; 140 campers
Clientele & fees: girls 5-15; Fees: B ☀ 🚐
Contact: Girl Scouts Susitna Counc, Day Camp Director at (907) 248-2250; fax: (907) 243-4819
Web site: www.girlscouts.ak.org
Operated by: Girl Scouts Susitna Council, 3911 Turnagain Blvd E, Anchorage, AK 99517 at (907) 248-2250 (#2649)

YMCA Camp Peggy Lake

(est 1975)

Willow, AK; (907) 244-2405
Heather Maisel, Director

Camp comments: Come grow in spirit, mind and body at the only YMCA camp in Alaska!
Activities: Aquatic Activities, Archery, Backpacking, Camping Skills/Outdoor Living, Canoeing, Drawing/Painting, Field Trips, Hiking, Riflery, Swimming — Recreational
Session lengths & capacity: 1 & 2 week sessions; 50 campers
Clientele & fees: coed 7-17; families; Fees: B △ 🚐
Contact: Heather Maisel, Camp Director at (907) 563-3211; fax: (907) 563-5739
e-mail: peggylake@hotmail.com
Operated by: Anchorage Community YMCA, 5353 Lake Otis, Anchorage, AK 99507 at (907) 563-3211

Group Rental Information
Seasons & Capacity: Spring 50, Summer 50, Fall 50
Facilities: Cabins, Double Occupancy, Hiking Trails, Kitchen Facilities, Lake, Meeting Rooms
Programs: Boating, Environmental Education, Swimming (#3101)

ICON LEGEND
☀ Day Camp
△ Resident Camp
🏠 Facilities Available To Rent
🚐 Transportation Available
🚌 Financial Aid Available

FEE RANGES PER WEEK
A $0-75
B $75-200
C $201-350
D $351-500
E $501-650
F over $650

Arizona

American Wilderness Leadership (est 1975)

Jackson, WY; (307) 730-3000
Donald J Brown, Director

Camp comments: "My time spent here, in the high mountains of WY, was one of the most exciting adventures I have ever experienced". AWLS student graduate, Webster Grove, MO
Activities: Archery, Backpacking, Camping Skills/Outdoor Living, Climbing/Rappelling, Fishing, Hiking, Nature/Environment Studies, Riflery, Wilderness Trips
Session lengths & capacity: June-August; 1 week sessions; 55 campers
Clientele & fees: coed 16-19; Fees: F △
Contact: Donald J Brown, Director of Education SCIF at (520) 620-1220 ext. 227; fax: (520) 618-3555
e-mail: dbrown@safariclub.org
Operated by: Safari Club International Fnd, 4800 West Gates Pass Road, Tucson, AZ 85745-9490 at (520) 620-1220

Group Rental Information
Site comments: Located in the historic mountain beauty of Bridger Teton National forest, AWLS is 33 miles SE of Jackson Hole, Wyoming.
Seasons & Capacity: Fall 70
Facilities: A/V Equipment, Cabins, Dorm-Style, Double Occupancy, Food Service, Hiking Trails, Kitchen Facilities, Linens, Lodges, Meeting Rooms, Playing Fields
Programs: Environmental Education (#30903)

Anytown Camp & Conference Ctr (est 1991)

Prescott, AZ (Yavapai Co.)
Vern Keaunui, Director
Contact: Web site: www.anytowncamp.org
Operated by: Anytown America Inc, 1951 W Camelback Rd Ste 445, Phoenix, AZ 85015 at (602) 995-1450

Group Rental Information
Site comments: Anytown promotes programs to enable youth respect for racial, religious, & cultural differences through education.
Facilities: Cabins, Food Service, Hiking Trails
Programs: Environmental Education (#2980)

Arizona Camp Sunrise

(est 1983)

Payson, AZ (Gila Co.); (520) 478-9913
Melissa Lee, Director

Camp comments: A camp for children ages 8-17 who have or have had cancer.24 hour medical staff, no fee to participate, great counselors
Activities: Archery, Arts/Crafts, Canoeing, Counselor Training (CIT), Dance, Fishing, Hiking, Horseback — Western, Nature/Environment Studies, Sports — Field & Team
Session lengths & capacity: July-July; 1 week sessions; 85 campers
Clientele & fees: coed 8-18; families; Fees: A △ 🚌
Contact: Barbara Nicholas, Manager/Programs at (602) 553-7129; fax: (602) 224-7466
Web site: www.azcampsunrise.org
Operated by: American Cancer Society SW, 2929 E Thomas Rd, Phoenix, AZ 85016 at (602) 553-7129 (#5426)

Camp Honor (est 1994)

Prescott, AZ (Yavapai Co.); (060) 295-5394
Michael Rosenthal, Director

Camp comments: Serving children with hemophilia and/or HIV, their siblings, and children of hemophiliacs.
Activities: Archery, Arts/Crafts, Camping Skills/Outdoor Living, Canoeing, Counselor Training (CIT), Drama, Hiking, Leadership Development, Music, Swimming — Recreational
Session lengths & capacity: 1 week sessions; 130 campers
Clientele & fees: coed 7-17; Fees: A △ 🚌
Contact: Michael Rosenthal, Executive Director at (602) 955-3947; fax: (602) 955-1962
e-mail: mike@hemophiliaz.org
Web site: www.hemophiliaz.org
Operated by: Hemophilia Association Inc, 4001 N 24th St, Phoenix, AZ 85016 at (602) 955-3947 (#2797)

Camp Ponderosa Ranch

Heber, AZ; (520) 535-5082
Neil Labarge, Director

Camp comments: This program offers a fun, safe, christian environment where children can meet friends and learn new skills
Activities: Archery, Community Service, Computer, Hiking, Leadership Development, Music, Nature/Environment Studies, Photography, Religious Study, Soccer
Session lengths & capacity: June-August; 1 & 2 week sessions; 130 campers
Clientele & fees: boys 7-14; girls 7-14; coed 7-14; families; single adults; Fees: B △ 🚌
Contact: Ivan Wild, Camp Director at (602) 267-4173; fax: (602) 267-4274
e-mail: ivan_wild@usw.salvationarmy.org
Operated by: The Salvation Army, 2707 E Van Buren, Phoenix, AZ 85072 at (602) 267-4100

Group Rental Information
Facilities: Cabins, Dorm-Style, Double Occupancy, Food Service, Hiking Trails, Meeting Rooms, Tents
Programs: Challenge/Ropes Course (#37360)

Camp Rainbow (est 1985)

Prescott, AZ (Yavapai Co.); (602) 239-4096
Renee Hunte, Director

Camp comments: A special camp for children who have or have had cancer. Caring staff. Great ratio. Medical team on-site.
Activities: Archery, Canoeing, Challenge/Rope Courses, Counselor Training (CIT), Horseback — Western, Music, Nature/Environment Studies, Swimming — Recreational, Tennis
Session lengths & capacity: 1 week sessions; 150 campers
Clientele & fees: boys 7-17; girls 7-17
Contact: Renee Hunte, Camp Director at (602) 546-0925; fax: (602) 546-0276
Operated by: Children's Cancer Center, 1919 E Thomas Rd, Phoenix, AZ 85006 at (602) 546-0925 (#438)

Camp Wamatochick (Camp Fire) (est 1924)

Prescott, AZ (Yavapai Co.); (520) 445-1434
Charlie Gantchoff, Director

Camp comments: Nestled in ponderosa pines and boulder outcroppings, campers have come to Camp Wamatochick since 1925 for an unforgettable and unique outdoor experience.
Activities: Archery, Arts/Crafts, Camping Skills/Outdoor Living, Counselor Training (CIT), Hiking, Leadership Development, Nature/Environment Studies, Sports — Field & Team, Swimming — Recreational, Team Building
Session lengths & capacity: June-August; 1 week sessions; 100 campers
Clientele & fees: coed 8-18; Fees: C △ 🚌
Contact: Taryn Lopez, Program Director at (800) 888-7954; fax: (602) 954-7352
e-mail: tlopez@campfireaz.org

Operated by: Kids Kamp, 5110 N 40th St Ste 107, Phoenix, AZ 85018-2143 at (602) 954-7544

Group Rental Information
Site comments: An ideal setting for large and small group gatherings such as: retreats, field trips, outdoor weddings, family reunions, and receptions. Accomodates up to 200.
Seasons & Capacity: Spring 100, Summer 1500, Fall 100
Facilities: Cabins, Double Occupancy, Lodges, Meeting Rooms, River
Programs: Challenge/Ropes Course, Environmental Education (#465)

Charles Pearlstein
(est 1975)
Prescott, AZ (Yavapai Co.); (520) 778-0091
Andrea P. Cohen; MSW, Director

Camp comments: Communal Jewish living in cool pines of Prescott, AZ. Friendly & caring environment. Emphasis on creative program. A summer of fun & a lifetime of memories.
Activities: Aquatic Activities, Archery, Arts/Crafts, Bicycling/Biking, Camping Skills/Outdoor Living, Challenge/Rope Courses, Drama, Leadership Development, Music, Religious Study
Session lengths & capacity: June-August; 1 & 3 week sessions; 180 campers
Clientele & fees: coed 7-15; Fees: E △
Contact: (480) 951-0323; fax: (480) 951-7150
Web site: www.camppearlstein.com
Operated by: Temple Beth Israel, 10460 N 56th St, Scottsdale, AZ 85253 at (480) 951-0323

Group Rental Information
Facilities: Cabins, Dorm-Style, Double Occupancy, Food Service, Meeting Rooms (#3680)

Chauncey Ranch (est 1975)
Mayer, AZ (Yavapai Co.); (520) 632-7704
Mike Spain, Director

Camp comments: YMCA Ranch & camp offering traditional activities & equestrian programs. 2 wk cowboy camp, lession, overnights. Paintball, high ropes, zipline & climbing wall.
Activities: Archery, Arts/Crafts, Challenge/Rope Courses, Counselor Training (CIT), Farming/Ranching/Gardening, Hiking, Horseback — Western, Leadership Development, Nature/Environment Studies, Riflery
Session lengths & capacity: May-August; 1, 2, 3 & 4 week sessions; 130 campers
Clientele & fees: coed 9-16; families; Fees: D △ 🐎
Contact: (800) 660-1385; fax: (520) 445-1908
e-mail: azcamps@cableone.net
Operated by: Valley of the Sun, Camping Services, HC 32 Box 292, Prescott, AZ 86303 at (928) 445-1385

Group Rental Information
Site comments: 5000 acres ranch/camp, Aquafria River basin. Cottonwood groves, 3 pastures. Specialties: equestrian, ropes, team challenge, corporate retreats & family events.
Seasons & Capacity: Spring 130, Fall 130, Winter 130
Facilities: A/V Equipment, Cabins, Food Service, Lodges, Meeting Rooms, Playing Fields
Programs: Challenge/Ropes Course, Environmental Education, Horseback Riding (#13409)

Faith Adventure Camp (est 1984) △
Payson, AZ (Gila Co.); (520) 478-4435
Duane Carr, Director

Camp comments: Mountain setting.Christian emphasis.Many outdoor activities.Caring atmosphere with trained,loving,caring counselors.

Activities: Archery, Arts/Crafts, Camping Skills/Outdoor Living, Drama, Fishing, Hiking, Music, Nature/Environment Studies, Religious Study, Riflery
Session lengths & capacity: 1 week sessions; 120 campers
Clientele & fees: boys 6-12; girls 6-12; Fees: B △
Contact: Joanne Winslow, Church Administrator at (480) 838-6559; fax: (480) 967-8839
e-mail: fcot@juno.com
Web site: www.feot.org
Operated by: Faith Church of Tempe, 1050 E Southern Ave D5, Tempe, AZ 85282 at (480) 838-6559 (#1505)

Friendly Pines Camp
(est 1941)
Prescott, AZ (Yavapai Co.); (928) 445-2128
Jack & Bebe Brown May, Director

Camp comments: Trad. 3rd generation camp in AZ. Tall cool pines, 30+ choices: horses, watrski, tennis, hikes, ropes course & more fun! A place for children to enjoy childhood.
Activities: Archery, Arts/Crafts, Challenge/Rope Courses, Climbing/Rappelling, Fishing, Horseback — English, Horseback — Western, Swimming — Instructional, Tennis
Session lengths & capacity: June-August; 2, 4 & 6 week sessions; 209 campers
Clientele & fees: coed 6-13; Fees: E △
Contact: Bebe Brown May, Owner/Director at (928) 445-2128;
e-mail: info@friendlypines.com
Web site: www.friendlypines.com
Operated by: Friendly Pines Camp, 933J Friendly Pines Road, Prescott, AZ 86303 at (928) 445-2128

Group Rental Information
Site comments: 130 mountain acres, sport, hiking, lake, nature study, ropes course, horseback riding. Full food service.
Seasons & Capacity: Spring 275, Summer 335, Fall 275, Winter 275
Facilities: Cabins, Dorm-Style, Food Service, Hiking Trails, Lake, Meeting Rooms, Playing Fields
Programs: Challenge/Ropes Course, Horseback Riding (#483)

Kids Kamp (est 1992)
Avondale, AZ (Maricopa Co.); (602) 932-0840
Jill Candland, Director
Activities: Arts/Crafts, Camping Skills/Outdoor Living, Community Service, Nature/Environment Studies, Sports — Field & Team, Team Building
Clientele & fees: Fees: A ☀
Contact: Taryn Lopez, Camp Administrator at (800) 888-7954; fax: (602) 954-7352
e-mail: camperaz@worldnet.att.net
Operated by: Kids Kamp, 5110 N 40th St Ste 107, Phoenix, AZ 85018-2143 at (602) 954-7544 (#5416)

Lions Camp Tatiyee Inc
(est 1958)
Lakeside, AZ; (520) 537-2421
Pamela Swanson, Director

Camp comments: Lions Camp Tatiyee provides a camping experience for challenged individuals among their peers. We provide self esteem among traditional camp experiences.
Activities: Arts/Crafts, Ceramics/Pottery, Drama, Fishing, Nature/Environment Studies, Swimming — Recreational, Team Building
Session lengths & capacity: May-August; 1 week sessions; 92 campers
Clientele & fees: coed 7-17; seniors
Contact: Pamela Swanson, Executive Director at (602) 275-2604;
e-mail: lionscampt@aol.com
Web site: www.geocities.com/lionscampt
Operated by: Lions Camp Tatiyee Inc, 1016 N 32nd St Ste 5, Phoenix, AZ 85008 at (480) 380-4254

Group Rental Information
Site comments: Lions Camp Tatiyee is located in the cool pines of the White Mountains of Arizona. We are available for use in the late spring and early fall.
Facilities: Cabins, Dorm-Style, Hiking Trails, Kitchen Facilities, Lodges, Meeting Rooms, Pool
Programs: Swimming (#30325)

Maripai (est 1934)
Prescott, AZ (Yavapai Co.); (602) 253-6359
Chris LeClair, Director

Camp comments: Rustic mountain setting, western trail riding program & backpacking trips.
Activities: Arts/Crafts, Backpacking, Camping Skills/Outdoor Living, Counselor Training (CIT), Hiking, Horseback — Western, Leadership Development, Nature/Environment Studies
Session lengths & capacity: June-August; 1 week sessions; 125 campers
Clientele & fees: girls 7-17; Fees: B △
Contact: Dee Dee Dodd & Lydia Martin, Program Area Manager at (602) 253-6359;
fax: (602) 252-1159
e-mail: deedeedodd@girlscoutsaz.org
Web site: www.girlscouts.org
Operated by: Arizona Cactus Pine GSC, PO Box 21776, Phoenix, AZ 85036 at (602) 253-6359 (#502)

Mingus Mountain Camp
(est 1950)
Prescott Valley, AZ (Yavapai Co.); (520) 634-5273
Contact: Brandon Hill, Manager at (520) 634-5273;
fax: (520) 634-5273
e-mail: mingusmtncmp@sedona.net
Web site: www.desertsw.org/camps/
Operated by: Desert Southwest Conf UMC, 1550 E Meadowbrook, Phoenix, AZ 85014 at (602) 266-6956

Group Rental Information
Site comments: 123 acre mountain top facility at 7600 ft in Ponderosa pines.
Seasons & Capacity: Spring 160, Summer 160, Fall 160
Facilities: Cabins, Dorm-Style, Food Service, Hiking Trails, Meeting Rooms (#481)

Mingus Springs Camp (est 1950)
Prescott, AZ (Yavapai Co.); (928) 445-3778
Henry Dahlberg, Director
Contact: Linda & Henry Dahlberg, Camp Managers at (928) 445-3778; fax: (928) 445-3778
e-mail: camp@mingussprings.org
Web site: www.mingussprings.org
Session lengths: April-October
Operated by: Henry Dahlberg Foundation, 2946 Darca Drive, Prescott, AZ 86305 at (928) 445-3778

Group Rental Information
Site comments: Serene mountain retreat,Cool Pines Lake for fishing & swimming. Pristine hiking trails along streamside habitat.
Seasons & Capacity: Spring 105, Summer 105, Fall 105
Facilities: Cabins, Dorm-Style, Food Service, Hiking Trails, Kitchen Facilities, Lake, Meeting Rooms
Programs: Swimming (#5791)

Orme Summer Camp (est 1929) △
Mayer, AZ; (928) 632-7601
Doug Bartlett, Director

Camp comments: West's best riding & rodeo camp on Orme Ranch: crafts, archery, riflery, survival, tennis, mtn biking, swimming, sports.
Activities: Archery, Arts/Crafts, Bicycling/Biking, Camping Skills/Outdoor Living, Climbing/Rappelling, Field Trips, Horseback — Western, Riflery, Tennis

Session lengths & capacity: June-August; 1, 2, 3, 4, 5, 6 & 7 week sessions; 150 campers
Clientele & fees: coed 7-16; Fees: E ⛺
Contact: Doug Bartlett, Camp Director at (520) 632-7601; fax: (520) 632-7605
e-mail: dbartlett@orme.k12.az.us
Web site: www.ormecamp.org
Operated by: Orme School, HC 63 Box 3040, Mayer, AZ 86333 at (928) 632-7601 (#487)

Pine Canyon Camp (est 1954)

Willcox, AZ (Yavapai Co.); (520) 824-3553
Marylou Chopelas, Director
Contact: MaryLou Chopelas, Manager at (520) 824-3553; fax: (520) 824-3553
e-mail: pinecanyon@vtc.net
Web site: www.desertsw.org/camps/
Operated by: Desert Southwest Conf UMC, 1550 E Meadowbrook, Phoenix, AZ 85014 at (602) 266-6956

Group Rental Information
Site comments: Located in the heart of the Chiricahua Mountains, where heaven and earth meet!
Seasons & Capacity: Spring 120, Summer 120, Fall 120
Facilities: Cabins, Dorm-Style, Food Service, Hiking Trails, Lodges, Meeting Rooms, Playing Fields
Programs: Environmental Education (#496)

Saguaro Camp Cherith

(est 1961)

Prescott, AZ (Maricopa Co.); (520) 778-2861
Vicki Lyding, Director

Camp comments: Christ centered outdoor program with craft and game electives based on age and interests. Experienced dedicated staff.
Activities: Archery, Arts/Crafts, Camping Skills/Outdoor Living, Counselor Training (CIT), Dance, Hiking, Horseback — Western, Nature/Environment Studies, Riflery
Session lengths & capacity: July-July; 1 & 2 week sessions; 90 campers
Clientele & fees: girls 6-18; Fees: C ⛺
Contact: Vicki Lyding, Camp Director at (602) 588-0731;
Operated by: Sagwaro Camp Cherith, 18420 N 56th Lane, Glendale, AZ 85308 (#456)

Shadow Rim Ranch

(est 1964)

Payson, AZ (Gila Co.); (602) 253-6359
Rebecca Manson, Director

ICON LEGEND

☀ Day Camp
⛺ Resident Camp
🏠 Facilities Available To Rent
🚐 Transportation Available
💰 Financial Aid Available

FEE RANGES PER WEEK

A	$0-75
B	$75-200
C	$201-350
D	$351-500
E	$501-650
F	over $650

Camp comments: Mountain ranch setting with program activities that are girl centered and foster self-esteem and cooperation
Activities: Archery, Arts/Crafts, Backpacking, Camping Skills/Outdoor Living, Canoeing, Counselor Training (CIT), Hiking, Leadership Development, Nature/Environment Studies, Sports — Field & Team
Session lengths & capacity: June-August; 1/2 & 1 week sessions; 105 campers
Clientele & fees: girls 7-17; Fees: B ⛺
Contact: Dee Dee Dodd & Lydia Martin, Program Area Manager at (602) 253-6359; fax: (602) 252-1159
e-mail: deedeedodd@girlscoutsaz.org
Web site: www.girlscouts.org
Operated by: Arizona Cactus Pine GSC, PO Box 21776, Phoenix, AZ 85036 at (602) 253-6359 (#486)

Sky Y Camp (est 1938)

Prescott, AZ; (602) 254-1571
Keith Crawley, Director

Camp comments: Traditional YMCA camp in Bradshaw Mountains. Forested setting. Program emphasizes fun, adventure and personal growth. Combine weeks to build your summer fun.
Activities: Archery, Arts/Crafts, Challenge/Rope Courses, Climbing/Rappelling, Hiking, Horseback — Western, Nature/Environment Studies, Riflery, Swimming — Recreational, Wilderness Trips
Session lengths & capacity: May-August; 1, 2, 3 & 4 week sessions; 230 campers
Clientele & fees: coed 7-16; families; Fees: D ⛺
Contact: Roxi Tuttle, Registrar at (800) 660-1385; fax: (520) 445-1908
e-mail: azcamps@cableone.net
Operated by: Valley of the Sun, Camping Services, HC 32 Box 292, Prescott, AZ 86303 at (928) 445-1385

Group Rental Information
Site comments: Schools, churches and groups find our remodeled facilities just right. Programs available include climbing tower, paintball, team challenge and more.
Seasons & Capacity: Spring 230, Fall 230, Winter 230
Facilities: A/V Equipment, Cabins, Double Occupancy, Food Service, Hiking Trails, Meeting Rooms
Programs: Challenge/Ropes Course, Environmental Education, Horseback Riding (#484)

Sombrero Day Camp

Phoenix, AZ (Maricopa Co.); (602) 253-6359
Fran Goudreau, Director

Camp comments: A fun-filled day camp for girls. Science exploration, outdoor adventures, arts & crafts, music & dance.
Activities: Archery, Arts/Crafts, Camping Skills/Outdoor Living, Dance, Hiking, Nature/Environment Studies, Swimming — Recreational, Team Building
Session lengths & capacity: June-August; 1 week sessions; 150 campers
Clientele & fees: girls 6-17; Fees: A ☀
Contact: Dee Dee Dodd, Program Area Manager at (602) 253-6359; fax: (602) 252-1159
Web site: www.girlscouts.org
Operated by: Arizona Cactus Pine GSC, PO Box 21776, Phoenix, AZ 85036 at (602) 253-6359 (#3497)

TJCC Summer Camps

Tucson, AZ; (520) 299-3000
Steve Tepper, Director

Camp comments: To provide a safe, inclusive, fun environment for all children.

Activities: Community Service, Counselor Training (CIT), Drama, Field Trips, Music, Performing Arts, Sports — Field & Team, Swimming — Instructional, Swimming — Recreational, Travel/Tour
Session lengths & capacity: June-August; 3 week sessions; 400 campers
Clientele & fees: coed 6-16; Fees: B ☀ Fees: B, C ⛺ 💰
Contact: Steve Tepper, Director Children, Youth, Camping Serves at (520) 299-3000; fax: (520) 529-0373
e-mail: stepper@tucsonjcc.org
Web site: www.tjccshalom.org
Operated by: Tucson Jewish Community Center, 3800 E River Road, Tucson, AZ 85718 at (520) 299-3000 (#43697)

Tonto Rim Baptist Camp

(est 1950)

Payson, AZ (Gila Co.); (520) 478-4630
Brian Crnadall, Director

Camp comments: Tonto Rim offers quality programming and modern winterized cabin facilities. It's your place for a great getaway.
Activities: Archery, Arts/Crafts, Backpacking, Canoeing, Counselor Training (CIT), Fishing, Hiking, Horseback — Western, Leadership Development, Nature/Environment Studies
Session lengths & capacity: 1 week sessions; 217 campers
Clientele & fees: coed 8-99; families; Fees: B ⛺
Contact: Brian Crandall, Executive Director at (928) 478-4630; fax: (928) 478-3000
e-mail: tontorim@theriver.com
Operated by: Am Baptist Churches of Pacific, HC 2 Box 95P, Payson, AZ 85541 at (602) 478-4630

Group Rental Information
Site comments: Located Northeast of Phoenix in the cool country below the Mogollon Rim in Eastern Arizona; Come try our award winning dinner rolls & cinnamon rolls.
Facilities: Cabins, Food Service, Hiking Trails, Meeting Rooms, Playing Fields
Programs: Boating, Horseback Riding (#476)

Willow Springs Program Center

(est 1971)

Prescott, AZ (Yavapai Co.); (602) 253-6359
Wayne Houk, Director

Camp comments: Noncompetitive, creative environment with extensive fine arts program & challenge/team building course.
Activities: Archery, Ceramics/Pottery, Challenge/Rope Courses, Drama, Drawing/Painting, Golf, Leadership Development
Session lengths & capacity: June-August; 1/2 & 1 week sessions; 150 campers
Clientele & fees: girls 7-17; Fees: B ⛺
Contact: Dee Dee Dodd & Lydia Martin, Program Area Manager at (602) 253-6359; fax: (602) 252-1159
e-mail: deedeedodd@girlscoutsaz.org
Web site: www.girlscouts.org
Operated by: Arizona Cactus Pine GSC, PO Box 21776, Phoenix, AZ 85036 at (602) 253-6359 (#3474)

YMCA Triangle Y Ranch Camp

(est 1949)

Oracle, AZ (Pinal Co.); (520) 825-2209
Tom Dinkins, Director

Camp comments: Focus on teaching responsibility, making new friends, learning to live away from home, and learn new skills.
Activities: Archery, Arts/Crafts, Bicycling/Biking, Challenge/Rope Courses, Horseback — Western, Leadership Development, Music, Nature/Environment Studies, Riflery, Swimming — Recreational

Session lengths & capacity: June-August; 1, 2, 3, 4, 5, 6, 7 & 8 week sessions; 230 campers
Clientele & fees: boys 8-14; girls 8-14; coed 8-14; Fees: **C** ▲ 🐷
Contact: Tom Dinkins, Executive Camp Director at (520) 884-0987; fax: (520) 624-1518
e-mail: campman@azstarnet.com
Web site: www.tucsonymca.org
Operated by: YMCA of Metropolitan Tucson, 60 W Alameda, Tucson, AZ 85702 at (520) 884-0987

Group Rental Information
Site comments: We have facilities to handle groups from 35 to 250. Please call with any special requests.
Seasons & Capacity: Spring 250, Fall 250, Winter 250
Facilities: A/V Equipment, Cabins, Double Occupancy, Food Service, Hiking Trails, Meeting Rooms, River
Programs: Environmental Education (#470)

Arkansas

Cahinnio (est 1967)　　　　▲ 🏠

Booneville, AR (Scott/Logan Co.); (501) 675-4620
Kelly Divine, Director

Camp comments: Camp Cahinnio offers girls the chance to: build character, gain leadership skills, gain a sence of belonging, have fun as they grow strong. Non scouts welcome.
Activities: Archery, Arts/Crafts, Camping Skills/Outdoor Living, Canoeing, Counselor Training (CIT), Horseback — Western, Leadership Development, Nature/Environment Studies, Swimming — Instructional, Swimming — Recreational
Session lengths & capacity: June-July; 1/2, 1 & 2 week sessions; 80 campers
Clientele & fees: girls 7-17; Fees: **B** ▲ 🐷
Contact: Kelly Divine, Camp Director at (501) 452-1290; fax: (501) 452-3365
e-mail: kellyd@gscmma.com
Web site: www.gscmma.org
Operated by: GS Council Mount Magazine Area, PO Box 3267, Fort Smith, AR 72913 at (479) 452-1290

Group Rental Information
Facilities: Cabins, Hiking Trails, Lake, Playing Fields, Tents
Programs: Swimming (#708)

Camp Aldersgate (est 1947)　　▲ 🏠

Little Rock, AR (Pulaski Co.); (501) 225-1444
Carey Walker, Director

Camp comments: Traditional camp for children & youth with physical disabilities & medical conditions.
Activities: Aerobics/Exercise, Aquatic Activities, Archery, Arts/Crafts, Camping Skills/Outdoor Living, Canoeing, Counselor Training (CIT), Hiking, Music, Nature/Environment Studies
Session lengths & capacity: May-August; 1 week sessions; 80 campers
Clientele & fees: coed 6-16; Fees: **D** ▲ 🐷
Contact: Carey Walker, Executive Director at (501) 225-1444; fax: (501) 225-2019
e-mail: info@campaldersgate.net
Web site: www.campaldersgate.net
Operated by: Camp Aldersgate Inc, 2000 Aldersgate Rd, Little Rock, AR 72205 at (501) 225-1444

Group Rental Information
Facilities: Cabins, Dorm-Style, Food Service, Lake, Lodges, Meeting Rooms, Pool (#720)

Camp Bear Track (est 1994)　▲ 🏠 🚐

Drasco, AR (Cleburne Co.); (501) 825-8222
Jack Dowell, Director

Camp comments: Teaching Christian values, Camp Bear Track is a place of individual achievement, adventure, fun, fellowship and friends.
Activities: Arts/Crafts, Basketball, Camping Skills/Outdoor Living, Canoeing, Challenge/Rope Courses, Climbing/Rappelling, Horseback — Western, Soccer, Swimming — Instructional, Waterskiing
Session lengths & capacity: June-August; 1 & 2 week sessions; 120 campers
Clientele & fees: coed 7-15; Fees: **E, F** ▲
Contact: Jack T Dowell, Owner/Director at (501) 825-8222; fax: (501) 825-8255
e-mail: campbear@aol.com
Web site: www.campbeartrack.com
Operated by: Camp Bear Track, 295 Prim Rd, Drasco, AR 72530 at (501) 825-8222

Group Rental Information
Site comments: Beautiful setting in Ozark Mtns of Arkansas. Modern facilities, awesome food, sporting gear provided, pavilion games, soccer, basketball, & tennis.
Seasons & Capacity: Spring 160, Fall 160
Facilities: A/V Equipment, Cabins, Food Service, Hiking Trails, Lake, Lodges, Meeting Rooms, Playing Fields, Pool, Tents
Programs: Challenge/Ropes Course, Environmental Education, Swimming (#26292)

Camp Noark (est 1967)　　　▲ 🏠

Huntsville, AR (Madison Co.); (501) 559-2509
Katie Dailey, Director

Camp comments: Traditional Girl Scout camp with excellent staff, fun, creative activities & beautiful Ozark scenery
Activities: Arts/Crafts, Bicycling/Biking, Camping Skills/Outdoor Living, Canoeing, Counselor Training (CIT), Hiking, Horseback — Western, Nature/Environment Studies, Swimming — Recreational
Session lengths & capacity: June-August; 1/2, 1 & 2 week sessions; 140 campers
Clientele & fees: girls 7-17; Fees: **B** ▲ 🐷
Contact: Katie Dailey, Camp Director at (800) 299-3914; fax: (501) 750-4699
e-mail: kdailey_noarkgsc@hotmail.com
Operated by: NOARK GSC, PO Box 6353, Springdale, AR 72766 at (501) 750-2442

Group Rental Information
Facilities: Hiking Trails, Lodges, Tents (#27851)

Joseph Pfeifer Kiwanis Camp

(est 1929)　　　　　　　　　▲ 🏠

Little Rock, AR; (501) 821-3714
Sanford Tollette, Director

Camp comments: Free. 24 hour supervision. Effective discipline model. Also have 6 week local school program for grades 3-5. At risk.
Activities: Academics, Arts/Crafts, Camping Skills/Outdoor Living, Challenge/Rope Courses, Community Service, Counselor Training (CIT), Farming/Ranching/Gardening, Hiking, Leadership Development, Swimming — Recreational
Session lengths & capacity: June-July; 1 & 6 week sessions; 80 campers
Clientele & fees: coed 9-14; Fees: **A** ▲
Contact: Sanford Tollette, Exec. Dir. at (501) 821-3714; fax: (501) 821-2629
e-mail: stollette@pfeifercamp.com
Web site: www.member.tripod.com/jpkcamp
Operated by: Joseph Pfeifer Kiwanis Camp, 5512 Ferndale Cutoff, Little Rock, AR 72223 at (501) 821-3714

Group Rental Information
Facilities: Cabins (#3546)

WOW Arkansas Youth Camp Inc

(est 1987)　　　　　　　　　▲ 🏠

Clinton, AR (Van Buren Co.); (501) 745-2909
A Lamar Harvey, Director

Camp comments: Camp offers fun filled activities for Woodmen Youth ages 8 through 15.
Activities: Archery, Arts/Crafts, Basketball, Golf, Leadership Development, Riflery, Sports — Field & Team, Swimming — Recreational, Team Building
Session lengths & capacity: June-August; 6 week sessions; 148 campers
Clientele & fees: coed 8-15; Fees: **A** ▲
Contact: A Lamar Harvey, Fraternal Coordinator at (501) 745-2909; fax: (501) 745-2909
Web site: www.woodmen.com
Operated by: WOW Life Insurance (HS), 1700 Farnam, Omaha, NE 68120 at (402) 271-7258 (#6252)

California

Academy bythe Sea/Camp Pacific (est 1943) ☀ ▲ ⌂ 🚐

Carlsbad, CA (San Diego Co.); (760) 434-7564
Jeff Barton, Director

Camp comments: Join us at our beachfront campus this summer for our five week academic program, three week recreational camp, or one week surf camps.
Activities: Academics, Aquatic Activities, Arts/Crafts, Basketball, Field Trips, Kayaking, Sports — Field & Team, Swimming — Recreational, Team Building, Tennis
Session lengths & capacity: June-August; 1, 2, 3, 4, 5, 6 week sessions; 150 campers
Clientele & fees: boys 8-16; girls 8-16; coed 8-16; Fees: E ☀ Fees: F ▲
Contact: Lori Adlfinger, Associate Director at (760) 434-7564; fax: (760) 729-1574
e-mail: info@abts.com
Web site: www.abts.com
Operated by: Army and Navy Academy, 2605 Carlsbad Blvd, Carlsbad, CA 92008 at (760) 729-2385

Group Rental Information
Site comments: Oceanfront campus, residential academic, recreational, or surf & bodyboard camp sessions. Ages 8-16.
Seasons & Capacity: Summer 300
Facilities: A/V Equipment, Cabins, Dorm-Style, Double Occupancy, Food Service, Kitchen Facilities, Linens, Meeting Rooms, Ocean, Playing Fields, Pool
Programs: Swimming (#208)

Adventure Day Camp

(est 1992) ☀ 🚐

Walnut Creek, CA; (925) 937-6500
Serafino Bianchi, Director

Camp comments: Our magnificently wooded site in Walnut Creek at Castle Rock Park offers all of the camp activities on the premises.
Activities: Archery, Baseball/Softball, Basketball, Canoeing, Counselor Training (CIT), Drama, Hiking, Horseback — Western, Soccer, Swimming — Instructional
Session lengths & capacity: 2, 4 & 6 week sessions; 150 campers
Clientele & fees: coed 3-11; Fees: C ☀ 🐖
Contact: Serafino Bianchi, Director/CFO at (510) 937-6500; fax: (510) 937-6590
e-mail: serafino@advcamp.com
Web site: www.adventuredaycamp.com

ICON LEGEND

☀ Day Camp
▲ Resident Camp
⌂ Facilities Available To Rent
🚐 Transportation Available
🐖 Financial Aid Available

FEE RANGES PER WEEK

A $0-75
B $75-200
C $201-350
D $351-500
E $501-650
F   over $650

Operated by: Adventure Day Camp, 3527 Mt Diablo Blvd 241, Lafayette, CA 94549 at (925) 937-6500 (#815)

Aldersgate Retreat Center

(est 1927) ⌂

Pacific Palisades, CA (Los Angeles Co.); (310) 454-6699
Bill Damerell, Director
Contact: Web site: www.cal-pac.org
Operated by: California Pacific Annual Conf, 110 S Euclid Ave, PO Box 6006, Pasadena, CA 91102 at (626) 568-7330

Group Rental Information
Site comments: Historic home, now retreat center. Comfortable beds and excellent meals for up to 47 persons. Lovely chapel and garden, great for weddings. Walk to the beach.
Seasons & Capacity: Spring 47, Summer 47, Fall 47, Winter 47
Facilities: A/V Equipment, Dorm-Style, Food Service, Hiking Trails, Lodges, Meeting Rooms, Ocean (#6568)

All Peoples Christian Center

(est 1949) ▲ 🚐

Mentone, CA (San Bernardino Co.); (213) 747-6357
Brad Carter, Director
Activities: Aquatic Activities, Archery, Arts/Crafts, Hiking, Swimming — Recreational
Session lengths & capacity: 1 week sessions; 65 campers
Clientele & fees: coed 8-12; Fees: B ▲ 🐖
Contact: Julio C Ramos, Camp Director at (213) 746-9866; fax: (213) 747-0541
e-mail: isaiah567@bigplanet.com
Operated by: All Peoples Christian Center, 822 E 20th St, Los Angeles, CA 90011 at (213) 747-6357 (#3266)

Aloha Beach Camp (est 1999) ☀ 🚐

Tarzana, CA (Los Angeles Co.); (818) 996-4780
Eric D. Naftulin, Director

Camp comments: Day trips to Los Angeles and Ventura County's best beaches, lakes and water parks. High-action and quality fun. 2-day, risk-free, 100% money-back guarantee.
Activities: Aquatic Activities, Boating, Field Trips, Fishing, Kayaking, Nature/Environment Studies, Sailing, Swimming — Recreational, Waterskiing, Windsurfing
Session lengths & capacity: June-August; 1/2, 1, 2, 3, 4, 5, 6, 7, 8 & 9 week sessions; 250 campers
Clientele & fees: coed 7-14; Fees: C ☀
Contact: Eric Naftulin, Executive Director at (818) 996-4780; fax: (818) 344-6841
e-mail: alohabeachcamp@aol.com
Web site: www.alohabeachcamp.com
Operated by: Aloha Day Camp LLC, PO Box 570812, Tarzana, CA 91357 at (818) 996-4780 (#44181)

Alpine Meadows Camp & Conf Ctr (est 1954) ⌂

Angelus Oaks, CA; (909) 794-3800
Dr Peter J Huber, Director
Contact: Susan Sostman at (909) 794-3800; fax: (909) 389-1148
e-mail: office@aplinecamps.com
Web site: www.alpinecamps.com
Operated by: Center for Reuniting Families, 42900 Jenks Lake Rd, Angelus Oaks, CA 92305 at (909) 794-3800

Group Rental Information
Site comments: $2 mil remodel-400 capacity, dorms w/bath-or sngls/dbls w/bath,4 meet lodges,56000 ac Big Pine Forest,lake,canoes,river. Group rental year round.
Seasons & Capacity: Spring 400, Winter 400

Facilities: A/V Equipment, Cabins, Dorm-Style, Food Service, Hiking Trails, Lake, Linens, Lodges, Meeting Rooms, Ocean, Playing Fields, Pool, River
Programs: Boating, Environmental Education, Swimming, Winter Sports (#3261)

Anaheim YMCA at Camp Arbolado ▲

Anaheim, CA
Activities: Archery, Arts/Crafts, Bicycling/Biking, Challenge/Rope Courses, Sports — Field & Team, Swimming — Recreational, Team Building
Contact: Web site: www.anaheimymca.org
Operated by: Anaheim YMCA Resident Camping, 240 S Euclid Ave, Anaheim, CA 92802-1065 at (714) 635-9622 (#48611)

Anaheim YMCA at Camp Fox

(est 1975) ▲ 🚐

Anaheim, CA (Orange Co.); (714) 635-9622
Carolyn Poulos, Director

Camp comments: Camp Fox ages 13-18 on Catalina Island. Camp Miehana ages 7-12 San Bernardino, no mountains.
Activities: Archery, Canoeing, Challenge/Rope Courses, Climbing/Rappelling, Counselor Training (CIT), Performing Arts, Riflery, Sailing, Swimming — Instructional
Session lengths & capacity: 2 week sessions; 300 campers
Clientele & fees: coed 7-18; families; Fees: C ▲ 🐖
Contact: Carolyn Poulos, Camping Program Director at (714) 635-9622 ext. 105; fax: (714) 635-8151
e-mail: cpoulos@anaheimymca.org
Web site: www.anaheimymca.org
Operated by: Anaheim YMCA Resident Camping, 240 S Euclid Ave, Anaheim, CA 92802-1065 at (714) 635-9622 (#194)

Apple Canyon Center (est 1994) ⌂

Mountain Center, CA (Riverside Co.); (909) 659-4609
Contact: Brian Carter, Director at (800) 625-7295; fax: (310) 473-3338
e-mail: info@campronaldmcdonald.org
Web site: www.campronaldmcdonald.org
Operated by: Ronald McDonald For Good Times, 1954 Cotner Avenue, Los Angeles, CA 90024 at (310) 268-8488

Group Rental Information
Site comments: Camps, conferences, retreats and reunions. Located near Idyllwild. Kosher meals available.
Seasons & Capacity: Spring 200, Fall 200, Winter 200
Facilities: A/V Equipment, Cabins, Dorm-Style, Food Service, Hiking Trails, Lake, Playing Fields, Pool
Programs: Challenge/Ropes Course (#6801)

Astro Camp (est 1990) ▲

Idyllwild, CA (San Bernardino Co.); (909) 659-6062
Brian Windrope, Director

Camp comments: Explore the wonders of the universe. Qualified staff lead campers on high tech, science adventures in a mountain setting.
Activities: Academics, Aquatic Activities, Arts/Crafts, Bicycling/Biking, Challenge/Rope Courses, Model Rocketry, Team Building
Session lengths & capacity: June-August; 1 & 2 week sessions; 85 campers
Clientele & fees: coed 8-14; Fees: F ▲ 🐖
Contact: (909) 625-6194; fax: (909) 625-7305
e-mail: info@guideddiscoveries.org
Web site: www.guideddiscoveries.org
Operated by: Guided Discoveries Inc, PO Box 1360, Claremont, CA 91711 at (909) 625-6194 (#1371)

Athenian Sport Camp

(est 1995)

Danville, CA (Contra Costa Co.); (925) 837-5375
Rebecca Good, Director

Camp comments: Age appropiate, skill building, non-competitive sport camp, wkly field trips, sm classes, transportation & extended care
Activities: Aquatic Activities, Archery, Baseball/Softball, Basketball, Counselor Training (CIT), Field Trips, Football, Soccer, Sports — Field & Team, Tennis
Session lengths & capacity: June-August; 2 week sessions; 70 campers
Clientele & fees: coed 7-15; Fees: **C, D**
Contact: Sondra Vander Meer, Associate Director,Special Programs at (925) 837-5375; fax: (925) 831-1120
e-mail: sondra_vandermeer@athenian.org
Web site: www.athenian.org
Operated by: The Athenian School, 2100 Mt Diablo Scenic Blvd, Danville, CA 94506 at (825) 837-5375 (#32975)

Azalea Trails Girl Scout Camp

(est 1940)

Idyllwild, CA (Riverside Co.); (909) 659-3524
Royce Rowe, Director

Camp comments: You can hike, sing, cookout, ride horses, ski on pine needles & more at our rustic campsite. Non Girl Scouts are welcome
Activities: Arts/Crafts, Camping Skills/Outdoor Living, Challenge/Rope Courses, Counselor Training (CIT), Hiking, Horseback — Western, Leadership Development, Nature/Environment Studies
Session lengths & capacity: June-August; 1/2, 1 & 2 week sessions; 125 campers
Clientele & fees: girls 6-17; Fees: **B, C, D**
Contact: Loyce Rowe, Program Manager at (909) 307-6555; fax: (909) 307-6526
e-mail: lrowe@gssgc.org
Web site: www.gssgc.org
Operated by: GSC of San Gorgonio, 1751 Plum Ln, Redlands, CA 92374-4505 at (909) 307-6555

Group Rental Information
Site comments: Rustic mountain camp. Tent camp or sleep in the lodge. Hiking trails, fishing, & idylwild are near by on site activities incl. hiking, chal. course, and more.
Seasons & Capacity: Spring 100, Fall 100
Facilities: Hiking Trails, Kitchen Facilities, Lodges
Programs: Challenge/Ropes Course (#87)

Balboa Cub Day Camp (est 1947)

San Diego, CA (San Diego Co.); (619) 298-6121
Marylyn Kitchens, Director

Camp comments: Program is based on Cub Scout activities & advancement program but is not limited to Scouts. All boys welcome.
Activities: Archery, Arts/Crafts, Counselor Training (CIT), Nature/Environment Studies, Riflery
Session lengths & capacity: July-August; 7 week sessions; 60 campers
Clientele & fees: boys 8-11; Fees: **B**
Contact: Darrell Watkins, Asst Scout Executive at (619) 298-6121 ext. 252; fax: (619) 298-5036
e-mail: dwatkin@bsamail.org
Web site: www.bsadpc.org
Operated by: Desert Pacific Council BSA, 1207 Upas St, San Diego, CA 92103 at (619) 298-6121 (#7720)

Bar 717 Ranch/Camp Trinity

(est 1930)

Hayfork, CA (Trinity Co.); (530) 628-5992
Kent Collard, Director

Camp comments: Beautiful mountain ranch camp teaching responsibility for oneself & others in a noncompetitive supportive environment.

Activities: Archery, Arts/Crafts, Backpacking, Ceramics/Pottery, Farming/Ranching/Gardening, Horseback — Western, Leadership Development, Nature/Environment Studies, Swimming — Recreational, Wilderness Trips
Session lengths & capacity: May-September; 2, 3 & 4 week sessions; 120 campers
Clientele & fees: coed 8-16; families; seniors; single adults; Fees: **E**
Contact: Kent Collard, Director at (530) 628-5992; fax: (530) 628-9392
e-mail: camptrinity@bar717.com
Web site: www.bar717.com
Operated by: The Bar 717 Ranch Inc, Star Route Box 150, Hayfork, CA 96041 at (530) 628-5992

Group Rental Information
Site comments: Beautiful, secluded location. Historic working ranch surrounded by national forest. Environmental education curriculum available.
Seasons & Capacity: Spring 140, Summer 30, Fall 140
Facilities: Double Occupancy, Hiking Trails, Kitchen Facilities, Lodges, Meeting Rooms, River
Programs: Challenge/Ropes Course, Horseback Riding, Swimming (#357)

Bearskin Meadow Camp

(est 1938)

Kings Canyon National, CA (Sierra Co.); (559) 335-2403

Camp comments: Recreation & Education for children & families living with diabetes. In High Sierra wilderness setting
Activities: Arts/Crafts, Backpacking, Camping Skills/Outdoor Living, Ceramics/Pottery, Counselor Training (CIT), Fishing, Hiking, Nature/Environment Studies, Swimming — Recreational, Wilderness Trips
Session lengths & capacity: June-September; 1 & 2 week sessions; 140 campers
Clientele & fees: coed 8-17; families; single adults; Fees: **F**
Contact: (925) 680-4994; fax: (925) 680-4863
Web site: www.dyf.org
Operated by: Diabetic Youth Foundation, 5167 Clayton Rd Ste F, Concord, CA 94521 at (925) 680-4994 (#286)

Big Bear Presbyterian Conf Ctr

(est 1937)

Big Bear Lake, CA (San Bernardino Co.); (909) 866-2360
Alan Herendich, Director

Camp comments: 20 acres of pine forest on Big Bear Lake. Open year round for all gropus of 18 to 190. Lake, hiking, ski, archery, riding.
Activities: Archery, Arts/Crafts, Canoeing, Challenge/Rope Courses, Fishing, Hiking, Leadership Development, Nature/Environment Studies, Religious Study, Swimming — Recreational
Session lengths & capacity: 1/2 & 1 week sessions; 190 campers
Clientele & fees: coed 6-17; Fees: **C**
Contact: Ana Nava, Registrar at (909) 866-2360; fax: (909) 866-2857
e-mail: ananava@synod.org
Operated by: Synod Of Southern California, 1501 Wilshire Blvd, Los Angeles, CA 90017 at (213) 483-3840

Group Rental Information
Site comments: Mtn top-lake front site provides year round opportunities for fun & spiritual renewal.
Seasons & Capacity: Spring 185, Summer 185, Fall 185, Winter 185
Facilities: Dorm-Style, Double Occupancy, Food Service, Lake, Lodges, Meeting Rooms (#7331)

Bloomfield (est 1953)

Malibu, CA (Los Angeles Co.); (310) 457-5330
John Martinez, Director

Camp comments: A unique, social & recreational opportunity with peers. International & American counselors provide caring guidance.
Activities: Aerobics/Exercise, Challenge/Rope Courses, Counselor Training (CIT), Drama, Hiking, Horseback — Western, Leadership Development, Music, Nature/Environment Studies, Swimming — Recreational
Session lengths & capacity: June-August; 1 & 2 week sessions; 150 campers
Clientele & fees: boys 5-18; girls 5-18; coed 5-18; families; single adults; Fees: **A**
Contact: John Martinez, Acting Director of Recreation/Camping at (323) 295-4555; fax: (323) 296-0424
Web site: www.fjb.org
Operated by: Foundation For The Jr Blind, 5300 Angeles Vista Blvd, Los Angeles, CA 90043 at (213) 295-4555

Group Rental Information
Facilities: Cabins, Food Service, Hiking Trails, Meeting Rooms, Pool (#197)

Bothin (est 1950)

Fairfax, CA (Marin Co.); (415) 453-5047

Camp comments: Wooded hills close to city. Arts, sports, drama, nature, swimming, indoor sleeping. Weekend for women of all ages.
Activities: Arts/Crafts, Ceramics/Pottery, Counselor Training (CIT), Drama, Gymnastics, Hiking, Leadership Development, Nature/Environment Studies, Performing Arts, Swimming — Recreational
Session lengths & capacity: June-August; 1/2 & 1 week sessions; 150 campers
Clientele & fees: girls 5-17; families; Fees: **C**
Contact: Sharon Kosch, Director of Programming at (510) 562-8470; fax: (510) 633-7925
e-mail: sharon@sfbgirlscouts.org
Web site: www.girlscoutsbayarea.org
Operated by: San Francisco Bay GSC, PO Box 2249, 7700 Edgewater Dr Ste 340, Oakland, CA 94621-2249 at (510) 562-8470

Group Rental Information
Site comments: Wooded hills close to city. Unique site.
Seasons & Capacity: Spring 200, Fall 200, Winter 160
Facilities: Cabins, Dorm-Style, Hiking Trails, Kitchen Facilities, Lodges, Meeting Rooms, Pool, Tents (#2993)

Cahito (est 1957)

San Diego, CA (San Diego Co.); (619) 291-8985
Nancy Thompson, Director

Camp comments: A diverse day camp atmosphere, with activities and programs designed to meet the interest and need of each camper.
Activities: Archery, Arts/Crafts, Camping Skills/Outdoor Living, Drama, Hiking, Leadership Development, Music, Swimming — Recreational
Session lengths & capacity: 9 week sessions; 150 campers
Clientele & fees: boys 5-12; girls 5-12; coed 5-12; Fees: **B**
Contact: Nancy Thompson, Program Director at (619) 291-8985; fax: (619) 891-8988
Operated by: Camp Fire Boys and Girls, PO Box 3275, San Diego, CA 92163-1275 at (619) 291-8985 (#5770)

Cali Camp Summer Day Camp

(est 1955)

Topanga, CA (Los Angeles Co.); (310) 455-0404
Saul Rowen, Director

Camp comments: Select the weeks you desire, select the days each week, transportation in fee, swim daily, be in same group with friends
Activities: Archery, Arts/Crafts, Computer, Drama, Gymnastics, Horseback — Western, Nature/Environment Studies, Tennis
Session lengths & capacity: 500 campers
Clientele & fees: boys 3-13; girls 3-13; coed 3-13; Fees: C
Contact: Saul Rowen, Director/Owner at (310) 455-0404; fax: (310) 455-0408
e-mail: info@calicamp.com
Web site: www.calicamp.com
Operated by: Cali Camp Summer Day Camp, 1717 Old Topanga Canyon Rd, Topanga, CA 90290-3934 at (310) 455-0404 (#83)

Camp A Lot (est 1964)

San Diego, CA (San Diego Co.); (858) 874-3243
Lin Taylor, Director

Camp comments: Summer resident camp for children & adults with developmental disabilities.
Activities: Arts/Crafts, Counselor Training (CIT), Drama, Hiking, Music, Sports — Field & Team, Swimming — Recreational
Session lengths & capacity: 1 week sessions; 65 campers
Clientele & fees: coed 6-99; Fees: F
Contact: Lin Taylor, Camp Director at (858) 874-3243; fax: (858) 874-3250
e-mail: palsarc@pacbell.net
Operated by: The Arc of San Diego, 9285 Chesapeake Dr Ste 0, San Diego, CA 92123 at (858) 874-3243 (#3574)

Camp Alonim (est 1951)

Simi Valley, CA (Ventura Co.); (805) 582-4450
Edward A Gelb, Director

Camp comments: We explore Jewish ideas, concepts, and artistic forms of expression celebrating the many facts of Jewish life. Kosher.
Activities: Arts/Crafts, Dance, Drama, Hiking, Horseback — Western, Leadership Development, Music, Nature/Environment Studies, Soccer, Swimming — Recreational
Session lengths & capacity: 1, 2 & 3 week sessions; 215 campers
Clientele & fees: boys 7-15; girls 7-15; coed 7-15; Fees: B Fees: D

ICON LEGEND

- ☀ Day Camp
- ▲ Resident Camp
- ⌂ Facilities Available To Rent
- 🚐 Transportation Available
- 🐷 Financial Aid Available

FEE RANGES PER WEEK

A	$0-75
B	$75-200
C	$201-350
D	$351-500
E	$501-650
F	over $650

Contact: Edward A Gelb, Director at (805) 582-4450; fax: (805) 526-1398
e-mail: alonim@brandeis-bardin.org
Web site: www.alonim.com
Operated by: The Brandeis-Bardin Institute, 1101 Peppertree Lane, Simi Valley, CA 93064 at (805) 582-4450 (#125)

Camp Arbolado (est 1977)

Yorba Linda, CA (San Berdnardino Co.); (714) 777-9622
Walid Durr, Director

Camp comments: Plenty of financial assistance to give. All No. Orange Cnty kids, Corona, D-Bar. Great CIT Program. Excellent Staff! #1
Activities: Archery, Arts/Crafts, Bicycling/Biking, Canoeing, Challenge/Rope Courses, Counselor Training (CIT), Hiking, Leadership Development, Nature/Environment Studies, Swimming — Recreational
Session lengths & capacity: July-July; 1 week sessions; 160 campers
Clientele & fees: coed 8-17; families; Fees: C
Contact: Walid Durr, Camp Director at (714) 777-9622; fax: (714) 777-1903
Operated by: Yorba Linda Placentia Fam YMCA, 18333 Lemon Dr, Yorba Linda, CA 92887 at (714) 777-9622 (#6548)

Camp Arroyo Grande (est 1885)

Arroyo Grande, CA (San Luis Obispo Co.); (805) 489-4139
Contact: Sylvia Miller, Camp Reservationist at (626) 568-7333; fax: (626) 568-7331
e-mail: smiller@cal-pack.org
Web site: www.cal-pac.org
Operated by: California Pacific Annual Conf, 110 S Euclid Ave, PO Box 6006, Pasadena, CA 91102 at (626) 568-7330

Group Rental Information

Site comments: Central coast near Pismo Beach. Historic tabernacle, cabins, pool, outdoor worship/meditation area. Meal service, small groups may self cook. Tent and RV areas.
Seasons & Capacity: Spring 92, Summer 92, Fall 92, Winter 92
Facilities: A/V Equipment, Cabins, Dorm-Style, Food Service, Kitchen Facilities, Lodges, Meeting Rooms, Ocean, Pool, River (#66)

Camp Augusta (est 1931)

Nevada City, CA (Nevada Co.); (530) 265-3702
David Lawell, Director

Camp comments: Camp Augusta offers boys & girls the opportunity to learn through specialized camp activities in an outdoor environment.
Activities: Aquatic Activities, Archery, Arts/Crafts, Backpacking, Canoeing, Challenge/Rope Courses, Climbing/Rappelling, Drama, Horseback — Western, Swimming — Recreational
Session lengths & capacity: April-October; 1, 2 & 3 week sessions; 100 campers
Clientele & fees: coed 8-17; families; seniors; single adults; Fees: E
Contact: David Lawell, Camp Director at (530) 265-3702; fax: (530) 265-3527
e-mail: dave@campaugusta.org
Web site: www.campaugusta.org
Operated by: Camp Augusta Inc, 17530 Lake Vera Road, Nevada City, CA 95959 at (530) 265-3702

Group Rental Information

Site comments: Rental to groups of 40-120. Cabins, lake, hot showers, flush toilets, ropes course, program and support staff.
Seasons & Capacity: Spring 110, Summer 110, Fall 110
Facilities: Cabins, Food Service, Hiking Trails, Lake, Meeting Rooms, River
Programs: Boating (#3577)

Camp Cedar Glen (est 1946)

Julian, CA (San Diego Co.); (760) 765-0477
Contact: Sylvia Miller, Camp Reservationist at (626) 568-7333; fax: (626) 568-7331
e-mail: smiller@cal-pac.org
Web site: www.cal-pac.org
Operated by: California Pacific Annual Conf, 110 S Euclid Ave, PO Box 6006, Pasadena, CA 91102 at (626) 568-7330

Group Rental Information

Site comments: Outdoor fun among the cedars! Near charming village of Julian. Small and large groups, self-cooking or meal service, hiking, swimming, unspoiled natural beauty.
Seasons & Capacity: Spring 151, Summer 151, Fall 151, Winter 151
Facilities: A/V Equipment, Cabins, Dorm-Style, Food Service, Hiking Trails, Kitchen Facilities, Lodges, Meeting Rooms, Playing Fields, Pool
Programs: Swimming (#7534)

Camp Colby (est 1945)

Palmdale, CA (Los Angeles Co.); (626) 792-2296
Contact: Sylvia Miller, Reservationist at (626) 568-7333; fax: (626) 568-7331
e-mail: smiller@cal-pac.org
Web site: www.cal-pac.org
Operated by: California Pacific Annual Conf, 110 S Euclid Ave, PO Box 6006, Pasadena, CA 91102 at (626) 568-7330

Group Rental Information

Site comments: Lush, secluded setting along Coldwater Creek in Angeles Forest. Cabins, dorms, museum, large dining and meeting areas. Meal service. One hour from Los Angeles.
Seasons & Capacity: Spring 177, Summer 177, Fall 177, Winter 177
Facilities: A/V Equipment, Cabins, Dorm-Style, Double Occupancy, Food Service, Hiking Trails, Kitchen Facilities, Lodges, Meeting Rooms, Pool, River (#138)

Camp Concord (est 1967)

South Lake Tahoe, CA (El Dorado Co.); (530) 541-1203
Brian Wills, Director

Camp comments: Lake Tahoe's best resident camping in a safe, fun, growth oriented environment. Superior staff, incredible locations!
Activities: Aquatic Activities, Archery, Arts/Crafts, Canoeing, Counselor Training (CIT), Field Trips, Hiking, Rafting, Swimming — Recreational
Session lengths & capacity: June-August; 1 week sessions; 100 campers
Clientele & fees: coed 8-14; families; Fees: C
Contact: General Info. Registration, Camp Registration Staff at (925) 671-3273; fax: (925) 671-3449
e-mail: bwills@ci.concord.ca.us
Operated by: City of Concord Leisure Serv, 1950 Parkside Dr MS 11, Concord, CA 94519 at (925) 671-3202

Group Rental Information

Site comments: Incredible Lake Tahoe location available to groups from 20 to 220. Full service main lodge serves delicious meals with adjacent meeting room and amenities.
Seasons & Capacity: Spring 200, Summer 200, Fall 200
Facilities: Cabins, Double Occupancy, Food Service, Hiking Trails, Kitchen Facilities, Lake, Lodges, Meeting Rooms, River
Programs: Boating, Challenge/Ropes Course, Horseback Riding, Swimming (#329)

Camp Conrad Chinnock

(est 1958)

Los Angeles, CA (San Diego Co.); (323) 966-2890
Rocky Wilson, Director

Camp comments: Camp designed for youth with diabetes, fun camp experiences including swimming & hiking in safe, nurturing atmosphere.
Activities: Arts/Crafts, Backpacking, Bicycling/Biking, Ceramics/Pottery, Counselor Training (CIT), Drama, Hiking, Nature/Environment Studies, Swimming — Recreational
Session lengths & capacity: 1 & 2 week sessions; 125 campers
Clientele & fees: boys 7-16; girls 7-16; coed 7-16; families; Fees: **D**
Contact: Tamara Smith, Director, Program Services at (323) 966-2890 ext. 244; fax: (323) 966-2790
Web site: www.dys.org
Operated by: Diabetic Youth Services, 6300 Wilshire Blvd 100, Los Angeles, CA 90048 at (323) 966-2890

Group Rental Information
Facilities: Cabins, Dorm-Style, Food Service, Kitchen Facilities, Lodges, Meeting Rooms, Pool (#122)

Camp Del Corazon Inc (est 1995)

Los Angeles, CA; (818) 754-0312

Camp comments: A free nonprofit camp for children with heart disease or with a history of heart disease. Our camp is held on beautiful Catalina Island in California.
Activities: Archery, Arts/Crafts, Boating, Canoeing, Challenge/Rope Courses, Climbing/Rappelling, Kayaking, Sports — Field & Team, Team Building, Tennis
Contact: Web site: www.campdelcorazon.org
Operated by: Camp Del Corazon Inc, 5655 Halbrent Ave 10, Van Nuys, CA 91411 at (818) 901-0323 (#30594)

Camp Eaton

Pasadena, CA (Los Angeles Co.); (626) 351-8815
Operated by: San Gabriel Valley Council Boy, 3450 Sierra Madre Blvd, Pasadena, CA 91107 at (626) 351-8815

Group Rental Information
Facilities: A/V Equipment, Cabins, Dorm-Style, Food Service, Hiking Trails, Lodges, Meeting Rooms, Playing Fields, Pool
Programs: Environmental Education, Swimming (#901432)

Camp Edwards (est 1927)

Angelus Oaks, CA (San Bernardino Co.); (909) 794-1702
Loren Werner, Director

Camp comments: Traditional YMCA program that focuses on Christian heritage of the YMCA in a rustic mountain setting.
Activities: Aquatic Activities, Archery, Basketball, Bicycling/Biking, Canoeing, Challenge/Rope Courses, Climbing/Rappelling, Hiking, International Culture, Performing Arts
Session lengths & capacity: 1/2 & 1 week sessions; 100 campers
Clientele & fees: coed 7-14; families; Fees: **B, C**
Contact: A.L. 'Alf' Ferreira, Camp Director at (909) 794-1702; fax: (909) 794-3157
e-mail: campedwards@pcinternet.net
Operated by: YMCA Movin-On Day Camp, 16 E Olive St, Redlands, CA 92373 at (909) 793-2957

Group Rental Information
Site comments: Traditional YMCA program that focuses on Christian heritage of the YMCA in a rustic mountain setting.
Seasons & Capacity: Spring 140, Summer 130, Fall 140, Winter 140

Facilities: Cabins, Food Service, Hiking Trails, Lake, Lodges
Programs: Challenge/Ropes Course (#192)

Camp Forrest (est 1996)

Joshua Tree, CA; (760) 320-7151
Dorie Polizzo, Director

Camp comments: We offer an integrated camp expereince with disabled & able-bodied campers in a unique desert surrounding. Explore abilities while overcoming social boundries.
Activities: Aquatic Activities, Archery, Arts/Crafts, Camping Skills/Outdoor Living, Challenge/Rope Courses, Counselor Training (CIT), International Culture, Leadership Development, Nature/Environment Studies, Team Building
Session lengths & capacity: June-August; 1/2 & 1 week sessions; 36 campers
Clientele & fees: coed 7-25; Fees: **A**
Contact: Dorie Polizzo, Camp Director at (760) 366-8129; fax: (760) 366-0146
e-mail: angelviewcamp@aol.com
Web site: www.angelview.org
Operated by: Angel View, 12379 Miracle Hill Rd, Desert Hot Springs, CA 92240 at (760) 329-6471

Group Rental Information
Site comments: Camp Forrest is available for group rentals & also hosts family retreats & theme retreats during the traditional school year.
Seasons & Capacity: Spring 48, Fall 48, Winter 48
Facilities: Cabins, Food Service, Hiking Trails, Meeting Rooms, Playing Fields, Pool
Programs: Challenge/Ropes Course, Environmental Education, Swimming (#30981)

Camp Funtime (est 1958)

Encino, CA (Los Angeles Co.); (818) 789-8405
Julie Blair, Director

Camp comments: Day camp offers warm supportive atmosphere for young campers. Special pre-teen adventure camp.
Activities: Arts/Crafts, Climbing/Rappelling, Counselor Training (CIT), Field Trips, Kayaking, Leadership Development, Nature/Environment Studies, Performing Arts, Sports — Field & Team, Swimming — Recreational
Session lengths & capacity: 4, 6 & 9 week sessions
Clientele & fees: coed 4-13; Fees: **C**
Contact: Julie Blair, Director at (818) 789-8405; fax: (818) 789-8405
e-mail: cmpfuntime@aol.com
Operated by: Westmarks Camp Funtime, 5461 Louise Ave, Encino, CA 91316 at (818) 789-8405 (#37)

Camp Gan Israel (est 1973)

San Diego, CA (San Diego Co.); (858) 566-1996
Rabbi David Smoller, Director

Camp comments: Campers make friends and learn about Jewish culture through games and activities in a fun-filled, enriching environment.
Activities: Arts/Crafts, Challenge/Rope Courses, Dance, Drama, Field Trips, Gymnastics, Music, Religious Study, Sports — Field & Team, Swimming — Recreational
Session lengths & capacity: 3 week sessions; 200 campers
Clientele & fees: coed 3-13; Fees: **B**
Contact: Rabbi Smoller, Director at (858) 566-1996; fax: (858) 547-8078
Operated by: CHABAD, 10785 Pomerado Rd, San Diego, CA 92131 at (858) 566-1996 (#4062)

Camp Gilmore (est 1968)

Calabasas, CA (Los Angeles Co.); (818) 222-6327
Don Mowery, Director

Camp comments: Christian camp serving inner city children primarily ages 7-12.

Activities: Aquatic Activities, Arts/Crafts, Basketball, Camping Skills/Outdoor Living, Challenge/Rope Courses, Football, Music, Soccer, Swimming — Recreational
Session lengths & capacity: June-August; 1 week sessions; 175 campers
Clientele & fees: coed 7-12; Fees: **B**
Contact: Don Mowery, Camp Administrator at (818) 222-6327; fax: (818) 222-6396
e-mail: dmowery@pacbell.net
Web site: www.campmtcrags.com
Operated by: The Salvation Army, 900 W James Wood Blvd, Los Angeles, CA 90015 at (213) 896-9160

Group Rental Information
Facilities: A/V Equipment, Cabins, Dorm-Style, Double Occupancy, Food Service, Hiking Trails, Kitchen Facilities, Linens, Lodges, Meeting Rooms, River
Programs: Challenge/Ropes Course, Environmental Education, Swimming (#33)

Camp Good in the Hood (est 1999)

Los Angeles, CA; (323) 935-8127

Camp comments: We offer a safe, caring place to play, build community, & experience love & acceptance through this camp ministry.
Activities: Arts/Crafts, Computer, Counselor Training (CIT), Dance, Drama, Field Trips, Music, Performing Arts, Swimming — Recreational
Session lengths & capacity: June-August; 1 week sessions; 120 campers
Clientele & fees: coed 5-17; Fees: **B**
Contact: Chris Haygood, Director at (323) 935-8127; fax: (323) 939-3547
e-mail: haygoodfun@aol.com
Web site: www.stagathas.org
Operated by: St Agatha Parish Family, 2646 S Mansfield Ave, Los Angeles, CA 90016 at (323) 935-8127 (#32711)

Camp Harmony (est 1990)

Malibu, CA
Robin G Segal, Director

Camp comments: An overnight camping experience for homeless & underprivileged children giving them a break from their daily struggles.
Activities: Climbing/Rappelling, Community Service, Counselor Training (CIT), Dance, Drama, Hiking, Leadership Development, Sports — Field & Team, Swimming — Recreational, Team Building
Session lengths & capacity: 1 week sessions; 200 campers
Clientele & fees: coed 7-10; Fees: **A**
Contact: Robin G Segal MSW, Executive Director at (310) 273-4775; fax: (310) 275-5786
Operated by: United In Harmony, 270 N Cannon Dr 1087, Beverly Hills, CA 90210 at (310) 273-4775 (#19145)

Camp Hillcrest Sports/Day Camp (est 1984)

Granada Hills, CA (Los Angeles Co.); (818) 368-7071
Heidi Ryan & Joshua Kendrick, Director

Camp comments: A Christian camp for children ages 5-14 focusing on various spiritual, emotional, social, and physical experiences.
Activities: Arts/Crafts, Baseball/Softball, Basketball, Field Trips, Football, Hockey, Religious Study, Soccer, Sports — Field & Team, Tennis
Session lengths & capacity: June-August
Clientele & fees: coed 5-14; Fees: **A**
Contact: Mrs Heidi Ryan, Day Camp Director at (818) 368-7071; fax: (818) 363-4455
Operated by: Hillcrest Christian School, 17531 Rinaldi St, Granada Hills, CA 91344-3399 at (818) 368-7071 (#32717)

Camp Hollywoodland (est 1925) ⚠ 🏠

Hollywood, CA (Los Angeles Co.); (323) 467-7193
Robin Smith, Director

Camp comments: Traditional camp for girls 6-17 with emphasis on nature, crafts and social skills. Parent-child weekends in the spring.
Activities: Archery, Arts/Crafts, Camping Skills/Outdoor Living, Ceramics/Pottery, Challenge/Rope Courses, Counselor Training (CIT), Drama, Field Trips, Nature/Environment Studies, Swimming — Recreational
Session lengths & capacity: 1 week sessions; 150 campers
Clientele & fees: girls 6-17; coed 4-7; families; Fees: B ⚠
Contact: Robin Smith, Program Director at (323) 467-7193; fax: (323) 957-1526
Operated by: City of LA Dept Rec & Parks, City Wide Serv Div - Camp Sec, 3900 W Chevy Chase Dr, Los Angeles, CA 90039 at (213) 485-4853 (#112)

Camp James (est 1997) ☀

Irvine, CA; (949) 585-0464
Theresa Collins, Director

Camp comments: Offers kids a summer of fun, packed with adventure; with convenient, flexible scheduling for busy parents.
Activities: Archery, Arts/Crafts, Climbing/Rappelling, Counselor Training (CIT), Dance, Nature/Environment Studies, Sports — Field & Team, Swimming — Recreational
Session lengths & capacity: June-August; 9 week sessions; 300 campers
Clientele & fees: coed 4-15; Fees: B ☀
Contact: Scottie Roach, Camp Director at (714) 239-6110; fax: (949) 585-0473
Web site: www.campjames.com
Operated by: James Productions Inc, 8790 Irvine Center Dr, Irvine, CA 92618 at (949) 585-0464 (#2319)

Camp Jaycee (est 1947) ☀ 🚐

LaJolla, CA; (858) 457-3030
Sandy Siperstein Rafner, Director

Camp comments: From 18-months to 11th grade, we offer everything from traditional camps to sports, specialty, theatre and teen camps.
Activities: Arts/Crafts, Basketball, Counselor Training (CIT), Drama, Field Trips, Music, Performing Arts, Sports — Field & Team, Swimming — Instructional, Swimming — Recreational
Session lengths & capacity: June-August; 1, 2, 4, 6 & 8 week sessions

ICON LEGEND

☀ Day Camp
⚠ Resident Camp
🏠 Facilities Available To Rent
🚐 Transportation Available
🐷 Financial Aid Available

FEE RANGES PER WEEK

A	$0-75
B	$75-200
C	$201-350
D	$351-500
E	$501-650
F	over $650

Clientele & fees: 🐷
Contact: Sandy Siperstein Rafner, Camp Jaycee Director at (858) 457-3030;
e-mail: sandysr@lfjcc.com
Web site: www.lfjcc.org
Operated by: Lawrence Family Jewish Comm Ce, 4126 Executive Street, LaJolla, CA 92037-1338 at (858) 457-3030 (#3402)

Camp Joan Mier (est 1960) ⚠ 🏠 🚐

Malibu, CA (Ventura Co.); (310) 457-9863
Kelly Privitt, Director

Camp comments: All facilities are wheelchair accessible.
Activities: Aquatic Activities, Archery, Arts/Crafts, Basketball, Dance, Drama, Horseback — Western, Music, Swimming — Recreational, Team Building
Session lengths & capacity: June-August; 1 week sessions; 50 campers
Clientele & fees: coed 7-70; Fees: F ⚠ 🐷
Contact: Kelly Privitt, Camp Director at (310) 457-9863; fax: (310) 457-6374
e-mail: kprivitt@abilityfirst.org
Web site: www.abilityfirst.org
Operated by: Ability First, 2555 E Colorado Boulevard, Pasadena, CA 91107-3745 at (626) 396-1010

Group Rental Information
Site comments: All facilities are wheelchair accessible.
Seasons & Capacity: Spring 100, Fall 100, Winter 84
Facilities: Cabins, Dorm-Style, Food Service, Hiking Trails, Meeting Rooms, Ocean, Pool (#130)

Camp Keystone (est 1995) ☀ 🚐

Agoura Hills, CA (Los Angeles Co.); (818) 889-2224
Larry Klein, Director

Camp comments: Camp Keystone is the complete camp that is completely for kids!!Call for brochure.
Activities: Archery, Arts/Crafts, Horseback — Western, Martial Arts, Nature/Environment Studies, Sports — Field & Team, Swimming — Recreational
Session lengths & capacity: 2, 4 & 9 week sessions
Clientele & fees: boys 3-14; girls 3-14; coed 3-13; Fees: C ☀
Contact: Larry Klein, Director at (818) 889-2224; fax: (818) 889-2416
Web site: www.campkeystone.com
Operated by: Camp Keystone, 2854 Triunfo Canyon Rd, Agoura, CA 91301 at (818) 889-2224 (#3823)

Camp Kids Inc ☀

Fresno, CA (Fresno Co.); (559) 298-9256
Activities: Horseback — Western, Swimming — Recreational
Operated by: Kids Inc, 7172 N Cedar Ave, Fresno, CA 93720 at (559) 298-9256 (#45556)

Camp Kinneret Day Camp
(est 1954) ☀ 🚐

Agoura, CA (Los Angeles Co.); (818) 706-8255
Harold Gordon, Director

Camp comments: Caring tradition builds confidence & esteem through fun, group centered program. Transportation provided.
Activities: Archery, Arts/Crafts, Challenge/Rope Courses, Horseback — Western, Leadership Development, Music, Nature/Environment Studies, Sports — Field & Team, Swimming — Instructional, Swimming — Recreational
Session lengths & capacity: June-August; 3, 4, 5 & 9 week sessions; 310 campers
Clientele & fees: coed 4-14; Fees: B, C, D ☀
Contact: Harold Gordon, Director at (818) 706-8255; fax: (818) 865-6262
e-mail: info@campkinneret.com

Operated by: Camp Kinneret Day Camp, PO Box 329, Agoura, CA 91376 at (818) 706-8255 (#184)

Camp Kochav at the JCCSF
(est 1877) ☀

San Francisco, CA (San Francisco Co.); (415) 292-1265

Camp comments: Open to all faiths & backgrounds. Four 2-week sessions. Swimming, overnights, sports, art, adventure challenge. Located in the Presidio National Park.
Activities: Aquatic Activities, Arts/Crafts, Camping Skills/Outdoor Living, Counselor Training (CIT), Field Trips, Leadership Development, Nature/Environment Studies, Sports — Field & Team, Swimming — Recreational, Team Building
Session lengths & capacity: 1 & 2 week sessions; 175 campers
Clientele & fees: coed 4-14; Fees: C ☀ 🚐
Contact: Alexandra Brucker, Director at (415) 750-1760; fax: (415) 346-4556
Operated by: Camp Kochav Jewish Comm Ctr, 1808 Wedemeyer St, San Francisco, CA 94129 (#2046)

Camp Krem Camping Unlimited
(est 1957) ⚠ 🏠 🚐

Boulder Creek, CA (Santa Cruz Co.); (510) 222-6662
Leon Wong, Director

Camp comments: Santa Cruz Mountains, residential summer camp for children and adults with disabilities. Traditional, free-choice programs, outddor and travel camp.
Activities: Aquatic Activities, Arts/Crafts, Camping Skills/Outdoor Living, Field Trips, Hiking, Music, Nature/Environment Studies, Sports — Field & Team, Swimming — Recreational, Travel/Tour
Session lengths & capacity: June-August; 1 & 2 week sessions; 125 campers
Clientele & fees: coed 5-70; Fees: B ☀
Fees: E ⚠ 🐷
Contact: Leon Wong, Director at (510) 222-6662; fax: (510) 223-3046
e-mail: campkrem@campingunlimited.com
Operated by: Camping Unltd for Children/Adt, PO Box 20774, El Sobrante, CA 94820 at (510) 222-6662

Group Rental Information
Seasons & Capacity: Spring 200, Fall 200, Winter 200
Facilities: Cabins, Hiking Trails, Kitchen Facilities, Meeting Rooms, Pool (#380)

Camp La Jolla (est 1979) ⚠

LaJolla, CA (San Diego Co.); (619) 435-7990
Nancy Lenhart, Director

Camp comments: Weight loss & fitness, beautiful beach setting. Exclusive facilities. Caring, specialized staff. Free follow-up. FUN!
Activities: Aerobics/Exercise, Basketball, Bicycling/Biking, Dance, Field Trips, Kayaking, Soccer, Sports — Field & Team, Tennis
Session lengths & capacity: June-August; 4, 7 & 9 week sessions; 250 campers
Clientele & fees: boys 8-16; girls 8-17; coed 8-16; families; seniors; single adults; Fees: F ⚠
Contact: Nancy Lenhart, Director & Founder at (800) 825-8746; fax: (619) 435-8188
e-mail: camplj@aol.com
Web site: www.camplajolla.com
Operated by: Camp La Jolla, 176 C Avenue, Coronado, CA 92118 at (619) 435-7990 (#3917)

Camp Lakota (est 1949) ⛺ 🏠

Frazier Park, CA (Kern Co.); (805) 245-3360

Camp comments: Beautiful mountain camp, sleep under the stars. Excellent horseback and leadership programs. Heated pool.
Activities: Aquatic Activities, Arts/Crafts, Backpacking, Camping Skills/Outdoor Living, Counselor Training (CIT), Hiking, Horseback — Western, Performing Arts, Swimming — Recreational, Travel/Tour
Session lengths & capacity: June-August; 1/2, 1 & 2 week sessions; 130 campers
Clientele & fees: girls 7-17; Fees: B, C, D ⛺
Contact: Constance Scharff, Program and Property Director at (818) 886-1801 ext. 31; fax: (818) 407-4840
e-mail: csharff@sfvgsc.org
Web site: www.sfvgsc.org
Operated by: SanFernando Valley GSC, 9421 Winnetka Ave, Chatsworth, CA 91311 at (818) 886-1801

Group Rental Information
Site comments: Pine forest environment near ski, hiking trails.Facilities to board horses during rental.In Natl forest 5800' elevation.
Seasons & Capacity: Spring 200, Fall 200, Winter 120
Facilities: Cabins, Double Occupancy, Food Service, Hiking Trails, Kitchen Facilities, Lodges
Programs: Environmental Education (#111)

Camp Laurel Foundation Inc

(est 1993) ⛺ 🚗

Los Angeles, CA (San Bernardino Co.); (323) 653-5005
Margot Andrew, Director

Camp comments: Camp Laurel is a camp for children living with HIV/AIDS. Camp Laurel strives to increase each child's self-esteem and self-worth.
Activities: Archery, Arts/Crafts, Backpacking, Challenge/Rope Courses, Drama, Drawing/Painting, Hiking, Horseback — Western
Session lengths & capacity: 1/2 & 1 week sessions; 120 campers
Clientele & fees: boys 6-16; girls 6-16; coed 6-16; families; Fees: A ⛺ 🐷
Contact: Margot Andrew, Executive Director at (323) 653-5005; fax: (323) 653-0558
e-mail: info@camplaurel.org
Operated by: Camp Laurel Foundation Inc, PO Box 93204, Los Angeles, CA 90093 at (323) 653-5005 (#1897)

ICON LEGEND

☀   Day Camp

⛺   Resident Camp

🏠   Facilities Available To Rent

🚗   Transportation Available

🐷   Financial Aid Available

FEE RANGES PER WEEK

A $0-75

B $75-200

C $201-350

D $351-500

E $501-650

F   over $650

Camp Max Straus (est 1938) ⛺ 🏠 🚗

Glendale, CA (Los Angeles Co.); (818) 957-4900
Gabriel Leon, Director

Camp comments: Residential Summer Camp serving underprivileged children between ages 7-12 who primarily come from single parent homes. Open to alll races and denominations.
Activities: Archery, Arts/Crafts, Camping Skills/Outdoor Living, Ceramics/Pottery, Farming/Ranching/Gardening, Hiking, Horseback — Western, Music, Nature/Environment Studies, Swimming — Instructional
Session lengths & capacity: June-August; 1 & 2 week sessions; 120 campers
Clientele & fees: coed 7-12; Fees: A, B, C ⛺ 🐷
Contact: Gabriel Leon, Camp Director at (818) 957-4900; fax: (818) 957-5885
e-mail: campmax@aol.com
Web site: www.campmaxstraus.org
Operated by: Jewish Big Brothers Assn, Suite 600, 6505 Wilshire Blvd 6th FL, Los Angeles, CA 90048-4918 at (323) 761-8675

Group Rental Information
Site comments: Convenient to metro LA. Large meeting rooms. Available for weekends and mid-week use.
Seasons & Capacity: Spring 144, Summer 180, Fall 144, Winter 144
Facilities: Cabins, Dorm-Style, Double Occupancy, Food Service, Hiking Trails, Kitchen Facilities, Lodges, Meeting Rooms, River (#170)

Camp Mendocino (est 1930) ⛺ 🏠 🚗

Fort Bragg, CA (Mendocino Co.); (707) 459-6458
Rob Conolly, Director

Camp comments: Rustic setting in Cal Redwoods on Noyo River. Cabins, teepees focus low income youth 160 mile north of San Francisco.
Activities: Archery, Arts/Crafts, Boating, Challenge/Rope Courses, Hiking, Horseback — Western, Leadership Development, Nature/Environment Studies, Photography, Swimming — Recreational
Session lengths & capacity: June-August; 2 week sessions; 250 campers
Clientele & fees: coed 6-14; Fees: D ⛺ 🐷
Contact: Rob Conolly, Camp Manager at (415) 445-5440; fax: (415) 445-5435
e-mail: campmend@pacific.net
Web site: www.bgcsf.org
Operated by: Boys & Girls Club SanFrancisco, 235 Montgomery St Ste 480, San Francisco, CA 94104 at (415) 445-5437

Group Rental Information
Facilities: Cabins, Food Service, Hiking Trails, Kitchen Facilities, Lodges, Playing Fields, River
Programs: Boating, Swimming (#321)

Camp Menzies (est 1947) ⛺ 🚗

Arnold, CA (Calaveras Co.); (209) 795-2081
Joy Galloway, Director

Camp comments: Sierra Mt setting, traditional specialized programs open to all girls with emphasis on self-esteem, team bldg & values.
Activities: Archery, Backpacking, Camping Skills/Outdoor Living, Canoeing, Caving, Counselor Training (CIT), Drama, Hiking, International Culture, Nature/Environment Studies
Session lengths & capacity: June-August; 1/2 & 1 week sessions; 120 campers
Clientele & fees: girls 7-17; Fees: C, D ⛺ 🐷
Contact: Joy Galloway, Camp Director at (916) 638-4475 ext. 40; fax: (916) 638-8452
e-mail: joy_galloway@tdogs.org
Web site: www.tdogs.org
Operated by: Girl Scouts of Tierra del Oro, 3005 Gold Canal Dr, Rancho Cordova, CA 95741 at (916) 638-4475 (#9)

Camp Metro (est 1994) ☀ 🚗

San Jose, CA (Santa Clara Co.); (408) 287-4170
Marla Howard, Director

Camp comments: Safe, supportive atmosphere. Runs M-F, 8am-6pm. Special global theme, emphasis on cultural sharing and the environment.
Activities: Climbing/Rappelling, Gymnastics, Horseback — English, Horseback — Western, Nature/Environment Studies, Performing Arts, Skating, Sports — Field & Team, Swimming — Instructional, Swimming — Recreational
Session lengths & capacity: June-August; 1 week sessions; 130 campers
Clientele & fees: girls 6-17; Fees: C ☀ 🚗
Contact: Marla Howard, Camp Director at (408) 287-4170 ext. 258;
e-mail: mhoward@girlscoutsofscc.org
Web site: www.girlscoutsofscc.org
Operated by: GSC of Santa Clara County, 1310 S Bascom Avenue, San Jose, CA 95128 at (408) 287-4170 (#3017)

Camp Oakes-YMCA Grt Long Beach (est 1954) ⛺ 🏠 🚗

Big Bear City, CA (San Bernardino Co.); (909) 585-2020
Martin Chandler, Director

Camp comments: At Camp Oakes character counts: caring, honesty, respect and responsibility are pillars to live by. All are welcome.
Activities: Archery, Arts/Crafts, Bicycling/Biking, Canoeing, Challenge/Rope Courses, Horseback — Western, Nature/Environment Studies, Riflery, Sailing, Wilderness Trips
Session lengths & capacity: Year-round; 6 week sessions; 300 campers
Clientele & fees: coed 8-14; families; Fees: C ⛺ 🐷
Contact: YMCA Camping Services at (562) 496-2756; fax: (562) 425-1169
e-mail: camp@lbymca.org
Web site: www.lbymca.org
Operated by: YMCA Of Greater Long Beach, PO Box 90095, Long Beach, CA 90809-0995 at (562) 496-2756

Group Rental Information
Site comments: Camp conference center, outdoor education, youth, adult groups.
Seasons & Capacity: Spring 250, Summer 300, Fall 250, Winter 250
Facilities: Cabins, Dorm-Style, Food Service, Hiking Trails, Lake, Meeting Rooms
Programs: Boating (#72)

Camp Okizu (est 1982) ⛺ 🏠 🚗

Berry Creek, CA; (530) 589-6985
Suzanne Randall, Director

Camp comments: A special place for children with cancer and their siblings. Family weekends
Activities: Aquatic Activities, Archery, Camping Skills/Outdoor Living, Canoeing, Challenge/Rope Courses, Counselor Training (CIT), Fishing, Hiking, Sports — Field & Team, Swimming — Recreational
Session lengths & capacity: June-August; 1 week sessions; 150 campers
Clientele & fees: coed 6-17; families; Fees: A ⛺ 🐷
Contact: Suzanne Randall, Executive Director at (415) 382-9083; fax: (415) 382-8384
e-mail: okizu@aol.com
Web site: www.okizu.org
Operated by: Okizu Foundation, 8 Digital Dr #102, Novato, CA 94949 at (415) 382-9083

Group Rental Information
Seasons & Capacity: Spring 256, Summer 256, Fall 256
Facilities: Cabins, Food Service, Hiking Trails, Lake, Meeting Rooms, Playing Fields
Programs: Boating, Challenge/Ropes Course, Swimming (#6188)

Camp Oliver (est 1953) ⛺ 🏠

Descanso, CA (San Diego Co.); (619) 445-6736
Joe Hamilton, Director

Camp comments: Rustic setting gives camping experience for youth of all backgrounds. Living together, exploring nature, develop skills
Activities: Archery, Arts/Crafts, Camping Skills/Outdoor Living, Counselor Training (CIT), Drama, Hiking, Leadership Development, Nature/Environment Studies, Swimming — Recreational
Session lengths & capacity: June-August; 1 week sessions; 70 campers
Clientele & fees: girls 6-16; coed 6-16; families; Fees: C ⛺ 🐴
Contact: Joe Hamilton, Executive Director at (858) 492-9171; fax: (858) 874-2939
Operated by: Camp Oliver, PO Box 206, Descanso, CA 91916 at (619) 445-5949
Group Rental Information
Seasons & Capacity: Spring 100, Fall 100, Winter 100
Facilities: A/V Equipment, Cabins, Food Service, Hiking Trails, Kitchen Facilities, Playing Fields, Pool (#225)

Camp Osito Rancho

(est 1937) ⛺ 🏠 🚌

Big Bear Lake, CA (San Bernardino Co.); (323) 933-4700
Mary Barstow, Director

Camp comments: Girl Scout resident camp over 65 years of tradition, girl planned program in Big Bear Lake. Serves girls grades 2-12.
Activities: Archery, Bicycling/Biking, Boating, Camping Skills/Outdoor Living, Canoeing, Challenge/Rope Courses, Hiking, Horseback — Western, Leadership Development, Swimming — Recreational
Session lengths & capacity: June-August; 1 week sessions; 168 campers
Clientele & fees: girls 6-17; Fees: C ⛺
Contact: Mary Barstow, Outdoor Program Specialist at (323) 933-4700; fax: (323) 933-3527
e-mail: marybarstow@angeles.org
Web site: www.angeles.org
Operated by: Angeles GSC, 2525 Ocean Park Blvd, Santa Monica, CA 90405 at (310) 450-3720
Group Rental Information
Facilities: Dorm-Style, Hiking Trails, Kitchen Facilities, Lake, Lodges, Meeting Rooms, Tents (#101)

Camp Paivika (est 1947) ⛺ 🏠 🚌

Crestline, CA (San Bernardino Co.); (909) 338-1102
Kelly Kunsek, Director

Camp comments: All facilities are wheelchair accessible.
Activities: Archery, Arts/Crafts, Basketball, Hiking, Horseback — Western, Nature/Environment Studies, Swimming — Recreational
Session lengths & capacity: June-August; 1 week sessions; 50 campers
Clientele & fees: coed 7-70; Fees: F ⛺ 🐴
Contact: Kelly Kunsek, Director at (909) 338-1102; fax: (909) 338-2502
e-mail: kkunsek@abilityfirst.org
Web site: www.abilityfirst.org
Operated by: Ability First, 2555 E Colorado Boulevard, Pasadena, CA 91107-3745 at (626) 396-1010
Group Rental Information
Site comments: All facilities are wheelchair accessible.
Seasons & Capacity: Spring 84, Winter 84
Facilities: A/V Equipment, Cabins, Dorm-Style, Food Service, Hiking Trails, Lodges, Meeting Rooms, Pool
Programs: Horseback Riding, Swimming (#36)

Camp Pine Mountain (est 1991) ⛺ 🏠

Angelus Oaks, CA
Dave Thompson, Director
Activities: Arts/Crafts, Bicycling/Biking, Field Trips, Fishing, Hiking, Leadership Development, Nature/Environment Studies, Sports — Field & Team, Swimming — Recreational
Session lengths & capacity: June-August; 1 week sessions; 50 campers
Clientele & fees: boys 9-13; Fees: B ⛺ 🐴
Contact: Dave Thompson at (626) 442-5470; fax: (626) 442-8803
e-mail: bgcsgv@pacbellnet
Operated by: Boys&Girls Club San Gabriel VI, 2740 Mountain View Rd, El Monte, CA 91732 at (626) 442-5470
Group Rental Information
Seasons & Capacity: Spring 80, Summer 50, Fall 50, Winter 80
Facilities: Cabins, Dorm-Style, Food Service, Hiking Trails, Kitchen Facilities, Meeting Rooms, Pool
Programs: Swimming (#48694)

Camp Rainbow (est 1984) ⛺

Glendale, CA (Los Angeles Co.); (818) 957-4900
Joanne Borromeo, Director
Activities: Archery, Arts/Crafts, Baseball/Softball, Ceramics/Pottery, Drama, Hiking, Horseback — Western, Nature/Environment Studies, Swimming — Recreational
Session lengths & capacity: August-August; 1 week sessions; 90 campers
Clientele & fees: coed 7-17; Fees: A ⛺
Contact: Joanne Borromeo, Camp Director at (310) 423-3186; fax: (310) 967-1141
e-mail: joanne.borromed@cshs.org
Operated by: Amie Karen Cancer Fund, 6535 Wilshire Blvd 120, Los Angeles, CA 90048 at (323) 655-5977 (#5431)

Camp Ronald McDonald at Eagle ⛺ 🏠

Susanville, CA; (916) 825-3158
Vicky Flaig, Director
Activities: Aquatic Activities, Archery, Arts/Crafts, Drama, Sports — Field & Team
Contact: Web site: www.campronald.org
Operated by: Ronald McDonald House Charitie, 2555 49th Street, Sacramento, CA 95817 at (916) 734-4230
Group Rental Information
Site comments: Programs include: arts & crafts, outdoor ed, sports, drama.
Seasons & Capacity: Spring 120, Summer 120, Fall 120
Facilities: Cabins, Food Service, Hiking Trails, Lake, Meeting Rooms
Programs: Boating, Swimming (#1667)

Camp Ronald McDonald GoodTimes (est 1982) ⛺ 🚌

Mountain Center, CA (Riverside Co.); (909) 659-4609
Brian Crater, Director
Camp comments: Cost free, medically supervised, year-round camps for children with cancer & their families.
Activities: Archery, Arts/Crafts, Backpacking, Camping Skills/Outdoor Living, Ceramics/Pottery, Challenge/Rope Courses, Drama, Horseback — Western, Swimming — Recreational, Team Building
Session lengths & capacity: January-December; 1 week sessions; 100 campers
Clientele & fees: coed 7-18; families; Fees: A ⛺ 🐴
Contact: Brian Crater, Director at (800) 625-7295; fax: (310) 473-3338
e-mail: brian@campronaldmcdonald.org
Web site: www.campronaldmcdonald.org

Operated by: Ronald McDonald For Good Times, 1954 Cotner Avenue, Los Angeles, CA 90024 at (310) 268-8488 (#5430)

Camp Ross Relles 🏠

Nevada City, CA (Nevada Co.); (530) 265-4353
Operated by: United Camps Conf & Retreats, 912 Lootens Pl, San Rafael, CA 94901 at (415) 456-5102
Group Rental Information
Site comments: Borders Malakoff Diggins State Park. Access to Blair Lake. Owned by Optimist Foundation for Handicapped Camping, Inc.
Facilities: Cabins, Dorm-Style, Food Service, Hiking Trails, Meeting Rooms, Playing Fields, Pool
Programs: Swimming (#3267)

Camp Scherman (est 1968) ⛺ 🚌

Mountain Center, CA (Riverside Co.); (714) 979-7900
Joyce Knoll, Director

Camp comments: Located in the High Desert outside Palm Springs. Cabins, lodge, 2 lakes, pool & tents nestled below Pacific Crest Trail.
Activities: Archery, Arts/Crafts, Backpacking, Climbing/Rappelling, Counselor Training (CIT), Hiking, Horseback — Western, Sailing, Swimming — Recreational
Session lengths & capacity: June-August; 1/2, 1 & 2 weeks sessions; 350 campers
Clientele & fees: girls 7-17; Fees: B ⛺ 🐴
Contact: Joyce Knoll, Program Specialist at (714) 979-7900 ext. 353; fax: (714) 850-1043
e-mail: jknoll@gscoc.org
Web site: www.gscoc.org
Operated by: GSC Orange County, PO Box 3739, Costa Mesa, CA 92626-3739 at (714) 979-7900 (#7038)

Camp St Michael (est 1963) ⛺ 🚌

Leggett, CA; (707) 984-6877
Agnes J Bailey, Director

Camp comments: Spiritual growth, leadership development & an experience of Christian living through a rugged & rustic camping program
Activities: Arts/Crafts, Backpacking, Camping Skills/Outdoor Living, Challenge/Rope Courses, Climbing/Rappelling, Horseback — Western, Leadership Development, Nature/Environment Studies, Swimming — Recreational, Wilderness Trips
Session lengths & capacity: June-August; 1 week sessions; 80 campers
Clientele & fees: boys 10-15; girls 10-15; Fees: C ⛺ 🐴
Contact: Agnes J Bailey, Director at (707) 542-5761; fax: (707) 566-4665
e-mail: campwizard@earthlink.net
Operated by: Roman Catholic Dioc Santa Rosa, PO Box 1297, Santa Rosa, CA 95402 at (707) 545-7610 (#7649)

Camp Stevens (est 1952) ⛺ 🏠 🚌

Julian, CA (San Diego Co.); (760) 765-0028
Peter Bergstrom, Director

Camp comments: Program emphasizes community, discovery & creativity. Beautiful 130 acre wooded site at 4200' in the Cuyamaca Mountains.
Activities: Archery, Arts/Crafts, Backpacking, Camping Skills/Outdoor Living, Hiking, Leadership Development, Music, Nature/Environment Studies, Swimming — Recreational
Session lengths & capacity: June-August; 1 week sessions; 91 campers
Clientele & fees: coed 8-16; families; Fees: C ⛺ 🐴
Contact: Anne Thatcher, Program Director at (760) 765-0028; fax: (760) 765-0153
e-mail: info@campstevens.org
Web site: www.ladiocese.org

Operated by: The Episcopal Diocese of LA, PO Box 512164, Los Angeles, CA 90051 at (213) 482-2040

Group Rental Information
Seasons & Capacity: Spring 120, Fall 120, Winter 120
Facilities: A/V Equipment, Cabins, Dorm-Style, Food Service, Hiking Trails, Lodges, Meeting Rooms, Pool
Programs: Challenge/Ropes Course, Environmental Education, Swimming (#142)

Camp Sugar Pine (est 1950) ▲ ⌂ 🚌

Camp Connell, CA (Calaveras Co.)
Frances Brown, Director

Camp comments: Friendly mountain camp, Horseback riding, crafts, camping, skills, swimming, and pioneer crafts. Family camp also.
Activities: Archery, Arts/Crafts, Camping Skills/Outdoor Living, Challenge/Rope Courses, Hiking, Horseback — Western, Nature/Environment Studies, Swimming — Recreational, Team Building
Session lengths & capacity: June-August; 1/2 & 1 week sessions; 100 campers
Clientele & fees: girls 6-17; families; Fees: B, D ▲ 🐷
Contact: Sharon Kosch, Director of Program at (510) 562-8470; fax: (510) 633-7925
e-mail: sharon@sfbgirlscouts.org
Web site: www.girlscoutsbayarea.org
Operated by: San Francisco Bay GSC, PO Box 2249, 7700 Edgewater Dr Ste 340, Oakland, CA 94621-2249 at (510) 562-8470

Group Rental Information
Facilities: Cabins (#6598)

Camp Summertime (est 1965) ☀ 🚌

Malibu, CA (Los Angeles Co.); (818) 706-7335
Jennifer or Mark Greenblatt, Director

Camp comments: A traditional day camp offering door to door transportation. Located at Calamigos Ranch on 120 private acres with 2 ponds.
Activities: Archery, Arts/Crafts, Boating, Horseback — Western, Leadership Development, Swimming — Recreational
Session lengths & capacity: June-August; 4, 5 & 9 week sessions; 200 campers
Clientele & fees: coed 4-14; Fees: B, C ☀
Contact: Jennifer or Mark Greenblatt, Directors at (818) 706-7335; fax: (818) 706-3099
e-mail: info@campsummertime.com
Web site: www.campsummertime.com
Operated by: Camp Summertime, PO Box 420, Agoura Hills, CA 91376 at (818) 706-7335 (#6267)

ICON LEGEND

☀	Day Camp
▲	Resident Camp
⌂	Facilities Available To Rent
🚌	Transportation Available
🐷	Financial Aid Available

FEE RANGES PER WEEK

A	$0-75
B	$75-200
C	$201-350
D	$351-500
E	$501-650
F	over $650

Camp Sunchasers - Echo Park ☀

Los Angeles, CA (Los Angeles Co.); (213) 847-0096
Rosa G Manriquez IHM, Director

Camp comments: Sunchasers is a safe nurturing environment where kids can learn, grow and be themselves in a positive diverse community.
Activities: Academics, Arts/Crafts, Baseball/Softball, Basketball, Field Trips, Nature/Environment Studies, Sports — Field & Team, Swimming — Recreational
Session lengths & capacity: July-August; 1, 2, 4 & 8 week sessions; 60 campers
Clientele & fees: coed 6-14; Fees: B ☀
Contact: Rosa G Manriquez IHM, Sr Recreation Director II at (213) 847-0095; fax: (213) 250-8946
e-mail: echobythelake@aol.com
Operated by: City of Los Angeles, Depart of Recreation & Parks, 3900 Chevy Chase Dr, Los Angeles, CA 90039 at (213) 485-1310 (#39204)

Camp Tawonga (est 1925) ▲ 🚌

Groveland, CA (Tuolumne Co.); (209) 962-7459
Deborah Newbrun, Director

Camp comments: Gorgeous camp next to Yosemite National Park. River,lake,pool,backpacking,ropes course,Judaism,arts,music,dance.
Activities: Arts/Crafts, Backpacking, Ceramics/Pottery, Challenge/Rope Courses, Drama, Music, Nature/Environment Studies, Swimming — Recreational, Travel/Tour, Wilderness Trips
Session lengths & capacity: April-September; 1, 2 & 3 week sessions; 250 campers
Clientele & fees: coed 7-17; families; single adults; Fees: F ▲
Contact: Jennifer Hoenigsberg, Office Manager at (415) 543-2267; fax: (415) 543-5417
e-mail: info@tawonga.org
Web site: www.tawonga.org
Operated by: Tawonga JCC, 131 Steuart Street Ste 460, San Francisco, CA 94105 at (415) 543-2267 (#3043)

Camp Tecuya (est 1952) ▲ ⌂

Frazier Park, CA (Kern Co.); (661) 245-3597
Linda L Reed, Director

Camp comments: Beautiful pines. Rustic mountain setting. Fun, safe, exciting environment. Girls will make friends and learn about Girl Scouting.
Activities: Archery, Arts/Crafts, Backpacking, Camping Skills/Outdoor Living, Canoeing, Counselor Training (CIT), Horseback — Western, Leadership Development, Nature/Environment Studies, Swimming — Recreational
Session lengths & capacity: June-August; 1/2, 1 & 2 week sessions; 125 campers
Clientele & fees: girls 6-17; Fees: B, C ▲ 🐷
Contact: Linda L Reed, Assistant Executive Director at (805) 564-4848 ext. 126; fax: (805) 965-5441
Operated by: Girl Scouts of Tres Condados, PO Box 30187, Santa Barbara, CA 93130-0187 at (805) 564-4848

Group Rental Information
Site comments: Rustic setting. Great retreat location. Nature at her best.
Facilities: Cabins, Food Service, Hiking Trails, Lodges, Meeting Rooms, Tents (#7248)

Camp Unalayee (est 1949) ▲ 🚌

Callahan, CA (Trinity Co.); (650) 696-6313
Lowell Fitch, Director

Camp comments: Multicultural, backpacking, wilderness skills, canoeing, leadership training, rock climbing, arts & crafts, fun.

Activities: Aquatic Activities, Archery, Arts/Crafts, Backpacking, Camping Skills/Outdoor Living, Climbing/Rappelling, Counselor Training (CIT), Nature/Environment Studies, Swimming — Recreational, Wilderness Trips
Session lengths & capacity: July-August; 2 week sessions; 100 campers
Clientele & fees: coed 10-17; families; Fees: B, C, D ▲ 🚌
Contact: Lowell Fitch, Director at (650) 969-6313; e-mail: director@unalayee.org
Web site: www.unalayee.org
Operated by: Camp Unalayee Association, 3921 E Bayshore Rd, Palo Alto, CA 94303 at (650) 969-6313 (#305)

Camp United Peace Officers Aga (est 1988) ▲ 🚌

Angeles Oaks, CA (Riverside Co.); (909) 794-3800
Anthony Campbell, Director

Camp comments: Law Enforcement Education Community Working together for a safe environment.
Activities: Baseball/Softball, Drama, Hiking, Swimming — Recreational, Team Building
Session lengths & capacity: 1 week sessions; 300 campers
Clientele & fees: coed 8-15; Fees: B ▲ 🐷
Contact: Sgt Tony Campbell, Director at (213) 300-3870; fax: (626) 965-5311
Operated by: UPAC, Ctr for Pre-Uniting Families, PO Box 514303, Los Angeles, CA 90051 at (213) 300-3870 (#2472)

Camp Venture Creek ☀ ▲

Nevada City, CA (Nevada Co.); (530) 265-4498

Camp comments: Traditional summer camp with a focus on entrepreneurship. Open to boys and girls 8-14 from all walks of life. Scholarships available.
Activities: Aquatic Activities, Archery, Basketball, Boating, Challenge/Rope Courses, Leadership Development, Sports — Field & Team, Team Building
Session lengths & capacity: June-August; 1 & 2 week sessions
Clientele & fees: coed 8-19; Fees: B, C, D, E, F ☀ Fees: B, C, D, E, F ▲ 🐷
Contact: Patrick Eagle, Director at (530) 265-4498; e-mail: patrick@campventurecreek.com
Web site: www.campventurecreek.com
Operated by: Lynch Operating Foundation, 20864 Rector Rd, Nevada City, CA 95959 at (530) 265-4498 (#9815)

Camp Virginia (est 1958) ⌂

Julian, CA (San Diego Co.); (760) 765-0424
Contact: Sylvia Miller, Reservationist at (626) 568-7333; fax: (626) 568-7331
e-mail: smiller@cal-pac.org
Web site: www.cal-pac.org
Operated by: California Pacific Annual Conf, 110 S Euclid Ave, PO Box 6006, Pasadena, CA 91102 at (626) 568-7330

Group Rental Information
Site comments: Walk to Julian. Unique Conestoga and teepee cabins. Rustic camp, great for kids and youth. Meal service for self-cooking. Nature trail, pool, tent area.
Seasons & Capacity: Spring 50, Summer 50, Fall 50, Winter 50
Facilities: A/V Equipment, Cabins, Dorm-Style, Food Service, Hiking Trails, Kitchen Facilities, Lodges, Meeting Rooms, Playing Fields, Pool, River (#7533)

Camp Wasewagan

(est 1936) ⛺ ⌂ �

Angelus Oaks, CA; (909) 794-2910
Brenda Holley, Director

Camp comments: Coed program, mountain setting, traditional camp program plus aquatics and wilderness hikes. Leadership training.
Activities: Aquatic Activities, Archery, Arts/Crafts, Canoeing, Hiking, International Culture, Nature/Environment Studies, Swimming — Recreational
Session lengths & capacity: 1 & 2 week sessions; 140 campers
Clientele & fees: coed 6-17; families; Fees: B ⛺ 🐷
Contact: Brenda Holley, Executive Director at (626) 305-1200; fax: (626) 305-1205
e-mail: campfire@artsci.net
Web site: www.aol.hometown.com/CampWasewagan
Operated by: Camp Fire USA Foothills Cncl, 1446 E Washington Blvd, Pasadena, CA 91104 at (626) 794-6361

Group Rental Information
Site comments: Mountain facility, tall pines adjacent to river. Offers dining lodge, kitchen, pool, cabins, health lodge and hiking.
Seasons & Capacity: Spring 150, Fall 150, Winter 150
Facilities: Cabins, Hiking Trails, Kitchen Facilities, Lake, Pool, River (#40)

Camp Wasiu II (est 1988) ⛺ ⌂ 🚙

Sierra City, CA (Sierra Co.); (530) 862-1409
Frances Brown, Director

Camp comments: Creating opportunities for all girls to fulfill their dreams and reach their potential
Activities: Archery, Arts/Crafts, Backpacking, Camping Skills/Outdoor Living, Canoeing, Counselor Training (CIT), Hiking, Horseback — Western, Nature/Environment Studies, Swimming — Recreational
Session lengths & capacity: June-August; 1/2, 1 & 2 week sessions; 120 campers
Clientele & fees: girls 7-17; families; Fees: A, B, C ⛺ 🐷
Contact: Frances Brown, Camp Director at (775) 322-0642 ext. 24; fax: (775) 322-0701
e-mail: fbrown@gssn.org
Web site: www.gssn.org
Operated by: GS of the Sierra Nevada, 605 Washington Street, Reno, NV 89503 at (775) 332-0642 (#6556)

Camp Whittier (est 1989) ⛺ ⌂ 🚙

Santa Barbara, CA (Santa Barbara Co.); (805) 962-6776
Steve Roberts, Director

Camp comments: Camp Whittier is a 55 acre retreat center offering teambuilding, outdoor education & children's summer camp. Join us in the beautiful Santa Barbara Mountains!
Activities: Archery, Arts/Crafts, Camping Skills/Outdoor Living, Challenge/Rope Courses, Climbing/Rappelling, Counselor Training (CIT), Hiking, Leadership Development, Nature/Environment Studies, Team Building
Session lengths & capacity: 1 week sessions; 135 campers
Clientele & fees: boys 5-15; girls 5-15; coed 5-15; families; Fees: C ⛺ 🐷
Contact: Steve Roberts, Camp Director at (805) 962-6776; fax: (805) 693-1686
e-mail: campwhittier@aol.com
Web site: www.campwhittier.org
Operated by: United Boys And Girls Clubs, 2400 Hwy 154, Santa Barbara, CA 93105 at (805) 962-6776

Group Rental Information
Site comments: Full service/youth/adult set in oaks, quiet, private, specialize in challenge course/rock climbing & sweat lodges.
Seasons & Capacity: Spring 150, Summer 150, Fall 150, Winter 150
Facilities: Double Occupancy, Kitchen Facilities, Lodges (#169)

Camp Winnarainbow (est 1972) ⛺

Laytonville, CA (Mendocino Co.); (707) 984-6507
Wavy Gravy & Jahanara Romney, Director

Camp comments: Circus & Performing Arts Camp. Juggling, unicycle, trapeze and stilts. Tipi living. A lake with large water slide.
Activities: Aquatic Activities, Arts/Crafts, Clowning, Dance, Drama, Gymnastics, Martial Arts, Music, Nature/Environment Studies, Performing Arts
Session lengths & capacity: June-August; 1, 2 & 4 week sessions; 130 campers
Clientele & fees: coed 7-14; Fees: E ⛺ 🐷
Contact: Camp Winnarainbow at (510) 525-4304; fax: (510) 528-8775
e-mail: arainbow@mcn.com
Web site: www.campwinnarainbow.org
Operated by: Camp Winnarainbow, 1301 Henry St, Berkeley, CA 94709 at (510) 525-4304 (#6427)

Camp Wrightwood (est 1946) ⌂

Wrightwood, CA (San Bernardino Co.); (760) 249-3453
Contact: Web site: www.cal-pac.org
Operated by: California Pacific Annual Conf, 110 S Euclid Ave, PO Box 6006, Pasadena, CA 91102 at (626) 568-7330

Group Rental Information
Site comments: Easy drive, near ski area. Huddle hut chalet, lodge, cabins, meal service and self cooking. Large and small groups. Pool, volleyball, hiking trails, fire ring.
Seasons & Capacity: Spring 182, Summer 182, Fall 182, Winter 182
Facilities: A/V Equipment, Cabins, Dorm-Style, Food Service, Hiking Trails, Kitchen Facilities, Linens, Lodges, Meeting Rooms, Pool
Programs: Swimming, Winter Sports (#145)

Canyon Creek Sports Camp

(est 2001) ⛺ ⌂ 🚙

Lake Hughes, CA (Los Angeles Co.); (661) 724-9184
Daryl Moss, Nathalie Shartin, Jeff Robinson, Director

Camp comments: CCSC is one of the only sleep-away sports camps in California. Campers build confidence, independence and learn teamwork in a non-competitive envirnment.
Activities: Archery, Arts/Crafts, Baseball/Softball, Basketball, Challenge/Rope Courses, Sports — Field & Team, Waterskiing
Session lengths & capacity: June-August; 1 & 2 week sessions; 150 campers
Clientele & fees: boys 7-14; girls 7-14; coed 7-14; Fees: F ⛺
Contact: Daryl Moss & Nathalie Shartin, Camp Directors at (661) 734-9184; fax: (661) 724-9182
e-mail: dmoss@canyoncreeksportscamp.com
Web site: www.canyoncreeksportscamps.com
Operated by: Canyon Creek Properties LLC, 41600 Lake Hughes Rd, Lake Hughes, CA 93532 at (661) 724-9184

Group Rental Information
Site comments: Swimming, gokarts, golf, baseball, football, soccer, basketball, tennis, art, archery, challenge course/wall, innertubing, jetskiing, wakeboarding, hockey, more
Facilities: Cabins, Dorm-Style, Food Service, Hiking Trails, Lodges, Meeting Rooms, Playing Fields, Pool
Programs: Challenge/Ropes Course, Swimming (#12583)

Catalina Island Camps

(est 1926) ⛺ ⌂

Two Harbors, CA (Los Angeles Co.)
Tom & Maria Horner, Director

Camp comments: Fun and friends on Catalina Island.
Activities: Aquatic Activities, Archery, Arts/Crafts, Boating, Challenge/Rope Courses, Climbing/Rappelling, Leadership Development, Riflery, Sailing, Waterskiing
Session lengths & capacity: June-August; 1, 2 & 4 week sessions; 190 campers
Clientele & fees: coed 8-15; Fees: F ⛺
Contact: Tom & Maria Horner, Director at (626) 296-4040; fax: (626) 794-1401
e-mail: info@catalinaislandcamps.com
Web site: www.catalinaislandcamps.com
Operated by: Catalina Island Camps, PO Box 94146, Pasadena, CA 91109 at (626) 296-4040

Group Rental Information
Facilities: Cabins, Hiking Trails, Kitchen Facilities, Ocean
Programs: Boating, Challenge/Ropes Course, Environmental Education, Swimming (#7166)

Catalina Sea Camp (est 1978) ⛺

Avalon, CA (Los Angeles Co.); (310) 510-1622
Ross Turner, Director

Camp comments: Learn marine biology scuba diving underwater photo & video, mountain bike across Catalina Island and much more.
Activities: Academics, Aquatic Activities, Challenge/Rope Courses, Climbing/Rappelling, Hiking, Nature/Environment Studies, Sailing, SCUBA, Windsurfing
Session lengths & capacity: June-August; 1 & 3 week sessions; 220 campers
Clientele & fees: coed 8-17; Fees: F ⛺ 🐷
Contact: Stacy Garrett, Seacamp Registrar at (909) 625-6194; fax: (909) 625-7305
e-mail: info@guideddiscoveries.org
Web site: www.guideddiscoveries.org
Operated by: Guided Discoveries Inc, PO Box 1360, Claremont, CA 91711 at (909) 625-6194 (#2899)

Cazadero ⌂

Cazadero, CA (Sonoma Co.); (707) 632-5276
Rebecca Mapes, Director
Operated by: United Camps Conf & Retreats, 912 Lootens Pl, San Rafael, CA 94901 at (415) 456-5102

Group Rental Information
Site comments: Near Russian River, recreational activities available. Owned by United Church of Christ, No. CA/NV Conference.
Seasons & Capacity: Spring 195, Summer 195, Fall 195, Winter 66
Facilities: Cabins, Dorm-Style, Food Service, Hiking Trails, Kitchen Facilities, Lodges, Meeting Rooms, Playing Fields, Pool (#361)

Cedar Lake Camp (est 1955) ⌂

Big Bear Lake, CA (San Bernardino Co.); (909) 866-5714
Ron Robillard, Director
Contact: Ron Robillard, Site Manager at (909) 866-5714; fax: (909) 866-5715
e-mail: cedarlake@bbv.net
Operated by: Cedar Lake Christian Camp, PO Box 1568, Big Bear Lake, CA 92315-1568 at (909) 866-5714

Group Rental Information
Site comments: 270-acre facility, 7000' elevation, excellent programs.
Facilities: Cabins, Dorm-Style, Double Occupancy, Food Service, Hiking Trails, Kitchen Facilities, Lake, Lodges, Meeting Rooms, Tents
Programs: Boating, Challenge/Ropes Course, Environmental Education, Swimming (#7773)

Central YMCA Day Camps

(est 1867) ☀

San Jose, CA (Santa Clara Co.); (408) 298-1717
Sarah Lilley, Director

Camp comments: Age-segmented program. Extended hours. Weekly themes, field trips, overnights, sports & specialty camps.
Activities: Arts/Crafts, Basketball, Dance, Drama, Field Trips, Nature/Environment Studies, Performing Arts, Swimming — Instructional, Swimming — Recreational
Session lengths & capacity: June-August; 1 week sessions; 300 campers
Clientele & fees: boys 6-14; girls 6-14; coed 6-14; Fees: **B** ☀ 🐷
Contact: Sarah Lilley, Senior Program Director at (408) 298-1717; fax: (408) 298-3237
e-mail: slilley@scuymca.org
Web site: www.scvymca.org
Operated by: YMCA of Santa Clara Valley, 1922 The Alameda 3rd Fl, San Jose, CA 95126 at (408) 298-3888 (#5787)

Chameleon

☀

Oakland, CA
Jean Fahy, Director

Camp comments: Dynamic like a chameleon & designed to meet the needs of each girl. Full of laughter, fun, creativity & adventure. Open to all girls.
Activities: Arts/Crafts, Camping Skills/Outdoor Living, Dance, Drama, Field Trips, Horseback — Western, Kayaking, Leadership Development, Nature/Environment Studies, Swimming — Recreational
Session lengths & capacity: 1 week sessions
Clientele & fees: Fees: **B** ☀
Contact: Web site: www.girlscoutsbayarea.org
Operated by: San Francisco Bay GSC, PO Box 2249, 7700 Edgewater Dr Ste 340, Oakland, CA 94621-2249 at (510) 562-8470 (#44785)

Channel Islands YMCA-Redwood

▲

Miramonte, CA; (209) 335-2886
Activities: Aquatic Activities, Archery, Arts/Crafts, Baseball/Softball, Challenge/Rope Courses, Climbing/Rappelling, Fishing
Contact: Web site: www.ciymca.org
Operated by: Channel Islands YMCA, 36 Hitchcock Way, Santa Barbara, CA 93105 at (805) 687-7727 (#331)

ICON LEGEND

☀ Day Camp

▲ Resident Camp

🏠 Facilities Available To Rent

🚐 Transportation Available

🐷 Financial Aid Available

FEE RANGES PER WEEK

A	$0-75
B	$75-200
C	$201-350
D	$351-500
E	$501-650
F	over $650

Channel Isls Y Camp Arbolado

▲ 🚐

(est 1993)

Santa Barbara, CA (Santa Barbara Co.); (805) 687-7727
Jody Taylor, Director
Activities: Archery, Arts/Crafts, Bicycling/Biking, Camping Skills/Outdoor Living, Challenge/Rope Courses, Hiking, Music
Session lengths & capacity: June-August; 7 week sessions
Clientele & fees: boys 8-17; girls 8-17; families; Fees: **C** ▲
Contact: Crystal Morgan, Program Director at (805) 687-7727; fax: (805) 687-7568
e-mail: crystal@ciymca.org
Web site: www.ciymca.org
Operated by: Channel Islands YMCA, 36 Hitchcock Way, Santa Barbara, CA 93105 at (805) 687-7727 (#4206)

Cherith At Sky Meadows

▲

(est 1946)

Angelus Oaks, CA (San Bernardino Co.); (909) 866-9366
Sharon M Livingston, Director

Camp comments: A unique Christian camp, offering separate camping experiences for girls & boys.
Activities: Archery, Arts/Crafts, Bicycling/Biking, Camping Skills/Outdoor Living, Canoeing, Hiking, Horseback — Western, Nature/Environment Studies, Photography, Swimming — Recreational
Session lengths & capacity: July-August; 1 week sessions; 120 campers
Clientele & fees: boys 6-16; girls 6-16; coed 6-12; Fees: **C** ▲
Contact: Sharon M Livingston, Executive Director at (760) 949-8504; fax: (760) 949-8652
e-mail: kmpkerith@aol.com
Web site: www.campcherithca.org
Operated by: Cherith At Sky Meadows, PO Box 400609, Hesperia, CA 92340-0609 at (760) 949-8504 (#2994)

Cherry Valley (est 1920)

▲ 🏠 🚐

Avalon, CA (Los Angeles Co.); (310) 510-2895
Gary Jensen, Director

Camp comments: Premier Oceanfront, with emphasis on self-esteem, confidence, cooperating with others. BSA, non-BSA groups welcome.
Activities: Aquatic Activities, Archery, Boating, Camping Skills/Outdoor Living, Counselor Training (CIT), Kayaking, Nature/Environment Studies, Riflery, Sailing, SCUBA
Session lengths & capacity: March-November; 1/2 & 1 week sessions; 350 campers
Clientele & fees: boys 7-18; girls 7-18; coed 7-21; families; seniors; single adults; Fees: **B, C** ▲
Contact: Gary Jensen, Program Director at (626) 351-8815 ext. 227; fax: (626) 351-9149
e-mail: garyj@sgvcbsa.org
Operated by: San Gabriel Valley Council Boy, 3450 Sierra Madre Blvd, Pasadena, CA 91107 at (626) 351-8815

Group Rental Information

Facilities: Cabins, Kitchen Facilities, Ocean, Tents
Programs: Environmental Education (#149)

Circle V Ranch (est 1945)

▲ 🏠 🚐

Santa Barbara, CA (Santa Barbara Co.); (805) 688-5252
Ricardo A Garcia, Director

Camp comments: A lay organization whose mission is to serve children by providing outdoor experiences that build self-esteem.
Activities: Arts/Crafts, Basketball, Counselor Training (CIT), Drama, Hiking, Leadership Development, Nature/Environment Studies, Sports — Field & Team, Swimming — Recreational

Session lengths & capacity: July-August; 8 week sessions; 160 campers
Clientele & fees: coed 7-13; Fees: **C** ▲ 🐷
Contact: Ricardo A Garcia, Camp Director at (323) 224-6213; fax: (323) 225-4997
Web site: www.svdpla.org
Operated by: Soc of St Vincent de Paul LA, 210 North Ave 21, Los Angeles, CA 90031 at (323) 224-6287

Group Rental Information

Site comments: A natural outdoor setting provides a perfect background for a retreat or getaway. Wonderful place to escape the city.
Seasons & Capacity: Spring 150, Fall 150, Winter 150
Facilities: Cabins, Dorm-Style, Food Service, Hiking Trails, Kitchen Facilities, Lake, Lodges, Meeting Rooms, Ocean, Playing Fields, Pool, River (#155)

Citylife (est 1995)

☀

Los Angeles, CA (Los Angeles Co.); (213) 687-2267
Jacki Breger, Director

Camp comments: For teenage children of people who work and live in downtown Los Angeles, strong in the arts, culture & leadership.
Activities: Dance, Drama, Drawing/Painting, Field Trips, Leadership Development, Music, Performing Arts, Photography, Radio/TV/Video, Sports — Field & Team
Session lengths & capacity: July-August; 5 week sessions; 25 campers
Clientele & fees: coed 11-17; Fees: **A, B, C** ☀ 🐷
Contact: Jacki Breger, Director at (213) 687-2267; fax: (213) 687-2191
e-mail: jackibreger@earthlink.net
Operated by: CityLife - Community Partners, PO Box 712574, Los Angeles, CA 90071-7574 at (213) 687-2267 (#3804)

CityTeam Camp May-Mac

▲ 🏠 🚐

(est 1935)

Felton, CA (Santa Cruz Co.); (831) 335-3019
John Scott, Director

Camp comments: Resident camp dedicated to providing a safe, affordable, unforgettable camp experience. Biking, swimming, and more.
Activities: Aquatic Activities, Archery, Arts/Crafts, Basketball, Bicycling/Biking, Fishing, Hiking, Nature/Environment Studies, Swimming — Recreational
Session lengths & capacity: July-August; 1/2 & 1 week sessions; 96 campers
Clientele & fees: coed 6-14; Fees: **A** ▲ 🐷
Contact: Betty Scott, Conference Registrar at (831) 335-3019; fax: (831) 335-7146
e-mail: bscott@cityteam.org
Web site: www.cityteam.org
Operated by: CityTeam Ministries, PO Box 357, Felton, CA 95018 at (831) 335-3019

Group Rental Information

Site comments: Beautiful 178 acre mountain site. 10 minutes from ocean.
Seasons & Capacity: Spring 144, Summer 144, Fall 144, Winter 144
Facilities: A/V Equipment, Cabins, Double Occupancy, Food Service, Meeting Rooms, Playing Fields, Pool
Programs: Swimming (#274)

Cloverleaf Ranch (est 1947)

☀ ▲

Santa Rosa, CA (Sonoma Co.); (707) 545-5906
Michaelo F. Pezet, Director

Camp comments: Traditional camp w/riding, pool, mtn bikes, archery, tennis, ropes course, batting cage. Resident RN. Coed fun, safe & challenging.
Activities: Aquatic Activities, Archery, Baseball/Softball, Basketball, Bicycling/Biking, Challenge/Rope Courses, Horseback — Western, Kayaking, Riflery, Tennis

Session lengths & capacity: 1 & 2 week sessions; 130 campers
Clientele & fees: boys 7-15; girls 7-15; coed 7-15; Fees: F ▲
Contact: Ginger De Grange, Director/Owner at (707) 545-5906; fax: (707) 545-5908
Web site: www.campchannel.com/cloverleaf
Operated by: Cloverleaf Ranch, 3892 Old Redwood Way, Santa Rosa, CA 95403 at (707) 545-5906 (#323)

COC YMCA at Camp Oakes   ▲

Newport Beach, CA; (949) 642-9990
Tina Fisher, Director
Activities: Archery, Bicycling/Biking, Challenge/Rope Courses, Counselor Training (CIT), Hiking, Horseback — Western, Nature/Environment Studies, Riflery, Swimming — Recreational, Team Building
Contact: Web site: www.ymcaoc.net
Operated by: Central Orange Coast YMCA, 2300 University Dr, Newport Beach, CA 92660 at (949) 642-9990 (#11496)

COC YMCA Camp Ta Ta Pochon   ▲

Angelus Oaks, CA (Orange Co.); (909) 794-2927
Nguyen Tong, Director
Activities: Archery, Arts/Crafts, Basketball, Canoeing, Challenge/Rope Courses, Counselor Training (CIT), Leadership Development, Riflery, Swimming — Recreational
Session lengths & capacity: 1 week sessions
Clientele & fees: coed 8-16; Fees: C ▲
Contact: Nguyen Tong, Program Director at (949) 262-0503;
Web site: www.ymcaoc.net
Operated by: Central Orange Coast YMCA, 2300 University Dr, Newport Beach, CA 92660 at (949) 642-9990 (#3290)

Community Of The Great Commission   ⌂

Foresthill, CA (Placer Co.); (530) 367-2370
Operated by: United Camps Conf & Retreats, 912 Lootens Pl, San Rafael, CA 94901 at (415) 456-5102
Group Rental Information
Site comments: Easy access to American River, Tahoe National Forest, cross-country skiing. Owned by Christian Church of No.CA/NV.
Facilities: Cabins, Dorm-Style, Double Occupancy, Food Service, Lodges, Meeting Rooms, Pool (#318)

Copley YMCA Summer Day Camp (est 1954)   ☀

San Diego, CA (San Diego Co.); (619) 283-2251
Phillip Sammuli, Director
Camp comments: Day camp offers nurturing environment to help build self-esteem, & leadership qualities. Join the adventures at Copley.
Activities: Aquatic Activities, Basketball, Computer, Counselor Training (CIT), Dance, Drama, Field Trips, Hiking, Swimming — Instructional, Swimming — Recreational
Session lengths & capacity: 1 week sessions; 150 campers
Clientele & fees: boys 5-15; girls 5-15; coed 5-15; Fees: B ☀ 🐷
Contact: Phillip Sammuli, Program Director at (619) 283-2251; fax: (619) 283-7586
e-mail: psammuli@ymca.org
Operated by: YMCA of San Diego County, 4715 Viewridge Ave Ste 100, San Diego, CA 92123 at (619) 292-4034 (#221)

Coppercreek Camp (est 1965)   ▲ 🚐

Greenville, CA (Plumas Co.); (530) 284-7617
Lauren Lindskog Allen, Director
Camp comments: Noncompetitive. 50+ activities. Free choice. Our staff know every camper. Rustic setting in California's North Sierra.
Activities: Arts/Crafts, Backpacking, Challenge/Rope Courses, Drama, Horseback — English, Horseback — Western, Riflery, Swimming — Recreational, Waterskiing, Wilderness Trips
Session lengths & capacity: June-August; 1, 2 & 4 week sessions; 100 campers
Clientele & fees: coed 7-17; families; Fees: F ▲
Contact: Lynne Evarts, Director at (530) 284-7617; fax: (530) 284-7497
e-mail: lynne_evarts@coppercreek.com
Web site: www.coppercreek.com
Operated by: Coppercreek Camp Inc, PO Box 749, Greenville, CA 95947 at (800) 350-0006 (#7019)

Costanoan (est 1954)   ▲ ⌂

Cupertino, CA (Santa Clara Co.); (408) 867-1115
Susan Berry, Director
Camp comments: Costanoan is a residential, respite & recreational camp for children & adults with disabilities. Our mission is to help campers achieve greater self-sufficiency
Activities: Arts/Crafts, Camping Skills/Outdoor Living, Dance, Drama, Farming/Ranching/Gardening, Hiking, Horseback — Western, Music, Nature/Environment Studies, Swimming — Recreational
Session lengths & capacity: June-August; 1/2 & 1 week sessions; 120 campers
Clientele & fees: boys 5-90; girls 5-90; coed 5-90; Fees: F ▲ 🐷
Contact: Susan Berry, Camp Director at (408) 243-7861; fax: (408) 243-0452
e-mail: sberry@viaservices.org
Web site: www.viaservices.org
Operated by: VIA Rehabilitation Services, 2851 Park Ave, Santa Clara, CA 95050 at (408) 243-7861
Group Rental Information
Site comments: 30 min. from SJ. 45 min. SF. Perfect for group retreats.
Seasons & Capacity: Spring 120, Summer 120, Fall 120, Winter 120
Facilities: Dorm-Style, Food Service, Hiking Trails, Lodges, Meeting Rooms, Pool
Programs: Horseback Riding, Swimming (#298)

Cottontail Ranch Club

(est 1957)   ▲ ⌂
Calibases, CA (Los Angeles Co.); (818) 880-3700
Lynn Pedroza, Director
Camp comments: Adj. 2500 Malibu Creek State Park, 5 mi from Malibu Beach. Horseback, waterskiing, rock climbing, surfing, & mini bikes.
Activities: Archery, Climbing/Rappelling, Field Trips, Horseback — English, Horseback — Western, Sailing, Tennis, Waterskiing, Windsurfing
Session lengths & capacity: 2, 4, 6 & 8 week sessions; 230 campers
Clientele & fees: coed 6-16; Fees: F ▲
Contact: Tess Cassel, Receptionist at (818) 880-3700; fax: (818) 880-3714
e-mail: cottontail@earthlink.net
Operated by: Pepperdine Univ Cottontail Rnh, 1666 Las Virgenes Canyon Rd, Calabasas, CA 91302 at (818) 880-3700
Group Rental Information
Site comments: Adj. 2500 acres Malibu Creek State Park. Ideal for retreats.
Seasons & Capacity: Spring 250, Fall 250, Winter 250
Facilities: A/V Equipment, Cabins, Dorm-Style, Food Service, Hiking Trails, Kitchen Facilities, Lodges, Playing Fields, Pool, River
Programs: Environmental Education, Swimming (#131)

Coulter Pines North

(est 1912)   ▲ ⌂ 🚐
Wrightwood, CA (Los Angeles Co.); (760) 249-6193
Ray Werhan, Manager, Director
Camp comments: A fun oriented camp surrounded by the beautiful national forest. The YMCA camping program builds strong kids, strong families, and strong communities.
Activities: Aquatic Activities, Archery, Arts/Crafts, Canoeing, Challenge/Rope Courses, Counselor Training (CIT), Nature/Environment Studies, Swimming — Recreational, Team Building
Session lengths & capacity: June-September; 1 week sessions; 125 campers
Clientele & fees: coed 5-17; families; Fees: B, C ▲ 🐷
Contact: Matthew Lancey, Director of Camp Services at (626) 339-6221; fax: (626) 339-4594
e-mail: mlancey@mjci.com
Web site: www.sangabrielvalleyymca.org
Operated by: YMCA San Gabriel Valley Family, 412 E Rowland St, Covina, CA 91723 at (626) 339-6221
Group Rental Information
Site comments: Great location to hold retreats, family reunions, ski parties, or just have the time of your life. Camp is great for youth, churches, families, business & more.
Seasons & Capacity: Spring 125, Summer 125, Fall 125
Facilities: Cabins, Dorm-Style, Double Occupancy, Food Service, Hiking Trails, Kitchen Facilities, Lake, Meeting Rooms, Pool, Tents
Programs: Challenge/Ropes Course, Environmental Education, Swimming, Winter Sports (#13)

Council Day Camps (est 1933)   ☀

San Diego, CA (San Diego Co.); (619) 610-0784
Christine Dreifuss, Director
Camp comments: Girl Scout day camps and summer specials are exciting places for girls to experience new adventures.
Activities: Aquatic Activities, Drama, Field Trips, Horseback — English, Leadership Development, Nature/Environment Studies, Sailing, Tennis, Windsurfing
Session lengths & capacity: 1/2 & 1 week sessions; 160 campers
Clientele & fees: girls 5-17; Fees: A, B ☀ 🐷
Contact: Christine Dreifuss, Director Day Camps at (619) 610-0784; fax: (619) 298-2031
e-mail: annadry@aol.com
Web site: www.girlscoutssdi.org
Operated by: San Diego Imperial GSC, 1231 Upas St, San Diego, CA 92103 at (619) 610-0726 (#210)

Creative Kids Summer Day Camp (est 1986)   ☀

Manhattan Beach, CA (Los Angeles Co.); (310) 546-6540
Josie Meade, Director
Activities: Academics, Arts/Crafts, Field Trips, Nature/Environment Studies
Session lengths & capacity: June-September; 1, 4 & 9 week sessions; 35 campers
Clientele & fees: coed 5-9; Fees: B ☀
Contact: Josie Meade, Camp Director at (310) 546-6540; fax: (310) 546-6660
e-mail: tiaoshie@peoplepc.com
Operated by: The Jemm Corp, 17719 Palora Street, Encino, CA 91316 at (818) 342-4905 (#6535)

Cub Resident Camp Mataquay

(est 1938)   ▲ ⌂
Santa Ysabel, CA (San Diego Co.); (760) 782-3642
Bob Oslie, Director

Camp comments: Camp is the perfect size for young boys. Program designed for Cub Scouts but participation of all boys is welcome.
Activities: Archery, Arts/Crafts, Camping Skills/Outdoor Living, Fishing, Hiking, Nature/Environment Studies, Riflery, Sports — Field & Team, Swimming — Recreational
Session lengths & capacity: July-August; 7 week sessions; 100 campers
Clientele & fees: boys 8-10; Fees: **C △ 🐷**
Contact: Bob Olsie, Ranger at (760) 782-3768;
Web site: www.bsadpc.org
Operated by: Desert Pacific Council BSA, 1207 Upas St, San Diego, CA 92103 at (619) 298-6121

Group Rental Information
Seasons & Capacity: Spring 90, Summer 90, Fall 90, Winter 90
Facilities: A/V Equipment, Cabins, Dorm-Style, Food Service, Hiking Trails, Lake, Meeting Rooms, Playing Fields
Programs: Boating, Challenge/Ropes Course (#7719)

CYO Camp Armstrong

(est 1950)   △ 🚐

Occidental, CA (Sonoma Co.); (707) 874-0200
Derrick Bullington, Director

Camp comments: CYO camp is a place where children can develop their own self worth, explore spirituality, have fun under the redwoods.
Activities: Archery, Arts/Crafts, Canoeing, Counselor Training (CIT), Hiking, Nature/Environment Studies, Swimming — Recreational, Team Building
Session lengths & capacity: June-August; 1 & 2 week sessions; 352 campers
Clientele & fees: coed 7-18; Fees: **C △ 🐷**
Contact: Paul Raia, Camp Registrar at (707) 874-0200; fax: (707) 874-0230
e-mail: pmraia@verio.com
Web site: www.cyocamp.org
Operated by: Catholic Youth Organization, 2255 Hayes Street 4th Floor, San Francisco, CA 94117 at (415) 592-9200 (#322)

Deer Crossing Camp Inc

(est 1982)   △ 🚐

Pollock Pines, CA (El Dorado Co.); (408) 996-9448
Jim Wiltens, Director

Camp comments: An exciting challenging true wilderness experience in the California High Sierra on a beautiful lake. Supportive and caring guidance. Structure and free choice.

ICON LEGEND

☀	Day Camp
△	Resident Camp
🏠	Facilities Available To Rent
🚐	Transportation Available
🐷	Financial Aid Available

FEE RANGES PER WEEK

A	$0-75
B	$75-200
C	$201-350
D	$351-500
E	$501-650
F	over $650

Activities: Aquatic Activities, Arts/Crafts, Backpacking, Camping Skills/Outdoor Living, Canoeing, Climbing/Rappelling, Leadership Development, Sailing, Wilderness Trips, Windsurfing
Session lengths & capacity: June-August; 1, 2 & 4 week sessions; 42 campers
Clientele & fees: coed 9-18; Fees: **E △**
Contact: Gwen Wiltens, Office Manager at (408) 996-9448; fax: (408) 973-8441
e-mail: mail@deercrossingcamp.com
Web site: www.deercrossingcamp.com
Operated by: Deer Crossing Inc, PO Box 486, Cupertino, CA 95015-0486 at (408) 996-9448 (#4103)

Deer Lake (est 1970)   △ 🚐

Soda Springs, CA (Placer Co.); (510) 562-8470
Shae Jewell, Director

Camp comments: Spectacular mountain, high adventure camp. Rock climbing, ropes course, boating, tripping, family camp.
Activities: Aquatic Activities, Camping Skills/Outdoor Living, Canoeing, Challenge/Rope Courses, Climbing/Rappelling, Horseback — Western, Leadership Development, Sailing, Wilderness Trips, Windsurfing
Session lengths & capacity: June-August; 1 week sessions; 150 campers

Clientele & fees: girls 8-17; families;
Fees: **B, D ⚠ 🐖**
Contact: Sharon Kosch, Director of Program at
(510) 562-8470; fax: (510) 633-7925
e-mail: sharon@sfbgirlscouts.org
Web site: www.girlscoutsbayarea.org
Operated by: San Francisco Bay GSC,
PO Box 2249, 7700 Edgewater Dr Ste 340,
Oakland, CA 94621-2249 at (510) 562-8470
(#3587)

Devil Mountain Summer Camp

(est 1992)   ☀ 🚗

Danville, CA (Contra Costa Co.); (925) 837-5375
Colleen Logan, Director

Camp comments: Credentialed teachers work
with campers in the morning doing art,math &
science Afternoons bring sports arts & swimming
Activities: Academics, Aquatic Activities,
Arts/Crafts, Counselor Training (CIT), Drama,
Drawing/Painting, Field Trips, Hiking, Leadership
Development, Nature/Environment Studies
Session lengths & capacity: June-August; 2 week
sessions; 60 campers
Clientele & fees: coed 4-15; Fees: **B, C ☀**
Contact: Sondra Vander Meer, Associate
Director,Special Programs at (925) 837-5375;
fax: (925) 831-1120
e-mail: sondra_vandermeer@athenian.org
Web site: www.athenian.org
Operated by: The Athenian School, 2100 Mt Diablo
Scenic Blvd, Danville, CA 94506 at (825) 837-5375
(#2130)

Douglas Ranch Camps Inc

(est 1925)   ⚠

Carmel Valley, CA (Monterey Co.); (831) 659-2761
Carole Douglas Ehrhardt, Director

Camp comments: 77 yr traditional, friendly,
structured, fun. Focus on building self-esteem &
growth in social & sport skills. 1:4 ratio
Activities: Archery, Arts/Crafts, Basketball, Drama,
Hiking, Horseback — Western, Riflery, Soccer,
Swimming — Instructional, Tennis
Session lengths & capacity: June-August; 2, 3 &
4 week sessions; 120 campers
Clientele & fees: boys 7-14; girls 7-14; Fees: **F ⚠**
Contact: Adam Smith, Assistant Director at
(510) 339-2706; fax: (510) 339-1932
e-mail: director@douglascamp.com
Web site: www.douglascamp.com
Operated by: Douglas Ranch Camps Inc, 33200 E
Carmel Valley Rd, Carmel Valley, CA 93924 at
(831) 659-2761 (#375)

East County YMCA Day Camp

(est 1964)   ☀

La Mesa, CA (San Diego Co.); (619) 464-1323
Aly Mancini, Director

Camp comments: Campers thrive in a
noncompetitive, fun environment with an emphasis
on caring, honesty, respect and responsibility.
Activities: Aquatic Activities, Arts/Crafts,
Climbing/Rappelling, Field Trips, Gymnastics,
Leadership Development, Nature/Environment
Studies, Sports — Field & Team, Travel/Tour
Session lengths & capacity: June-August; 1 week
sessions; 250 campers
Clientele & fees: boys 4-15; girls 4-15; coed 4-15;
Fees: **B ☀ 🐖**
Contact: Aly Mancini, Program Director at
(619) 464-1323; fax: (619) 464-1361
Operated by: YMCA of San Diego County, 4715
Viewridge Ave Ste 100, San Diego, CA 92123 at
(619) 292-4034 (#207)

Easter Seal Camp Harmon

(est 1963)   ⚠ 🏠

Boulder Creek, CA; (408) 338-3383
Jane Carr, Director

Camp comments: A resident coed camp for
disabled children and adults. Provides experience
in independence and increased self-esteem.
Activities: Arts/Crafts, Computer, Golf, Music,
Nature/Environment Studies, Swimming —
Recreational
Session lengths & capacity: 1 & 2 week sessions;
80 campers
Clientele & fees: boys 6-70; girls 6-70; coed 6-70
Contact: Mike Mooney, Director of Camping
Services at (831) 338-3383; fax: (831) 338-0200
e-mail: mmooney@scruznet.com
Operated by: Easter Seals Central CA, 9010
Soquel Drive Ste 1, Aptos, CA 95003-4002 at
(831) 684-2166

Group Rental Information
Site comments: Loc in Redwood Forest, 20 miles
to ocean. Top quality food.
Seasons & Capacity: Spring 140, Fall 140
Facilities: Cabins, Food Service, Hiking Trails,
Meeting Rooms, Playing Fields, Pool (#288)

El Camino Pines (est 1958)   ⚠ 🏠

Frazier Park, CA (Kern Co.); (805) 245-3519
Connie Wolfe, Director

Camp comments: Christian camp, serves all
denominations, mountain site, open all year for all
ages & interests.
Activities: Archery, Arts/Crafts, Camping
Skills/Outdoor Living, Challenge/Rope Courses,
Climbing/Rappelling, Hiking, Leadership
Development, Nature/Environment Studies,
Religious Study, Swimming — Recreational
Session lengths & capacity: 1/2 & 1 week
sessions; 130 campers
Clientele & fees: coed 8-18; families;
Fees: **B ⚠ 🐖**
Contact: Kris W Turk, Office Manager at
(661) 245-3519; fax: (661) 245-2047
e-mail: elcamino@frazmtn.com
Web site: www.lrccsca.org
Operated by: Lutheran Retreats Camps & Conf,
PO Box 2027, Santa Clarita, CA 91386-2027 at
(661) 250-2880

Group Rental Information
Site comments: Christian camp serves all
denominations, mountain site, open all year for all
ages and interests.
Facilities: A/V Equipment, Cabins, Food Service,
Hiking Trails, Lodges, Meeting Rooms, Playing
Fields, Pool, Tents
Programs: Challenge/Ropes Course,
Environmental Education, Swimming (#57)

El-O-Win (est 1959)   ⚠ 🏠 🚗

Shaver Lake, CA (Fresno Co.); (559) 841-7799
Joyce Jones, Director

Camp comments: High Sierra adventure on Dinkey
Creek. Self-esteem, independence, team work
along with fun and new friends.
Activities: Arts/Crafts, Backpacking, Camping
Skills/Outdoor Living, Canoeing, Counselor Training
(CIT), Horseback — Western, Leadership
Development, Nature/Environment Studies,
Performing Arts
Session lengths & capacity: June-August; 1/2, 1 &
2 week sessions; 125 campers
Clientele & fees: girls 7-17; Fees: **B, C, D ⚠**
Contact: Sarah Flores, Assistant Director of Camp
& Program at (559) 291-5078; fax: (559) 291-5079
e-mail: sflores@sgvc.yahoo.com
Web site: www.girlscoutsgvc.org
Operated by: Girl Scouts Golden Valley Cncl, 4910
E Ashlan Ave 105, Fresno, CA 93726-3021 at
(559) 291-5078

Group Rental Information
Facilities: Cabins, Food Service, Kitchen Facilities
Programs: Horseback Riding, Swimming (#384)

Emandal A Farm On A River

(est 1965)   ⚠ 🚗

Willits, CA (Mendocin Co.); (707) 459-5439
Tamara Adams, Director

Camp comments: Being responsible is making
new friends, swimming, creating something you
never dreamed before & even doing farm chores!
Activities: Arts/Crafts, Basketball, Camping
Skills/Outdoor Living, Counselor Training (CIT),
Farming/Ranching/Gardening, Fishing, Music,
Nature/Environment Studies, Swimming —
Recreational, Team Building
Session lengths & capacity: June-July; 1, 2, 3, 4 &
5 week sessions; 80 campers
Clientele & fees: coed 6-17; families; seniors;
Fees: **E ⚠**
Contact: Tamara Adams, Director at
(707) 459-5439; fax: (707) 459-1808
e-mail: emandal@pacific.net
Web site: www.emandal.com
Operated by: Emandal A Farm on a River, 16500
Hearst P O Rd, Willits, CA 95490 at (707) 459-5439
(#3616)

Embarcadero YMCA   ☀

San Francisco, CA (San Francisco Co.);
(415) 957-9622
Tiffany Patterson, Director

Camp comments: Youth ages 5-17 spend your
summer at our day camp discovering hidden
talents,seeking adventures & building friendships
by engaging in fun & exciting trips.
Activities: Arts/Crafts, Computer, Dance, Drama,
Field Trips, Leadership Development,
Nature/Environment Studies, Sports — Field &
Team, Swimming — Recreational
Session lengths & capacity: 1 week sessions;
145 campers
Clientele & fees: boys 5-17; girls 5-17; coed 5-17;
Fees: **A, B ☀ 🐖**
Contact: Youth Program Director, Community
Program Director at (415) 957-9622;
fax: (415) 957-1260
e-mail: tpatterson@ymcasf.org
Operated by: YMCA San Francisco Day Camps,
1877 S Grant Street, San Mateo, CA 94402 at
(650) 286-9622 (#148)

Emerson (est 1919)   ⚠ 🏠

Idyllwild, CA (Riverside Co.); (909) 659-2690
David Kline, Director

Camp comments: Three new shower & restroom
facilities. Near town. Full-time ranger on premises.
Week or weekend rentals available.
Activities: Aquatic Activities, Archery, Arts/Crafts,
Camping Skills/Outdoor Living, Hiking,
Nature/Environment Studies, Riflery, Swimming —
Instructional, Swimming — Recreational
Session lengths & capacity: July-August; 1 week
sessions; 200 campers
Clientele & fees: boys 11-18; families; Fees: **B ⚠**
Contact: Tracy Youden, Program at (909) 825-8844
ext. 113; fax: (909) 793-0306
Web site: www.bsa-ciec.org
Operated by: California Inland Empire Cncl, 1230
Indiana Court, Redlands, CA 92374-2896 at
(909) 825-8844

Group Rental Information
Site comments: Newly constructed rifle range. To
add to a great facility loacted by Idyllwild. Historic
country landmark #1. Improved restrooms,
barbeque area. Large groups OK
Seasons & Capacity: Spring 300, Summer 300,
Fall 300, Winter 100

Facilities: Cabins, Hiking Trails, Kitchen Facilities, Lake, Lodges
Programs: Boating, Environmental Education (#180)

Enchanted Hills Camp

(est 1947) 🏠 🚐

Napa, CA (Napa Co.); (707) 224-4023
Cynthia Diggs, Director
Contact: Tony Fletcher, Camp Director at (415) 431-1481 ext. 219; fax: (415) 863-7568
e-mail: afletcher@lighthouse-sf.org
Operated by: United Camps Conf & Retreats, 912 Lootens Pl, San Rafael, CA 94901 at (415) 456-5102
Group Rental Information
Site comments: Enchanted Hills Camp has been working small miracles for over 50 years. We build community, independence & self esteem. All ages welcome. Serves non-profits.
Seasons & Capacity: Spring 56, Fall 56, Winter 56
Facilities: A/V Equipment, Cabins, Dorm-Style, Double Occupancy, Food Service, Hiking Trails, Linens, Lodges, Meeting Rooms, Playing Fields, Pool
Programs: Environmental Education (#293)

Enchanted Hills Camp for Blind

(est 1950) △

Napa, CA
Tony Fletcher, Director
Camp comments: Serving people of all ages and varying degrees of vision loss, Enchanted Hills offers traditional camp programs in an accessible way.
Activities: Arts/Crafts, Counselor Training (CIT), Dance, Drama, Farming/Ranching/Gardening, Fishing, Hiking, Horseback — Western, Nature/Environment Studies, Swimming — Recreational
Session lengths & capacity: 1/2, 1 & 2 week sessions
Clientele & fees: Fees: A △
Contact: Anthony Fletcher, Ed/Rec Director at (415) 431-1481; fax: (415) 863-7568
e-mail: afletcher@lighthouse-sf.org
Operated by: Lighthouse for the Blind, 214 Van Ness Avenue, San Francisco, CA 94102 at (415) 431-1481 (#48676)

Episcopal Diocese of El Camino

(est 1988) △

Boulder Creek, CA (Santa Cruz Co.); (831) 338-2128
Cartenna Robohm, Director

ICON LEGEND

☀ Day Camp
△ Resident Camp
🏠 Facilities Available To Rent
🚐 Transportation Available
🐷 Financial Aid Available

FEE RANGES PER WEEK

A	$0-75
B	$75-200
C	$201-350
D	$351-500
E	$501-650
F	over $650

Camp comments: Thrive in noncompetitive Christian community. Enjoy creative adventures, fun in the faith. Learn to make a difference.
Activities: Archery, Arts/Crafts, Challenge/Rope Courses, Community Service, Counselor Training (CIT), Hiking, Leadership Development, Swimming — Recreational
Session lengths & capacity: June-August; 1 week sessions; 65 campers
Clientele & fees: coed 7-18; Fees: C △
Contact: Fr. Fritz & Carteena Robohm, Camp Directors at (831) 663-6218; fax: (831) 663-4867
e-mail: jfriii@concentric.net
Operated by: Episcopal Diocese El Camino, 17940 Berta Canyon Road, Prunedale, CA 93907-3323 at (831) 663-6218 (#6285)

Extreme Sports Beach Camp

(est 1989) ☀

Dana Point, CA; (949) 496-1609
Matt Johnson, Director

Camp comments: Build ocean sports skills in a fun, safe environment, with a focus on building character and friendships.
Activities: Aquatic Activities, Arts/Crafts, Nature/Environment Studies, Swimming — Recreational
Session lengths & capacity: June-August; 1 week sessions; 70 campers
Clientele & fees: coed 6-14; Fees: B ☀ 🐷
Contact: Capistrano Beach Cities YMCA at (949) 496-1609; fax: (949) 496-2712
Operated by: Extreme Sports Beach Camp, 31411 La Matanza B, San Juan Capistrano, CA 92675 at (949) 496-1609 (#27215)

Fairfield Family YMCA Day Camp

(est 1978) ☀

Long Beach, CA (Los Angeles Co.); (310) 423-0491

Camp comments: YMCA day camping for children entering grades K-8. All activities are age appropriate & based on weekly themes.
Activities: Academics, Arts/Crafts, Community Service, Drama, Field Trips, Leadership Development, Music, Nature/Environment Studies, Swimming — Recreational
Session lengths & capacity: 1 week sessions; 175 campers
Clientele & fees: coed 4-14; Fees: B ☀ 🐷
Contact: BT Tuggle, Director at (310) 423-0491; fax: (310) 984-9611
Web site: www.lbymca.org
Operated by: YMCA Of Greater Long Beach, PO Box 90095, Long Beach, CA 90809-0995 at (562) 496-2756 (#6659)

Fairmont Private Schools

(est 1953) ☀

Anaheim, CA; (714) 774-9500
Teri Kidder, Director

Camp comments: Providing children with an educational, recreational, positive camp experience! Program options include, Summer School, Day, Computer, Science & Sports Camp.
Session lengths & capacity: June-August; 1 & 2 week sessions
Clientele & fees: coed 3-14; Fees: B, C ☀
Contact: Web site: www.fairmontschools.com
Operated by: Fairmont Private Schools, 1275 Mable St, Anaheim, CA 92802 at (714) 234-2720 (#41710)

Forest Home (est 1938) △ 🏠

Forest Falls, CA (San Bernardino Co.); (909) 389-2300
Ridge Burns, Director

Camp comments: Camping in tipis or safari tents, kids experience the magic of camp while mastering life skills from a biblical view.

Activities: Archery, Canoeing, Challenge/Rope Courses, Fishing, Kayaking, Nature/Environment Studies, Photography, Radio/TV/Video, Religious Study, Swimming — Recreational
Session lengths & capacity: June-August; 1 week sessions; 220 campers
Clientele & fees: coed 7-12; Fees: C △
Contact: (909) 389-2300; fax: (909) 389-3482
e-mail: reg@foresthome.org
Web site: www.foresthome.org
Operated by: Forest Home Inc, 40000 Valley of the Falls Dr, Forest Falls, CA 92339 at (909) 389-2300
Group Rental Information
Site comments: Escape to one of 5 unique camps-from rustic to deluxe nestled in a scenic canyon of the San Bernardino Mountains.
Seasons & Capacity: Spring 900, Summer 1500, Fall 900, Winter 900
Facilities: Cabins, Food Service, Lake, Lodges, Meeting Rooms, Pool
Programs: Environmental Education (#6699)

Gallagher's High Adventure Camp (est 1996) △ 🚐

Meadow Valley, CA (Plumas Co.); (530) 283-5502
John Champion Gallagher, Director

Camp comments: Wilderness campers have fun learning traditional lifelong skills:whitewater rafting,backpacking,climbing & rapelling. Great ropes course & mature staff.
Activities: Backpacking, Camping Skills/Outdoor Living, Challenge/Rope Courses, Climbing/Rappelling, Counselor Training (CIT), Leadership Development, Nature/Environment Studies, Rafting, Team Building, Wilderness Trips
Session lengths & capacity: June-August; 2, 4 & 8 week sessions; 24 campers
Clientele & fees: boys 8-14; Fees: F △
Contact: John C Gallagher, Director at (530) 283-5502;
e-mail: highcamp@psln.com
Web site: www.psln.comlhighcamp/
Operated by: Gallaghers High Adventure Camp, Drawer 240, Meadow Valley, CA 95956 at (530) 283-5502 (#6564)

Gold Arrow Camp (est 1933) △ 🚐

Lakeshore, CA; (559) 893-6641
Audrey & Steve Monke, Director

Camp comments: A traditional, fun, and non-competitive program with a variety of activities on the shore of beautiful Huntington Lake, Sierra National Forest, since 1933.
Activities: Archery, Backpacking, Ceramics/Pottery, Challenge/Rope Courses, Climbing/Rappelling, Horseback — Western, Kayaking, Sailing, Waterskiing, Windsurfing
Session lengths & capacity: June-August; 1, 2, 3 & 4 week sessions; 260 campers
Clientele & fees: coed 6-14; Fees: F △
Contact: Audrey & Steve Monke, Camp Directors at (800) 554-2267; fax: (714) 424-0844
e-mail: mail@goldarrowcamp.com
Web site: www.goldarrowcamp.com
Operated by: Gold Arrow Enterprises Inc, 2900 Bristol St Ste A107, Costa Mesa, CA 92626 at (800) 554-2267 (#110)

Griffith Park Boys Camp

(est 1920) △ 🏠

Los Angeles, CA (Los Angeles Co.); (323) 664-0571
Roger Williams or David Johnson, Director

Camp comments: Rewarding summer adv. for boys! Dynamic camp surrounded by the amenities of Griffith Park and the exciting city of LA.
Activities: Aquatic Activities, Archery, Arts/Crafts, Camping Skills/Outdoor Living, Challenge/Rope Courses, Climbing/Rappelling, Field Trips, Hiking, Nature/Environment Studies
Session lengths & capacity: June-September; 1 week sessions; 100 campers

Clientele & fees: boys 6-14; Fees: **B** △ 🚤
Contact: Roger S Williams, Sr Rec Dir II - Camp
Director at (323) 664-0571; fax: (323) 913-4170
Operated by: City of LA Dept Rec & Parks, City
Wide Serv Div - Camp Sec, 3900 W Chevy Chase
Dr, Los Angeles, CA 90039 at (213) 485-4853
Group Rental Information
Seasons & Capacity: Spring 110, Winter 110
Facilities: Cabins, Dorm-Style, Food Service,
Hiking Trails, Kitchen Facilities, Lodges, Meeting
Rooms, Playing Fields
Programs: Challenge/Ropes Course,
Environmental Education, Horseback Riding (#132)

Gualala

Annapolis, CA (Sonoma Co.); (707) 886-5351
Operated by: United Camps Conf & Retreats, 912
Lootens Pl, San Rafael, CA 94901 at (415) 456-5102
Group Rental Information
Site comments: 9 mi.to coast; near historical Fort
Ross. Recreational activities available. Owned by
the Berkeley-Albany YMCA.
Facilities: Cabins, Dorm-Style, Food Service,
Hiking Trails, Lodges, Meeting Rooms, River (#281)

Harker Summer Programs

(est 1956)

San Jose, CA (Santa Clara Co.); (408) 871-4600
Kelly Espinosa, Director

Camp comments: Qualified staff & beautiful facility
morning academic program, afternoon sports
recreation & all camp activities group & individual
activities. Coed Day Camp.
Activities: Academics, Archery, Arts/Crafts,
Camping Skills/Outdoor Living, Computer,
Counselor Training (CIT), Skating, Sports — Field &
Team, Swimming — Instructional, Tennis
Session lengths & capacity: June-August; 3 & 5
week sessions; 800 campers
Clientele & fees: coed 4-13; Fees: **C, D** ☀
Fees: **E** △
Contact: Cindi Gonsalves, Office Coordinator at
(408) 871-4611; fax: (408) 871-4320
e-mail: campinfo@harker.org
Web site: www.harker.org
Operated by: The Harker School, PO Box 9067,
San Jose, CA 95157 at (408) 871-4600 (#5641)

Harmony Pines Christian Center

Wrightwood, CA; (760) 249-6102
Robert D Sstradley, Director
Contact: Web site: www.angelescrest.com
Operated by: Angeles Crest Christian Camp, 2555
E Chapman Ave Suite 605, Fullerton, CA 92831 at
(714) 870-9190
Group Rental Information
Seasons & Capacity: Spring 80, Summer 80, Fall
80, Winter 80
Facilities: A/V Equipment, Cabins, Dorm-Style,
Food Service, Hiking Trails, Meeting Rooms
Programs: Boating, Challenge/Ropes Course,
Swimming, Winter Sports (#11740)

Helendade Scout Reservation

(est 1960)

Running Springs, CA (San Bernardino Co.);
(909) 867-2480
Tracy Youden, Director

Camp comments: Full time ranger on premises.
We have lakefront, ranges, lodges for program plus
large campfire ring, barbeque pits, indoor
restrooms and shower facilities.
Activities: Aquatic Activities, Archery, Arts/Crafts,
Canoeing, Hiking, Leadership Development,
Nature/Environment Studies, Riflery, Swimming —
Recreational
Session lengths & capacity: June-August; 1/2 &
1 week sessions; 150 campers

Clientele & fees: boys 7-11; families;
Fees: **B** △
Contact: Volunteer Services at (909) 825-8844 ext.
129; fax: (909) 793-0306
Web site: www.bsa-ciec.org
Operated by: California Inland Empire Cncl, 1230
Indiana Court, Redlands, CA 92374-2896 at
(909) 825-8844
Group Rental Information
Site comments: Large kitchen, lodges, campsites
with shower & restroom facility. Fire rings also in
campsites. Winter camp program available in
addition to existing schedule.
Seasons & Capacity: Spring 200, Summer 200,
Fall 200, Winter 100
Facilities: Cabins, Hiking Trails, Kitchen Facilities,
Lake, Lodges, Meeting Rooms
Programs: Boating (#134)

Hidden Falls Camp

(est 1957)

Soquel, CA (Santa Cruz Co.)
Sari VanOtegham, Director

Camp comments: Rustic camp near the Pacific
Ocean! Supportive atmosphere. Specialty
programs in snorkeling, surfing & performance art
Activities: Archery, Arts/Crafts, Camping
Skills/Outdoor Living, Dance, Hiking, Kayaking,
Nature/Environment Studies, Performing Arts,
Sports — Field & Team, Swimming — Recreational
Session lengths & capacity: June-August; 1/2 &
1 week sessions; 130 campers
Clientele & fees: girls 7-17; Fees: **C** △
Contact: Sari VanOtegham, Outdoor Program
Director at (408) 287-4170 ext. 257;
e-mail: svanotegham@girlscoutsofscc.org
Web site: www.girlscoutsofscc.org
Operated by: GSC of Santa Clara County, 1310 S
Bascom Avenue, San Jose, CA 95128 at
(408) 287-4170
Group Rental Information
Facilities: Hiking Trails, Kitchen Facilities, Pool
(#303)

Hidden Villa Summer Camp

(est 1945)

Los Altos Hills, CA (Santa Clara Co.);
(650) 949-8641
Jill Kilty-Newburn, Director

Camp comments: Nonprofit ranch & wilderness.
Animals, organic gardens, ropes course &
swimming. Program emphasis on multicultural
understanding & environmental awareness.
Activities: Arts/Crafts, Backpacking, Camping
Skills/Outdoor Living, Challenge/Rope Courses,
Farming/Ranching/Gardening, Hiking, Leadership
Development, Nature/Environment Studies, Team
Building
Session lengths & capacity: June-August; 1 & 2
week sessions; 150 campers
Clientele & fees: coed 6-18; Fees: **C** ☀
Fees: **D** △ 🚤
Contact: Jill Kilty-Newburn, Camp Director at
(650) 949-8641; fax: (650) 948-1916
e-mail: camp@hiddenvilla.org
Web site: www.hiddenvilla.org
Operated by: Trust For Hidden Villa, 26870 Moody
Rd, Los Altos Hills, CA 94022 at (650) 949-8641
(#7723)

Hollenbeck Park Day Camp

Los Angeles, CA (Los Angeles Co.); (213) 261-0113
Activities: Aquatic Activities, Counselor Training
(CIT), Dance, Drama, Field Trips, Fishing,
Leadership Development, Music, Soccer,
Swimming — Recreational
Contact: Karen Fox, Director at (323) 261-0113;
fax: (323) 261-0113
Operated by: City of LA Rec and Parks Dept, 415
So St Louis Street, Los Angeles, CA 90033 at
(213) 261-0113 (#6794)

Id Tech Camps - So Cal

(est 1999)

Los Angeles, CA; (888) 709-8324

Camp comments: Summer technology camps for
ages 8-17 at top universities nation wide. Learn to
create digital movies, video games, websites,
programming, robotics and more!
Activities: Academics, Basketball, Computer,
Drawing/Painting, Performing Arts, Photography,
Radio/TV/Video, Sports — Field & Team, Swimming
— Recreational, Team Building
Session lengths & capacity: June-August; 1 &
2 week sessions; 40 campers
Clientele & fees: coed 8-17; 🚤
Contact: Cari Flood, Client Service Manager at
(888) 709-8324; fax: (408) 626-9505
e-mail: info@internaldrive.com
Web site: www.internaldrive.com
Operated by: InternalDrive, 2103 S Bascom Ave,
Campbell, CA 95008 at (408) 626-9500 (#14880)

Idyllwild Pines Camp and Conf

(est 1923)

Idyllwild, CA (Riverside Co.)
Paul W Schlenz, Director
Operated by: Idyllwild Pines Camp and Conf,
PO Box 425, Idyllwild, CA 92549 at (909) 659-2605
Group Rental Information
Site comments: Beautiful mile high mountain
camp rental facility serving Christ and Christians
since 1923.
Seasons & Capacity: Spring 380, Summer 500,
Fall 380, Winter 380
Facilities: A/V Equipment, Cabins, Dorm-Style,
Food Service, Hiking Trails, Kitchen Facilities,
Lodges, Meeting Rooms, Playing Fields, Pool
Programs: Horseback Riding, Swimming (#3603)

Jackie Robinson YMCA Day

(est 1995)

San Diego, CA (San Diego Co.); (619) 264-0144
Chip Robinson, Director

Camp comments: Day camp offers warm
supportive atmosphere. For young campers. We
strive to provide a safe fun day camp for everyone.
Activities: Academics, Aquatic Activities,
Arts/Crafts, Baseball/Softball, Basketball, Computer,
Counselor Training (CIT), Field Trips, Soccer,
Sports — Field & Team
Clientele & fees: boys 5-13; girls 5-13; coed 5-13;
families; single adults; Fees: **A, B** ☀ 🚤
Contact: (619) 264-0144; fax: (619) 264-7356
Operated by: YMCA of San Diego County, 4715
Viewridge Ave Ste 100, San Diego, CA 92123 at
(619) 292-4034 (#4032)

Jameson Ranch Camp (est 1935) △

Glennville, CA (Kern Co.); (805) 536-8888
Ross Jameson, Director

Camp comments: Close family atmosphere on a
mountain ranch. Home grown food, positive role
model staff, a wide choice of activities.
Activities: Archery, Arts/Crafts, Bicycling/Biking,
Climbing/Rappelling, Drama,
Farming/Ranching/Gardening, Horseback —
Western, Kayaking, Sailing, Swimming —
Recreational
Session lengths & capacity: June-August; 2, 4, 6
& 8 week sessions; 80 campers
Clientele & fees: coed 6-14; Fees: **E** △
Contact: Ross & Debby Jameson, Owner at
(805) 536-8888; fax: (805) 536-8896
e-mail: thejamesons@jamesonranchcamp.com
Web site: www.jamesonranchcamp.com
Operated by: Jameson Ranch, PO Box ACA,
Glennville, CA 93226 at (661) 536-8888 (#190)

JCC Camp Komaroff (est 1953) ☀

Long Beach, CA (Los Angeles Co.); (562) 426-7601
Linda Keiles, Director

Camp comments: New campus with arts and craft rooms. Full size gym, outdoor play area for kids in K-6th.
Activities: Aquatic Activities, Arts/Crafts, Basketball, Drama, Drawing/Painting, Field Trips, Performing Arts, Swimming — Recreational
Session lengths & capacity: June-September; 1 week sessions; 120 campers
Clientele & fees: boys 4-12; girls 4-12; Fees: B ☀ 🐷
Contact: Susan Paletz, Camp Director at (562) 426-7601; fax: (562) 424-3915
e-mail: jcclb@aol.com
Operated by: Long Beach JCC, 3801 East Willow Ave, Long Beach, CA 90815 at (562) 426-7601 (#204)

Jefunira Camp (est 1990) ☀

Palo Alto, CA (Santa Clara Co.); (650) 365-6429
Jeff Gamble, Ira Lit, Director

Camp comments: Our exciting well-rounded program and talented staff will provide an extraordinary summer experience for your child
Activities: Arts/Crafts, Field Trips, Hiking, Sports — Field & Team
Session lengths & capacity: June-August; 2 week sessions; 100 campers
Clientele & fees: coed 6-14; Fees: C ☀ 🐷 🚐
Contact: Ira Lit, Director at (650) 365-6429; fax: (650) 694-4650
e-mail: jefunira@aol.com
Web site: www.jefuniracamp.com
Operated by: Jefunira, 2494 Palm Ave, Redwood City, CA 94062 at (650) 365-6429 (#14085)

Joe & Mary Mottino Family YMCA (est 1975) ☀

Oceanside, CA (San Diego Co.); (760) 758-0808
Sharon Plathe, Director

Camp comments: Day Camp offers traditional & speciality camps including gymnastics, sports & other fun, camps in the North County.
Activities: Aquatic Activities, Arts/Crafts, Baseball/Softball, Basketball, Climbing/Rappelling, Counselor Training (CIT), Field Trips, Gymnastics, Leadership Development, Nature/Environment Studies
Session lengths & capacity: June-September; 1 week sessions; 150 campers
Clientele & fees: boys 4-16; girls 4-16; coed 4-16; families; Fees: B ☀
Contact: Sharon Plathe, Program Coordinator at (760) 758-0808; fax: (760) 758-8058

ICON LEGEND

☀ Day Camp
⛺ Resident Camp
🏠 Facilities Available To Rent
🚐 Transportation Available
🐷 Financial Aid Available

FEE RANGES PER WEEK

A	$0-75
B	$75-200
C	$201-350
D	$351-500
E	$501-650
F	over $650

Operated by: YMCA of San Diego County, 4715 Viewridge Ave Ste 100, San Diego, CA 92123 at (619) 292-4034 (#2009)

Kennolyn Camps (est 1946) ☀ ⛺ 🚐

Soquel, CA (Santa Cruz Co.); (831) 479-6714
Andrew Townsend, Director

Camp comments: In the Redwoods, 5 miles from Monterey Bay. Great high ropes/climbing facility . 56 summers with original owners. Coed.
Activities: Aquatic Activities, Archery, Backpacking, Ceramics/Pottery, Challenge/Rope Courses, Fencing, Horseback — English, Photography, Riflery
Session lengths & capacity: June-September; 1, 2, 3 & 4 week sessions; 245 campers
Clientele & fees: boys 6-14; girls 6-14; coed 6-14; families; Fees: D ☀ Fees: F ⛺
Contact: Andrew Townsend, Director at (831) 479-6714; fax: (831) 479-6718
e-mail: camp@kennolyn.com
Web site: www.kennolyn.com
Operated by: Kennolyn Camps Inc, 8205 Glen Haven Rd, Soquel, CA 95073 at (831) 479-6714 (#335)

LA County 4H Summer Camp

(est 1946) ⛺ 🚐

Crestline, CA (San Bernardino Co.); (909) 338-9002
Activities: Aquatic Activities, Arts/Crafts, Camping Skills/Outdoor Living, Hiking, Leadership Development, Nature/Environment Studies
Session lengths & capacity: 1 week sessions
Clientele & fees: coed 9-19; Fees: B ⛺ 🐷
Contact: Judith E Kingston, 4H Youth Development Advisor at (323) 838-8335; fax: (323) 838-7449
e-mail: jekingston@ucdavis.edu
Web site: celosangeles.ucdavis.edu
Operated by: 4H Youth Program Coop Ext, 2 Coral Circle, Monterey Park, CA 91755 at (323) 838-4557 (#7043)

La Jolla YMCA (est 1969) ☀

La Jolla, CA (San Diego Co.); (858) 453-3483
Kristyn Valentino, Director

Camp comments: Day camp & caravan trips. Serving children (4-16 yrs) through a large variety of exciting camp options. Specialty sports
Activities: Baseball/Softball, Counselor Training (CIT), Dance, Drama, Golf, Horseback — English, Skating, Soccer, Swimming — Instructional, Tennis
Session lengths & capacity: June-August; 1 week sessions; 700 campers
Clientele & fees: boys 4-16; girls 4-16; coed 4-16; families; Fees: B ☀ 🐷
Contact: Kristyn Valentino, Camp Director at (858) 453-3483; fax: (858) 452-3761
e-mail: kvalentino@ymca.org
Operated by: YMCA of San Diego County, 4715 Viewridge Ave Ste 100, San Diego, CA 92123 at (619) 292-4034 (#3037)

Lake Mission Viejo Day Camp ☀

Mission Viejo, CA (Orange Co.); (949) 770-1313

Camp comments: LMV Camps offer members 3-14 an exciting menu of activities in 1 of 4 separate, age-appropriate groups. Classic summer fun in a 1st rate resort-style atmosphere
Activities: Arts/Crafts, Boating, Counselor Training (CIT), Fishing, Sports — Field & Team, Swimming — Recreational, Team Building
Session lengths & capacity: June-August; 1/2, 1, 2, 3, 4, 5, 6, 7, 8 & 9 week sessions
Clientele & fees: coed 3-14; Fees: B ☀
Contact: Laurel Jacoby, Recreation Supervisor at (949) 770-1313 ext. 222;
Web site: www.lakemissionviejo.org

Operated by: Lake Mission Viejo Assoc, 22555 Olympiad Road, Mission Viejo, CA 92692 at (949) 770-1313 (#31561)

Lakewood YMCA Day Camp ☀

Lakewood, CA; (562) 425-7431
Sue Gevedon, Director

Camp comments: Day camp offers a fun, safe, environment for all children. We offer a variety of activities that children love.
Activities: Arts/Crafts, Field Trips, Leadership Development, Nature/Environment Studies
Session lengths & capacity: 1 week sessions; 230 campers
Clientele & fees: coed 5-12; Fees: B ☀ 🐷
Contact: Sue Gevedon, Program Director at (310) 425-7431; fax: (310) 425-5451
Web site: www.lbymca.org
Operated by: YMCA Of Greater Long Beach, PO Box 90095, Long Beach, CA 90809-0995 at (562) 496-2756 (#6656)

Las Posas Children's Ctr Inc ☀

Ventura, CA; (805) 659-4115
Robert Alfino, Director
Activities: Arts/Crafts, Basketball, Drama, Field Trips, Football, Soccer, Swimming — Recreational
Contact: Web site: www.lpcc.com
Operated by: Las Posas Children's Center In, 4435 McGrath St Ste 308, Ventura, CA 93003 at (805) 644-4344 (#25227)

Lazy J Ranch Camp

(est 1945) ⛺ 🏠 🚐

Malibu, CA (Los Angeles Co.); (310) 457-5572
Craig 'Crazzy' Johnson, Director

Camp comments: Visit our 140-acre Malibu. CA ranch camp. Kids enjoy horseback riding, archery, kayaking, and more. Free tours available.
Activities: Archery, Camping Skills/Outdoor Living, Farming/Ranching/Gardening, Fencing, Hiking, Horseback — Western, Kayaking, Riflery, Swimming — Recreational, Tennis
Session lengths & capacity: 1, 2 & 9 week sessions; 120 campers
Clientele & fees: coed 5-15; families; Fees: F ⛺
Contact: Craig Johnson, Executive Director at (310) 457-5572; fax: (310) 457-8882
e-mail: crazzycraig@earthlink.net
Web site: www.LazyJRanchCamp.com
Operated by: Lazy J Ranch Camp, Box 505 Route 2, Malibu, CA 90265 at (310) 457-5572

Group Rental Information
Site comments: 140 Acre Malibo Ranch. Weekend youth groups summer camps. Horses animal care, archery, riflery, fencing, tennis, kayaking, pool, call for more info tours avail.
Facilities: Cabins, Double Occupancy, Food Service, Hiking Trails, Kitchen Facilities, Ocean, Pool
Programs: Environmental Education, Horseback Riding, Swimming (#8399)

Lazy W Ranch (est 1948) 🏠

San Juan Capistrano, CA (Orange Co.); (949) 728-0141
Contact: Sylvia Miller, Reservationist at (626) 568-7333; fax: (626) 568-7331
e-mail: smiller@cal-pac.org
Web site: www.cal-pac.org
Operated by: California Pacific Annual Conf, 110 S Euclid Ave, PO Box 6006, Pasadena, CA 91102 at (626) 568-7330

Group Rental Information
Site comments: Charming camp in Oak Canyon setting, southern Orange County. Cabins, lodge, pool, excellent meal service or small group self-cooking. Tent area, craft hall.
Seasons & Capacity: Spring 159, Summer 159, Fall 159, Winter 159

Facilities: A/V Equipment, Cabins, Dorm-Style, Food Service, Hiking Trails, Kitchen Facilities, Lodges, Meeting Rooms, Pool
Programs: Swimming (#100)

Lions Camp at Teresita Pines

(est 1929)

Wrightwood, CA; (800) 585-3245
John Bauer, Director
Contact: Lee Thorneycroft, Program Director at (800) 585-3245; fax: (619) 249-1063
e-mail: leethorn@cheerful.com
Web site: www.socalionscamp.com
Operated by: Lions Camp At Teresita Pines, PO Box 98, Wrightwood, CA 92397 at (760) 249-3580

Group Rental Information
Seasons & Capacity: Spring 100, Summer 200, Fall 100, Winter 100
Facilities: Cabins, Dorm-Style, Double Occupancy, Food Service, Hiking Trails, Lodges, Meeting Rooms, Pool, Tents
Programs: Boating, Swimming (#74)

Loch Leven Christian Camp/Conf (est 1957)

Mentone, CA (San Bernardino Co.); (909) 794-2507
Brad Carter, Director
Contact: Brad Carter, Operations Manager at (909) 794-2507; fax: (909) 794-2232
e-mail: llcc@gte.net
Operated by: Christian Church Disciples, 2401 N Lake Ave, Altadena, CA 91001 at (626) 296-0385

Group Rental Information
Site comments: Mountain canyon setting. Serving adults, families and youth. A Christian camp providing a place to renew your spirit.
Facilities: A/V Equipment, Cabins, Dorm-Style, Double Occupancy, Food Service, Hiking Trails, Kitchen Facilities, Lodges, Meeting Rooms, Pool
Programs: Environmental Education, Swimming (#34)

Lodestar

Wilseyville, CA (Calaveras Co.); (209) 293-4980
Operated by: United Camps Conf & Retreats, 912 Lootens Pl, San Rafael, CA 94901 at (415) 456-5102

Group Rental Information
Site comments: In historical Gold Country, near High Sierras. Owned by CA/NV Annual Conference of the United Methodist Church.
Seasons & Capacity: Summer 142, Winter 108
Facilities: Dorm-Style, Double Occupancy, Food Service, Hiking Trails, Kitchen Facilities, Lodges, Pool (#7114)

Los Altos YMCA Day Camp

(est 1960)

Long Beach, CA (Los Angeles Co.); (562) 596-3394
Joe Bergfalk, Director

Camp comments: Mix & match from week-week, based on your favorite activities, 23 speciality camps offered summer, spring & winter.
Activities: Arts/Crafts, Baseball/Softball, Basketball, Camping Skills/Outdoor Living, Field Trips, Leadership Development, Skating, Swimming — Recreational
Session lengths & capacity: 1 week sessions; 300 campers
Clientele & fees: boys 5-18; girls 5-18; coed 5-18; Fees: B
Contact: Joe Bergfalk, Executive Director at (310) 596-3394; fax: (310) 596-7911
Web site: www.lbymca.org
Operated by: YMCA Of Greater Long Beach, PO Box 90095, Long Beach, CA 90809-0995 at (562) 496-2756 (#6658)

Los Cerritos YMCA Day Camp

(est 1966)

Belflower, CA (Los Angeles Co.); (310) 925-1292
Jeremy Echnoz, Director

Camp comments: Develop positive values, make new friends. Learn new skills, have fun & feel good about yourself, the YMCA way.
Activities: Arts/Crafts, Baseball/Softball, Basketball, Camping Skills/Outdoor Living, Dance, Drawing/Painting, Field Trips, Hiking
Session lengths & capacity: 1 week sessions
Clientele & fees: boys 5-16; girls 5-16; coed 5-16; Fees: A, B
Contact: Cindy Bopp/ Janice Bopp, Office Manager/Receptionist at (562) 925-1292;
Web site: www.lbymca.org
Operated by: YMCA Of Greater Long Beach, PO Box 90095, Long Beach, CA 90809-0995 at (562) 496-2756 (#6657)

Lost Valley Scout Reservation

(est 1964)

Warner Springs, CA (San Diego Co.); (909) 767-1183
Bob Williams, Director

Camp comments: Boy Scout summer camp, open weekends and some holidays, family camps, new log cabins sleep 8; beautiful high desert.
Activities: Aquatic Activities, Archery, Bicycling/Biking, Challenge/Rope Courses, Climbing/Rappelling, Hiking, Horseback — Western, Leadership Development, Nature/Environment Studies, Riflery
Session lengths & capacity: June-August; 1 week sessions; 500 campers
Clientele & fees: boys 11-17; Fees: C
Contact: Steve Adams, Camping Director at (714) 546-4990; fax: (714) 546-0415
e-mail: stevea@ocbsa.org
Operated by: Orange County Council BSA, 3590 Harbor Gateway North, Costa Mesa, CA 92626-1425 at (714) 546-4990

Group Rental Information
Facilities: Cabins, Food Service, Hiking Trails, Meeting Rooms
Programs: Environmental Education (#96)

Luther Village Camp Yolijwa

(est 1957)

Oak Glen, CA; (909) 797-9183
Loretta E. Clark, Director

Camp comments: Warm, supportive, caring staff. Christian values. Located a mile high in beautiful Oak Glen.
Activities: Aquatic Activities, Archery, Arts/Crafts, Basketball, Counselor Training (CIT), Hiking, Music, Nature/Environment Studies, Religious Study, Swimming — Recreational
Session lengths & capacity: 1 week sessions; 100 campers
Clientele & fees: boys 7-18; girls 7-18; coed 7-18; Fees: B
Contact: Loretta Clark, Site Director at (909) 797-9183; fax: (909) 797-9184
e-mail: luthervillage@lrccsca.org
Web site: www.lrccsca.org
Operated by: Lutheran Retreats Camps & Conf, PO Box 2027, Santa Clarita, CA 91386-2027 at (661) 250-2880

Group Rental Information
Site comments: Old fashion camp fun-led by spirit filled counselors. Campfire nightly confirmation & beach camp available.
Seasons & Capacity: Spring 96, Summer 96, Fall 96, Winter 80
Facilities: Dorm-Style, Food Service (#60)

Lyle Mc Leod (est 1947)

Tahuya, WA (Mason Co.); (360) 275-6396
Activities: Aquatic Activities, Archery, Arts/Crafts, Boating, Canoeing, Hiking
Session lengths & capacity: June-August; 160 campers
Contact: Jan Viney, Director of Outdoor Program Services at (080) 088-4682; fax: (425) 333-6236
e-mail: jancv@girlscoutstotem.org
Web site: www.girlscoutstotem.org
Operated by: Totem GSC, 3611 Woodland Park Ave N, Seattle, WA 98103 at (206) 633-5600

Group Rental Information
Site comments: Rustic setting, modern kitchen, private 60 acre lake.
Seasons & Capacity: Spring 200, Summer 200, Fall 200, Winter 54
Facilities: Cabins, Hiking Trails, Kitchen Facilities, Lake, Lodges, Tents
Programs: Boating, Swimming (#435)

Magdalena Ecke YMCA Camps

Encinitas, CA (San Diego Co.); (760) 942-9622
Chris Wiseman, Director
Activities: Baseball/Softball, Basketball, Fishing, Gymnastics, Kayaking, Leadership Development, Sailing, Soccer, Waterskiing
Session lengths & capacity: June-August; 1 week sessions; 1000 campers
Clientele & fees: coed 2-13; families; Fees: B, C
Contact: Bill Campbell, Camp Director at (760) 942-9622; fax: (760) 944-9329
Operated by: YMCA of San Diego County, 4715 Viewridge Ave Ste 100, San Diego, CA 92123 at (619) 292-4034 (#6279)

Mariastella (est 1946)

Wrightwood, CA (San Bernardino Co.); (760) 249-3530
Jennifer Gaeta SSS, Director

Camp comments: Focus is outdoor recreation in a Christian ecumenical setting. Fun, caring, staff, diverse economic, ethnic backgrounds
Activities: Arts/Crafts, Camping Skills/Outdoor Living, Drama, Hiking, Leadership Development, Nature/Environment Studies, Swimming — Recreational
Session lengths & capacity: 1 week sessions; 120 campers
Clientele & fees: girls 7-15; Fees: B
Contact: Jennifer Gaeta, Director at (213) 745-7870; fax: (213) 745-7871
Web site: www.campmariastella.com
Operated by: Camp Mariastella Inc, 2303 S Figueroa Way, Los Angeles, CA 90007 at (213) 745-7870

Group Rental Information
Site comments: We strive to introduce young women to nature & to their own inner strength through a safe & nurturing experience.
Facilities: Cabins, Dorm-Style, Double Occupancy, Food Service, Hiking Trails, Lodges, Meeting Rooms (#91)

Marin YMCA Day Camp

(est 1948)

San Rafael, CA (Marin Co.); (415) 492-9622
Stephanie Reed, Director

Camp comments: Day camp offers warm, supportive atmosphere for young campers. Outstanding staff.
Activities: Arts/Crafts, Drawing/Painting, Field Trips, Hiking, International Culture, Leadership Development, Nature/Environment Studies, Sports — Field & Team, Swimming — Recreational
Session lengths & capacity: June-September; 1 week sessions; 400 campers
Clientele & fees: boys 5-14; girls 5-14; coed 5-14

Contact: Stephanie Reed, CAmp and Family Director at (415) 492-9622; fax: (415) 492-9703 e-mail: sreed@ymcasf.org
Operated by: YMCA San Francisco Day Camps, 1877 S Grant Street, San Mateo, CA 94402 at (650) 286-9622 (#7394)

Mataguay Scout Reservation

(est 1961)   ▲ ⌂

Santa Ysabel, CA (San Diego Co.); (760) 782-3616
Bob Oslie, Director

Camp comments: Nationally recognized riflery program plus mountain bikes, golf, climbing, rappelling & glider flight!
Activities: Archery, Aviation, Camping Skills/Outdoor Living, Challenge/Rope Courses, Climbing/Rappelling, Golf, Riflery, Sports — Field & Team
Session lengths & capacity: July-August; 7 week sessions; 500 campers
Clientele & fees: boys 11-18; coed 14-21; Fees: **C** ▲ 🚐
Contact: Sean Roy, Director at (760) 782-3616; Web site: www.bsadpc.org
Operated by: Desert Pacific Council BSA, 1207 Upas St, San Diego, CA 92103 at (619) 298-6121

Group Rental Information
Seasons & Capacity: Spring 200, Fall 200, Winter 200
Facilities: A/V Equipment, Hiking Trails, Kitchen Facilities, Lake, Meeting Rooms, Playing Fields, Pool, Tents
Programs: Boating, Challenge/Ropes Course, Swimming (#7721)

Mission Valley YMCA Camp Marst

▲

Julian, CA (Los Angeles Co.); (760) 765-0642
Jennifer Naylor, Director

Camp comments: Come spend a week in the Julian mountains with the Mission Valley YMCA. Staff and activities are all top notch!
Activities: Archery, Arts/Crafts, Leadership Development, Nature/Environment Studies, Sports — Field & Team, Swimming — Recreational
Session lengths & capacity: August-August; 1 week sessions; 250 campers
Clientele & fees: coed 7-15; Fees: **C** ▲ 🚐
Contact: Jennifer Naylor, Community Program Director at (619) 298-3576; fax: (619) 298-9262 e-mail: jnaylor@ymca.org
Operated by: YMCA of San Diego County, 4715 Viewridge Ave Ste 100, San Diego, CA 92123 at (619) 292-4034 (#4306)

ICON LEGEND

☼   Day Camp

▲   Resident Camp

⌂   Facilities Available To Rent

🚐   Transportation Available

🚐   Financial Aid Available

FEE RANGES PER WEEK

A	$0-75
B	$75-200
C	$201-350
D	$351-500
E	$501-650
F	over $650

Mission Valley YMCA Day Camp

(est 1982)   ☼ 🚐

San Diego, CA (San Diego Co.); (619) 298-3576
Jennifer Naylor, Director

Camp comments: Day camp offers over 30 specialty camps ranging from surfing to laser tag.We also offer teen caravans,& 2 one week resident camps at Camp Marston & Camp Wolahi.
Activities: Basketball, Climbing/Rappelling, Football, Golf, Gymnastics, Horseback — English, Leadership Development, Nature/Environment Studies, Swimming — Recreational
Session lengths & capacity: 1 week sessions; 1000 campers
Clientele & fees: coed 3-16; Fees: **B, C** ☼ 🚐
Contact: Jennifer Naylor, Community Program Director at (619) 298-3576; fax: (619) 298-4341 e-mail: jnaylor@ymca.org
Operated by: YMCA of San Diego County, 4715 Viewridge Ave Ste 100, San Diego, CA 92123 at (619) 292-4034 (#4233)

Mission YMCA Day Camp

(est 1995)   ☼

San Francisco, CA (San Francisco Co.); (415) 586-6900
Activities: Baseball/Softball, Basketball, Field Trips, Hiking, Soccer, Sports — Field & Team, Swimming — Recreational
Operated by: YMCA San Francisco Day Camps, 1877 S Grant Street, San Mateo, CA 94402 at (650) 286-9622 (#2576)

Monte Toyon (est 1929)

⌂

Aptos, CA (Santa Cruz Co.); (408) 688-5420
Toby Pope, Director
Operated by: United Camps Conf & Retreats, 912 Lootens Pl, San Rafael, CA 94901 at (415) 456-5102

Group Rental Information
Facilities: A/V Equipment, Dorm-Style, Food Service, Hiking Trails, Meeting Rooms, Playing Fields
Programs: Environmental Education (#370)

Mount Hermon's Redwood Camp (est 1921)

▲ ⌂

Mount Hermon, CA (Santa Cruz Co.); (831) 335-4466
Ron Taylor, Director

Camp comments: Redwood provides junior and junior-high students week long camp experiences that are fun, safe, and relational.
Activities: Archery, Camping Skills/Outdoor Living, Canoeing, Challenge/Rope Courses, Counselor Training (CIT), Hiking, Music, Nature/Environment Studies, Riflery, Team Building
Session lengths & capacity: June-August; 1/2 & 1 week sessions; 140 campers
Clientele & fees: coed 7-13; families; Fees: **D** ▲ 🚐
Contact: Ron Taylor, Camp Director at (831) 430-1251; fax: (831) 335-9218 e-mail: rtaylor@mhcamps.org
Operated by: Mount Hermon Association Inc, PO Box 413, Mount Hermon, CA 95041 at (831) 335-4466

Group Rental Information
Site comments: Redwood Camp offers an ideal setting for a mid-week or weekend retreat in the non-summer months. Friendly staff, affordable accomodations, & delightful facility
Seasons & Capacity: Spring 140, Fall 140, Winter 140
Facilities: A/V Equipment, Cabins, Food Service, Hiking Trails, Playing Fields, Pool, River
Programs: Challenge/Ropes Course, Swimming (#346)

Mount Kare (est 1972)

⌂

Wrightwood, CA (San Bernardino Co.); (760) 249-3807
Pat Taylor, Director
Contact: Charles Parsons, Resident Manager at (760) 249-3807; e-mail: mtkare@uia.net
Session lengths: January-December
Operated by: Kare Youth League, 5150 Farna Ave, Arcadia, CA 91066-2080 at (626) 442-1160

Group Rental Information
Site comments: Excellent facility available to small and moderately sized groups. Beautiful mountain setting with easy access.
Seasons & Capacity: Spring 100, Summer 110, Fall 100, Winter 100
Facilities: Cabins, Food Service, Hiking Trails, Lodges, Meeting Rooms (#7625)

Mountain Camp (est 1987)

▲ 🚐

Pollock Pines, CA (Lassen Co.); (415) 351-2267
Jeff Lamb, Director

Camp comments: High Sierra adventure. Beautiful lakeside mountain setting. Noncompetitive, focus on outdoor & challenge activities.
Activities: Aquatic Activities, Archery, Arts/Crafts, Backpacking, Bicycling/Biking, Challenge/Rope Courses, Kayaking, Music, Sailing
Session lengths & capacity: 1, 2 & 3 week sessions; 160 campers
Clientele & fees: coed 8-15; Fees: **F** ▲
Contact: Scott Whipple, Director at (415) 351-2267; fax: (415) 351-3939
e-mail: scott@mountaincamp.com
Web site: www.mountaincamp.com
Operated by: Mountain Camp, 3717 Buchanan St Suite 300, San Francisco, CA 94123-1720 at (415) 351-2267 (#6353)

Mountain Meadow Ranch

(est 1955)   ▲ 🚐

Susanville, CA (Lassen Co.); (530) 257-4419
Chip, Jody, Director

Camp comments: Gorgeous forest ranch; acres of lush lawns; family envir. Build self-esteem; indvl activitie choices. Limited enrollment
Activities: Archery, Arts/Crafts, Backpacking, Ceramics/Pottery, Challenge/Rope Courses, Counselor Training (CIT), Drama, Horseback — Western, Riflery, Waterskiing
Session lengths & capacity: June-August; 1, 3 & 6 week sessions; 110 campers
Clientele & fees: coed 7-17; Fees: **E** ▲
Contact: Chip & Jody Ellena, Owner/Directors at (530) 257-4419; fax: (530) 257-7155
e-mail: chip@mountainmeadow.com
Web site: www.mountainmeadow.com
Operated by: Mountain Meadow Ranch, PO Box 610, Susanville, CA 96130 at (530) 257-4419 (#157)

Mt Crags Camp (est 1939)

▲ ⌂

Calabasas, CA (Los Angeles Co.); (818) 222-6327
Don Mowery, Director

Camp comments: Christian camp. Located in the beautiful Santa Monica Mountains. Offer traditional camping with outstanding staff.
Activities: Arts/Crafts, Baseball/Softball, Basketball, Challenge/Rope Courses, Drama, Hiking, Music, Performing Arts, Soccer
Session lengths & capacity: June-August; 1 & 2 week sessions; 125 campers
Clientele & fees: coed 7-16; Fees: **B, C** ▲
Contact: Don Mowery, Director at (818) 222-6327; fax: (818) 222-6396
e-mail: dmowery@pacbell.net
Web site: www.campmtcrags.com
Operated by: The Salvation Army, 900 W James Wood Blvd, Los Angeles, CA 90015 at (213) 896-9160

Group Rental Information

Site comments: Christian camp in Santa Monica Mtns close to Los Angeles metro area. Great facility for retreats with a friendly staff.
Seasons & Capacity: Spring 200, Fall 200
Facilities: A/V Equipment, Cabins, Dorm-Style, Double Occupancy, Food Service, Hiking Trails, Linens, Lodges, Meeting Rooms, Playing Fields, Pool
Programs: Challenge/Ropes Course, Environmental Education (#6106)

Mt Madonna YMCA

Morgan Hill, CA (Santa Clara Co.); (408) 779-0208
Tina Holloway, Director

Camp comments: Character building through healthy activities under leadership of child care professional YMCA staff.
Activities: Arts/Crafts, Camping Skills/Outdoor Living, Ceramics/Pottery, Community Service, Field Trips, Swimming — Instructional, Swimming — Recreational
Session lengths & capacity: June-September; 1 week sessions; 100 campers
Clientele & fees: coed 5-13; Fees: B
Contact: Tina Holloway, Program Director at (408) 779-0208; fax: (408) 779-5040
Web site: www.scvymca.org
Operated by: YMCA of Santa Clara Valley, 1922 The Alameda 3rd Fl, San Jose, CA 95126 at (408) 298-3888 (#2339)

Nawakwa (est 1947)

Angelus Oaks, CA (San Bernardino Co.);
(909) 794-3668
Letty Hernandez, Director

Camp comments: Boys and girls, ages 9-12, will enjoy 5 fun-filled days of a great outdoor experience. Children are separated by age & gender and sleep in fully enclosed cabins.
Activities: Archery, Arts/Crafts, Canoeing, Challenge/Rope Courses, Counselor Training (CIT), Dance, Drama, Nature/Environment Studies, Swimming — Recreational, Team Building
Session lengths & capacity: August-August; 1/2 week sessions; 185 campers
Clientele & fees: coed 9-12; Fees: C
Contact: Francie Rodgers, Administrative Assistant at (909) 624-5076; fax: (909) 626-2747
Web site: www.campfireusamsac.com
Operated by: Camp Fire USA, Mt San Antonio Council, 4959 Palo Verde St 208C, Montclair, CA 91763-2330 at (909) 624-5076

Group Rental Information

Site comments: Camp Nawakwa is ideal for large groups year round. Nice hike to lake. Heated pool, archery, climing wall, canoeing, hiking. FUN!
Seasons & Capacity: Spring 210, Summer 210, Fall 210, Winter 210
Facilities: Cabins, Double Occupancy, Hiking Trails, Kitchen Facilities, Lake, Lodges, Meeting Rooms, Pool
Programs: Boating, Challenge/Ropes Course, Environmental Education, Swimming (#129)

New Image Camp at Ojai

(est 1992)

Ojai, CA (Ventura Co.); (800) 365-0556
Tony Sparber, Director

Camp comments: Trad weight loss camp prog, upscale modern facilities. Sports & culture act inc. Motto: Weight loss, self-esteem & fun.
Activities: Aerobics/Exercise, Arts/Crafts, Baseball/Softball, Basketball, Drama, Field Trips, Horseback — Western, Soccer, Sports — Field & Team, Tennis
Session lengths & capacity: June-August; 2, 4 & 8 week sessions; 150 campers
Clientele & fees: coed 8-18; Fees: F

Contact: Tony Sparber, Owner/Director at (800) 365-0556; fax: (201) 750-1558
e-mail: sparber@newimagecamp.com
Operated by: Tony Sparbers New Image Camps, PO Box 417, Norwood, NJ 07648 at (800) 365-0556 (#1896)

North Bay YMCA

Swison, CA; (707) 421-8746
Veronica Roberson, Director

Camp comments: North Bay YMCA offers summer daycamp/daycare for children 6 to 13 years old. Children develip skills, grow personally & claify values through fun activities.
Activities: Arts/Crafts, Basketball, Field Trips, Football, Soccer, Swimming — Recreational, Team Building
Session lengths & capacity: June-August; 1, 2, 3, 4, 5, 6, 7, 8 & 9 week sessions; 100 campers
Clientele & fees: Fees: B
Contact: Veronica Robinson, Camp Director at (707) 421-8746; fax: (707) 121-9635
e-mail: vrobinson@ymcasf.org
Operated by: YMCA San Francisco Day Camps, 1877 S Grant Street, San Mateo, CA 94402 at (650) 286-9622 (#48303)

Northwest YMCA Day Camp

(est 1960)

Cupertino, CA (Santa Clara Co.); (408) 257-7160
Katie Bondelie, Director

Camp comments: Campers thrive in noncompetitive, caring atmosphere. Opportunities to build self-esteem, belong, learn & make friends.
Activities: Arts/Crafts, Camping Skills/Outdoor Living, Community Service, Drawing/Painting, Field Trips, Hiking, Leadership Development, Nature/Environment Studies
Session lengths & capacity: June-August; 1 week sessions; 350 campers
Clientele & fees: boys 6-15; girls 6-15; coed 6-15; families; Fees: B
Contact: Katie Bondelie, Youth & Family Program Dir. at (408) 257-7160; fax: (408) 257-6448
Web site: www.scvymca.org
Operated by: YMCA of Santa Clara Valley, 1922 The Alameda 3rd Fl, San Jose, CA 95126 at (408) 298-3888 (#5789)

Ojai Vley Summer School & Camp (est 1943)

Ojai, CA (Ventura Co.); (805) 646-1423
Gary Gartrell, Director

Camp comments: Loc. near Pacific Ocean & Los Padres Forest, campers strengthen or enrich academic skills while enjoying trad camp prog.
Activities: Academics, Arts/Crafts, Camping Skills/Outdoor Living, Ceramics/Pottery, Challenge/Rope Courses, Computer, Horseback — English, Swimming — Recreational, Tennis
Session lengths & capacity: June-July; 2, 4 & 6 week sessions; 175 campers
Clientele & fees: coed 8-18; Fees: D Fees: F
Contact: John Williamson, Director of Admission at (805) 646-1423; fax: (805) 646-0362
e-mail: jhw@ovs.org
Web site: www.ous.org
Operated by: Ojai Valley School, 723 El Paseo Rd, Ojai, CA 93023 at (805) 646-1423 (#140)

Olympian Day Camp

(est 1962)

Burlingame, CA (San Mateo Co.); (415) 692-6400
Kim O'Malley, Director

Camp comments: Olympian Day Camp gives your child a satisfying experience through effective leadership, activities & modern facilities.

Activities: Arts/Crafts, Baseball/Softball, Basketball, Drawing/Painting, Field Trips, Nature/Environment Studies, Skating, Soccer, Swimming — Instructional, Swimming — Recreational
Session lengths & capacity: 1 week sessions; 185 campers
Clientele & fees: boys 5-12; girls 5-12; coed 5-12; Fees: C
Contact: Len Beatie, Owner at (650) 692-6400; fax: (650) 552-9535
Operated by: Olympian Day Camp, PO Box 1515, Burlingame, CA 94011-1515 at (650) 692-6400 (#615)

Olympic Sports Camp

(est 1957)

West Los Angeles, CA (Los Angeles Co.); (310) 477-6864
Rob & Steve Bloom and Tom Anderson, Director

Camp comments: All sports program with individual attention given to each child. A staff ratio of 1:6 campers.
Activities: Baseball/Softball, Basketball, Dance, Football, Golf, Skating, Soccer, Swimming — Instructional, Tennis
Session lengths & capacity: June-August; 2 & 4 week sessions; 250 campers
Clientele & fees: boys 5-14; girls 5-14; Fees: C
Contact: Rob Bloom, Camp Director at (310) 477-6864; fax: (818) 385-1344
Web site: www.olysportscamp.com
Operated by: Olympic Sports Camp, PO Box 492404, Los Angeles, CA 90049 at (310) 477-6864 (#6332)

Orange YMCA at Camp Oakes

Big Bear City, CA (San Bernardino Co.); (714) 633-9622
Session lengths & capacity: 1 week sessions
Clientele & fees: coed 8-16; Fees: D
Fees: D
Contact: Web site: www.ymcaoforange.org
Operated by: YMCA of Orange, 2241 E Palmyra, Orange, CA 92869 at (714) 633-9622 (#14324)

Osher Marin JCC Day Camp

(est 1953)

San Rafael, CA (Marin Co.); (415) 444-8055
Barbara Schwartz, Director

Camp comments: Safety a priority! outstanding staff, supportive atmosphere, diverse programming, teen programs, specialty camps too!
Activities: Arts/Crafts, Camping Skills/Outdoor Living, Challenge/Rope Courses, Drama, Field Trips, Music, Nature/Environment Studies, Sports — Field & Team, Swimming — Recreational
Session lengths & capacity: June-August; 1, 2 & 3 week sessions; 300 campers
Clientele & fees: coed 3-16; Fees: B
Contact: (415) 444-8055; fax: (415) 491-1235
Operated by: Martin JCC Day Camps, 200 N San Pedro Rd, San Rafael, CA 94903 at (415) 444-8052 (#2337)

Pali Adventures (est 1991)

Running Springs, CA; (909) 867-5743
Elisa Becker, Director
Activities: Aquatic Activities, Boating, Challenge/Rope Courses, Drama, Horseback — Western, Leadership Development, Performing Arts, SCUBA, Skating
Session lengths & capacity: June-August; 1 & 3 week sessions; 165 campers
Clientele & fees: coed 9-16; Fees: F
Contact: Donna Head, Camp Director at (909) 867-5743; fax: (909) 867-7643
e-mail: director@paliadventures.com
Web site: www.palicamp.com

Operated by: Pali Camps, 12924 San Vicente Blvd, Los Angeles, CA 90049 at (310) 477-2700

Group Rental Information
Seasons & Capacity: Spring 200, Summer 200, Fall 200, Winter 200
Facilities: A/V Equipment, Cabins, Dorm-Style, Double Occupancy, Food Service, Hiking Trails, Lodges, Meeting Rooms, Playing Fields, Pool
Programs: Boating, Challenge/Ropes Course, Swimming (#47884)

Pali Camp (est 1990)
Pacific Palisades, CA (Los Angeles Co.); (310) 477-2700
Debbie Rudman, Director

Camp comments: Travel camp with over 100 activities & field trips. Door to door service: Westside & part of San Fernando Valley.
Activities: Aquatic Activities, Arts/Crafts, Drama, Field Trips, Gymnastics, Martial Arts, Soccer, Waterskiing
Session lengths & capacity: June-September; 1 & 2 week sessions; 225 campers
Clientele & fees: coed 3-16; Fees: D ☼ Fees: F ▲
Contact: Lindy Bazan, Camp Director at (310) 477-2700; fax: (310) 575-3237
e-mail: palicamp@palicamp.com
Web site: www.palicamp.com
Operated by: Pali Camps, 12924 San Vicente Blvd, Los Angeles, CA 90049 at (310) 477-2700 (#2475)

Palomar Family YMCA Day Camp (est 1970)
Escondido, CA (San Diego Co.); (619) 745-7490
Joseph Paul Olguin III, Director

Camp comments: The Palomar YMCA is dedicated to providing a safe, fun camping experience for youth and teens.
Activities: Camping Skills/Outdoor Living, Climbing/Rappelling, Counselor Training (CIT), Field Trips, Fishing, Golf, Gymnastics, Horseback — Western, Leadership Development, Wilderness Trips
Session lengths & capacity: 1 week sessions; 200 campers
Clientele & fees: boys 4-17; girls 4-17; Fees: B ☼ 🐖
Contact: Joseph Paul Olguin III at (760) 293-8916; fax: (760) 745-7942
e-mail: jolguin@ymca.org
Operated by: YMCA of San Diego County, 4715 Viewridge Ave Ste 100, San Diego, CA 92123 at (619) 292-4034 (#3045)

ICON LEGEND
☼ Day Camp
▲ Resident Camp
🏠 Facilities Available To Rent
🚗 Transportation Available
🐖 Financial Aid Available

FEE RANGES PER WEEK
A	$0-75
B	$75-200
C	$201-350
D	$351-500
E	$501-650
F	over $650

Pathfinder Ranch (est 1967)   ☼ ▲ 🏠
Mountain Center, CA (Riverside Co.); (909) 659-2455
Chris Fife, Director

Camp comments: Southern California Boys & Girls Club Camp in mountains above Palm Springs.
Activities: Archery, Arts/Crafts, Canoeing, Challenge/Rope Courses, Climbing/Rappelling, Counselor Training (CIT), Drama, Horseback — Western, Nature/Environment Studies, Swimming — Recreational
Session lengths & capacity: 1 week sessions; 130 campers
Clientele & fees: coed 7-17; Fees: B ▲ 🐖
Contact: Chris Fife, Director at (909) 659-2455; fax: (909) 659-0351
e-mail: director@pathfinderranch.com
Web site: www.bgcps.org
Operated by: Boys & Girls Club of Palm Sprg, 450 S Sunrise Way, Palm Springs, CA 92262 at (760) 325-3160

Group Rental Information
Site comments: Warm days & cool nights are the usual at this low cost high quality retreat. 1 hour southeast of Riverside.
Seasons & Capacity: Spring 130, Summer 130, Fall 130, Winter 130
Facilities: Cabins, Dorm-Style, Food Service, Hiking Trails, Lake, Lodges, Meeting Rooms, Pool
Programs: Boating, Environmental Education, Horseback Riding, Swimming (#30)

Peninsula Bay Cities Day Camp (est 1995)   ☼ 🚗
Rancho Palos Verdes, CA (Los Angeles Co.); (310) 541-3664
Greg Schneider/Adam Hibbeler, Director

Camp comments: Summer day camp. Fun & enrichment for children in the South Bay & Palos Verdes Peninsula area of southern California.
Activities: Academics, Aquatic Activities, Arts/Crafts, Climbing/Rappelling, Horseback — English, Horseback — Western, Sailing, Swimming — Instructional, Swimming — Recreational, Tennis
Session lengths & capacity: June-August; 1, 2 & 8 week sessions; 200 campers
Clientele & fees: coed 5-14; Fees: C ☼
Contact: Greg Schneider/Adam Hibbeler, Directors at (310) 541-3664; fax: (310) 541-3125
e-mail: pencamps@aol.com
Web site: www.peninsuladaycamp.com
Operated by: Peninsula Activities, PO Box 5245, Playa Del Rey, CA 90296 at (310) 541-3664 (#3298)

Peninsula Family YMCA   ☼
San Diego, CA (San Diego Co.); (619) 226-8888
Alison Saxe, Director
Activities: Aquatic Activities, Arts/Crafts, Counselor Training (CIT), Field Trips, Skating, Soccer, Sports — Field & Team, Swimming — Instructional
Session lengths & capacity: June-August; 1 week sessions; 300 campers
Clientele & fees: coed 5-16; Fees: B ☼ 🐖
Contact: Alison Saxe, Program Director at (619) 226-8888; fax: (619) 226-1675
e-mail: asaxe@ymca.org
Operated by: YMCA of San Diego County, 4715 Viewridge Ave Ste 100, San Diego, CA 92123 at (619) 292-4034 (#3147)

Peninsula Family YMCA Day Camp (est 1983)   ☼ 🚗
San Mateo, CA (San Mateo Co.); (650) 286-9622
Marisa Picchi, Director

Camp comments: Day camp offers caring experienced leaders to lead sports, crafts, games & field trips. Financial assistance available.

Activities: Arts/Crafts, Basketball, Camping Skills/Outdoor Living, Community Service, Counselor Training (CIT), Drawing/Painting, Field Trips, Leadership Development, Nature/Environment Studies, Swimming — Recreational
Session lengths & capacity: 1 week sessions; 450 campers
Clientele & fees: coed 5-14; Fees: B ☼ 🐖
Contact: Marisa Picchi, Camp Director at (650) 286-9622; fax: (650) 286-0128
Operated by: YMCA San Francisco Day Camps, 1877 S Grant Street, San Mateo, CA 94402 at (650) 286-9622 (#7686)

Peninsula Jewish Community Ctr (est 1956)   ☼
Belmont, CA (San Mateo Co.); (650) 591-4438
Stephanie Levin, Director

Camp comments: Campers make friends, learn new skills, develop appreciation of the Jewish culture in a supportive, safe atmosphere.
Activities: Arts/Crafts, Camping Skills/Outdoor Living, Community Service, Dance, Drama, Drawing/Painting, Field Trips, Music, Nature/Environment Studies, Swimming — Instructional
Session lengths & capacity: 3 week sessions; 200 campers
Clientele & fees: coed 3-15; Fees: B, C ☼ 🐖
Contact: Stephanie Levin, Camp Director at (650) 591-4438; fax: (650) 591-6902
e-mail: pjccyouth@aol.com
Web site: www.pjcc.org/camp
Operated by: Peninsula JCC, 2440 Carlmont Dr, Belmont, CA 94002 at (650) 591-4438 (#332)

Piedmont Choirs Music Camp (est 1983)   ▲ 🚗
Occidental, CA
Robert Geary, Director

Camp comments: We specialize in choral music instruction including theory, small group lessons, exploration of varied repertoire.
Activities: Aquatic Activities, Arts/Crafts, Basketball, Counselor Training (CIT), Drama, Drawing/Painting, Hiking, Music, Swimming — Recreational
Session lengths & capacity: August-August; 2 week sessions; 110 campers
Clientele & fees: coed 7-15; Fees: D ▲ 🐖
Contact: Arthur Kelly, Executive Director at (510) 547-4441; fax: (510) 547-7449
e-mail: akelly@piedmontchoirs.org
Web site: www.piedmontchoirs.org
Operated by: Piedmont Choirs Music Camp, 401A Highland Ave, Piedmont, CA 94611 at (510) 547-4441 (#128)

Pilgrim Pines Camp & Conf Ctr (est 1944)   ▲ 🏠
Yucaipa, CA (San Bernardino Co.); (909) 797-1821
Mickey Stone, Director

Camp comments: God-centered, life enriching, loving community for children ages 7-18 and developmentally challenged children and adults. Beautiful mtn setting. Good food, fun!
Activities: Arts/Crafts, Basketball, Camping Skills/Outdoor Living, Challenge/Rope Courses, Field Trips, Hiking, Leadership Development, Nature/Environment Studies, Swimming — Recreational, Team Building
Session lengths & capacity: July-August; 1 week sessions; 250 campers
Clientele & fees: boys 7-18; girls 7-18; coed 7-18; families; Fees: C ▲ 🐖
Contact: Mickey Stone, Executive Director at (909) 797-1821; fax: (909) 797-2691
e-mail: mickeystone@earthlink.net
Web site: www.pilgrimpinescamp.org

Operated by: United Church of Christ, Southern Calif Nevada Conf, 39570 Glen Rd, Yucaipa, CA 92399 at (909) 797-1821
Group Rental Information
Site comments: Easy access from I10 & I79. Great food. Beautiful pines. Team building and community at its finest.
Facilities: A/V Equipment, Cabins, Double Occupancy, Food Service, Hiking Trails, Linens, Lodges, Meeting Rooms, Playing Fields
Programs: Challenge/Ropes Course, Environmental Education, Swimming (#202)

Pine Springs Ranch Christian
(est 1961)
Mountain Center, CA (Riverside Co.); (909) 659-3173
Winston Morgan, Director
Camp comments: Christian camp providing quality program and emphasis on self-esteem. Mtn setting. A place to make and keep friends.
Activities: Aquatic Activities, Archery, Arts/Crafts, Backpacking, Bicycling/Biking, Challenge/Rope Courses, Drama, Horseback — Western, Waterskiing
Session lengths & capacity: June-August; 7 & 8 week sessions; 220 campers
Clientele & fees: coed 8-17; families; Fees: B
Fees: C
Contact: Winston Morgan, Asst Mgr/Summer Camp Director at (909) 659-3173; fax: (909) 659-5692
e-mail: wmorgan@pinespringsranch.org
Operated by: Southeastern Calif Conf SDA, PO Box 38, Mountain Center, CA 92561 at (909) 659-3173
Group Rental Information
Facilities: Cabins, Double Occupancy, Food Service, Hiking Trails, Linens, Meeting Rooms, Ocean, Pool
Programs: Challenge/Ropes Course, Environmental Education (#95)

Pine Valley Bible Conf Assoc
(est 1947)
Pine Valley, CA (San Diego Co.); (619) 473-8879
Jeff Darling, Director
Activities: Aerobics/Exercise, Archery, Arts/Crafts, Basketball, Hiking, Swimming — Recreational, Tennis
Session lengths & capacity: 1 week sessions; 300 campers
Clientele & fees: boys 1-18; girls 1-18; coed 1-18; families; seniors; single adults; Fees: B
Contact: (619) 473-8879; fax: (619) 473-8891
e-mail: info@pvbc.net
Web site: www.pvbc.net
Operated by: Pine Valley Bible Conf Assoc, PO Box 400, Pine Valley, CA 91962 at (619) 473-8879
Group Rental Information
Site comments: "Challenging campers for Christ"
Seasons & Capacity: Spring 300, Summer 300, Fall 300, Winter 300
Facilities: Dorm-Style, Double Occupancy, Food Service, Hiking Trails, Linens, Lodges, Meeting Rooms, Playing Fields, Pool
Programs: Swimming (#16624)

Plantation Farm Camp
(est 1952)
Cazadero, CA (Sonoma Co.); (707) 847-3494
David V Brown PhD, Director
Camp comments: Old-fashioned fun & adventure. Noncompetitive family atmosphere. Farm life, choice of daily activities. Sonoma Coast.

Activities: Archery, Arts/Crafts, Camping Skills/Outdoor Living, Drama, Farming/Ranching/Gardening, Hiking, Horseback — Western, Kayaking, Sports — Field & Team, Swimming — Recreational
Session lengths & capacity: June-August; 3 week sessions; 100 campers
Clientele & fees: coed 8-14; Fees: F
Contact: Suzanne Brown, Co-Director at (707) 847-3494; fax: (707) 847-3132
e-mail: info@plantationcamp.com
Web site: www.plantationcamp.com
Operated by: Plantation Farm Camp, 34285 Kruse Ranch Rd, Cazadero, CA 95421 at (707) 847-3494 (#3688)

Presidio YMCA Day Camp
(est 1993)
San Francisco, CA (San Francisco Co.); (415) 447-9622
Lara Farrell/Welcome Bisson, Director
Camp comments: Day camp with daily field trips. Highlights are swimming, overnight camping, values in a diverse, caring atmosphere.
Activities: Basketball, Camping Skills/Outdoor Living, Drama, Field Trips, Hiking, International Culture, Skating, Soccer, Sports — Field & Team, Tennis
Session lengths & capacity: 1 week sessions; 120 campers
Clientele & fees: coed 5-14; Fees: B
Contact: (415) 666-9622; fax: (415) 668-3370
Operated by: YMCA San Francisco Day Camps, 1877 S Grant Street, San Mateo, CA 94402 at (650) 286-9622 (#2406)

Quest Camp (est 1991)
Alamo, CA (Contra Costa Co.); (925) 743-1370
Robert Field, PhD, Director
Camp comments: Unique day camp providing individualized psychological treatment & camp activities. Campers improve selfesteem, behavior & social skills, parent assist. as well
Activities: Arts/Crafts, Baseball/Softball, Field Trips, Leadership Development, Soccer, Sports — Field & Team, Swimming — Recreational, Team Building
Session lengths & capacity: June-August; 3, 4, 5, 6, 7, 8 week sessions; 50 campers
Clientele & fees: coed 6-15; Fees: D
Contact: Robert Field, PhD, Director at (925) 743-1370; fax: (925) 743-1937
e-mail: bfield12@aol.com
Web site: www.questcamps.com
Operated by: Quest Camp, 2333 San Ramon Valley Blvd, Ste 200, San Ramon, CA 94583 at (925) 743-1370 (#2186)

Raintree Ranch YMCA
(est 1969)
Julian, CA
Tom Madeyski, Director
Camp comments: Western horseback specialty camp in mountains east of San Diego. Spectacular trails, excellent instruction, all levels.
Activities: Archery, Arts/Crafts, Challenge/Rope Courses, Climbing/Rappelling, Dance, Horseback — Western, Nature/Environment Studies
Session lengths & capacity: June-August; 1 week sessions; 70 campers
Clientele & fees: coed 9-15; families; Fees: D
Contact: (760) 765-0642; fax: (760) 765-0183
e-mail: camp@ymca.org
Operated by: YMCA of San Diego County, 4715 Viewridge Ave Ste 100, San Diego, CA 92123 at (619) 292-4034
Group Rental Information
Seasons & Capacity: Spring 100, Fall 100, Winter 100 (#43445)

Ramah In California
(est 1956)
Ojai, CA (Ventura Co.); (805) 646-4301
Rabbi Daniel Greyber, Director
Camp comments: Jewish environment provides perfect setting for a fun, exciting summer. We also have family & special needs programs.
Activities: Arts/Crafts, Baseball/Softball, Basketball, Challenge/Rope Courses, Community Service, Drama, Hiking, Leadership Development, Nature/Environment Studies, Swimming — Recreational
Session lengths & capacity: June-August; 1, 4 & 8 week sessions; 575 campers
Clientele & fees: coed 8-16; families; Fees: F
Contact: Rabbi Daniel Greyber, Executive Director at (310) 476-8571; fax: (310) 472-3810
e-mail: info@ramah.org
Web site: www.ramah.org
Operated by: The Univ of Judaism, 15600 Mulholland Dr, Los Angeles, CA 90077 at (310) 476-8571
Group Rental Information
Seasons & Capacity: Spring 0, Fall 0, Winter 0
Facilities: Cabins, Double Occupancy, Food Service, Hiking Trails, Linens, Lodges, Meeting Rooms (#121)

Rancho Family YMCA (est 1989)
San Diego, CA
Marissa Edwards, Director
Camp comments: The Rancho YMCA offers 40 speciality camps & aquatic programs. Camps range from rock climbing to surf to sport camps.
Activities: Aquatic Activities, Basketball, Counselor Training (CIT), Field Trips, Golf, Gymnastics, Horseback — English, Skating, Sports — Field & Team
Session lengths & capacity: June-September; 1 & 2 week sessions; 400 campers
Clientele & fees: coed 5-14; Fees: B, C
Contact: Jennifer Naylor, Program Director at (619) 484-8788; fax: (619) 484-8869
Operated by: YMCA of San Diego County, 4715 Viewridge Ave Ste 100, San Diego, CA 92123 at (619) 292-4034 (#24291)

Rancho La Scherpa Presbyterian (est 1960)
Goleta, CA; (805) 688-5360
Rev. Barbara Lee, Director
Contact: Ana Nava, Registrar at (213) 483-3840; fax: (213) 483-4275
e-mail: ananava@synod.org
Operated by: Synod Of Southern California, 1501 Wilshire Blvd, Los Angeles, CA 90017 at (213) 483-3840
Group Rental Information
Site comments: 27 miles No. of Sta Barbara with an unmatched mtn top view-210 acres offer abundant space for activities and meditation.
Facilities: Dorm-Style, Food Service, Hiking Trails, Lodges, Meeting Rooms, Pool
Programs: Environmental Education (#7333)

Rawhide Ranch (est 1963)
Bonsall, CA (San Diego Co.); (760) 758-0083
Tom and Val Ewan, Director
Camp comments: Rawhide Ranch provides campers from all over the world a taste of the old west, riding, vaulting, animal care and much more.
Activities: Aquatic Activities, Archery, Arts/Crafts, Counselor Training (CIT), Drama, Farming/Ranching/Gardening, Horseback — Western, Music, Riflery, Swimming — Recreational
Session lengths & capacity: June-August; 1 week sessions; 220 campers

Clientele & fees: coed 7-16; Fees: E △
Contact: Valeria Ewan, Co-Camp Director at (760) 758-0083; fax: (760) 758-0440
e-mail: info@rawhideranch.com
Web site: www.rawhideranch.com
Operated by: Rawhide Ranch Enterprises LLC, PO Box 216, Bonsall, CA 92003 at (760) 758-0083

Group Rental Information
Seasons & Capacity: Spring 150, Fall 150, Winter 150
Facilities: Playing Fields, Pool
Programs: Swimming (#16440)

Reach For The Sky (est 1982) △ 🚐

San Diego, CA (San Diego Co.); (619) 682-7427
Rocco Diubaldi, Director
Camp comments: Special camp for children who have, oFr have had cancer. Focused on building self-esteem through camping experiences
Activities: Aquatic Activities, Archery, Camping Skills/Outdoor Living, Canoeing, Climbing/Rappelling, Leadership Development, Riflery, Soccer, Sports — Field & Team, Swimming — Recreational
Session lengths & capacity: August-August; 1 week sessions; 100 campers
Clientele & fees: coed 8-18; Fees: A △ 🐖
Contact: Jeanne Sereff, Administrative Assistant at (619) 682-7411; fax: (619) 296-0928
Web site: www.cancer.org
Operated by: Am Cancer Society Border Reg, 2655 Camino del Rio N Ste 100, San Diego, CA 92108 at (619) 682-7427 (#13260)

Reach For The Sky Day Camp

(est 1983) ☀

San Diego, CA (San Diego Co.); (619) 298-8393
Barbara Wiggins, Director

Camp comments: A day camp for childhood cancer patients & their siblings ages 4-10. Emphasis: a normal camp experience, fun & friends.
Activities: Archery, Arts/Crafts, Baseball/Softball, Camping Skills/Outdoor Living, Dance, Field Trips, Music, Nature/Environment Studies, Soccer, Swimming — Recreational
Session lengths & capacity: July-July; 1 week sessions; 75 campers
Clientele & fees: coed 4-10; Fees: A ☀ 🐖
Contact: Barbara Wiggins/Jeanie Seref, Camp Director/Camp Secretary at (619) 682-7427; fax: (619) 296-0928
Web site: www.cancer.org
Operated by: Am Cancer Society Border Reg, 2655 Camino del Rio N Ste 100, San Diego, CA 92108 at (619) 682-7427 (#4504)

ICON LEGEND
☀ Day Camp
△ Resident Camp
🏠 Facilities Available To Rent
🚐 Transportation Available
🐖 Financial Aid Available

FEE RANGES PER WEEK
A $0-75
B $75-200
C $201-350
D $351-500
E $501-650
F over $650

Redwood Glen △ 🏠

Scotts Valley, CA; (408) 439-5131
Mark Morton, Director
Activities: Aquatic Activities, Archery, Backpacking, Challenge/Rope Courses, Performing Arts, Religious Study
Operated by: The Salvation Army, 3100 Bear Creek Rd, Scotts Valley, CA 95066 at (415) 553-3500

Group Rental Information
Seasons & Capacity: Spring 25, Summer 30, Fall 25, Winter 25
Facilities: A/V Equipment, Cabins, Dorm-Style, Double Occupancy, Food Service, Hiking Trails, Linens, Lodges, Meeting Rooms, Playing Fields, Pool
Programs: Challenge/Ropes Course, Swimming (#311)

Redwood Glen Baptist Camp

(est 1958) △ 🏠

Loma Mar, CA (San Mateo Co.); (650) 879-0320
Jay Nordgaard, Director
Activities: Backpacking, Basketball, Drama, Religious Study, Soccer, Swimming — Recreational
Session lengths & capacity: January-December; 1 week sessions; 150 campers
Clientele & fees: boys 1-18; girls 1-18; coed 1-18; families; seniors; single adults; Fees: B △
Operated by: Amer Baptist Churches of West, 2420 Camino Ramon Ste 140, San Ramon, CA 94583 at (925) 277-3980

Group Rental Information
Site comments: Year round camp and conference center. Guest groups from 20 - 200 are welcome.
Seasons & Capacity: Spring 200, Summer 200, Fall 200, Winter 200
Facilities: A/V Equipment, Cabins, Dorm-Style, Double Occupancy, Food Service, Hiking Trails, Kitchen Facilities, Lake, Lodges, Meeting Rooms, Playing Fields, Pool, Tents
Programs: Swimming (#316)

River Way Ranch Camp

(est 1966) △ 🚐

Sanger, CA (Fresno Co.); (559) 787-2551
Nancy Oken Nighbert, Director

Camp comments: Family owned & operated. 60 activities, emphasis on 1st time camper, memories to last a lifetime, highly trained staff. Wonder Valley Family Camp avail in Aug.
Activities: Aquatic Activities, Arts/Crafts, Challenge/Rope Courses, Drama, Horseback — English, Horseback — Western, Martial Arts, Performing Arts, Sports — Field & Team, Waterskiing
Session lengths & capacity: June-August; 2, 4 & 6 week sessions; 300 campers
Clientele & fees: coed 7-16; families; single adults; Fees: F △
Contact: Nancy Oken Nighbert, Camp Director at (559) 787-2551; fax: (559) 787-3851
e-mail: rwrcamp@aol.com
Operated by: River Way Ranch Camp, 6450 Elwood Rd, Sanger, CA 93657 at (209) 787-2551 (#38)

Riverside YMCA at Camp Tatapoc (est 1923) △

Alhambra, CA (San Bernardino Co.); (818) 576-9097
Stacy Rossi-Kollar, Director

Camp comments: Mountain setting. Traditional program. Christian emphasis. 8 day 7 nights. Chapels, campfires daily. Competition day.
Activities: Archery, Arts/Crafts, Backpacking, Challenge/Rope Courses, Hiking, Leadership Development, Nature/Environment Studies, Riflery
Session lengths & capacity: 1 week sessions; 120 campers

Clientele & fees: coed 8-14; Fees: C △ 🚐
Contact: Stacy Rossi-Kollar, Program Director at (909) 689-9622; fax: (909) 689-7543
Operated by: YMCA Riverside City and County, 9254 Galena Street, Riverside, CA 92509 at (909) 685-5241 (#81)

Riverside YMCA Day Camp ☀

Riverside, CA (Riverside Co.); (909) 689-9622

Camp comments: Day camp offers a wide variety of activities while under direct supervision of trained leaders. Extended hours available
Activities: Arts/Crafts, Basketball, Field Trips, Leadership Development, Nature/Environment Studies
Session lengths & capacity: June-August; 1 & 2 week sessions; 100 campers
Clientele & fees: coed 5-14; Fees: B ☀ 🐖
Contact: Stacy Rossi-Kollar, Program Director at (909) 689-9622; fax: (909) 689-7543
Operated by: YMCA Riverside City and County, 9254 Galena Street, Riverside, CA 92509 at (909) 685-5241 (#90)

RM Pyles Boys Camp (est 1949) △ 🏠

Kernville, CA (Los Angeles Co.)
Sean Mc Enulty, Director

Camp comments: Participants are disadvantaged, at-risk boys 12-14, selected through law enforcement agencies and local school districts.
Activities: Archery, Camping Skills/Outdoor Living, Challenge/Rope Courses, Counselor Training (CIT), Hiking, Horseback — Western, Leadership Development, Nature/Environment Studies, Wilderness Trips
Session lengths & capacity: June-August; 2 week sessions; 72 campers
Clientele & fees: coed 12-14; Fees: A △
Contact: Sean P McEnulty, Executive Director at (661) 294-1394; fax: (661) 294-1397
e-mail: beaver@pylescamp.com
Operated by: RM Pyles Boys Camp, 27211 Henry Mayo Drive, Valencia, CA 91355-1009 at (661) 294-1394

Group Rental Information
Seasons & Capacity: Fall 75
Facilities: Cabins, Dorm-Style, Food Service, Hiking Trails
Programs: Challenge/Ropes Course (#12412)

Roughing It Day Camp

(est 1972) ☀ 🚐

Orinda, CA (Contra Costa Co.); (510) 283-3795
Ann & Hobie Woods, Director

Camp comments: Traditional camp with camper growth & group centered focus. All outdoor prog lakefront site in SF Bay area, 30th year.
Activities: Arts/Crafts, Camping Skills/Outdoor Living, Canoeing, Climbing/Rappelling, Fishing, Horseback — English, International Culture, Leadership Development, Soccer, Swimming — Instructional
Session lengths & capacity: 4 & 8 week sessions; 300 campers
Clientele & fees: coed 4-16; Fees: C ☀ 🐖
Contact: Ann & Hobie Woods, Founder/Owner/Director at (510) 283-3795; fax: (510) 283-1619
e-mail: ann@roughingit.com
Web site: www.roughinit.com
Operated by: Roughing It, PO Box 1266, Orinda, CA 94563 at (925) 283-3795 (#7724)

Saddleback Valley YMCA △ 🚐

Angelus Oaks, CA (San Bernadino Co.); (949) 859-9622

Activities: Archery, Arts/Crafts, Bicycling/Biking, Camping Skills/Outdoor Living, Canoeing, Challenge/Rope Courses, Hiking, Nature/Environment Studies, Swimming — Recreational
Session lengths & capacity: July-July; 1 week sessions; 230 campers
Clientele & fees: coed 8-17; Fees: C △ 🐷 🚐
Contact: Terry Palhidai, Program Director II at (949) 859-9622 ext. 122; fax: (949) 380-2447 e-mail: tpalhidai@ymcaoc.net
Operated by: Saddleback Valley YMCA, 27431 Trabuco Circle, Mission Viejo, CA 92692 at (949) 859-9622 (#19148)

Saddleback Valley YMCA Day Cmp

Mission Viejo, CA (Orange Co.); (949) 859-9622
Activities: Archery, Arts/Crafts, Basketball, Drama, Field Trips, Hiking, Leadership Development, Nature/Environment Studies, Sports — Field & Team, Swimming — Recreational
Session lengths & capacity: June-September; 1 week sessions; 120 campers
Clientele & fees: coed 6-15; Fees: B ☀ 🐷 🚐
Contact: Annette Perry, Program Director II at (949) 859-9622 ext. 121; fax: (949) 380-2447 e-mail: aperry@ymcaoc.net
Operated by: Saddleback Valley YMCA, 27431 Trabuco Circle, Mission Viejo, CA 92692 at (949) 859-9622 (#19155)

Salvation Army Sierra Del Mar

(est 1995) △ ⌂ 🚐

Ramona, CA (San Diego Co.); (760) 788-3311
Dianne Doom, Director

Camp comments: A Christian camp emphasizing character development & social skills primarily serving children from lower economic areas.
Activities: Archery, Arts/Crafts, Baseball/Softball, Basketball, Hiking, Leadership Development, Music, Nature/Environment Studies, Religious Study, Swimming — Recreational
Session lengths & capacity: June-September; 1 week sessions; 200 campers
Clientele & fees: coed 6-12; seniors; Fees: B △ 🚐
Contact: Dianne Doom, Camp Director at (619) 231-6000 ext. 215; fax: (619) 446-0497 e-mail: dianne_doom@usw.salvationarmy.org
Operated by: Salvation Army Sierra Del Mar, 2320 Fifth Avenue, San Diego, CA 92101 at (619) 231-6000

Group Rental Information
Facilities: A/V Equipment, Cabins, Dorm-Style, Food Service, Hiking Trails, Kitchen Facilities, Lodges, Meeting Rooms, Playing Fields, Pool
Programs: Swimming (#4254)

San Diego Youth Aquatics Ctr

(est 1991) △

San Diego, CA (San Diego Co.); (619) 275-3384
Christine Higueria-Street, Director

Camp comments: Beautiful weather and many local attractions makes our camp something special. Fun in, on & out of the water.
Activities: Aquatic Activities, Boating, Camping Skills/Outdoor Living, Canoeing, Kayaking, Sailing, Windsurfing
Session lengths & capacity: July-August; 7 week sessions; 100 campers
Clientele & fees: boys 7-21; coed 14-21; Fees: C △ 🚐

Contact: Christine Higueria Street, Ranger/Summer Camp Director at (619) 298-6121 ext. 308; fax: (619) 298-5036
Web site: www.bsadpc.org
Operated by: Desert Pacific Council BSA, 1207 Upas St, San Diego, CA 92103 at (619) 298-6121 (#2810)

Santa Susana School (est 1978) ☀

Chatsworth, CA (Los Angeles Co.); (818) 709-9854
Activities: Academics, Arts/Crafts, Baseball/Softball, Basketball, Computer, Field Trips, Performing Arts, Soccer, Sports — Field & Team, Swimming — Recreational
Session lengths & capacity: July-August; 1, 4 & 8 week sessions; 300 campers
Clientele & fees: coed 2-11; Fees: B ☀
Contact: Dr Marilyn Luckey, Owner/Administrator at (818) 709-9854; fax: (818) 709-1722
Operated by: Santa Susana School, 22280 Devonshire Street, Chatsworth, CA 91311 at (818) 709-9854 (#27012)

SeaWorld Adventure Camps

(est 1982) ☀ △

San Diego, CA (San Diego Co.); (800) 380-3202
Mike Dunn, Director

Camp comments: A splash of summer excitement at SeaWorld's Adventure camps. Shamu, penguins, sharks and more. the thrills are non-stop in this animal experience of a lifetime.
Activities: Academics, Aquatic Activities, Arts/Crafts, Field Trips, Kayaking, Nature/Environment Studies
Session lengths & capacity: June-August; 1/2 & 1 week sessions; 24 campers

Clientele & fees: coed 5-18; Fees: **A, B** ☀
Fees: **F** ⛺
Contact: Sea World Education Department, Reservationists at (800) 380-3202;
fax: (619) 226-3634
e-mail: education.swc@seaworld.com
Web site: www.seaworld.org
Operated by: SeaWorld San Diego, 500 Sea World Dr, San Diego, CA 92109 at (800) 380-3202 (#3855)

Shaffer's High Sierra Camp Inc

(est 2000) ⛺

Sattley, CA (Marin Co.); (800) 516-3513
Scott & Lisa Shaffer, Director

Camp comments: Wilderness adventure in the Tahoe Natl Forest for 9-16 yr-olds. Small, noncompetitive, near 70+ lakes & miles of trails.
Activities: Aquatic Activities, Arts/Crafts, Backpacking, Bicycling/Biking, Challenge/Rope Courses, Horseback — Western, Rafting, Swimming — Recreational, Team Building, Wilderness Trips
Session lengths & capacity: June-August; 1 & 2 week sessions; 48 campers
Clientele & fees: coed 9-16; Fees: **F** ⛺
Contact: Scott/Lisa Shaffer, Directors at (800) 516-3513; fax: (415) 897-0316
e-mail: highsierracamp@hotmail.com
Web site: www.highsierracamp.com
Operated by: Shaffer's High Sierra Camp Inc, 248 San Marin Drive, Novato, CA 94945-1221 at (800) 516-3513 (#46258)

Shalom Institute Camp & Conf

(est 1951) ☀ ⛺ 🏠 🚐

Sherman Oaks, CA (Los Angeles Co.); (818) 374-7077

Camp comments: Beautiful Malibu; caring environment, every camper counts; emphasis on Jewish culture; outdoor adventure, nature & fun!
Activities: Aquatic Activities, Archery, Arts/Crafts, Challenge/Rope Courses, Horseback — Western, Leadership Development, Nature/Environment Studies, Performing Arts, Sports — Field & Team
Session lengths & capacity: 1, 2 & 4 week sessions; 230 campers
Clientele & fees: coed 6-17; families; seniors; single adults; Fees: **C** ☀ Fees: **D** ⛺ 🐷
Contact: Bill Kaplan, Director at (818) 889-5500; fax: (818) 889-5132
e-mail: billkap@aol.com
Web site: www.shalominstitute.com
Operated by: Shalom Institute Camp & Conf, 34342 Mulholland Hwy, Malibu, CA 90265 at (818) 889-5500

ICON LEGEND

☀   Day Camp
⛺   Resident Camp
🏠   Facilities Available To Rent
🚐   Transportation Available
🐷   Financial Aid Available

FEE RANGES PER WEEK

A	$0-75
B	$75-200
C	$201-350
D	$351-500
E	$501-650
F	over $650

Group Rental Information

Site comments: Nestled in rustic, wooded canyon; few miles from ocean & 45 minutes from LA. Shalom Institute: an ideal retreat facility
Seasons & Capacity: Spring 350, Summer 350, Fall 350, Winter 350
Facilities: Cabins, Dorm-Style, Double Occupancy, Food Service, Kitchen Facilities
Programs: Challenge/Ropes Course, Environmental Education (#7203)

Shasta Camp Cherith (est 1959) ⛺

Alta, CA (Nevada Co.); (530) 389-2277
Bobbie Gilchrist, Director

Camp comments: Shasta Camp Cherith is a non-denominational Christian camp. Our program consists of small cabin groups and mature staff.
Activities: Archery, Arts/Crafts, Camping Skills/Outdoor Living, Canoeing, Counselor Training (CIT), Drama, Hiking, Religious Study, Riflery, Swimming — Recreational
Session lengths & capacity: June-July; 1 week sessions; 100 campers
Clientele & fees: boys 8-18; girls 8-18; Fees: **C** ⛺ 🐷
Contact: Bobbie Jean Gilchrist, Co Director at (408) 997-3639;
Operated by: Shasta Camp Cherith, 1225 PoppY Lane Dr, Hollister, CA 95023 at (831) 636-5482 (#306)

Shiwaka (est 1930) ☀ 🏠

Long Beach, CA (Los Angeles Co.); (310) 421-2725
Shirlee Jackert, Director

Camp comments: Cooking over the campfire & outdoor skills. Sleep-over camp on the edge of the city for boys and girls near 605 Fwy.
Activities: Archery, Arts/Crafts, Camping Skills/Outdoor Living, Challenge/Rope Courses, Counselor Training (CIT), Field Trips, Hiking, Leadership Development, Nature/Environment Studies, Team Building
Session lengths & capacity: 1 week sessions; 100 campers
Clientele & fees: boys 5-12; girls 5-12; coed 5-12; Fees: **B** ☀ 🐷
Contact: Shirlee Jackert, Executive Director at (562) 421-2725; fax: (562) 421-4056
e-mail: campfirelb@earthlink.net
Web site: www.campfirelb.net
Operated by: Camp Fire Boys & Girls, 7070 E Carson St, Long Beach, CA 90808 at (562) 421-2725

Group Rental Information

Facilities: Kitchen Facilities, Lodges, Meeting Rooms, Tents (#161)

Sierra Adventure Camps

(est 1965) ☀ ⛺ 🚐

Los Angeles, CA (Los Angeles Co.); (310) 826-7000
Kent D. Newell and Heather Hibbeler, Director

Camp comments: Life long aquatic skills taught, beautiful lake & ocean settings. Lmtd Enrollment. Much Individual guidance & attention.
Activities: Aquatic Activities, Boating, Camping Skills/Outdoor Living, Canoeing, Counselor Training (CIT), Kayaking, Sailing, Swimming — Recreational, Waterskiing
Session lengths & capacity: June-August; 2 & 3 week sessions; 60 campers
Clientele & fees: coed 7-16; Fees: **C** ☀ Fees: **D** ⛺
Contact: Kent D Newell or Heather Hibbeler, Directors at (310) 826-7000; fax: (310) 826-0474
e-mail: sierracamp@earthlink.net
Web site: www.sierraadventurecamps.com
Operated by: Sierra Ski And Pack Club Inc, 2633 Lincoln Blvd 604, Santa Monica, CA 90405 at (310) 392-3100 (#58)

Sierra Canyon Day Camp

(est 1972) ☀ 🚐

Chatsworth, CA (Los Angeles/SFV Co.); (818) 882-8121
Shosh Byron & Adam Horwitz, Director

Camp comments: A special place for children. Rustic setting, outstanding staff. Many activities, including 105 ft waterslide, schedule flexibilty.
Activities: Academics, Archery, Arts/Crafts, Computer, Counselor Training (CIT), Dance, Drama, Gymnastics, Nature/Environment Studies, Skating
Session lengths & capacity: June-August; 4 & 5 week sessions; 500 campers
Clientele & fees: coed 4-14; Fees: **C** ☀
Contact: Shosh Byron, Director at (818) 882-8121; fax: (818) 882-8218
e-mail: shosh@sierracanyon.com
Web site: www.sierracanyon.com
Operated by: Sierra Canyon Day Camp, 11052 Sierra Canyon Way, Chatsworth, CA 91311 at (818) 882-8121 (#3407)

Sierra Pines Baptist (est 1977) 🏠

Twin Bridges, CA (El Dorado Co.); (530) 659-7111
Rev. Douglas L. Siden, Director
Operated by: Amer Baptist Churches of West, 2420 Camino Ramon Ste 140, San Ramon, CA 94583 at (925) 277-3980

Group Rental Information

Site comments: In the High Sierra near Lake Tahoe. Guest groups welcome.
Facilities: Cabins, Dorm-Style, Food Service, Kitchen Facilities, Meeting Rooms, Pool (#8390)

Silver Gan Israel Day Camp

(est 1972) ☀ 🚐

Huntington Beach, CA (Orange Co.); (714) 898-0051
Rabbi Moishe B Rodman, Director

Camp comments: Day camp offering exciting trips and activities. Emphasizes sports, swim program & Jewish culture. Pool on premisses.
Activities: Arts/Crafts, Basketball, Computer, Field Trips, Hockey, Music, Sports — Field & Team, Swimming — Instructional, Swimming — Recreational
Session lengths & capacity: 2 week sessions; 500 campers
Clientele & fees: coed 2-13; Fees: **D** ☀ 🐷
Contact: Rabbi Moishe B Rodman, Director at (714) 898-0051; fax: (714) 898-0633
e-mail: moisherodman@hotmail.com
Web site: www.hebrewacademyhb.com
Operated by: Hebrew Academy, 14401 Willow Lane, Huntington Beach, CA 92647 at (714) 898-0051 (#7310)

Skylake Yosemite Camp

(est 1945) ⛺ 🚐

Wishon, CA (Madera Co.); (559) 642-3720
Jeff Portnoy, Director

Camp comments: Traditional style camp with 58 years of tradtionals. Located on a warm water lake in a pine forest. Small cabin groups and high counselor/camper ratio.
Activities: Aquatic Activities, Archery, Arts/Crafts, Canoeing, Challenge/Rope Courses, Drama, Golf, Horseback — Western, Waterskiing, Wilderness Trips
Session lengths & capacity: June-August; 2, 4, 6 & 8 week sessions; 210 campers
Clientele & fees: coed 7-16; Fees: **F** ⛺
Contact: Jeffery Portnoy, Director/Owner at (559) 642-3720; fax: (559) 642-3395
e-mail: jpskylake@aol.com
Web site: www.skylakeyosemite.com
Operated by: Skylake Yosemite Camp, 37976 Road 222, Wishon, CA 93669 at (559) 642-3720 (#368)

Skylark Ranch (est 1953)

San Jose, CA (Santa Cruz Co.); (408) 287-4170

Camp comments: Coastal redwoods. Supportive atmosphere; tents. Traditional program plus beach. Llamas, horseback riding (E/W vault).
Activities: Archery, Arts/Crafts, Backpacking, Camping Skills/Outdoor Living, Challenge/Rope Courses, Field Trips, Hiking, Horseback — English, Horseback — Western, Nature/Environment Studies
Session lengths & capacity: June-August; 1/2, 1 & 2 week sessions; 150 campers
Clientele & fees: girls 7-17; Fees: C ⚐ 🚌
Contact: Sari VanOtegham, Director of Outdoor Program at (408) 287-4170 ext. 257; fax: (408) 287-8025
e-mail: pchappars@girlscoutsofscc.org
Web site: www.girlscoutsofscc.org
Operated by: GSC of Santa Clara County, 1310 S Bascom Avenue, San Jose, CA 95128 at (408) 287-4170
Group Rental Information
Facilities: Hiking Trails, Kitchen Facilities, Ocean, Tents (#296)

Snow Mountain Camp

(est 1969)

Nevada City, CA (Nevada County Co.); (530) 265-4439
Kelly Newell, Director

Camp comments: Mature, caring staff. Guides campers daily. Choices from carefully structured program. Diverse int'l staff & clientele.
Activities: Arts/Crafts, Bicycling/Biking, Challenge/Rope Courses, Drama, Horseback — English, Horseback — Western, Leadership Development, Waterskiing
Session lengths & capacity: June-August; 1, 2, 3, 4, 5, 6, 7 & 8 week sessions; 75 campers
Clientele & fees: coed 7-16; Fees: F ⚐
Contact: Kelly Newell, Director at (530) 265-4439; fax: (530) 265-4435
e-mail: smcamp@nccn.net
Web site: www.snowmountaincamp.com
Operated by: Snow Mountain Camp, PO Box 476, Nevada City, CA 95959 at (916) 265-4439
Group Rental Information
Site comments: Site available for groups - 43 acre facility in the Sierra Nevada foothills - year round program & food service staff, heated cabins & meeting room.
Seasons & Capacity: Spring 40, Fall 125, Winter 40
Facilities: Cabins, Food Service, Hiking Trails, Kitchen Facilities, Meeting Rooms, Pool
Programs: Challenge/Ropes Course, Swimming (#377)

Sonoma Cty YMCA Dunbar Elmntry (est 1995)

Glen Ellen, CA (Sonoma Co.); (707) 996-9220
Activities: Counselor Training (CIT), Field Trips, Leadership Development, Music, Performing Arts, Swimming — Recreational, Team Building
Session lengths & capacity: June-August
Clientele & fees: coed 6-12; Fees: B ☀
Contact: Michelle Head, Program Director at (707) 544-1829; fax: (707) 544-4432
Operated by: Sonoma County YMCA, 1111 College Ave, Santa Rosa, CA 95404 at (707) 544-1829 (#3120)

Sonoma Cty YMCA Grant Day Camp

Petaluma, CA; (707) 544-1829
Michelle Head, Director

Activities: Baseball/Softball, Basketball, Counselor Training (CIT), Drama, Drawing/Painting, Field Trips, Nature/Environment Studies, Soccer, Swimming — Recreational, Team Building
Operated by: Sonoma County YMCA, 1111 College Ave, Santa Rosa, CA 95404 at (707) 544-1829 (#45986)

Sonoma Cty YMCA Guerneville

Guerneville, CA; (707) 544-1829
Michelle Head, Director
Activities: Baseball/Softball, Basketball, Counselor Training (CIT), Drama, Drawing/Painting, Field Trips, Music, Soccer, Swimming — Recreational, Team Building
Operated by: Sonoma County YMCA, 1111 College Ave, Santa Rosa, CA 95404 at (707) 544-1829 (#45985)

Sonoma Cty YMCA Hahn Elmntry (est 1995)

Rohnert Park, CA (Sonoma Co.); (707) 544-1829
Michelle Head, Director
Activities: Arts/Crafts, Baseball/Softball, Basketball, Drama, Drawing/Painting, Field Trips, Music, Nature/Environment Studies, Soccer, Swimming — Recreational
Contact: Michelle Head, Program Director at (707) 544-1829; fax: (707) 544-4432
Operated by: Sonoma County YMCA, 1111 College Ave, Santa Rosa, CA 95404 at (707) 544-1829 (#3106)

Sonoma Cty YMCA Monte Vista

(est 1991)

Rohnert Park, CA (Sonoma Co.); (707) 544-1829
Michelle Head, Director
Activities: Arts/Crafts, Baseball/Softball, Basketball, Drama, Drawing/Painting, Field Trips, Music, Nature/Environment Studies, Soccer, Swimming — Recreational
Contact: Michelle Head, Program Director at (707) 544-1829; fax: (707) 544-4432
Operated by: Sonoma County YMCA, 1111 College Ave, Santa Rosa, CA 95404 at (707) 544-1829 (#1617)

Sonoma Cty YMCA Olivet Day Cmp (est 1994)

Santa Rosa, CA (Sonoma Co.); (707) 544-1829
Activities: Arts/Crafts, Baseball/Softball, Basketball, Counselor Training (CIT), Drama, Drawing/Painting, Field Trips, Nature/Environment Studies, Soccer, Swimming — Recreational
Contact: Michelle Head, Program Director at (707) 544-1829; fax: (707) 544-4432
Operated by: Sonoma County YMCA, 1111 College Ave, Santa Rosa, CA 95404 at (707) 544-1829 (#2761)

Sonoma Cty YMCA Piner

Rohnert Park, CA (Sonoma Co.); (707) 544-1829
Michelle Head, Director

Camp comments: Day camp provides safe, caring and fun environment for youth. Activities focus on self-esteem and social development.
Activities: Aquatic Activities, Arts/Crafts, Camping Skills/Outdoor Living, Drama, Field Trips, Leadership Development, Nature/Environment Studies, Performing Arts, Sports — Field & Team, Swimming — Recreational
Session lengths & capacity: 2 week sessions; 65 campers
Clientele & fees: coed 6-12; Fees: B ☀ 🚌
Contact: Michelle Head, Program Director at (707) 544-1829; fax: (707) 544-4432

Operated by: Sonoma County YMCA, 1111 College Ave, Santa Rosa, CA 95404 at (707) 544-1829 (#3961)

Sonoma Cty YMCA Prestwood Day (est 1994)

Sonoma, CA (Sonoma Co.); (707) 544-1829
Contact: Michelle Head, Program Director at (707) 544-1829; fax: (707) 544-4432
Operated by: Sonoma County YMCA, 1111 College Ave, Santa Rosa, CA 95404 at (707) 544-1829 (#2789)

Sonoma Cty YMCA Schaefer Day (est 1985)

Santa Rosa, CA (Sonoma Co.); (707) 544-1829
Activities: Arts/Crafts, Counselor Training (CIT), Drawing/Painting, Field Trips, Music, Nature/Environment Studies, Swimming — Recreational
Contact: Michelle Head, Program Director at (707) 544-1829; fax: (707) 544-4432
Operated by: Sonoma County YMCA, 1111 College Ave, Santa Rosa, CA 95404 at (707) 544-1829 (#1613)

Sonoma Cty YMCA Steele Ln Perf (est 1975)

Santa Rosa, CA (Sonoma Co.); (707) 544-9817
Activities: Arts/Crafts, Clowning, Drama, Drawing/Painting, Field Trips, Leadership Development, Performing Arts, Swimming — Recreational
Contact: Michelle Head, Program Director at (707) 544-1829; fax: (707) 544-4432
Operated by: Sonoma County YMCA, 1111 College Ave, Santa Rosa, CA 95404 at (707) 544-1829 (#1273)

Sonoma Cty YMCA Strawberry

Santa Rosa, CA (Sonoma County Co.)
Michelle Head, Director
Activities: Baseball/Softball, Basketball, Counselor Training (CIT), Field Trips, Hockey, Leadership Development, Soccer, Sports — Field & Team, Swimming — Recreational, Team Building
Session lengths & capacity: June-August; 2 week sessions; 50 campers
Clientele & fees: coed 5-6; Fees: B ☀
Contact: Michelle Head, Program Director at (707) 544-1829; fax: (707) 544-4432
Operated by: Sonoma County YMCA, 1111 College Ave, Santa Rosa, CA 95404 at (707) 544-1829 (#32725)

Sonoma Cty YMCA Yulupa Day Cmp (est 1973)

Santa Rosa, CA (Sonoma Co.); (707) 544-1829
Michelle Head, Director

Camp comments: Day camp offers fun, safe activities for youth. Also available are sports & performing arts camps.
Activities: Drama, Field Trips, Soccer, Swimming — Recreational
Session lengths & capacity: 2 week sessions; 66 campers
Clientele & fees: coed 6-13; Fees: B ☀ 🚌
Contact: Michelle Head, Associate Program Director at (707) 544-1829; fax: (707) 544-4432
Operated by: Sonoma County YMCA, 1111 College Ave, Santa Rosa, CA 95404 at (707) 544-1829 (#1633)

South Bay Fmly YMCA Summer Cmp (est 1958)

Chula Vista, CA (San Diego Co.); (619) 421-8805
Debbie Apfel, Director

Camp comments: Our responsibility is to be caring to all, treating all with honesty and respect in a fun, safe and exciting atmosphere.
Activities: Arts/Crafts, Baseball/Softball, Climbing/Rappelling, Field Trips, Gymnastics, Horseback — English, Skating, Soccer, Sports — Field & Team, Swimming — Instructional
Session lengths & capacity: June-August; 1 week sessions; 200 campers
Clientele & fees: coed 5-13; Fees: **B** ☀
Contact: Debbie Apfel, Program Director at (619) 422-8354; fax: (619) 422-4412
Operated by: YMCA of San Diego County, 4715 Viewridge Ave Ste 100, San Diego, CA 92123 at (619) 292-4034 (#1639)

South Coast Day Camps

(est 1986)   ☀

Laguna Niguel, CA (Orange Co.); (714) 495-9622
Paul Giguere, Director

Camp comments: Entering 1st-6th graders. Experience activities to learn, grow and create memories, including trips, swimming and more.
Activities: Arts/Crafts, Basketball, Climbing/Rappelling, Field Trips, Leadership Development, Sports — Field & Team, Swimming — Recreational
Session lengths & capacity: 8 & 9 week sessions; 150 campers
Clientele & fees: coed 6-12; Fees: **B** ☀ 🐖
Contact: Kendall Romero & Ariel Mendoza at (714) 495-9622; fax: (714) 495-6397
Operated by: South Coast YMCA, 29831 Crown Valley Pkwy, Laguna Niguel, CA 92677 at (714) 495-9622 (#5785)

South Coast YMCA Camp Fox ⛺

Laguna Niguel, CA (Orange Co.); (949) 495-9622
Randy Smith, Director

Camp comments: Camp Fox is located on Catalina Island. It's a coed high school camp focusing on good, clean, creative fun.
Activities: Archery, Arts/Crafts, Boating, Challenge/Rope Courses, Counselor Training (CIT), Drama, Kayaking, Leadership Development, Sports — Field & Team, Swimming — Recreational
Session lengths & capacity: 1 week sessions; 320 campers
Clientele & fees: coed 13-18; Fees: **C ⛺** 🐖
Contact: Kendall Romero & Randy Smith, Program Director at (714) 495-9622; fax: (714) 495-6397
Operated by: South Coast YMCA, 29831 Crown Valley Pkwy, Laguna Niguel, CA 92677 at (714) 495-9622 (#2402)

ICON LEGEND

☀   Day Camp

⛺   Resident Camp

🏠   Facilities Available To Rent

🚐   Transportation Available

🐖   Financial Aid Available

FEE RANGES PER WEEK

A	$0-75
B	$75-200
C	$201-350
D	$351-500
E	$501-650
F	over $650

South Coast YMCA Camp Oakes ⛺

Big Bear, CA (San Bernadino Co.); (909) 585-2020
Staci Chambers, Director

Camp comments: Mountain setting. Campers thrive in an atmosphere that is caring, fun & noncompetitive.
Activities: Archery, Arts/Crafts, Challenge/Rope Courses, Horseback — Western, Leadership Development, Nature/Environment Studies, Riflery
Session lengths & capacity: 1 week sessions; 170 campers
Clientele & fees: coed 9-15; Fees: **C ⛺** 🐖
Contact: Staci Chambers, Program Director at (949) 495-4619; fax: (949) 249-6114
Operated by: South Coast YMCA, 29831 Crown Valley Pkwy, Laguna Niguel, CA 92677 at (714) 495-9622 (#6417)

Springlake Nature Camp ☀

Santa Rosa, CA (Sonoma Co.); (707) 544-1829
Activities: Arts/Crafts, Counselor Training (CIT), Field Trips, Hiking, Leadership Development, Nature/Environment Studies, Swimming — Recreational, Team Building
Contact: Michelle Head, Program Director at (707) 544-1829; fax: (707) 544-4432
Operated by: Sonoma County YMCA, 1111 College Ave, Santa Rosa, CA 95404 at (707) 544-1829 (#1619)

St Michaels Summer Camp

(est 1962)   ⛺

Silverado, CA (Orange Co.); (949) 858-0222
Rev Anthony M Kopp, Director
Activities: Aquatic Activities, Arts/Crafts, Baseball/Softball, Basketball, Hiking, Nature/Environment Studies, Soccer, Sports — Field & Team, Swimming — Instructional, Swimming — Recreational
Session lengths & capacity: July-August; 5 week sessions; 100 campers
Clientele & fees: boys 7-13; Fees: **B ⛺** 🐖
Contact: Rev Anthony M Kopp, Camp Director at (949) 858-0222; fax: (949) 858-4583
Operated by: Norbertine Fathers of Orange, 19292 El Toro Road, Silverado, CA 92676 at (949) 858-0222 (#8)

Stonestown Family YMCA Day Cmp (est 1954) ☀ 🚐

San Francisco, CA (San Francisco Co.); (415) 242-7101
Rachel Del Monte, Director

Camp comments: Day camp offers fun safe environment for campers to grow and explore. Well trained qualified staff and low ratios.
Activities: Arts/Crafts, Basketball, Camping Skills/Outdoor Living, Field Trips, Hiking, International Culture, Leadership Development, Nature/Environment Studies, Swimming — Recreational, Tennis
Session lengths & capacity: 9 week sessions; 250 campers
Clientele & fees: coed 5-16; Fees: **B** ☀ 🐖
Contact: Julie Humphrey, Teen & Family Program Dir at (415) 242-7130; fax: (415) 759-9630
e-mail: jhumphrey@ymcasf.org
Operated by: YMCA San Francisco Day Camps, 1877 S Grant Street, San Mateo, CA 94402 at (650) 286-9622 (#6807)

Sturtevant's Camp (est 1893) 🏠

Sierra Madre, CA (Los Angeles Co.); (760) 249-4626
Contact: Sylvia Miller, Camp Reservationist at (626) 568-7333; fax: (626) 568-7331
e-mail: smiller@cal-pac.org
Web site: www.cal-pac.org

Operated by: California Pacific Annual Conf, 110 S Euclid Ave, PO Box 6006, Pasadena, CA 91102 at (626) 568-7330
Group Rental Information
Site comments: Last trail resort from great hiking era. Hike 4 miles along stream to lodge and cabins in scenic canyon. Full baths, kitchen, heaters.Served by pack mule train.
Seasons & Capacity: Spring 44, Summer 44, Fall 44, Winter 44
Facilities: Cabins, Dorm-Style, Hiking Trails, Kitchen Facilities, Lodges, Meeting Rooms, River (#7537)

Summer Day Camp ☀

Yorba Linda, CA; (714) 777-9622
Clare McKenna, Director
Activities: Arts/Crafts, Computer, Field Trips, Hiking, Leadership Development, Nature/Environment Studies, Sports — Field & Team, Swimming — Recreational, Team Building
Session lengths & capacity: 1 week sessions; 120 campers
Clientele & fees: coed 5-14; Fees: **B** ☀
Contact: Clare McKenna, Program Director at (714) 777-9622; fax: (714) 777-1903
Operated by: Yorba Linda Placentia Fam YMCA, 18333 Lemon Dr, Yorba Linda, CA 92887 at (714) 777-9622 (#29522)

Sunny Skies Day Camp

(est 1974)   ☀ 🚐

Agoura, CA; (818) 889-8383
Harold Gordon & Jeff Salzman, Director

Camp comments: Tradition of friendly, caring, counselors in dynamic outdoor program. 23 oak covered ac with creek. Transportation.
Activities: Archery, Arts/Crafts, Basketball, Fishing, Horseback — Western, Leadership Development, Music, Nature/Environment Studies, Swimming — Instructional
Session lengths & capacity: 3, 4, 5 & 9 week sessions; 300 campers
Clientele & fees: coed 4-14; Fees: **B, C, D** ☀
Contact: Harold Gordon, Jeff Salzman, Directors at (818) 889-8383; fax: (818) 865-0920
e-mail: info@sunnyskies.com
Operated by: Camp Kinneret Day Camp, PO Box 329, Agoura, CA 91376 at (818) 706-8255 (#3092)

SuperCamp (est 1982) ⛺

Oceanside, CA (San Diego Co.); (760) 722-0072
Bobbi DePorter, Director

Camp comments: SuperCamp ten day academic adventure in life long learning & personal growth skills raise grades-motivation-confidence
Activities: Academics, Basketball, Challenge/Rope Courses, Leadership Development, Soccer, Swimming — Recreational, Team Building
Session lengths & capacity: June-August; 2 week sessions; 120 campers
Clientele & fees: coed 9-24; Fees: **F ⛺**
Contact: (800) 285-3276 ext. 1; fax: (760) 722-3507
e-mail: info@supercamp.com
Web site: www.supercamp.com
Operated by: SuperCamp, 1725 South Coast Hwy, Oceanside, CA 92054-5319 at (800) 285-3276 (#6239)

Tautona Girl Scout Camp

(est 1945)   ⛺ 🏠 🚐

Angelus Oaks, CA (San Bernardino Co.); (909) 794-4155

Camp comments: Swimming, canoeing, hiking, mtn biking, cookouts, campfires & crafts - a few of the things you can do at Camp Tautona.

Activities: Arts/Crafts, Bicycling/Biking, Camping Skills/Outdoor Living, Canoeing, Counselor Training (CIT), Hiking, Nature/Environment Studies, Sports — Field & Team, Swimming — Recreational
Session lengths & capacity: June-August; 1/2, 1 & 2 week sessions; 100 campers
Clientele & fees: girls 6-17; Fees: **B, C, D** ⚠ 🚐
Contact: Loyce Rowe, Program Manager at (909) 307-6555; fax: (909) 307-6526
e-mail: lrowe@gssgc.org
Web site: www.gssgc.org
Operated by: GSC of San Gorgonio, 1751 Plum Ln, Redlands, CA 92374-4505 at (909) 307-6555
Group Rental Information
Site comments: Rustic mountain camp. Lodges & "sleep under the stars" site. Located close to hiking trails, Jenks Lake and Big Bear.
Seasons & Capacity: Spring 150, Summer 150, Fall 150
Facilities: Hiking Trails, Kitchen Facilities, Lake, Lodges (#141)

The Episcopal Cmp @ Wrightwood (est 1990) ⚠ 🏠

Wrightwood, CA (Los Angeles Co.); (760) 249-3615
Mitch Jones, Director

Camp comments: Prog combine trad camp act, coping skills, leadership develop. We encourage stewardship for creation. Episcopal Theology
Activities: Aquatic Activities, Archery, Arts/Crafts, Basketball, Canoeing, Community Service, Hiking, Leadership Development, Nature/Environment Studies
Session lengths & capacity: July-August; 1 week sessions; 50 campers
Clientele & fees: coed 8-18; families; seniors; single adults; Fees: **B** ⚠ 🚐
Contact: Mitch Jones, Camp Manager at (760) 249-3615; fax: (760) 249-9057
Web site: www.ladiocese.org
Operated by: The Episcopal Diocese of LA, PO Box 512164, Los Angeles, CA 90051 at (213) 482-2040
Group Rental Information
Facilities: Cabins, Dorm-Style, Food Service, Lake, Lodges, Meeting Rooms, Pool (#2258)

THE Horse Camp (est 1996) ☀

Granada Hills, CA (Los Angeles Co.); (818) 832-8788
Gayle Paperno, Director

Camp comments: Focusing daily on serious classical riding as well as safety, team building skills, cooperation, understanding, horse games, crafts, trips, and more.
Activities: Community Service, Counselor Training (CIT), Drama, Field Trips, Horseback — English, Horseback — Western, Leadership Development, Nature/Environment Studies, Team Building
Session lengths & capacity: July-August; 1 week sessions; 20 campers
Clientele & fees: Fees: **C** ☀
Contact: Gayle Paperno, Owner/Director at (818) 317-7203;
e-mail: famequestrian@aol.com
Operated by: Family Equestrian Connection, 11630 Zelzah, Granada Hills, CA 91344 at (818) 832-8788 (#46508)

The Phoenix Ranch Day Camp

(est 1982) ☀ 🚐

Simi Valley, CA (Ventura Co.); (805) 526-0136
Joni Wade, Director

Camp comments: A warm, safe and exciting environment. Explorative activities with an emphasis on skill development. Summer fun for all.

Activities: Arts/Crafts, Camping Skills/Outdoor Living, Challenge/Rope Courses, Computer, Drama, Field Trips, Horseback — English, Nature/Environment Studies, Sports — Field & Team, Swimming — Recreational
Session lengths & capacity: June-August; 1, 2, 3, 4, 5, 6, 7, 8 & 9 week sessions; 200 campers
Clientele & fees: coed 5-12; Fees: **B** ☀
Contact: Frances Alascano/ Amy Brown, Owner at (805) 526-0136; fax: (805) 526-5002
Operated by: The Phoenix Consultants Inc, 1845 Oak Rd, Simi Valley, CA 93063 at (805) 526-0136 (#4174)

The Rowdy Ridge Gang Camp

(est 1994) ⚠ 🚐

Torrance, CA (Los Angeles Co.)

Camp comments: Our camp serves families, mothers & children who have suffered thru substance abuse & domestic violence. Invitation only.
Activities: Archery, Arts/Crafts, Basketball, Canoeing, Counselor Training (CIT), Dance, Drama, Hiking, Radio/TV/Video, Swimming — Recreational
Session lengths & capacity: June-August; 6 week sessions; 250 campers
Clientele & fees: coed 1-15; Fees: **A** ⚠
Contact: Ruben Barajas, Executive Director at (310) 791-7627; fax: (310) 791-7631
e-mail: ruben@scottnewmancenter.org
Web site: www.scottnewmancenter.org
Operated by: Scott Newman Center, 3701 Skypark Dr Bldg 6 Ste 130, Torrance, CA 90505 at (800) 783-6396 (#16100)

Thousand Pines Christian Camp

(est 1939) ⚠ 🏠

Crestline, CA (San Bernadino Co.); (909) 338-2705
Mike Pate, Director

Camp comments: 70 Miles from LA, summer & winter programs for 1st - 12th grades. Rental facilities for church and para-church groups.
Activities: Arts/Crafts, Baseball/Softball, Basketball, Bicycling/Biking, Challenge/Rope Courses, Hiking, Swimming — Recreational
Session lengths & capacity: 1/2 & 1 week sessions; 360 campers
Clientele & fees: boys 6-99; girls 6-99; coed 6-99; families; Fees: **B, C** ⚠ 🚐
Contact: Bonnie Keller at (909) 338-2705; fax: (909) 338-3511
e-mail: info@thousandpines.com
Web site: www.thousandpines.com
Operated by: Thousand Pines Christian Camp, PO Box 3288, Crestline, CA 92325-3288 at (909) 338-2705
Group Rental Information
Site comments: 70 miles from LA. Serving church & parachurch groups of men, women, children, and youth. Beautiful mountain setting!
Facilities: A/V Equipment, Cabins, Double Occupancy, Food Service, Lodges, Meeting Rooms, Playing Fields, Pool
Programs: Challenge/Ropes Course, Environmental Education, Swimming, Winter Sports (#195)

Thunderbird Ranch (est 1962) ☀ ⚠

Healdsburg, CA (Sonoma Co.); (707) 433-3729
Bruce Johnson, Director

Camp comments: 'Where the fun never sets' Traditional program. Limited enrollment. Family like atmosphere 75 mi north of San Francisco, in the heart of Sonomo Cy Wine Country
Activities: Aquatic Activities, Archery, Arts/Crafts, Bicycling/Biking, Farming/Ranching/Gardening, Hiking, Horseback — Western, Soccer, Swimming — Instructional, Waterskiing
Session lengths & capacity: June-August; 1, 2 & 8 week sessions; 45 campers

Clientele & fees: coed 6-15; Fees: **C** ☀ Fees: **F** ⚠
Contact: Bruce Johnson, Owner/Director at (707) 433-3729; fax: (707) 433-2960
Web site: www.campchannel.com/thunderbird
Operated by: Thunderbird Ranch, 9455A Hwy 128, Healdsburg, CA 95448 at (707) 433-3729 (#3611)

Tocaloma Summer Day Camp

(est 1945) ☀ 🚐

Los Angeles, CA (Los Angeles Co.); (310) 399-2267
Tiffany Romero, Director

Camp comments: Traditional camp nestled on private site, SM Mts. Supportive caring staff, transportation available to westside & valley
Activities: Archery, Arts/Crafts, Basketball, Sailing, Swimming — Instructional, Tennis, Waterskiing
Session lengths & capacity: June-August; 3, 6 & 9 week sessions; 300 campers
Clientele & fees: boys 3-13; girls 3-13; coed 3-13; Fees: **C** ☀
Contact: Tiffany Romero, Director at (310) 399-2267; fax: (310) 399-5198
e-mail: campoffice@tocaloma.com
Web site: www.tocaloma.com
Operated by: Tocaloma Summer Day Camp, PO Box 1460, Santa Monica, CA 90406 at (310) 399-2267 (#3339)

Tom Sawyer Camps Inc (est 1926) ☀

Altadena, CA (Los Angeles Co.); (626) 794-1156
Sally L Horner, Director

Camp comments: Campers experience carefree, constructive activities in the out-of-doors like Tom Sawyer & Becky Thatcher!
Activities: Archery, Challenge/Rope Courses, Climbing/Rappelling, Counselor Training (CIT), Hiking, Horseback — Western, Kayaking, Swimming — Recreational, Team Building, Windsurfing
Session lengths & capacity: June-August; 3, 4 & 6 week sessions; 500 campers
Clientele & fees: boys 3-14; girls 3-14; coed 3-14; Fees: **C** ☀ 🚐
Contact: Tom Sawyer Inc at (626) 794-1156; fax: (626) 794-1401
e-mail: info@tomsawyercamps.com
Web site: www.tomsawyercamps.com
Operated by: Tom Sawyer Camps, 707 W Woodbury Road F, Altadena, CA 91001 at (626) 794-1156 (#85)

Trask Scout Reservation ☀ ⚠ 🏠

Monrovia, CA; (626) 359-4949
Gary Jensen, Director

Camp comments: Never have you felt so far away, so close before: a unique wilderness camp serving the urban Los Angeles community
Activities: Archery, Boating, Camping Skills/Outdoor Living, Canoeing, Leadership Development, Nature/Environment Studies, Riflery, Swimming — Recreational, Team Building
Session lengths & capacity: 1 week sessions
Clientele & fees: boys 7-18; families; Fees: **A** ⚠ 🚐
Contact: Gary Jensen, Program Director at (626) 351-8815 ext. 227; fax: (626) 351-9149
e-mail: garyj@sgvcbsa.org
Operated by: San Gabriel Valley Council Boy, 3450 Sierra Madre Blvd, Pasadena, CA 91107 at (626) 351-8815
Group Rental Information
Facilities: A/V Equipment, Food Service, Hiking Trails, Kitchen Facilities, Lake, Meeting Rooms, Playing Fields, Pool, Tents
Programs: Boating, Environmental Education, Swimming (#29366)

Tumbleweed Day Camp

(est 1954)

Los Angeles, CA (Los Angeles Co.); (310) 472-7474
John Beitner, Director

Camp comments: Rustic site, modern/traditional activities. Door-to-door transportation. Safety, fun, personal attention for your child. Established 1954.
Activities: Aquatic Activities, Archery, Arts/Crafts, Challenge/Rope Courses, Counselor Training (CIT), Horseback — Western, Nature/Environment Studies, Radio/TV/Video, Sports — Field & Team, Swimming — Instructional
Session lengths & capacity: June-August; 1, 2, 4, 6 & 8 week sessions; 550 campers
Clientele & fees: coed 4-13; Fees: **B, C, D**
Contact: John Beitner, Executive Director at (310) 472-7474 ext. 110; fax: (310) 476-7788
e-mail: jbeitner@tumbleweed4ever.com
Web site: www.twforever.com
Operated by: Tumbleweed Educ Enterprises, 1024 Hanley Avenue, Los Angeles, CA 90049 at (310) 472-7474

Group Rental Information
Seasons & Capacity: Spring 30, Fall 30, Winter 30
Facilities: Hiking Trails, Playing Fields, Pool
Programs: Challenge/Ropes Course, Environmental Education, Horseback Riding, Swimming (#107)

UAHC Camp Newman (est 1997)

Santa Rosa, CA (Sonoma Co.)
Ruben Arquilevich, Director

Camp comments: Build friendships & enjoy excellent recreation & art program in reform Jewish community. Entering 2nd-8th grade.
Activities: Archery, Arts/Crafts, Ceramics/Pottery, Challenge/Rope Courses, Counselor Training (CIT), Dance, Drama, Music, Religious Study, Swimming — Recreational
Session lengths & capacity: June-August; 1, 2 & 3 weeks sessions; 300 campers
Clientele & fees: coed 7-16; families; Fees: **E, F**
Contact: David May, Registrar at (415) 392-7080 ext. 10; fax: (415) 392-1182
Web site: www.campnewmanswig.org
Operated by: Union American Hebrew Congreg, 703 Market St Ste 1300, San Francisco, CA 94103 at (415) 392-7070

Group Rental Information
Site comments: Available for weekday or weekend groups.
Seasons & Capacity: Spring 200, Fall 300, Winter 200
Facilities: A/V Equipment, Cabins, Double Occupancy, Food Service, Hiking Trails, Lake, Linens, Meeting Rooms, Playing Fields, Pool

ICON LEGEND

☀ Day Camp

⛰ Resident Camp

🏠 Facilities Available To Rent

🚐 Transportation Available

🐷 Financial Aid Available

FEE RANGES PER WEEK

A	$0-75
B	$75-200
C	$201-350
D	$351-500
E	$501-650
F	over $650

Programs: Boating, Challenge/Ropes Course, Swimming (#27036)

UCLA Uni Camp (est 1935)

Los Angeles, CA (Los Angeles Co.); (310) 203-8023

Camp comments: Summer resident camp program for children from low income families in Los Angeles County. Children 8-14; teens 14-17.
Activities: Aquatic Activities, Archery, Arts/Crafts, Camping Skills/Outdoor Living, Community Service, Hiking, Leadership Development, Nature/Environment Studies, Swimming — Recreational
Session lengths & capacity: 1 week sessions; 132 campers
Clientele & fees: coed 8-17; Fees: **A**
Contact: Shirley Walch, Director of Constituancy Services at (310) 206-4586; fax: (310) 206-3861
e-mail: unicamp@ucla.edu
Operated by: UCLA UniCamp, 900 Hilgard Ave 301, Los Angeles, CA 90024 at (310) 203-8023 (#206)

Unique (est 1978)

Portola Valley, CA (San Mateo Co.); (650) 851-8224
Bob Cavalli, Director

Camp comments: Boarding and Day Camp. Emphasis on fun. Mature staff provides expert instruction in athletics, the arts, horsebackriding, biking, & outdoor living skills.
Activities: Archery, Arts/Crafts, Bicycling/Biking, Counselor Training (CIT), Dance, Drama, Horseback — English, Soccer, Swimming — Instructional, Tennis
Session lengths & capacity: June-August; 1, 2, 3, 4, 5, 6 week sessions; 200 campers
Clientele & fees: boys 7-15; girls 7-15; coed 7-15; Fees: **D** Fees: **E**
Contact: Bob Cavalli, owner at (415) 381-5615; fax: (415) 381-2922
e-mail: bobcavalli@sbcglobal.net
Operated by: Camp Unique, 491 Green Glen Way, Mill Valley, CA 94941 at (415) 381-5615 (#6650)

Univ of San Diego Sports Camps

San Diego, CA; (619) 260-4593
Mary Johnson, MS, Director

Camp comments: Celebrating 25 years, USD knows about kids & what is important for their growth & development. USD prides itself in providing a values based prog. w/Div 1 Prof.
Activities: Baseball/Softball, Basketball, Field Trips, Soccer, Sports — Field & Team, Swimming — Recreational, Tennis
Session lengths & capacity: June-August; 1 & 2 week sessions; 350 campers
Clientele & fees: boys 6-18; girls 6-18; coed 6-18; seniors; single adults; Fees: **B, D**
Contact: Judy Stokes, Adm Asst Summer Sports Camps at (619) 260-4593; fax: (619) 260-4185
e-mail: sportscamps@sandiego.edu
Web site: camps.sandiego.edu
Operated by: University of San Diego, 5998 Alcala Park, San Diego, CA 92110-2213 at (619) 260-4593 (#10339)

Upward Bound (est 1983)

San Diego, CA; (619) 594-6184
Peter Larson, Director

Camp comments: Upward Bound Summer Residential Camp prepares students for the psychological, social and academic rigors of college.
Activities: Academics, Aerobics/Exercise, Aquatic Activities, Camping Skills/Outdoor Living, Field Trips, International Culture, Leadership Development, Team Building
Session lengths & capacity: June-August; 6 week sessions; 140 campers

Clientele & fees: coed 15-18; Fees: **F**
Contact: Peter Larson, Director at (619) 594-6184; fax: (619) 594-7821
e-mail: plarson@projects.sdsu.edu
Web site: wwwrohan.sdsu.edu/dept/sdsutrio
Operated by: SDSU College of Education, Pre-College Institute, San Diego, CA 92182-1106 at (619) 594-2349 (#41602)

Valley Of The Moon Camp

Glen Ellen, CA (Sonoma Co.); (707) 996-6987
Operated by: United Camps Conf & Retreats, 912 Lootens Pl, San Rafael, CA 94901 at (415) 456-5102

Group Rental Information
Site comments: Near Jack London State Park & other historical landmarks. Owned by the Presbytery of San Francisco.
Facilities: Cabins, Dorm-Style, Double Occupancy, Food Service, Hiking Trails, Meeting Rooms, Pool (#309)

Valley Trails Summer Camp

(est 1969)

Tarzana, CA (Los Angeles Co.); (818) 345-3002
Michael Stillson, Director

Camp comments: Valley Trails offers a traditional camp experience for campers grades K-9. Safe campus setting with low camper to counselor ratios providing great memories.
Activities: Academics, Arts/Crafts, Challenge/Rope Courses, Computer, Field Trips, Golf, Music, SCUBA, Swimming — Recreational
Session lengths & capacity: June-September; 1, 2 & 4 week sessions; 250 campers
Clientele & fees: coed 5-14; Fees: **B**
Contact: Michael Stillson, Director at (818) 345-3002; fax: (818) 345-7880
e-mail: info@valleytrails.com
Web site: www.valleytrails.com
Operated by: Woodcrest Schools Inc, 6043 Tampa Ave, Tarzana, CA 91356 at (818) 345-3002 (#3221)

Venice Camp (est 1968)

Los Angeles, CA (Los Angeles Co.)
Jeanette James, Director

Camp comments: Primarily serves economically disadvantaged, ethnically diverse and children with disabilities.
Activities: Arts/Crafts, Baseball/Softball, Camping Skills/Outdoor Living, Drama, Field Trips, Hiking, Swimming — Recreational
Session lengths & capacity: July-August; 2 week sessions; 120 campers
Clientele & fees: coed 5-15; Fees: **A**
Contact: Alex Nunez, Camp Director at (310) 574-6061; fax: (310) 574-1360
e-mail: alexlayp@aol.com
Web site: www.layp.org
Operated by: Los Angeles Youth Programs Inc, 5301 Beethoven St Ste 120, Los Angeles, CA 90066 at (310) 574-6061 (#3571)

Verdugo Pines Bible Camp

(est 1963)

Wrightwood, CA (Los Angeles Co.); (760) 249-3532
Don Butcher, Director

Camp comments: A Christ centered camp located in the mountains of the Angeles National Forest without the mountain driving.
Activities: Archery, Arts/Crafts, Basketball, Canoeing, Hiking, Religious Study, Swimming — Recreational
Session lengths & capacity: June-August; 1 week sessions; 180 campers
Clientele & fees: boys 8-12; girls 8-12; coed 8-18; Fees: **B**
Contact: Chris Butcher, Office Manager at (760) 249-3532; fax: (760) 249-4447
e-mail: verdugopines@snowline.net

Operated by: Southern California Bible Conf, PO Box 1989, Wrightwood, CA 92397 at (760) 249-3532

Group Rental Information
Facilities: Cabins, Hiking Trails, Lake, Meeting Rooms, Pool
Programs: Boating, Swimming (#41)

Voorhis Viking (est 1929) ▲ 🚐

Mammoth Lakes, CA (Mono Co.); (626) 442-5470
Clayton Hollopeter, Director

Camp comments: Campers are exposed to adventures, discovery and excitement, tempered with responsibility and self-discipline.
Activities: Arts/Crafts, Bicycling/Biking, Field Trips, Fishing, Hiking, Leadership Development, Nature/Environment Studies, Photography, Swimming — Recreational
Session lengths & capacity: June-September; 1 week sessions; 40 campers
Clientele & fees: boys 12-19; coed 12-19; Fees: C ▲ 🚌
Contact: Clayton Hollopeter, Executive Director at (626) 442-5470; fax: (626) 442-8803
Operated by: Boys&Girls Club San Gabriel VI, 2740 Mountain View Rd, El Monte, CA 91732 at (626) 442-5470 (#185)

Waltons Grizzly Lodge Inc

(est 1926) ▲

Portola, CA (Plumas Co.); (530) 832-4834
Adam Stein, Director

Camp comments: A family tradition since 1926. 4th generation directors. Private lake! Tremendous activities! Mature and caring counselors. Join us!
Activities: Aquatic Activities, Archery, Arts/Crafts, Challenge/Rope Courses, Horseback — Western, Riflery, Sailing, Waterskiing, Windsurfing
Session lengths & capacity: June-August; 1, 2, 4 & 6 week sessions; 160 campers
Clientele & fees: coed 7-14; Fees: F ▲
Contact: Adam & Julie Stein, Directors at (530) 832-4834; fax: (530) 832-4195
e-mail: wgl4u@aol.com
Web site: www.grizzlylodge.com
Operated by: Waltons Grizzly Lodge Inc, PO Box 519, Portola, CA 96122 at (530) 832-4834 (#302)

Wawona (est 1929) ▲ 🏠

Wawona, CA (Mariposa Co.); (209) 375-6231
Dan Kittle, Director

Camp comments: Yosemite! Quality rock climbing, horsemanship & waterskiing. Value based program builds self-esteem, teamwork & trust.
Activities: Archery, Camping Skills/Outdoor Living, Challenge/Rope Courses, Climbing/Rappelling, Golf, Gymnastics, Horseback — Western, Nature/Environment Studies, Waterskiing
Session lengths & capacity: June-August; 1 week sessions; 225 campers
Clientele & fees: coed 8-16; families; Fees: C ▲ 🚌
Contact: Cynthia Ordonez, Secretary at (209) 291-7700 ext. 148; fax: (209) 291-9636
e-mail: cordonez@cccsda.org
Web site: www.campwawona.org
Operated by: Central California Conference, PO Box 770, Clovis, CA 93613 at (209) 291-7700 (#344)

Westminster Woods Camp/Conf

(est 1946) ▲ 🏠 🚐

Occidental, CA (Sonoma Co.); (707) 874-2426
Steve Coons, Director

Camp comments: The Woods helps the local church & community in fulfilling their ministry & mission to youth & families.

Activities: Archery, Arts/Crafts, Basketball, Bicycling/Biking, Canoeing, Challenge/Rope Courses, Hiking, Leadership Development, Religious Study, Swimming — Recreational
Session lengths & capacity: 1 week sessions; 320 campers
Clientele & fees: boys 7-18; girls 7-18; coed 7-18; Fees: C ▲ 🚌
Contact: Jane Lawler, Guest Relations Manager at (707) 874-2426 ext. 629; fax: (707) 823-3382
e-mail: janel@westminsterwoods.org
Web site: www.westminsterwoods.org
Operated by: Presbytery of the Redwoods, 8 4th St, Petaluma, CA 94952 at (707) 874-2426

Group Rental Information
Site comments: A path in the Redwoods,in the heart of the woods.Serves churches and local community through camp, retreat, conferences, envir ed.
Facilities: A/V Equipment, Cabins, Double Occupancy, Food Service, Hiking Trails, Linens, Lodges, Meeting Rooms, Playing Fields, Pool, River, Tents
Programs: Challenge/Ropes Course, Environmental Education, Swimming (#5896)

Whispering Oaks (est 1997) ▲ 🏠 🚐

Julian, CA (San Diego Co.)
Katie Greksouk, Director

Camp comments: Mountain setting w/ all the comforts of home. Sports, hiking, team building, art programs, first time & general camping
Activities: Baseball/Softball, Basketball, Camping Skills/Outdoor Living, Challenge/Rope Courses, Drawing/Painting, Hiking, Nature/Environment Studies, Soccer, Sports — Field & Team, Team Building
Session lengths & capacity: June-August; 1/2 & 1 week sessions; 120 campers
Clientele & fees: girls 7-17; Fees: B ▲
Contact: Madhu Narayan, Camp Coordinator at (619) 298-8393 ext. 226; fax: (619) 298-2031
Web site: www.girlscoutssdi.org
Operated by: San Diego Imperial GSC, 1231 Upas St, San Diego, CA 92103 at (619) 610-0726

Group Rental Information
Site comments: Available weekdays only
Seasons & Capacity: Spring 140, Fall 140, Winter 140
Facilities: Cabins, Hiking Trails, Kitchen Facilities, Lodges, Meeting Rooms, Playing Fields (#5602)

Wilshire Blvd Temple Camps

(est 1952) ▲ 🏠

Malibu, CA (Ventura Co.); (310) 457-7861
Howard Kaplan, Director

Camp comments: Excellence in Jewish camping. Sports and arts are a large part of our program. Join us for the magic in Malibu.
Activities: Archery, Arts/Crafts, Challenge/Rope Courses, Dance, Drama, Golf, Radio/TV/Video, SCUBA, Soccer, Tennis
Session lengths & capacity: June-August; 1, 2, 3 & 4 week sessions; 340 campers
Clientele & fees: coed 8-15; Fees: E ▲
Contact: Howard Kaplan, Director at (310) 457-7861; fax: (310) 457-4614
e-mail: wbtcamps@aol.com
Web site: www.wbtcamps.org
Operated by: Wilshire Blvd Temple Camps, 3663 Wilshire Blvd, Los Angeles, CA 90010 at (213) 388-2401

Group Rental Information
Site comments: Ocean views, ROPES Course, tennis courts, golf area, fine food and Malibu sunsets.
Seasons & Capacity: Spring 250, Fall 250, Winter 250
Facilities: A/V Equipment, Cabins, Double Occupancy, Food Service, Linens, Meeting Rooms, Ocean, Playing Fields, Pool

Programs: Challenge/Ropes Course, Environmental Education, Swimming (#133)

Winacka (est 1976) ▲ 🏠 🚐

Julian, CA (San Diego Co.); (619) 298-8393
Madhu Narayan, Director

Camp comments: Mountain setting with open-air living, CIT, high adventure programs, riding & general camping.
Activities: Arts/Crafts, Backpacking, Challenge/Rope Courses, Horseback — Western, Leadership Development, Nature/Environment Studies, Photography, Swimming — Recreational, Wilderness Trips
Session lengths & capacity: June-August; 1/2, 1 & 2 week sessions; 192 campers
Clientele & fees: girls 7-17; Fees: B ▲ 🚌
Contact: Madhu Narayan, Camp Coordinator at (619) 298-8393 ext. 226; fax: (619) 298-2031
Web site: www.girlscoutssdi.org
Operated by: San Diego Imperial GSC, 1231 Upas St, San Diego, CA 92103 at (619) 610-0726

Group Rental Information
Site comments: Available weekdays only. No heated buildings.
Seasons & Capacity: Spring 250, Summer 250, Fall 250, Winter 250
Facilities: Cabins, Kitchen Facilities, Lodges (#219)

Wintaka (est 1958) ▲ 🚐

Running Springs, CA (San Bernardio Co.); (909) 867-7037
Kristin Harlocker, Director

Camp comments: Mountain setting. Traditional program plus specialty activities for 7th-11th grades. Trips to Green Valley & overnights.
Activities: Archery, Arts/Crafts, Camping Skills/Outdoor Living, Counselor Training (CIT), Dance, Drama, Hiking, Leadership Development, Nature/Environment Studies, Swimming — Recreational
Session lengths & capacity: 1 week sessions; 165 campers
Clientele & fees: coed 7-17; Fees: C ▲ 🚌
Contact: Shirlee Jackert, Executive Director at (562) 421-2725; fax: (562) 421-4056
e-mail: campfirelb@earthlink.net
Web site: www.campfirelb.net
Operated by: Camp Fire Boys & Girls, 7070 E Carson St, Long Beach, CA 90808 at (562) 421-2725 (#143)

Wolahi (est 1933) ▲ 🏠

Julian, CA (San Diego Co.); (619) 765-0710
Chris Orahead, Director

Camp comments: Unique outdoor experience where experiences become skills to share and the environment becomes a meaningful commitment.
Activities: Archery, Arts/Crafts, Basketball, Camping Skills/Outdoor Living, Canoeing, Challenge/Rope Courses, Counselor Training (CIT), Fishing, Leadership Development, Swimming — Recreational
Session lengths & capacity: 1, 2, 3, 4, 5, 6, 7 & 8 week sessions; 180 campers
Clientele & fees: coed 8-17; Fees: C ▲ 🚌
Contact: Nancy Thompson, Program Director at (619) 291-8985; fax: (619) 291-8988
Operated by: Camp Fire Boys and Girls, PO Box 3275, San Diego, CA 92163-1275 at (619) 291-8985

Group Rental Information
Site comments: Located 55 miles east of San Diego amid tall pines and oaks.
Seasons & Capacity: Summer 110
Facilities: Cabins, Kitchen Facilities, Pool
Programs: Boating, Challenge/Ropes Course (#217)

Woodcraft Rangers Camps

(est 1945)

Castaic, CA (Los Angeles Co.); (661) 257-0266
Chris Vargas, Director

Camp comments: Caring, rustic setting serving economically disadvantaged youth.
Activities: Archery, Arts/Crafts, Baseball/Softball, Camping Skills/Outdoor Living, Challenge/Rope Courses, Hiking, Nature/Environment Studies, Swimming — Recreational, Team Building
Session lengths & capacity: June-August; 1 week sessions; 180 campers
Clientele & fees: coed 7-14; Fees: **C ∆ ⬤**
Contact: Cathie Mostovoy, Director of Camping Services at (213) 749-3031 ext. 232;
fax: (213) 749-0409
Web site: www.woodcraftrangers.org
Operated by: Woodcraft Rangers, 2111 Park Grove Ave, Los Angeles, CA 90007 at (213) 749-3031

Group Rental Information

Site comments: 200+ acres year-round access, one hour from LA, Ventura.
Seasons & Capacity: Spring 150, Summer 60, Fall 120, Winter 80
Facilities: Cabins, Double Occupancy, Food Service, Hiking Trails, Kitchen Facilities, Lodges, Pool
Programs: Challenge/Ropes Course, Environmental Education, Swimming (#163)

Wylie Woods Presbyterian Conf (est 1949)

Skyforest, CA (San Bernardino Co.);
(909) 337-3360
Donna Ward, Director
Contact: Ana Nava, Registrar at (909) 337-3360;
fax: (909) 337-8111
e-mail: ananava@synod.org
Operated by: Synod Of Southern California, 1501 Wilshire Blvd, Los Angeles, CA 90017 at (213) 483-3840

Group Rental Information

Site comments: Comfortable historic mtn lodge in rustic setting. Groups may be strengthened through renewal & learning experiences.
Facilities: A/V Equipment, Cabins, Double Occupancy, Food Service, Hiking Trails, Linens, Lodges, Meeting Rooms, Playing Fields
Programs: Challenge/Ropes Course, Environmental Education, Winter Sports (#7332)

ICON LEGEND

☼ Day Camp
∆ Resident Camp
⌂ Facilities Available To Rent
🚐 Transportation Available
⬤ Financial Aid Available

FEE RANGES PER WEEK

A	$0-75
B	$75-200
C	$201-350
D	$351-500
E	$501-650
F	over $650

YMCA Adventure Day Camp ☼

San Bernardino, CA (San Bernardino Co.);
(909) 881-9622
Teresa A. Grant, Director

Camp comments: COED;92es7-12. Serves San Bernardino Co. Safe & secure environment, fun activities including arts & crafts, swimming, basketball, field trips & teamwork, etc.
Activities: Aquatic Activities, Arts/Crafts, Basketball, Community Service, Drawing/Painting, Farming/Ranching/Gardening, Gymnastics, Martial Arts, Swimming — Instructional, Team Building
Clientele & fees: boys 7-12; girls 7-12; coed 7-12; families; Fees: **F ☼**
Contact: Teresa A Grant, Day Camp Coordinator at (909) 881-9622; fax: (909) 886-3151
e-mail: tgrant75@yahoo.com
Operated by: YMCA Movin-On Day Camp, 16 E Olive St, Redlands, CA 92373 at (909) 793-2957 (#12123)

YMCA Camp Big Bear (est 1938) ∆ ⌂

Big Bear Lake, CA; (909) 866-3977
Dean A. Hastings, Director

Camp comments: Mtn setting on the shores of beautiful Big Bear Lake. Active waterfront program. Spring through fall. Winter sports.
Activities: Archery, Arts/Crafts, Bicycling/Biking, Boating, Horseback — Western, Nature/Environment Studies, Riflery, Sailing, Swimming — Recreational
Session lengths & capacity: 1/2, 1 & 2 week sessions
Clientele & fees: boys 7-15; girls 7-15; coed 7-99; families; single adults; Fees: **C, D ∆**
Contact: Dean A. Hastings, Director at (909) 866-3977; fax: (909) 878-3368
Operated by: YMCA Santa Monica Family, PO Box 1516, Big Bear Lake, CA 92315 at (909) 866-3977

Group Rental Information

Site comments: Lakeside camp, full water front activities, winter sports.
Facilities: Cabins, Dorm-Style, Food Service, Hiking Trails, Lake, Meeting Rooms, Pool
Programs: Boating, Environmental Education, Horseback Riding, Swimming, Winter Sports (#174)

YMCA Camp Jones Gulch

(est 1934) ∆ ⌂

La Honda, CA (San Mateo Co.); (415) 747-1200
David Somers, Director

Camp comments: YMCA Camp Jones Gulch offers high quality resident camp in the coastal Santa Cruz Mountains south of San Francisco CA
Activities: Archery, Arts/Crafts, Backpacking, Bicycling/Biking, Challenge/Rope Courses, Climbing/Rappelling, Counselor Training (CIT), Horseback — Western, Swimming — Recreational, Wilderness Trips
Session lengths & capacity: July-August; 1 week sessions; 200 campers
Clientele & fees: coed 8-18; families; Fees: **D ∆ ⬤**
Contact: Elizabeth Jordan, Executive Director at (415) 747-1200; fax: (415) 747-0986
e-mail: jonesgulch@ymcasf.org
Operated by: YMCA San Francisco Day Camps, 1877 S Grant Street, San Mateo, CA 94402 at (650) 286-9622

Group Rental Information

Site comments: Beautiful coastal redwood forest 1 hour from San Francisco. Year round accomodations.
Seasons & Capacity: Spring 400, Winter 400
Facilities: Cabins, Dorm-Style, Food Service, Hiking Trails, Lodges, Meeting Rooms, Playing Fields, Pool

Programs: Boating, Challenge/Ropes Course, Environmental Education, Horseback Riding, Swimming (#320)

YMCA Camp Loma Mar ∆ ⌂ 🚐

Loma Mar, CA (San Mateo Co.); (650) 879-0223
Niki Roussopoulos, Director

Camp comments: Located in the beautiful redwoods of the Santa Cruz Mountains. Busing available from the East Bay. Call for more info about camp and rentals.
Activities: Aquatic Activities, Archery, Arts/Crafts, Basketball, Bicycling/Biking, Climbing/Rappelling, Counselor Training (CIT), Nature/Environment Studies
Session lengths & capacity: July-August; 6 week sessions; 160 campers
Clientele & fees: coed 7-17; families; seniors; single adults; Fees: **C ∆ ⬤**
Contact: (510) 451-9009;
e-mail: ymca@grin.net
Web site: www.ymcaeastbay.org
Operated by: YMCA of the East Bay, 2330 Broadway, Oakland, CA 94612-2415 at (510) 451-8039

Group Rental Information

Site comments: Available for all organized groups. Bring your program/agenda we'll provide food service,housekeeping & redwood forest.
Facilities: Cabins, Food Service, Hiking Trails, Pool
Programs: Swimming (#3356)

YMCA Camp Marston

(est 1921) ☼ ∆ ⌂ 🚐

Julian, CA (San Diego Co.); (760) 765-0642
Darin Borgstadter, Director

Camp comments: Traditional YMCA mtn resident camp. Spectacular site in San Diego's high mountains. Character building experiences.
Activities: Archery, Arts/Crafts, Backpacking, Canoeing, Challenge/Rope Courses, Climbing/Rappelling, Counselor Training (CIT), Nature/Environment Studies, Riflery, Wilderness Trips
Session lengths & capacity: June-August; 1 & 2 week sessions; 240 campers
Clientele & fees: coed 7-15; families; Fees: **C ∆ ⬤**
Contact: (760) 765-0642; fax: (760) 765-0183
e-mail: camp@ymca.org
Operated by: YMCA of San Diego County, 4715 Viewridge Ave Ste 100, San Diego, CA 92123 at (619) 292-4034

Group Rental Information

Seasons & Capacity: Spring 296, Fall 296, Winter 296
Facilities: Cabins, Dorm-Style, Food Service, Hiking Trails, Lake, Playing Fields
Programs: Boating, Challenge/Ropes Course, Environmental Education (#224)

YMCA Camp Round Meadow

(est 1925) ∆ ⌂ 🚐

Fawnskin, CA (San Bernardino Co.);
(909) 794-2929
Emily Cheng, Director

Camp comments: YMCA camp located on the edge of wilderness area. Rich history of camping dedicated to serving the youth & families of the greater Los Angeles area.
Activities: Archery, Arts/Crafts, Bicycling/Biking, Challenge/Rope Courses, Hiking, Horseback — Western, Leadership Development, Nature/Environment Studies, Sports — Field & Team, Swimming — Recreational
Session lengths & capacity: 1/2 & 1 week sessions; 180 campers
Clientele & fees: coed 7-17; families; Fees: **A, B, C ∆ ⬤**

Contact: Brian Bost, Director, Camping Services at (909) 866-3000; fax: (909) 866-5065
e-mail: brianbost@ymcala.org
Operated by: YMCA Metropolitan Los Angeles, PO Box 70, Fawnkin, CA 92533 at (909) 866-3000 (#70)

YMCA Camp Surf

(est 1969)

Imperial Beach, CA (San Diego Co.); (619) 423-5850
Mark Thompson, Director

Camp comments: Beautiful oceanfront camp. Surfing, body boarding, sea kayaking, San Diego, CA.Travel groups served. Beach camping.
Activities: Aquatic Activities, Archery, Arts/Crafts, Challenge/Rope Courses, Fishing, Kayaking, Leadership Development, Nature/Environment Studies, Sailing, Swimming — Recreational
Session lengths & capacity: June-August; 1 & 2 week sessions; 180 campers
Clientele & fees: coed 7-17; Fees: C A 🚌
Contact: Mark Thompson, Camp Director at (619) 423-5850; fax: (619) 423-4141
e-mail: mthompson@ymca.org
Operated by: YMCA of San Diego County, 4715 Viewridge Ave Ste 100, San Diego, CA 92123 at (619) 292-4034

Group Rental Information
Seasons & Capacity: Spring 250, Summer 100, Fall 250, Winter 250
Facilities: Cabins, Dorm-Style, Food Service, Meeting Rooms, Ocean, Tents
Programs: Boating, Challenge/Ropes Course, Environmental Education, Swimming (#3605)

YMCA Camp Ta Ta Pochon

(est 1923)

Angelus Oaks, CA; (909) 794-2927
Dave Branconier, Director

Camp comments: Dedicated adult staff lead traditional YMCA camp activities. Self-esteem, self-confidence, social skills & fun!
Activities: Archery, Arts/Crafts, Backpacking, Bicycling/Biking, Canoeing, Challenge/Rope Courses, Riflery, Swimming — Recreational
Session lengths & capacity: 1/2 & 1 week sessions; 150 campers
Clientele & fees: coed 7-17; families; Fees: C A 🚌
Contact: Dave Branconier, Dir of Camping Services at (909) 794-2927; fax: (909) 794-8567
e-mail: tatapochon@aol.com
Operated by: YMCA West San Gabriel Valley, 401 E Corto St, Alhambra, CA 91801 at (626) 576-0226

Group Rental Information
Site comments: High quality food service, beautiful high mountain setting, 1/4 mile from Jenks Lake; pool, low ropes, archery and more.
Facilities: Cabins, Food Service, Hiking Trails, Lake, Meeting Rooms, Pool
Programs: Boating, Challenge/Ropes Course, Swimming, Winter Sports (#51)

YMCA Camp Tulequoia

(est 1914)

Miramonte, CA (Fresno Co.); (209) 335-2603

Camp comments: Since 1914 our summer campers have enjoyed an environment that encourages heartfelt laughter, interactive learning, & personal growth through fun YMCA programs.
Activities: Aquatic Activities, Archery, Bicycling/Biking, Boating, Canoeing, Challenge/Rope Courses, Kayaking, Sailing, Swimming — Instructional, Swimming — Recreational
Session lengths & capacity: May-October; 1 week sessions; 120 campers

Clientele & fees: boys 5-17; girls 5-17; coed 5-17; families; Fees: C A 🚌
Contact: Karen Michigian, Camping Services Director at (559) 627-0700; fax: (559) 739-7819
e-mail: info@sequoialakeymca.org
Web site: www.visaliaymca.org
Operated by: Visalia YMCA, 211 W Tulare Ave, Visalia, CA 93277 at (559) 627-0700

Group Rental Information
Facilities: Cabins, Food Service, Hiking Trails, Lake, Playing Fields
Programs: Boating, Swimming (#13485)

YMCA Harold F Whittle

(est 1958)

Fawnskin, CA (San Bernardino Co.); (909) 866-3000
Brian Bost, Director

Camp comments: YMCA camp located in beautiful mountain area. Year-round modern facility dedicated to serving the youth and families of Los Angeles.
Activities: Archery, Bicycling/Biking, Camping Skills/Outdoor Living, Canoeing, Challenge/Rope Courses, Climbing/Rappelling, Horseback — Western, Leadership Development, Nature/Environment Studies, Swimming — Recreational
Session lengths & capacity: 1/2, 1 & 2 week sessions; 380 campers
Clientele & fees: coed 7-17; families; seniors; single adults; Fees: A, B, C A 🚌
Contact: Brian Bost, Director, Camping Services at (909) 866-3000; fax: (909) 866-5065
e-mail: brianbost@ymcala.org
Operated by: YMCA Metropolitan Los Angeles, PO Box 70, Fawnkin, CA 92533 at (909) 866-3000

Group Rental Information
Facilities: A/V Equipment, Cabins, Dorm-Style, Food Service, Hiking Trails, Linens, Lodges, Meeting Rooms, Playing Fields, Pool, Tents
Programs: Challenge/Ropes Course, Environmental Education, Horseback Riding, Winter Sports (#50)

YMCA Jack Hazard (est 1924)

Dardanelle, CA (Tvolumne Co.); (209) 578-9622
Jason Poisson, Director

Camp comments: A "Beautiful High Sierra Camp. Learn about the environment & self. Overnight packtrips are a specialty!"
Activities: Arts/Crafts, Backpacking, Camping Skills/Outdoor Living, Challenge/Rope Courses, Climbing/Rappelling, Horseback — Western, Leadership Development, Nature/Environment Studies
Session lengths & capacity: 1 week sessions; 108 campers
Clientele & fees: boys 8-18; girls 8-18; coed 8-18; families; Fees: C A 🚌
Contact: Jason Poison, Camp Director at (209) 578-9622; fax: (209) 578-1502
Operated by: YMCA of Stanislaus County, 2700 Mc Henry Ave, Modesto, CA 95350 at (209) 578-9622 (#371)

YMCA Mayfair Day Camp

(est 1995)

San Jose, CA (Santa Clara Co.); (408) 715-6518

Camp comments: Day Camp promotes community pride through activities for all children.
Activities: Arts/Crafts, Basketball, Community Service, Counselor Training (CIT), Drawing/Painting, Field Trips, Leadership Development, Nature/Environment Studies, Soccer, Swimming — Recreational
Session lengths & capacity: June-August; 7 week sessions; 64 campers
Clientele & fees: coed 5-12; Fees: A ☀ 🚌

Contact: Enrique Ortiz, Director at (408) 258-4419; fax: (408) 258-4496
Web site: www.scvymca.org
Operated by: YMCA of Santa Clara Valley, 1922 The Alameda 3rd Fl, San Jose, CA 95126 at (408) 298-3888 (#3274)

YMCA Milpitas Day Camp

(est 1986)

San Jose, CA (Santa Clara Co. Co.); (408) 715-6547
Elena Jolly, Director

Camp comments: Self-esteem specialty. Campers thrive in noncompetitive, caring atmosphere with opportunities to belong, learn, contribute. Outstanding staff.
Activities: Arts/Crafts, Basketball, Camping Skills/Outdoor Living, Climbing/Rappelling, Field Trips, Golf, Hockey, Nature/Environment Studies, Soccer, Team Building
Session lengths & capacity: June-August; 9 week sessions; 200 campers
Clientele & fees: coed 5-13; families; Fees: B, C ☀
Contact: Elena Jolly, Program Director at (408) 945-0919; fax: (408) 945-7621
e-mail: ejolly66@aol.com
Web site: www.scvymca.org
Operated by: YMCA of Santa Clara Valley, 1922 The Alameda 3rd Fl, San Jose, CA 95126 at (408) 298-3888 (#6603)

YMCA Movin-On Day Camp

Redlands, CA; (909) 793-2957
Sheila Healy, Director

Camp comments: Enjoy before & after school activities w/other 6-8th graders. Learn skills in arts & crafts, sports, recreation, homework tutoring is available.
Activities: Arts/Crafts, Baseball/Softball, Basketball, Community Service, Computer, Field Trips, Swimming — Recreational
Session lengths & capacity: 1/2, 1, 2, 3, 4, 5, 6, 7, 8 & 9 week sessions; 75 campers
Clientele & fees: boys 12-14; girls 12-14; Fees: B ☀
Contact: Sheila Healy, Camp Director at (909) 793-2957; fax: (909) 793-8788
Operated by: YMCA Movin-On Day Camp, 16 E Olive St, Redlands, CA 92373 at (909) 793-2957 (#12116)

YMCA of Mid-Peninsula Camps

Palo Alto, CA; (650) 856-9622
Erika Buck, Sue Corteposi, Tavia Harwell, Director
Activities: Aquatic Activities, Basketball, Climbing/Rappelling, Field Trips, Fishing, Golf, Hiking, Leadership Development, Nature/Environment Studies, Sports — Field & Team
Session lengths & capacity: June-August; 1 & 2 week sessions; 700 campers
Clientele & fees: coed 4-15; Fees: B ☀ 🚌
Contact: Web site: www.ymcamidpeninsula.org
Operated by: YMCA of the Mid Peninsula, 4151 Middlefield Road, Palo Alto, CA 94303 at (650) 856-3955 (#40741)

YMCA of Orange Day Camp

(est 1971)

Orange, CA (Orange Co.); (714) 633-9622
Kathleen Murphy, Director

Camp comments: Highlight of the summer. Excursions to amusement parks, beaches, museums & sporting events. Fills up fast. Fun, fun!

Activities: Arts/Crafts, Baseball/Softball, Basketball, Counselor Training (CIT), Field Trips, Swimming — Recreational
Session lengths & capacity: June-August; 2 week sessions; 80 campers
Clientele & fees: boys 6-12; girls 6-12; coed 6-12; Fees: B ☀ ☛
Contact: Dolores Marikian, Director at (714) 633-9622; fax: (714) 633-4337
Web site: www.ymcaoforange.org
Operated by: YMCA of Orange, 2241 E Palmyra, Orange, CA 92869 at (714) 633-9622 (#3253)

YMCA of Redwoods Camp Campbell (est 1936) ☀ ▲ ⌂ 🚐

Boulder Creek, CA (Santa Cruz Co.); (831) 338-2128
Mike Wentz, Director

Camp comments: Beautiful redwoods in Santa Cruz Mtns. Traditional YMCA program. Ages 7-18. Adventure activities. Backpacking, challenge courses, rock climbing, caring staff.
Activities: Archery, Backpacking, Camping Skills/Outdoor Living, Ceramics/Pottery, Challenge/Rope Courses, Climbing/Rappelling, Counselor Training (CIT), Leadership Development, Nature/Environment Studies, Photography
Session lengths & capacity: June-August; 1/2, 1 & 2 week sessions; 1800 campers
Clientele & fees: boys 7-18; girls 7-18; coed 7-18; families; Fees: D ▲ ☛
Contact: Mike Wentz, Executive Director at (831) 338-2128; fax: (831) 338-9486
Web site: www.scvymca.org
Operated by: YMCA of Santa Clara Valley, 1922 The Alameda 3rd Fl, San Jose, CA 95126 at (408) 298-3888

Group Rental Information
Site comments: Beautiful redwood forest 20 miles south of San Jose in the Santa Cruz Mtns. Lodges, pool, hiking, climbing wall, challenge courses, year-round activities.
Seasons & Capacity: Spring 224, Winter 224
Facilities: A/V Equipment, Cabins, Dorm-Style, Food Service, Hiking Trails, Lodges, Meeting Rooms, Playing Fields, Pool, River
Programs: Boating, Challenge/Ropes Course, Environmental Education, Swimming (#343)

YMCA Point Bonita ☀ ⌂ 🚐

Sausalito, CA (Marin Co.); (415) 331-9622
Andrew M. Boyd-Goodrich, Director

Camp comments: Environmental day camp by ocean in National Park by GG Bridge. Trips to nat. areas, climbing, kayaking, and overnights.

ICON LEGEND

☀ Day Camp
▲ Resident Camp
⌂ Facilities Available To Rent
🚐 Transportation Available
☛ Financial Aid Available

FEE RANGES PER WEEK

A	$0-75
B	$75-200
C	$201-350
D	$351-500
E	$501-650
F	over $650

Activities: Arts/Crafts, Camping Skills/Outdoor Living, Challenge/Rope Courses, Counselor Training (CIT), Field Trips, Hiking, Kayaking, Nature/Environment Studies, Swimming — Recreational, Team Building
Session lengths & capacity: June-August; 1 week sessions; 70 campers
Clientele & fees: coed 7-14; ☛
Operated by: YMCA San Francisco Day Camps, 1877 S Grant Street, San Mateo, CA 94402 at (650) 286-9622

Group Rental Information
Seasons & Capacity: Spring 150, Summer 150, Fall 150, Winter 150 (#4536)

YMCA Redlands Adventure ☀

Redlands, CA (San Bernardino Co.); (909) 793-2161

Camp comments: The YMCA Day Camp provides games, activities, and field trips for children 5-11. We operate Mon-Fri, 6:30am-6:30pm year-round. Please call for more information.
Session lengths & capacity: 1 week sessions
Clientele & fees: coed 5-11; Fees: B ☀
Contact: Amy Larson, Day Camp Director at (909) 798-9622; fax: (909) 335-2007
Operated by: YMCA Movin-On Day Camp, 16 E Olive St, Redlands, CA 92373 at (909) 793-2957 (#12111)

YMCA S Vley Family Day & Sport (est 1969) ☀

San Jose, CA (Santa Clara Co.); (408) 226-9622
Nancy Grove, Director

Camp comments: Day camp program with special emphasis on character skill development - excellent, safe, well-trained staff.
Activities: Arts/Crafts, Camping Skills/Outdoor Living, Counselor Training (CIT), Field Trips, Football, Golf, Hiking, Leadership Development, Nature/Environment Studies, Swimming — Recreational
Session lengths & capacity: June-August; 1 week sessions; 130 campers
Clientele & fees: boys 6-11; girls 6-11; coed 6-11; families; Fees: B ☀ ☛
Contact: Susan Cartopassi, Program Director at (408) 226-9622 ext. 18; fax: (408) 226-3324
Web site: www.scvymca.org
Operated by: YMCA of Santa Clara Valley, 1922 The Alameda 3rd Fl, San Jose, CA 95126 at (408) 298-3888 (#3296)

YMCA Southwest Day Camps ☀

(est 1851)

Saratoga, CA (Santa Clara Co.); (408) 370-1877
Jacqueline Hawkes, Director

Camp comments: Specialty day camps offering a wide variety for campers age appropriate in skills & activities great value safe and fun
Activities: Aquatic Activities, Arts/Crafts, Camping Skills/Outdoor Living, Climbing/Rappelling, Counselor Training (CIT), Field Trips, Horseback — English, Sports — Field & Team, Swimming — Instructional, Travel/Tour
Session lengths & capacity: 1/2, 1 & 2 week sessions; 1000 campers
Clientele & fees: boys 5-12; girls 5-12; coed 5-14; families; Fees: A, B, C ☀ ☛
Contact: Jacqueline Hawkes, Associate Executive Director at (408) 370-1877; fax: (408) 370-1333
e-mail: jhawkes@scoymca.org
Web site: www.scvymca.org
Operated by: YMCA of Santa Clara Valley, 1922 The Alameda 3rd Fl, San Jose, CA 95126 at (408) 298-3888 (#6610)

Yosemite Sierra Summer Camp ▲ ⌂

Bass Lake, CA
Contact: Web site: www.yssc.com
Operated by: Emerald Cove Camp, PO Box 449, Bass Lake, CA 93604 at (559) 642-2267 (#35480)

Young Set Club (est 1969) ☀ 🚐

Thousand Oaks, CA; (805) 495-2104
Robin Dean, Director

Camp comments: Year round day camp offers fun filled, exciting days,full and part-time available. Camp is open 6:30am - 6:30pm.
Activities: Archery, Challenge/Rope Courses, Climbing/Rappelling, Computer, Field Trips, Hiking, Leadership Development, Nature/Environment Studies, Swimming — Instructional, Swimming — Recreational
Session lengths & capacity: 1/2 & 1 week sessions; 150 campers
Clientele & fees: boys 5-12; girls 5-12; coed 5-12; Fees: B ☀
Contact: Robin Dean, Program Director at (805) 495-2104; fax: (805) 495-0397
e-mail: YoungSet3@aol.com
Web site: www.cdicdc.org
Operated by: Young Set Club, 400 E Rolling Oaks Dr, Thousand Oaks, CA 91361 at (805) 495-2104 (#103)

Colorado

Adventure Unlimited Ranches ▲ ⌂ 🚐

(est 1955)

Buena Vista, CO; (719) 395-2468
Bobby Lewis, Director

Camp comments: Program for Christian Science kids, all abilities. Safe, loving, environment, spiritual growth & personal challenge.
Activities: Arts/Crafts, Backpacking, Boating, Camping Skills/Outdoor Living, Challenge/Rope Courses, Climbing/Rappelling, Counselor Training (CIT), Horseback — Western, Rafting, Swimming — Instructional
Session lengths & capacity: June-September; 2 week sessions; 200 campers
Clientele & fees: coed 8-17; families; seniors; single adults; Fees: D, E ▲ ☛
Contact: Bobby Lewis, Ranch Director at (719) 395-2468; fax: (719) 395-2460
e-mail: bobby@adventureunlimited.org
Web site: www.adventureunlimited.org
Operated by: Adventure Unlimited Inc, PO Box 2036, Buena Vistan, CO 81211 at (719) 395-2468

Group Rental Information
Seasons & Capacity: Spring 120, Fall 120
Facilities: Cabins, Double Occupancy, Hiking Trails, Kitchen Facilities, Lodges, Meeting Rooms, River (#646)

Americas Adventure Venture Euro (est 1976) ▲

Golden, CO; (800) 222-3595
Abbott Wallis, Director

Camp comments: Outstanding leadership, 3-6 weeks, hands on. Camping,outdoor adventure for teens in Western USA, Hawaii, Alaska & Europe
Activities: Backpacking, Bicycling/Biking, Camping Skills/Outdoor Living, Climbing/Rappelling, Hiking, Horseback — Western, Leadership Development, Rafting, Travel/Tour, Wilderness Trips
Session lengths & capacity: June-August; 3, 4 & 6 week sessions; 650 campers
Clientele & fees: coed 11-19; Fees: E ▲ ☛
Contact: Abbott Wallis, Owner at (800) 222-3595; fax: (303) 526-0806

e-mail: info@aave.com
Web site: www.aave.com
Operated by: Americas Adventure Venture, 2245 Stonecrop Way, Golden, CO 80401 at (800) 222-3595 (#1301)

Anderson Western Colorado Camp (est 1962)

Gypsum, CO (Eagle Co.); (970) 524-7766
Christopher Porter, Director

Camp comments: Fun in the majestic Colorado Rockies!Individual noncompetitive emphasis. Daily activity choices-rafting/riding & more!
Activities: Backpacking, Caving, Challenge/Rope Courses, Climbing/Rappelling, Horseback — Western, Kayaking, Rafting, Riflery, Swimming — Recreational, Wilderness Trips
Session lengths & capacity: June-August; 2, 3 & 4 week sessions; 125 campers
Clientele & fees: coed 7-17; Fees: B ▲
Contact: Christopher Porter, Director at (970) 524-7766; fax: (970) 524-7107
e-mail: chrisp@rof.net
Web site: www.andersoncamps.com
Operated by: Porter Trading Company, 7177 Colorado River Rd, Gypsum, CO 81637 at (970) 524-7766 (#599)

Blue Mountain Ranch (est 1947) ▲ ⌂

Florissant, CO (Park Co.); (719) 748-3279
Suzie Graf, Director

Camp comments: Traditional program in a cool mountain setting emphasis on the child as an individual outstanding staff field trips.
Activities: Archery, Basketball, Challenge/Rope Courses, Field Trips, Fishing, Football, Hiking, Horseback — Western, Nature/Environment Studies, Tennis
Session lengths & capacity: June-September; 2, 4 & 6 week sessions; 120 campers
Clientele & fees: coed 7-16; Fees: F ☼ Fees: F ▲
Contact: Suzie Graf, Director at (719) 748-3279; fax: (719) 748-3472
e-mail: campbluemt@aol.com
Web site: www.bluemountainranch.com
Operated by: Allen Family Real Estate LP, PO Box 146, Florissant, CO 80816 at (719) 748-3279

Group Rental Information
Site comments: Traditional program in a cool mountain setting emphasis on the child as an individual outstanding staff field trips.
Seasons & Capacity: Spring 150, Fall 150
Facilities: A/V Equipment, Dorm-Style, Food Service, Hiking Trails, Lake, Lodges, Meeting Rooms, Playing Fields, Pool
Programs: Boating, Challenge/Ropes Course, Environmental Education, Swimming (#598)

Briargate Family YMCA ☼

Colorado Springs, CO; (719) 282-9622
Jill Sutton, Director
Activities: Aquatic Activities, Bicycling/Biking, Camping Skills/Outdoor Living, Counselor Training (CIT), Field Trips, Hiking, Martial Arts, Sports — Field & Team
Operated by: Briargate Family YMCA, 4025 Family Pl, Colorado Springs, CO 80920 at (719) 282-9622 (#10220)

C Bar T Trail Ranch (est 1958) ▲

Idledale, CO (Jefferson Co.); (303) 674-6477
Dr. Roger N. Felch, Director

Camp comments: Specializing in wilderness camping & horsemanship. Continuous horse backpack trips in the Colorado National forests.
Activities: Camping Skills/Outdoor Living, Farming/Ranching/Gardening, Fishing, Hiking, Horseback — Western, Nature/Environment Studies, Wilderness Trips

Session lengths & capacity: June-August; 3, 4 & 7 week sessions; 9 campers
Clientele & fees: coed 11-17; Fees: D ▲
Contact: Roger N Felch, Director at (303) 674-6477;
Operated by: C Bar T Trail Ranch, PO Box 158, Idledale, CO 80453 at (303) 674-5149 (#617)

Camp Chief Ouray YMCA
(est 1907) ▲ ⌂

Granby, CO (Grand Co.); (970) 887-2152
Trueman Hoffmeister, Director

Camp comments: Traditional camp programs to help children grow in spirit,mind & body.Located in Rocky Mountains 80 miles NW of Denver.
Activities: Archery, Backpacking, Camping Skills/Outdoor Living, Challenge/Rope Courses, Hiking, Horseback — Western, Leadership Development, Riflery, Swimming — Recreational, Travel/Tour
Session lengths & capacity: June-August; 1, 2 & 3 week sessions; 230 campers
Clientele & fees: coed 8-18; seniors; Fees: C ▲ ⌂
Contact: Trueman Hoffmeister, Director at (970) 887-2152 ext. 4172; fax: (303) 449-6781
e-mail: thoffmeister@ymcarockies.org
Web site: www.ymcarockies.org/cco
Operated by: Camp Chief Ouray YMCA, PO Box 169, Winter Park, CO 80482-0169 at (970) 887-2152 (#8383)

Camp Paha Rise Above
(est 1980) ☼ ⌂

Lakewood, CO
Jan Greer, Director

Camp comments: Special day camp for children&young adults with all disabilities. Provide 1:4 ratio camper/staff. Activities include field trips, sports & games,arts & crafts.
Activities: Arts/Crafts, Dance, Drama, Field Trips, Nature/Environment Studies, Sports — Field & Team, Swimming — Recreational, Team Building
Session lengths & capacity: June-August; 3 & 7 week sessions; 100 campers
Clientele & fees: boys 6-99; girls 6-99; coed 6-30; Fees: B ☼
Contact: Jo Burns, Coordinator at (303) 274-6659 ext. 12; fax: (303) 237-0762
Operated by: City of Lakewood, 12100 W Alameda Pkwy, Lakewood, CO 80228 at (303) 987-4866 (#5441)

Camp Santa Maria Del Monte
(est 1930) ▲ ⌂ ⌂

Shawnee, CO; (303) 838-5268
Ralph Lowder, Director

Camp comments: Fees: Sliding scale based on income.
Activities: Archery, Boating, Camping Skills/Outdoor Living, Counselor Training (CIT), Fishing, Hiking, Nature/Environment Studies
Session lengths & capacity: 1 week sessions; 96 campers
Clientele & fees: coed 6-13; seniors
Contact: Ralph Lowder, Director at (303) 742-0823 ext. 130; fax: (303) 742-1181
e-mail: ralphcsm@juno.com
Web site: www.archden.org/archden
Operated by: Catholic Charities, 2525 W Alameda, Denver, CO 80219 at (303) 742-0828

Group Rental Information
Seasons & Capacity: Spring 110, Summer 110, Fall 110, Winter 110
Facilities: A/V Equipment, Cabins, Dorm-Style, Food Service, Hiking Trails, Lake, Playing Fields, Pool, River (#630)

Challenger Middle School ☼

Colorado Springs, CO; (719) 598-1007
Jenny Bell, Director
Activities: Aquatic Activities, Arts/Crafts, Counselor Training (CIT), Field Trips, Leadership Development, Nature/Environment Studies, Sports — Field & Team, Swimming — Recreational
Operated by: Briargate Family YMCA, 4025 Family Pl, Colorado Springs, CO 80920 at (719) 282-9622 (#10228)

Cheley Colorado Camps
(est 1921) ▲ ⌂ ⌂

Estes Park, CO (Larimer Co.); (970) 586-4244
Don & Carole Cheley, Director

Camp comments: Rocky Mountain beauty, outstanding staff. Time tested program of riding, hiking, & backpacking. Caring, warm, fun camp!
Activities: Arts/Crafts, Backpacking, Bicycling/Biking, Climbing/Rappelling, Hiking, Horseback — Western, Leadership Development, Sports — Field & Team, Wilderness Trips
Session lengths & capacity: 4 week sessions; 494 campers
Clientele & fees: boys 9-17; girls 9-17; families; Fees: E ▲
Contact: Don & Carole Cheley, Executive Directors at (303) 377-3616; fax: (303) 377-3020
e-mail: don@cheley.com
Operated by: Cheley Colorado Camps Inc, PO Box 6525, Denver, CO 80206-0525 at (303) 377-3616 (#610)

Colorado Camp Cherith
(est 1950) ▲ ⌂

Greeley, CO (Fremont Co.); (970) 353-3170
Jeanette Meis, Director

Camp comments: Mountain setting. Christian camp serving girls ages 6 to 18. Leadership training. Bible based outdoor program.
Activities: Aquatic Activities, Archery, Arts/Crafts, Camping Skills/Outdoor Living, Counselor Training (CIT), Hiking, Nature/Environment Studies, Religious Study, Riflery, Team Building
Session lengths & capacity: July-July; 1 week sessions; 140 campers
Clientele & fees: girls 6-18; Fees: C ⚠ 🚐
Contact: Jeanette Meis, Director at (970) 353-3170; fax: (970) 353-3170
e-mail: j.meis@alpha.psd.k12.co.us
Operated by: Colorado Camp Cherith, 432 Sumac Ct, Louisville, CO 80027 at (720) 890-1655 (#614)

Colorado Mountain Camps   ⚠

Oak Creek, CO (Routt Co.); (800) 651-8336
Farley Kautz, Director

Camp comments: Rewarding,challenging and FUN summer camps in Colorado, and wilderness adventure/travel programs across the US & Canada
Activities: Backpacking, Climbing/Rappelling, Counselor Training (CIT), Horseback — Western, Leadership Development, Rafting, Snow Sports, Team Building, Travel/Tour, Wilderness Trips
Session lengths & capacity: June-August; 1, 2 & 3 week sessions; 150 campers
Clientele & fees: coed 9-21; Fees: F ⚠ 🐖
Contact: Farley Kautz, Owner/Director at (800) 651-8336; fax: (970) 736-8311
e-mail: info@apadventures.com
Web site: www.coloradomountaincamps.com
Operated by: Colorado Mountain Camps, PO Box 658, Oak Creek, CO 80467 at (970) 736-8336 (#2527)

Colvig Silver Camps

(est 1969)   ⚠ 🏠 🚐

Durango, CO (La Plata Co.); (800) 858-2850
Clay Colvig, Director

Camp comments: 30 year residential program mixing traditional camp activities & wilderness adventures.
Activities: Arts/Crafts, Backpacking, Camping Skills/Outdoor Living, Challenge/Rope Courses, Climbing/Rappelling, Horseback — Western, Leadership Development, Nature/Environment Studies, Rafting, Wilderness Trips
Session lengths & capacity: June-August; 2, 4 & 8 week sessions; 150 campers
Clientele & fees: boys 11-13; girls 11-13; coed 7-17; Fees: D, F ⚠ 🐖
Contact: Clay Colvig, Director at (800) 858-2850; fax: (970) 247-2547
e-mail: colvigsilvercamps@compuserve.com
Web site: www.colvigsilvercamps.com

ICON LEGEND

☀ Day Camp
⚠ Resident Camp
🏠 Facilities Available To Rent
🚐 Transportation Available
🐖 Financial Aid Available

FEE RANGES PER WEEK

A	$0-75
B	$75-200
C	$201-350
D	$351-500
E	$501-650
F	over $650

Operated by: Colvig Silver Camps Inc, 9665 Florida Road, Durango, CO 81301 at (970) 247-2564

Group Rental Information

Site comments: Rustic site surrounded by San Juan National Forest available in late spring and late summer for site rental or some programming.
Facilities: A/V Equipment, Cabins, Food Service, Hiking Trails, Kitchen Facilities, Lake, Lodges, Meeting Rooms, River
Programs: Challenge/Ropes Course, Environmental Education, Horseback Riding (#459)

Eagle Lake Camp   (est 1957)   ⚠

Colorado Springs, CO (El Paso Co.); (719) 472-1260
Jack McQueeney, Director

Camp comments: Something for every kid, so every kid succeeds!
Activities: Archery, Bicycling/Biking, Canoeing, Challenge/Rope Courses, Climbing/Rappelling, Hiking, Horseback — English, Horseback — Western, Riflery, Wilderness Trips
Session lengths & capacity: June-September; 1 & 2 week sessions; 240 campers
Clientele & fees: boys 8-18; girls 8-18; coed 8-18; families; Fees: D ⚠ 🐖
Contact: Craig Dunham, Associate Director at (719) 472-1260; fax: (719) 472-1208
e-mail: useagle@navyouth.com
Web site: www.eaglelake.org
Operated by: The Navigators, PO Box 6000, Colorado Springs, CO 80934 at (719) 472-1260 (#638)

Easter Seals Colorado Rocky Mt   (est 1951)   ⚠ 🏠

Empire, CO (Clear Creek Co.); (303) 892-6063
Christine Newell, Director

Camp comments: Residential camp for children & adults with disabilities. Outdoor accessible experiences in a challenging setting.
Activities: Baseball/Softball, Basketball, Bicycling/Biking, Computer, Golf, Horseback — Western, Swimming — Recreational
Session lengths & capacity: June-August; 1 week sessions; 70 campers
Clientele & fees: coed 7-70; families; single adults; Fees: E ⚠ 🐖
Contact: Melissa Huber, Director at (303) 569-2333; fax: (303) 569-3857
e-mail: campinfo@cess.org
Operated by: Easter Seal Colorado, 5755 W Alameda Ave, Lakewood, CO 80226 at (303) 233-1666

Group Rental Information

Facilities: A/V Equipment, Cabins, Dorm-Style, Double Occupancy, Food Service, Hiking Trails, Kitchen Facilities, Linens, Lodges, Meeting Rooms, Playing Fields
Programs: Challenge/Ropes Course, Horseback Riding, Swimming (#612)

Estes Park Ctr YMCA of Rockies   (est 1960)   ☀

Estes Park, CO (Larimer Co.); (970) 586-3341
Shelly Coerver, Director

Camp comments: Day camp serves guests of family resort, conf center & YMCA members. Beautiful setting bordering Rocky Mtn Natl Park.
Activities: Aquatic Activities, Archery, Arts/Crafts, Backpacking, Bicycling/Biking, Camping Skills/Outdoor Living, Challenge/Rope Courses, Climbing/Rappelling, Hiking, Horseback — Western
Session lengths & capacity: June-August; 1 week sessions; 300 campers
Clientele & fees: coed 5-18; Fees: B ☀ 🚐
Contact: Shelly Coerver, Youth Program Coordinator at (970) 586-3341 ext. 1280; fax: (970) 577-1255

e-mail: info@ymcarockies.org
Operated by: YMCA of the Rockies, Schlessman Executive Offices, PO Box 20800, Estes Park, CO 80511-2800 at (970) 586-4444 (#2057)

Flying G Ranch   (est 1945)   ⚠ 🏠

Sedalia, CO (Jefferson Co.); (303) 647-2312
Rhonda Mickelson, Director

Camp comments: Mountain setting. Focus on developing social relationships, leadership skills, enhancing self-esteem, and building communities.
Activities: Arts/Crafts, Backpacking, Camping Skills/Outdoor Living, Challenge/Rope Courses, Counselor Training (CIT), Hiking, Horseback — Western, Leadership Development, Nature/Environment Studies, Team Building
Session lengths & capacity: June-August; 1 & 2 week sessions; 150 campers
Clientele & fees: girls 9-17; Fees: C, D ⚠ 🐖
Contact: Rhonda Mickelson, Camp Administrator at (303) 778-8774; fax: (303) 733-6345
e-mail: rhondam@gsmhc.org
Web site: www.girlscoutsmilehi.org
Operated by: Girl Scouts - Mile Hi Council, PO Box 9407, Denver, CO 80209 at (303) 778-8774 (#618)

Genesee Day Camp

(est 1968)   ☀ 🏠 🚐

Golden, CO (Jefferson Co.); (303) 778-8774
Shorty Sutterlin, Director

Camp comments: Girls learn self-reliance, develop leadership skills & learn to care about others in a natural environment.
Activities: Archery, Arts/Crafts, Camping Skills/Outdoor Living, Field Trips, Hiking, Leadership Development, Nature/Environment Studies
Session lengths & capacity: June-August; 1 week sessions; 125 campers
Clientele & fees: girls 6-12; Fees: B ☀ 🚐
Contact: Shorty Sutterlin, Day Camp Administrator at (303) 778-8774; fax: (303) 733-6345
e-mail: Pattys@gsmhc.org
Web site: www.girlscoutsmilehi.org
Operated by: Girl Scouts - Mile Hi Council, PO Box 9407, Denver, CO 80209 at (303) 778-8774 (#1628)

Geneva Glen Camp Inc

(est 1922)   ⚠ 🏠

Indian Hills, CO (Jefferson Co.); (303) 697-4621
Ken & Nancy Atkinson, Director

Camp comments: Continuous seasons since 1922, offering theme prog for campers of all backgrounds. Rich heritage; leadership emphasis.
Activities: Archery, Arts/Crafts, Climbing/Rappelling, Drama, Horseback — Western, Leadership Development, Nature/Environment Studies, Photography, Riflery, Swimming — Recreational
Session lengths & capacity: 2 week sessions; 220 campers
Clientele & fees: coed 6-16; Fees: E ⚠
Contact: Ken & Nancy Atkinson, Directors at (303) 697-4621; fax: (303) 697-9429
e-mail: ggcamp@genevaglen.org
Web site: www.genevaglen.org
Operated by: Geneva Glen Camp Inc, Box 248, Indian Hills, CO 80454 at (303) 697-4621 (#620)

Girl Scout Camp Lazy Acres

(est 1947)   ☀ 🏠

Pueblo, CO (Rye Co.); (719) 489-3373
Cheryl Scott, Director

Camp comments: Girl Scout camp - open to rental.

Activities: Arts/Crafts, Camping Skills/Outdoor Living, Dance, Drama, Field Trips, Hiking, Horseback — Western, Leadership Development, Photography
Session lengths & capacity: June-October; 1/2 & 5 week sessions; 75 campers
Clientele & fees: girls 5-17; families; Fees: A ☀
Contact: Cheryl Scott, Program Director
Operated by: Girls Scouts Columbine Council, 21 Montebello Rd, Pueblo, CO 81001 at (719) 543-4690
Group Rental Information
Seasons & Capacity: Spring 60, Summer 85, Winter 40
Facilities: Cabins, Hiking Trails, Kitchen Facilities, Lodges, Tents
Programs: Environmental Education (#4229)

Glacier View Ranch (est 1949) ▲ ⌂

Ward, CO (Boulder Co.); (303) 459-0771
Vern Jewett, Director

Camp comments: Changing Lives--Making Memories
Activities: Aquatic Activities, Bicycling/Biking, Ceramics/Pottery, Challenge/Rope Courses, Climbing/Rappelling, Gymnastics, Horseback — Western, Sailing, Swimming — Recreational, Waterskiing
Session lengths & capacity: June-July; 1 week sessions; 162 campers
Clientele & fees: coed 7-17; Fees: B ▲
Contact: Vern Jewett, Ranch Manager at (303) 459-0771; fax: (303) 459-3325
e-mail: vajewett@juno.com
Operated by: Rocky Mountain Conference, 2520 S Downing, Denver, CO 80210 at (303) 733-3771
Group Rental Information
Site comments: Changing Lives--Making Memories
Facilities: A/V Equipment, Cabins, Dorm-Style, Double Occupancy, Food Service, Hiking Trails, Kitchen Facilities, Lake, Linens, Lodges, Meeting Rooms, Playing Fields, Pool
Programs: Horseback Riding, Swimming (#650)

High Peak Camp and Conference (est 1985) ▲

Estes Park, CO; (970) 586-3311
Shea Simms, Director
Activities: Boating, Challenge/Rope Courses, Fishing
Session lengths & capacity: Year-round; 1 week sessions; 150 campers
Clientele & fees: coed 7-16; Fees: B ▲ 🐷
Contact: Shea Simms, Administrative Director at (970) 586-3311; fax: (970) 586-0595
e-mail: covertsy@aol.com
Operated by: The Salvation Army, PO Box 2369, Denver, CO 80201-2369 at (303) 861-4833 (#39940)

Highlands Pby Camp & Retreat (est 1945) ☀ ▲ ⌂

Allenspark, CO (Boulder Co.); (303) 747-2888
Russell Napier, Director

Camp comments: 8500' Mountain setting providing Christian programing open to all faiths coed.Resident&day camp,horse camps,backpacking,mountain biking,canoeing,hiking,archery.
Activities: Archery, Arts/Crafts, Bicycling/Biking, Camping Skills/Outdoor Living, Canoeing, Counselor Training (CIT), Field Trips, Hiking, Horseback — Western, Religious Study
Session lengths & capacity: January-December; 1/2 & 1 week sessions; 1500 campers
Clientele & fees: coed 5-18; families; seniors; single adults; Fees: A ☀ Fees: C ▲
Contact: Russell Napier, Executive Director at (303) 747-2888; fax: (303) 747-2889
e-mail: highlands_co@bemail.com

Web site: www.highlandscamp.org
Operated by: Highlands Pby Camp, PO Box 533, Allenspark, CO 80510 at (303) 747-2888
Group Rental Information
Site comments: Majestic 285 acre setting at 8500 ft. Close to national park&Estes park. Unlimited higking&streams, 28 miles from poplular skiing area,cabins or dorm,good food.
Seasons & Capacity: Spring 240, Summer 320, Fall 240, Winter 240
Facilities: A/V Equipment, Cabins, Dorm-Style, Double Occupancy, Food Service, Hiking Trails, Kitchen Facilities, Lake, Linens, Lodges, Meeting Rooms, Playing Fields, River
Programs: Boating, Challenge/Ropes Course (#28142)

Horizon Adventures Inc (est 1985) ▲

Denver, CO (Denver Co.); (303) 393-7297
Paul Woodward, Director

Camp comments: Colorado Back Country Adventures for Teens. Fun, exciting courses that stress Mtn. Safety, Environ Educ. & Skills Inst. Capacity of 10 persons per course.
Activities: Backpacking, Bicycling/Biking, Camping Skills/Outdoor Living, Climbing/Rappelling, Hiking, Leadership Development, Nature/Environment Studies, Rafting, Travel/Tour, Wilderness Trips
Session lengths & capacity: June-August; 1 & 2 week sessions; 100 campers
Clientele & fees: coed 13-17; Fees: D, E ▲ 🐷
Contact: Paul Woodward at (303) 393-7297; fax: (303) 393-7296
e-mail: horizon@earthnet.net
Web site: www.horizonadventures.com
Operated by: Horizon Adventures Inc, 1370 Birch St, Denver, CO 80220 at (303) 393-7297 (#6685)

J Bar CC Ranch Camp (est 1953) ▲ 🚗

Elbert, CO; (303) 841-2137
Juli Kramer, Director

Camp comments: Creating memories in Colorado since 1953! Horseback riding, mt. biking, outdoor heated swimming pool! Fun, safe, caring environment! Teen Adventures too!
Activities: Arts/Crafts, Bicycling/Biking, Camping Skills/Outdoor Living, Climbing/Rappelling, Drama, Horseback — Western, Swimming — Recreational, Wilderness Trips
Session lengths & capacity: June-August; 2, 3 & 4 week sessions; 195 campers
Clientele & fees: coed 7-16; families; Fees: D ▲
Contact: Juli Kramer, Director at (303) 316-6384; fax: (303) 320-0042
e-mail: jkramer@jccranch.org
Web site: www.ranchcamp.org
Operated by: Robert E Loup JCC, 350 S Dahlia, Denver, CO 80246 at (303) 316-6384 (#3813)

La Foret Conference Center (est 1946) ▲ ⌂ 🚗

Colorado Springs, CO (El Paso Co.); (719) 495-2743
Susan R Lander, Director

Camp comments: Week long Christian youth camps in summer. Available cabins, meeting space, and full meal service for rentals year round.
Activities: Arts/Crafts, Baseball/Softball, Basketball, Challenge/Rope Courses, Dance, Drama, Nature/Environment Studies, Sports — Field & Team, Swimming — Recreational, Tennis
Session lengths & capacity: 1/2 & 1 week sessions; 180 campers
Clientele & fees: families; seniors; Fees: B, C ▲
Contact: Susan r Lander, Director at (719) 495-2743; fax: (719) 495-9016
e-mail: mail@laforet.org
Web site: www.laforet.org

Operated by: La Foret Conf and Retreat Ctr, PO Box 88229, Colorado Springs, CO 80908 at (719) 495-2743
Group Rental Information
Site comments: LaForet, a beautiful, historic site w/ a view of Pikes Peak. Offers a variety of camping experiences. La Foret boasts one of the finest ropes crses in Colorado.
Facilities: A/V Equipment, Cabins, Double Occupancy, Food Service, Hiking Trails, Kitchen Facilities, Lodges, Meeting Rooms, Playing Fields, Pool, River, Tents
Programs: Environmental Education, Swimming, Winter Sports (#10381)

Meadow Mountain Ranch (est 1961) ▲

Allenspark, CO (Boulder Co.); (303) 747-2416
Jamili Omar, Director

Camp comments: Colorado Rocky Mtns. Horses, backpacking, climbing, arts & crafts, archery and more.
Activities: Archery, Arts/Crafts, Backpacking, Camping Skills/Outdoor Living, Canoeing, Challenge/Rope Courses, Climbing/Rappelling, Hiking, Horseback — Western, Nature/Environment Studies
Session lengths & capacity: June-August; 1/2, 1 & 2 week sessions; 100 campers
Clientele & fees: girls 6-17; Fees: C ▲ 🐷
Contact: Jamili Omar, Camp Director at (970) 493-1844; fax: (970) 493-6838
e-mail: camp@gsmpc.org
Web site: www.gsmpc.org
Operated by: GS Mountain Prairie Council, 1600 Specht Point Ste A, Fort Collins, CO 80525 at (970) 493-1844 (#641)

Poulter Colorado Camps (est 1966) ▲ 🚐

Steamboat Springs, CO (Routt Co.); (888) 879-4816
Jay B Poulter, Director

Camp comments: Over 35 years with the Poulter family. Our life adventures focus on individual growth, wilderness appreciation. Traditional programs, mountaineering, world trav
Activities: Backpacking, Camping Skills/Outdoor Living, Climbing/Rappelling, Fishing, Hiking, Horseback — Western, Leadership Development, Rafting, Team Building, Wilderness Trips
Session lengths & capacity: March-August; 1, 2 & 4 week sessions; 80 campers
Clientele & fees: coed 10-17; Fees: B ☀ Fees: E, F ▲
Contact: Jay Poulter, Director at (888) 879-4816; e-mail: poulter@poultercamps.com
Web site: www.poultercamps.com
Operated by: Poulter Colorado Camps, PO Box 772947, Steamboat Springs, CO 80477 at (970) 879-4816 (#16846)

Rainbow Trail Lutheran Camp (est 1957) ▲ ⌂

Hillside, CO (Custer Co.); (719) 942-4220
David K Jarvis, Director

Camp comments: Located in the Southern Rockies of Colorado. Christian backpacking, hiking, Bible study, worship. Outstanding staff.
Activities: Archery, Arts/Crafts, Camping Skills/Outdoor Living, Challenge/Rope Courses, Hiking, Leadership Development, Nature/Environment Studies, Religious Study, Wilderness Trips
Session lengths & capacity: June-August; 1 week sessions; 105 campers
Clientele & fees: coed 6-18; families; Fees: C ▲ 🐷
Contact: David K Jarvis, Executive Director at (719) 276-5233; fax: (719) 276-5235
e-mail: dave@rainbowtrail.org

Web site: www.rainbowtrail.org
Operated by: Lutheran Outdoor Ministries, 107 south Ninth St Ste B, Canon City, CO 81212 at (719) 276-5233
Group Rental Information
Site comments: Located in the Southern Rockies of Colorado. Homestyle meals, fresh bread & wonderful hospitality. Located near Monarch ski area.
Seasons & Capacity: Spring 100, Winter 50
Facilities: A/V Equipment, Cabins, Dorm-Style, Double Occupancy, Food Service, Hiking Trails, Linens, Lodges, Meeting Rooms, Playing Fields
Programs: Challenge/Ropes Course, Environmental Education, Winter Sports (#7475)

Sanborn Western Camps
(est 1948)   ▲

Florissant, CO (Teller Co.); (719) 748-3341
Mike MacDonald and Jan Sanborn van West, Director

Camp comments: Adventurous program. Personal growth emphasis. Mature, caring staff. Exciting wilderness trips, plus outstanding in-camp program in the Colorado Rockies.
Activities: Aquatic Activities, Arts/Crafts, Backpacking, Camping Skills/Outdoor Living, Climbing/Rappelling, Hiking, Horseback — Western, Nature/Environment Studies, Swimming — Recreational, Wilderness Trips
Session lengths & capacity: June-August; 2 & 5 week sessions; 340 campers
Clientele & fees: boys 7-16; girls 7-16; Fees: E ▲
Contact: Jerry McLain, Director at (719) 748-3341; fax: (719) 748-3259
e-mail: info@sanbornwesterncamps.com
Web site: www.sanbornwesterncamps.com
Operated by: Sanborn Western Camps, PO Box 167, Florissant, CO 80816 at (719) 748-3341 (#642)

Shwayder Camp Of Temple Emanue (est 1948)   ▲ ⌂ 🚗

Idaho Springs, CO; (303) 567-2722
Zim Zimmerman, Director

Camp comments: Jewish camp located 10,200 feet high in the Colorado Rocky Mtns. Outdoor program, sports, creative arts, and lots more.
Activities: Arts/Crafts, Basketball, Camping Skills/Outdoor Living, Challenge/Rope Courses, Counselor Training (CIT), Drama, Hiking, Horseback — Western, Music, Religious Study
Session lengths & capacity: June-August; 1, 2 & 4 week sessions; 120 campers
Clientele & fees: coed 8-15; Fees: E ▲ 🐷

ICON LEGEND

☀   Day Camp

▲   Resident Camp

⌂   Facilities Available To Rent

🚗   Transportation Available

🐷   Financial Aid Available

FEE RANGES PER WEEK

A	$0-75
B	$75-200
C	$201-350
D	$351-500
E	$501-650
F	over $650

Contact: Zim Zimmerman, Director at (303) 388-4013; fax: (303) 388-6328
e-mail: camp@congregationemanuel.com
Web site: www.shwayder.com
Operated by: Congregation Emanuel, 51 Grape Street, Denver, CO 80220 at (303) 388-4013
Group Rental Information
Facilities: Cabins, Dorm-Style, Food Service, Hiking Trails, Playing Fields, Tents
Programs: Challenge/Ropes Course, Horseback Riding (#619)

Sky High Ranch (est 1952)   ▲ 🚗

Woodland Park, CO (Teller Co.); (719) 597-8603

Camp comments: Beautiful 880 acres. Rustic camp in CO Rockies 8200 ft. Varied programs, horses, low rope course, canoeing, camping etc.
Activities: Archery, Arts/Crafts, Backpacking, Camping Skills/Outdoor Living, Canoeing, Counselor Training (CIT), Hiking, Horseback — Western, Leadership Development, Nature/Environment Studies
Session lengths & capacity: June-August; 1/2, 1 & 2 week sessions; 130 campers
Clientele & fees: girls 7-17; Fees: B, C ▲
Contact: Valerie Williamson, Director/Outdoor Program & Property at (719) 597-8603 ext. 39; fax: (719) 597-5986
e-mail: vwilliamson@girlscouts-wwc.org
Web site: www.girlscouts-wwc.org
Operated by: Wagon Wheel GSC, 3535 Parkmoor Village Dr, Colorado Springs, CO 80917 at (719) 597-8603 (#634)

Sonlight Christian Camp
(est 1979)   ▲ ⌂

Pagosa Springs, CO (Archuleta Co.); (970) 264-4379
Winston and Mary Marugg, Director

Camp comments: Our goal is to build self-esteem, create community, develop respect for others&the environment in a Christian atmosphere
Activities: Archery, Arts/Crafts, Backpacking, Bicycling/Biking, Challenge/Rope Courses, Leadership Development, Nature/Environment Studies, Soccer, Team Building, Wilderness Trips
Session lengths & capacity: June-August; 1 week sessions; 64 campers
Clientele & fees: coed 8-18; Fees: C ▲ 🐷
Contact: Winston or Mary Marugg, Directors at (970) 264-4379; fax: (970) 264-4383
Web site: www.sonlightcamp.org
Operated by: Sonlight Christian Camp, PO Box 536, Pagosa Springs, CO 81147 at (970) 264-4379
Group Rental Information
Facilities: Cabins, Dorm-Style, Food Service, Hiking Trails, Meeting Rooms
Programs: Challenge/Ropes Course, Winter Sports (#5515)

Timberview Middle School   ☀

Colorado Springs, CO; (719) 282-1144
Jennifer Bell, Director
Activities: Aquatic Activities, Arts/Crafts, Counselor Training (CIT), Field Trips, Leadership Development, Swimming — Recreational
Operated by: Briargate Family YMCA, 4025 Family Pl, Colorado Springs, CO 80920 at (719) 282-9622 (#10224)

Tomahawk Ranch (est 1953)   ▲ ⌂

Bailey, CO (Park Co.); (303) 838-5311
Angela Langhus, Director

Camp comments: Girls learn self reliance, develop leadership skills and learn to care for others in a natural mountain setting.

Activities: Archery, Arts/Crafts, Camping Skills/Outdoor Living, Counselor Training (CIT), Dance, Drama, Farming/Ranching/Gardening, Hiking, Leadership Development, Nature/Environment Studies
Session lengths & capacity: June-August; 1/2 & 1 week sessions; 150 campers
Clientele & fees: girls 6-14; Fees: B ▲
Contact: Debbie Speicher, Camp Administrator at (303) 778-8774; fax: (303) 733-6345
e-mail: debbies@hsmhc.org
Web site: www.girlscoutsmilehi.org
Operated by: Girl Scouts - Mile Hi Council, PO Box 9407, Denver, CO 80209 at (303) 778-8774
Group Rental Information
Facilities: Double Occupancy, Food Service, Kitchen Facilities, Lodges, Meeting Rooms
Programs: Environmental Education (#622)

YMCA Camp Jackson (est 1916) ▲ ⌂

Rye, CO (Pueblo Co.); (719) 489-3822
Douglas Lauritzen, Director

Camp comments: YMCA Camp Jackson builds confidence & independence in youth at our co-ed mountain camp. We provide the opportunity to develope team work & outdoor experiences.
Activities: Archery, Arts/Crafts, Camping Skills/Outdoor Living, Challenge/Rope Courses, Hiking, Horseback — Western, Leadership Development, Nature/Environment Studies, Riflery, Team Building
Session lengths & capacity: June-August; 1 week sessions; 100 campers
Clientele & fees: coed 7-17; families; seniors; single adults; Fees: C ▲ 🐷
Contact: Douglas Lauritzen, Camp/Program Director at (719) 543-5151; fax: (719) 543-7960
e-mail: lauritzen@campjackson.com
Web site: www.campjackson.com
Operated by: YMCA of Pueblo, 700 N Albany Ave, Pueblo, CO 81003 at (719) 543-5151
Group Rental Information
Site comments: YMCA Camp Jackson is nestled in the beautiful San Isabel National Forest. Come be our guest and experience a community of solitude and peace.
Seasons & Capacity: Spring 100, Fall 100
Facilities: A/V Equipment, Cabins, Dorm-Style, Double Occupancy, Food Service, Hiking Trails, Kitchen Facilities, Lodges, Meeting Rooms, Playing Fields, River, Tents
Programs: Challenge/Ropes Course, Environmental Education, Horseback Riding, Winter Sports (#629)

YMCA Camp Shady Brook
(est 1948)   ▲ ⌂ 🚗

Sedalia, CO; (303) 647-2313
Chris Pierce, Director

Camp comments: Our mission encourages development of mind, body & spirit with fun, challenging programs that respect the environment.
Activities: Archery, Arts/Crafts, Backpacking, Camping Skills/Outdoor Living, Challenge/Rope Courses, Climbing/Rappelling, Hiking, Horseback — Western, Riflery
Session lengths & capacity: 1 week sessions; 150 campers
Clientele & fees: boys 7-16; girls 7-16; families; seniors; single adults; Fees: C ▲ 🐷
Contact: Cathy Dodyes, Administrative Assistant at (719) 593-9622 ext. 203; fax: (719) 593-2299
Web site: www.ppymca.org
Operated by: YMCA of the Pikes Peak Region, PO Box 1694, Colorado Springs, CO 80901 at (719) 473-9622
Group Rental Information
Facilities: A/V Equipment, Hiking Trails, Lodges, Tents
Programs: Boating, Challenge/Ropes Course, Environmental Education, Swimming (#639)

YMCA Pike Peak Day Camp ☀

Colorado Springs, CO; (719) 329-7253
Wendy Motch, Director

Camp comments: YMCA Day Camp offers wide variety of camps to meet the needs of your family. Camps are for ages 5-16. We build strong kids, strong families & strong communities
Activities: Arts/Crafts, Backpacking, Bicycling/Biking, Climbing/Rappelling, Counselor Training (CIT), Field Trips, Golf, Rafting, Sports — Field & Team, Swimming — Recreational
Session lengths & capacity: June-August; 1 week sessions; 325 campers
Clientele & fees: coed 5-17; Fees: B ☀ 🐖
Contact: Wendy Motch, Youth Director at (719) 329-7264; fax: (719) 471-1723
e-mail: wmotch@ppymca.org
Web site: www.ppymca.org
Operated by: YMCA of the Pikes Peak Region, PO Box 1694, Colorado Springs, CO 80901 at (719) 473-9622 (#40730)

Connecticut

Aspetuck (est 1939) ☀ 🚗

Weston, CT (Fairfield Co.); (203) 226-6536
Lin Walsh, Director

Camp comments: Great staff. Supportive environment encouraging girls to reach their fullest experiences and be their best.
Activities: Arts/Crafts, Camping Skills/Outdoor Living, Counselor Training (CIT), Field Trips, Hiking, Leadership Development, Nature/Environment Studies, Swimming — Instructional, Swimming — Recreational
Session lengths & capacity: 2, 4 & 6 week sessions; 150 campers
Clientele & fees: girls 5-17; Fees: B, C ☀ 🐖
Contact: Anita Hausheer, Program Manager at (203) 762-0557; fax: (203) 762-0688
e-mail: ahausheer@webquill.com
Web site: www.councilweb.girlscouts.org/gscswct
Operated by: GSC of Southwestern CT Inc, 529 Danbury Road, Wilton, CT 06897 at (203) 762-5557 (#3962)

Awosting Chinqueka (est 1900) ▲

Bantam, CT (Litchfield Co.); (860) 567-9678
The Ebners, Director

Camp comments: A pioneer in the camping industry for over 100 yrs. Great 1st time camp. 25+ specialty activities, elective prog daily.
Activities: Ceramics/Pottery, Challenge/Rope Courses, Fencing, Gymnastics, Horseback — English, Sailing
Session lengths & capacity: June-August; 2, 4, 6 & 8 week sessions; 250 campers
Clientele & fees: boys 6-16; girls 6-16; Fees: F ▲
Contact: The Ebner Family, Owners/Directors at (860) 567-9678; fax: (860) 567-1215
e-mail: info@awosting.com
Web site: www.awosting.com
Operated by: Ebner Camps Inc, Box 355, Bantam, CT 06750 at (860) 567-9678 (#2146)

Bucks Rock Camp (est 1943) ▲

New Milford, CT (Litchfield Co.); (860) 354-5030
Mickey & Laura Morris, Director

Camp comments: A unique program for teens emphasizing: freedom of choice, prof. instructors, impressive facilities. Theater, music, dance, glassblowing, recording studio & mor
Activities: Arts/Crafts, Ceramics/Pottery, Clowning, Computer, Dance, Drama, Music, Performing Arts, Photography, Radio/TV/Video
Session lengths & capacity: 4 & 8 week sessions; 350 campers

Clientele & fees: coed 12-16; Fees: F ▲ 🚐
Contact: Mickey Morris, Directors at (860) 354-5030; fax: (860) 354-1355
e-mail: bucksrock@mindspring.com
Web site: www.bucksrockcamp.com
Operated by: Bucks Rock Camp, 59 Bucks Rock Rd, New Millford, CT 06776 at (860) 354-5030 (#2224)

Camp Chase YMCA ☀ 🏠 🚗

Unionville, CT; (860) 673-4321
Kevin Eddy, Director

Camp comments: We build strong kids, strong families, strong communitites.
Activities: Archery, Arts/Crafts, Nature/Environment Studies, Sports — Field & Team, Swimming — Instructional, Swimming — Recreational
Session lengths & capacity: June-August; 2 week sessions; 320 campers
Clientele & fees: coed 6-13; Fees: B ☀ 🚐
Contact: (860) 673-4321; fax: (860) 793-9631
e-mail: camp.chaseymca@ghymca.org
Operated by: YMCA of Greater Hartford, 160 Jewell St, Hartford, CT 06103 at (860) 522-4183

Group Rental Information
Facilities: Food Service, Hiking Trails, Playing Fields, Pool
Programs: Swimming (#46422)

Camp Discovery (est 1996) ☀

South Windsor, CT (Hartford Co.); (860) 648-6355
Michael McCarty, Director

Camp comments: The South Windsor Recreation Department - the benefits are endless!
Activities: Aquatic Activities, Arts/Crafts, Baseball/Softball, Drama, Drawing/Painting, Field Trips, Football, Nature/Environment Studies, Soccer, Sports — Field & Team
Session lengths & capacity: 1 & 2 week sessions
Clientele & fees: Fees: B ☀
Contact: Michael McCarty, Assistant Director of Recreation at (860) 648-6351 ext. 258; fax: (860) 648-9366
e-mail: mccarty@southwindsor.org
Web site: www.southwindsor.org
Operated by: Town of South Windsor Rec Dept, 150 Nevers Rd, South Windsor, CT 06074 at (860) 648-6355 (#25563)

Camp Downtown ☀

Hartford, CT; (860) 379-2782
Mia Randolph, Director

Camp comments: Swimming, sports leagues, mentoring enrichment, field trips, computer club, bible club, nutrition, theme days, community projects, drills dance.
Activities: Academics, Arts/Crafts, Basketball, Community Service, Computer, Field Trips, Football, Leadership Development, Religious Study, Swimming — Recreational
Session lengths & capacity: July-August; 8 week sessions; 110 campers
Clientele & fees: boys 6-13; girls 6-13; Fees: A ☀ 🚐
Contact: Mia Randolph, Youth Services Director at (860) 522-4183; fax: (860) 724-9858
e-mail: mia.randolph@ghymca.org
Operated by: YMCA of Greater Hartford, 160 Jewell St, Hartford, CT 06103 at (860) 522-4183 (#2226)

Camp Gan Israel ☀

Greenwich, CT
Maryashie Deren, Rabbi Yoseph Deren, Director
Activities: Ceramics/Pottery, Computer, Dance, Drama, Field Trips, Horseback — Western, Music, Performing Arts, Swimming — Instructional, Tennis
Operated by: Chabad of Greenwich, 75 Mason St, Greenwich, CT 06831 at (203) 629-9059 (#30625)

Camp Hazen YMCA (est 1920) ☀ ▲ 🏠

Chester, CT (Middlesex Co.); (860) 526-9529
Paul E Bryant, Director

Camp comments: Caring committed staff, individual camper attention, beautiful CT river valley location, great general camp program!!
Activities: Aquatic Activities, Archery, Arts/Crafts, Bicycling/Biking, Camping Skills/Outdoor Living, Challenge/Rope Courses, Sailing, Skating, Sports — Field & Team, Wilderness Trips
Session lengths & capacity: June-August; 1 & 2 week sessions; 230 campers
Clientele & fees: coed 8-16; families; Fees: B ☀ Fees: D ▲ 🚐
Contact: Denise P Learned, Executive Director at (800) 248-8244; fax: (860) 526-9520
e-mail: office@camphazenymca.org
Web site: www.camphazenymca.org
Operated by: Camp Hazen YMCA Inc, 204 W Main St, Chester, CT 06412 at (860) 526-9529

Group Rental Information
Site comments: Camp Hazen is a multiple-use educational & recreational facility. Great for schools, colleges, youth groups, workshops, corporate retreats and banquets.
Seasons & Capacity: Spring 300, Fall 300, Winter 60
Facilities: A/V Equipment, Cabins, Double Occupancy, Hiking Trails, Lake, Playing Fields, Tents
Programs: Boating, Challenge/Ropes Course, Environmental Education (#4160)

Camp Horizons (est 1979) ▲

South Windham, CT (Windham Co.);
(860) 456-1032
Lauren Perrotti, Director

Camp comments: Excellent program for people who are mentally handicapped! We support, challenge campers in fun supportive environment!
Activities: Arts/Crafts, Boating, Camping Skills/Outdoor Living, Ceramics/Pottery, Drama, Horseback — Western, Music, Nature/Environment Studies, Swimming — Instructional, Swimming — Recreational
Session lengths & capacity: June-August; 2, 4, 6 & 8 week sessions; 112 campers
Clientele & fees: coed 8-40; seniors; Fees: E ▲
Contact: Lauren Perrotti, Director of Operations at (860) 456-1032; fax: (860) 456-4721
e-mail: lauren.perrotti@camphorizons.org
Web site: www.camphorizons.org
Operated by: Camp Horizons Inc, PO Box 323, South Windham, CT 06266 at (860) 456-1032 (#12101)

Camp Jewell YMCA

(est 1901) ☀ ▲ 🏠

Colebrook, CT (Litchfield Co.); (860) 379-2782
Brian Rupe/Paul Kamin, Director

Camp comments: Programs that build spirit, mind & body. Beautiful, year-round 500 acre Berkshire Mtn site, (bathrooms in the cabins!)
Activities: Archery, Arts/Crafts, Bicycling/Biking, Climbing/Rappelling, Horseback — Western, Kayaking, Photography, Sailing, Tennis, Wilderness Trips
Session lengths & capacity: 2 week sessions; 285 campers
Clientele & fees: boys 8-16; girls 8-16; coed 8-16; families; Fees: D ▲ 🚐
Contact: Paul Kamin, Camp Director at (888) 412-2267; fax: (860) 379-2782
e-mail: camp.jewell@ghymca.org
Operated by: YMCA of Greater Hartford, 160 Jewell St, Hartford, CT 06103 at (860) 522-4183

Group Rental Information
Facilities: Cabins, Dorm-Style, Food Service, Hiking Trails, Lake, Lodges, Meeting Rooms, Playing Fields

Programs: Boating, Challenge/Ropes Course, Environmental Education, Horseback Riding, Swimming, Winter Sports (#4440)

Camp Laurelwood (est 1937) ▲ ⌂

Madison, CT; (203) 421-3736
Dan Oren, M.D., Director

Camp comments: Warm & sensitive staff. Traditional program in beautiful scenic environment. Excellent athletic & art facility.
Activities: Arts/Crafts, Basketball, Boating, Challenge/Rope Courses, Drama, Martial Arts, Photography, Soccer, Swimming — Instructional, Tennis
Session lengths & capacity: June-August; 2, 4, 6 & 8 week sessions; 300 campers
Clientele & fees: coed 7-15; Fees: F ▲
Contact: Dan Oren MD, Executive Director at (203) 397-2267; fax: (203) 397-0122
Web site: www.camplaurelwood.org
Operated by: Camp Laurelwood, 360 Amity Rd, Woodbridge, CT 06525 at (203) 397-2267
Group Rental Information
Site comments: A perfect setting for a retreat or conference. Conveniently between New York and Boston.
Seasons & Capacity: Spring 200, Summer 200, Fall 200
Facilities: Cabins, Dorm-Style, Double Occupancy, Food Service, Hiking Trails, Kitchen Facilities, Lake, Meeting Rooms, Playing Fields, Pool, River, Tents
Programs: Swimming (#2161)

Camp Pelican (est 1965) ☀ 🚐

Greenwich, CT; (203) 869-4243
Pat Hellwig, Jr, Director

Camp comments: Transportation included, indoor and outdoor pools, optional lunch available, flexible dates.
Activities: Archery, Arts/Crafts, Basketball, Computer, Drama, Soccer, Sports — Field & Team, Swimming — Instructional, Swimming — Recreational, Tennis
Session lengths & capacity: June-August; 4, 5, 6, 7 & 8 week sessions; 500 campers
Clientele & fees: coed 3-13; Fees: D ☀
Contact: Pat Hellwig, Director at (203) 869-4243; fax: (203) 227-1668
Operated by: The Hellwig Family, 19 Broad St, Weston, CT 06883 at (203) 227-5470 (#3841)

ICON LEGEND

☀	Day Camp
▲	Resident Camp
⌂	Facilities Available To Rent
🚐	Transportation Available
🐷	Financial Aid Available

FEE RANGES PER WEEK

A	$0-75
B	$75-200
C	$201-350
D	$351-500
E	$501-650
F	over $650

Camp Sloane YMCA

(est 1928)   ☀ ▲ ⌂ 🚐

Lakeville, CT (Litchfield Co.); (860) 435-2557
Kathleen H Woods, Director

Camp comments: A place to grow in the Berkshires where character development occurs plus skill development, friendships and fun.
Activities: Challenge/Rope Courses, Counselor Training (CIT), Horseback — English, Nature/Environment Studies, Performing Arts, Radio/TV/Video, Sailing, Tennis, Waterskiing, Windsurfing
Session lengths & capacity: 2, 4, 6 & 8 week sessions
Clientele & fees: coed 5-15; families; Fees: C ☀ Fees: D ▲ 🚐
Contact: John H Hedbavny, Exec Director at (800) 545-9367; fax: (860) 435-2599
e-mail: jhh@mohawk.net
Web site: www.camp-sloane.org
Operated by: Camp Sloane YMCA Inc, 124 Indian Mountain Road, PO Box 1950, Lakeville, CT 06039-1950 at (860) 435-2557
Group Rental Information
Site comments: Year-round programs for schools, families, church & corporate groups with activities designed to meet the group's goals. A place to grow and learn.
Seasons & Capacity: Spring 250, Summer 150, Fall 250, Winter 100
Facilities: A/V Equipment, Cabins, Dorm-Style, Food Service, Hiking Trails, Kitchen Facilities, Lake, Linens, Meeting Rooms, Playing Fields, Pool, Tents
Programs: Boating, Challenge/Ropes Course, Environmental Education, Swimming, Winter Sports (#2003)

Camp Washington (est 1917) ▲

Lakeside, CT (Litchfield Co.); (860) 567-9623
Jean V Handler, Director

Camp comments: Christian community.300 acres Berkshire mtns. Caring atmosphere where team-work,self-esteem, and belonging are stressed.
Activities: Aquatic Activities, Archery, Arts/Crafts, Camping Skills/Outdoor Living, Challenge/Rope Courses, Counselor Training (CIT), Drama, Performing Arts, Photography, Wilderness Trips
Session lengths & capacity: June-August; 1/2, 1 & 2 week sessions; 112 campers
Clientele & fees: coed 7-18; families; Fees: C ▲ 🐷
Contact: Jean V Handler, Camp Director at (860) 567-9623; fax: (860) 567-3037
e-mail: elia_v@hotmail.com
Web site: www.campwashington.org
Operated by: Episcopal Diocese Connecticut, Camp Washington, 190 Kenyon Rd, Lakeside, CT 06758 at (860) 567-9623 (#3998)

Campus Kids - CT (est 1990) ▲ 🚐

South Kent, CT (Litchfield Co.); (860) 927-5331
Brad Finkelstein, Director

Camp comments: Mon-Fri sleep-away camp; home on the weekends; transportation provided. Campers choose activities daily. Fun & Friendly.
Activities: Aquatic Activities, Archery, Arts/Crafts, Camping Skills/Outdoor Living, Fencing, Golf, Gymnastics, Horseback — English, Performing Arts, Sports — Field & Team
Session lengths & capacity: June-August; 2, 4, 6 & 8 week sessions; 200 campers
Clientele & fees: coed 7-15; Fees: F ▲
Contact: Brad J Finkelstein, Director at (973) 243-9970; fax: (973) 243-1312
e-mail: ckconnecticut@aol.com
Web site: www.campuskids.com
Operated by: Campus Kids Summer Camps, PO Box 422, Mahopac, NY 10541 at (845) 621-2193 (#6783)

Candlewood (est 1962)   ☀ ▲ ⌂ 🚐

New Fairfield, CT (Fairfield Co.); (203) 762-5557
Karen Wen, Director

Camp comments: Great staff. Supportive environment, encouraging girls to reach their fullest potential. Try new experiences and be their best.
Activities: Camping Skills/Outdoor Living, Leadership Development, Sailing, Travel/Tour
Session lengths & capacity: 1/2, 1 & 2 week sessions; 150 campers
Clientele & fees: girls 5-17; Fees: C ☀
Contact: Anita Hausheer, Program Manager at (203) 762-5557; fax: (203) 762-0688
e-mail: ahausheer@webquilll.com
Web site: www.councilweb.girlscouts.org/gscswct
Operated by: GSC of Southwestern CT Inc, 529 Danbury Road, Wilton, CT 06897 at (203) 762-5557 (#2887)

Center Church Camp Asto Wamah (est 1910) ▲ ⌂

Columbia, CT (Tolland Co.); (860) 228-3489
Nancy Maclean, Director

Camp comments: Traditional prog, small resident camp. Cooperative living skills & independence are developed & recreational skills.
Activities: Aquatic Activities, Archery, Arts/Crafts, Boating, Canoeing, Leadership Development, Sailing, Sports — Field & Team, Swimming — Instructional, Tennis
Session lengths & capacity: June-August; 1 & 2 week sessions; 80 campers
Clientele & fees: boys 8-14; girls 8-14; coed 8-14; Fees: C ▲
Contact: Nancy T. Maclean, Director at (860) 649-8614; fax: (860) 647-7829
Operated by: First Church Christ Hartford, 42 W Route 87, Columbia, CT 06237 at (860) 249-5631 (#3480)

Connri (est 1978) ▲

Ashford, CT (Windham Co.); (860) 429-6401
Captain Tonie Cameron, Director
Activities: Arts/Crafts, Camping Skills/Outdoor Living, Drama, Hiking, Music, Nature/Environment Studies, Religious Study, Swimming — Recreational
Session lengths & capacity: 7 week sessions; 180 campers
Clientele & fees: coed 7-11; Fees: C ▲
Contact: Captain Tonie Cameron, Camp Director at (203) 543-8400 ext. 135; fax: (203) 543-8412
Operated by: The Salvation Army, PO Box 628, Hartford, CT 06105 at (860) 543-8400 (#3753)

Delaware Outdoor Adventure Ctr (est 2000) ▲ ⌂

Winsted, CT; (860) 379-6517
Alexandra Thomas, Director

Camp comments: Perfect setting for fun & learning. Non-competative, traditional prgm. Caring professional staff. Specialty - 1st timers
Activities: Archery, Arts/Crafts, Camping Skills/Outdoor Living, Challenge/Rope Courses, Leadership Development, Photography, Swimming — Instructional, Swimming — Recreational, Team Building
Session lengths & capacity: June-August; 2, 4 & 8 week sessions; 175 campers
Clientele & fees: coed 8-15; Fees: F ▲
Contact: Alexandra Thomas, Director/Owner at (860) 379-6517; fax: (860) 379-6539
e-mail: DelawareOAC@aol.com
Web site: www.delawareoac.com
Operated by: Delaware Outdoor Adventure Ctr, 390 Winchester Road, Winsted, CT 06098 at (860) 379-6517
Group Rental Information
Facilities: Cabins, Dorm-Style, Food Service, Meeting Rooms, Pool, River

Programs: Boating (#40587)

Easter Seals Camp Hemlocks

(est 1950)

Hebron, CT (Tolland Co.); (860) 228-9496
Sharon Nichols, Director

Camp comments: Year round recreation and camping programs for children and adults with or without disabilities. Programs include activities adapted for all ability levels.
Activities: Arts/Crafts, Camping Skills/Outdoor Living, Challenge/Rope Courses, Computer, Leadership Development, Nature/Environment Studies, Swimming — Recreational, Team Building, Travel/Tour
Session lengths & capacity: June-August; 1 & 2 week sessions; 90 campers
Clientele & fees: coed 6-80; families; seniors; single adults; Fees: B ☀ Fees: E ⚠ 🚗
Contact: Helen Miner, Adm. Asst. at (860) 228-9496 ext. 100; fax: (860) 228-2091
e-mail: helenm@easterealsofct.org
Web site: www.ct.easter-seals.org
Operated by: Easter Seals of CT Inc, PO Box 100, Amston, CT 06231 at (860) 228-9438

Group Rental Information
Site comments: Easter Seals Camp Hemlocks is owned/operated by Easter Seals of CT. It's a fully accessible, full service, year round facility loc. on 160 ac. of beautiful wood
Seasons & Capacity: Spring 150, Winter 150
Facilities: A/V Equipment, Dorm-Style, Double Occupancy, Food Service, Linens, Meeting Rooms, Playing Fields, Pool
Programs: Challenge/Ropes Course (#2746)

High Meadow Day Camp

(est 1960)

Granby, CT (Hartford Co.); (860) 653-9325
Chuck Washer, Director

Camp comments: High Meadow is a traditional camp. Our foundation is based on the belief that children grow best when inspired & challenged in a caring & nurturing environment.
Activities: Archery, Arts/Crafts, Ceramics/Pottery, Challenge/Rope Courses, Counselor Training (CIT), Horseback — Western, Nature/Environment Studies, Riflery, Swimming — Instructional, Tennis
Session lengths & capacity: July-August; 4, 5, 6, 7 & 8 week sessions; 350 campers
Clientele & fees: coed 4-13; Fees: D ☀
Contact: Chuck Washer, Director at (860) 653-9325; fax: (806) 653-7055
e-mail: hmdaycamp@aol.com
Web site: www.holidayhilldaycamp.com
Operated by: Holiday Hill Day Camp, 947 Mountain Road, Cheshire, CT 06410 at (203) 272-5358 (#18761)

Holiday Hill (est 1954)

Prospect, CT (New Haven Co.); (203) 272-9636
William Cunningham, Director

Camp comments: Optimum development of each child in a safe outdoor environment. Our 47th year offering a dynamic camp experience. Diversified program of sports and acts.
Activities: Archery, Arts/Crafts, Boating, Counselor Training (CIT), Horseback — Western, Music, Nature/Environment Studies, Riflery, Swimming — Instructional, Tennis
Session lengths & capacity: July-August; 4, 5, 6, 7 & 8 week sessions; 400 campers
Clientele & fees: coed 4-13; Fees: D ☀
Contact: William E Cunningham, Director at (203) 272-9636; fax: (203) 272-3157
e-mail: hhdaycamp@aol.com
Web site: www.holidayhilldaycamp.com
Operated by: Holiday Hill Day Camp, 947 Mountain Road, Cheshire, CT 06410 at (203) 272-5358 (#4381)

Incarnation Center

(est 1886)

Ivoryton, CT (Middlesex Co.); (860) 767-0848
Jennifer Carpenter, Director

Camp comments: Traditional camp experience in a safe, caring Christian environment. 650 acres &a mile long, private lake.
Activities: Aquatic Activities, Archery, Arts/Crafts, Basketball, Boating, Canoeing, Nature/Environment Studies, Soccer, Swimming — Instructional, Team Building
Session lengths & capacity: June-August; 2, 4 & 6 week sessions; 348 campers
Clientele & fees: coed 6-15; seniors; Fees: B ☀ Fees: C ⚠ 🚗
Contact: Danita Ballantyne at (860) 767-0848; fax: (860) 767-8432
e-mail: incarctr@connix.com
Web site: www.incarnationcenter.org
Operated by: Incarnation Center Inc, PO Box 577, Ivoryton, CT 06442-0577 at (860) 767-0848

Group Rental Information
Facilities: A/V Equipment, Cabins, Dorm-Style, Double Occupancy, Food Service, Hiking Trails, Kitchen Facilities, Lake, Linens, Lodges, Meeting Rooms, Playing Fields
Programs: Boating, Swimming (#2098)

Joel Ross Tennis & Sports Camp (est 1991)

Kent, CT; (860) 927-5773
Joel Ross, Director

Camp comments: An intensive tennis program including instruction, drilling, match play. Plus a wide range of instructional electives.
Activities: Arts/Crafts, Baseball/Softball, Basketball, Bicycling/Biking, Canoeing, Hiking, Soccer, Swimming — Recreational, Tennis
Session lengths & capacity: 2 week sessions; 140 campers
Clientele & fees: coed 8-18; Fees: F ⚠
Contact: Joel Ross, Owner/Director at (914) 668-3258; fax: (914) 723-4579
e-mail: rosstennis@aol.com
Web site: www.joelrosstennis.com
Operated by: Joel Ross Tennis & Sports, PO Box 62H, Scarsdale, NY 10583 at (914) 668-3258 (#1714)

Katoya Day Camp (est 1952)

Milford, CT (New Haven Co.); (203) 334-3145
Sue E. Stevens, Director

Camp comments: Campers share in planning their program with guidance from caring counselors. Transportation available, a place for fun.
Activities: Arts/Crafts, Camping Skills/Outdoor Living, Counselor Training (CIT), Hiking, Horseback — English, Leadership Development, Nature/Environment Studies, Swimming — Instructional, Team Building
Session lengths & capacity: June-August; 1, 2 & 3 week sessions; 200 campers
Clientele & fees: girls 5-14; Fees: B ☀ 🚗
Contact: Linda Bresky, Camp Administrator at (203) 334-3145 ext. 3015; fax: (203) 334-4475
e-mail: lbresky@hcgs103.org
Web site: www.gsofhousatonic.org
Operated by: Housatonic GSC, 87 Washington Avenue, Bridgeport, CT 06604 at (203) 334-3145

Group Rental Information
Facilities: Hiking Trails, Kitchen Facilities, Lodges (#2793)

KenMont and KenWood Camps

(est 1924)

Kent, CT; (860) 927-3042
David & Sharon Miskit, Director

Camp comments: Premier 4 wk boys camp & girls camp with world class

sports/adventure/creative programs. 200 beautiful acres on lake. Warm family atmosphere/traditional values.
Activities: Aquatic Activities, Arts/Crafts, Camping Skills/Outdoor Living, Golf, Gymnastics, Performing Arts, Radio/TV/Video, Sports — Field & Team, Tennis, Waterskiing
Session lengths & capacity: June-August; 4 week sessions; 350 campers
Clientele & fees: boys 8-14; girls 8-14; Fees: F ⚠
Contact: David & Sharon Miskit, Directors at (305) 673-3310; fax: (305) 673-4131
e-mail: david@kencamp.com
Web site: www.kenmontkenwood.com
Operated by: KenMont and KenWood Camps, PO Box 398596, Miami Beach, FL 33239-8596 at (305) 673-3310

Group Rental Information
Site comments: 200 acres w/ state-of-the-art sports & creative facilities, lake, pool, 9 hole golf course, 18 tennis courts. Lodging & dining for 500. 2 hrs NYC, 3 hrs Boston.
Seasons & Capacity: Spring 500, Fall 500
Facilities: Cabins, Kitchen Facilities, Lake, Lodges, Meeting Rooms, Playing Fields, Pool
Programs: Boating, Challenge/Ropes Course, Swimming (#2193)

Laurel Girl Scout Resident Cmp

(est 1955)

Lebanon, CT (New London Co.)
Terrie Campbell, Director

Camp comments: Contemporary programs for girls 7 to 17. We help girls develop into young women with strong values, self confidence and life skills while having fun.
Activities: Aquatic Activities, Arts/Crafts, Camping Skills/Outdoor Living, Challenge/Rope Courses, Counselor Training (CIT), Farming/Ranching/Gardening, Horseback — English, Nature/Environment Studies, Swimming — Instructional
Session lengths & capacity: July-August; 1/2, 1, 2 & 3 week sessions; 200 campers
Clientele & fees: girls 7-17; families; Fees: C ⚠ 🚗
Contact: Terrie Campbell, Director Outdoor Program at (203) 239-2922; fax: (203) 239-7220
e-mail: Terrie@cttrails.org
Operated by: GSCTC, 20 Washington Avenue, North Haven, CT 06473 at (203) 239-2922 (#14398)

Mahackeno Summer Camps

(est 1938)

Westport, CT (Fairfield Co.); (203) 226-4221
Nick Willeh, Director

Camp comments: A 42 acre outdoor center serves as a local day camp & outdoor recreational area.
Activities: Archery, Arts/Crafts, Camping Skills/Outdoor Living, Canoeing, Counselor Training (CIT), Nature/Environment Studies, Performing Arts, Sports — Field & Team, Swimming — Recreational
Session lengths & capacity: 2 week sessions
Clientele & fees: coed 5-15; Fees: B ☀ 🚗
Contact: (203) 226-4221; fax: (203) 227-1945
Web site: www.westportymca.org
Operated by: Westport\Weston YMCA, PO Box 190, Westport, CT 06881 at (203) 226-4221

Group Rental Information
Facilities: Meeting Rooms, Pool
Programs: Boating (#2773)

Mansfield's Holiday Hill

(est 1960)

Mansfield Center, CT (Tolland Co.); (860) 423-1375
Dudley & Wendy Duff Hamlin, Director

Camp comments: Eastern Connecticut's summer tradition for fresh air, fun and friendship.

Activities: Archery, Arts/Crafts, Canoeing, Challenge/Rope Courses, Counselor Training (CIT), Nature/Environment Studies, Sports — Field & Team, Swimming — Instructional, Swimming — Recreational, Tennis
Session lengths & capacity: June-August; 2 week sessions; 350 campers
Clientele & fees: coed 4-15; Fees: C ☀
Contact: Dudley Hamlin, Director at (860) 423-1375; fax: (860) 456-2444
e-mail: dudley.hamlin@snet.net
Web site: www.mansfieldsholidayhilldaycamp.bunk1.com
Operated by: Mansfields Holiday Hill, 41 Chaffeeville Road, Mansfield Center, CT 06250 at (860) 423-1375 (#2823)

Maria Pratt (est 1947) ▲

Torrington, CT (Litchfield Co.); (860) 489-9481
Jane Bielefield, Director

Camp comments: All girls welcome in supportive, noncompetitive, democratic environment. Beautiful rustic camp in Northwest Hills of CT
Activities: Camping Skills/Outdoor Living, Challenge/Rope Courses, Leadership Development, Nature/Environment Studies, Swimming — Recreational, Team Building
Session lengths & capacity: June-August; 1/2, 1 & 2 week sessions; 100 campers
Clientele & fees: girls 6-16; Fees: B ☀ Fees: C ▲
Contact: Jane Bielefield, Outdoor Program Specialist at (860) 482-4495; fax: (860) 489-8936
Operated by: GSC Northwestern CT Inc, 26 Prescott St, Torrington, CT 06790-5235 at (860) 482-4495 (#2732)

Middlesex County Camp

(est 1962) ☀ ▲

Moodus, CT (Middlesex Co.); (860) 873-2294
Beth Owen-Mishou, Director
Activities: Archery, Arts/Crafts, Camping Skills/Outdoor Living, Challenge/Rope Courses, Climbing/Rappelling, Horseback — Western, Nature/Environment Studies, Sports — Field & Team, Swimming — Instructional, Team Building
Session lengths & capacity: July-August; 1 week sessions; 100 campers
Clientele & fees: coed 7-15; Fees: B ☀ Fees: C ▲
Contact: (860) 873-2294;
e-mail: lzanelli@snet.net
Web site: www.middlesexcountycamp.org
Operated by: Middlesex County Camp, PO Box 687, Moodus, CT 06469 at (860) 873-2294 (#2605)

ICON LEGEND

☀   Day Camp

▲   Resident Camp

🏠   Facilities Available To Rent

🚗   Transportation Available

🚐   Financial Aid Available

FEE RANGES PER WEEK

A	$0-75
B	$75-200
C	$201-350
D	$351-500
E	$501-650
F	over $650

New London County 4H Camp

(est 1931) ▲

North Franklin, CT (New London Co.); (860) 642-6131
Chuck Lester, Director

Camp comments: Self-esteem building, campers thrive in noncompetitive atmosphere with opportunities to belong, learn, contribute.
Activities: Archery, Arts/Crafts, Camping Skills/Outdoor Living, Canoeing, Dance, Drama, Fishing, Leadership Development, Nature/Environment Studies, Swimming — Recreational
Session lengths & capacity: 1 week sessions; 140 campers
Clientele & fees: boys 6-17; girls 6-17; Fees: B, C ▲ 🚐
Contact: Donald Beebe, President at (860) 889-5266; fax: (860) 887-1378
Operated by: New London Co 4 H Foundation, 335 Washington St Box 6002, Norwich, CT 06360 at (860) 886-7476 (#2676)

S J Ranch (est 1956) ▲

Ellington, CT (Tolland Co.); (860) 872-4742
Pat Haines, Director

Camp comments: Extensive riding and horse care. Our priorities are safety, having fun, and learning. Girls choose activities daily.
Activities: Archery, Arts/Crafts, Basketball, Boating, Camping Skills/Outdoor Living, Counselor Training (CIT), Horseback — English, Horseback — Western, Swimming — Recreational, Tennis
Session lengths & capacity: June-August; 2 & 3 week sessions; 48 campers
Clientele & fees: girls 8-15; Fees: F ▲
Contact: Pat Haines, Director at (860) 872-4742; fax: (860) 870-4914
e-mail: sjranch@erols.com
Web site: www.kidscamps.com/specialty/sports/sjranch
Operated by: SJ Ranch Inc, 130 Sandy Beach Road, Ellington, CT 06029-3110 at (860) 872-4742 (#2754)

Shoreline Foundation Day Camp (est 1986) ☀ 🚗

Killingworth, CT (Middlesex Co.); (203) 421-3115
Dylan Clough, Director

Camp comments: 250 acres with 2 private lakes. Children have fun, make friends, learn new skills in safe day camp setting.
Activities: Archery, Arts/Crafts, Camping Skills/Outdoor Living, Counselor Training (CIT), Hiking, Leadership Development, Nature/Environment Studies, Sports — Field & Team, Swimming — Instructional
Session lengths & capacity: 1 & 2 week sessions; 290 campers
Clientele & fees: coed 4-15; Fees: B ☀ 🚐
Contact: Richard E Ward, Recreation Director at (203) 458-6612; fax: (203) 453-4994
e-mail: reward.sf@snet.net
Web site: www.shoreline.org
Operated by: Shoreline Foundation Inc, 2415 Boston Post Rd, Guilford, CT 06437 at (203) 458-6612 (#2334)

The Hole In The Wall Gang Camp (est 1987) ▲

Ashford, CT (Windham Co.); (860) 429-3444
Matthew Cook, Director

Camp comments: Providing a normal camp experience for children with life threatening illness's,from June to August with 9-1 week sessions each summer.

Activities: Aquatic Activities, Arts/Crafts, Boating, Camping Skills/Outdoor Living, Challenge/Rope Courses, Horseback — Western, Music, Nature/Environment Studies, Performing Arts, Sports — Field & Team
Session lengths & capacity: June-August; 1 week sessions; 120 campers
Clientele & fees: coed 7-15; Fees: A ▲
Contact: Ingrid Schamko, Director of Camper Admissions at (860) 429-3444 ext. 123; fax: (860) 429-7295
e-mail: ashford@holeinthewallgang.org
Web site: www.holeinthewallgang.org
Operated by: The Hole in the Wall Gang Fund, 565 Ashford Center Rd, Ashford, CT 06278 at (860) 429-3444 (#6582)

Windham Tolland 4H Camp

(est 1954) ☀ ▲ 🏠

Pomfret Center, CT (Pomfret Co.); (860) 974-3379
Amy Bennett, Director

Camp comments: Caring staff; TLC for each child; strong environmental commitment; variety of activities for campers to choose from; great price; wonderful setting.
Activities: Archery, Arts/Crafts, Basketball, Bicycling/Biking, Camping Skills/Outdoor Living, Canoeing, Challenge/Rope Courses, Counselor Training (CIT), Leadership Development, Nature/Environment Studies
Session lengths & capacity: June-August; 1 week sessions; 200 campers
Clientele & fees: coed 7-17; Fees: B ☀ Fees: B ▲
Contact: (860) 974-3379; fax: (860) 974-3327
e-mail: windham4h@yahoo.com
Web site: www.windhamtolland4hcamp.com
Operated by: Windham County 4H Fndtn, Inc, 326 Taft Pond Rd, Pomfret Center, CT 06259 at (860) 974-3379

Group Rental Information

Facilities: Cabins, Hiking Trails, Kitchen Facilities, Lake, Lodges, Meeting Rooms, Playing Fields, River
Programs: Boating, Challenge/Ropes Course, Horseback Riding, Swimming (#8248)

Winding Trails Summer Day Camp (est 1947) ☀ 🚗

Farmington, CT (Hartford Co.); (860) 678-9582
Scott Brown, Director

Camp comments: Camp offers warm supportive atmosphere for children; outstanding staff, located on 350 ac recreation area, 100 ac lake.
Activities: Archery, Basketball, Camping Skills/Outdoor Living, Challenge/Rope Courses, Drama, Hockey, Nature/Environment Studies, Soccer, Sports — Field & Team, Tennis
Session lengths & capacity: June-August; 2 week sessions; 550 campers
Clientele & fees: boys 3-13; girls 3-13; coed 3-13; Fees: B ☀
Contact: Scott Brown, Camp Director at (860) 678-9582; fax: (860) 676-9407
e-mail: camp@windingtrails.com
Operated by: Winding Trails Inc, 50 Winding Trails Drive, Farmington, CT 06032 at (860) 678-9582 (#7443)

YMCA Camp Mohawk Inc

(est 1919) ▲ 🏠

Litchfield, CT; (203) 672-6655
Fran Marchand, Director

Camp comments: Girls camp, emphasis on personal growth, fun, friendship. Beautiful! Located in Foot Hills of Berkshires. 2 hrs to NYC.

Activities: Archery, Arts/Crafts, Camping Skills/Outdoor Living, Ceramics/Pottery, Counselor Training (CIT), Drama, Horseback — English, Nature/Environment Studies, Photography, Tennis
Session lengths & capacity: June-August; 1 & 2 week sessions; 187 campers
Clientele & fees: girls 7-15; Fees: D △
Contact: Fran Marchand, Director at (860) 672-6655; fax: (860) 482-3878
Web site: www.campmohawk.org
Operated by: YMCA Camp Mohawk Inc, PO Box 1209, Litchfield, CT 06759 at (860) 672-6655
Group Rental Information
Seasons & Capacity: Spring 200, Summer 164, Fall 200
Facilities: A/V Equipment, Cabins, Double Occupancy, Food Service, Hiking Trails, Lake, Lodges, Playing Fields
Programs: Boating, Challenge/Ropes Course, Horseback Riding, Swimming (#2734)

YMCA Camp Woodstock
(est 1922)
Woodstock Valley, CT (Windham Co.);
(860) 974-1336
Michael Sherman, Director
Camp comments: The friendship camp, more fun than you can imagine, located in beautiful north eastern CT.
Activities: Archery, Arts/Crafts, Basketball, Bicycling/Biking, Canoeing, Leadership Development, Sailing, Swimming — Recreational, Wilderness Trips, Windsurfing
Session lengths & capacity: June-August; 1, 2 & 4 week sessions; 250 campers
Clientele & fees: coed 7-15; Fees: D △ 🐗
Contact: Steve Heiny, Asst Director at (860) 974-1336; fax: (860) 974-0754
e-mail: camp.woodstockymca@ghymca.org
Operated by: YMCA of Greater Hartford, 160 Jewell St, Hartford, CT 06103 at (860) 522-4183
Group Rental Information
Site comments: One of New England's premier youth retreat centers.
Facilities: A/V Equipment, Cabins, Dorm-Style, Food Service, Hiking Trails, Kitchen Facilities, Lake, Lodges, Meeting Rooms, Playing Fields
Programs: Boating, Challenge/Ropes Course, Swimming, Winter Sports (#2610)

YWCA Camp Aya PO
(est 1923)
Somers, CT (Hartford Co.); (860) 763-6444
Camp comments: Traditional day camp with Native American roots on 193 wooded acres with lake. Specialty overnight & field trip programs. Known for diversity of staff & campers
Activities: Aquatic Activities, Archery, Arts/Crafts, Boating, Canoeing, Drama, Music, Nature/Environment Studies, Sports — Field & Team, Swimming — Instructional
Session lengths & capacity: May-October; 2 week sessions; 260 campers
Clientele & fees: coed 5-14; Fees: B, D 🔆 🐗
Contact: (860) 525-1163 ext. 293;
fax: (860) 543-8919
Web site: www.ywcahartford.org
Operated by: YWCA of the Hartford Region In, 135 Broad St, Hartford, CT 06105 at (860) 525-1163
Group Rental Information
Facilities: Cabins, Dorm-Style, Kitchen Facilities, Lake
Programs: Boating, Swimming (#27658)

Delaware

Bear Glasgow YMCA Camp Cassey (est 1995)
Newark, DE
Camp comments: A values-based camp focusing on the development of character in a safe, fun, enriching, outdoor environment.
Activities: Arts/Crafts, Baseball/Softball, Basketball, Boating, Canoeing, Counselor Training (CIT), Leadership Development, Sports — Field & Team, Swimming — Recreational, Team Building
Session lengths & capacity: June-August; 1 & 2 week sessions; 300 campers
Clientele & fees: coed 5-13; Fees: B 🔆 🐗
Contact: (302) 832-8464;
Web site: www.ymcade.org
Operated by: YMCA Camp Quoowant, 3 Mt Lebanon Rd, Wilmington, DE 19810 at (302) 478-8303 (#27839)

Central Delaware Branch YMCA (est 1980)
Wyoming, DE (Kent Co.); (302) 674-3000
Mary Servon, Director
Activities: Arts/Crafts, Basketball, Computer, Counselor Training (CIT), Field Trips, Football, Performing Arts, Soccer, Sports — Field & Team, Swimming — Recreational
Contact: Max Drzymalski, Family & Youth Director at (302) 674-3000; fax: (302) 674-2906
e-mail: mdrzymalski@ymcade.org
Web site: www.ymcade.org
Operated by: YMCA Camp Quoowant, 3 Mt Lebanon Rd, Wilmington, DE 19810 at (302) 478-8303 (#2694)

Childrens Beach House
(est 1936)
Lewes, DE (Sussex Co.); (302) 645-9184
Diane O'Hara, Director
Camp comments: Beach-side facility serves Delaware residents only. Normal potential with communication disorders.
Activities: Arts/Crafts, Field Trips, Nature/Environment Studies, Swimming — Instructional, Swimming — Recreational
Session lengths & capacity: June-August; 4 week sessions; 30 campers
Clientele & fees: coed 6-12; Fees: F △ 🐗
Contact: Diane B O'Hara, Program Director/Family Coor at (302) 645-9184; fax: (302) 645-9467
e-mail: childrens.beach.house@dol.net
Web site: www.cbhinc.org
Operated by: Childrens Beach House Inc, 100 W 10th Street Ste 411, Willmington, DE 19801-1674 at (302) 655-4288 (#2566)

Western Family YMCA (est 1955)
Newark, DE (New Castle Co.); (302) 453-1482
Mary Servon, Director
Camp comments: A diverse atmosphere where campers have fun, make friends & are challenged by exciting activities.
Activities: Arts/Crafts, Baseball/Softball, Basketball, Counselor Training (CIT), Field Trips, Hockey, Leadership Development, Nature/Environment Studies, Soccer, Swimming — Recreational
Session lengths & capacity: June-August; 1 week sessions
Clientele & fees: boys 5-13; girls 5-13; Fees: B 🔆
Contact: Crystal Himes, Senior Program Director at (302) 453-1482; fax: (302) 453-1610
e-mail: chimes@ymcade.org
Web site: www.ymcade.org

Operated by: YMCA Camp Quoowant, 3 Mt Lebanon Rd, Wilmington, DE 19810 at (302) 478-8303 (#2568)

YMCA Camp Quoowant
(est 1958)
Wilmington, DE (New Castle Co.); (302) 475-0700
Bridget O'Connor, Director
Camp comments: Traditional outdoor day camp on 96 acre facility. Large teaching pool. Teen trip program. Transportation available. Contact on-site director with questions.
Activities: Arts/Crafts, Counselor Training (CIT), Drama, Field Trips, Nature/Environment Studies, Swimming — Instructional, Swimming — Recreational, Travel/Tour
Session lengths & capacity: June-August; 1 & 2 week sessions; 420 campers
Clientele & fees: boys 5-15; girls 5-15; Fees: B 🔆 🐗
Contact: Tina Rydgren, Associate Executive Director at (302) 478-8303; fax: (302) 478-2260
Web site: www.ymcade.org
Operated by: YMCA Camp Quoowant, 3 Mt Lebanon Rd, Wilmington, DE 19810 at (302) 478-8303
Group Rental Information
Seasons & Capacity: Spring 200, Summer 50, Fall 200
Facilities: Hiking Trails, Playing Fields, Pool, Tents
Programs: Swimming (#2563)

District of Columbia

G W Summer Tour (est 1993)
Washington, DC (DC Co.); (202) 994-6251
Bridget Cooper, Director
Camp comments: Campers customize their summer experience by selecting from over 70 enrichment activities & recreational athletics utilizing the unique facilites & instructors.
Activities: Aerobics/Exercise, Aquatic Activities, Arts/Crafts, Basketball, Computer, Performing Arts, Photography, Radio/TV/Video
Session lengths & capacity: July-August; 2 week sessions; 200 campers
Clientele & fees: coed 7-12; Fees: C 🔆
Contact: Bridget Cooper, Director at (202) 994-2267; fax: (202) 994-0475
e-mail: bcurious@gwu.edu
Web site: www.gwired.gwu.edu/curiousmindsrock
Operated by: George Washington University, 2121 Eye St NW 403, Washington, DC 20052 at (202) 994-2267 (#2545)

Moss Hollow (est 1966)
Washington, DC; (202) 289-1510
Activities: Aquatic Activities, Arts/Crafts, Camping Skills/Outdoor Living, Computer, Dance, Hiking, Nature/Environment Studies
Session lengths & capacity: 7 week sessions; 120 campers
Clientele & fees: coed 7-14; Fees: A △
Contact: Randolph Dorsey, Program Director at (202) 289-1510 ext. 131; fax: (202) 371-0863
Operated by: Family And Child Services, 929 L St NW, Washington, DC 20001 at (202) 289-1510 (#2491)

TIC Computer Camp
(est 1983)
Washington, DC (Washington DC Co.); (202) 333-3041
Dr Karen J Rosenbaum, Director
Camp comments: The Washington area's premiere technology/sports day camp. Staff ratio 4:1. The

excitement of learning and the fun of sports for kids 7-16.
Activities: Baseball/Softball, Basketball, Computer, Drama, Football, Hockey, Soccer, Sports — Field & Team, Swimming — Instructional, Tennis
Session lengths & capacity: June-August; 2 week sessions; 200 campers
Clientele & fees: coed 7-16; Fees: **C** ☀
Contact: Dr Karen J Rosenbaum, Director at (703) 241-5542; fax: (703) 534-0616
e-mail: kjrtic@radix.net
Operated by: TIC Computer Camp, 4620 Dittmar Road, Arlington, VA 22207 at (703) 241-5542 (#4243)

Florida

Busch Gardens Adventure Camps (est 1997) ☀ ▲ 🚐

Tampa, FL (Hillsborough Co.); (813) 987-5252
Linda Burdick, Director

Camp comments: Busch Gardens Adventure Camps offer unique zoo experiences from face-to-face animal encounters to hands on zoo husbandry
Activities: Academics, Aquatic Activities, Field Trips, Nature/Environment Studies, Swimming — Recreational, Team Building
Session lengths & capacity: May-September; 1/2, 1, 2 & 3 week sessions; 30 campers
Clientele & fees: coed 4-22; families; single adults; Fees: **B, C** ☀ Fees: **E, F** ▲
Contact: e-mail: buschgardens.zoocamps@buschgardens.com
Web site: www.buschgardens.org
Operated by: Busch Gardens Tampa Bay, Anheuser Busch Theme Park, PO Box 9158, Tampa, FL 33674 at (800) 372-1797 (#26211)

Camp Crystal Lake (est 1948) ▲ 🏠

Starke, FL (Clay Co.); (352) 475-1414
Michael A Oyenarte (Tony), Director

Camp comments: Beautiful camp. 144 acres on 2 sand bottom lakes. Year-round environmental ed program. Weekend leadership & ropes program. 'A classroom without walls.'
Activities: Aquatic Activities, Boating, Camping Skills/Outdoor Living, Canoeing, Challenge/Rope Courses, Counselor Training (CIT), Kayaking, Sailing, Waterskiing, Wilderness Trips
Session lengths & capacity: June-August; 1 & 2 week sessions; 160 campers
Clientele & fees: coed 7-14; Fees: **B** ▲

ICON LEGEND

☀ Day Camp
▲ Resident Camp
🏠 Facilities Available To Rent
🚐 Transportation Available
🐷 Financial Aid Available

FEE RANGES PER WEEK

A	$0-75
B	$75-200
C	$201-350
D	$351-500
E	$501-650
F	over $650

Contact: Tony Oyenarte, Camp Director at (352) 475-1414; fax: (352) 473-2402
e-mail: oyenart@sbac.edu
Web site: www.campcrystal.sbac.edu
Operated by: Alachua County School Board, Camp Crystal Lake, 6724 Camp Crystal Road, Starke, FL 32091 at (352) 475-1414
Group Rental Information
Facilities: Cabins, Double Occupancy, Hiking Trails, Kitchen Facilities, Lodges, Meeting Rooms
Programs: Boating, Challenge/Ropes Course (#820)

Camp Gan Israel (est 1999) ☀

Palm City, FL; (561) 288-0606
Rabbi Shlomo Uminer, Director

Camp comments: Provide Jewish children ages 3-12 with a comprehensive and meaningful summer program, fostering their growth individually, socially and Jewishly.
Activities: Aquatic Activities, Arts/Crafts, Drawing/Painting, Field Trips, Gymnastics, Martial Arts, Religious Study, Sports — Field & Team, Swimming — Recreational, Team Building
Session lengths & capacity: June-July; 1, 2, 3 & 4 week sessions
Clientele & fees: Fees: **B** ☀
Contact: Rabbi Shlomo Uminer & Daniella, Directors at (561) 288-0606; fax: (561) 219-0111
e-mail: chabadm@aol.com
Operated by: Chabad Jewish Center, 3571 SW Thistlewood Ln, Palm City, FL 34990 at (561) 288-0606 (#39937)

Camp JCC ☀

Sarasota, FL (Sarasota Co.); (941) 378-5568
Wendy Fogel, Director
Activities: Arts/Crafts, Counselor Training (CIT), Drama, Field Trips, Gymnastics, Nature/Environment Studies, Performing Arts, Sports — Field & Team, Swimming — Instructional, Swimming — Recreational
Session lengths & capacity: June-August; 2 & 3 week sessions; 300 campers
Clientele & fees: coed 3-14; Fees: **B, C** ☀ 🐷
Contact: Web site: www.flanzerjcc.org
Operated by: Flanzer Jewish Community Ctr, 582 S Macintosh Rd, Sarasota, FL 34232 at (941) 378-5568 (#44434)

Camp Kulaqua (est 1953) ▲ 🏠

High Springs, FL (Alachua Co.); (386) 454-1351
Rick Faber, Director

Camp comments: Modeling a joyous christian lifestyle by providing campers w/exciting activities, programs, classes & special features.
Activities: Archery, Arts/Crafts, Basketball, Canoeing, Golf, Gymnastics, Horseback — Western, Model Rocketry, Nature/Environment Studies, Swimming — Recreational
Session lengths & capacity: 1 week sessions; 250 campers
Clientele & fees: coed 8-17; families; seniors; single adults; Fees: **C, D** ▲
Contact: Joyce Davis, Marketing Director at (386) 454-1351; fax: (386) 454-4748
e-mail: groups@campkulaqua.com
Web site: www.campkulaqua.com
Operated by: FL Conf Seventh Day Adventist, 700 NW Cheeota Ave, High Springs, FL 32643 at (904) 454-1351
Group Rental Information
Facilities: Cabins, Food Service, Hiking Trails, Lodges, Meeting Rooms, River
Programs: Horseback Riding (#32534)

Camp La-no-che ▲ 🏠

Paisley, FL (Lake Co.); (352) 669-8558
Matthew Ragan, Director
Activities: Aquatic Activities, Boating, Camping Skills/Outdoor Living, Canoeing, Challenge/Rope Courses, Counselor Training (CIT), Leadership Development, Nature/Environment Studies, Riflery, Sailing
Session lengths & capacity: June-August; 1 week sessions; 450 campers
Clientele & fees: boys 6-17; coed 14-20; families
Contact: Matthew Ragan, Director of Camps & Properties at (352) 669-8558; fax: (352) 669-7636
e-mail: adventure@camplanoche.com
Operated by: Central Florida Cncl Boy Scout, PO Box 323, Paisley, FL 32767 at (332) 669-8558
Group Rental Information
Seasons & Capacity: Spring 1000, Summer 600, Fall 1000, Winter 1000
Facilities: A/V Equipment, Cabins, Double Occupancy, Food Service, Hiking Trails, Kitchen Facilities, Lake, Lodges, Meeting Rooms, Playing Fields, Pool, River, Tents
Programs: Boating, Challenge/Ropes Course, Environmental Education, Swimming (#43894)

Camp Live Oak (est 1989) ☀

Fort Lauderdale, FL (Broward Co.); (954) 491-2917
Ken Evans, Director

Camp comments: 180 acres on Ft Lauderdale Beach. Environmental hands on science program and noncompetitive sports. Certified teachers as counselors. Exciting canoe trips.
Activities: Archery, Arts/Crafts, Camping Skills/Outdoor Living, Canoeing, Field Trips, Hiking, Nature/Environment Studies, Photography, Sports — Field & Team, Swimming — Recreational
Session lengths & capacity: 3 week sessions; 151 campers
Clientele & fees: coed 5-13; Fees: **B** ☀
Contact: Ken Evans, Camp Director at (954) 491-2917; fax: (954) 491-2297
e-mail: kevans922@aol.com
Web site: www.kidscamp.com/daycamps/live-oak
Operated by: Camp Live Oak Inc, 1915 NE 45th St Suite 202, Fort Lauderdale, FL 33308 at (954) 491-2917 (#6566)

Camp Live Oak South (est 2000) ☀

North Miami Beach, FL

Camp comments: 1,043 acres in N Miami Beach. Environmental hands on science program and noncompetitive sports. Certified teachers as counselors. Swim in our blue lagoon.
Activities: Arts/Crafts, Camping Skills/Outdoor Living, Hiking, Nature/Environment Studies, Photography, Sports — Field & Team
Session lengths & capacity: 3 week sessions; 150 campers
Clientele & fees: coed 5-13; Fees: **B** ☀
Contact: Web site: www.kidscamp.com/daycamps/live-oak
Operated by: Camp Live Oak Inc, 1915 NE 45th St Suite 202, Fort Lauderdale, FL 33308 at (954) 491-2917 (#43181)

Camp Neshama-Jacksonville Jewi ☀

Jacksonville, FL (Duval Co.); (904) 292-1000
Kelly M. Waeltz, Director
Activities: Aquatic Activities, Camping Skills/Outdoor Living, Community Service, Computer, Counselor Training (CIT), Field Trips, Religious Study, Swimming — Instructional, Swimming — Recreational, Team Building
Contact: Web site: www.jaxjewishcenter.com
Operated by: Jacksonville Jewish Center, 3662 Crown Point Rd, Jacksonville, FL 32257-5955 at (904) 292-1000 (#45622)

Camp Nova (est 1978) ☀

Fort Lauderdale, FL (Broward Co.); (954) 262-4517
Lynn Stern, Director

Camp comments: Professional adult staff
provide campers with distinctive format designed to
challenge, motivate & promote creativity.
Activities: Arts/Crafts, Dance, Drama, Field Trips,
Golf, Performing Arts, Sports — Field & Team,
Swimming — Instructional, Tennis
Session lengths & capacity: June-August; 1 &
3 week sessions; 500 campers
Clientele & fees: coed 3-13; Fees: B ☀
Contact: Shirley Thebaud, Administrative Assistant
at (954) 262-4517; fax: (954) 262-3974
e-mail: sthebaud@nsu.nova.edu
Operated by: Univ School Nova SE University,
7500 SW 36th St, Fort Lauderdale, FL 33314 at
(954) 262-4500 (#5250)

Camp Thunderbird (est 1968) ▲ ⌂

Apopka, FL (Orange Co.); (407) 889-8088
Dr. Shirley O'Brien, Director

Camp comments: Serve developmentally disabled,
all ages. Orlando area, lakefront forest preserve.
Focus on self-esteem & socialization.
Activities: Hiking, Nature/Environment Studies
Session lengths & capacity: June-August; 1 &
2 week sessions; 100 campers
Clientele & fees: coed 8-80; Fees: D ▲ 🚌
Contact: Ann Anderson, Director at
(407) 889-8088; fax: (407) 889-8072
e-mail: campthunder@questinc.org
Operated by: FL Fnd for Special Children, Camp
Thunderbird, PO Box 1300, Apopka, FL 32704 at
(407) 889-8088 (#5447)

Cedarkirk (est 1970) ▲ ⌂ 🚌

Lithia, FL (Hillsborough Co.); (813) 685-4224
John Bronkema, Director

Camp comments: Christian camp nestled in trees
with the Alafia River running through it. Counselor
based program serving South Florida.
Activities: Aquatic Activities, Archery, Arts/Crafts,
Camping Skills/Outdoor Living, Canoeing,
Challenge/Rope Courses, Kayaking, Music,
Religious Study, Swimming — Recreational
Session lengths & capacity: June-August; 1 &
2 week sessions; 140 campers
Clientele & fees: coed 7-18; families; seniors;
single adults; Fees: B ▲
Contact: Helen Harrell Howard, Office Manager at
(813) 685-4224; fax: (813) 689-9170
e-mail: cedarkirk@juno.com
Web site: www.cedarkirk.com
Operated by: Presbyterian Camp/Conf Ministr,
1920 Streetman Drive, Lithia, FL 33547 at
(813) 685-4224
Group Rental Information
Seasons & Capacity: Spring 190, Fall 190, Winter
190
Facilities: A/V Equipment, Cabins, Dorm-Style,
Double Occupancy, Food Service, Hiking Trails,
Linens, Lodges, Meeting Rooms, Playing Fields,
Pool, River
Programs: Challenge/Ropes Course, Swimming
(#14242)

Dorothy Thomas (est 1954) ☀ ▲ ⌂

Riverview, FL (Hillsborough Co.); (813) 689-8061
Laura Foster, Director

Camp comments: Beautiful Florida back-country
trails, wildlife. Platform tents. CIT program.
Progressive riding program.
Activities: Archery, Arts/Crafts, Ceramics/Pottery,
Challenge/Rope Courses, Hiking, Horseback —
English, Horseback — Western, Sports — Field &
Team, Tennis
Session lengths & capacity: June-July; 1/2, 1 &
2 week sessions; 125 campers
Clientele & fees: girls 6-17; Fees: B ▲

Contact: Gloria Hartness, Outdoor Education
Director at (813) 281-4475 ext. 203;
fax: (813) 282-8285
e-mail: ghartnes@sgsc.org
Web site: www.suncoastgirlscouts.org
Operated by: Suncoast GSC Inc, PO Drawer
18066, Tampa, FL 33679-8066 at (800) 881-4475
Group Rental Information
Facilities: A/V Equipment, Cabins, Dorm-Style,
Double Occupancy, Food Service, Hiking Trails,
Kitchen Facilities, Lodges, Pool, Tents
Programs: Challenge/Ropes Course,
Environmental Education, Horseback Riding,
Swimming (#830)

Dovewood (est 1977) ▲ 🚌

OBrien, FL (Suwannee Co.); (904) 935-0863
Roberta Richmond, Director

Camp comments: Camp Dovewood is a dynamic
Christian camp for girls 7-14. Fabulous equestrian
program, Christian leadership, cheerleading, Bible,
water ballet.
Activities: Arts/Crafts, Dance, Drama, Gymnastics,
Horseback — English, Horseback — Western,
Leadership Development, Religious Study,
Swimming — Instructional, Tennis
Session lengths & capacity: 1, 2 & 3 week
sessions; 56 campers
Clientele & fees: girls 7-17; Fees: C ▲
Contact: Roberta Richmond, Director at
(904) 935-0863;
e-mail: campdovewood@alltel.net
Web site: www.campdovewood.org
Operated by: Dovewood, 23221 101st Road,
O'Brien, FL 32071 at (904) 935-0863 (#2036)

Easter Seals Camp Challenge

(est 1960) ☀ ▲ ⌂ 🚌

Sorrento, FL (Lake Co.); (352) 383-4711
Michael Currence, Director

Camp comments: Self-esteem specialty. Campers
thrive in noncompetitive, caring atmosphere,
opportunities to belong, learn, contribute.
Activities: Arts/Crafts, Camping Skills/Outdoor
Living, Computer, Farming/Ranching/Gardening,
Leadership Development, Nature/Environment
Studies, Sports — Field & Team, Swimming —
Recreational
Session lengths & capacity: 1 & 2 week sessions;
90 campers
Clientele & fees: boys 6-99; girls 6-99; families;
Fees: A ☀ Fees: E ▲
Contact: Michael Currence, Director, Camping &
Recreation at (352) 383-4711; fax: (352) 383-0744
e-mail: mikec@esfl.org
Web site: www.fl.easter-seals.org
Operated by: Easter Seals Camp Challenge, 31600
Camp Challenge Road, Sorrento, FL 32776 at
(352) 383-4711 (#828)

Everglades Youth Conservation

(est 1965) ▲ ⌂

West Palm Beach, FL; (561) 624-6929
Janice Kerber, Director

Camp comments: Summer programs focus on
wildlife & habatat issues unique to south Fla.
Activities inc swimming, fishing, archery, nature
hikes, wildlife presentation & more.
Activities: Aquatic Activities, Camping
Skills/Outdoor Living, Canoeing, Fishing, Hiking,
Nature/Environment Studies, Swimming —
Recreational
Session lengths & capacity: June-August; 1 week
sessions; 124 campers
Clientele & fees: coed 8-14; Fees: C ▲
Contact: Janice Kerber, Camp Director at
(561) 624-6929; fax: (561) 624-6928
e-mail: jtkerber@aol.com
Web site:
www.floridaconservation.org/join-us/eyc.htm

Operated by: FL Fish & Wildlife Conservatio, 12100
Seminole Pratt Whitney R, West Palm Beach, FL
33412 at (561) 624-6929
Group Rental Information
Site comments: Weekend gropu rental facility from
September to April. Environmental education must
be component of group's program.
Seasons & Capacity: Fall 160, Winter 160
Facilities: Cabins, Dorm-Style, Food Service,
Hiking Trails, Lake
Programs: Environmental Education, Swimming
(#11065)

Florida Diabetes Camp (est 1970) ▲

De Leon Springs, FL (Volusia Co.); (386) 985-4544
Rosalie Bandyopadhyay, Director

Camp comments: Youngsters with insulin
dependent diabetes enjoy camping activities while
learning diabetes management. Camp Motto is 'I
can handle it.'
Activities: Archery, Arts/Crafts, Bicycling/Biking,
Camping Skills/Outdoor Living, Challenge/Rope
Courses, Nature/Environment Studies, Sailing,
Soccer, Swimming — Recreational
Session lengths & capacity: June-August; 1 &
2 week sessions; 140 campers
Clientele & fees: coed 6-18; families;
Fees: D ▲ 🚌
Contact: Rosalie Bandyopadhyay, Executive
Director at (352) 334-1323; fax: (352) 334-1326
e-mail: fccyd@hotmail.com
Web site: www.floridadiabetescamp.org
Operated by: Florida Diabetes Camp, University
Station, PO Box 14136, Gainesville, FL 32604 at
(352) 334-1323 (#1230)

Florida Elks Youth Camp

(est 1995) ▲ ⌂

Umatilla, FL (Marion Co.); (352) 669-9443
Lynn Warburton, Director

Camp comments: Pristine setting. Non-threatening
environment with superior staff plus exciting trips in
the Ocala National Forest. Florida residents only.
Activities: Archery, Baseball/Softball, Basketball,
Canoeing, Challenge/Rope Courses, Leadership
Development, Nature/Environment Studies, Sports
— Field & Team, Tennis
Session lengths & capacity: June-August; 1, 2 & 4
week sessions; 168 campers
Clientele & fees: boys 9-13; girls 9-13;
Fees: B ▲ 🚌
Contact: Elaine, Reservations Rep at
(352) 669-9443; fax: (352) 669-0135
e-mail: feyc2@aol.com
Operated by: Florida Elks Youth Camp, PO Box 49,
Umatilla, FL 32784 at (352) 669-9443 (#3626)

Florida Lions Camp (est 1974) ▲

Lake Wales, FL (Polk Co.); (863) 696-1948
Barbara Cage, Director

Camp comments: FLC serves campers who are
challenged by a variety of special
needs-(developmental, physical, visual) and their
siblings. Ages 5-adult.
Activities: Arts/Crafts, Baseball/Softball, Camping
Skills/Outdoor Living, Canoeing, Music,
Nature/Environment Studies, Performing Arts,
Swimming — Recreational, Team Building
Session lengths & capacity: June-August; 1 week
sessions; 60 campers
Clientele & fees: coed 5-21; Fees: B ▲
Contact: Barb Cage, Administrator at
(941) 696-1948; fax: (941) 692-2398
e-mail: flc@gtc.net
Web site: www.lionscampfl.org
Operated by: Lions of Multiple District 35, 2819
Tiger Lake Rd, Lake Wales, FL 33853 at
(941) 696-1948 (#23146)

Florida Sheriffs Caruth Camp

(est 1998) ▲ 🏠

Inglis, FL; (352) 447-2259
Jodi Saks, Director

Camp comments: Camp's purpose is to provide a wholesome & positive camping opportunity for troubled & underprivileged youth.
Activities: Archery, Bicycling/Biking, Canoeing, Challenge/Rope Courses, Hiking, Leadership Development, Swimming — Recreational, Team Building
Session lengths & capacity: 1 week sessions; 50 campers
Clientele & fees: coed 10-15; Fees: B ▲ 🐷
Contact: Jodi Saks, Camp Director at (352) 447-2259; fax: (352) 447-0400
e-mail: meneli@xtalwind.net
Operated by: Florida Sheriffs Youth Ranches, 1170 Youth Camp Rd, Barberville, FL 32105 at (386) 749-9999

Group Rental Information

Facilities: Cabins, Food Service, Hiking Trails, Meeting Rooms, Playing Fields, Pool
Programs: Challenge/Ropes Course, Swimming (#28894)

Florida Sheriffs Youth Camp

(est 1982) ☀ ▲ 🏠

Barberville, FL (Volusia Co.); (386) 749-9999
Greg Dodd, Director

Camp comments: Camps purpose is to provide a wholesome atmosphere & positive camping opportunity for troubled & underprivileged youth.
Activities: Archery, Arts/Crafts, Basketball, Canoeing, Challenge/Rope Courses, Horseback — Western, Leadership Development, Nature/Environment Studies, Team Building
Session lengths & capacity: January-December; 1 week sessions; 50 campers
Clientele & fees: coed 6-15; Fees: A ▲
Contact: Greg Dodd, Camp Director at (386) 749-9999; fax: (386) 749-9020
e-mail: gdodd@youthranches.org
Operated by: Florida Sheriffs Youth Ranches, 1170 Youth Camp Rd, Barberville, FL 32105 at (386) 749-9999 (#4602)

Florida WMU Camps (est 1946) ▲

Marianna, FL; (904) 526-3676
Dr Sharon Thompson, Director

Camp comments: Sunny Florida! Christian girls camp offers self-esteem building, multicultural simulations, fun, We love children!!

ICON LEGEND

☀	Day Camp
▲	Resident Camp
🏠	Facilities Available To Rent
🚐	Transportation Available
🐷	Financial Aid Available

FEE RANGES PER WEEK

A	$0-75
B	$75-200
C	$201-350
D	$351-500
E	$501-650
F	over $650

Activities: Arts/Crafts, Canoeing, Challenge/Rope Courses, Clowning, Community Service, Dance, Drama, Leadership Development, Performing Arts, Sailing
Session lengths & capacity: June-July; 1 week sessions; 250 campers
Clientele & fees: girls 8-18; Fees: B ▲
Contact: Dr Sharon Thompson, Camp Director at (904) 396-2351 ext. 8282; fax: (904) 396-6470
e-mail: vcornaire@flbaptist.org
Operated by: Florida Baptist Convention, 1230 Hendricks Avenue, Jacksonville, FL 32207 at (800) 226-8584 (#2749)

GS of Gateway Cncl Camp Kateri

▲ 🏠

Orange Springs, FL (Putnam Co.); (352) 546-2253
Ginny Miller, Director

Activities: Aquatic Activities, Arts/Crafts, Canoeing, Drama, Field Trips, Horseback — English, Nature/Environment Studies, Sailing, Swimming — Instructional, Swimming — Recreational
Session lengths & capacity: June-July; 1/2, 1 & 2 week sessions; 160 campers
Clientele & fees: girls 6-17; Fees: B ▲ 🐷
Contact: Betsy Paulson at (904) 388-4653; fax: (904) 384-1542
e-mail: bpaulson@girlscouts-gateway.org
Operated by: GS of Gateway Council Inc, 1000 Shearer Street, Jacksonville, FL 32205 at (904) 388-4653

Group Rental Information

Facilities: Cabins, Double Occupancy, Food Service, Hiking Trails, Lodges, Meeting Rooms
Programs: Boating, Environmental Education, Swimming (#1299)

Happy Acres Ranch Inc (est 1953) ☀

Jacksonville, FL (Duval Co.); (904) 725-1410
Mary Anne Adams, Director

Camp comments: Located in city limits, 10 acres with woodlands, small lake and a pool. A place to play, to learn, to discover, to grow.
Activities: Archery, Arts/Crafts, Canoeing, Fishing, Horseback — English, Horseback — Western, Kayaking, Soccer, Swimming — Instructional
Session lengths & capacity: 2 week sessions; 170 campers
Clientele & fees: coed 3-13; Fees: B ☀
Contact: Brenda Harris, Receptionist at (904) 725-1410;
e-mail: HAR@happyacresranch.com
Web site: www.happyacresranch.com
Operated by: Happy Acres Ranch Inc, 7117 Crane Ave, Jacksonville, FL 32216 at (904) 725-1410 (#837)

JCC of Greater Orlando

☀

(est 1973)

Maitland, FL (Orange Co.); (407) 645-5933
Sylvia Pasnak, Director

Camp comments: Caring, nurturing and safe environment. Opportunities to explore new interest. Age appropriate programs, fun and games.
Activities: Arts/Crafts, Basketball, Computer, Drama, Field Trips, Gymnastics, Performing Arts, Swimming — Instructional, Swimming — Recreational, Travel/Tour
Session lengths & capacity: June-August; 1, 2, 3, 4, 5, 6, 7 & 8 week sessions; 400 campers
Clientele & fees: coed 5-14; Fees: B ☀ 🚐
Contact: Sylvia Pasnak, Camp Director at (407) 645-5933; fax: (407) 645-1172
Web site: www.orlandojcc.org
Operated by: JCC of Greater Orlando Inc, 851 N Maitland Avenue, Maitland, FL 32751 at (407) 645-5933 (#6034)

Jewish Community Alliance ☀

Jacksonville, FL; (904) 730-2100
Activities: Aquatic Activities, Arts/Crafts, Basketball, Boating, Ceramics/Pottery, Climbing/Rappelling, Dance, Drama, Field Trips, Football
Operated by: Jewish Community Alliance, 8505 San Jose Blvd, Jacksonville, FL 32217 at (904) 730-2100 (#47870)

Land O'Sunshine Camp Cherith

(est 1983) ▲

Lutz, FL; (904) 658-5100
Jane Fenby, Director

Camp comments: Nondenominational Christ-centered outdoor program that focuses on relationships and develops skills.
Activities: Archery, Arts/Crafts, Basketball, Bicycling/Biking, Camping Skills/Outdoor Living, Canoeing, Challenge/Rope Courses, Counselor Training (CIT), Riflery, Swimming — Instructional
Session lengths & capacity: February-November; 1 & 2 week sessions; 100 campers
Clientele & fees: boys 8-18; girls 8-18; Fees: B ▲ 🐷
Contact: Jane Fenby, Executive Director at (813) 949-8241; fax: (813) 949-7942
e-mail: jfenby@edifymin.org
Operated by: Land o'Sunshine Camp Cherith, 7312 Summerbridge Drive, Tampa, FL 33634 at (813) 882-8636 (#5799)

Magicamp Inc (est 1989) ☀

Miami, FL (Dade Co.); (800) 570-7273
David Gindy, Director

Camp comments: Since 1989 MagiCamp has brought over 5000 children into the exciting worlds of Magic, Dinosaurs and Space & Rockets.
Activities: Arts/Crafts, Clowning, Drama, Field Trips, Model Rocketry, Performing Arts, Sports — Field & Team, Swimming — Recreational
Session lengths & capacity: June-August; 2, 3 & 4 week sessions; 200 campers
Clientele & fees: coed 5-12; Fees: B ☀
Contact: David Gindy, Owner at (800) 570-7273; fax: (305) 665-4212
Web site: www.funcamps.com
Operated by: Magicamp Inc, 7615 SW 62nd Ave, Miami, FL 33143 at (800) 570-7273 (#24475)

Montgomery Presbyterian Center (est 1955) ☀ ▲ 🏠

Starke, FL; (352) 473-4516
Activities: Aquatic Activities, Arts/Crafts, Challenge/Rope Courses, Climbing/Rappelling, Kayaking, Leadership Development, Religious Study, Sailing, Swimming — Recreational, Waterskiing
Session lengths & capacity: June-August; 1 & 2 week sessions; 135 campers
Clientele & fees: coed 16-18; Fees: C, D ▲
Contact: Philip & Helen Saltzgiver, Directors at (352) 473-4516; fax: (352) 473-4723
e-mail: mpc@campmontgomery.org
Operated by: Presbytery Of St Augustine, 1937 University Blvd West, Jacksonville, FL 32217 at (904) 733-8277

Group Rental Information

Seasons & Capacity: Spring 175, Summer 140, Fall 175, Winter 175
Facilities: Cabins, Dorm-Style, Double Occupancy, Food Service, Hiking Trails, Kitchen Facilities, Lake, Linens, Lodges, Meeting Rooms, Playing Fields, Tents
Programs: Boating, Challenge/Ropes Course, Environmental Education, Swimming (#3843)

New Image Camp at Vanguard

(est 1996)

Lake Wales, FL (Polk Co.); (800) 365-0556
Tony Sparber, Director

Camp comments: A camp that features weight loss, self-esteem and fun in a stress-free environment. Campers ages 8-18.
Activities: Aerobics/Exercise, Arts/Crafts, Baseball/Softball, Basketball, Drama, Field Trips, Soccer, Sports — Field & Team, Swimming — Recreational, Tennis
Session lengths & capacity: June-August; 2, 4 & 8 week sessions; 150 campers
Clientele & fees: coed 8-18; Fees: F ▲
Contact: Tony Sparber, Owner/Director at (800) 365-0556; fax: (201) 750-1558
e-mail: sparber@newimagecamp.com
Operated by: Tony Sparbers New Image Camps, PO Box 417, Norwood, NJ 07648 at (800) 365-0556 (#11284)

Pine Tree Camps (est 1978)

Boca Raton, FL (Palm Beach Co.); (561) 237-7310
Diane Dicerbo, Director

Camp comments: Coed day camp, ages 3-14. Beautiful facility in Boca Raton. Friendly, warm, caring counselors. Exciting programs. Day and resident programs available.
Activities: Arts/Crafts, Clowning, Computer, Dance, Drama, Music, Soccer, Swimming — Instructional, Tennis
Session lengths & capacity: June-August; 3, 6 & 9 week sessions; 950 campers
Clientele & fees: coed 3-14; Fees: C ☀ Fees: E ▲
Contact: Diane Di Cerbo, Director at (561) 237-7310; fax: (561) 237-7962
e-mail: ddicerbo@lynn.edu
Web site: www.pinetreecamp.com
Operated by: Pine Tree Camps at Lynn Univ, 3601 North Military Trail, Boca Raton, FL 33431 at (561) 237-7310 (#3902)

Scoutcrest Camp (est 1940)

Odessa, FL (Hillsborough Co.); (813) 920-2873
Joyce Barnett, Director

Camp comments: Rustic camp on lake near Tampa. Older girl programs in sailing, windsurfing, canoeing. Special trips.
Activities: Aquatic Activities, Arts/Crafts, Boating, Camping Skills/Outdoor Living, Canoeing, Drama, Kayaking, Nature/Environment Studies, Sailing, Windsurfing
Session lengths & capacity: June-July; 1 & 2 week sessions; 76 campers
Clientele & fees: girls 10-17; Fees: B ▲
Contact: Gloria Hartness, Outdoor Education Director at (813) 281-4475 ext. 203; fax: (813) 282-8285
e-mail: ghartnes@sgsc.org
Web site: www.suncoastgirlscouts.org
Operated by: Suncoast GSC Inc, PO Drawer 18066, Tampa, FL 33679-8066 at (800) 881-4475

Group Rental Information
Seasons & Capacity: Spring 124, Summer 124, Fall 124, Winter 124
Facilities: Cabins, Double Occupancy, Hiking Trails, Lake, Lodges, Tents
Programs: Boating, Environmental Education, Swimming (#284)

Seacamp (est 1966)

Big Pine Key, FL (Monroe Co.); (305) 872-2331
Chuck Brand, Director

Camp comments: Marine science/SCUBA camp in FL Keys for teens. Gain knowledge & respect for the fragile marine environment.
Activities: Arts/Crafts, Drawing/Painting, Kayaking, Nature/Environment Studies, Photography, Sailing, SCUBA, Windsurfing

Session lengths & capacity: June-August; 3 week sessions; 160 campers
Clientele & fees: coed 12-17; Fees: B ☀ Fees: F ▲
Contact: Chuck Brand, Camp Director at (305) 872-2331; fax: (305) 872-2555
e-mail: info@seacamp.org
Web site: seacamp.org
Operated by: Seacamp Association Inc, 1300 Big Pine Ave, Big Pine Key, FL 33043 at (305) 872-2331 (#826)

Seaworld Adventure Camps

(est 1992)

Orlando, FL (Orange Co.); (800) 406-2244
Josh Kennedy, Director

Camp comments: Camp SeaWorld and Adventure Camp offer up close animal encounters, crafts, songs, games, marine field adventures & fun.
Activities: Academics, Aquatic Activities, Arts/Crafts, Canoeing, Field Trips, Nature/Environment Studies, Photography, Travel/Tour
Session lengths & capacity: June-August; 1/2, 1 & 2 week sessions; 400 campers
Clientele & fees: coed 3-18; families; seniors; single adults; Fees: B ☀
Contact: Education Reservations at (800) 406-2244; fax: (407) 363-2399
e-mail: education@seaworld.org
Operated by: SeaWorld Adventure Park, 7007 SeaWorld Dr, Orlando, FL 32821 at (407) 363-2380 (#3176)

Space Camp Florida

(est 1988)

Titusville, FL (Brevard Co.); (321) 267-3184
Charlene Neuterman, Director

Camp comments: Our mission is to inspire people of all ages to discover the excitement of space through hands-on, minds-on education experiences.
Activities: Academics, Model Rocketry, Team Building
Session lengths & capacity: February-December; 1 week sessions; 264 campers
Clientele & fees: coed 9-12; Fees: F ▲
Contact: Charlene Neuterman, Manager at (321) 269-6101 ext. 6110; fax: (321) 269-6116
e-mail: cneuterman@spacecamp.com
Web site: www.spacecamp.com
Operated by: US Space Camp Foundation, One Tranquility Base, Huntsville, AL 35805-3399 at (205) 837-3400

Group Rental Information
Facilities: Dorm-Style, Food Service, Linens (#762)

The Boggy Creek Gang Camp

(est 1996)

Eustis, FL; (352) 483-4200
Dorcas Tomasek, Director

Camp comments: BCGC is a year-round camp for children with chronic & life threatening illnesses through summer camp & family retreats.
Activities: Archery, Arts/Crafts, Challenge/Rope Courses, Drama, Fishing, Horseback — Western, Nature/Environment Studies, Sports — Field & Team, Swimming — Recreational
Session lengths & capacity: January-December; 1 week sessions; 140 campers
Clientele & fees: coed 7-16; Fees: A ▲
Contact: Kathleen Bladen, Office Manager at (352) 483-4200 ext. 215; fax: (352) 483-0358
Web site: www.boggycreek.org
Operated by: Boggy Creek Gang Inc, 30500 Brantley Branch Road, Eustis, FL 32736 at (352) 483-4200 (#2617)

Wai Lani (est 1968)

Palm Harbor, FL (Pinellas Co.); (813) 937-0203
Cheryl Warnock, Director

Camp comments: Located on Gulf of Mexico Estuary. Expert instruction in boating and marine biology.
Activities: Aquatic Activities, Arts/Crafts, Boating, Canoeing, Drama, Kayaking, Nature/Environment Studies, Performing Arts, Sailing, Swimming — Recreational
Session lengths & capacity: June-July; 1/2, 1 & 2 week sessions; 82 campers
Clientele & fees: girls 6-17; Fees: B ▲
Contact: Gloria Hartness, Outdoor Education Director at (813) 281-4475 ext. 203; fax: (813) 282-8285
e-mail: ghartnes@sgcs.org
Web site: www.suncoastgirlscouts.org
Operated by: Suncoast GSC Inc, PO Drawer 18066, Tampa, FL 33679-8066 at (800) 881-4475

Group Rental Information
Facilities: Cabins, Dorm-Style, Double Occupancy, Food Service, Hiking Trails, Lodges, Meeting Rooms, Ocean, Pool
Programs: Environmental Education, Swimming (#275)

Welaka (est 1959)

Jupiter, FL; (561) 746-8000

Camp comments: Minutes from the ocean. South Florida environment and aquatic activities explored!
Activities: Aquatic Activities, Arts/Crafts, Camping Skills/Outdoor Living, Canoeing, Counselor Training (CIT), Drama, Hiking, Nature/Environment Studies, SCUBA, Tennis
Session lengths & capacity: 1/2, 1 & 2 week sessions; 150 campers

Clientele & fees: girls 5-17; Fees: **B** ⚠
Contact: Elisa Royall, Camp Administrator at (561) 582-5362; fax: (561) 547-2169
Operated by: Palm Glades GSC, 2728 Lake Worth Rd, Lake Worth, FL 33461 at (561) 582-5362

Group Rental Information
Facilities: Cabins, Food Service, Kitchen Facilities, Lodges, Meeting Rooms, Tents
Programs: Boating (#827)

Wildwood (est 1961) ⚠ 🏠

Wildwood, FL (Sumter Co.); (352) 748-2825
Cindy Lackey, Director

Camp comments: Equestrian program for all levels & seats. Programs for girls who don't want to ride. Non Girl Scouts welcome!
Activities: Arts/Crafts, Camping Skills/Outdoor Living, Canoeing, Challenge/Rope Courses, Hiking, Horseback — English, Horseback — Western, Nature/Environment Studies
Session lengths & capacity: 1 & 2 week sessions; 90 campers
Clientele & fees: girls 6-17; Fees: **B** ⚠
Contact: Cindy Lackey, Director of Outdoor Program at (352) 748-2825; fax: (352) 748-0808
e-mail: gscamp@scia.net
Web site: www.hfgsc.org
Operated by: Heart of Florida GSC, 1831 N Gilmore Ave, Lakeland, FL 33805-3017 at (863) 688-7648

Group Rental Information
Facilities: Cabins, Dorm-Style
Programs: Environmental Education, Horseback Riding (#818)

WOW N FL Youth Assoc ⚠ 🏠

Hosford, FL; (904) 379-8314
Tom Monahan, Director
Activities: Archery, Arts/Crafts, Baseball/Softball, Basketball, Canoeing, Swimming — Recreational, Team Building
Contact: Thomas Monahan, Fraternal Coordinator at (904) 379-8314;
Operated by: WOW Life Insurance (SE), 1700 Farnam, Omaha, NE 68120 at (402) 271-7258 (#3934)

YMCA Camp Indian Springs ⚠

Crawfordville, FL; (850) 926-3361
Derek Hart, Director

Camp comments: Where a summer will last a lifetime.

ICON LEGEND

☀ Day Camp
⚠ Resident Camp
🏠 Facilities Available To Rent
🚍 Transportation Available
🐷 Financial Aid Available

FEE RANGES PER WEEK

A	$0-75
B	$75-200
C	$201-350
D	$351-500
E	$501-650
F	over $650

Activities: Bicycling/Biking, Canoeing, Challenge/Rope Courses, Counselor Training (CIT), Dance, Horseback — English, Horseback — Western, Swimming — Recreational
Session lengths & capacity: 1, 2 & 3 week sessions; 168 campers
Clientele & fees: coed 7-15; Fees: **C, D** ⚠
Contact: Anna Woodey, Assistant Director at (850) 926-3361; fax: (850) 926-3624
e-mail: campregistration@aol.com
Web site: www.campindiansprings.com
Operated by: YMCA Camp Indian Springs, 2387 Bloxham Cut Off Rd, Crawfordville, FL 32327 at (850) 926-3361 (#27486)

YMCA Camp Winona (est 1919) ⚠ 🏠

Deleon Springs, FL (Volusia Co.); (386) 985-4544
David Larrabee, Director

Camp comments: Camp offers traditional program in a supportive, nurturing environment for campers to grow in spirit, mind & body. Beautiful rustic setting on a spring-fed lake
Activities: Archery, Arts/Crafts, Camping Skills/Outdoor Living, Canoeing, Challenge/Rope Courses, Counselor Training (CIT), Horseback — Western, Nature/Environment Studies, Sailing, Swimming — Recreational
Session lengths & capacity: May-August; 1/2, 1 & 2 week sessions; 180 campers
Clientele & fees: coed 7-15; Fees: **C** ⚠ 🐷
Contact: David Larrabee, Executive Director at (386) 985-4544; fax: (386) 985-6553
e-mail: ycwinona@bellsouth.net
Operated by: Greater Daytona Beach YMCA, 825 Derbyshire Rd, Daytona Beach, FL 32117 at (386) 253-5675

Group Rental Information
Site comments: A beautiful place for weekend retreats & conferences, outdoor education, ropes course/leadership training or company picnics.
Seasons & Capacity: Spring 220, Fall 220, Winter 220
Facilities: A/V Equipment, Cabins, Double Occupancy, Food Service, Lodges, Meeting Rooms, Playing Fields
Programs: Boating, Challenge/Ropes Course, Environmental Education, Swimming (#836)

Georgia

Adahi (est 1965) ⚠ 🏠

Cloudland, GA (Chattanooga Co.); (706) 862-2722
Erin Kenner, Director

Camp comments: A quality camping program open to all girls 6 to 17 on Lookout Mtn where the smiles begin and the friendships never end.
Activities: Archery, Camping Skills/Outdoor Living, Canoeing, Challenge/Rope Courses, Hiking, Horseback — Western, International Culture, Nature/Environment Studies, Swimming — Recreational
Session lengths & capacity: June-July; 1/2, 1 & 2 week sessions; 140 campers
Clientele & fees: girls 6-17; Fees: **B, C, D** ⚠
Contact: Erin Kenner, Camp Director at (423) 877-2688; fax: (423) 877-5581
Web site: www.mbgsc.org
Operated by: Girl Scouts Moccesin Bend Cncl, PO Box 15969, Chattanooga, TN 37415 at (423) 877-2688 (#686)

Athens Y Camp for Boys

(est 1898) ⚠ 🏠

Tallulah Falls, GA (Rabun Co.)
Harmon Tison, Director

Camp comments: AYC was established on faith in Jesus Christ, the true rock, 100 yr old camp that excels through Christian truths, varied physical activities, & brotherly inter
Activities: Aquatic Activities, Archery, Basketball, Challenge/Rope Courses, Climbing/Rappelling, Counselor Training (CIT), Religious Study, Riflery, Soccer, Sports — Field & Team
Session lengths & capacity: Year-round; 1 week sessions; 250 campers
Clientele & fees: boys 7-15; Fees: **D** ⚠ 🚍
Contact: Harmon Tison, Director at (706) 754-6912; fax: (706) 754-7014
e-mail: ayccamp@alltel.net
Web site: www.athensycamp.org
Operated by: Athens YMCA Camps, 915 Hawthorne Avenue, Athens, GA 30606 at (706) 754-6912

Group Rental Information
Facilities: Cabins, Food Service, Hiking Trails, Lake, Lodges (#6261)

Athens YWCO Camp For Girls

(est 1925) ⚠ 🏠

Clarkesville, GA (Habersham Co.); (706) 754-8528
Nanette Baughman, Director

Camp comments: Magical, fun place for a child to build lifetime memories and friendships.
Activities: Arts/Crafts, Camping Skills/Outdoor Living, Canoeing, Counselor Training (CIT), Dance, Drama, Horseback — English, Horseback — Western, Swimming — Recreational
Session lengths & capacity: June-August; 1 & 2 week sessions; 104 campers
Clientele & fees: girls 7-15; Fees: **D** ⚠ 🐷
Contact: Nanette Baughman, Director at (706) 754-8528; fax: (706) 754-3868
e-mail: ycamp@alltel.net
Web site: www.kidscamps.com/traditional/athens-ywco
Operated by: Athens YWCO Camp for Girls, 445 Athens Y Camp Rd, Clarkesville, GA 30523 at (706) 754-8528

Group Rental Information
Seasons & Capacity: Spring 140, Winter 80
Facilities: Cabins, Double Occupancy, Food Service, Hiking Trails, Lake, Meeting Rooms, Playing Fields, Pool
Programs: Boating, Swimming (#10464)

Blue Ridge Camp (est 1969) ⚠ 🚍

Mountain City, GA (Rabun Co.); (706) 746-5491
Coach J.I. Montgomery/Joey & Sheila Waldman, Director

Camp comments: In the scenic mountains of N. GA. with 37 camper selected activities. Teen program-Shabatt services-family run camp.
Activities: Aerobics/Exercise, Aquatic Activities, Arts/Crafts, Climbing/Rappelling, Golf, Performing Arts, Rafting, Sports — Field & Team, Tennis, Waterskiing
Session lengths & capacity: June-August; 4 & 8 week sessions; 200 campers
Clientele & fees: coed 8-15; Fees: **D** ⚠
Contact: Sheila Waldman & Joey Waldman, Director at (800) 878-2267; fax: (305) 532-3152
e-mail: CBRCamp@aol.com
Web site: www.blueridgecamp.com
Operated by: Blue Ridge Camp and Resort Inc, PO Box 2888, Miami Beach, FL 33140 at (305) 538-3434 (#3762)

Calvin Center (est 1960) ☀ ⚠ 🏠

Hampton, GA (Clayton Co.); (770) 946-4276
John Hicks, Director

Camp comments: A place to grow spiritually.548 acres of woods & meadows, lake for boating, equestrian program incl therapeutic riding, year round facilites for groups.
Activities: Archery, Canoeing, Challenge/Rope Courses, Climbing/Rappelling, Counselor Training (CIT), Horseback — Western, Religious Study, Swimming — Recreational, Wilderness Trips

Session lengths & capacity: June-August; 1 & 2 week sessions; 160 campers
Clientele & fees: coed 6-18; families; Fees: B ☀
Fees: C ⚠
Contact: John Hicks, Executive Director at (770) 946-7276 ext. 23; fax: (770) 946-4191
e-mail: presbyjohns@aol.com
Web site: www.calvincenter.org
Operated by: Presbytery of Greater Atlanta, 1024 Ponce de Leon NE, Atlanta, GA 30306 at (770) 946-4276

Group Rental Information
Site comments: A place to grow spiritually. 548 acres of woods & meadows, lake for boating, equestrian program incl therapeutic riding, year round facilities for group.
Facilities: Cabins, Dorm-Style, Double Occupancy, Food Service, Hiking Trails, Kitchen Facilities, Lake, Linens, Lodges, Meeting Rooms, Playing Fields, Pool
Programs: Boating, Challenge/Ropes Course, Environmental Education, Horseback Riding, Swimming (#743)

Camp Barney Medintz

(est 1963) ⚠ ⌂ 🚐

Cleveland, GA (White Co.); (706) 865-2715
Jim Mittenthal, MSW, Director

Camp comments: 500 acres in Blue Ridge Mtns. 2 lakes. Exhilarating age-appropriate program. Fabulous staff. Dynamic facility. Kosher.
Activities: Challenge/Rope Courses, Climbing/Rappelling, Horseback — Western, Performing Arts, Rafting, Sports — Field & Team, Swimming — Recreational, Tennis, Waterskiing, Wilderness Trips
Session lengths & capacity: June-August; 2 & 4 week sessions; 450 campers
Clientele & fees: coed 8-16; families; Fees: D, E ⚠
Contact: Jim Mittenthal, MSW, Director at (770) 396-3250; fax: (770) 481-0101
e-mail: summer@campbarney.org
Operated by: Marcus Jewish Community Ctr, 5342 Tilly Mill Rd, Dunwoody, GA 30338 at (770) 396-3250

Group Rental Information
Facilities: A/V Equipment, Cabins, Double Occupancy, Food Service, Lake, Lodges, Meeting Rooms, Playing Fields, Pool
Programs: Boating, Challenge/Ropes Course, Environmental Education, Swimming (#747)

Camp Big Creek

☀ 🚐

Alpharetta, GA; (770) 664-1220
Debra Beauford, Director

Camp comments: Outdoor rustic day camp for campers to explore crafts,teambuilding, outdoor living, water sports, rollerblading, biking, & fun in the sun atmosphere.
Activities: Archery, Canoeing, Challenge/Rope Courses, Climbing/Rappelling, Community Service, Fishing, Nature/Environment Studies, Riflery, Skating, Swimming — Recreational
Session lengths & capacity: June-August; 2 week sessions; 300 campers
Clientele & fees: coed 5-14; Fees: C ☀ 🐷
Contact: Debra Beauford, Camp Director at (770) 664-1220; fax: (770) 664-0337
Web site: www.ymcaatlanta.org
Operated by: Metro Atlanta YMCA, 100 Edgewood Ave NE Ste 1100, Atlanta, GA 30303 at (404) 588-9622 (#40788)

Camp Breathe Easy (est 1981) ⚠

Rutledge, GA; (706) 557-9070

Camp comments: The self-management camp for kids with asthma.

Activities: Archery, Bicycling/Biking, Canoeing, Challenge/Rope Courses, Clowning, Drawing/Painting, Nature/Environment Studies, Sports — Field & Team, Swimming — Instructional, Waterskiing
Session lengths & capacity: June-August; 1 week sessions; 200 campers
Clientele & fees: coed 8-13; Fees: B, C ⚠ 🐷
Contact: Chanda Mobley, Director at (770) 434-5864; fax: (770) 319-0349
e-mail: cmobley@alaga.org
Web site: www.alaga.org
Operated by: American Lung Association, 2452 Spring Rd, Smyrna, GA 30080 at (770) 434-5864 (#1721)

Camp Concharty (est 1956)

⚠ ⌂

Shiloh, GA (Harris Co.); (706) 628-5283

Camp comments: Camp Concharty, 196 acres of woodland at the base of Pine Mtn, Ga. Girl Scout Camp offers variety of programs to girls.
Activities: Arts/Crafts, Baseball/Softball, Basketball, Camping Skills/Outdoor Living, Canoeing, Field Trips, Hiking, Horseback — English, Performing Arts, Swimming — Recreational
Session lengths & capacity: June-August; 1/2, 1 & 2 week sessions; 130 campers
Clientele & fees: girls 6-17; Fees: B, C, D ⚠
Contact: Brad Baker, Director of Program at (706) 327-2646; fax: (706) 327-9689
e-mail: program@girlscoutsconcharty.org
Operated by: Concharty GSC, 1344 13th Ave, Columbus, GA 31901 at (706) 327-2646

Group Rental Information
Seasons & Capacity: Spring 46, Fall 46, Winter 46
Facilities: Cabins, Dorm-Style, Lake
Programs: Horseback Riding (#10459)

Camp Glisson (est 1925)

⚠ ⌂

Dahlonega, GA (Lumpkin Co.); (706) 864-6181
Rev. Gary Greenwald, Director

Camp comments: United Methodist Camp, North Georgia Mtns. Small group, spiritual emphasis, cabin, tent, wilderness. Mentally challenged
Activities: Backpacking, Basketball, Camping Skills/Outdoor Living, Challenge/Rope Courses, Climbing/Rappelling, Hiking, Kayaking, Team Building, Wilderness Trips
Session lengths & capacity: 1 week sessions; 275 campers
Clientele & fees: boys 10-18; girls 10-18; Fees: C ⚠
Contact: Donna Collins, Registrar at (706) 864-6181; fax: (706) 864-9352
e-mail: glissonregistrar@alltel.net
Web site: www.campglisson.org
Operated by: United Methodist Church, 865 Camp Glisson Rd, Dahlonega, GA 30533 at (706) 864-6181

Group Rental Information
Site comments: An ideal location in the mountains, quiet setting, 1 hour north of Atlanta. Mountain streams, waterfalls and excellent retreat facilities for chuch youth groups
Seasons & Capacity: Spring 350, Summer 350, Fall 350, Winter 350
Facilities: A/V Equipment, Cabins, Food Service, Hiking Trails, Kitchen Facilities, Lake, Lodges, Meeting Rooms, Pool, River
Programs: Challenge/Ropes Course, Swimming (#7299)

Camp Juliette Low Inc

(est 1922) ⚠ ⌂

Cloudland, GA (Chattooga Co.); (706) 862-2169
Nancy Brim & Kathy Switzer, Director

Camp comments: Program focuses on living in, enjoying and appreciating the outdoors. Emphasis on building self-confidence.

Activities: Archery, Arts/Crafts, Camping Skills/Outdoor Living, Canoeing, Challenge/Rope Courses, Counselor Training (CIT), Horseback — English, Sailing, Swimming — Instructional, Swimming — Recreational
Session lengths & capacity: June-August; 1 & 2 week sessions; 112 campers
Clientele & fees: girls 7-17; Fees: D ⚠
Contact: Peggy Holbrook, Business Manager at (770) 428-1062; fax: (770) 428-1302
Web site: www.cji.org
Operated by: Camp Juliette Low Inc, Board of Trustees, PO Box 5113, Marietta, GA 30061-0352 at (770) 428-1062

Group Rental Information
Facilities: Hiking Trails, Playing Fields, River, Tents (#754)

Camp Kaleo (est 1987)

⚠ ⌂

Forsyth, GA (Monroe Co.); (478) 994-5333

Camp comments: Wilderness based program. Emphasis on cooperation, self-esteem, personal and spiritual growth.
Activities: Archery, Camping Skills/Outdoor Living, Canoeing, Challenge/Rope Courses, Climbing/Rappelling, Nature/Environment Studies, Wilderness Trips
Session lengths & capacity: June-August; 1/2 & 1 week sessions; 130 campers
Clientele & fees: boys 6-18; Fees: B ⚠
Contact: A Glen Mc Call, Camp Director at (800) 746-4422 ext. 256; fax: (770) 452-6575
e-mail: gmccall@gabaptist.org
Web site: www.gabaptist.org/mem.campkaleo.html
Operated by: GA Baptist Convention, 2930 Flowers Rd South, Atlanta, GA 30341 at (800) 746-4422

Group Rental Information
Seasons & Capacity: Spring 120, Fall 120, Winter 120
Facilities: Cabins, Food Service, Lake, Meeting Rooms
Programs: Challenge/Ropes Course (#6264)

Camp Kiwanis (est 1951)

⚠

Danielsville, GA; (706) 795-2098
Mike Miller, Director

Camp comments: To provide a quality developmental program which empowers Metro Atlanta Youth to become productive adults.
Activities: Archery, Camping Skills/Outdoor Living, Canoeing, Counselor Training (CIT), Fishing, Kayaking, Nature/Environment Studies, Riflery, Swimming — Recreational, Team Building
Session lengths & capacity: June-August; 1 week sessions; 40 campers
Clientele & fees: coed 9-14; Fees: A ⚠
Contact: Lee Fox, Assistant Director at (706) 795-2098; fax: (706) 795-0976
Operated by: Boys And Girls Club of Atlanta, 100 Edgewood Ave Ste 700, Atlanta, GA 30303 at (706) 795-2098 (#28990)

Camp Lookout Inc (est 1956) ⚠ ⌂

Rising Fawn, GA (Walker Co.); (706) 820-1163
Don Washburn, Director

Camp comments: Come experience the joys of creation through exploration at Camp Lookout.
Activities: Bicycling/Biking, Camping Skills/Outdoor Living, Canoeing, Caving, Challenge/Rope Courses, Climbing/Rappelling, Hiking, Kayaking, Nature/Environment Studies, Team Building
Session lengths & capacity: 1/2 & 1 week sessions; 80 campers
Clientele & fees: coed 7-18; Fees: B, C ⚠
Contact: Don Washburn, Director/Manager at (706) 820-1163; fax: (706) 820-9911
e-mail: info@camplookout.com
Operated by: Holston Conference Camping, PO Box 1178, Johnson City, TN 37605-1178 at (423) 928-2156

Group Rental Information
Seasons & Capacity: Spring 140, Summer 100, Winter 120
Facilities: Cabins, Food Service, Kitchen Facilities, Lodges, Pool
Programs: Environmental Education (#3980)

Camp Martha Johnston
(est 1925) ☀ ▲ ⌂

Lizella, GA (Crawford Co.); (478) 836-3646
Activities: Archery, Arts/Crafts, Camping Skills/Outdoor Living, Challenge/Rope Courses, Climbing/Rappelling, Horseback — English, Rafting, Swimming — Recreational, Tennis, Travel/Tour
Session lengths & capacity: May-August; 1 & 2 week sessions; 96 campers
Clientele & fees: girls 6-15; Fees: **B** ▲ 🐷
Contact: Lyn Hicks, Camp Director at (912) 836-3646; fax: (912) 935-2224
e-mail: mnature100@aol.com
Web site: www.gsmginc.com
Operated by: GS of Middle Georgia Inc, 6869 Columbus Rd, Lizella, GA 31052 at (912) 935-2221

Group Rental Information
Facilities: A/V Equipment, Cabins, Dorm-Style, Food Service, Hiking Trails, Kitchen Facilities, Lodges, Meeting Rooms, Pool, Tents
Programs: Challenge/Ropes Course, Swimming (#3012)

Camp Mikell (est 1941) ▲ ⌂ 🚐

Toccoa, GA (Stephens Co.); (706) 886-7515
Robin Dake, Director

Camp comments: An Episcopal church camp in the woods, open to all, offering Christian education, adventure and creative arts programs, and a whole lot of fun.
Activities: Arts/Crafts, Backpacking, Canoeing, Challenge/Rope Courses, Drama, Hiking, Music, Religious Study, Sports — Field & Team, Swimming — Recreational
Session lengths & capacity: June-August; 1 week sessions; 120 campers
Clientele & fees: coed 8-18; Fees: **C, D** ▲ 🐷
Contact: Robin Dake, Assistant Director at (706) 886-7515;
e-mail: mikell@alltel.net
Web site: www.campmikell.com
Operated by: Episcopal Diocese of Atlanta, Rt 3 Box 3495, Toccoa, GA 30577 at (706) 886-7515

Group Rental Information
Site comments: An Episcopal center, open to all, offering space for gatherings, meetings, retreats, and professionally-staffed adventure and environmental education programs.

ICON LEGEND
☀ Day Camp
▲ Resident Camp
⌂ Facilities Available To Rent
🚐 Transportation Available
🐷 Financial Aid Available

FEE RANGES PER WEEK
A	$0-75
B	$75-200
C	$201-350
D	$351-500
E	$501-650
F	over $650

Seasons & Capacity: Spring 200, Summer 20, Fall 200, Winter 200
Facilities: A/V Equipment, Cabins, Dorm-Style, Double Occupancy, Food Service, Hiking Trails, Linens, Lodges, Meeting Rooms, Playing Fields
Programs: Challenge/Ropes Course, Environmental Education (#10488)

Camp Misty Mountain
(est 1995) ▲ ⌂

Armuchee, GA (Floyd Co.); (706) 629-1030
Jill Allison, Director

Camp comments: Two-week camp focusing on interests of girls, their growth and potential. Helping girls grow strong.
Activities: Aquatic Activities, Archery, Arts/Crafts, Canoeing, Challenge/Rope Courses, Horseback — English, Horseback — Western, Leadership Development, Riflery, Swimming — Recreational
Session lengths & capacity: June-August; 2 week sessions; 140 campers
Clientele & fees: girls 9-16; Fees: **C** ▲ 🐷
Contact: Jill Allison, Program Center Director at (706) 629-1030; fax: (706) 629-2676
e-mail: jalllison@girlscoutsnwga.org
Web site: www.girlscoutsnwga.org
Operated by: Girl Scout Cncl Northwest GA, 1577 Northeast Expressway, Atlanta, GA 30329 at (404) 527-7500 (#4209)

Camp Odako (est 1993) ☀

Avondale, GA (DeKalb Co.); (404) 527-7125
Jimmy Thomas, Director

Camp comments: Day camp with childcare capabilities. Outdoor skills, field trips and team building.
Activities: Aerobics/Exercise, Archery, Arts/Crafts, Community Service, Field Trips, Leadership Development, Swimming — Recreational
Session lengths & capacity: June-August; 1 week sessions; 50 campers
Clientele & fees: coed 6-15; Fees: **B** ☀
Contact: Marian Long, Senior Program Director at (404) 527-7125 ext. 134; fax: (404) 527-7139
e-mail: info@campfireusaga.org
Web site: /www.campfireusaga.org
Operated by: Camp Fire USA, 100 Edgewood Ave NE Suite 528, Atlanta, GA 30303-3030 at (404) 527-7125 (#4223)

Camp Pacer (est 1985) ☀

Savannah, GA (Chatham Co.); (912) 927-7089
Donna Stembridge, Director

Camp comments: Self-esteem speciality campers thrive in non-competitive caring atmosphere. Leadership programs. Every child is special.
Activities: Arts/Crafts, Camping Skills/Outdoor Living, Challenge/Rope Courses, Counselor Training (CIT), Drama, Leadership Development, Nature/Environment Studies, Sports — Field & Team, Swimming — Recreational
Session lengths & capacity: 9 week sessions
Clientele & fees: coed 7-14; seniors;
Fees: **A** ☀ 🐷
Contact: Jean Norris, Project Director at (912) 927-9537; fax: (912) 927-9537
Operated by: Camp Pacer, 204 Tibet Ave, Savannah, GA 31406 at (912) 927-9537 (#6321)

Camp Pine Valley (est 1966) ▲ ⌂

Meansville, GA (Pike Co.); (770) 567-3402
Terri R Ison, Director

Camp comments: Fantastic 643 acre Girl Scout camp empowering girls for success through art, science, and self esteem.
Activities: Arts/Crafts, Camping Skills/Outdoor Living, Canoeing, Challenge/Rope Courses, Counselor Training (CIT), Horseback — English, Nature/Environment Studies, Swimming — Recreational, Team Building

Session lengths & capacity: June-August; 1/2 & 1 week sessions; 96 campers
Clientele & fees: girls 6-17; families;
Fees: **C** ▲ 🐷
Contact: (770) 227-2524; fax: (770) 228-2272
e-mail: pinevalleygs@mindspring.com
Operated by: Pine Valley GSC Inc, 350 Airport Rd, Griffin, GA 30224-1569 at (770) 227-2524

Group Rental Information
Facilities: Cabins, Dorm-Style, Hiking Trails, Kitchen Facilities, Lake, Lodges, Playing Fields, Pool, Tents
Programs: Boating (#3372)

Camp Pinnacle (est 1947) ▲ ⌂

Clayton, GA; (706) 782-3231
LeAnn Gunter, Director

Camp comments: Camp Pinnacle is dedicated to God to lead people to Christ to develope christian character & to promote world missions.
Activities: Arts/Crafts, Canoeing, Community Service, Hiking, Leadership Development, Music, Religious Study, Swimming — Recreational
Session lengths & capacity: June-August; 1/2 & 1 week sessions; 168 campers
Clientele & fees: girls 6-18; Fees: **B** ▲
Contact: (800) 746-4422 ext. 326;
fax: (770) 452-6572
e-mail: dcox@gabaptist.org
Web site: www.georgiawmu.org
Operated by: Baptist Womans Missionary, 2930 Flowers Road South, Atlanta, GA 30341-5512 at (800) 746-4422

Group Rental Information
Site comments: Camp Pinnacle conference and retreat center is dedicated to God and developing Christian character and to promote world missions.
Seasons & Capacity: Spring 331, Fall 331, Winter 135
Facilities: Cabins, Double Occupancy, Food Service, Hiking Trails, Lake, Linens, Lodges, Meeting Rooms, Playing Fields, Pool
Programs: Swimming (#41451)

Camp Tanglewood (est 1946) ☀ ▲ ⌂

Martinez, GA (Columbia Co.); (706) 863-0764
Teresa Morris, Director

Camp comments: Girl Scout camping is exciting & fun. Girls thrive on creative educational learning experiences in the outdoors.
Activities: Aquatic Activities, Archery, Camping Skills/Outdoor Living, Canoeing, Hiking, Horseback — English, Horseback — Western, Nature/Environment Studies, Rafting, Travel/Tour
Session lengths & capacity: June-August; 1/2, 1 & 2 week sessions; 125 campers
Clientele & fees: girls 6-17; Fees: **A** ☀
Fees: **B, C** ▲
Contact: Teresa Morris, Camp Director at (706) 774-0505; fax: (706) 774-0045
e-mail: tmorris@girlscoutscsra.org
Operated by: Girl Scouts Ctrl Savannah Rvr, 1325 Greene Street, Augusta, GA 30901-1031 at (706) 774-0505

Group Rental Information
Site comments: Camp Tanglewood is packed with fun-filled programs and activities for girls entering 1st through 12th grades.
Seasons & Capacity: Spring 125, Summer 150, Fall 125
Facilities: Cabins, Hiking Trails, Kitchen Facilities, Lake, Lodges, Pool, Tents
Programs: Boating, Challenge/Ropes Course, Horseback Riding (#730)

Camp Timber Ridge (est 1924) ▲ ⌂

Mableton, GA (Cobb Co.); (770) 948-8200
Kate Kearney, Director

Camp comments: Girl Scout Camp located near Atlanta. Team building & challenging choice for all age levels.

Activities: Archery, Arts/Crafts, Camping Skills/Outdoor Living, Canoeing, Challenge/Rope Courses, Counselor Training (CIT), Dance, Drama, Leadership Development, Nature/Environment Studies
Session lengths & capacity: June-August; 1/2, 1 & 2 week sessions; 144 campers
Clientele & fees: girls 7-17; Fees: B ⚠ 🚐
Contact: Kate Kearney, Timber Ridge Program Center Director at (770) 948-8200; fax: (770) 745-6473
e-mail: kkearney@girlscoutsnwga.org
Web site: www.girlscoutsnwga.org
Operated by: Girl Scout Cncl Northwest GA, 1577 Northeast Expressway, Atlanta, GA 30329 at (404) 527-7500 (#728)

Camp Toccoa (est 1927) ⚠ 🏠 🚗

Toccoa, GA (Stephens Co.); (706) 886-2457
Sue K Edwards, Director

Camp comments: Beautiful scenery. Traditional program plus exciting adventure programs. A place where every child is special.
Activities: Archery, Arts/Crafts, Backpacking, Camping Skills/Outdoor Living, Canoeing, Challenge/Rope Courses, Climbing/Rappelling, Drama, Horseback — Western, Nature/Environment Studies
Session lengths & capacity: June-August; 1, 2 & 4 week sessions; 150 campers
Clientele & fees: coed 7-17; families; single adults; Fees: C, E ⚠ 🚐
Contact: Sue Edwards, Director at (706) 886-2457; fax: (706) 886-5123
e-mail: camptoccoa@alltel.net
Web site: /www.campfireusaga.org
Operated by: Camp Fire USA, 100 Edgewood Ave NE Suite 528, Atlanta, GA 30303-3030 at (404) 527-7125

Group Rental Information
Site comments: Mountain scenery,waterfall,trails.Rustic cabin clusters combine flexibly;nature;team building programs available.
Seasons & Capacity: Spring 175, Summer 175, Fall 175, Winter 88
Facilities: Cabins, Food Service, Hiking Trails, Kitchen Facilities, Lake, Lodges, Meeting Rooms, Pool
Programs: Challenge/Ropes Course, Environmental Education, Horseback Riding, Swimming (#735)

Camp Twin Lakes Inc (est 1992) ⚠ 🏠

Atlanta, GA; (404) 231-9887
Larry Melnick, Director

Camp comments: Camp for children with medical problems. Only camp in Georgia providing this program. Allowing children to experience joys of camping.
Activities: Aquatic Activities, Archery, Arts/Crafts, Bicycling/Biking, Canoeing, Ceramics/Pottery, Challenge/Rope Courses, Horseback — Western, Nature/Environment Studies, Tennis
Session lengths & capacity: June-August; 1 week sessions; 370 campers
Clientele & fees: coed 8-18; Fees: B ⚠
Contact: Larry Melnick, Executive Director at (404) 892-1206; fax: (770) 351-0475
e-mail: camptwinlakes@mindspring.com
Web site: camptwinlakes.org
Operated by: Camp Twin Lakes Inc, 5909 Peachtree Dunwoody 802, Atlanta, GA 30328 at (404) 231-9887

Group Rental Information
Site comments: CTL is the perfect blend of modern conveniences,quiet fun,serving children with special medical needs & business groups.
Seasons & Capacity: Spring 370, Summer 370, Fall 370, Winter 370

Facilities: A/V Equipment, Cabins, Dorm-Style, Double Occupancy, Food Service, Hiking Trails, Kitchen Facilities, Lake, Linens, Lodges, Meeting Rooms, Playing Fields, Pool, River
Programs: Boating, Challenge/Ropes Course, Environmental Education, Swimming (#1437)

Camp Wieuca (est 1994) ☀

Atlanta, GA (Fulton Co.); (404) 814-4467
April Walker, Director

Camp comments: Christ centered, adventure filled fun!
Activities: Archery, Arts/Crafts, Climbing/Rappelling, Field Trips, Music, Religious Study, Skating, Sports — Field & Team, Swimming — Recreational
Session lengths & capacity: June-August; 1 week sessions; 100 campers
Clientele & fees: boys 6-13; girls 6-13; coed 6-13; Fees: B ☀
Contact: April Walker, Camp Director at (404) 814-4467; fax: (404) 814-4468
Web site: www.wieuca.org
Operated by: Wieuca Rd Baptist Church, 3626 Peachtree Rd, Atlanta, GA 30326 at (404) 814-4460 (#7204)

Camp Wo He Lo (est 1991) ☀

Roswell, GA (Fulton Co.); (404) 527-7125
Cheryl Gans, CCD, Director

Camp comments: A day camp in suburbs with emphasis on outdoors, full child care capabilities.
Activities: Archery, Arts/Crafts, Basketball, Camping Skills/Outdoor Living, Field Trips, Nature/Environment Studies, Sports — Field & Team, Swimming — Recreational
Session lengths & capacity: June-July; 1 week sessions; 40 campers
Clientele & fees: coed 5-12; Fees: B ☀
Contact: Annemarie Brown, Registrar at (404) 527-7125; fax: (404) 527-7139
e-mail: info@campfireusaga.org
Web site: /www.campfireusaga.org
Operated by: Camp Fire USA, 100 Edgewood Ave NE Suite 528, Atlanta, GA 30303-3030 at (404) 527-7125 (#555)

Camp Woodmont (est 1980) ⚠

Cloudland, GA (Walker Co.); (706) 398-0739
Tyran Bennett, Director

Camp comments: Beautiful Lookout Mtn. NW GA. 1-2 Weeks. Caring counselors & warm Christian atmosphere-campers feel secure, welcome & reassured. Cabins. 1000+ pics at web site.
Activities: Aquatic Activities, Archery, Arts/Crafts, Challenge/Rope Courses, Climbing/Rappelling, Dance, Hiking, Horseback — Western, Nature/Environment Studies, Swimming — Recreational
Session lengths & capacity: June-August; 1, 2, 3, 4, 6, 8 week sessions; 100 campers
Clientele & fees: coed 6-14; Fees: D ⚠
Contact: Jane or Jim Bennett, Owners/Directors at (770) 457-0862; fax: (770) 457-2189
e-mail: campdirector@campwoodmont.com
Web site: www.campwoodmont.com
Operated by: Camp Woodmont, 2339 Welton Place, Dunwoody, GA 30338 at (770) 457-0862 (#6370)

Girl Scout Camp Low
(est 1957) ☀ ⚠ 🏠

Savannah, GA (Chatham Co.); (912) 925-6645
Michelle Anderson, Director

Camp comments: Private Island camp, serving girls 5-17. Swimming, hiking, archery, canoeing, horseback riding and laughter.

Activities: Aquatic Activities, Archery, Arts/Crafts, Camping Skills/Outdoor Living, Canoeing, Counselor Training (CIT), Field Trips, Hiking, Horseback — English, Swimming — Recreational
Session lengths & capacity: June-August; 1/2, 1, 2 & 4 week sessions; 100 campers
Clientele & fees: girls 5-17; Fees: A ☀
Fees: B ⚠ 🚐
Contact: (800) 750-6468; fax: (912) 236-5703
e-mail: amy@girlscouting.org
Web site: www.girlscouting.org
Operated by: GSC of Savannah, 127 Abercorn St Ste 400, Savannah, GA 31401 at (912) 236-1571

Group Rental Information
Site comments: Beautiful private island filled with laughter, friendships, and girl scouting. Camp Low is "where girls grow strong".
Seasons & Capacity: Spring 150, Summer 150, Fall 150, Winter 150
Facilities: Cabins, Hiking Trails, Kitchen Facilities, Lodges, Playing Fields, Pool, Tents
Programs: Swimming (#768)

High Meadows (est 1973) ☀ 🚗

Roswell, GA (Fulton Co.); (770) 993-2940
John Milan Dovic, Director

Camp comments: Farm & forest setting. Buses from Metro Atlanta. Traditional active and reflective camp activities in the out-of-doors. Non-competitive, nurturing atmosphere.
Activities: Archery, Arts/Crafts, Canoeing, Challenge/Rope Courses, Counselor Training (CIT), Nature/Environment Studies, Performing Arts, Swimming — Instructional, Swimming — Recreational, Team Building
Session lengths & capacity: June-August; 2 & 3 week sessions; 270 campers
Clientele & fees: coed 3-14; Fees: C ☀
Contact: John M Dovic, Camp Director at (770) 993-2940; fax: (770) 993-8331
e-mail: jdovic@highmeadows.org
Web site: www.highmeadows.org
Operated by: Friends of High Meadows Inc, 1055 Willeo Road, Roswell, GA 30075-4131 at (770) 993-2940 (#3906)

Joe Corley American Karate ☀

Dunwoody, GA (DeKalb Co.); (770) 451-9900
Steve Voelkel, Director

Camp comments: A martial arts focused day camp. Art history forms kata weapons and more. Beginners welcome!
Activities: Arts/Crafts, Gymnastics, Martial Arts, Performing Arts
Session lengths & capacity: June-August; 1 & 2 week sessions; 45 campers
Clientele & fees: coed 5-12; Fees: B ☀
Contact: Steve Voelkel, Owner/Director at (770) 451-9900; fax: (770) 451-9225
e-mail: jckdunwoody@earthlink.net
Web site: www.TheDojoInfo.com
Operated by: American Karate Centers, 4478B Chamblee-Dunwoody Rd, Dunwoody, GA 30338 at (770) 451-9900 (#46719)

Lane Creek Farms Summer Camp (est 1990) ☀

Bogart, GA (Oconee Co.); (706) 769-9223
Mike Zacker-Co-director, Director

Camp comments: Come join the fun at Lane Creek Farms for a great summer! Daily activities include horseback riding, arts & crafts, swimming, nature trails, outdoor games, more
Activities: Arts/Crafts, Counselor Training (CIT), Farming/Ranching/Gardening, Field Trips, Horseback — English, Horseback — Western, Leadership Development, Music, Sports — Field & Team, Swimming — Recreational
Session lengths & capacity: June-August; 9 week sessions; 60 campers
Clientele & fees: coed 5-14; Fees: B ☀

Contact: e-mail: lanecreekfarm@aol.com
Operated by: Lane Creek Farms Summer Camp, 1950 Lane Creek Rd, Bogart, GA 30622 at (706) 769-9223 (#1591)

Pine Acres (est 1960)

Acworth, GA (Bartow Co.); (770) 975-9330
Laurel Martin, Director

Camp comments: Girl Scout camp near Atlanta. Located on beautiful lake. Campers enjoy strong aquatic and equestrian programs.
Activities: Archery, Arts/Crafts, Camping Skills/Outdoor Living, Canoeing, Drama, Horseback — English, Horseback — Western, Leadership Development, Sailing, Windsurfing
Session lengths & capacity: 1/2, 1 & 2 week sessions; 96 campers
Clientele & fees: girls 8-17; Fees: B, D
Contact: Laurel Martin, Camp Director at (770) 975-9330;
e-mail: nwggsc4@mindspring.com
Web site: www.girlscoutsnwga.org
Operated by: Girl Scout Cncl Northwest GA, 1577 Northeast Expressway, Atlanta, GA 30329 at (404) 527-7500 (#782)

Ramah Darom Inc

Clayton, GA
Rabbi Loren Sykes, Director
Activities: Aquatic Activities, Archery, Boating, Camping Skills/Outdoor Living, Canoeing, Challenge/Rope Courses, Climbing/Rappelling, Counselor Training (CIT), Field Trips, Swimming — Recreational
Contact: (404) 531-0801; fax: (404) 531-0450
e-mail: darom@inners.net
Web site: www.ramahdarom.org
Operated by: Ramah Darom Inc, 6075 Roswell Rd Ste 410, Atlanta, GA 30328 at (405) 531-0801
Group Rental Information
Site comments: 2 hours N of Atlanta, Ramah Darom is nestled in 122 beautiful acres in the GA mountains. The site has an inspiring waterfall, picturesque lake and modern accom.
Seasons & Capacity: Spring 600, Winter 80
Facilities: Cabins, Dorm-Style, Double Occupancy, Food Service, Hiking Trails, Lake, Linens, Lodges, Meeting Rooms, Playing Fields, Pool
Programs: Boating, Challenge/Ropes Course, Swimming (#30469)

Sandy Creek Day Camp (est 1989)

Athens, GA (Clarke Co.); (706) 613-3615

Camp comments: Focus: environmental education, natural science, land-based recreation &

outdoor skills, individual & team building opportunity.
Activities: Academics, Aquatic Activities, Archery, Boating, Camping Skills/Outdoor Living, Fishing, Hiking, Nature/Environment Studies, Swimming — Recreational, Team Building
Session lengths & capacity: 1 week sessions; 75 campers
Clientele & fees: coed 7-12; Fees: A
Contact: Mike Wharton, Day Camp Asst Director at (706) 613-3615; fax: (706) 613-3618
Operated by: Athens Clarke Co Leisure Servi, 205 Old Commerce Road, Athens, GA 30607 at (706) 613-3615 (#6559)

UAHC Camp Coleman (est 1962)

Cleveland, GA (White Co.); (706) 865-4111
Bobby Harris, Director

Camp comments: Program focuses on enriching young Jewish lives with an abundance of cultural, social, religious & recreational programs
Activities: Aquatic Activities, Arts/Crafts, Basketball, Bicycling/Biking, Challenge/Rope Courses, Hockey, Nature/Environment Studies, Team Building
Session lengths & capacity: June-August; 2, 4 & 8 week sessions; 400 campers
Clientele & fees: coed 7-16; Fees: E
Contact: Bobby Harris, Camp Director at (770) 671-8971; fax: (770) 671-0241
e-mail: campcole@aol.com
Operated by: Union American Hebrew Cong, 1580 Spalding Dr, Dunwoody, GA 30350 at (770) 671-8971
Group Rental Information
Facilities: Lake, Pool
Programs: Challenge/Ropes Course (#753)

Westminster Summer Camp

(est 1964)
Atlanta, GA (Fulton Co.); (404) 367-5108
Damian Kavanagh, Director
Activities: Archery, Arts/Crafts, Camping Skills/Outdoor Living, Canoeing, Challenge/Rope Courses, Counselor Training (CIT), Nature/Environment Studies, Riflery, Swimming — Instructional
Session lengths & capacity: June-July; 2 week sessions; 220 campers
Clientele & fees: coed 4-13; Fees: C
Contact: Damian Kavanagh, Director at (404) 609-6265;
e-mail: damiankavanagh@westminster.net
Operated by: The Westminster Schools, 1424 West Paces Ferry Rd, Atlanta, GA 30327 at (404) 355-8673 (#764)

WinShape for Boys and Girls

(est 1985)
Mt Berry, GA (Floyd Co.); (706) 238-7717
Rick Johnson, Director

Camp comments: Recreational program offering many activities with emphasis on Christian growth & character development.
Activities: Archery, Arts/Crafts, Basketball, Bicycling/Biking, Challenge/Rope Courses, Climbing/Rappelling, Horseback — English, Soccer, Swimming — Recreational, Tennis
Session lengths & capacity: June-August; 1 & 2 week sessions
Clientele & fees: boys 7-16; girls 7-16; Fees: F
Contact: Rick Johnson, Director at (800) 448-6955; fax: (706) 238-7742
e-mail: nhardin@berry.edu
Web site: www.winshape.com
Operated by: Winshape Foundation, Box 490009, Mt Berry, GA 30149 at (800) 448-6955 (#6422)

WOW Camp Glynn South Georgia (est 1987)

Brunswick, GA (Glynn Co.); (912) 261-0606
Eddie Cook, Director

Camp comments: Camp is located on a beautiful island. Emphasis placed on confidence-building and self-esteem. Outstanding staff.
Activities: Archery, Arts/Crafts, Basketball, Drama, Hiking, Leadership Development, Riflery, Sports — Field & Team, Swimming — Recreational, Team Building
Session lengths & capacity: June-August; 1 week sessions; 144 campers
Clientele & fees: coed 8-15; families; seniors; Fees: A
Contact: Eddie Cook, Fraternal Coordinator at (229) 436-8496; fax: (229) 438-8232
e-mail: ecook@woodmen.com
Operated by: WOW Life Insurance (SE), 1700 Farnam, Omaha, NE 68120 at (402) 271-7258 (#6251)

WOW Central GA (est 1965)

Gainesville, GA
James Jeffries, Director

Camp comments: Open to Woodmen Of the World members only.
Activities: Archery, Arts/Crafts, Canoeing, Challenge/Rope Courses, Counselor Training (CIT), Riflery, Swimming — Recreational
Session lengths & capacity: June-September; 1 week sessions; 150 campers
Clientele & fees: coed 8-15; seniors; Fees: A
Contact: James Jeffries, Fraternal Coordinator at (912) 746-4072; fax: (912) 746-5138
Operated by: WOW Life Insurance (SE), 1700 Farnam, Omaha, NE 68120 at (402) 271-7258 (#6258)

WOW I L Knight Youth Camp N GA

Gainsville, GA (Hall Co.)
Curtis Waters, Director
Activities: Aquatic Activities, Archery, Arts/Crafts, Baseball/Softball, Basketball, Canoeing, Riflery, Sports — Field & Team, Swimming — Recreational, Tennis
Session lengths & capacity: June-July; 150 campers
Clientele & fees: coed 8-15; families; seniors
Operated by: WOW Life Insurance (SE), 1700 Farnam, Omaha, NE 68120 at (402) 271-7258 (#32255)

YMCA Camp High Harbour Service (est 1942)

Clayton, GA (Rabun Co.); (706) 702-6311
Ken O Kelley, Director

Camp comments: Premier mountain and lakeside camp, providing a fun, safe, quality outdoor experience developing mind, body and spirit.
Activities: Archery, Boating, Horseback — English, Kayaking, Nature/Environment Studies, Rafting, Riflery, Tennis, Travel/Tour, Waterskiing
Session lengths & capacity: June-August; 1 week sessions; 250 campers
Clientele & fees: coed 7-17; Fees: E
Contact: Ken O Kelley, Director at (770) 532-2267; fax: (800) 954-5586
Web site: www.ymcaatlanta.org
Operated by: Metro Atlanta YMCA, 100 Edgewood Ave NE Ste 1100, Atlanta, GA 30303 at (404) 588-9622
Group Rental Information
Seasons & Capacity: Spring 250, Winter 250
Facilities: A/V Equipment, Cabins, Double Occupancy, Food Service, Hiking Trails, Kitchen Facilities, Lake, Lodges, Meeting Rooms, Ocean, Playing Fields

---

ICON LEGEND

☀ Day Camp
▲ Resident Camp
🏠 Facilities Available To Rent
🚐 Transportation Available
🐷 Financial Aid Available

FEE RANGES PER WEEK

A	$0-75
B	$75-200
C	$201-350
D	$351-500
E	$501-650
F	over $650

Programs: Boating, Challenge/Ropes Course, Horseback Riding (#5776)

Hawaii

Aloha Adventure Photo Camp

(est 1995)

Makawao, HI; (877) 755-2267
Kate Stanley, Director

Camp comments: Learn photography while exploring the 'Magic Isle' of Maui. Our photography instructors are all professionals photographers. Learn to Hula Dance too!
Activities: Boating, Caving, Field Trips, Hiking, Kayaking, Photography, SCUBA, Swimming — Recreational
Session lengths & capacity: July-August; 1, 2, 3 & 4 week sessions; 50 campers
Clientele & fees: coed 11-18; families; single adults; Fees: F ▲
Contact: Llew Lazarus, Camp Operations at (877) 755-2267; fax: (310) 391-7738
e-mail: llew@hawaiicamps.com
Web site: www.hawaiicamps.com
Operated by: Aloha Adventure Camps, 3825 McLaughlin Ave 201, Los Angeles, CA 90066-4081 at (877) 755-2267 (#39898)

Camp Mokuleia (est 1947)

Waialua, HI (Honolulu Co.); (808) 637-6241
David Close, Director

Camp comments: On scenic north shore off Oahu; Camp for all ages; conf center in splendid setting; food unbeatable. See you soon.
Activities: Aquatic Activities, Archery, Arts/Crafts, Camping Skills/Outdoor Living, Challenge/Rope Courses, Hiking, Horseback — English, International Culture, Leadership Development, Nature/Environment Studies
Session lengths & capacity: 1 & 2 week sessions; 100 campers
Clientele & fees: boys 7-17; girls 7-17; Fees: B ☀
Fees: C ▲ 🚌
Contact: Verta Betancours, Assistant Director at (808) 637-6241; fax: (808) 637-5505
e-mail: mokuleia@pixi.com
Web site: wwwcampmokuleia.com
Operated by: Camp Mokuleia Inc, 1418 5th Ave W, Henderson, NC 28739 at (808) 637-6241

Group Rental Information
Site comments: Ocean front cabins & lodge rooms on Oahu's north shore.
Facilities: Cabins, Food Service, Lodges, Ocean, Pool
Programs: Boating, Horseback Riding (#7731)

Camp Timberline

Kapolei, HI (Honolulu Co.); (808) 672-5441
Aaron Haneline, Director
Activities: Camping Skills/Outdoor Living, Challenge/Rope Courses, Hiking, Leadership Development, Nature/Environment Studies, SCUBA, Swimming — Recreational, Team Building, Travel/Tour, Wilderness Trips
Contact: Web site: www.kamaainakids.com
Operated by: Kama'aina Kids, 156 C Hamakua Dr, Kailua, HI 96734 at (808) 262-4538

Group Rental Information
Site comments: Environmental Ed & retreat programs help your group learn more about yourselves, others & the earth around you.
Facilities: Cabins, Hiking Trails, Kitchen Facilities, Meeting Rooms, Pool, Tents
Programs: Environmental Education (#12853)

Homelani (est 1942)

Waialua, HI (Oahu Co.); (808) 637-4131
Joe Harvey-Hall, Director

Camp comments: Beach camp in Hawaii. Christian emphasis, loving staff. Campers build self-esteem and recreational skills.
Activities: Arts/Crafts, Baseball/Softball, Basketball, Camping Skills/Outdoor Living, Drama, Football, Music, Religious Study, Soccer, Swimming — Recreational
Session lengths & capacity: 1 week sessions; 90 campers
Clientele & fees: boys 7-12; girls 7-12; coed 7-12; Fees: B ▲ 🚌
Contact: Barbie Harvey-Hall, Conference Director at (808) 637-4131; fax: (808) 637-7170
e-mail: homelani@aol.com
Web site: www.camphomelani.org
Operated by: The Salvation Army, 68-243 Olohio St, Waialua, HI 96791 at (808) 637-4131

Group Rental Information
Site comments: Quiet north shore beach setting. Large meeting room, great group getaway.
Seasons & Capacity: Spring 120, Fall 120, Winter 120
Facilities: Cabins, Double Occupancy, Food Service, Meeting Rooms, Ocean, Playing Fields, Tents
Programs: Environmental Education (#21)

Kama'aina Kids (est 1987)

Kailua, HI (Honolulu Co.); (808) 262-4538
Gregory S Harris, Director

Camp comments: Giving Children a greater sense of self, community, and earth thru hands-on activities, aquatics camp-outs and more!
Activities: Aquatic Activities, Arts/Crafts, Camping Skills/Outdoor Living, Canoeing, Drama, Field Trips, Kayaking, Nature/Environment Studies, Sailing, Swimming — Instructional
Session lengths & capacity: June-August; 1, 7 & 9 week sessions; 675 campers
Clientele & fees: coed 5-14; Fees: B ☀
Contact: Greg Harris, Program Director at (808) 262-4538; fax: (808) 261-2051
e-mail: info@kamaainakids.com
Web site: www.kamaainakids.com
Operated by: Kama'aina Kids, 156 C Hamakua Dr, Kailua, HI 96734 at (808) 262-4538 (#600)

Paumalu (est 1954)

Haleiwa, HI (Honolulu Co.); (808) 595-8400
Activities: Aquatic Activities, Arts/Crafts, Camping Skills/Outdoor Living, Counselor Training (CIT), Drawing/Painting, Leadership Development
Contact: Web site: www.girlscouts-hawaii.org
Operated by: GSC of Hawaii, 420 Wyllie St, Honolulu, HI 96817 at (808) 595-8400

Group Rental Information
Site comments: Located north shore of Oahu, 135 acres, 1 mile to main highway.
Facilities: Cabins, Food Service, Hiking Trails, Lodges, Pool, Tents (#22)

YWCA Camp Sloggett (est 1937)

Lihue, HI (Kauai Co.); (808) 245-5959
Roslynne Lowry, Director
Contact: Julia Krieger, Administrative Asst at (808) 245-5959; fax: (808) 245-5961
e-mail: info@campingkauai.com
Web site: www.campingkauai.com
Operated by: YWCA Camp Sloggett, Koke's State Park, 3094 Elua St, Lihue, HI 96766 at (808) 245-5959

Group Rental Information
Site comments: Mountain setting at 4000 ft. elevation on west side of Kauai. Close to 45 miles of maintained trails.

Facilities: Dorm-Style, Hiking Trails, Kitchen Facilities, Lodges, Meeting Rooms (#25599)

Idaho

Ascent

Sandpoint, ID; (208) 265-0607
Activities: Backpacking, Camping Skills/Outdoor Living, Challenge/Rope Courses, Climbing/Rappelling, Hiking, Leadership Development, Team Building, Wilderness Trips
Contact: Web site: www.cedu.com
Operated by: CEDU, 110 Main St, Sandpoint, ID 83864 at (208) 265-0607 (#11562)

Camp Cross (est 1923)

Coeur D Alene, ID; (208) 667-9596
Evita M Krislock, Director

Camp comments: Located on beautiful Lake Coeur D'Alene where individuals grow and share in their faith, while having an incredible time
Activities: Dance, Hiking, Leadership Development, Music, Nature/Environment Studies, Religious Study, Sailing, Sports — Field & Team, Swimming — Recreational, Waterskiing
Session lengths & capacity: 3 & 7 week sessions; 120 campers
Clientele & fees: boys 11-18; girls 11-18; coed 11-18; families; Fees: A, B ▲ 🚌
Contact: Evita M Krislock, Executive Director at (509) 624-5780; fax: (509) 747-0049
e-mail: theark4u@aol.com
Web site: www.campcross.com
Operated by: Episcopal Diocese of Spokane, 245 E 13th, Spokane, WA 99202 at (509) 624-3191

Group Rental Information
Facilities: Cabins, Food Service, Hiking Trails, Lake, Lodges, Meeting Rooms
Programs: Boating, Swimming (#14056)

Camp Hodia (est 1978)

Ketchum, ID; (208) 342-2774
Don Scott, Director

Camp comments: Sawtooth Mountains, loads of fun, friendship, one camp for teens, one for school age. Learn to live with diabetes.
Activities: Arts/Crafts, Bicycling/Biking, Canoeing, Climbing/Rappelling, Hiking, Horseback — Western, Rafting
Session lengths & capacity: 1 week sessions; 80 campers
Clientele & fees: coed 8-18; Fees: C ▲ 🚌
Contact: Don Scott, Director at (208) 336-6829; fax: (208) 387-2398
e-mail: info@hodia.com
Web site: www.hodia.com
Operated by: Idaho Diabetes Youth Programs, 2875 Mountain View Dr, Boise, ID 83704 at (208) 375-4333 (#5436)

Camp Lutherhaven (est 1945)

Coeur D Alene, ID (Kootenai Co.); (208) 667-3459
Bob Baker, Director

Camp comments: Christ-centered camp program on beautiful Lake Coeur d'Alene in North Idaho. Traditional programs plus outpost villages, high adventure, challenge course, & fun
Activities: Canoeing, Challenge/Rope Courses, Counselor Training (CIT), Leadership Development, Music, Nature/Environment Studies, Religious Study, Sailing, Swimming — Recreational
Session lengths & capacity: June-August; 1/2, 1 & 2 week sessions; 200 campers
Clientele & fees: boys 4-18; girls 4-18; coed 4-18; families; seniors; single adults; Fees: B, C ▲ 🚌
Contact: Robert Baker, Executive Director at (208) 667-3459; fax: (208) 765-1713

e-mail: onmicabay@juno.com
Web site: www.lutherhaven.com
Operated by: Inland NW Lutheran Outdoor Min, 3258 West Lutherhaven Rd, Coeur D Alene, ID 83814 at (208) 667-3459

Group Rental Information
Site comments: Christ-centered camp program on beautiful Lake Coeur d'Alene in North Idaho. Youth programs, challenge course, family retreats, outdoor education, group events.
Seasons & Capacity: Spring 200, Summer 200, Fall 200, Winter 200
Facilities: Cabins, Food Service, Hiking Trails, Lake, Lodges, Meeting Rooms, Playing Fields, Tents
Programs: Boating, Challenge/Ropes Course, Environmental Education, Swimming, Winter Sports (#7782)

Camp Rainbow Gold (est 1982) △

Ketchum, ID; (208) 726-4640
Tim Tyree, Director

Camp comments: Camp Rainbow Gold, a one week camp for children with cancer, accepts ages 6-16 from Idaho free of charge. Newly accredited in 2002 with score of 100%!
Activities: Archery, Arts/Crafts, Bicycling/Biking, Counselor Training (CIT), Fishing, Hiking, Horseback — Western, Sports — Field & Team, Swimming — Recreational, Team Building
Session lengths & capacity: August-August; 1 week sessions; 75 campers
Clientele & fees: boys 6-16; girls 6-16; coed 6-16; Fees: A △ 🐷
Contact: Sharon Buckle, Camp Manager at (208) 734-2425; fax: (208) 734-2425
e-mail: sharonbu@mvrmc.org
Operated by: ACS Camp Rainbow Gold, 357 Edwards Drive, Twin Falls, ID 83301 at (208) 734-2425 (#9016)

Luther Heights Bible Camp

(est 1952)   △ 🏠
Shoshone, ID (Blaine Co.); (208) 886-7657
Eric Olsen, Director

Camp comments: Traditional Bible camp + adventure camps and servant events located in beautiful mountains outstanding Christian staff.
Activities: Archery, Backpacking, Bicycling/Biking, Canoeing, Community Service, Horseback — English, Rafting, Religious Study, Team Building, Wilderness Trips
Session lengths & capacity: May-August; 1/2 & 1 week sessions; 90 campers
Clientele & fees: coed 6-18; Fees: B △
Contact: (208) 886-7657; fax: (208) 886-7657

ICON LEGEND

☀ Day Camp
△ Resident Camp
🏠 Facilities Available To Rent
🚐 Transportation Available
🐷 Financial Aid Available

FEE RANGES PER WEEK

A	$0-75
B	$75-200
C	$201-350
D	$351-500
E	$501-650
F	over $650

e-mail: lheights@micron.net
Web site: www.netnow.micron.net/~lheights
Operated by: Intermountain Lutheran Camping, HC 64 Box 9381, Ketchum, ID 83340 at (208) 774-3556

Group Rental Information
Site comments: Traditional Bible Camp + adventure camps and servant events located in beautiful mountains outstanding Christian Staff.
Seasons & Capacity: Summer 100, Winter 8
Facilities: Cabins, Food Service, Hiking Trails, Kitchen Facilities
Programs: Boating, Horseback Riding (#19207)

Sawtooth United Methodist Camp (est 1948) △ 🏠 🚐

Fairfield, ID (Camas Co.)
David Hargreaves, Director

Camp comments: Spectacular mountain setting. Rustic cabins; beautiful log lodge. Mountain bikes& trail onsite. On the Boise River.
Activities: Aquatic Activities, Arts/Crafts, Backpacking, Bicycling/Biking, Camping Skills/Outdoor Living, Counselor Training (CIT), Fishing, Hiking, Wilderness Trips
Session lengths & capacity: June-August; 1/2 & 1 week sessions; 100 campers
Clientele & fees: coed 8-18; families; single adults; Fees: B, C △ 🐷
Contact: Lisa Jean Hoefner, Executive Director at (503) 226-7931; fax: (503) 226-4158
e-mail: lisajean@umoi.org
Web site: www.gocamping.org
Operated by: UM Camps of OR-ID Conference, 1505 SW 18th Ave, Portland, OR 97201 at (503) 226-7931

Group Rental Information
Seasons & Capacity: Summer 100, Fall 100
Facilities: A/V Equipment, Cabins, Food Service, Hiking Trails, Kitchen Facilities, Meeting Rooms, Playing Fields, River (#12598)

Sweyolakan (est 1922) ☀ △ 🏠 🚐

Coeur D Alene, ID (Kootenai Co.); (208) 664-9327
Peggy Clark, Director

Camp comments: Coed camp on lake open to anyone looking for fun, excitement and great outdoor opportunities and special programs!
Activities: Archery, Arts/Crafts, Canoeing, Challenge/Rope Courses, Counselor Training (CIT), Hiking, Horseback — Western, Nature/Environment Studies, Sailing, Swimming — Recreational
Session lengths & capacity: June-August; 1/2, 1 & 2 week sessions; 200 campers
Clientele & fees: boys 6-18; girls 6-18; coed 6-18; families; Fees: C, D △ 🐷
Contact: Vi Martin, Executive Director at (509) 747-6191; fax: (509) 747-4913
Web site: www.campfireiec.org
Operated by: Camp Fire USA Inland Northwest, 524 N Mullan Road, Spokane, WA 99206-3864 at (509) 747-6191

Group Rental Information
Facilities: Kitchen Facilities, Lodges, Meeting Rooms
Programs: Boating, Challenge/Ropes Course, Swimming (#411)

Illinois

4H Camp Shaw-Waw-Nas-See

(est 1946)   △ 🏠
Manteno, IL (Kankakee Co.); (815) 933-3011
Jeff Althoff, Director

Camp comments: 50 yrs quality camping. Pool,adventure, nature, rec, crafts, farm, camp, garden, canoe, horseback, counselor training.

Activities: Archery, Arts/Crafts, Challenge/Rope Courses, Climbing/Rappelling, Counselor Training (CIT), Farming/Ranching/Gardening, Horseback — Western, Nature/Environment Studies, Team Building
Session lengths & capacity: June-August; 1/2 & 1 week sessions; 216 campers
Clientele & fees: coed 8-15; families; seniors; Fees: B △ 🐷
Contact: Jeff Althoff, Camp Director at (815) 933-3011; fax: (815) 933-3028
e-mail: campshaw@keynet.net
Web site: www.campshaw.org
Operated by: Northern Illinois 4H Camp Assn, 6641 N 6000W Road, Manteno, IL 60950 at (815) 933-3011

Group Rental Information
Seasons & Capacity: Spring 250, Summer 250, Fall 250, Winter 20
Facilities: Cabins, Food Service, Hiking Trails, Kitchen Facilities, Meeting Rooms, Playing Fields, Pool
Programs: Challenge/Ropes Course, Swimming (#4291)

4H Memorial Camp (est 1946) △ 🏠

Monticello, IL (Piatt Co.); (217) 762-2741
Curt Sinclair, Director

Camp comments: The finest in group camping. Beautiful setting adjacent to Robert Allerton Park. New log cabins. References available
Activities: Archery, Arts/Crafts, Basketball, Boating, Challenge/Rope Courses, Fishing, Hiking, Nature/Environment Studies, Swimming — Recreational, Team Building
Session lengths & capacity: 1/2 & 1 week sessions; 360 campers
Clientele & fees: coed 8-16; families; Fees: B △
Contact: Curt Sinclair, Camp Director at (217) 762-2741; fax: (217) 762-8613
e-mail: sinclairc@mail.aces.uiuc.edu
Operated by: University of Illinois, 499 Old Timber Road, Monticello, IL 61856

Group Rental Information
Site comments: The finest in traditional camping. Beautiful central IL.
Seasons & Capacity: Spring 75, Summer 360, Fall 75, Winter 75
Facilities: Cabins, Food Service, Lake, Lodges, Meeting Rooms
Programs: Boating, Environmental Education (#3556)

ADA Northern Illinois Day Camp

(est 1989)   ☀
Chicago, IL; (312) 346-1805
Suzanne Apsey, Director

Camp comments: Provides children opportunity to participate in summer activities while developing confidence in caring for their diabetes.
Activities: Arts/Crafts, Nature/Environment Studies, Swimming — Recreational, Team Building
Session lengths & capacity: June-August; 1 week sessions; 60 campers
Clientele & fees: coed 4-8; Fees: B ☀ 🐷
Contact: Suzanne Apsey, Program Director at (312) 346-1805 ext. 6567; fax: (312) 346-5342
e-mail: sapsey@diabetes.org
Operated by: Northern Illinois ADA, 30 N Michigan Ave Ste 2015, Chicago, IL 60602 at (312) 346-1805 (#31841)

ADA Triangle D Camp (est 1949) △

Ingleside, IL (Lake Co.); (847) 546-8086
Sue Apsey, Director

Camp comments: A special camp program combining summer activities, diabetes education and medical supervision.
Activities: Archery, Arts/Crafts, Baseball/Softball, Boating, Challenge/Rope Courses, Soccer, Swimming — Recreational

Session lengths & capacity: August-August;
1 week sessions; 110 campers
Clientele & fees: boys 8-13; girls 8-13; coed 8-13;
Fees: D △ 🐷
Contact: Sue Apsey, Program Director at
(312) 346-1805 ext. 6567; fax: (312) 346-5342
e-mail: sapsey@diabetes.org
Operated by: Northern Illinois ADA, 30 N Michigan
Ave Ste 2015, Chicago, IL 60602 at (312) 346-1805
(#14906)

Albany Park Community Center

(est 1975)

Chicago, IL; (773) 509-9139
Goyce Rates & Tim O'Donahue, Director

Camp comments: Day camp is conducted at the
beautiful wooded Bunker Hill Forest Preserve. The
program emphasis is social development.
Activities: Arts/Crafts, Baseball/Softball, Basketball,
Computer, Drama, Drawing/Painting, Field Trips,
Soccer, Swimming — Recreational
Session lengths & capacity: June-August; 8 week
sessions; 70 campers
Clientele & fees: coed 6-12; Fees: A ☀ 🐷
Contact: Scott McNally, Program Director at
(773) 583-5111; fax: (773) 583-5062
e-mail: scott@gateway.net
Web site: www.albanyparkcommunitycenter.org
Operated by: Albany Park Community Center, 3403
W Lawerence, Chicago, IL 60625 at (773) 583-5111
(#3124)

Alfred Campanelli YMCA Day Cmp

Schaumburg, IL (Cook Co.); (847) 891-9622
Glynn Walker, Youth & Family Director, Director

Camp comments: YMCA Camp Campanelli is
for campers who want a traditional setting with
many activities available. For ages 5-14 we have
something for everyone!
Activities: Aquatic Activities, Arts/Crafts,
Community Service, Drama, Field Trips,
International Culture, Nature/Environment Studies,
Sports — Field & Team, Swimming — Recreational,
Team Building
Session lengths & capacity: June-August; 9 week
sessions
Clientele & fees: coed 5-14; Fees: B ☀ 🐷
Contact: Glynn Walker, Youth and Family Director
at (847) 891-9622; fax: (847) 891-8901
e-mail: glynnw@campanelliymca.org
Web site: www.alfredcampanelli.org
Operated by: Alfred Campanelli YMCA, 300 W
Wise Rd, Schaumburg, IL 60193 at (847) 891-9622
(#47666)

Anita M Stone JCC Day Camp

(est 1972)

Flossmoor, IL (Cook Co.); (708) 799-7650
Laurie Goldberg, Director

Camp comments: Stone Camp offers innovative
programming on 10 acres of wooded land. Swim
lessons, art, sports and adventure programs.
Activities: Baseball/Softball, Basketball,
Ceramics/Pottery, Challenge/Rope Courses,
Climbing/Rappelling, Drama, Field Trips, Sports —
Field & Team, Swimming — Instructional,
Swimming — Recreational
Session lengths & capacity: 4, 6 & 8 week
sessions; 500 campers
Clientele & fees: coed 5-15; Fees: B ☀ 🐷
Contact: Laura M Goldberg &Ari Riekes, Camp
Directors at (708) 799-7650; fax: (708) 799-7673
Operated by: JCC of Chicago, 3050 Woodridge
Rd, Northbrook, IL 60062 at (847) 272-7050
(#3829)

Austin YMCA

Chicago, IL (Cook Co.); (773) 287-9120
Lashawnda Loyd, Director
Activities: Academics, Arts/Crafts,
Baseball/Softball, Basketball, Counselor Training
(CIT), Field Trips, Nature/Environment Studies,
Swimming — Recreational
Session lengths & capacity: August-August; 1, 2
& 4 week sessions; 80 campers
Clientele & fees: boys 5-12; girls 5-12; coed 5-12;
Fees: B ☀
Contact: Lashawnda Loyd, Youth Development
Director at (773) 287-9120; fax: (773) 287-3661
e-mail: lashawndaloydymca@hotmail.com
Operated by: YMCA Of Metropolitan Chicago, 801
N Dearborn St, Chicago, IL 60610 at
(312) 932-1200 (#28871)

Banner Day Camp Inc

(est 1964)

Lake Forest, IL (Lake Co.); (847) 295-4900
Allen & Helen Schwartz, Director

Camp comments: A dynamic, spirited program
emphasizes self-esteem thru skill development in a
non-competitive, fun environment. Adventure thru
aquatics, climbing walls & more!
Activities: Arts/Crafts, Baseball/Softball, Basketball,
Gymnastics, Music, Performing Arts, Soccer, Sports
— Field & Team, Swimming — Instructional,
Swimming — Recreational
Session lengths & capacity: June-August; 4 &
8 week sessions
Clientele & fees: coed 3-12
Contact: Camp Office at (847) 295-4900;
fax: (847) 295-0995
e-mail: bannercamp@aol.com
Operated by: Banner Day Camp Inc, 1225
Riverwoods Road, Lake Forest, IL 60045-3461 at
(847) 295-4900 (#8335)

Buehler YMCA Day Camp

(est 1969)

Palatine, IL (Cook Co.); (847) 359-2400
Robin Wagner, Director
Activities: Aquatic Activities, Baseball/Softball,
Basketball, Counselor Training (CIT), Field Trips,
Football, Gymnastics, Nature/Environment Studies,
Sailing, Team Building
Contact: Robin Wagner, Teen & Family Director at
(847) 359-2400 ext. 326; fax: (847) 359-5098
Operated by: YMCA Of Metropolitan Chicago, 801
N Dearborn St, Chicago, IL 60610 at
(312) 932-1200 (#1644)

Burbank Park District Day Camp

Burbank, IL (Cook Co.); (708) 599-2070
April Samonski, Director
Activities: Academics, Aquatic Activities,
Arts/Crafts, Counselor Training (CIT), Field Trips,
Performing Arts, Soccer, Swimming — Recreational
Session lengths & capacity: June-August; 9 week
sessions
Clientele & fees: coed 3-12; Fees: A ☀ 🐷
Contact: Tammy Stefanatos, Recreation Supervisor
at (708) 599-2070; fax: (708) 599-2063
Operated by: Burbank Park District Day Camp,
8050 South Newcastle, Burbank, IL 60459 at
(708) 559-2070 (#31772)

Camp Algonquin (est 1907)

Algonquin, IL (McHenry Co.); (708) 658-8212
Penny Friedberg, Director

Camp comments: Residential program offers a
unique multicultural experience for low income
populations,1-90.Year round retreat/educ ctr

Activities: Aquatic Activities, Arts/Crafts, Boating,
Canoeing, Challenge/Rope Courses,
Nature/Environment Studies, Swimming —
Recreational, Team Building
Session lengths & capacity: June-August; 8 week
sessions; 120 campers
Clientele & fees: boys 1-14; girls 1-14; coed 1-14;
families; seniors; single adults; Fees: A △ 🐷
Contact: Penyy Friedberg, Summer Camp Director
at (847) 658-8212; fax: (847) 658-8431
e-mail: info@campalgonquin.org
Web site: www.campalgonquin.org
Operated by: Camp Algonquin, 1889 Cary Rd,
Algonquin, IL 60102 at (847) 658-8212
Group Rental Information
Seasons & Capacity: Summer 100
Facilities: Cabins, Dorm-Style, Food Service,
Hiking Trails, Pool, River (#8329)

Camp Dean (est 1947)

Big Rock, IL (Kane Co.); (630) 556-3122
Joy Rosenberg, Director

Camp comments: Beautifully wooded 160 acre
camp 50 miles from chicago with pool; lake access
for boating/canoeing. Girls live in platform tents;
both GS and non-GS are welcome
Activities: Aquatic Activities, Archery, Arts/Crafts,
Boating, Camping Skills/Outdoor Living, Canoeing,
Golf, Nature/Environment Studies, Sports — Field &
Team, Swimming — Recreational
Session lengths & capacity: June-August; 1/2 &
1 week sessions; 84 campers
Clientele & fees: girls 7-11; Fees: B △ 🐷
Contact: Joy Rosenberg, Outdoor Program &
Education Director at (630) 897-1565;
fax: (630) 466-7018
e-mail: joy@fvgsc.org
Web site: www.fvgsc.org
Operated by: Girl Scouts of Fox Valley Cncl, 200
New Bond St, Aurora, IL 60506 at (630) 897-1565
Group Rental Information
Facilities: Cabins, Hiking Trails, Tents (#1681)

Camp Forever (est 1949)

Yorkville, IL; (630) 553-7361
Laura G. McNeece, Director

Camp comments: A special camp for children with
disabilities with activities adapted to their abilities in
a safe environment.
Activities: Arts/Crafts, Counselor Training (CIT),
Music, Nature/Environment Studies, Sports — Field
& Team, Swimming — Recreational
Session lengths & capacity: August-August;
1 week sessions; 50 campers
Clientele & fees: coed 5-18; Fees: D △
Contact: Laura G McNeece, Camp Director at
(630) 844-5040 ext. 203; fax: (630) 859-1229
e-mail: lmcneece@the-association.org
Web site: www.the-association.org
Operated by: Association for Individual Dev, 309 W
New Indian Trail Ct, Aurora, IL 60506 at
(630) 844-5040 (#3867)

Camp Greene Wood

Naperville, IL (DuPage Co.); (630) 963-6050

Camp comments: The program offered at Camp
Greene Wood aspires to help the Girl Scouts of
DuPage County Council "discover the fun,
friendship and power of girls together."
Activities: Arts/Crafts, Backpacking,
Bicycling/Biking, Camping Skills/Outdoor Living,
Canoeing, Hiking, Leadership Development,
Nature/Environment Studies, Snow Sports, Team
Building
Session lengths & capacity: June-August; 1 week
sessions; 400 campers
Clientele & fees: girls 6-17; Fees: B ☀ 🐷
Contact: Leslie Worcester, Program Manager at
(630) 544-5900 ext. 5976; fax: (630) 544-5999
e-mail: leslie@girlscoutsofdupage.org
Web site: www.girlscoutsofdupage.org

Operated by: GS of DuPage County Council, 8S 021 Route 53, Naperville, IL 60540 at (630) 963-6050 (#45199)

Camp Little Giant (est 1953) ⚊ 🏠

Carbondale, IL (Jackson Co.); (618) 453-1121
Randwick Osborn, Director

Camp comments: 45 yrs of service enabling people with disabilities to experience nature, build self-esteem make friends & enjoy life.
Activities: Arts/Crafts, Boating, Camping Skills/Outdoor Living, Hiking, Horseback — Western, Leadership Development, Nature/Environment Studies, Swimming — Recreational, Travel/Tour, Wilderness Trips
Session lengths & capacity: 1, 2 & 4 week sessions; 110 campers
Clientele & fees: boys 8-80; girls 8-80; coed 8-80; families; seniors; single adults; Fees: D, E, F ⚊ 🐖
Contact: Chilang Lawless, Registrar at (618) 453-1121; fax: (618) 453-1188
e-mail: tonec@siu.edu
Web site: www.pso.siu.edu/tonec
Operated by: Southern Illinois University, Touch of Nature Environmental, Mailcode 6888, Carbondale, IL 62901-6888 at (618) 453-1121

Group Rental Information
Site comments: We provide a 48 year tradition of recreation, education, and community to people of special needs.
Seasons & Capacity: Spring 50, Summer 50, Fall 50, Winter 50
Facilities: A/V Equipment, Cabins, Dorm-Style, Double Occupancy, Food Service, Hiking Trails, Lake, Linens, Lodges, Meeting Rooms, Playing Fields, Tents
Programs: Boating, Challenge/Ropes Course, Environmental Education, Horseback Riding, Swimming (#1)

Camp Medill McCormick

(est 1940) ☀ ⚊ 🏠

Stillman Valley, IL (Ogle Co.); (815) 234-8622
Vickie Thomas, Director

Camp comments: Beautiful woodland. Trained, supportive staff. Learning environment, emphasis on friends, teamwork, nature, independence
Activities: Aquatic Activities, Archery, Arts/Crafts, Camping Skills/Outdoor Living, Canoeing, Dance, Drama, Horseback — Western, Nature/Environment Studies, Team Building
Session lengths & capacity: June-August; 1/2 & 1 week sessions; 150 campers
Clientele & fees: girls 5-17; families; seniors; Fees: B ☀ Fees: B, C, D ⚊

ICON LEGEND

☀	Day Camp
⚊	Resident Camp
🏠	Facilities Available To Rent
🚗	Transportation Available
🐖	Financial Aid Available

FEE RANGES PER WEEK

A	$0-75
B	$75-200
C	$201-350
D	$351-500
E	$501-650
F	over $650

Contact: Vickie Thomas, Camp Director/Program Specialist at (815) 962-5591 ext. 133; fax: (815) 962-5658
e-mail: vthomas@girlscoutsrrv.org
Operated by: Girl Scout Rock Rvr Valley Cnl, 2101 Auburn St, Rockford, IL 61103 at (815) 962-5591

Group Rental Information
Site comments: Beautiful wooded site, varied ecosystems,pools,tepees,teams course,platform,tents,lodges,dining hall with kitchen.
Seasons & Capacity: Spring 60, Summer 60, Fall 60, Winter 60
Facilities: A/V Equipment, Cabins, Dorm-Style, Food Service, Hiking Trails, Kitchen Facilities, Lodges, Meeting Rooms, Pool, River, Tents
Programs: Swimming (#1548)

Camp Ondessonk (est 1959) ⚊ 🏠 🚗

Ozark, IL (Johnson Co.); (618) 695-2489
Patrick R Higgins, Director

Camp comments: Catholic camping in the Shawnee National Forest. Rustic adventuresome program. Live in treehouses, cabins, horses, hiking, caves, and water fun!
Activities: Aquatic Activities, Archery, Arts/Crafts, Camping Skills/Outdoor Living, Challenge/Rope Courses, Hiking, Horseback — Western, Nature/Environment Studies, Riflery
Session lengths & capacity: June-August; 1/2 & 1 week sessions; 396 campers
Clientele & fees: boys 9-15; girls 9-15; coed 9-15; Fees: C ⚊ 🐖
Contact: Carol Simmons, Office Manager at (618) 695-2489; fax: (618) 695-3593
e-mail: camp@midwest.net
Web site: www.ondessonk.com
Operated by: Camp Ondessonk, 3760 Ondessonk Road, Ozark, IL 62972 at (618) 695-2489

Group Rental Information
Site comments: Camping in the Shawnee National Forest! Outdoor edcuation & recreation programs. Retreats and time to explore the beauty of God's creation in southern Illinois.
Seasons & Capacity: Spring 400, Summer 400, Fall 400, Winter 100
Facilities: Cabins, Dorm-Style, Double Occupancy, Food Service, Hiking Trails, Kitchen Facilities, Lake, Lodges
Programs: Boating, Challenge/Ropes Course, Environmental Education, Horseback Riding (#408)

Camp Tu-Endie-Wei

(est 1929) ☀ ⚊ 🏠

Elgin, IL (Kane Co.); (847) 742-2169
Laura Nolan de Galindo, Director
Activities: Archery, Camping Skills/Outdoor Living, Canoeing, Challenge/Rope Courses, Counselor Training (CIT), Field Trips, Horseback — English, Nature/Environment Studies
Contact: Web site: www.geocities.com/tuendiewei
Operated by: Young Womens Christian Assoc, 220 E Chicago St, Elgin, IL 60120 at (847) 742-7930

Group Rental Information
Site comments: The lodge is nestled in a natural forest area. Camp program emphasizes nature exploration, friendship, & self-esteem.
Seasons & Capacity: Spring 110, Summer 110, Fall 80, Winter 80
Facilities: Cabins, Dorm-Style, Hiking Trails, Kitchen Facilities, Lake, Lodges, Meeting Rooms, Playing Fields, Tents
Programs: Environmental Education (#1631)

Camp Tuckabatchee

(est 1927) ☀ ⚊ 🏠

Ottawa, IL (LaSalle Co.); (815) 433-2984
Kelly Bunnell, Director

Camp comments: Independent, not for profit, co-ed youth camp. Rustic cabins; traditional camping program.150 acres of unspoiled nature.
Activities: Archery, Arts/Crafts, Camping Skills/Outdoor Living, Canoeing, Counselor Training (CIT), Hiking, Horseback — Western, Nature/Environment Studies, SCUBA, Swimming — Recreational
Session lengths & capacity: June-August; 1 week sessions; 120 campers
Clientele & fees: coed 7-15; families; Fees: A, B ☀ Fees: C ⚊
Contact: Kelly Bunnell, Executive Director at (815) 433-2984; fax: (815) 433-3493
e-mail: tuckabatchee@indianvalley.com
Operated by: Camp Tuckabatchee, 1973 N 35th Rd, Ottawa, IL 61350 at (815) 433-2984

Group Rental Information
Site comments: Limited area for winter retreats, spring and fall, full access, reasonable rates,rustic setting, cabins and lodges.
Seasons & Capacity: Spring 120, Fall 30, Winter 30
Facilities: Cabins, Hiking Trails, Kitchen Facilities, Pool
Programs: Horseback Riding, Swimming (#1593)

Camp White Eagle Inc

(est 1950) ⚊ 🏠

Leaf River, IL (Ogle Co.); (815) 738-2754
Erin V. DeVore, Director
Activities: Archery, Arts/Crafts, Boating, Canoeing, Climbing/Rappelling, Hiking, Nature/Environment Studies, Riflery, Swimming — Recreational
Session lengths & capacity: March-October; 1 & 2 week sessions; 145 campers
Clientele & fees: coed 8-15
Operated by: Camp White Eagle Inc, 6903 W White Ealge Rd, Leaf River, IL 61047 at (815) 738-2754

Group Rental Information
Site comments: Custom designed camp, tripping and retreat programs. Organizational team-building is our specialty.
Seasons & Capacity: Spring 60, Summer 145, Fall 60
Facilities: Cabins, Food Service, Hiking Trails, Lake, Lodges, Meeting Rooms, Playing Fields, Pool, River
Programs: Boating, Challenge/Ropes Course, Swimming (#4289)

Camp Widjiwagan (est 1936) ☀ ⚊ 🏠

Springfield, IL (Sangamon Co.); (217) 529-2212
Cathy Annerino, Director

Camp comments: Program emphasis on teaching & encouraging cooperation, responsibility & creativity. GS values in the outdoors.
Activities: Arts/Crafts, Bicycling/Biking, Camping Skills/Outdoor Living, Canoeing, Counselor Training (CIT), Hiking, Horseback — English, Leadership Development, Swimming — Recreational
Session lengths & capacity: June-August; 1/2, 1 & 2 week sessions; 120 campers
Clientele & fees: girls 7-17; Fees: B ⚊
Contact: Cathy Annerino, Camp Administrator at (217) 523-8159; fax: (217) 523-8321
e-mail: gsllc@girlscoutsllc.org
Web site: www.girlscoutsllc.org
Operated by: Land of Lincoln GSC, 3020 Baker Drive, Springfield, IL 62703 at (217) 523-8159

Group Rental Information
Seasons & Capacity: Spring 220, Winter 64
Facilities: Kitchen Facilities, Lodges, Tents (#1056)

Carew (est 1952) ☀ ⚊ 🏠

Makanda, IL (Williamson Co.); (618) 457-5596
Dr. Richard Ryman, Director

Camp comments: A Presbyterian Camp for Southeastern Illinois.

Activities: Aquatic Activities, Camping Skills/Outdoor Living, Climbing/Rappelling, Counselor Training (CIT), Hiking, Horseback — Western, Leadership Development, Nature/Environment Studies, Religious Study, Sailing
Session lengths & capacity: 1/2 & 1 week sessions; 48 campers
Clientele & fees: coed 6-18; families; Fees: **B** ▲
Contact: Dr. Richard Ryman, Director at (618) 893-2039;
Operated by: Camp Carew Office, PO Box 172, Cobden, IL 62920 at (618) 893-2039
Group Rental Information
Facilities: Cabins, Dorm-Style, Hiking Trails, Kitchen Facilities, Lake, Meeting Rooms, Playing Fields (#3800)

Crystal Lake Park Dist Camp ☼

Crystal Lake, IL (mchenry Co.); (815) 459-0680
Activities: Archery, Arts/Crafts, Canoeing, Counselor Training (CIT), Field Trips, Fishing, Leadership Development, Soccer, Swimming — Instructional, Team Building
Session lengths & capacity: June-August; 2 week sessions; 450 campers
Clientele & fees: coed 5-14; Fees: **B** ☼ 🚌
Contact: Sam Thompson or S Chase, Recreation Supervisor and Asst Director at (815) 459-0680 ext. 220; fax: (815) 477-5005
Web site: www.crystallakeparks.org
Operated by: Crystal Lake Park District, 1 E Crystal Lake Ave, Crystal Lake, IL 60014 at (815) 459-0680 (#46703)

Decoma Day Camp Inc ☼ 🚌

(est 1949)
Northbrook, IL (Cook Co.); (847) 272-2267
Gary and Eugene Deutsch, Director
Camp comments: Non-competitive, warm and genuine attitude in working with children.Teaching of skills is an easy way to reach children.
Activities: Arts/Crafts, Baseball/Softball, Basketball, Dance, Drama, Gymnastics, Soccer, Sports — Field & Team, Swimming — Instructional, Tennis
Session lengths & capacity: June-August; 4, 6 & 8 week sessions; 320 campers
Clientele & fees: coed 3-13; Fees: **C, D** ☼
Contact: Gary or Eugene Deutsch, Owners at (847) 272-2267; fax: (847) 945-2131
e-mail: decomadaycamp@aol.com
Operated by: Decoma Day Camp Inc, 3851 N Mission Hills Rd Apt405, Northbrook, IL 60062 at (847) 272-2267 (#1683)

Discovery Day Camp Inc ☼ 🚌

(est 1984)
Lincolnshire, IL (Lake Co.); (847) 367-2267
David & Ilise Schwartzwald, Director
Camp comments: Fun while gaining skills & self-esteem. Supportive environment emphasizes swimming, fine arts, sports, nature, ropes course and special events.
Activities: Arts/Crafts, Basketball, Challenge/Rope Courses, Gymnastics, Nature/Environment Studies, Sports — Field & Team, Swimming — Instructional, Swimming — Recreational
Session lengths & capacity: June-August; 4 & 8 week sessions; 282 campers
Clientele & fees: coed 4-11; Fees: **D** ☼
Contact: Ilise & David Schwartzwald, Executive Directors at (847) 367-2267; fax: (847) 367-4202
e-mail: inquiry@campdiscovery.com
Web site: www.CampDiscovery.com
Operated by: Discovery Day Camp Inc, PO Box 753, Lincolnshire, IL 60069 at (847) 367-2267 (#6571)

DuBois Center (est 1965) ▲ 🏠

Du Bois, IL (Washington Co.); (618) 787-2202
Kerry Bean, Director
Camp comments: Year-round retreat & conference center. Serving schools, churches & other groups. We offer outdoor education.
Activities: Archery, Arts/Crafts, Canoeing, Challenge/Rope Courses, Horseback — Western, Nature/Environment Studies, Swimming — Recreational, Team Building, Travel/Tour
Session lengths & capacity: June-August; 1/2 & 1 week sessions; 100 campers
Clientele & fees: coed 7-18; Fees: **B** ▲
Contact: Rev Kerry Bean, Director of Outdoor Ministry at (618) 787-2202; fax: (618) 787-7701
e-mail: duboisce@midwest.net
Web site: www.duboiscenter.org
Operated by: Illinois South Conference UCC, PO Box 325, Highland, IL 62249 at (618) 654-2125
Group Rental Information
Site comments: We provice a wide variety of opportunities for spiritual growth and recreation.
Facilities: A/V Equipment, Cabins, Food Service, Hiking Trails, Kitchen Facilities, Lake, Linens, Lodges, Meeting Rooms, Playing Fields, Tents
Programs: Boating, Challenge/Ropes Course, Environmental Education, Horseback Riding, Swimming (#1052)

Duncan YMCA Day Camp

(est 1851) ☼ 🚐

Chicago, IL (Cook Co.); (312) 421-7800
John Perkins, Director
Camp comments: A day camp where children take part in activities that broaden horizons and encourage creative expression.
Activities: Academics, Computer, Dance, Drama, Drawing/Painting, Field Trips, Leadership Development, Music, Nature/Environment Studies, Swimming — Recreational
Session lengths & capacity: 1 week sessions; 130 campers
Clientele & fees: boys 6-13; girls 6-13; coed 6-13; Fees: **B** ☼ 🚌
Contact: Mary Irvin, Administrative Director at (312) 421-7800; fax: (312) 421-1805
e-mail: mary.irvin@ymcachgo.org
Operated by: YMCA Of Metropolitan Chicago, 801 N Dearborn St, Chicago, IL 60610 at (312) 932-1200 (#5449)

East Bay Camp ▲ 🏠

Hudson, IL; (309) 365-7531
Marshall Fowler, Director
Activities: Aquatic Activities, Arts/Crafts, Canoeing, Community Service, Counselor Training (CIT), Leadership Development, Religious Study, Sailing, Team Building
Operated by: Illinois Great Rivers Conf, 2144 S MacArthur Blvd Ste 2B, Springfield, IL 61704 at (217) 747-0720
Group Rental Information
Seasons & Capacity: Spring 275, Summer 500, Fall 275, Winter 250
Facilities: A/V Equipment, Cabins, Dorm-Style, Double Occupancy, Food Service, Hiking Trails, Kitchen Facilities, Lake, Linens, Lodges, Meeting Rooms, Playing Fields, Pool
Programs: Boating, Challenge/Ropes Course, Swimming (#47322)

Elmhurst Family YMCA ☼

Elmhurst, IL (Dupage Co.); (630) 834-9220
Lori Riley, Director
Camp comments: To build mind, body, and spirit
Activities: Arts/Crafts, Baseball/Softball, Basketball, Counselor Training (CIT), Field Trips, Leadership Development, Nature/Environment Studies, Soccer, Swimming — Instructional

Session lengths & capacity: June-August; 1 week sessions; 100 campers
Clientele & fees: coed 5-12; Fees: **B** ☼
Contact: Lori Riley, Child Care & Family Service Director at (630) 834-9220;
Operated by: YMCA Of Metropolitan Chicago, 801 N Dearborn St, Chicago, IL 60610 at (312) 932-1200 (#27105)

Farm & Ranch Camps at the Ctr (est 1936) ▲

Palos Park, IL (Cook Co.); (708) 361-3650
Lois Lauer, Director
Camp comments: 60 acre farm in suburban Chicago with horses, farm animals, woods, creeks, nature study, crafts, and outdoor fun. All learn to ride. Teens get their own horse.
Activities: Arts/Crafts, Camping Skills/Outdoor Living, Counselor Training (CIT), Farming/Ranching/Gardening, Horseback — Western, Nature/Environment Studies
Session lengths & capacity: June-August; 2 week sessions; 32 campers
Clientele & fees: coed 9-15; Fees: **D** ▲ 🚌
Contact: Lois Lauer, Camp Director at (708) 361-3650; fax: (708) 361-2811
e-mail: centerpalospark@aol.com
Web site: www.thecenter-palospark.org
Operated by: The Center, 12700 Southwest Hwy, Palos Park, IL 60464-1812 at (708) 361-3650 (#1570)

Foglia YMCA Day Camp ☼

Lake Zurich, IL; (847) 438-5300
Angie Flesch, Director
Activities: Arts/Crafts, Camping Skills/Outdoor Living, Counselor Training (CIT), Golf, Leadership Development, Sports — Field & Team, Swimming — Recreational
Contact: Angie Flesh, Youth & Family Director at (847) 438-5300; fax: (847) 438-4605
Operated by: YMCA Of Metropolitan Chicago, 801 N Dearborn St, Chicago, IL 60610 at (312) 932-1200 (#29660)

Granada (est 1976) ▲

Monticello, IL (Piatt Co.); (217) 762-2741
Ken Cook, Director
Camp comments: A special camp for children with diabetes. 2 to 1 camper/staff ratio.
Activities: Archery, Arts/Crafts, Canoeing, Challenge/Rope Courses, Counselor Training (CIT), Dance, Nature/Environment Studies, Swimming — Recreational
Session lengths & capacity: 1 week sessions; 120 campers
Clientele & fees: boys 8-17; girls 8-17; Fees: **C** ▲ 🚌
Contact: Donna Scott, Executive Director at (217) 875-9011; fax: (217) 875-6849
Operated by: Am Diabetes Assn Downstate, 2580 Federal Drive Suite 403, Decatur, IL 62526 at (217) 875-9011 (#14315)

Greater Roseland YMCA Day Camp (est 1996) ☼

Chicago, IL (Cook Co.); (773) 785-9210
Eric Johnson, Director
Camp comments: Pure excitement would be the best description of Greater Roseland Family YMCA Adventure Camp.
Activities: Academics, Basketball, Field Trips, Football
Session lengths & capacity: June-August; 9 week sessions; 50 campers
Clientele & fees: coed 6-13; families; seniors; single adults; Fees: **B** ☼ 🚌
Contact: Marcla Wright, Day Camp Director at (773) 785-9210; fax: (773) 785-9407

Operated by: YMCA Of Metropolitan Chicago, 801 N Dearborn St, Chicago, IL 60610 at (312) 932-1200 (#27099)

Hastings Lake YMCA Camps

(est 1922) ☀ ᴀ ⌂ 🚐

Lake Villa, IL (Lake Co.); (847) 356-4001
Shawn Bacon, Director

Camp comments: On 350 acres & 80 acre lake, our many activities give campers a chance to learn & grow in a safe, nurturing environment.
Activities: Boating, Climbing/Rappelling, Counselor Training (CIT), Golf, Horseback — English, Horseback — Western, Skating, Swimming — Instructional, Waterskiing, Windsurfing
Session lengths & capacity: June-August; 1, 2 & 4 week sessions; 220 campers
Clientele & fees: coed 8-16; Fees: **B** ☀
Fees: **C, D** ᴀ 🐖
Contact: Shawn Bacon, Camp Director at (847) 356-4001; fax: (847) 356-7591
e-mail: hastings@lnd.com
Operated by: YMCA Of Metropolitan Chicago, 801 N Dearborn St, Chicago, IL 60610 at (312) 932-1200

Group Rental Information

Site comments: 1 hr north of Chicago. Facilities for group camping year round, professional staff. Complete food service.
Seasons & Capacity: Spring 700, Summer 200, Fall 700, Winter 700
Facilities: Cabins, Food Service, Hiking Trails, Lake, Linens, Lodges, Meeting Rooms, Playing Fields, Pool
Programs: Boating, Challenge/Ropes Course, Environmental Education, Horseback Riding, Swimming, Winter Sports (#1680)

High Ridge YMCA Day Camp ☀

Chicago, IL (Cook Co.); (773) 262-8300
Michiye Morishige, Director
Activities: Aquatic Activities, Arts/Crafts, Counselor Training (CIT), Field Trips, Leadership Development, Swimming — Instructional, Swimming — Recreational
Session lengths & capacity: June-August; 1, 2 & 9 week sessions; 250 campers
Clientele & fees: coed 6-16; Fees: **B** ☀ 🐖
Contact: Mickie Morishige, Senior Program Director at (773) 262-8300; fax: (773) 262-7902
Operated by: YMCA Of Metropolitan Chicago, 801 N Dearborn St, Chicago, IL 60610 at (312) 932-1200 (#27102)

ICON LEGEND

☀	Day Camp
ᴀ	Resident Camp
⌂	Facilities Available To Rent
🚐	Transportation Available
🐖	Financial Aid Available

FEE RANGES PER WEEK

A	$0-75
B	$75-200
C	$201-350
D	$351-500
E	$501-650
F	over $650

Illinois Fire Safety Alliance

(est 1991) ᴀ 🚐

Ingleside, IL (Lake Co.)
Kathleen Haage, Director

Camp comments: IFSA Burn Camp is the setting for burn survivors to share common experiences, make new friends and enjoy camp activities
Activities: Aquatic Activities, Archery, Arts/Crafts, Basketball, Bicycling/Biking, Challenge/Rope Courses, Climbing/Rappelling, Horseback — Western, Radio/TV/Video, Swimming — Recreational
Session lengths & capacity: June-June; 1 week sessions; 100 campers
Clientele & fees: coed 8-16; Fees: **A** ᴀ 🐖
Contact: Mary Werderitch, Executive Director,IFSA at (847) 390-0911; fax: (847) 390-0920
e-mail: mwerder@ifsa.org
Web site: www.ifsa.org
Operated by: Illinois Fire Safety Alliance, PO Box 911, Mt Prospect, IL 60056 at (847) 390-0911 (#3897)

Indian Boundary YMCA Day Camp ☀

Downers Grove, IL (Du Page Co.); (630) 968-8400
Sandy Wildermuth, Director

Camp comments: Camp offers creative learning experiences for children entering grades 1-9. The focus is on a well rounded experience.
Activities: Arts/Crafts, Basketball, Climbing/Rappelling, Field Trips, Soccer, Swimming — Instructional, Swimming — Recreational
Session lengths & capacity: 1 week sessions
Clientele & fees: Fees: **B** ☀
Contact: Sandra Wildermuth, Camp Director at (630) 968-8400; fax: (630) 968-8389
Operated by: YMCA Of Metropolitan Chicago, 801 N Dearborn St, Chicago, IL 60610 at (312) 932-1200 (#14017)

Irving Park YMCA Day Camp

(est 1990) ☀

Chicago, IL (Cook Co.); (773) 777-7500
Stephanie Michl, Director

Camp comments: Our YMCA Day Camp offers urban outdoor camping experiences and projects designed to bring out the leader in all.
Activities: Arts/Crafts, Drama, Field Trips, Hockey, Leadership Development, Nature/Environment Studies, Performing Arts, Sports — Field & Team, Swimming — Recreational, Team Building
Session lengths & capacity: June-August; 9 week sessions; 200 campers
Clientele & fees: coed 6-12; Fees: **B** ☀ 🐖
Contact: Stephanie Michl, Child Care Director at (773) 777-7500 ext. 286; fax: (773) 777-8892
Operated by: YMCA Of Metropolitan Chicago, 801 N Dearborn St, Chicago, IL 60610 at (312) 932-1200 (#27100)

JCYS Camp Henry Horner

(est 1940) ☀ ᴀ ⌂ 🚐

Ingleside, IL (Lake Co.); (847) 740-5010
Chuck Kahalnik, Johanna Sievers & Jonathan Fields, Director

Camp comments: Offers fun, friendship, excitement, surprise, discovery & adventure, a place campers can learn independence, new activities, and enjoy a safe camp vacation.
Activities: Archery, Arts/Crafts, Basketball, Climbing/Rappelling, Counselor Training (CIT), Drama, Field Trips, Hiking, Nature/Environment Studies
Session lengths & capacity: 2, 4, 6 & 8 week sessions; 250 campers
Clientele & fees: coed 4-14; Fees: **C** ☀ Fees: **E** ᴀ
Contact: Chuck Kahalnik & Johanna Sievers, Directors at (847) 740-5010; fax: (847) 740-5014

e-mail: jcyschh@iwc.net or ckahalnik@jcys.org
Operated by: JCYS Camp Henry Horner, PO Box 297, Ingleside, IL 60041 at (847) 740-5010

Group Rental Information

Facilities: Cabins, Hiking Trails, Kitchen Facilities, Lake, Lodges, Meeting Rooms
Programs: Boating (#1560)

JCYS Camp Red Leaf (est 1961) ᴀ

Ingleside, IL
Carissa Miller, Director

Camp comments: Camp Red Leaf is a special place for special people.
Activities: Arts/Crafts, Drama, Drawing/Painting, Hiking, Kayaking, Music, Nature/Environment Studies, Performing Arts
Session lengths & capacity: 1 & 2 week sessions
Clientele & fees: Fees: **D** ᴀ
Contact: Carissa Miller, Director at (847) 740-5010; fax: (847) 740-5014
e-mail: jcyschh@iwc.net or cmiller@jcys.org
Operated by: JCYS Camp Henry Horner, PO Box 297, Ingleside, IL 60041 at (847) 740-5010 (#48570)

JCYS North Shore Day Camp

(est 1976) ☀ 🚐

Deerfield, IL (Lake Co.); (847) 267-9001
Micky Aaronson, Director

Camp comments: Relaxed, supportive setting. Flexible, child centered program. Great field trips.
Activities: Arts/Crafts, Baseball/Softball, Basketball, Counselor Training (CIT), Dance, Drama, Field Trips, Soccer, Sports — Field & Team, Swimming — Instructional
Session lengths & capacity: June-August; 2, 4, 6 & 8 week sessions; 250 campers
Clientele & fees: coed 5-15; Fees: **B** ☀ 🐖
Contact: Micky Aaronson, Director at (847) 433-6001 ext. 5; fax: (847) 433-6003
Operated by: JCYS Camp Henry Horner, PO Box 297, Ingleside, IL 60041 at (847) 740-5010 (#1611)

Kellys Camp Inc (est 1939) ☀ 🚐

Vernon Hills, IL (Lake Co.); (847) 634-9393
Jeff Ford/Anni Ford, Director

Camp comments: Celebrating 60 years Kelly's philosophy is to have fun while learning new skills and making new friends.
Activities: Boating, Dance, Field Trips, Golf, Gymnastics, Horseback — English, Performing Arts, Sports — Field & Team, Swimming — Instructional, Tennis
Session lengths & capacity: June-August; 4, 6 & 8 week sessions
Clientele & fees: coed 4-13; Fees: **C** ☀
Contact: Jeff & Anni Ford, Owners at (847) 634-9393; fax: (847) 634-9683
e-mail: info@kellyscamp.com
Web site: www.kellyscamp.com
Operated by: Kellys Camp Inc, PO Box 875, Lincolnshire, IL 60069 at (847) 634-9393 (#7810)

Lake Co. Forest Pres. Day Camp ☀

Libertyville, IL; (847) 367-6640

Camp comments: Summer Learning cleverly discuised as outdoor adventures. Structured activities that are educational and fun.
Activities: Camping Skills/Outdoor Living, Canoeing, Fishing, Hiking, Kayaking, Nature/Environment Studies
Session lengths & capacity: June-August; 1 week sessions; 84 campers
Clientele & fees: coed 4-14; Fees: **A, B** ☀
Contact: Eileen Davis, Environmental Educator at (847) 968-3482; fax: (847) 918-9017
e-mail: edurkin@co.lake.il.us

Operated by: Lake County Forest Preserve, 2000 N Milwaukee Ave, Libertyville, IL 60048 at (847) 367-6640 (#14271)

Lake View YMCA Day Camp ☀

Chicago, IL; (773) 248-3333
Lori Johanson, Director
Activities: Aquatic Activities, Arts/Crafts, Baseball/Softball, Basketball, Counselor Training (CIT), Field Trips, Nature/Environment Studies, Soccer, Sports — Field & Team, Swimming — Recreational
Session lengths & capacity: June-September; 1 week sessions; 80 campers
Clientele & fees: coed 6-12; Fees: **B** ☀
Contact: Kelley Cross, Day Camp Coordinator at
Operated by: YMCA Of Metropolitan Chicago, 801 N Dearborn St, Chicago, IL 60610 at (312) 932-1200 (#32419)

Land O Lincoln Camp Cherith ▲

(est 1962)

Dixon, IL (Bureau Co.); (815) 284-6979
Sue Murphy, Director
Camp comments: A special activity-centered Bible camp for girls 2nd grade - H.S. Beautiful location - excellent food, pool & lake.
Activities: Archery, Arts/Crafts, Counselor Training (CIT), Drama, Hiking, Music, Nature/Environment Studies, Religious Study, Riflery, Swimming — Instructional
Session lengths & capacity: July-August; 1 & 2 week sessions; 110 campers
Clientele & fees: girls 7-17; Fees: **C** ▲
Contact: Mrs Sue Murphy, Director at (309) 682-8196;
e-mail: murphy1949@yahoo.com
Operated by: Land O'Lincoln Camp Cherith, 4132 Hollyridge Circle, Peoria, IL 61614 at (309) 682-8196 (#1589)

Lattof YMCA Day Camp ☀

Des Plaines, IL (Cook Co.); (847) 296-3376
Sabrina Ferguson, Director

Camp comments: A place to grow physically, spiritually & mentally. Experience success & excitement through outdoor exploration.
Activities: Aquatic Activities, Arts/Crafts, Challenge/Rope Courses, Climbing/Rappelling, Counselor Training (CIT), Field Trips, Gymnastics, Soccer, Sports — Field & Team, Team Building
Session lengths & capacity: June-August; 1 week sessions; 175 campers
Clientele & fees: coed 5-15; Fees: **B** ☀ 🐷
Contact: Sabrina Ferguson, Program Director at (847) 296-3376; fax: (847) 296-9431
e-mail: sabrina_ferguson@ymcachgo.org
Operated by: YMCA Of Metropolitan Chicago, 801 N Dearborn St, Chicago, IL 60610 at (312) 932-1200 (#3838)

Leaning Tower YMCA Day Camp (est 1955) ☀

Niles, IL (Cook Co.); (847) 647-8222
Mary Wiltgen, Director

Camp comments: Self-esteem specialty. Campers thrive in non-competitive, caring atmosphere with opportunities to belong and contribute.
Activities: Aquatic Activities, Arts/Crafts, Community Service, Field Trips, Leadership Development, Soccer, Sports — Field & Team, Swimming — Instructional, Swimming — Recreational, Team Building
Session lengths & capacity: June-August; 1 week sessions; 200 campers
Clientele & fees: boys 5-15; girls 5-15; coed 5-15; Fees: **B** ☀ 🐷
Contact: Mary Wiltgen, Camp Director at (847) 647-8222 ext. 2275; fax: (847) 647-7736

Operated by: YMCA Of Metropolitan Chicago, 801 N Dearborn St, Chicago, IL 60610 at (312) 932-1200 (#1553)

Little Grassy United Methodist ▲ ⌂

(est 1953)

Makanda, IL (Jackson Co.); (618) 457-6030
Donald Terry, Director
Activities: Aquatic Activities, Canoeing, Caving, Climbing/Rappelling, Horseback — Western, Religious Study, Swimming — Recreational
Operated by: Illinois Great Rivers Conf, 2144 S MacArthur Blvd Ste 2B, Springfield, IL 61704 at (217) 747-0720

Group Rental Information
Site comments: Located on 190 acres of wooded, lakefront property, 7 miles south of Carbondale IL near the crab orchard NWR.
Seasons & Capacity: Spring 230, Summer 412, Fall 230
Facilities: A/V Equipment, Cabins, Dorm-Style, Food Service, Hiking Trails, Lake, Lodges, Meeting Rooms
Programs: Boating, Environmental Education, Swimming (#14577)

Lutheran Outdoor Center ☀ ▲ ⌂

(est 1927)

Oregon, IL (Ogle Co.); (815) 732-2220
Pastor Bill Beyer, Director
Camp comments: Church in outdoor settings connecting the Word of God with the World of God.
Activities: Camping Skills/Outdoor Living, Canoeing, Caving, Drama, Drawing/Painting, Golf, Music, Nature/Environment Studies, Performing Arts, Religious Study
Session lengths & capacity: 1 week sessions; 150 campers
Clientele & fees: coed 6-18; seniors; single adults; Fees: **C** ▲ 🐗
Contact: Pastor Bill Beyer, Executive Director at (815) 732-2220; fax: (815) 732-7282
e-mail: lomc@essex1.com
Web site: www.ebl.org\lomc
Operated by: Evangelical Lutheran Church in, Box 239, Oregon, IL 61061 at (815) 732-2220 (#2982)

Mary Sears Summer Day Camp ☀

Orland Park, IL; (708) 460-4414
Activities: Aquatic Activities, Baseball/Softball, Basketball, Computer, Drawing/Painting, Field Trips, Music, Soccer, Sports — Field & Team, Swimming — Recreational
Operated by: Mary Sears Childrens Academy, 16807 S 108th Ave, Orland Park, IL 60467 at (708) 460-4414 (#14290)

McCormick Tribune YMCA Day Cmp ☀

Chicago, IL (Cook Co.); (773) 235-5150
Ina Anthony, Director
Activities: Academics, Basketball, Community Service, Counselor Training (CIT), Dance, Drawing/Painting, Sports — Field & Team, Team Building
Contact: Ian Anthony, Day Camp Director at (773) 235-5150; fax: (773) 235-4489
Operated by: YMCA Of Metropolitan Chicago, 801 N Dearborn St, Chicago, IL 60610 at (312) 932-1200 (#40460)

New City YMCA Camp ☀

Chicago, IL (Cook Co.); (312) 440-7272
Janelle Fitzpatrick, Director

Activities: Aquatic Activities, Arts/Crafts, Baseball/Softball, Basketball, Drawing/Painting, Field Trips, Sports — Field & Team, Swimming — Recreational
Session lengths & capacity: May-August; 1, 2, 3, 4, 5, 6, 7, 8 & 9 week sessions; 150 campers
Clientele & fees: coed 6-12; Fees: **B** ☀
Contact: Janelle Fitzpatrick, Day Camp Director at (312) 440-7287; fax: (312) 266-6084
Operated by: YMCA Of Metropolitan Chicago, 801 N Dearborn St, Chicago, IL 60610 at (312) 932-1200 (#27329)

North Lawndale YMCA Day Camp ☀

Chicago, IL (Cook Co.); (773) 638-0773
Kim George, Director

Camp comments: We build strong kids,strong families and strong communities.
Activities: Academics, Arts/Crafts, Basketball, Computer, Field Trips, Leadership Development, Sports — Field & Team
Session lengths & capacity: June-August; 1 week sessions; 100 campers
Clientele & fees: boys 6-13; Fees: **A, B** ☀
Contact: Kim George, Program Director at (773) 638-0773; fax: (773) 638-7925
Operated by: YMCA Of Metropolitan Chicago, 801 N Dearborn St, Chicago, IL 60610 at (312) 932-1200 (#32421)

Park District of Oak Park ☀

(est 1970)

Oak Park, IL; (708) 725-2000
Charity W. Luter, Director

Camp comments: The Park District of Oak Park Day Camps strive to provide diverse recreational activities for children ages 4-13.
Activities: Arts/Crafts, Baseball/Softball, Basketball, Field Trips, Football, Golf, Performing Arts, Sports — Field & Team, Swimming — Recreational
Session lengths & capacity: June-August; 1, 2 & 3 week sessions
Clientele & fees: coed 4-13; Fees: **A, B** ☀ 🐗
Contact: Charity W Luter, Recreation Program Manager at (708) 725-2000 ext. 2250; fax: (708) 383-5702
Operated by: Park District of Oak Park, 218 Madison, Oak Park, IL 60302 at (708) 725-2000 (#26370)

Pilgrim Park Camp Conf Center ▲ ⌂

Princeton, IL (Bureau Co.); (815) 447-2390
Wendy Croisant, Director
Activities: Aquatic Activities, Challenge/Rope Courses, Leadership Development, Religious Study
Session lengths & capacity: 1/2 & 1 week sessions
Clientele & fees: coed 2-18; families; seniors; single adults; Fees: **C** ▲
Contact: Wendy Croisant, Camp Manager at (815) 447-2390; fax: (815) 447-2205
e-mail: pilgrimpark@hotmail.com
Web site: www.ilucc.org
Operated by: Illinois Conference UCC, 1840 Westchester Blvd Ste 200, Westchester, IL 60154 at (708) 344-4470

Group Rental Information
Seasons & Capacity: Spring 158, Summer 174, Fall 158, Winter 158
Facilities: A/V Equipment, Cabins, Dorm-Style, Double Occupancy, Food Service, Hiking Trails, Kitchen Facilities, Linens, Lodges, Meeting Rooms, Playing Fields, Tents
Programs: Challenge/Ropes Course (#45217)

Pilsen YMCA Day Camp ☀

Chicago, IL (Cook Co.); (312) 738-0282
Rose Dominguez, Director

Camp comments: 2001 site: St Adalbert Convent, 1628 W 17th Street, rear patio.
Activities: Academics, Arts/Crafts, Community Service, Field Trips
Session lengths & capacity: 2 & 8 week sessions
Clientele & fees: Fees: B ☀
Contact: Rose Dominguez, Program Director at (312) 738-0282; fax: (312) 738-2827
e-mail: rose_marie_dominguez@ymcachigo.org
Operated by: YMCA Of Metropolitan Chicago, 801 N Dearborn St, Chicago, IL 60610 at (312) 932-1200 (#40457)

Reynoldswood Christ. Cmp & Ret (est 1959) ▲ ⌂

Dixon, IL (Lee Co.); (815) 284-6979
Stephen Luse, Director

Activities: Archery, Basketball, Canoeing, Challenge/Rope Courses, Hiking, Nature/Environment Studies, Religious Study, Team Building
Session lengths & capacity: 1 week sessions
Clientele & fees: Fees: C ▲
Operated by: Outdoor and Retreat Ministries, 200 Stam Street, Williams Bay, WI 53191 at (262) 245-6706

Group Rental Information

Seasons & Capacity: Spring 124, Summer 188, Fall 124, Winter 108
Facilities: A/V Equipment, Cabins, Dorm-Style, Food Service, Linens, Meeting Rooms, Playing Fields, Pool, River
Programs: Challenge/Ropes Course, Swimming, Winter Sports (#5473)

Rich Port YMCA Day Camp ☀

La Grange, IL (Cook Co.); (708) 352-7600
Leanna Hartung, Director

Activities: Aquatic Activities, Arts/Crafts, Drawing/Painting, Field Trips, Hiking, Nature/Environment Studies, Sports — Field & Team, Swimming — Recreational
Session lengths & capacity: 1 week sessions
Clientele & fees: coed 6-12; Fees: B ☀
Contact: Leanna Hartung, Camp Director at (708) 352-7600; fax: (708) 352-7635
Operated by: YMCA Of Metropolitan Chicago, 801 N Dearborn St, Chicago, IL 60610 at (312) 932-1200 (#14029)

ICON LEGEND

☀ Day Camp
▲ Resident Camp
⌂ Facilities Available To Rent
🚐 Transportation Available
🐷 Financial Aid Available

FEE RANGES PER WEEK

A	$0-75
B	$75-200
C	$201-350
D	$351-500
E	$501-650
F	over $650

Riverwoods Christian Center

(est 1976) ☀ ▲ ⌂ 🚐

St Charles, IL (Kane Co.); (630) 584-2222
Jay Curtis, Director

Camp comments: A special camp for economically disadvantaged children in the Fox River Valley.
Activities: Arts/Crafts, Basketball, Camping Skills/Outdoor Living, Canoeing, Counselor Training (CIT), Hiking, Leadership Development, Nature/Environment Studies, Religious Study, Swimming — Recreational
Session lengths & capacity: June-August; 1, 2 & 8 weeks sessions; 70 campers
Clientele & fees: coed 6-16; Fees: A ☀
Fees: A ▲ 🐷
Contact: Brian Heinrich, Camp Program Manager at (630) 584-2222 ext. 216; fax: (630) 584-2267
e-mail: riverwds@mcs.net
Operated by: Riverwoods Christian Center, 35 W 701 Riverwoods Lane, St Charles, IL 60174 at (630) 584-2222

Group Rental Information

Seasons & Capacity: Spring 70, Winter 70
Facilities: A/V Equipment, Cabins, Hiking Trails, Kitchen Facilities, Meeting Rooms, Playing Fields (#3679)

Round Lake Area Park District ☀

Round Lake, IL (Lake Co.); (847) 546-8558
Activities: Arts/Crafts, Drama, Field Trips, Golf, Nature/Environment Studies, Swimming — Recreational
Contact: Peggy Dohr, Manager Child Dev Center at (847) 546-8558; fax: (847) 740-8180
Operated by: Round Lake Area Park District, 814 Hart Road, Round Lake, IL 60073 at (847) 546-8558 (#41818)

Seton Summer Day Camp

(est 1965) ☀

Clarendon Hills, IL (DuPage Co.); (630) 655-1066
Anna Perry, Director

Camp comments: Beautiful setting on 3 wooded acres. Trained & experienced staff combining learning & outdoor fun for ages 2 to 9.
Activities: Academics, Arts/Crafts, Basketball, Computer, Field Trips, Language Studies, Leadership Development, Swimming — Instructional, Swimming — Recreational, Team Building
Session lengths & capacity: June-August; 3 week sessions; 175 campers
Clientele & fees: coed 2-9; Fees: B ☀
Contact: Anna Perry, Director at (630) 655-1066; fax: (630) 654-0182
e-mail: meca1seton@aol.com
Web site: www.meca-seton.com
Operated by: Montessori Educ Ctrs Assoc, 5728 Virginia Street, Clarendon Hills, IL 60514 at (630) 654-0151 (#3673)

Skokie Park District Camps ☀ 🚐

Skokie, IL; (847) 674-1500
Cheryl Toohey/Kathy Benson, Director

Camp comments: Excellence in everything we do. We will amaze you.
Activities: Arts/Crafts, Camping Skills/Outdoor Living, Counselor Training (CIT), Field Trips, Leadership Development, Nature/Environment Studies, Performing Arts, Sports — Field & Team, Swimming — Recreational, Team Building
Session lengths & capacity: June-August; 4 week sessions
Clientele & fees: Fees: C, D ☀ 🐷
Contact: Cheryl Toohey, Director at (847) 933-4966; e-mail: catoohey@skokieparkdistrict.org
Web site: www.skokieparkdistrict.org

Operated by: Skokie Park District, 9300 Weber Park Pl, Skokie, IL 60077 at (847) 674-1500 (#32994)

South Side YMCA ☀

Chicago, IL (Cook Co.); (773) 947-0700
Dana Robinson, Director

Camp comments: Our full day summer program is designed to enrich campers' personal growth and increase awareness of their environment.
Activities: Academics, Arts/Crafts, Basketball, Community Service, Golf, Nature/Environment Studies, Swimming — Instructional, Swimming — Recreational
Session lengths & capacity: June-August; 2 week sessions; 200 campers
Clientele & fees: coed 3-16; Fees: A ☀ 🐷
Contact: Danyell Taylor, Youth & Family Director at (773) 947-0700 ext. 251; fax: (773) 947-8983
Operated by: YMCA Of Metropolitan Chicago, 801 N Dearborn St, Chicago, IL 60610 at (312) 932-1200 (#27098)

South Suburban YMCA ☀

Harvey, IL (Cook Co.); (708) 331-6500
Kyna Simpson, Director

Camp comments: Our camp offers many different activities for all campers. The camp is challenging fun and meaningful. Ask for details.
Activities: Arts/Crafts, Baseball/Softball, Basketball, Field Trips, Soccer, Swimming — Instructional, Swimming — Recreational
Session lengths & capacity: June-August; 2 week sessions; 90 campers
Clientele & fees: coed 6-13; Fees: B ☀ 🐷
Contact: Daniel Kasambira, Executive Director at (708) 331-6500; fax: (708) 331-1560
e-mail: danielkasambira@ymcachgo.org
Operated by: YMCA Of Metropolitan Chicago, 801 N Dearborn St, Chicago, IL 60610 at (312) 932-1200 (#40463)

Tamarak Day Camp (est 1946) ☀ 🚐

Lincolnshire, IL (Lake Co.); (847) 634-3168
Lucia and Dave Thoensen, Director

Camp comments: Tamarak Day Camp has a tradition of excellence for over 50 years. Excellent programs, beautiful facilites & highly trained staff provide a safe & fun experience
Activities: Ceramics/Pottery, Field Trips, Gymnastics, Horseback — English, Nature/Environment Studies, Performing Arts, Sports — Field & Team, Swimming — Instructional, Team Building, Tennis
Session lengths & capacity: June-August; 4 & 8 week sessions
Clientele & fees: coed 4-11; Fees: C ☀
Contact: Lucia and Dave Thoensen, Directors, Owners at (847) 634-3168; fax: (847) 634-8262
e-mail: DPThoensen1@aol.com
Web site: www.tamarekDayCamp.com
Operated by: Tamarak Day Camp, 23970 N Elm Road, Lincolnshire, IL 60069 at (847) 634-3168 (#1586)

Tapawingo (est 1957) ☀ ▲ ⌂

Metamora, IL (Woodford Co.); (309) 367-4775
Lara Campbell, Director

Camp comments: A quality experience with super staff. Sessions offer many choices. All stress girl planning & teamwork plus fun!
Activities: Arts/Crafts, Camping Skills/Outdoor Living, Canoeing, Challenge/Rope Courses, Counselor Training (CIT), Horseback — Western, Leadership Development, Nature/Environment Studies, Swimming — Recreational, Team Building
Session lengths & capacity: June-August; 1/2, 1 & 2 week sessions; 120 campers
Clientele & fees: girls 7-17; Fees: A ☀
Fees: B, C ▲

Contact: Lara Campbell, Director of Program & Property at (309) 688-8671 ext. 24; fax: (309) 688-7358 e-mail: campbell@girlscouts-kickapoocouncil.org Web site: www.girlscouts-kickapoocouncil.org **Operated by:** Girl Scouts Kickapoo Council, 1103 W Lake Ave, Peoria, IL 61614 at (309) 688-8671

Group Rental Information
Site comments: Setting includes woods, meadows, small lake & trails. Builds knowledge, skills, competencies through outdoor education. **Seasons & Capacity:** Spring 176, Summer 155, Fall 176, Winter 136 **Facilities:** Cabins, Hiking Trails, Lodges, Meeting Rooms (#1652)

The Road Less Traveled (est 1991) ▲

Chicago, IL (Cook Co.); (773) 342-5200 Jim & Donna Stein, Director

Camp comments: Our purpose is to enrich young people's lives by offering a life experience in a challenging and supportive environment **Activities:** Backpacking, Camping Skills/Outdoor Living, Climbing/Rappelling, Hiking, Kayaking, Leadership Development, Nature/Environment Studies, Rafting, Travel/Tour, Wilderness Trips **Session lengths & capacity:** May-August; 3, 4 & 6 week sessions; 300 campers **Clientele & fees:** coed 13-19; families; Fees: F ▲ 🚐 **Contact:** Jim and Donna Stein, Directors at (773) 342-5200; fax: (773) 342-5703 e-mail: rlt1road@aol.com Web site: www.theroadlesstraveled.com **Operated by:** The Road Less Traveled Inc, 2331 North Elston Ave, Chicago, IL 60614 at (773) 342-5200 (#2385)

Timber Pointe Outdoor Center

(est 1989) ▲ ⌂

Hudson, IL (McLean Co.); (309) 365-8021 Kurt R Podeszwa, Director

Camp comments: Beautiful wooded setting on Lake Bloomington offering accessible, challenging & fun outdoor programming. **Activities:** Aquatic Activities, Archery, Arts/Crafts, Camping Skills/Outdoor Living, Canoeing, Counselor Training (CIT), Nature/Environment Studies, Swimming — Recreational **Session lengths & capacity:** 1 & 2 week sessions; 90 campers **Clientele & fees:** boys 6-99; girls 6-99; coed 6-99; families; Fees: D ▲ 🚐 **Contact:** Kurt Podeszwa, Director of Camping at (309) 365-8021; fax: (309) 365-8934 e-mail: kpodeszwa@easterseals-ucp.org **Operated by:** Easter Seals-UCP, 20 Timber Pointe Lane, Hudson, IL 61748 at (309) 365-8021

Group Rental Information
Seasons & Capacity: Spring 160, Fall 160, Winter 160 **Facilities:** A/V Equipment, Cabins, Food Service, Hiking Trails, Lake, Meeting Rooms, Playing Fields, Pool, Tents **Programs:** Boating, Challenge/Ropes Course, Environmental Education, Horseback Riding, Swimming (#2247)

TNI Summer Day Camp ☀ 🚐

Godfrey, IL; (618) 467-2521 Sherry Droste, Director **Activities:** Arts/Crafts, Hiking, Nature/Environment Studies **Session lengths & capacity:** June-August; 1 week sessions; 45 campers **Clientele & fees:** coed 4-13; Fees: B ☀ **Contact:** Sherry Droste, Camp Director at (618) 466-9930; fax: (618) 466-9948 e-mail: tnil@piasanet.com **Operated by:** The Nature Institute, 2213 S Levis Ln, Godfrey, IL 62035 at (618) 466-9930 (#38753)

United Youth Camps ▲

Troy, IL; (618) 667-4722 **Camp comments:** Variety camps in the US & abroad. Specialty is team building & relationship development. Visit us on the web at www.ucgyouth.org to request our camp magazine. **Activities:** Arts/Crafts, Backpacking, Canoeing, Counselor Training (CIT), Horseback — Western, Religious Study **Session lengths & capacity:** 1 & 2 week sessions **Clientele & fees:** coed 12-18; Fees: C ▲ **Contact:** Larry Greider, National Director at (618) 667-4722; fax: (618) 667-4750 e-mail: lwg73@aol.com **Operated by:** United Church of God, PO Box 541027, Cincinnati, OH 45254 at (513) 576-9796 (#40125)

Walcamp Outdoor Ministries Inc (est 1964) ▲ ⌂

Kingston, IL (DeKalb Co.); (815) 784-5141 Jeffrey Meinz, Director

Camp comments: Providing opportunities to experience Christ in the outdoors through experiential learning, teamwork, & personal growth. **Activities:** Camping Skills/Outdoor Living, Canoeing, Challenge/Rope Courses, Climbing/Rappelling, Hiking, Leadership Development, Nature/Environment Studies, Religious Study, Sports — Field & Team, Team Building **Session lengths & capacity:** June-August; 1 week sessions; 130 campers **Clientele & fees:** coed 5-16; families; Fees: B ▲ **Contact:** (815) 784-5141; fax: (815) 784-4085 Web site: www.walcamp.org **Operated by:** Walcamp Outdoor Ministries, 32653 Five Points Rd, Kingston, IL 60145 at (815) 784-5141

Group Rental Information
Facilities: A/V Equipment, Cabins, Dorm-Style, Food Service, Hiking Trails, Lake, Lodges, Meeting Rooms, Playing Fields, River, Tents **Programs:** Boating, Challenge/Ropes Course, Environmental Education, Swimming (#10873)

Wartburg ☀ ▲ ⌂

Waterloo, IL; (618) 939-7715 **Activities:** Archery, Challenge/Rope Courses, Nature/Environment Studies, Religious Study, Swimming — Recreational **Operated by:** LCFS Camp Wartburg, 2408 Lebanon Ave, Belleville, IL 62221 at (618) 234-8904

Group Rental Information
Seasons & Capacity: Spring 150, Summer 150, Fall 150, Winter 130 **Facilities:** A/V Equipment, Cabins, Dorm-Style, Food Service, Meeting Rooms, Playing Fields, Pool, Tents **Programs:** Challenge/Ropes Course, Environmental Education, Swimming (#10878)

YMCA Camp Benson (est 1928) ▲ ⌂

Mt Carroll, IL (Whiteside Co.); (815) 244-8722 Michael Rule, Director

Camp comments: Camp Benson is located in scenic NW IL. We offer traditional and unique actvities. Program focuses on 4 core values: caring, honesty, respect & responsibility. **Activities:** Archery, Bicycling/Biking, Caving, Climbing/Rappelling, Hiking, Leadership Development, Nature/Environment Studies, Performing Arts, Riflery, Wilderness Trips **Session lengths & capacity:** June-August; 1/2, 1 & 2 week sessions; 80 campers **Clientele & fees:** coed 6-16; families; Fees: B, C ▲ 🚐 **Contact:** Michael Rule, Camp Director at (815) 244-8722; e-mail: ycampbenson@aol.com

Operated by: Sterling Rock Falls Fam YMCA, 2505 YMCA Way, Sterling, IL 61081 at (815) 535-9622
Group Rental Information
Facilities: A/V Equipment, Cabins, Double Occupancy, Food Service, Hiking Trails, Kitchen Facilities, Lodges, Meeting Rooms, Playing Fields, River **Programs:** Environmental Education (#1590)

YMCA Camp Duncan ☀ ▲ ⌂ 🚐

(est 1921)

Ingleside, IL (Lake Co.); (847) 546-8086 Kim Kiser, Executive, Director

Camp comments: Beautiful setting. Staff are carefully selected & trained as role models to lead campers in a variety of safe activities. **Activities:** Boating, Challenge/Rope Courses, Climbing/Rappelling, Counselor Training (CIT), Field Trips, Horseback — Western, Leadership Development **Session lengths & capacity:** 1, 2 & 3 week sessions; 450 campers **Clientele & fees:** boys 7-15; girls 7-15; coed 7-15; families; Fees: B ☀ Fees: D ▲ 🚐 **Contact:** Rona Roffey, Camp Director at (847) 546-8086; fax: (847) 546-3550 e-mail: rkr@ymcacampduncan.org **Operated by:** YMCA Of Metropolitan Chicago, 801 N Dearborn St, Chicago, IL 60610 at (312) 932-1200

Group Rental Information
Seasons & Capacity: Spring 500, Summer 80, Fall 500, Winter 500 **Facilities:** A/V Equipment, Cabins, Dorm-Style, Food Service, Lake, Meeting Rooms, Playing Fields, Pool **Programs:** Boating, Challenge/Ropes Course, Environmental Education, Horseback Riding, Swimming, Winter Sports (#1587)

YMCA Camp Winnebago ☀ ⌂ 🚐

(est 1965)

Rockford, IL (Winnebago Co.) Susie Johnson, Director

Camp comments: To develop leadership and life skills through fun progressive prog. delivered in nature's learning environment for Rock River Valley. **Activities:** Archery, Backpacking, Camping Skills/Outdoor Living, Canoeing, Challenge/Rope Courses, Climbing/Rappelling, Hiking, Leadership Development, Nature/Environment Studies, Swimming — Recreational **Session lengths & capacity:** June-August; 1 & 2 week sessions; 200 campers **Clientele & fees:** coed 6-14; Fees: B ☀ 🚐 **Contact:** Susie Johnson, Program Director at (815) 489-1212; fax: (815) 987-3767 **Operated by:** YMCA of Rock River Valley, 200 Y Blvd, Rockford, IL 61107 at (815) 489-1212

Group Rental Information
Facilities: A/V Equipment, Hiking Trails, Lodges, Meeting Rooms, Playing Fields **Programs:** Environmental Education (#5087)

YMCA Summer Day Camp ☀ 🚐

(est 1987)

Quincy, IL (Adams Co.); (217) 222-1400 Mrs Debbie Wort, Director

Camp comments: Provide a quality & safe program while developing the family in body, mind & spirit with Christian values. **Activities:** Arts/Crafts, Camping Skills/Outdoor Living, Counselor Training (CIT), Field Trips, Leadership Development, Nature/Environment Studies, Swimming — Recreational **Session lengths & capacity:** June-August; 70 campers **Clientele & fees:** boys 6-14; girls 6-14; Fees: A, B ☀ 🚐

Contact: Debbie Wort, Youth Program Director at (217) 222-9622; fax: (217) 222-8596
e-mail: ymca@quincyymca.com
Web site: www.quincyymca.net
Operated by: Quincy Family YMCA, 3101 Maine, Quincy, IL 62301 at (217) 222-1400 (#6578)

Z Frank Apachi Day Camp

(est 1987) ☀ 🚗

Northbrook, IL (Cook Co.); (847) 272-7050
Gayle Malvin, Director

Camp comments: We're big enough to give your children the time of their lives, yet small enough to know who they are!
Activities: Arts/Crafts, Baseball/Softball, Basketball, Field Trips, Sports — Field & Team, Swimming — Instructional, Tennis
Session lengths & capacity: 4, 6 & 8 week sessions; 700 campers
Clientele & fees: coed 4-12; Fees: C ☀ 🐷
Contact: Gayle Malvin, Director at (708) 272-7050; fax: (708) 272-5357
Operated by: JCC of Chicago, 3050 Woodridge Rd, Northbrook, IL 60062 at (847) 272-7050 (#6226)

Indiana

Boys and Girls Club Camp

(est 1913) ⛺ 🏠

Noblesville, IN; (317) 877-2628
Rick Crosslin, Director

Camp comments: Educational Science Program; boys & girls grades 4-8 explore caves, archeology, fossils, space, past & future and science experiments.
Activities: Academics, Arts/Crafts, Challenge/Rope Courses, Community Service, Computer, Field Trips, Leadership Development, Model Rocketry, Nature/Environment Studies, Swimming — Recreational
Session lengths & capacity: June-August; 1 week sessions; 100 campers
Clientele & fees: boys 10-14; girls 10-14; coed 10-14; Fees: C ⛺
Contact: Tricia Napier, Secretary at (317) 920-4700; fax: (317) 920-4701
e-mail: bgcindy@nonline.com
Web site: www.bgcindy.org
Operated by: Boys & Girls Clubs ndianapolis, 300 E Fall Crk Prkwy N Dr 300, Indianapolis, IN 46205-4279 at (317) 920-4700

ICON LEGEND

☀	Day Camp
⛺	Resident Camp
🏠	Facilities Available To Rent
🚗	Transportation Available
🐷	Financial Aid Available

FEE RANGES PER WEEK

A	$0-75
B	$75-200
C	$201-350
D	$351-500
E	$501-650
F	over $650

Group Rental Information

Facilities: Cabins, Double Occupancy, Food Service, Hiking Trails, Kitchen Facilities, Playing Fields, Pool
Programs: Challenge/Ropes Course, Swimming (#1519)

Bradford Woods/Camp Riley

(est 1955) ⛺ 🏠

Martinsville, IN (Morgan Co.); (765) 342-2915
Gary Robb, Director

Camp comments: Recreation & camping experiences for youth/adults with physical disabilities. Promote growth, independence & fun.
Activities: Aquatic Activities, Archery, Arts/Crafts, Camping Skills/Outdoor Living, Challenge/Rope Courses, Horseback — Western, Leadership Development, Nature/Environment Studies, Travel/Tour
Session lengths & capacity: June-August; 1 & 2 weeks sessions; 100 campers
Clientele & fees: coed 8-18; Fees: D, E ⛺ 🐷
Contact: Carol Stone, Coordinator/Camping Programs at (765) 342-2915; fax: (765) 349-1086
e-mail: castone@indiana.edu
Web site: www.bradwoods.org
Operated by: Indiana Univ-Bradford Woods, 5040 St Road 67 North, Martinsville, IN 46151 at (765) 342-2915

Group Rental Information

Facilities: A/V Equipment, Cabins, Dorm-Style, Double Occupancy, Food Service, Hiking Trails, Kitchen Facilities, Lake, Linens, Lodges, Meeting Rooms, Pool, Tents
Programs: Challenge/Ropes Course, Environmental Education, Horseback Riding, Swimming (#1537)

Camp Alexander Mack

(est 1924) ⛺ 🏠

Milford, IN (Kosciusko Co.); (219) 658-4831
Rex M. Miller, Director

Camp comments: Beautiful, peaceful facility on lake with dedicated caring Christian staff.
Activities: Arts/Crafts, Canoeing, Counselor Training (CIT), Hiking, Leadership Development, Nature/Environment Studies, Sailing, Soccer
Session lengths & capacity: June-August; 1/2 & 1 week sessions; 400 campers
Clientele & fees: coed 8-18; families; seniors; single adults; Fees: B ⛺
Contact: Rex M Miller, CCCP, Executive Director at (219) 658-4831; fax: (219) 658-4765
e-mail: campmack@npcc.net
Web site: www.campmack.org
Operated by: Church Of The Brethren, PO Box 158, Milford, IN 46542-0158 at (219) 658-4831

Group Rental Information

Site comments: Camp Alexander Mack, a camp & retreat center, is a Christ-centered ministry of the Church of the Brethren in Indiana providing holy hospitality for God's people
Seasons & Capacity: Spring 200, Summer 400, Fall 200, Winter 200
Facilities: A/V Equipment, Cabins, Dorm-Style, Food Service, Hiking Trails, Lake, Lodges, Meeting Rooms, Playing Fields
Programs: Boating, Challenge/Ropes Course, Swimming (#1540)

Camp at the Woods (est 1979) ☀ ⛺

St Mary of the Woods, IN (Vigo Co.); (812) 535-5148
Veronica Dougherty, Director

Camp comments: Summer camp at the woods is dedicated to providing young campers ages 7-14 with a positive, supportive experience in which their individuality is appreciated.

Activities: Academics, Archery, Canoeing, Drama, Hiking, Horseback — Western, Music, Photography, Swimming — Recreational
Session lengths & capacity: June-July; 1 week sessions; 100 campers
Clientele & fees: coed 7-14; Fees: C ☀
Fees: C ⛺
Contact: Cindy Van Duyn, Summer Camp Director at (812) 535-5148; fax: (812) 535-4613
e-mail: reserve@smwc.edu
Operated by: St Mary Of The Woods College, Conferences & Non Credit Prog, 209 Guerin Hall, St Mary of the Woods, IN 47876 at (812) 535-5148 (#4131)

Camp Crosley YMCA

(est 1921) ☀ ⛺ 🏠

North Webster, IN; (877) 811-6189
Richard Armstrong, Director

Camp comments: Dynamic program, caring staff, beautiful lakefront setting combine to give children a safe place to grow and have fun!
Activities: Archery, Challenge/Rope Courses, Drama, Horseback — English, Horseback — Western, Nature/Environment Studies, Riflery, Sailing, Soccer, Waterskiing
Session lengths & capacity: June-August; 1/2, 1, 2 & 3 week sessions; 200 campers
Clientele & fees: coed 7-17; families; seniors; Fees: A ☀ Fees: C, D ⛺ 🐷
Contact: Richard Armstrong, Exec Dir at (877) 811-6189; fax: (219) 834-3313
e-mail: info@campcrosley.org
Operated by: Muncie Family YMCA, 500 S Mullberry St, Muncie, IN 47305-2493 at (765) 288-4448

Group Rental Information

Site comments: Dynamic outdoor education, retreat and conference program that will ensure a successful trip! The right place for your group...naturally!
Seasons & Capacity: Spring 250, Fall 250, Winter 200
Facilities: A/V Equipment, Cabins, Double Occupancy, Food Service, Hiking Trails, Lake, Linens, Lodges, Meeting Rooms, Playing Fields
Programs: Boating, Challenge/Ropes Course, Environmental Education, Swimming (#1510)

Camp Little Eagle (est 1981) ☀ 🚗

Warsaw, IN; (219) 269-9622
Ryan T Finney, Director

Camp comments: A summer adventure for children ages 5-16. All of the benefits of camp and they come home each night.
Activities: Archery, Camping Skills/Outdoor Living, Canoeing, Counselor Training (CIT), Golf, Leadership Development, Swimming — Recreational
Session lengths & capacity: June-August; 1 week sessions; 200 campers
Clientele & fees: coed 5-16; Fees: A ☀ 🐷
Contact: Ryan T Finney, Teen & Family Director at (219) 269-9622; fax: (219) 269-1396
e-mail: kosymca@kconline.com
Web site: www.kcymca.org
Operated by: Kosciusko Community YMCA, 1401 East Smith Street, Warsaw, IN 46580 at (219) 269-9622 (#40395)

Camp Millhouse (est 1937) ⛺ 🏠

South Bend, IN (St Joseph Co.); (219) 287-9833
Lea Anne Pitcher, Director

Camp comments: Our residential summer camp offers fun-filled adventurous outdoor activities for persons with special needs.
Activities: Arts/Crafts, Counselor Training (CIT), Nature/Environment Studies, Swimming — Recreational
Session lengths & capacity: 1 week sessions; 60 campers

Clientele & fees: coed 5-99; Fees: **C** ⚠ 🚐
Contact: Lea Anne Pitcher, Executive Director at (219) 233-2202; fax: (219) 233-2511
Operated by: Camp Millhouse Inc, 25600 Kelly Road, South Bend, IN 46614 at (574) 233-2202

Group Rental Information
Facilities: Cabins, Dorm-Style, Hiking Trails, Kitchen Facilities, Lodges, Meeting Rooms, Pool (#1534)

Camp Pyoca (est 1953) ⚠ 🏠

Brownstown, IN (Jackson Co.); (812) 358-3413
Richard Swartwood, Director

Camp comments: Pyoca is a place from the busy world where people can grow in their relationship with Christ w/others & with themselves.
Activities: Arts/Crafts, Camping Skills/Outdoor Living, Canoeing, Challenge/Rope Courses, Hiking, Leadership Development, Music, Nature/Environment Studies, Religious Study, Team Building
Session lengths & capacity: June-August; 1/2 & 1 week sessions; 130 campers
Clientele & fees: boys 7-18; girls 7-18; coed 7-18; families; Fees: **B, C** ⚠
Contact: Richard Swartwood, Executive Director at (812) 358-3413; fax: (812) 358-5501
e-mail: camppyoca@aol.com
Web site: www.camppyoca.org
Operated by: Presbytery Whitewater Valley, 886 E County Rd 100 S, Brownstown, IN 47220 at (812) 358-3413

Group Rental Information
Site comments: Adult freindly accomodations adjacent to Jackson Washington State Forest. Call for more information.
Seasons & Capacity: Spring 153, Fall 153, Winter 48
Facilities: A/V Equipment, Cabins, Dorm-Style, Double Occupancy, Food Service, Hiking Trails, Lake, Lodges, Meeting Rooms, Playing Fields, Tents
Programs: Boating, Challenge/Ropes Course, Environmental Education, Swimming (#1511)

Camp Tecumseh YMCA

(est 1924) ☀ ⚠ 🏠

Brookston, IN (Carroll Co.); (765) 564-2898
David Wright, Director

Camp comments: Midwest's premiere camp. Fills before Christmas for next year. Outstanding staff & facilities.
Activities: Arts/Crafts, Challenge/Rope Courses, Climbing/Rappelling, Counselor Training (CIT), Horseback — English, Horseback — Western, Leadership Development, Riflery, Swimming — Recreational, Wilderness Trips
Session lengths & capacity: June-August; 1 & 2 week sessions; 420 campers
Clientele & fees: coed 8-15; families; Fees: **D** ⚠ 🚐
Contact: David Wright, Executive Director at (765) 564-2898; fax: (765) 564-3210
e-mail: info@camptecumseh.org
Operated by: YMCA Camp Tecumseh, 12635 W Tecumseh Bend Road, Brookston, IN 47923 at (765) 564-2898

Group Rental Information
Site comments: Midwest's premiere retreat & conference center. Excellent food, facilites, staff and programs for groups & schools. Very reasonable fees.
Seasons & Capacity: Spring 420, Summer 68, Fall 420, Winter 420
Facilities: A/V Equipment, Cabins, Food Service, Hiking Trails, Lake, Meeting Rooms, Playing Fields, River
Programs: Boating, Challenge/Ropes Course, Environmental Education, Horseback Riding (#1513)

Country Lake Christian Rtr Ctr ☀ ⚠ 🏠

Underwood, IN; (812) 294-4789
Activities: Arts/Crafts, Canoeing, Challenge/Rope Courses, Fishing, Music, Religious Study, Swimming — Recreational
Session lengths & capacity: August-August; 180 campers
Clientele & fees: Fees: **C** ⚠
Contact: David Baird, Executive Director at (812) 294-4789;
Web site: www.southeastchristian.org
Operated by: Southeast Christian Church, 920 Blankenbaker Rd, Louisville, KY 40243-1845 at (812) 253-8000

Group Rental Information
Facilities: Cabins, Dorm-Style, Food Service, Lake, Meeting Rooms
Programs: Boating (#38662)

Culver Summer Camps

(est 1902) ⚠ 🚐

Culver, IN (Marshall Co.); (800) 221-2020
Anthony T. Mayfield, Director

Camp comments: Culver Summer Camps unique camp experience offer campers, from around the world, a summer of fun, leadership and memories.
Activities: Academics, Aviation, Boating, Fencing, Hockey, Horseback — English, Sailing, Sports — Field & Team, Tennis, Waterskiing
Session lengths & capacity: June-August; 2 & 6 week sessions; 1250 campers
Clientele & fees: coed 9-17; Fees: **E** ⚠ 🚐
Contact: Anthony T Mayfield, Director at (800) 221-2020; fax: (219) 842-8462
e-mail: summer@culver.org
Web site: www.culver.org
Operated by: Culver Educational Foundation, 1300 Academy Rd #138, Culver, IN 46511 at (800) 221-2020 (#1512)

CYO Camp Lawrence (est 1959) ⚠

Merrillville, IN (Lake Co.); (219) 736-8931

Camp comments: Campers grow physically, intellectually, spiritually, sharing adventures in the great outdoors, by campfire, on a nature hike, or during an afternoon swim.
Activities: Aquatic Activities, Arts/Crafts, Baseball/Softball, Basketball, Camping Skills/Outdoor Living, Hiking, Leadership Development, Nature/Environment Studies, Soccer
Session lengths & capacity: June-August; 8 week sessions; 160 campers
Clientele & fees: coed 7-14; Fees: **B** ⚠
Contact: Northwest Indiana CYO, Office Staff at (219) 736-8931; fax: (219) 736-9457
e-mail: nwicyo@mcleodusa.net
Operated by: CYO Camp Lawrence, 7725 Broadway Ste G, Merrillville, IN 46410-4787 at (219) 736-8931 (#1492)

CYO Camp Rancho Framasa

(est 1946) ⚠ 🏠 🚐

Nashville, IN (Brown Co.); (812) 988-2839
Kevin J Sullivan, Director

Camp comments: Inclusive camp. Mass 1 time a week. Cabins with bath. St. John Bosco Philosophy wtih campers.
Activities: Archery, Arts/Crafts, Bicycling/Biking, Camping Skills/Outdoor Living, Canoeing, Caving, Challenge/Rope Courses, Counselor Training (CIT), Horseback — Western, Leadership Development
Session lengths & capacity: June-August; 1/2 & 1 week sessions; 200 campers
Clientele & fees: coed 7-17; families; Fees: **B, C** ⚠ 🚐
Contact: Kevin J Sullivan, Camp Director at (888) 988-2839; fax: (812) 988-4842
e-mail: cyocamp@aol.com

Web site: www.campranchoframasa.org
Operated by: CYO of the Archdiocese Indpls, 2230 N Clay Lick Rd, Nashville, IN 47448 at (812) 988-2839

Group Rental Information
Site comments: Outdoor Ed and Challenge programs offered for school and youth groups. Full services.
Seasons & Capacity: Spring 100, Fall 100, Winter 50
Facilities: A/V Equipment, Cabins, Dorm-Style, Double Occupancy, Food Service, Hiking Trails, Lake, Meeting Rooms, Playing Fields, Pool, Tents
Programs: Boating, Challenge/Ropes Course, Environmental Education, Swimming (#3453)

Ella J Logan (est 1928) ⚠ 🏠

Syracuse, IN (Kosciusko Co.); (219) 457-2841
Sandy Kohne, Director

Camp comments: Beautiful, rustic lakefront camp for girls. Progressive programming includes adult & child programs. Great staff. This creates a summer you won't want to miss.
Activities: Aquatic Activities, Arts/Crafts, Camping Skills/Outdoor Living, Canoeing, Horseback — Western, Leadership Development, Nature/Environment Studies, Sailing, Team Building, Wilderness Trips
Session lengths & capacity: June-August; 1/2, 1 & 2 week sessions; 100 campers
Clientele & fees: girls 7-17; families; Fees: **B, C** ⚠ 🚐
Contact: Deborah Dilley, Director of Membership at (260) 422-3417; fax: (260) 422-0084
e-mail: camplogan@hotmail.com
Web site: www.gslimberlost.org
Operated by: Logan GS of Limberlost Cncl, 2135 Spy Run Avenue, Fort Wayne, IN 46805 at (800) 283-4812

Group Rental Information
Site comments: Tucked in a corner of northern Indiana, Camp Logan offers 220 acres of woods and meadows over looking Dewart Lake - Perfect for day trips, trainings, retreats.
Seasons & Capacity: Spring 150, Fall 150, Winter 25
Facilities: Cabins, Hiking Trails, Kitchen Facilities, Lake, Playing Fields, Tents
Programs: Boating, Challenge/Ropes Course, Environmental Education, Swimming, Winter Sports (#1541)

Flat Rock River YMCA Camps

(est 1946) ⚠ 🏠

St Paul, IN (Decatur Co.); (765) 525-6730
Arthur W. Spriggs, Director

Camp comments: Traditional camping program with a focus on teaching the core values of caring, honesty, respect & responsibility.
Activities: Archery, Bicycling/Biking, Canoeing, Challenge/Rope Courses, Climbing/Rappelling, Horseback — Western, Leadership Development, Nature/Environment Studies, Riflery, Team Building
Session lengths & capacity: June-August; 1/2, 1 & 2 week sessions; 210 campers
Clientele & fees: coed 7-17; Fees: **C, D** ⚠ 🚐
Contact: Arthur W Spriggs, Executive Director at (317) 525-6730; fax: (317) 525-2265
e-mail: aspriggs@indymca.org
Web site: www.indymca.org
Operated by: YMCA of Greater Indianapolis, 615 N Alabama St, Indianapolis, IN 46204 at (317) 266-9622

Group Rental Information
Seasons & Capacity: Spring 186, Fall 186, Winter 186
Facilities: Cabins, Food Service, Hiking Trails, Meeting Rooms, Playing Fields, Pool, River
Programs: Boating, Challenge/Ropes Course, Environmental Education, Horseback Riding, Swimming (#1491)

Gnaw Bone Camp Inc (est 1943) ▲

Nashville, IN (Brown Co.); (812) 988-4852
Alice Lorenz, Director

Camp comments: 1650 acres/2 lakes/25 miles of trails to explore. Experience yrs of traditions & a caring staff in a relaxed atmosphere.
Activities: Archery, Arts/Crafts, Bicycling/Biking, Camping Skills/Outdoor Living, Ceramics/Pottery, Hiking, Horseback — Western, Leadership Development, Nature/Environment Studies, Swimming — Recreational
Session lengths & capacity: June-July; 2 week sessions; 75 campers
Clientele & fees: girls 8-12; Fees: C ▲
Contact: Alice Lorenz at (812) 988-4852;
Operated by: Gnaw Bone Camp Inc, 1888 S State Road 135, Nashville, IN 47448 at (812) 988-4852 (#1546)

Happy Hollow Childrens Camp

(est 1951) ▲ ⌂

Nashville, IN (Brown Co.); (812) 988-4900
Bernard Schrader, CCD, Director

Camp comments: Residential camp for central Indiana youth. Special progs for under-privileged, asthmatics, diabetics & burn survivors.
Activities: Archery, Arts/Crafts, Bicycling/Biking, Camping Skills/Outdoor Living, Canoeing, Challenge/Rope Courses, Farming/Ranching/Gardening, Horseback — Western, Nature/Environment Studies, Swimming — Recreational
Session lengths & capacity: June-August; 1 & 2 week sessions; 128 campers
Clientele & fees: coed 7-15; Fees: A, C ▲ �
Contact: Bernard Schrader, CCD, Executive Director at (812) 988-4900; fax: (812) 988-7505
e-mail: hhcdir@aol.com
Operated by: Happy Hollow Children Camp Inc, 615 N Alabama Room 325, Indianapolis, IN 46204 at (317) 638-3849

Group Rental Information
Site comments: Available for outdoor education programs. 800 acres,creek,lake,forest. South Central Indiana-easy access to I65. Spring and fall dates available.
Facilities: Dorm-Style, Double Occupancy, Food Service, Hiking Trails, Kitchen Facilities, Lodges, Meeting Rooms, Playing Fields (#1517)

Howe Military Sch Summer Camp (est 1925) ▲

Howe, IN (LaGrange Co.); (219) 562-2131
Duane Van Orden, Director

ICON LEGEND
☀ Day Camp
▲ Resident Camp
⌂ Facilities Available To Rent
🚗 Transportation Available
🐷 Financial Aid Available

FEE RANGES PER WEEK
A	$0-75
B	$75-200
C	$201-350
D	$351-500
E	$501-650
F	over $650

Camp comments: Military & academic prog with sports, rope course, full water front activities . Fun in a structured camp environment.
Activities: Archery, Arts/Crafts, Baseball/Softball, Basketball, Boating, Challenge/Rope Courses, Leadership Development, Riflery, Sailing, SCUBA
Session lengths & capacity: June-August; 3 & 6 week sessions; 122 campers
Clientele & fees: boys 9-15; Fees: D ▲
Contact: Dr Brent Smith, Director of Admission at (219) 562-2131; fax: (219) 562-3678
e-mail: dvanorden@howemilitary.com
Operated by: Howe Military School, PO Box 240, Howe, IN 46746 at (260) 562-2131 (#1494)

Indian Creek Baptist Camp ▲ ⌂

Bedford, IN (Lawrence Co.); (812) 279-2161
Paul Scott, Director
Activities: Archery, Basketball, Canoeing, Counselor Training (CIT), Hiking, Leadership Development, Music, Nature/Environment Studies, Religious Study, Swimming — Recreational
Contact: Web site:
www.ABC-Indiana.org/camps.htm
Operated by: American Baptist Churches Ind, 1350 N Delaware, Indianapolis, IN 46202 at (317) 635-3552 (#42107)

Indiana Baptist Assembly

(est 1965) ▲ ⌂

Reelsville, IN (Putnam Co.); (765) 795-4400
Jim Walter, Director

Camp comments: Changing lives and creating leaders for the church - today and tomorrow.
Activities: Aquatic Activities, Canoeing, Challenge/Rope Courses, Drama, Leadership Development, Music, Nature/Environment Studies, Performing Arts, Religious Study, Swimming — Recreational
Session lengths & capacity: June-August; 1/2 & 1 week sessions; 75 campers
Clientele & fees: coed 8-18; families; Fees: B ▲
Contact: Jim Walter, Director at (765) 795-4400; fax: (765) 795-4400
e-mail: iba@abc-indiana.org
Web site: www.ABC-Indiana.org/camps.htm
Operated by: American Baptist Churches Ind, 1350 N Delaware, Indianapolis, IN 46202 at (317) 635-3552 (#12327)

InPursuit (est 2000) ▲ ⌂

Seymour, IN (Jackson Co.); (812) 497-0008
David Grout, Director

Camp comments: Fun. Challenge. Life-changing. A new SpringHill Initiatives camp, InPursuit offers 1-3 wk programs for kids 7-17 Jun-Aug. All-season retreat accom. for 500+
Activities: Aquatic Activities, Basketball, Challenge/Rope Courses, Climbing/Rappelling, Dance, Drama, Horseback — Western, Team Building
Session lengths & capacity: June-August; 1, 2 & 3 week sessions; 425 campers
Clientele & fees: boys 7-17; girls 7-17; coed 7-17; Fees: C, D, E, F ▲
Contact: Keith Rudge, Director of Guest Services at (812) 497-0008; fax: (812) 497-0195
e-mail: krudge@inpursuit.org
Web site: www.springhillcamps.com
Operated by: Spring Hill Initiatives, PO Box 100, Evart, MI 49631 at (231) 734-2616

Group Rental Information
Site comments: Offering facilities for small groups to 550+ person retreats w/partial to full program facilitation, creative housing, meals, & limitless activity options.
Seasons & Capacity: Spring 0, Summer 550, Fall 550, Winter 550

Facilities: A/V Equipment, Cabins, Food Service, Hiking Trails, Lake, Meeting Rooms, Playing Fields, Tents
Programs: Boating, Challenge/Ropes Course, Horseback Riding, Swimming (#41441)

Isanogel Center (est 1962) ☀ ▲ ⌂

Muncie, IN (Delaware Co.); (765) 288-1073
Monica Sauter, Director

Camp comments: Isanogel strives to provide recreational and educational opportunities through progressive programming for individuals with disabilities and their families.
Activities: Aquatic Activities, Arts/Crafts, Basketball, Camping Skills/Outdoor Living, Challenge/Rope Courses, Dance, Drama, Nature/Environment Studies, Swimming — Instructional, Swimming — Recreational
Session lengths & capacity: June-August; 1 & 2 week sessions; 48 campers
Clientele & fees: coed 5-99; Fees: B ☀ Fees: D, E ▲ 🐷
Contact: Monica Sauter, Recreation Director at (765) 288-1073; fax: (765) 288-3103
e-mail: isanogel@iquest.net
Web site: www.isanogelcenter.org
Operated by: Isanogel Center, 7601 W Isanogel Rd 50N, Muncie, IN 47304-9339 at (765) 288-1073

Group Rental Information
Facilities: Kitchen Facilities, Linens, Pool, Tents
Programs: Challenge/Ropes Course, Swimming (#1536)

Jameson Inc (est 1928) ▲ ⌂ 🚗

Indianapolis, IN (Marion Co.); (317) 241-2661
Sherri Brown, Director

Camp comments: Programs for at-risk and special needs youth to increase self-esteem. Variety of activities offered. Campers attend on referral basis.
Activities: Archery, Arts/Crafts, Basketball, Camping Skills/Outdoor Living, Challenge/Rope Courses, Counselor Training (CIT), Leadership Development, Nature/Environment Studies, Swimming — Recreational
Session lengths & capacity: 1 & 2 week sessions; 80 campers
Clientele & fees: boys 7-17; girls 7-17; coed 7-17; Fees: C ▲
Contact: Sherri Brown, Program Manager at (317) 241-2661; fax: (317) 241-2760
e-mail: jcprogram@comcast.net
Operated by: Jameson Inc, PO Box 31156, 2001 S Bridgeport Rd, Indianapolis, IN 46231-0156 at (317) 241-2661 (#1535)

Kid City Original (est 1993) ☀

Bloomington, IN (Monroe Co.); (812) 349-3731
Anna Gilmore/David Weigand, Director

Camp comments: Children experience camp through fun & exciting weekly theemes. Kid City - where everyone learns, grows, & belongs. Arts/crafts, field trips, sports, nature.
Activities: Arts/Crafts, Basketball, Caving, Climbing/Rappelling, Counselor Training (CIT), Field Trips, Hiking, Nature/Environment Studies, Sports — Field & Team, Swimming — Recreational
Session lengths & capacity: May-August; 1 week sessions; 130 campers
Clientele & fees: coed 3-15; Fees: B ☀ 🐷
Contact: Anna Gilmore at (812) 349-3731; fax: (812) 349-3785
e-mail: gilmorea@city.bloomington.in.us
Web site: www.city.blommington.in.us
Operated by: Bloomington Parks & Recreation, PO Box 848, Bloomington, IN 47402 at (812) 349-3700 (#11364)

Lake Luther Bible Camp

(est 1966) ▲ ⌂

Angola, IN (Steuben Co.); (219) 833-2383
Rev Mark Radloff, Director

Camp comments: Lake Luther is owned &
operated by the Indiana-Kentucky Synod of the
Evangelical Lutheran Church in America.
Activities: Arts/Crafts, Basketball, Canoeing,
Challenge/Rope Courses, Music,
Nature/Environment Studies, Religious Study,
Soccer, Swimming — Recreational
Session lengths & capacity: 1/2 & 1 week
sessions; 65 campers
Clientele & fees: coed 7-18; families; Fees: B ▲
Contact: Rev Mark Radloff, Director at
(317) 253-3522; fax: (317) 254-5666
e-mail: markradloff@juno.comt.org
Operated by: Lutheran Outdoor Ministries, 911 E
86th Suite 200, Indianapolis, IN 46240-1860 at
(317) 253-3522 (#13933)

Lutheran Hills (est 1966) ▲ ⌂

Morgantown, IN (Brown Co.); (812) 988-2519
Rev Mark Radloff, Director

Camp comments: Lutheran Hills is owned &
operated by the Evangelical Lutheran Church in
America Indiana-Kentucky Synod
Activities: Aquatic Activities, Arts/Crafts,
Backpacking, Camping Skills/Outdoor Living,
Music, Nature/Environment Studies
Session lengths & capacity: 1/2 & 1 week
sessions; 100 campers
Clientele & fees: coed 7-18; families; Fees: B ▲
Contact: Rev Mark Radloff, Director at
(317) 253-3522; fax: (317) 254-5666
e-mail: markradloff@juno.com
Operated by: Lutheran Outdoor Ministries, 911 E
86th Suite 200, Indianapolis, IN 46240-1860 at
(317) 253-3522 (#5668)

Lutherwald (est 1955) ▲ ⌂

Howe, IN (LaGrange Co.); (317) 562-2102
Rev. Mark Radloff, Director

Camp comments: Lutherwald is owned & operated
by the Indiana-Kentucky Synod of the Evangelical
Lutheran Church in America.
Activities: Arts/Crafts, Basketball, Canoeing,
Drama, Music, Nature/Environment Studies,
Swimming — Recreational
Session lengths & capacity: 1/2 & 1 week
sessions; 150 campers
Clientele & fees: coed 7-18; families; Fees: B ▲
Contact: Rev. Mark Radloff, Director at
(317) 253-3522; fax: (317) 254-5666
e-mail: markradloff@juno.com
Operated by: Lutheran Outdoor Ministries, 911 E
86th Suite 200, Indianapolis, IN 46240-1860 at
(317) 253-3522 (#12329)

McMillen Program Center

(est 1948) ☀ ⌂ 🚐

Huntertown, IN (Allen Co.); (219) 637-6279
Jill Frey, Director

Camp comments: Day camp in a sleep-away
setting. Transportation available. Traditional
program in a caring supportive atmosphere.
Activities: Archery, Arts/Crafts, Camping
Skills/Outdoor Living, Challenge/Rope Courses,
Climbing/Rappelling, Hiking, Leadership
Development, Sports — Field & Team
Session lengths & capacity: June-August; 1 week
sessions; 125 campers
Clientele & fees: girls 5-17; Fees: B ☀ 🐷
Contact: Jill Frey, Center Day Camp Director at
(219) 637-6279; fax: (219) 637-0010
e-mail:
girlscoutsmcmillenprogramcenter@yahoo.com
Web site: www.gslimberlost.org

Operated by: Logan GS of Limberlost Cncl, 2135
Spy Run Avenue, Fort Wayne, IN 46805 at
(800) 283-4812

Group Rental Information
Site comments: A peaceful setting with modern
facilities where you can open the door to
communications and enjoyment while closing the
door on distractions & interruptions.
Seasons & Capacity: Spring 178, Winter 94
Facilities: A/V Equipment, Cabins, Dorm-Style,
Hiking Trails, Kitchen Facilities, Meeting Rooms,
Tents (#1506)

Myron S Goldman Union Cmp Inst

☀ ▲ ⌂

Zionsville, IN (Marion Co.)
Rabbi Ron Klotz, Director
Activities: Aquatic Activities, Arts/Crafts,
Challenge/Rope Courses, Dance, Field Trips,
Language Studies, Performing Arts, Religious
Study, Sports — Field & Team, Swimming —
Recreational
Session lengths & capacity: June-August; 2 &
4 week sessions
Clientele & fees: Fees: E ▲
Contact: Ronald Klotz, Director at (317) 873-3361;
fax: (317) 873-3742
e-mail: guciron@aol.com
Operated by: Goldman Union Camp, 9349 Moore
Road, Zionsville, IN 46077 at (317) 873-3361

Group Rental Information
Facilities: Dorm-Style, Food Service, Hiking Trails,
Meeting Rooms, Playing Fields (#22636)

Ransburg Branch YMCA Day Camps

☀

Indianapolis, IN (Marion Co.); (317) 266-9622
Jeanette M Randall, Director

Camp comments: YMCA camps are building
strong kids strong families and strong communities.
Specialty camps.Half-day & daily programs.Ages
3-16
Activities: Aquatic Activities, Arts/Crafts, Camping
Skills/Outdoor Living, Community Service, Field
Trips, Fishing, Leadership Development,
Nature/Environment Studies, Sports — Field &
Team, Swimming — Recreational
Session lengths & capacity: May-August; 1 week
sessions
Clientele & fees: coed 3-16; Fees: B ☀ 🐷
Contact: Karin Ogden, Senior Program Director at
(317) 357-8441; fax: (317) 322-2793
e-mail: kogden@indymca.org
Web site: www.indymca.org
Operated by: YMCA of Greater Indianapolis, 615 N
Alabama St, Indianapolis, IN 46204 at
(317) 266-9622 (#20377)

The Outpost (est 1970) ▲ ⌂

Santa Claus, IN (Spencer Co.); (812) 937-2723
John E 'Jack' Thompson, Director

Camp comments: Unique camping experience.
Camping program is based on Roman Catholic
thought & life. 1 to 5 staff to camper ratio.
Activities: Aquatic Activities, Archery, Arts/Crafts,
Camping Skills/Outdoor Living, Community
Service, Field Trips, Leadership Development,
Nature/Environment Studies, Team Building
Session lengths & capacity: Year-round; 1 week
sessions; 40 campers
Clientele & fees: boys 12-16; girls 12-16;
coed 10-11; Fees: B ▲ 🐷
Contact: Michael Eppler, Dir. Youth Ministry at
(812) 424-5536; fax: (812) 421-1334
e-mail: marknoah@aol.com
Operated by: Catholic Diocese of Evansville,
PO Box 4169, Evansville, IN 47724 at
(812) 424-5536 (#3806)

Tippecanoe Baptist Camp

(est 1941) ▲ ⌂

N Webster, IN (Kosiosko Co.); (219) 834-4184

Camp comments: Changing lives and creating
leaders for the church - today and tomorrow.
Activities: Aquatic Activities, Camping
Skills/Outdoor Living, Canoeing, Counselor Training
(CIT), Leadership Development,
Nature/Environment Studies, Performing Arts,
Religious Study, Swimming — Recreational, Team
Building
Session lengths & capacity: June-August; 1/2 &
1 week sessions; 120 campers
Clientele & fees: coed 8-18; families;
Fees: B ▲ 🐷
Contact: Dennis Judy, Manager at (219) 834-4184;
fax: (219) 834-1904
e-mail: camptippy@hoosierlink.net
Web site: www.ABC-Indiana.org/camps.htm
Operated by: American Baptist Churches Ind, 1350
N Delaware, Indianapolis, IN 46202 at
(317) 635-3552 (#22495)

Waycross Camp (est 1957) ▲ ⌂

Morgantown, IN (Brown Co.); (812) 597-4241
Joan Amati, Director

Camp comments: Waycross Episcopal camp
provides an opportunity for campers to discover
and grow in their awareness of God thru adventure,
community, creation, reflection
Activities: Archery, Arts/Crafts, Camping
Skills/Outdoor Living, Canoeing, Counselor Training
(CIT), Hiking, Leadership Development, Music,
Swimming — Recreational, Team Building
Session lengths & capacity: June-August; 1 week
sessions; 70 campers
Clientele & fees: coed 8-16; Fees: C ▲ 🐷
Contact: Rita Allender, Camp Coordinator at
(812) 597-4241; fax: (812) 597-4291
e-mail: info@waycrosscamp.org
Web site: www.waycrosscamp.org
Operated by: Waycross Inc, 7363 Bear Creek Rd,
Morgantown, IN 46160 at (812) 597-4241

Group Rental Information
Site comments: Waycross camp hosts retreats for
the Episcopal church and for other religious,
educational, and charitable not-for-profit groups
Seasons & Capacity: Spring 130, Summer 130,
Fall 130, Winter 130
Facilities: A/V Equipment, Cabins, Dorm-Style,
Food Service, Hiking Trails, Linens, Meeting
Rooms, Pool (#6425)

YMCA A. Jordan Y Day Camps

(est 1959) ☀

Indianapolis, IN (Marion Co.); (317) 253-3206

Camp comments: YMCA camp can spell
leadership, quality instruction, and values to last a
lifetime!
Activities: Arts/Crafts, Camping Skills/Outdoor
Living, Counselor Training (CIT), Field Trips,
Nature/Environment Studies, Performing Arts,
Sports — Field & Team
Session lengths & capacity: 1 week sessions;
600 campers
Clientele & fees: coed 3-16; Fees: B ☀ 🐷
Contact: Lashanda Fitzgerald, Youth Director at
(317) 253-3206; fax: (317) 259-5652
Web site: www.indymca.org
Operated by: YMCA of Greater Indianapolis, 615 N
Alabama St, Indianapolis, IN 46204 at
(317) 266-9622 (#12406)

YMCA Camp Carson

☀ ▲ ⌂

Evansville, IN (Gibson Co.); (812) 423-8622
Mark Scoular, Director

Camp comments: Committed to providing safe,
fun-filled summers, where the friendships and
memories built are the kind that last a lifetime.

Activities: Aquatic Activities, Archery, Arts/Crafts, Ceramics/Pottery, Challenge/Rope Courses, Horseback — Western, Nature/Environment Studies, Riflery, Sports — Field & Team, Wilderness Trips
Session lengths & capacity: April-November; 1/2, 1 & 2 week sessions; 120 campers
Clientele & fees: coed 7-16; Fees: C, D ⚠ 🐷
Contact: Mark Scoular, Executive Director at (812) 385-3597; fax: (812) 386-1654
e-mail: scoular@sigemcon.net
Operated by: YMCA of South West Indiana, 272 NW Sixth St, Evansville, IN 47708 at (812) 423-8622
Group Rental Information
Seasons & Capacity: Spring 160, Summer 40, Fall 160, Winter 40 (#22796)

YMCA Camp Potawotami
(est 1920) ⚠ 🏠
South Milford, IN (La Grange Co.); (800) 966-9622
Sonny Adkins, Director

Camp comments: Premiere camp on nrthern Indiana. Great activities, excellent staff. Building character, friends, and memories since 1920.
Activities: Arts/Crafts, Basketball, Camping Skills/Outdoor Living, Canoeing, Challenge/Rope Courses, Climbing/Rappelling, Leadership Development, Nature/Environment Studies, Sports — Field & Team, Travel/Tour
Session lengths & capacity: 1/2, 1 & 2 week sessions; 200 campers
Clientele & fees: boys 7-16; girls 7-16; coed 7-16; families; seniors; Fees: C ⚠ 🐷
Contact: Jim Parry, Executive Director at (800) 966-9622; fax: (260) 351-3915
e-mail: ymcacamp@camp-potawotami.org
Web site: www.camp-potawotami.org
Operated by: YMCA of Greater Fort Wayne, 1020 Barr Street, Fort Wayne, IN 46802 at (260) 422-6486
Group Rental Information
Site comments: Over 80 years of building character...One child at a time. Do great things!
Facilities: A/V Equipment, Cabins, Dorm-Style, Food Service, Hiking Trails, Kitchen Facilities, Lake, Linens, Lodges, Meeting Rooms, Playing Fields
Programs: Boating, Challenge/Ropes Course, Environmental Education, Swimming (#4042)

YMCA-B. Harrison Y Day Camps
(est 1997) ☀
Indianapolis, IN (Marion Co.); (317) 547-9622
Robin Heugel, Director

Camp comments: Our goal is to help participants grow spiritually, mentally, & physically. To help build memories that last a lifetime.

ICON LEGEND
☀ Day Camp
⚠ Resident Camp
🏠 Facilities Available To Rent
🚐 Transportation Available
🐷 Financial Aid Available

FEE RANGES PER WEEK
A $0-75
B $75-200
C $201-350
D $351-500
E $501-650
F over $650

Activities: Basketball, Drama, Field Trips, Hiking, Nature/Environment Studies, Soccer, Sports — Field & Team, Swimming — Recreational, Tennis
Session lengths & capacity: June-August; 1 week sessions; 125 campers
Clientele & fees: coed 6-12; Fees: B ☀ 🚐
Contact: Sharon Griffin, Senior Program Director at (317) 547-9622 ext. 18; fax: (317) 547-9640
e-mail: sgriffin@indymca.org
Web site: www.indymca.org
Operated by: YMCA of Greater Indianapolis, 615 N Alabama St, Indianapolis, IN 46204 at (317) 266-9622 (#22670)

YMCA-Baxter Y Day Camps
(est 1963) ☀
Indianapolis, IN (Marion Co.); (317) 881-9347
Andrew McFarlane, Director

Camp comments: We build strong kids, strong families, strong communities.
Activities: Archery, Arts/Crafts, Camping Skills/Outdoor Living, Community Service, Counselor Training (CIT), Field Trips, Leadership Development, Sports — Field & Team, Swimming — Recreational
Session lengths & capacity: June-August; 1 week sessions
Clientele & fees: coed 4-15; Fees: B ☀ 🐷 🚐
Contact: Greg Wegesin, Teen Director at (317) 881-9347; fax: (317) 887-8787
e-mail: gwegesin@indymca.org
Web site: www.indymca.org
Operated by: YMCA of Greater Indianapolis, 615 N Alabama St, Indianapolis, IN 46204 at (317) 266-9622 (#901535)

YMCA-Fall Creek Y Day Camps
☀
Indianapolis, IN (Marion Co.); (317) 634-2478
Activities: Aerobics/Exercise, Arts/Crafts, Ceramics/Pottery, Counselor Training (CIT), Drama, Drawing/Painting, Swimming — Recreational, Team Building
Contact: Fred Dorsey, Youth and Teen Director at (317) 634-2478; fax: (317) 687-3693
e-mail: fdorsey@indymca.org
Web site: www.indymca.org
Operated by: YMCA of Greater Indianapolis, 615 N Alabama St, Indianapolis, IN 46204 at (317) 266-9622 (#22822)

YMCA-Hamilton Co. Y Day Camps (est 1990) ☀ 🚐
Fishers, IN (Hamilton Co.); (317) 595-9622
Fritz Harbridge, Director

Camp comments: Day camp serves all of Hamilton Co. Sport Art Teen Preschool camps. Character development emphasis team building & fun.
Activities: Aquatic Activities, Archery, Arts/Crafts, Basketball, Camping Skills/Outdoor Living, Canoeing, Challenge/Rope Courses, Drama, Hiking, Sports — Field & Team
Session lengths & capacity: June-August; 1 week sessions; 350 campers
Clientele & fees: boys 3-15; girls 3-15; coed 3-15; Fees: B ☀ 🚐 🐷
Contact: Geoffrey Mertens, Program Director at (317) 577-2070; fax: (317) 577-2075
e-mail: gmertens@indymca.org
Web site: www.indymca.org
Operated by: YMCA of Greater Indianapolis, 615 N Alabama St, Indianapolis, IN 46204 at (317) 266-9622 (#901541)

YMCA-West District Y Day Camps (est 1987) ☀
Indianapolis, IN (Marion Co.); (317) 484-9622
Greg Gundersen, Director

Camp comments: Your child will have fun activities teaching fair play, caring, honesty,respect, responsibility. Lifetime memories.
Activities: Aquatic Activities, Camping Skills/Outdoor Living, Community Service, Drawing/Painting, Hiking, Leadership Development, Sports — Field & Team, Swimming — Recreational
Session lengths & capacity: June-August; 1 week sessions; 400 campers
Clientele & fees: coed 5-14; Fees: B ☀ 🐷 🚐
Contact: Joshua Brown, Youth and Teen Director at (317) 484-9622; fax: (317) 484-2360
e-mail: jbrown@indymca.org
Web site: www.indymca.org
Operated by: YMCA of Greater Indianapolis, 615 N Alabama St, Indianapolis, IN 46204 at (317) 266-9622 (#20375)

Iowa

Abe Lincoln (est 1922) ☀ ⚠ 🏠
Blue Grass, IA; (563) 381-3053
Dave Phelps, Director

Camp comments: In addition to fun learning and enhancing self esteem skills Camp Abe Lincolns major focus is character development.
Activities: Archery, Canoeing, Challenge/Rope Courses, Counselor Training (CIT), Horseback — Western, Nature/Environment Studies, Swimming — Instructional, Swimming — Recreational, Team Building
Session lengths & capacity: June-August; 1 week sessions; 140 campers
Clientele & fees: coed 4-17; Fees: B ☀
Fees: C ⚠ 🚐
Contact: Dave Phelps Patrick Telman, Director/Assistant Director at (319) 381-3053; fax: (319) 381-3056
e-mail: ymca@campabelincoln.org
Operated by: Scott County Family Y, 1624 W Front St, Blue Grass, IA 52726 at (563) 322-7171
Group Rental Information
Seasons & Capacity: Spring 140, Summer 140, Fall 140, Winter 140
Facilities: Cabins, Food Service, Hiking Trails, Kitchen Facilities, Lake, Lodges, Meeting Rooms, Playing Fields, Pool
Programs: Challenge/Ropes Course, Horseback Riding, Swimming (#3422)

Albrecht Acres of the Midwest
(est 1975) ⚠ 🏠
Sherrill, IA; (563) 552-1771
Daniel King, Director
Activities: Arts/Crafts, Ceramics/Pottery, Dance, Drama, Fishing, Hiking, International Culture, Music, Nature/Environment Studies
Session lengths & capacity: June-August; 1 week sessions; 70 campers
Clientele & fees: coed 2-99; Fees: C ☀
Fees: C ⚠
Contact: Daniel King, Administrative Director at (563) 552-1771; fax: (563) 552-2732
e-mail: albrecht@mwci.net
Web site: www.albrechtacres.org
Operated by: Albrecht Acres of the Midwest, PO Box 50, Sherrill, IA 52073 at (563) 552-1771
Group Rental Information
Site comments: A residental camp for individuals with mental and physical disabilities. Campers age 2 and older.
Facilities: Cabins, Dorm-Style, Food Service, Hiking Trails, Lake, Lodges, Meeting Rooms, Pool
Programs: Swimming (#6715)

Aldersgate UM Camp (est 1957) ▲ ⌂

Villisca, IA (Montgomery Co.); (712) 826-8121
Jackie & Oscar Cordon, Director

Camp comments: Emphasis on Christian community living. Theme weeks & field trips. Zoo overnight camp in Omaha. CIT/Leadership Program.
Activities: Aquatic Activities, Archery, Camping Skills/Outdoor Living, Canoeing, Counselor Training (CIT), Field Trips, Leadership Development, Music, Nature/Environment Studies, Team Building
Session lengths & capacity: 1/2 & 1 week sessions; 90 campers
Clientele & fees: coed 3-18; families;
Fees: A, B ▲ 🐷
Contact: Jackie & Oscar Cordon, Executive Directors at (712) 826-8121;
Web site: www.iaumc/camps
Operated by: Iowa Conf United Methodist, 500 E Court Ave Ste C, Des Moines, IA 50309 at (515) 283-1991

Group Rental Information
Site comments: Retreat facility set in rolling woodland and prairie.
Seasons & Capacity: Spring 80, Winter 80
Facilities: Dorm-Style, Double Occupancy, Food Service, Hiking Trails, Kitchen Facilities, Lodges, Meeting Rooms
Programs: Environmental Education (#3282)

Camp Courageous of Iowa

(est 1972) ▲ ⌂

Monticello, IA (Jones Co.); (319) 465-5916
Jeanne Muellerleile, Director

Camp comments: Year-round respite care & recreational program for children & adults with disabilities. Traditional & adventure activities offered. Trip/Travel programs also.
Activities: Aquatic Activities, Archery, Arts/Crafts, Camping Skills/Outdoor Living, Canoeing, Caving, Challenge/Rope Courses, Climbing/Rappelling, Nature/Environment Studies, Swimming — Recreational
Session lengths & capacity: May-August; 1/2 & 1 week sessions; 75 campers
Clientele & fees: coed 3-99; families;
Fees: C ▲ 🐷
Contact: Jeanne Muellerleile, Camp Director at (319) 465-5916 ext. 206; fax: (319) 465-5919
e-mail: jmuellerleile@campcourageous.org
Web site: www.campcourageous.org
Operated by: Camp Courageous Of Iowa, 12007 190th St, Monticello, IA 52310 at (319) 465-5916

Group Rental Information
Site comments: Camp Courageous is fully winterized & air conditioned. Great place for any event from a few hours to a few days. Indoor swimming pools are very popular!
Seasons & Capacity: Spring 100, Summer 100, Fall 100, Winter 100
Facilities: Cabins, Dorm-Style, Food Service, Hiking Trails, Kitchen Facilities, Linens, Lodges, Meeting Rooms, Pool
Programs: Challenge/Ropes Course, Swimming (#3159)

Camp Fire Day Camps

(est 1946) ☀ ▲ ⌂

Des Moines, IA (Polk Co.); (515) 274-1501
D.D. Gass, Director

Camp comments: Day camps for school-age boys & girls. Several sites in Central Iowa: Des Moines, Ames, Fort Dodge. Zoo Day Camp in Des Moines. Theme weeks and field trips.
Activities: Arts/Crafts, Camping Skills/Outdoor Living, Drama, Field Trips, Hiking, Leadership Development, Nature/Environment Studies, Sports — Field & Team, Swimming — Recreational
Session lengths & capacity: June-August; 1 week sessions; 75 campers
Clientele & fees: coed 5-16; Fees: B ☀ 🐷

Contact: (515) 274-1501; fax: (515) 274-1502
e-mail: campfiredm@aol.com
Web site: www.iowacampfire.com
Operated by: Camp Fire USA, 5615 Hickman Rd, Des Moines, IA 50310 at (515) 274-1501

Group Rental Information
Site comments: Day camp programs for school-age boys & girls. Theme weeks, field trips, swimming. Locations in Central Iowa: Des Moines, Ames, and Fort Dodge.
Facilities: Dorm-Style, Lodges, Meeting Rooms (#4014)

Camp Hertko Hollow

(est 1968) ▲ 🚐

Boone, IA; (515) 432-7558
Vivian Murray, Director

Camp comments: Our mission is to prevent and cure diabetes an to improve the lives of all people affected by diabetes.
Activities: Archery, Canoeing, Challenge/Rope Courses, Climbing/Rappelling, Horseback — English, Leadership Development, Nature/Environment Studies, Riflery, Swimming — Recreational, Team Building
Session lengths & capacity: June-June; 1/2 & 1 week sessions; 250 campers
Clientele & fees: coed 6-16; Fees: D ▲
Contact: Sheryl Rolfe, District Manager - Programs at (800) 678-4232; fax: (515) 276-2662
e-mail: srolfe@diabetes.com
Operated by: Camp Hertko Hollow Inc, 1701 E Schwartz Blvd, Lady Lake, FL 32159 at (352) 750-6759 (#6314)

Camp Little Cloud (est 1950) ☀ ▲ ⌂

Epworth, IA (Dubuque Co.); (563) 583-0081
Debra Stork, Director

Camp comments: Traditional Girl Scout program.
Activities: Arts/Crafts, Camping Skills/Outdoor Living, Canoeing, Counselor Training (CIT), Hiking, Horseback — Western, Leadership Development, Nature/Environment Studies, Photography, Swimming — Recreational
Session lengths & capacity: June-August; 1/2, 1 & 2 week sessions; 100 campers
Clientele & fees: girls 6-17; Fees: B ☀ Fees: B ▲ 🐷
Contact: Jan Firzlaff, Camp Reservations Manager at (563) 583-9169 ext. 11; fax: (563) 588-3630
e-mail: girlscouts@littlecloud.org
Web site: www.littlecloud.org
Operated by: Girl Scouts Little Cloud Cncl, 2644 Pennsylvania Ave, Dubuque, IA 52001 at (563) 583-9169

Group Rental Information
Site comments: Near Dubuque, five winterized cabins, four tent units, flush toilets, showers, sleeping is mainly with mats on floor.
Seasons & Capacity: Spring 210, Summer 210, Fall 210, Winter 145
Facilities: Cabins, Dorm-Style, Hiking Trails, Kitchen Facilities, Lake, Lodges, Meeting Rooms, Pool, Tents
Programs: Swimming, Winter Sports (#1469)

Camp Sacajawea (est 1963) ▲ ⌂

Boone, IA (Boone Co.); (515) 432-2948
Wanda Armstrong, Director

Camp comments: Iowa highlands. Horseback riding, swimming, sports,nature. Fun-loving capable staff set the pace, girls 3rd grade & up.
Activities: Arts/Crafts, Canoeing, Challenge/Rope Courses, Counselor Training (CIT), Horseback — Western, International Culture, Nature/Environment Studies, Performing Arts, Photography
Session lengths & capacity: June-August; 1/2 & 1 week sessions; 160 campers
Clientele & fees: girls 6-17; families; Fees: B ▲
Contact: Wanda Armstrong, Camp Director at (515) 278-2881; fax: (515) 278-5988

e-mail: campsac@aol.com
Web site: www.moingonagirlscouts.org
Operated by: Girl Scouts Moingona Council, 10715 Hickman Rd, Des Moines, IA 50322 at (515) 278-2881

Group Rental Information
Site comments: Program center, dining hall, winterized lodge facilities.
Seasons & Capacity: Spring 200, Fall 200, Winter 144
Facilities: Cabins, Double Occupancy, Hiking Trails, Kitchen Facilities, Lodges, Meeting Rooms, River, Tents (#1489)

Camp Shalom, Inc (est 1976) ▲ ⌂

Maquoketa, IA (Jackson Co.); (319) 652-3311
Rev. Eric Elkin, Director

Camp comments: A Christ-centered outdoor ministry that inspires all people to live fully in thespirit.
Activities: Archery, Arts/Crafts, Caving, Challenge/Rope Courses, Hiking, Leadership Development, Music, Sports — Field & Team
Session lengths & capacity: June-August; 1/2 & 1 week sessions; 64 campers
Clientele & fees: coed 8-18; families;
Fees: C ▲ 🐷
Contact: Eric Elkin, Director at (563) 323-2790; fax: (563) 326-1422
e-mail: shalom@netexpress.net
Operated by: Camp Shalom Inc, 2136 Brady St, Davenport, IA 52803 at (563) 323-2790

Group Rental Information
Site comments: Camp Shalom is a Christian camp located near Maquoketa, IA. It offers trails, ropes course, canoeing, soccer fields and space for retreat.
Seasons & Capacity: Spring 99, Summer 84, Fall 99
Facilities: A/V Equipment, Cabins, Dorm-Style, Food Service, Hiking Trails, Lodges, Meeting Rooms, Playing Fields, Tents
Programs: Challenge/Ropes Course, Environmental Education (#3449)

Camp Wyoming (est 1960) ▲ ⌂

Wyoming, IA (Jones Co.); (319) 488-3893
Dean E Nelson, Director

Camp comments: All season Christian camp & conf. center. Located east central Iowa. Adult & youth retreat facilities. Full summer program. Programming help available.
Activities: Archery, Camping Skills/Outdoor Living, Canoeing, Caving, Counselor Training (CIT), Leadership Development, Nature/Environment Studies, Religious Study, Swimming — Recreational, Team Building
Session lengths & capacity: June-August; 1/2 & 1 week sessions; 160 campers
Clientele & fees: coed 5-18; families; seniors;
Fees: B, C ▲ 🐷
Contact: Dean E Nelson, Camp Administrator at (319) 488-3893; fax: (319) 488-3895
e-mail: campwyo@netins.net
Web site: www.netins.net/showcase/campwyoming
Operated by: Camp Wyoming, 9106 42nd Ave, Wyoming, IA 52362-7647 at (319) 488-3893

Group Rental Information
Site comments: All season Christian camp & conf. center. Located east central Iowa. Adult & youth retreat facilities. Full summer program. Programming help available.
Seasons & Capacity: Spring 130, Summer 160, Fall 130, Winter 130
Facilities: Cabins, Double Occupancy, Food Service, Hiking Trails, Kitchen Facilities, Linens, Lodges, Meeting Rooms, Playing Fields, Pool, River
Programs: Challenge/Ropes Course, Environmental Education, Swimming (#1474)

Conestoga (est 1948)
☀ ▲ 🏠

New Liberty, IA; (309) 843-2950
Camp comments: Traditional and trip camping. Focus on self-esteem, skill and team building. Make friends for a lifetime of memories.
Activities: Archery, Arts/Crafts, Camping Skills/Outdoor Living, Challenge/Rope Courses, Climbing/Rappelling, Field Trips, Hiking, Leadership Development, Team Building, Wilderness Trips
Session lengths & capacity: 1/2, 1 & 2 week sessions; 160 campers
Clientele & fees: girls 8-18; Fees: **B, C** ▲ 🐷
Contact: Janet Kington, Director at (319) 363-8335; fax: (319) 363-1620
Operated by: Mississippi Valley GSC, 2011 Second Avenue, Rock Island, IL 61201 at (309) 788-0833 (#1486)

Des Moines YMCA Camp
(est 1919)
▲ 🏠 🚐

Boone, IA; (515) 432-7558
David Sherry, Director
Camp comments: Beautiful Des Moines River Valley setting.Rich 80 year history of kids learning and having fun.Come 🐷 be a part of it.
Activities: Archery, Arts/Crafts, Canoeing, Challenge/Rope Courses, Climbing/Rappelling, Horseback — Western, Leadership Development, Nature/Environment Studies, Riflery, Swimming — Recreational
Session lengths & capacity: January-December; 1/2, 1 & 2 week sessions; 350 campers
Clientele & fees: boys 6-16; girls 6-16; coed 6-16; families; Fees: **C** ▲ 🐷
Contact: David Sherry, Exec Director at (515) 432-7558; fax: (515) 432-5414
e-mail: d.sherry@dmymca.org
Operated by: YMCA of Greater Des Moines, 101 Locust St, Des Moines, IA 50309 at (515) 288-0131

Group Rental Information
Site comments: Come experience the beautiful Des Moines River Valley. Great for youth, adult & business retreats.
Seasons & Capacity: Spring 350, Summer 350, Fall 350, Winter 350
Facilities: A/V Equipment, Cabins, Food Service, Hiking Trails, Lodges, Meeting Rooms, Playing Fields, Pool, River, Tents
Programs: Boating, Challenge/Ropes Course, Environmental Education, Horseback Riding, Swimming, Winter Sports (#1481)

ICON LEGEND
☀   Day Camp
▲   Resident Camp
🏠   Facilities Available To Rent
🚐   Transportation Available
🐷   Financial Aid Available

FEE RANGES PER WEEK
A	$0-75
B	$75-200
C	$201-350
D	$351-500
E	$501-650
F	over $650

Easter Seals Camp Sunnyside
(est 1961)
☀ ▲ 🏠

Des Moines, IA (Polk Co.); (515) 289-1933
Paul Thorne, Director
Camp comments: Providing the standard of excellence in recreation and respite services to children & adults with disabilities in Iowa.
Activities: Archery, Arts/Crafts, Camping Skills/Outdoor Living, Challenge/Rope Courses, Horseback — Western, Music, Nature/Environment Studies, Riflery, Swimming — Recreational
Session lengths & capacity: 1 & 2 week sessions; 120 campers
Clientele & fees: coed 4-95; seniors; single adults; Fees: **B** ▲ Fees: **D** ▲ 🐷
Contact: Paul Thorne, Director of Camp and Recreation at (515) 289-1933 ext. 205; fax: (515) 289-1281
e-mail: pthorne@eastersealsia.org
Operated by: Easter Seal Iowa, 401 NE 66th Ave, Des Moines, IA 50313 at (515) 289-1933

Group Rental Information
Site comments: Cabin & dorm style living on 130 wooded acres with lake & nature trails. Large & small meeting rooms. Great food svc.
Facilities: Double Occupancy, Food Service, Kitchen Facilities, Lodges, Pool, River
Programs: Environmental Education, Swimming (#1463)

Ewalu Camp and Retreat Center (est 1961)
▲ 🏠 🚐

Strawberry Point, IA (Clayton Co.); (319) 933-4700
Dale L. Goodman, Director
Camp comments: Year-round Lutheran affiliated camp,Christ-centered summer Bible camp program,youth & family retreats, high & low ropes course, environmental education program.
Activities: Archery, Arts/Crafts, Backpacking, Canoeing, Challenge/Rope Courses, Community Service, Counselor Training (CIT), Hiking, Nature/Environment Studies, Swimming — Recreational
Session lengths & capacity: 1/2 & 1 week sessions; 200 campers
Clientele & fees: coed 8-18; families; seniors; single adults; Fees: **B** ▲ 🐷
Contact: Lisa Krieg, Administrative Assistant at (563) 933-4700; fax: (563) 933-6022
e-mail: ewalu@mwci.net
Operated by: Ewalu Camp and Retreat Center, 37776 Alpha Ave, Strawberry Point, IA 52076 at (319) 933-4700

Group Rental Information
Site comments: Year-round, high comfort adult retreat center on 250 acre site. High and low ropes course nearby, canoe rental.
Facilities: Cabins, Food Service, Hiking Trails, Lodges, Meeting Rooms, Pool, River (#2911)

Foster YMCA (est 1912)
☀ ▲ 🏠 🚐

Spirit Lake, IA (Dickinson Co.); (712) 336-3272
Brian A Petersen CEO, Director
Camp comments: Mission driven YMCA camp. Values of honesty, respect, responsibility, fairness, caring. 60 college-age staff. Traditional yet progressive programming.
Activities: Archery, Arts/Crafts, Boating, Challenge/Rope Courses, Horseback — Western, Nature/Environment Studies, Riflery, Sailing, Swimming — Recreational, Waterskiing
Session lengths & capacity: 1/2 & 1 week sessions; 210 campers
Clientele & fees: boys 5-16; girls 5-16; families; Fees: **B** ☀ Fees: **C** ▲
Contact: Ellen Tischer, Office Manager at (800) 456-9622; fax: (712) 336-2026
e-mail: foster@ncn.net
Web site: www.campfoster.org
Operated by: Camp Foster YMCA Inc, PO Box 296, Spirit Lake, IA 51360 at (712) 336-3272

Group Rental Information
Facilities: Cabins, Double Occupancy, Hiking Trails, Kitchen Facilities, Lake, Playing Fields, Pool
Programs: Boating, Challenge/Ropes Course, Environmental Education, Horseback Riding, Swimming (#1462)

Girl Scout Camp Tanglefoot
(est 1947)
▲ 🏠

Clear Lake, IA (Cerro Gordo Co.); (641) 357-2481
Cynthia Findley, Director
Camp comments: Premier Iowa camp for 54 yrs. Sail,canoe,challenge course,CIT,campfires,music,skills! Strong traditions,super staff,and fun gives you the magic of camp.
Activities: Archery, Arts/Crafts, Camping Skills/Outdoor Living, Canoeing, Challenge/Rope Courses, Counselor Training (CIT), Music, Nature/Environment Studies, Sailing, Swimming — Recreational
Session lengths & capacity: June-August; 1/2, 1 & 2 week sessions; 120 campers
Clientele & fees: girls 6-18; families; Fees: **B, C** ▲ 🐷
Contact: Cynthia Findley, Camp Director at (641) 357-2481; fax: (641) 357-7735
e-mail: cindy@niowagirlscouts.org
Web site: www.niowagirlscouts.org
Operated by: Girl Scout Council North Iowa, 601 South Illinois Ave, Mason City, IA 50401 at (800) 657-5853

Group Rental Information
Site comments: Tanglefoot is available for limited rental use. Beautiful setting,well-appointed,and quiet. Groups,families will enjoy the special Tanglefoot spirit!
Seasons & Capacity: Spring 80, Fall 80, Winter 80
Facilities: Cabins, Hiking Trails, Kitchen Facilities, Lodges, Meeting Rooms, Playing Fields, Tents
Programs: Winter Sports (#1490)

Golden Valley Camp & Rtr Ctr
▲ 🏠

Lockridge, IA (Jefferson Co.); (319) 696-2573
Dawn Wright, Director
Camp comments: Challenge/ropes course, CIT, outdoor skills, swimming, western horseback, music, christian studies, canoeing, and hiking.
Activities: Camping Skills/Outdoor Living, Challenge/Rope Courses, Horseback — Western, Leadership Development, Music, Religious Study, Team Building
Session lengths & capacity: June-August; 1/2 & 1 week sessions; 84 campers
Clientele & fees: boys 3-90; girls 3-90; coed 3-90; families; Fees: **C, D** ▲
Contact: Dawn Wright, Site Director at (866) 231-2686; fax: (319) 686-2575
e-mail: goldenvalley.camp@iaumc.org
Web site: www.iaumc.org/camps
Operated by: Iowa Conf United Methodist, 500 E Court Ave Ste C, Des Moines, IA 50309 at (515) 283-1991

Group Rental Information
Site comments: Dorm style, food service, hiking trails, kitchen facilities, ropes/challenge course, and a pond.
Seasons & Capacity: Spring 92, Summer 62, Fall 92, Winter 92
Facilities: Cabins, Dorm-Style, Food Service, Hiking Trails, Kitchen Facilities, Lodges, Meeting Rooms
Programs: Challenge/Ropes Course, Horseback Riding, Swimming (#1757)

Hantesa (est 1919)   ☀ ⛺ 🏠 🚐

Boone, IA (Boone Co.); (515) 432-1417
Suz Welch, Director

Camp comments: Noncompetitive, small group activities, decision-making & leadership skills emphasized. Traditional camp.
Activities: Archery, Arts/Crafts, Camping Skills/Outdoor Living, Canoeing, Challenge/Rope Courses, Climbing/Rappelling, Drama, Horseback — English, Nature/Environment Studies, Photography
Session lengths & capacity: 1 week sessions; 150 campers
Clientele & fees: coed 5-17; families; seniors; single adults; Fees: B ☀ Fees: C ⛺ 🚐
Contact: Suz Welch, Director at (515) 432-1417; fax: (515) 432-1294
e-mail: hantesa@opencominc.com
Web site: www.iowacampfire.com
Operated by: Camp Fire USA, 5615 Hickman Rd, Des Moines, IA 50310 at (515) 274-1501

Group Rental Information
Site comments: Located near I-80 & I-35.Easy access.All seasons programs. Housing & meeting rooms. Staff and meals available.
Seasons & Capacity: Spring 225, Summer 300, Fall 225, Winter 195
Facilities: Cabins, Dorm-Style, Food Service, Hiking Trails, Lodges, Meeting Rooms, Tents
Programs: Challenge/Ropes Course, Environmental Education (#1465)

Iowa 4H Center (est 1950)   ⛺ 🏠

Madrid, IA (Boone Co.); (515) 795-3338
Donna MacNeir, Director

Camp comments: 1100 ac, woods creeks & prairie. Caring & creative staff, science, field schools; challenge course & wilderness trips.
Activities: Aquatic Activities, Archery, Backpacking, Camping Skills/Outdoor Living, Canoeing, Challenge/Rope Courses, Climbing/Rappelling, Counselor Training (CIT), Team Building
Session lengths & capacity: 1/2, 1 & 2 week sessions
Clientele & fees: coed 5-18; families; seniors; Fees: B ⛺ 🚐
Contact: Michele Thompson, Secretary at (515) 795-2389; fax: (515) 795-2107
e-mail: ia4hctr@iastate.edu
Web site: www.extension.iastate.ed/4hcenter
Operated by: Iowa State University Extensio, 1991 Peach Ave, Madvid, IA 50156 at (515) 795-3338

Group Rental Information
Site comments: Nestled in woods, many activities, great for retreats & camps.
Seasons & Capacity: Spring 250, Summer 360, Fall 360, Winter 250
Facilities: A/V Equipment, Cabins, Food Service, Hiking Trails, Linens, Lodges, Meeting Rooms, Playing Fields, Pool, River
Programs: Challenge/Ropes Course, Winter Sports (#1487)

L-Kee-Ta (est 1945)   ⛺ 🏠

Danville, IA (Des Moines Co.); (319) 392-4505
Becky Godfrey, Director

Camp comments: Theme weeks, specialties as listed stress community living skills. Tents, cabins, treehouses, pool, horses, games court
Activities: Aquatic Activities, Arts/Crafts, Camping Skills/Outdoor Living, Drama, Hiking, Horseback — Western, Nature/Environment Studies, Performing Arts, Swimming — Recreational
Session lengths & capacity: June-August; 1/2 & 1 week sessions; 16 campers
Clientele & fees: girls 7-18; families; Fees: B ⛺
Contact: Becky Godfrey, Director at (319) 752-3639; fax: (319) 753-1410
e-mail: camplkeeta@yahoo.com

Operated by: Girl Scouts of Shining Trail, 1308 Broadway, West Burlington, IA 52655-0190 at (319) 752-3639

Group Rental Information
Seasons & Capacity: Spring 120, Fall 120, Winter 120
Facilities: Dorm-Style, Hiking Trails, Kitchen Facilities, Lodges, Pool, Tents (#1472)

Lake Okoboji UM Camp

(est 1915)   ☀ ⛺ 🏠

Spirit Lake, IA (Dickinson Co.); (712) 336-2936
Keith Shew, Director

Camp comments: Campers & families grow in Jesus as they swim, boat, sing around campfires, do crafts, & much more! Safe, comfortable facilities & caring staff to serve you!
Activities: Arts/Crafts, Boating, Canoeing, Challenge/Rope Courses, Counselor Training (CIT), Field Trips, Music, Religious Study, Swimming — Recreational, Team Building
Session lengths & capacity: 1/2 & 1 week sessions; 200 campers
Clientele & fees: coed 5-18; families; seniors; single adults; Fees: A ☀ Fees: A, B, C ⛺ 🚐
Contact: Keith Shew, Executive Director at (712) 336-2936; fax: (712) 336-1822
e-mail: okoboji@ncn.net
Web site: www.iaumc/camps
Operated by: Iowa Conf United Methodist, 500 E Court Ave Ste C, Des Moines, IA 50309 at (515) 283-1991

Group Rental Information
Facilities: A/V Equipment, Cabins, Dorm-Style, Food Service, Hiking Trails, Kitchen Facilities, Lake, Lodges, Meeting Rooms, Playing Fields
Programs: Boating, Challenge/Ropes Course, Horseback Riding, Swimming, Winter Sports (#34044)

Lakota Camp (est 1960)   ☀ ⛺ 🏠

Dayton, IA; (515) 547-2502
Activities: Aquatic Activities, Arts/Crafts, Camping Skills/Outdoor Living, Hiking, Horseback — Western, Nature/Environment Studies, Soccer, Swimming — Recreational
Operated by: Lakota GSC, 112 South 3rd Street, Fort Dodge, IA 50501 at (515) 573-8141 (#7774)

Lutheran Lakeside Camp

(est 1960)   ⛺ 🏠 🚐

Spirit Lake, IA (Dickinson Co.); (712) 336-2109
Judy Engh, Director

Camp comments: Lake & pool, prairie & woods are ideal setting for spiritual growth & adventure for families & youth of all ages.
Activities: Aquatic Activities, Archery, Arts/Crafts, Canoeing, Counselor Training (CIT), Kayaking, Music, Sailing, SCUBA, Swimming — Recreational
Session lengths & capacity: 1/2 & 1 week sessions; 200 campers
Clientele & fees: boys 8-18; girls 8-18; coed 8-18; families; single adults; Fees: C, D ⛺ 🚐
Contact: Judy Engh, Executive Director at (712) 336-2109; fax: (712) 336-0638
e-mail: luthlake@ncn.net
Operated by: Lutheran Lakeside Camp, 2491 170th Street, Spirit Lake, IA 51360 at (712) 336-2109

Group Rental Information
Seasons & Capacity: Spring 40, Fall 40, Winter 40
Facilities: A/V Equipment, Cabins, Dorm-Style, Hiking Trails, Lake, Lodges, Playing Fields, Tents
Programs: Challenge/Ropes Course, Environmental Education, Winter Sports (#2215)

Pictured Rocks Camp (est 1960)   ⛺ 🏠

Monticello, IA (Jones Co.)
Steve Kalb, Director

Camp comments: Variety of programs for all ages. Music, archery, rock climbing, Bible studies. Fun, caring, accepting, Christian environment.
Activities: Aquatic Activities, Archery, Camping Skills/Outdoor Living, Canoeing, Caving, Climbing/Rappelling, Counselor Training (CIT), Hiking, Martial Arts, Religious Study
Session lengths & capacity: May-August; 1/2 & 1 week sessions; 70 campers
Clientele & fees: boys 5-18; girls 5-18; coed 5-18; Fees: C ⛺ 🚐
Contact: Steve Kalb, Site Director at (319) 465-4194; fax: (319) 465-6022
e-mail: picturedrocks.camp@iaumc.org
Web site: www.iaumc/camps
Operated by: Iowa Conf United Methodist, 500 E Court Ave Ste C, Des Moines, IA 50309 at (515) 283-1991

Group Rental Information
Site comments: Year round retreat cabins. Equipped with kitchen, fireplace, TV & VCR. Rock climbing, caving, rappelling, available seasonally. Food service also available. ♦
Seasons & Capacity: Spring 80, Summer 80, Fall 80, Winter 80
Facilities: A/V Equipment, Cabins, Dorm-Style, Food Service, Hiking Trails, Kitchen Facilities, Lodges, Meeting Rooms, Playing Fields, River, Tents
Programs: Challenge/Ropes Course (#6721)

Presbyterian Camp On Okoboji (est 1954)   ☀ ⛺ 🏠

Milford, IA (Dickinson Co.); (712) 337-3313
Rev David Feltman, Director

Camp comments: Christian emphasis. Facility on lake. Music/performance/nature/sailing. Singles & adult camps. Handicapped facility.
Activities: Aquatic Activities, Boating, Drama, Music, Nature/Environment Studies, Performing Arts, Religious Study, Sailing, Swimming — Recreational
Session lengths & capacity: April-September; 1 week sessions; 80 campers
Clientele & fees: boys 5-18; girls 5-18; families; seniors; Fees: A, B ⛺ 🚐
Contact: David Feltman, Rev at (712) 337-3313; fax: (712) 337-0104
Operated by: Presbyterian Camp on Okoboji, 1864 Hwy 86, Milford, IA 51351 at (712) 337-3313

Group Rental Information
Site comments: Christian emphasis facility on lake,Music/performance Nature/sailing Singles & adults camping Handicapped facility
Seasons & Capacity: Spring 54, Summer 80, Fall 54, Winter 54
Facilities: Cabins, Double Occupancy, Kitchen Facilities, Lake, Lodges, Meeting Rooms, Playing Fields, River
Programs: Boating (#7392)

Tahigwa (est 1965)   ⛺ 🚐

Dorchester, IA; (319) 546-7755
Susan Kerns and Gene Averhoff, Director

Camp comments: 315 wooded acres. CIT. Campers develop skills in non-competitive, cooperative setting. GS focus. Adventure programs.
Activities: Aquatic Activities, Archery, Camping Skills/Outdoor Living, Canoeing, Caving, Challenge/Rope Courses, Climbing/Rappelling, Counselor Training (CIT), Horseback — Western, Leadership Development
Session lengths & capacity: June-August; 1/2, 1 & 3 week sessions; 120 campers
Clientele & fees: girls 6-17; Fees: B, C ⛺ 🚐

Contact: Gene Averhoff, Camp Director at
(319) 232-6601; fax: (319) 232-3942
e-mail: rangergene@oneota.net
Operated by: Conestoga GSC, 321 Tahigwa Dr,
Dorchester, IA 52140 at (319) 232-6601 (#1483)

Village Creek Bible Camp & Ret

(est 1972) ▲ ⌂

Lansing, IA (Allamakee Co.); (319) 535-7320
Tom Treptau/Camie Treptau, Director

Camp comments: Beautiful farming valley
w/streams & wooded hillsides, quiet loving
atmosphere. Christ-centered teaching.
Activities: Aerobics/Exercise, Archery,
Baseball/Softball, Basketball, Camping
Skills/Outdoor Living, Canoeing, Drama, Horseback
— Western, Model Rocketry, Swimming —
Recreational
Session lengths & capacity: 1 week sessions;
166 campers
Clientele & fees: coed 8-19; families; seniors;
single adults; Fees: **B, C** ▲
Contact: Tom or Camie Treptau, Directors at
(563) 535-7320; fax: (563) 535-7561
e-mail: tom@villagecreek.net
Web site: www.villagecreek.net
Operated by: N Amer Baptist 4 State Assoc, 1588
Drake Rd, Lansing, IA 52151 at (563) 535-7320
Group Rental Information
Site comments: Beautiful valley, streams, lake &
hills. Quietness of God's creation. Caring staff,
exciting Bible teaching & fun!
Seasons & Capacity: Spring 180, Summer 180,
Fall 180, Winter 180
Facilities: Cabins, Dorm-Style, Food Service,
Hiking Trails, Lake, Lodges
Programs: Horseback Riding (#2301)

Wesley Woods Camp and Retreat (est 1956)

▲ ⌂ 🚐

Indianola, IA (Warren Co.); (515) 961-4523
Art & Nan Allen, Director

Camp comments: Jesus's love experienced
through life together in an outdoor atmosphere.
Many opportunities for Christian birth, growth, and
renewal.
Activities: Aquatic Activities, Camping
Skills/Outdoor Living, Canoeing, Counselor Training
(CIT), Hiking, Horseback — Western, Leadership
Development, Music, Nature/Environment Studies,
Team Building
Session lengths & capacity: June-August; 1/2 &
1 week sessions; 225 campers
Clientele & fees: boys 4-99; girls 4-99; coed 4-99;
families; single adults; Fees: **B, C** ▲ 🐷

ICON LEGEND

☀ Day Camp

▲ Resident Camp

⌂ Facilities Available To Rent

🚐 Transportation Available

🐷 Financial Aid Available

FEE RANGES PER WEEK

A $0-75

B $75-200

C $201-350

D $351-500

E $501-650

F over $650

Contact: Suzie Orr, Retreat and Volunteer Director
at (515) 961-4523; fax: (515) 961-4162
Web site: www.iaumc/camps
Operated by: Iowa Conf United Methodist, 500 E
Court Ave Ste C, Des Moines, IA 50309 at
(515) 283-1991
Group Rental Information
Site comments: Enjoy Jesus's love in an outdoor
atmosphere.
Seasons & Capacity: Spring 185, Summer 250,
Fall 185, Winter 185
Facilities: A/V Equipment, Cabins, Food Service,
Hiking Trails, Kitchen Facilities, Lake, Lodges,
Meeting Rooms, Playing Fields, Pool, River, Tents
Programs: Boating, Environmental Education,
Horseback Riding (#1476)

YMCA Camp Wapsie

(est 1918) ☀ ▲ ⌂

Coggon, IA; (319) 435-2577
Carl Lipke, Director

Camp comments: Outstanding & well-trained staff.
Self-esteem specialty, friendly, warm, free choice
adventures.
Activities: Aquatic Activities, Canoeing,
Climbing/Rappelling, Horseback — Western,
Leadership Development, Model Rocketry,
Photography, Riflery, Travel/Tour, Wilderness Trips
Session lengths & capacity: 1/2 & 1 week
sessions; 200 campers
Clientele & fees: coed 6-18; families; Fees: **B** ☀
Fees: **C** ▲ 🐷
Contact: Carl Lipke, Director at (319) 435-2577;
fax: (319) 435-2578
Operated by: YMCA Cedar Rapids Metro Area,
2174 Wapsie Rd, Coggon, IA 52218 at
(319) 435-2577
Group Rental Information
Seasons & Capacity: Spring 175, Summer 250,
Fall 175, Winter 175
Facilities: Cabins, Dorm-Style, Food Service, Lake,
Meeting Rooms, Pool
Programs: Boating (#1485)

Kansas

Camp Chippewa (est 1955)

▲ ⌂

Ottawa, KS (Franklin Co.); (785) 242-6797
Lawrence Wiliford, Director
Activities: Archery, Arts/Crafts, Camping
Skills/Outdoor Living, Canoeing, Challenge/Rope
Courses, Counselor Training (CIT), Fishing,
Horseback — Western, Swimming — Recreational
Session lengths & capacity: 1 week sessions
Clientele & fees: coed 6-99; Fees: **C** ▲
Contact: Web site: www.campchippewa.org
Operated by: Kansas East Conference,
PO Box 4187, Topeka, KS 66604 at (785) 272-9111
Group Rental Information
Seasons & Capacity: Spring 120, Summer 144,
Fall 144, Winter 120
Facilities: A/V Equipment, Cabins, Food Service,
Hiking Trails, Lake, Lodges, Meeting Rooms,
Playing Fields, Pool
Programs: Boating, Challenge/Ropes Course,
Horseback Riding, Swimming (#14147)

Camp Discovery (est 1974)

▲

Junction City, KS; (316) 257-3318
Diana Rhiley, Director

Camp comments: Camp teaches Diabetes care
while providing recreational fun. Qualified Medical
staff are present.
Activities: Archery, Canoeing, Challenge/Rope
Courses, Counselor Training (CIT), Horseback —
Western, Nature/Environment Studies, Riflery,
Swimming — Recreational

Session lengths & capacity: 1 week sessions;
85 campers
Clientele & fees: coed 8-18; Fees: **C** ▲ 🐷
Contact: Lindsay Giles, District Manager at
(316) 684-6091 ext. 6905; fax: (316) 684-5675
e-mail: lgiles@diabetes.org
Web site: www.diabetes.org
Operated by: American Diabetes Assn KS, 837 S
Hillside, Wichita, KS 67211-3005 at (316) 684-6091
(#4182)

Camp Hope (est 1982)

▲

Claflin, KS
Will Williams, Director

Camp comments: To provide a normal, active and
safe camp experience where children can celebrate
life while living with, through, and beyond the
diagnosis of cancer.
Activities: Archery, Baseball/Softball, Basketball,
Field Trips, Fishing, Football, Golf, Soccer, Sports
— Field & Team, Swimming — Recreational
Session lengths & capacity: 1 week sessions
Clientele & fees: boys 8-21; girls 8-21; Fees: **A** ▲
Contact: Stephanie Weiter, Regional Vice President
at (785) 273-4422; fax: (785) 273-1503
e-mail: stephanie.weiter@cancer.org
Operated by: American Cancer Society, 1100
Pennsylvania Ave, Kansas City, MO 64105 at
(785) 273-4422 (#11827)

Camp Wood YMCA (est 1915)

☀ ▲ ⌂

Elmdale, KS (Chase Co.); (316) 273-8641
Kenneth Wold, Director

Camp comments: Set on 630 acres of Tallgrass
Prairie. Camp Wood YMCA offers traditional
residence camping to youth, 7-17 years of age.
Activities: Archery, Arts/Crafts, Basketball, Hiking,
Horseback — Western, Nature/Environment
Studies, Swimming — Recreational, Team Building,
Tennis, Travel/Tour
Session lengths & capacity: June-August; 1 &
2 week sessions; 112 campers
Clientele & fees: coed 7-18; families; Fees: **B** ☀
Fees: **C** ▲ 🐷
Contact: Kenneth Wold, Executive Director at
(620) 273-6435; fax: (620) 273-8676
e-mail: campwood@bulldognet.com
Web site: www.campwood.org
Operated by: Camp Wood YMCA, RR 1 Box 78,
Elmdale, KS 66850 at (620) 273-8641
Group Rental Information
Facilities: Cabins, Food Service, Hiking Trails,
Lake, Lodges
Programs: Boating, Horseback Riding (#3778)

Lakeside United Methodist Ctr

(est 1947) ▲ ⌂

Scott City, KS (Scott Co.); (316) 872-2021
H Lee Walz, Director

Camp comments: Beautiful canyon setting for
Christian nurture & growth; serving youth & adults;
horse riding; wheelchair accessible.
Activities: Camping Skills/Outdoor Living,
Canoeing, Challenge/Rope Courses, Field Trips,
Horseback — Western, Nature/Environment
Studies, Performing Arts, Religious Study, Sailing,
Swimming — Recreational
Session lengths & capacity: 1/2 & 1 week
sessions; 135 campers
Clientele & fees: coed 8-18; families; seniors;
single adults; Fees: **B** ▲ 🐷
Operated by: Lakeside United Methodist Ctr, 300 E
Scott Lake Dr, Scott City, KS 67871 at
(620) 872-2021
Group Rental Information
Site comments: Unique year round Christian
camping for youth, adults and families. Wheelchair
accessible. Aquatic, equine, low ropes activities.
Beautiful lakeside setting.
Seasons & Capacity: Spring 80, Summer 140, Fall
115, Winter 90

Facilities: A/V Equipment, Cabins, Dorm-Style, Double Occupancy, Food Service, Hiking Trails, Kitchen Facilities, Lake, Lodges, Pool
Programs: Boating, Challenge/Ropes Course, Environmental Education, Horseback Riding, Swimming (#17468)

Tall Oaks Conference Center

(est 1961)

Linwood, KS (Leavenworth Co.); (913) 301-3004
Activities: Arts/Crafts, Challenge/Rope Courses, Horseback — Western, Leadership Development, Religious Study, Swimming — Recreational, Team Building
Session lengths & capacity: June-August; 1/2 week sessions; 120 campers
Clientele & fees: coed 6-18; families; seniors; single adults; Fees: B, C △
Contact: (913) 301-3004; fax: (913) 301-3005
e-mail: sharon@talloaks.org
Operated by: Christian Church of Gtr Kansas, 5700 Broadmoor Ste 702, Mission, KS 66202 at (913) 432-1414

Group Rental Information
Site comments: Yearround camp/conference center. Retreats, youth facilities, ropes course, equestrain programs, motel units, dorm cabins, full food service, meeting space.
Seasons & Capacity: Spring 174, Summer 174, Fall 174, Winter 174
Facilities: A/V Equipment, Cabins, Dorm-Style, Double Occupancy, Food Service, Hiking Trails, Linens, Lodges, Meeting Rooms, Playing Fields, Pool
Programs: Challenge/Ropes Course, Horseback Riding, Swimming (#7093)

Theodore Naish Scout Reservat.

Kansas City, KS; (913) 422-1035
Activities: Archery, Arts/Crafts, Bicycling/Biking, Camping Skills/Outdoor Living, Challenge/Rope Courses, Climbing/Rappelling, Model Rocketry, Nature/Environment Studies, Swimming — Recreational
Operated by: Heart of America Council BSA, 10210 Holmes Road, Kansas City, MO 64131 at (816) 942-9333

Group Rental Information
Facilities: Hiking Trails, Meeting Rooms, Tents
Programs: Challenge/Ropes Course (#12217)

Kentucky

Bear Creek Aquatic Camp

(est 1940)

Benton, KY (Marshall Co.); (502) 354-6557
Camp comments: Kentucky's only Girl Scout aquatic camp. Located on Kentucky Lake. Features sailing, kayaking, canoeing, swimming & adventure challenge. All girls welcome.
Activities: Aquatic Activities, Arts/Crafts, Camping Skills/Outdoor Living, Caving, Climbing/Rappelling, Counselor Training (CIT), Kayaking, Sailing, Windsurfing
Session lengths & capacity: 1/2 & 1 week sessions; 75 campers
Clientele & fees: girls 12-18; Fees: C, D △
Contact: Lisa Gunterman, Camping Administrator at (502) 636-0900; fax: (502) 634-0837
e-mail: lgunterman@kyanags.org
Web site: www.kyanags.org
Operated by: Girl Scouts of Kentuckiana, PO Box 32335, Louisville, KY 40232 at (502) 636-0900

Group Rental Information
Facilities: Cabins, Hiking Trails, Kitchen Facilities, Lake, Lodges, Playing Fields, Tents
Programs: Challenge/Ropes Course (#4266)

Camp CEDAR (est 1989)

Scottsville, KY (Allen Co.); (270) 622-6004
Linda Larson, Director

Camp comments: Dedicated to the conservation of & the appreciation for nature, both wild & domestic, while enriching lives of people.
Activities: Aquatic Activities, Archery, Arts/Crafts, Camping Skills/Outdoor Living, Canoeing, Farming/Ranching/Gardening, Fishing, Hiking, Nature/Environment Studies, Swimming — Recreational
Session lengths & capacity: April-October; 1/2 & 1 week sessions; 1005 campers
Clientele & fees: coed 6-99; families; seniors; Fees: A ☀ 🚌
Contact: Linda Larson, President & CEO at (270) 622-6004;
Operated by: McLars Enterprises Inc, 3576 Pitchford Ridge Rd, Scottsville, KY 42164 at (270) 622-6004

Group Rental Information
Facilities: Kitchen Facilities, Lake, Playing Fields
Programs: Environmental Education (#46224)

Camp Paradise Valley

Burkesville, KY; (270) 433-5801
Major Algerome Newsome, Director
Activities: Aquatic Activities, Baseball/Softball, Basketball, Boating, Camping Skills/Outdoor Living, Fishing, Hiking, Music, Religious Study, Swimming — Recreational
Session lengths & capacity: June-August; 1, 5 & 9 week sessions; 250 campers
Clientele & fees: boys 6-12; girls 6-12; coed 13-18; Fees: B △ 🚌
Contact: Capt Keath Biggers, Divisional Youth Secretary at (502) 583-5391; fax: (502) 625-1199
e-mail: ktdys@aol.com
Operated by: Salvation Army, 216 W Chestnut Street, Louisville, KY 40202 at (502) 583-5391 (#42703)

Cathedral Domain (est 1946)

Irvine, KY (Lee Co.); (606) 464-8254
Andy Sigmon, Director

Camp comments: Adventure based programs in a loving Christ like environment.
Activities: Archery, Arts/Crafts, Climbing/Rappelling, Hiking, Leadership Development, Nature/Environment Studies, Swimming — Recreational
Session lengths & capacity: 1 week sessions; 200 campers
Clientele & fees: boys 8-13; girls 8-13; coed 6-18; families; seniors; single adults; Fees: C △
Contact: Andy Sigmon, Director at (606) 464-8254; fax: (606) 464-0759
e-mail: andysigmon@aol.com
Operated by: Episcopal Diocese of Lexington, 800 Highway 1746, Irvine, KY 40336 at (606) 252-6527

Group Rental Information
Facilities: A/V Equipment, Cabins, Dorm-Style, Double Occupancy, Food Service, Hiking Trails, Kitchen Facilities, Linens, Lodges, Meeting Rooms, Playing Fields, Pool
Programs: Environmental Education, Swimming (#14806)

Cedar Ridge (est 1960)

Louisville, KY (Jefferson Co.); (502) 267-5848
Andrew Hartmans, Director

Camp comments: Building a diverse community of faith each week, inclusive of special needs. Resident day and adventure camps.

Activities: Aquatic Activities, Archery, Arts/Crafts, Canoeing, Challenge/Rope Courses, Hiking, Nature/Environment Studies, Religious Study, Swimming — Recreational, Team Building
Session lengths & capacity: 1/2, 1 & 2 week sessions; 80 campers
Clientele & fees: boys 6-17; girls 6-17; coed 6-17; Fees: B ☀ Fees: C △ 🚌
Contact: Andrew Hartmans, Executive Director at (502) 267-5848; fax: (502) 267-0116
e-mail: cedrrdg@aol.com
Operated by: Cedar Ridge Inc, 4010 Routt Rd, Louisville, KY 40299 at (502) 267-5848

Group Rental Information
Site comments: Building a diverse community of faith each week, inclusive of special needs. Resident day and adventure camps.
Seasons & Capacity: Spring 180, Summer 180, Fall 180, Winter 120
Facilities: Cabins, Double Occupancy, Hiking Trails, Kitchen Facilities, Lake, Lodges, Meeting Rooms, Playing Fields, Pool
Programs: Boating, Challenge/Ropes Course, Environmental Education, Horseback Riding, Swimming (#3830)

Easter Seal Camp Kysoc

(est 1961)

Carrollton, KY (Carroll Co.); (502) 732-5333
Sallie Price, Director

Camp comments: Traditional outdoor camp program. Woodland setting with quality trained staff. Quality care for campers.
Activities: Arts/Crafts, Canoeing, Ceramics/Pottery, Challenge/Rope Courses, Climbing/Rappelling, Farming/Ranching/Gardening, Fishing, Nature/Environment Studies, Photography, Swimming — Instructional
Session lengths & capacity: May-August; 1/2, 1 & 2 week sessions; 80 campers
Clientele & fees: boys 6-99; girls 6-99; coed 6-99; families; seniors; Fees: C, D, E △ 🚌
Contact: Sallie Price, Director of Camping/Recreation at (502) 732-5333; fax: (502) 732-0783
e-mail: fun@kysoc.org
Web site: www.cardinalhill.org
Operated by: Easter Seal Camp Kysoc, 1902 Easterday Rd, Carrollton, KY 41008 at (606) 254-5701

Group Rental Information
Facilities: Kitchen Facilities, Lake, Pool (#1445)

Hendon (est 1965)

Louisville, KY (Bullitt Co.); (502) 452-6072
Susan Abell, Director

Camp comments: To provide a fun, medically safe camping experience for children with diabetes while teaching diabetes management.
Activities: Aquatic Activities, Archery, Arts/Crafts, Canoeing, Sports — Field & Team, Swimming — Recreational, Team Building
Session lengths & capacity: August-August; 1/2 & 1 week sessions; 115 campers
Clientele & fees: coed 8-17; Fees: B, C △ 🚌
Contact: Tracy Esarey, District Director at (502) 452-6072; fax: (502) 452-2705
e-mail: tesarey@diabetes.org
Operated by: American Diabetes Association, 1941 Bishop Ln Suite 110, Louisville, KY 40218 at (502) 452-6072 (#5421)

Life Adventure Camp Inc

(est 1977)

Lexington, KY (Estill Co.); (859) 252-4733

Camp comments: Primitive wilderness camp for children w/ emotional/behavioral challenges. Simple living in a highly structured setting

Activities: Backpacking, Camping Skills/Outdoor Living, Caving, Challenge/Rope Courses, Hiking, Leadership Development, Nature/Environment Studies, Team Building, Wilderness Trips
Session lengths & capacity: June-August; 1/2 & 1 week sessions; 32 campers
Clientele & fees: boys 9-18; girls 9-18; Fees: **D, E** ⛺ 🚐
Contact: Susan Ownby, Program Director at (859) 252-4733; fax: (859) 225-5115
e-mail: lac@lifeadventurecamp.org
Web site: www.lifeadventure.org
Operated by: Life Adventure Camp, 1122 Oak Hill Drive, Lexington, KY 40505 at (859) 252-4733 (#4073)

Pennyroyal (est 1956)   ⛺ 🏠 🚐

Utica, KY (Daviess Co.); (502) 275-4521
Lisa Leonard, Director

Camp comments: An all around Girl Scout Camp located on a small lake. Programs feature swimming, canoeing, arts & crafts, horseback riding & more! Open to all girls.
Activities: Aquatic Activities, Arts/Crafts, Camping Skills/Outdoor Living, Canoeing, Challenge/Rope Courses, Counselor Training (CIT), Hiking, Horseback — Western, Swimming — Instructional, Team Building
Session lengths & capacity: 1/2 & 1 week sessions; 120 campers
Clientele & fees: girls 6-13; Fees: **C** ⛺
Contact: Lisa Gunterman, Camp Administrator at (502) 636-0900; fax: (502) 634-0837
e-mail: lgunterman@kyanags.org
Web site: www.kyanags.org
Operated by: Girl Scouts of Kentuckiana, PO Box 32335, Louisville, KY 40232 at (502) 636-0900

Group Rental Information
Facilities: A/V Equipment, Cabins, Hiking Trails, Kitchen Facilities, Lake, Lodges, Tents
Programs: Boating, Challenge/Ropes Course, Swimming (#1450)

Sheltered Risks Inc   ⛺

Frankfort, KY; (502) 553-2423
Activities: Arts/Crafts, Camping Skills/Outdoor Living, Horseback — English, Horseback — Western, Leadership Development, Music, Nature/Environment Studies, Team Building
Contact: Web site: www.kampkessa.org
Operated by: Sheltered Risks Inc, 758 Beechridge Rd, Frankfort, KY 40601 at (502) 599-6363 (#9454)

ICON LEGEND

☀ Day Camp

⛺ Resident Camp

🏠 Facilities Available To Rent

🚐 Transportation Available

🐷 Financial Aid Available

FEE RANGES PER WEEK

A	$0-75
B	$75-200
C	$201-350
D	$351-500
E	$501-650
F	over $650

WOW Blue Grass Youth Camp
(est 1975)   ⛺ 🏠

Lexington, KY (Jessamine Co.); (859) 263-8656
Mike Phillips, Director

Camp comments: Eligibility to Woodmen Insurance policy holders only.
Activities: Archery, Arts/Crafts, Basketball, Camping Skills/Outdoor Living, Canoeing, Challenge/Rope Courses, Climbing/Rappelling, Counselor Training (CIT), Dance, Nature/Environment Studies
Session lengths & capacity: June-July; 6 week sessions; 125 campers
Clientele & fees: coed 8-15; seniors; Fees: **A** ⛺
Contact: Michael Phillips, Camp Director at (859) 263-8656; fax: (859) 264-9697
Web site: www.woodmen.com
Operated by: WOW Life Insurance (5IN), 1700 Farnam, Omaha, NE 68120 at (402) 271-7258

Group Rental Information
Facilities: A/V Equipment, Cabins, Dorm-Style, Food Service, Kitchen Facilities, Lake, Lodges, Meeting Rooms, Playing Fields, Pool
Programs: Challenge/Ropes Course, Swimming (#4494)

WOW Camp West Kentucky
(est 1983)   ⛺ 🏠 🚐

Murray, KY (Calloway Co.); (270) 753-2319
Colleen Anderson, Director

Camp comments: Educational adventure with emphasis on building self-esteem, fully certified staff located in heart of Jackson Purchase.
Activities: Aquatic Activities, Archery, Basketball, Challenge/Rope Courses, Climbing/Rappelling, Counselor Training (CIT), Riflery, Swimming — Instructional, Swimming — Recreational, Tennis
Session lengths & capacity: May-July; 1/2 & 1 week sessions; 136 campers
Clientele & fees: coed 8-15; seniors; Fees: **A** ⛺
Contact: Colleen Anderson, Camp Director at (270) 753-2319; fax: (270) 753-2319
e-mail: campwowky@ldd.net
Web site: www.woodmen.com
Operated by: WOW Life Insurance (5IN), 1700 Farnam, Omaha, NE 68120 at (402) 271-7258

Group Rental Information
Site comments: Camp now offers that special rental experience for band or sports camps, reunions, receptions, & much more. Call Today!
Seasons & Capacity: Spring 136, Summer 136, Fall 136, Winter 136
Facilities: Double Occupancy, Food Service, Kitchen Facilities, Playing Fields, Pool
Programs: Challenge/Ropes Course, Swimming (#3072)

YMCA Camp Ernst
(est 1928)   ⛺ 🏠 🚐

Burlington, KY (Boone Co.); (859) 586-6181
Jon Perry, Director

Camp comments: A safe, fun filled environment in which kids can learn about themselves & others & the world in which they live
Activities: Archery, Arts/Crafts, Canoeing, Challenge/Rope Courses, Horseback — Western, Leadership Development, Nature/Environment Studies, Riflery, Sports — Field & Team
Session lengths & capacity: April-October; 1 week sessions; 200 campers
Clientele & fees: coed 7-16; families
Contact: Jon Perry, Camp Director at (859) 586-6181; fax: (859) 586-6214
e-mail: jperry@cincinnatiymca.org
Operated by: YMCA of Greater Cincinnati, 1105 Elm St, Cincinnati, OH 45210 at (513) 651-2100

Group Rental Information
Seasons & Capacity: Spring 100, Summer 250, Fall 100

Facilities: Cabins, Dorm-Style, Food Service, Hiking Trails, Lake
Programs: Boating, Horseback Riding (#3348)

YMCA Camp Piomingo
(est 1938)   ⛺ 🏠 🚐

Brandenburg, KY (Meade Co.); (800) 411-5822
Larry Maxwell, Director

Camp comments: From zipping down a mudslide to growing as an individual, your experience at YMCA Camp Piomingo will last a lifetime.
Activities: Archery, Backpacking, Camping Skills/Outdoor Living, Challenge/Rope Courses, Climbing/Rappelling, Golf, Horseback — English, Horseback — Western, Wilderness Trips
Session lengths & capacity: June-August; 1, 2 & 8 week sessions; 250 campers
Clientele & fees: coed 7-15; families; seniors; Fees: **C** ⛺
Contact: Mike de Ridder, Program Coordinator at (800) 411-5822; fax: (502) 942-2637
e-mail: ypiomingo@aol.com
Web site: www.ypiomingo.org
Operated by: YMCA of Greater Louisville, 545 S 2nd Street, Louisville, KY 40202-1801 at (502) 587-9622

Group Rental Information
Site comments: Family reunions, church groups, corporate groups, schools. Everyone is welcome at YMCA Camp Piomingo, we customize outings.
Seasons & Capacity: Spring 250, Summer 300, Fall 250, Winter 40
Facilities: Cabins, Food Service, Hiking Trails, Meeting Rooms, Pool, River
Programs: Challenge/Ropes Course, Environmental Education, Horseback Riding (#1436)

Louisiana

Camp Bon Coeur Inc (est 1985)   ⛺

Lafayette, LA (Lafayette Paris Co.); (318) 233-8437
Susannah Craig, Director

Camp comments: 2 week resident cardiac rehab camp located in South LA for children with congenital or acquired heart defects, ages 8 - 16 from across the US.
Activities: Arts/Crafts, Canoeing, Drama, Horseback — English, Sports — Field & Team, Swimming — Instructional, Swimming — Recreational, Team Building
Session lengths & capacity: July-July; 2 week sessions; 50 campers
Clientele & fees: coed 8-16; Fees: **E** ⛺ 🐷
Contact: Susannah Craig, Executive Director at (337) 233-8437; fax: (337) 233-4160
e-mail: susannah@heartcamp.com
Web site: www.heartcamp.com
Operated by: Camp Bon Coeur Inc, PO BOx 53765, Lafayette, LA 70501 at (337) 233-8437 (#6500)

Camp Challenge (est 1987)   ⛺

Harvey, LA; (050) 434-7147
Cathy Allain, Director

Camp comments: A bright light in summer till a cure for cancer is found.
Activities: Aquatic Activities, Arts/Crafts, Boating, Canoeing, Counselor Training (CIT), Nature/Environment Studies, Sports — Field & Team, Swimming — Recreational
Session lengths & capacity: 1 week sessions
Clientele & fees: boys 6-18; girls 6-18
Contact: Cathy Allain, Camp Director at (504) 347-2267;
e-mail: campdirector@campchallenge.org

Operated by: Camp Challenge Inc,
PO Box 641253, Kenner, LA 70064 at
(504) 347-2267 (#6705)

Camp Fire Camp Wi-Ta-Wentin

(est 1950)

Lake Charles, LA; (318) 478-6550
Wendy Sonnier, Director

Camp comments: Beautiful 96 acre site on bay.
Coed. Quality staff, canoeing, archery, swimming,
nature activities, skills development.
Activities: Archery, Arts/Crafts, Baseball/Softball,
Basketball, Camping Skills/Outdoor Living,
Canoeing, Hiking, Nature/Environment Studies,
Soccer, Swimming — Recreational
Session lengths & capacity: 1 week sessions;
125 campers
Clientele & fees: coed 5-14; families; seniors;
single adults; Fees: B 💥 Fees: B ⚠
Contact: Katheleen Mayo, Executive Director at
(337) 478-6550; fax: (337) 478-6551
e-mail: kmkmayo@bellsouth.net
Web site: www.cfsowela.bigstep.com
Operated by: Camp Fire Council Of Sowela, 2126
Oak Park Blvd, Lake Charles, LA 70601-7896 at
(318) 478-6550

Group Rental Information
Site comments: Rustic fully equipped camp
over-looking a bay.Ideal for all groups.full
kitchen,canoes,pool,hiking,sports. Close to I10
Seasons & Capacity: Spring 130, Fall 130,
Winter 130
Facilities: Cabins, Hiking Trails, Kitchen Facilities,
Lodges (#854)

Camp Hardtner

Pollock, LA (Grant Co.); (318) 765-3794
Robert (Bob) Hansbrough, Director

Camp comments: Our basic program is designed
to build community that encourages individual
expression of ability, attitude and faith.
Activities: Arts/Crafts, Canoeing, Counselor
Training (CIT), Drama, Fishing, Leadership
Development, Nature/Environment Studies,
Swimming — Recreational, Tennis
Session lengths & capacity: 1/2 & 1 week
sessions
Clientele & fees: Fees: C ⚠
Contact: Gena Kendrew, Administrative Assistant at
(318) 765-3794; fax: (318) 765-0603
e-mail: camphardtner@aol.com
Web site: www.diocesewl.org
Operated by: Hardtner Camp & Conf Center, 2393
Camp Hardtner Rd, Pollock, LA 71467 at
(318) 765-3794 (#26851)

Camp Marydale (est 1947)

St Francisville, LA (W Feliciana Co.); (504) 635-3112
Jill Pollard, Director

Camp comments: Beautiful facility in plantation
area of South Louisiana. All girls 8-17 welcome.
Activities: Archery, Arts/Crafts, Camping
Skills/Outdoor Living, Canoeing, Counselor Training
(CIT), Drama, Hiking, Horseback — Western,
Nature/Environment Studies, Swimming —
Recreational
Session lengths & capacity: June-July; 1/2, 1 &
2 week sessions; 130 campers
Clientele & fees: girls 8-17; Fees: B ⚠
Contact: (504) 927-8946; fax: (504) 927-8402
Operated by: Girl Scouts - Audubon Council, 545
Colonial, Baton Rouge, LA 70806 at (225) 927-8946

Group Rental Information
Facilities: Food Service, Hiking Trails, Lake,
Meeting Rooms, Pool, Tents
Programs: Environmental Education, Horseback
Riding, Swimming (#859)

Camp Whispering Pines

(est 1971)

Independence, LA (Tangipahoa Co.);
(504) 878-9598
Hillary Hatcher, Director

Camp comments: Fun, balanced camp program
for girls. Set in a beautiful wooded site that is a
recognized threatened habitat.
Activities: Aquatic Activities, Boating, Camping
Skills/Outdoor Living, Canoeing, Leadership
Development, Nature/Environment Studies, Sailing,
Swimming — Instructional, Swimming —
Recreational, Travel/Tour
Session lengths & capacity: June-July; 1/2, 1 &
2 week sessions; 120 campers
Clientele & fees: girls 7-17; Fees: B ⚠ 🚌
Contact: Megan Hougard, Resident Camp
Director/Prog Specialist at (504) 733-8220;
fax: (504) 733-8219
e-mail: jfahr@girlscoutssela.org
Operated by: Girl Scout Cncl SE Louisiana,
PO Box 10800, New Orleans, LA 70181 at
(504) 733-8220

Group Rental Information
Site comments: Rustic camp nestled in a
threatened long leaf pine habitat.Special emphasis
is aquatics and nature exploration.
Facilities: Cabins, Hiking Trails, Kitchen Facilities,
Lake, Lodges, Meeting Rooms, Pool, River, Tents
Programs: Environmental Education (#3738)

Feliciana Retreat Center

(est 1980)

Norwood, LA (E Feliciana Co.); (225) 683-9420
John Crane, Director

Camp comments: Programming goal is to
introduce campers to an environment of Christian
community in an outdoor setting.
Activities: Arts/Crafts, Canoeing, Hiking,
Nature/Environment Studies, Religious Study,
Swimming — Recreational, Travel/Tour
Session lengths & capacity: 1 week sessions
Clientele & fees: coed 8-18; Fees: B ⚠
Contact: Presbytery of South Louisiana at
(225) 926-4562; fax: (225) 926-4573
Operated by: Presbytery of South Louisiana, 928
Rodin Dr, Baton Rouge, LA 70761 at (225) 926-4562

Group Rental Information
Site comments: To nurture and revitalize Christian
growth of individuals and mission of churches in a
beautiful retreat setting.
Facilities: Cabins, Double Occupancy, Kitchen
Facilities, Lake, Meeting Rooms, River
Programs: Boating, Environmental Education
(#14194)

Indian Creek Girl Scout Camp

(est 1983)

Chatham, LA (Jackson Co.); (318) 249-4193
Stephanie Lewis Ellett, Director

Camp comments: Outdoor experiences to help
girls develop self-potential, social skills,
environmental awareness while having fun!
Activities: Archery, Arts/Crafts, Camping
Skills/Outdoor Living, Canoeing, Counselor Training
(CIT), Horseback — Western, Leadership
Development, Nature/Environment Studies,
Swimming — Instructional, Travel/Tour
Session lengths & capacity: June-July; 1 &
2 week sessions; 60 campers
Clientele & fees: girls 7-18; Fees: B ⚠ 🚌
Contact: Charlotte Crawford, Registrar at
(318) 325-2691; fax: (318) 325-7903
e-mail: girlscoutssw@bayou.com
Web site: www.girlscoutsswc.org
Operated by: Girl Scouts Silver Waters Cncl, 102
Arkansas Ave, Monroe, LA 71201 at (318) 325-2691
(#479)

LA Lions Camps-Disabled/
Diabet (est 1961)

Leesville, LA (Vernon Co.); (318) 239-6567
Raymond Cecil III, CCD, Director

Camp comments: All campers sponsored by local
Lions Clubs
Activities: Archery, Arts/Crafts, Baseball/Softball,
Basketball, Canoeing, Golf, Nature/Environment
Studies, Riflery, Swimming — Recreational, Tennis
Session lengths & capacity: June-August; 1 week
sessions; 80 campers
Clientele & fees: coed 7-25; Fees: A ⚠
Contact: Raymond Cecil III, CCD, Camp Director at
(800) 348-6567; fax: (318) 239-9975
e-mail: lalions@lionscamp.org
Operated by: LA Lions League Crippled Child, 292
L Beauford Dr, Leesville, LA 71496 at
(318) 239-6567

Group Rental Information
Site comments: 292 L Beauford Rd. PO Box 171.
Leesville LA 71496.
Seasons & Capacity: Summer 700
Facilities: Cabins, Dorm-Style, Food Service, Pool
(#17548)

Ruth Lee (est 1948)

Norwood, LA; (225) 683-8800
Erin Curry, Director

Camp comments: Set in the beautiful rolling hills of
E Feliciana Parish. Emphasis on fun in a caring
atmosphere.
Activities: Archery, Arts/Crafts, Camping
Skills/Outdoor Living, Canoeing, Challenge/Rope
Courses, Counselor Training (CIT), Hiking,
Horseback — Western, Swimming — Recreational,
Team Building
Session lengths & capacity: June-July; 6 week
sessions; 98 campers
Clientele & fees: coed 6-16; families;
Fees: B ⚠ 🚌
Contact: Erin Curry, Camp Director at
(504) 924-1344; fax: (504) 924-1774
e-mail: brcampfiresb@mindspring.com
Web site: www.campfire-campruthlee.com
Operated by: Big River Council of Camp Fire, 4874
Constitution Ave Ste 1E, Baton Rouge, LA 70808 at
(225) 924-2267

Group Rental Information
Site comments: 204 beautiful acres of pine &
hardwood forest,seven miles of hiking trails & 18
acre lake with rustic cabins.
Seasons & Capacity: Spring 120, Summer 120,
Fall 120
Facilities: Double Occupancy, Food Service,
Hiking Trails, Kitchen Facilities, Lake, Meeting
Rooms, Playing Fields, Pool, Tents
Programs: Boating, Challenge/Ropes Course,
Environmental Education, Horseback Riding,
Swimming (#850)

Tulane Univ Ripples
Summer Day (est 1989)

New Orleans, LA (Orleans Parish Co.);
(504) 865-5431
Bruce Bershad, Director

Camp comments: Our staff of caring educators
creates a family atmosphere where campers
self-esteem & parental trust are priority #1.
Activities: Archery, Arts/Crafts, Baseball/Softball,
Canoeing, Field Trips, Gymnastics, Horseback —
Western, Music, Sports — Field & Team, Swimming
— Instructional
Session lengths & capacity: 4 week sessions;
200 campers
Clientele & fees: coed 5-13; Fees: B 💥 🚌
Contact: Missie McGuire, Director of Campus
Recreation at (504) 865-5431; fax: (504) 862-8764
e-mail: mmcguir@mailhost.tcs.tulane.edu
Operated by: Tulane Univ Dept of Campus Rec,
Reily Student Recreation Cente, New Orleans, LA
70118 at (504) 865-5431 (#27385)

Wawbansee (est 1946) ⚠

Simsboro, LA; (318) 263-8895
Sandra Wrenn E.D., Director
Activities: Aquatic Activities, Archery, Arts/Crafts, Canoeing, Counselor Training (CIT), Nature/Environment Studies, Swimming — Recreational
Session lengths & capacity: June-July; 1/2, 1 & 2 week sessions; 90 campers
Clientele & fees: girls 5-17; Fees: B ⚠ 🚐
Contact: Sandra Wrenn, Camp Director at (318) 688-5788; fax: (318) 687-1515
Operated by: GS of Pelican Council, PO Box 3740, Shreveport, LA 71133-3740 at (318) 220-0254 (#4105)

WOW South Louisiana Youth Camp (est 1992) ⚠ 🏠

Abbeville, LA
Gretchen Varnell, Director
Camp comments: Our mission is to pro more fun & edu. activities which strengthens family life respect for God, Country, body, & mind.
Activities: Archery, Arts/Crafts, Canoeing, Challenge/Rope Courses, Climbing/Rappelling, Nature/Environment Studies, Riflery, Swimming — Recreational, Team Building
Session lengths & capacity: June-July; 1 week sessions; 168 campers
Clientele & fees: coed 8-15; Fees: A ⚠
Contact: Gretchen Varnell, Camp Director at (337) 268-9661; fax: (337) 268-9664
e-mail: gvarnell@woodmen.com
Web site: www.woodmen.com
Operated by: WOW Life Insurance (HS), 1700 Farnam, Omaha, NE 68120 at (402) 271-7258

Group Rental Information

Site comments: S-LA WOW Youth Camp does not provide any programs. Usage of canoes and pool require extra charge. Contact state office for rental fees and contracts.
Seasons & Capacity: Spring 200, Winter 200
Facilities: Cabins, Kitchen Facilities, Lake, Playing Fields, Pool (#526)

Maine

Agassiz Village (est 1935) ⚠ 🏠 🚐

Poland, ME (Androscoggin Co.); (207) 998-4340
Latasha Harris, Director
Camp comments: Multicultural & inclusive in a beautiful lakefront setting. Private not for profit 66th season. Fun, safe, supportive.

ICON LEGEND

☀	Day Camp
⚠	Resident Camp
🏠	Facilities Available To Rent
🚐	Transportation Available
🐷	Financial Aid Available

FEE RANGES PER WEEK

A	$0-75
B	$75-200
C	$201-350
D	$351-500
E	$501-650
F	over $650

Activities: Aquatic Activities, Archery, Ceramics/Pottery, Challenge/Rope Courses, Kayaking, Performing Arts, Photography, Soccer, Sports — Field & Team, Tennis
Session lengths & capacity: June-August; 2 & 3 week sessions; 250 campers
Clientele & fees: coed 7-14; Fees: A, B ⚠ 🚐
Contact: Joanne Lucas, Office Manager at (781) 860-0200; fax: (781) 860-0352
Web site: www.agassizvillage.com
Operated by: Agassiz Village Inc, 238 Bedford St Ste 8, Lexington, MA 02420 at (781) 860-0200 (#2766)

Alford Lake Camp (est 1907) ⚠ 🚐

Hope, ME (Knox Co.); (207) 785-2400
Sue or Jean McMullan, Director
Camp comments: A place of sensitivity, challenge, respect, appreciation, warmth & citizenship - where values matter & people thrive!
Activities: Arts/Crafts, Drama, Gymnastics, Horseback — English, International Culture, Leadership Development, Sailing, Tennis, Travel/Tour, Wilderness Trips
Session lengths & capacity: June-August; 3 & 7 week sessions; 175 campers
Clientele & fees: girls 8-18; coed 14-16; families; Fees: B, E ⚠ 🚐
Contact: Sue McMullan, Owner/Director at (207) 799-3005; fax: (207) 799-5044
e-mail: alc@alfordlake.com
Operated by: Alford Lake Camp, 5 Salt Marsh Way, Cape Elizabeth, ME 04107 at (207) 799-3005 (#2713)

Androscoggin (est 1907) ⚠ 🚐

Wayne, ME (Kennebec Co.); (207) 685-4441
Peter & Roberta Hirsch, Director
Camp comments: Diverse individualized program incl: sports,waterfront & trips.Excellent instruction.Mature & caring staff. A fun-filled summer to remember.
Activities: Baseball/Softball, Basketball, Camping Skills/Outdoor Living, Challenge/Rope Courses, Radio/TV/Video, Sailing, Soccer, Swimming — Instructional, Tennis, Waterskiing
Session lengths & capacity: June-August; 8 week sessions; 250 campers
Clientele & fees: boys 8-15; Fees: F ⚠
Contact: Peter Hirsch, Director at (914) 835-5800; fax: (914) 777-2718
e-mail: directors@campandro.com
Web site: www.campandro.com
Operated by: Androscoggin, 601 West Street, Harrison, NY 10528 at (914) 835-5800 (#2079)

Birch Rock Camp ⚠ 🚐

Waterford, ME (Oxford Co.); (207) 583-4478
Richard Deering/Michael Mattson, Director
Camp comments: Diverse noncompetitive 90 campers+staff encourage confidence, cooperation, appreciation of natural environment & spirited fun.
Activities: Academics, Aquatic Activities, Archery, Camping Skills/Outdoor Living, Hiking, Sailing, Sports — Field & Team, Swimming — Instructional, Wilderness Trips
Session lengths & capacity: June-August; 2, 3, 4 & 7 week sessions; 75 campers
Clientele & fees: boys 7-15; Fees: F ⚠ 🐷
Contact: Richard Deering, Director at (207) 741-2930; fax: (207) 741-2959
e-mail: birchrock@aol.com
Web site: www.birchrock.org
Operated by: Birch Rock Camp, 30 Bellevue Ave, South Portland, ME 04106 at (207) 741-2930 (#4210)

Bishopswood (est 1962) ⚠ 🏠

Hope, ME (Knox Co.); (207) 763-3148
Georgia L Koch, Director
Camp comments: Commitment to community living skills & respect for self & others. General camp activities.
Activities: Aquatic Activities, Arts/Crafts, Camping Skills/Outdoor Living, Community Service, Counselor Training (CIT), Leadership Development, Swimming — Instructional
Session lengths & capacity: June-August; 1, 2, 3, 4, 5, 6 & 7 week sessions; 100 campers
Clientele & fees: coed 7-15; Fees: C ⚠
Contact: Georgia L Koch, Director at (207) 772-1953; fax: (207) 773-0095
e-mail: gkoch@diomaine.org
Web site: www.diomaine.org
Operated by: Diocese Of Maine Episcopal, 143 State St, Portland, ME 04101-3799 at (207) 772-1953

Group Rental Information

Seasons & Capacity: Spring 0, Fall 0
Facilities: Cabins, Dorm-Style, Food Service, Kitchen Facilities, Lodges, Meeting Rooms, Playing Fields (#3716)

Camp Agawam (est 1919) ⚠ 🏠

Raymond, ME (Cumberland Co.); (207) 627-4780
Garth Nelson, Director
Camp comments: Broad activity program stimulates personal achievement; inter-personal skills grow within the warm camp community.
Activities: Arts/Crafts, Baseball/Softball, Basketball, Camping Skills/Outdoor Living, Challenge/Rope Courses, Hiking, Sailing, Soccer, Tennis
Session lengths & capacity: June-August; 7 week sessions; 125 campers
Clientele & fees: boys 8-15; Fees: F ⚠ 🐷
Contact: Garth Nelson, Director at (781) 826-5913; fax: (781) 829-0208
e-mail: chief@campagawam.org
Web site: www.campagawam.org
Operated by: Agawam Council, 30 Fieldstone Lane, Hanover, MA 02339 at (781) 826-5913

Group Rental Information

Site comments: Lakes region, southern Maine; 25 mi-Portland; 2 1/2 hrs-Boston.
Programs: Boating (#2721)

Camp Arcadia Inc (est 1916) ⚠ 🏠 🚐

Casco, ME (Oxford Co.); (207) 627-4605
Anne Fritts/Louise Henderson/Louise Fritts Johnson, Director
Camp comments: A warm family atmosphere & close guidance fosters the development of personal growth and confidence. Extensive program.
Activities: Aquatic Activities, Arts/Crafts, Camping Skills/Outdoor Living, Canoeing, Counselor Training (CIT), Hiking, Horseback — English, Performing Arts, Sailing, Tennis
Session lengths & capacity: June-August; 1, 2, 4 & 7 week sessions; 165 campers
Clientele & fees: girls 6-17; Fees: D, E ⚠
Contact: Anne Fritts, Director at (973) 538-5409; fax: (973) 540-1555
e-mail: cmparcadia@aol.com
Operated by: Camp Arcadia, Pleasantville Rd Box 225, New Vernon, NJ 07976 at (973) 538-5409

Group Rental Information

Seasons & Capacity: Fall 100
Facilities: Cabins, Dorm-Style, Double Occupancy, Food Service, Hiking Trails, Lake, Lodges, Playing Fields
Programs: Environmental Education, Horseback Riding, Swimming (#2770)

Camp Beech Cliff (est 1994)

Mount Desert, ME (Hancock Co.); (207) 244-0365
Vance O'Donnell, Director

Camp comments: The most imp aspect of camp is the opp. for campers to develop soc skills and relationships with each other and the staff
Activities: Archery, Camping Skills/Outdoor Living, Challenge/Rope Courses, Community Service, Counselor Training (CIT), Nature/Environment Studies, Sailing, Sports — Field & Team, Swimming — Recreational, Wilderness Trips
Session lengths & capacity: 1 week sessions; 110 campers
Clientele & fees: coed 8-14; Fees: **B**
Contact: Sandy del Castillo, Office Manager at (207) 244-0365; fax: (207) 244-3355
e-mail: campbeechcliff2@acadia.net
Web site: www.campbeechcliff.org
Operated by: Camp Beech Cliff, PO Box 381, Mount Desert, ME 04660 at (207) 244-0365

Group Rental Information
Site comments: Challenge courses are not just for kids it is not all about fear of heights it is about life skills.
Seasons & Capacity: Spring 100, Fall 100
Facilities: Cabins, Hiking Trails, Lodges, Meeting Rooms, Playing Fields, Tents
Programs: Boating, Challenge/Ropes Course, Environmental Education, Swimming (#46274)

Camp Cedar (est 1954)

Casco, ME (Cumberland Co.); (207) 627-4266
Jeff Hacker, Sue Hacker-Wolf, Director

Camp comments: Happy, well cared for campers - superior facilities and excellent instruction in a family camp atmosphere.
Activities: Baseball/Softball, Basketball, Camping Skills/Outdoor Living, Challenge/Rope Courses, Climbing/Rappelling, Sailing, Soccer, Swimming — Instructional, Tennis, Waterskiing
Session lengths & capacity: June-August; 7 week sessions; 280 campers
Clientele & fees: boys 7-15; Fees: **F**
Contact: Jeff Hacker & Sue Hacker-Wolf, Directors at (617) 277-8080; fax: (617) 277-1488
e-mail: campcedar@aol.com
Web site: www.campcedar.com
Operated by: Camp Cedar, 1758 Beacon St, Brookline, MA 02445 at (617) 277-8080

Group Rental Information
Facilities: A/V Equipment, Cabins, Dorm-Style, Food Service, Kitchen Facilities, Lake, Linens, Meeting Rooms, Playing Fields
Programs: Boating, Challenge/Ropes Course, Swimming (#2752)

Camp Fernwood (est 1921)

Poland, ME (Androscoggin Co.); (207) 998-4346
Fritz Seving and Maxine B. King, Director

Camp comments: Friendly & welcoming. Great staff. Strong instructional program. Land & water, team & individual sports, arts & trips.
Activities: Archery, Canoeing, Ceramics/Pottery, Horseback — English, Performing Arts, Riflery, Sailing, Tennis, Waterskiing
Session lengths & capacity: June-August; 8 week sessions; 175 campers
Clientele & fees: girls 8-15; Fees: **F**
Contact: Fritz Seving, Director at (610) 695-0169; fax: (610) 695-0905
e-mail: fernwood@campfernwood.com
Web site: www.campfernwood.com
Operated by: Camp Fernwood, 733 Providence Road, Mavern, PA 19355 at (610) 695-0169 (#2104)

Camp Jordan (est 1908)

Ellsworth, ME; (207) 667-8708
Jim Bentley, Director

Camp comments: Traditional YMCA program. Teen leadership & adventure trips, building self-esteem, honesty, caring, respect, & responsibility on beautiful Branch Lake in Maine.
Activities: Aquatic Activities, Archery, Arts/Crafts, Challenge/Rope Courses, Climbing/Rappelling, Leadership Development, Sailing, Sports — Field & Team, Waterskiing, Wilderness Trips
Session lengths & capacity: 1 week sessions; 140 campers
Clientele & fees: coed 8-17; Fees: **C, D**
Contact: Allen Archer, Camp Director at (207) 941-2815; fax: (207) 941-2819
e-mail: bangory@mint.net
Web site: www.bangorymca.org
Operated by: Bangor YMCA, 127 Hammond St, Bangor, ME 04401 at (207) 941-2815

Group Rental Information
Facilities: Cabins, Double Occupancy, Food Service, Hiking Trails, Kitchen Facilities, Lake, Lodges, Meeting Rooms, Ocean, Playing Fields, River
Programs: Boating, Challenge/Ropes Course (#6244)

Camp Kawanhee (est 1921)

Weld, ME; (207) 585-2210
Mark Nelson and Walter & Jane Estabrook, Director

Camp comments: Fun with a purpose finish what you start, learn to do by doing. 82 year tradtional liberal arts camp founded as a character building force for boys.
Activities: Archery, Baseball/Softball, Basketball, Kayaking, Riflery, Sailing, Soccer, Sports — Field & Team, Tennis, Wilderness Trips
Session lengths & capacity: June-August; 4 & 7 week sessions; 150 campers
Clientele & fees: boys 7-15; Fees: **E**
Contact: Mark Nelson & Walter Estabrook, Directors at (336) 794-2400; fax: (336) 659-3511
e-mail: mjnelson88@hotmail.com
Operated by: Camp Kawanhee, 121 Pennsylvania Ave, Winston Salem, NC 27104 at (336) 794-2400 (#3472)

Camp Mechuwana

(est 1948)

Winthrop, ME (Kennebec Co.); (207) 377-2924
Norman R Thombs, Director

Camp comments: Beautiful surroundings on 200 acres of land with 2 lakes. Come share in the fun as we explore God's world.
Activities: Arts/Crafts, Backpacking, Camping Skills/Outdoor Living, Drama, Hiking, Music, Nature/Environment Studies
Session lengths & capacity: 1 week sessions; 200 campers
Clientele & fees: coed 5-90; single adults; Fees: **A** Fees: **B**
Contact: Norman Thombs, Director at (207) 377-2924; fax: (207) 377-4388
e-mail: nthombs@bpddeford.com
Operated by: Camp Mechuwana, PO Box 277, Winthrop, ME 04364 at (207) 377-2924

Group Rental Information
Seasons & Capacity: Spring 100, Summer 250, Fall 250, Winter 100
Facilities: Cabins, Food Service, Hiking Trails, Lake, Lodges, Meeting Rooms, Playing Fields
Programs: Boating, Challenge/Ropes Course, Environmental Education, Swimming (#4204)

Camp Natarswi (est 1936)

Millinocket, ME (Piscataquis Co.); (207) 723-4156
Pam Weinle-Tower, Director

Camp comments: Wilderness site in Baxter Park with focus on high adventure, outdoor living, hiking, camp craft skills, Jr Maine Guide.
Activities: Aquatic Activities, Archery, Backpacking, Camping Skills/Outdoor Living, Hiking, Kayaking, Leadership Development, Nature/Environment Studies, Sailing, Wilderness Trips

Session lengths & capacity: July-August; 1, 2 & 4 week sessions; 130 campers
Clientele & fees: girls 8-17; Fees: **B, C**
Contact: Roberta Smart, Director of Camping Services at (207) 989-7474; fax: (207) 989-7478
e-mail: abnaki@midmaine.com
Operated by: Abnaki GSC, 156 N Main St, Brewer, ME 04412-2012 at (207) 989-7474 (#4670)

Camp Peirce Webber

Bangor, ME (Penobscot Co.); (207) 941-2815
Lisa Wicks, Director

Camp comments: Cam Peirce Webber is a 55 acre traditional day camp for children ages 5-12. Campers swim twice daily and particpate in crafts, nature, sports and archery.
Activities: Aquatic Activities, Archery, Arts/Crafts, Baseball/Softball, Counselor Training (CIT), Field Trips, Leadership Development, Nature/Environment Studies, Soccer, Sports — Field & Team
Session lengths & capacity: 1 week sessions; 150 campers
Clientele & fees: coed 3-15; Fees: **B**
Contact: Lisa Wicks, Camp Director at (207) 941-2815 ext. 360; fax: (207) 941-2819
Web site: www.bangorymca.org
Operated by: Bangor YMCA, 127 Hammond St, Bangor, ME 04401 at (207) 941-2815

Group Rental Information
Facilities: Pool (#3161)

Camp Runoia (est 1907)

Belgrade Lakes, ME (Kennebec Co.); (207) 495-2228
Pamela Cobb, Director

Camp comments: Friendly camp, strong traditions. Dynamic staff. 4th generation director. Lake region, cabins, free-choice, family style dining.
Activities: Archery, Camping Skills/Outdoor Living, Challenge/Rope Courses, Horseback — English, Kayaking, Riflery, Sailing, Tennis, Wilderness Trips, Windsurfing
Session lengths & capacity: June-August; 3, 4 & 7 week sessions; 100 campers
Clientele & fees: girls 8-15; Fees: **F**
Contact: Pamela Cobb, Director at (617) 547-4676; fax: (617) 661-1964
e-mail: info@runoia.com
Web site: www.runoia.com
Operated by: Camp Runoia, 56 Jackson Street, Cambridge, MA 02140 at (617) 547-4676 (#4250)

Camp Samoset (est 1944)

Casco, ME (Cumberland Co.); (207) 627-4275
Arthur & Barbara Savage, Director

Camp comments: Hand chosen staff. Excellent lakefront facility. Diverse program. Individual instruction. Intercamp teams. Exciting special events.
Activities: Arts/Crafts, Baseball/Softball, Basketball, Canoeing, Hockey, Sailing, Soccer, Swimming — Instructional, Tennis, Waterskiing
Session lengths & capacity: June-August; 4 & 8 week sessions; 170 campers
Clientele & fees: boys 7-16; Fees: **F**
Contact: Arthur Savage, Director at (781) 237-3017; fax: (781) 237-7269
e-mail: campsamoset@aol.com
Web site: www.campsamoset.com
Operated by: Camp Samoset, 15 Cornell Road, Wellesley, MA 02482 at (781) 237-3017 (#2838)

Camp Sunshine (est 1984)

Casco, ME (Cumberland Co.); (207) 655-3800
Michael Katz, Director

Camp comments: The mission of camp sunshine is to provide terminally and critically ill children & their families a retreat & respite, all at no expense to the family.

Activities: Aquatic Activities, Archery, Baseball/Softball, Boating, Canoeing, Climbing/Rappelling, Computer, Soccer, Sports — Field & Team, Swimming — Recreational
Session lengths & capacity: May-October; 40 campers
Clientele & fees: families
Contact: Michael Katz, Campus Director at (207) 655-3800; fax: (207) 655-3825
e-mail: mkatz@campsunshine.org
Web site: www.campsunshine.org
Operated by: Camp Sunshine Inc, 35 Acadia Road, Casco, ME 04015 at (207) 655-3800 (#32390)

Camp Susan Curtis (est 1974) ▲

Stoneham, ME (Oxford Co.); (207) 928-2955
Michael Procter, Director

Camp comments: Camp for disadvantaged ME children, including leadership training. Self-esteem focus. Income eligibility.
Activities: Arts/Crafts, Boating, Camping Skills/Outdoor Living, Canoeing, Drama, Field Trips, Hiking, Leadership Development, Sports — Field & Team, Swimming — Instructional
Session lengths & capacity: June-August; 2 week sessions; 100 campers
Clientele & fees: boys 8-12; girls 8-12; coed 8-12; Fees: A ▲ 🐷
Contact: Mary Ellen Deschenes, Executive Director at (207) 774-1552; fax: (207) 774-4240
e-mail: campsue@maine.rr.com
Web site: www.campsusancurtis.com
Operated by: Susan L Curtis Foundation, PO Box 821, Portland, ME 04104 at (207) 774-1552 (#7732)

Camp Takajo (est 1947) ▲

Naples, ME; (207) 693-6675
Jeffrey Konigsberg, Director

Camp comments: Magnificent lakefront setting, exceptional facilities, diversified program of athletics, waterfront, tripping & hobbies.
Activities: Arts/Crafts, Baseball/Softball, Basketball, Camping Skills/Outdoor Living, Climbing/Rappelling, Drama, Nature/Environment Studies, Sailing, Sports — Field & Team, Tennis
Session lengths & capacity: 8 week sessions; 395 campers
Clientele & fees: boys 7-15; Fees: F ▲
Contact: Jeffrey A Konigsberg, Director at (914) 273-5020; fax: (914) 273-5352
Operated by: Tripp Lake Camp, 34 Maple Ave, Armonk, NY 10504 at (914) 273-4065 (#2180)

ICON LEGEND

☀ Day Camp
▲ Resident Camp
🏠 Facilities Available To Rent
🚐 Transportation Available
🐷 Financial Aid Available

FEE RANGES PER WEEK

A	$0-75
B	$75-200
C	$201-350
D	$351-500
E	$501-650
F	over $650

Camp Tapawingo (est 1919) ▲ 🏠

Sweden, ME (Oxford Co.); (207) 647-3351
Jane Lichtman, Director

Camp comments: Improving self-confidence of girls. Trad. camp balances creative arts & athletics. Mountains overlook beautiful lake.
Activities: Arts/Crafts, Basketball, Drama, Gymnastics, Hiking, Horseback — English, Swimming — Instructional, Tennis, Waterskiing, Wilderness Trips
Session lengths & capacity: June-August; 4 & 7 week sessions; 175 campers
Clientele & fees: girls 8-16; Fees: F ▲
Contact: Jane Lichtman, Director at (973) 275-1139; fax: (973) 275-1182
e-mail: camptap@aol.com
Web site: www.camptosawings.com
Operated by: Camp Tapawingo, PO Box 248, Maplewood, NJ 07040 at (973) 275-1139

Group Rental Information
Facilities: Double Occupancy, Hiking Trails, Kitchen Facilities, Lake, Lodges, Playing Fields
Programs: Boating, Challenge/Ropes Course, Swimming (#2637)

Camp Walden (est 1916) ▲

Denmark, ME (Oxford Co.); (207) 452-2901
Wendy Cohen, Director

Camp comments: Honor system. Long standing traditions, small family atmosphere. Individual scheduling. Long-lasting friendships. Trips.
Activities: Arts/Crafts, Challenge/Rope Courses, Drama, Gymnastics, Horseback — English, Leadership Development, Soccer, Swimming — Instructional, Tennis, Waterskiing
Session lengths & capacity: June-August; 4, 5 & 8 week sessions; 150 campers
Clientele & fees: girls 9-15; Fees: F ▲ 🐷
Contact: Wendy S Cohen, Director at (804) 293-3730; fax: (804) 293-8802
e-mail: wendycohen@aol.com
Web site: www.campwalden.com
Operated by: Camp Walden, Box 3427, Charlottesville, VA 22903-0427 at (804) 293-3730 (#1747)

Camp Waziyatah (est 1922) ▲ 🏠 🚐

Waterford, ME (Oxford Co.); (207) 583-6781
Penny & Peter Kerns, Director

Camp comments: The Experience: Make Good Choices, Live Your Dreams! Develop independent thought, respect for others and self-esteem.
Activities: Arts/Crafts, Basketball, Climbing/Rappelling, Horseback — English, Performing Arts, Soccer, Sports — Field & Team, Tennis, Waterskiing, Wilderness Trips
Session lengths & capacity: June-August; 3, 4 & 7 week sessions; 200 campers
Clientele & fees: coed 8-15; families; single adults; Fees: E, F ▲
Contact: The Kerns Family, Directors at (508) 668-9758; fax: (508) 668-2665
e-mail: info@wazi.com
Web site: www.wazi.com
Operated by: Camp Waziyatah Inc, 19 Vose Lane, East Walpole, MA 02032 at (508) 668-9758

Group Rental Information
Facilities: Cabins, Kitchen Facilities, Lake, Playing Fields
Programs: Horseback Riding, Swimming (#1605)

Camps Newfound Owatonna (est 1914) ▲ 🏠

Harrison, ME; (207) 583-6711
Anne McCauley & Peter Martin, Director

Camp comments: Lakeside setting. Traditional prog for young Christian Scientists. Emphasis: character, team building & lasting friends.

Activities: Aquatic Activities, Arts/Crafts, Backpacking, Boating, Challenge/Rope Courses, Climbing/Rappelling, Soccer, Sports — Field & Team, Swimming — Recreational, Waterskiing
Session lengths & capacity: June-August; 3, 4 & 7 week sessions; 200 campers
Clientele & fees: boys 6-16; girls 6-16; Fees: D ▲
Contact: Amy Sparkman, Business Director at (800) 646-6711; fax: (860) 434-3481
e-mail: newfowat@cs.com
Operated by: Camps Newfound/Owatonna, 4 Camp Newfound Road, Harrison, ME 04040 at (800) 646-6711 (#7170)

Caribou For Boys (est 1922) ▲

Winslow, ME (Kennebec Co.); (207) 872-9313
Bill & Martha Lerman, Director

Camp comments: Warm, nurturing, challenging environment. 200 ac private peninsula. Individual instruction, outstanding-mature staff.
Activities: Archery, Baseball/Softball, Basketball, Challenge/Rope Courses, Golf, Sailing, Soccer, Tennis, Waterskiing
Session lengths & capacity: June-August; 3 week sessions; 185 campers
Clientele & fees: boys 7-15; Fees: F ▲
Contact: Bill Lerman, Director/Owner at (508) 358-5050; fax: (508) 358-5876
e-mail: campcaribou@aol.com
Web site: www.campcaribou.com
Operated by: Caribou for Boys, PO Box 129, Wayland, MA 01778 at (508) 358-5050 (#2702)

Chewonki (est 1915) ▲ 🏠 🚐

Wiscasset, ME (Lincoln Co.); (207) 882-7323
Dick Thomas, Director

Camp comments: Located on 400 ac coastal peninsula, emphasizing nature study & wilderness trips for all. Nonprofit; year-round environmental education programs.
Activities: Archery, Camping Skills/Outdoor Living, Challenge/Rope Courses, Farming/Ranching/Gardening, Kayaking, Nature/Environment Studies, Photography, Sailing, Tennis, Wilderness Trips
Session lengths & capacity: June-August; 1, 3 & 7 week sessions; 215 campers
Clientele & fees: boys 8-18; girls 12-18; coed 13-18; families; seniors; single adults; Fees: D, E, F ▲ 🐷
Contact: Dick Thomas, Camp Director at (207) 882-7323; fax: (207) 882-4074
e-mail: dthomas@chewonki.org
Web site: www.chewonki.org
Operated by: The Chewonki Foundation Inc, 485 Chewonki Neck Rd, Wiscasset, ME 04578-9980 at (207) 882-7323

Group Rental Information
Site comments: Our center for environmental education offers meeting spaces and food service for day use for up to 100 people.
Seasons & Capacity: Spring 100, Summer 100, Fall 100, Winter 100
Facilities: A/V Equipment, Food Service, Hiking Trails, Meeting Rooms
Programs: Challenge/Ropes Course, Environmental Education (#2830)

Chop Point (est 1966) ▲ 🏠 🚐

Woolwich, ME; (207) 443-5860
David Wilkinson, Director

Camp comments: Just for teens. Great counselors. Trips are specialty. International. Great food. Lobster bakes.
Activities: Aquatic Activities, Backpacking, Bicycling/Biking, Hiking, Sailing, Soccer, Tennis, Waterskiing, Wilderness Trips, Windsurfing
Session lengths & capacity: June-August; 3 & 6 week sessions; 85 campers
Clientele & fees: coed 12-18; Fees: E ▲ 🐷

Contact: Jean Willard, Office Manager at (207) 443-5860; fax: (207) 443-6760
e-mail: jean@choppoint.org
Web site: www.choppoint.org
Operated by: Chop Point Inc, 420 Chop Point Rd, Woolwich, ME 04579 at (207) 443-5860
Group Rental Information
Facilities: Cabins, Dorm-Style, Hiking Trails, Kitchen Facilities, Meeting Rooms, Playing Fields, River (#2606)

Cobbossee (est 1902)

Winthrop, ME; (207) 933-4503
Steve & Nancy Rubin, Director

Camp comments: Excellent instruction-all sports-top adventure program climb, hike, camp, scenic lake, full water sports. Personalized programs; structured & elective.
Activities: Baseball/Softball, Basketball, Climbing/Rappelling, Hiking, Hockey, Sailing, Soccer, Swimming — Instructional, Tennis, Waterskiing
Session lengths & capacity: June-August; 4, 5, 6 & 7 week sessions; 225 campers
Clientele & fees: boys 7-15; Fees: F ▲
Contact: Steve or Nancy Rubin, Owner/Director at (914) 533-6104; fax: (914) 533-6069
e-mail: cobbacheif@aol.com
Web site: www.campcobbossee.com
Operated by: Cobbossee, 10 Silvermine Dr, South Salem, NY 10590 at (914) 533-6104 (#2102)

Darrow Wilderness Trip Camp

(est 1957)

Grand Lake Stream, ME (Washington Co.); (888) 854-0810
John & Carolyn Houghton, Director

Camp comments: Life-changing experiences in the wilderness. Canoe and backpack trips, Maine and eastern Canada. Small groups. Two expereinced staff (5:1 ratio) per trip group.
Activities: Backpacking, Camping Skills/Outdoor Living, Canoeing, Fishing, Hiking, Nature/Environment Studies, Team Building, Wilderness Trips
Session lengths & capacity: June-August; 1, 2, 4, 6 & 7 week sessions; 10 campers
Clientele & fees: coed 10-17; families; seniors; single adults; Fees: E, F ▲ 🚐
Contact: John or Carolyn Houghton, Directors at (888) 854-0810; fax: (207) 725-2114
e-mail: info@darrowcamp.com
Operated by: Darrow Wilderness Trip Camp, 24 Lunt Rd, Brunswick, ME 04011-7288 at (888) 854-0810
Group Rental Information
Seasons & Capacity: Summer 20
Facilities: Dorm-Style, Food Service, Lake, Meeting Rooms, Tents (#2801)

Encore Coda (est 1950)

Sweden, ME (Oxford Co.); (207) 647-3947
James Saltman, Director

Camp comments: Noncompetitive, daily music instruction all styles, traditional camp atmosphere, includes swimming, sports, trips.
Activities: Arts/Crafts, Drama, Drawing/Painting, Field Trips, Music, Performing Arts, Sailing, Soccer, Swimming — Instructional, Tennis
Session lengths & capacity: July-August; 3 & 7 week sessions; 160 campers
Clientele & fees: coed 9-17; Fees: D ☼
Fees: F ▲ 🚐
Contact: James Saltman, Director at (617) 325-1541; fax: (617) 325-7278
e-mail: jamie@encore-coda.com
Web site: encore-coda.com
Operated by: Encore Coda, 32 Grassmere Rd, Brookline, MA 02467 at (617) 325-1541 (#4432)

Fernwood Cove

Harrison, ME (Oxford Co.)
Claire R. King, Director

Camp comments: Super staff spirited welcoming community! Build skills, friendships, and traditions. Choice instructional program.
Activities: Archery, Arts/Crafts, Camping Skills/Outdoor Living, Climbing/Rappelling, Gymnastics, Horseback — English, Performing Arts, Sports — Field & Team, Swimming — Instructional, Tennis
Session lengths & capacity: June-August; 3 week sessions; 150 campers
Clientele & fees: girls 7-15; Fees: F ▲
Contact: Claire R King, Director at (978) 369-0572; fax: (978) 369-0920
e-mail: cove@fernwoodcove.com
Web site: www.campfernwood.com
Operated by: Camp Fernwood, 733 Providence Road, Mavern, PA 19355 at (610) 695-0169 (#41397)

Forest Acres Camp for Girls

(est 1924)

Fryeburg, ME; (207) 935-2305
Lisa & Geoffrey Newman, Director

Camp comments: Traditional camp located in White Mountains. Mature staff with lots of choice in a nurturing, warm, caring environment.
Activities: Archery, Ceramics/Pottery, Challenge/Rope Courses, Drama, Gymnastics, Horseback — English, Sailing, Soccer, Swimming — Recreational, Tennis
Session lengths & capacity: June-August; 4 & 7 week sessions; 150 campers
Clientele & fees: girls 6-16; Fees: F ▲
Contact: Lisa & Geoffrey Newman, Directors at (954) 385-3545; fax: (954) 349-7812
e-mail: geoff@indianacres.com
Web site: www.indianacres.com
Operated by: Forest/Indian Acres, 2914 Medinah, Weston, FL 33332 at (954) 385-3545
Group Rental Information
Facilities: Cabins, Kitchen Facilities, Lodges, Playing Fields, Pool
Programs: Swimming (#2798)

Four Winds (est 1946)

Sargentville, ME (Hancock Co.); (207) 359-8823
Amey Dodge, Director

Camp comments: Traditional, non-competitive girl's program: Elected, twice daily, land, lake & ocean activities. Penobscot Bay. International populace. 2,3 1/2 & 7 wk sessions
Activities: Aquatic Activities, Archery, Arts/Crafts, Camping Skills/Outdoor Living, Ceramics/Pottery, Horseback — English, Kayaking, Sailing, Tennis, Waterskiing
Session lengths & capacity: June-August; 2, 3 & 7 week sessions; 105 campers
Clientele & fees: girls 8-16; Fees: F ▲
Contact: Amey Dodge, Director at (207) 374-5267; fax: (207) 374-5478
e-mail: cfw@acadia.net
Operated by: Camp Four Winds, PO Box 195, Blue Hill, ME 04614-0195 at (207) 374-5267 (#2714)

Hidden Valley Camp

(est 1968)

Freedom, ME (Waldo Co.); (800) 922-6737
Meg & Peter Kassen, Director

Camp comments: Non-competitive, non-traditional, international. Live in a peaceful farmlike community setting, and choose your own activities. Private lake & heated pool.

Activities: Aquatic Activities, Arts/Crafts, Bicycling/Biking, Camping Skills/Outdoor Living, Challenge/Rope Courses, Horseback — English, Music, Performing Arts, Photography, Sports — Field & Team
Session lengths & capacity: June-August; 4 & 8 week sessions; 225 campers
Clientele & fees: coed 8-13; Fees: F ▲
Contact: Peter & Meg Kassen, Owner/Director at (800) 922-6737; fax: (207) 342-5685
e-mail: summer@hiddenvalleycamp.com
Web site: www.hiddenvalleycamp.com
Operated by: Hidden Valley Camp, RR 1 Box 2360, Freedom, ME 04941 at (800) 922-6737 (#7049)

Indian Acres Camp for Boys

(est 1924)

Fryeburg, ME (Oxford Co.); (207) 935-2300
Lisa & Geoffrey Newman, Director

Camp comments: Traditional camp,mature staff,individualized program teaching skills & values in relaxed,caring,supportive atmosphere.
Activities: Archery, Baseball/Softball, Basketball, Ceramics/Pottery, Drama, Hiking, Sailing, Soccer, Tennis, Waterskiing
Session lengths & capacity: June-August; 4 & 7 week sessions; 150 campers
Clientele & fees: boys 7-16; Fees: F ▲
Contact: Lisa & Geoffrey Newman, Directors at (954) 385-3545; fax: (954) 349-7812
e-mail: geoff@indianacres.com
Web site: www.indianacres.com
Operated by: Forest/Indian Acres, 2914 Medinah, Weston, FL 33332 at (954) 385-3545

Group Rental Information
Seasons & Capacity: Summer 200, Fall 200
Facilities: Cabins, Kitchen Facilities, Playing Fields, Pool
Programs: Swimming (#2799)

JCC Camp Kingswood

(est 1948) ▲ ▭

Bridgton, ME (Cumberland Co.); (207) 647-3969
Ava Goldman, Director

Camp comments: Beautiful lakes-region setting. Culture & experience. Wide variety of activities. Warm, caring staff. Kosher.
Activities: Archery, Basketball, Camping Skills/Outdoor Living, Ceramics/Pottery, Drama, Hiking, Soccer, Sports — Field & Team, Tennis, Waterskiing
Session lengths & capacity: June-August; 2, 4 & 8 week sessions; 240 campers
Clientele & fees: coed 8-16; Fees: **D** ▲ ▭
Contact: Ava Goldman, Director at (617) 244-5124; fax: (617) 244-1289
e-mail: info@kingswood.org
Web site: www.kingswood.org
Operated by: JCC Camp Kingswood, 333 Nahanton St, Newton Center, MA 02459 at (617) 244-5124 (#2856)

Kamp Kohut (est 1907)   ▲

Oxford, ME (Oxford Co.); (207) 539-0966
Ms. Lisa Tripler, Director

Camp comments: Warm & friendly four week camp; individualized skill-oriented program. Comprehensive range of activities & trips.
Activities: Arts/Crafts, Baseball/Softball, Challenge/Rope Courses, Drama, Field Trips, Gymnastics, Radio/TV/Video, Tennis, Waterskiing, Windsurfing
Session lengths & capacity: June-August; 4 week sessions; 150 campers
Clientele & fees: coed 7-16; Fees: **F** ▲
Contact: Ms Lisa Tripler, Owner/Director at (207) 767-2406; fax: (207) 767-0604
e-mail: kampkohut@aol.com
Web site: www.kampkohut.com
Operated by: Kamp Kohut, 2 Tall Pine Rd, Cape Elizabeth, ME 04107-2323 at (207) 767-2406 (#1946)

Kingsley Pines Camp

(est 1984) ▲ ▭

Raymond, ME (Cumberland Co.); (207) 655-7181
Alan Kissack, Director

ICON LEGEND

☼ Day Camp
▲ Resident Camp
⌂ Facilities Available To Rent
▭ Transportation Available
🐷 Financial Aid Available

FEE RANGES PER WEEK

A	$0-75
B	$75-200
C	$201-350
D	$351-500
E	$501-650
F	over $650

Camp comments: Positive reinforcement in a noncompetitive atmosphere, excellent staff role models, high quality instruction & fun!
Activities: Aquatic Activities, Archery, Arts/Crafts, Climbing/Rappelling, Kayaking, Performing Arts, Sailing, Sports — Field & Team, Tennis, Waterskiing
Session lengths & capacity: June-August: 2, 3, 5, 6 & 8 week sessions; 200 campers
Clientele & fees: coed 8-15; families; Fees: **F** ▲ 🐷
Contact: Alan Kissack, Director at (800) 480-1533; fax: (207) 761-1817
e-mail: info@kingsleypines.com
Web site: www.kingsleypines.com
Operated by: Kingsley Pines Camp, 75 Pearl St, Portland, ME 04101 at (207) 773-4621 (#4402)

Kippewa For Girls (est 1957)   ▲

Monmouth, ME; (207) 933-2993
Marty, Sylvia and Jon Silverman, Director

Camp comments: Caring, nurturing ambiance, arts, athletics, water sports, horses, wilderness trips. Individualized scheduling. Lakeside
Activities: Arts/Crafts, Dance, Drama, Gymnastics, Horseback — English, Sailing, Swimming — Instructional, Tennis, Waterskiing, Wilderness Trips
Session lengths & capacity: 4 & 8 week sessions; 140 campers
Clientele & fees: girls 7-16; Fees: **F** ▲
Contact: Marty or Jon Silverman, Directors at (781) 762-8291; fax: (781) 255-7167
e-mail: kippewa@tiac.net
Web site: www.kippewa.com
Operated by: Kippewa for Girls, 60 Mill St, Westwood, MA 02090-0340 at (781) 762-8291 (#2668)

Laurel (est 1949)   ▲ ⌂ ▭

Readfield, ME (Kennebec Co.); (207) 685-4945
Keith Klein, Director

Camp comments: Fine, coed 8 week camping. Full program of watersports, athletics, arts, adventure, riding & tennis w/family atmosphere.
Activities: Baseball/Softball, Basketball, Camping Skills/Outdoor Living, Drama, Gymnastics, Horseback — English, Soccer, Tennis, Waterskiing
Session lengths & capacity: June-August; 8 week sessions; 460 campers
Clientele & fees: coed 7-16; Fees: **F** ▲
Contact: Keith Klein, Owner/Director at (201) 750-0515; fax: (201) 750-0665
e-mail: summer@camplaurel.com
Web site: www.camplaurel.com
Operated by: Coastal Camps, Box 327, Readfield, ME 04355 at (201) 750-0515 (#2196)

Laurel South (est 1921)   ▲ ⌂ ▭

Casco, ME (Cumberland Co.); (207) 627-4334
Roger & Dagni Christian, Director

Camp comments: 4 wk Resident Camp offers top instruction in a family atmosphere. We take care of children! Beautiful setting on a lake.
Activities: Aquatic Activities, Arts/Crafts, Ceramics/Pottery, Challenge/Rope Courses, Performing Arts, Sports — Field & Team, Swimming — Instructional, Tennis, Waterskiing
Session lengths & capacity: 4 week sessions; 325 campers
Clientele & fees: coed 7-15; Fees: **F** ▲
Contact: Roger Christian, Director at (352) 331-4600; fax: (352) 331-0014
e-mail: fun@camplaurelsouth.com
Web site: www.camplaurel.com
Operated by: Coastal Camps, Box 327, Readfield, ME 04355 at (201) 750-0515 (#2782)

Maine Teen Camp (est 1984)   ▲ ▭

Porter, ME (Oxford Co.); (207) 625-8581
Bob Briskin, Director

Camp comments: Adult staff offers professional instruction in over 40 activities. Come join us, remember MTC is for teens only!
Activities: Challenge/Rope Courses, Dance, Drama, Drawing/Painting, Leadership Development, Music, Sports — Field & Team, Tennis, Travel/Tour, Waterskiing
Session lengths & capacity: June-August; 4, 6 & 8 week sessions; 300 campers
Clientele & fees: coed 13-17; Fees: **D, E, F** ▲ ▭
Contact: Robert Briskin, Owner/Director at (800) 752-2267; fax: (610) 520-0182
e-mail: mtc@teencamp.com
Web site: www.teencamp.com
Operated by: The Maine Teen Camp, 180 Upper Gulph Rd, Radnor, PA 19087 at (610) 527-6759 (#2849)

Manitou (est 1947)   ▲ ⌂

Oakland, ME; (207) 465-2271
Jason Silberman/David Schiff/Jon Deren, Director

Camp comments: Spectacular 250 acre campus. 42 sports & creative programs. Warm atmosphere. Structured so boys feel good about themselves.
Activities: Baseball/Softball, Basketball, Challenge/Rope Courses, Climbing/Rappelling, Fishing, Hiking, Radio/TV/Video, SCUBA, Soccer, Waterskiing
Session lengths & capacity: June-August; 4 & 8 week sessions; 275 campers
Clientele & fees: boys 7-16; Fees: **F** ▲
Contact: Jason Silberman, Director/Owner at (617) 928-1916; fax: (617) 928-1918
e-mail: Campmanito@aol.com
Web site: www.campmanitou.com
Operated by: Manitou, 84 Rachel Road, Newton Center, MA 02459-2913 at (617) 928-1916
Group Rental Information
Seasons & Capacity: Summer 400
Facilities: A/V Equipment, Cabins, Food Service, Lake, Linens, Meeting Rooms, Playing Fields
Programs: Boating, Challenge/Ropes Course, Swimming (#2719)

Mataponi Inc (est 1950)   ▲ ▭

Naples, ME (Cumberland Co.); (207) 787-3221
Dan & Marcy Isdaner, Director

Camp comments: Traditional high spirited warm focuses on self-esteem You don't have to be the best but you have to try your best Fun
Activities: Aquatic Activities, Arts/Crafts, Challenge/Rope Courses, Dance, Drama, Horseback — English, Sports — Field & Team, Swimming — Instructional, Tennis, Waterskiing
Session lengths & capacity: June-August; 7 week sessions; 300 campers
Clientele & fees: girls 7-16; Fees: **F** ▲
Contact: Marcy & Dan Isdaner, Owners/Directors at (856) 787-2240; fax: (856) 787-2242
e-mail: info@campmataponi.com
Web site: www.campmataponi.com
Operated by: Mataponi Inc, 520 Fellowship Rd Ste A104, Mt Laurel, NJ 08054 at (888) 684-2267 (#6221)

Matoaka For Girls (est 1951)   ▲ ⌂ ▭

Smithfield, ME (Kennebec Co.); (207) 362-2500
Michael & Paula Nathanson, Director

Camp comments: Second generation Directors impart individual attention to all areas of camp, professional staff & the best facilities.
Activities: Arts/Crafts, Challenge/Rope Courses, Dance, Drama, Gymnastics, Horseback — English, Sailing, Tennis, Waterskiing
Session lengths & capacity: 4 & 8 week sessions; 275 campers
Clientele & fees: girls 6-15; Fees: **F** ▲
Contact: Michael Nathanson, Director at (561) 488-6363; fax: (561) 488-6386
e-mail: matoaka@matoaka.com
Web site: www.matoaka.com

Operated by: Matoaka for Girls, 8751 Horseshoe Lane, Boca Raton, FL 33496-1235 at (561) 488-6363

Group Rental Information
Seasons & Capacity: Spring 225, Fall 225
Facilities: A/V Equipment, Cabins, Dorm-Style, Double Occupancy, Food Service, Hiking Trails, Lake, Linens, Meeting Rooms, Playing Fields, Pool
Programs: Boating, Challenge/Ropes Course, Swimming (#2737)

Med O Lark Camp (est 1922)

Washington, ME (Knox Co.); (207) 845-2441
Jay Stager, Director

Camp comments: Arts program-theatre & dance plus culinary arts + 12 studios. Nontraditional, noncompetitive.
Activities: Arts/Crafts, Ceramics/Pottery, Challenge/Rope Courses, Dance, Drama, Fencing, Horseback — English, Sailing, Tennis, Waterskiing
Session lengths & capacity: June-August; 4 & 8 week sessions; 220 campers
Clientele & fees: coed 11-15; Fees: F ▲ 🐖
Contact: Carly Cross, Director at (800) 292-7757; fax: (207) 338-0848
e-mail: medolark@acadia.net
Web site: www.medolark.com
Operated by: Med O Lark Camp, 214 Atlantic Hwy, Northport, ME 04849 at (207) 338-5733 (#2682)

Modin (est 1922)

Belgrade, ME (Kennebec Co.); (207) 465-4444
Howard Salzberg, Director

Camp comments: Oldest Jewish camp in New England. Nurturing noncompetitive environment. Over 60 program options. Warm, caring staff.
Activities: Arts/Crafts, Challenge/Rope Courses, Climbing/Rappelling, Performing Arts, Sailing, Sports — Field & Team, Tennis, Waterskiing, Wilderness Trips
Session lengths & capacity: June-August; 4 & 8 week sessions; 340 campers
Clientele & fees: coed 7-16; Fees: F ▲
Contact: Howard Salzberg, Director/Owner at (212) 570-1600; fax: (212) 570-1677
e-mail: modin@modin.com
Web site: www.modin.com
Operated by: Modin, 401 E 80th St Ste 28E/F, New York, NY 10021-0654 at (212) 570-1600 (#7660)

Nashoba North (est 1933)

Raymond, ME (Cumberland Co.); (207) 655-7170
The Seaward Family, Director

Camp comments: Beautiful facility on crystal clear waters. International clientele. Elective program. Outstanding staff & programs.
Activities: Archery, Ceramics/Pottery, Golf, Hiking, Horseback — English, Performing Arts, Sailing, Soccer, Tennis, Waterskiing
Session lengths & capacity: 4, 7 & 8 week sessions; 195 campers
Clientele & fees: coed 7-15; Fees: F ▲
Contact: The Seaward Family at (978) 486-8236; fax: (978) 952-2442
e-mail: nashobafun@aol.com
Web site: www.campnashoba.com
Operated by: The Seaward Family, 140 Nashoba Rd, Littleton, MA 01460 at (978) 486-8236

Group Rental Information
Facilities: Cabins, Food Service, Lake (#2787)

New England Camp Cherith

(est 1945)

Alfred, ME (York Co.); (207) 247-5251
Sue Miller, Director

Camp comments: Beautiful southern Maine. Christian (Interdenominational) residential camping for girls ages 8-17.

Activities: Archery, Arts/Crafts, Counselor Training (CIT), Kayaking, Leadership Development, Riflery, Sailing, Swimming — Instructional, Waterskiing, Wilderness Trips
Session lengths & capacity: June-August; 1 week sessions; 150 campers
Clientele & fees: girls 8-18; Fees: C ▲ 🐖
Contact: Sue Miller, Camp Director at (207) 247-5251; fax: (207) 247-8139
e-mail: necamp.cherith@juno.com
Web site: www.ultranet.com/~necc
Operated by: New England Camp Cherith, PO Box 154, Alfred, ME 04002 at (207) 247-5251

Group Rental Information
Site comments: Rustic facilities in southern Maine available for group rental, late summer through early spring. Food service provided.
Seasons & Capacity: Spring 50, Summer 250, Fall 50, Winter 50
Facilities: A/V Equipment, Cabins, Dorm-Style, Food Service, Lake, Lodges, Meeting Rooms, Playing Fields
Programs: Boating, Swimming, Winter Sports (#2655)

New England Music Camp

(est 1937)

Sidney, ME (Kennebec Co.); (207) 465-3025
Davis Wiggin, Director

Camp comments: Exceptional musical training by professional staff, weekly performances, water & land sports on beautiful lake; supervised social activities; 66th yr.
Activities: Aquatic Activities, Archery, Basketball, Canoeing, Drama, Music, Performing Arts, Sailing, Soccer, Tennis
Session lengths & capacity: June-August; 4 & 8 week sessions; 195 campers
Clientele & fees: coed 11-18; Fees: E 🐖
Contact: Davis & Jeanette Wiggin, Co-Directors at (860) 646-1642; fax: (860) 646-2128
e-mail: playatnemc@aol.com
Web site: www.nemusiccamp.com
Operated by: New England Music Camp, 8 Golden Rd Ln, Sidneyster, ME 04330-1954 at (860) 646-1642

Group Rental Information
Facilities: Cabins, Dorm-Style, Double Occupancy, Food Service, Lake, Lodges, Meeting Rooms (#4435)

O-AT-KA Inc (est 1906)

Sebago, ME (Cumberland Co.); (800) 818-8455
Keith Reinhardt, Director

Camp comments: O-At-Ka offers limitless opportunities for boys to develop their abilities.Emphasis on building character & good values.
Activities: Archery, Arts/Crafts, Basketball, Camping Skills/Outdoor Living, Counselor Training (CIT), Riflery, Sailing, Sports — Field & Team, Swimming — Instructional
Session lengths & capacity: June-September; 2, 3, 4 & 7 week sessions; 160 campers
Clientele & fees: boys 7-16; families; Fees: E ▲
Contact: Ron Hall, Director at (800) 818-8455; fax: (207) 787-3930
e-mail: campoatka@aol.com
Web site: www.campoatka.com
Operated by: Camp O-AT-KA Inc, 593 Sebago Road, Sebago, ME 04029-9713 at (800) 818-8455

Group Rental Information
Seasons & Capacity: Spring 200, Summer 200, Fall 200, Winter 200
Facilities: A/V Equipment, Cabins, Food Service, Lake, Linens, Lodges, Meeting Rooms, Playing Fields
Programs: Boating, Challenge/Ropes Course, Swimming, Winter Sports (#4530)

OMNI Camp (est 1989)

Poland Spring, ME (Androscoggin Co.); (207) 998-4777
Betsy & Gar Roper, Director

Camp comments: Lake setting, friendly community. Exciting choices in visual arts, drama, outdoor challenge, trips, awareness workshops.
Activities: Arts/Crafts, Aviation, Climbing/Rappelling, Community Service, Dance, Drama, Hiking, Horseback — English, Performing Arts, Waterskiing
Session lengths & capacity: June-August; 2, 4 & 8 week sessions; 220 campers
Clientele & fees: coed 9-15; Fees: F ▲
Contact: Betsy & Gar Roper, Directors at (888) 417-6664; fax: (207) 998-4722
e-mail: info@omnicamp.com
Web site: www.omnicamp.com
Operated by: OMNI Camp, 15 Merganser Way, Freeport, ME 04032 at (207) 865-0788

Group Rental Information
Seasons & Capacity: Spring 200, Fall 200
Facilities: Cabins, Dorm-Style, Double Occupancy, Hiking Trails, Kitchen Facilities, Lake, Lodges, Meeting Rooms, Playing Fields
Programs: Boating (#6407)

Pinecliffe (est 1917)

Harrison, ME; (207) 583-2201

Camp comments: Outstanding staff, beautiful facility. Cabins, warm cooperative atmosphere, lake setting. 4th generation leadership.
Activities: Aquatic Activities, Boating, Camping Skills/Outdoor Living, Canoeing, Field Trips, Horseback — English, Soccer, Swimming — Instructional, Tennis, Waterskiing
Session lengths & capacity: 7 week sessions; 200 campers
Clientele & fees: girls 8-15; Fees: F ▲
Contact: Susan R Lifter, Director at (614) 236-5698; fax: (614) 235-2267
e-mail: pinecliffe@msn.com
Web site: www.pinecliff.com
Operated by: Pinecliffe, 277 S Cassingham Rd, Columbus, OH 43209 at (614) 236-5698 (#2050)

Pondicherry Kennebec GSC

(est 1969)

Bridgton, ME (Cumberland Co.); (207) 647-5575
Tracey Graffam, Director

Camp comments: At Girl Scout camp, your daughter will learn new skills that will last a lifetime, make new friends and discover the wonders of outdoor living.
Activities: Arts/Crafts, Camping Skills/Outdoor Living, Challenge/Rope Courses, Counselor Training (CIT), Dance, Field Trips, Hiking, Leadership Development, Nature/Environment Studies, Swimming — Instructional
Session lengths & capacity: June-August; 1, 2, 3 & 4 week sessions; 155 campers
Clientele & fees: girls 7-17; Fees: C ▲ 🐖
Contact: Tracey Graffam, Director of Program at (207) 772-1177; fax: (207) 874-2646
e-mail: jeanh@kgsc.org
Web site: www.kgsc.org
Operated by: Kennebec GSC, PO Box 9421, South Portland, ME 04116-9421 at (207) 772-1177

Group Rental Information
Facilities: Dorm-Style, Hiking Trails, Kitchen Facilities, Lake, Playing Fields, Tents
Programs: Boating, Challenge/Ropes Course, Swimming (#4200)

Sebago (est 1957)

Sebago Lake, ME (Cumberland Co.); (207) 642-3771
Captain Paul Moore, Director

Camp comments: Camp Sebago provides a rural encounter, hiking & nature trails, lake front, recreational facilities & rustic buildings.
Activities: Aquatic Activities, Arts/Crafts, Basketball, Boating, Leadership Development, Nature/Environment Studies, Soccer, Swimming — Recreational, Tennis
Session lengths & capacity: 7 week sessions; 200 campers
Clientele & fees: boys 7-11; girls 7-11; coed 7-11; 🐘
Contact: Capt Everett Henry, Camp Director at (207) 642-3771;
Operated by: The Salvation Army, PO Box 3647, Portland, ME 04101 at (207) 774-6304
Group Rental Information
Facilities: Cabins, Dorm-Style, Food Service, Lake, Meeting Rooms
Programs: Boating (#2780)

Seeds of Peace Interntnl Camp

(est 1921)   ▲

Otisfield, ME (Oxford Co.); (207) 627-7500
Timothy Wilson, Director

Camp comments: Seeds of Peace equips the next generation with the leadership capabilities required to end the cycles of violence.
Activities: Aquatic Activities, Arts/Crafts, Basketball, Boating, Canoeing, Challenge/Rope Courses, International Culture, Leadership Development, Soccer, Team Building
Session lengths & capacity: June-September; 3 week sessions; 160 campers
Clientele & fees: coed 14-18; Fees: **F** ▲
Contact: e-mail: info@seedsofpeace.org
Web site: www.seedsofpeace.org
Operated by: Seeds of Peace, 370 Lexington Ave Ste 401, New York, NY 10017 at (212) 573-8040 (#4620)

Skylemar (est 1948)   ▲ 🏠

Naples, ME (Cumberland Co.); (207) 693-6414
Arleen & Pat Shepherd, Director

Camp comments: Sports-oriented program with 2-1 instruction in tennis & golf. Specialized clinics in basketball, soccer, & lacrosse.
Activities: Aquatic Activities, Baseball/Softball, Basketball, Challenge/Rope Courses, Golf, Hockey, Soccer, Sports — Field & Team, Tennis, Waterskiing
Session lengths & capacity: June-August; 4 & 7 week sessions; 170 campers
Clientele & fees: boys 7-16; Fees: **F** ▲
Contact: Arleen & Shep Shepherd, Directors at (410) 337-9697; fax: (410) 337-5250
e-mail: campskylemar@aol.com

ICON LEGEND

☀ Day Camp

▲ Resident Camp

🏠 Facilities Available To Rent

🚐 Transportation Available

🐘 Financial Aid Available

FEE RANGES PER WEEK

A	$0-75
B	$75-200
C	$201-350
D	$351-500
E	$501-650
F	over $650

Operated by: Skylemar, 2331 Old Court Rd Apt 310, Baltimore, MD 21208 at (410) 337-9697
Group Rental Information
Site comments: 200 acre site, with open fields, quiet lake and mountain views. 3 large indoor buildings for up to 300 people. 25 cabins with restrooms.
Seasons & Capacity: Summer 300
Facilities: A/V Equipment, Cabins, Food Service, Hiking Trails, Kitchen Facilities, Lake, Linens, Lodges, Meeting Rooms, Playing Fields
Programs: Swimming (#2496)

Skylodge Camp (est 1989)   ▲

Moose River, ME (Somerset Co.); (207) 668-2171
Valerie Paradise, Director

Camp comments: To build an attitude of self-respect develop self-confidence & instill leadership qualities in the lives of all campers.
Activities: Arts/Crafts, Bicycling/Biking, Camping Skills/Outdoor Living, Canoeing, Challenge/Rope Courses, Hiking, Nature/Environment Studies, Rafting, Sports — Field & Team, Swimming — Recreational
Session lengths & capacity: June-August; 1 week sessions; 16 campers
Clientele & fees: coed 10-12; Fees: **A** ▲
Contact: Catherine S Church, Executive Director at (203) 431-5762; fax: (203) 438-2472
Operated by: Couri Foundation Inc., 63 Copps Hill Rd, Ridgefield, CT 06877 at (203) 431-5762 (#5268)

State YMCA Camp of Maine

(est 1915)   ☀ ▲ 🏠

Winthrop, ME; (207) 395-4200
John C Bennett, Director

Camp comments: Since 1915 providing campers with opportunities to grow and build self-confidence through traditional programs and cabin life.
Activities: Aquatic Activities, Archery, Arts/Crafts, Camping Skills/Outdoor Living, Canoeing, Leadership Development, Sailing, Sports — Field & Team, Swimming — Instructional, Wilderness Trips
Session lengths & capacity: June-August; 1, 2, 3, 4, 5, 6, 7, 8 & 9 week sessions; 220 campers
Clientele & fees: coed 8-16; Fees: **B** ☀
Fees: **C** ▲
Contact: e-mail: ymcacamp@ctel.net
Web site: www.ctel.net/~ymcacamp
Operated by: State YMCA Of Maine, 305 Winthrop Center Rd, Winthrop, ME 04364-0090 at (207) 395-4200
Group Rental Information
Seasons & Capacity: Spring 220, Summer 220, Fall 220
Facilities: Cabins, Double Occupancy, Food Service, Lake, Lodges, Meeting Rooms, Playing Fields
Programs: Boating, Challenge/Ropes Course, Swimming (#6757)

The Summer Camp Inc (est 1986)   ▲

Washington, ME; (207) 845-2050
Tracy St Onge-May, Director

Camp comments: Campers are selected by social service agencies and school.
Activities: Arts/Crafts, Canoeing, Dance, Drama, Sports — Field & Team, Team Building, Tennis
Session lengths & capacity: 2 week sessions; 100 campers
Clientele & fees: girls 8-14; Fees: **A** ▲ 🐘
Contact: Tracy St Onge-May, Camp Director at (207) 647-5278; fax: (207) 647-5278
Web site: www.thesummercamp.org
Operated by: The Summer Camp Inc, 8 Church St, Bridgton, ME 04009 at (207) 647-5278 (#6671)

The Wavus Camps

(est 1922)   ☀ ▲ 🏠 🚐

Jefferson, ME (Lincoln Co.); (207) 549-5719
Carol Montgomery, Director

Camp comments: Noncompetitive,traditional Camp Wavus campers learn actively through experience. Our program is designed to promote progressive skills in many areas.
Activities: Aquatic Activities, Archery, Arts/Crafts, Boating, Canoeing, Challenge/Rope Courses, Kayaking, Nature/Environment Studies, Sailing, Swimming — Instructional
Session lengths & capacity: June-August; 2, 4, 6 & 8 week sessions; 135 campers
Clientele & fees: coed 5-16; Fees: **C** ☀
Fees: **E** ▲ 🐘
Contact: Carol A Montgomery, Camp Director at (207) 549-5719; fax: (207) 549-3693
e-mail: wavus@mint.net
Web site: www.wavus.org
Operated by: The Wavus Foundation, PO Box 350, Jefferson, ME 04348 at (207) 549-5719
Group Rental Information
Site comments: Our year round Jewell Lodge Dining Hall and Meeting Place is available from mid-August - mid-June with a capacity for 200 - sleeping accomodations for 60 fall/s
Seasons & Capacity: Spring 60, Fall 60
Facilities: Cabins, Dorm-Style, Hiking Trails, Kitchen Facilities, Lake, Lodges, Meeting Rooms
Programs: Boating, Challenge/Ropes Course, Environmental Education, Swimming, Winter Sports (#1020)

Timanous (est 1917)   ▲

Raymond, ME (Cumberland Co.); (207) 655-4569
David & Linda Suitor, Director

Camp comments: Counselors avg. 8 yrs of service.50 2nd,3rd,4th,5th generation campers,21 states,9 foreign countries,80% return rate
Activities: Aquatic Activities, Archery, Arts/Crafts, Camping Skills/Outdoor Living, Riflery, Sailing, Soccer, Swimming — Instructional, Tennis, Waterskiing
Session lengths & capacity: June-August; 3 & 7 week sessions; 115 campers
Clientele & fees: boys 7-15; Fees: **E** ▲ 🚐
Contact: David & Linda Suitor, Directors at (508) 485-8020; fax: (508) 460-6164
e-mail: camptiman@aol.com
Web site: www.timanous.com
Operated by: Timanous, St Marks School, Southborough, MA 01772 at (508) 485-8020 (#2687)

Trailmark Outdoor Adventures

(est 1984)   ▲ 🚐

Nyack, NY (Rockland Co.); (845) 358-0262
Rusty Pedersen, Director

Camp comments: Trailmark offers adventure trips to Maine, Pennsylvania, Colorado, Wyoming and Washington. Trips are grouped by age.
Activities: Backpacking, Bicycling/Biking, Camping Skills/Outdoor Living, Caving, Challenge/Rope Courses, Climbing/Rappelling, Kayaking, Rafting, Travel/Tour, Wilderness Trips
Session lengths & capacity: June-August; 1, 2 & 3 week sessions; 450 campers
Clientele & fees: coed 10-18; Fees: **F** ▲ 🐘
Contact: Rusty & Donna Pedersen, Owners/Directors at (800) 229-0262; fax: (845) 348-0437
e-mail: info@trailmark.com
Web site: www.trailmark.com
Operated by: Trailmark Outdoor Adventures, 16 Schuyler Rd, Nyack, NY 10960 at (800) 229-0262 (#3461)

Tripp Lake Camp (est 1911) ▲

Poland, ME; (207) 998-4347
Leslie K Levy, Director

Camp comments: Steeped in tradition. Active, spirited, structured, diverse program builds self esteem, skills: tennis, swim, ski, team sports, arts, drama, and more.
Activities: Arts/Crafts, Challenge/Rope Courses, Climbing/Rappelling, Gymnastics, Horseback — English, Performing Arts, Sports — Field & Team, Swimming — Instructional, Tennis, Waterskiing
Session lengths & capacity: June-August; 8 week sessions; 330 campers
Clientele & fees: girls 8-16; Fees: F ▲
Contact: Leslie Levy, Directors at (914) 273-4065; fax: (914) 273-5963
e-mail: tripplakecamp@aol.com
Operated by: Tripp Lake Camp, 34 Maple Ave, Armonk, NY 10504 at (914) 273-4065 (#3362)

Vega (est 1936) ▲ 🚐

Kents Hill, ME (Kennebec Co.); (207) 685-3707
Dick & Linda Courtiss, Director

Camp comments: Outstanding staff. Top facilities. We emphasize wholesome living relationships and skill achievement.
Activities: Academics, Canoeing, Climbing/Rappelling, Gymnastics, Horseback — English, Sailing, Soccer, Sports — Field & Team, Tennis, Waterskiing
Session lengths & capacity: June-August; 8 week sessions; 300 campers
Clientele & fees: girls 8-15; Fees: F ▲
Contact: Dick or Linda Courtiss, Owner/Directors at (781) 934-6536; fax: (781) 934-6544
e-mail: dick@campvega.com
Web site: www.campvega.com
Operated by: Vega, 19 Depot St, PO Box 1771, Duxbury, MA 02332 at (781) 934-6536 (#2014)

Wawenock (est 1910) ▲

Raymond, ME (Cumberland Co.); (207) 655-4657
June Gray & Patricia Smith, Director

Camp comments: Program of choice gives maximum attention to the individual girl. Emphasis on personal development in group living.
Activities: Archery, Arts/Crafts, Camping Skills/Outdoor Living, Canoeing, Drama, Horseback — English, Leadership Development, Sailing, Swimming — Instructional, Tennis
Session lengths & capacity: June-August; 7 week sessions; 110 campers
Clientele & fees: girls 8-16; Fees: F ▲
Contact: June W Gray or Patricia A Smith, Directors at (207) 655-4657;
e-mail: info@campwawenock.com
Web site: www.campwawenock.com
Operated by: Wawenock, 33 Wawenock Rd, Raymond, ME 04071-6824 at (207) 655-4657 (#2587)

Wekeela For Boys And Girls

(est 1922) ▲ 🏠 🚐

Canton, ME (Oxford Co.); (207) 224-7878
Eric Scoblionko, Director

Camp comments: Flexible sessions, traditional camp. Terrific facilities & staff of specialists. Campers from 27 states, 19 countries.
Activities: Arts/Crafts, Baseball/Softball, Basketball, Drama, Gymnastics, Horseback — English, Soccer, Swimming — Instructional, Tennis, Waterskiing
Session lengths & capacity: June-August; 4, 6 & 8 week sessions; 300 campers
Clientele & fees: coed 6-16; Fees: F ▲
Contact: Eric Scoblionko, Director at (614) 253-3177; fax: (614) 253-3661
e-mail: wekeela1@aol.com
Web site: www.campwekeela.com
Operated by: Wekeela for Boys and Girls, 2807C Delmar Dr, Columbus, OH 43209 at (614) 253-3177

Group Rental Information
Site comments: Fabulous facility for retreats, reunions and meetings. Available spring and fall.
Seasons & Capacity: Spring 300, Fall 300
Facilities: A/V Equipment, Cabins, Food Service, Hiking Trails, Lake, Linens, Meeting Rooms, Playing Fields
Programs: Boating, Challenge/Ropes Course, Horseback Riding, Swimming (#2821)

Wigwam (est 1910) ▲

Waterford, ME (Oxford Co.); (207) 583-2300
Robert W Strauss, Director

Camp comments: In the foothills of White Mountains, very personalized, emphasis on golf, tennis & outstanding waterfront programs.
Activities: Baseball/Softball, Basketball, Field Trips, Golf, Model Rocketry, Music, Sailing, Swimming — Recreational, Tennis, Waterskiing
Session lengths & capacity: June-August; 5 & 7 week sessions; 150 campers
Clientele & fees: boys 6-16; Fees: F ▲
Contact: Robert & Jane Strauss, Directors at (207) 583-2300; fax: (207) 583-6242
e-mail: wigwam@maine.com
Web site: www.campwigwam.com
Operated by: Wigwam, 57 Wigwam Pass, Waterford, ME 04088 at (207) 583-2300 (#6124)

Wildwood (est 1953) ▲ 🚐

Bridgton, ME; (207) 647-8864
Mark & Peter Meyer, Director

Camp comments: Warm & traditional sports camp for boys, offer all team sports, lots of tennis. Especially watchful of 1st yr campers.
Activities: Baseball/Softball, Basketball, Golf, Hockey, Skating, Soccer, Swimming — Instructional, Tennis, Waterskiing
Session lengths & capacity: 4 & 7 week sessions; 175 campers
Clientele & fees: boys 7-15; Fees: F ▲ 🚌
Contact: Mark Meyer, Director at (212) 316-1419; fax: (212) 316-1279
e-mail: lmeyer8@cs.com
Web site: www.campwildwood.com
Operated by: Camp Wildwood, 838 West End Ave, New York, NY 10025 at (212) 316-1419 (#2065)

Winnebago (est 1919) ▲ 🚐

Kents Hill, ME (Kennebec Co.); (207) 685-4918
Phil Lilienthal & Andy Lilienthal, Director

Camp comments: How do yo measure value at camp? Kids say 'Fun'. We say fun plus values & healthy relationships. We have stayed small, yet expanded our already top facilities.
Activities: Archery, Camping Skills/Outdoor Living, Canoeing, Challenge/Rope Courses, Sailing, Sports — Field & Team, Team Building, Tennis, Waterskiing, Wilderness Trips
Session lengths & capacity: 4 & 8 week sessions; 160 campers
Clientele & fees: boys 8-15; Fees: F ▲
Contact: Phil Lilienthal, Director/Owner at (703) 437-0808; fax: (703) 437-8620
e-mail: unkphilwc@aol.com
Web site: www.campwinnebago.com
Operated by: Winnebago, 1606 Washington Plaza, Reston, VA 22090-4300 at (703) 437-0808 (#2131)

Winona Camps For Boys

(est 1908) ▲ 🏠 🚐

Bridgton, ME (Cumberland Co.); (207) 647-3721
Alan B Ordway, Director

Camp comments: Traditional camping at its best! 95th Anniversary season, 30 states, 20 countries, 90% staff return rate, daily choice of activities.
Activities: Aquatic Activities, Archery, Camping Skills/Outdoor Living, Climbing/Rappelling, Hiking, Horseback — English, Kayaking, Leadership Development, Riflery, Sailing

Session lengths & capacity: 3 & 7 week sessions; 275 campers
Clientele & fees: boys 6-16; Fees: F ▲
Contact: Alan B Ordway, Director at (207) 647-3721; fax: (207) 647-2750
e-mail: uncleal@winonacamps.com
Web site: www.winonacmaps.com
Operated by: Winona Inc, RR 1 Box 868, Bridgton, ME 04009 at (207) 647-3721

Group Rental Information
Facilities: Cabins, Dorm-Style, Food Service, Hiking Trails, Lake, Meeting Rooms
Programs: Boating (#2748)

Wohelo Luther Gulick Camps

(est 1907) ▲

South Casco, ME (Cumberland Co.); (207) 655-4739
Davis & Louise Gulick Van Winkle, Director

Camp comments: Diverse activities, lifelong friendships, relaxed atmosphere on beautiful Sebago Lake - 3rd largest lake in New England.
Activities: Archery, Arts/Crafts, Canoeing, Dance, Drama, Nature/Environment Studies, Sailing, Swimming — Instructional, Tennis, Waterskiing
Session lengths & capacity: 3 & 7 week sessions; 200 campers
Clientele & fees: girls 6-16; families; Fees: F ▲ 🚌
Contact: Davis & Louise VanWinkle, Directors at (207) 655-4739; fax: (207) 655-2292
Web site: www.wohelo.com
Operated by: Wohelo Luther Gulick Camps, PO Box 39, South Casco, ME 04077-4739 at (207) 655-4739 (#2593)

Wyonegonic Camps (est 1902) ▲

Denmark, ME (Oxford Co.); (207) 452-2051
Carol Suddeth & Steven Suddeth, Director

Camp comments: Noncompetitive atmosphere, campers choose from traditional activities with focus on wilderness trips & waterfront.
Activities: Arts/Crafts, Camping Skills/Outdoor Living, Canoeing, Challenge/Rope Courses, Drama, Horseback — English, Leadership Development, Sailing, Swimming — Recreational, Tennis
Session lengths & capacity: 3 & 7 week sessions; 190 campers
Clientele & fees: girls 8-18; families; Fees: E ▲ 🚌
Contact: Carol Suddeth, Owner/Director at (207) 452-2051; fax: (207) 452-2611
e-mail: wyonegonic@maine.com
Web site: www.wyonegonic.com
Operated by: Wyonegonic Camps, 215 Wyonegonic Rd, Denmark, ME 04022 at (207) 452-2051 (#2686)

Maryland

4-H Teen Extreme Camp ▲ 🚐

Clinton, MD (Prince George's Co.); (301) 868-9366
Activities: Aquatic Activities, Camping Skills/Outdoor Living, Community Service, Counselor Training (CIT), Hiking, Leadership Development, Nature/Environment Studies, Photography, Swimming — Recreational, Team Building
Session lengths & capacity: 1 week sessions
Clientele & fees: coed 12-17; Fees: B ▲
Contact: Lenora Harper, Camp Manager at (301) 868-9636; fax: (301) 599-6714
e-mail: lh91@umail.umd.edu
Operated by: Maryland Coop Ext 4H Youth Dev, 8020 Greenmead Dr, College Park, MD 20740 at (301) 403-4248 (#13200)

Airy (est 1924) ⛰ 🏠

Thurmont, MD (Frederick Co.); (301) 271-4636
Stan Brodsky, Director

Camp comments: Diversity is the key. Sports, swim, outdoors, arts, etc. Super facility & staffing Jewish boys, over 75 summers!
Activities: Arts/Crafts, Basketball, Camping Skills/Outdoor Living, Challenge/Rope Courses, Drama, Hiking, Music, Photography, Soccer, Sports — Field & Team
Session lengths & capacity: June-August; 2 & 4 week sessions; 400 campers
Clientele & fees: boys 7-17; Fees: D ⛰
Contact: Mike Schneider, Executive Director at (410) 466-9010; fax: (410) 466-0560
e-mail: airlou@airylouise.org
Operated by: Camp Airy & Camp Louise Fnd, 5750 Park Heights Ave, Baltimore, MD 21215 at (410) 466-9010

Group Rental Information
Facilities: Cabins, Dorm-Style, Double Occupancy, Food Service, Hiking Trails, Kitchen Facilities, Linens, Playing Fields, Pool (#2516)

Bar T Ranch ☀ 🚗

Gaithersburg, MD (Montgomery Co.); (301) 948-3819
Mark Orens, Director

Camp comments: Offering broad range of activities for ages 4 to 16. Adventure & travel is offered to campers ages 10+
Activities: Aquatic Activities, Archery, Arts/Crafts, Ceramics/Pottery, Challenge/Rope Courses, Horseback — Western, Performing Arts, Sports — Field & Team, Tennis
Session lengths & capacity: June-August; 3 week sessions; 460 campers
Clientele & fees: coed 4-13; Fees: C ☀
Contact: Mark Orens, Camp Director at (301) 948-3819; fax: (301) 948-1602
Operated by: Bar T Camps, 6530 Olney Laytonsville Rd, Gaithersburg, MD 20882 at (301) 948-3819 (#4244)

Barrie Day Camp (est 1932) ☀ 🚗

Silver Spring, MD (Montgomery Co.); (301) 871-6200
Peter Vogdes, Director

Camp comments: Perfect setting for traditional, all-in-one program, including on-site riding, swimming & boating.
Activities: Computer, Counselor Training (CIT), Field Trips, Horseback — English, Nature/Environment Studies, Performing Arts, Sports — Field & Team, Swimming — Instructional, Swimming — Recreational

ICON LEGEND

☀	Day Camp
⛰	Resident Camp
🏠	Facilities Available To Rent
🚗	Transportation Available
🐷	Financial Aid Available

FEE RANGES PER WEEK

A	$0-75
B	$75-200
C	$201-350
D	$351-500
E	$501-650
F	over $650

Session lengths & capacity: June-August; 4, 5, 6, 7 & 8 week sessions; 600 campers
Clientele & fees: coed 3-14; Fees: C ☀ 🚗
Contact: Peter Vogdes, Director at (301) 871-6200 ext. 215; fax: (301) 871-1177
e-mail: pvogdes@barrie.org
Web site: www.barrie.org
Operated by: Barrie School, 13500 Layhill Rd, Silver Spring, MD 20906 at (301) 871-6200 (#2515)

Beth Tfiloh Camps (est 1942) ☀ 🚗

Reisterstown, MD (Baltimore County Co.); (410) 517-3451
Steve Eller,LCSW, Director

Camp comments: 1:4 staff-camper ratio, counselors are teachers; all activities are taught by certified instructors, free bus service.
Activities: Aquatic Activities, Arts/Crafts, Camping Skills/Outdoor Living, Challenge/Rope Courses, Computer, Counselor Training (CIT), Drama, Music, Nature/Environment Studies, Sports — Field & Team
Session lengths & capacity: June-August; 4, 5, 6 & 8 week sessions; 800 campers
Clientele & fees: coed 2-14; Fees: B, C ☀
Contact: Steve Eller, Director at (410) 517-3451; fax: (410) 517-3453
e-mail: steve@camps.org
Web site: www.btfiloh.org
Operated by: Beth Tfiloh Camps, 400 Delight Meadows Rd, Reisterstown, MD 21136 at (410) 517-3451 (#2483)

Camp Conowingo (est 1956) ⛰ 🏠 🚗

Conowingo, MD (Cecil Co.); (410) 378-4242
Laura VanBrunt, Director

Camp comments: Resident girls camp offers 5 day sessions in beautiful outdoor environment. Builds self-esteem and group cooperation.
Activities: Aquatic Activities, Arts/Crafts, Camping Skills/Outdoor Living, Canoeing, Challenge/Rope Courses, Counselor Training (CIT), Drama, Horseback — English, Nature/Environment Studies, Swimming — Recreational
Session lengths & capacity: June-August; 1 & 2 week sessions; 150 campers
Clientele & fees: girls 6-17; Fees: B, C ⛰
Contact: Adam Rubin, Outdoor Program and Property Manager at (410) 358-9711 ext. 241; fax: (410) 358-9918
e-mail: arubin@gscm.org
Web site: www.gscm.org
Operated by: GS of Central Maryland, 4806 Seton Drive, Baltimore, MD 21215 at (410) 358-9711

Group Rental Information
Seasons & Capacity: Spring 300, Summer 300, Fall 300, Winter 96
Facilities: Cabins, Hiking Trails, Lake, Lodges, Meeting Rooms, Playing Fields, Pool, River, Tents
Programs: Boating, Challenge/Ropes Course, Swimming (#2511)

Camp Farthest Out Inc (est 1962) ⛰

Sykesville, MD (Carroll Co.); (410) 795-2760
Brian Carter, Director

Camp comments: Residential camp for inner city children. Offering swimming, arts&craft, cookouts, basketball, baseball hiking outdoors.
Activities: Arts/Crafts, Baseball/Softball, Camping Skills/Outdoor Living, Drawing/Painting, Leadership Development, Nature/Environment Studies, Swimming — Recreational
Session lengths & capacity: June-August; 2 & 8 week sessions; 100 campers
Clientele & fees: coed 7-12; Fees: A ⛰ 🐷
Contact: Dr Virginia Johns, Chair Personnel Committee at (410) 233-0117;
Operated by: Douglas Memorial Comm Church, 1325 Madison Ave, Baltimore, MD 21217 at (410) 523-1700 (#8285)

Camp Glyndon (est 1952) ⛰ 🏠

Nanjemoy, MD; (301) 870-5858
Robert Rainey, Director

Camp comments: Residential camp. Provides activities, teaching diabetes management by medical & counseling staff, while among peers.
Activities: Archery, Baseball/Softball, Basketball, Boating, Canoeing, Challenge/Rope Courses, Climbing/Rappelling, Leadership Development, Music, Tennis
Session lengths & capacity: July-August; 1 & 2 week sessions; 80 campers
Clientele & fees: coed 8-16; families; Fees: E ⛰ 🐷
Contact: Jody Kakacek, District Manager at (410) 663-6785; fax: (410) 663-6789
e-mail: jkakacek@diabetes.org
Web site: www.diabetes.org
Operated by: American Diabetes Association, 3120 Timanus Lane Ste 106, Baltimore, MD 21244 at (410) 265-0075

Group Rental Information
Facilities: Cabins, Double Occupancy, Hiking Trails, Meeting Rooms, Pool, River
Programs: Boating (#3022)

Camp JCC (est 1968) ☀ 🚗

Rockville, MD (Montgomery Co.); (301) 230-3759
Sara Portman Milner, LCSW-C, Director

Camp comments: Convenient location, Jewish values, general & spec prog; teen trips & CITs. Onsite pool. Great trips! Total inclusion. Camp JCC is the place to be!
Activities: Arts/Crafts, Baseball/Softball, Basketball, Counselor Training (CIT), Field Trips, Music, Performing Arts, Sports — Field & Team, Swimming — Instructional, Swimming — Recreational
Session lengths & capacity: June-August; 4 & 8 week sessions; 750 campers
Clientele & fees: coed 2-15; Fees: B, C ☀ 🐷
Contact: Diane Kendall, Camp Administrator at (301) 230-3759; fax: (301) 881-6549
e-mail: jcccamp@jccgw.org
Web site: www.jccgw.org
Operated by: JCC of Greater Washington, 6125 Montrose Rd, Rockville, MD 20852 at (301) 881-0100 (#7424)

Camp Pecometh (est 1946) ☀ ⛰ 🏠

Centreville, MD (Queen Anne's Co.); (410) 758-0304
Rev. John Ky Shitama, Director

Camp comments: Our mission is to provide an environment that promotes positive life-changing experiences.
Activities: Arts/Crafts, Camping Skills/Outdoor Living, Canoeing, Challenge/Rope Courses, Counselor Training (CIT), Music, Nature/Environment Studies, Sports — Field & Team, Swimming — Recreational, Team Building
Session lengths & capacity: June-August; 1/2 & 1 week sessions; 200 campers
Clientele & fees: coed 6-17; Fees: B ☀ Fees: C, D ⛰
Contact: Richelle Darrell, Registrar at (410) 758-0304; fax: (410) 758-0413
e-mail: campinfo@juno.com
Web site: www.pecometh.org
Operated by: Peninsula Delaware Conference, 136 Bookers Wharf Rd, Centreville, MD 21617 at (410) 758-0304

Group Rental Information
Site comments: Our mission is to provide an environment that promotes positive life-changing experiences.
Seasons & Capacity: Spring 336, Summer 72, Fall 336, Winter 96

Facilities: A/V Equipment, Cabins, Dorm-Style, Double Occupancy, Food Service, Kitchen Facilities, Meeting Rooms, Playing Fields, Pool, River, Tents
Programs: Boating, Challenge/Ropes Course, Environmental Education, Swimming (#2524)

Camp Saint Charles (est 1951)

Rock Point, MD (Charles Co.); (301) 259-2645
Stephen Blaine, Director

Camp comments: Kids share in caring for earth, sea, nature & each other, water sports, petting zoo & fun.
Activities: Archery, Arts/Crafts, Boating, Camping Skills/Outdoor Living, Challenge/Rope Courses, Horseback — Western, Riflery, Sailing, Soccer, Swimming — Instructional
Session lengths & capacity: June-August; 2 week sessions; 155 campers
Clientele & fees: boys 8-15; Fees: C
Contact: Mr Stephen Blaine, Camp Director at (301) 858-7110; fax: (301) 577-1146
Web site: www.campstcharles.org
Operated by: Camp St Charles, 15375 Stella Maris Dr, Newburg, MD 20664 at (301) 259-2645

Group Rental Information
Facilities: Cabins, Dorm-Style, Food Service, Kitchen Facilities, Meeting Rooms
Programs: Boating, Environmental Education (#2468)

Camp Sonshine (est 1981)

Silver Spring, MD (Montgomery Co.); (301) 989-2267
David Black, Director

Camp comments: The quality of our staff keeps 100's of campers coming back! Safe/exciting adventures/personal growth. GREAT MEMORIES!
Activities: Archery, Arts/Crafts, Camping Skills/Outdoor Living, Canoeing, Challenge/Rope Courses, Counselor Training (CIT), Drama, Nature/Environment Studies, Sports — Field & Team, Swimming — Recreational
Session lengths & capacity: June-August; 2, 4, 8 & 9 week sessions; 900 campers
Clientele & fees: boys 4-16; girls 4-16; coed 4-16; Fees: B
Contact: Beth Sebastion, Executive Secretary at (301) 989-2267; fax: (301) 989-7116
e-mail: beth.sebastian@immanuels.org
Web site: www.campsonshine.org
Operated by: Immanuel's Church, 16819 New Hampshire Ave, Silver Spring, MD 20905 at (301) 989-4673 (#228)

Camp Sunrise (est 1986)

Port Deposit, MD (Baltimore Co.); (410) 378-2267
Ms Carole Sharp, Director

Camp comments: 1 week residential day camp for children ages 4-18 who have or have had cancer . No cost.
Activities: Archery, Arts/Crafts, Challenge/Rope Courses, Counselor Training (CIT), Drama, Field Trips, Leadership Development, Nature/Environment Studies, Sports — Field & Team, Swimming — Recreational
Session lengths & capacity: 1 week sessions; 150 campers
Clientele & fees: boys 4-18; girls 4-18; coed 4-18
Contact: Carole Sharp, Manager, Patient Services at (410) 933-5139; fax: (410) 931-6875
e-mail: csharp1@cancer.org
Operated by: American Cancer Soc Maryland, 8219 Town Center Dr, Baltimore, MD 21236-0026 at (410) 931-6850 (#6362)

Camp Wright (est 1930)

Stevensville, MD (Queen Anne's Co.); (410) 643-4171
Mr. Van E Beers, Director

Camp comments: Chesapeake Bay camp; Sail, canoe, sports, nature & art. Adventure trips. Christian community, caring & safe since 1930.
Activities: Arts/Crafts, Canoeing, Leadership Development, Nature/Environment Studies, Rafting, Sailing, Soccer, Swimming — Recreational, Tennis, Wilderness Trips
Session lengths & capacity: May-September; 1 week sessions; 120 campers
Clientele & fees: coed 7-17; families; Fees: B
Fees: D
Contact: Van Beers, Director at (410) 643-4171; fax: (410) 643-8421
e-mail: campwri@shore.intercom.net
Web site: www.campwright4life.org
Operated by: Episcopal Diocese of Easton, PO Box 1027, Easton, MD 21601 at (410) 822-1919 (#1842)

Capital Camps (est 1988)

Waynesboro, PA; (717) 794-2177
David M Phillips MSW, Director

Camp comments: Warm Jewish environment, Kosher dining, teen leadership, wide variety of group & individual activities Israel trip.
Activities: Archery, Arts/Crafts, Camping Skills/Outdoor Living, Challenge/Rope Courses, Leadership Development, Photography
Session lengths & capacity: May-November; 2, 4 & 8 week sessions; 350 campers
Clientele & fees: coed 8-18; Fees: E
Contact: David Phillips, Executive Director at (301) 468-2267; fax: (301) 468-1719
e-mail: info@capitalcamps.org
Web site: www.capitalcamps.org
Operated by: Jewish Camp & Conf Services, 133 Rollins Ave Ste 4, Rockville, MD 20852 at (301) 468-2267 (#787)

Carroll County 4H Youth Devel

(est 1960)

Westminster, MD (Carroll Co.); (410) 386-2760
Denise Frebertshauser, Director

Camp comments: Program focuses on life skill development, responsibility, team building, self-esteem, leadership, and cooperation.
Activities: Aquatic Activities, Arts/Crafts, Camping Skills/Outdoor Living, Canoeing, Challenge/Rope Courses, Hiking, Leadership Development, Nature/Environment Studies, Swimming — Recreational, Team Building
Session lengths & capacity: July-August; 1 week sessions; 160 campers
Clientele & fees: coed 8-14; Fees: B
Contact: Jennifer Reynolds, Extension Educator at (410) 386-2760; fax: (410) 876-0132
e-mail: jr208@umail.umd.edu
Operated by: Maryland Coop Ext 4H Youth Dev, 8020 Greenmead Dr, College Park, MD 20740 at (301) 403-4248 (#4501)

Carroll County YMCA Day Camp

Westminister, MD (Carroll Co.); (410) 876-1194
Mike Walters, Director

Camp comments: Whatever your child's age and interests, look to YMCA camping for a safe and fun summer experience.
Activities: Arts/Crafts, Community Service, Counselor Training (CIT), Field Trips, Leadership Development, Nature/Environment Studies, Performing Arts, Sports — Field & Team, Swimming — Recreational, Team Building
Session lengths & capacity: June-August; 1 & 2 week sessions; 189 campers
Clientele & fees: coed 5-15; Fees: B
Contact: Mike Walters, Associate Executive Director at (410) 848-3660 ext. 227; fax: (410) 876-9319
e-mail: mikewalters@ymcamd.org

Operated by: Harford County Family YMCA, 309 Thomas Run Rd, Bel Air, MD 21015 at (410) 893-5025 (#34637)

Columbia Association Camps

(est 1970)

Columbia, MD (Howard Co.); (410) 715-3168
Charlie Thomas, Director

Camp comments: Our top priority is children & we specialize in fun! Variety of activities, we have something for every child. Ages 3-15
Activities: Archery, Backpacking, Bicycling/Biking, Ceramics/Pottery, Sailing, Tennis, Travel/Tour
Session lengths & capacity: 1 & 2 week sessions; 785 campers
Clientele & fees: coed 3-15; Fees: B, C
Contact: Charlie Thomas, Camp Manager at (410) 715-3168; fax: (410) 715-3043
Operated by: Columbia Association, 10221 Wincopin Cir Ste 100, Columbia, MD 21044-3410 at (410) 715-3168 (#6605)

Druid Hill YMCA Summer Camp

Baltimore, MD (Baltimore Co.); (410) 728-1600
Steve Vassor, Director

Camp comments: Give your child an experience to last a lifetime.
Activities: Arts/Crafts, Camping Skills/Outdoor Living, Community Service, Computer, Counselor Training (CIT), Field Trips, Leadership Development, Sports — Field & Team, Swimming — Instructional, Swimming — Recreational
Session lengths & capacity: June-August; 1 week sessions; 250 campers
Clientele & fees: coed 5-14; Fees: B
Contact: Rodney Dunton, Community & Youth Director at (410) 728-1600; fax: (410) 462-4591
e-mail: rodneydunton@ymcamd.org
Operated by: Harford County Family YMCA, 309 Thomas Run Rd, Bel Air, MD 21015 at (410) 893-5025 (#45573)

Eastern Shore Camp Horn Point

Princess Anne, MD (Somerset Co.); (410) 651-1350
Lisa Dennis, Director

Camp comments: Environmental education
Activities: Academics, Archery, Canoeing
Session lengths & capacity: 1/2 week sessions; 40 campers
Clientele & fees: coed 8-10; Fees: B
Operated by: Maryland Coop Ext 4H Youth Dev, 8020 Greenmead Dr, College Park, MD 20740 at (301) 403-4248 (#13202)

Echo Hill Camp (est 1944)

Worton, MD (Kent Co.); (410) 348-5303
Peter P Rice Jr, Director

Camp comments: Echo Hill fosters an unusual amount of love and kindness which leads to lasting friendships and unforgettable memories.
Activities: Archery, Arts/Crafts, Challenge/Rope Courses, Horseback — English, Sailing, Swimming — Instructional, Waterskiing, Windsurfing
Session lengths & capacity: June-August; 2, 4 & 8 week sessions; 140 campers
Clientele & fees: coed 7-16; Fees: D, E, F
Contact: Peter P Rice Jr, Director/Owner at (410) 348-5303; fax: (410) 348-2010
e-mail: echohillcamp@hotmail.com
Web site: www.echohillcamp.com
Operated by: Echo Hill Inc, 13655 Bloomingneck Rd, Worton, MD 21678 at (410) 348-5303 (#2513)

Elks Camp Barrett (est 1952) ⚠ 🏠 🚐

Annapolis, MD; (410) 224-2945
Jason Pittman, Director

Camp comments: Provide a safe & healthy experience while learning about nature & team work, develop physical skills & foster attitutues of patriotism & establish self esteem.
Activities: Baseball/Softball, Basketball, Nature/Environment Studies, Soccer, Swimming — Recreational, Team Building
Session lengths & capacity: 7 week sessions; 120 campers
Clientele & fees: boys 9-13; girls 9-13; Fees: A ⚠ 🐷
Contact: Stu Kerr at (410) 224-2945; fax: (410) 224-4558
e-mail: elkscb@erols.com
Web site: www.users.erols.com/elkscb/
Operated by: MD DEL DC Elks Assoc, PO Box 258, Crownsville, MD 21032 at (410) 224-2945

Group Rental Information

Site comments: Facilities available for rental year round for camping, meetings, weddings, reunions, picnics, swimming May - September. We never close.
Seasons & Capacity: Spring 300, Summer 300, Fall 300, Winter 200
Facilities: Cabins, Food Service, Hiking Trails, Kitchen Facilities, Meeting Rooms, Playing Fields, Pool
Programs: Swimming (#25203)

Fairlee Manor Rec & Educ Ctr (est 1954) ⚠ 🏠 🚐

Chestertown, MD (Kent Co.); (410) 778-0566
Sean Proa, Director

Camp comments: Summer camp and year recreational opportunities for people with disabilities.
Activities: Archery, Arts/Crafts, Canoeing, Computer, Farming/Ranching/Gardening, Horseback — Western, Nature/Environment Studies, Sports — Field & Team, Swimming — Recreational
Session lengths & capacity: June-August; 1 week sessions; 40 campers
Clientele & fees: boys 8-99; girls 8-99; coed 8-99; families; seniors; single adults; Fees: B ☀
Fees: F ⚠
Contact: Sean Proa, Director at (410) 778-0566; fax: (410) 778-0567
e-mail: fairlee@dmv.com
Web site: www.fairleemanor.org
Operated by: Easter Seals DE/MD Eastern Shr, 22242 Bay Shore Rd, Chestertown, MD 21620 at (410) 778-0566

ICON LEGEND

☀ Day Camp
⚠ Resident Camp
🏠 Facilities Available To Rent
🚐 Transportation Available
🐷 Financial Aid Available

FEE RANGES PER WEEK

A	$0-75
B	$75-200
C	$201-350
D	$351-500
E	$501-650
F	over $650

Group Rental Information

Facilities: A/V Equipment, Cabins, Dorm-Style, Double Occupancy, Food Service, Hiking Trails, Lodges, Meeting Rooms, Playing Fields, Pool, River
Programs: Boating, Challenge/Ropes Course, Horseback Riding, Swimming (#2569)

Frederick County 4H Camp ⚠

Frederick, MD; (301) 695-1509
Larry Cromwell, Director

Camp comments: Resident camp for ages 8-18 offering crafts, swimming, & nature. Located just 5 minutes south of the city of Frederick.
Activities: Arts/Crafts, Camping Skills/Outdoor Living, Leadership Development, Nature/Environment Studies, Sports — Field & Team, Swimming — Instructional, Swimming — Recreational, Team Building
Session lengths & capacity: July-August; 1 week sessions; 150 campers
Clientele & fees: coed 8-18; Fees: B ⚠
Contact: Larry Cromwell, Extension Educator at (301) 694-1594; fax: (301) 694-1588
e-mail: lc30@umail.umd.edu
Operated by: Maryland Coop Ext 4H Youth Dev, 8020 Greenmead Dr, College Park, MD 20740 at (301) 403-4248 (#4500)

Greentop (est 1937) ⚠ 🚐

Sabillasville, MD (Frederick Co.); (411) 323-0500
Katrina Johnson, Director

Camp comments: Great camp for people with disabilities! 1:2 staff:camper ratio, outstanding staff, beautiful, accessible facility. Travel and adventure programs.
Activities: Aquatic Activities, Archery, Arts/Crafts, Canoeing, Counselor Training (CIT), Drama, Field Trips, Fishing, Hiking, Horseback — Western
Session lengths & capacity: June-August; 1 & 2 week sessions; 60 campers
Clientele & fees: coed 7-99; families; Fees: D, F ⚠ 🐷
Contact: Thea Mardaga, Administrative Assistant at (410) 323-0500; fax: (410) 323-3298
e-mail: dmardaga@leagueforpeople.org
Web site: www.campgreentop.org
Operated by: The League, 1111 E Cold Spring Lane, Baltimore, MD 21239 at (410) 323-0500 (#2523)

Grove Point (est 1948) ⚠ 🏠

Earleville, MD (Cecil Co.); (410) 275-2800
Peg D Reynolds, Director

Camp comments: 265 beautiful wooded acres, located on Chesapeake Bay at mouth of Sassafras River. All girls 6-17 welcome, resident camp
Activities: Camping Skills/Outdoor Living, Canoeing, Counselor Training (CIT), Dance, Drama, Horseback — English, Sailing, Swimming — Recreational, Tennis, Windsurfing
Session lengths & capacity: 1/2, 1 & 2 week sessions; 130 campers
Clientele & fees: girls 6-17; families; Fees: B, C, D ⚠ 🐷
Contact: Barbara Fallat, Camp Programs Assistant at (302) 456-7150 ext. 7173; fax: (302) 456-7188
e-mail: barb@cbgsc.org
Web site: www.cbgsc.org
Operated by: Chesapeake Bay GSC Inc, 501 South College Avenue, Newark, DE 19713 at (302) 456-7150

Group Rental Information

Facilities: Cabins, Hiking Trails, Kitchen Facilities, Lodges, Pool, Tents (#2567)

Habonim Dror Camp Moshava

(est 1935) ⚠ 🚐

Street, MD (Harford Co.); (410) 893-7079
Rachel Glaser, Director

Camp comments: Kibbutz atmosphere, Kosher, Hebrew language, featuring creative Jewish activities.
Activities: Baseball/Softball, Basketball, Camping Skills/Outdoor Living, Community Service, Counselor Training (CIT), Dance, Field Trips, Language Studies, Leadership Development, Soccer
Session lengths & capacity: June-August; 2, 4 & 8 week sessions; 150 campers
Clientele & fees: coed 9-15; Fees: D ⚠ 🐷
Contact: Tammy Schmidt, Registrar at (800) 454-2205;
e-mail: moshava@aol.com
Operated by: Habonim Camp Association, 3755 Spring Lake Rd, Owings Mills, MD 21117 at (410) 654-5629 (#2546)

Harford County 4H Camp Inc

(est 1921) ⚠ 🏠

Street, MD (Harford Co.); (301) 838-1671
Cynthia Warner, Director

Camp comments: Resident camp, ages 8-18, offering crafts, swimming,& nature. Located along Deer Creek. 30 minutes north of Baltimore.
Activities: Aquatic Activities, Archery, Arts/Crafts, Camping Skills/Outdoor Living, Leadership Development, Model Rocketry, Music, Nature/Environment Studies
Session lengths & capacity: June-August; 1/2 & 1 week sessions; 130 campers
Clientele & fees: coed 8-18; Fees: B ⚠ 🐷
Contact: Cynthia Warner, Extension Educator at (410) 638-3255; fax: (410) 638-3053
e-mail: cw103@email.umd.edu
Operated by: Maryland Coop Ext 4H Youth Dev, 8020 Greenmead Dr, College Park, MD 20740 at (301) 403-4248 (#4503)

Harford County Family YMCA Day ☀ 🚐

Joppa, MD (Harford Co.); (410) 877-9171
Tracy Moran Ashman, Director

Camp comments: Whatever your child's age and interests, look to YMCA camping for a safe and fun summer experience.
Activities: Aquatic Activities, Arts/Crafts, Camping Skills/Outdoor Living, Climbing/Rappelling, Counselor Training (CIT), Field Trips, Hiking, Nature/Environment Studies, Sports — Field & Team, Swimming — Instructional
Session lengths & capacity: June-September; 1 week sessions; 300 campers
Clientele & fees: coed 5-16; Fees: B ☀
Fees: C ⚠
Contact: Tracy Moran Ashman, Program Director at (410) 893-5025; fax: (410) 893-5089
e-mail: tracymoran@ymcamd.org
Operated by: Harford County Family YMCA, 309 Thomas Run Rd, Bel Air, MD 21015 at (410) 893-5025 (#37647)

Howard County Family YMCA Day ☀

Ellicott City, MD (Howard Co.); (410) 465-4334
Amy Maloy, Director

Camp comments: Whatever your child's age and interests, look to YMCA camping for a safe and fun summer experience.
Activities: Aquatic Activities, Arts/Crafts, Community Service, Field Trips, Leadership Development, Nature/Environment Studies, Swimming — Recreational, Team Building
Session lengths & capacity: June-August; 1 & 2 week sessions; 400 campers
Clientele & fees: coed 3-17; Fees: B ☀ 🐷
Contact: Dawn Chrystal, Family Youth Services Director at (410) 465-4334; fax: (410) 750-9553
e-mail: dawnchrystal@ymcamd.org

Operated by: Harford County Family YMCA, 309 Thomas Run Rd, Bel Air, MD 21015 at (410) 893-5025 (#34640)

Kamp A-Kom-plish (est 1974) ▲ ⌂

Nanjemoy, MD (Charles Co.); (301) 870-3226
Heidi Aldous, Director

Camp comments: The sleepaway camp in Nanjemoy, MD that feels like home. With modern air conditioned cabins, great food and caring staff we specialize in first-time campers.
Activities: Archery, Arts/Crafts, Canoeing, Challenge/Rope Courses, Horseback — Western, Nature/Environment Studies, Sports — Field & Team, Swimming — Recreational
Session lengths & capacity: 1, 2, 3 & 4 week sessions; 45 campers
Clientele & fees: coed 8-16
Contact: Heidi Aldous, Director at (301) 870-3226; fax: (301) 870-2620
e-mail: haldous@melwood.com
Web site: www.kampakomplish.com
Operated by: Melwood Horticultural Training, 5606 Dower House Rd, Upper Marlboro, MD 20772 at (301) 599-8000

Group Rental Information

Site comments: Air conditioning, fireplaces, skylights & mini kitchens make these cabins perfect for any event. Located on 108 acres in beautiful/historic Nanjemoy, MD.
Seasons & Capacity: Spring 75, Fall 75, Winter 75
Facilities: Double Occupancy, Food Service, Hiking Trails, Kitchen Facilities, Linens, Lodges, Meeting Rooms
Programs: Challenge/Ropes Course, Environmental Education, Horseback Riding (#4488)

Lakeside Day Camp (est 1972) ☼

Cockeysville, MD; (410) 252-8095
Fred Rigger, Director

Camp comments: Fun weekly themes. 30 country acres min from I83 N. Weekly & daily regist. options. Extended care incl. Swim lessons & recreational swimming, arts & sports.
Activities: Arts/Crafts, Counselor Training (CIT), Field Trips, Nature/Environment Studies, Performing Arts, Swimming — Instructional, Swimming — Recreational
Session lengths & capacity: June-August; 1 week sessions; 225 campers
Clientele & fees: coed 5-13
Contact: Fred Rigger, General Manager at (410) 252-2046; fax: (410) 561-1560
e-mail: camp@padoniaparkclub.psemail.com
Web site: www.padoniaparkclub.com
Operated by: Child Care International Ltd, PO Box 426, Timonium, MD 21094-0426 at (410) 252-8095 (#6335)

Lions Camp Merrick Inc

(est 1980) ▲ ⌂

Nanjemoy, MD; (301) 870-5858
Robert J Rainey, Director

Camp comments: 3 programs offered. Deaf/hard of hearing, 4 1 week sessions.Diabetes 1 family wk 3 1 wk sessions. 1 wk blind children
Activities: Aquatic Activities, Archery, Boating, Canoeing, Challenge/Rope Courses, Climbing/Rappelling, Counselor Training (CIT), Drama, Drawing/Painting, Swimming — Recreational
Session lengths & capacity: April-November; 8 week sessions; 100 campers
Clientele & fees: coed 6-15; Fees: D, E ▲
Contact: Robert J Rainey, Camp Administrator at (301) 870-5858;
e-mail: RJRainey@aol.com
Web site: www.lionscampmerrick.org
Operated by: Lions Camp Merrick Inc, PO Box 56, Nanjemoy, MD 20662 at (301) 870-5858

Group Rental Information

Seasons & Capacity: Spring 115, Summer 115, Fall 115
Facilities: Cabins, Food Service, Hiking Trails, Kitchen Facilities, Lodges, Meeting Rooms, Playing Fields, River
Programs: Boating, Challenge/Ropes Course, Swimming (#32010)

Louise (est 1922) ▲ ⌂

Cascade, MD (Washington Co.); (301) 241-3661
Jessie Reter-Choate, Director

Camp comments: Serving Jewish Girls for over 75 years.
Activities: Arts/Crafts, Camping Skills/Outdoor Living, Ceramics/Pottery, Challenge/Rope Courses, Dance, Drama, Martial Arts, Performing Arts, Photography, Sports — Field & Team
Session lengths & capacity: June-August; 2 & 4 week sessions; 430 campers
Clientele & fees: girls 7-17; Fees: D ▲
Contact: Bobbie Miller, Associate Director at (410) 466-9010; fax: (410) 466-0560
e-mail: airlou@airylouise.org
Operated by: Camp Airy & Camp Louise Fnd, 5750 Park Heights Ave, Baltimore, MD 21215 at (410) 466-9010

Group Rental Information

Seasons & Capacity: Spring 400, Fall 400
Facilities: Cabins, Dorm-Style, Double Occupancy, Food Service, Hiking Trails, Kitchen Facilities, Playing Fields, Pool
Programs: Swimming (#6141)

Mar-Lu-Ridge (est 1959) ▲ ⌂

Jefferson, MD (Frederick Co.); (301) 874-5544
Rod Pearce, Director

Camp comments: An exciting Christian camp encouraging spiritual growth and self awareness with a fun well-trained staff.
Activities: Archery, Arts/Crafts, Bicycling/Biking, Canoeing, Counselor Training (CIT), Hiking, Horseback — English, Nature/Environment Studies, Performing Arts, Swimming — Recreational
Session lengths & capacity: June-August; 1/2, 1 & 2 week sessions; 150 campers
Clientele & fees: coed 7-15; families; seniors; single adults; Fees: B, C ▲ 🚐
Contact: Rod Pearce, Executive Administrator at (800) 238-9974; fax: (301) 874-5545
e-mail: mlr@mar-lu-ridge.org
Web site: www.mar-lu-ridge.org
Operated by: Delaware MD & Metro DC Synods, 3200 Mar-Lu-Ridge, Jefferson, MD 21755 at (301) 874-5544

Group Rental Information

Site comments: A place apart on mountaintop ridge-watch sunset and sunrise from same spot-however we're more than a view. Motel-style rooms, meeting rooms, near major airport.
Seasons & Capacity: Spring 200, Summer 150, Fall 150, Winter 200
Facilities: A/V Equipment, Cabins, Dorm-Style, Double Occupancy, Food Service, Hiking Trails, Linens, Lodges, Meeting Rooms, Pool, River
Programs: Challenge/Ropes Course, Environmental Education, Winter Sports (#24870)

Maryland 4H Day Camps

(est 1990) ☼ 🚐

College Park, MD; (301) 403-4248
Denise Frebertshauser, Director

Camp comments: 4H camps are open to all youth includes traditional camp activities boys and girs.
Activities: Arts/Crafts, Camping Skills/Outdoor Living, Counselor Training (CIT), Leadership Development, Nature/Environment Studies, Team Building
Session lengths & capacity: 1 week sessions

Clientele & fees: coed 8-12; families; Fees: B ☼ Fees: B ▲
Contact: Rick Byrne, 4H Program Leader at (301) 403-4248; fax: (301) 422-7914
e-mail: rb237@umail.umd.edu
Operated by: Maryland Coop Ext 4H Youth Dev, 8020 Greenmead Dr, College Park, MD 20740 at (301) 403-4248 (#28891)

Milldale Camp (est 1966) ☼ 🚐

Reisterstown, MD (Baltimore Co.); (410) 429-4900
Roz Goldberg, Director

Camp comments: Day camp on 155 acres. Additional specialty programs are: sports camp, arts camp, teen camp & special needs camp.
Activities: Arts/Crafts, Camping Skills/Outdoor Living, Drama, Field Trips, Leadership Development, Martial Arts, Music, Performing Arts, Sports — Field & Team
Session lengths & capacity: June-August; 4 & 8 week sessions; 900 campers
Clientele & fees: boys 5-15; girls 5-15; coed 11-15; Fees: B ☼
Contact: Roz Goldberg, Camp Director at (410) 356-5200 ext. 315; fax: (410) 581-0561
Operated by: JCC of Baltimore, 3506 Gwynnbrook Ave, Owings Mills, MD 21117 at (410) 356-5200 (#2517)

Mount Aetna Camp (est 1949) ☼ ▲

Hagerstown, MD (Washington Co.); (301) 824-2729
Pete Braman, Director

Camp comments: Enjoy our modern facilities and rustic setting, our caring, dynamic staff offers the most class options in the state of MD
Activities: Arts/Crafts, Canoeing, Challenge/Rope Courses, Climbing/Rappelling, Drama, Gymnastics, Horseback — English, Nature/Environment Studies, Swimming — Instructional, Waterskiing
Session lengths & capacity: June-August; 1, 2 & 3 week sessions; 140 campers
Clientele & fees: boys 7-16; girls 7-16; coed 7-16; Fees: B, C ▲ 🚐
Contact: Samantha Young, Marketing Director at (301) 824-6045; fax: (301) 824-6373
e-mail: mtaetnacamp@aol.com
Web site: www.mtaetnacamp.com
Operated by: Chesapeake Conference of SDA, 6600 Martin Rd, Columbia, MD 21044 at (410) 995-1910 (#1107)

Patuxent River 4H Center

(est 1965) ☼ ▲ ⌂

Upper Marlboro, MD (Prince Georges Co.); (301) 390-7259
Bonnie Dunn, Director

Camp comments: Our camp is open to all youth; traditional program with focus on environmental awareness.
Activities: Archery, Arts/Crafts, Camping Skills/Outdoor Living, Canoeing, Challenge/Rope Courses, Farming/Ranching/Gardening, Hiking, Leadership Development, Nature/Environment Studies
Session lengths & capacity: 1/2 & 1 week sessions; 80 campers
Clientele & fees: boys 8-14; girls 8-14; coed 8-14; Fees: B ☼ Fees: B ▲
Contact: Nancy Canter at (301) 390-7259; fax: (301) 390-7883
e-mail: bonniedunn@erols.com
Operated by: Patuxent River 4H Center Fnd, 18405 Queen Anne Road, Upper Marlboro, MD 20774 at (301) 390-7259

Group Rental Information

Site comments: 134 acres facility located along the Patuxent River. Program focus on environmental ed and cooperative learning.

Facilities: Dorm-Style, Food Service, Hiking Trails, Meeting Rooms, River
Programs: Boating, Environmental Education (#1578)

Saint Joseph (est 1946)

Baltimore, MD (Baltimore Co.); (410) 644-3300
David Lee Norton, Director

Camp comments: 50 years of continued service to the Baltimore area.
Activities: Arts/Crafts, Baseball/Softball, Basketball, Field Trips, Football, Hiking, Soccer, Sports — Field & Team, Swimming — Instructional, Tennis
Session lengths & capacity: 1 & 7 week sessions
Clientele & fees: boys 5-12; Fees: B ☀
Contact: David Lee Norton, Director at (410) 644-3300; fax: (410) 646-6221
Operated by: Mount Saint Joseph High School, 4403 Frederick Avenue, Baltimore, MD 21229 at (410) 644-3300 (#3772)

Sandy Hill Camp (est 1951)

North East, MD (Cecil Co.); (410) 287-5554
Greg & Kathy Ann Joseph, Director
Activities: Aquatic Activities, Archery, Arts/Crafts, Challenge/Rope Courses, Climbing/Rappelling, Horseback — English, Sailing, Sports — Field & Team, Team Building, Waterskiing
Contact: Web site: www.sandyhillcamp.com
Operated by: Sandy Hill LLC, 3380 Turkey Pt Rd, North East, MD 21901-6048 at (410) 287-5554

Group Rental Information

Site comments: 215 acres, upper Chesapeake between Baltimore & Philadelphia
Seasons & Capacity: Spring 340, Summer 340, Fall 340
Facilities: A/V Equipment, Cabins, Food Service, Hiking Trails, Meeting Rooms, Playing Fields, Pool, River
Programs: Boating, Challenge/Ropes Course, Environmental Education, Horseback Riding, Swimming (#1618)

The Marsh (est 2001)

North East, MD (Cecil Co.); (410) 287-5433
Jenny Riley, Director

Camp comments: The Marsh is a Christian summer day camp for boys & girls between the ages of 6 & 11 years old. Make summer memorable.
Activities: Aquatic Activities, Archery, Arts/Crafts, Basketball, Camping Skills/Outdoor Living, Climbing/Rappelling, Field Trips, Nature/Environment Studies, Religious Study, Swimming — Instructional

Session lengths & capacity: June-August; 1 & 2 week sessions; 30 campers
Clientele & fees: coed 6-11; Fees: B ☀
Contact: Jenny Riley, Director at (410) 287-5433 ext. 454; fax: (410) 287-3196
e-mail: themarsh@sandycove.org
Web site: ww.sandycove.org/camp.htm
Operated by: Morning Cheer Inc, 60 Sandy Cove Road, North East, MD 21901 at (410) 287-5433 (#46266)

The Salvation Army Camp Puhtok (est 1942)

Monkton, MD (Baltimore Co.); (410) 329-6590
Robert Eldredge, Director

Camp comments: A rustic, nondenominational, international camp. Indian lore, ecology, sailing, canoeing, horses, cycling, wilderness trips, and American Heritage skills.
Activities: Arts/Crafts, Camping Skills/Outdoor Living, Canoeing, Challenge/Rope Courses, Horseback — English, Nature/Environment Studies, Sailing, Swimming — Instructional, Travel/Tour
Session lengths & capacity: June-August; 1, 2 & 4 week sessions; 200 campers
Clientele & fees: coed 5-16; families; Fees: B ☀ Fees: B, C ▲ 🐷
Contact: Robert Elderdge, Director at (410) 329-6590; fax: (410) 329-6034
e-mail: director@camppuhtok.org
Operated by: The Salvation Army, 814 Light St, Baltimore, MD 21230 at (410) 347-9944

Group Rental Information

Facilities: Cabins, Food Service, Hiking Trails, Kitchen Facilities, Playing Fields, River (#146)

Valley Mill Camp Inc

(est 1956)
Germantown, MD; (301) 948-0220
Evelyn McEwen, Director

Camp comments: It's like a going away camp at home.
Activities: Archery, Camping Skills/Outdoor Living, Canoeing, Climbing/Rappelling, Horseback — English, Kayaking, Swimming — Instructional
Session lengths & capacity: June-August; 3, 6 & 9 week sessions; 400 campers
Clientele & fees: boys 6-15; girls 6-15; coed 4-5; Fees: C ☀
Contact: Evelyn McEwen, Director at (301) 948-0220; fax: (301) 948-6835
e-mail: valleymill@aol.com
Web site: www.valleymill.com
Operated by: Valley Mill Camp Inc, 1405 Dublin Drive, Silver Spring, MD 20902 at (301) 593-1576 (#25554)

Western Maryland 4H Center

(est 1956)
Swanton, MD (Garrett Co.); (301) 245-4103
James W Simms, Director

Camp comments: Center offers traditional rustic camping, specialty/adventure & family camps. Emphasis on education. Rental available.
Activities: Aquatic Activities, Archery, Backpacking, Basketball, Canoeing, Challenge/Rope Courses, Counselor Training (CIT), Leadership Development, Nature/Environment Studies, Riflery
Session lengths & capacity: April-October; 1 week sessions; 155 campers
Clientele & fees: boys 8-18; girls 8-18; coed 8-18; families; Fees: B ▲
Contact: James W Simms, Camp Supervisor at (301) 334-6960; fax: (301) 334-6961
e-mail: js63@umail.umd.edu
Operated by: Maryland Coop Ext 4H Youth Dev, 8020 Greenmead Dr, College Park, MD 20740 at (301) 403-4248

Group Rental Information

Seasons & Capacity: Spring 150, Summer 150, Fall 150
Facilities: Cabins, Food Service, Hiking Trails, Lake, Lodges, Meeting Rooms, Playing Fields
Programs: Boating, Challenge/Ropes Course, Environmental Education, Swimming (#3950)

Whitemarsh YMCA Family Day Cmp

Baltimore, MD (Baltimore Co.); (410) 661-5600
Angie Fiorito, Director

Camp comments: Whatever your child's age or interests, look to YMCA camping for a safe and fun summer experience.
Activities: Aquatic Activities, Community Service, Counselor Training (CIT), Field Trips, Leadership Development, Performing Arts, Sports — Field & Team, Swimming — Instructional, Swimming — Recreational, Team Building
Session lengths & capacity: June-August; 1, 2 & 4 week sessions; 300 campers
Clientele & fees: coed 4-15; Fees: B ☀ 🚌
Contact: Jean Fiorito, Site Director at (410) 661-5741; fax: (410) 882-9913
e-mail: jeanfiorito@ymcamd.org
Operated by: Harford County Family YMCA, 309 Thomas Run Rd, Bel Air, MD 21015 at (410) 893-5025 (#45571)

YMCA Camp Letts

(est 1906)
Edgewater, MD; (410) 798-0440
Scott Peckins, Director

Camp comments: Co-ed residential YMCA camp on the Chesapeake Bay near Annapolis, MD, offering horse programs, sailing, BMX biking, rope challenge course & lots more.
Activities: Aquatic Activities, Archery, Canoeing, Challenge/Rope Courses, Horseback — English, Horseback — Western, Sailing, Tennis, Waterskiing, Wilderness Trips
Session lengths & capacity: June-August; 1, 2, 3, 4, 5, 6, 7 & 8 week sessions; 340 campers
Clientele & fees: coed 8-16; Fees: E, F ▲ 🐷
Contact: Gloria Brown, Registrar at (410) 919-1400; fax: (301) 261-7336
e-mail: info@campletts.org
Web site: www.ymcawashdc.org
Operated by: YMCA Metropolitan Washington, PO Box 208, Edgewater, MD 21037 at (202) 232-6700

Group Rental Information

Site comments: Beautiful 219 acre facility on Chesapeake Bay, 15 minutes from Annapolis. Offer rentals for day groups or overnight, Horse rides, canoeing, ropes course & more.
Seasons & Capacity: Spring 350, Fall 350, Winter 350
Facilities: A/V Equipment, Cabins, Dorm-Style, Double Occupancy, Food Service, Hiking Trails, Kitchen Facilities, Lodges, Meeting Rooms, Playing Fields, Pool, River, Tents
Programs: Boating, Challenge/Ropes Course, Environmental Education, Horseback Riding, Swimming (#8286)

YMCA Camp Tockwogh

(est 1938)
Worton, MD; (410) 348-6000
Phil Mc Govern, Director

Camp comments: Located on the Chesapeake Bay. Waterfront program is our specialty, including sailing, waterskiing, boating & canoeing!
Activities: Archery, Arts/Crafts, Canoeing, Challenge/Rope Courses, Horseback — English, Sailing, Tennis, Waterskiing, Windsurfing
Session lengths & capacity: June-August; 1, 2 & 4 week sessions; 440 campers

ICON LEGEND

☀ Day Camp
▲ Resident Camp
🏠 Facilities Available To Rent
🚗 Transportation Available
🐷 Financial Aid Available

FEE RANGES PER WEEK

A $0-75
B $75-200
C $201-350
D $351-500
E $501-650
F over $650

Clientele & fees: coed 8-15; families; seniors; Fees: D ☀ ⛟
Contact: Janie Schultz, Registrar at (410) 348-6000; fax: (410) 348-6023
e-mail: jschultz@ymcade.org
Web site: www.ymcade.org
Operated by: YMCA Camp Quoowant, 3 Mt Lebanon Rd, Wilmington, DE 19810 at (302) 478-8303

Group Rental Information

Site comments: Located on Chesapeake Bay, we offer varied land&water based programs speciality sailing&racing camp for 12-15 year olds.
Seasons & Capacity: Spring 500, Fall 500, Winter 95
Facilities: A/V Equipment, Cabins, Double Occupancy, Food Service, Hiking Trails, Lake, Lodges, Meeting Rooms, Playing Fields, Pool, River
Programs: Boating, Challenge/Ropes Course, Environmental Education, Horseback Riding, Swimming, Winter Sports (#2561)

YMCA Camp-Sandy Point St Park ☀ ⛟

Annapolis, MD (Anne Arundel Co.)
Caran Tolliver, Director

Camp comments: Whatever your child's age and interests, look to YMCA camping for a safe and fun summer experience.
Activities: Arts/Crafts, Canoeing, Counselor Training (CIT), Drama, Field Trips, Fishing, Leadership Development, Nature/Environment Studies, Sports — Field & Team, Swimming — Recreational
Session lengths & capacity: June-August; 1 week sessions; 125 campers
Clientele & fees: coed 5-12; Fees: B ☀ 🐷 ⛟
Contact: Lana Smith, Program Executive Director at (410) 760-4363; fax: (410) 760-4980
e-mail: lanasmith@ymcamd.org
Operated by: Harford County Family YMCA, 309 Thomas Run Rd, Bel Air, MD 21015 at (410) 893-5025 (#34628)

Massachusetts

4H Camp Howe (est 1928) ☀ ⛟

Goshen, MA; (413) 238-7635

Camp comments: Enthusiastic, caring staff offer a range of quality experiences in highly supportive community. Excellent teen program.
Activities: Arts/Crafts, Canoeing, Challenge/Rope Courses, Climbing/Rappelling, Drama, Fishing, Leadership Development, Model Rocketry, Nature/Environment Studies, Swimming — Recreational
Session lengths & capacity: June-August; 1 & 2 week sessions; 150 campers
Clientele & fees: coed 7-17; Fees: B ☀ Fees: C ⛟ ⛟
Contact: (413) 268-7635; fax: (413) 549-6337
Web site: www.camphowe.com
Operated by: 4H Camp Howe, PO Box 362, Hathorne, MA 01937 at (413) 549-3969 (#164)

4H Camp Leslie (est 1939) ☀ ⛟

Georgetown, MA (Essex Co.); (978) 352-8060
Jenny Goudreau, Director

Camp comments: 4-H camping builds valuable life skills such as decision making, peer relations , cooperation & independent living.
Activities: Archery, Arts/Crafts, Boating, Camping Skills/Outdoor Living, Challenge/Rope Courses, Counselor Training (CIT), Nature/Environment Studies, Sports — Field & Team, Swimming — Recreational, Team Building
Session lengths & capacity: 1 week sessions; 92 campers

Clientele & fees: coed 7-14; Fees: B ☀ Fees: C ⛟
Contact: Jenny Goudreau, Camp Director at (978) 352-8060; fax: (978) 750-0565
e-mail: campleslie@aol.com
Operated by: 4H Club Camp Inc, PO Box 362, Hathorne, MA 01937 at (978) 352-8060 (#115)

4H Camp Marshall Mass State Ho (est 1931) ☀ ⛟

Spencer, MA (Worcester Co.); (508) 885-4891
Ken Presley, Director

Camp comments: Noncompetitive environment for youth development.
Activities: Archery, Arts/Crafts, Boating, Challenge/Rope Courses, Horseback — English, Horseback — Western, Leadership Development, Nature/Environment Studies, Riflery, Swimming — Instructional
Session lengths & capacity: 1 week sessions; 125 campers
Clientele & fees: coed 6-15; Fees: C, D ⛟ ⛟
Contact: Ken Presley, Executive at (508) 885-4891; fax: (508) 885-4019
e-mail: KSPresley@earthlink.net
Operated by: Worcester County 4H Center Inc, PO Box 362, Hawthorne, MA 01937-0362 at (508) 885-4891 (#10233)

4H Camp Middlesex (est 1940) ☀ ⛟

Ashby, MA; (978) 386-7704
Paul Meani, Director

Camp comments: Self-esteem specialty. Campers thrive in noncompetitive, caring atmosphere with opportunities to belong, learn, contribute.
Activities: Aquatic Activities, Archery, Boating, Challenge/Rope Courses, Counselor Training (CIT), Dance, Farming/Ranching/Gardening, Horseback — English, Model Rocketry, Nature/Environment Studies
Session lengths & capacity: July-August; 1 & 2 week sessions; 100 campers
Clientele & fees: coed 8-14; Fees: B ☀ Fees: C ⛟ ⛟
Contact: David Z Freedman, Executive Director at (978) 386-7704; fax: (978) 750-0565
e-mail: info@campmiddlesex.com
Web site: www.campmiddlesex.com
Operated by: Middlesex Cty Foundation Inc, 1031 Erickson Road, Ashby, MA 01431 at (978) 386-7704 (#3455)

4H Farley Outdoor Ed Center (est 1934) ☀ ⛟

Mashpee, MA (Barnstable Co.); (508) 477-0181
Mike Campbell, Director

Camp comments: Self-esteem specialty. Campers thrive in noncompetitive, caring atmosphere, opportunities to belong, learn, contribute.
Activities: Aquatic Activities, Archery, Arts/Crafts, Canoeing, Challenge/Rope Courses, Counselor Training (CIT), Horseback — English, Kayaking, Nature/Environment Studies, Swimming — Recreational
Session lengths & capacity: 1 week sessions; 150 campers
Clientele & fees: coed 4-14; Fees: B ☀ Fees: C ⛟
Contact: Michael Campbell, Executive Director at (508) 477-0181; fax: (508) 539-0080
e-mail: office@campfarley.com
Web site: www.campfarley.com
Operated by: Cape Cod 4H Camp Corporation, 615 Route 130, Mashpee, MA 02649 at (508) 477-0181 (#1454)

Animal Friends Summer Camp ☀

(est 1947)

Cataumet, MA (Barnstable Co.); (508) 563-6116
Laura Sheehan, Director

Camp comments: Cape Cod. Focused on encouraging proper attitudes & respect for all living things. Hands on experience working with animals.
Activities: Arts/Crafts, Drama, Farming/Ranching/Gardening, Nature/Environment Studies, Sports — Field & Team
Session lengths & capacity: June-August; 1, 3 & 4 week sessions; 130 campers
Clientele & fees: coed 6-12; Fees: B ☀ 🐷 ⛟
Contact: Laura Sheehan, Camp Director at (617) 338-1138; fax: (781) 461-9493
e-mail: lsheehan@arlboston.org
Operated by: Animal Rescue League Of Boston, PO Box 265, Boston, MA 02117 at (617) 338-1138 (#2949)

Arcadia Nature Day Camp ☀

(est 1946)

Easthampton, MA (Hampshire Co.); (413) 584-3009
Cyndee Frere, Director

Camp comments: Active, outdoor natural history-based camp. Mature, talented staff. Low counselor to camper ratios.
Activities: Arts/Crafts, Canoeing, Counselor Training (CIT), Drawing/Painting, Hiking, Nature/Environment Studies
Session lengths & capacity: June-August; 1 & 2 week sessions; 52 campers
Clientele & fees: coed 3-17; Fees: B ☀
Contact: Cyndee Frere, Camp Director at (413) 584-3009 ext. 14; fax: (413) 584-0250
e-mail: cfrere@massaudubon.org
Web site: www.massaudubon.org
Operated by: Mass Audubon, 472 West Mountain Rd, Lenox, MA 01240 at (413) 637-0320 (#3054)

Atwater (est 1921) ⛟

North Brookfield, MA (Worcester Co.); (508) 867-6916
Devonia Thomas, Director

Camp comments: Afro-centric setting. Focusing on leadership development, recreation education and culture.
Activities: Aquatic Activities, Arts/Crafts, Computer, Drama, Golf, Horseback — English, Leadership Development, Nature/Environment Studies, Swimming — Instructional, Tennis
Session lengths & capacity: June-August; 2 & 4 week sessions; 150 campers
Clientele & fees: boys 8-15; girls 8-15; Fees: D ⛟
Contact: Devonia Thomas at (508) 867-6916; e-mail: league3626@aol.com
Web site: www.campatwater.org
Operated by: Urban League of Springfield, 756 State Street, Springfield, MA 01109 at (413) 739-7211 (#8276)

AU Kamp for Kids (est 1975) ☀ ⛟

Westfield, MA (Hampden Co.); (413) 562-5678
Debby Clarke, Director

Camp comments: Integrated camp serving able & disabled for 20 years. Focus on fun, inclusion & respect for similarities. 1:2 staffing.
Activities: Aquatic Activities, Arts/Crafts, Basketball, Camping Skills/Outdoor Living, Challenge/Rope Courses, Counselor Training (CIT), Nature/Environment Studies, Soccer, Team Building
Session lengths & capacity: July-August; 2 week sessions; 120 campers
Clientele & fees: coed 3-22; Fees: C ☀ ⛟
Contact: Debby Clarke, Camp Director at (413) 562-5678; fax: (413) 562-1239
Operated by: Abilities Unlimited, 61 Union St, Westfield, MA 01085 at (413) 562-5678 (#14598)

Avoda (est 1927) ▲

Middleboro, MA (Plymouth Co.); (508) 947-3800
Paul G. Davis, Director

Camp comments: Non-religious Jewish boys' camp. Caring, warm supportive staff. Trad. all around prog. Vari. of activities. Kosher food, 2 exper. nurses; 3 on-call pediatrician
Activities: Aquatic Activities, Baseball/Softball, Basketball, Challenge/Rope Courses, Photography, Sailing, Soccer, Sports — Field & Team, Tennis, Waterskiing
Session lengths & capacity: June-August; 3, 4 & 7 week sessions; 150 campers
Clientele & fees: boys 7-15; Fees: E ▲ 🐘
Contact: Paul G Davis, Director at (781) 334-6275; fax: (781) 334-4779
e-mail: campavoda@aol.com
Web site: www.campavoda.org
Operated by: Camp Avoda Inc, 11 Essex St, Lynnfield, MA 01940 at (781) 334-6275 (#4470)

Bauercrest (est 1931) ▲

Amesbury, MA (Amesbury Co.); (978) 388-4732
Robert C Stone, Director

Camp comments: Our emphasis is in helping a well rounded child, we offer excellent athletics, unique elective system, superior waterfront.
Activities: Arts/Crafts, Baseball/Softball, Basketball, Canoeing, Golf, Sailing, Soccer, Sports — Field & Team, Swimming — Instructional, Tennis
Session lengths & capacity: 4 & 8 week sessions; 270 campers
Clientele & fees: boys 6-17; Fees: D ▲ 🐘
Contact: Robert Stone, Executive Director at (781) 784-5230;
e-mail: Bob@Bauercrest.org
Web site: www.bauercrest.org
Operated by: Bauercrest, 25 Owl Drive, Sharon, MA 02067 at (784) 784-5577 (#4610)

Beaver Summer Programs

(est 1946) ☀ 🚐

Chestnut Hill, MA (Suffolk Co.); (617) 738-2750
Nat Saltonstall, Director

Camp comments: Traditional noncompetitive day camp: outstanding instruction; high counselor/camper ratio. Programs incl. nature, soccer, daytrips, CIT, drama, detectives,ropes
Activities: Archery, Arts/Crafts, Challenge/Rope Courses, Counselor Training (CIT), Nature/Environment Studies, Performing Arts, Soccer, Sports — Field & Team, Swimming — Instructional, Wilderness Trips
Session lengths & capacity: June-August; 1 & 2 week sessions; 650 campers
Clientele & fees: coed 3-15; Fees: D ☀

ICON LEGEND

☀ Day Camp

▲ Resident Camp

🏠 Facilities Available To Rent

🚐 Transportation Available

🐘 Financial Aid Available

FEE RANGES PER WEEK

A	$0-75
B	$75-200
C	$201-350
D	$351-500
E	$501-650
F	over $650

Contact: Linda Harding, Office Manager at (617) 738-2750; fax: (617) 738-2790
Web site: www.beavercds.org
Operated by: Beaver Country Day School, 791 Hammond St, Chestnut Hill, MA 02467 at (617) 738-2750 (#4375)

Becket Chimney Corners YMCA

(est 1994) ☀

Becket, MA; (413) 623-8991
Dee Ward, Director

Camp comments: Our camp encourages children to grow socially, physically, and intellectually in a safe and nurturing environment. We offer many activities for the campers.
Activities: Aquatic Activities, Archery, Arts/Crafts, Boating, Camping Skills/Outdoor Living, Counselor Training (CIT), Field Trips, Hiking, Nature/Environment Studies, Team Building
Session lengths & capacity: June-August; 1 week sessions; 46 campers
Clientele & fees: coed 3-12; Fees: B ☀ 🐘
Contact: Jessie Vogt, Camp Director at (413) 623-8991; fax: (413) 623-5890
e-mail: jvogt@bccymca.org
Web site: www.bccymca.org
Operated by: Becket Chimney Corners YMCA, 748 Hamilton Rd, Becket, MA 01223 at (413) 623-8991 (#3141)

Becket Chimney Corners YMCA ▲ 🏠

Becket, MA
Angel Krimm, Director

Camp comments: A variety of team building, leadership, recreation programs for families, teens, scouts, religious institutions, schools
Activities: Aquatic Activities, Archery, Arts/Crafts, Boating, Canoeing, Challenge/Rope Courses, Kayaking, Leadership Development, Nature/Environment Studies, Team Building
Session lengths & capacity: 1/2 & 1 week sessions; 800 campers
Clientele & fees: coed 1-99; families; seniors; single adults; Fees: C ▲
Contact: Angel Krimm, Outdoor Education Director at (413) 623-8991; fax: (413) 623-5890
e-mail: akrimm@bccymca.org
Web site: www.bccymca.org
Operated by: Becket Chimney Corners YMCA, 748 Hamilton Rd, Becket, MA 01223 at (413) 623-8991
Group Rental Information
Seasons & Capacity: Spring 800, Fall 800, Winter 170 (#43916)

Belmont Day School Camp

(est 1946) ☀ 🚐

Belmont, MA (Middlesex Co.); (617) 484-3078
Tony Vine, CCD, Director

Camp comments: BDS camp provides a positive, safe and creative learning environment for children. Support and challenge growth!
Activities: Aquatic Activities, Archery, Arts/Crafts, Drama, Field Trips, Nature/Environment Studies, Sailing, Swimming — Instructional, Swimming — Recreational, Tennis
Session lengths & capacity: 2, 4 & 8 week sessions; 256 campers
Clientele & fees: boys 4-12; girls 4-12; coed 4-12; Fees: C ☀
Contact: Tony Vine, CCD at (617) 484-3078 ext. 225; fax: (617) 489-1942
e-mail: tvine@belmontday.org
Web site: www.belmontday.org
Operated by: Belmont Day School, 55 Day School Lane, Belmont, MA 02478 at (617) 484-3078 (#2745)

Belvoir Terrace Arts Ctr

(est 1954) ▲ 🚐

Lenox, MA (Berkshire Co.); (413) 637-0555
Nancy Goldberg/Diane Marcus, Director

Camp comments: Individually structured program: art, dance, music, theater, individual sports. Professional staff, estate living.
Activities: Arts/Crafts, Ceramics/Pottery, Dance, Drama, Drawing/Painting, Horseback — English, Music, Photography, Swimming — Instructional, Tennis
Session lengths & capacity: June-August; 7 week sessions; 185 campers
Clientele & fees: girls 9-17; Fees: F ▲ 🐘
Contact: Diane Marcus, Directors at (212) 580-3398; fax: (212) 579-7282
e-mail: Belvoirt@aol.com
Operated by: Belvoir Terrace Fine Perform, 101 W 79th St, New York, NY 10024 at (212) 580-3398 (#3103)

Bement Camp & Conference Ctr (est 1948) ▲ 🏠

Charlton Depot, MA (Worcester Co.); (508) 248-7811
Mark D Rourke, Director

Camp comments: Christian emphasis, nondenominational, campers thrive in noncompetitive, caring atmosphere. Ropes & Challenge facilities
Activities: Aquatic Activities, Archery, Backpacking, Boating, Challenge/Rope Courses, Community Service, Leadership Development, Religious Study, Team Building
Session lengths & capacity: June-August; 1 & 2 week sessions; 135 campers
Clientele & fees: boys 6-17; girls 6-17; coed 6-17; Fees: C ▲ 🐘
Contact: Mark Rourke, Director at (508) 248-7811; fax: (508) 248-5012
e-mail: mrourke555@aol.com
Web site: www.bementcenter.com
Operated by: Episcopal Diocese Western MA, 37 Chestnut St, Springfield, MA 01103 at (413) 737-4786
Group Rental Information
Facilities: Cabins, Dorm-Style, Food Service, Lake, Lodges, Meeting Rooms, Pool (#6121)

Brewster Day Camp (est 1981) ☀

Brewster, MA; (508) 896-6555
Milisa M Galazzi, Director

Camp comments: BDC welcomes 280 campers and 85 staff from 14 countries + 22 U.S. to 4.5 acre campus on Cape Cod. All share Courage, Hope, Good Spirit and Peace!
Activities: Archery, Arts/Crafts, Boating, Drama, Field Trips, Leadership Development, Sailing, Sports — Field & Team, Swimming — Instructional, Team Building
Session lengths & capacity: June-August; 1/2, 1, 2, 3, 4, 5, 6, 7 & 8 week sessions; 280 campers
Clientele & fees: coed 1-13; Fees: B, C ☀
Contact: Milisa Galazzi, Camp Director at (888) 396-2267; fax: (401) 461-4647
e-mail: brewsterdaycamp@cs.com
Web site: www.brewsterdaycamp.com
Operated by: The Family Schools Inc, 3570 Main St, Brewster, MA 02631 at (508) 896-6555 (#45625)

Broadmoor Natural History Day ☀

South Natick, MA; (508) 655-2296
Daniel Farber, Director
Activities: Arts/Crafts, Camping Skills/Outdoor Living, Canoeing, Counselor Training (CIT), Drawing/Painting, Hiking, Nature/Environment Studies

Contact: Daniel Farber, Camp Director at (508) 655-2296;
Web site: www.massaudubon.org
Operated by: Mass Audubon, 472 West Mountain Rd, Lenox, MA 01240 at (413) 637-0320 (#31324)

Brooks School Day Camp

(est 1970)

North Andover, MA; (978) 686-6101
Bobbie Crump-Burbank, Director

Camp comments: Traditional day camp offering a variety of activities on water and land that will enrich your child's summer.
Activities: Archery, Arts/Crafts, Boating, Counselor Training (CIT), Drama, Music, Nature/Environment Studies, Swimming — Instructional, Tennis
Session lengths & capacity: June-August; 2 week sessions; 360 campers
Clientele & fees: coed 4-12; Fees: **C** ☀
Contact: Bobbie Crump-Burbank, Director at (978) 725-6253; fax: (978) 725-6254
e-mail: daycamp@brooksschool.org
Web site: www.brooksschool.org/summer
Operated by: Brooks School, 1160 Great Pond Rd, North Andover, MA 01845 at (978) 725-6253 (#6214)

Burgess/Hayward (est 1928)

Sandwich, MA (Barnstable Co.); (508) 428-2571
Bruce Netherwood, Director

Camp comments: Located on beautiful Cape Cod. We build skills, confidence & cooperation in a challenging, caring, fun environment.
Activities: Aquatic Activities, Archery, Arts/Crafts, Challenge/Rope Courses, Counselor Training (CIT), Horseback — English, Sailing, Tennis, Travel/Tour, Windsurfing
Session lengths & capacity: June-August; 1 & 2 week sessions; 160 campers
Clientele & fees: boys 7-15; girls 7-15; coed 13-17; Fees: **D** △ 🚍
Contact: Leon Emplit, Administrative Assistant at (508) 428-2571; fax: (508) 420-3545
Operated by: South Shore YMCA Camps, 75 Stowe Rd, Sandwich, MA 02563 at (508) 428-2571

Group Rental Information
Site comments: Our year-round center is uniquely located to offer lake, forest & ocean teaching environments and will shape the program to suit your group's needs.
Seasons & Capacity: Spring 120, Fall 120
Facilities: Cabins, Hiking Trails, Lake, Lodges, Meeting Rooms, Playing Fields, Tents
Programs: Boating, Challenge/Ropes Course, Environmental Education, Swimming (#7677)

Cambridge Adventure Day Camp (est 1967)

Belmont, MA (Middlesex Co.); (617) 864-0960
Syrl Silberman, Director

Camp comments: Day camp for urban children from Cambridge. Growth promoting summer adventure. Sliding scale fee.
Activities: Arts/Crafts, Baseball/Softball, Basketball, Counselor Training (CIT), Field Trips, Leadership Development, Music, Nature/Environment Studies, Swimming — Instructional
Session lengths & capacity: July-August; 2 week sessions; 165 campers
Clientele & fees: coed 6-13; Fees: **A** ☀
Contact: J.L. Woodward, Office Manager/Registrar at (617) 864-0960; fax: (617) 876-8187
Operated by: Cambridge Camping Association, 99 Bishop Richard Allen Dr, Cambridge, MA 02139 at (617) 864-0960 (#7474)

Cambridge School Day Camp

(est 1951) ☀ 🚍

Weston, MA (Middlesex Co.); (781) 642-8666
Kaye Glass, Director

Camp comments: A noncompetitive camp which offers flexibility within a structured environment. 1:5 staff to camper ratio.
Activities: Archery, Ceramics/Pottery, Computer, Counselor Training (CIT), Drama, Field Trips, Nature/Environment Studies, Performing Arts, Photography, Swimming — Instructional
Session lengths & capacity: 2 week sessions; 300 campers
Clientele & fees: coed 4-14; Fees: **D** ☀
Contact: Kaye Glass, Camp Director at (781) 642-8666; fax: (781) 899-3870
e-mail: camp@csw.org
Web site: www.csw.org
Operated by: Cambridge School Of Weston, Georgian Road, Weston, MA 02493 at (781) 642-8600 (#7376)

Camp Becket YMCA

(est 1903) △ ⌂ 🚍

Becket, MA (Berkshire Co.); (413) 623-8991
Dave De Luca, Director

Camp comments: Character education based upon the small-group living environment. More than 90 yrs of excellence in YMCA camping.
Activities: Ceramics/Pottery, Challenge/Rope Courses, Community Service, Drama, Horseback — English, Leadership Development, Nature/Environment Studies, Sailing, Tennis, Travel/Tour
Session lengths & capacity: June-August; 4 week sessions; 280 campers
Clientele & fees: boys 8-16; Fees: **E** △ 🚍
Contact: David DeLuca, Director at (413) 623-8991; fax: (413) 623-5890
e-mail: DDeLuca@bccymca.org
Web site: www.bccymca.org
Operated by: Becket Chimney Corners YMCA, 748 Hamilton Rd, Becket, MA 01223 at (413) 623-8991

Group Rental Information
Facilities: Food Service, Hiking Trails, Lake, Lodges, Meeting Rooms
Programs: Boating, Environmental Education (#2666)

Camp Bonnie Brae (est 1919) △ ⌂

East Otis, MA (Berkshire Co.); (413) 269-4481
Emily Bedaw, Director

Camp comments: The oldest Girl Scout camp in the U.S. Located in the Berkshires on a scenic lake. Girls 2nd-12th grade are welcome to attend.
Activities: Aquatic Activities, Arts/Crafts, Boating, Camping Skills/Outdoor Living, Counselor Training (CIT), Hiking, Leadership Development, Nature/Environment Studies, Sailing, Waterskiing
Session lengths & capacity: July-August; 1/2, 1 & 2 week sessions; 120 campers
Clientele & fees: girls 6-16; Fees: **B, C** △ 🚍
Contact: Emily Bedaw, Outdoor Ed. Director at (413) 525-4124; fax: (413) 525-5901
e-mail: ebedaw@pvgsc.org
Web site: www.pvgsc.org
Operated by: Pioneer Valley GSC, 40 Harkness Avenue, East Longmeadow, MA 01028 at (413) 525-4124

Group Rental Information
Site comments: Camp Bonnie Brae is located on a scenic lake in the Berkshires. Comfortable and beautiful setting with lots of program opportunities.
Seasons & Capacity: Spring 150, Summer 150, Fall 150, Winter 150
Facilities: Cabins, Hiking Trails, Kitchen Facilities, Lake, Playing Fields, Tents
Programs: Boating, Challenge/Ropes Course, Swimming, Winter Sports (#4158)

Camp Emerson

(est 1968) △ 🚍

Hinsdale, MA (Berkshire Co.); (413) 655-8123
Marv, Addie & Sue Lein & Kevin McDonough, Director

Camp comments: Premiere multi-specialty camp, outstanding instruction, new sports center, heated pool, home of Camp Odyssey (Odyssey of the mind), The unique creative thinking
Activities: Arts/Crafts, Challenge/Rope Courses, Drama, Hockey, Model Rocketry, Sailing, Sports — Field & Team, Swimming — Instructional, Tennis, Waterskiing
Session lengths & capacity: June-August; 4 & 8 week sessions; 220 campers
Clientele & fees: coed 8-15; Fees: **F** △
Contact: Marvin, Lein, Directors/Owners at (914) 779-9406; fax: (914) 793-9334
e-mail: cmpemerson@aol.com
Operated by: Camp Emerson, 5 Brassie Road, Eastchester, NY 10709-5407 at (914) 779-9406 (#2125)

Camp Frank A Day (est 1916) △

East Brookfield, MA (Worcester Co.); (508) 867-3780
Richard & Sonya McKnight, Director

Camp comments: Located on a beautiful lake in central MA; high staff to camper ratio; most land & water activities; promote positive self image; family atmosphere.
Activities: Archery, Arts/Crafts, Boating, Drama, Field Trips, Sailing, Sports — Field & Team, Swimming — Instructional, Team Building, Waterskiing
Session lengths & capacity: 2, 4, 6 & 8 week sessions; 180 campers
Clientele & fees: coed 7-15; Fees: **D, E** △ 🚍
Contact: Richard or Sonya McKnight, Co-Directors at (617) 527-6492; fax: (617) 965-8832
e-mail: sonymc@aol.com
Operated by: YMCA West Suburban, 276 Church St Newton YMCA, Newton, MA 02458 at (617) 244-6050 (#2603)

Camp Frederick Douglass

☀ 🚍

New Bedford, MA; (508) 997-0734
Maxine Hebert, Director

Camp comments: Our YMCA offers daily swim lessons, a climbing tower, basketball, and sports programming.
Activities: Arts/Crafts, Baseball/Softball, Basketball, Climbing/Rappelling, Sports — Field & Team, Swimming — Instructional, Swimming — Recreational, Team Building
Session lengths & capacity: July-August; 2 week sessions; 80 campers
Clientele & fees: boys 6-13; girls 6-13; coed 6-13; Fees: **B** ☀
Contact: Maxine Hebert, Program Director at (508) 997-0734;
Operated by: YMCA of Greater New Bedford, 25 South Water St, New Bedford, MA 02740 at (508) 997-0734 (#9167)

Camp Greylock for Boys

(est 1916) △ 🚍

Becket, MA (Berkshire Co.); (413) 623-8921
Michael Marcus and Lukas Horn, Director

Camp comments: Traditional values, advanced instruction in individual and team sports. Excellent water front, nature & hiking programs.
Activities: Backpacking, Baseball/Softball, Basketball, Golf, Hiking, Hockey, Soccer, Sports — Field & Team, Swimming — Instructional, Tennis
Session lengths & capacity: 8 week sessions; 350 campers
Clientele & fees: boys 6-16; Fees: **F** △

Contact: Camp Greylock at (212) 582-1042; fax: (212) 765-8177
e-mail: info@campgreylock.com
Operated by: Camp Greylock, 1525 Main St, Becket, MA 01223 at (413) 623-8921 (#1986)

Camp Kingsmont (est 1971) ▲

West Stockbridge, MA (Berkshire Co.); (413) 232-8518
Keith Zucker, Director

Camp comments: Active summer in beautiful Berkshires. Weight loss w/ emphasis on fun. Interactive net year round. Owner former camper.
Activities: Aerobics/Exercise, Aquatic Activities, Bicycling/Biking, Boating, Challenge/Rope Courses, Drama, Horseback — Western, Sports — Field & Team, Tennis
Session lengths & capacity: June-August; 3, 6 & 8 week sessions; 260 campers
Clientele & fees: coed 7-18; Fees: **F** ▲
Contact: Keith Zucker, Owner at (800) 854-1377; fax: (914) 777-3709
e-mail: info@campkingsmont.com
Web site: www.campkingsmont.com
Operated by: Camp Kingsmont, 48 W Alford Road, West Stockbridge, MA 01266 at (800) 854-1377 (#7053)

Camp Lewis Perkins

(est 1926)
S Hadley, MA; (413) 584-2602
Megan Kennedy, Director

Camp comments: Girl Scout day camp offering timeless camp activities! Open to all girls ages 6 to 16. Girl Scouts discover the fun, friendship, and power of girls together.
Activities: Aquatic Activities, Archery, Arts/Crafts, Camping Skills/Outdoor Living, Hiking, Nature/Environment Studies, Sports — Field & Team, Swimming — Recreational, Team Building
Session lengths & capacity: June-August; 1 & 2\ week sessions; 150 campers
Clientele & fees: girls 6-17; Fees: **B**
Contact: Elizabeth Brooke-Willbanks, Program Director at (413) 584-2602; fax: (413) 586-7937
e-mail: wmgsc.elizabeth@the-spa.com
Web site: www.the-spa.com/wmgsc
Operated by: Girl Scouts of Western Mass, PO Box 558, Leeds, MA 01053 at (413) 584-2602

Group Rental Information
Seasons & Capacity: Spring 100
Facilities: Cabins, Double Occupancy, Hiking Trails, Kitchen Facilities, Meeting Rooms, Playing Fields, Pool, Tents (#16304)

ICON LEGEND

☀	Day Camp
▲	Resident Camp
⌂	Facilities Available To Rent
🚐	Transportation Available
🐖	Financial Aid Available

FEE RANGES PER WEEK

A	$0-75
B	$75-200
C	$201-350
D	$351-500
E	$501-650
F	over $650

Camp Marion White ☀ ⌂ 🚐

Richmond, MA
Kim Hyman, Director

Camp comments: Girl Scouts day camp in the Berkshires. Offering sailing, canoeing, and traditional camping. Open to all girls ages 6 to 16. Beautiful lakefront property!
Activities: Aquatic Activities, Archery, Arts/Crafts, Boating, Camping Skills/Outdoor Living, Canoeing, Nature/Environment Studies, Sailing, Swimming — Instructional, Swimming — Recreational
Session lengths & capacity: June-August; 1 & 2 weeks sessions; 120 campers
Clientele & fees: girls 6-17; Fees: **B** ☀ 🐖
Contact: Elizabeth Brooke-Willbanks, Program Director at (413) 584-2602 ext. 11; fax: (413) 586-7937
e-mail: wmgsc.elizabeth@the-spa.com
Web site: www.the-spa.com/wmgsc
Operated by: Girl Scouts of Western Mass, PO Box 558, Leeds, MA 01053 at (413) 584-2602

Group Rental Information
Facilities: Kitchen Facilities, Lake, Lodges, Tents (#17028)

Camp Massasoit (est 1932) ☀

Springfield, MA (Hampden Co.); (413) 750-5011
Michael Boulden, Director

Camp comments: Focus on noncompetitive outdoor recreation and environmental awareness activities in a safe supportive environment.
Activities: Arts/Crafts, Boating, Camping Skills/Outdoor Living, Challenge/Rope Courses, Climbing/Rappelling, Hiking, Kayaking, Nature/Environment Studies, Wilderness Trips
Session lengths & capacity: June-August; 1 & 2 week sessions; 200 campers
Clientele & fees: coed 5-15; Fees: **C** ☀
Contact: Michael Boulden, Camp Director at (413) 750-5011;
Web site: www.spfldcol.edu
Operated by: Springfield College, Recreation and Leisure Service, 263 Alden Street, Springfield, MA 01109-3707 at (413) 748-3693 (#2763)

Camp Metacomet ☀ 🚐

Dartmouth, MA; (508) 997-0734
Karen Binder, Director

Camp comments: Our 60 acre field, forest, wetland site is a beautiful place to swim, make new friends, learn about nature, and challenge yourselves, on the ropes course.
Session lengths & capacity: June-August; 2 week sessions; 300 campers
Clientele & fees: coed 6-13; Fees: **B** ☀
Operated by: YMCA of Greater New Bedford, 25 South Water St, New Bedford, MA 02740 at (508) 997-0734 (#9166)

Camp Mishannock (est 1947) ☀ ▲

Kingston, MA (Plymouth Co.); (781) 585-8592
Sr. Jacqueline Meyer, Director
Activities: Archery, Arts/Crafts, Boating, Counselor Training (CIT), Drama, Field Trips, Horseback — English, Sports — Field & Team, Swimming — Instructional, Tennis
Session lengths & capacity: June-August; 1, 2, 3, 4, 5, 6 week sessions; 140 campers
Clientele & fees: girls 6-15; Fees: **C** ☀ Fees: **D** ▲
Contact: Sr Jacqueline Meyer CDP, Director at (781) 585-8592; fax: (781) 582-1596
e-mail: campmish@adelphia.net
Web site: www.campmishannock.com
Operated by: Congreg of Divine Providence, 363 Bishops Highway, Kingston, MA 02364 at (781) 585-7707 (#29520)

Camp Mishnoah (est 1928) ▲ 🚐

Holland, MA (Hampden Co.); (413) 245-3455
Audri Victory, Director

Camp comments: Resident camp for girls. Located on 100 acres on lake. Cabins, infirmary, dining & rec hall. Indian ceremonies & lore.
Activities: Arts/Crafts, Basketball, Camping Skills/Outdoor Living, Counselor Training (CIT), Drama, Hiking, Leadership Development, Nature/Environment Studies, Sports — Field & Team, Tennis
Session lengths & capacity: July-August; 6 week sessions; 65 campers
Clientele & fees: girls 6-13; Fees: **C** ▲ 🐖
Contact: (413) 739-4743; fax: (413) 739-4744
Operated by: Springfield Girls Club Family, 100 Acorn St, Springfield, MA 01109 at (413) 739-4743 (#2703)

Camp Mitchman (est 1945) ☀ 🚐

Beverly, MA (Essex Co.); (978) 927-6582
Joe Boccia, Director

Camp comments: Unique family atmosphere. Varied activities give each child chance to shine. Let your child be part of something special
Activities: Archery, Basketball, Challenge/Rope Courses, Field Trips, Nature/Environment Studies, Soccer, Sports — Field & Team, Swimming — Instructional, Team Building, Tennis
Session lengths & capacity: June-August; 2 week sessions; 140 campers
Clientele & fees: coed 5-13; Fees: **B** ☀
Contact: Joe Boccia, Director at (978) 927-6582; fax: (978) 927-7988
e-mail: boccia@mediaone.net
Operated by: Mitchman Inc, 36 Foster St, Beverly, MA 01915 at (978) 927-6582 (#10354)

Camp Nawaka (est 1967) ▲ ⌂ 🚐

East Otis, MA (Berkshire Co.); (413) 269-4296
Christopher Egan, Director

Camp comments: Camp Nawaka is a small resident camp in the Berkshires of Western Massachusetts serving a diverse population of children in an atmosphere of mutual respect.
Activities: Archery, Arts/Crafts, Camping Skills/Outdoor Living, Canoeing, Ceramics/Pottery, Leadership Development, Soccer, Swimming — Instructional
Session lengths & capacity: June-August; 1, 2 & 3 week sessions; 120 campers
Clientele & fees: coed 7-16; Fees: **D** ▲ 🐖
Contact: Christopher Egan, Director at (617) 523-6006 ext. 41; fax: (617) 523-6290
e-mail: info@nawaka.org
Web site: www.campfireusa-emass.org
Operated by: Camp Fire USA Eastern MA Cncl, 108 Union Wharf, Boston, MA 02109 at (617) 523-6006

Group Rental Information
Seasons & Capacity: Spring 120, Fall 120
Facilities: A/V Equipment, Cabins, Dorm-Style, Food Service, Hiking Trails, Kitchen Facilities, Lake, Playing Fields
Programs: Boating, Swimming (#2613)

Camp Romaca (est 1929) ▲ 🚐

Hinsdale, MA (Berkshire Co.); (413) 655-2715
Jeannine & Jeff Saltz, Director

Camp comments: Amidst Berkshire culture. Outstanding staff & program. Emphasis on swim, tennis & drama. Positive, loving & traditional.
Activities: Arts/Crafts, Basketball, Camping Skills/Outdoor Living, Drama, Gymnastics, Sailing, Soccer, Swimming — Recreational, Tennis, Waterskiing
Session lengths & capacity: June-August; 8 week sessions; 160 campers
Clientele & fees: girls 6-16; Fees: **F** ▲

Contact: Jeannine & Jeff Saltz, Owners/Directors at (800) 779-2070; fax: (518) 581-2600
e-mail: summer@romaca.com
Web site: www.romaca.com
Operated by: Camp Romaca, 9 Winding Brook Drive, Saratoga Springs, NY 12866 at (800) 779-2070 (#1900)

Camp Rotary (est 1921)

Boxford, MA (Essex Co.); (978) 352-9952
Rich Cowdell, Director

Camp comments: Providing residential camping opportunities for over 80 years! We offer a great mix of traditional and novel camp activities. Come try our BMX bike race track!
Activities: Aquatic Activities, Archery, Bicycling/Biking, Challenge/Rope Courses, Counselor Training (CIT), Field Trips, Riflery, Sailing, Sports — Field & Team
Session lengths & capacity: June-August; 1, 2, 4 & 8 week sessions; 200 campers
Clientele & fees: coed 7-15; Fees: D ⛺
Contact: Rich Cowdell, Director at (978) 352-9952; fax: (781) 593-5431
e-mail: camprotaryma@aol.com
Web site: www.camprotary.org
Operated by: Greater Lynn Rotary Club, 122 Woodland Avenue, Lynn, MA 01904 at (781) 593-4247

Group Rental Information
Facilities: Cabins, Dorm-Style, Food Service, Hiking Trails, Lake, Playing Fields
Programs: Boating, Challenge/Ropes Course, Swimming (#26584)

Camp Sewataro (est 1960)

Sudbury, MA (Middlesex Co.); (978) 443-3100
The Taylor Family, Director

Camp comments: North woods setting, diverse, noncompetitive program, fishing, riding, etc!
Activities: Archery, Arts/Crafts, Canoeing, Fishing, Horseback — English, Sports — Field & Team, Swimming — Instructional
Session lengths & capacity: June-August; 4 & 8 week sessions; 550 campers
Clientele & fees: coed 4-12; Fees: D ☀
Contact: Christine Taylor, Director at (978) 443-3100; fax: (978) 443-8153
e-mail: camp@sewataro.com
Web site: www.sewataro.com
Operated by: The Taylor Family, 1 Liberty Ledge, Sudbury, MA 01776 at (978) 443-3100 (#2575)

Camp Thoreau Day Camp

(est 1951)

Concord, MA (Middlesex Co.); (978) 369-4095
Jennifer Bush, Director

Camp comments: Noncompet. outdoor emphasis w/small groups.We are based in character development & provide a warm,friendly atmosphere.CIT program,electives,riding,trip/travel.
Activities: Archery, Arts/Crafts, Camping Skills/Outdoor Living, Challenge/Rope Courses, Horseback — English, Leadership Development, Nature/Environment Studies, Sailing, Swimming — Instructional, Tennis
Session lengths & capacity: June-August; 2, 4 & 8 week sessions; 400 campers
Clientele & fees: coed 4-15; Fees: D ☀
Contact: Jackie Croteau, Administrative Assistant at (978) 369-4095; fax: (978) 369-8078
e-mail: camp@thoreau.com
Web site: www.thoreau.com
Operated by: Camp Thoreau Inc, 275 Forest Ridge Road, Concord, MA 01742-0536 at (978) 369-4095 (#2628)

Cape Cod Sea Camps

(est 1922)

Brewster, MA; (508) 896-3451
Nancy W Garran, Director

Camp comments: Directly on Cape Cod Bay and freshwater lake. Programs blend tradition and innovation in a safe supportive community.
Activities: Aquatic Activities, Archery, Arts/Crafts, Counselor Training (CIT), Photography, Riflery, Sailing, Sports — Field & Team, Swimming — Instructional, Tennis
Session lengths & capacity: June-August; 1, 4 & 7 week sessions; 370 campers
Clientele & fees: coed 4-15; Fees: D ☀ Fees: F ⛺
Contact: David Peterson, Resident Camp Director at (508) 896-3451; fax: (508) 896-8272
e-mail: info@capecodseacamps.com
Web site: www.capecodseacamps.com
Operated by: Cape Cod Sea Camps, Box 1880, Brewster, MA 02631 at (508) 896-3451

Group Rental Information
Site comments: Convenient base to tour Cape Cod & islands. Clambake special.
Seasons & Capacity: Spring 500, Fall 500
Facilities: Cabins, Dorm-Style, Double Occupancy, Food Service, Lake, Linens, Meeting Rooms, Ocean, Playing Fields (#2634)

Cathedral Camp (est 1915)

East Freetown, MA (Bristol Co.); (508) 763-8874
Sister Joseph Marie Levesque, O.P., Director

Camp comments: 80 yr camp. Safe, well-supervised prog. 90 scenic acres bordering Long Pond.Nondiscrimination. Wheelchair accessible.
Activities: Archery, Arts/Crafts, Baseball/Softball, Basketball, Boating, Camping Skills/Outdoor Living, Canoeing, Counselor Training (CIT), Dance, Swimming — Instructional
Session lengths & capacity: July-August; 2 week sessions; 525 campers
Clientele & fees: coed 4-13; Fees: B ☀
Contact: Sis Joseph Marie Levesque, Director at (508) 763-8874; fax: (508) 763-3768
e-mail: joseph_marie2@juno.com
Operated by: Roman Catholic Bishop Fall Rvr, PO Box 428, East Freetown, MA 02717 at (508) 763-8874

Group Rental Information
Site comments: Cathedral Camp Retreat Center is available for group retreats, conferences, picnics, private retreats and other functions.
Facilities: A/V Equipment, Double Occupancy, Food Service, Lake, Linens, Meeting Rooms, Playing Fields
Programs: Swimming (#2689)

Cedar Hill Day Camp

(est 1980)

Waltham, MA (Middlesex Co.); (617) 482-1078
Pat Stens, Director

Camp comments: 72 acres including 2 pools, pond, ropes course, nature center. Transportation available from many Greater Boston communities.
Activities: Arts/Crafts, Camping Skills/Outdoor Living, Challenge/Rope Courses, Drama, Drawing/Painting, Gymnastics, Leadership Development, Music, Nature/Environment Studies, Swimming — Recreational
Session lengths & capacity: June-August; 1 & 2 week sessions; 350 campers
Clientele & fees: girls 6-12; Fees: C ☀
Contact: Pat Stens, Program Manager at (617) 482-1078; fax: (617) 350-5246
e-mail: pstens@ptgirlscouts.org
Web site: www.ptgirlscouts.org
Operated by: Patriots Trail GSC, 95 Berkeley St, Boston, MA 02116 at (617) 350-8335

Group Rental Information
Site comments: Facilities available to groups. Must provide own equipment. No smoking or alcohol permitteed.
Seasons & Capacity: Spring 300, Fall 300, Winter 180
Facilities: Cabins, Meeting Rooms, Playing Fields, Tents (#2813)

Chickatawbut Hill Summer Natur (est 1988)

Milton, MA (Norfolk Co.); (617) 333-0690
Patti Steinman, Director

Camp comments: Specialized nature day camp. Learn through nature games, crafts and hikes.
Activities: Arts/Crafts, Backpacking, Camping Skills/Outdoor Living, Hiking, Nature/Environment Studies
Session lengths & capacity: July-August; 1 & 2 week sessions; 50 campers
Clientele & fees: coed 4-14; Fees: B ☀
Contact: Patti Steinman, Camp Director at (617) 333-0690; fax: (617) 333-0814
Web site: www.massaudubon.org
Operated by: Mass Audubon, 472 West Mountain Rd, Lenox, MA 01240 at (413) 637-0320

Group Rental Information
Site comments: Hilltop facility available for small rental groups during spring and fall.
Seasons & Capacity: Spring 50, Winter 50
Facilities: Dorm-Style, Hiking Trails, Kitchen Facilities
Programs: Environmental Education (#12711)

Chimney Corners Camp YMCA

(est 1931)

Becket, MA (Berkshire Co.); (413) 623-8991
Shannon Donovan-Monti, Director

Camp comments: Traditional program for girls. Focus on individual growth in a small group setting. Character building through values centered prog. Beautiful Berkshire site.
Activities: Arts/Crafts, Challenge/Rope Courses, Dance, Horseback — English, International Culture, Leadership Development, Nature/Environment Studies, Performing Arts, Sailing, Tennis
Session lengths & capacity: June-August; 4 week sessions; 250 campers
Clientele & fees: girls 8-15; Fees: E ⛺ 🚌
Contact: Shannon Donovan-Monti, Camp Director at (413) 623-8991; fax: (413) 623-5890
e-mail: sdonovan-monti@bccymca.org
Web site: www.bccymca.org
Operated by: Becket Chimney Corners YMCA, 748 Hamilton Rd, Becket, MA 01223 at (413) 623-8991

Group Rental Information
Site comments: Outdoor rec. & character building through group living.
Seasons & Capacity: Spring 470, Summer 470, Fall 470, Winter 160
Facilities: A/V Equipment, Cabins, Dorm-Style, Double Occupancy, Food Service, Hiking Trails, Kitchen Facilities, Lake, Linens, Lodges, Meeting Rooms, Playing Fields, Tents
Programs: Boating, Challenge/Ropes Course, Environmental Education, Horseback Riding, Swimming, Winter Sports (#7301)

Clara Barton Diabetes Camp

(est 1932)

N Oxford, MA (Worcester Co.); (508) 987-2056
Brooke Beverly, Director

Camp comments: Year round programs, resident summer camp, day camp, & adventure camp that encourages children/families to live well with diabetes.
Activities: Aquatic Activities, Arts/Crafts, Canoeing, Counselor Training (CIT), Horseback — English, Sports — Field & Team, Team Building, Wilderness Trips

Session lengths & capacity: 1 & 2 week sessions; 80 campers
Clientele & fees: girls 3-17; coed 3-17; families; Fees: F ▲ 🚗
Contact: Brooke Beverly, Resident Camps Director at (508) 987-3856; fax: (508) 987-2002
e-mail: bcdecamp@aol.com
Web site: www.bartoncenter.org
Operated by: Clara Barton for Girls w/Diab, PO Box 356, North Oxford, MA 01537 at (508) 987-2056

Group Rental Information
Site comments: Clara Barton Camp boasts winterized cabins, athletic fields, ropes course, and kitchen facilties. It is available for rental groups when camp is not in session.
Seasons & Capacity: Spring 150, Summer 250, Fall 150, Winter 150
Facilities: Cabins, Dorm-Style, Food Service, Hiking Trails, Kitchen Facilities, Lake, Meeting Rooms, Playing Fields
Programs: Boating, Challenge/Ropes Course, Swimming, Winter Sports (#2866)

CNS Camp New Connections ☀

Belmont, MA; (617) 855-2736
Liana P. Morgens, Director

Camp comments: Pragmatic language (social) skills training for Aspergers,NLD,HFA. Develop peer relationships w/fun, interactive activities & drama. www.campnewconnections.com
Activities: Ceramics/Pottery, Drama, Drawing/Painting, Field Trips, Swimming — Recreational, Team Building
Session lengths & capacity: June-August; 6 week sessions; 16 campers
Clientele & fees: coed 6-14; Fees: F ☀
Contact: CNS at (617) 855-2736; fax: (617) 855-3691
e-mail: cnsserv@mcleanpo.cmlean.org
Web site: www.mcleanhospital.org
Operated by: McLean Hospital/CNS, 115 Mill Street, Belmont, MA 02478 at (617) 855-2736 (#43064)

Computer High Tech Camps
(est 1982) ☀ ▲ 🚗

Newton, MA (Middlesex Co.); (888) 226-6733
Francesca Foti, Director

Camp comments: Technology meets traditional summer camps. Web design/broadcasting, 3D animation, digital photo, video, music, build & repair PC's, RC cars, rocketry & more.

ICON LEGEND
☀ Day Camp
▲ Resident Camp
🏠 Facilities Available To Rent
🚗 Transportation Available
🐷 Financial Aid Available

FEE RANGES PER WEEK
A $0-75
B $75-200
C $201-350
D $351-500
E $501-650
F over $650

Activities: Basketball, Computer, Counselor Training (CIT), Drama, Field Trips, Model Rocketry, Music, Photography, Radio/TV/Video, Swimming — Recreational
Session lengths & capacity: June-August; 2, 4, 6 & 8 week sessions; 250 campers
Clientele & fees: coed 8-17; Fees: D ☀ Fees: F ▲
Contact: Francesca Foti, Camp Director at (617) 625-2525; fax: (617) 625-5900
e-mail: camp@computered.com
Web site: www.computercamps.com
Operated by: Education Holdings Inc, 5 Middlesex Ave, Box 108, Somerville, MA 02145 at (617) 625-2525 (#4573)

Concord Academy Summer Camp (est 1970) ☀

Concord, MA (USA Co.); (978) 402-2284
Samantha Eustace, Director

Camp comments: We offer flexible one week sessions, camper choice & nurturing, fun adult head counselors. Tons of activities & events.
Activities: Archery, Arts/Crafts, Canoeing, Ceramics/Pottery, Field Trips, Leadership Development, Performing Arts, Sports — Field & Team, Swimming — Instructional, Tennis
Session lengths & capacity: June-August; 1 week sessions; 240 campers
Clientele & fees: coed 3-15; Fees: C ☀
Contact: Samantha Eustace, Camp Director at (978) 402-2284; fax: (978) 369-3452
e-mail: camp@concordacademy.org
Operated by: Concord Academy, 166 Main St, Concord, MA 01742 at (978) 369-6080 (#27990)

Danbee for Girls (est 1950) ▲ 🚗

Hinsdale, MA (Berkshire Co.); (413) 655-8115
Jay Toporoff, Director

Camp comments: Danbee features a caring staff that combine individual concern for each child & expert instruction in assigned programs.
Activities: Arts/Crafts, Challenge/Rope Courses, Dance, Gymnastics, Horseback — English, Soccer, Tennis, Waterskiing
Session lengths & capacity: 8 week sessions; 375 campers
Clientele & fees: girls 7-15; Fees: E ▲
Contact: Jay Toporoff, Director at (973) 402-0606; fax: (973) 402-1771
e-mail: campdanbee@aol.com
Web site: www.campgrp.com
Operated by: CampGroup, LLC, 3 New King St, White Plains, NY 10604 at (914) 997-2177 (#3240)

Drumlin Farm Day Camp
(est 1958) ☀

Lincoln, MA (Middlesex Co.); (781) 259-9506
Hannah M Freedberg, Director

Camp comments: A hands-on farm and nature experience. Campers explore farm, forest, and pond environments through age-appropriate activities.
Activities: Backpacking, Camping Skills/Outdoor Living, Canoeing, Counselor Training (CIT), Farming/Ranching/Gardening, Field Trips, Hiking, Nature/Environment Studies, Travel/Tour, Wilderness Trips
Session lengths & capacity: June-August; 1 & 2 week sessions; 200 campers
Clientele & fees: coed 4-15; families; Fees: B, C ☀ 🐷
Contact: Hannah Freedberg, Director at (781) 259-9506 ext. 7725; fax: (781) 259-1242
e-mail: hfreedberg@massaudubon.org
Web site: www.massaudubon.org
Operated by: Mass Audubon, 472 West Mountain Rd, Lenox, MA 01240 at (413) 637-0320 (#3808)

East Boston Camps (est 1937) ☀ ▲ 🏠

Westford, MA (Middlesex Co.); (978) 692-5126
Gloria DeVine, Director

Camp comments: 400 rustic acres w/private lake. General recreation camp emphasizing team building, self-esteem, promote a safe, healthy, relaxed atmosphere. Skilled staff.
Activities: Aquatic Activities, Archery, Arts/Crafts, Canoeing, Counselor Training (CIT), Nature/Environment Studies, Soccer, Swimming — Instructional, Swimming — Recreational
Session lengths & capacity: June-August; 1, 2 & 8 week sessions; 150 campers
Clientele & fees: boys 8-14; girls 8-14; coed 6-14; Fees: B ☀ Fees: B ▲ 🐷
Contact: Gloria DeVine, Camp Director at (617) 569-3221; fax: (617) 569-9862
e-mail: gloria.devine@bsoc.org
Web site: www.ebsoc.org
Operated by: East Boston Social Centers Inc, 68 Central Square, East Boston, MA 02128 at (617) 569-3221 (#2611)

Edith Read Girl Scout Center ☀ 🚗

Norton, MA (Bristol Co.); (508) 222-2585
Gail Sim, Director

Camp comments: Open to any girl,we offer programs to develop skills, confidence and encourage proactive learning. Fun that counts.
Activities: Aquatic Activities, Arts/Crafts, Boating, Camping Skills/Outdoor Living, Hiking, Leadership Development, Nature/Environment Studies, Swimming — Recreational, Team Building
Session lengths & capacity: June-August; 1 & 2 week sessions; 150 campers
Clientele & fees: girls 6-14; Fees: B ☀ 🐷
Contact: Sandra DeCosta, Info. Systems Asst at (508) 923-0800 ext. 46; fax: (508) 923-7676
e-mail: sdecosta@gscsm.org
Web site: www.gscsm.org
Operated by: GSC Southeastern Massachusetts, 111 East Grove St, Middleboro, MA 02346 at (508) 923-0800 (#10929)

Eisner Camp for Living Judaism
(est 1958) ☀ ▲ 🏠 🚗

Great Barrington, MA (Berkshire Co.); (413) 528-1652
Louis Bordman, Director

Camp comments: Beautiful Berkshire Mtn setting for Reform Jewish Camp. Full range of sports/arts & cultural programs.
Activities: Arts/Crafts, Bicycling/Biking, Canoeing, Challenge/Rope Courses, Drama, Leadership Development, Soccer, Swimming — Instructional, Swimming — Recreational, Tennis
Session lengths & capacity: 2, 4 & 8 week sessions; 425 campers
Clientele & fees: coed 7-17; families; Fees: B ☀ Fees: E ▲ 🐷
Contact: Louis Bordman, Director at (212) 650-4130; fax: (212) 650-4139
e-mail: eisnerguy@aol.com
Operated by: Union Of American Hebrew Cong, 633 Third Ave, New York, NY 10017 at (212) 650-4208

Group Rental Information
Facilities: Dorm-Style, Food Service, Lodges, Meeting Rooms, Playing Fields
Programs: Challenge/Ropes Course (#1894)

Elliott P. Joslin Camps
(est 1925) ▲ 🚗

Charlton, MA (Worcester Co.); (508) 248-5220
Brad MacDougall, Director

Camp comments: Camp emphasizing recreation, FUN, education, leadership for children with diabetes.

Activities: Basketball, Computer, Hockey, Radio/TV/Video, Skating, Sports — Field & Team, Tennis, Wilderness Trips
Session lengths & capacity: June-August; 1, 2 & 3 week sessions; 90 campers
Clientele & fees: boys 7-16; coed 4-18; Fees: F ⚠ 🐷
Contact: Stephanie Holloway, Camp Coordinator at (617) 732-2455; fax: (617) 735-1925
e-mail: camp@joslin.harvard.edu
Web site: www.joslin.org
Operated by: Joslin Camp Office and Clinic, One Joslin Place, Boston, MA 02215 at (617) 732-2455 (#4290)

Favorite (est 1962) ⚠ 🏠 🚗

Brewster, MA (Barnstable Co.); (617) 896-3431

Camp comments: Biking, sailing, and ocean exploration. Emphasis on cooperation not competition. Girls don't need to be Girl Scouts.
Activities: Bicycling/Biking, Boating, Camping Skills/Outdoor Living, Canoeing, Counselor Training (CIT), Leadership Development, Sailing, Swimming — Instructional, Swimming — Recreational, Windsurfing
Session lengths & capacity: June-August; 1 & 2 week sessions; 100 campers
Clientele & fees: girls 7-16; Fees: D ⚠ 🐷
Contact: Pat Stens, Program Manager at (617) 482-1078; fax: (617) 350-5246
e-mail: pstens@ptgirlscouts.org
Web site: www.ptgirlscouts.org
Operated by: Patriots Trail GSC, 95 Berkeley St, Boston, MA 02116 at (617) 350-8335
Group Rental Information
Site comments: Facilities available for youth groups. Must provide own equipment. No alcohol or smoking allowed.
Seasons & Capacity: Spring 200, Fall 200
Facilities: Lodges, Tents (#4126)

Felix Neck Natural History Cmp ☀

Vinyard Haven, MA; (508) 627-4850
Rebecca Taylor, Director
Activities: Aquatic Activities, Arts/Crafts, Canoeing, Hiking, Kayaking, Nature/Environment Studies, Team Building
Session lengths & capacity: June-August
Clientele & fees: 🐷
Contact: Rebecca Taylor, Camp Director at (508) 627-4850; fax: (508) 627-6052
e-mail: rtaylor@massaudbon.org
Web site: www.massaudubon.org
Operated by: Mass Audubon, 472 West Mountain Rd, Lenox, MA 01240 at (413) 637-0320 (#31323)

Fenn School Summer Day Camp ☀ 🚗

Concord, MA (Middlesex Co.); (978) 318-3614
David Platt, Director

Camp comments: General Camps: arts, adventure, sports, swim. Specialty Camps: ceramics, painting, wood, photo, vidoe. Trip Camps: Nature, adventure. Ropes, rock wall, pool.
Activities: Academics, Arts/Crafts, Ceramics/Pottery, Challenge/Rope Courses, Climbing/Rappelling, Community Service, Photography, Radio/TV/Video, Swimming — Instructional, Swimming — Recreational
Session lengths & capacity: June-August; 1/2, 1 & 2 week sessions; 200 campers
Clientele & fees: coed 6-15; Fees: D ☀ 🐷
Contact: David Platt, Director of Summer Programs at (978) 318-3614; fax: (978) 371-7520
e-mail: summercamp@fenn.org
Web site: www.fenn.org
Operated by: The Fenn School, 516 Monument Street, Concord, MA 01742-1894 at (978) 318-3614 (#43126)

Fessenden Day Camp

(est 1942) ☀ 🚗

West Newton, MA (Middlesex Co.); (617) 630-2373
Peter Sanderson, Director

Camp comments: Acclaimed all around program, specializing in the arts, sports, and swimming. Mature staff. 55 years of service.
Activities: Archery, Arts/Crafts, Ceramics/Pottery, Counselor Training (CIT), Dance, Drama, Music, Sports — Field & Team, Swimming — Instructional, Tennis
Session lengths & capacity: 4 & 8 week sessions; 320 campers
Clientele & fees: boys 4-12; girls 4-12; Fees: B, C ☀
Contact: Peter Sanderson, Director at (617) 630-2373; fax: (617) 630-2374
Operated by: Fessenden School, 250 Waltham Street, West Newton, MA 02465 at (617) 630-2373 (#4460)

Friendship (est 1995) ☀ 🚗

Boston, MA
Pat Stens, Director

Camp comments: General camp program. Swimming, arts, games. Explore the land and water on beautiful Duxbury Bay. Work on Girl Scout badges.
Activities: Aquatic Activities, Arts/Crafts, Camping Skills/Outdoor Living, Canoeing, Drama, Nature/Environment Studies, Swimming — Recreational
Session lengths & capacity: June-August; 1 week sessions; 125 campers
Clientele & fees: girls 6-12; Fees: B ☀ 🐷
Contact: Pat Stens, Program Manager at (617) 482-1078; fax: (617) 350-5246
e-mail: pstens@ptgirlscouts.org
Web site: www.ptgirlscouts.org
Operated by: Patriots Trail GSC, 95 Berkeley St, Boston, MA 02116 at (617) 350-8335 (#26)

Good News (est 1935) ☀ ⚠ 🏠

Forestdale, MA (Barnstable Co.); (508) 477-9731
Faith Willard, Director

Camp comments: Emphasize positive Christian values. Help young people discover the relevance of the Bible in our culture.
Activities: Aquatic Activities, Arts/Crafts, Boating, Computer, Music, Sailing, Soccer, Swimming — Instructional, Tennis
Session lengths & capacity: 2, 3 & 7 week sessions; 200 campers
Clientele & fees: boys 6-16; girls 6-16; coed 6-16; Fees: B ☀ Fees: C ⚠
Contact: Faith Willard, Director at (508) 477-9731; fax: (508) 477-8016
e-mail: faithwill@capecode.net
Operated by: Soc for Christian Activities, PO Box 1295, Forestdale, MA 02644 at (508) 477-9731 (#2607)

Green Eyrie (est 1925) ⚠ 🏠

Harvard, MA (Worcester Co.); (508) 456-3518

Camp comments: Outstanding staff to provide creative program on lakeside camp.
Activities: Aquatic Activities, Arts/Crafts, Boating, Camping Skills/Outdoor Living, Canoeing, Counselor Training (CIT), Swimming — Recreational
Session lengths & capacity: June-August; 1/2, 1 & 2 week sessions; 100 campers
Clientele & fees: girls 6-17; Fees: B ⚠ 🐷
Contact: Donna Lockington, Camp Administrator at (508) 853-1070; fax: (508) 852-7674
Operated by: Montachusett GSC, 81 Gold Star Blvd, Worcester, MA 01606 at (508) 853-1070 (#2577)

Hale Reservation Day Camp

(est 1987) ☀ 🏠

Westwood, MA (Norfolk Co.); (617) 326-1770
Maryellen Gill, Director

Camp comments: Beautiful 1200 acre setting. Traditional program which promotes a safe, warm environment where campers learn & have fun
Activities: Archery, Arts/Crafts, Boating, Challenge/Rope Courses, Music, Swimming — Instructional, Swimming — Recreational
Session lengths & capacity: June-August; 2 week sessions; 120 campers
Clientele & fees: coed 4-13; Fees: B ☀ 🐷
Contact: Maryellen Gill, Director at (781) 329-8107; fax: (781) 326-0676
e-mail: haleresrv@aol.com
Operated by: Hale Reservation Inc, PO Box 310, Westwood, MA 02090 at (781) 326-1770 (#254)

Handi Kids (est 1972) ☀

Bridgewater, MA (Plymouth Co.); (508) 697-7557
Mary Gallant, Director

Camp comments: Handi Kids offers a summer day camp to special children & yound adults. Camp runs Jul & Aug with 4 2-week sessions geared towards specific disabilities.
Activities: Boating, Computer, Counselor Training (CIT), Fishing, Horseback — English, Horseback — Western, Music, Soccer, Swimming — Recreational
Session lengths & capacity: July-August; 2 week sessions; 150 campers
Clientele & fees: coed 4-35; Fees: C ☀ 🐷
Contact: Denise Blumenthal, Executive Director at (508) 697-7557; fax: (508) 697-1529
e-mail: deniseb@handikids.com
Web site: www.handikids.com
Operated by: Handi Kids, 470 Pine Street, Bridgewater, MA 02324 at (508) 697-7557 (#4492)

Horizons For Youth ⚠ 🏠 🚗

(est 1938)

Sharon, MA (Norfolk Co.); (781) 828-7550
Allison McDonagh, Director

Camp comments: Supportive environment for children from challenging family situations. Individual attention/emphasis on group process.
Activities: Arts/Crafts, Camping Skills/Outdoor Living, Challenge/Rope Courses, Community Service, Hiking, Leadership Development, Nature/Environment Studies, Sports — Field & Team, Swimming — Instructional, Team Building
Session lengths & capacity: June-August; 1/2 & 2 week sessions; 200 campers
Clientele & fees: coed 7-14; Fees: D ⚠ 🐷
Contact: Allison McDonagh, Summer Program Director at (781) 828-7550; fax: (781) 784-1287
e-mail: ally@hfy.org
Web site: www.hfy.org
Operated by: Horizons For Youth Inc, 121 Lakeview St, Sharon, MA 02067 at (781) 828-7550
Group Rental Information
Site comments: Affordable rustic meeting space near Boston. Environmental education & team building available. Customized plans for your group.
Seasons & Capacity: Spring 175, Summer 20, Fall 175, Winter 80
Facilities: Cabins, Dorm-Style, Food Service, Hiking Trails, Lake, Lodges, Playing Fields, Tents
Programs: Challenge/Ropes Course, Environmental Education, Swimming (#4450)

Ipswich River Day Camp

(est 1951) ☀

Topsfield, MA (Essex Co.); (978) 887-9264
Bob Speare, Director

Camp comments: Ipswich River Day Camp offers natural history programs for children with emphasis on field, forest & pond communities.

Activities: Arts/Crafts, Canoeing, Counselor Training (CIT), Field Trips, Hiking, Nature/Environment Studies
Session lengths & capacity: June-August; 1 & 2 week sessions; 45 campers
Clientele & fees: coed 4-14; Fees: **B, C** ☀ 🚐
Contact: Bob Speare, Camp Coordinator at (978) 887-9264; fax: (978) 887-0875
e-mail: bspeare@massaudubon.org
Web site: www.massaudubon.org
Operated by: Mass Audubon, 472 West Mountain Rd, Lenox, MA 01240 at (413) 637-0320 (#3048)

Lakeside Christian Camp

(est 1980) ⛺ 🏠

Pittsfield, MA (Berkshire Co.); (413) 447-8930
Mark Watkins, Director

Camp comments: Caring staff providing a fun, varied program in a Christ-centered setting. On Richmond Pond in the beautiful Berkshires.
Activities: Aquatic Activities, Arts/Crafts, Canoeing, Drama, Model Rocketry, Sailing, Sports — Field & Team, Swimming — Recreational, Waterskiing
Session lengths & capacity: June-August; 1/2, 1 & 2 week sessions; 170 campers
Clientele & fees: coed 5-18; families; Fees: **C** ⛺ 🚐
Contact: Cindy Morgan, Director of Guest Services at (413) 447-8930; fax: (413) 447-8934
e-mail: guestservices@lakesideonline.org
Web site: www.lakesideonline.org
Operated by: Northeast Baptist Conf BGC, 195 Cloverdale Street, Pittsfield, MA 01201 at (413) 447-8930

Group Rental Information
Site comments: Retreat facilities in a beautiful setting. Comfortable lodging, flexible meeting spaces, excellent meals, and recreational options.
Seasons & Capacity: Spring 180, Winter 180
Facilities: A/V Equipment, Dorm-Style, Double Occupancy, Food Service, Lake, Linens, Lodges, Meeting Rooms, Playing Fields
Programs: Boating, Challenge/Ropes Course, Swimming (#2177)

Lapham (est 1936) ⛺ 🚗

Ashby, MA (Middlesex Co.); (978) 386-5633
Aileen Traynor, Director

Camp comments: Small, family-like community which builds self-concept & self awareness in a peaceful camp setting.
Activities: Academics, Archery, Arts/Crafts, Bicycling/Biking, Boating, Leadership Development, Nature/Environment Studies, Swimming — Instructional, Team Building

---

ICON LEGEND

☀ Day Camp

⛺ Resident Camp

🏠 Facilities Available To Rent

🚗 Transportation Available

🚐 Financial Aid Available

FEE RANGES PER WEEK

A $0-75

B $75-200

C $201-350

D $351-500

E $501-650

F over $650

Session lengths & capacity: 2 & 3 week sessions; 50 campers
Clientele & fees: coed 7-12;
Fees: **A, B, C, D** ⛺ 🚐
Contact: Aileen Orrego, Director at (781) 834-2700; fax: (781) 834-2701
e-mail: aorrego@crossroads4kids.org
Web site: www.crossroads4kids.org
Operated by: Crossroads For Kids Inc, 119 Myrtle St, Duxbury, MA 02332 at (781) 834-2700 (#4320)

Laughing Brook Natural History

(est 1979) ☀

Hampden, MA (Hampden Co.); (413) 566-8034
Jane McCarry, Director

Camp comments: Nature education camp at wildlife sanctuary. Encourages noncompetitive, age-appropriate outdoor activities.
Activities: Arts/Crafts, Counselor Training (CIT), Hiking, Nature/Environment Studies
Session lengths & capacity: June-August; 1 & 2 week sessions; 52 campers
Clientele & fees: coed 4-11; Fees: **A, B** ☀ 🚐
Contact: Jane McCarry, Camp Director at (413) 566-8034; fax: (413) 566-5322
e-mail: laughbrook@massaudubon.org
Web site: www.massaudubon.org
Operated by: Mass Audubon, 472 West Mountain Rd, Lenox, MA 01240 at (413) 637-0320 (#3061)

Lenox (est 1918) ⛺ 🚗

Lee, MA (Berkshire Co.); (413) 243-2223
Richard Moss, Director

Camp comments: Top level instruction in all team & indiv sports. Camp spirit, warmth - full aquatics on Mt Lake. Emphasis on values & community.
Activities: Baseball/Softball, Basketball, Golf, Hockey, Sailing, Soccer, Tennis, Waterskiing, Windsurfing
Session lengths & capacity: 6 & 8 week sessions; 330 campers
Clientele & fees: boys 7-16; girls 7-16; Fees: **F** ⛺
Contact: Richard Moss, Director at (954) 340-6634; fax: (954) 340-8282
Operated by: Camp Lenox, PO Box 75-9900, Coral Springs, FL 33075 at (954) 340-6634 (#2004)

Mah-Kee-Nac (est 1929) ⛺ 🏠 🚗

Lenox, MA (Berkshire Co.); (413) 637-0781
Danny & Nancy Metzger, Director

Camp comments: An all around, traditional camp with an emphasis on sports & instruction in a warm, supportive atmosphere.
Activities: Baseball/Softball, Basketball, Bicycling/Biking, Challenge/Rope Courses, Field Trips, Golf, Soccer, Swimming — Instructional, Tennis, Waterskiing
Session lengths & capacity: June-August; 8 week sessions; 375 campers
Clientele & fees: boys 7-16; Fees: **F** ⛺
Contact: Danny Metzger, Owner/Director at (973) 429-8522; fax: (973) 429-1394
e-mail: campmkn@campmkn.com
Web site: www.campgrp.com
Operated by: CampGroup, LLC, 3 New King St, White Plains, NY 10604 at (914) 997-2177 (#2116)

Maplewood Country Day Camp

(est 1965) ☀ 🚗

S Easton, MA (Bristol Co.); (508) 238-2387
Lee & Susan Pinstein, Director

Camp comments: Outstanding facilities & staff. Active program including land & water sports. Effort - not competition is stressed.
Activities: Arts/Crafts, Boating, Dance, Golf, Gymnastics, Horseback — English, Martial Arts, Sports — Field & Team, Swimming — Instructional, Tennis

Session lengths & capacity: June-August; 2, 4, 6 & 8 week sessions; 250 campers
Clientele & fees: coed 4-14; Fees: **C** ☀
Contact: Susan Pinstein, Co-Director at (508) 238-6758; fax: (508) 230-9872
e-mail: funatmaplewood@mediaone.net
Web site: www.maplewooddaycamp.com
Operated by: Maplewood Country Day Camp, 15 Aspen Hollow Drive, North Easton, MA 02356 at (508) 238-6758 (#2622)

Mass Audubon Discovery Day Cmp

☀

Marshfield, MA; (781) 837-9400
Ellyn Einhorn, Director
Activities: Arts/Crafts, Canoeing, Field Trips, Hiking, Kayaking, Nature/Environment Studies
Contact: Web site: www.massaudubon.org
Operated by: Mass Audubon, 472 West Mountain Rd, Lenox, MA 01240 at (413) 637-0320 (#44829)

Maude Eaton (est 1940) ☀ 🏠

Andover, MA; (978) 689-8015
Peg Juppe, Director

Camp comments: Nestled in a beautiful pine forest on a pond. Program focuses on helping girls grow strong with opportunity to try new skills & share within a safe environment.
Activities: Aquatic Activities, Archery, Arts/Crafts, Boating, Camping Skills/Outdoor Living, Canoeing, Challenge/Rope Courses, Hiking, Nature/Environment Studies, Swimming — Recreational
Session lengths & capacity: June-August; 1 & 2 week sessions; 184 campers
Clientele & fees: girls 5-14; Fees: **B** ☀
Contact: Karyn L Martin, Director of Outdoor Program at (978) 689-8015; fax: (978) 688-1846
e-mail: kmartin@ssgsc.org
Web site: www.ssgsc.org
Operated by: Girl Scouts Spar & Spindle, 1740 Turnpike Street, North Andover, MA 01845 at (978) 689-8015

Group Rental Information
Seasons & Capacity: Spring 75, Summer 75, Fall 75, Winter 75
Facilities: Cabins, Double Occupancy, Hiking Trails, Kitchen Facilities, Lake, Lodges, Meeting Rooms
Programs: Boating, Challenge/Ropes Course, Environmental Education, Swimming (#1785)

Meadowbrook Day Camp

(est 1950) ☀ 🚗

Weston, MA (Middlesex Co.); (781) 647-0546
Daniel E Hanlon IV, Director

Camp comments: Meadowbrook offers a warm, supportive environment. Mature staff, superior facilites. Structured, varied, high quality program with outstanding swim program.
Activities: Archery, Arts/Crafts, Camping Skills/Outdoor Living, Ceramics/Pottery, Challenge/Rope Courses, Drama, Music, Nature/Environment Studies, Sports — Field & Team, Swimming — Instructional
Session lengths & capacity: 4 & 8 week sessions; 375 campers
Clientele & fees: coed 5-13; Fees: **C** ☀ 🚐
Contact: Daniel Hanlon at (781) 647-0546; fax: (781) 894-0557
e-mail: meadowbrook@excite.com
Web site: www.meadowbrook-ma.org/daycamp
Operated by: Meadowbrook School Of Weston, 10 Farm Rd, Weston, MA 02493 at (781) 647-0546 (#2800)

Meadowcroft (est 1938)

Norwell, MA (Plymouth Co.); (781) 659-2362
James & Eileen Kelly, Director

Camp comments: Strong swimming, soccer, arts, music, nature, woodworking, gymnastics, theater, trips. Voted best camp on South Shore for 2000.
Activities: Archery, Arts/Crafts, Counselor Training (CIT), Drama, Field Trips, Music, Nature/Environment Studies, Soccer, Swimming — Instructional, Tennis
Session lengths & capacity: June-August; 2 & 3 week sessions; 350 campers
Clientele & fees: coed 4-15; Fees: C
Contact: James & Eileen Kelly, Directors at (781) 659-2362; fax: (781) 659-7434
Operated by: Meadowcroft, 260 Bowker St, Norwell, MA 02061 at (781) 659-2362 (#2600)

Moose Hill Nature Day Camp
(est 1945)

Sharon, MA (Norfolk Co.); (781) 784-5691
Kay Andberg, Director

Camp comments: Weekly themes focus on the environment through hands-on exploration. Specialty art or adventure programs for ages 9-15.
Activities: Arts/Crafts, Boating, Canoeing, Drawing/Painting, Hiking, Nature/Environment Studies
Session lengths & capacity: June-August; 1 & 2 week sessions; 88 campers
Clientele & fees: coed 4-17; Fees: B, C
Contact: Kay Andberg, Director at (781) 784-5691; fax: (781) 784-9153
e-mail: kandberg@massaudubon.org
Web site: www.massaudubon.org
Operated by: Mass Audubon, 472 West Mountain Rd, Lenox, MA 01240 at (413) 637-0320

Group Rental Information
Seasons & Capacity: Spring 120, Summer 120, Fall 120, Winter 120
Facilities: Hiking Trails, Meeting Rooms
Programs: Environmental Education (#3542)

Morgan Memorial Fresh Air Camp (est 1906)

South Athol, MA (Worcester Co.); (508) 249-4001
Diana Donnelly, Director

Camp comments: Philosophy: provide a creative, recreational, learning experience, create a positive sense of community, foster personal growth.
Activities: Academics, Aquatic Activities, Arts/Crafts, Bicycling/Biking, Drama, Fishing, Leadership Development, Nature/Environment Studies, Swimming — Recreational
Session lengths & capacity: 2 week sessions; 150 campers
Clientele & fees: coed 8-16; Fees: B
Contact: Diana Donnelly, Director Camp & Community Serv at (617) 541-1408 ext. 1434;
Operated by: Morgan Memorial Goodwill Ind, 1010 Harrison Avenue, Boston, MA 02119 at (617) 541-1408 (#7454)

Mount Ida Day Camp (est 1930)

Newton Center, MA (Middlesex Co.);
(617) 969-8334
Steve D'Arcy, Director

Camp comments: Day Camp offers warm atmosphere, sports activities, arts & crafts. Strong swim program on beautiful secluded 85 acre campus.
Activities: Archery, Arts/Crafts, Baseball/Softball, Basketball, Drawing/Painting, Soccer, Sports — Field & Team, Swimming — Instructional, Tennis
Session lengths & capacity: June-August; 2, 3, 4, 5, 6, 7 & 8 week sessions; 450 campers
Clientele & fees: boys 4-13; girls 4-13; Fees: C
Contact: Steve D'Arcy, Director at (617) 969-8334; fax: (617) 928-4049

e-mail: scdarcy@mountida.edu
Web site: www.mountida.edu
Operated by: Mount Ida College, 777 Dedham St, Newton Centre, MA 02459 at (617) 969-8334 (#4110)

Nashoba Day Camp (est 1957)

Littleton, MA (Midddlesex Co.); (978) 486-3916
Jean Seaward, Director

Camp comments: A traditional camp with professional and caring staff. Transportation included, extended day p.m
Activities: Aquatic Activities, Archery, Arts/Crafts, Ceramics/Pottery, Drama, Horseback — English, Nature/Environment Studies, Soccer, Swimming — Instructional, Tennis
Session lengths & capacity: 4 & 8 week sessions; 250 campers
Clientele & fees: coed 4-14; Fees: D
Contact: Bob & Jean Seaward, Co-Owner Directors at (978) 486-3916; fax: (978) 486-9812
e-mail: nashobaday@aol.com
Operated by: The Seaward Family I, 140 Nashoba Rd, Littleton, MA 01460 at (978) 486-3916 (#2661)

New England Keswick (est 1941)

Monterey, MA (Berkshire Co.); (413) 528-3604
Richard Haapenen, Director

Camp comments: Nondenominational Christian youth camp, 253 high elevation acres in the Berkshire Hills. Ages 7-18.
Activities: Aquatic Activities, Archery, Arts/Crafts, Canoeing, Challenge/Rope Courses, Hiking, Horseback — Western, Music, Sports — Field & Team, Waterskiing
Session lengths & capacity: June-August; 1 week sessions; 110 campers
Clientele & fees: coed 7-18; Fees: C
Contact: Richard Haapanen, Executive Director at (413) 528-3604; fax: (413) 528-3604
e-mail: keswickt@berkshire.net
Web site: www.nekeswick.com
Operated by: New England Keswick Inc, PO Box 156, Monterey, MA 01245-0156 at (413) 528-3604

Group Rental Information
Site comments: Nondenominational Christian retreat center for youth, men, women, and families who are in keeping with our statement of faith.
Seasons & Capacity: Spring 160, Fall 160, Winter 160
Facilities: A/V Equipment, Cabins, Dorm-Style, Food Service, Hiking Trails, Kitchen Facilities, Lake, Lodges, Meeting Rooms, Playing Fields, Pool
Programs: Boating, Challenge/Ropes Course, Swimming, Winter Sports (#585)

Newman YMCA Summer Camp

Seekonk, MA; (508) 336-7103
Laurie Pansa, Director

Camp comments: To put christian principles into practice through programs that build a healthy spirit, mind and body for all.
Activities: Arts/Crafts, Clowning, Computer, Counselor Training (CIT), Drawing/Painting, Leadership Development, Nature/Environment Studies, Sports — Field & Team, Swimming — Recreational, Travel/Tour
Session lengths & capacity: June-August; 1 week sessions; 450 campers
Clientele & fees: coed 5-15; Fees: B
Contact: Laurie Pansa, Camping Services Director at (508) 336-7103; fax: (508) 336-2166
e-mail: lpansa@gpymca.org
Operated by: YMCA Gtr Providence Camping, 70 Ship St, Providence, RI 02903 at (401) 521-9622 (#40112)

Newton Community Day Camp

Westwood, MA; (781) 326-7380
Jennifer Capello, Director

Camp comments: Located at Hale Reservation. Campers benefit from a beautiful 1200 acre setting. Program promotes confidence & independence, learn to make friends & have fun.
Activities: Archery, Arts/Crafts, Canoeing, Counselor Training (CIT), Kayaking, Swimming — Instructional, Swimming — Recreational
Session lengths & capacity: June-August; 9 week sessions; 90 campers
Clientele & fees: coed 5-14; Fees: B
Contact: Jennifer Capello, Camp Director at (617) 969-5906 ext. 131; fax: (617) 964-3975
e-mail: jennifercapello@hotmail.com
Web site: www.ncsc.org
Operated by: Newton Community Service Ctr, 492 Waltham St, West Newton, MA 02465-1920 at (617) 969-5906 (#10595)

Nobles Day Camp (est 1948)

Dedham, MA (Norfolk Co.); (781) 320-1320
John Lee, Director

Camp comments: Multi-specialty camp. Children make choices. Swim program. Noncompetitive atmosphere. Popular Owl's nest for 4&5 yrs old
Activities: Archery, Ceramics/Pottery, Challenge/Rope Courses, Dance, Gymnastics, Music, Nature/Environment Studies, Soccer, Swimming — Instructional, Swimming — Recreational
Session lengths & capacity: June-August; 2, 4, 6 & 8 week sessions; 720 campers
Clientele & fees: coed 4-14; Fees: D
Contact: B.J. Caouette, Associate Director at (781) 320-1320; fax: (781) 329-8118
e-mail: bj_caouette@nobles.edu
Web site: www.nobles.edu/summer/ndc
Operated by: Noble and Greenough School, 10 Campus Drive, Dedham, MA 02026 at (781) 320-1320 (#10386)

OVERLAND (est 1985)

Williamstown, MA; (413) 458-9672
Tom Costley and Brooks Follansbee, Director

Camp comments: Overland offers hiking, bicycle touring & mountain biking to boys & girls ages 13-18 in New England, the West & Europe.
Activities: Backpacking, Bicycling/Biking, Camping Skills/Outdoor Living, Community Service, Hiking, Kayaking, Leadership Development, Rafting, Team Building, Wilderness Trips
Session lengths & capacity: June-August; 2, 4 & 6 week sessions; 650 campers
Clientele & fees: coed 13-18; Fees: F
Contact: Tom Costley, Director at (413) 458-9672; fax: (413) 458-5208
e-mail: overland@adelphia.net
Web site: www.overlandadventures.com
Operated by: Overland Travel, Inc, PO Box 31, Williamstown, MA 01267 at (413) 458-9672 (#383)

Pembroke (est 1936)

Pembroke, MA (Plymouth Co.); (781) 294-8006
Leslie Brenner, Director

Camp comments: Warm caring environment/heated Olympic pool/Judaic prog/kosher/modern facilities/located at gateway to Cape Cod.
Activities: Arts/Crafts, Ceramics/Pottery, Dance, Drama, Field Trips, Horseback — Western, Sailing, Swimming — Instructional, Tennis, Waterskiing
Session lengths & capacity: 4 & 8 week sessions; 275 campers
Clientele & fees: girls 7-15; Fees: D

Contact: Pearl W Lourie, Executive Director at (508) 881-1002; fax: (508) 881-1006 e-mail: cohencamps@aol.com
Operated by: Cohen Foundation, 30 Main Street, Ashland, MA 01721 at (508) 881-1002 (#4490)

Pennacook

Rowley, MA; (978) 689-8015
Kelly Porcaro, Director

Camp comments: 200 acres of forest with nice facilities incl. a pool. Program focuses on helping girls to grow strong through skill development & sharing in a safe environment
Activities: Archery, Arts/Crafts, Camping Skills/Outdoor Living, Nature/Environment Studies, Sports — Field & Team, Swimming — Instructional, Swimming — Recreational
Session lengths & capacity: July-August; 1 & 2 week sessions; 184 campers
Clientele & fees: girls 7-17; Fees: **B**
Contact: Karyn L Martin, Director of Outdoor Program at (978) 689-8015; fax: (978) 688-1846 e-mail: kmartin@ssgsc.org
Web site: www.ssgsc.org
Operated by: Girl Scouts Spar & Spindle, 1740 Turnpike Street, North Andover, MA 01845 at (978) 689-8015
Group Rental Information
Seasons & Capacity: Spring 80, Summer 80, Fall 80, Winter 80
Facilities: Cabins, Hiking Trails, Kitchen Facilities, Lodges, Meeting Rooms, Pool, Tents
Programs: Environmental Education, Swimming (#3249)

Pingree Experience (est 1985)

South Hamilton, MA (Essex Co.); (978) 468-5121
Greg West & Eileen Araneo, Director

Camp comments: Pingree experience offers an outstanding staff, a wide range of activity & a beautiful country location.
Activities: Archery, Arts/Crafts, Boating, Ceramics/Pottery, Computer, Dance, Drama, Gymnastics, Sports — Field & Team, Swimming — Instructional
Session lengths & capacity: June-August; 2 week sessions; 280 campers
Clientele & fees: coed 4-15; Fees: **B**
Contact: Greg West or Eileen Araneo, Camp Directors at (978) 468-5121; fax: (978) 468-3758 e-mail: gwest@massed.net
Web site: www.homepage.mac.com/pingreecamp
Operated by: The Pingree School, 537 Highland St, South Hamilton, MA 01982 at (978) 468-4415 (#2189)

ICON LEGEND

☀	Day Camp
▲	Resident Camp
⌂	Facilities Available To Rent
🚗	Transportation Available
🐷	Financial Aid Available

FEE RANGES PER WEEK

A	$0-75
B	$75-200
C	$201-350
D	$351-500
E	$501-650
F	over $650

Pleasant Valley Day Camp

(est 1948)

Lenox, MA (Berkshire Co.); (413) 637-0320
Rene Laubach, Director

Camp comments: Since 1948, set on 1400 acres of forest, meadows, brooks, mountains and exciting beaver lodges. Related nature games, songs and crafts. Outdoor labs for kids.
Activities: Arts/Crafts, Backpacking, Camping Skills/Outdoor Living, Counselor Training (CIT), Hiking, Nature/Environment Studies, Team Building, Wilderness Trips
Session lengths & capacity: June-August; 1 & 2 week sessions; 48 campers
Clientele & fees: coed 6-18; Fees: **C**
Contact: Deborah Rawson, Office Manager at (413) 637-0320; fax: (413) 637-0499 e-mail: drawson@massaudubon.org
Web site: www.massaudubon.org
Operated by: Mass Audubon, 472 West Mountain Rd, Lenox, MA 01240 at (413) 637-0320

Group Rental Information
Site comments: Newly renovated barn with deck provides a comfortable atmosphere in a spectacular nature setting. Includes sanctuary admission fees, setup of tables & chairs.
Seasons & Capacity: Spring 80, Summer 80, Fall 80, Winter 80
Facilities: A/V Equipment, Hiking Trails, Meeting Rooms, River
Programs: Boating, Environmental Education, Winter Sports (#25272)

Pompositticut Farm Day Camp

(est 1980)

Hudson, MA (Middlesex Co.); (978) 562-0968
Jacqueline Kane, Director

Camp comments: Small private camp on farm all inclusive activities staff ratio of 3:1 experiential learning philosophy with prof staff.
Activities: Archery, Arts/Crafts, Challenge/Rope Courses, Climbing/Rappelling, Counselor Training (CIT), Drama, Horseback — English, Performing Arts, Sports — Field & Team, Swimming — Instructional
Session lengths & capacity: June-August; 2, 4 & 8 week sessions; 96 campers
Clientele & fees: coed 4-12; Fees: **C**
Contact: Jacqueline Kane, Owner/Director at (978) 562-0968; fax: (978) 568-8831 e-mail: mail@pompositticutfarm.com
Web site: www.pompositticutfarm.com
Operated by: Pompositticut Farm Day Camp, 25 Lewis St, Hudson, MA 01749 at (978) 562-0968 (#27155)

Ponkapoag Outdoor Center

(est 1929)

Boston, MA; (781) 575-9905
Jennifer Christian, Director

Camp comments: Values programming at our 25 wooded acres in Blue Hills, 20 min. from Boston. Transportation and lunch provided
Activities: Archery, Arts/Crafts, Basketball, Dance, Hiking, Leadership Development, Nature/Environment Studies, Sports — Field & Team, Swimming — Instructional, Swimming — Recreational
Session lengths & capacity: June-August; 1, 2, 3, 4, 5, 6, 7, 8 & 9 week sessions; 190 campers
Clientele & fees: coed 6-15; Fees: **B**
Contact: Jennifer Christian, Director at (781) 575-9905; fax: (781) 575-1222 e-mail: jchristian@ymcaboston.org
Web site: www.ymcaboston.org
Operated by: YMCA Grtr Boston Camp Serv Br, 316 Huntington Ave, Boston, MA 02115 at (617) 927-8220 (#27464)

Ponkawissett (est 1975)

Westwood, MA (Norfolk Co.); (781) 329-8547
Dianne Allen, Director

Camp comments: Camp Ponkawissett is a traditional outdoor day camp serving a diverse poplation of children in a community that fosters self-esteem and social skills.
Activities: Arts/Crafts, Basketball, Boating, Canoeing, Counselor Training (CIT), Leadership Development, Nature/Environment Studies, Soccer, Swimming — Instructional, Swimming — Recreational
Session lengths & capacity: July-August; 2 week sessions; 100 campers
Clientele & fees: coed 7-13; Fees: **B**
Contact: (617) 523-6006 ext. 21; fax: (617) 523-6290 e-mail: info@campfireusa-emass.org
Web site: www.campfireusa-emass.org
Operated by: Camp Fire USA Eastern MA Cncl, 108 Union Wharf, Boston, MA 02109 at (617) 523-6006 (#2650)

Ramah In New England

(est 1954)

Palmer, MA; (413) 283-9771
Billy Mencow, Director

Camp comments: Jewish educational camp in a fun setting. Conservative movement.
Activities: Arts/Crafts, Camping Skills/Outdoor Living, Field Trips, Language Studies, Leadership Development, Performing Arts, Sports — Field & Team
Session lengths & capacity: 4 & 8 week sessions
Clientele & fees: coed 9-16; Fees: **D** ▲
Contact: Raylea Pemstein, Registrar at (781) 449-7090; fax: (781) 449-6331 e-mail: rayleap@campramahne.org
Operated by: Ramah In New England, 35 Highland Circle, Needham Heights, MA 02494 at (718) 449-7090
Group Rental Information
Facilities: A/V Equipment, Cabins, Dorm-Style, Food Service, Hiking Trails, Kitchen Facilities, Lake, Lodges, Meeting Rooms, Playing Fields
Programs: Boating, Swimming (#2191)

Rice Moody (est 1963)

Reading, MA (Middlesex Co.); (617) 482-1078

Camp comments: Wooded suburban site including swimming pool. Emphasis on cooperation not competition.
Activities: Arts/Crafts, Camping Skills/Outdoor Living, Drama, Music, Nature/Environment Studies, Swimming — Recreational
Session lengths & capacity: June-August; 1 week sessions; 100 campers
Clientele & fees: girls 6-12; Fees: **C**
Contact: Pat Stens, Program Manager at (617) 482-1078; fax: (617) 350-5246 e-mail: pstens@ptgirlscouts.org
Web site: www.ptgirlscouts.org
Operated by: Patriots Trail GSC, 95 Berkeley St, Boston, MA 02116 at (617) 350-8335
Group Rental Information
Seasons & Capacity: Spring 45, Fall 45, Winter 45
Facilities: Lodges (#4330)

Rivers Day Camp (est 1963)

Weston, MA (Middlesex Co.); (781) 235-9300
Paul & Mark Licht, Director

Camp comments: Located on a 52 acre spring-fed pond. General camp with CIT program, transportation, extended day, and hot lunches.
Activities: Archery, Arts/Crafts, Canoeing, Computer, Counselor Training (CIT), Sailing, Sports — Field & Team, Swimming — Instructional, Tennis
Session lengths & capacity: June-August; 4, 6 & 8 week sessions; 450 campers

Clientele & fees: coed 4-15; Fees: **C** ☀
Contact: Kathy Bass, Managing Director at
(781) 235-9300 ext. 293; fax: (781) 239-3614
e-mail: k.bass@rivers.org
Web site: www.rivers.org
Operated by: The Rivers School Corp, 333 Winter
St, Weston, MA 02493-1040 at (781) 235-9300
(#2706)

Salvation Army Camp Wonderland (est 1924) ⛺ 🚗

Sharon, MA (Norfolk Co.); (781) 784-5934
Captain Eduardo Zuniga, Director

Camp comments: Christian emphasis traditional
camp program serving the disadvantaged &
underprivileged youth of Massachusetts.
Activities: Arts/Crafts, Basketball, Camping
Skills/Outdoor Living, Canoeing, Challenge/Rope
Courses, Music, Nature/Environment Studies,
Soccer, Sports — Field & Team, Swimming —
Recreational
Session lengths & capacity: June-August; 1 week
sessions; 216 campers
Clientele & fees: boys 6-12; girls 6-12; coed 6-12;
Fees: **B** ⛺
Contact: Eduardo Zuniga, Camp Director at
(617) 542-5420; fax: (617) 542-6356
Operated by: The Salvation Army, 147 Berkeley St,
Boston, MA 02116 at (617) 542-5420 (#4380)

Sayre ☀ 🚗

Milton, MA (Norfolk Co.); (617) 482-1078
Donna Lee Washburn, Director

Camp comments: Located in Miltons Blue Hills.
Transportation from Greater Boston communities.
Emphasis on cooperation not competition.
Activities: Arts/Crafts, Camping Skills/Outdoor
Living, Hiking, Music, Nature/Environment Studies,
Swimming — Recreational
Session lengths & capacity: June-August; 1 week
sessions; 100 campers
Clientele & fees: girls 6-12; Fees: **C** ☀ 🚐
Contact: Pat Stens, Program Manager at
(617) 482-1078; fax: (617) 350-5246
e-mail: pstens@ptgirlscouts.org
Web site: www.ptgirlscouts.org
Operated by: Patriots Trail GSC, 95 Berkeley St,
Boston, MA 02116 at (617) 350-8335 (#18151)

Shady Hill Day Camp ☀

Cambridge, MA; (617) 520-9390
Activities: Swimming — Instructional, Swimming —
Recreational
Contact: Web site: www.shs.org
Operated by: Shady Hill School, 178 Coolidge Hill,
Cambridge, MA 02138 at (617) 868-1260 (#49325)

Sharon Country Day Camp

(est 1963) ☀ 🚗

Walpole, MA (Norfolk Co.); (781) 784-3057
Charles A Hershman, Director

Camp comments: 'We are family'-mature,caring
staff;beautiful camp
setting,aquatics,sports,arts,nature,ropes
course,overnights.We build skills & self-reliance
through fun & adv
Activities: Archery, Arts/Crafts, Baseball/Softball,
Basketball, Challenge/Rope Courses, Gymnastics,
Nature/Environment Studies, Performing Arts,
Soccer, Swimming — Instructional
Session lengths & capacity: July-August; 4 &
8 week sessions; 300 campers
Clientele & fees: coed 5-14; Fees: **C** ☀
Contact: Charles A Hershman, Director at
(617) 784-3057; fax: (617) 784-4139
Web site: www.shacounda.com
Operated by: Sharon Country Day Camp, 438 S
Main St, Sharon, MA 02067 at (781) 784-3057
(#2772)

Shire Village Camp (est 1972) ⛺

Cummington, MA; (413) 634-2281
Margaret Lopez and David Arnstein, Director

Camp comments: Non-competitive and inter-racial
camp that encourages humanistic values.
Activities: Arts/Crafts, Camping Skills/Outdoor
Living, Canoeing, Drama,
Farming/Ranching/Gardening, Horseback —
English, Nature/Environment Studies, Photography,
Sports — Field & Team, Swimming — Recreational
Session lengths & capacity: 3, 4 & 7 week
sessions; 90 campers
Clientele & fees: coed 8-14; Fees: **E** ⛺ 🚐
Contact: Beth Schneider, Registrar at
(718) 622-8204;
e-mail: beths@mmcl.net
Operated by: Shire Village Camp Inc, 175 Eastern
Parkway Apt 65, Brooklyn, NY 11238 at
(718) 622-8204 (#7056)

Springfield Boys Club Camp

(est 1920) ⛺

Brimfield, MA (Hampden Co.); (413) 245-7616

Camp comments: Recreational camping for youth
with a special emphasis for youth from
disadvantaged circumstances.
Activities: Aquatic Activities, Arts/Crafts, Camping
Skills/Outdoor Living, Hiking, Nature/Environment
Studies, Swimming — Instructional, Swimming —
Recreational, Team Building
Session lengths & capacity: July-August; 2 week
sessions; 90 campers
Clientele & fees: coed 7-13; Fees: **E** ⛺
Contact: Charles Hollins, Assistant Executive
Director at (413) 732-7201; fax: (413) 736-2620
e-mail: hollins@sbgc.org
Operated by: Springfield Boys & Girls Club, 481
Carew St, Springfield, MA 01104 at (413) 732-7201
(#2615)

Stony Brook Nat'l Hsty Day Camp (est 1967) ☀

Norfolk, MA; (508) 528-3140
Marla Cohen, Director

Camp comments: Campers discover nature's
beauty & complexity through trail explorations,
hands-on activities, and noncompetitive games.
Activities: Arts/Crafts, Counselor Training (CIT),
Hiking, Nature/Environment Studies
Session lengths & capacity: June-August; 1 week
sessions; 45 campers
Clientele & fees: coed 5-12; Fees: **B** ☀ 🚐
Contact: Michelle Grzenda, Day Camp
Director/Naturalist at (508) 528-3140;
fax: (508) 553-3864
e-mail: stonybrook@massaudbon.org
Web site: www.massaudbon.org
Operated by: Mass Audubon, 472 West Mountain
Rd, Lenox, MA 01240 at (413) 637-0320 (#10150)

Student Hosteling Program Inc

(est 1970) ⛺ 🚗

Conway, MA (Franklin Co.); (800) 343-6132
Ted Lefkowitz, Director

Camp comments: Bicycle touring adventures
through the countrysides and cultural centers of the
world for teenagers.
Activities: Aerobics/Exercise, Bicycling/Biking,
Camping Skills/Outdoor Living, Hiking, International
Culture, Leadership Development, Travel/Tour,
Wilderness Trips
Session lengths & capacity: June-August; 2, 3, 4,
5, 6, 7 & 8 week sessions; 500 campers
Clientele & fees: coed 12-18; Fees: **D, E, F** ⛺
Contact: Ted Lefkowitz, Director at (800) 343-6132;
fax: (413) 369-4257
e-mail: shpbike@aol.com
Web site: www.bicycletrips.com

Operated by: Student Hosteling Program,
PO Box 419, Conway, MA 01341-0419 at
(800) 343-6132 (#3262)

Summers Edge Day Camp

(est 1991) ☀

Waltham, MA (Middlesex Co.); (781) 391-3343
Ann Marie Gallo, Director

Camp comments: Warm & friendly atmosphere,
professional certified caring staff. Extended day
services available from 7:30am to 5:30pm.
Activities: Aerobics/Exercise, Archery, Arts/Crafts,
Camping Skills/Outdoor Living, Golf, Leadership
Development, Soccer, Sports — Field & Team,
Swimming — Instructional, Tennis
Session lengths & capacity: 2, 4 & 8 week
sessions; 90 campers
Clientele & fees: coed 3-14; Fees: **B** ☀
Contact: Ann Marie Gallo, Owner/Camp Director at
(781) 391-3343;
Operated by: Summers Edge Day Camp, 342 Main
Street, Medford, MA 02155 at (781) 391-3343 (#92)

Sunset Point Camp (est 1919) ⛺ 🚗

Hull, MA (Plymouth Co.); (781) 925-0710
Jeff Menice, Director

Camp comments: Located on Hull Bay, camp
provides fun, safe and nurturing environment for
low-income children from Gtr Boston area.
Activities: Aquatic Activities, Arts/Crafts,
Basketball, Boating, Counselor Training (CIT),
Drama, Music, Swimming — Recreational, Team
Building
Session lengths & capacity: June-August; 1 week
sessions; 75 campers
Clientele & fees: boys 6-12; girls 6-12;
Fees: **A** ⛺ 🚐
Contact: Jeff Menice, Camp Director at
(781) 925-0710; fax: (781) 925-3840
Web site: www.ccab.org
Operated by: Gtr Boston Catholic Charities, 35 Bird
Street, Dorchester, MA 02125 at (617) 287-1150
(#41108)

Taconic (est 1932) ⛺ 🏠 🚗

Hinsdale, MA (Berkshire Co.); (413) 655-2717
Barbara & Robert Ezrol, Director

Camp comments: Make new friends & have fun.
Individually elected activities. Caring staff.
Intercamp games & sensational trips.
Activities: Aquatic Activities, Arts/Crafts, Camping
Skills/Outdoor Living, Drama, Horseback —
English, Performing Arts, Sports — Field & Team,
Tennis, Waterskiing
Session lengths & capacity: June-August; 7 week
sessions; 280 campers
Clientele & fees: coed 7-15; Fees: **F** ⛺
Contact: Barbara or Robert Ezrol, Directors at
(914) 762-2820; fax: (914) 762-4437
e-mail: ctaconic@aol.com
Web site: www.camptaconic.com
Operated by: Taconic, 66 Chestnut Hill Lane,
Briarcliff Manor, NY 10510 at (914) 762-2820
Group Rental Information
Facilities: Cabins, Food Service, Hiking Trails,
Kitchen Facilities, Lake, Meeting Rooms, Pool
(#2105)

Tenacre Day Camp (est 1968) ☀

Wellesley, MA (Norfolk Co.); (781) 235-3238
Libby LaBruzzo, Director

Camp comments: Private school site. 4-6 & 5-12
yrs. Programmed activities. High ratio
staff:campers. Swim 2X daily, heated pools.
Activities: Archery, Arts/Crafts, Challenge/Rope
Courses, Drama, Music, Nature/Environment
Studies, Sports — Field & Team, Swimming —
Instructional
Session lengths & capacity: June-August; 2, 4, 6
& 8 week sessions; 350 campers

Clientele & fees: coed 4-12; Fees: **D** ☀
Contact: Barbara Kaufman, Registrar at
(781) 235-3238; fax: (781) 237-5825
e-mail: tenacrcamp@aol.com
Operated by: Tenacre Country Day School, 80
Benvenue St, Wellesley, MA 02482 at
(781) 235-2282 (#14722)

The Ultimate Sports Camp

(est 1994) ☀

Dedham, MA; (781) 326-2900
Steve Lempert, Director

Camp comments: Emphasizes building
self-esteem through sports and physical fitness.
Having fun is a must!
Activities: Aerobics/Exercise, Basketball,
Climbing/Rappelling, Soccer, Sports — Field &
Team, Swimming — Instructional, Swimming —
Recreational, Tennis
Session lengths & capacity: June-August; 1 week
sessions
Clientele & fees: coed 6-14; Fees: **C** ☀
Contact: Steve Lempert & Michelle St. George,
Camp Director at (781) 326-2900;
fax: (781) 329-1629
e-mail: camps@dedhamhealth.com
Web site: www.dedhamhealth.com
Operated by: Econo Tennis Management, 200
Providence Hwy, Dedham, MA 02026 at
(781) 326-2900 (#32268)

UAHC Crane Lake Camp

(est 1922) 🅰 🚐

West Stockbridge, MA (Berkshire Co.);
(413) 232-4257
Louis Bordman or Herb May, Director

Camp comments: Beautiful Berkshire camp on
private lake. Supportive mature staff for an
outstanding camp experience.
Activities: Aquatic Activities, Basketball,
Challenge/Rope Courses, Gymnastics, Horseback
— English, Religious Study, Sailing, Tennis,
Waterskiing, Windsurfing
Session lengths & capacity: June-August; 4 &
8 week sessions; 325 campers
Clientele & fees: coed 6-15; Fees: **E** 🅰 🐷
Contact: Louis Bordman or Herb May, Senior
Director/Site Director at (212) 650-4208;
fax: (212) 650-4139
e-mail: iluvcamp@aol.com
Operated by: Union Of American Hebrew Cong,
633 Third Ave, New York, NY 10017 at
(212) 650-4208 (#1948)

ICON LEGEND

☀	Day Camp
🅰	Resident Camp
🏠	Facilities Available To Rent
🚐	Transportation Available
🐷	Financial Aid Available

FEE RANGES PER WEEK

A	$0-75
B	$75-200
C	$201-350
D	$351-500
E	$501-650
F	over $650

Virginia (est 1953) ☀ 🏠 🚐

Bolton, MA (Worchester Co.); (978) 779-2759
Pat Stens, Director

Camp comments: Located on West Pond in
Bolton. Emphasis on cooperation not competition.
Transportation provided.
Activities: Aquatic Activities, Arts/Crafts, Camping
Skills/Outdoor Living, Canoeing, Drama, Hiking,
Nature/Environment Studies, Swimming —
Recreational
Session lengths & capacity: June-August; 1 &
2 week sessions; 150 campers
Clientele & fees: girls 6-13; Fees: **C** ☀ 🐷
Contact: Pat Stens, Program Manager at
(617) 482-1078; fax: (617) 350-5246
e-mail: pstens@ptgirlscouts.org
Web site: www.ptgirlscouts.org
Operated by: Patriots Trail GSC, 95 Berkeley St,
Boston, MA 02116 at (617) 350-8335

Group Rental Information
Site comments: Facilities available to youth
groups. Must provide own equipment. No alcohol
or smoking permitted.
Seasons & Capacity: Spring 160, Fall 160
Facilities: Lodges, Tents (#4400)

Waltham Family YMCA Day Camp

☀

Waltham, MA; (781) 894-5295

Camp comments: Come be a part of the YMCA
family and join in the fun! Swim lessons daily - 30
minutes, archery, drama.
Activities: Archery, Arts/Crafts, Baseball/Softball,
Counselor Training (CIT), Drama, Sports — Field &
Team, Swimming — Instructional, Swimming —
Recreational
Session lengths & capacity: June-September; 1 &
2 week sessions; 190 campers
Clientele & fees: coed 5-11; Fees: **B** ☀ 🐷
Contact: Web site: www.ymcaboston.org
Operated by: YMCA Grtr Boston Camp Serv Br,
316 Huntington Ave, Boston, MA 02115 at
(617) 927-8220 (#12574)

Watitoh (est 1937) 🅰

Becket, MA (Berkshire Co.); (413) 623-8951
Sandy, Bill & Suzanne Hoch, Director

Camp comments: Traditional family-run camp with
a wide variety of land & water sports.
Activities: Arts/Crafts, Basketball,
Ceramics/Pottery, Challenge/Rope Courses,
Drama, Gymnastics, Sailing, Swimming —
Instructional, Tennis, Waterskiing
Session lengths & capacity: June-August; 8 week
sessions; 200 campers
Clientele & fees: coed 7-16; Fees: **E** 🅰
Contact: Sandy, Bill & Suzanne Hoch, Directors at
(914) 428-1894; fax: (914) 428-1648
e-mail: watitoh@msn.com
Web site: www.campwatitoh.com
Operated by: Camp Watitoh, 28 Sammis Lane,
White Plains, NY 10605 at (914) 428-1894 (#18192)

Wellfleet Bay Wildlife Sanctua

(est 1962) ☀

South Wellfleet, MA; (508) 349-2615
Amy Kiebala, Director

Camp comments: Our goal is to instill awareness
and appreciation of the natural world and to
promote understanding of our place in nature.
Activities: Arts/Crafts, Canoeing, Counselor
Training (CIT), Field Trips, Music,
Nature/Environment Studies, Team Building
Session lengths & capacity: June-August; 1 week
sessions; 55 campers
Clientele & fees: coed 4-15; Fees: **B, C** ☀ 🐷
Contact: Amy Kiebala, Education Coordinator at
(508) 349-2615 ext. 111; fax: (508) 349-2632
e-mail: akiebala@massaudubon.org

Web site: www.massaudubon.org
Operated by: Mass Audubon, 472 West Mountain
Rd, Lenox, MA 01240 at (413) 637-0320 (#25846)

Wildwood (est 1950) 🅰

Ridge, NH (Worcester Co.); (978) 632-6115
Charlotte Shire, Director

Camp comments: 1000 acres of forests, fields,
wetlands. Nature exploration, wilderness adventure,
and aquatic activities.
Activities: Aquatic Activities, Backpacking, Boating,
Canoeing, Challenge/Rope Courses, Counselor
Training (CIT), Hiking, Leadership Development,
Wilderness Trips
Session lengths & capacity: June-August; 1 &
2 week sessions; 108 campers
Clientele & fees: coed 7-18; families; Fees: **B** ☀
Fees: **C** 🅰 🐷
Contact: Charlotte Shire, Director at (781) 259-9506
ext. 7253; fax: (781) 259-8899
e-mail: cshire@massaudubon.org
Web site: www.massaudubon.org
Operated by: Mass Audubon, 472 West Mountain
Rd, Lenox, MA 01240 at (413) 637-0320 (#414)

Winadu (est 1927) 🅰 🚐

Pittsfield, MA; (413) 447-8900
Shelley & Arleen Weiner, Director

Camp comments: Character training through
sports. Great facilities and specialized staff. Winadu
spirit is 'caring for others.'
Activities: Baseball/Softball, Basketball,
Bicycling/Biking, Golf, Hockey, Sailing, Soccer,
Tennis, Waterskiing, Windsurfing
Session lengths & capacity: 8 week sessions;
430 campers
Clientele & fees: boys 7-16; Fees: **F** 🅰
Contact: Mr & Mrs Shelley & Arle, Directors at
(413) 447-8900; fax: (413) 447-8905
Web site: www.campgrp.com
Operated by: CampGroup, LLC, 3 New King St,
White Plains, NY 10604 at (914) 997-2177 (#1969)

Wind in the Pines

(est 1929) ☀ 🅰 🏠 🚐

Plymouth, MA (Plymouth Co.); (508) 224-2002
Jill Massa, Director

Camp comments: Girls grow strong through new
experiences. They can go beyond their perceived
limits, gain confidence in themselves and support
one another in a community.
Activities: Aquatic Activities, Arts/Crafts,
Backpacking, Bicycling/Biking, Boating, Camping
Skills/Outdoor Living, Challenge/Rope Courses,
Horseback — English, Leadership Development,
Nature/Environment Studies
Session lengths & capacity: June-August; 1/2, 1 &
2 week sessions; 120 campers
Clientele & fees: girls 6-17; families; Fees: **B** ☀
Fees: **C** 🅰 🐷
Contact: Debbie Lewis, Executive Assistant at
(508) 923-0800 ext. 25; fax: (508) 923-7676
e-mail: dlewis@gscsm.org
Web site: www.gscsm.org
Operated by: GSC Southeastern Massachusetts,
111 East Grove St, Middleboro, MA 02346 at
(508) 923-0800

Group Rental Information
Seasons & Capacity: Spring 200, Fall 200,
Winter 30
Facilities: Hiking Trails, Kitchen Facilities, Lake,
Lodges, Meeting Rooms, Playing Fields, Tents
Programs: Boating, Challenge/Ropes Course,
Environmental Education, Swimming (#7642)

Wing Duxbury Stockade

(est 1936)   ☀ ▲ ⌂ 🚐

Duxbury, MA (Plymouth Co.); (781) 834-2700
Deborah Donohoe, Director

Camp comments: Program builds a positive self-image, teaches new skills, encourages racial harmony, and is fun. Excellent facilities.
Activities: Archery, Arts/Crafts, Basketball, Boating, Challenge/Rope Courses, Climbing/Rappelling, Farming/Ranching/Gardening, Fishing, Nature/Environment Studies, Swimming — Instructional
Session lengths & capacity: 2 & 3 week sessions; 240 campers
Clientele & fees: boys 7-16; girls 7-16; Fees: D ▲ 🚐
Contact: Deborah Donohoe, Director at (781) 834-2700; fax: (781) 834-2701
e-mail: ddonohoe@crossroads4kids.org
Web site: www.crossroads4kids.org
Operated by: Crossroads For Kids Inc, 119 Myrtle St, Duxbury, MA 02332 at (781) 834-2700
Group Rental Information
Seasons & Capacity: Spring 200, Fall 200, Winter 200
Facilities: Cabins, Dorm-Style, Food Service, Lake, Lodges, Meeting Rooms, Playing Fields, Pool
Programs: Boating, Challenge/Ropes Course, Environmental Education, Swimming (#2751)

Wingate Kirkland (est 1957)   ▲ ⌂ 🚐

Yarmouth, MA (Barnstable Co.); (508) 362-3798
Jim & Barb Wolfson, Director

Camp comments: Program of daily choice in a caring community atmosphere. Kids build character & self-esteem while having loads of fun.
Activities: Archery, Arts/Crafts, Basketball, Challenge/Rope Courses, Community Service, Drama, Nature/Environment Studies, Soccer, Sports — Field & Team, Tennis
Session lengths & capacity: June-August; 3 & 7 week sessions; 175 campers
Clientele & fees: coed 7-15; Fees: E ▲ 🚐
Contact: Jim or Barb Wolfson, Directors at (508) 358-5816; fax: (508) 358-0249
e-mail: office@campwk.com
Web site: www.campwk.com
Operated by: Wingate Kirkland, 18 Woodridge Rd, Wayland, MA 01778 at (508) 358-5816
Group Rental Information
Seasons & Capacity: Spring 200, Fall 200
Facilities: A/V Equipment, Cabins, Dorm-Style, Food Service, Lake, Meeting Rooms
Programs: Boating, Challenge/Ropes Course, Environmental Education (#2988)

Winnekeag (est 1951)   ▲ ⌂

Ashburnham, MA (Worcester Co.); (978) 827-4455
Bob Saunders, Director

Camp comments: Lake setting with Christian emphasis. A noncompetitive, caring atmosphere with opportunities to learn new skills.
Activities: Aquatic Activities, Arts/Crafts, Camping Skills/Outdoor Living, Horseback — Western, Photography, Radio/TV/Video, Sailing, Swimming — Instructional, Swimming — Recreational, Waterskiing
Session lengths & capacity: 1 & 2 week sessions; 96 campers
Clientele & fees: boys 8-16; girls 8-16; coed 8-16; families; seniors; Fees: C ▲
Contact: Bob Saunder, Camp Director at (978) 365-4551; fax: (978) 365-3838
Operated by: Southern New England Conf, PO Box 1169, South Lancaster, MA 01561 at (978) 365-4551
Group Rental Information
Seasons & Capacity: Spring 170, Fall 170, Winter 170

Facilities: A/V Equipment, Cabins, Dorm-Style, Food Service, Hiking Trails, Kitchen Facilities, Lake, Lodges, Meeting Rooms, Playing Fields, Tents
Programs: Boating, Horseback Riding, Swimming, Winter Sports (#7690)

Winnetaska (est 1967)   ☀ ⌂ 🚐

Ashland, MA (Middlesex Co.); (617) 482-1078
Pat Stens, Director

Camp comments: Located on the Ashland Reservoir. Emphasis on cooperation, not competition. Excellent horseback riding for beginner riders.
Activities: Arts/Crafts, Boating, Camping Skills/Outdoor Living, Canoeing, Drama, Horseback — English, Music, Nature/Environment Studies
Session lengths & capacity: June-August; 1 & 2 week sessions; 130 campers
Clientele & fees: girls 6-13; Fees: C ☀ 🚐
Contact: Pat Stens, Program Manager at (617) 482-1078; fax: (617) 350-5246
e-mail: pstens@ptgirlscouts.org
Web site: www.ptgirlscouts.org
Operated by: Patriots Trail GSC, 95 Berkeley St, Boston, MA 02116 at (617) 350-8335
Group Rental Information
Site comments: Facilities available to youth groups. Must provide own equipment. No alcohol or smoking permited.
Seasons & Capacity: Spring 100, Fall 120, Winter 20
Facilities: Cabins, Tents (#2786)

YMCA Camp Hi-Rock

(est 1948)   ☀ ▲ 🚐

Mount Washington, MA (Bershire Co.);
(413) 528-1227
Scott Elliott, Director

Camp comments: Exceptionally supportive staff. Traditional prog. Adventure course, state-of-the-art. Waterskiing. On Appalachian Trail.
Activities: Camping Skills/Outdoor Living, Challenge/Rope Courses, Climbing/Rappelling, Horseback — Western, Kayaking, Leadership Development, Riflery, Waterskiing, Wilderness Trips, Windsurfing
Session lengths & capacity: 1 & 2 week sessions; 400 campers
Clientele & fees: boys 4-15; girls 4-15; coed 4-15; families; Fees: B ☀ ▲
Contact: Scott Elliott, Camping Director at (413) 528-1227 ext. 14; fax: (413) 528-4234
e-mail: summer@camphirock.com
Web site: www.camhirock.com
Operated by: Central Connecticut Coast YMCA, 1240 Chapel Street, New Haven, CT 06511 at (203) 777-9622 (#2733)

YMCA Camp Lowe (est 1957)   ☀ 🚐

Lancaster, MA; (978) 537-8477
Michael Quinn, Director

Camp comments: Pre-camp and post camp hours available.
Activities: Archery, Boating, Canoeing, Sailing, Sports — Field & Team, Swimming — Instructional, Swimming — Recreational
Session lengths & capacity: June-August; 2 week sessions; 200 campers
Clientele & fees: coed 6-13; Fees: C ☀ 🚐
Contact: Michael Quinn, Director at (978) 343-4847;
e-mail: mquinn@montymca.org
Operated by: Montachusett Regional YMCA, 55 Wallace Ave, Fitchburg, MA 01420 at (978) 343-4847 (#39760)

YMCA Camp Massasoit

(est 1963)   ☀ 🚐

Mattapoisett, MA (Bristol Co.); (508) 758-4203
Carl Robidoux, Director

Camp comments: Beautiful harbor setting. General camp program with a warm caring staff. Transportation available.
Activities: Aquatic Activities, Archery, Arts/Crafts, Basketball, Challenge/Rope Courses, Nature/Environment Studies, Sailing, Soccer, Tennis, Travel/Tour
Session lengths & capacity: 1 & 2 week sessions; 450 campers
Clientele & fees: boys 4-14; girls 4-14; coed 4-14; Fees: B ☀ 🚐
Contact: Doreen Murphy, Center Director at (508) 758-4203; fax: (508) 758-9889
Operated by: YMCA of Greater New Bedford, 25 South Water St, New Bedford, MA 02740 at (508) 997-0734 (#2598)

YMCA Camp Wakanda   ☀ 🚐

Boxford, MA; (978) 352-2188
Ben Clapp, Director

Activities: Aquatic Activities, Arts/Crafts, Boating, Challenge/Rope Courses, Counselor Training (CIT), Drama, Sports — Field & Team, Swimming — Recreational, Team Building
Session lengths & capacity: June-August; 1 & 2 week sessions; 175 campers
Clientele & fees: coed 6-15; Fees: B ☀ 🚐
Contact: Ben Clapp, Youth Development Director at (781) 944-9622 ext. 229; fax: (781) 942-1130
e-mail: bclapp@ymcaboston.org
Web site: www.ymcaboston.org
Operated by: YMCA Grtr Boston Camp Serv Br, 316 Huntington Ave, Boston, MA 02115 at (617) 927-8220 (#4220)

Michigan

ADA Teen Adventure Camp

(est 1984)   ▲ 🚐

Iron River, MI (Iron Co.); (906) 265-2117
Suzanne Apsey, Director

Camp comments: Campers meet other young adults with diabetes. Learn about diabetes while enjoying a variety of activities.
Activities: Aquatic Activities, Boating, Challenge/Rope Courses, Swimming — Recreational, Waterskiing
Session lengths & capacity: 1 week sessions; 70 campers
Clientele & fees: coed 14-18; Fees: D ▲ 🚐
Contact: Suzanne Apsey, Program Director at (312) 346-1805 ext. 6567; fax: (312) 346-5342
e-mail: sapsey@diabetes.org
Operated by: Northern Illinois ADA, 30 N Michigan Ave Ste 2015, Chicago, IL 60602 at (312) 346-1805 (#4431)

Adventure Learning Center

(est 1969)   ☀ ▲ ⌂

Hersey, MI (Osceola Co.); (231) 832-1424
Tamara McLeod, Director

Camp comments: The Adventure Learning Center provides a safe, fun camp environment for youth experiencing emotional and behavioral disorders or challenges.
Activities: Arts/Crafts, Backpacking, Camping Skills/Outdoor Living, Canoeing, Challenge/Rope Courses, Climbing/Rappelling, Hiking, Swimming — Recreational, Team Building, Wilderness Trips
Session lengths & capacity: June-August; 1/2, 1 & 2 week sessions; 30 campers
Clientele & fees: boys 13-16; girls 13-16; coed 5-17; Fees: A ☀ Fees: F ▲
Contact: Marsha Kehr, Intake Coordinator at (800) 748-0061 ext. 262; fax: (231) 832-1468
e-mail: mkehr@eaglevillage.org
Web site: www.eaglevillage.org
Operated by: Eagle Village, 4507 170th Ave, Hersey, MI 49639 at (231) 832-2234

Group Rental Information
Site comments: The Adventure Learning Center is available to provide teambuilding and high adventure activities. Programs are tailored to meet group goals.
Seasons & Capacity: Spring 300, Summer 300, Fall 300, Winter 300
Facilities: Cabins, Dorm-Style, Double Occupancy, Food Service, Hiking Trails, Linens, Meeting Rooms, Playing Fields, Pool, Tents
Programs: Challenge/Ropes Course, Environmental Education, Swimming (#7748)

Al-Gon-Quian (est 1968)　▲ 🚐

Burt Lake, MI (Chebeygan Co.); (734) 663-0536
C L Walker, Director
Activities: Archery, Arts/Crafts, Climbing/Rappelling, Horseback — Western, Photography, Riflery, Sailing, Sports — Field & Team, Waterskiing, Wilderness Trips
Session lengths & capacity: 1 & 2 week sessions; 170 campers
Clientele & fees: coed 8-17; Fees: D ▲ 🐷
Contact: Christopher Walker, Director of Camping Services at (734) 663-0536; fax: (734) 663-8232
Operated by: Ann Arbor 'Y', 350 S Fifth Ave, Ann Arbor, MI 48104-2294 at (734) 663-0536 (#8351)

Anna Behrens (est 1960)　▲ 🏠

Greenville, MI (Montcalm Co.); (616) 754-4782
Kate Krueger, Director

Camp comments: A safe, totally experiential, rustic outdoor experience for girls to grow into strong young women.
Activities: Aquatic Activities, Archery, Backpacking, Bicycling/Biking, Camping Skills/Outdoor Living, Canoeing, Counselor Training (CIT), Hiking, Horseback — Western, Swimming — Recreational
Session lengths & capacity: June-August; 1/2, 1 & 2 week sessions; 150 campers
Clientele & fees: girls 6-16; Fees: B, C, D ▲ 🐷
Contact: Kate Krueger, Director Outdoor Programming & Property at (616) 784-3341; fax: (616) 784-8187
e-mail: kkrueger@gsmt.org
Web site: www.campannabehrens.bunk.com
Operated by: GS of Michigan Trails, 3275 Walker Ave NW, Grand Rapids, MI 49544 at (616) 784-3341
Group Rental Information
Facilities: Cabins, Dorm-Style, Hiking Trails, Kitchen Facilities, Lake, Lodges, Meeting Rooms, Playing Fields, River, Tents
Programs: Boating, Challenge/Ropes Course, Swimming, Winter Sports (#7590)

ICON LEGEND

☀ Day Camp

▲ Resident Camp

🏠 Facilities Available To Rent

🚐 Transportation Available

🐷 Financial Aid Available

FEE RANGES PER WEEK

A	$0-75
B	$75-200
C	$201-350
D	$351-500
E	$501-650
F	over $650

Au Sable (est 1948)　▲ 🏠

Grayling, MI; (517) 348-5491
Elder James Michoff, Director
Activities: Aquatic Activities, Arts/Crafts, Bicycling/Biking, Challenge/Rope Courses, Climbing/Rappelling, Gymnastics, Horseback — Western, Nature/Environment Studies, Photography
Session lengths & capacity: 1 & 9 week sessions; 211 campers
Clientele & fees: coed 8-16; families; seniors; Fees: B ▲
Contact: James Micheff, Camp Director at (517) 485-2226; fax: (517) 485-0672
Operated by: Michigan Conference of SDA, PO Box 19009, Lansing, MI 48901 at (517) 485-2226
Group Rental Information
Facilities: Dorm-Style, Food Service, Hiking Trails, Kitchen Facilities, Lake
Programs: Environmental Education, Horseback Riding (#3149)

Black River Farm & Ranch Inc　▲

Croswell, MI; (810) 679-2505
Activities: Basketball, Boating, Canoeing, Ceramics/Pottery, Challenge/Rope Courses, Counselor Training (CIT), Horseback — Western, Kayaking, Soccer, Swimming — Recreational
Session lengths & capacity: June-August; 1 & 2 week sessions; 135 campers
Clientele & fees: coed 7-15; Fees: F ▲
Contact: (810) 679-2505;
Operated by: Black River Farm & Ranch Inc, 5040 Sheridan Line, Croswell, MI 48422 at (810) 679-2505 (#7149)

Brook Cherith Camp (est 1961)　▲ 🏠

Pierson, MI (Montcalm Co.); (616) 937-5305

Camp comments: Camp Cherith program is nondenominational.300 acres on private lake.Holiday family camp wkds.Available for church rentals.
Activities: Archery, Arts/Crafts, Camping Skills/Outdoor Living, Counselor Training (CIT), Fishing, Horseback — Western, Leadership Development, Religious Study, Riflery, Swimming — Recreational
Session lengths & capacity: April-October; 1/2 & 1 week sessions; 90 campers
Clientele & fees: boys 7-18; girls 7-18; families; Fees: B ▲
Contact: David Dufendach, Executive Director at (616) 937-5305;
Web site: www.brookcherithcamp.org
Operated by: Brook Cherith Camp Inc, PO Box 7342, Grand Rapids, MI 49510 at (231) 937-5305
Group Rental Information
Facilities: Cabins, Hiking Trails, Kitchen Facilities, Lake, Lodges
Programs: Boating (#1291)

Camp Beechpoint

(est 1959)　☀ ▲ 🏠 🚐

Allegan, MI (Allegan Co.); (616) 673-5767
Mark Davidhizar, Director

Camp comments: Lives are changed at camp!
Activities: Aquatic Activities, Archery, Boating, Canoeing, Challenge/Rope Courses, Religious Study, Riflery, Swimming — Recreational, Team Building
Session lengths & capacity: 1 week sessions; 100 campers
Clientele & fees: coed 8-13; Fees: B ☀ Fees: B ▲
Contact: Mark Davidhizar, Director at (000) 080-0991;
e-mail: beechpoint@datawise.net
Operated by: Camp Beechpoint Inc, 3212 125th Ave, Allegan, MI 49010-9260 at (616) 673-6155

Group Rental Information
Seasons & Capacity: Spring 120, Summer 120, Fall 120, Winter 120
Facilities: Cabins, Dorm-Style, Food Service, Hiking Trails, Lake, Meeting Rooms, Playing Fields
Programs: Boating, Challenge/Ropes Course, Swimming (#11694)

Camp Daggett (est 1925)　▲ 🏠

Petoskey, MI (Charlevoix Co.); (231) 347-9742
Scott J Okerlund, Director

Camp comments: On the shore of beautiful Walloon Lake. Traditional character building activities for boys and girls 7-14 years old
Activities: Aquatic Activities, Arts/Crafts, Canoeing, Challenge/Rope Courses, Nature/Environment Studies, Sailing, Sports — Field & Team
Session lengths & capacity: June-August; 1 week sessions; 120 campers
Clientele & fees: coed 7-14; Fees: C ▲
Contact: Scott J Okerlund, Executive Director at (231) 347-9742; fax: (231) 347-5899
e-mail: campdaggett@northlink.net
Web site: www.campdaggett.com
Operated by: Camp Daggett, 3001 Church Rd, Petoskey, MI 49770-9101 at (231) 347-9742
Group Rental Information
Site comments: On the shore of beautiful Walloon Lake, 106 acres. Outdoor education & adventure education center. Ideal retreat center.
Seasons & Capacity: Spring 150, Fall 150, Winter 150
Facilities: Dorm-Style, Food Service, Hiking Trails, Kitchen Facilities, Lake, Lodges, Meeting Rooms, River
Programs: Challenge/Ropes Course, Environmental Education (#4152)

Camp Henry (est 1937)　▲ 🏠

Newaygo, MI (Newaygo Co.); (231) 652-6472
Judy Astle, Director

Camp comments: Specialty camps: Teen travel, teen challenge, horses, waterski, rock climbing, ropes. Multi-week enrollment welcome.
Activities: Canoeing, Challenge/Rope Courses, Climbing/Rappelling, Horseback — Western, Leadership Development, Swimming — Recreational, Travel/Tour, Waterskiing, Wilderness Trips
Session lengths & capacity: 1/2 & 1 week sessions; 190 campers
Clientele & fees: coed 7-17; Fees: B, C, E ▲
Contact: Judy Astle, Exec Dir at (616) 459-2267; fax: (616) 732-6374
e-mail: info@camphenry.org
Web site: www.camphenry.org
Operated by: Westminster Presbyterian, 47 Jefferson SE, Grand Rapids, MI 49503 at (616) 459-2267
Group Rental Information
Site comments: Fantastic wetland trail & environmental education program. Team building for any age & group size. Perfect for school camps & youth groups.
Seasons & Capacity: Spring 190, Fall 190, Winter 85
Facilities: A/V Equipment, Cabins, Dorm-Style, Food Service, Hiking Trails, Lake, Lodges, Meeting Rooms, Playing Fields, Tents
Programs: Boating, Challenge/Ropes Course, Environmental Education, Swimming, Winter Sports (#11116)

Camp Kidwell (est 1949)　☀ ▲ 🏠

Bloomingdale, MI (Allegan Co.); (616) 521-3559
Lynne Seibert, Director

Camp comments: Giving the opportunity to expand your mind, explore team building through social activities, make friends, create memories that 'LAST' the rest of your life.

Activities: Archery, Canoeing, Challenge/Rope Courses, Climbing/Rappelling, Hiking, Horseback — Western, Kayaking, Nature/Environment Studies, Swimming — Recreational, Team Building
Session lengths & capacity: April-October; 1/2, 1 & 2 week sessions; 64 campers
Clientele & fees: coed 5-15; families; Fees: B ☀ Fees: C ⚠
Contact: Marvin King, Executive Director at (616) 686-2335; fax: (616) 686-0804
e-mail: mlkck@btc-bci.net
Operated by: Camp Kidwell, 39000 1st Avenue, Bloomingdale, MI 49026 at (616) 521-3559

Group Rental Information
Site comments: The use of our entire facility is available to guests. Camp staff ill tailor programs to meet guest needs.
Seasons & Capacity: Spring 70, Summer 70, Fall 70, Winter 70
Facilities: Cabins, Food Service, Hiking Trails, Kitchen Facilities, Lake, Lodges, Playing Fields
Programs: Boating, Challenge/Ropes Course, Environmental Education, Horseback Riding, Swimming, Winter Sports (#13754)

Camp Kinawind ⚠

Boyne Falls, MI; (231) 549-2149
Heather Rafanan, Director
Activities: Backpacking, Camping Skills/Outdoor Living, Hiking, Religious Study, Swimming — Recreational, Travel/Tour, Wilderness Trips
Contact: Web site: www.camping.umc-detconf.org
Operated by: Detroit Conference-UMC, 1309 N Ballenger Hwy Ste 1, Flint, MI 48504 at (810) 233-5500 (#11745)

Camp Living Waters (est 1967) ⚠ ⌂

Luther, MI (Lake Co.); (231) 797-5107
Olinda Barnes, Director

Camp comments: Christian camping in the midst of the Pere Marquette State Forest. Learn about God's love in the great outdoors.
Activities: Archery, Arts/Crafts, Basketball, Canoeing, Drama, Hiking, Horseback — Western, Nature/Environment Studies, Riflery, Swimming — Recreational
Session lengths & capacity: 1 week sessions; 137 campers
Clientele & fees: coed 8-17; Fees: B, C ⚠
Contact: Olinda Barnes, Executive Director at (231) 797-5107; fax: (231) 797-5552
e-mail: camplwa@netonecom.net
Web site: www.campclw.org
Operated by: Church of the United Brethren, 536 E 6 Mile Rd, Luther, MI 49656 at (231) 797-5107

Group Rental Information
Facilities: A/V Equipment, Cabins, Food Service, Hiking Trails, Lake, Meeting Rooms, Playing Fields
Programs: Boating, Horseback Riding, Swimming, Winter Sports (#2963)

Camp Merrie Woode
(est 1926) ☀ ⚠ ⌂

Plainwell, MI (Barry Co.); (616) 664-4435
Stephanie Klaassen/Jill Hosbein, Director

Camp comments: Girl Scout camp housed on 216 wooded and hilly acres. Girls can spend their days swimming, horseback riding, hiking and having fun. Non-Girl Scouts welcome.
Activities: Aerobics/Exercise, Aquatic Activities, Boating, Canoeing, Horseback — Western, Nature/Environment Studies, Swimming — Recreational, Travel/Tour
Session lengths & capacity: 1/2, 1 & 2 week sessions
Clientele & fees: girls 7-17; Fees: B, C, D ⚠
Contact: Stephanie Klaassen, Camp Director at (269) 343-1516; fax: (269) 343-0370
e-mail: sklaassen@gegsc.org

Operated by: GS of Glowing Embers Council, 1011 W Maple St, Kabmazoo, MI 49008 at (269) 343-1516

Group Rental Information
Site comments: Aquatic activities, archery, canoeing, hiking, horseback riding (Western). Adventure travel, arts and crafts, camping skills, nature study.
Facilities: Playing Fields, Tents
Programs: Environmental Education (#42073)

Camp O' The Hills (est 1928) ☀ ⚠ ⌂

Brooklyn, MI (Jackson Co.); (517) 592-6373
Activities: Archery, Arts/Crafts, Bicycling/Biking, Camping Skills/Outdoor Living, Counselor Training (CIT), Hiking, Horseback — Western, Nature/Environment Studies, Sailing, Swimming — Recreational
Session lengths & capacity: June-August; 1/2, 1 & 2 week sessions; 70 campers
Clientele & fees: Fees: A ☀ Fees: B, C ⚠
Contact: Nancy Webster, Director at (517) 592-6373; fax: (517) 592-3203
Operated by: Girl Scouts Irish Hills Cncl, 209 E Washington #355, PO Box 1362, Jackson, MI 49201 at (517) 784-8543

Group Rental Information
Facilities: Dorm-Style, Food Service, Hiking Trails, Kitchen Facilities, Meeting Rooms, Playing Fields, Tents
Programs: Boating, Environmental Education, Swimming, Winter Sports (#1231)

Camp O'Fair Winds (est 1930) ⚠ ⌂

Columbiaville, MI (LaPeer Co.); (810) 793-4130
Nancy Burger, Director

Camp comments: Girl Scout program emphasis. Rustic environment & recreational group living skills. Non-members welcome!
Activities: Archery, Arts/Crafts, Backpacking, Bicycling/Biking, Camping Skills/Outdoor Living, Challenge/Rope Courses, Field Trips, Horseback — Western, Nature/Environment Studies, Swimming — Recreational
Session lengths & capacity: June-August; 1/2, 1 & 2 week sessions; 150 campers
Clientele & fees: girls 7-12; Fees: B, C ⚠ 🐃
Contact: Nancy Burger, Camp Director at (800) 482-6734; fax: (810) 230-0955
e-mail: nburger@fwgsc.org
Web site: www.fwgsc.org
Operated by: Fair Winds GSC, PO Box 349, Swartz Creek, MI 48473 at (800) 482-6734

Group Rental Information
Seasons & Capacity: Spring 150, Fall 150
Facilities: Lodges, Meeting Rooms (#1249)

Camp Oak Hills (est 1949) ⚠ ⌂

Harrison, MI (Clare Co.); (989) 539-7267
Tish Llewellyn, Director

Camp comments: Beautiful, wooded Girl Scout camp, lower peninsula of Michigan. Private lake. Family weekends. Non Girl Scouts welcome!
Activities: Aquatic Activities, Camping Skills/Outdoor Living, Canoeing, Field Trips, Horseback — Western, Leadership Development, Nature/Environment Studies, Performing Arts, Sports — Field & Team
Session lengths & capacity: June-August; 1/2, 1 & 2 week sessions; 124 campers
Clientele & fees: girls 6-17; families; Fees: B, C ⚠ 🐃
Contact: Tish Llewellyn, Camp Director/Outdoor Program Specialist at (517) 799-9565 ext. 31; fax: (517) 799-1450
e-mail: lallew@mittenbay.org
Web site: www.mittenbay.org
Operated by: Girl Scouts of Mitten Bay, 5470 Davis Rd, Saginaw, MI 48604 at (989) 799-9565 (#6421)

Camp Paradise (est 1976) ⚠

Newberry, MI (Luce Co.); (847) 765-5000
Tim Vanden Bos, Director

Camp comments: Among majestic trees, unspoiled air & star filled skies. Sessions for junior high students & dad's with son or daughter.
Activities: Archery, Basketball, Canoeing, Challenge/Rope Courses, Climbing/Rappelling, Hiking, Kayaking, Swimming — Recreational, Waterskiing
Session lengths & capacity: 120 campers
Clientele & fees: boys 7-16; girls 7-15; Fees: C ⚠ 🐃
Contact: Tim Vanden Bos, Director at (847) 765-5000 ext. 1940; fax: (847) 765-9225
Operated by: Willow Creek Community Church, 67 E Algonquin Rd, South Barrington, IL 60010 at (847) 765-5000 (#901526)

Camp Playfair (est 1947) ⚠ ⌂

Lexington, MI (Sanilac Co.); (810) 359-7500
Molly Middel, Director

Camp comments: Campers thrive in noncompetitive, caring environment. Environmental progs & self-esteem building. Tents & a-frames.
Activities: Aquatic Activities, Arts/Crafts, Camping Skills/Outdoor Living, Counselor Training (CIT), Drama, Horseback — English, Nature/Environment Studies
Session lengths & capacity: June-August; 1/2, 1 & 2 week sessions; 80 campers
Clientele & fees: girls 7-17; families; Fees: B ⚠ 🐃
Contact: Molly Middel, Camping Director/Program Specialist at (810) 984-3189; fax: (810) 984-2206
e-mail: dusty@advnet.net
Operated by: Michigan Waterways GSC, 2186 Water St, Port Huron, MI 48060 at (810) 984-3189 (#4469)

Camp Roger (est 1941) ⚠ ⌂

Rockford, MI (Kent Co.); (616) 874-7286
Jim Van Wingerden, Director

Camp comments: Explore God's world,discover God's love! Providing Christian growth-adventures;nurturing relationships with God,others,creation,and developing independence.
Activities: Archery, Arts/Crafts, Backpacking, Camping Skills/Outdoor Living, Challenge/Rope Courses, Hiking, Nature/Environment Studies, Riflery, Swimming — Recreational, Team Building
Session lengths & capacity: June-August; 1/2 & 1 week sessions; 160 campers
Clientele & fees: coed 8-14; Fees: C ⚠
Contact: Jim Van Wingerden, Camp Director at (616) 874-7286; fax: (616) 874-5734
e-mail: jimvwg@juno.com
Web site: www.camproger.org
Operated by: Camp Roger, 8356 Belding Road, Rockford, MI 49341 at (616) 874-7286

Group Rental Information
Programs: Challenge/Ropes Course, Environmental Education (#1363)

Camp Shawadasee (est 1956) ⚠ ⌂

Lawton, MI (Van Buren Co.); (616) 624-6312
Donna Lockington, Director

Camp comments: Beautiful lake setting where girls experience the fun, adventures and traditions of camp. Committed and caring staff.
Activities: Arts/Crafts, Boating, Camping Skills/Outdoor Living, Counselor Training (CIT), Horseback — English, Leadership Development, Nature/Environment Studies, Swimming — Recreational, Team Building
Session lengths & capacity: June-August; 1/2, 1 & 2 week sessions; 100 campers
Clientele & fees: girls 6-17; Fees: B ⚠ 🐃

Contact: Donna Lockington, Camp Director/Program Specialis at (219) 273-3021; fax: (219) 273-4944
e-mail: dindigo@aol.com
Web site: www.gsssc.org
Operated by: Singing Sands GSC, 3620 Deahl Court, South Bend, IN 46628 at (219) 273-3021 (#1305)

Camp Tall Turf (est 1968) 🜊 🏠 🚗

Walkerville, MI (Kent Co.); (231) 854-3466
Denise Fase, Director

Camp comments: Christian ministry of reconciliation providing camps & community based follow-up programs primarily for inner-city youth and single parent families.
Activities: Aquatic Activities, Archery, Camping Skills/Outdoor Living, Canoeing, Challenge/Rope Courses, Community Service, Leadership Development, Music, Nature/Environment Studies, Team Building
Session lengths & capacity: June-August; 1 & 2 week sessions; 130 campers
Clientele & fees: boys 8-16; girls 8-16; coed 8-16; families; Fees: **A, B, C** 🜊 🚲
Contact: Jack Kooyman, President & CEO at (616) 459-7206; fax: (616) 456-8595
e-mail: tallturf@iserv.net
Web site: www.tallturf.org
Operated by: Christian Camps Inner City Yth, 935 Baxter St SE, Grand Rapids, MI 49506-2599 at (616) 459-7206

Group Rental Information
Site comments: New retreat and conference center available to user groups at reasonable rates from September - May.
Seasons & Capacity: Spring 150, Fall 150, Winter 75
Facilities: A/V Equipment, Cabins, Double Occupancy, Hiking Trails, Kitchen Facilities, Lake, Lodges, Meeting Rooms, Playing Fields, River (#13827)

Camp Timbers (est 1967) ☀ 🜊 🏠

West Branch, MI (Ogemaw Co.); (517) 345-2630
Steve Meyer, Director

Camp comments: Beautiful Northern Michigan camp on historic site surrounding private lake. Mature staff. Exciting program options.
Activities: Aquatic Activities, Archery, Camping Skills/Outdoor Living, Canoeing, Challenge/Rope Courses, Climbing/Rappelling, Drama, Horseback — Western, Nature/Environment Studies, Swimming — Instructional
Session lengths & capacity: June-August; 1 week sessions; 140 campers

---

ICON LEGEND

☀ Day Camp

🜊 Resident Camp

🏠 Facilities Available To Rent

🚗 Transportation Available

🚲 Financial Aid Available

FEE RANGES PER WEEK

A	$0-75
B	$75-200
C	$201-350
D	$351-500
E	$501-650
F	over $650

Clientele & fees: coed 7-16; Fees: **C** 🜊
Contact: Camp Office at (517) 753-7721; fax: (517) 755-9329
e-mail: timbers@saginawymca.org
Web site: www.camptimbers.org
Operated by: Saginaw YMCA, 1915 Fordney, Saginaw, MI 48601 at (517) 753-7721

Group Rental Information
Seasons & Capacity: Spring 160, Summer 160, Fall 160, Winter 160
Facilities: Cabins, Food Service, Hiking Trails, Lake, Lodges, Playing Fields
Programs: Boating, Challenge/Ropes Course, Environmental Education, Horseback Riding, Swimming, Winter Sports (#3235)

Camp Walden (est 1959) 🜊 🏠 🚗

Cheboygan, MI (Cheboygan Co.); (231) 625-2050
Larry Stevens, Director

Camp comments: Camp Walden offers a noncompetitive, supportive environment where children learn to play together, build social skills and gain self-esteem.
Activities: Archery, Arts/Crafts, Backpacking, Fencing, Horseback — English, Sailing, Soccer, Swimming — Instructional, Tennis, Waterskiing
Session lengths & capacity: June-August; 2, 4, 6 & 8 week sessions; 400 campers
Clientele & fees: boys 7-17; girls 7-17; coed 7-17; Fees: **F** 🜊
Contact: Larry or Ina Stevens, Directors at (248) 661-1890; fax: (248) 661-1891
e-mail: waldenmi@aol.com
Web site: www.campwaldenmi.com
Operated by: Camp Walden Inc, 31070 Applewood Lane, Farmington Hills, MI 48331 at (248) 661-1890

Group Rental Information
Site comments: Choice and structure combine with fun and adventure in a beautiful natural setting. Est. 1959.
Facilities: Cabins, Dorm-Style, Food Service, Lake, Meeting Rooms
Programs: Swimming (#1262)

Camp Watoto (est 1993) ☀ 🚗

Flint, MI (Genesee Co.); (810) 736-0211
Roberta Cox, Director

Camp comments: Join kids of other UAW-represented GM employees at Camp Watoto this summer. You'll have great fun & meet new friends.
Activities: Aquatic Activities, Archery, Arts/Crafts, Baseball/Softball, Basketball, Counselor Training (CIT), Field Trips, Football, Soccer, Team Building
Session lengths & capacity: 100 campers
Clientele & fees: coed 5-13; Fees: **B** ☀
Contact: Roberta Cox, Camp Director at (810) 736-0211 ext. 320; fax: (810) 736-1623
Operated by: Camp Watoto, 4358 Richfield Rd, Flint, MI 48506-2016 at (810) 736-0211 (#2456)

Camp Westminster Higgins Lake (est 1925) ☀ 🜊 🏠 🚗

Roscommon, MI (Crawford Co.); (517) 821-9474
Suzanne G Bates, Director

Camp comments: Develop faith, self-esteem and teamwork in a caring Christian community on beautiful Higgins Lake. Sail! Swim! Travel!
Activities: Archery, Canoeing, Challenge/Rope Courses, Climbing/Rappelling, Counselor Training (CIT), Fishing, Sailing, Swimming — Recreational, Tennis, Travel/Tour
Session lengths & capacity: June-August; 1, 2 & 7 week sessions; 110 campers
Clientele & fees: boys 7-17; girls 7-17; coed 7-17; families; seniors; single adults; Fees: **B** ☀ Fees: **C** 🜊 🚲
Contact: Suzanne Getz Bates, Director at (313) 341-2697 ext. 204; fax: (313) 341-1514
e-mail: Suzanne_Bates@ureach.com
Web site: www.campwestminster.com

Operated by: Camp Westminster Higgins Lake, 17567 Hubbell Ave, Detroit, MI 48235 at (313) 341-2697

Group Rental Information
Facilities: Cabins, Food Service, Hiking Trails, Kitchen Facilities, Lake, Playing Fields
Programs: Challenge/Ropes Course, Swimming (#1331)

Catch A Rainbow (est 1986) 🜊 🚗

Montague, MI (Muskegon Co.); (800) 723-0360
Debra Dillingham, Director

Camp comments: Camp Catch-A-Rainbow offers a week of fun for kids with cancer. This free program is sponsored by the American Cancer Society, Great Lakes Division.
Activities: Archery, Arts/Crafts, Canoeing, Challenge/Rope Courses, Hiking, Horseback — Western, Music, Riflery, Sailing, Swimming — Recreational
Session lengths & capacity: July-July; 1 week sessions; 100 campers
Clientele & fees: coed 7-18; Fees: **A** 🜊
Contact: American Cancer Society, Cancer Response System at (800) 723-0360; fax: (517) 664-1497
e-mail: deb.dillingham@cancer.org
Web site: www.gl.cancer.org
Operated by: American Cancer Society, 1755 Abbey Rd, East Lansing, MI 48823 at (517) 332-2222 (#6409)

Cavell YWCA Metro Detroit (est 1914) ☀ 🜊 🏠 🚗

Lexington, MI (Sanilac Co.); (810) 359-2267
Jill Laidlaw, Director

Camp comments: A great place to learn new skills & meet new friends. Interact with international counselors, collect shells on our beach & visit our petting farm.
Activities: Archery, Arts/Crafts, Backpacking, Camping Skills/Outdoor Living, Counselor Training (CIT), Dance, Horseback — English, Kayaking
Session lengths & capacity: June-August; 1, 2, 3, 4 & 5 week sessions; 60 campers
Clientele & fees: girls 7-17; Fees: **C** 🜊 🚲
Contact: Jill Laidlaw, Camp Director at (810) 359-2267; fax: (810) 359-2430
e-mail: cavell@greatlakes.net
Web site: ww.campcavell.org
Operated by: YWCA of Metroit Detroit, Cavell YWCA Metro Detroit, 3335 Lakeview, Lexington, MI 48450 at (313) 259-9922

Group Rental Information
Site comments: The perfect place for a retreat, meeting, or camp experience. We are located 90 miles north of Detroit on beautiful Lake Huron. We offer country cooking and fun
Seasons & Capacity: Spring 250, Summer 250, Fall 250
Facilities: A/V Equipment, Cabins, Food Service, Hiking Trails, Lake, Meeting Rooms, Playing Fields
Programs: Boating, Challenge/Ropes Course, Horseback Riding, Swimming (#1368)

Cedar Lodge (est 1964) ☀ 🜊

Lawrence, MI (Van Buren Co.); (616) 674-8071
Amy Edwards, Director

Camp comments: Family operated, top horsemanship prog. Lake, sports, crafts & more. 55 campers. Rustic setting. Visit our web site.
Activities: Aquatic Activities, Archery, Arts/Crafts, Bicycling/Biking, Camping Skills/Outdoor Living, Drama, Horseback — English, Horseback — Western, Music, Swimming — Recreational
Session lengths & capacity: June-August; 2, 4 & 8 week sessions; 55 campers
Clientele & fees: coed 7-16; Fees: **D** 🜊
Contact: Stella Edwards, Camp Director at (616) 674-8071; fax: (616) 674-3143
e-mail: info@cedarlodge.com

Web site: www.cedarlodge.com
Operated by: Cedar Lodge, PO Box 218, Lawrence, MI 49064 at (616) 674-8071 (#11733)

Circle Pines Center

(est 1938)

Delton, MI (Barry Co.); (616) 623-5555
Traci Furman, Director

Camp comments: Peace, Justice, ecology and cooperation. Co-op camp on 300 acres. Safe and accepting environment.
Activities: Arts/Crafts, Canoeing, Ceramics/Pottery, Community Service, Counselor Training (CIT), Drama, Farming/Ranching/Gardening, Hiking, Nature/Environment Studies, Swimming — Recreational
Session lengths & capacity: 1, 2 & 4 week sessions; 55 campers
Clientele & fees: coed 7-17; families; Fees: C △ 🐗
Contact: Traci Furman, Camp Director at (616) 623-5555; fax: (616) 623-9054
e-mail: circle@net-link.net
Web site: www.circlepinescenter.org
Operated by: Circle Pines Summer Camp, 8650 Mullen Rd, Delton, MI 49046-9751 at (616) 623-5555
Group Rental Information
Facilities: Cabins, Food Service, Lake, Meeting Rooms (#1377)

Covenant Point Bible Camp

(est 1926)

Iron River, MI; (906) 265-2117
Chuck Frasier, Director

Camp comments: Christian emphasis. Counselors modeling their relationship with Jesus Christ. Northwoods, Michigan. Spec. Island camp.
Activities: Aquatic Activities, Archery, Arts/Crafts, Backpacking, Bicycling/Biking, Challenge/Rope Courses, Nature/Environment Studies, Sports — Field & Team, Waterskiing, Wilderness Trips
Session lengths & capacity: 8 week sessions; 150 campers
Clientele & fees: coed 8-18; families; Fees: B △ 🐗
Contact: Chuck Frasier, Executive Director at (906) 265-2117; fax: (906) 265-5123
e-mail: cpbc@up.net
Web site: www.covenantharbor.org
Operated by: Harbor Point Ministries, 3311 W Foster Ave, Chicago, IL 60625 at (773) 583-0220
Group Rental Information
Site comments: 8 acre island adds to mainland experience, special camping.
Seasons & Capacity: Spring 110, Summer 115, Fall 130, Winter 10
Facilities: Cabins, Dorm-Style, Food Service, Hiking Trails, Lake, Meeting Rooms
Programs: Boating, Challenge/Ropes Course, Environmental Education, Winter Sports (#3167)

CYO Boys' Camp (est 1946)

Carsonville, MI (Sanilac Co.); (810) 622-9297

Camp comments: Traditional camp on shores of Lake Huron. Small group living, age group based programming. Canoe trip for teens, 14-16.
Activities: Aquatic Activities, Archery, Arts/Crafts, Camping Skills/Outdoor Living, Challenge/Rope Courses, Climbing/Rappelling, Kayaking, Nature/Environment Studies, Wilderness Trips
Session lengths & capacity: 1 & 2 week sessions; 144 campers
Clientele & fees: boys 7-17; Fees: C △ 🐗
Contact: (313) 963-7172; fax: (313) 963-7179
Web site: www.cyocamps.org
Operated by: Catholic Youth Organization, 305 Michigan Ave, Detroit, MI 48226 at (313) 963-7172

Group Rental Information
Site comments: A natural setting for any group. CYO off-season patrons use our camps for everything from extensive study, sports training, religious reflection to outdoor ed.
Seasons & Capacity: Spring 120, Fall 120
Facilities: Cabins, Food Service, Lake, Meeting Rooms, Playing Fields
Programs: Challenge/Ropes Course, Swimming (#1287)

CYO Camp For Girls (est 1950)

Port Sanilac, MI (Sanilac Co.); (810) 622-8883
Heather Kearns, Director

Camp comments: Traditional camp on shores of Lake Huron. Small group living, age group based programming. Canoe trip for teens, 14-16.
Activities: Aquatic Activities, Archery, Arts/Crafts, Camping Skills/Outdoor Living, Challenge/Rope Courses, Climbing/Rappelling, Hiking, Kayaking, Nature/Environment Studies, Wilderness Trips
Session lengths & capacity: 1 & 2 week sessions; 166 campers
Clientele & fees: girls 7-17; Fees: C △
Contact: (313) 963-7172; fax: (313) 963-7179
Web site: www.cyocamps.org
Operated by: Catholic Youth Organization, 305 Michigan Ave, Detroit, MI 48226 at (313) 963-7172

Group Rental Information
Site comments: A natural, tranquil setting for any group. CYO off-season patrons use our facilites for everything from extensive study, sports training, religious reflection.
Seasons & Capacity: Spring 166, Fall 166
Facilities: Cabins, Food Service, Lake, Meeting Rooms, Playing Fields
Programs: Challenge/Ropes Course (#1288)

Deer Trails (est 1938)

Harrison, MI (Clare Co.); (989) 539-6595
Amy Kremkow, Director

Camp comments: Over 200 beautiful wooded acres/one half mile lakefront provide many opportunities for discovery adventure/water sports.
Activities: Aquatic Activities, Archery, Arts/Crafts, Boating, Camping Skills/Outdoor Living, Canoeing, Hiking, Leadership Development, Nature/Environment Studies, Swimming — Recreational
Session lengths & capacity: 1/2, 1 & 2 week sessions; 150 campers
Clientele & fees: girls 6-17; Fees: B △ 🐗
Contact: Amy Kremkow, Outdoor Program Director at (517) 699-9400 ext. 45; fax: (517) 699-9405
e-mail: akremkow@michcom.net
Web site: www.mcgsc.org
Operated by: Michigan Capitol GSC, 1974 Cedar Street, Holt, MI 48842 at (517) 699-9400 (#1229)

Fortune Lake Lutheran Camp

(est 1930)

Crystal Falls, MI (Iron Co.); (906) 875-3697
Rev. Eric T. Ackerman, Director

Camp comments: A place of grace in the beautiful Northwoods, Christian community for life long learning. Nourish body, mind, soul.
Activities: Arts/Crafts, Camping Skills/Outdoor Living, Canoeing, Challenge/Rope Courses, Leadership Development, Religious Study, Swimming — Recreational
Session lengths & capacity: January-December; 1 week sessions; 200 campers
Clientele & fees: coed 9-17; families; seniors; single adults; Fees: A ☀ Fees: A, B △
Contact: Rev. Eric T Ackerman, Executive Director at (906) 875-3697; fax: (906) 875-4829
e-mail: biblecmp@up.net
Web site: www.fortunelake.org
Operated by: Fortune Lake Lutheran Camp, 138 Fortune Lake Camp Rd, Crystal Falls, MI 49920 at (906) 875-3697

Group Rental Information
Seasons & Capacity: Spring 130, Winter 130
Facilities: A/V Equipment, Cabins, Dorm-Style, Double Occupancy, Food Service, Kitchen Facilities, Lake, Linens, Lodges, Meeting Rooms, Playing Fields, River, Tents
Programs: Challenge/Ropes Course, Environmental Education, Swimming, Winter Sports (#21400)

Gordonwood (est 1981)

Ortonville, MI (Oakland Co.); (248) 627-2558
Tammi-Jo Slieff, Director

Camp comments: A place apart to experience the loving Christian family in all it's diversity. Learning, worshipping and playing within God's creation.
Activities: Canoeing, Counselor Training (CIT), Leadership Development, Music, Nature/Environment Studies, Religious Study, Swimming — Instructional, Swimming — Recreational, Team Building, Wilderness Trips
Session lengths & capacity: June-August; 1 & 2 week sessions; 95 campers
Clientele & fees: coed 5-17; Fees: B ☀ Fees: C, D △ 🐗
Contact: Tammi-Jo Slieff, Camp Director at (248) 627-2558; fax: (248) 627-3005
e-mail: grdnwood@gordonwood.org
Operated by: Episcopal Diocese of Michigan, 4800 Woodward, Detroit, MI 48201 at (313) 832-4400
Group Rental Information
Site comments: Private lake on 175 acres of rolling hills & pine forests.Outdoor ed program in Spring. Team building nature center.
Seasons & Capacity: Spring 100, Fall 150, Winter 100
Facilities: A/V Equipment, Dorm-Style, Food Service, Hiking Trails, Lake, Lodges, Playing Fields
Programs: Boating, Environmental Education, Swimming (#1235)

Greenwood Presbyterian Camp

(est 1952)

Gowen, MI (Kent Co.); (616) 754-7258
Rev. Robert W. Vodra, Director

Camp comments: Camping in a Christian community. Worship & Bible study mix with canoeing, swimming, archery, crafts & recreation.
Activities: Aquatic Activities, Archery, Arts/Crafts, Camping Skills/Outdoor Living, Canoeing, Challenge/Rope Courses, Music, Religious Study, Swimming — Recreational, Team Building
Session lengths & capacity: June-August; 1/2, 1 & 2 week sessions; 100 campers
Clientele & fees: boys 5-18; girls 5-18; coed 5-18; families; Fees: C △ 🐗
Contact: Rev Robert W Vodra, Director at (616) 754-7258; fax: (616) 754-0906
e-mail: robvodra@iserv.net
Web site: www.lakemichiganpresbytery.org
Operated by: Presbytery of Lake Michigan, 1511 Helen Ave, Portage, MI 49002 at (616) 381-6337
Group Rental Information
Seasons & Capacity: Spring 100, Fall 100, Winter 80
Facilities: Cabins, Dorm-Style, Food Service, Hiking Trails, Kitchen Facilities, Lake, Meeting Rooms, Playing Fields
Programs: Boating, Swimming (#11105)

Greenwoods Camp For Boys

(est 1935)

Decatur, MI; (616) 423-3091
Dayna Hardin, Director

Camp comments: We promote individual growth & achievement. 40+ activities, campers customize their own program 1:3 staff/camper ratio
Activities: Archery, Basketball, Canoeing, Climbing/Rappelling, Golf, Horseback — Western, Sailing, Tennis, Waterskiing, Windsurfing

Session lengths & capacity: June-August; 3, 4 & 8 week sessions; 120 campers
Clientele & fees: boys 7-15; families; Fees: E ▲
Contact: Dayna Glasson Hardin, Owner/Director at (888) 459-2492; fax: (580) 515-3698
e-mail: lwcgwc@aol.com
Web site: www.lakeofthewoodscamps.com
Operated by: Greenwood Camps, 227 Mary Street, Winnetka, IL 60093 at (888) 459-2492 (#1634)

Hawthorn Hollow (est 1996)   ▲ 🏠

Columbus Twp, MI (St Clair Co.); (810) 367-3318
Jenny Fehn, Director

Camp comments: Great opportunity for a girl to meet friends & try new challenges in a fun-filled & supportive natural environment.
Activities: Archery, Arts/Crafts, Camping Skills/Outdoor Living, Counselor Training (CIT), Hiking, Horseback — Western, Leadership Development, Nature/Environment Studies, Performing Arts, Swimming — Recreational
Session lengths & capacity: June-August; 1/2, 1 & 2 week sessions; 128 campers
Clientele & fees: girls 6-17; Fees: B, C ▲
Contact: Jenny Fehn, Resident Camp Director at (810) 263-0220 ext. 210; fax: (810) 263-6320
e-mail: jfehn@gsmc-oc.org
Web site: www.gsmc-oc.org
Operated by: GS of Macomb County, 42804 Garfield, Clinton Twp, MI 48038 at (810) 263-0220

Group Rental Information
Seasons & Capacity: Spring 225, Fall 225, Winter 225
Facilities: Cabins, Dorm-Style, Hiking Trails, Kitchen Facilities, Lodges, Meeting Rooms, Playing Fields, Pool, River, Tents
Programs: Swimming (#1310)

High Scope Institute for IDEAS   ▲ 🏠

(est 1963)

Clinton, MI (Washtenaw Co.); (517) 456-7300
John Weiss, Director

Camp comments: A powerful learning experience for youth. Leadership opportunities & active engagement with peers & supportive adults.
Activities: Academics, Ceramics/Pottery, Community Service, Dance, Drama, Drawing/Painting, International Culture, Leadership Development, Music, Photography
Session lengths & capacity: 4 week sessions; 60 campers
Clientele & fees: coed 14-17; Fees: E ▲ 🐷
Contact: John K Weiss, Director/Adolescent Division at (734) 485-2000; fax: (734) 485-0704
e-mail: johnw@highscope.org
Web site: www.highscope.org/adol/intro.htm

ICON LEGEND

☀	Day Camp
▲	Resident Camp
🏠	Facilities Available To Rent
🚐	Transportation Available
🐷	Financial Aid Available

FEE RANGES PER WEEK

A	$0-75
B	$75-200
C	$201-350
D	$351-500
E	$501-650
F	over $650

Operated by: High Scope Foundation, 600 N River St, Ypsilanti, MI 48198 at (734) 485-2000
Group Rental Information
Site comments: Located on 450 acres of beautiful rolling terrain. Two country estate homes serve as dorms. Features a barn & several indoor & outdoor meeting spaces.
Seasons & Capacity: Spring 0, Summer 80, Fall 0, Winter 80
Facilities: A/V Equipment, Dorm-Style, Double Occupancy, Food Service, Hiking Trails, Lake, Linens, Meeting Rooms, Playing Fields
Programs: Swimming (#1295)

Huron Forest Camp Cherith   ▲

(est 1941)

Oscoda, MI (Iosco Co.); (517) 739-3571
Linda Gillies, Director

Camp comments: Christian camp, pool, horses, rustic, river fun. Kids feel safe & cared for. Parent-child wknds Homeschoolers, Science
Activities: Archery, Arts/Crafts, Camping Skills/Outdoor Living, Canoeing, Horseback — Western, Leadership Development, Nature/Environment Studies, Religious Study, Riflery, Swimming — Instructional
Session lengths & capacity: June-September; 1 week sessions; 120 campers
Clientele & fees: boys 7-17; girls 7-17; families; Fees: B ▲
Contact: Linda Gillies, Executive Director at (248) 615-9844; fax: (248) 615-4932
e-mail: HFCC-TuKi@juno.com
Web site: www.cherith.com
Operated by: Huron Forest Cmp Cherith Metro, 36208 Freedom Rd, Farmington, MI 48335 at (248) 615-9844 (#1381)

Indian Trails Camp Inc (est 1953)   ▲

Grand Rapids, MI (Ottawa Co.); (616) 677-5251
Lynn Gust, Director

Camp comments: A magical experience, state of the art facility & program allowing for camper growth, independence & development.
Activities: Aquatic Activities, Archery, Arts/Crafts, Camping Skills/Outdoor Living, Canoeing, Drama, Leadership Development, Music, Nature/Environment Studies, Sports — Field & Team
Session lengths & capacity: 1 & 2 week sessions; 84 campers
Clientele & fees: coed 6-70; families; Fees: D, E, F ▲ 🐷
Contact: Lynn Gust, Executive Director at (616) 677-5251; fax: (616) 677-2955
Operated by: Indian Trails Camp Inc, 4335 Lake Michigan Dr Ste 146, Grand Rapids, MI 49544 at (616) 677-5251 (#1365)

Jcc Summer Camp (est 1935)   ☀ 🚐

W Bloomfield, MI (Oakland Co.); (248) 661-1010
Nancie Furgang, Director

Camp comments: JCC camps combine preschool thru high school specialty camps art, hiking, CIT, travel, pro sports, with Jewish education
Activities: Aquatic Activities, Arts/Crafts, Baseball/Softball, Canoeing, Challenge/Rope Courses, Computer, Counselor Training (CIT), Drama, Field Trips, Golf
Session lengths & capacity: June-August; 1, 2, 4 & 8 week sessions; 1000 campers
Clientele & fees: boys 2-14; girls 2-14; coed 2-14; Fees: B, C ☀ 🐷
Contact: Nancie Fargang, Day Camp Director at (248) 432-5578; fax: (248) 432-5552
e-mail: nfurganag@jcc.org
Operated by: JCC of Metro Detroit, Accounts Payable, 6600 West Maple Rd, West Bloomfield, MI 48322 at (248) 432-5578 (#28732)

Judson Collins Center   ☀ ▲ 🏠

(est 1952)

Onsted, MI (Lenawee Co.); (517) 467-7711
Larry Kalas, Director

Camp comments: Experience a Christian community at Judson Collins Center, a United Methodist year-round camping and retreat ministry, on the shores of Wamplers Lake.
Activities: Camping Skills/Outdoor Living, Canoeing, Challenge/Rope Courses, Counselor Training (CIT), Farming/Ranching/Gardening, Fishing, Horseback — Western, Religious Study, Swimming — Recreational, Team Building
Session lengths & capacity: June-August; 1/2 & 1 week sessions; 278 campers
Clientele & fees: coed 5-99; families; seniors; single adults; Fees: C ▲
Contact: Larry Kalas, Director at (517) 467-7711; fax: (517) 467-6650
e-mail: jccume@tc3net.com
Web site: www.camping.umc-detconf.org
Operated by: Detroit Conference-UMC, 1309 N Ballenger Hwy Ste 1, Flint, MI 48504 at (810) 233-5500

Group Rental Information
Site comments: Experience a Christian community at Judson Collins Center, a United Methodist year-round camping and retreat ministry, on the shores of Wamplers Lake.
Seasons & Capacity: Spring 278, Summer 278, Fall 278, Winter 96
Facilities: Cabins, Dorm-Style, Food Service, Hiking Trails, Lake, Lodges, Meeting Rooms, Playing Fields
Programs: Boating, Challenge/Ropes Course, Swimming (#1296)

Lake Ann Baptist Camp   ▲ 🏠

(est 1948)

Lake Ann, MI (Benzie Co.); (616) 275-7329
Ken Riley, Director

Camp comments: Discover life at its best at Lake Ann! Age-distinct and graded programming for 4th to 12th grades. 18 miles from Traverse City, Lake Ann is your up-north home!
Activities: Archery, Arts/Crafts, Basketball, Canoeing, Challenge/Rope Courses, Climbing/Rappelling, Nature/Environment Studies, Swimming — Recreational, Team Building, Wilderness Trips
Session lengths & capacity: June-August; 1 week sessions; 508 campers
Clientele & fees: coed 9-18; seniors; single adults; Fees: C ▲
Contact: Dan Good, Guest Relations at (231) 275-7329; fax: (231) 275-5174
e-mail: dgood@lakeanncamp.com
Operated by: Lake Ann Baptist Camp, PO Box 109, Lake Ann, MI 49650 at (231) 275-7329

Group Rental Information
Site comments: State of the art cabin styled conference facilities for 500 guests. Nestled in the pride of the upnorth region-Michigan's Grand Traverse community.
Seasons & Capacity: Spring 400, Summer 557, Fall 400, Winter 400
Facilities: Cabins, Dorm-Style, Double Occupancy, Food Service, Hiking Trails, Lake, Lodges, Meeting Rooms, Playing Fields, River
Programs: Boating, Challenge/Ropes Course, Environmental Education, Swimming, Winter Sports (#2290)

Lake Huron Retreat Center   🏠

Lakeport, MI (Saint Clair Co.); (810) 327-6272
Ann Emerson, Director
Contact: Ann Emerson, Director at (810) 327-6272; fax: (810) 327-6223
e-mail: aemerson@tir.com
Web site: www.camping.umc-detconf.org

Operated by: Detroit Conference-UMC, 1309 N Ballenger Hwy Ste 1, Flint, MI 48504 at (810) 233-5500
Group Rental Information
Facilities: Double Occupancy, Food Service, Linens, Lodges, Meeting Rooms (#46609)

Lake Of The Woods Camp

(est 1935)

Decatur, MI; (616) 423-3091
Dayna Hardin, Director

Camp comments: Over 40 activities on beautiful lake. We promote individual growth & achievement.1:3 staff to camper ratio.
Activities: Arts/Crafts, Climbing/Rappelling, Drama, Gymnastics, Horseback — English, Horseback — Western, Sailing, Tennis, Waterskiing, Windsurfing
Session lengths & capacity: June-August; 3, 4 & 8 week sessions; 130 campers
Clientele & fees: boys 7-15; girls 7-15; families; Fees: E ▲
Contact: Dayna Glasson Hardin, Owner/Director at (888) 459-2492; fax: (480) 515-3698
e-mail: Lwcgwc@aol.com
Web site: www.lakeofthewoodscamps.com
Operated by: Greenwood Camps, 227 Mary Street, Winnetka, IL 60093 at (888) 459-2492 (#1573)

Leelanau Kohahna Camps

(est 1921)

Maple City, MI (Leelanau Co.); (616) 334-3808
Clark Shutt, Director

Camp comments: Camps for children attending the Christian Science Sunday School.
Activities: Archery, Arts/Crafts, Horseback — English, Leadership Development, Nature/Environment Studies, Sailing, Tennis, Waterskiing, Wilderness Trips, Windsurfing
Session lengths & capacity: 3, 4 & 7 week sessions; 160 campers
Clientele & fees: boys 6-17; girls 6-17; Fees: D ▲
Contact: Clark Shutt, Director at (616) 334-3808; fax: (616) 334-6238
e-mail: kohahna@traverse.com
Operated by: Leelanau Kohahna Foundation, 1653 Port Oneida Rd, Maple City, MI 49664-9631 at (616) 334-3808
Group Rental Information
Facilities: Cabins, Food Service, Hiking Trails, Lodges
Programs: Environmental Education (#7434)

Linden (est 1961)

Linden, MI (Livingston Co.); (810) 735-5427
Alison May, Director

Camp comments: Make your summer count! Girls laughing, playing and having fun. Come horseback riding, swimming, climbing and hiking with us this summer!
Activities: Aquatic Activities, Archery, Arts/Crafts, Camping Skills/Outdoor Living, Challenge/Rope Courses, Counselor Training (CIT), Hiking, Horseback — Western, Leadership Development, Nature/Environment Studies
Session lengths & capacity: June-August; 1/2, 1 & 2 week sessions; 250 campers
Clientele & fees: girls 6-17; families; Fees: B ☀
Fees: B, C ▲
Contact: Theresa Bizoe, Camp Director at (734) 971-8800; fax: (734) 971-2160
e-mail: camplinden@aol.com
Operated by: Girl Scouts-Huron Valley Cncl, PO Box 969, Ann Arbor, MI 48106 at (734) 971-8800 (#1263)

Lions Bear Lake Camp

(est 1982)

Lapeer, MI (Lapeer Co.); (810) 245-0726
Dennis Tomkins, Director

Camp comments: Offering outdoor programs and facilities for physically challenged individuals and groups.
Activities: Arts/Crafts, Canoeing, Counselor Training (CIT), Drama, Fishing, Horseback — Western, Nature/Environment Studies, Swimming — Instructional
Session lengths & capacity: June-August; 3 week sessions; 160 campers
Clientele & fees: coed 6-15; families; Fees: A ▲ 🚌
Contact: Dennis Tomkins, Director at (810) 245-0726; fax: (810) 245-0750
e-mail: bearlakecamp@fir.com
Operated by: Lions Visually Impaired Youth, 3409 N Five Lakes Rd, Lapeer, MI 48446 at (810) 245-0721
Group Rental Information
Site comments: Modern, Accessible and comfortable facilities are available for rental all year round. Facilities can accomodate 160 person overnight and 250 day.
Facilities: A/V Equipment, Cabins, Food Service, Hiking Trails, Lake, Meeting Rooms (#46027)

Little Pine Island Camp

(est 1929)

Comstock Park, MI (Kent Co.); (616) 784-1404
Curtis Britcher, Director

Camp comments: West Michigan's best kept secret for year round retreats & summer camping for children in need.
Activities: Aquatic Activities, Camping Skills/Outdoor Living, Challenge/Rope Courses, Leadership Development, Music, Nature/Environment Studies, Religious Study, Sports — Field & Team, Swimming — Recreational, Team Building
Session lengths & capacity: June-August; 1/2, 1 & 2 week sessions; 140 campers
Clientele & fees: coed 7-16; families; seniors; 🚌
Contact: Curtis Britcher, Director at (616) 784-1404; fax: (616) 784-3432
e-mail: lpicamp@usc.salvationarmy.org
Operated by: The Salvation Army, 6889 Pine Island Drive, Comstock Park, MI 49321 at (616) 784-1404
Group Rental Information
Seasons & Capacity: Spring 270, Summer 190, Fall 270, Winter 270
Facilities: A/V Equipment, Cabins, Dorm-Style, Food Service, Hiking Trails, Kitchen Facilities, Lake, Lodges, Meeting Rooms, Playing Fields
Programs: Boating, Challenge/Ropes Course, Winter Sports (#1281)

Maplehurst (est 1955)

Kewadin, MI; (231) 264-9675
Dr Laurence Cohn, Director

Camp comments: Campers develop responsibility and decision making skills by choosing from a variety of well supervised activities.
Activities: Archery, Arts/Crafts, Ceramics/Pottery, Drama, Fishing, Horseback — English, Horseback — Western, SCUBA, Tennis, Waterskiing
Session lengths & capacity: June-September; 2, 4 & 8 week sessions; 120 campers
Clientele & fees: coed 7-17; Fees: E ▲
Contact: Dr Laurence Cohn, Director at (248) 647-2646; fax: (248) 647-6716
e-mail: campmaple@aol.com
Web site: www.campmaplehurst.com
Operated by: Maplehurst Inc, 1455 Quarton Rd, Birmingham, MI 48009 at (248) 647-2646 (#1330)

MMGSC Camp Innisfree

(est 1963)

Howell, MI (Livingston Co.); (313) 878-5133
Julie A Yeager, Director

Camp comments: Girls who love horses & animals camp here! 40+ horses, 5 miles trail. Fun & conscientious staff. Non Girl Scouts welcome
Activities: Aquatic Activities, Boating, Camping Skills/Outdoor Living, Canoeing, Hiking, Horseback — English, Horseback — Western, Nature/Environment Studies, Swimming — Recreational
Session lengths & capacity: June-August; 1/2, 1 & 2 week sessions; 100 campers
Clientele & fees: girls 6-17; Fees: B, C ☀
Fees: D, E ▲
Contact: Julie Yeager, Director of Outdoor Program at (313) 972-4475 ext. 248; (313) 870-2576
e-mail: jyeager@mmgsc.org
Web site: www.mmgsc.org
Operated by: Michigan Metro GSC, 500 Fisher Building, 3011 W Grand Blvd, Detroit, MI 48202-3012 at (313) 972-4475
Group Rental Information
Seasons & Capacity: Spring 150, Summer 150, Fall 150, Winter 150
Facilities: Cabins, Double Occupancy, Hiking Trails, Kitchen Facilities, Lake, Meeting Rooms
Programs: Boating, Environmental Education, Horseback Riding (#7733)

MMGSC Camp Metamora

(est 1936)

Metamora, MI (Lapeer Co.); (810) 678-3333
Julie Yeager, Director

Camp comments: The best camp for girls. Resident and family camps including sisters/best friends. Non Girl Scouts welcome.
Activities: Aquatic Activities, Arts/Crafts, Boating, Camping Skills/Outdoor Living, Canoeing, Ceramics/Pottery, Nature/Environment Studies, Photography, Swimming — Recreational
Session lengths & capacity: June-August; 1/2, 1 & 2 week sessions; 104 campers
Clientele & fees: girls 6-17; families; Fees: B, C, D, E ▲ 🚌
Contact: Julie Yeager, Director, Outdoor Program at (313) 972-4475 ext. 248; fax: (313) 870-2578
e-mail: jyeager@mmgsc.org
Web site: www.mmgsc.org
Operated by: Michigan Metro GSC, 500 Fisher Building, 3011 W Grand Blvd, Detroit, MI 48202-3012 at (313) 972-4475
Group Rental Information
Facilities: Cabins, Hiking Trails, Lake, Lodges, Tents (#1328)

Mystic Lake Ymca Camp

(est 1926)

Lake, MI (Clare Co.); (517) 544-2844
Ian Longman, Director

Camp comments: 600 acress private land 90 acre private lake campers thrive in noncompetitive atmosphere traditional camping programs specialty camps technical tree climbing
Activities: Archery, Arts/Crafts, Boating, Challenge/Rope Courses, Climbing/Rappelling, Counselor Training (CIT), Horseback — Western, Nature/Environment Studies, Swimming — Recreational, Wilderness Trips
Session lengths & capacity: 1, 2, 3 & 8 week sessions; 183 campers
Clientele & fees: coed 5-17; families; Fees: C, D ▲ 🚌
Contact: Ricky Wright, Program Director at (989) 544-2844; fax: (989) 544-2722
e-mail: mlcamp@ymcaoflansing.org
Web site: www.ymcaoflansing.org
Operated by: Mystic Lake Camp, PO Box 100, Lake, MI 48632 at (989) 544-2844

Group Rental Information

Site comments: 600 acres of private land 90 acre private lake. A variety of natural resources & facilities meeting room and lodging. One of the finest facilities of its kind
Facilities: A/V Equipment, Cabins, Double Occupancy, Food Service, Hiking Trails, Kitchen Facilities, Lake, Lodges, Meeting Rooms, Playing Fields
Programs: Boating, Challenge/Ropes Course, Environmental Education, Horseback Riding, Swimming, Winter Sports (#1240)

NCCS Camp Newaygo

(est 1926)

Newaygo, MI (Newaygo Co.); (616) 652-1184
Jane Vitek, Director

Camp comments: Fantastic girls only programs which foster exploration, creativity and cooperation among individuals and communities in the natural environment.
Activities: Aquatic Activities, Archery, Arts/Crafts, Boating, Camping Skills/Outdoor Living, Horseback — English, Music, Photography, Waterskiing, Wilderness Trips
Session lengths & capacity: June-September; 1, 2 & 4 week sessions; 140 campers
Clientele & fees: girls 7-17; coed 5-9; families; seniors; Fees: **B** ☀ Fees: **C, D, E** ⚠ 🐷
Contact: Jane Vitek, Camp Director at (231) 924-0641; fax: (231) 924-5594
e-mail: campnewaygo@ncats.net
Web site: wwwcampnewaygo.org
Operated by: Newaygo County Comm Services, 4 W Oak St, Fremont, MI 49412 at (616) 924-0641

Group Rental Information

Site comments: Our Conference & Retreat Center is ideal for groups up to 200. Visit our "Conference & Retreat Center" page at www.campnewaygo.org for complete details.
Seasons & Capacity: Spring 200, Fall 200
Facilities: A/V Equipment, Cabins, Food Service, Hiking Trails, Lake, Lodges, Meeting Rooms, Tents
Programs: Boating, Challenge/Ropes Course, Environmental Education, Horseback Riding, Swimming (#1222)

Pine Trail Camp (est 1961)

Saugatuck, MI (Allegan Co.); (616) 857-2564
Scott Klingberg, Director
Activities: Archery, Boating, Canoeing, Fishing, Hiking, Religious Study, Snow Sports, Sports — Field & Team, Swimming — Instructional, Swimming — Recreational
Session lengths & capacity: June-August; 1 week sessions; 160 campers

---

ICON LEGEND

☀   Day Camp

⚠   Resident Camp

🏠   Facilities Available To Rent

🚐   Transportation Available

🐷   Financial Aid Available

FEE RANGES PER WEEK

A	$0-75
B	$75-200
C	$201-350
D	$351-500
E	$501-650
F	over $650

Clientele & fees: coed 7-17; Fees: **B** ⚠
Contact: Scott Klingberg, Executive Director at (616) 857-7564; fax: (616) 857-7821
e-mail: info@pinetrailcamp.org
Web site: www.pinetrailcamp.org
Operated by: Pine Trail Camp & Conf Ctr, PO Box 35, Saugatuck, MI 49453 at (616) 857-2564

Group Rental Information

Seasons & Capacity: Spring 160, Summer 200, Fall 160, Winter 160
Facilities: A/V Equipment, Cabins, Dorm-Style, Food Service, Hiking Trails, Lodges, Meeting Rooms, Playing Fields, Pool, River
Programs: Boating, Swimming, Winter Sports (#40516)

Presbyterian Camps (est 1899)

Saugatuck, MI (Allegan Co.); (616) 857-2531
Joe Hill, Director

Camp comments: Lake Michigan Shorefront. Special rustic setting within the city limits of Saugatuck.
Activities: Arts/Crafts, Camping Skills/Outdoor Living, Canoeing, Hiking, Leadership Development, Nature/Environment Studies, Religious Study, Swimming — Recreational, Team Building
Session lengths & capacity: June-August; 1/2 & 1 week sessions; 220 campers
Clientele & fees: boys 7-18; girls 7-18; coed 7-18; families; seniors; single adults; Fees: **B, C** ⚠
Contact: Joseph Hill, Director at (616) 857-2531; fax: (616) 857-3107
e-mail: prescamps@sprynet.com
Web site: www.chicagopresbytery.org
Operated by: Presbytery of Chicago, 100 S Morgan, Chicago, IL 60607 at (312) 243-8300 (#1635)

Salvation Army Echo Grove Camp (est 1921)

Leonard, MI (Oakland Co.); (248) 628-3108
Scott R Barger Sr, Director

Camp comments: Christian camping on the cutting edge for youth, families & visually impaired. Quality staff with a heart for ministry.
Activities: Aquatic Activities, Archery, Arts/Crafts, Baseball/Softball, Basketball, Canoeing, Challenge/Rope Courses, Hiking, Music, Nature/Environment Studies
Session lengths & capacity: 1/2, 1 & 2 week sessions; 450 campers
Clientele & fees: boys 6-18; girls 6-18; coed 6-18; families; seniors; Fees: **B** ⚠
Contact: Dale Johnson, Director at (248) 628-3108; fax: (248) 628-7055
e-mail: echogrovecamp@hotmail.com
Operated by: Salvation Army Echo Grove Camp, 1101 Camp Rd, Leonard, MI 48367 at (248) 628-3108

Group Rental Information

Facilities: Cabins, Food Service, Hiking Trails, Meeting Rooms, Pool
Programs: Boating (#1244)

Sancta Maria (est 1933)

Gaylord, MI (Otsego Co.); (231) 546-3878
Michael Hickey, Director

Camp comments: North Michigan, 2 inland lakes. Catholic framework builds self-esteem, teamwork through ropes course, horsemanship, OLS
Activities: Archery, Arts/Crafts, Backpacking, Basketball, Challenge/Rope Courses, Football, Horseback — Western, Nature/Environment Studies, Wilderness Trips
Session lengths & capacity: June-August; 2 & 3 week sessions; 170 campers
Clientele & fees: boys 8-16; Fees: **C** ⚠ 🐷
Contact: Jim Berigan, Assoc. Director at (231) 546-3878; fax: (231) 546-3171
e-mail: jberigan@campsantamaria.org

Operated by: Camp Sancta Maria Trust, PO Box 338, Gaylord, MI 49734 at (231) 546-3878 (#11311)

Sea Gull (est 1955)

Charlevoix, MI (Charlevoix Co.); (231) 547-6556
Jack and Bill Schulman, Director

Camp comments: All girls camp, located in Charlevoix, Michigan. Sea-Gull provides a supportive environment in which girls can experience success, accomplishment & fun.
Activities: Arts/Crafts, Challenge/Rope Courses, Golf, Horseback — English, Kayaking, Performing Arts, Sailing, Sports — Field & Team, Tennis, Waterskiing
Session lengths & capacity: June-August; 2, 4 & 6 week sessions; 100 campers
Clientele & fees: girls 7-16; Fees: **E, F** ⚠
Contact: Bill Schulman, Director at (231) 547-6556; fax: (231) 547-0461
e-mail: seagull@freeway.net
Web site: www.campseagull.com
Operated by: Camp Sea Gull, 301 Mercer Blvd, Charlevoix, MI 49720 at (231) 547-6556

Group Rental Information

Seasons & Capacity: Spring 200, Summer 200, Fall 200
Facilities: A/V Equipment, Cabins, Dorm-Style, Double Occupancy, Food Service, Lake, Lodges, Meeting Rooms, Playing Fields, Tents
Programs: Boating, Challenge/Ropes Course, Environmental Education, Swimming, Winter Sports (#1264)

Sherman Lake YMCA Outdoor Ctr (est 1995)

Augusta, MI (Kalamazoo Co.); (616) 731-3000
Luke Austenfeld, Director

Camp comments: All programs at this new YMCA camp reinforce four principles: honesty, caring, respect, and responsibility.
Activities: Aquatic Activities, Archery, Arts/Crafts, Aviation, Challenge/Rope Courses, Sailing, Skating, Soccer, Sports — Field & Team, Wilderness Trips
Session lengths & capacity: June-August; 1/2, 1 & 2 week sessions; 300 campers
Clientele & fees: coed 6-15; families; seniors; Fees: **C** ☀ Fees: **C, D** ⚠ 🐷
Contact: Bob Campbell, Director of Camping Services at (616) 731-3021; fax: (616) 731-3020
e-mail: RobertC@ymcaSL.org
Operated by: Sherman Lake YMCA Camp, 6225 N 39th Street, Augusta, MI 49012-9722 at (616) 731-3021

Group Rental Information

Site comments: Imagine a mile of lakefront,wooded setting,brand-new state of the art facilities,and a staff that cares about people.
Seasons & Capacity: Winter 200
Facilities: A/V Equipment, Cabins, Double Occupancy, Food Service, Hiking Trails, Kitchen Facilities, Lake, Linens, Lodges, Meeting Rooms, Ocean, Playing Fields, Pool
Programs: Boating, Challenge/Ropes Course, Environmental Education, Swimming, Winter Sports (#901376)

Skyline Camp (est 1964)

Almont, MI (Lapeer Co.); (810) 798-8240
Joel Thiebaut, Director

Camp comments: Skyline, 156-acre country site, rolling hills with wildlife & natural beauty. We try to model life the way it should be.
Activities: Archery, Arts/Crafts, Bicycling/Biking, Camping Skills/Outdoor Living, Canoeing, Challenge/Rope Courses, Nature/Environment Studies, Religious Study, Soccer, Swimming — Recreational
Session lengths & capacity: June-August; 1/2, 1 & 2 week sessions; 72 campers

Clientele & fees: coed 6-18; families; seniors; single adults; Fees: **C** △
Contact: Mary Cupples, Registrar Admin.-Asst. at (248) 644-2040; fax: (248) 644-8047
e-mail: cskyline@hotmail.com
Operated by: First Presbyterian Church, 1669 W Maple Rd, Birmingham, MI 48009-1298 at (248) 644-2040

Group Rental Information
Site comments: Cabin groups of 6-8.Highly qualified staff. 72 campers/week. Noncompetitive. Rec. Christian values. Aquatics, outdoor skills.
Seasons & Capacity: Spring 104, Summer 184, Fall 104, Winter 104
Facilities: Cabins, Food Service, Hiking Trails, Lake, Lodges, Meeting Rooms, Pool (#3945)

Spring Hill Camps Inc
(est 1969)   ☀ △ ⌂

Evart, MI (Osceola Co.); (231) 734-2616
Michael Perry, Director

Camp comments: Helping parents raise better kids!
Activities: Aquatic Activities, Arts/Crafts, Basketball, Challenge/Rope Courses, Climbing/Rappelling, Drama, Horseback — Western, Soccer, Tennis, Wilderness Trips
Session lengths & capacity: June-August; 1, 2 & 3 week sessions; 460 campers
Clientele & fees: boys 7-17; girls 7-17; coed 7-17; Fees: **A, C, D** △ 🐎
Contact: David Grout, Director of Marketing/Dev at (231) 734-2616; fax: (231) 734-9870
e-mail: dgrout@springhillcamps.com
Web site: www.springhillcamps.com
Operated by: Spring Hill Initiatives, PO Box 100, Evart, MI 49631 at (231) 734-2616

Group Rental Information
Facilities: Cabins, Food Service, Meeting Rooms, Pool
Programs: Boating, Environmental Education, Horseback Riding (#11328)

Summer Impressions Day Camp
☀

West Bloomfield, MI (Oakland Co.); (248) 661-3630
Libby & Art White, Director

Camp comments: Specialty day camp, pro instructors, in-ground pools,tennis & basketball, sports fields, arts/crafts bldg, fitness trail
Activities: Arts/Crafts, Baseball/Softball, Basketball, Computer, Drama, Nature/Environment Studies, Sports — Field & Team, Swimming — Instructional, Swimming — Recreational, Tennis
Session lengths & capacity: June-August; 1 & 3 week sessions
Clientele & fees: boys 4-9; girls 4-9; coed 4-9; Fees: **C** ☀
Contact: Libby & Art White, Directors at (248) 661-3630; fax: (248) 357-6361
Operated by: Summer Impressions Day Camp, 6280 Carroll, W Bloomfield, MI 48322 at (248) 661-3630 (#6680)

Tamarack Camps (est 1902)   △ ⌂ 🚗

Ortonville, MI; (248) 627-2821
Harvey Finkelberg, Director

Camp comments: Jewish community camp offering all sports, water activities, fine arts, horseback riding, ropes course & always a fun, exciting summer.
Activities: Aquatic Activities, Arts/Crafts, Camping Skills/Outdoor Living, Ceramics/Pottery, Challenge/Rope Courses, Gymnastics, Hiking, Horseback — Western, Sports — Field & Team, Waterskiing
Session lengths & capacity: June-August; 1, 2, 3, 4, 6, 7 week sessions; 750 campers
Clientele & fees: coed 7-16; families; Fees: **D** △ 🐎

Contact: Harvey Finkelberg, Executive Director at (248) 647-1100; fax: (248) 647-1493
e-mail: tamarack@tamarackcamps.com
Operated by: Fresh Air Society, 6735 Telegraph Road Suite 380, Bloomfield, MI 48301 at (248) 647-1100

Group Rental Information
Seasons & Capacity: Spring 400, Summer 200, Fall 400, Winter 400
Facilities: A/V Equipment, Cabins, Double Occupancy, Food Service, Hiking Trails, Kitchen Facilities, Lake, Lodges, Meeting Rooms, Playing Fields, Pool, River
Programs: Boating, Challenge/Ropes Course, Environmental Education, Horseback Riding, Swimming, Winter Sports (#3309)

Tannadoonah (est 1921)   ☀ △ ⌂

Vandalia, MI (Cass Co.); (616) 476-2177
Jane Goldsberry, Director

Camp comments: Tannadoonah has always been dedicated to fun for the camper in a well supervised outdoor atmosphere. Rich in tradition.
Activities: Archery, Camping Skills/Outdoor Living, Canoeing, Kayaking, Sailing, Soccer, Swimming — Instructional, Swimming — Recreational, Tennis
Session lengths & capacity: May-August; 7 week sessions; 104 campers
Clientele & fees: boys 6-13; girls 6-16; Fees: **B** ☀ Fees: **C** △
Contact: Jane Goldsberry, Director at (219) 234-4145;
Operated by: Camp Fire USA River Bend Cnl, 2828 E Jefferson Blvd, South Bend, IN 46615-2726 at (219) 234-4145

Group Rental Information
Seasons & Capacity: Spring 150, Summer 150, Fall 150
Facilities: Cabins, Kitchen Facilities, Lake
Programs: Boating (#1497)

The Fowler Center (est 1957)   △ ⌂

Mayville, MI (Lapeer Co.); (989) 673-2050
Thomas Hussmann, Director

Camp comments: Supported recreation. Barrier free campus with a wide variety of opportunities. Promoting independence & personal growth.
Activities: Aquatic Activities, Arts/Crafts, Backpacking, Baseball/Softball, Camping Skills/Outdoor Living, Farming/Ranching/Gardening, Hiking, Horseback — English, Nature/Environment Studies, Soccer
Session lengths & capacity: June-August; 1/2, 1 & 2 week sessions; 90 campers
Clientele & fees: boys 6-99; girls 6-99; coed 6-99; families; seniors; Fees: **D** △ 🐎
Contact: Patricia Jordan, Program Registrar at (517) 673-2050; fax: (517) 635-6355
e-mail: info@thefowlercenter.org
Web site: www.thefowlercenter.org
Operated by: The Fowler Center, 2315 Harmon Lake Road, Mayville, MI 48744 at (989) 673-2050

Group Rental Information
Site comments: Barrier free camping for group homes and assisted living homes. Supported recreation that your residents can cherish and remember for a lifetime!
Seasons & Capacity: Spring 100, Fall 100, Winter 100
Facilities: Cabins, Food Service, Hiking Trails, Kitchen Facilities, Lake, Meeting Rooms, Playing Fields
Programs: Boating, Environmental Education, Horseback Riding, Swimming, Winter Sports (#1350)

The Timbers Girl Scout Camp
(est 1962)   △ ⌂ 🚗

Traverse City, MI (Grand Traverse Co.); (231) 946-8981
Abby Wattenberg, Director

Camp comments: Wilderness adventure and challenge camping for girls.
Activities: Aquatic Activities, Arts/Crafts, Backpacking, Bicycling/Biking, Camping Skills/Outdoor Living, Canoeing, Challenge/Rope Courses, Climbing/Rappelling, Sailing, Wilderness Trips
Session lengths & capacity: June-August; 2, 3 & 4 week sessions; 110 campers
Clientele & fees: girls 12-17; Fees: **B, C, D** △
Contact: Joann Downing, Director at (810) 230-0244; fax: (810) 230-0955
Web site: www.fwgsc.org
Operated by: Fair Winds GSC, PO Box 349, Swartz Creek, MI 48473 at (800) 482-6734

Group Rental Information
Facilities: Hiking Trails
Programs: Winter Sports (#1250)

Tower Hill Camp & Retreat Ctr
△ ⌂

Sawyer, MI (Berrien Co.); (269) 426-3881
Robert Schmidt, Director
Activities: Arts/Crafts, Dance, Drama, Music, Religious Study, Sports — Field & Team
Session lengths & capacity: 1/2 & 1 week sessions
Clientele & fees: coed 2-18; families; seniors; single adults; Fees: **C** △
Contact: Robert Schmidt, Camp Manager at (616) 426-3881; fax: (616) 426-8255
e-mail: rsch49125@aol.com
Web site: www.ilucc.org
Operated by: Illinois Conference UCC, 1840 Westchester Blvd Ste 200, Westchester, IL 60154 at (708) 344-4470

Group Rental Information
Seasons & Capacity: Spring 187, Summer 310, Fall 187, Winter 150
Facilities: A/V Equipment, Cabins, Dorm-Style, Double Occupancy, Food Service, Hiking Trails, Kitchen Facilities, Lake, Linens, Lodges, Meeting Rooms, Playing Fields, Tents
Programs: Challenge/Ropes Course, Swimming (#11734)

UMC at Lake Louise (est 1936)   △

Boyne Falls, MI; (231) 549-2728
Dean Ozment, Director

Camp comments: Detroit Conf United Methodist Camps are avail to all regardless of race,color,religion,national origin,sex,age or handicapp.
Activities: Arts/Crafts, Swimming — Recreational
Session lengths & capacity: June-August; 1 week sessions; 120 campers
Clientele & fees: coed 9-18; Fees: **C** △ 🐎
Contact: Steffanie Schwartz, Camp Registrar at (800) 334-0544 ext. 354; fax: (810) 233-5700
e-mail: campregistrar@umc-detconf.org
Web site: www.camping.umc-detconf.org
Operated by: Detroit Conference-UMC, 1309 N Ballenger Hwy Ste 1, Flint, MI 48504 at (810) 233-5500 (#46616)

Van Buren Youth Camp
(est 1950)   △ ⌂

Bloomingdale, MI (Van Buren Co.); (616) 521-3855
Tricia Merson, Director

Camp comments: Traditional recreational youth camp with leadership focus.
Activities: Archery, Arts/Crafts, Canoeing, Leadership Development, Nature/Environment Studies, Riflery, Swimming — Recreational
Session lengths & capacity: 1 week sessions; 125 campers
Clientele & fees: coed 8-17; Fees: **B** △ 🐎
Contact: Tricia Merson, Executive Director at (616) 521-3855; fax: (616) 521-6668
e-mail: amosmoses@btc-bci.com
Web site: www.vbyc.org

Operated by: Van Buren Youth Camp, 12370 45th St, Bloomingdale, MI 49026 at (616) 521-3855

Group Rental Information
Facilities: Cabins, Dorm-Style, Food Service, Hiking Trails, Kitchen Facilities, Lake, Linens, Lodges, Meeting Rooms, Playing Fields, Tents
Programs: Boating, Challenge/Ropes Course, Environmental Education, Swimming, Winter Sports (#1293)

Willoway Day Camp Inc

(est 1969)

W Bloomfield, MI (Oakland Co.); (248) 932-2123
Lorraine & Arnold Fisher, Director

Camp comments: Exciting noncompetitive program in a warm & caring environment. Beautiful pools, pond & lake in a natural setting. 33 yrs of self esteem building & great fun.
Activities: Aquatic Activities, Archery, Arts/Crafts, Counselor Training (CIT), Fishing, Nature/Environment Studies, Photography, Sports — Field & Team, Swimming — Instructional, Swimming — Recreational
Session lengths & capacity: June-August; 1, 4 & 8 week sessions; 250 campers
Clientele & fees: coed 5-14; Fees: C ☀
Contact: Lorraine or Arnold Fisher, Directors at (248) 932-2123;
e-mail: willowaydc@aol.com
Web site: www.willowaydaycamp.com
Operated by: Willoway Day Camp, PO Box 250933, West Bloomfield, MI 48325 at (248) 932-2123 (#16961)

Y Camp Pendalouan

(est 1924)

Montague, MI (Muskegon Co.); (231) 894-4538
June de Lorme, Director

Camp comments: 76 years of camping excellence! Forest & lake setting provide beautiful place for strong, traditional, YMCA camping pgm.
Activities: Archery, Boating, Canoeing, Challenge/Rope Courses, Horseback — Western, Nature/Environment Studies, Photography, Riflery, Sailing, Swimming — Recreational
Session lengths & capacity: June-August; 1/2, 1 & 2 week sessions; 150 campers
Clientele & fees: coed 7-17; families; Fees: B ☀
Fees: B, C ⛺ 🚐
Contact: June de Lorme, Executive Director at (231) 894-4538; fax: (231) 894-4448
e-mail: ycamp@pendalouan.org
Web site: www.muskegonymca.org
Operated by: Muskegon Family YMCA, 900 W Western Ave, Muskegon, MI 49441 at (231) 722-9322

ICON LEGEND

☀	Day Camp
⛺	Resident Camp
🏠	Facilities Available To Rent
🚐	Transportation Available
🐷	Financial Aid Available

FEE RANGES PER WEEK

A	$0-75
B	$75-200
C	$201-350
D	$351-500
E	$501-650
F	over $650

Group Rental Information
Site comments: A quiet, secluded retreat for your group in beautiful western Michigan. Many activities and a dedicated staff to enhance your experience.
Seasons & Capacity: Spring 170, Fall 170, Winter 170
Facilities: A/V Equipment, Cabins, Dorm-Style, Food Service, Hiking Trails, Lake, Lodges, Meeting Rooms, Playing Fields, River
Programs: Boating, Challenge/Ropes Course, Environmental Education, Horseback Riding, Swimming, Winter Sports (#1320)

YMCA Camp Algonquin

(est 1947)

Hastings, MI (Barry Co.); (616) 945-4574
Catherine Deyo, Director

Camp comments: A place where the focus is not on getting to the top or winning, but rather on building each individual's self-esteem and group-worth.
Activities: Archery, Arts/Crafts, Boating, Camping Skills/Outdoor Living, Challenge/Rope Courses, Climbing/Rappelling, Field Trips, International Culture, Nature/Environment Studies
Session lengths & capacity: June-August; 1/2 & 1 week sessions; 49 campers
Clientele & fees: coed 6-13; Fees: B ☀
Fees: C ⛺ 🐷
Contact: Cathi Deyo, Executive Director at (616) 945-4574; fax: (616) 945-2631
Operated by: Barry County YMCA, PO Box 252, Hastings, MI 49058 at (616) 945-4574 (#1375)

YMCA Camp Arbutus-Hayo-Went-Ha

(est 1914)

Traverse City, MI (Grand Traverse Co.); (231) 946-8589
Amanda Macaluso, Director

Camp comments: YMCA Camp Arbutus/Hayo-Went-Ha offers great wilderness trips, individualized programs, worldwide staff, long traditions and a large equestrian program.
Activities: Arts/Crafts, Camping Skills/Outdoor Living, Challenge/Rope Courses, Counselor Training (CIT), Field Trips, Hiking, Horseback — English, Kayaking, Nature/Environment Studies, Wilderness Trips
Session lengths & capacity: June-September; 2 & 4 week sessions; 130 campers
Clientele & fees: girls 9-17; Fees: D ⛺ 🐷
Contact: Amanda Macaluso, Camp Director at (231) 946-8589; fax: (231) 946-8677
e-mail: amacaluso@hayowentha.org
Web site: www.hayowentha.org
Operated by: State YMCA of Michigan, 919 N East Torch Lake Dr, Central Lake, MI 49622 at (231) 544-5915 (#1232)

YMCA Camp Copneconic

(est 1915)

Fenton, MI (Genesee Co.); (810) 629-9622
Frederick (Fritz) Cheek, Director

Camp comments: For anyone who likes the water, horses or high adventure. There's sailing, boating, fishing, swimming and an Aqua Jump. We offer day and resident camps.
Activities: Aquatic Activities, Archery, Arts/Crafts, Camping Skills/Outdoor Living, Challenge/Rope Courses, Horseback — Western, Sailing, Swimming — Recreational
Session lengths & capacity: June-August; 1 week sessions; 180 campers
Clientele & fees: coed 3-16; seniors; Fees: B ☀
Fees: C ⛺
Contact: Frederick (Fritz) Cheek, Executive Director at (810) 629-9622; fax: (810) 629-2128
e-mail: fritzcheek@campcopneconic.org

Operated by: Flint Michigan YMCA, 411 E 3rd Street, Flint, MI 48503 at (810) 232-9622

Group Rental Information
Facilities: Cabins, Dorm-Style, Double Occupancy, Food Service, Hiking Trails, Lake
Programs: Boating, Challenge/Ropes Course, Environmental Education, Horseback Riding, Swimming, Winter Sports (#1344)

YMCA Camp Eberhart

(est 1909)

Three Rivers, MI (St Joseph Co.); (616) 244-5125
Brice Emanuel, Director

Camp comments: Recreational skill proficiency development. Astronomy observatory, windsurfing, sailing, horseback, waterskiing.
Activities: Canoeing, Challenge/Rope Courses, Horseback — Western, Model Rocketry, Photography, Riflery, Sailing, Swimming — Recreational, Waterskiing, Windsurfing
Session lengths & capacity: June-August; 1/2 & 1 week sessions; 275 campers
Clientele & fees: boys 7-16; girls 7-16; coed 7-16; families; Fees: B ☀ Fees: D ⛺ 🐷
Contact: Brice Emanuel, Director of Camping Services at (616) 244-5125; fax: (616) 244-5000
e-mail: emanueleb@aol.com
Web site: www.campeb.org
Operated by: YMCA of Michiana, 1201 Northside Blvd, South Bend, IN 46615 at (219) 287-9622

Group Rental Information
Seasons & Capacity: Spring 160, Summer 245, Fall 160, Winter 160
Facilities: Cabins, Dorm-Style, Food Service, Hiking Trails, Lake, Lodges, Meeting Rooms, Playing Fields
Programs: Boating, Challenge/Ropes Course, Environmental Education, Horseback Riding, Swimming, Winter Sports (#1526)

YMCA Camp Hayo-Went-Ha

(est 1904)

Central Lake, MI (Antrim Co.); (231) 544-5915
David Martin, Director

Camp comments: Traditional YMCA program. Outstanding water activities. Wilderness setting & trips. Character development-100 year tradition.
Activities: Camping Skills/Outdoor Living, Challenge/Rope Courses, Counselor Training (CIT), Hiking, Nature/Environment Studies, Sailing, SCUBA, Sports — Field & Team, Team Building, Wilderness Trips
Session lengths & capacity: June-September; 2 & 4 week sessions; 210 campers
Clientele & fees: boys 10-17; coed 5-9; families; Fees: B ☀ Fees: D ⛺ 🐷
Contact: David R Martin, Camp Director at (231) 544-5915; fax: (231) 544-2916
e-mail: dmartin@hayowentha.org
Web site: www.hayowentha.org
Operated by: State YMCA of Michigan, 919 N East Torch Lake Dr, Central Lake, MI 49622 at (231) 544-5915

Group Rental Information
Site comments: Perfect conference setting for groups located on beautiful Torch Lake. Near Traverse City, Michigan. Dormitory-style housing and excellent meal service.
Facilities: Cabins, Dorm-Style, Food Service, Hiking Trails, Lake, Playing Fields
Programs: Boating, Challenge/Ropes Course, Environmental Education, Winter Sports (#1362)

YMCA Camp Manitou Lin

(est 1913)

Middleville, MI; (616) 891-9160
Jay Turpin, Executive Director, Director

Camp comments: YMCA Camp Manitou Lin provides a rich tradition of camping experience for youth. Transportation provided for Day Camp.

Activities: Arts/Crafts, Bicycling/Biking, Camping Skills/Outdoor Living, Canoeing, Challenge/Rope Courses, Counselor Training (CIT), Horseback — Western, Nature/Environment Studies, Team Building
Session lengths & capacity: January-December; 1 week sessions; 220 campers
Clientele & fees: coed 4-17; families; Fees: B ☀ Fees: C ⚠ 🐷
Contact: Jay Turpin, Executive Director at (888) 909-2267; fax: (616) 795-1629
e-mail: jturpin@grymca.org
Web site: www.grymca.org
Operated by: Grand Rapids Metropolitan YMCA, 1095 Briggs Rd, Middleville, MI 49333 at (616) 795-9163 (#14335)

YMCA Camp Nissokone

(est 1914)   ⚠ 🏠

Oscoda, MI (Iosco Co.); (989) 739-2801
David E Marks, Director

Camp comments: High adventure camp for teens. Specializing in horses, water sports, off camp trips, leadership training, voyager canoes.
Activities: Challenge/Rope Courses, Drama, Horseback — Western, Leadership Development, Nature/Environment Studies, Sailing, Swimming — Instructional
Session lengths & capacity: 1 & 2 week sessions; 220 campers
Clientele & fees: boys 10-17; girls 10-17; coed 10-17; families; Fees: C ⚠ 🐷
Contact: David Marks, Executive Director at (248) 887-4533; fax: (248) 887-5203
e-mail: campymca@ymcametrodetroit.org
Operated by: YMCA Camping Services, 7300 Hickory Ridge Rd, Holly, MI 48442 at (248) 887-4533

Group Rental Information
Facilities: Cabins, Food Service, Lake, Lodges
Programs: Boating, Environmental Education, Horseback Riding (#6629)

YMCA Camp Ohiyesa

(est 1918)   ☀ ⚠ 🏠 🚗

Holly, MI (Oakland Co.); (248) 887-4533
David E Marks, Director

Camp comments: Small group work philosophy camp w/high quality trained staff, professional year round leadership challenging activities
Activities: Aquatic Activities, Archery, Camping Skills/Outdoor Living, Canoeing, Climbing/Rappelling, Drama, Farming/Ranching/Gardening, Hiking, Music, Nature/Environment Studies
Session lengths & capacity: June-August; 1 week sessions; 200 campers
Clientele & fees: coed 5-13; Fees: B ☀ 🐷
Contact: David Marks, Executive Director at (248) 887-4533; fax: (248) 887-5203
e-mail: campymca@ymcametrodetroit.org
Operated by: YMCA Camping Services, 7300 Hickory Ridge Rd, Holly, MI 48442 at (248) 887-4533

Group Rental Information
Facilities: Cabins, Food Service, Hiking Trails, Lake, Meeting Rooms
Programs: Boating, Environmental Education (#31609)

YMCA Camp Pinewood

(est 1925)   ⚠ 🏠 🚗

Twin Lake, MI; (231) 821-2421
Dean Buntley, Director

Camp comments: Co-ed outdoor adventure camp in Michigan's Manistec National Forest. Rental groups & family camps also available.

Activities: Backpacking, Camping Skills/Outdoor Living, Challenge/Rope Courses, Climbing/Rappelling, Horseback — Western, Leadership Development, Sailing, Swimming — Instructional, Travel/Tour
Session lengths & capacity: 1, 2 & 3 week sessions; 230 campers
Clientele & fees: boys 7-15; girls 7-15; coed 7-15; families; single adults; Fees: D ⚠ 🐷
Contact: Dean Buntley, Executive Director at (231) 821-2421; fax: (231) 821-0487
e-mail: dbuntley@ymcachgo.org
Operated by: YMCA Of Metropolitan Chicago, 801 N Dearborn St, Chicago, IL 60610 at (312) 932-1200

Group Rental Information
Seasons & Capacity: Spring 200, Winter 150
Facilities: A/V Equipment, Cabins, Food Service, Hiking Trails, Lake, Lodges, Meeting Rooms, Playing Fields
Programs: Boating, Challenge/Ropes Course, Environmental Education, Horseback Riding, Swimming, Winter Sports (#1581)

YMCA Storer Camps

(est 1918)   ☀ ⚠ 🏠

Jackson, MI (Jackson Co.); (517) 536-8607
Nancy Burger, Director

Camp comments: Traditional program plus wilderness trips. Leadership training, warm supportive environment for all campers. FUN!
Activities: Aquatic Activities, Archery, Backpacking, Challenge/Rope Courses, Horseback — Western, Leadership Development, Nature/Environment Studies, Sailing, Swimming — Recreational, Travel/Tour
Session lengths & capacity: January-December; 1, 2 & 3 week sessions; 450 campers
Clientele & fees: boys 15-17; girls 15-17; coed 8-15; families; Fees: D ⚠ 🐷
Contact: Dawn Mayett, Administrative Assistant at (517) 536-8607; fax: (517) 536-4922
e-mail: ystorer@dmci.net
Web site: www.ymcastorercamps.org
Operated by: YMCA of Greater Toledo, YMCA Storer Camps, 7260 South Stony Lake Road, Jackson, MI 49201 at (517) 536-8607

Group Rental Information
Seasons & Capacity: Spring 580, Summer 630, Fall 580, Winter 580
Facilities: A/V Equipment, Cabins, Dorm-Style, Food Service, Hiking Trails, Lake, Lodges, Meeting Rooms, Playing Fields
Programs: Boating, Challenge/Ropes Course, Environmental Education, Horseback Riding, Swimming, Winter Sports (#1349)

Minnesota

Big Sandy Camp and Retreat Ctr (est 1959)

⚠ 🏠 🚗

Mc Gregor, MN (Aitkin Co.); (218) 426-3389
Gordie Fisher, Director

Camp comments: Beautiful N. MN setting, tall pines, excellent waterfront. Christ-centered, highly relational program. Great facilities.
Activities: Archery, Arts/Crafts, Bicycling/Biking, Canoeing, Challenge/Rope Courses, Counselor Training (CIT), Nature/Environment Studies, Riflery, Swimming — Recreational
Session lengths & capacity: June-September; 1/2 & 1 week sessions; 220 campers
Clientele & fees: coed 7-18; families; seniors; single adults; Fees: B ⚠ 🐷
Contact: Gordie Fisher, Executive Director at (218) 426-3389; fax: (218) 426-3394
e-mail: bsc@lcp2.net

Operated by: Big Sandy Camp and Retreat Ctr, 52511 185th Place, Mc Gregor, MN 55760 at (218) 426-3389

Group Rental Information
Seasons & Capacity: Spring 250, Summer 250, Fall 250, Winter 250
Facilities: A/V Equipment, Dorm-Style, Food Service, Hiking Trails, Lake, Lodges, Meeting Rooms, Playing Fields
Programs: Boating, Challenge/Ropes Course, Winter Sports (#13852)

Bovey (est 1949)

⚠ 🏠 🚗

Solon Springs, WI (Douglas Co.); (715) 378-2914
Kathy Jurichko, Director

Camp comments: For over 50 years Camp Bovey has been providing a safe, fun and meaningful camp experience for youth. Become a part of the tradition!
Activities: Arts/Crafts, Backpacking, Boating, Camping Skills/Outdoor Living, Canoeing, Fishing, Leadership Development, Swimming — Instructional, Swimming — Recreational, Team Building
Session lengths & capacity: June-August; 1 & 2 week sessions; 48 campers
Clientele & fees: coed 8-14; Fees: C ⚠ 🐷
Contact: Kathy Jurichko, Camp Director at (612) 787-4030; fax: (612) 787-4002
e-mail: campbovey@esns.org
Operated by: East Side Neighborhood Service, 1700 2nd St NE, Minneapolis, MN 55413 at (612) 781-6011

Group Rental Information
Site comments: Camp Bovey offers a rustic, quiet setting for retreats, ideal for civic, academic or faith based groups.
Seasons & Capacity: Fall 30
Facilities: Cabins, Double Occupancy, Food Service, Kitchen Facilities, Lake, Lodges
Programs: Boating, Swimming (#1215)

Camp Birchwood (est 1959)

⚠ 🚗

La Porte, MN; (218) 335-6706
Terry Bredemus and Rachel Wagman, Director

Camp comments: Gorgeous girls camp offers 30+ exciting activities that build confidence and outstanding memories of fun and friendship. Quality staff. Independent daily signup
Activities: Archery, Arts/Crafts, Ceramics/Pottery, Climbing/Rappelling, Dance, Horseback — Western, Sailing, Tennis, Waterskiing, Wilderness Trips
Session lengths & capacity: June-August; 2, 4, 6 & 8 week sessions; 144 campers
Clientele & fees: girls 8-18; Fees: E ⚠ 🐷
Contact: Terry Bredemus Rachel Wagman, Director at (218) 335-6706; fax: (218) 335-7866
e-mail: cbgwc@aol.com
Web site: www.campbirchwood.com
Operated by: Camp Birchwood, 6983 N Steamboat Lake Dr, LaPorte, MN 56461 at (218) 335-2809 (#1183)

Camp Buckskin (est 1959)

⚠

Ely, MN; (218) 365-2121
Thomas Bauer, CCD, Director

Camp comments: Our therapeutic program promotes social and academic growth. This growth produces greater success at home and in school.
Activities: Academics, Archery, Arts/Crafts, Canoeing, Nature/Environment Studies, Riflery, Swimming — Instructional, Team Building, Wilderness Trips
Session lengths & capacity: June-August; 4 week sessions; 160 campers
Clientele & fees: coed 6-18; Fees: E ⚠
Contact: Thomas Bauer, CCD, Director at (952) 930-3544; fax: (952) 938-6996
e-mail: buckskin@spacestar.net
Web site: www.campbuckskin.com

Operated by: Camp Buckskin, 8700 W 36th St Suite 6W, St Louis Park, MN 55426 at (952) 930-3544 (#1179)

Camp Chippewa For Boys

(est 1935) △

Cass Lake, MN (Beltrami Co.); (218) 335-8807
John Endres, Director

Camp comments: Limited enrollment, unlimited opportunities, traditional pgm & Canada canoe trips, fish from our Canadian island lodge.
Activities: Archery, Canoeing, Fencing, Fishing, Kayaking, Riflery, Sailing, Waterskiing, Wilderness Trips
Session lengths & capacity: June-August; 2, 4 & 8 week sessions; 72 campers
Clientele & fees: boys 7-17; Fees: E △ 🐷
Contact: John Endres or Michael Thompson, Director at (414) 241-5733; fax: (414) 241-3893
e-mail: campchip@aol.com
Web site: www.campchippewa.com
Operated by: Camp Chippewa Foundation, 15 E 5th St Ste 4022, Tulsa, OK 74103 at (918) 599-7968 (#934)

Camp Cormorant

△ 🏠

Lake Park, MN (Cass Co.)
Activities: Archery, Arts/Crafts, Boating, Canoeing, Challenge/Rope Courses, Drama, Horseback — Western, Leadership Development, Photography, Swimming — Recreational
Contact: Web site: www.campcormorant.org
Operated by: YMCA Camp Cormorant, 4243 19th Ave SW, Fargo, ND 58103 at (701) 281-0126

Group Rental Information
Facilities: Cabins, Kitchen Facilities, Lake, Playing Fields
Programs: Swimming (#48506)

Camp Foley (est 1924)

△ 🏠 🚗

Pine River, MN (Crow Wing Co.); (218) 543-6161
Marie Schmid, Director

Camp comments: Make your summer sizzle! It's awesome! It's fun! Lake setting; traditional prog. Talented staff guide in making new friends & learning new skills.
Activities: Archery, Bicycling/Biking, Climbing/Rappelling, Nature/Environment Studies, Riflery, Sailing, Tennis, Waterskiing, Wilderness Trips, Windsurfing
Session lengths & capacity: June-August; 2 & 4 week sessions; 160 campers
Clientele & fees: coed 8-16; Fees: F △
Contact: Marie Schmid, Director at (218) 543-6161; fax: (218) 543-4269

ICON LEGEND

☀ Day Camp
△ Resident Camp
🏠 Facilities Available To Rent
🚗 Transportation Available
🐷 Financial Aid Available

FEE RANGES PER WEEK

A	$0-75
B	$75-200
C	$201-350
D	$351-500
E	$501-650
F	over $650

e-mail: fun@campfoley.com
Web site: www.campfoley.com
Operated by: Camp Foley, Trail Properties Inc, 9303 Father Foley Dr, Pine River, MN 56474 at (218) 543-6161 (#1143)

Camp Friendship (est 1965)

△ 🏠

Annandale, MN (Wright Co.); (952) 852-0101
Laurie Tschetter, Director

Camp comments: Beautiful site in Central MN., offers services for children/adults with disabilities. Travel program & family camp.
Activities: Archery, Arts/Crafts, Canoeing, Challenge/Rope Courses, Counselor Training (CIT), Drama, Leadership Development, Music, Nature/Environment Studies, Travel/Tour
Session lengths & capacity: 1/2, 1, 2 & 3 week sessions; 125 campers
Clientele & fees: coed 5-90; families; seniors; single adults; Fees: D, E △ 🐷
Contact: Laurie Tschetter, Program Director at (952) 852-0101; fax: (952) 852-0123
e-mail: fv@friendshipventures.org
Web site: www.friendshipventures.org
Operated by: Friendship Ventures, 10509 108th Ave NW, Annandale, MN 55302 at (952) 852-0101

Group Rental Information
Site comments: 60 miles NW of Twin Cities. Beautiful site. High & low ropes challenge course.
Seasons & Capacity: Spring 205, Fall 205, Winter 205
Facilities: A/V Equipment, Cabins, Dorm-Style, Food Service, Hiking Trails, Lake, Linens, Lodges, Meeting Rooms, Playing Fields, Pool
Programs: Challenge/Ropes Course, Environmental Education, Swimming, Winter Sports (#1191)

Camp Greenwood (est 1925)

△ 🏠

Buffalo, MN (Wright Co.); (763) 684-4243
Heather Farber, Director

Camp comments: Where girls grow strong. A beautiful camp,2 lakes,trips,general camp program. Excitement and adventure await you at Camp Greenwood!
Activities: Arts/Crafts, Bicycling/Biking, Boating, Camping Skills/Outdoor Living, Canoeing, Counselor Training (CIT), Nature/Environment Studies, Swimming — Recreational, Team Building, Wilderness Trips
Session lengths & capacity: June-August; 1/2, 1 & 2 week sessions; 120 campers
Clientele & fees: girls 7-17; Fees: C △ 🐷
Contact: Heather Farber, Camp Director at (763) 971-4050; fax: (763) 535-7524
e-mail: hfarber@girlscoutsmpls.org
Web site: www.girlscoutsmpls.org
Operated by: GSC Greater Minneapolis, 5601 Brooklyn Blvd, Minneapolis, MN 55429 at (763) 535-4602

Group Rental Information
Facilities: Cabins, Hiking Trails, Kitchen Facilities, Lake, Lodges, Meeting Rooms, Tents
Programs: Boating, Challenge/Ropes Course, Environmental Education, Swimming (#1140)

Camp Kamaji (est 1914)

△

Cass Lake, MN (Hubbard Co.); (218) 335-6612
Mike & Kathy Jay, Director

Camp comments: Because Kamaji values childhood simply for what it is, its campers grow up one day at a time in a structured, supportive, supervised and child-centered setting.
Activities: Aquatic Activities, Archery, Arts/Crafts, Dance, Horseback — English, Sailing, Tennis, Waterskiing, Wilderness Trips, Windsurfing
Session lengths & capacity: 4 & 8 week sessions; 165 campers
Clientele & fees: girls 7-15; Fees: F △
Contact: Mike or Kathy Jay, Owners at (800) 752-6254; fax: (314) 721-5309

e-mail: mike@kamaji.com
Web site: www.kamaji.com
Operated by: Camp Kamaji, 7436 Byron Pl, St Louis, MO 63105-2917 at (314) 721-0475 (#7042)

Camp Kici Yapi (est 1963)

☀ 🚗

Prior Lake, MN (Scott Co.); (952) 445-4700

Camp comments: Day camp that offers a great outdoor experience.
Activities: Archery, Arts/Crafts, Canoeing, Challenge/Rope Courses, Counselor Training (CIT), Horseback — Western, Swimming — Recreational
Session lengths & capacity: June-August; 1, 2 & 3 week sessions; 280 campers
Clientele & fees: coed 4-12; Fees: B ☀ 🐷
Contact: Tom Carlberg, Director at (612) 835-2567; fax: (612) 835-0221
Operated by: Southdale YMCA, 7355 York Ave S, Edina, MN 55435 at (612) 835-2567 (#1155)

Camp Lakamaga (est 1927)

△ 🏠 🚗

Marine On St Croix, MN; (651) 251-1227
Julie Hoeft, Director

Camp comments: The Girl Scouts help girls grow up to be caring, competent, confident women.
Activities: Archery, Arts/Crafts, Boating, Camping Skills/Outdoor Living, Ceramics/Pottery, Nature/Environment Studies
Session lengths & capacity: June-August; 1/2, 1 & 2 week sessions; 125 campers
Clientele & fees: girls 6-13; Fees: B, C △ 🐷
Contact: Julie Hoeft, Camp Director at (612) 227-8835; fax: (612) 227-7533
e-mail: jhoeft@girlscoutscv.org
Web site: www.girlscoutscv.org
Operated by: GSC of St Croix Valley, 400 S Robert Street, St Paul, MN 55107 at (651) 227-8835 (#1216)

Camp Lake Hubert For Girls

(est 1927) △ 🏠

Lake Hubert, MN (Crow Wing Co.); (218) 963-2281
Sam Cote & Bill Jones, Director

Camp comments: 800 ac in MN Lakes, land/water activ. 1:3 staff/camper ratio; 2-8 wks + golf, tennis, fishing/family wk. video/brochure.
Activities: Aquatic Activities, Archery, Bicycling/Biking, Challenge/Rope Courses, Golf, Horseback — Western, Riflery, Sailing, Tennis, Windsurfing
Session lengths & capacity: June-September; 2, 3 & 4 week sessions; 200 campers
Clientele & fees: girls 7-17; coed 7-17; families; Fees: F △
Contact: Sam Cote & Bill Jones, Directors at (800) 242-1909; fax: (952) 922-7149
e-mail: home@lincoln-lakehubert.com
Web site: www.lincoln-lakehubert.com
Operated by: Camp Lincoln/Camp Lake Hubert, 10179 Crosstown Circle, Eden Prairie, MN 55344 at (952) 922-2545 (#1203)

Camp Lincoln For Boys

(est 1909) △ 🏠 🚗

Lake Hubert, MN (Crow Wing Co.); (218) 963-2339
Sam Cote & Bill Jones, Director

Camp comments: 800 ac in MN lakes. Land/water activ. 1:3 staff/camper ratio; 2-8 wks + golf, tennis, fishing/family wk. video/brochure.
Activities: Aquatic Activities, Archery, Golf, Horseback — Western, Riflery, Sailing, Tennis, Wilderness Trips, Windsurfing
Session lengths & capacity: June-September; 2, 3 & 4 week sessions; 200 campers
Clientele & fees: boys 7-17; coed 7-17; families; Fees: F △
Contact: Sam Cote/Bill Jones, Director at (800) 242-1909; fax: (952) 922-7149
e-mail: home@lincoln-lakehubert.com
Web site: www.lincoln-lakehubert.com

Operated by: Camp Lincoln/Camp Lake Hubert, 10179 Crosstown Circle, Eden Prairie, MN 55344 at (952) 922-2545 (#1192)

Camp New Hope Inc

(est 1968)   ▲ ⌂ 🚗

Mc Gregor, MN (Aitkin Co.); (218) 426-3560
Lori Czarneski, Director

Camp comments: Camp New Hope is a non-profit camp that offers vacation opportunities in the outdoors for individuals with disabilities.
Activities: Arts/Crafts, Dance, Drama, Drawing/Painting, Farming/Ranching/Gardening, Field Trips, Music, Nature/Environment Studies, Swimming — Recreational
Session lengths & capacity: June-September; 1/2 & 1 week sessions; 40 campers
Clientele & fees: boys 6-99; girls 6-99; coed 6-99; families; seniors; single adults; Fees: E ▲ 🚌
Contact: Lori A Czarneski, Executive Director at (218) 426-3560; fax: (218) 426-3560
e-mail: cnewhope@lcp2.net
Web site: www.campnewhopemn.org
Operated by: Camp New Hope Inc, 53035 Lake Avenue, Mc Gregor, MN 55760 at (218) 426-3560

Group Rental Information
Seasons & Capacity: Spring 60, Summer 60, Fall 60, Winter 40
Facilities: A/V Equipment, Cabins, Double Occupancy, Food Service, Hiking Trails, Kitchen Facilities, Lake, Linens, Lodges, Meeting Rooms, Playing Fields, Tents
Programs: Boating, Swimming (#3299)

Camp Omega (est 1964)   ▲ ⌂

Waterville, MN (Rice Co.); (507) 685-4266
Kevin Hall, Director

Camp comments: Challenging & fun programs that promote solid Christian values/self-esteem development & spiritual growth!
Activities: Aquatic Activities, Archery, Basketball, Bicycling/Biking, Canoeing, Nature/Environment Studies, Religious Study, Soccer, Swimming — Recreational, Team Building
Session lengths & capacity: June-August; 1/2 & 1 week sessions; 158 campers
Clientele & fees: coed 6-17; families; Fees: B ▲
Contact: Kevin Hall, Director at (507) 685-4266; fax: (507) 685-4401
e-mail: info@campomego.org
Web site: www.campomega.org
Operated by: Camp Omeaga Inc, 22750 Lind Avenue, Waterville, MN 56096 at (507) 685-4266

Group Rental Information
Site comments: Quality facilities for your year round retreat and meeting needs. Located one hour south of Minneapolis. Visit our Web site or call for more information.
Seasons & Capacity: Spring 160, Fall 160, Winter 160
Facilities: A/V Equipment, Cabins, Dorm-Style, Food Service, Hiking Trails, Lake, Meeting Rooms, Playing Fields, Pool
Programs: Boating, Environmental Education, Swimming, Winter Sports (#1141)

Camp Thunderbird For Boys

(est 1946)   ▲

Bemidji, MN (Hubbard Co.); (218) 751-5171
Roger Bristowe, Director

Camp comments: Individualized prog, multi-specialty land & water sports, wilderness trips, designed to have fun & feel great. Try us.
Activities: Aquatic Activities, Arts/Crafts, Bicycling/Biking, Horseback — Western, Sailing, Sports — Field & Team, Tennis, Waterskiing, Wilderness Trips, Windsurfing
Session lengths & capacity: June-August; 4 & 8 week sessions; 190 campers
Clientele & fees: boys 8-16; Fees: E ▲

Contact: Allen Sigoloff, Director at (314) 567-3167; fax: (314) 567-7218
e-mail: tbirdcamp@primary.net
Web site: www.camptbird.com
Operated by: Camp Thunderbird Inc, 941 Gardenview Office Parkway, St Louis, MO 63141 at (314) 567-3167 (#1041)

Camp Thunderbird For Girls

(est 1970)   ▲ 🚗

Bemidji, MN (Hubbard Co.); (218) 751-6761
Carol A Sigoloff, Director

Camp comments: Diverse individual choice program in pristine Northwoods lake setting. Girls experience unconditional acceptance in an exciting challenging nurturing community.
Activities: Aquatic Activities, Bicycling/Biking, Climbing/Rappelling, Gymnastics, Horseback — English, Sailing, Team Building, Waterskiing, Wilderness Trips, Windsurfing
Session lengths & capacity: June-August; 4 & 8 week sessions; 150 campers
Clientele & fees: girls 8-16; Fees: E ▲
Contact: Carol A Sigoloff, Director at (314) 567-3167; fax: (314) 567-7218
e-mail: tbird camp@primary.net
Web site: www.camptbird.com
Operated by: Camp Thunderbird Inc, 941 Gardenview Office Parkway, St Louis, MO 63141 at (314) 567-3167 (#1040)

Camp Trowbridge (est 1929)   ▲ ⌂ 🚗

Vergas, MN (Otter Tail Co.); (218) 342-2811
Myrna Johnson, Director

Camp comments: Beautiful facility, lakes area, outstanding trained staff, friendly, warm, varied program, camp outs, nourishing meals.
Activities: Archery, Arts/Crafts, Camping Skills/Outdoor Living, Canoeing, Counselor Training (CIT), Hiking, Leadership Development, Nature/Environment Studies, Swimming — Recreational
Session lengths & capacity: May-October; 1/2 & 1 week sessions; 120 campers
Clientele & fees: boys 5-21; girls 5-21; coed 5-21; Fees: B ☀ Fees: B ▲
Contact: Myrna Johnson, Executive Director at (218) 236-1090; fax: (218) 236-1094
e-mail: nscampfire@juno.com
Operated by: Northern Star Camp Fire Cncl, 725 Center Avenue, Moorhead, MN 56560 at (218) 236-1090

Group Rental Information
Site comments: Modern cabins, handicap accessible, meadow & trees, clean lake, noncompetitive group activities,encourages cooperation.
Seasons & Capacity: Spring 120, Summer 120, Fall 120
Facilities: Cabins, Double Occupancy, Hiking Trails, Lake, Lodges, Meeting Rooms
Programs: Boating, Environmental Education, Swimming (#1207)

Camp Voyageur (est 1951)   ▲ ⌂

Ely, MN (Lake Co.); (218) 365-6042
John C Erdmann, Director

Camp comments: In-camp program of land & water sports plus wilderness trips, hiking & canoeing in Boundary Waters. One counselor to four campers.
Activities: Archery, Backpacking, Canoeing, Hiking, Kayaking, Sailing, Soccer, Swimming — Recreational, Waterskiing, Wilderness Trips
Session lengths & capacity: June-August; 4 & 8 week sessions; 75 campers
Clientele & fees: boys 10-17; Fees: E ▲
Contact: Deb Erdmann, Director at (800) 950-7291; fax: (218) 365-5901
e-mail: cvspirit@campvoyageur.com
Web site: www.campvoyageur.com

Operated by: Camp Voyageur, PO Box 420, Ely, MN 55731 at (218) 365-6042

Group Rental Information
Site comments: Our camp is perfect for group retreats or wilderness canoe outfitting. Call Deb for details.
Seasons & Capacity: Spring 30, Summer 30, Fall 30, Winter 30
Facilities: A/V Equipment, Cabins, Dorm-Style, Food Service, Lake, Meeting Rooms, Tents
Programs: Boating, Swimming, Winter Sports (#11523)

Catholic Youth Camp

(est 1947)   ▲ ⌂ 🚗

Mc Gregor, MN (Aitkin Co.); (218) 426-3383
Maggie and Bob Braun, Director

Camp comments: All are welcome to 'Share the Spirit' at CYC on Big Sandy Lake in northern Minnesota. Traditional camp experiences for children, teens and families.
Activities: Archery, Arts/Crafts, Boating, Canoeing, Counselor Training (CIT), Fishing, Nature/Environment Studies, Soccer, Swimming — Recreational, Wilderness Trips
Session lengths & capacity: June-August; 1/2, 1 & 2 week sessions; 154 campers
Clientele & fees: coed 8-18; families; Fees: C ▲ 🚌
Contact: Bob and Maggie Braun, Co-Director at (651) 636-1645; fax: (651) 628-9323
e-mail: camp@cycamp.org
Web site: www.cycamp.org
Operated by: Catholic Youth Camps Inc, 2131 Fairview Ave N Ste 200, Roseville, MN 55113 at (651) 636-1645

Group Rental Information
Seasons & Capacity: Spring 150, Fall 150, Winter 25
Facilities: Cabins, Dorm-Style, Kitchen Facilities, Lake, Lodges, Playing Fields
Programs: Boating, Swimming, Winter Sports (#6403)

Circle R Ranch (est 1969)   ▲

Long Prairie, MN (Todd Co.); (320) 547-2176
Jack Mc Coy, Director

Camp comments: Kids get their own horse for the week. Ride approx. 50 miles during week. Other activities include dance night, archery, tennis, heated swimming pool & more!
Activities: Aquatic Activities, Archery, Basketball, Boating, Camping Skills/Outdoor Living, Canoeing, Counselor Training (CIT), Horseback — Western, Sports — Field & Team, Tennis
Session lengths & capacity: June-August; 1, 2 & 3 week sessions; 80 campers
Clientele & fees: girls 7-16; coed 7-16; Fees: D ▲
Contact: Jack McCoy, Owner/Director at (320) 547-2176; fax: (320) 547-2176
e-mail: circler97@aol.com
Web site: www.circlerranch.com
Operated by: Circle R Ranch, Rt 1 Box 120, Long Prairie, MN 56347 at (612) 547-2176 (#7699)

Concordia Language Villages

(est 1961)   ▲ ⌂ 🚗

Moorhead, MN (Clay Co.); (800) 450-2214
Christine Schulze, Director

Camp comments: Concordia Language Villages offers culture & language immersion in 12 languages. High school credit & abroad programs also available.
Activities: Academics, Arts/Crafts, Camping Skills/Outdoor Living, International Culture, Language Studies, Leadership Development, Music, Nature/Environment Studies, Sports — Field & Team, Wilderness Trips
Session lengths & capacity: June-August; 1, 2 & 4 week sessions; 154 campers

Clientele & fees: coed 7-18; Fees: E ▲ 🐷
Contact: Pat Hesby, Receptionist at
(800) 222-4750; fax: (218) 299-3807
e-mail: clvoffice@village.cord.edu
Operated by: Concordia Language Villages, 901 S
Eighth St, Moorhead, MN 56560 at (800) 222-4750
Group Rental Information
Site comments: Concordia Language Villages
operates four facilities for workshops, retreats &
conferences Spet. to May. Call 450-2214 for more
information.
Seasons & Capacity: Spring 200, Fall 200,
Winter 200
Facilities: A/V Equipment, Cabins, Dorm-Style,
Food Service, Hiking Trails, Lake, Linens, Meeting
Rooms, Playing Fields (#7278)

Courage (est 1955) ▲ 🏠 🚐

Maple Lake, MN (Wright Co.); (612) 963-3121
Roger Upcraft, Director

Camp comments: Also serve children with
burns/blind/cancer. Run special needs sport camp
& college preview focusing on computer use.
Activities: Arts/Crafts, Boating, Camping
Skills/Outdoor Living, Computer, Horseback —
Western, Leadership Development,
Nature/Environment Studies, Photography, Sports
— Field & Team, Swimming — Recreational
Session lengths & capacity: June-August; 1, 2 &
3 week sessions; 150 campers
Clientele & fees: coed 6-99; families; seniors;
Fees: D ▲
Contact: Bob Pollard, Camping Secretary at
(612) 520-0504; fax: (612) 520-0577
e-mail: camping@courage.org
Operated by: Courage Center I, 3915 Golden
Valley Road, Golden Valley, MN 55422 at
(612) 566-0811 (#1132)

Courage North (est 1972) ▲ 🏠 🚐

Lake George, MN; (218) 266-3658
Tom Fogarty, Director

Camp comments: Focus on ability not disability.
Opportunities for personal growth and leadership
development through camping.
Activities: Arts/Crafts, Backpacking,
Bicycling/Biking, Camping Skills/Outdoor Living,
Counselor Training (CIT), Leadership Development,
Nature/Environment Studies, Photography,
Waterskiing, Wilderness Trips
Session lengths & capacity: June-September; 1 &
2 week sessions; 60 campers
Clientele & fees: coed 7-70; Fees: D ▲ 🐷
Contact: Tom Fogarty, Camp Director at
(218) 266-3658; fax: (218) 266-3458
e-mail: couragen@wcta.net

ICON LEGEND

☀	Day Camp
▲	Resident Camp
🏠	Facilities Available To Rent
🚐	Transportation Available
🐷	Financial Aid Available

FEE RANGES PER WEEK

A	$0-75
B	$75-200
C	$201-350
D	$351-500
E	$501-650
F	over $650

Operated by: Courage Center I, 3915 Golden
Valley Road, Golden Valley, MN 55422 at
(612) 566-0811 (#6330)

Decision Hills Camp ☀ ▲ 🏠

(est 1957)

Spicer, MN (Kandiyohi Co.); (320) 796-5510
Activities: Aquatic Activities, Bicycling/Biking,
Canoeing, Challenge/Rope Courses, Hiking,
Religious Study, Sailing, Team Building
Clientele & fees: Fees: C ☀
Contact: Kim Embretson, Director at
(320) 796-5510; fax: (320) 796-6786
e-mail: dhcnice@midstate.tds.net
Web site: www.campminnesota.org
Operated by: United Methodist Church, 122
Franklin Ave W Rm 400, Minneapolis, MN 55404 at
(612) 870-0058
Group Rental Information
Site comments: We specialize in small group
adventure and cabin camps.
Facilities: Cabins, Dorm-Style, Food Service,
Hiking Trails, Lake, Meeting Rooms
Programs: Boating (#11525)

Eagle Lake Camp & Retreat Cntr (est 1969) 🏠

Brainerd, MN (Crow Wing Co.); (218) 764-2985
Contact: Vern Hill, Business Manager at
(651) 633-4871;
e-mail: elc@eaglelakecamp.org
Web site: eaglelakecamp.org
Session lengths: April-October
Operated by: Community Of Christ, 17040 County
Rd 102, Brainerd, MN 56401
Group Rental Information
Site comments: Beautiful, secluded, wooded
camping area for RV or tent shower, laundry
facilities. Lake access.
Seasons & Capacity: Spring 120, Summer 120,
Fall 120
Facilities: Dorm-Style, Double Occupancy, Kitchen
Facilities, Lake, Lodges, Meeting Rooms
Programs: Boating (#6804)

Eden Wood (est 1958) ▲ 🏠

Eden Prairie, MN (Hennepin Co.); (952) 852-0101
Georgann Rumsey, Director

Camp comments: Beautiful site in an urban setting
offers resident & day camp services to children &
adults with disabilities.
Activities: Aquatic Activities, Archery,
Challenge/Rope Courses, Counselor Training (CIT),
Drama, Fishing, Leadership Development, Music,
Nature/Environment Studies, Swimming —
Recreational
Session lengths & capacity: 1/2, 1, 2 & 3 week
sessions; 35 campers
Clientele & fees: coed 5-99; families; seniors;
single adults; Fees: D, E ▲ 🐷
Contact: Georgann Rumsey, President/CEO at
(320) 274-8376; fax: (320) 274-3238
e-mail: fv@friendshipventures.org
Web site: www.friendshipventures.org
Operated by: Friendship Ventures, 10509 108th
Ave NW, Annandale, MN 55302 at (952) 852-0101
Group Rental Information
Site comments: Beautiful site in urban setting
conviently located near metro area landmarks great
for day group and overnight meetings and retreats.
Challenge course on site.
Seasons & Capacity: Spring 50, Summer 80, Fall
50, Winter 50
Facilities: A/V Equipment, Cabins, Dorm-Style,
Food Service, Hiking Trails, Meeting Rooms,
Playing Fields
Programs: Challenge/Ropes Course (#1142)

Girl Scout Camp Singing Hills ▲ 🏠

(est 1966)

Waterville, MN (Waseca Co.); (507) 362-4660
Jennifer Tschida, Director

Camp comments: Girl Scout Camp Singing Hills
offfers a traditional camp environment with exciting
programs to meet contemporary girl need and
enable girls to grow strong.
Activities: Archery, Arts/Crafts, Bicycling/Biking,
Camping Skills/Outdoor Living, Canoeing,
Horseback — Western, Nature/Environment
Studies, Sailing, Swimming — Recreational
Session lengths & capacity: June-September; 1/2,
1 & 3 week sessions; 100 campers
Clientele & fees: girls 6-16; families;
Fees: B ▲ 🐷
Contact: Cori Sendle, Program Director at
(800) 344-4757; fax: (507) 645-6605
e-mail: cori@gsccv.org
Web site: www.gsccv.org
Operated by: GSC of Cannon Valley, 1025 Hwy 3
North, Northfield, MN 55057 at (507) 645-6603
Group Rental Information
Seasons & Capacity: Spring 150, Fall 150,
Winter 30
Facilities: Cabins, Hiking Trails, Kitchen Facilities,
Lodges, Meeting Rooms, Tents
Programs: Boating (#1201)

Good Earth Village (est 1969) ☀ ▲ 🏠

Spring Valley, MN (Fillmore Co.); (507) 346-2494
David Herder, Director

Camp comments: A beautiful 500 acre Christian
camp and retreat center tucked into the bluffs of SE
Minnesota.
Activities: Arts/Crafts, Camping Skills/Outdoor
Living, Canoeing, Challenge/Rope Courses, Hiking,
Leadership Development, Nature/Environment
Studies, Religious Study, Sports — Field & Team,
Team Building
Session lengths & capacity: 1/2 & 1 week
sessions; 125 campers
Clientele & fees: coed 6-18; families; seniors;
single adults; Fees: C ▲ 🐷
Contact: David Herder, Executive Director at
(507) 346-2494; fax: (507) 346-2035
e-mail: goodearth@deskmedia.com
Operated by: Good Earth Village, Rt 1 Box 258,
Spring Valley, MN 55975 at (507) 346-2494
Group Rental Information
Site comments: An excellent setting for retreats
and group getaways--Root River bike trail, Old
Town Village, miles of hiking trails, comfortable
meeting & lodging space.
Seasons & Capacity: Spring 100, Summer 150,
Fall 100, Winter 100
Facilities: A/V Equipment, Cabins, Double
Occupancy, Food Service, Hiking Trails, Kitchen
Facilities, Lodges, Meeting Rooms, Playing Fields,
River, Tents
Programs: Challenge/Ropes Course,
Environmental Education, Winter Sports (#3654)

Grindstone Lake Bible Camp

(est 1932) ▲ 🏠

Sandstone, MN (Pine Co.); (320) 245-2777
Doug Sikkink, Director

Camp comments: Evangelical, interdenominational
camp committed to keeping the cost low for
all campers.
Activities: Aquatic Activities, Arts/Crafts,
Baseball/Softball, Basketball, Canoeing, Fishing,
Religious Study, Soccer, Sports — Field & Team,
Swimming — Recreational
Session lengths & capacity: June-September;
1 week sessions; 180 campers
Clientele & fees: coed 6-18; families; Fees: A ▲
Contact: Doug Sikkink, Director at (763) 560-1364;
Operated by: Grindstone Lake Bible Camp,
PO Box 523, Sandstone, MN 55072-0523 at
(320) 245-2777

Group Rental Information
Seasons & Capacity: Summer 180
Facilities: Cabins, Food Service, Kitchen Facilities, Lake, Meeting Rooms, Playing Fields
Programs: Boating, Swimming (#2920)

Gunflint Wilderness Camp

(est 1968)

Grand Marais, MN; (218) 388-4402
Tim Edmonds, Director

Camp comments: Wilderness experience, Boundary Waters Canoe Area. Variety trips: canoe, sea kayak, backpack, mtn. bike & climb. 44th operating season.
Activities: Backpacking, Bicycling/Biking, Camping Skills/Outdoor Living, Canoeing, Climbing/Rappelling, Kayaking, Leadership Development, Nature/Environment Studies, Wilderness Trips
Session lengths & capacity: June-August; 2 & 4 week sessions; 40 campers
Clientele & fees: coed 10-17; families; Fees: E ▲
Contact: Tim Edmonds, Director at (888) 744-2101; fax: (952) 967-0110
e-mail: gunflintcamp@aol.com
Web site: www.campbirchwood.com
Operated by: Camp Birchwood, 6983 N Steamboat Lake Dr, LaPorte, MN 56461 at (218) 335-2809 (#13268)

Hidden Pines Ranch (est 1983)

Stillwater, MN (Washington Co.); (651) 430-1282
Gregg Ellingson, Director

Camp comments: Hidden Pines Ranch offers a wide variety of outdoor activities all led by experienced counselors in a supportive and fun-filled environment.
Activities: Archery, Arts/Crafts, Basketball, Camping Skills/Outdoor Living, Canoeing, Drama, Horseback — Western, Sports — Field & Team, Swimming — Instructional, Tennis
Session lengths & capacity: 2, 4 & 8 week sessions; 100 campers
Clientele & fees: coed 4-13; Fees: C
Contact: Gregg Ellingson and Robin Ellingson, Directors at (651) 430-1282; fax: (651) 430-0545
e-mail: hpr@minn.net
Web site: www1.minn.net~hpr
Operated by: Hidden Pines Ranch, 10670 75th Street North, Stillwater, MN 55082 at (651) 430-1282 (#4495)

Jack Butwin Memorial Camp

(est 1953)

Eagan, MN (Dakota Co.); (651) 423-1485
Michael Waldman, Director

Camp comments: Camp Butwin creates a friendly and cooperative atmosphere which fosters individual growth at the campers own pace.
Activities: Aquatic Activities, Arts/Crafts, Camping Skills/Outdoor Living, Canoeing, Challenge/Rope Courses, Climbing/Rappelling, Drama, Horseback — Western, Nature/Environment Studies, Sports — Field & Team
Session lengths & capacity: June-August; 4 week sessions; 275 campers
Clientele & fees: coed 6-12; Fees: B
Contact: Michael Waldman, Camp Director at (651) 698-0751; fax: (651) 698-8591
Operated by: Jewish Community Ctr St Paul, 1375 St Paul Ave, St Paul, MN 55116 at (612) 698-0751 (#1122)

JCC Camp Olami (est 1965)

Minneapolis, MN (Hennepin Co.); (952) 381-3421
Benjamin Davis, Director

Camp comments: JCC Camp Olami - A World of Adventure!

Activities: Drama, Field Trips, Nature/Environment Studies, Performing Arts, Religious Study, Sports — Field & Team, Swimming — Instructional, Swimming — Recreational, Travel/Tour, Wilderness Trips
Session lengths & capacity: June-August; 3 week sessions; 190 campers
Clientele & fees: Fees: D
Contact: Ben Davis, Camp Director at (952) 381-3421; fax: (952) 381-3401
e-mail: bdavis@jccminneapolis.org
Web site: www.jccminneapolis.org
Operated by: Sabes JCC, 4330 S Cedar Lake Rd, Minneapolis, MN 55416 at (952) 381-3421 (#29049)

Jeanette Polley Program Center

(est 1927)

Duluth, MN (St Louis Co.); (218) 726-4710
Karen Kjolhaug, Director
Contact: Karen Kjolhaug, Director Outdoor Program at (218) 726-4710; fax: (218) 726-4715
e-mail: gscout@cpinternet.com
Operated by: Northern Pine GSC, Ordean Bldg Ste G3, Duluth, MN 55802 at (218) 726-4710 (#46419)

Kingswood

Mound, MN; (952) 472-3586
Activities: Backpacking, Canoeing, Challenge/Rope Courses, Climbing/Rappelling, Community Service, Religious Study, Team Building
Contact: Web site: www.campminnesota.org
Operated by: United Methodist Church, 122 Franklin Ave W Rm 400, Minneapolis, MN 55404 at (612) 870-0058
Group Rental Information
Seasons & Capacity: Spring 84, Summer 70, Fall 84, Winter 70 (#46034)

Kooch-I-Ching (est 1924)

International Falls, MN (Koochiching Co.); (218) 286-3141
David M Plain, Director

Camp comments: Renowned wilderness tripping program build self-esteem group cooperation through challenging adventures 600 acre island.
Activities: Archery, Backpacking, Camping Skills/Outdoor Living, Canoeing, Climbing/Rappelling, Riflery, Sailing, Swimming — Instructional, Tennis, Wilderness Trips
Session lengths & capacity: June-August; 4 & 8 week sessions; 150 campers
Clientele & fees: boys 8-18; Fees: E, F ▲
Contact: David M Plain, Director at (513) 772-7479; fax: (513) 772-5673
e-mail: office@koochiching.org
Web site: www.kooch-i-ching.org
Operated by: Camping & Education Foundation, 230 Northland Blvd Ste 206, Cincinnati, OH 45246 at (513) 772-7479 (#1210)

Lake Koronis Assembly Grounds

(est 1921)

Paynesville, MN; (320) 243-4544
Wayne L Walther, Director

Camp comments: Christian camp, retreat, conference center. Provides program and facility in setting of natural beauty for refreshment, recreation, and renewal.
Activities: Aquatic Activities, Archery, Arts/Crafts, Boating, Canoeing, Counselor Training (CIT), Drama, Fishing, Horseback — Western, Religious Study
Session lengths & capacity: June-August; 1/2 & 1 week sessions; 500 campers
Clientele & fees: boys 7-17; girls 7-17; coed 7-17; Fees: B, C ▲
Contact: Wayne Walther, Executive Director at (320) 243-4544; fax: (320) 243-7334
e-mail: lkag@lkdllink.net
Web site: www.campminnesota.org

Operated by: United Methodist Church, 122 Franklin Ave W Rm 400, Minneapolis, MN 55404 at (612) 870-0058
Group Rental Information
Site comments: Christian camp, retreat, conference center. Provides program and facility in setting of natural beauty for refreshment, recreation, and renewal.
Seasons & Capacity: Spring 200, Summer 500, Fall 200, Winter 200
Facilities: A/V Equipment, Cabins, Dorm-Style, Double Occupancy, Food Service, Hiking Trails, Lake, Linens, Lodges, Meeting Rooms, Playing Fields
Programs: Boating, Challenge/Ropes Course, Swimming, Winter Sports (#40525)

Laketrails Base Camp Inc

(est 1952)

Oak Island, MN (Lake of the Woods Co.); (218) 223-8281
Jeff Odendahl, Director

Camp comments: Laugh, love, live and learn at Laketrails Base Camp. Wilderness canoe tripping for teenagers on Lake of the Woods in Ontario, Canada.
Activities: Boating, Camping Skills/Outdoor Living, Canoeing, Fishing, Leadership Development, Nature/Environment Studies, Swimming — Recreational, Team Building, Wilderness Trips
Session lengths & capacity: June-August; 1 week sessions; 45 campers
Clientele & fees: coed 12-18; Fees: D ▲
Contact: Jeff Odendahl, Camp Director at (800) 450-6460;
e-mail: laketrl@uslink.net
Web site: www.laketrails.org
Operated by: Laketrails Base Camp, 107 2nd St SE 203, Little Falls, MN 56345 at (320) 632-6460 (#1120)

Little Elk Youth Ranch Inc

(est 1975)

Browerville, MN (Todd Co.); (320) 594-2750
Ron & Sheila Johnston, Director

Camp comments: Have your own horse! Riding inst., trail riding, swimming, canoeing,archery,sports,crafts, Indian village. Big modern bunkhouse. Greatest riding camp in midwest
Activities: Archery, Arts/Crafts, Canoeing, Horseback — Western, Sports — Field & Team, Swimming — Recreational
Session lengths & capacity: June-August; 1 week sessions; 80 campers
Clientele & fees: coed 8-16; Fees: D ▲
Contact: Ron Johnston, Camp Director at (320) 594-2750;
e-mail: littleelkr@aol.com
Web site: www.littleelkranch.com
Operated by: Little Elk Youth Ranch Inc, RR 3 Box 78, Browerville, MN 56438 at (320) 594-2750 (#3174)

Luther Crest Bible Camp

(est 1945)

Alexandria, MN (Douglas Co.); (320) 846-2431
Arden L Norum, Director

Camp comments: A place to grow in understanding, appreciation & knowledge of God, others, self and creation.
Activities: Aquatic Activities, Arts/Crafts, Basketball, Camping Skills/Outdoor Living, Canoeing, Challenge/Rope Courses, Nature/Environment Studies, Religious Study
Session lengths & capacity: June-September; 1/2 & 1 week sessions; 144 campers
Clientele & fees: boys 10-18; girls 10-18; coed 10-18; Fees: A Fees: C ▲

Contact: Arden L. Norum, Executive Director at (320) 846-2431; fax: (320) 846-0201
e-mail: lcbc@luthercrest.org
Web site: www.luthercrest.org
Operated by: Luther Crest Bible Camp Assn, 8231 Co Rd 11 NE, Alexandria, MN 56308 at (320) 846-2431

Group Rental Information
Seasons & Capacity: Spring 100, Winter 100
Facilities: Double Occupancy, Food Service, Hiking Trails, Linens, Lodges, Meeting Rooms, Playing Fields
Programs: Challenge/Ropes Course, Environmental Education (#1171)

Mishawaka For Boys And Girls

(est 1910)   ⚑ ⌂

Grand Rapids, MN (Itasca Co.); (800) 308-5011
Steve Purdum, Director

Camp comments: Mature staff help develop lifetime skills. Brother/Sister camp offer best in traditional camping. Residential & tripping
Activities: Aquatic Activities, Archery, Arts/Crafts, Drama, Horseback — English, Sailing, Soccer, Tennis, Waterskiing, Wilderness Trips
Session lengths & capacity: June-August; 2, 4, 6 & 8 week sessions; 120 campers
Clientele & fees: boys 8-16; girls 8-16; families; Fees: **D** ⚑
Contact: Sonia Larsen, Office Manager at (218) 326-5011; fax: (218) 326-9228
e-mail: campmi@aol.com
Web site: www.campmishawaka.com
Operated by: New Camps Inc, PO Box 368 Mishawaka Road, Grand Rapids, MN 55744 at (800) 308-5011 (#1672)

MN National Guard Youth Camp

(est 1990)   ⚑

Little Falls, MN; (612) 632-6631
Rich Kemp, Director

Camp comments: An exciting camp experience for dependents of the Minnesota Nat'l Guard, ages 10-12.
Activities: Archery, Bicycling/Biking, Canoeing, Counselor Training (CIT), Hiking, Swimming — Recreational, Team Building
Session lengths & capacity: August-August; 2 week sessions; 125 campers
Clientele & fees: coed 10-12; Fees: **A** ⚑
Contact: Susan Rasmussen, State Coordinator at (651) 450-8534; fax: (651) 552-7637
e-mail: srasmus@inverhills.mnscu.edu
Web site: www.dma.state.mn.us/youthcamp

ICON LEGEND

☀ Day Camp

⚑ Resident Camp

⌂ Facilities Available To Rent

🚐 Transportation Available

🐖 Financial Aid Available

FEE RANGES PER WEEK

A $0-75

B $75-200

C $201-350

D $351-500

E $501-650

F   over $650

Operated by: National Guard Training Center, 211 North McCarron Blvd, Roseville, MN 55113-6998 at (651) 296-4469 (#1846)

Moraine Day Camp (est 1985)   ☀ 🚐

Albert Lea, MN (Freeborn Co.); (507) 373-8228
James Smith/Ben Smith, Director

Camp comments: Y day camp offers fine camp experience outdoors. Themes for each week. Varied activities & special events, swim daily.
Activities: Aquatic Activities, Archery, Arts/Crafts, Camping Skills/Outdoor Living, Canoeing, Drawing/Painting, Field Trips, Hiking, Leadership Development, Nature/Environment Studies
Session lengths & capacity: June-August; 1 week sessions; 80 campers
Clientele & fees: boys 6-12; girls 6-12; coed 6-12; Fees: **B** ☀ 🐖
Contact: James Smith, Community Program Director at (507) 373-8228; fax: (507) 373-1053
Operated by: Albert Lea Family Y, 2021 West Main St, Albert Lea, MN 56007 at (507) 373-8228 (#11489)

North Central Camp Cherith Inc

(est 1947)   ⚑ ⌂ 🚐

Frazee, MN (Ottertail Co.); (218) 334-8454
Becky Nelson, Director

Camp comments: Christ-centered outdoor program, with small group focus. 1 week session for boys; 6-1 week sessions for girls.
Activities: Archery, Arts/Crafts, Canoeing, Counselor Training (CIT), Horseback — Western, Leadership Development, Riflery, Sailing, Swimming — Instructional, Waterskiing
Session lengths & capacity: June-August; 1 week sessions; 100 campers
Clientele & fees: boys 7-18; girls 7-18; Fees: **B** ⚑
Contact: Becky Nelson, Administrative Director at (952) 884-1451;
Web site: www.cherith.com
Operated by: North Central Camp Cherith Inc, 10039 James Circle, Bloomington, MN 55431 at (952) 884-1451

Group Rental Information
Facilities: Cabins, Kitchen Facilities, Lake, Lodges, Meeting Rooms, Playing Fields
Programs: Boating, Swimming (#1127)

Northwoods (est 1957)   ⚑ ⌂ 🚐

Mason, WI (Bayfield Co.); (715) 372-8820
Ann Palzer, Director

Camp comments: High adventure wilderness trips for girls. Beautiful rustic setting. Fun with an emphasis on earth friendly travel.
Activities: Backpacking, Bicycling/Biking, Camping Skills/Outdoor Living, Canoeing, Counselor Training (CIT), Horseback — Western, Kayaking, Wilderness Trips
Session lengths & capacity: June-August; 1, 2 & 3 week sessions; 125 campers
Clientele & fees: girls 10-17; Fees: **C** ⚑ 🐖
Contact: Ann Palzer, Camp Director at (651) 227-8835; fax: (651) 227-7533
e-mail: camps@girlscoutscv.org
Web site: www.girlscoutscv.org
Operated by: GSC of St Croix Valley, 400 S Robert Street, St Paul, MN 55107 at (651) 227-8835

Group Rental Information
Seasons & Capacity: Spring 100, Summer 125, Fall 100, Winter 100
Facilities: Cabins, Hiking Trails, Kitchen Facilities, Lake, Tents
Programs: Boating, Environmental Education, Swimming (#1157)

Ojiketa (est 1926)   ☀ ⌂

Chicago City, MN (Chisago Co.); (651) 257-0600
Lori Johnson & Sue Winter, Director

Camp comments: Summer Day Camp outstanding staff modern facilities on beautiful lake shore. Avail yr round for rental programs run by user groups.
Activities: Aquatic Activities, Archery, Arts/Crafts, Camping Skills/Outdoor Living, Canoeing, Fishing, Hiking, Nature/Environment Studies, Swimming — Recreational
Session lengths & capacity: 1/2, 1 & 2 week sessions; 120 campers
Clientele & fees: coed 6-12; Fees: **B** ☀ 🐖
Contact: Council Registrar at (651) 647-4407; fax: (651) 647-5717
e-mail: info@minnesotacouncil.org
Web site: www.camp-fire.org
Operated by: Camp Fire USA Minnesota Cncl, 2610 University Ave W, St Paul, MN 55114 at (651) 647-4407

Group Rental Information
Site comments: Open yr round for family vacations & groups up to 150.Over 20 summer activities skiing & sledding in winter great rates.
Seasons & Capacity: Spring 120, Summer 120, Fall 120, Winter 80
Facilities: Cabins, Food Service, Hiking Trails, Kitchen Facilities, Lake, Lodges, Meeting Rooms
Programs: Boating, Challenge/Ropes Course, Environmental Education, Swimming (#1124)

Presbyterian Clearwater Forest

(est 1954)   ☀ ⚑ ⌂

Deerwood, MN (Crowning Co.); (218) 678-2325
David Jeremiason, Director

Camp comments: 1000 acre camp & retreat center w/3.5 miles of lake shore, great facilities & outstanding camps & other programs for youth, families & adults.
Activities: Archery, Arts/Crafts, Canoeing, Golf, Horseback — English, Religious Study, Sailing, Soccer, Swimming — Recreational, Team Building
Session lengths & capacity: June-August; 1 & 2 week sessions; 200 campers
Clientele & fees: coed 8-17; families; seniors; Fees: **C** ⚑ 🐖
Contact: David Jeremiason, Director of Summer Camp & Youth Programs at (218) 678-2325; fax: (218) 678-3196
e-mail: dj@clearwaterforest.org
Web site: www.clearwaterforest.org
Operated by: Presbyterian Clearwater Forest, 16595 Crooked Lake Rd, Deerwood, MN 56444-8173 at (218) 678-2325

Group Rental Information
Seasons & Capacity: Spring 96, Summer 56, Fall 96, Winter 96
Facilities: A/V Equipment, Cabins, Double Occupancy, Food Service, Hiking Trails, Kitchen Facilities, Lake, Linens, Lodges, Meeting Rooms, Playing Fields, Tents
Programs: Boating, Challenge/Ropes Course, Environmental Education, Swimming, Winter Sports (#1149)

Shetek Lutheran Ministries

(est 1947)   ⚑ ⌂

Slayton, MN (Murray Co.); (507) 763-3567
Jon Hoyme, Director

Camp comments: Lake setting! Programs and facilities for all ages all year around. Beautiful island with medium & high comfort living.
Activities: Arts/Crafts, Camping Skills/Outdoor Living, Canoeing, Challenge/Rope Courses, Community Service, Leadership Development, Nature/Environment Studies, Religious Study, Swimming — Recreational, Wilderness Trips
Session lengths & capacity: 1 week sessions; 140 campers

Clientele & fees: coed 8-18; families; seniors;
Fees: **B** ⛺ �
Contact: Jon Hoyme, Director at (507) 763-3567;
fax: (507) 763-3567
e-mail: slbc@rconnect.com
Operated by: Sheteck Lutheran Ministries, 14
Keeley Island Dr, Slayton, MN 56172 at
(507) 763-3567

Group Rental Information
Seasons & Capacity: Spring 20, Summer 20, Fall
20, Winter 15
Facilities: A/V Equipment, Cabins, Food Service,
Hiking Trails, Kitchen Facilities, Lake, Linens,
Meeting Rooms, Playing Fields
Programs: Boating, Challenge/Ropes Course,
Environmental Education, Swimming, Winter Sports
(#3491)

Star Lake (est 1963)

Pequot Lakes, MN (Crow Wing Co.);
(218) 543-4871

Camp comments: Have fun, make friends, and
experience a simpler way of life. Weeklong
adventures for youth. Trips to BWCA and superior
hiking trail for older youth. Ages 9-18.
Activities: Arts/Crafts, Backpacking, Camping
Skills/Outdoor Living, Canoeing, Challenge/Rope
Courses, Hiking, Nature/Environment Studies,
Religious Study, Swimming — Instructional,
Swimming — Recreational
Session lengths & capacity: June-August; 1/2, 1 &
2 week sessions; 75 campers
Clientele & fees: coed 9-18; families;
Fees: **B, C** ⛺ �
Contact: David Mc Donald, Board of Management
at (612) 940-7346; fax: (651) 490-7809
e-mail: starlake@campminnesota.org
Web site: www.campminnesota.org
Operated by: United Methodist Church, 122
Franklin Ave W Rm 400, Minneapolis, MN 55404 at
(612) 870-0058

Group Rental Information
Seasons & Capacity: Spring 60, Summer 40, Fall
60, Winter 18
Facilities: Hiking Trails, Lake, Tents
Programs: Challenge/Ropes Course,
Environmental Education, Horseback Riding,
Swimming (#46037)

Tanadoona (est 1924)

Excelsior, MN (Carver Co.); (612) 474-8085
Lori Johnson & Beth Osborne, Director

Camp comments: Traditional day and resident
camp plus wilderness adventure trips 100 wooded
acres near metro outstanding staff.
Activities: Aquatic Activities, Archery, Backpacking,
Camping Skills/Outdoor Living, Canoeing,
Challenge/Rope Courses, Climbing/Rappelling,
Hiking, Nature/Environment Studies
Session lengths & capacity: 1/2, 1 & 2 week
sessions; 120 campers
Clientele & fees: coed 6-18; Fees: **B** ☀
Fees: **C** ⛺ �
Contact: Camp Reservations at (651) 647-4407;
fax: (651) 647-5717
e-mail: info@minnesotacouncil.org
Web site: www.camp-fire.org
Operated by: Camp Fire USA Minnesota Cncl,
2610 University Ave W, St Paul, MN 55114 at
(651) 647-4407

Group Rental Information
Site comments: Available yr round to groups.
Modern facilities, 100 acres of mature forest,
lkshore&meadows near twin city metro area.
Seasons & Capacity: Spring 100, Summer 100,
Fall 100, Winter 50
Facilities: Cabins, Food Service, Hiking Trails,
Kitchen Facilities, Lake, Lodges, Meeting Rooms
Programs: Boating, Challenge/Ropes Course,
Environmental Education, Swimming (#1133)

Whispering Hills (est 1972)

Houston, MN (Houston/Filmore Co.);
(507) 896-3173
Jennifer Bollo, Director

Camp comments: Emphasis on development of
self-confidence & skills through challenge,
progressive experiences in variety of areas.
Activities: Arts/Crafts, Camping Skills/Outdoor
Living, Canoeing, Dance, Drama, Hiking,
Horseback — Western, Nature/Environment
Studies, Swimming — Instructional, Swimming —
Recreational
Session lengths & capacity: June-August; 1/2, 1 &
2 week sessions; 124 campers
Clientele & fees: girls 9-17; families;
Fees: **A, B, C** ⛺ �
Contact: Carolyn Stalnaker, Director of Outdoor
Program & Property at (507) 288-4703;
fax: (507) 288-7702
e-mail: cstalnaker@rivertrails.org
Web site: www.rivertrails.org
Operated by: River Trails GSC, PO Box 9338,
Rochester, MN 55903 at (507) 288-4703

Group Rental Information
Site comments: Access to bike & canoe trips.
Abundant wildlife. Beautiful setting on 800 acres of
Minnesota Bluff country.
Seasons & Capacity: Spring 125, Fall 125,
Winter 40
Facilities: Cabins, Double Occupancy, Hiking
Trails, Kitchen Facilities, Lodges, Meeting Rooms,
River (#7017)

Wilderness Canoe Base (est 1956) ⛺

Grand Marais, MN (Cook Co.); (218) 388-2241
Tim Knutson, Director

Camp comments: Leadership development &
personal & spiritual growth on BWCA canoe trips.
Activities: Backpacking, Camping Skills/Outdoor
Living, Canoeing, Climbing/Rappelling, Community
Service, Hiking, Leadership Development,
Nature/Environment Studies, Team Building,
Wilderness Trips
Session lengths & capacity: June-August; 1, 2 &
4 week sessions; 180 campers
Clientele & fees: boys 8-99; girls 8-99; coed 8-99;
families; seniors; single adults; Fees: **C** ⛺ �
Contact: Tim Knutson, Director at (218) 388-2241;
fax: (218) 388-2241
Web site: www.spacestar.net/~campwapo
Operated by: Lake Wapogasset Lutheran Bible,
738 Hickory Point Lane, Amery, WI 54001-5129 at
(715) 268-8434 (#1165)

YMCA Camp Christmas Tree

(est 1958)

Mound, MN (Hennepin Co.); (612) 472-1018
Kerry Pioske, Director

Camp comments: Serving western Mpls. suburbs.
Camp Christmas Tree provides an introductory
outdoor experience for children ages 4-16.
Activities: Archery, Arts/Crafts, Camping
Skills/Outdoor Living, Canoeing,
Climbing/Rappelling, Counselor Training (CIT),
Horseback — Western, Nature/Environment
Studies, Swimming — Recreational, Team Building
Session lengths & capacity: June-August; 1, 2 &
3 week sessions; 300 campers
Clientele & fees: coed 4-16; Fees: **B** ☀ �
Contact: Kerry Pioske, Camp/Community Prgm
Director at (612) 544-7708; fax: (612) 544-4765
Operated by: Ridgedale Branch YMCA, 12301
Ridgedale Dr, Minnetonka, MN 55343 at
(952) 544-7708

Group Rental Information
Site comments: Enjoy a meeting, company picnic
or family reunion in the great outdoors.
Facilities: Meeting Rooms, Playing Fields
Programs: Boating, Challenge/Ropes Course,
Horseback Riding, Swimming (#1135)

YMCA Camp Guy Robinson

(est 1969)

Oak Grove, MN (Ramsey Co.); (612) 770-4948
Dave Lundell, Director

Camp comments: We provide safe & exciting
adventures in a variety of traditional & specialty
camps based in a wilderness setting.
Activities: Archery, Arts/Crafts, Camping
Skills/Outdoor Living, Canoeing, Horseback —
Western, Leadership Development,
Nature/Environment Studies, Swimming —
Recreational
Session lengths & capacity: June-August; 1, 2 &
3 week sessions; 166 campers
Clientele & fees: coed 6-12; single adults;
Fees: **B** ☀
Contact: Dave Lundell, Camp Director at
(763) 717-1836;
Operated by: Emma B Howe YMCA, 8950
Springbrook Dr, Coon Rapids, MN 55433 at
(612) 785-7882 (#7325)

YMCA Camp Ihduhapi

(est 1930)

Loretto, MN (Hennepin Co.); (763) 479-1146
Erik Dussault, Director

Camp comments: Camp Ihduhapi fosters
transformational experiences in an outdoor setting.
Activities: Aquatic Activities, Archery, Arts/Crafts,
Boating, Camping Skills/Outdoor Living,
Challenge/Rope Courses, Horseback — Western,
Nature/Environment Studies, Sailing, Wilderness
Trips
Session lengths & capacity: June-August; 1/2, 1 &
2 week sessions; 150 campers
Clientele & fees: coed 7-16; Fees: **B** ☀
Fees: **D** ⛺ �
Contact: (763) 479-1146; fax: (763) 479-1333
e-mail: info@campihuduhapi.org
Web site: www.ymcacamping.org
Operated by: Minneapolis YMCA Camping Serv, 4
W Rustic Lodge, Minneapolis, MN 55409 at
(612) 822-2267

Group Rental Information
Site comments: Come stay in our conference or
retreat center. Play and learn at our Adventure
Leanrning Center.
Seasons & Capacity: Spring 223, Fall 223,
Winter 223
Facilities: A/V Equipment, Cabins, Food Service,
Hiking Trails, Lake, Lodges, Meeting Rooms,
Playing Fields, Tents
Programs: Boating, Challenge/Ropes Course,
Environmental Education, Swimming, Winter Sports
(#1128)

YMCA Camp Menogyn

(est 1922)

Grand Marais, MN (Cook Co.); (218) 388-4497
Paul Danicic, Director

Camp comments: Menogyn-YMCA wilderness
adventures offers young men and women 13 to 18
years old a chance to grow fully on canoeing,
backpacking, and rock climbing trips.
Activities: Backpacking, Camping Skills/Outdoor
Living, Canoeing, Climbing/Rappelling, Wilderness
Trips
Session lengths & capacity: June-August; 1, 2 &
3 week sessions; 80 campers
Clientele & fees: boys 13-18; girls 13-18; families;
single adults; Fees: **D** ⛺ �
Contact: (612) 822-2267; fax: (612) 823-2482
e-mail: info@campmenogyn.org
Web site: www.ymcacamping.org
Operated by: Minneapolis YMCA Camping Serv, 4
W Rustic Lodge, Minneapolis, MN 55409 at
(612) 822-2267

Group Rental Information
Site comments: Menogyn is a leader in wilderness adventures & introductory programs year-round. Learn about the beauty, solitude & power of a wilderness experience at Menogyn.
Seasons & Capacity: Spring 50, Summer 100, Fall 100, Winter 50
Facilities: Cabins, Dorm-Style, Food Service, Hiking Trails, Lake, Lodges (#1172)

YMCA Camp Miller (est 1898) ☀ ▲ ⌂

Sturgeon Lake, MN (Pine Co.); (218) 372-3188
Tracie Clanaugh, Director

Camp comments: Located in tall pine country of NE MN. Camper thrives in caring noncompetitive atmosphere with opportunities to belong.
Activities: Aquatic Activities, Arts/Crafts, Canoeing, Challenge/Rope Courses, Counselor Training (CIT), Horseback — Western, Kayaking, Riflery, Sailing, Team Building
Session lengths & capacity: 1/2, 1 & 2 week sessions; 130 campers
Clientele & fees: boys 9-16; girls 9-16; coed 9-16; families; Fees: C ▲ 🐷
Contact: Tracie Clanaugh, Camp Director at (218) 722-4745; fax: (218) 722-4746
Operated by: Duluth Area Family YMCA, 302 W 1st St, Duluth, MN 55802 at (218) 722-4745

Group Rental Information
Facilities: Dorm-Style, Food Service, Hiking Trails, Lake, Meeting Rooms
Programs: Boating, Environmental Education (#1221)

YMCA Camp Olson (est 1954) ☀ ▲ 🚐

Longville, MN (Cass Co.); (218) 363-2207
Andrew Healy, Director

Camp comments: 1200 acres on 5 lakes. Wilderness setting. Riding, sailing, trips, leadership development & traditional crafts.
Activities: Archery, Farming/Ranching/Gardening, Horseback — Western, Nature/Environment Studies, Riflery, Sailing, Wilderness Trips
Session lengths & capacity: May-September; 1, 2 & 3 week sessions; 130 campers
Clientele & fees: coed 8-16; families; Fees: C, D ▲ 🐷
Contact: Andrew T Healy, Executive Director at (800) 320-2917; fax: (218) 363-2490
e-mail: mgmt@campolson.org
Operated by: YMCA Camp Olson, PO Box 118, Longville, MN 56655 at (218) 363-2207 (#1162)

ICON LEGEND

☀	Day Camp
▲	Resident Camp
⌂	Facilities Available To Rent
🚐	Transportation Available
🐷	Financial Aid Available

FEE RANGES PER WEEK

A	$0-75
B	$75-200
C	$201-350
D	$351-500
E	$501-650
F	over $650

YMCA Camp Pepin (est 1934) ▲ ⌂

Stockholm, WI (Pepin Co.); (715) 442-3811
Clint Knox, Director

Camp comments: Nestled in the Northern Hills, we are a beautiful camp with outstanding programs and exceptional staff, promoting safety, creativity, and BIG FUN!
Activities: Aquatic Activities, Archery, Arts/Crafts, Camping Skills/Outdoor Living, Canoeing, Challenge/Rope Courses, Counselor Training (CIT), Drama, Kayaking, Sailing
Session lengths & capacity: June-August; 1 & 2 week sessions; 120 campers
Clientele & fees: coed 7-18; Fees: C ▲ 🐷
Contact: Mark Hennessy, Executive Director at (651) 388-4724; fax: (651) 388-5340
e-mail: camp@redwingymca.org
Web site: www.redwingymca.org
Operated by: Red Wing Family YMCA, 434 Main Street, Red Wing, MN 55066 at (651) 388-4724

Group Rental Information
Site comments: Whether you're looking for a highflying experience to bring out the energy of your group or a formal setting for meetings we have everything you need.
Seasons & Capacity: Spring 150, Summer 150, Fall 150, Winter 100
Facilities: A/V Equipment, Cabins, Food Service, Kitchen Facilities, Lake, Lodges, Meeting Rooms, Playing Fields, River
Programs: Boating, Challenge/Ropes Course, Environmental Education, Horseback Riding, Swimming, Winter Sports (#417)

YMCA Camp St Croix

(est 1909) ☀ ▲ ⌂

Hudson, WI (St Croix Co.); (651) 436-8428
Rob Schultz, Director

Camp comments: St. Croix national scenic river way, canoe tripping & sailing, small group focus. Mature & caring staff.
Activities: Archery, Arts/Crafts, Camping Skills/Outdoor Living, Canoeing, Challenge/Rope Courses, Horseback — Western, Leadership Development, Nature/Environment Studies, Sailing, Swimming — Recreational
Session lengths & capacity: 1 & 2 week sessions; 300 campers
Clientele & fees: coed 8-17; Fees: B ☀ Fees: C, E ▲ 🐷
Contact: Robert Schultz, Director at (651) 436-8428; fax: (715) 386-4382
e-mail: info@campstcroix.org
Operated by: YMCA of Greater St Paul, Camping Services, 2233 Energy Park Dr, St Paul, MN 55108 at (651) 292-4115

Group Rental Information
Site comments: St. Croix Scenic River way 25 miles east of Mpls.St. Paul Metro. Adventure courses & environmental ed programs.
Seasons & Capacity: Spring 203, Summer 240, Fall 203, Winter 203
Facilities: A/V Equipment, Cabins, Dorm-Style, Food Service, Hiking Trails, Lake, Lodges, Meeting Rooms, Playing Fields
Programs: Challenge/Ropes Course, Environmental Education, Winter Sports (#1123)

YMCA Camp Streefland

(est 1979) ☀ ⌂ 🚐

Lakeville, MN (Dakota Co.); (612) 435-2859
Jeremy Kersten, Director

Camp comments: Day camp with some overnight sessions. Emphasis on building self-esteem, values education and working as a team. 9:1 ratio.
Activities: Arts/Crafts, Camping Skills/Outdoor Living, Canoeing, Challenge/Rope Courses, Field Trips, Horseback — Western, Leadership Development, Nature/Environment Studies, Swimming — Recreational

Session lengths & capacity: 1 & 2 week sessions; 175 campers
Clientele & fees: coed 5-15; Fees: B ☀ 🚐
Contact: Jeremy Kersten, Program Director at (952) 898-9622; fax: (952) 898-5007
Operated by: Minnesota Valley YMCA, 13850 Portland Ave So, Burnsville, MN 55337 at (952) 898-9622 (#6392)

YMCA Camp Warren

(est 1928) ▲ ⌂ 🚐

Eveleth, MN (St Louis Co.); (218) 744-4222
Cheri Harder-Keepers, Director

Camp comments: Long term, single gender camp offers unique setting with old world charm. Programs focus on leadership & independence skills.
Activities: Aquatic Activities, Canoeing, Horseback — Western, Kayaking, Photography, Sailing, Windsurfing
Session lengths & capacity: June-August; 1, 2 & 4 week sessions; 135 campers
Clientele & fees: boys 8-16; girls 8-16; families; Fees: D, F ▲ 🐷
Contact: (612) 822-2267; fax: (612) 823-2482
e-mail: info@campwarren.org
Web site: www.ymcacamping.org
Operated by: Minneapolis YMCA Camping Serv, 4 W Rustic Lodge, Minneapolis, MN 55409 at (612) 822-2267

Group Rental Information
Site comments: Camp Warren is located on the shores of Half Moon Lake. Warren, just 3 hrs north of the Twin Cities, is conducive to teambuilding, planning and leadership.
Seasons & Capacity: Spring 164, Fall 164, Winter 92
Facilities: Cabins, Food Service, Kitchen Facilities, Lake, Lodges, Meeting Rooms, Playing Fields
Programs: Boating, Swimming, Winter Sports (#1160)

YMCA Camp Widjiwagan

(est 1929) ▲ ⌂ 🚐

Ely, MN (St Louis Co.); (218) 365-2117
Karen Pick, Director

Camp comments: Building respect for self, others & the environment through wilderness adventure and environmental education.
Activities: Backpacking, Camping Skills/Outdoor Living, Canoeing, Hiking, Leadership Development, Nature/Environment Studies, Wilderness Trips
Session lengths & capacity: June-August; 2, 3 & 7 week sessions; 60 campers
Clientele & fees: boys 12-18; girls 12-18; Fees: D ▲ 🐷
Contact: Tim Gravelle, Registrar at (651) 645-6605; fax: (651) 646-5521
e-mail: tim@widji.org
Operated by: YMCA of Greater St Paul, Camping Services, 2233 Energy Park Dr, St Paul, MN 55108 at (651) 292-4115 (#1177)

YMCA Day Camp Kitchigami

(est 1970) ☀ 🚐

Duluth, MN (St Louis Co.); (218) 722-4745
Sarah Henrickson and Gina Miller, Director

Camp comments: It is our goal to provide fun and rewarding experiences where campers can make new friends and learn new skills.
Activities: Archery, Arts/Crafts, Camping Skills/Outdoor Living, Canoeing, Counselor Training (CIT), Nature/Environment Studies, Swimming — Recreational
Session lengths & capacity: June-August; 1 & 2 week sessions; 75 campers
Clientele & fees: boys 4-11; girls 4-11; Fees: B ☀

Contact: Sarah Hendrickson, Camp Director at (218) 722-4745; fax: (218) 722-4746
Operated by: Duluth Area Family YMCA, 302 W 1st St, Duluth, MN 55802 at (218) 722-4745 (#3868)

YMCA Day Camp Manitou

(est 1950)

Monticello, MN (Hennepin Co.); (763) 295-5454
Brian Burns, Director

Camp comments: 1400 acres just outside the Twin cities offers excellent horseback riding & other outdoor activities for youth.
Activities: Archery, Arts/Crafts, Hiking, Horseback — Western, International Culture, Leadership Development, Nature/Environment Studies, Swimming — Recreational
Session lengths & capacity: June-August; 1, 2 & 3 week sessions; 250 campers
Clientele & fees: coed 4-15; Fees: C
Contact: Stephanie Thomas, Manager at (612) 535-4800; fax: (612) 535-7005
Operated by: Northwest YMCA, 7601 42nd Ave No, New Hope, MN 55427 at (763) 535-4800 (#7139)

Mississippi

Camp Hidden Lake (est 1983)

Lexington, MS (Holmes Co.); (662) 834-2149
Fred McKay, Director
Activities: Arts/Crafts, Basketball, Canoeing, Fishing, Hiking, Music, Religious Study, Swimming — Recreational
Session lengths & capacity: June-July; 1/2, 1 & 4 week sessions; 150 campers
Clientele & fees: boys 7-14; girls 7-16; coed 7-16; Fees: B
Contact: Capt Mark A Woodcock, Camp Director at (601) 969-7560; fax: (601) 968-0272
Operated by: The Salvation Army, PO Box 4857, Jackson, MS 39296-4857 at (601) 969-7560
Group Rental Information
Seasons & Capacity: Spring 210, Summer 210, Fall 210, Winter 210
Facilities: A/V Equipment, Cabins, Dorm-Style, Double Occupancy, Food Service, Hiking Trails, Lake, Lodges, Meeting Rooms, Playing Fields, Pool
Programs: Boating, Swimming (#40046)

Camp Lake Stephens (est 1946)

Oxford, MS (Lafayette Co.); (662) 234-3350
Joe E. Paslay, Director

Camp comments: Owned by United Methodist Church but open to all persons regardless of religious preference, racial or social backgrnd.
Activities: Archery, Arts/Crafts, Camping Skills/Outdoor Living, Climbing/Rappelling, Hiking, Horseback — Western, Leadership Development, Swimming — Instructional, Team Building, Tennis
Session lengths & capacity: June-August; 1 week sessions; 150 campers
Clientele & fees: boys 9-17; girls 9-17; coed 9-17; families; Fees: B
Contact: Joe E Paslay, Director at (662) 234-3350; fax: (662) 234-3883
e-mail: cls@camplakestephens.com
Web site: www.camplakestephens.com
Operated by: Miss Conf United Methodist, 117 Lake Stephens Drive, Oxford, MS 38655 at (662) 234-3350
Group Rental Information
Site comments: Located in the rolling hills of North Mississippi.
Facilities: A/V Equipment, Cabins, Double Occupancy, Food Service, Lake, Meeting Rooms, Pool
Programs: Boating, Challenge/Ropes Course, Horseback Riding, Swimming (#3196)

Camp Of The Rising Son

(est 1980)

French Camp, MS (Choctaw Co.); (662) 547-6169
Larry Littlejohn, Director

Camp comments: Beautiful site, quality staff, Christian emphasis, nondenominational. Campers thrive in challenging, loving atmosphere.
Activities: Aquatic Activities, Archery, Arts/Crafts, Camping Skills/Outdoor Living, Canoeing, Ceramics/Pottery, Challenge/Rope Courses, Horseback — Western, Rafting, Sailing
Session lengths & capacity: June-July; 1 week sessions; 200 campers
Clientele & fees: coed 7-14; Fees: C
Contact: Larry Littlejohn, Director at (662) 547-6169; fax: (662) 547-6169
e-mail: llittlejohn@frenchcamp.org
Web site: www.frenchcamp.org
Operated by: French Camp Academy, 1 Fine Place, French Camp, MS 39745 at (662) 547-6169
Group Rental Information
Site comments: Beautiful rural setting. Great for church retreats, family reunions, Christian ladies, men, or youth retreats.
Seasons & Capacity: Spring 200, Winter 32
Facilities: A/V Equipment, Cabins, Food Service, Hiking Trails, Lake, Linens, Lodges, Meeting Rooms, Tents
Programs: Challenge/Ropes Course, Horseback Riding, Swimming (#5485)

Camp Wahi GSCMM

(est 1949)

Brandon, MS; (601) 825-5165
Lisa Gabriel, Director

Camp comments: In an all girl outdoor setting, trained staff & specialty programs offer new challenges & add to learned skills.
Activities: Archery, Canoeing, Ceramics/Pottery, Counselor Training (CIT), Hiking, Kayaking, Nature/Environment Studies, Swimming — Instructional, Team Building, Wilderness Trips
Session lengths & capacity: June-August; 1/2, 1 & 2 week sessions; 120 campers
Clientele & fees: girls 6-17; Fees: A, B, C, D
Contact: Lisa Gabriel, Program Services Director at (601) 366-0607 ext. 241; fax: (601) 366-0664
e-mail: spice@gscmm.com
Web site: www.gscmm.org
Operated by: Girl Scout Coun Middle Miss, 1471 W County Line Rd, Jackson, MS 39213 at (601) 366-0607
Group Rental Information
Facilities: Cabins, Food Service, Hiking Trails, Lake, Pool, Tents
Programs: Challenge/Ropes Course, Swimming (#28067)

Hopewell Camp & Conf Center

(est 1949)

Oxford, MS (Lafayette Co.); (662) 234-2254
Robert & Karen Allen, Director

Camp comments: Christian program gives caring support so campers belong, contribute, and grow. Open year-round for retreat rentals.
Activities: Archery, Arts/Crafts, Camping Skills/Outdoor Living, Caving, Challenge/Rope Courses, Horseback — Western, Leadership Development, Music, Nature/Environment Studies, Swimming — Recreational
Session lengths & capacity: June-August; 1 week sessions; 100 campers
Clientele & fees: coed 6-15; seniors; Fees: C
Contact: Robert & Karen Allen, Directors at (662) 234-2254; fax: (662) 234-4150
e-mail: hopewell@dixie-net.com
Operated by: The Presbytery of St Andrew, 24 Country Road 231, Oxford, MS 38655 at (662) 234-6069

Group Rental Information
Seasons & Capacity: Spring 120, Winter 120
Facilities: Cabins, Dorm-Style, Food Service, Hiking Trails, Kitchen Facilities, Lake, Linens, Lodges, Meeting Rooms
Programs: Challenge/Ropes Course (#715)

Phoenix Boys & Girls Clubs

(est 1970)

Como, MS (Panola Co.); (662) 526-5970
Joe Sing, Director

Camp comments: Resident camp is offered to members of the Boys & Girls Clubs of Greater Memphis.
Activities: Archery, Arts/Crafts, Canoeing, Farming/Ranching/Gardening, Fishing, Hiking, Nature/Environment Studies, Sailing, Swimming — Recreational
Session lengths & capacity: June-August; 1 week sessions; 95 campers
Clientele & fees: coed 7-12; Fees: A
Contact: Joe Sing, Camp Director at (901) 278-2947;
Web site: www.BGCM.org
Operated by: Boys Girls Clubs Gtr Memphis, 189 So Barksdale, Memphis, TN 38104 at (901) 278-2947 (#2954)

South MS WOW Youth Camp

Hathesburg, MS
Darryl Mc Han, Director
Activities: Archery, Arts/Crafts, Baseball/Softball, Basketball, Canoeing, Challenge/Rope Courses, Counselor Training (CIT), Riflery, Swimming — Recreational
Contact: Web site: www.woodmen.com
Operated by: WOW Life Insurance (HS), 1700 Farnam, Omaha, NE 68120 at (402) 271-7258
Group Rental Information
Facilities: Cabins, Kitchen Facilities, Meeting Rooms, Playing Fields, Pool (#45488)

Tik-A-Witha (est 1970)

Van Vleet, MS (Chickasaw Co.); (662) 447-3250
Jenny Holley Jones, Director

Camp comments: Rich with traditions, fun, friends and laughter. Where everyone is treated with dignity and respect.
Activities: Aquatic Activities, Arts/Crafts, Camping Skills/Outdoor Living, Canoeing, Challenge/Rope Courses, Counselor Training (CIT), Hiking, Horseback — Western, Nature/Environment Studies, Team Building
Session lengths & capacity: June-July; 1 & 2 week sessions; 100 campers
Clientele & fees: girls 6-17; Fees: B
Contact: Jenny Holley, Camp Director at (662) 844-7577; fax: (662) 680-3164
e-mail: shine@girlscoutsnems.org
Web site: www.girlscoutsnems.org
Operated by: Girl Scouts of Northeast Miss, PO Box 1087, Tupelo, MS 38802 at (662) 844-7577
Group Rental Information
Facilities: Hiking Trails
Programs: Environmental Education (#711)

Uahc Henry S Jacobs Camp

(est 1970)

Utica, MS (Hinds Co.); (601) 885-6042
Jonathan Cohen, Director

Camp comments: Reform Jewish camping with a purpose. Fun, friendship, community. Focus on healthy development. Great specialty activities. Experience it!

Activities: Aerobics/Exercise, Arts/Crafts, Challenge/Rope Courses, Music, Nature/Environment Studies, Performing Arts, Religious Study, Sports — Field & Team, Swimming — Recreational, Team Building
Session lengths & capacity: June-August; 2, 4 & 6 week sessions; 240 campers
Clientele & fees: coed 7-16; Fees: E ⛺ 🚐
Contact: Jonathan Cohen, Camp Director at (601) 885-6042; fax: (601) 885-6269
e-mail: jc@hsjacobscamp.org
Web site: www.hsjacobscamp.org
Operated by: UAHC Henry S Jacobs Camp, PO Box 327, Utica, MS 39175 at (601) 885-6042

Group Rental Information
Site comments: Hold your next retreat in the country! Modern camp/retreat center in beautiful wooded, rural setting. Close to Jackson, MS.
Facilities: A/V Equipment, Dorm-Style, Double Occupancy, Food Service, Hiking Trails, Lake, Linens, Meeting Rooms, Playing Fields, Pool
Programs: Boating, Challenge/Ropes Course, Environmental Education, Swimming (#42075)

WOW North MS Youth Camp
(est 1970) ⛺

Ackerman, MS (Choctaw Co.); (601) 285-3235
Billy Donaldson, Director

Camp comments: Beautiful wooded area in Choctaw County. Limited to Woodmen of the World Life Insurance society members only.
Activities: Archery, Arts/Crafts, Baseball/Softball, Basketball, Canoeing, Challenge/Rope Courses, Counselor Training (CIT), Leadership Development, Nature/Environment Studies, Riflery
Session lengths & capacity: June-July; 1/2 & 1 week sessions; 86 campers
Clientele & fees: coed 8-15; seniors; Fees: A ⛺
Contact: Billy Donaldson, Camp Director at (622) 844-4199; fax: (622) 844-4199
Web site: www.woodmen.com
Operated by: WOW Life Insurance (HS), 1700 Farnam, Omaha, NE 68120 at (402) 271-7258 (#6246)

Missouri

Camp Cedarledge (est 1927) ⛺ 🏠
Pevely, MO (Jefferson Co.); (636) 475-5359

Camp comments: Wide variety of learning experiences: camp crafts, canoeing, arts & crafts, swimming, trails & more.

ICON LEGEND
☀ Day Camp
⛺ Resident Camp
🏠 Facilities Available To Rent
🚐 Transportation Available
🐷 Financial Aid Available

FEE RANGES PER WEEK
A	$0-75
B	$75-200
C	$201-350
D	$351-500
E	$501-650
F	over $650

Activities: Archery, Arts/Crafts, Bicycling/Biking, Camping Skills/Outdoor Living, Hiking, Horseback — Western, Leadership Development, Nature/Environment Studies
Session lengths & capacity: 1, 2 & 4 week sessions; 350 campers
Clientele & fees: girls 7-17; Fees: B, C ⛺ 🐷
Contact: Jennifer Morgan, Camping Services Director at (314) 592-2363; fax: (314) 423-5297
Web site: www.gscgsl.org
Operated by: GSC of Greater St Louis, 2130 Kratky Road, St Louis, MO 63114 at (314) 890-9569

Group Rental Information
Facilities: Cabins, Hiking Trails, Kitchen Facilities, Lodges, Pool, Tents
Programs: Boating (#1051)

Camp Emeth (est 1987) ☀
St Louis, MO (St Louis Co.); (314) 569-1273
Beth MacLean, Director

Camp comments: Campers learn & grow through activities, spirituality & a sense of community.
Activities: Aquatic Activities, Arts/Crafts, Camping Skills/Outdoor Living, Community Service, Dance, Drama, Field Trips, Music, Nature/Environment Studies
Session lengths & capacity: 3, 6 & 8 week sessions; 130 campers
Clientele & fees: coed 5-13; Fees: B ☀
Contact: Beth MacLean, Camp Director at (314) 569-1273; fax: (314) 569-0271
e-mail: bmaclean@shaare-emeth.org
Web site: www.shaare-emeth.org
Operated by: Shaare Emeth Congregation, 11645 Ladue Rd, St Louis, MO 63141-8201 at (314) 569-1273 (#189)

Camp Fiddlecreek (est 1956) ⛺ 🏠
Labadie, MO (Franklin Co.); (636) 451-5604

Camp comments: Eight, 3 day & 2 night sessions. Teaches self-reliance, confidence & is fun!
Activities: Arts/Crafts, Camping Skills/Outdoor Living, Canoeing, Hiking, Nature/Environment Studies, Swimming — Recreational
Session lengths & capacity: 1/2 week sessions; 100 campers
Clientele & fees: girls 6-10; Fees: A ⛺ 🐷
Contact: Jennifer Morgan, Camping Services Director at (314) 592-2363; fax: (314) 423-5297
Web site: www.gscgsl.org
Operated by: GSC of Greater St Louis, 2130 Kratky Road, St Louis, MO 63114 at (314) 890-9569 (#7237)

Camp Finbrooke (est 1950) ⛺ 🏠
Rogersville, MO (Christian Co.); (417) 581-4943
Peggy Oney, Director

Camp comments: Girl Scout camp in rustic setting with river access. Activities include pool, mountain bikes, challenge course, pioneer living.
Activities: Aquatic Activities, Arts/Crafts, Bicycling/Biking, Camping Skills/Outdoor Living, Challenge/Rope Courses, Climbing/Rappelling, Horseback — Western, Leadership Development, Nature/Environment Studies, Swimming — Recreational
Session lengths & capacity: June-July; 1/2, 1 & 2 week sessions; 140 campers
Clientele & fees: girls 7-17; Fees: B ⛺
Contact: Linda DuBrul, Outdoor Program Director at (417) 862-0004; fax: (417) 862-4120
e-mail: camp@dogwoodtrails.org
Web site: www.dogwoodtrails.org
Operated by: Girl Scouts of Dogwood Trails, 210 S Ingram Mill Rd, Springfield, MO 65802-6100 at (417) 862-0004

Group Rental Information
Seasons & Capacity: Spring 100, Summer 160, Fall 100

Facilities: Hiking Trails, Kitchen Facilities, Lodges, Pool, River, Tents
Programs: Challenge/Ropes Course (#3191)

Camp Heritage (est 1965) ⛺ 🏠
Climax Springs, MO; (573) 345-3760
Elden Ramirez, Director

Activities: Aquatic Activities, Archery, Ceramics/Pottery, Climbing/Rappelling, Gymnastics, Horseback — English, Horseback — Western, Swimming — Instructional, Swimming — Recreational, Waterskiing
Session lengths & capacity: June-August; 1, 2 & 3 week sessions; 150 campers
Clientele & fees: coed 7-17; families; seniors; single adults; Fees: B ⛺
Contact: Tammy Micheff, Secretary at (515) 223-1197 ext. 100; fax: (515) 223-5692
e-mail: tamichef@ucollege.edu
Web site: www.campheritage.org
Operated by: Iowa Missouri Conf of SDA, PO Box 65665, West Des Moines, IA 50265 at (515) 223-1197

Group Rental Information
Facilities: A/V Equipment, Cabins, Double Occupancy, Food Service, Hiking Trails, Kitchen Facilities, Lake, Lodges, Meeting Rooms, River
Programs: Boating, Environmental Education, Horseback Riding, Swimming (#847)

Camp Hickory Hill (est 1974) ⛺
Columbia, MO (Boone Co.); (573) 884-6633
Bob Buckwalter, Director

Camp comments: Camp Hickory Hill provides recreation, emotional support & a strong educational program for children with diabetes.
Activities: Aquatic Activities, Archery, Arts/Crafts, Camping Skills/Outdoor Living, Caving, Climbing/Rappelling, Counselor Training (CIT), Nature/Environment Studies, Riflery, Sports — Field & Team
Session lengths & capacity: June-August; 1 & 2 week sessions; 75 campers
Clientele & fees: coed 8-17; Fees: C ⛺
Contact: Pete Bakutes, Agency Director at (573) 698-2510; fax: (573) 698-2710
e-mail: camphickoryhill@juno.com
Web site: www.camphickoryhill.com
Operated by: Central Missouri Diabetic Chil, PO Box 1942, Columbia, MO 65205-1942 at (573) 445-9146 (#4265)

Camp Kee Tov (est 1974) ⛺ 🚐
Silex, MO (Lincoln Co.); (636) 528-5796
Michah Turner, Director

Camp comments: An opportunity to experience Reform Jewish living at its best. A great first time overnight camp experience.
Activities: Archery, Arts/Crafts, Camping Skills/Outdoor Living, Drama, Language Studies, Music, Nature/Environment Studies, Sports — Field & Team, Swimming — Recreational, Team Building
Session lengths & capacity: 1, 2 & 3 week sessions; 40 campers
Clientele & fees: coed 9-11; Fees: D ⛺
Contact: Michah Turner, Director at (314) 432-0020; fax: (314) 432-6150
e-mail: mturner@cajestl.org
Operated by: Central Agency for Jewish Educ, 12 Millstone Campus Drive, St Louis, MO 63146 at (314) 432-0020 (#3821)

Camp MITIOG (est 1969) ⛺ 🚐
Excelsior Springs, MO (Ray Co.); (816) 221-4450
Brenda O'Dell, Director

Camp comments: For children with spina bifida. One to one camper/counselor ratio. Twenty-four hour nursing staff.

Activities: Aquatic Activities, Arts/Crafts, Bicycling/Biking, Boating, Canoeing, Music, Nature/Environment Studies, Swimming — Instructional, Swimming — Recreational
Session lengths & capacity: July-July; 1 week sessions; 60 campers
Clientele & fees: coed 6-16; Fees: A ▲ 🚐
Contact: Nancy Krahl, Executive Director at (816) 221-4450; fax: (816) 221-1420
Operated by: Share Inc, 600 Broadway Ste 430, Kansas City, MO 64105-1536 at (816) 221-6268 (#6389)

Camp Shawnee (est 1953)   ☀ ▲ 🏠

Waldron, MO; (816) 891-1075
July Holley, Director

Camp comments: Camp Shawnee is nestled in 290 acres of beautiful rolling hills overlooking the Missouri River near Parkville, Missouri.
Activities: Archery, Basketball, Bicycling/Biking, Camping Skills/Outdoor Living, Challenge/Rope Courses, Community Service, Counselor Training (CIT), Leadership Development, Swimming — Recreational
Session lengths & capacity: 1/2 & 1 week sessions; 125 campers
Clientele & fees: coed 5-18; families; seniors; single adults; Fees: A ☀ Fees: B, C ▲ 🚐
Contact: Judy Holley, Outdoor Director at (913) 648-2121 ext. 118; fax: (913) 648-2197
Operated by: Camp Shawnee, 7930 State Line Rd, Prairie Village, KS 66208 at (913) 648-2121

Group Rental Information
Seasons & Capacity: Spring 0, Fall 0, Winter 0
Facilities: Cabins, Dorm-Style, Double Occupancy, Hiking Trails, Kitchen Facilities, Pool
Programs: Challenge/Ropes Course, Environmental Education (#1101)

Camp Tuckaho (est 1966)   ▲ 🚐

Troy, MO (Lincoln Co.); (636) 462-7272

Camp comments: Six, 1 week special interest programs plus camping skills, canoeing, making friends.
Activities: Archery, Arts/Crafts, Bicycling/Biking, Camping Skills/Outdoor Living, Hiking, Leadership Development, Nature/Environment Studies
Session lengths & capacity: 1 week sessions; 200 campers
Clientele & fees: girls 7-17; Fees: B ▲ 🚐
Contact: Jennifer Morgan, Camping Services Director at (314) 592-2363; fax: (314) 423-5297
Web site: www.gscgsl.org
Operated by: GSC of Greater St Louis, 2130 Kratky Road, St Louis, MO 63114 at (314) 890-9569 (#3648)

Cedars Camps (est 1962)   ▲ 🏠 🚐

Lebanon, MO (Laclede Co.); (417) 532-6699
Warren Huff, Director

Camp comments: Spiritual growth for Christian Scientists in beautiful setting. Great staff ratio, 300' waterslide, lake, aquatic & sports centers, 60 horses, cabins w/baths.
Activities: Archery, Challenge/Rope Courses, Counselor Training (CIT), Horseback — English, Horseback — Western, Sports — Field & Team, Swimming — Instructional, Swimming — Recreational, Waterskiing
Session lengths & capacity: May-November; 1/2, 1, 2 & 3 week sessions; 250 campers
Clientele & fees: boys 6-12; girls 6-12; coed 13-18; families; seniors; single adults; Fees: C, D, F ▲ 🚐
Contact: Warren Huff, Executive Director at (314) 394-6162; fax: (314) 227-0815
e-mail: warrenhuff@aol.com
Web site: www.cedarscamp.org
Operated by: The Cedars Camps Office, 1314 Parkview Valley, Manchester, MO 63011 at (636) 394-6162

Group Rental Information
Site comments: Private lake, 300' waterslide, aquatic & sports centers, 60 horses, private rooms or bunks in cabins. Many indoor & decked meeting areas in beautiful settings.
Seasons & Capacity: Spring 180, Summer 340, Fall 180, Winter 100
Facilities: A/V Equipment, Cabins, Dorm-Style, Double Occupancy, Food Service, Hiking Trails, Kitchen Facilities, Lake, Linens, Lodges, Meeting Rooms, Playing Fields, Pool, River
Programs: Boating, Challenge/Ropes Course, Environmental Education, Horseback Riding, Swimming (#1074)

Concerned Care Inc Day Camp

(est 1990)   ☀ 🚐

North Kansas City, MO (Clay Co.); (816) 474-3026
John Whalen, Director
Activities: Aerobics/Exercise, Aquatic Activities, Arts/Crafts, Drawing/Painting, Field Trips, Fishing, Swimming — Recreational
Session lengths & capacity: July-August; 5 week sessions; 10 campers
Clientele & fees: coed 7-16; Fees: A ☀
Contact: John Whalen or Jim Huffman, Camp Coordinator at (816) 474-3026; fax: (816) 474-3029
Operated by: Concerned Care Inc, 320 Armour Road Ste 101, North Kansas City, MO 64116 at (816) 474-3026 (#25470)

Edison Retreat Center   🏠

Silex, MO (Lincoln Co.); (314) 528-5796
Contact: Mark Shook, Director at (314) 432-8050; fax: (314) 432-8053
Operated by: Temple Israel, 1 Rabbi Alvan D Rubin Dr, St Louis, MO 63141 at (314) 432-8050

Group Rental Information
Seasons & Capacity: Spring 50, Summer 50, Fall 50
Facilities: Dorm-Style, Food Service, Kitchen Facilities, Lodges, Meeting Rooms, Pool (#6292)

H Roe Bartle Scout Reservation

(est 1929)   ▲

S B Osceola, MO (St Clair Co.); (417) 646-8115
Roger Hoyt, Director

Camp comments: Scout camping for young men ages 11 to 18. Outpost programs and lakefront facilities on site. Older boy programs available. Venturing activities for 2002.
Activities: Aquatic Activities, Boating, Camping Skills/Outdoor Living, Challenge/Rope Courses, Climbing/Rappelling, Hiking, Leadership Development, Riflery, Swimming — Instructional, Team Building
Session lengths & capacity: June-August; 1 week sessions; 1700 campers
Clientele & fees: boys 11-18; Fees: B ▲
Operated by: Heart of America Council BSA, 10210 Holmes Road, Kansas City, MO 64131 at (816) 942-9333 (#43732)

Kansas City Rotary Youth Camp

(est 1922)   🏠

Lees Summit, MO; (816) 524-0923
Operated by: Kansas City Rotary 13, 1228 Baltimore Ste 722, Kansas City, MO 64105 at (816) 842-2322

Group Rental Information
Site comments: Youth groups only. No kitchen in school-year season.
Facilities: Cabins, Food Service, Hiking Trails, Meeting Rooms, Pool, Tents (#1095)

Kiwanis Camp Wyman

(est 1898)   ▲ 🏠 🚐

Eureka, MO (St Louis Co.); (636) 938-5245
Ken Keusen Kothen, Director

Camp comments: Respect theme in program: responsibility; environment; self-discovery; peace; enjoyment; challenge; tolerance.
Activities: Arts/Crafts, Camping Skills/Outdoor Living, Canoeing, Caving, Challenge/Rope Courses, Counselor Training (CIT), Hiking, Leadership Development, Nature/Environment Studies, Team Building
Session lengths & capacity: June-August; 1 & 2 week sessions; 120 campers
Clientele & fees: coed 7-16; families; Fees: C ▲ 🚐
Contact: Rachel Crosetto, Branch Director at (636) 938-5245 ext. 228; fax: (636) 938-5289
e-mail: rachelc@wymancenter.org
Web site: www.wymancenter.org
Operated by: Wyman Center Inc, 600 Kiwanis Dr, Eureka, MO 63025 at (636) 938-5245

Group Rental Information
Site comments: St.Louis area & beyond-youth development, special needs, environmental & adventure programs, leadership training. Conference & retreat services. Estab. 1898.
Seasons & Capacity: Spring 180, Fall 180, Winter 180
Facilities: A/V Equipment, Cabins, Dorm-Style, Double Occupancy, Food Service, Hiking Trails, Kitchen Facilities, Lake, Linens, Meeting Rooms, Playing Fields, Pool, River
Programs: Boating, Challenge/Ropes Course, Environmental Education, Swimming (#1067)

Lake Of The Woods   🏠

Kansas City, MO (Jackson Co.); (816) 513-8962
Payt Bergert, Director
Contact: Marci Jones at (816) 513-8965; e-mail: Marci_Jones@kcmo.org
Operated by: Kansas City Parks & Recreation, 4701 E Gregory, Kansas City, MO 64132 at (816) 513-8962

Group Rental Information
Site comments: The central location & beautiful forest setting is ideal for workshops, receptions, reunions, camp outs & picnics.
Facilities: Hiking Trails, Pool
Programs: Environmental Education (#1105)

Lions Den Outdoor Learning Ctr (est 1926)   ☀ ▲ 🏠

Imperial, MO; (636) 296-4480
Becky Brendel, Director

Camp comments: Mane Event Adventure Camp offers challenges in an outdoor learning environment-caving, climbing wall, backpacking, high ropes-that increase skills & self-esteem
Activities: Backpacking, Camping Skills/Outdoor Living, Canoeing, Caving, Challenge/Rope Courses, Climbing/Rappelling, Nature/Environment Studies, Swimming — Recreational, Team Building, Wilderness Trips
Session lengths & capacity: July-July; 1 week sessions; 100 campers
Clientele & fees: coed 11-16; Fees: C ▲
Contact: Dave Knobbe, Branch Director at (636) 296-4480; fax: (636) 296-4476
e-mail: davek@wymancenter.org
Web site: www.wymancenter.org
Operated by: Wyman Center Inc, 600 Kiwanis Dr, Eureka, MO 63025 at (636) 938-5245

Group Rental Information
Site comments: St Louis area.Handicap accessible.Youth development, adventure, environmental education & special needs programming.
Seasons & Capacity: Spring 150, Summer 150, Fall 150

Facilities: Cabins, Dorm-Style, Double Occupancy, Food Service, Hiking Trails, Kitchen Facilities, Lodges
Programs: Environmental Education (#2030)

Mattie Rhodes Camp (est 1968) ▲

Lees Summit, MO (Jackson Co.); (816) 524-0923
Janelle Arnett Campbell, Director

Camp comments: Supportive therapeutic residential camp for at-risk inner city youth. One week-long session only. Closed enrollment.
Activities: Archery, Arts/Crafts, Camping Skills/Outdoor Living, Counselor Training (CIT), Hiking, Leadership Development, Nature/Environment Studies, Swimming — Recreational, Team Building
Session lengths & capacity: June-July; 1 week sessions; 100 campers
Clientele & fees: coed 7-18; Fees: A ▲
Contact: Janelle Arnett Campbell, Camp Director at (816) 471-2536; fax: (816) 471-2521
e-mail: jarnettcampbell@mattierhodes.org
Operated by: Mattie Rhodes Cnsl & Arts Ctr, 1740 Jefferson, Kansas City, MO 64108 at (816) 471-2536 (#3409)

Mihaska (est 1948) ▲ 🏠

Bourbon, MO (Crawford Co.); (573) 732-5239
Mike Delashmit, Director

Camp comments: From June-Aug all campers register for camp thru their local S.Army Corps. Sept-May camp & conference center is available for groups of 12-400. Write for info.
Activities: Arts/Crafts, Camping Skills/Outdoor Living, Challenge/Rope Courses, Fishing, Golf, Music, Performing Arts, Swimming — Recreational
Contact: Mike Delashmit, Camp Manager at (573) 732-5239; fax: (573) 732-5027
e-mail: mihaska@fidnet.com
Operated by: The Salvation Army, Mihaska 1466 Hwy N, Bourbon, MO 65441 at (573) 732-5239
Group Rental Information
Site comments: Camp Mihaska is nestled in the Ozarks @ 1.5 hours SW of St Louis.It is rich with natural beauty and has springs & trails. Groups of 12-400 are able to come.
Seasons & Capacity: Spring 250, Fall 250, Winter 250
Facilities: Dorm-Style, Food Service, Hiking Trails, Kitchen Facilities, Lodges, Meeting Rooms, Tents (#1071)

ICON LEGEND

☀ Day Camp
▲ Resident Camp
🏠 Facilities Available To Rent
🚌 Transportation Available
🐷 Financial Aid Available

FEE RANGES PER WEEK

A	$0-75
B	$75-200
C	$201-350
D	$351-500
E	$501-650
F	over $650

Mintahama (est 1946) ▲ 🏠

Joplin, MO (Jasper Co.); (417) 623-2140
Beth Hunt, Director

Camp comments: Ozark setting. Variety in terrain. Interpretative trail. Tree houses, cabins, lodge, tents. Beautiful spring fed lake.
Activities: Aquatic Activities, Backpacking, Camping Skills/Outdoor Living, Canoeing, Counselor Training (CIT), Horseback — Western, Photography, Sailing, Swimming — Recreational
Session lengths & capacity: June-July; 1/2, 1 & 2 week sessions; 130 campers
Clientele & fees: girls 6-18; families; Fees: B ▲
Contact: Julie Jones, Director Office Services at (417) 623-8277; fax: (417) 625-1261
e-mail: jjones@gscoa.org
Web site: www.girlscoutsozark.org
Operated by: GSC of the Ozark Area, PO Box 2400, Joplin, MO 64804 at (417) 623-8277
Group Rental Information
Site comments: 7 miles from I-44 in Ozark scenic area. Modern kitchen.
Seasons & Capacity: Spring 160, Summer 160, Fall 160, Winter 70
Facilities: Cabins, Double Occupancy, Hiking Trails, Kitchen Facilities, Lake, Pool, Tents
Programs: Boating, Environmental Education, Horseback Riding, Swimming (#1113)

Missouri Military Academy
(est 1889) ▲

Mexico, MO (Audrain Co.); (573) 581-1776
Major Mark Vaughan, Director

Camp comments: MMA leadership confidence camps are adventurous training sessions in the basics of group effort, personal responsibility and leadership.
Activities: Aquatic Activities, Archery, Boating, Camping Skills/Outdoor Living, Canoeing, Challenge/Rope Courses, Horseback — Western, Leadership Development, Riflery, Team Building
Session lengths & capacity: July-July; 1 & 2 week sessions; 150 campers
Clientele & fees: boys 8-16; Fees: F ▲
Contact: Captain Dennis Diederich, Director of Admissions at (573) 581-1776; fax: (573) 581-0081
e-mail: ddie@mma.mexico.mo.us
Operated by: Missouri Military Academy, 204 Grand Ave, Mexico, MO 65265 at (573) 581-1776 (#34750)

NeKaMo Camp Cherith (est 1966) ▲

Warsaw, MO; (816) 438-5253
Debbie Morris, Director

Camp comments: Traditional program Christian camp. In Ozarks near Truman Lake. Small group activities focused on personal development.
Activities: Archery, Arts/Crafts, Canoeing, Counselor Training (CIT), Hiking, Leadership Development, Riflery, Sailing, Swimming — Instructional, Waterskiing
Session lengths & capacity: 1/2 & 1 week sessions; 85 campers
Clientele & fees: boys 7-14; girls 7-18; Fees: B ▲ 🐷
Contact: Debbie Morris, Director at (913) 764-7240; e-mail: genedebmorris@juno.com
Web site: www.nekamo.org
Operated by: NeKaMo Camp Cherith, 440 W 61st St, Kansas City, MO 64113 at (816) 444-4221 (#3431)

Oakledge (est 1947) ▲ 🏠 🚌

Warsaw, MO (Benton Co.); (816) 438-7768
Robyn E. Ratcliff, Director

Camp comments: Help girls become confident, responsible women. Come join the fun on the Lake of the Ozarks. Rustic camp setting.

Activities: Archery, Backpacking, Camping Skills/Outdoor Living, Canoeing, Climbing/Rappelling, Counselor Training (CIT), Hiking, Kayaking, Sailing, Swimming — Recreational
Session lengths & capacity: June-August; 2 week sessions; 180 campers
Clientele & fees: girls 10-18; Fees: B, C ▲ 🐷
Contact: Robyn E Ratcliff, Director at (660) 438-7768; fax: (660) 438-6828
e-mail: rratcliff@girlscoutsmcc.org
Operated by: Girl Scouts of Mid Continent, 8383 Blue Parkway Drive, Kansas City, MO 64133 at (816) 358-8750 (#1103)

Prairie Schooner (est 1947) ▲

Kansas City, MO (Jackson Co.); (816) 373-6517
Jennifer Wellman, Director

Camp comments: Helping girls become confident, responsible women. A general camp program full of fun and adventure just for girls.
Activities: Archery, Arts/Crafts, Camping Skills/Outdoor Living, Climbing/Rappelling, Computer, Counselor Training (CIT), Hiking, Performing Arts, Swimming — Recreational
Session lengths & capacity: June-August; 1 week sessions; 160 campers
Clientele & fees: girls 6-10; Fees: B ▲
Contact: Lisa Nichols, Director at (816) 358-8750 ext. 3020; fax: (816) 358-5714
e-mail: lnichols@plugged-in.org
Operated by: Girl Scouts of Mid Continent, 8383 Blue Parkway Drive, Kansas City, MO 64133 at (816) 358-8750 (#1098)

Rocky Point Day Camp
(est 1952) ☀ 🚌

Kansas City, MO; (816) 513-8962
Payt Bergert, Director

Camp comments: Provides children the opportunity to hike, explore the forest, discover wildlife, learn to swim & make new friends.
Activities: Archery, Arts/Crafts, Camping Skills/Outdoor Living, Counselor Training (CIT), Field Trips, Fishing, Hiking, Nature/Environment Studies, Swimming — Instructional, Swimming — Recreational
Session lengths & capacity: June-August; 2 week sessions; 100 campers
Clientele & fees: coed 5-12; Fees: A ☀ 🐷
Contact: Marci Jones at (816) 513-8965; e-mail: Marci_Jones@kcmo.org
Operated by: Kansas City Parks & Recreation, 4701 E Gregory, Kansas City, MO 64132 at (816) 513-8962 (#4211)

S-F Scout Ranch (est 1965) ▲

Knob Lick, MO (St Francois Co.); (573) 756-5738
Pat Martchink, Director

Camp comments: Camp for Boy Scouts & Venturers. Located in the Missouri Ozarks, 5200 acres with a 270 acre lake.
Activities: Archery, Bicycling/Biking, Camping Skills/Outdoor Living, Climbing/Rappelling, Horseback — Western, Nature/Environment Studies, Riflery, Sailing, Swimming — Instructional, Swimming — Recreational
Session lengths & capacity: 1/2 & 1 week sessions
Clientele & fees: boys 11-18; coed 14-20; Fees: B ▲
Contact: Pat Martchink, Director of Camping at (314) 361-0600; fax: (314) 361-5165
Operated by: Greater St Louis Area Council, 4568 West Pine Blvd, St Louis, MO 63108 at (314) 361-0600 (#6102)

Sabra (est 1970) ⛺ ⌂ 🚗

Rocky Mount, MO; (573) 365-1591
Randy Comensky, Director

Camp comments: Caring & talented staff, dynamic activities incl waterskiing, sailing & riding. 960 acre campus, 3 mi shoreline, Kosher.
Activities: Arts/Crafts, Bicycling/Biking, Climbing/Rappelling, Drama, Horseback — Western, Photography, Sailing, Tennis, Waterskiing
Session lengths & capacity: June-August; 2 & 4 week sessions; 350 campers
Clientele & fees: boys 8-15; girls 8-15; coed 8-15; Fees: D ⛺ 🐃
Contact: Randy Comensky, Director at (314) 442-3426; fax: (314) 442-3404
e-mail: sabra1@concentric.net
Operated by: JCC, 2 Millstone Campus Dr, St Louis, MO 63146 at (314) 432-5700

Group Rental Information
Facilities: Double Occupancy, Kitchen Facilities, Lake (#1034)

Sherwood Forest Camp Inc

(est 1937) ⛺ ⌂ 🚗

Lesterville, MO (Reynolds Co.); (573) 637-2476
Michael Castulik, Director

Camp comments: We create healthy, caring communitoes where children, primarily from disadvantaged families, develop characher & competence. School year programs also.
Activities: Aquatic Activities, Archery, Arts/Crafts, Camping Skills/Outdoor Living, Climbing/Rappelling, Counselor Training (CIT), Hiking, Leadership Development, Team Building
Session lengths & capacity: June-August; 1 & 2 week sessions; 100 campers
Clientele & fees: boys 7-16; girls 7-16; Fees: A, B ⛺ 🐃
Contact: Michelle Metzler, Administrative Assistant at (314) 644-3322; fax: (314) 644-3330
e-mail: mmetzler-sfc@qwest.net
Web site: www.sherwoodforestcamp.com
Operated by: Sherwood Forest Camp Inc, 2708 Sutton Blvd, St Louis, MO 63143 at (314) 644-3322

Group Rental Information
Site comments: Nestled in a Mo Ozark Valley on 487 acres. We offer programs & assistance taylored to the needs of schools & organizations that serve youth & families.
Seasons & Capacity: Spring 200, Fall 200
Facilities: Cabins, Food Service, Hiking Trails, Lake, Linens, Lodges, Playing Fields
Programs: Boating, Challenge/Ropes Course, Environmental Education (#1062)

Sidney R Baer Day Camp

(est 1945) ☀ 🚗

St Louis, MO (St Louis Co.); (314) 432-5700
Sally Lang, Director

Camp comments: Integrates variety of traditional camp sport cultural activities including Judaic programs for children of all abilities
Activities: Aquatic Activities, Arts/Crafts, Counselor Training (CIT), Dance, Field Trips, Leadership Development, Music, Nature/Environment Studies, Sports — Field & Team, Swimming — Instructional
Session lengths & capacity: June-August; 2, 4 & 8 week sessions; 250 campers
Clientele & fees: coed 5-12; Fees: B ☀ 🐃
Contact: Lisa Cohen, Director at (314) 432-5700 ext. 150; fax: (314) 432-5825
Operated by: JCC, 2 Millstone Campus Dr, St Louis, MO 63146 at (314) 432-5700 (#1026)

St Mark's Day Camp

(est 1971) ☀ 🚗

Kansas City, MO; (816) 444-5156
Maurice Parrish, Director

Camp comments: We provide fun sustained experiences including a variety of activities allows growth in abilities/socialization skills
Activities: Aerobics/Exercise, Arts/Crafts, Basketball, Camping Skills/Outdoor Living, Counselor Training (CIT), Dance, Field Trips, Golf, Hiking, Music
Session lengths & capacity: 9 week sessions; 160 campers
Clientele & fees: boys 6-13; girls 6-13; coed 6-13; Fees: B ☀
Contact: Rhonda Robinson, Admin. Assist. at (816) 842-5454; fax: (816) 842-3247
Operated by: St Marks Church, 1101 Euclid, Kansas City, MO 64127 at (816) 842-5454 (#3145)

Sunnyhill Adventure Center

(est 1979) ⛺ ⌂ 🚗

Dittmer, MO (Jefferson Co.); (636) 274-9044
Jennifer Schicker, Director

Camp comments: Adventure theme programs, youth, children & adults with special needs, groups. A/C heat available - group rentals.
Activities: Archery, Arts/Crafts, Boating, Camping Skills/Outdoor Living, Canoeing, Caving, Challenge/Rope Courses, Climbing/Rappelling, Fishing, Swimming — Recreational
Session lengths & capacity: June-August; 1/2, 1 & 2 week sessions; 70 campers
Clientele & fees: coed 8-99; Fees: C, E, F ⛺ 🐃
Contact: Jennifer Schicker, Director at (636) 274-9044; fax: (636) 285-1305
e-mail: dropin4fun@aol.com
Operated by: Council For Extended Care, 5257 Shaw Ave Ste 305, St Louis, MO 63110 at (314) 781-4950

Group Rental Information
Site comments: Year round lodge in rustic setting, lake, pool, challenge course, float streams and caving opportunities.
Seasons & Capacity: Spring 0, Fall 0, Winter 0
Facilities: Dorm-Style, Food Service, Hiking Trails, Kitchen Facilities, Lake, Lodges, Meeting Rooms, Playing Fields, Pool, River, Tents
Programs: Boating, Challenge/Ropes Course, Environmental Education, Swimming (#12460)

Taum Sauk (est 1946) ⛺ 🚗

Lesterville, MO (Reynolds Co.); (573) 637-2489
Nick Smith, Director

Camp comments: Dedicated to creating positive lasting impressions. Strong concern for safety & individual attention. Family atmosphere.
Activities: Archery, Arts/Crafts, Bicycling/Biking, Canoeing, Challenge/Rope Courses, Climbing/Rappelling, Horseback — Western, Radio/TV/Video, Sailing, Swimming — Instructional
Session lengths & capacity: June-August; 2, 3, 5, 6 & 8 week sessions; 130 campers
Clientele & fees: boys 8-15; girls 8-15; coed 8-15; Fees: D ⛺
Contact: Nick Smith, Director at (314) 961-5538; fax: (314) 961-5538
e-mail: nsmithcts@aol.com
Web site: www.taumsauk.com
Operated by: Taum Sauk, 13 Litzsinger Lane, St Louis, MO 63124 at (314) 961-5538 (#8361)

Wonderland Camp Foundation

(est 1971) ⛺ ⌂ 🚗

Rocky Mount, MO (Morgan Co.); (573) 392-1000

Camp comments: Wonderland Camp provides recreation for mentally and physically challenged people and respite care for parents.
Activities: Aquatic Activities, Arts/Crafts, Basketball, Boating, Camping Skills/Outdoor Living, Counselor Training (CIT), Hiking, Nature/Environment Studies, Riflery, Swimming — Recreational
Session lengths & capacity: May-November; 1 week sessions; 80 campers

Clientele & fees: coed 6-80; families; seniors; single adults; Fees: C ⛺ 🐃
Contact: Allen Moore, CEO at (573) 392-1000; fax: (573) 392-3605
e-mail: amoore@usmo.com
Operated by: Wonderland Camp, 18591 Miller Circle, Rocky Mount, MO 65072-0760 at (573) 392-1000

Group Rental Information
Site comments: Handicapped
Seasons & Capacity: Spring 153, Fall 153
Facilities: Dorm-Style, Hiking Trails, Lake, Meeting Rooms, Pool
Programs: Boating (#3170)

Woodland Girl Scouts (est 1948) ⛺ ⌂

Albany, MO; (816) 726-3314
Devera Lambing, Director

Activities: Aquatic Activities, Archery, Arts/Crafts, Camping Skills/Outdoor Living, Canoeing, Counselor Training (CIT), Hiking, Horseback — Western, Nature/Environment Studies, Swimming — Recreational
Session lengths & capacity: June-August; 1/2, 1 & 2 week sessions; 74 campers
Clientele & fees: girls 6-18; Fees: A ☀ Fees: B ⛺
Contact: Devera Lambing, Program Director at (816) 279-7438; fax: (816) 279-7443
e-mail: megsc@ponyexpress.net
Operated by: Girl Scouts Midland Empire, 1702 Buckingham, St Joseph, MO 64506 at (816) 279-7438

Group Rental Information
Facilities: Cabins, Kitchen Facilities, Lake, Lodges, Pool, Tents
Programs: Boating (#1093)

YMCA Camp Lakewood

(est 1947) ⛺ 🚗

Potosi, MO (Washington Co.); (088) 864-5841
Randy Grayson, Director

Camp comments: Come play in nature's 5000 acre backyard within the beautiful Ozark foothills at Missouri's premiere residence camp!!
Activities: Aquatic Activities, Archery, Boating, Caving, Challenge/Rope Courses, Horseback — Western, Leadership Development, Sailing, Sports — Field & Team, Tennis
Session lengths & capacity: June-August; 1, 2 & 3 week sessions; 400 campers
Clientele & fees: coed 6-18; Fees: D ⛺ 🐃
Contact: Roxana Hall, Camp Registrar at (000) 000-0888; fax: (314) 438-3913
e-mail: rhall@ymcastlouis.org
Web site: www.ymcastlouis.org
Operated by: YMCA of the Ozarks, Rt 2 Box 240, Potosi, MO 63664 at (888) 386-9622 (#1046)

YMCA Camp Wakonda

(est 1953) ☀ ⛺ ⌂

Ash Grove, MO (Lawrence Co.); (417) 491-4206
Casey Holck, Director

Camp comments: Ozark Mountain getaway. Lots of one-on-one time for campers. New experiences are a regular part of our schedule.
Activities: Aquatic Activities, Archery, Arts/Crafts, Bicycling/Biking, Challenge/Rope Courses, Climbing/Rappelling, Counselor Training (CIT), Nature/Environment Studies, Sports — Field & Team
Session lengths & capacity: 1 week sessions; 90 campers
Clientele & fees: coed 7-18; Fees: B ⛺ 🐃
Contact: Casey Holck, Camp Director at (417) 491-4206; fax: (417) 862-4004
e-mail: campwakonda@aol.com
Web site: www.ymcaspringfield.org
Operated by: YMCA Camp Wakonda, 417 South Jefferson, Springfield, MO 65806 at (417) 862-7456

Group Rental Information
Facilities: Cabins, Food Service, Hiking Trails, Kitchen Facilities, Meeting Rooms, Playing Fields, Pool
Programs: Challenge/Ropes Course, Environmental Education, Swimming (#3696)

Montana

Alpengirl

Manhattan, MT
Alissa Farley, Director

Camp comments: TEEN GIRLS! Wilderness adventure fitness camps in Montana, Alaska & Washington! National Parks, horses, backpacking, biking, rafting, sea kayaking.
Activities: Aerobics/Exercise, Backpacking, Bicycling/Biking, Canoeing, Climbing/Rappelling, Horseback — Western, Kayaking, Rafting, Sailing, Wilderness Trips
Session lengths & capacity: June-August; 2 & 3 week sessions; 12 campers
Clientele & fees: girls 12-16; Fees: F
Contact: Alissa Farley, Owner at (800) 585-7476; e-mail: alissa@alpengirl.com
Web site: www.alpengirl.com
Operated by: Alpengirl, PO Box 1138, Manhattan, MT 59741 at (800) 585-7476 (#27064)

Christikon (est 1951)

Mc Leod, MT (Park Co.); (406) 932-6300
Robert L Quam, Director

Camp comments: Serving all on behalf of area ELCA Lutherans, Christikon offers residential, backpack & CreationCare programs in the Rocky Mountains near Yellowstone Park.
Activities: Arts/Crafts, Backpacking, Camping Skills/Outdoor Living, Community Service, Dance, Hiking, Music, Wilderness Trips
Session lengths & capacity: June-August; 1/2 & 1 week sessions; 75 campers
Clientele & fees: coed 10-18; families; seniors; Fees: B, C
Contact: Rev Robert L Quam, Pastor/Director at (406) 656-1969; fax: (406) 656-1969
e-mail: christikon@aol.com
Web site: www.christikon.org
Operated by: Lutheran Bible Camp Inc, 1108 24th St West, Billings, MT 59102-3810 at (406) 656-1969
Group Rental Information
Facilities: Cabins, Food Service, Hiking Trails, Kitchen Facilities, Linens, Lodges, Meeting Rooms (#3140)

ICON LEGEND

☀ Day Camp

▲ Resident Camp

🏠 Facilities Available To Rent

🚐 Transportation Available

🐷 Financial Aid Available

FEE RANGES PER WEEK

A	$0-75
B	$75-200
C	$201-350
D	$351-500
E	$501-650
F	over $650

Glacier Camp & Conference Ctr

Lakeside, MT (Lake Co.); (406) 844-2114
Keith Newman, Director

Camp comments: Glacier Camp is located on the shores of Flathead Lake about 40 miles from Glacier National Park. The camp has been offering programs for youth since 1928.
Activities: Backpacking, Challenge/Rope Courses, Climbing/Rappelling, Counselor Training (CIT), Leadership Development, Rafting, Religious Study, Snow Sports, Swimming — Recreational, Wilderness Trips
Session lengths & capacity: June-August; 1/2, 1, 2 & 4 week sessions; 50 campers
Clientele & fees: coed 7-18; families; Fees: B
Contact: Keith Newman, Director at (406) 844-2114; fax: (406) 844-0551
e-mail: keithn@digisys.net
Web site: www.glaciercamp.org
Operated by: Glacier Presbytery, 538 University Ave, Missoula, MT 59801 at (888) 465-4187
Group Rental Information
Seasons & Capacity: Spring 80, Fall 80, Winter 80
Facilities: Cabins, Food Service, Kitchen Facilities, Lake, Lodges, Meeting Rooms
Programs: Boating, Challenge/Ropes Course, Winter Sports (#6732)

Trails End Ranch (est 1978)

Ekalaka, MT (Carter Co.); (406) 775-6401
Bob Anderson, Director

Camp comments: Christian sports and adventure camp in ranch setting. Individual centered with exciting program. Every age, every week.
Activities: Arts/Crafts, Basketball, Camping Skills/Outdoor Living, Challenge/Rope Courses, Climbing/Rappelling, Drama, Horseback — Western, Leadership Development, Music, Riflery
Session lengths & capacity: June-August; 1 & 4 week sessions; 150 campers
Clientele & fees: coed 8-18; families; Fees: B
Contact: Bob or Pat Anderson, Directors at (406) 775-6401; fax: (416) 775-6441
e-mail: ter@midrivers.com
Operated by: New Life Fellowship of MT Inc, Box 460, Ekalaka, MT 59324 at (406) 775-6401
Group Rental Information
Site comments: Christian retreat center. We provide full programming or will work with you for a tailor-made retreat.
Seasons & Capacity: Spring 100, Fall 100
Facilities: A/V Equipment, Cabins, Dorm-Style, Double Occupancy, Food Service, Hiking Trails, Lodges, Meeting Rooms, Playing Fields
Programs: Challenge/Ropes Course, Environmental Education, Horseback Riding (#13910)

Nebraska

Calvin Crest Camp Conf Ctr

(est 1962)

Fremont, NE (Saunders Co.); (402) 628-6455
Lynne Morton, Director

Camp comments: Christian centered curriculum, scenic hiking w/wild turkey & deer. 5 ranch camps/horses/ great staff for fun camping.
Activities: Arts/Crafts, Camping Skills/Outdoor Living, Challenge/Rope Courses, Counselor Training (CIT), Hiking, Horseback — Western, Leadership Development, Nature/Environment Studies, Religious Study, Swimming — Recreational
Session lengths & capacity: 1/2 & 1 week sessions; 200 campers

Clientele & fees: boys 6-18; girls 6-18; coed 6-18; families; Fees: B, C
Contact: Doug Morton, Administrator at (402) 628-6455; fax: (402) 628-8255
e-mail: calvin_crest@alltel.net
Operated by: Homestead Presbytery, 2870 County Road 13, Fremont, NE 68025 at (402) 474-0612
Group Rental Information
Site comments: On a bluff overlooking the Platte River, Calvin Crest serves churches and communities by providing camp,retreat and conference opportunities
Facilities: A/V Equipment, Cabins, Double Occupancy, Hiking Trails, Kitchen Facilities, Linens, Lodges, Meeting Rooms, Playing Fields, River
Programs: Challenge/Ropes Course, Environmental Education, Swimming (#1083)

Camp Comeca (est 1950)

Cozad, NE (Dawson Co.); (308) 784-2808

Camp comments: A distraction-free environment for religious, personal, and business retreats.
Activities: Basketball, Boating, Canoeing, Challenge/Rope Courses, Fishing, Religious Study, Tennis
Session lengths & capacity: June-September; 1/2 & 1 week sessions; 200 campers
Clientele & fees: coed 6-19; families; seniors; single adults; Fees: B
Contact: Mary Garner, Manager at (308) 784-2808; fax: (308) 784-4208
e-mail: mgarner507@aol.com
Operated by: NE Annual Conference, Box 4553, Lincoln, NE 68503 at (402) 464-5994
Group Rental Information
Site comments: A place where you can feel good about yourself have fun and learn about God's love.
Seasons & Capacity: Spring 200, Summer 250, Fall 200, Winter 200
Facilities: Cabins, Food Service, Lake, Meeting Rooms, Pool
Programs: Boating (#18796)

Camp Easter Seals (est 1968)

Nebraska City, NE (Otoe Co.)
Sara Masten, Director

Camp comments: Residential camp for people w/disabilities. Encourages independence, social development & self-confidence. Terrific opportunity for growth.
Activities: Arts/Crafts, Camping Skills/Outdoor Living, Challenge/Rope Courses, Computer, Drama, Music, Nature/Environment Studies, Sports — Field & Team, Swimming — Recreational, Team Building
Session lengths & capacity: June-August; 1 week sessions; 30 campers
Clientele & fees: coed 6-99; seniors; single adults; Fees: E
Contact: Sara Masten, Director of Camping/Recreation at (402) 345-2200; fax: (402) 345-2500
e-mail: smasten@ne.easter-seals.org
Web site: www.ne.easter-seals.org
Operated by: Easter Seals Nebraska, 7171 Mercy Rd Ste 102, Omaha, NE 68106 at (402) 345-2200 (#7784)

Camp Maha Girl Scouts

(est 1945)

Omaha, NE; (402) 339-8443
Liz Martin, Director

Camp comments: Beautiful river bluff setting for girls K-6. Transportation. Hiking songs swimming environmental education center.
Activities: Archery, Arts/Crafts, Camping Skills/Outdoor Living, Hiking, Leadership Development, Nature/Environment Studies, Swimming — Recreational
Session lengths & capacity: 1/2 & 1 week sessions; 150 campers
Clientele & fees: girls 5-14; Fees: B

Contact: Liz Martin, Outdoor Program Specialist at (402) 558-8189; fax: (402) 558-8060
e-mail: emartin@gpgirlscouts.org
Web site: www.gpgirlscouts.org
Operated by: Great Plains GSC, 2121 S 44th Street, Omaha, NE 68105-2800 at (402) 558-8189
Group Rental Information
Site comments: Environmental education center, river setting, lodges, perma tents, platform tents.
Seasons & Capacity: Spring 150, Summer 150, Fall 150, Winter 50
Facilities: Hiking Trails, Kitchen Facilities, Lodges, Meeting Rooms, Pool, Tents
Programs: Challenge/Ropes Course, Environmental Education, Swimming (#1091)

Carol Joy Holling Camp, Conf &

(est 1974)

Ashland, NE (Cass Co.); (402) 944-2544
Roger Sasse, Director

Camp comments: Scenic 300 acre Christian Camp. Between Omaha & Lincoln. Cabins, tents, tipis, retreat and conference facilities.
Activities: Aquatic Activities, Backpacking, Boating, Challenge/Rope Courses, Counselor Training (CIT), Horseback — Western, Leadership Development, Nature/Environment Studies, Religious Study, Team Building
Session lengths & capacity: June-August; 1/2 & 1 week sessions; 225 campers
Clientele & fees: coed 3-18; families; Fees: C ▲ 🐖
Contact: Roger L Sasse, Executive Director at (402) 944-2544; fax: (402) 944-2544
e-mail: rsasse@nlom.org
Operated by: Nebraska Luth Outdoor Ministry, 27416 Ranch Rd, Ashland, NE 68003-3518 at (402) 944-2544 (#12199)

Catron Camp and Retreat Center (est 1940)

Nebraska City, NE; (402) 873-4285
Debbie Salansky, Director
Activities: Archery, Backpacking, Community Service, Dance, Leadership Development, Team Building
Session lengths & capacity: January-December; 1/2 & 1 week sessions
Clientele & fees: girls 5-18; Fees: A 🌞 Fees: B ▲
Contact: Debbie Salansky, Director of Catron Operations at (402) 873-4285; fax: (402) 873-5196
e-mail: debbiecatron@yahoo.com
Web site: www.homesteadgsc.com
Operated by: Girl Scouts-Homestead Council, 1701 S 17, Lincoln, NE 68502 at (402) 476-7539
Group Rental Information
Seasons & Capacity: Spring 45, Summer 125, Fall 45, Winter 45
Facilities: A/V Equipment, Dorm-Style, Food Service, Hiking Trails, Kitchen Facilities, Meeting Rooms, Pool, River, Tents
Programs: Challenge/Ropes Course, Environmental Education, Swimming (#1090)

Eastern Nebraska 4H Center

(est 1976)

Gretna, NE (Sarpy Co.); (402) 332-4496
Kelly Krambeck, Director

Camp comments: Eastern NE 4-H Center provides a unique setting for kids to discover, learn & grow while having a great time in the outdoors.
Activities: Archery, Arts/Crafts, Camping Skills/Outdoor Living, Canoeing, Challenge/Rope Courses, Leadership Development, Nature/Environment Studies, Riflery, Swimming — Recreational, Team Building
Session lengths & capacity: January-December; 1/2 & 1 week sessions; 150 campers
Clientele & fees: coed 6-18; families; Fees: A 🌞 Fees: B ▲

Contact: Kelly Krambeck, Camp Director at (402) 332-4496; fax: (402) 332-2580
e-mail: eastern4hcenter@unl.edu
Web site: www.4h.unl.edu
Operated by: Nebraska 4H Youth Development, 114 Ag Hall, Lincoln, NE 68583-0700 at (402) 472-6717
Group Rental Information
Seasons & Capacity: Spring 150, Summer 150, Fall 150, Winter 150
Facilities: A/V Equipment, Cabins, Dorm-Style, Double Occupancy, Food Service, Hiking Trails, Lodges, Meeting Rooms, Playing Fields, River
Programs: Challenge/Ropes Course, Environmental Education (#4242)

Elkhorn River YMCA Camp

(est 1987)

Papillion, NE; (402) 339-9861
Staci Gowan, Director
Activities: Archery, Arts/Crafts, Bicycling/Biking, Canoeing, Challenge/Rope Courses, Counselor Training (CIT), Leadership Development, Nature/Environment Studies, Soccer, Sports — Field & Team
Session lengths & capacity: June-August; 1 week sessions; 120 campers
Clientele & fees: coed 5-17; Fees: B 🌞 🐖
Contact: Staci Gowan, Executive Director at (402) 339-9861;
Operated by: Elkhorn River YMCA Camp, 1111 E First Street, Papillion, NE 68046 at (402) 332-4279
Group Rental Information
Facilities: Dorm-Style, Hiking Trails, Kitchen Facilities, Lodges, Meeting Rooms, Pool (#1955)

Floyd Rogers (est 1931)

Omaha, NE (Douglas Co.); (402) 341-0866
Sherman Poska, PhD, Director

Camp comments: No child with diabetes denied because of lack of funds, exceptional experienced staff.
Activities: Aquatic Activities, Boating, Canoeing, Fishing, Hiking, Leadership Development, Performing Arts, Sports — Field & Team, Swimming — Recreational
Session lengths & capacity: June-June; 1 week sessions; 100 campers
Clientele & fees: coed 8-18; Fees: C ▲ 🐖
Contact: Sherman Poska, PHD, Director at (402) 341-0866; fax: (402) 341-0866
e-mail: sposka@radiks.net
Web site: www.campfloydrogers.com
Operated by: Floyd Rogers Foundation, PO Box 31536, Omaha, NE 68131-0536 at (402) 341-0866 (#4277)

Jewish Community Center Day Camp (est 1927)

Omaha, NE (Douglas Co.); (402) 334-6409
Laura Wine, Director

Camp comments: Fun & exciting activities in a safe, friendly environment. We emphasize building skills, self-esteem, & Jewish values.
Activities: Arts/Crafts, Bicycling/Biking, Drama, Field Trips, Golf, Horseback — Western, Nature/Environment Studies, Sports — Field & Team, Swimming — Instructional, Swimming — Recreational
Session lengths & capacity: June-August; 2 week sessions; 150 campers
Clientele & fees: coed 5-13; Fees: B 🌞
Contact: Laura Wine, Director at (402) 334-6409; fax: (402) 334-6466
e-mail: lwine@jewishomaha.org
Web site: www.jewishomaha.org
Operated by: JCC of Omoha, 333 South 132nd St, Omaha, NE 68154 at (402) 334-6409 (#3593)

Kamp Kaleo (est 1965)

Burwell, NE; (308) 346-5083
Judie L Luther, Director

Camp comments: Remote peaceful setting. Over 200 acres of wood, grassland and westland in Nebraska sandhills. Summer canoeing and tubing on the N Loup River.
Activities: Aquatic Activities, Arts/Crafts, Canoeing, Challenge/Rope Courses, Field Trips, Hiking, Religious Study, Swimming
Session lengths & capacity: May-August; 1/2 & 1 week sessions; 80 campers
Clientele & fees: boys 9-18; girls 9-18; coed 9-18; families; seniors; single adults; Fees: A 🌞 Fees: B ▲
Contact: Judie L Luther, Administrator at (308) 346-5083; fax: (308) 346-5083
e-mail: kamp@micrord.com
Web site: www.uccnebraska.org
Operated by: Nebraska Conference of the UCC, 825 M St Ste 201, Lincoln, NE 68508-2246 at (402) 477-4131
Group Rental Information
Seasons & Capacity: Spring 80, Summer 80, Fall 80, Winter 15
Facilities: A/V Equipment, Cabins, Double Occupancy, Food Service, Hiking Trails, Kitchen Facilities, Linens, Lodges, Meeting Rooms, Playing Fields, River
Programs: Boating, Challenge/Ropes Course, Environmental Education, Swimming (#13374)

Nebraska State 4H Camp

(est 1963)

Halsey, NE (Thomas Co.); (308) 533-2224
Kimberly Kelly, Director

Camp comments: Nestled in the NE Nat'l Forest, State 4-H Camp is an ideal setting for kids to learn about themselves, others, and the outdoors.
Activities: Aquatic Activities, Archery, Canoeing, Challenge/Rope Courses, Climbing/Rappelling, Counselor Training (CIT), Nature/Environment Studies, Riflery, Swimming — Recreational, Team Building
Session lengths & capacity: January-December; 1/2 & 1 week sessions; 170 campers
Clientele & fees: coed 6-18; families; Fees: B ▲
Contact: Kimberly Kelly, Camp Director at (308) 533-2224; fax: (308) 533-2228
e-mail: state4hcamps@unl.edu
Web site: www.4h.unl.edu
Operated by: Nebraska 4H Youth Development, 114 Ag Hall, Lincoln, NE 68583-0700 at (402) 472-6717
Group Rental Information
Seasons & Capacity: Spring 170, Summer 170, Fall 170, Winter 170
Facilities: A/V Equipment, Cabins, Dorm-Style, Double Occupancy, Food Service, Hiking Trails, Linens, Lodges, Meeting Rooms, Playing Fields
Programs: Challenge/Ropes Course, Environmental Education (#1084)

Nebraska/Iowa Camp Woodmen

(est 1993)

Nebraska City, NE (Otoe Co.); (402) 873-3220
Justin M Baylor, Director

Camp comments: Nebraska/Iowa Camp Woodmen. 'Where memories are made.'
Activities: Archery, Basketball, Camping Skills/Outdoor Living, Challenge/Rope Courses, Climbing/Rappelling, Riflery, Sports — Field & Team, Swimming — Recreational
Session lengths & capacity: June-September; 5 week sessions; 64 campers
Clientele & fees: coed 8-15; seniors; Fees: A ▲
Contact: Justin M Baylor, Fraternal Coordinator/Camp Director at (402) 873-3220; fax: (402) 873-3220
Operated by: WOW Life Insurance (GR), 1700 Farnam, Omaha, NE 68120 at (402) 271-7258

Group Rental Information
Site comments: Nebraska/Iowa Camp Woodmen. 'Where memories are made.'
Seasons & Capacity: Spring 64, Summer 64, Fall 64
Facilities: Cabins, Double Occupancy, Hiking Trails, Meeting Rooms, Playing Fields
Programs: Challenge/Ropes Course (#2678)

Norwesca Camp & Retreat Center
Chadron, NE; (308) 432-3872

Camp comments: Located in Pine Forest. Emphasis on Christian growth & character development. Trails, quiet area, environmental education. Near historical attractions.
Activities: Arts/Crafts, Backpacking, Hiking, Horseback — Western, Performing Arts, Religious Study, Snow Sports, Swimming — Recreational, Team Building
Session lengths & capacity: May-August; 1/2 & 1 week sessions; 140 campers
Contact: DJ Winebrinner, Manager at (308) 432-3872;
e-mail: norwesca@bbc.net
Web site: www.campnorwesca.com
Operated by: Norwesca Camp and Retreat Ctr, 79 Camp Norwesca Rd, Chadron, NE 69337 at (308) 432-3872

Group Rental Information
Seasons & Capacity: Spring 104, Summer 104, Fall 104, Winter 38
Facilities: Cabins, Dorm-Style, Food Service, Hiking Trails, Linens, Lodges, Meeting Rooms, Tents
Programs: Environmental Education, Winter Sports (#27384)

Salvation Army Gene Eppley Cmp (est 1944)
Omaha, NE (Sarpy Co.); (402) 291-1912
Heather Caldwell, Director

Camp comments: Emphasis on Christian growth and character development. Summer Camp attendace is coordinated through local Salvation Army Corps. For all ages.
Activities: Arts/Crafts, Basketball, Camping Skills/Outdoor Living, Canoeing, Drama, Hiking, Music, Swimming — Instructional, Swimming — Recreational, Tennis
Session lengths & capacity: 1/2 & 1 week sessions; 300 campers
Clientele & fees: boys 9-18; girls 9-18; coed 9-18; families; seniors; single adults; Fees: A ▲ 🐖

ICON LEGEND
☀ Day Camp
▲ Resident Camp
🏠 Facilities Available To Rent
🚐 Transportation Available
🐖 Financial Aid Available

FEE RANGES PER WEEK
A $0-75
B $75-200
C $201-350
D $351-500
E $501-650
F over $650

Contact: Heather Caldwell & Scott Lewis, Conference Ctr Manager & Plant Manager at (402) 291-1912; fax: (402) 291-1936
e-mail: heather_caldwell@use.slavationarmy.org
Web site: www.GeneEppleyCamp.org
Operated by: Gene Eppley Camp of the SA, 915 Allied Rd, Omaha, NE 68123-3693 at (402) 291-1912

Group Rental Information
Site comments: Where Christ can be seen in nature, hospitality, and service.
Seasons & Capacity: Spring 224, Summer 380, Fall 224, Winter 224
Facilities: A/V Equipment, Cabins, Dorm-Style, Double Occupancy, Food Service, Hiking Trails, Kitchen Facilities, Lake, Linens, Lodges, Meeting Rooms, Playing Fields, Pool, Tents
Programs: Boating, Swimming (#1089)

YMCA Camp Kitaki (est 1903)
Louisville, NE (Cass Co.); (402) 234-4141
Chris Klingenberg, Director

Camp comments: One of Midwest's best camps. Christian values & quality have built our reputation. Teen leadership a specialty.
Activities: Archery, Arts/Crafts, Camping Skills/Outdoor Living, Canoeing, Challenge/Rope Courses, Climbing/Rappelling, Horseback — Western, Leadership Development, Swimming — Recreational, Team Building
Session lengths & capacity: May-September; 1 & 2 week sessions; 200 campers
Clientele & fees: boys 7-17; girls 7-17; coed 7-17; families; Fees: C, D ▲ 🐖
Contact: Chris Klingenberg, Exec Dir at (402) 434-9223; fax: (402) 434-9226
e-mail: campkitaki@aol.com
Web site: www.ymcalincoln.org
Operated by: Lincoln YMCA, 6000 Cornhusker Highway, Lincoln, NE 68507-3110 at (402) 434-9205

Group Rental Information
Facilities: A/V Equipment, Cabins, Dorm-Style, Food Service, Hiking Trails, Lake, Meeting Rooms, Pool, River
Programs: Challenge/Ropes Course, Environmental Education, Horseback Riding, Swimming (#1078)

Nevada

Camp Dat-So-La-Lee
(est 1990)
Elko County, NV; (702) 433-5762
B. Dennis Hugh, Director

Camp comments: Children are spons. by Lions Clubs in Nevada. Attendance must be coordinated through a local club. Inquiries encouraged.
Activities: Archery, Arts/Crafts, Drawing/Painting, Hiking, Nature/Environment Studies, Riflery
Session lengths & capacity: June-June; 1 week sessions; 50 campers
Clientele & fees: coed 9-10; Fees: A ▲ 🐖
Contact: Dennis Hugh, President/Camp Administrator at (702) 433-5762;
fax: (702) 433-2632
e-mail: dennish@skylink.net
Operated by: Lions District 4N, 5018 Wright View Dr, Las Vegas, NV 89120 at (702) 433-5762 (#26870)

Foxtail Girl Scout Camp
(est 1953)
Las Vegas, NV (Clark County Co.); (702) 872-5485
Stafanie Lawhorn, Director

Camp comments: Every Girl Everywhere
Activities: Arts/Crafts, Camping Skills/Outdoor Living, Counselor Training (CIT), Hiking

Session lengths & capacity: June-August; 1/2, 1 & 2 week sessions; 100 campers
Clientele & fees: girls 7-17; Fees: B, C, D ▲
Contact: Madalaine Calovini, Camp Administrator at (702) 385-3677 ext. 231; fax: (702) 385-9278
Operated by: Frontier GSC, 2941 Harris Avenue, Las Vegas, NV 89101 at (702) 385-3677

Group Rental Information
Facilities: Cabins, Hiking Trails, Kitchen Facilities, Lodges (#462)

New Hampshire

Barry Conservation Camp
(est 1984)
Berlin, NH (Coos Co.); (603) 449-2591

Camp comments: Programs emphasize conservation ed & shooting sports safety. Operated by NH Fish &Game & UNH Cooperative Extension. Small camp offering individualized attn.
Activities: Archery, Camping Skills/Outdoor Living, Canoeing, Fishing, Hiking, Nature/Environment Studies, Riflery, Swimming — Recreational
Session lengths & capacity: June-August; 1 week sessions; 30 campers
Clientele & fees: coed 11-15; Fees: C ▲ 🐖
Contact: Ann Dolloff, CTRS, Extension Specialist at (603) 862-2198; fax: (603) 862-2157
e-mail: ann.dolloff@unh.edu
Web site: www.ceinfo.unh.edu
Operated by: UNH Cooperative Extension, Moiles House, 180 Main St, Durham, NH 03824 at (603) 624-2184 (#2497)

Bear Hill 4H Camp
(est 1936)
Allenstown, NH (Merrimack Co.); (603) 485-9046
Sheila Fabrizio, Director

Camp comments: Programs encourage life skills development & stewardship thru hands on activities. The learning lasts a lifetime.
Activities: Archery, Arts/Crafts, Canoeing, Counselor Training (CIT), Fishing, Hiking, Leadership Development, Nature/Environment Studies, Swimming — Instructional, Swimming — Recreational
Session lengths & capacity: June-August; 1/2 & 1 week sessions; 150 campers
Clientele & fees: coed 6-15; Fees: B ☀ Fees: C ▲ 🐖
Contact: Ann Dolloff, CTRS, Extension Specialist at (603) 862-2198; fax: (603) 862-2157
e-mail: ann.dolloff@unh.edu
Web site: www.ceinfo.unh.edu
Operated by: UNH Cooperative Extension, Moiles House, 180 Main St, Durham, NH 03824 at (603) 624-2184

Group Rental Information
Site comments: Rustic site for small group get-aways. Near Concord and Machester, NH.
Seasons & Capacity: Spring 100, Fall 100
Facilities: Cabins, Hiking Trails, Kitchen Facilities, Lake, Lodges
Programs: Boating, Swimming (#2486)

Berea Inc (est 1945)
Bristol, NH (Grafton Co.); (603) 744-6344
Ron Ward, Director

Camp comments: Christian emphasis, nondenominational, committed staff, labeled by the state of NH as the Rolls Royce of camps.
Activities: Aquatic Activities, Archery, Challenge/Rope Courses, Riflery, Sailing, Soccer, Tennis, Waterskiing
Session lengths & capacity: 1 & 2 week sessions; 171 campers

Clientele & fees: boys 7-18; girls 7-18; coed 7-18; families; Fees: **C, D ▲**
Contact: Secretary at (603) 774-6344; fax: (603) 744-6346
e-mail: office@berea.org
Web site: www.berea.org
Operated by: Berea Inc, RR1 Box 452, Bristol, NH 03222 at (603) 744-6344
Group Rental Information
Seasons & Capacity: Spring 250, Winter 250
Facilities: A/V Equipment, Cabins, Dorm-Style, Double Occupancy, Food Service, Hiking Trails, Lake, Lodges, Meeting Rooms, Playing Fields
Programs: Boating, Challenge/Ropes Course, Winter Sports (#10810)

Birch Hill Camp (est 1993)   ▲ 🚗

New Durham, NH; (603) 859-4525
Richard & Jayne Morell, Director

Camp comments: Traditional coed sleep away camp. Family atmosphere, an elective program guided by caring & competent staff.
Activities: Arts/Crafts, Dance, Drama, Golf, Horseback — English, Sailing, Sports — Field & Team, Tennis, Waterskiing, Windsurfing
Session lengths & capacity: June-August; 2, 4 & 6 week sessions; 165 campers
Clientele & fees: coed 6-16; Fees: **F ▲**
Contact: Richard & Jayne Morell, Owners/Directors at (603) 868-7821; fax: (603) 868-7355
e-mail: birchhill@aol.com
Web site: www.campbirchhill.com
Operated by: Birch Hill Camp, 8 Sunnyside Dr, Durham, NH 03824 at (603) 868-7821 (#28319)

Birchmont A Pierce Camp

(est 1951)   ▲ 🚗

Wolfeboro, NH (Carroll Co.); (603) 569-1337
Greg & Laura Pierce, Director

Camp comments: The Birchmont difference: Trad sports, values & skill. Great mix of kids. Superb staff, top notch environment. Join us!
Activities: Arts/Crafts, Baseball/Softball, Basketball, Golf, Horseback — English, Nature/Environment Studies, Soccer, Swimming — Instructional, Tennis, Waterskiing
Session lengths & capacity: June-August; 4 & 8 week sessions; 400 campers
Clientele & fees: boys 8-15; girls 8-15; coed 8-15; Fees: **F ▲**
Contact: Greg & Laura Pierce, Directors at (516) 621-5035; fax: (516) 621-0489
e-mail: gpierce@campbirchmont.com
Web site: www.campbirchmont.com
Operated by: Birchmont A Pierce Camp, 37 Mineola Avenue, Roslyn, NY 11576 at (516) 621-5085 (#2019)

Brantwood Camp (est 1904)   ▲ 🏠

Peterborough, NH; (603) 924-3542
Activities: Aquatic Activities, Baseball/Softball, Basketball, Challenge/Rope Courses, Hiking, Leadership Development, Soccer
Session lengths & capacity: 2 week sessions
Clientele & fees: coed 11-14; Fees: **B ▲**
Contact: Web site: www.brantwood.org
Operated by: Trustees of Brantwood Camp, PO Box 3350, Peterborough, NH 03458 at (603) 924-3542
Group Rental Information
Facilities: Cabins, Double Occupancy, Food Service, Hiking Trails, Kitchen Facilities, Meeting Rooms (#3312)

Brookwoods Deer Run

(est 1944)   ▲ 🏠 🚗

Alton, NH (Belknap Co.); (603) 875-3600
Bob Strodel, Director

Camp comments: Christian camping for those with a taste for innovation and excellence. Over 300 acres on New Hampshire's largest lake.
Activities: Aquatic Activities, Archery, Boating, Challenge/Rope Courses, Hiking, Leadership Development, Riflery, Sailing, Waterskiing, Wilderness Trips
Session lengths & capacity: 2 & 4 week sessions; 270 campers
Clientele & fees: boys 8-16; girls 8-16; coed 8-16; Fees: **D ▲** 🚗
Contact: Bob Strodel, Executive Director at (603) 875-3600; fax: (603) 875-4606
e-mail: brook@worldpath.net
Web site: www.brookwoods.org
Operated by: Christian Camps and Conf Inc, Chestnut Cove Road, RR1 Box 47, Alton, NH 03809 at (603) 875-3600
Group Rental Information
Site comments: Located on the shores of Lake Winnipesaukee, Brookwoods offers accommodations and facilities that are ideal for church retreats and special school activities.
Seasons & Capacity: Spring 200, Winter 200
Facilities: A/V Equipment, Cabins, Dorm-Style, Double Occupancy, Food Service, Kitchen Facilities, Lake, Meeting Rooms, Ocean, Playing Fields, River
Programs: Boating, Challenge/Ropes Course, Swimming (#7735)

Camp Bernadette (est 1953)   ▲ 🏠 🚗

Wolfeboro, NH (Belknap Co.); (603) 364-5851
Sue Marcoux, Director

Camp comments: Traditional residential summer camp offering diverse activities with a Christian foundation
Activities: Aquatic Activities, Arts/Crafts, Boating, Counselor Training (CIT), Horseback — Western, Sports — Field & Team
Session lengths & capacity: June-August; 2, 4 & 8 week sessions; 265 campers
Clientele & fees: girls 6-15; Fees: **C ▲**
Contact: Michael Drumm, Marketing & Development Director at (603) 364-5851; fax: (603) 364-5038
e-mail: mdrumm@diocamps.org
Web site: www.diocamps.org
Operated by: Diocese of Manchester Camping, PO Box 206, Gilmanton IW, NH 03837 at (603) 364-5851
Group Rental Information
Facilities: Cabins, Kitchen Facilities, Lake, Meeting Rooms (#2817)

Camp Calumet Lutheran

(est 1960)   ☀ ▲ 🏠 🚗

West Ossipee, NH (Carroll Co.); (603) 539-4773
Donald G Johnson, Director

Camp comments: A place of friendship, great fun, spiritual growth & renewal. Outdoor activities in beautiful setting: Lake & mountains.
Activities: Arts/Crafts, Canoeing, Challenge/Rope Courses, Hiking, Nature/Environment Studies, Sports — Field & Team, Swimming — Instructional, Team Building, Wilderness Trips
Session lengths & capacity: 1 & 2 week sessions; 240 campers
Clientele & fees: coed 8-18; families; seniors; single adults; Fees: **B** ☀ Fees: **C ▲** 🚗
Contact: Donald G Johnson, Executive Director at (603) 539-4773; fax: (603) 539-5343
e-mail: calumet@landmarknet.net
Web site: www.calumet.org
Operated by: Lutheran Outdoor Ministries NE, PO Box 236, West Ossipee, NH 03890 at (603) 539-4773
Group Rental Information
Site comments: Fun/friends/faith develop in a great setting: lake & mtns.
Seasons & Capacity: Spring 200, Summer 800, Fall 200, Winter 100

Facilities: Cabins, Double Occupancy, Food Service, Hiking Trails, Lake
Programs: Boating (#2783)

Camp Carefree (est 1976)   ▲

Wolfeboro, NH (Shafford Co.); (603) 859-0410
Phyllis Woestemeyer, Director

Camp comments: OUR MISSION: Provide a fun, educational camping experience for children with diabetes that will help them to develop & maintain active, healthy life styles.
Activities: Archery, Arts/Crafts, Canoeing, Challenge/Rope Courses, Counselor Training (CIT), Hiking, Nature/Environment Studies, Photography, Swimming — Instructional
Session lengths & capacity: August-August; 2 week sessions; 120 campers
Clientele & fees: boys 8-15; girls 8-15; Fees: **F ▲**
Contact: Beth Rowe, Administrative Assistant at (603) 659-7061; fax: (603) 659-8891
e-mail: BR45ox@aol.com
Operated by: Camp Carefree, 7 Washington Square, Albany, NY 12205 at (518) 218-1755 (#1233)

Camp Fatima (est 1949)   ▲ 🏠 🚗

Gilmanton IW, NH (Belknap Co.); (603) 364-5851
Dave Coffey, Resident Director, Director

Camp comments: Traditional residential summer camp. Also offering speciality programs for 5-9 yr olds and Special Needs campers.
Activities: Basketball, Boating, Challenge/Rope Courses, Climbing/Rappelling, Radio/TV/Video, Sailing, Sports — Field & Team, Swimming — Instructional
Session lengths & capacity: June-August; 1, 2 & 6 week sessions; 310 campers
Clientele & fees: boys 6-15; coed 5-9; Fees: **C ▲**
Contact: Michael Drumm, Marketing & Development Director at (603) 364-5851; fax: (603) 364-5038
e-mail: mdrumm@diocamps.org
Web site: www.diocamps.org
Operated by: Diocese of Manchester Camping, PO Box 206, Gilmanton IW, NH 03837 at (603) 364-5851
Group Rental Information
Facilities: Cabins, Meeting Rooms (#2818)

Camp Hale (est 1900)   ▲ 🏠 🚗

Center Sandwich, NH (Carroll Co.); (603) 284-6494
Jake Jagel, Director

Camp comments: In 30 acres of forest with about one third mile of lake shoreline for inner city boys dedicated to creating a community.
Activities: Archery, Arts/Crafts, Boating, Camping Skills/Outdoor Living, Canoeing, Hiking, Leadership Development, Soccer, Swimming — Instructional, Team Building
Session lengths & capacity: June-September; 3 & 4 week sessions; 65 campers
Clientele & fees: boys 8-15; Fees: **A, B ▲** 🚗
Contact: Jake Jagel, Director at (978) 456-8385; fax: (978) 456-8385
e-mail: jakejagel@aol.com
Operated by: United South End Settlements, 566 Columbus Avenue, Boston, MA 02118-1195 at (617) 536-8610
Group Rental Information
Facilities: Cabins, Kitchen Facilities, Lake, Meeting Rooms, Playing Fields
Programs: Swimming (#4230)

Camp Kaleidoscope (est 1989)   ☀

Lebanon, NH (Grafton Co.); (603) 448-1963
Elizabeth Burdette, Director

Camp comments: Accommodating public day camp focusing on the whole growth and development of each camper.

Activities: Arts/Crafts, Field Trips, Hiking, Leadership Development, Music, Nature/Environment Studies, Sports — Field & Team, Swimming — Instructional, Swimming — Recreational, Team Building
Session lengths & capacity: June-August; 1, 2 & 6 week sessions; 120 campers
Clientele & fees: coed 5-12; Fees: B ☀ 🚐
Contact: Cindy Heath, Recreation Director at (603) 448-5121; fax: (603) 448-4891
e-mail: recreation@lebcity.com
Operated by: City of Lebanon, NH, 51 N Park St, Lebanon, NH 03766 at (603) 448-5121 (#4060)

Camp Marist (est 1949)   ☀ ⚠ 🏠 🚐

Center Ossipee, NH (Caroll Co.); (603) 539-4552
Brother Jim Halliday, Director

Camp comments: 300 acres in the White Mtns. Outstanding staff. 1:3 ratio, select your own schedule from over 35 activities. Fully equipped cabins.
Activities: Archery, Baseball/Softball, Basketball, Bicycling/Biking, Horseback — Western, Riflery, Sailing, Soccer, Tennis, Waterskiing
Session lengths & capacity: June-August; 2, 3, 7 & 8 week sessions; 250 campers
Clientele & fees: boys 6-16; Fees: C ⚠ 🐷
Contact: Dayna Rousseau, Secretary at (603) 539-4552; fax: (603) 539-8318
e-mail: marist@ix.netcom.com
Web site: www.campmarist.org
Operated by: Camp Marist, Rt 25 East, Center Ossipee, NH 03814 at (603) 539-4552

Group Rental Information
Site comments: Retreat lodge and youth group bunk house available throughout school year.
Facilities: Cabins, Dorm-Style, Hiking Trails, Kitchen Facilities, Lake, Linens, Lodges, Meeting Rooms, Playing Fields
Programs: Challenge/Ropes Course, Swimming, Winter Sports (#7298)

Camp Merriwood (est 1949)   ⚠ 🚐

Orford, NH (Grafton Co.); (603) 353-9882
Judy & Gary Miller, Director

Camp comments: Traditional girls camp, mature staff lead strong instructional program, friendly environment, third generation owners.
Activities: Aquatic Activities, Climbing/Rappelling, Drama, Gymnastics, Horseback — English, Sailing, Soccer, Tennis, Waterskiing, Windsurfing
Session lengths & capacity: June-August; 3, 4 & 7 week sessions; 130 campers
Clientele & fees: girls 8-15; Fees: E ⚠
Contact: Judy/Gary Miller or Susan Miller Hild, Directors/Owners or Assistant Director at (800) 997-8006; fax: (203) 637-5132

ICON LEGEND

☀	Day Camp
⚠	Resident Camp
🏠	Facilities Available To Rent
🚐	Transportation Available
🐷	Financial Aid Available

FEE RANGES PER WEEK

A	$0-75
B	$75-200
C	$201-350
D	$351-500
E	$501-650
F	over $650

e-mail: cmerriwood@aol.com
Operated by: Camp Merriwood, 51 Forest Ave 107, Old Greenwich, CT 06870 at (203) 637-4674 (#1999)

Camp Quinebarge

(est 1936)   ☀ ⚠ 🏠 🚐

Moultonboro, NH (Carroll Co.); (603) 253-6029
David R Hurley, Director

Camp comments: Quinebarge is a trad coed residential camp in the lakes region of NH. Ages 7-15 non-competitive fostering growth, friendships, riding, trips, waterfront, ropes.
Activities: Aquatic Activities, Archery, Arts/Crafts, Backpacking, Canoeing, Challenge/Rope Courses, Field Trips, Hiking, Horseback — English, Swimming — Instructional
Session lengths & capacity: June-August; 2, 3, 4, 5, 6, 7 week sessions; 100 campers
Clientele & fees: coed 7-15; Fees: E ⚠
Contact: David Hurley, Director at (603) 253-6029; fax: (603) 253-6027
e-mail: adventures@campquinebarge.com
Web site: www.campquinebarge.com
Operated by: Camp Quinebarge Inc, PO Box 608, Center Harbor, NH 03226 at (603) 253-6029

Group Rental Information
Site comments: Quinebarge, w/75 acres-great for school groups, scouts, weddings, corp team building using our ropes course.Housing & meals for 100+.Hiking, waterfront,tennis.
Seasons & Capacity: Spring 100, Fall 100
Facilities: Cabins, Kitchen Facilities, Lake, Meeting Rooms, Playing Fields
Programs: Boating, Challenge/Ropes Course, Swimming (#12128)

Camp Robin Hood (est 1927)   ⚠ 🚐

Freedom, NH (Carroll Co.); (603) 539-4500
John Klein, Director

Camp comments: Sail our lake, climb a mountain, play sports on wide-open fields, ride, throw a pot, act in a play, make friends, ENJOY!
Activities: Arts/Crafts, Baseball/Softball, Basketball, Camping Skills/Outdoor Living, Drama, Horseback — English, Sailing, Soccer, Sports — Field & Team, Tennis
Session lengths & capacity: June-August; 4, 6 & 8 week sessions; 275 campers
Clientele & fees: boys 7-16; girls 7-16; Fees: F ⚠
Contact: John Klein, Director at (440) 646-1911; fax: (440) 646-1972
e-mail: robinhdnh@aol.com
Web site: www.camprobinhood.com
Operated by: Camp Robin Hood, 344 Thistle Trail, Mayfield Hts, OH 44124 at (440) 646-1911 (#2169)

Camp Squanto (est 1957)   ⚠ 🏠

West Swanzey, NH (Cheshire Co.); (603) 352-1337
Steve Carter, Director

Camp comments: Traditional lakeside program with outstanding leadership and caring staff in a life changing Christian environment.
Activities: Archery, Arts/Crafts, Drama, Hiking, Leadership Development, Religious Study
Session lengths & capacity: 1/2, 1 & 2 week sessions; 153 campers
Clientele & fees: coed 7-17; Fees: C ⚠ 🐷
Contact: Robert DeJong, Camp Director at (603) 352-0443; fax: (603) 357-7660
e-mail: squanto@pilgrimpines.com
Operated by: East Coast Conf Evangelical, 220 W Shore Rd, Swanzey, NH 03446-3112 at (603) 352-0443

Group Rental Information
Facilities: A/V Equipment, Cabins, Food Service, Lake, Playing Fields
Programs: Boating, Swimming (#19771)

Camp Takodah (est 1921)   ⚠ 🏠

Richmond, NH (Cheshire Co.); (603) 239-4781
William Therrien, Director

Camp comments: Camp Takodah is a traditional residential summer camp program affiliated with the Cheshire County YMCA. Our motto is 'Friendly to all.' Serving youth since 1921
Activities: Arts/Crafts, Boating, Challenge/Rope Courses, Counselor Training (CIT), Nature/Environment Studies, Riflery, Sports — Field & Team, Swimming — Instructional, Swimming — Recreational, Wilderness Trips
Session lengths & capacity: June-August; 1, 2 & 4 week sessions; 230 campers
Clientele & fees: boys 8-17; girls 8-17; coed 7-10; families; Fees: C, D ⚠
Contact: Melinda Glenn, Camp Registrar at (603) 352-0447; fax: (603) 352-0516
e-mail: info@camptakodah.com
Operated by: Cheshire County YMCA Inc, PO Box 647, Keene, NH 03431 at (603) 352-0447

Group Rental Information
Seasons & Capacity: Spring 100, Winter 30
Facilities: Cabins, Hiking Trails, Kitchen Facilities, Lake, Meeting Rooms
Programs: Boating, Challenge/Ropes Course, Swimming, Winter Sports (#2832)

Camp Tecumseh (est 1903)   ⚠

Center Harbor, NH (Carroll Co.); (603) 253-4010
Jim Talbot, Director

Camp comments: Founded in 1903,Tecumseh flourishes on the shore of Lake Winnip Esaukee.Building character in boys through athletics,mountain trips with a professional staff.
Activities: Aquatic Activities, Baseball/Softball, Basketball, Drama, Football, Soccer, Sports — Field & Team, Team Building, Tennis, Waterskiing
Session lengths & capacity: June-August; 5 & 7 week sessions; 175 campers
Clientele & fees: boys 8-16; Fees: E ⚠ 🐷
Contact: Jim Talbot, Director at (610) 275-6634; fax: (610) 275-6635
e-mail: chtecumseh@aol.com
Operated by: Camp Tecumseh, 1906 Johnson Road, Plymouth Meeting, PA 19462 at (610) 275-6634 (#1326)

Camp Yavneh (est 1944)   ⚠ 🏠 🚐

West Nottingham, NH (Rockingham Co.); (603) 942-5593
Debbie Sussman, Director

Camp comments: Located on beautiful lake in NH. Hebrew, Judaic classes, sports, swimming, arts. Shabbat observant & kosher. New: 1 week hiking camp 8/17-8/25.
Activities: Academics, Aquatic Activities, Archery, Baseball/Softball, Basketball, Camping Skills/Outdoor Living, Dance, Drama, Field Trips, Sailing
Session lengths & capacity: 2, 4 & 8 week sessions; 300 campers
Clientele & fees: coed 8-16; Fees: D ⚠ 🐷
Contact: Debbie Sussman, Director at (617) 739-0363; fax: (617) 264-9264
e-mail: debbie@campyavneh.org
Web site: www.campyavneh.org
Operated by: Hebrew College, 160 Herrick Rd, Newton, MA 02459 at (617) 559-8860

Group Rental Information
Facilities: Cabins, Dorm-Style, Double Occupancy, Food Service, Hiking Trails, Lake, Lodges, Meeting Rooms, Playing Fields
Programs: Boating, Challenge/Ropes Course, Swimming (#11810)

Camp Young Judaea (est 1939) ▲

Amherst, NH (Hillsborough Co.); (603) 673-3710
Kenneth J Kornreich, Director

Camp comments: Jewish overnight camp offers water sports, athletics program & performing arts. Great staff, great place, great fun!
Activities: Aquatic Activities, Arts/Crafts, Camping Skills/Outdoor Living, Performing Arts, Swimming — Instructional, Tennis, Waterskiing
Session lengths & capacity: 4 & 8 week sessions; 350 campers
Clientele & fees: coed 8-15; Fees: D ▲
Contact: Ken Kornreich, Director at (781) 237-9410; fax: (781) 431-7336
e-mail: cyjnh@aol.com
Operated by: Friends of Young Judaea Inc, 22 Priscilla Circle, Wellesley Hills, MA 02481 at (603) 673-3710 (#2639)

Camps Kenwood and Evergreen

(est 1930) ▲ 🚐

Potter Place, NH (Merrimack Co.); (603) 735-5189
Scott Brody/Phyllis Dank, Director

Camp comments: High quality individual instruction in land & water sports, arts, combined with a warm family atmosphere ratio 2.5:1.
Activities: Aquatic Activities, Baseball/Softball, Basketball, Ceramics/Pottery, Challenge/Rope Courses, Drama, Gymnastics, Soccer, Tennis, Waterskiing
Session lengths & capacity: June-August; 4 & 7 week sessions; 280 campers
Clientele & fees: boys 7-15; girls 7-15; Fees: F ▲
Contact: Scott Brody, Director at (781) 793-0091; fax: (781) 793-0606
Web site: www.kenwood-evergreen.com
Operated by: Camp Kenwood and Evergreen, PO Box 501, Potter Place, NH 03216 at (781) 793-0091 (#2664)

Chenoa (est 1994) ▲ 🏠

Antrim, NH (Hillsborough Co.); (603) 588-8008
Missy Long, Director

Camp comments: Fun, creative and varied program planned by girls & staff in small groups to build self-esteem & sense of community
Activities: Aquatic Activities, Camping Skills/Outdoor Living, Drama, Hiking, Horseback — English, Leadership Development, Nature/Environment Studies, Sailing, Swimming — Instructional, Team Building
Session lengths & capacity: June-August; 1/2, 1 & 2 week sessions; 125 campers
Clientele & fees: girls 6-17; Fees: B, C, D ▲
Contact: Missy Long, Director of Program & Outdoor Education at (800) 654-1270 ext. 135; fax: (603) 627-4169
e-mail: camping@swgirlscouts.org
Web site: www.swgirlscouts.org
Operated by: Girl Scouts Swift Water Cncl, 8 Perimeter Road, Manchester, NH 03103-3307 at (603) 627-4158

Group Rental Information
Seasons & Capacity: Spring 200, Fall 200
Facilities: Cabins, Hiking Trails, Kitchen Facilities, Lake (#7547)

Fleur-De-Lis Camp (est 1929) ▲

Fitzwilliam, NH (Cheshire Co.); (603) 585-7751
Elizabeth V Young, Director

Camp comments: Fleur-De-Lis camp is for the girl who is looking for summer fun, lasting friendships, & confidence in her own ability.
Activities: Archery, Arts/Crafts, Canoeing, Drama, Riflery, Sailing, Swimming — Instructional, Tennis, Waterskiing, Windsurfing
Session lengths & capacity: June-August; 4, 6 & 8 week sessions; 110 campers
Clientele & fees: girls 8-15; Fees: D, E ▲

Contact: Elizabeth V Young, Director at (603) 585-7751; fax: (603) 585-7751
e-mail: fdlcamp@aol.com
Web site: www.fleurdeliscamp.org
Operated by: Fleur de Lis Camp Inc, PO Box 659, Lincoln, MA 01773 at (508) 757-1402 (#4420)

Geneva Point Center

(est 1919) ☀ ▲ 🏠

Center Harbor, NH (Carolle Co.); (603) 253-4366
Jess Schload, Director

Camp comments: A beautiful site on Lake Winnipesaukee offering day camp and resident camp programs as well as rental facilities for religious and non-profit groups.
Activities: Aquatic Activities, Camping Skills/Outdoor Living, Canoeing, Challenge/Rope Courses, Kayaking, Nature/Environment Studies, Swimming — Instructional, Swimming — Recreational
Session lengths & capacity: July-August; 1 & 2 week sessions; 50 campers
Clientele & fees: coed 9-15; families; Fees: C ☀ Fees: C ▲
Contact: Jess Schload, Executive Director at (603) 253-4366; fax: (603) 253-4883
e-mail: geneva@genevapoint.org
Web site: www.genevapoint.org
Operated by: Geneva Point Center Inc, HCR 62 Box 469, Center Harbor, NH 03226 at (603) 253-4366

Group Rental Information
Site comments: Beautiful site on Lake Winnipesaukee for retreats, camp, & conferences. Range of housing & meeting options.
Seasons & Capacity: Spring 150, Summer 400, Fall 150, Winter 30
Facilities: Cabins, Double Occupancy, Food Service, Lodges, Meeting Rooms
Programs: Boating, Environmental Education (#2997)

Glen Brook (est 1946) ▲ 🏠

Marlborough, NH (Cheshire Co.); (603) 876-3342
James Madsen, Director

Camp comments: Joy, enthusiasm & respect for self, others & earth in a warm, caring atmosphere. Strength to lead and faith to follow.
Activities: Archery, Arts/Crafts, Camping Skills/Outdoor Living, Canoeing, Challenge/Rope Courses, Horseback — English, Music, Nature/Environment Studies, Swimming — Instructional, Tennis
Session lengths & capacity: June-August; 3 & 6 week sessions; 75 campers
Clientele & fees: coed 8-14; Fees: E ▲
Contact: James Madsen, Director at (603) 876-3342; fax: (603) 876-3763
e-mail: glenbrook@glenbrook.org
Web site: www.glenbrook.org
Operated by: Waldorf School of Garden City, Cambridge Ave, Garden City, NY 11530 at (516) 742-3434

Group Rental Information
Facilities: Dorm-Style, Hiking Trails, Kitchen Facilities, Lake, Meeting Rooms (#2760)

Interlocken International Camp

(est 1961) ▲ 🚐

Windsor, NH (Hillsborough Co.); (603) 478-3166
Richard Herman, Director

Camp comments: Creative, caring community, campers choose their own activities. Respect, responsibility and risk are Interlocken's 3 'R's.
Activities: Archery, Bicycling/Biking, Challenge/Rope Courses, Climbing/Rappelling, Community Service, Drama, Music, Sports — Field & Team, Tennis

Session lengths & capacity: 4 & 8 week sessions; 160 campers
Clientele & fees: coed 9-15; families; Fees: E ▲ 🏕
Contact: Richard Herman, Director at (603) 478-3166; fax: (603) 478-5260
e-mail: richard@interlocken.org
Web site: www.interlocken.org
Operated by: Interlocken International Camp, 19 Interlocken Way, Windsor, NH 03244 at (603) 478-3166 (#3245)

Kettleford (est 1958) ☀ 🚐

Bedford, NH (Hillsborough Co.); (603) 625-5421
Sandy McCarthy, Director

Camp comments: Fun, creative & varied program planned by girls & staff in small groups to build self-esteem and sense of community.
Activities: Aquatic Activities, Arts/Crafts, Camping Skills/Outdoor Living, Drama, Hiking, Leadership Development, Nature/Environment Studies, Swimming — Instructional
Session lengths & capacity: June-August; 1 & 2 week sessions; 170 campers
Clientele & fees: girls 6-16; Fees: B ☀
Contact: Swift Water GSC/ Becky Hadley, Director of Day Camping at (603) 627-4158 ext. 125; fax: (603) 627-4169
e-mail: camping@swgirlscouts.org
Web site: www.swgirlscouts.org
Operated by: Girl Scouts Swift Water Cncl, 8 Perimeter Road, Manchester, NH 03103-3307 at (603) 627-4158 (#4186)

Kingswood Camp (est 1909) ▲ 🏠

Piermont, NH (Grafton Co.); (603) 989-5556
Bob Wipfler, Director

Camp comments: Balanced approach to waterfront, team sports, individual activities. Daily scheduling from menu of choices.
Activities: Backpacking, Baseball/Softball, Basketball, Camping Skills/Outdoor Living, Golf, Hiking, Sailing, Soccer, Tennis, Waterskiing
Session lengths & capacity: 4, 6 & 8 week sessions; 140 campers
Clientele & fees: boys 7-16; Fees: F ▲
Contact: Bob Wipfler, Director at (301) 656-8406; fax: (301) 656-8406
e-mail: wiff5@aol.com
Web site: www.kingswoodcamp.com
Operated by: Kingswood Camp, 7101 Clarden Rd, Bethesda, MD 20814 at (301) 656-8406 (#1923)

Lions Camp Pride (est 1989) 🏠

New Durham, NH (Strafford Co.); (603) 859-0417
Richard W Elliott, Director
Contact: Richard Elliott, Administrative Director at (603) 859-0417; fax: (603) 859-0418
e-mail: campride@worldpath.net
Web site: www.campride.nhlions.org
Operated by: Lions District 44 H, PO Box 543, Farmington, NH 03835-0543 at (603) 859-0417

Group Rental Information
Site comments: Modern full service 22 bldg complex. Scenic, many amenities, capacity 220. Excellent camp & conference site.
Seasons & Capacity: Spring 220, Summer 220, Fall 220
Facilities: A/V Equipment, Cabins, Dorm-Style, Double Occupancy, Food Service, Hiking Trails, Lake, Meeting Rooms, Playing Fields
Programs: Boating, Challenge/Ropes Course, Swimming (#6599)

Menotomy (est 1923) ▲ 🏠

Meredith, NH (Belknap Co.); (603) 279-6022

Camp comments: Rustic outdoor setting on Lake Winnipesaukee. Emphasis on cooperation, not competition.

Activities: Aquatic Activities, Arts/Crafts, Camping Skills/Outdoor Living, Field Trips, Hiking, Leadership Development, Nature/Environment Studies, Sailing, Team Building
Session lengths & capacity: June-August; 1 week sessions; 100 campers
Clientele & fees: girls 8-15; families; Fees: D ▲ 🐷
Contact: Pat Stens, Program Manager at (617) 482-1078; fax: (617) 350-5246
e-mail: pstens@ptgirlscouts.org
Web site: www.ptgirlscouts.org
Operated by: Patriots Trail GSC, 95 Berkeley St, Boston, MA 02116 at (617) 350-8335

Group Rental Information
Site comments: Rustic outdoor setting on Lake Winnipesaukge. No smoking or alchohol permitted. Must provide own equipment.
Seasons & Capacity: Spring 100, Fall 100
Facilities: Tents
Programs: Boating, Environmental Education (#2742)

Merrowvista (est 1924) ▲ 🏠 🚐

Center Tuftonboro, NH (Carroll Co.); (603) 539-6607
Heather Kiley, Director

Camp comments: Outstanding staff; beautiful mountain setting. Coed, residential program focuses responsibility, cooperation, leadership
Activities: Arts/Crafts, Backpacking, Bicycling/Biking, Canoeing, Challenge/Rope Courses, Climbing/Rappelling, Leadership Development, Sailing, Wilderness Trips, Windsurfing
Session lengths & capacity: June-August; 1, 2, 3 & 4 week sessions; 220 campers
Clientele & fees: coed 8-17; families; Fees: E, F ▲ 🐷
Contact: Lisa Boucher, Camp Registrar at (603) 539-6607; fax: (603) 539-7504
e-mail: merrowvistacamps@ayf.com
Web site: www.ayf.com
Operated by: Merrowvista, 147 Canaan Rd, Center Tuftonboro, NH 03816 at (603) 539-6607

Group Rental Information
Site comments: Year-round customized programs: Cooperative learning, community building, leadership, environment. 6th grade through adult groups. Comfortable lodge for retreat
Seasons & Capacity: Spring 200, Summer 50, Fall 200, Winter 70
Facilities: Cabins, Dorm-Style, Double Occupancy, Food Service, Hiking Trails, Lake, Lodges, Meeting Rooms, Playing Fields
Programs: Boating, Challenge/Ropes Course, Environmental Education, Swimming, Winter Sports (#4040)

ICON LEGEND

☀   Day Camp

▲   Resident Camp

🏠   Facilities Available To Rent

🚐   Transportation Available

🐷   Financial Aid Available

FEE RANGES PER WEEK

A $0-75

B $75-200

C $201-350

D $351-500

E $501-650

F   over $650

Moosilauke (est 1904) ▲ 🚐

Orford, NH (Grafton Co.); (603) 353-4545
Bill McMahon, Director

Camp comments: Our unique program of sports/waterfront/outdoor adventure, incredible campus & extraordinary attn to individuals combine to create an extraordinary growth exper
Activities: Baseball/Softball, Basketball, Bicycling/Biking, Kayaking, Sailing, Soccer, Sports — Field & Team, Swimming — Instructional, Wilderness Trips, Windsurfing
Session lengths & capacity: 2, 4 & 7 week sessions; 150 campers
Clientele & fees: boys 7-16; Fees: F ▲ 🐷
Contact: Sabina & Bill McMahon, Directors at (603) 353-4545; fax: (603) 353-9103
e-mail: cmoosilauk@aol.com
Web site: www.moosilauke.com
Operated by: Moosilauke Merriwood Inc, PO Box E, Orford, NH 03777 at (603) 353-4545 (#2000)

Naticook Day Camp (est 1995) ☀

Merrimack, NH (Hillsborough Co.); (603) 882-1046
Michael Housman, Director

Camp comments: Trained counselors guide campers in a relaxed atmosphere increasing self confidence, respect and good sportsmanship.
Activities: Arts/Crafts, Counselor Training (CIT), Dance, Drama, Gymnastics, International Culture, Sports — Field & Team, Swimming — Instructional, Team Building
Session lengths & capacity: June-August; 2 week sessions; 130 campers
Clientele & fees: boys 5-12; girls 5-12; coed 5-12; Fees: B ☀
Contact: Michael Housman, Director Parks & Recreation at (603) 882-1046; fax: (603) 883-5335
Operated by: Town of Merrimack Parks & Rec, PO Box 940, Merrimack, NH 03054 at (603) 882-1046 (#2599)

North Woods & Pleasant Valley
(est 1929) ▲ 🏠 🚐

Mirror Lake, NH (Carroll Co.); (603) 569-2725
Jill Gary and David Goodwin, Director

Camp comments: Breathtaking Lake Winnipesqukee site. Character development, group living combined with diverse activity choices.
Activities: Aquatic Activities, Archery, Arts/Crafts, Challenge/Rope Courses, Hiking, Horseback — Western, Photography, Riflery, Tennis, Waterskiing
Session lengths & capacity: June-August; 2, 4, 6 & 8 week sessions; 260 campers
Clientele & fees: boys 8-18; girls 8-18; Fees: D ▲ 🐷
Contact: Jill Gary or David Goodwin, Camp Directors at (617) 927-8032; fax: (617) 927-8156
e-mail: jgary@ymcaboston.org
Web site: www.ymcaboston.org
Operated by: YMCA Grtr Boston Camp Serv Br, 316 Huntington Ave, Boston, MA 02115 at (617) 927-8220

Group Rental Information
Seasons & Capacity: Spring 100
Facilities: Cabins, Double Occupancy, Kitchen Facilities, Lake, Lodges, Meeting Rooms, Playing Fields
Programs: Boating, Challenge/Ropes Course, Horseback Riding (#8279)

Pemigewassett (est 1908) ▲ 🚐

Wentworth, NH (Grafton Co.); (603) 764-5833
Robert Grabill, Director

Camp comments: Traditional camp program with broad range of activities. Outstanding veteran staff & happy positive spirit. Superb location and facilites. Private lake.

Activities: Archery, Baseball/Softball, Hiking, Music, Nature/Environment Studies, Sailing, Soccer, Sports — Field & Team, Tennis, Waterskiing
Session lengths & capacity: June-August; 3 & 7 week sessions; 170 campers
Clientele & fees: boys 8-15; Fees: F ▲ 🚐
Contact: Robert L Grabill, Director at (603) 643-8055; fax: (603) 643-9601
e-mail: robert.grabill@valley.net
Web site: www.camppemi.com
Operated by: Camp Pemigewassett Inc, 25 Rayton Road, Hanover, NH 03755 at (603) 643-8055 (#2740)

Pony Farm Inc (est 1971) ▲ 🏠

Temple, NH (Hillsborough Co.); (603) 654-6308
Boo McDaniel, Director

Camp comments: In a small, caring farm setting. Each girl has total care of a 'horse of her own.' Instruct beg-adv, games, shows. FUN!
Activities: Arts/Crafts, Horseback — English, Swimming — Recreational
Session lengths & capacity: June-August; 2 & 4 week sessions; 42 campers
Clientele & fees: girls 8-14; Fees: F ▲
Contact: Boo McDaniel, Director at (603) 654-6308; fax: (603) 654-4077
e-mail: boo@ponyfarm.com
Web site: www.ponyfarm.com
Operated by: Pony Farm, 13 Pony Farm Ln, Temple, NH 03084 at (603) 654-6308 (#3941)

Robindel For Girls (est 1951) ▲ 🏠 🚐

Center Harbor, NH; (603) 253-9271
Nat & Ann Greenfield, Director

Camp comments: Fun with a purpose! Teach skills to develop self worth. Warm caring staff. Strong arts, water, land sports programs.
Activities: Camping Skills/Outdoor Living, Challenge/Rope Courses, Drama, Golf, Gymnastics, Horseback — English, Sailing, Soccer, Tennis, Waterskiing
Session lengths & capacity: 8 week sessions; 290 campers
Clientele & fees: girls 7-15; Fees: F ▲
Contact: Ann & Nat Greenfield, Owner/Directors at (800) 325-3396; fax: (215) 887-2325
e-mail: natman@home.com
Web site: www.robindel.com
Operated by: Camp Robindel, 1271 Mill Road, Meadowbrook, PA 19046 at (215) 884-3326

Group Rental Information
Seasons & Capacity: Summer 260, Fall 260
Facilities: Cabins, Food Service, Kitchen Facilities, Lake, Linens, Lodges, Meeting Rooms, Playing Fields
Programs: Boating, Swimming (#2164)

Runels/Machagamee
(est 1930) ☀ ▲ 🏠

Pelham, NH; (603) 635-2366
Karyn Martin/Karen Provost, Director

Camp comments: 300 acres of pine forest on a lake. Program focuses on helping girls grow strong with opportunity to try new skills and share within a safe environment.
Activities: Aquatic Activities, Archery, Arts/Crafts, Camping Skills/Outdoor Living, Canoeing, Horseback — English, Nature/Environment Studies
Session lengths & capacity: July-August; 1/2, 1 & 2 week sessions; 316 campers
Clientele & fees: girls 7-17; Fees: B ☀
Fees: C, D ▲
Contact: Karyn L Martin, Director of Outdoor Program/Marketing at (978) 689-8015; fax: (978) 688-1846
e-mail: kmartin@ssgsc.org
Web site: www.ssgsc.org
Operated by: Girl Scouts Spar & Spindle, 1740 Turnpike Street, North Andover, MA 01845 at (978) 689-8015

Group Rental Information
Seasons & Capacity: Spring 230, Summer 230, Fall 230, Winter 40
Facilities: Cabins, Hiking Trails, Kitchen Facilities, Lake, Meeting Rooms, Tents
Programs: Boating, Environmental Education, Swimming (#2803)

Tel Noar (est 1946) ▲ ⌂

Hampstead, NH (Rockingham Co.); (603) 329-6931
Mitchell Stern, Director

Camp comments: Individual attention,electives,Judaic prog.Kosher,cabins are lodge style with lounges/fireplaces,warm intimate setting.
Activities: Arts/Crafts, Basketball, Bicycling/Biking, Dance, Drama, Sailing, Swimming — Instructional, Tennis, Waterskiing
Session lengths & capacity: 3, 4, 7 & 8 week sessions; 265 campers
Clientele & fees: coed 8-16; Fees: **D** ▲ 🚌
Contact: Pearl W Lourie, Executive Director at (508) 881-1002; fax: (508) 881-1006
e-mail: cohencamps@aol.com
Operated by: Cohen Foundation, 30 Main Street, Ashland, MA 01721 at (508) 881-1002 (#2718)

Tevya (est 1940) ▲

Brookline, NH (Hillsborough Co.); (603) 673-4010
Adina Ziegler, Director

Camp comments: All around program, child centered emphasis. On 650 acres. Dietary laws observed. Counselor training & Israel programs.
Activities: Archery, Arts/Crafts, Drama, Field Trips, Sailing, Swimming — Instructional, Tennis, Waterskiing, Windsurfing
Session lengths & capacity: 4 & 8 week sessions; 325 campers
Clientele & fees: coed 8-16; Fees: **D** ▲ 🚌
Contact: Pearl W Lourie, Executive Director at (508) 881-1002; fax: (508) 881-1006
e-mail: cohencamps@aol.com
Operated by: Cohen Foundation, 30 Main Street, Ashland, MA 01721 at (508) 881-1002 (#2862)

Tohkomeupog (est 1932) ▲ 🚐

East Madison, NH (Carroll Co.); (603) 367-8362
Andrew Mahoney, Director

Camp comments: Warm supportive staff, exciting prog, fun friendships, responsibility, leadership, sucess, sportsmanship, self-esteem
Activities: Archery, Basketball, Bicycling/Biking, Camping Skills/Outdoor Living, Hiking, Riflery, Sailing, Soccer, Tennis, Waterskiing
Session lengths & capacity: June-August; 2, 4 & 8 week sessions; 120 campers
Clientele & fees: boys 8-16; families;
Fees: **E** ▲ 🚌
Contact: Andrew Mahoney & Bobbi Hoyt, Director's at (603) 367-8362; fax: (603) 367-8664
e-mail: tohko@tohko.com
Web site: www.tohko.com
Operated by: Camp Tohkomeupog, Route 153, East Madison, NH 03849 at (603) 367-8362 (#2777)

Wa-Klo (est 1938) ▲ 🚐

Jaffrey, NH (Cheshire Co.); (603) 563-8531
Marie J Jensen, Director

Camp comments: Superb facilities all land and water sports. Individualized programing - excellent instruction. Trips & special events.
Activities: Drama, Gymnastics, Horseback — English, Leadership Development, Sailing, Skating, Sports — Field & Team, Tennis, Waterskiing
Session lengths & capacity: June-August; 4 & 8 week sessions; 135 campers
Clientele & fees: girls 6-17; Fees: **E** ▲

Contact: Marie J Jensen, Director at (516) 678-3174; fax: (516) 594-9234
Web site: www.campwaklo.com
Operated by: Wa-Klo, 3638 Lorrie Dr, Oceanside, NY 11572 at (516) 678-3174 (#3475)

Wabasso (est 1956) ▲ ⌂ 🚐

Bradford, NH (Merrimac Co.); (603) 938-2240

Camp comments: Develop horseback riding and drama skills in a safe supportive environment.
Activities: Arts/Crafts, Boating, Camping Skills/Outdoor Living, Canoeing, Drama, Hiking, Horseback — English, Swimming — Instructional, Swimming — Recreational
Session lengths & capacity: June-August; 1 & 2 week sessions; 150 campers
Clientele & fees: girls 6-16; Fees: **D** ▲ 🚌
Contact: Pat Stens, Program Manager at (617) 482-1078; fax: (617) 350-5246
e-mail: pstens@ptgirlscouts.org
Web site: www.ptgirlscouts.org
Operated by: Patriots Trail GSC, 95 Berkeley St, Boston, MA 02116 at (617) 350-8335

Group Rental Information
Site comments: Facilities available for youth groups. Must provide own equipment. No smoking or alcohol permitted.
Seasons & Capacity: Spring 150, Fall 150, Winter 70
Facilities: Cabins, Lodges, Playing Fields
Programs: Boating (#2591)

Walt Whitman (est 1948) ▲ ⌂ 🚐

Piermont, NH (Grafton Co.); (603) 764-5521
Jancy and Bill Dorfman, Director

Camp comments: White Mountains. Outstanding staff, facilities, program. Tripping, gymnastics, boating, heated pool, caring environment.
Activities: Aquatic Activities, Arts/Crafts, Baseball/Softball, Basketball, Boating, Camping Skills/Outdoor Living, Ceramics/Pottery, Drama, Sports — Field & Team, Tennis
Session lengths & capacity: June-August; 4 & 8 week sessions; 350 campers
Clientele & fees: coed 7-15; Fees: **F** ▲
Contact: Jancy/Bill Dorfman, Directors at (914) 234-5484; fax: (914) 234-5484
e-mail: cww@campwalt.com
Web site: www.campgrp.com
Operated by: CampGroup, LLC, 3 New King St, White Plains, NY 10604 at (914) 997-2177

Group Rental Information
Site comments: White Mountains. Excellent fall retreat facility.
Seasons & Capacity: Fall 250
Facilities: Cabins, Double Occupancy, Food Service, Hiking Trails, Playing Fields, Pool (#1924)

Waukeela (est 1922) ▲ 🚐

Eaton Center, NH (Carroll Co.); (603) 447-2260
Phil Steele, Director

Camp comments: Premier girls camp, in White Mtns. strong general program designed for fun and development of life-long skills & friendships.
Activities: Aquatic Activities, Arts/Crafts, Camping Skills/Outdoor Living, Canoeing, Ceramics/Pottery, Drama, Hiking, Horseback — English, Wilderness Trips
Session lengths & capacity: June-August; 4 & 8 week sessions; 115 campers
Clientele & fees: girls 8-16; Fees: **F** ▲ 🚌
Contact: Phil Steele, Director at (800) 626-0207; fax: (914) 713-0393

e-mail: phil@waukeela.com
Operated by: Waukeela, 19 Greenacres Ave, Scarsdale, NY 10583 at (800) 626-0207 (#2850)

White Mountain Ranch

(est 1957)   ▲ 🚗

Rumney, NH (Grafton Co.); (603) 786-2208
Patrick Mc Nally, Director

Camp comments: Christian camp in White Mts on lake. A safe place with staff committed to caring atmosphere and fun activities.
Activities: Archery, Bicycling/Biking, Hiking, Horseback — Western, Religious Study, Sailing, Skating, Waterskiing
Session lengths & capacity: June-August; 2, 3 & 4 week sessions; 120 campers
Clientele & fees: coed 7-17; Fees: C ▲ 🐷
Contact: Patrick McNally, Director at (603) 786-9504; fax: (603) 786-9505
e-mail: pmcnally@rumneybible.org
Web site: www.whitemountainranch.org
Operated by: NE Fellowship of Evangelicals, PO Box 99, Rumney, NH 03266 at (603) 786-9504 (#15849)

Wicosuta (est 1920)

                                               ▲ 🏠 🚗

Bristol, NH (Grafton Co.); (603) 744-3301
Lauren & Michael Bogart, Director

Camp comments: Warm, caring, nurturing atmosphere. Semi structured program, safe environment, sports, arts, wilderness.
Activities: Arts/Crafts, Camping Skills/Outdoor Living, Drama, Gymnastics, Horseback — English, Sailing, Soccer, Swimming — Instructional, Tennis, Waterskiing
Session lengths & capacity: 3, 4 & 7 week sessions; 250 campers
Clientele & fees: girls 6-16; Fees: E ▲ 🐷
Contact: Michael Bogart, Director at (617) 964-9633; fax: (781) 455-1486
e-mail: wicocamp@ultranet.com
Web site: www.campgrp.com
Operated by: CampGroup, LLC, 3 New King St, White Plains, NY 10604 at (914) 997-2177

Group Rental Information
Facilities: Cabins, Food Service, Lake, Linens, Lodges, Meeting Rooms, Playing Fields, Pool, Tents
Programs: Boating, Horseback Riding, Swimming (#2211)

ICON LEGEND

☀ Day Camp

▲ Resident Camp

🏠 Facilities Available To Rent

🚗 Transportation Available

🐷 Financial Aid Available

FEE RANGES PER WEEK

A $0-75

B $75-200

C $201-350

D $351-500

E $501-650

F over $650

William Lawrence Camp

(est 1913)   ▲ 🏠

Center Tuftonboro, NH (Carroll Co.); (603) 569-3698
Nat Crane, Director

Camp comments: A balanced program, William Lawrence offers fun, adventure and growth in a caring, supportive and value based community
Activities: Aquatic Activities, Archery, Arts/Crafts, Camping Skills/Outdoor Living, Challenge/Rope Courses, Counselor Training (CIT), Riflery, Sports — Field & Team, Swimming — Instructional, Wilderness Trips
Session lengths & capacity: June-August; 2, 4 & 8 week sessions; 112 campers
Clientele & fees: boys 8-16; families; Fees: D, E ▲ 🐷
Contact: Nat Crane, Director at (603) 569-3698; fax: (603) 569-5468
e-mail: wlc@worldpath.net
Web site: www.wlcamp.org
Operated by: William Lawrence Camp Inc, 139 Federal Corner Road, Center Tuftonboro, NH 03816 at (603) 569-3698 (#6119)

Winaukee Winaukee Island Camp (est 1920)

                                               ▲ 🚗

Center Harbor, NH; (603) 253-9272
John & Dr Bart Sobel, Director

Camp comments: Superb sports instruction program. Great outdoor tripping program. Mature supportive staff. Warm friendly atmosphere.
Activities: Baseball/Softball, Basketball, Challenge/Rope Courses, Football, Sailing, Soccer, Tennis, Waterskiing
Session lengths & capacity: June-August; 8 week sessions; 360 campers
Clientele & fees: boys 6-16; Fees: F ▲
Contact: John & Dr Bart Sobel, Directors at (800) 487-9157; fax: (203) 356-1545
Web site: www.campgrp.com
Operated by: CampGroup, LLC, 3 New King St, White Plains, NY 10604 at (914) 997-2177 (#12561)

Wiyaka (est 1921)

                                               ▲ 🏠

Richmond, NH (Cheshire Co.); (603) 239-4841
Al Benjamin, Director

Camp comments: Tenting with nature. Well rounded program on fresh water lake in heart of Richmond Hills. Memorable outdoor adventures.
Activities: Archery, Arts/Crafts, Camping Skills/Outdoor Living, Counselor Training (CIT), Hiking, Nature/Environment Studies, Riflery, Sailing, Swimming — Instructional
Session lengths & capacity: June-August; 1, 2 & 3 week sessions; 70 campers
Clientele & fees: boys 7-15; girls 7-15; Fees: B ▲
Contact: Athol Area YMCA, Joseph Hawkins at (978) 249-3305; fax: (978) 249-7215
Web site: www.wiyaka.org
Operated by: Athol Area YMCA, 545 Main St, Athol, MA 01331 at (978) 249-3305

Group Rental Information
Facilities: Cabins, Dorm-Style, Double Occupancy, Kitchen Facilities, Lake, Tents
Programs: Boating (#7478)

YMCA Camp Belknap (est 1903) ▲ 🏠

Wolfeboro, NH (Carroll Co.); (603) 569-3475
Eugene & Caryn Clark, Director

Camp comments: Leadership development with a rich tradition grounded in the philosophy of spirit, mind & body for each boy.
Activities: Aquatic Activities, Archery, Baseball/Softball, Basketball, Challenge/Rope Courses, Leadership Development, Riflery, Sailing, Soccer, Sports — Field & Team
Session lengths & capacity: May-October; 2 & 4 week sessions; 285 campers
Clientele & fees: boys 8-16; Fees: D ▲ 🐷

Contact: Gene & Caryn Clark, Directors at (603) 569-3475; fax: (603) 569-1471
e-mail: clarks@campbelknap.org
Web site: www.campbelknap.org
Operated by: YMCA Camp Belknap Inc, Rt 109 Box 1546, Wolfeboro, NH 03894 at (603) 569-3475

Group Rental Information
Seasons & Capacity: Spring 100, Fall 100
Facilities: Cabins, Food Service, Kitchen Facilities, Lake, Lodges
Programs: Boating, Swimming (#4270)

YMCA Camp Coniston Inc

(est 1964)   ▲ 🏠

Grantham, NH (Sullivan Co.); (603) 863-1160
John Tilley, Director

Camp comments: Trad. YMCA camp on 1100 acres, own lake, values oriented, campers choose activities with skills emphasized. Safety & fun
Activities: Archery, Arts/Crafts, Challenge/Rope Courses, Climbing/Rappelling, Drama, Horseback — English, Soccer, Tennis, Waterskiing, Wilderness Trips
Session lengths & capacity: June-August; 2 & 4 week sessions; 320 campers
Clientele & fees: coed 8-15; families; seniors; Fees: D ▲ 🐷
Contact: John Tilley, Director at (603) 863-1160; fax: (603) 863-1620
e-mail: info@coniston.org
Web site: www.coniston.org
Operated by: YMCA Camp Coniston Inc, PO Box 185, Grantham, NH 03753 at (603) 863-1160

Group Rental Information
Facilities: Cabins, Food Service, Meeting Rooms
Programs: Boating (#2648)

YMCA Camp Foss (est 1923)   ▲

Barnstead, NH (Strafford Co.); (603) 269-3800
Renee Hapgood, Director

Camp comments: Warm, friendly atmosphere in a small camp environment. Beautiful lakeside setting in central New Hampshire pine forest.
Activities: Aquatic Activities, Archery, Arts/Crafts, Canoeing, Challenge/Rope Courses, Drama, Horseback — English, Leadership Development, Tennis
Session lengths & capacity: June-August; 1 & 2 week sessions; 150 campers
Clientele & fees: girls 7-15; Fees: C ▲ 🐷
Contact: Deborah J Farmer, Camp Adminstrator at (603) 623-3559 ext. 242; fax: (603) 623-5934
e-mail: dfarmer@gmymca.org
Operated by: Greater Manchester Family YMCA, 30 Mechanic St, Manchester, NH 03101 at (603) 623-3558 (#2767)

YMCA Camp Halfmoon (est 1960) ☀

Goffstown, NH (Hillsborough Co.); (603) 497-4663
Chris Beaulieu, Director

Camp comments: Creating memories to last a lifetime!
Activities: Aquatic Activities, Archery, Challenge/Rope Courses, Farming/Ranching/Gardening, Field Trips, Hiking, Leadership Development, Soccer, Sports — Field & Team, Swimming — Instructional
Session lengths & capacity: June-August; 1 week sessions; 250 campers
Clientele & fees: coed 5-13; Fees: B ☀ 🐷
Contact: Rick Wilhelmi, Sr. Program Director at (603) 497-4663; fax: (603) 497-4837
e-mail: rwilhelmi@gmymca.org
Operated by: Greater Manchester Family YMCA, 30 Mechanic St, Manchester, NH 03101 at (603) 623-3558 (#14602)

YMCA Camp Huckins (est 1928) ▲

Freedom, NH (Carroll Co.); (603) 539-4710
Judith W Snell, Director

Camp comments: A traditional friendship camp with an accent on leadership development & a caring environment.
Activities: Archery, Arts/Crafts, Canoeing, Challenge/Rope Courses, Horseback — Western, Sailing, Sports — Field & Team, Swimming — Instructional, Waterskiing, Windsurfing
Session lengths & capacity: June-August; 2 & 4 week sessions; 353 campers
Clientele & fees: girls 8-16; families; seniors; single adults; Fees: C ▲
Contact: Judith Snell, Executive Director at (603) 539-4710; fax: (603) 539-6724
e-mail: huckins.camp@rscs.net
Operated by: Huckins Carroll County YMCA, 17 Camp Huckins Rd, Freedom, NH 03836 at (603) 539-4710 (#2595)

YMCA Camp Lawrence

(est 1907) ▲ ⌂ 🚐

Laconia, NH (Belknap Co.); (603) 279-6488
David Hetherly, Director

Camp comments: The camp covers 70 acres of picturesque Bear Island on Lake Winnipesaukee, amid the breathtaking White Mountains.
Activities: Aquatic Activities, Archery, Basketball, Canoeing, Challenge/Rope Courses, Kayaking, Sailing, Waterskiing, Windsurfing
Session lengths & capacity: June-August; 2, 4, 6 & 8 week sessions; 150 campers
Clientele & fees: boys 8-15; Fees: D ▲ 🐷
Contact: John Shandorf, Exec Dir Camping Services at (978) 975-1330; fax: (978) 681-1126
e-mail: campexec@bica.org
Web site: www.bica.org
Operated by: Merrimack Valley YMCA, 7 Ballard Way, Lawrence, MA 01843 at (978) 975-1330 (#2579)

YMCA Camp Lincoln

(est 1924) ☀ ⌂ 🚐

Kingston, NH (Rockingham Co.); (603) 642-3361
Eric Tucker, Director

Camp comments: Located along the sandy shores of Kingston Lake. Coed, traditional based day and adventure camp that offers fun-filled adventures with great, caring staff.
Activities: Aquatic Activities, Archery, Boating, Challenge/Rope Courses, Counselor Training (CIT), Fishing, Nature/Environment Studies, Soccer, Wilderness Trips
Session lengths & capacity: June-August; 1 & 2 week sessions; 340 campers
Clientele & fees: coed 5-15; Fees: B ☀ 🐷
Contact: Eric Tucker, Camp Director at (603) 642-3361; fax: (603) 642-4340
e-mail: eric@ymcacamplincoln.com
Web site: www.ymcacamplincoln.com
Operated by: Southern District YMCA, Camp Lincoln Inc, PO Box 729, Kingston, NH 03848 at (603) 642-3361

Group Rental Information
Seasons & Capacity: Spring 300, Summer 300, Fall 300, Winter 100
Facilities: Cabins, Double Occupancy, Hiking Trails, Lake, Lodges, Meeting Rooms, Ocean, Playing Fields
Programs: Boating, Challenge/Ropes Course, Environmental Education, Swimming, Winter Sports (#2631)

YMCA Camp Mi-Te-Na

(est 1913) ▲ ⌂

Alton, NH (Belknap Co.); (603) 776-3000
Richard J Ross, Director

Camp comments: An experience that lasts a lifetime.
Activities: Aquatic Activities, Archery, Basketball, Canoeing, Challenge/Rope Courses, Climbing/Rappelling, Hiking, Leadership Development, Riflery, Sailing
Session lengths & capacity: June-August; 1, 2 & 4 week sessions; 153 campers
Clientele & fees: boys 7-15; Fees: C ▲ 🐷
Contact: Deb Farmer, Camping Services Branch Adminstrator at (603) 623-3559 ext. 242; fax: (603) 623-5934
e-mail: dfarmer@gmfymca.org
Operated by: Greater Manchester Family YMCA, 30 Mechanic St, Manchester, NH 03101 at (603) 623-3558

Group Rental Information
Facilities: Cabins, Food Service, Hiking Trails, Lake, Lodges
Programs: Boating, Environmental Education (#2790)

YMCA Camp Nokomis (est 1952) ▲ ⌂

Laconia, NH (Belknap Co.); (603) 279-4918
Debbie Parker, Director

Camp comments: The island camp setting of Sandy Beach and Wooded trails is located on Bear Island on spectacular Lake Winnpesaukee.
Activities: Aquatic Activities, Arts/Crafts, Counselor Training (CIT), Drama, Hiking, Leadership Development, Sailing, Tennis, Waterskiing, Windsurfing
Session lengths & capacity: June-August; 2, 4, 6 & 8 week sessions; 150 campers
Clientele & fees: girls 8-15; Fees: D ▲ 🐷
Contact: John Shandorf, Executive Director Camping Ser at (978) 975-1330; fax: (978) 681-1126
e-mail: campexed@bica.org
Web site: www.bica.org
Operated by: Merrimack Valley YMCA, 7 Ballard Way, Lawrence, MA 01843 at (978) 975-1330

Group Rental Information
Site comments: Main objective of YMCA camping shall be to aid in the development of Judeao Christian standards of living conduct and life purpose in it's campers and staff.
Facilities: Cabins, Food Service, Lake, Lodges
Programs: Swimming (#2580)

YMCA Coney Pines ☀ 🚐

Rochester, NH; (603) 332-7334
Kelly Morse, Director

Camp comments: YMCA Camp Coney Pine creates memories to last a lifetime! Swim, learn crafts, sing songs, and make new friends!
Activities: Archery, Arts/Crafts, Basketball, Challenge/Rope Courses, Drama, Field Trips, Nature/Environment Studies, Swimming — Instructional, Swimming — Recreational
Session lengths & capacity: June-August; 1 & 2 week sessions; 150 campers
Clientele & fees: coed 6-14; Fees: B ☀ 🐷
Contact: Kelly Morse, Camp Director at (603) 332-7334; fax: (603) 332-7349
Operated by: Greater Manchester Family YMCA, 30 Mechanic St, Manchester, NH 03101 at (603) 623-3558 (#31417)

YMCA Day Camp Otter

(est 1957) ☀ 🚐

Salem, NH (Rockingham Co.); (603) 893-4911
Lynn Wappel, Director

Camp comments: Camp Otter is located on the tree lined shore of Captains Pond, Salem, NH. Perfect summer location for your children. ACA certified well trained staff.
Activities: Aquatic Activities, Archery, Arts/Crafts, Challenge/Rope Courses, Counselor Training (CIT), Leadership Development, Nature/Environment Studies, Riflery, Swimming — Instructional

Session lengths & capacity: June-August; 1, 2, 3, 4, 5, 6, 7, 8 & 9 week sessions; 160 campers
Clientele & fees: coed 6-13; Fees: B ☀ 🐷
Contact: John Shandorf, Executive Director of Camping Services at (978) 975-1330; fax: (978) 681-1126
e-mail: campexec@bica.org
Web site: www.bica.org
Operated by: Merrimack Valley YMCA, 7 Ballard Way, Lawrence, MA 01843 at (978) 975-1330 (#4271)

New Jersey

Aldersgate Center (est 1961) ▲

Newton, NJ (Sussex Co.); (973) 383-5978
Declan Thompson, Director

Camp comments: Christian camp that offers a diverse & challenging program to children, youth and adults with special needs.Relax, warm, and friendly atmosphere.
Activities: Aquatic Activities, Archery, Arts/Crafts, Boating, Camping Skills/Outdoor Living, Canoeing, Challenge/Rope Courses, Counselor Training (CIT), Horseback — English, Music
Session lengths & capacity: June-August; 1 & 8 week sessions; 95 campers
Clientele & fees: boys 6-18; girls 6-18; coed 6-18; families; single adults; Fees: C ▲ 🐷
Contact: Declan Thompson, Executive Director at (973) 383-5978; fax: (973) 383-4428
e-mail: aldersgate@garden.net
Web site: www.aldersgatenj.com
Operated by: Commission on Camps Conf Ret, PO Box 122, Swartswood, NJ 07877 at (973) 383-5978 (#2930)

Amity Acres (est 1979) ☀ 🚐

Waretown, NJ (Ocean Co.); (609) 698-0565
Diane Douglas, Director

Camp comments: Traditional program plus weekly themes, choice of activities, outstanding trained staff. Non Girl Scouts welcome.
Activities: Arts/Crafts, Boating, Canoeing, Challenge/Rope Courses, Counselor Training (CIT), Horseback — Western, Music, Nature/Environment Studies, Swimming — Recreational
Session lengths & capacity: June-August; 8 week sessions; 175 campers
Clientele & fees: girls 6-13; Fees: B ☀ 🐷
Contact: Betty Lou Cox, Outdoor Director at (732) 349-4499; fax: (732) 349-4690
e-mail: ocgsc@vitinc.com
Web site: www.ocgsc.org
Operated by: Ocean County GSC, 1405 Old Freehold Road, Toms River, NJ 08753 at (732) 349-4499 (#6235)

Appel Farm Arts & Music Center

(est 1960) ▲

Elmer, NJ; (609) 358-2472
Matt Sisson, Director

Camp comments: Fine & performing arts in a noncompetitive setting for children ages 9-17.
Activities: Arts/Crafts, Ceramics/Pottery, Dance, Drama, Drawing/Painting, Music, Photography, Radio/TV/Video, Swimming — Instructional, Tennis
Session lengths & capacity: June-August; 4 & 8 week sessions; 200 campers
Clientele & fees: boys 9-17; girls 9-17; coed 9-17; Fees: E, F ▲ 🐷
Contact: Matt Sisson, Camp Director at (856) 358-2472; fax: (856) 358-6513
e-mail: appelcamp@aol.com
Web site: www.appelfarm.org
Operated by: Appel Farm Arts & Music Center, PO Box 888, Elmer, NJ 08318-0888 at (856) 358-2472 (#2382)

Baptist Camp Lebanon

(est 1949)   ▲ 🏠

Lebanon, NJ (Hunterdon Co.); (908) 236-2638
Donald E Smith, Director

Camp comments: Religious affiliation noncompetitive. Focusing on living in community with others
Activities: Archery, Arts/Crafts, Boating, Canoeing, Ceramics/Pottery, Challenge/Rope Courses, Model Rocketry, Music, Sailing
Session lengths & capacity: June-August; 1/2 & 1 week sessions; 135 campers
Clientele & fees: coed 7-18; families; Fees: **B, C** ▲
Contact: Penny Kenyon, Registrar at (908) 236-2638; fax: (908) 236-0550
Web site: www.camplebanon.com
Operated by: American Baptist Churches NJ, 79 Blossom Hill Road, Lebanon, NJ 08833 at (908) 236-2638
Group Rental Information
Facilities: Cabins, Dorm-Style, Food Service, Kitchen Facilities, Lodges, Meeting Rooms, Tents (#2306)

Blue Mountain Day Camp YMCA

(est 1979)   ☀ 🚐

Newton, NJ (Sussex Co.); (973) 383-8000
Frank Kelly, Director

Camp comments: The program takes full advantage of the 660 acres and gorgeous lake. A caring staff that provides plenty of laughter with learning to create lasting memories.
Activities: Archery, Arts/Crafts, Canoeing, Climbing/Rappelling, Fishing, Horseback — Western, Riflery, Sailing, Swimming — Instructional, Tennis
Session lengths & capacity: June-August; 1, 2, 3 & 9 week sessions; 150 campers
Clientele & fees: boys 4-14; girls 4-14; coed 4-14; Fees: **C** ☀
Contact: Frank Kelly, Day Camp Director at (973) 383-9282; fax: (973) 383-6386
Web site: www.metroymcas.org
Operated by: Metro YMCA of The Oranges, 139 E McClellan Ave, Livingston, NJ 07039 at (973) 758-9622 (#3691)

Breenes Camp Riverbend

(est 1962)   ☀ 🚐

Warren Township, NJ (Somerset Co.);
(908) 580-2267
Harold & Marianne Breene, Director

ICON LEGEND

☀   Day Camp

▲   Resident Camp

🏠   Facilities Available To Rent

🚐   Transportation Available

🐷   Financial Aid Available

FEE RANGES PER WEEK

A $0-75

B $75-200

C $201-350

D $351-500

E $501-650

F   over $650

Camp comments: 'Classic' program with sports, crafts, nature awareness. Mature responsible staff. Fun, noncompetitive approach.
Activities: Archery, Arts/Crafts, Baseball/Softball, Canoeing, Ceramics/Pottery, Drama, Swimming — Instructional, Swimming — Recreational, Tennis
Session lengths & capacity: June-August; 3, 4 & 7 week sessions; 900 campers
Clientele & fees: coed 4-14; Fees: **E** ☀
Contact: Harold Breene, Director at (908) 580-2267; fax: (908) 647-2435
e-mail: rvrbnd1@aol.com
Operated by: The Breene Family, 116 Hillcrest Rd, Warren Township, NJ 07059-5328 at (908) 580-2267 (#2252)

Camp Cannundus (est 1930)   ☀ 🚐

Summit, NJ (Union Co.); (908) 273-3330
Amy Ketcham, Director

Camp comments: We build character in kids! Campers learn new skills, make friends and expand their horizons in a natural environment.
Activities: Arts/Crafts, Counselor Training (CIT), Drama, Field Trips, Hiking, Nature/Environment Studies, Sports — Field & Team, Swimming — Instructional, Swimming — Recreational
Session lengths & capacity: June-August; 1 week sessions; 160 campers
Clientele & fees: coed 6-11; Fees: **B** ☀ 🐷
Contact: Amy Ketcham, Camp & Family Director at (908) 273-3330; fax: (908) 273-0258
e-mail: amy_ketcham@hotmail.com
Operated by: Summit Area YMCA, 67 Maple St, Summit, NJ 07901 at (908) 273-3330 (#26365)

Camp Cedar Knoll (est 1950)   ▲ 🏠

Millville, NJ (Cumberland Co.); (609) 825-5531
Samuel Hull, Director

Camp comments: A Christian camp located in the beautiful pine forests of southern New Jersey. Excellent trained staff serving all humanity.
Activities: Aerobics/Exercise, Arts/Crafts, Basketball, Boating, Dance, Drama, Field Trips, Music, Nature/Environment Studies, Swimming — Recreational
Session lengths & capacity: 1 week sessions; 60 campers
Clientele & fees: coed 6-14; families; Fees: **B** ▲
Contact: Samuel C Hull, Camp Director at (856) 881-1546; fax: (856) 881-0499
e-mail: bethany@JIL.net
Web site: www.bba-SJ.org
Operated by: Bethany Baptist Assoc of NJ, Schooner Landing Road, PO Box 804, Millville, NJ 08332 at (856) 825-5531
Group Rental Information
Site comments: A Christian camp for boys & girls between ages 6 & 14, located in the beautiful pine forests of New Jersey.
Seasons & Capacity: Spring 100, Summer 2000, Fall 100, Winter 100
Facilities: Dorm-Style, Food Service, Hiking Trails, Kitchen Facilities, Lake, Lodges, Meeting Rooms, Playing Fields, Pool, River, Tents
Programs: Boating, Environmental Education, Swimming (#2325)

Camp Dark Waters (est 1928)   ▲ 🏠

Medford, NJ (Burlington Co.); (609) 654-8846
Travis W Simmons, Director

Camp comments: Caring Quaker atmosphere where we believe a child's summer vacation should be a time for play, to venture forth in learning new skills, and to grow.
Activities: Archery, Arts/Crafts, Baseball/Softball, Camping Skills/Outdoor Living, Canoeing, Challenge/Rope Courses, Horseback — English, Music, Performing Arts, Swimming — Instructional
Session lengths & capacity: June-August; 1, 2 & 8 week sessions; 94 campers
Clientele & fees: coed 7-14; Fees: **C** ▲ 🐷

Contact: Travis W Simmons, Director at (609) 654-8846;
Web site: www.campdarkwaters.org
Operated by: Camp Dark Waters Inc, PO Box 263, Medford, NJ 08055 at (609) 654-8846
Group Rental Information
Site comments: Rustic, wooded setting nestled along a meandering creek provides the perfect atmosphere for your next outing or retreat. Call for more information or brochure.
Seasons & Capacity: Spring 100, Fall 100
Facilities: Cabins, Dorm-Style, Food Service, Kitchen Facilities, Meeting Rooms, Playing Fields, Pool, River
Programs: Boating, Challenge/Ropes Course, Environmental Education, Swimming (#3247)

Camp Gan Israel   ☀

New Brunswick, NJ; (732) 296-1800
Activities: Field Trips, Swimming — Instructional, Swimming — Recreational
Operated by: Chabad House, 170 College Ave, New Brunswick, NJ 08901 at (732) 296-1800 (#45098)

Camp Harmony (est 1926)   ☀ 🚐

Warren, NJ; (800) 842-2842
Jerry Amedeo, Director
Activities: Challenge/Rope Courses, Computer, Drama, Gymnastics, Music, Nature/Environment Studies, Sports — Field & Team, Swimming — Instructional, Swimming — Recreational, Tennis
Session lengths & capacity: June-August; 8 week sessions; 300 campers
Clientele & fees: coed 3-12; Fees: **D** ☀
Contact: Carol Amedeo, Director at (732) 469-6900; fax: (732) 469-9444
e-mail: carol@campharmony.com
Web site: www.campharmony.com
Operated by: Camp Harmony, 206 Mt Horeb Rd, PO Box 4305, Warren, NJ 07059 at (732) 469-6900 (#34252)

Camp Horizons (est 1984)   ☀ 🚐

Livingston, NJ (Essex Co.); (973) 992-7767
Alan Pressman, Director

Camp comments: Campers select their entire schedule. This gives them the opportunity to be independent and develope decision making skills. Children love Camp Horizons.
Activities: Ceramics/Pottery, Computer, Dance, Drama, Gymnastics, Model Rocketry, Performing Arts, Photography, Sports — Field & Team, Swimming — Instructional
Session lengths & capacity: June-August; 4, 6 & 8 week sessions; 300 campers
Clientele & fees: coed 6-14; Fees: **E** ☀
Contact: Neil Rothstein, Owner at (973) 992-7767; fax: (973) 992-6997
Operated by: Camp Horizons, 33 Hemlock Road, Livingston, NJ 07039 at (973) 992-7767 (#6278)

Camp Jotoni (est 1973)   ☀ ▲

Warren, NJ (Somerset Co.); (908) 753-4244
Chris Reagan, Director
Activities: Arts/Crafts, Baseball/Softball, Basketball, Drama, Music, Nature/Environment Studies, Soccer, Swimming — Recreational
Session lengths & capacity: 7 week sessions; 100 campers
Clientele & fees: coed 5-99; Fees: **B** ☀ Fees: **C** ▲ 🐷
Contact: Barbara Lutzsky, Program Assistant at (908) 725-8544;
Operated by: ARC of Somerset, 141 S Main Street, Warren, NJ 08835 at (908) 725-8544 (#3229)

Camp Louemma Inc ▲ ⌂

Sussex, NJ (sussex Co.); (973) 875-4403
Hal Pugach, Director

Camp comments: A summer of fun, a lifetime of memories. Diverse program, modern cabins, excellent staff, Kosher. Ideal for 1st. timers.
Activities: Arts/Crafts, Baseball/Softball, Basketball, Boating, Drama, Hockey, Soccer, Sports — Field & Team, Swimming — Instructional, Tennis
Session lengths & capacity: 1, 2 & 3 week sessions
Clientele & fees: Fees: D ▲
Contact: Hal Pugach, Director at (973) 316-0362; fax: (973) 316-0980
Operated by: Camp Louemma Inc, 214 45 42nd Ave, Bayside, NY 11361 at (718) 631-3747 (#13171)

Camp Nehemiah ☀

Lindenwold, NJ (Camden Co.); (856) 784-2220
Activities: Academics, Arts/Crafts, Counselor Training (CIT), Field Trips, Religious Study, Skating, Swimming — Recreational
Contact: Web site: www.abundantharvest.com
Operated by: Bethany Baptist Church, 1115 Gibbsboro Rd, Lindenwold, NJ 08021 at (856) 784-2220 (#49025)

Camp Oakhurst (est 1906) ▲ ⇋

Oakhurst, NJ (Monmouth Co.); (732) 531-0215
James Grande, Director

Camp comments: Disabled children gain self-esteem & independence in a Camp where it's easy to participate in activities, make friends & be accepted.
Activities: Arts/Crafts, Baseball/Softball, Basketball, Camping Skills/Outdoor Living, Drama, Field Trips, Music, Photography, Swimming — Instructional, Swimming — Recreational
Session lengths & capacity: July-August; 2, 4 & 6 week sessions; 90 campers
Clientele & fees: coed 8-18; Fees: E ▲ 🚌
Contact: Marvin Raps, Executive Director at (212) 533-4020; fax: (212) 533-4023
e-mail: oakhurst06@aol.com
Web site: www.campchannel.com/campoakhurst
Operated by: NY Service for the Handicapped, 853 Broadway Suite 605, New York, NY 10003 at (212) 533-4020 (#11693)

Camp Ockanickon Matollionequay (est 1906) ☀ ⌂

Medford, NJ (Burlington Co.); (609) 654-8225
Tom Rapine, Director

Camp comments: Situated on 560 scenic acres of lakes & pinelands, day & overnight camps. A quality experience in the great outdoors.
Activities: Aquatic Activities, Archery, Arts/Crafts, Baseball/Softball, Boating, Canoeing, Counselor Training (CIT), Drawing/Painting, Horseback — English, Nature/Environment Studies
Session lengths & capacity: June-August; 1 & 2 week sessions; 250 campers
Clientele & fees: coed 5-15; families; Fees: B ☀ Fees: D ▲ 🚌
Contact: Tom Rapine, Summer Camp Director at (609) 654-8225; fax: (609) 654-8895
e-mail: info@ycamp.org
Web site: www.ycamp.org
Operated by: YMCA Camps, 1303 Stokes Rd, Medford, NJ 08055 at (609) 654-8225

Group Rental Information
Site comments: Over 560 acres of lakes & pinelands provides a unique backdrop for your next conference, banquet or retreat. Specialized programs, diverse accomodations.
Seasons & Capacity: Spring 500, Fall 500, Winter 100

Facilities: Cabins, Double Occupancy, Food Service, Hiking Trails, Lake, Lodges, Meeting Rooms
Programs: Boating, Challenge/Ropes Course, Environmental Education, Swimming (#2260)

Camp Sun N Fun/Arc Gloucester

(est 1957) ▲

Williamstown, NJ (Gloucester Co.); (856) 629-4502

Camp comments: Residential camp for developmentally disabled children-adults ages 8 and up. One and two week sessions. Financial assistance.
Activities: Arts/Crafts, International Culture, Nature/Environment Studies, Performing Arts, Sports — Field & Team, Swimming — Instructional, Swimming — Recreational
Session lengths & capacity: June-August; 1 & 2 week sessions; 45 campers
Clientele & fees: coed 8-88; Fees: D ▲
Contact: Brenda Powell Homan, Team Leader at (856) 848-8648; fax: (856) 848-7753
e-mail: bpowell.homan@thearcgloucester.org
Operated by: The Arc Gloucester Resid Camp, 1555 Gateway Blvd, Woodbury, NJ 08096 at (856) 848-8648 (#2288)

Camp Sussex Inc (est 1923) ▲ ⌂ ⇋

Sussex, NJ (Sussex Co.); (973) 875-3694
Gary E Cardamone, Director

Camp comments: We foster a warm family spirit and offer children an opportunity to live with others from varied backgrounds.
Activities: Academics, Arts/Crafts, Basketball, Boating, Computer, Drama, Fishing, Soccer, Swimming — Instructional, Tennis
Session lengths & capacity: 3 week sessions; 280 campers
Clientele & fees: boys 7-14; girls 7-14; coed 7-14; Fees: B ▲ 🚌
Contact: Savodnik/Linda, Office Manager Administrator at (718) 261-8700; fax: (718) 793-2857
e-mail: Campsussex@aol.com
Web site: www.campsussex.org
Operated by: Camp Sussex Inc, 110-11 Queens Blvd, Forest Hills, NY 11375 at (718) 261-8700

Group Rental Information
Facilities: Cabins, Food Service, Lake, Lodges, Meeting Rooms
Programs: Swimming (#2297)

Camp Tecumseh (est 1964) ▲

Pittstown, NJ (Hunterdon Co.); (908) 735-4136
Captain Evan Hickman, Director

Camp comments: Christian emphasis for disadvantaged children.
Activities: Aquatic Activities, Archery, Arts/Crafts, Camping Skills/Outdoor Living, Canoeing, Challenge/Rope Courses, Nature/Environment Studies, Soccer, Sports — Field & Team, Swimming — Recreational
Session lengths & capacity: June-August; 1 week sessions; 165 campers
Clientele & fees: coed 7-12; seniors; Fees: B ▲ 🚌
Contact: Chris McCloskey, Director at (908) 851-9300; fax: (908) 688-4460
e-mail: njtecumseh@aol.com
Web site: www.CampTecumseh.com
Operated by: The Salvation Army, 4 Gary Road, Union, NJ 07083 at (908) 851-8216 (#2284)

Campus Kids - NJ (est 1991) ▲ ⇋

Hackettstown, NJ (Warren Co.); (908) 850-5872
Tom Riddleberger, Director

Camp comments: Mon-Fri sleep-away camp; home on the weekends; transportation provided. Campers choose their activities individually.

Activities: Archery, Arts/Crafts, Basketball, Ceramics/Pottery, Drama, Gymnastics, Horseback — English, Swimming — Instructional, Tennis
Session lengths & capacity: June-August; 2, 4, 6 & 8 week sessions; 220 campers
Clientele & fees: coed 7-15; Fees: F ▲
Contact: Tom Riddleberger, Owner-Director at (973) 635-2300; fax: (973) 635-1217
e-mail: campuskids@aol.com
Web site: www.campuskids.com
Operated by: CK Summer Camps Inc, PO Box 1058, Chatham, NJ 07928 at (973) 635-2300 (#6785)

Country Roads Day Camp

(est 1970) ☀ ⇋

Manalapan, NJ (Monmouth Co.); (908) 446-4100
Joan & Ed Klein, Director

Camp comments: Family owned 30 yrs heated pools & waterpark, sports clinics, trapeze, theater, dance, fine arts, site & travel programs. Ages 3-15
Activities: Arts/Crafts, Drawing/Painting, Gymnastics, Performing Arts, Photography, Skating, Sports — Field & Team, Travel/Tour
Session lengths & capacity: June-August; 4, 6 & 8 week sessions
Clientele & fees: boys 3-15; girls 3-15; Fees: D ☀
Contact: Scott Kuzmic, Marketing Director at (732) 446-4100; fax: (732) 786-1072
e-mail: scott.countryroads@starband.net
Web site: www.countryroadsdaycamp.com
Operated by: Country Roads Day Camp, 139 Pinebrook Rd, Manalapan, NJ 07726 at (732) 446-4100 (#4541)

Cromwell (est 1983) ☀ ▲ ⇋

Bound Brook, NJ (Somerset Co.); (732) 469-4333
Anthony Blake, Director

Camp comments: Available only to boys who are members of the Boys Club of New York
Activities: Academics, Archery, Arts/Crafts, Baseball/Softball, Basketball, Challenge/Rope Courses, Nature/Environment Studies, Soccer, Swimming — Recreational
Session lengths & capacity: 2, 4 & 6 week sessions; 250 campers
Clientele & fees: boys 7-14; Fees: A ☀ Fees: A ▲ 🚌
Contact: Anthony Blake, Director at (732) 469-4333; fax: (732) 469-8542
Operated by: The Boys Club of New York, PO Box 671, Bound Brook, NJ 08805-0671 at (732) 469-4333 (#12126)

Cross Roads Camp (est 2000) ▲ ⌂

Port Murray, NJ (Hunterdon Co.); (908) 832-7264
Peggy Mellors, Director

Camp comments: Camping which focuses on the relationships between the Creator, the creature, and the care of the creation.
Activities: Aquatic Activities, Arts/Crafts, Backpacking, Counselor Training (CIT), Leadership Development, Nature/Environment Studies, Religious Study, Swimming — Recreational
Session lengths & capacity: June-August; 1 week sessions; 180 campers
Clientele & fees: coed 7-15; families; Fees: C ▲ ⇋
Contact: Peggy Mellors, Executive Director at (908) 832-7264; fax: (908) 832-6593
e-mail: crossroadsom@mindspring.com
Web site: www.crossroadsoutdoorministries.org
Operated by: Cross Roads Outdoor Ministries, 29 Pleasant Grove Road, Port Murray, NJ 07865 at (908) 832-7264

Group Rental Information
Seasons & Capacity: Spring 250, Fall 90, Winter 90

Facilities: A/V Equipment, Cabins, Dorm-Style, Double Occupancy, Food Service, Hiking Trails, Kitchen Facilities, Lake, Meeting Rooms, Playing Fields, Pool
Programs: Boating, Swimming (#3157)

CYO Day Camp (est 1958) ☀ 🚐

Yardeville, NJ (Mercer Co.); (609) 585-4280
Kevin Walsh, Director

Camp comments: The goal of the CYO Day Camp is to help each camper have a healthy, happy summer while developing body, mind and spirit. We stress safety first.
Activities: Aquatic Activities, Arts/Crafts, Baseball/Softball, Basketball, Field Trips, Fishing, Nature/Environment Studies, Sports — Field & Team, Swimming — Instructional, Swimming — Recreational
Session lengths & capacity: June-August; 3, 6 & 9 week sessions; 310 campers
Clientele & fees: coed 5-12; Fees: B ☀ 🐷
Contact: Kevin Walsh, Camp Director at (609) 396-8383; fax: (609) 392-8419
e-mail: cyomercer@aol.com
Operated by: Catholic Youth Org of Mercer, 920 S Broad St, Trenton, NJ 08611 at (609) 396-8383 (#26649)

Eagle Springs at the Shore ⚠

Ocean City, NJ; (609) 399-3758
Activities: Aquatic Activities, Arts/Crafts, Baseball/Softball, Basketball, Field Trips, International Culture, Sports — Field & Team
Operated by: Eagle Springs Programs, 58 Eagle Springs Ln, Pine Grove, PA 17963 at (570) 345-8705 (#11301)

ESNJ Camp Merry Heart

(est 1949) ☀ ⚠ 🏠

Hackettstown, NJ (Warren Co.); (908) 852-3896
Alex Humanick, Director

Camp comments: A special camp for people with disabilities. Activities typical of camps but adapted to meet the campers needs.
Activities: Arts/Crafts, Boating, Challenge/Rope Courses, Dance, Kayaking, Leadership Development, Music, Nature/Environment Studies, Swimming — Recreational, Travel/Tour
Session lengths & capacity: June-August; 1 & 2 week sessions; 70 campers
Clientele & fees: coed 5-80; families; seniors; Fees: B ☀ Fees: D, F ⚠ 🐷
Contact: Alex Humanick, Director of Camping & Recreation at (908) 852-3896; fax: (908) 852-9263
e-mail: A.Humanick@eastersealsnj.org
Web site: www.eastersealsnj.org

ICON LEGEND

☀	Day Camp
⚠	Resident Camp
🏠	Facilities Available To Rent
🚐	Transportation Available
🐷	Financial Aid Available

FEE RANGES PER WEEK

A	$0-75
B	$75-200
C	$201-350
D	$351-500
E	$501-650
F	over $650

Operated by: ESNJ Camp Merry Heart, 21 O'Brien Road, Hackettstown, NJ 07840-9802 at (908) 852-3896
Group Rental Information
Site comments: Beautiful, quiet site close to city, meet any groups needs.
Seasons & Capacity: Spring 150, Fall 80, Winter 80
Facilities: Cabins, Dorm-Style, Hiking Trails, Kitchen Facilities, Meeting Rooms
Programs: Boating (#2298)

Fairview Lake YMCA Camp & Conf (est 1915) ⚠ 🏠

Newton, NJ (Sussex Co.); (201) 383-9282
Marc Koch, Director

Camp comments: Traditional camp on 600 acres w/110 acre lake. A place where children can learn & grow in a caring environment.
Activities: Arts/Crafts, Drama, Horseback — Western, Music, Performing Arts, Sailing, Sports — Field & Team, Swimming — Instructional, Tennis, Windsurfing
Session lengths & capacity: June-August; 1, 2, 3 & 6 week sessions; 200 campers
Clientele & fees: boys 7-16; girls 7-16; coed 7-16; families; Fees: D ⚠
Contact: Marc Koch, Summer Camp Director at (201) 383-9282; fax: (201) 383-6386
e-mail: mkoch@metroymcas.org
Web site: www.metroymcas.org
Operated by: Metro YMCA Of The Oranges, 139 E McClellan Ave, Livingston, NJ 07039 at (973) 758-9622
Group Rental Information
Seasons & Capacity: Spring 300, Summer 300, Fall 300, Winter 300
Facilities: Cabins, Food Service, Hiking Trails, Lake, Lodges, Meeting Rooms, Playing Fields
Programs: Boating, Challenge/Ropes Course, Environmental Education, Swimming, Winter Sports (#7085)

Frogbridge Day Camp

(est 1999) ☀ 🏠 🚐

Millstone Township, NJ (Monmouth Co.); (609) 208-9050
Peter Normandia, Director

Camp comments: 86 Acres of fun! A/C facilities, horses, boating, 3 lakes, performing arts, sports, 52,000 sq ft indoor space. Much more
Activities: Aquatic Activities, Boating, Challenge/Rope Courses, Fishing, Golf, Gymnastics, Hockey, Horseback — English, Horseback — Western, Performing Arts
Session lengths & capacity: June-August; 4, 6 & 8 week sessions; 600 campers
Clientele & fees: coed 3-15; Fees: D ☀
Contact: Mary Magarine, Office Manager at (609) 208-9050; fax: (609) 208-9052
e-mail: info@frogbridge.com
Web site: www.frogbridge.com
Operated by: Frogbridge Inc, 7 Yellow Meeting House Rd, Millstone Township, NJ 08514 at (609) 208-9050 (#29651)

Gan Israel Day Camp ☀

Old Bridge, NJ
Activities: Arts/Crafts, Baseball/Softball, Field Trips, Language Studies, Soccer
Operated by: Chabad Lubavitch W Monmouth Co, 26 Wickatunk Rd, Manalapan, NJ 07726 at (732) 972-3688 (#38995)

Happiness Is Camping

(est 1958) ⚠ 🏠 🚐

Blairstown, NJ (Warren Co.); (908) 362-6733
Keely Gibbs, Director

Camp comments: A 'normal' camp experience for children with cancer.
Activities: Aquatic Activities, Archery, Arts/Crafts, Camping Skills/Outdoor Living, Challenge/Rope Courses, Dance, Sailing, Swimming — Recreational
Session lengths & capacity: 1, 2 & 6 week sessions; 100 campers
Clientele & fees: coed 7-15; Fees: A ⚠ 🐷
Contact: Rich Campbell, Executive Director at (908) 362-6733; fax: (908) 362-5197
e-mail: hicamping@nac.net
Web site: wwwhappinessiscamping.org
Operated by: Happiness Is Camping Inc, 2169 Grand Concorse, Bronx, NY 10453 at (718) 295-3100
Group Rental Information
Facilities: A/V Equipment, Cabins, Dorm-Style, Food Service, Hiking Trails, Kitchen Facilities, Lake, Lodges, Meeting Rooms, Playing Fields, Pool
Programs: Boating, Challenge/Ropes Course, Environmental Education, Swimming (#2035)

Harbor Haven (est 1996) ☀ 🚐

West Orange, NJ (Essex Co.); (973) 669-0800
Robyn Tanne, Director

Camp comments: Harbor Haven is a nurturing place where success is a daily occurrence. Children participate in typical camp activities while improving social & attention skills
Activities: Academics, Arts/Crafts, Music, Performing Arts, Sports — Field & Team, Swimming — Instructional, Tennis
Session lengths & capacity: June-August; 3, 4, 5, 6 & 7 week sessions; 150 campers
Clientele & fees: boys 3-15; girls 3-15; coed 3-15
Contact: Robyn Tanne, Director at (973) 669-0800; fax: (973) 669-3246
e-mail: info@harborhaven.com
Web site: www.harborhaven.com
Operated by: Harbor Haven LLC, PO Box 1654, Livingston, NJ 07039 at (973) 669-0800 (#14309)

Harbor Hills Day Camp

(est 1963) ☀ 🚐

Mt Freedom, NJ (Morris Co.); (973) 895-3200
Charlie Zetterstrom, Director

Camp comments: Outstanding age appropriate programs emphasizing personal growth and skills development. Limited enrollment.
Activities: Arts/Crafts, Baseball/Softball, Basketball, Bicycling/Biking, Challenge/Rope Courses, Climbing/Rappelling, Photography, Swimming — Recreational, Tennis, Travel/Tour
Session lengths & capacity: 4, 6 & 8 week sessions; 500 campers
Clientele & fees: boys 3-15; girls 3-15; coed 3-15; Fees: D ☀
Contact: Charlie Zetterstrom, Director at (973) 895-3200; fax: (973) 895-7239
e-mail: info@hhdc.com
Web site: www.hhdc.com
Operated by: Harbor Hills Day Camp Inc, 75 Doby Road Box 516, Mt Freedom, NJ 07970 at (973) 895-3200 (#5434)

Hi Hills Day Camp (est 1966) ☀ 🚐

Gladstone, NJ (Somerset Co.); (908) 234-0067
Bunny & Marv Goldberg, Director

Camp comments: Mature staff, great 'New England type' setting. Warm, supportive atmosphere. All activities, door to door transportation
Activities: Aquatic Activities, Archery, Arts/Crafts, Dance, Drama, Horseback — English, Nature/Environment Studies, Sports — Field & Team, Tennis, Travel/Tour
Session lengths & capacity: June-August; 4, 6 & 8 week sessions; 400 campers
Clientele & fees: coed 3-14; Fees: C ☀
Contact: Marv Goldberg, Director at (908) 234-0067; fax: (609) 683-7973

Operated by: Hi Hills Day Camp, c/o Gill St Bernards School, PO Box 604, Gladstone, NJ 07934 at (908) 234-0067 (#2268)

Hope Conference & Renewal Ctr

Hope, NJ; (908) 459-4435
Wilmer Hassler, Director
Activities: Aquatic Activities, Arts/Crafts, Baseball/Softball, Basketball, Boating, Canoeing, Religious Study
Contact: Rev Tammie Rinker at (908) 686-5262; fax: (908) 459-5571
e-mail: trinkeraz@aol.com
Operated by: Moravian Church Eastern Dist, PO Box 165, Hope, NJ 07844 at (908) 459-4435
Group Rental Information
Seasons & Capacity: Spring 60, Summer 150, Fall 60, Winter 60
Facilities: Cabins, Food Service, Hiking Trails, Kitchen Facilities, Meeting Rooms, Playing Fields, Pool
Programs: Boating, Swimming (#2372)

Inawendiwin Program Center

(est 1950)

Tabernacle, NJ (Burlington Co.); (609) 859-3179
HL Ransom, Director

Camp comments: Located in Pine Barrens, special choices each day. Day Camp offers 1 sleep over night. Outstanding staff.
Activities: Aquatic Activities, Archery, Arts/Crafts, Camping Skills/Outdoor Living, Canoeing, Counselor Training (CIT), Hiking, Leadership Development, Nature/Environment Studies, Swimming — Recreational
Session lengths & capacity: 1 week sessions; 100 campers
Clientele & fees: girls 6-18; Fees: **B**
Fees: **B A**
Contact: Laura Perez, Membership/Program Director at (856) 795-1560; fax: (856) 354-8425
e-mail: lperez@gscamden.org
Operated by: Girl Scouts Camden County NJ, 40 Brace Road, Cherry Hill, NJ 08034 at (856) 795-1560
Group Rental Information
Facilities: Cabins, Hiking Trails, Kitchen Facilities, Lake, Tents
Programs: Boating, Challenge/Ropes Course, Swimming (#6583)

Ivy League Day Camp

(est 1972)

Manalapan, NJ (Monmouth Co.); (732) 446-7035
Ron & Sandy Leiser, Director

Camp comments: Big league fun, through self esteem building activities. Campers make friends. Nurturing staff as role models. Half & full day. Teen travel.
Activities: Aquatic Activities, Arts/Crafts, Computer, Field Trips, Hockey, Performing Arts, Swimming — Recreational, Tennis, Travel/Tour
Session lengths & capacity: July-August; 4, 6 & 8 week sessions; 500 campers
Clientele & fees: boys 3-15; girls 3-15; coed 3-15; Fees: **D**
Contact: Ron & Sandy Leiser, Owner/Director at (732) 446-7035; fax: (732) 446-5623
e-mail: mail@ivyleggvedaycamp.com
Web site: www.ivyleaguedaycamp.com
Operated by: Ivy League Day Camp, 140 Gordons Corner Road, Manalapan, NJ 07726 at (732) 446-7035 (#2987)

JCC Camp Deeny Riback-MetroWst (est 1885)

Flanders, NJ (Morris Co.); (973) 584-6060
Diana Ackerman, Director

Camp comments: Super staff promotes integrity, self-esteem, positive values. Skill development & sportsmanship in a Jewish environment.
Activities: Aquatic Activities, Archery, Arts/Crafts, Boating, Ceramics/Pottery, Challenge/Rope Courses, Counselor Training (CIT), Performing Arts, Photography, Sports — Field & Team
Session lengths & capacity: June-August; 4, 6 & 8 week sessions; 500 campers
Clientele & fees: coed 3-15; Fees: **C**
Contact: Diana Ackerman, Director of Camping Services at (973) 428-9300; fax: (973) 428-6068
e-mail: dackerman@ujfmetrowest.org
Operated by: JCC Metro West, 760 Northfield Ave, West Orange, NJ 07052 at (973) 736-3200 (#17758)

JCC Camps at Medford

(est 1942)

Medford, NJ; (609) 654-5192
Aaron Greenberg, Director

Camp comments: On 120 wooded acres, outstanding staff provide instruction in arts, aquatics & athletics. 5 pools & many fields/courts.
Activities: Aquatic Activities, Arts/Crafts, Boating, Counselor Training (CIT), Drama, Nature/Environment Studies, Performing Arts, Sports — Field & Team, Travel/Tour
Session lengths & capacity: June-August; 4, 6, 7 & 8 week sessions; 1500 campers
Clientele & fees: coed 3-16; Fees: **C**
Contact: Deena Sherman, Asst. Camp Director at (856) 424-4444 ext. 233; fax: (856) 489-8230
e-mail: dsherman@jfedsnj.org
Web site: www.katzjcc.org
Operated by: Jewish Federation of South NJ, 1301 Springdale Rd, Cherry Hill, NJ 08003 at (856) 424-4444 (#27502)

Jefferson Lakes Day Camp

(est 1958)

Stanhope, NJ (Sussex/Morris Co.); (973) 347-1230
Ira R Fish, I. Dudley Edge, Susan Rynar, Director

Camp comments: Supportive & nurturing atmosphere 300 acres, 4 pools, 50 acre lake, water slide program & facilities like an overnight camp
Activities: Archery, Arts/Crafts, Baseball/Softball, Basketball, Boating, Challenge/Rope Courses, Drama, Gymnastics, Soccer, Tennis
Session lengths & capacity: 4, 6 & 8 week sessions
Clientele & fees: boys 3-15; girls 3-15; coed 3-15; Fees: **D**
Contact: Ira R Fish, Director at (973) 347-1230; fax: (973) 691-4813
Web site: www.jefflakecamp.com
Operated by: Jefferson Lakes Day Camp, PO Box 426, Stanhope, NJ 07874 at (973) 568-0454 (#4214)

Jockey Hollow (est 1939)

Mendham, NJ (Morris Co.); (973) 543-2156
Janet Thomas, Director
Activities: Arts/Crafts, Camping Skills/Outdoor Living, Challenge/Rope Courses, Hiking, Horseback — English, Nature/Environment Studies, Swimming — Instructional
Session lengths & capacity: July-August; 1, 2 & 6 week sessions; 200 campers
Clientele & fees: girls 5-14; Fees: **B**
Contact: Janet Thomas, Director of Program & Property at (973) 927-7722; fax: (973) 927-7683
e-mail: janet@magsc.org
Web site: www.magsc.org
Operated by: Morris Area GSC, 1579 Sussex Turnpike, Randolph, NJ 07869-1811 at (973) 927-7722 (#3213)

Johnsonburg Presbyterian Ctr

(est 1959)

Johnsonburg, NJ (Frelinghuysen Co.); (908) 852-2349
Howard Miller, Director

Camp comments: Noncompetitive camp with 1/2 to 2 week sessions for youth 8-18. Kids learn to make good choices. Self-esteem specialty.
Activities: Archery, Canoeing, Challenge/Rope Courses, Clowning, Hiking, Horseback — Western, Leadership Development, Nature/Environment Studies, Religious Study, Swimming — Recreational
Session lengths & capacity: June-September; 1/2, 1 & 2 week sessions; 225 campers
Clientele & fees: coed 7-17; families; seniors; single adults; Fees: **C A**
Contact: Dr Howard Miller, Executive Director at (908) 852-2349; fax: (908) 852-0045
e-mail: campjburg@campjburg.org
Web site: www.campjburg.org
Operated by: Presbyterian Camps & Conf Inc, PO Box 475, Johnsonburg, NJ 07846 at (908) 852-2349
Group Rental Information
Facilities: A/V Equipment, Cabins, Dorm-Style, Double Occupancy, Food Service, Hiking Trails, Lake, Lodges, Meeting Rooms, Playing Fields, Pool
Programs: Boating, Challenge/Ropes Course, Swimming (#7115)

Kettle Run (est 1959)

Medford, NJ (Burlington Co.); (856) 983-5705

Camp comments: This all girls camp is in the Pine Barrens of Medford NJ. Enjoy arts & crafts, archery, swimming, canoeing, and our nature trails. Where girls grow strong.
Activities: Aquatic Activities, Archery, Arts/Crafts, Camping Skills/Outdoor Living, Canoeing, Hiking, Leadership Development, Nature/Environment Studies, Swimming — Instructional, Swimming — Recreational
Session lengths & capacity: July-August; 1 week sessions; 120 campers
Clientele & fees: girls 6-15; Fees: **B**
Contact: Web site: www.gssjp.org
Operated by: South Jersey Pines GSC, 2944 Victoria Ave, Newfield, NJ 08344 at (856) 697-3900
Group Rental Information
Site comments: Located in the Pine Barrens of Medford NJ. Enjoy arts,crafts,archery,swimming,canoeing and walking the nature trails.
Seasons & Capacity: Spring 230, Summer 230, Fall 104, Winter 104
Facilities: Cabins, Hiking Trails, Lake, Lodges
Programs: Boating, Environmental Education (#7004)

Kiddie Keep Well Camp (est 1924)

Edison, NJ (Middlesex Co.); (732) 548-6542
Kevin Cullum, Director

Camp comments: Nonprofit camp for 6-13 yr old boys & girls, from low income families in Middlesex Co.
Activities: Arts/Crafts, Baseball/Softball, Basketball, Camping Skills/Outdoor Living, Dance, Drama, Nature/Environment Studies, Soccer, Sports — Field & Team, Swimming — Recreational
Session lengths & capacity: June-August; 2 week sessions; 170 campers
Clientele & fees: coed 6-15; seniors; Fees: **A A**
Contact: Kevin Cullum, Camp Director at (732) 548-6542; fax: (732) 548-9535
e-mail: kcullum@yahoo.com
Operated by: Middlesex County Recreation Co, 35 Roosevelt Dr, Edison, NJ 08837-2333 at (732) 548-6542 (#2267)

Lake Rickabear (est 1980) ☀ 🏠 🚗

Kinnelon, NJ (Morris Co.); (973) 334-6187

Camp comments: Beautiful facility, outstanding staff. Focus on fun activities to meet girls needs. Transportation available.
Activities: Archery, Arts/Crafts, Canoeing, Field Trips, Nature/Environment Studies, Soccer, Swimming — Instructional, Swimming — Recreational
Session lengths & capacity: June-August; 1 & 2 week sessions; 240 campers
Clientele & fees: girls 6-12; Fees: B ☀
Contact: Kim Trem, Outdoor Program Mngr at (973) 248-8200; fax: (973) 248-8050
Web site: www.gsllc.org
Operated by: Lenni Lenape GSC, 95 Newark Pompton Tpk, Riverdale, NJ 07457 at (973) 248-8200

Group Rental Information
Facilities: Lake, Meeting Rooms
Programs: Boating (#2276)

Lake Stockwell Day Camp YMCA (est 1990) ☀ 🏠 🚗

Medford, NJ; (609) 654-8225
Judy Martin, Director
Activities: Arts/Crafts, Camping Skills/Outdoor Living, Nature/Environment Studies
Session lengths & capacity: June-August; 1 week sessions; 225 campers
Clientele & fees: coed 5-15; Fees: B ☀
Contact: Judy Martin, Day Camp Director at (609) 953-5663 ext. 220;
e-mail: judy@ycamps.org
Web site: www.ycamp.org
Operated by: YMCA Camps, 1303 Stokes Rd, Medford, NJ 08055 at (609) 654-8225

Group Rental Information
Seasons & Capacity: Spring 500, Fall 500, Winter 100
Facilities: A/V Equipment, Cabins, Dorm-Style, Food Service, Hiking Trails, Kitchen Facilities, Lake, Lodges, Meeting Rooms, Playing Fields
Programs: Boating, Challenge/Ropes Course, Environmental Education, Horseback Riding, Swimming (#48287)

Lake Vu Day Camp (est 1939) ☀ 🚗

East Brunswick, NJ (Middlesex Co.); (732) 821-8933
Amy & Barry Wasserman, Director

Camp comments: 20 acre shaded campus on a lake. Family run since 1939. Hot lunch, mature staff, door to door transportation.

ICON LEGEND

☀ Day Camp
▲ Resident Camp
🏠 Facilities Available To Rent
🚗 Transportation Available
🚌 Financial Aid Available

FEE RANGES PER WEEK

A $0-75
B $75-200
C $201-350
D $351-500
E $501-650
F over $650

Activities: Archery, Arts/Crafts, Boating, Drama, Gymnastics, Nature/Environment Studies, Sports — Field & Team, Swimming — Instructional, Tennis, Travel/Tour
Session lengths & capacity: June-August; 4, 6 & 8 week sessions; 750 campers
Clientele & fees: coed 3-15; Fees: D, E, F ☀
Contact: Amy & Barry Wasserman, Director at (732) 821-8933; fax: (732) 821-9456
e-mail: mailbag@lakevu.com
Web site: www.lakevu.com
Operated by: Lake Vu Day Camp, 505 Riva Ave, East Brunswick, NJ 08816 at (732) 821-8933 (#2932)

Lou Henry Hoover (est 1953) ▲ 🏠

Middleville, NJ (Sussex Co.); (973) 383-3220
Deborah Hooker, Director

Camp comments: Outstanding staff & facility! Enjoy the program of your choice combined with cookouts, swimming, boating & more!
Activities: Arts/Crafts, Backpacking, Canoeing, Challenge/Rope Courses, Drama, Gymnastics, Hiking, Horseback — Western, Leadership Development, Sailing
Session lengths & capacity: July-August; 1/2, 1 & 2 week sessions; 200 campers
Clientele & fees: girls 7-18; Fees: C ▲
Contact: Washington Rock GSC, Outdoor Program Director at (908) 232-3236; fax: (908) 232-2140
Operated by: GS of Washington Rock Council, 201 Grove St E, Westfield, NJ 07090 at (908) 232-3236

Group Rental Information
Facilities: Cabins, Hiking Trails, Kitchen Facilities, Lake, Playing Fields, Tents
Programs: Boating, Challenge/Ropes Course, Swimming (#2257)

Meadowbrook Country Day Camp (est 1990) ☀

Long Valley, NJ (Morris Co.); (908) 876-3429

Camp comments: Create memories that last lifetime. Diversified program, warm, caring, camp atmosphere. Emphasis on building self-esteem
Activities: Archery, Arts/Crafts, Basketball, Challenge/Rope Courses, Nature/Environment Studies, Soccer
Session lengths & capacity: 4, 6 & 8 week sessions; 400 campers
Clientele & fees: coed 3-15; Fees: C ☀
Contact: Jonathan Gold, Director at (908) 876-3429; fax: (908) 876-9635
e-mail: dilithiuml@aol.com
Web site: www.ivyleaguedaycamp.com
Operated by: Ivy League Day Camp, 140 Gordons Corner Road, Manalapan, NJ 07726 at (732) 446-7035 (#6647)

Mill Road Day Camp (est 1972) ☀ 🚗

North Brunswick, NJ (Middlesex Co.); (732) 821-9155
Burt Blittner/George Novick, Director

Camp comments: Campers thrive in a safe, caring, fun setting, where activities and facilities are designed for growth and enjoyment.
Activities: Archery, Baseball/Softball, Basketball, Challenge/Rope Courses, Counselor Training (CIT), Drama, Music, Photography, Swimming — Instructional, Swimming — Recreational
Session lengths & capacity: July-August; 4, 5, 6, 7 & 8 week sessions; 600 campers
Clientele & fees: coed 3-15; Fees: D ☀
Contact: Burt Blittner/Geo. Novick, Directors at (732) 821-9155; fax: (732) 821-5196
e-mail: MillrdCamp@aol.com
Web site: www.millroaddaycamp.com
Operated by: Mill Road Day Camp, 74 Davidsons Mill Rd, North Brunswick, NJ 08902 at (732) 821-9155 (#3166)

Montclair YMCA Day Camp (est 1970) ☀ 🏠

West Milford, NJ (Passaic Co.); (973) 697-2929
Gina Stravic, Director

Camp comments: We combine adventure, learning and fun to express creativity, learn new skills and build meaningful relationships.
Activities: Aquatic Activities, Challenge/Rope Courses, Hiking, Leadership Development, Nature/Environment Studies, SCUBA, Soccer, Sports — Field & Team, Swimming — Instructional, Swimming — Recreational
Session lengths & capacity: June-August; 1 week sessions; 350 campers
Clientele & fees: coed 6-15; Fees: B ☀ 🚌
Contact: Gina Stravic, Camp Director at (973) 744-3400; fax: (973) 744-1917
Web site: www.montclairymca.org
Operated by: Montclair YMCA, 25 Park St, Montclair, NJ 07042 at (973) 744-3400

Group Rental Information
Seasons & Capacity: Summer 100, Fall 100
Facilities: Hiking Trails, Lake, Lodges
Programs: Boating, Environmental Education, Swimming (#27593)

Nejeda (est 1957) ▲ 🏠

Stillwater, NJ (Sussex Co.); (973) 383-2611
James Daschbach, Director

Camp comments: A special camp providing an active, safe camping experience with emphasis on sound medical management of diabetes.
Activities: Archery, Arts/Crafts, Boating, Challenge/Rope Courses, Hiking, Model Rocketry, Nature/Environment Studies, Photography, Sports — Field & Team, Swimming — Recreational
Session lengths & capacity: June-August; 1 & 2 week sessions; 77 campers
Clientele & fees: boys 7-15; girls 7-15; families; Fees: F ▲ 🚌
Contact: Janis M Woersching, Executive Director at (973) 383-2611; fax: (973) 383-9891
e-mail: nejeda@nac.net
Web site: www.campnejeda.com
Operated by: Camp Nejeda Foundation Inc, 910 Saddleback Rd, Stillwater, NJ 07875 at (973) 383-2611

Group Rental Information
Facilities: Cabins, Hiking Trails, Lake, Playing Fields, Pool
Programs: Challenge/Ropes Course, Swimming (#2265)

Oak Crest Day Camp (est 1962) ☀ 🚗

Somerset, NJ (Somerset Co.); (732) 297-2000
Amy Schulman, Director

Camp comments: Oak Crest is more than a camp, it's an experience. 35 acres of beautiful facilities. Offers fun friendship & much more.
Activities: Arts/Crafts, Challenge/Rope Courses, Drama, Field Trips, Hockey, Photography, Soccer, Swimming — Instructional, Swimming — Recreational
Session lengths & capacity: June-August; 4, 5, 6, 7 & 8 week sessions; 600 campers
Clientele & fees: boys 3-15; girls 3-15; coed 3-5; Fees: C ☀
Contact: Amy Schulman or Jill Farkas, Camp Director/Office Administrator at (732) 297-2000; fax: (732) 821-5017
e-mail: oakcrestdaycamp@aol.com
Web site: www.oakcrestdaycamp.com
Operated by: Oak Crest Day Camp, 92 Cortelyou Ln, Somerset, NJ 08873 at (732) 297-2000 (#3317)

Oak Knoll School

Summit, NJ (Union Co.); (908) 522-8151
Ed Bell, Director

Camp comments: Day Camp for age 3-11. Sports, Performing Arts and Travel Camps for ages 8-14. Certified teachers and nurses, hot lunch, trips, carnivals, and family barbecues.
Session lengths & capacity: June-August; 2 week sessions; 450 campers
Clientele & fees: boys 3-17; girls 3-17; coed 3-17; Fees: C
Contact: Mary Sullivan, Administrative Assistant at (908) 522-8186;
e-mail: adventures@oakknoll.org
Web site: www.oakknoll.org
Operated by: Oak Knoll School, 44 Blackburn Rd, Summit, NJ 07901 at (908) 522-8151 (#9068)

Oak Spring Program EE Center

(est 1980)

Somerset, NJ (Somerset Co.); (732) 469-6061
Maryann Polefka, Director

Camp comments: Day camp on Delaware-Raritan Canal offers activities that provide progressive skill-building & Girl Scout program.
Activities: Aquatic Activities, Arts/Crafts, Camping Skills/Outdoor Living, Drawing/Painting, Hiking, Leadership Development, Nature/Environment Studies, Performing Arts, Photography
Session lengths & capacity: June-August; 1/2, 1 & 6 week sessions; 150 campers
Clientele & fees: girls 6-16; Fees: B
Contact: Vicky Allen, Program/Property Director at (732) 821-9090 ext. 125; fax: (732) 821-4211
Web site: www.gsofdr.org
Operated by: Delaware Raritan GSC, 108 Church Ln, East Brunswick, NJ 08816 at (732) 821-9090

Group Rental Information

Facilities: Hiking Trails, Tents
Programs: Boating, Environmental Education, Swimming (#2967)

Palisades Country Day Camp

(est 1994)

Closter, NJ (Bergen Co.); (201) 784-7600
Maryann Hubschman, Director

Camp comments: A unique and innovative state-of-the-art facility designed & built especially for the young child ages 3-6 years of age.
Activities: Basketball, Dance, Gymnastics, Nature/Environment Studies, Sports — Field & Team, Swimming — Instructional, Swimming — Recreational
Session lengths & capacity: June-August; 4 & 8 week sessions
Clientele & fees: coed 3-6; Fees: D, E
Contact: Pat Luttrell, Camp Director at (201) 784-7600; fax: (201) 784-1885
Operated by: Palisades Country Day Camp, 212 Herbert Ave, Closter, NJ 07624 at (201) 784-7600 (#178)

Pine Grove Day Camp

(est 1972)

Brick, NJ (Monmouth Co.); (732) 938-3760
Marty & Bernice Spielman, Director

Camp comments: Day camp as complete as sleep-away blending sports, science & the arts. Opt. progs incl a 2wk sleep-a-way & 2-1wk trips.
Activities: Aquatic Activities, Baseball/Softball, Basketball, Bicycling/Biking, Challenge/Rope Courses, Dance, Gymnastics, Hockey, Soccer, Tennis
Session lengths & capacity: July-August; 4, 6 & 8 week sessions; 600 campers
Clientele & fees: boys 4-15; girls 4-15; Fees: D
Contact: Marty or Bernice Spielman, Directors at (732) 938-3760; fax: (732) 938-2088
e-mail: spielmanb@aol.com

Web site: www.pinegrovedaycamp.com
Operated by: Mar Bern Associates Inc, 4010 Herbertsville Rd, Brick, NJ 08724 at (732) 938-3760 (#7072)

Pioneer Trails Day Camp

(est 1939)

Caldwell, NJ (Essex Co.); (973) 228-6300
Robert M Lampf, Director

Camp comments: An 'old-fashioned' day camp experience. Nondenominational with beautiful air conditioned indoor facilities great staff & program.
Activities: Aquatic Activities, Arts/Crafts, Baseball/Softball, Basketball, Ceramics/Pottery, Drama, Football, Soccer, Sports — Field & Team, Tennis
Session lengths & capacity: June-August; 3, 4 & 7 week sessions; 175 campers
Clientele & fees: coed 4-12; Fees: C
Contact: Robert M Lampf, Camp Director at (973) 994-7160; fax: (973) 994-7160
Web site: www.metroymcas.org
Operated by: Metro YMCA of The Oranges, 139 E McClellan Ave, Livingston, NJ 07039 at (973) 758-9622 (#3053)

Rambling Pines Day Camp

(est 1975)

Hopewell, NJ (Hunterdon Co.); (609) 466-1212

Camp comments: Fun summers since '76
Activities: Archery, Arts/Crafts, Boating, Computer, Dance, Drama, Golf, Performing Arts, Swimming — Instructional, Tennis
Session lengths & capacity: 4, 6 & 8 week sessions; 400 campers
Clientele & fees: coed 3-13; Fees: D
Contact: Robert Jordan, Director at (609) 466-1212; fax: (609) 466-1196
Web site: www.ramblingpines.com
Operated by: Rambling Pines Day Camp, Box 3, Hopewell, NJ 08525 at (609) 466-1212 (#3570)

Ranney In The Summer

(est 1980)

Tinton Falls, NJ (Monmouth Co.); (732) 542-4777
Tom Moriau, Director
Activities: Aquatic Activities, Arts/Crafts, Computer, Drama, Music, Nature/Environment Studies, Sports — Field & Team
Clientele & fees: Fees: C
Operated by: Ranney In The Summer, 119 Lillie Road, Toms River, NJ 08753 at (732) 270-6891 (#1152)

Rolling Hills Country Day Camp

(est 1986)

Freehold, NJ (Monmouth Co.); (732) 308-0405

Camp comments: Day camp; each child is made to feel good about themselves. Emphasis on swimming & athletics, fun runs through prog
Activities: Arts/Crafts, Baseball/Softball, Basketball, Challenge/Rope Courses, Climbing/Rappelling, Hockey, Horseback — English, Soccer, Sports — Field & Team, Swimming — Instructional
Session lengths & capacity: June-August; 4, 6 & 8 week sessions
Clientele & fees: boys 3-14; girls 3-14; coed 3-14; Fees: D
Contact: Bill & Stan Breitner, Owner Director at (732) 308-0405; fax: (732) 780-4726
e-mail: rollinghillscamp@aol.com
Web site: www.rollinghillsdaycamp.com
Operated by: Rolling Hills Country Day Camp, Dittmar Rd PO Box 6623, Freehold, NJ 07728-6623 at (732) 308-0405 (#3226)

Sacajawea (est 1950)

Newfield, NJ (Gloucester Co.); (856) 697-2323
Catherine Boyce, Director

Camp comments: This all girls camp is located in southern NJ. Enjoy arts & crafts, archery, swimming in our pool, canoeing on our lake, & our nature trails & exercise course.
Activities: Archery, Boating, Camping Skills/Outdoor Living, Canoeing, Counselor Training (CIT), Hiking, Leadership Development, Nature/Environment Studies, Sports — Field & Team, Swimming — Recreational
Session lengths & capacity: July-August; 1 week sessions; 144 campers
Clientele & fees: girls 6-17; families; Fees: B Fees: C
Contact: Dawn Durkee, Outdoor Program Manager/Camp Admin. at (856) 697-3900; fax: (856) 697-3900
e-mail: camping@gssjp.org
Web site: www.gssjp.org
Operated by: South Jersey Pines GSC, 2944 Victoria Ave, Newfield, NJ 08344 at (856) 697-3900

Group Rental Information

Site comments: Where girls grow strong.
Facilities: Cabins, Hiking Trails, Kitchen Facilities, Lake, Lodges, Meeting Rooms, Playing Fields, Pool, Tents
Programs: Boating (#2330)

Sacajawea Camp (est 1960)

Farmingdale, NJ (Monmouth Co.); (732) 938-7724
Jane Smetts, Director

Camp comments: Sacajawea provides girls with opportunities to grow, make new friends, and participate in fun and exciting activities.
Activities: Aquatic Activities, Canoeing, Challenge/Rope Courses, Field Trips, Horseback — English, Swimming — Recreational
Session lengths & capacity: June-August; 1 & 2 week sessions; 200 campers
Clientele & fees: girls 6-16; Fees: B
Contact: Patricia J Kurz, Director at (732) 938-5454 ext. 25; fax: (732) 938-7463
e-mail: pkurz@mcgirlscouts.org
Web site: www.mcgirlscouts.org
Operated by: Monmouth GSC, 242 Adelphia Road, Farmingdale, NJ 07727-3525 at (732) 938-5454

Group Rental Information

Facilities: Hiking Trails, Lake, Lodges, Pool, Tents
Programs: Boating, Challenge/Ropes Course, Swimming (#11)

SOMapY Day Camp

(est 1971)

Maplewood, NJ (Essex Co.)
David Berry, Director

Camp comments: Trad Day Camp; variety of activities, fun safe environment. Features choice & group time, day trips/events, mini sports clinics.
Activities: Arts/Crafts, Baseball/Softball, Basketball, Field Trips, Hockey, Soccer, Sports — Field & Team, Swimming — Instructional, Swimming — Recreational, Tennis
Session lengths & capacity: June-August; 1 & 3 week sessions; 132 campers
Clientele & fees: coed 5-13; Fees: B, C
Contact: David Berry, Camp Director at (973) 762-4145; fax: (973) 762-2064
e-mail: dberry@metroymcas.org
Web site: www.metroymcas.org
Operated by: Metro YMCA of The Oranges, 139 E McClellan Ave, Livingston, NJ 07039 at (973) 758-9622 (#2058)

Spring Lake Day Camp

(est 1989)

Ringwood, NJ; (097) 383-1900

Camp comments: Spring Lake Day Camp offers a well-rounded program including sports, arts and performing arts for campers' ages 3-15.
Activities: Arts/Crafts, Challenge/Rope Courses, Climbing/Rappelling, Fishing, Gymnastics, Martial Arts, Soccer, Sports — Field & Team, Swimming — Instructional, Tennis
Session lengths & capacity: July-August; 4, 6, 7 & 8 week sessions; 500 campers
Clientele & fees: coed 3-15; Fees: D ☀
Contact: Mitchell Kessler, Director at (973) 831-9000; fax: (973) 831-9174
e-mail: info@springlakedaycamp.com
Web site: www.springlakedaycamp.com
Operated by: Spring Lake Day Camp, Conklintown Rd, PO Box 176, Ringwood, NJ 07456 at (973) 831-9000 (#6679)

Stonybrook Day Camp

(est 1940)

Randolph, NJ (Morris Co.); (973) 584-0078
Stephen & JoAnn Pine, Director

Camp comments: Our goal is to create a happy place for our campers and we succeed! Outstanding staff gorgeous campus.
Activities: Archery, Arts/Crafts, Boating, Challenge/Rope Courses, Golf, Nature/Environment Studies, Performing Arts, Sports — Field & Team, Swimming — Instructional, Tennis
Session lengths & capacity: 4, 6 & 8 week sessions; 500 campers
Clientele & fees: coed 3-14
Contact: JoAnn Pine, Director at (973) 994-3897; fax: (973) 922-3584
Web site: www.stonybrookdaycamp.com
Operated by: Stonybrook Day Camp, 9 Bennington Road, Livingston, NJ 07039 at (973) 994-3897 (#18482)

Super Summer Day Camp

(est 1981)

Livingston, NJ (Essex Co.); (973) 533-9731
Bonnie L Narciso, Director

Camp comments: A day camp that offers a variety of educational and fun activities. A safe and caring environment
Activities: Archery, Arts/Crafts, Computer, Counselor Training (CIT), Dance, Field Trips, Nature/Environment Studies, Sports — Field & Team, Swimming — Instructional, Swimming — Recreational

ICON LEGEND

☀ Day Camp
▲ Resident Camp
🏠 Facilities Available To Rent
🚐 Transportation Available
🖐 Financial Aid Available

FEE RANGES PER WEEK

A	$0-75
B	$75-200
C	$201-350
D	$351-500
E	$501-650
F	over $650

Session lengths & capacity: June-August; 1 week sessions; 150 campers
Clientele & fees: coed 5-13; Fees: C ☀ 🚐
Contact: Bonnie L Narciso, Director at (973) 992-7500; fax: (973) 992-7680
Web site: www.metroymcas.org
Operated by: Metro YMCA of The Oranges, 139 E McClellan Ave, Livingston, NJ 07039 at (973) 758-9622 (#26877)

Tall Pines Day Camp Inc

(est 1996)

Williamstown, NJ (Gloucester Co.); (856) 262-3900
Andrew Yankowitz, AICP, Director

Camp comments: We capture the magic of summer & create opportunities to build memories that last a lifetime.
Activities: Archery, Arts/Crafts, Challenge/Rope Courses, Computer, Counselor Training (CIT), Golf, Horseback — Western, Kayaking, Model Rocketry, Sports — Field & Team
Session lengths & capacity: June-August; 4, 6 & 8 week sessions; 500 campers
Clientele & fees: coed 3-14; Fees: D ☀
Contact: Andrew Yankowitz, Director at (856) 262-3900; fax: (856) 262-0195
e-mail: tpinesdaycamp@aol.com
Web site: www.tallpinesdaycamp.com
Operated by: Tall Pines Day Camp Inc, 1349 Sykesville Rd, Williamstown, NJ 08094 at (856) 262-3900 (#3259)

The Youth Center Day Camp ☀

Glen Gardner, NJ; (908) 537-4594
Colleen Rountree, Director

Camp comments: Small & personal, we know our campers.Arts & crafts,nature,games,swimming,field trips & talent shows.Creativity & indiv. growth is highly emphasized in camp.
Activities: Aquatic Activities, Counselor Training (CIT), Dance, Drama, Field Trips, Fishing, Nature/Environment Studies, Performing Arts, Swimming — Instructional, Swimming — Recreational
Session lengths & capacity: June-August; 1, 2, 3, 4, 5, 6, 7, 8 & 9 week sessions; 80 campers
Clientele & fees: coed 4-12; Fees: B ☀ 🖐
Contact: Colleen Rountree, Director at (908) 537-4594; fax: (908) 537-6549
e-mail: theyouth@earthlink.net
Operated by: The Youth Center, PO Box 92, Glen Gardner, NJ 08826 at (908) 537-4594 (#30380)

Trail Blazers (est 1887) ▲ 🚐

Montague, NJ (Sussex Co.); (973) 875-4116
Dennis Kramer-Wine; Lindsay Slabich, Director

Camp comments: Disadvantaged youngsters referred by social service agencies and schools. Are taught social skills and are provided with academic enrichment.
Activities: Arts/Crafts, Backpacking, Camping Skills/Outdoor Living, Farming/Ranching/Gardening, Hiking, Leadership Development, Nature/Environment Studies, Swimming — Recreational, Team Building, Wilderness Trips
Session lengths & capacity: 3 week sessions; 125 campers
Clientele & fees: boys 9-17; girls 8-17; 🖐
Contact: Sharon Griffin, Agency Coordinator at (212) 529-5113; fax: (212) 529-2704
e-mail: tbcny@aol.com
Web site: www.trailblazers.org
Operated by: Trail Blazers, 45 E 20th St Fl 9, New York, NY 10003-1308 at (212) 529-5113 (#2181)

Vacamas Programs for Youth

(est 1924) ▲ 🏠 🚐

West Milford, NJ (Passaic Co.); (973) 838-1394
Sandra I Friedman, Director

Camp comments: Overnight capacity 140. Day trips, 300 ropes course, food service customized service to meet your conference needs, environmental programs for youth at risk.
Activities: Aquatic Activities, Arts/Crafts, Farming/Ranching/Gardening, Nature/Environment Studies, Photography, Sports — Field & Team
Session lengths & capacity: 3 & 6 week sessions
Clientele & fees: boys 7-16; girls 7-16; coed 7-16; Fees: B, C, D ▲ 🖐
Contact: Sandra I Friedman, Director of Camping Operations at (973) 838-1394 ext. 1412; fax: (973) 838-7534
e-mail: sandi@vacamas.org
Web site: www.vacamas.org
Operated by: Camp Vacamas Assn Inc, 256 Macopin Rd, West Milford, NJ 07480-9971 at (973) 838-1394

Group Rental Information

Seasons & Capacity: Spring 250, Fall 250, Winter 175
Facilities: Cabins, Dorm-Style, Food Service, Hiking Trails, Kitchen Facilities, Lake, Linens, Meeting Rooms, Tents
Programs: Boating, Challenge/Ropes Course, Swimming, Winter Sports (#1945)

Watershed (est 1973) ☀ 🚐

West Milford, NJ (Passaic Co.); (973) 697-9018
Valerie James CCD, Director

Camp comments: On pristine Pequannock watershed providing Newark residents only comprehensive, exciting, activities, peer-comradery.
Activities: Archery, Arts/Crafts, Camping Skills/Outdoor Living, Canoeing, Challenge/Rope Courses, Computer, Hiking, Sports — Field & Team, Swimming — Recreational
Session lengths & capacity: July-August; 8 week sessions; 250 campers
Clientele & fees: coed 7-20
Contact: Valerie James CCD, Camp Director at (973) 733-3940; fax: (973) 424-4030
Operated by: City of Newark, Dept of Neighborhood & Rec, 94 William St 2nd Fl, Newark, NJ 07102-2677 at (973) 733-3940 (#5089)

Willow Lake Day Camp ☀ 🚐

(est 1975)

Lake Hopatcong, NJ (Morris Co.); (973) 663-2732
Wendy Saiff, Director

Camp comments: Mature staff encourages cooperation & building of confidence and self esteem. Beautiful mountain/lake setting. Age 3-15.
Activities: Arts/Crafts, Baseball/Softball, Basketball, Boating, Ceramics/Pottery, Challenge/Rope Courses, Drama, Sports — Field & Team, Swimming — Instructional, Tennis
Session lengths & capacity: 4, 6 & 8 week sessions; 700 campers
Clientele & fees: coed 3-15; Fees: D ☀
Contact: Wendy Saiff, Owner/Director at (732) 846-3811; fax: (732) 545-1704
Web site: w.willowlakedaycamp.com
Operated by: Willow Lake Day Camp, PO Box 1266, Highland Park, NJ 08904 at (732) 846-3811 (#5566)

Winnewald Day Camp ☀ 🚐

(est 1951)

Lebanon, NJ (Hunterdon Co.); (908) 735-8336
Bob Jones, Director

Camp comments: A natural setting with heated pools, playfields & tennis court. Program for 4-12. Transportation & extended hours. Caring mature staff, owner operated 51st year

Activities: Archery, Arts/Crafts, Challenge/Rope Courses, Computer, Field Trips, Fishing, Leadership Development, Nature/Environment Studies, Sports — Field & Team, Swimming — Instructional
Session lengths & capacity: June-August; 2, 4, 6 & 8 week sessions; 225 campers
Clientele & fees: boys 4-12; girls 4-12; coed 4-12; Fees: C ☀
Contact: Bob Jones, Owner/Director at (908) 735-8336; fax: (908) 730-7196
e-mail: winneday@ptd.net
Web site: www.winnewald.com
Operated by: Winnewald Day Camp, 21 Cratetown Rd, Lebanon, NJ 08833-9605 at (908) 735-8336 (#2279)

Y Knots Day Camp (est 1981) ☀

Maplewood, NJ (Essex Co.); (973) 762-4145
Dave Berry, Director

Camp comments: Trained & caring staff provide variety of safe, fun, educational activities for this preschool camp to grade 2 camp.
Activities: Aquatic Activities, Arts/Crafts, Drawing/Painting, Field Trips, Music, Nature/Environment Studies, Soccer, Swimming — Instructional, Swimming — Recreational
Session lengths & capacity: June-August; 1 & 3 week sessions; 72 campers
Clientele & fees: coed 3-7; Fees: B ☀ 🐷
Contact: David Berry, Camp Director at (973) 762-4145; fax: (973) 762-2064
e-mail: dberry@metroymcas.org
Web site: www.metroymcas.org
Operated by: Metro YMCA of The Oranges, 139 E McClellan Ave, Livingston, NJ 07039 at (973) 758-9622 (#2069)

YMCA Camp Bernie (est 1957) ▲ 🏠

Port Murray, NJ; (908) 832-5315
David Parfitt, Director

Camp comments: Self-esteem specialty. Campers thrive in noncompetitive, caring atmosphere w/opportunities to belong, learn, contribute.
Activities: Archery, Arts/Crafts, Bicycling/Biking, Camping Skills/Outdoor Living, Climbing/Rappelling, Counselor Training (CIT), Horseback — Western, Sports — Field & Team, Swimming — Instructional, Travel/Tour
Session lengths & capacity: June-August; 2 & 4 week sessions; 200 campers
Clientele & fees: coed 7-15; Fees: D ▲ 🐷
Contact: David Parfitt, Executive Director at (908) 832-5315; fax: (908) 832-9078
e-mail: campbernie@campbernieymca.org
Web site: www.campbernieymca.org
Operated by: Ridgewood YMCA, 112 Oak St, Ridgewood, NJ 07450 at (201) 444-5600

Group Rental Information
Facilities: Cabins, Dorm-Style, Food Service, Hiking Trails, Lodges, Meeting Rooms, Playing Fields, Pool
Programs: Boating, Challenge/Ropes Course, Environmental Education, Horseback Riding, Swimming (#2302)

YMCA Camp Ken-Etiwa-Pec

(est 1996) 🏠

Hardwick, NJ; (908) 362-8217
Marcus Forester, Director
Contact: Marcus Forester at (908) 362-8217; fax: (908) 362-5767
e-mail: information@campmason.org
Web site: www.campmason.org
Operated by: YMCA Camp Ralph S Mason Inc, 23 Birch Ridge Road, Hardwick, NJ 07825 at (908) 362-8217

Group Rental Information
Site comments: School,group&organizational camping with basic or full services. Located in Delaware Water Gap National Recreation Area.

Seasons & Capacity: Spring 100, Summer 130, Fall 100
Facilities: Cabins, Food Service, Hiking Trails, Kitchen Facilities, Lake, Lodges, Meeting Rooms, Ocean, Playing Fields
Programs: Boating, Challenge/Ropes Course, Environmental Education, Swimming (#10526)

YMCA Camp Ralph S Mason

(est 1900) ▲ 🏠

Hardwick, NJ (Warren Co.); (908) 362-8217
Jerry Waldron, Director

Camp comments: Traditional program since 1900. We specialize in first timers. Modern 600 acre campus.
Activities: Aquatic Activities, Archery, Bicycling/Biking, Camping Skills/Outdoor Living, Horseback — Western, Nature/Environment Studies, Riflery, Sports — Field & Team, Swimming — Instructional, Wilderness Trips
Session lengths & capacity: 2 & 4 week sessions; 250 campers
Clientele & fees: coed 7-16; Fees: B ☀ Fees: D ▲
Contact: Jerry Waldron, Camp Director at (908) 362-8217; fax: (908) 362-5767
e-mail: information@campmason.org
Web site: www.campmason.org
Operated by: YMCA Camp Ralph S Mason Inc, 23 Birch Ridge Road, Hardwick, NJ 07825 at (908) 362-8217

Group Rental Information
Seasons & Capacity: Spring 400, Fall 400, Winter 280
Facilities: A/V Equipment, Cabins, Dorm-Style, Food Service, Hiking Trails, Lake, Meeting Rooms, Playing Fields, Pool
Programs: Boating, Challenge/Ropes Course, Environmental Education, Swimming (#7163)

YMCA Camp Worth (est 1953) ☀ 🚐

Tabernacle, NJ (Burlington Co.); (856) 234-6200
Flo Crowley, Director

Camp comments: We provide a trad. day camp which encourages and recognizes the values of honesty, caring, respect, & responsibility.
Activities: Aquatic Activities, Archery, Arts/Crafts, Camping Skills/Outdoor Living, Canoeing, Drama, Nature/Environment Studies, Sports — Field & Team, Swimming — Instructional, Swimming — Recreational
Session lengths & capacity: June-August; 1 week sessions; 115 campers
Clientele & fees: coed 6-12; Fees: B ☀ 🐷 🐷
Contact: Flo Crowley, Camp Director at (856) 234-6200; fax: (856) 234-6560
Operated by: Family 'Y' Burlington County, 5001 Centerton Rd, Mt Laurel, NJ 08054 at (856) 234-6200 (#2300)

Young Peop Day Camp-Ocean Cty ☀ 🚐

Jackson, NJ; (732) 938-6928
Larry Marantz, Director

Camp comments: Traditional camp combines swimming, sports, karate, arts & crafts, & music with daily trips and special events. Adult counselors and free transportation.
Activities: Arts/Crafts, Dance, Field Trips, Football, Music, Soccer, Sports — Field & Team, Swimming — Recreational
Session lengths & capacity: June-August; 2, 3, 4, 5, 6, 7 & 8 week sessions; 250 campers
Clientele & fees: coed 4-14; Fees: A ☀
Contact: Larry Marantz, Director at (732) 972-7400; fax: (732) 761-9323
e-mail: larryscamp@aol.com
Web site: www.ypdc.com
Operated by: YPDC of Middlesex Co, 20 Highland Ct, Freehold, NJ 07728 at (732) 761-1970 (#42464)

YPDC of Momouth County

(est 1996) ☀ 🚐

Old Bridge, NJ (Middlesex Co.); (732) 972-7400
Larry Marantz, Director

Camp comments: Traditional camp combines sports, swimming, karate, music with daily special events and trips, free transportation.
Activities: Aquatic Activities, Arts/Crafts, Basketball, Dance, Field Trips, Gymnastics, Martial Arts, Swimming — Recreational
Session lengths & capacity: June-August; 2, 3, 4, 5, 6, 7 & 8 week sessions; 200 campers
Clientele & fees: coed 4-15; Fees: A, B ☀
Contact: Larry Marantz, Director at (732) 972-7400; fax: (732) 761-9323
Web site: www.ypdc.com
Operated by: YPDC of Middlesex Co, 20 Highland Ct, Freehold, NJ 07728 at (732) 761-1970 (#27250)

New Mexico

Brush Ranch Camps (est 1956) ▲ 🏠

Tererro, NM (San Miquel Co.); (800) 722-2843
Kay & Scott Rice, Director

Camp comments: Join us for summer fun in mtns. Learn fly fishing, dance, riding & more! Beautiful setting, top facility, super staff.
Activities: Archery, Ceramics/Pottery, Challenge/Rope Courses, Dance, Drama, Fencing, Fishing, Horseback — English, Horseback — Western, Rafting
Session lengths & capacity: June-August; 1, 2 & 4 week sessions; 150 campers
Clientele & fees: boys 6-16; girls 6-16; coed 6-16; families; Fees: F ▲
Contact: Kay or Scott Rice, Co-Directors at (800) 722-2843; fax: (505) 757-8822
e-mail: info@brushranchcamps.com
Web site: www.brushranchcamps.com
Operated by: Brush Ranch Camps for Girls, PO Box 5759, Santa Fe, NM 87502-5759 at (505) 757-8821

Group Rental Information
Facilities: Cabins, Double Occupancy, Kitchen Facilities, Linens, Meeting Rooms, Playing Fields, Pool, Tents
Programs: Challenge/Ropes Course, Swimming (#523)

Camp Challenge ▲

Santa Fe, NM; (505) 983-5610
Helen Pino, Director

Camp comments: Camp Challenge, the only camp in New Mexico for children with diabetes, sponsored by the New Mexico Area American Diabetes Association.
Activities: Aquatic Activities, Archery, Arts/Crafts, Baseball/Softball, Challenge/Rope Courses, Hiking, Sports — Field & Team, Swimming — Recreational, Team Building
Session lengths & capacity: 1 week sessions; 65 campers
Clientele & fees: coed 8-13; Fees: D ▲ 🐷
Contact: Christine Rocha, District Manager at (505) 266-5716 ext. 7132; fax: (505) 268-4533
e-mail: crocha@diabetes.org
Operated by: American Diabetes Assn NM Area, 525 San Pedro NE Ste 101, Albuquerque, NM 87108 at (505) 266-5716 (#5478)

Camp Elliott Barker

(est 1963) ☀ ▲ 🏠

Eagle Nest, NM (Colfax Co.); (505) 377-6129

Camp comments: Stunning mountain setting. Excellent outdoor Girl Scout program building self-esteem in an all-girl environment.

Activities: Archery, Arts/Crafts, Backpacking, Bicycling/Biking, Camping Skills/Outdoor Living, Challenge/Rope Courses, Counselor Training (CIT), Hiking, Horseback — Western, Leadership Development
Session lengths & capacity: June-August; 1/2, 1 & 2 week sessions; 90 campers
Clientele & fees: girls 7-17; families; Fees: **A** ☀ Fees: **B** ▲
Contact: Lauren Rubinson, Program Director at (505) 983-6339; fax: (505) 983-6671
e-mail: sdcgsc@earthlink.net
Operated by: GS Sangre De Cristo Council, 450 St Michaels Dr, Santa Fe, NM 87505 at (505) 983-6339

Group Rental Information
Site comments: Stunning site near Angel Fire Ski area & Eagle Nest Lake.
Seasons & Capacity: Summer 90, Fall 90
Facilities: Cabins, Tents
Programs: Horseback Riding (#472)

Camp Enchantment   ▲ 🚐
Alamogordo, NM; (505) 437-3505
Adrian Guerrero, Director

Camp comments: Week long overnight camp for children who have ever had cancer.Free camp&supported by donations&the American Cancer Soc
Activities: Aquatic Activities, Arts/Crafts, Counselor Training (CIT), Dance, Field Trips, Music, Team Building
Session lengths & capacity: June-June; 1 week sessions; 80 campers
Clientele & fees: coed 7-18; Fees: **A** ▲
Contact: Rossi Burns, Manager, Childhood Cancer Support Prog at (505) 260-2105; fax: (505) 266-9513
e-mail: rburns@cancer.org
Web site: www.campenchantment.org
Operated by: American Cancer Society, 5800 Lomas Blvd NE, Albuquerque, NM 87110 at (505) 260-2105 (#30214)

Camp Stoney   ▲ 🏠
Santa Fe, NM (Santa Fe Co.); (505) 983-5610
Heather Gaunie, Director
Activities: Archery, Backpacking, Camping Skills/Outdoor Living, Challenge/Rope Courses, Counselor Training (CIT), Dance, Drama, Hiking, Religious Study, Sports — Field & Team
Contact: Heather Gaunie, Camp Director at (505) 983-5610; fax: (505) 983-9150
e-mail: campstoney@aol.com
Operated by: Camp Stoney, 7855 Old Santa Fe Trail, Santa Fe, NM 87505 at (505) 983-5610

ICON LEGEND
☀ Day Camp
▲ Resident Camp
🏠 Facilities Available To Rent
🚐 Transportation Available
💰 Financial Aid Available

FEE RANGES PER WEEK
A $0-75
B $75-200
C $201-350
D $351-500
E $501-650
F over $650

Group Rental Information
Facilities: Dorm-Style, Food Service, Hiking Trails, Lodges, Meeting Rooms (#39944)

Easter Seal Camp (est 1984)   ▲
Vanderwagen, NM (McKinley Co.); (505) 778-5234
Jane Carr, Director

Camp comments: Easter Seal campers with disabilities achieve equality, dignity and independence.
Activities: Aquatic Activities, Arts/Crafts, Basketball, Camping Skills/Outdoor Living, Dance, Field Trips, Fishing, Nature/Environment Studies, Swimming — Recreational, Team Building
Session lengths & capacity: July-August; 1 & 5 week sessions; 60 campers
Clientele & fees: boys 6-99; girls 6-99; coed 6-99; Fees: **D** ▲
Contact: Marlis Hadley, President at (800) 279-5261; fax: (505) 888-0490
e-mail: essnm@tarrnet.com
Operated by: Easter Seal Society New Mexico, 430 W Grant Street, Healdsburg, CA 95448 at (707) 433-3530 (#4982)

Fort Lone Tree (est 1991)   ▲ 🏠
Capitan, NM (lincoln Co.); (505) 354-4265
Tim Worrell, Director

Camp comments: A replica Fort Stockade, Fort Lone Tree offers horses, archery, rifles, rockwall, etc. in a safe christian setting. 1 to 4 leader to camper ratio.
Activities: Archery, Arts/Crafts, Camping Skills/Outdoor Living, Climbing/Rappelling, Counselor Training (CIT), Horseback — Western, Leadership Development, Nature/Environment Studies, Religious Study, Riflery
Session lengths & capacity: May-October; 1 week sessions; 100 campers
Clientele & fees: coed 8-12; families; Fees: **C** ▲
Contact: Ed Kaczmarek, Camp Director at (505) 354-4265; fax: (505) 354-5301
e-mail: nmfort@lonetree.org
Web site: www.lonetree.org
Operated by: Lone Tree Inc, PO Box 713, Capitan, NM 83316 at (505) 354-3322

Group Rental Information
Facilities: A/V Equipment, Cabins, Hiking Trails, Lodges
Programs: Challenge/Ropes Course, Environmental Education, Horseback Riding (#3089)

Lone Tree Lakeshore Camp   ▲
(est 1990)
Elephant Butte, NM (Sierra Co.); (505) 744-9164
Aaron Hansen, Director

Camp comments: Adventure camp specializing in water fun: tube the Rio Grande, ride the SeaWasp. Christ-centered program and staff.
Activities: Aquatic Activities, Boating, Counselor Training (CIT), Hiking, Nature/Environment Studies, Religious Study, Swimming — Recreational, Waterskiing
Session lengths & capacity: June-October; 1 week sessions; 50 campers
Clientele & fees: coed 13-18; families; Fees: **E** ▲
Contact: Carrie Koch, Camp Director at (505) 744-9164; fax: (505) 744-9164
Web site: www.lonetree.org
Operated by: Lone Tree Inc, PO Box 713, Capitan, NM 83316 at (505) 354-3322 (#18393)

Lone Tree Ranch (est 1982)   ▲
Capitan, NM (Lincoln Co.); (505) 354-2523
Steve Dirks, Director

Camp comments: Year rnd Christian based high adventure. Horses, western setting. High rope course, team building, goal setting emphasis

Activities: Backpacking, Basketball, Bicycling/Biking, Challenge/Rope Courses, Climbing/Rappelling, Counselor Training (CIT), Hiking, Horseback — Western, Nature/Environment Studies, Riflery
Session lengths & capacity: 1 week sessions; 120 campers
Clientele & fees: coed 13-18; families; single adults; Fees: **C** ▲
Contact: Steve Dirks, Director at (505) 354-2523; fax: (505) 354-2961
Web site: www.lonetree.org
Operated by: Lone Tree Inc, PO Box 713, Capitan, NM 83316 at (505) 354-3322 (#890)

Manzano Mountain Retreat   🏠
(est 1991)
Torreon, NM; (505) 384-4467
Kim Simmons, Director
Contact: Kim Simmons, Camp Director at (505) 384-4467; fax: (505) 384-0472
e-mail: kimsim@qwest.net
Web site: www.manzanomountain.com
Operated by: Manzano Mountain Retreat, 7120 Wyoming Blvd NE Ste 5, Albuquerque, NM 87109 at (505) 858-1533

Group Rental Information
Site comments: Group Rentals, food service, challenge course, team building, soccer, basketball, softball, volleyball, pool, hiking, 100 acres bordering national forest.
Seasons & Capacity: Spring 200, Summer 200, Fall 200, Winter 100
Facilities: Dorm-Style, Food Service, Hiking Trails, Lodges, Meeting Rooms, Playing Fields, Pool
Programs: Challenge/Ropes Course, Swimming (#37617)

Philmont Scout Ranch BSA   ▲ 🏠 🚐
(est 1938)
Cimarron, NM (Colfax Co.); (505) 376-2281
Mark Anderson, Director

Camp comments: High adventure program of the Boy Scouts of America. Builds character, citizenship, physical, mental & emotional fitness
Activities: Archery, Backpacking, Bicycling/Biking, Camping Skills/Outdoor Living, Challenge/Rope Courses, Climbing/Rappelling, Hiking, Horseback — Western, Leadership Development, Wilderness Trips
Session lengths & capacity: June-August; 2 week sessions; 350 campers
Clientele & fees: boys 14-20; girls 14-20; coed 14-20; Fees: **B** ▲ 💰
Contact: Mark Anderson, Director of Program at (505) 376-2281; fax: (505) 376-2636
Web site: www.scouting.org/philmont
Operated by: National Council BSA, Philmont Scout Ranch, Cimarron, NM 87714 at (505) 376-2281

Group Rental Information
Site comments: Conference facilities in fall and spring. BSA camping yr-rd.
Facilities: Cabins, Dorm-Style, Double Occupancy, Food Service, Hiking Trails, Lake, Lodges, Meeting Rooms, River, Tents
Programs: Environmental Education, Horseback Riding (#461)

Rancho Del Chaparral   ▲ 🏠 🚐
(est 1969)
Cuba, NM; (505) 289-3720

Camp comments: Horses, canoes, arts, friends, hiking. Great summers in the Rockies. Girl Scout camp for all girls, including non Scouts
Activities: Archery, Arts/Crafts, Backpacking, Camping Skills/Outdoor Living, Ceramics/Pottery, Hiking, Horseback — Western, Leadership Development, Nature/Environment Studies

Session lengths & capacity: June-August; 1/2, 1 & 2 week sessions; 225 campers
Clientele & fees: girls 6-17; families;
Fees: **A, B, C** △
Contact: Sheryl-Lynn Wilkeson, Camp Administrator at (505) 343-1040 ext. 3201; fax: (505) 343-1050
e-mail: swilkeson@chaparralgirlscouts.org
Web site: www.ranchogs.org
Operated by: Chaparral GSC Inc, 4000 Jefferson Plaza NE, Albuquerque, NM 87109-3404 at (505) 343-1050
Group Rental Information
Facilities: Cabins, Hiking Trails, Kitchen Facilities, Meeting Rooms, River, Tents (#485)

Starfire Day Camp Inc

(est 1982)

Tijeras, NM (Bernalillo Co.); (505) 281-9577
Eric Sallach, Director

Camp comments: Adventure and challenge! Quality instruction! Small groups! Beautiful mountains!Home pick-up included! Fun! Fun! Fun!
Activities: Archery, Arts/Crafts, Bicycling/Biking, Camping Skills/Outdoor Living, Climbing/Rappelling, Counselor Training (CIT), Horseback — Western, Nature/Environment Studies, Riflery, Swimming — Recreational
Session lengths & capacity: June-August; 1 & 3 week sessions; 225 campers
Clientele & fees: coed 5-13; Fees: **C** ☀
Contact: Eric Sallach, Director at (505) 281-9577; e-mail: esallach@flash.net
Web site: www.starfiredaycamp.com
Operated by: Starfire Day Camp Inc, 4612 Overland Dr NE, Albuquerque, NM 87109 at (505) 837-1263
Group Rental Information
Seasons & Capacity: Spring 30
Facilities: Hiking Trails, Playing Fields, Pool, Tents
Programs: Challenge/Ropes Course, Environmental Education (#4245)

New York

4H Camp Bristol Hills

(est 1931)

Canandaigua, NY (Ontario Co.); (716) 394-7838
Mary Gleason, Director

Camp comments: Located in the beautiful Bristol Hills region of the Finger Lakes/coed camp for youth and adults ages 5 & up. 70 season.
Activities: Arts/Crafts, Backpacking, Challenge/Rope Courses, Counselor Training (CIT), Fishing, Horseback — Western, Model Rocketry, Nature/Environment Studies, Sports — Field & Team, Swimming — Recreational
Session lengths & capacity: July-August; 1/2 & 1 week sessions; 150 campers
Clientele & fees: coed 5-16; Fees: **B** ☀ Fees: **B** △
Contact: Carol Young, Secretary at (716) 394-3977 ext. 11; fax: (716) 394-0377
e-mail: cmy4@cornell.edu
Operated by: Cornell Coop Ext Ontario Co, 480 N Main Street, 4H Camp Bristol Hills, Canandaigua, NY 14424-1049 at (716) 394-3977
Group Rental Information
Site comments: 65th season serving youths and adults
Seasons & Capacity: Spring 159, Summer 150, Fall 150
Facilities: Cabins, Food Service, Kitchen Facilities, Lodges, Meeting Rooms, Playing Fields
Programs: Challenge/Ropes Course (#1864)

92nd St Y Camps (est 1878)

New York, NY (New York Co.); (212) 415-5600
Alan Saltz, Director

Camp comments: For children of all ages, interest & needs. Rustic Rockland Co setting, 20 min from G.W.Bridge. Convenient pickups. Diverse program.
Activities: Archery, Ceramics/Pottery, Climbing/Rappelling, Horseback — Western, Martial Arts, Nature/Environment Studies, Sports — Field & Team, Swimming — Recreational, Tennis
Session lengths & capacity: June-August; 2, 4, 6 & 8 week sessions; 700 campers
Clientele & fees: coed 5-16; Fees: **E** ☀ 🐷
Contact: Steve Levin, Assistant Director of Camp Programs at (212) 415-5620; fax: (212) 415-5637
e-mail: slevin@92ndsty.org
Operated by: 92nd St Y Camps, 1395 Lexington Avenue, New York, NY 10128 at (212) 415-5600 (#2163)

A Long Lake Camp for the Arts

(est 1969)

Long Lake, NY (Hamilton Co.); (518) 624-4831
Marc & Susan Katz, Director

Camp comments: Rich full program culminating in performances. Campers choose from performing/fine arts while enjoying traditional fun.
Activities: Arts/Crafts, Dance, Drama, Horseback — English, Music, Performing Arts, Radio/TV/Video, Sailing, Swimming — Recreational, Waterskiing
Session lengths & capacity: 3, 6 & 9 week sessions; 160 campers
Clientele & fees: coed 7-16; Fees: **E** △
Contact: Marc & Susan Katz, Directors at (914) 693-7111; fax: (914) 693-7684
e-mail: marc@longlakecamp.com
Operated by: Long Lake Camp for the Arts, 33 Western Dr, Ardsley, NY 10502 at (800) 767-7111 (#7129)

AGBU Camp Nubar (est 1963)

Andes, NY; (914) 676-3101
Margarit Casaceli, Director

Camp comments: Catskill mountain setting with a spring-fed lake. Emphasizing Armenian ethnic and cultural studies
Activities: Aquatic Activities, Arts/Crafts, Basketball, Boating, Ceramics/Pottery, Computer, Horseback — Western, Photography, Swimming — Instructional, Waterskiing
Session lengths & capacity: June-August; 2, 4 & 6 week sessions; 125 campers
Clientele & fees: coed 8-15; Fees: **D** △
Contact: Margarit Casaceli, Director at (212) 319-6383; fax: (212) 486-6196
e-mail: director@campnubar.org
Web site: www.campnubar.org
Operated by: Armenian Gen Benevolent Union, 55 East 59th St 7th Fl, New York, NY 10022 at (212) 319-6383 (#3952)

Aldersgate Camp & Retreat Ctr

(est 1948)

Brantingham, NY (Lewis Co.); (315) 348-8833
Julie Lautt, Director

Camp comments: Christian growth in Jesus-centered community. Adirondack summer camp, year-roundretreat for families, teens, adults & children. A place where lives are changed.
Activities: Aquatic Activities, Backpacking, Bicycling/Biking, Canoeing, Dance, Music, Nature/Environment Studies, Religious Study, Swimming — Recreational, Wilderness Trips
Session lengths & capacity: 1/2, 1 & 2 week sessions; 200 campers
Clientele & fees: coed 5-18; families; Fees: **C** △ 🐷
Contact: Tammy Davidson, Office Administrator/Registrar at (315) 348-8833; fax: (315) 348-4279

e-mail: info@AldersgateNY.org
Web site: www.ncnyumc.org
Operated by: North Central NY Conf UMC, PO Box 1515, 8422 N Main, Cicero, NY 13039 at (800) 699-8715
Group Rental Information
Site comments: Be our guest year-round! Enjoy Christian hospitality in the Adirondacks of Upstate New York, featuring a bog, excellent snow cover & spectacular fall foliage.
Seasons & Capacity: Spring 125, Summer 225, Fall 200, Winter 100
Facilities: A/V Equipment, Cabins, Dorm-Style, Double Occupancy, Food Service, Hiking Trails, Lake, Lodges, Meeting Rooms, Playing Fields, Tents
Programs: Boating, Challenge/Ropes Course, Environmental Education, Swimming, Winter Sports (#5948)

Alvernia (est 1888)

Centerport, NY (Suffolk Co.); (631) 261-5730
Brother Robert La Fave, O.S.F., Director

Camp comments: Day camp located on Centerport Harbor in a country setting. Strong staff and strong program,Great waterfront. Est 1888
Activities: Arts/Crafts, Basketball, Canoeing, Kayaking, Nature/Environment Studies, Performing Arts, Sailing, Soccer, Sports — Field & Team, Swimming — Recreational
Session lengths & capacity: June-August; 2, 4, 6 & 8 week sessions; 500 campers
Clientele & fees: boys 4-14; girls 4-14; Fees: **C** ☀
Contact: Brother Robert La Fave, DSF, Director at (631) 261-5730; fax: (631) 754-4204
e-mail: camp1888@juno.com
Web site: www.alvernia.org
Operated by: Franciscan Brothers, St Francis Monastery, 105 Prospect Rd Box 301, Centerport, NY 11721 at (631) 261-5730
Group Rental Information
Seasons & Capacity: Spring 60, Fall 60, Winter 60
Facilities: Dorm-Style, Meeting Rooms (#1922)

Amer Diabetes Assn Summer Camp (est 1981)

Rush, NY; (716) 533-2080

Camp comments: Provide children who have diabetes with a fun and safe camping experience. Achieving good control of diabetes.
Activities: Archery, Arts/Crafts, Boating, Camping Skills/Outdoor Living, Challenge/Rope Courses, Drama, Radio/TV/Video, Swimming — Recreational
Session lengths & capacity: 2 week sessions
Clientele & fees: coed 7-17; Fees: **D** △
Contact: Beverly J Gaines, Director at (716) 458-3040 ext. 3475; fax: (716) 458-3138
e-mail: bgaines@diabetes.org
Operated by: ADA Eastern Region, 20 Ramona St, Rochester, NY 14613-1144 at (716) 458-3040 (#12228)

Baco for Boys Che-Na-Wah for G (est 1923)

Minerva, NY (Essex Co.); (518) 251-2919
The Wortman Family, Director

Camp comments: Separate activity programs with nurturing, caring supervision. Located in the beautiful Adirondacks.
Activities: Arts/Crafts, Baseball/Softball, Basketball, Challenge/Rope Courses, Drama, Hiking, Soccer, Swimming — Instructional, Tennis, Waterskiing
Session lengths & capacity: 8 week sessions; 360 campers
Clientele & fees: boys 6-16; girls 6-16; Fees: **F** △
Contact: Bob Wortman, Director at (516) 867-3895; fax: (516) 868-3819
e-mail: campbaco@aol.com chenawah@aol.com
Web site: www.campbaco.com

Operated by: Baco For Boys, 484 Southwood Rd, Rockville, NY 11570-2250 at (516) 867-3895 (#7320)

Bay View YMCA Summer Camp

(est 1963)

Webster, NY (Montoe Co.); (716) 671-8414
Kelly Bilow, Director

Camp comments: Bay View YMCA Summer Camp is an experience for youngsters to challenge themselves, to develop new skills, and build friendships.
Activities: Arts/Crafts, Canoeing, Counselor Training (CIT), Field Trips, Kayaking, Sailing, Sports — Field & Team
Session lengths & capacity: 2 week sessions
Clientele & fees: coed 6-15; Fees: **B**
Contact: Kelly Bilow, Youth Program Director at (716) 671-8414; fax: (716) 671-7246
Web site: www.rochesterymca.org
Operated by: YMCA of Greater Rochester, 444 E Main St, Rochester, NY 14604 at (716) 546-5500 (#3818)

Bayside YMCA Day Camp

(est 1988)

Bayside, NY (Queens Co.); (718) 229-5972
Laura Fosco, Director

Camp comments: We have an exciting summer planned for you. Including recreational social and educational activities.
Activities: Arts/Crafts, Baseball/Softball, Basketball, Dance, Drama, Field Trips, Football, Skating, Soccer, Swimming — Recreational
Session lengths & capacity: 8 week sessions
Clientele & fees: boys 5-15; girls 5-15; Fees: **B**
Contact: Laura Fosco, Youth Coordinator at (718) 229-5972; fax: (718) 229-1924
e-mail: lfosco@ymcanyc.org
Operated by: Flushing YMCA, 138-46 Northern Blvd, Flushing, NY 11354 (#1959)

Beaver Camp (est 1969)

Lowville, NY (Lewis Co.); (315) 376-2640
Emanuel Gingerich, Director

Camp comments: Christian emphasis. Adirondack Lake & ropes course.
Activities: Aquatic Activities, Boating, Canoeing, Challenge/Rope Courses, Climbing/Rappelling, Counselor Training (CIT), Hiking, Leadership Development, Nature/Environment Studies, Wilderness Trips
Session lengths & capacity: July-August; 1 week sessions; 96 campers

---

ICON LEGEND

☀ Day Camp

▲ Resident Camp

⌂ Facilities Available To Rent

🚐 Transportation Available

🐷 Financial Aid Available

FEE RANGES PER WEEK

A	$0-75
B	$75-200
C	$201-350
D	$351-500
E	$501-650
F	over $650

Clientele & fees: coed 6-18; families; Fees: **B ▲**
Contact: Emanuel Gingerich, Administrator at (315) 376-2640; fax: (315) 376-7011
e-mail: emanuel@beavercamp.org
Web site: www.beavercamp.org
Operated by: Adirondack Mennonite Camping, 8884 Buck Point Rd, Lowville, NY 13367 at (315) 376-2640

Group Rental Information

Seasons & Capacity: Spring 110, Summer 140, Fall 110, Winter 110
Facilities: A/V Equipment, Cabins, Dorm-Style, Double Occupancy, Food Service, Hiking Trails, Kitchen Facilities, Lake, Meeting Rooms
Programs: Boating, Challenge/Ropes Course, Environmental Education, Swimming, Winter Sports (#3090)

Berkshire Hills - Emanuel Camp

(est 1931)

Copake, NY (Columbia Co.); (518) 329-3303
Elaine & Art Weingarten, Director

Camp comments: All American staff. Family atmosphere. Excellent facilities. Make life long friends, learn new skills & have fun. Modern, air-conditioned facilities.
Activities: Arts/Crafts, Basketball, Bicycling/Biking, Challenge/Rope Courses, Dance, Hockey, Nature/Environment Studies, Skating, Swimming — Instructional, Tennis
Session lengths & capacity: June-August; 2, 4 & 7 week sessions; 230 campers
Clientele & fees: coed 7-14; Fees: **C, D, E ▲ 🐷**
Contact: Elaine Weingarten, Asst Exec Director at (914) 693-8952; fax: (914) 674-8952
e-mail: bhecamps@aol.com
Web site: www.bhecamps.com
Operated by: BHEC Inc, 547 Saw Mill River Rd Ste 3D, Ardsley, NY 10502 at (914) 693-8952 (#533)

Beth El Summer Session

New Rochelle, NY (Westchester Co.); (914) 235-2700
Julie Rockowitz, Director

Camp comments: Caring, nurturing, and safe environment. Varied age appropriate programs, fun and games. Strong swim program.
Activities: Arts/Crafts, Dance, Music, Nature/Environment Studies, Swimming — Instructional, Swimming — Recreational
Session lengths & capacity: June-August; 8 week sessions; 275 campers
Clientele & fees: coed 3-7; Fees: **C ☀**
Contact: Julie Rockowitz, Summer Session Director at (914) 235-2700 ext. 256; fax: (914) 235-2718
Operated by: Beth El Synagogue, Northfield Rd at N Ave, New Rochelle, NY 10804 at (914) 235-2700 (#46226)

Beth Sholom Day Camp

(est 1965)

Roslyn Heights, NY (Nassau Co.); (516) 621-9257
Ginger Bloom, Director

Camp comments: Exceptional variety of supervised athletics/cultural activities/special events and trips in a Jewish oriented atmosphere
Activities: Baseball/Softball, Basketball, Ceramics/Pottery, Challenge/Rope Courses, Counselor Training (CIT), Field Trips, Leadership Development, Sports — Field & Team, Swimming — Instructional, Swimming — Recreational
Session lengths & capacity: July-August; 4, 6 & 8 week sessions; 600 campers
Clientele & fees: coed 3-15; Fees: **C ☀**
Contact: Ginger Bloom, Director at (516) 621-9257; fax: (516) 621-2438
Operated by: Temple Beth Sholom, 401 Roslyn Road, Roslyn Heights, NY 11577 at (516) 621-9257 (#1956)

Blue Bay (est 1947) ▲ ⌂ 🚐

East Hampton, NY (Suffolk Co.); (631) 324-4435
Catherine Mottola, Director

Camp comments: At Camp Blue Bay girls explore a variety of recreational, cultural & educational activities in a fun, safe environment.
Activities: Aquatic Activities, Arts/Crafts, Boating, Camping Skills/Outdoor Living, Canoeing, Kayaking, Leadership Development, Nature/Environment Studies, Sailing, Swimming — Instructional
Session lengths & capacity: July-August; 1 & 2 week sessions; 152 campers
Clientele & fees: girls 6-16; Fees: **C, D ▲ 🐷**
Contact: Laura Bissett-Carr, Program & Adult Development at (516) 741-2550 ext. 233; fax: (516) 741-2207
e-mail: bissett@gsnc.org
Web site: www.gsnc.org
Operated by: GS of Nassau County, 110 Ring Road West, Garden City, NY 11530 at (516) 741-2550 (#2044)

Blue Rill Day Camp (est 1951) ☀ 🚐

Monsey, NY (Rockland Co.); (845) 352-3521
Howard & Susan Gulker, Director

Camp comments: Small groups, warm caring atmosphere. Most campers & staff return year after year.
Activities: Arts/Crafts, Challenge/Rope Courses, Computer, Nature/Environment Studies, Performing Arts, Sports — Field & Team, Swimming — Instructional, Swimming — Recreational, Tennis
Session lengths & capacity: June-August; 4, 6 & 8 week sessions
Clientele & fees: coed 3-15
Contact: Howard & Susan Gulker, Owners/Directors at (845) 352-3521; fax: (845) 352-0168
e-mail: bluerill1@aol.com
Operated by: Blue Rill Day Camp, 444 Saddle River Rd, Monsey, NY 10952 at (845) 352-3521 (#2167)

Brant Lake Camp (est 1916) ▲ 🚐

Brant Lake, NY (Warren Co.)
Robert Gersten and Richard Gersten, Director

Camp comments: Traditional camp with large, mature key staff. Excellent instruction emphasizing team sports, waterfront, tennis, etc.
Activities: Aquatic Activities, Arts/Crafts, Baseball/Softball, Basketball, Challenge/Rope Courses, Golf, Hockey, Soccer, Tennis
Session lengths & capacity: June-August; 8 week sessions; 60 campers
Clientele & fees: boys 12-16; Fees: **F ▲**
Contact: Richard Gersten, Director at (914) 273-5401; fax: (914) 273-1587
e-mail: brantlakec@aol.com
Web site: www.brantlake.com
Operated by: Brant Lake Camp Inc, 7586 State Route 8, Brant Lake, NY 12815 at (914) 273-5401 (#1992)

Breezemont Day Camp

(est 1936) ☀ 🚐

Armonk, NY (Westchester Co.); (914) 273-3162
John Richard Tesone, Director

Camp comments: Day camp with sleep-away atmosphere, campers thrive in noncompetitive setting under direction of mature staff.
Activities: Archery, Drama, Music, Nature/Environment Studies, Soccer, Swimming — Recreational, Tennis
Session lengths & capacity: June-August; 4, 6, 7 & 8 week sessions; 750 campers
Clientele & fees: coed 3-13; Fees: **E ☀**
Contact: John Richard Tesone, Director at (914) 273-3162;
e-mail: info@breezemont.com

Web site: www.breezemont.com
Operated by: Breezemont Day Camp, 62 64 Cox Ave, Armonk, NY 10504 at (914) 273-3162 (#2120)

Brockport YMCA Day Camp

(est 1984)

Brockport, NY; (716) 637-8121
Margaret Ramsey Boyle, Director

Camp comments: YMCA day camp offers an opportunity for campers to learn new skills, face new challenges and make memories and friendships that last a lifetime.
Activities: Arts/Crafts, Canoeing, Counselor Training (CIT), Field Trips, Hiking, Nature/Environment Studies, Sports — Field & Team, Swimming — Recreational
Session lengths & capacity: June-August; 1 week sessions
Clientele & fees: coed 6-14; Fees: **B** ☀ 🐖
Contact: Margaret Ramsey Boyle, Center Director at (716) 637-8121; fax: (716) 637-7626
Web site: www.rochesterymca.org
Operated by: YMCA of Greater Rochester, 444 E Main St, Rochester, NY 14604 at (716) 546-5500 (#5483)

Bronx YMCA of Greater NY

Bronx, NY (Bronx Co.); (718) 792-9736
Mary Thomas, Director

Camp comments: Our camp is offered to boys & girls 5-13 yrs, we offer a diversity of programs by trained & qualified staff in a safe place.
Activities: Arts/Crafts, Baseball/Softball, Basketball, Computer, Dance, Field Trips, Nature/Environment Studies, Swimming — Recreational
Session lengths & capacity: 9 week sessions; 350 campers
Clientele & fees: coed 5-15; Fees: **B** ☀ 🐖
Contact: Mary Thomas, Day Camp Director at (718) 792-9736; fax: (718) 792-9740
e-mail: mthomas@ymcany.org
Operated by: Bronx YMCA, 2 Castle Hill Ave, Bronx, NY 10473 at (718) 792-9736 (#577)

Brookhaven Roe YMCA

(est 1979)

Holtsville, NY (Suffolk Co.); (631) 289-4440
Deborah L Belzak, Director

Camp comments: Provide opportunity for children to develop in a safe, secure atmosphere. Allowing social, emotional, physical, intellectual growth.
Activities: Aquatic Activities, Arts/Crafts, Basketball, Challenge/Rope Courses, Counselor Training (CIT), Leadership Development, Music, Nature/Environment Studies, Soccer, Swimming — Instructional
Session lengths & capacity: June-August; 1 & 3 week sessions; 350 campers
Clientele & fees: boys 3-16; girls 3-16; coed 3-16; Fees: **B** ☀ 🐖
Contact: Laura Hermann, Administrative Assistant at (631) 289-4440; fax: (631) 289-4451
Operated by: YMCA Long Island, 155 Buckley Road, Holtsville, NY 11742 at (631) 289-4440 (#4154)

Brooklyn Expansion YMCA Summer

Brooklyn, NY

Activities: Arts/Crafts, Baseball/Softball, Basketball, Community Service, Counselor Training (CIT), Drawing/Painting, Field Trips, Leadership Development, Swimming — Recreational, Team Building
Session lengths & capacity: July-August; 6 week sessions
Clientele & fees: coed 5-99; Fees: **B** ☀
Contact: Diane Rizzolo, Camp Director at (718) 491-1449; fax: (718) 491-2583
e-mail: drizzolo@ymcanyc.org

Operated by: Brooklyn Expansion YMCA Summer, PO Box 090 410, Brooklyn, NY 11209 at (718) 491-1449 (#38167)

Buckley Country Day Camp

Roslyn, NY (Nassau Co.); (516) 365-7760
Mr. Greg Schreiner, Director

Camp comments: Life is camp...Let's play. There is no place like Buckley
Activities: Academics, Aquatic Activities, Arts/Crafts, Camping Skills/Outdoor Living, Drama, Hockey, Model Rocketry, Sports — Field & Team, Tennis
Session lengths & capacity: June-August; 4, 6 & 8 week sessions; 500 campers
Clientele & fees: coed 3-16; Fees: **D, E** ☀
Contact: Donna Kocis, Admin. Assist. at (516) 365-7760; fax: (516) 869-0964
e-mail: gregcamp@optonline.net
Web site: www.Buckleycamp.com
Operated by: Buckley Country Day School, IU Willets Rd, Roslyn, NY 11576 at (516) 627-1910 (#18822)

Camp Addisone Boyce

(est 1952)

Tomkins Cove, NY (Rockland Co.); (845) 786-5800
Julie Favreau Schwartz, Director

Camp comments: Noncompetitive, progressive, outdoor program, relaxed atmosphere, rustic wooded setting. Non Girl Scouts welcomed.
Activities: Arts/Crafts, Backpacking, Camping Skills/Outdoor Living, Canoeing, Challenge/Rope Courses, Counselor Training (CIT), Hiking, Leadership Development, Nature/Environment Studies, Swimming — Instructional
Session lengths & capacity: July-August; 1, 2 & 3 week sessions; 150 campers
Clientele & fees: girls 5-15; Fees: **B** ☀
Contact: Julie Favreau Schwartz, Director of Outdoor Program at (845) 638-0438 ext. 24; fax: (845) 638-2804
e-mail: camp@gscrc.org
Web site: www.gscrc.org/cab
Operated by: Girl Scouts of Rockland County, 211 Red Hill Rd, New City, NY 10956 at (845) 634-0438

Group Rental Information
Site comments: Rustic setting:tents, cabins, tepee; Lake for swimming, boating. Ropes course, hiking trails. Available weekdays.
Seasons & Capacity: Spring 200, Summer 200, Fall 200, Winter 60
Facilities: Cabins, Hiking Trails, Kitchen Facilities, Lake, Lodges, Playing Fields, Tents
Programs: Boating, Challenge/Ropes Course, Environmental Education, Swimming (#2094)

Camp Adventure

Shelter Island, NY; (631) 436-7071
Marianne Esolen, Director
Activities: Aquatic Activities, Arts/Crafts, Drama, Music, Nature/Environment Studies, Sports — Field & Team, Team Building
Operated by: American Cancer Society, 75 Davids Dr, Hauppauge, NY 11788 at (631) 436-7070 (#34753)

Camp Chateaugay

(est 1946)

Merrill, NY (Clinton Co.); (518) 425-6888

Camp comments: Enjoy memories for a lifetime on picturesque Chateaugay Lake in the Adiron Mtns.Our 2.5:1 staff ratio offers children a caring environment & fine instruction
Activities: Baseball/Softball, Basketball, Golf, Gymnastics, Horseback — English, Soccer, Sports — Field & Team, Tennis, Waterskiing, Wilderness Trips

Session lengths & capacity: June-August; 4 & 7 week sessions; 250 campers
Clientele & fees: coed 7-15; Fees: **F** ⚠
Contact: Hal Lyons/ Laurie Roland, Directors at (800) 431-1184; fax: (203) 396-0686
e-mail: chateaugay@aol.com
Web site: www.chateaugay.com
Operated by: Chateaugay Lake Camp Inc, 165 Short Hill Lane, Fairfield, CT 06432 at (203) 396-0688
Group Rental Information
Site comments: Doctors & nurses live on site. (#3674)

Camp Cherokee (est 1963)

Saranac Lake, NY (Franklin Co.); (518) 891-3520
Daniel Whitlow, Director

Camp comments: Discovering, experiencing and sharing the joy of knowing Jesus.
Activities: Aquatic Activities, Archery, Canoeing, Ceramics/Pottery, Counselor Training (CIT), Horseback — Western, Sports — Field & Team, Swimming — Recreational, Waterskiing
Session lengths & capacity: June-August; 1 & 2 week sessions; 70 campers
Clientele & fees: coed 8-17; families; seniors; single adults; Fees: **C** ⚠
Contact: Daniel Whitlow, Director, Youth Ministries at (315) 469-6921; fax: (315) 469-6924
e-mail: DanLisaWhitlow@compuserve.com
Operated by: New York Conference of SDAs, 4930 W Seneca Trpk, Syracuse, NY 13215 at (315) 469-6921 (#18752)

Camp DeBaun (est 1949)

Oceanside, NY; (516) 764-1044
Edyth, Craig, Annette DeBaun, Pamela DeBaun Lucas, Director

Camp comments: Family operated for 49 years. Trips off camp. Activities, cabins, arena, specialty buildings. Limited size groups.
Activities: Arts/Crafts, Boating, Ceramics/Pottery, Computer, Dance, Drama, Gymnastics, Sports — Field & Team, Tennis
Session lengths & capacity: 4 & 8 week sessions; 650 campers
Clientele & fees: coed 3-13; Fees: **D** ☀
Contact: Edyth DeBaun, Director at (516) 764-1044; fax: (516) 764-6450
Web site: www.campdebaun.com
Operated by: Camp DeBaun Inc, 465 Atlantic Avenue, Oceanside, NY 11572 at (516) 764-1044 (#1684)

Camp Deer Run (est 1996)

Pine Bush, NY; (845) 733-5494
Giro De Roover, Director

Camp comments: 110 wooded acres. Int'l staff. Traditional program plus ropes challenge course, nature studies, hiking, drug prevention.
Activities: Academics, Camping Skills/Outdoor Living, Ceramics/Pottery, Challenge/Rope Courses, Climbing/Rappelling, International Culture, Nature/Environment Studies, Swimming — Instructional, Team Building
Session lengths & capacity: July-August; 1/2, 1 & 2 week sessions; 65 campers
Clientele & fees: coed 8-14; families; seniors; single adults; Fees: **D** ⚠
Contact: Cam Cheema, Coordinator at (845) 733-5494; fax: (845) 733-5471
e-mail: cheema@campdeerrun.org
Web site: www.dianova.org
Operated by: Dianova USA Inc, 218 E 30th Street, New York, NY 10016 at (212) 686-5331 (#901445)

Camp Dudley YMCA Inc

(est 1885)   △

Westport, NY (Essex Co.); (518) 962-4720
Mr Andrew Bisselle, Director

Camp comments: Diverse Christian community. All sports, hiking/canoeing, music, & theater arts. Emphasizing excellence in leadership.
Activities: Baseball/Softball, Basketball, Canoeing, Counselor Training (CIT), Drama, Hiking, Leadership Development, Music, Soccer, Team Building
Session lengths & capacity: June-August; 4 & 8 week sessions; 350 campers
Clientele & fees: boys 10-15; Fees: E △
Contact: Andrew Bisselle, Camp Director at (518) 962-4720; fax: (518) 962-4320
e-mail: andy@campdudley.org
Operated by: Camp Dudley YMCA Inc, RR 1 Box 1034, Westport, NY 12993 at (518) 962-4720 (#1935)

Camp Eagle Hill (est 1963)   △ 🏠 🚐

Elizaville, NY (Columbia Co.); (845) 756-2426
Murray and Jesse Scherer, Director

Camp comments: One summer in a child's life should be unforgettable. Camp Eagle Hill is where it happens.
Activities: Aquatic Activities, Arts/Crafts, Bicycling/Biking, Climbing/Rappelling, Counselor Training (CIT), Drama, Field Trips, Sports — Field & Team, Swimming — Recreational, Tennis
Session lengths & capacity: 4, 6 & 8 week sessions; 250 campers
Clientele & fees: coed 6-16; Fees: E △
Contact: Jesse Scherer, Owner-Director at (914) 395-0045; fax: (914) 395-0056
e-mail: ceaglehill@aol.com
Web site: www.campeaglehill.com
Operated by: Camp Eagle Hill, White Oak Rd, PO Box 12, Elizaville, NY 12523 at (518) 537-4000

Group Rental Information
Facilities: Cabins, Dorm-Style, Food Service, Meeting Rooms, Pool (#11951)

Camp Eagle Island (est 1938)   △ 🚐

Saranac Lake, NY (Franklin Co.); (518) 891-0928
Traci Soileau, Director

Camp comments: Warm, caring staff; noncompetitive atmosphere. Adventure & challenge, fun & friendship in a beautiful island setting.
Activities: Aquatic Activities, Archery, Arts/Crafts, Camping Skills/Outdoor Living, Canoeing, Counselor Training (CIT), Hiking, Sailing, Swimming — Recreational, Waterskiing

ICON LEGEND

☀	Day Camp
△	Resident Camp
🏠	Facilities Available To Rent
🚐	Transportation Available
🐷	Financial Aid Available

FEE RANGES PER WEEK

A	$0-75
B	$75-200
C	$201-350
D	$351-500
E	$501-650
F	over $650

Session lengths & capacity: June-August; 1, 2 & 4 week sessions; 125 campers
Clientele & fees: girls 8-17; families; single adults; Fees: C △
Contact: Carol Chu, Outdoor Program Manager at (973) 746-8200; fax: (973) 746-4163
e-mail: camp@gscgehc.org
Operated by: GSC of Gtr Essex & Hudson Co, 120 Valley Rd, Montclair, NJ 07042 at (888) 746-8200 (#2261)

Camp Echo-Coleman High Country (est 1924)   △ 🚐

Burlingham, NY; (845) 733-4567
Jordon Coleman & Robert Ednick, Director

Camp comments: 'Discover the Adventure.' Children discover their talents & live out their dreams as they have fun, make new friends, develop new skills & experience adventure.
Activities: Aquatic Activities, Baseball/Softball, Basketball, Boating, Canoeing, Ceramics/Pottery, Drama, Swimming — Instructional, Swimming — Recreational, Tennis
Session lengths & capacity: July-August; 4 & 8 week sessions; 350 campers
Clientele & fees: boys 7-16; girls 7-16; coed 7-16; Fees: F △
Contact: Coleman Family, Owners/Directors at (516) 223-2267; fax: (516) 868-7449
e-mail: mailbox@campecho.com
Web site: www.colemancountry.com
Operated by: Coleman Family Camps, PO Box 34, Merrick, NY 11566 at (516) 223-2267 (#2168)

Camp Edey (est 1945)   ☀ 🏠 🚐

Bayport, NY (Suffolk Co.); (516) 472-1625
Claudia Bowers, Director

Camp comments: Girl Scout camp located on the beautiful San Souci Lakes on Long Island; traditional program.
Activities: Arts/Crafts, Boating, Camping Skills/Outdoor Living, Canoeing, Counselor Training (CIT), Dance, Drama, Horseback — English, Leadership Development, Swimming — Recreational
Session lengths & capacity: June-August; 1 week sessions; 200 campers
Clientele & fees: girls 6-15; Fees: B ☀ Fees: C △
Contact: Brenda Manfredi, Camp Director at (516) 472-1625; fax: (516) 472-8199
Operated by: Suffolk County GSC, 1500 Lakeview Ave, Bayport, NY 11725 at (516) 472-1625

Group Rental Information
Seasons & Capacity: Spring 130, Fall 130, Winter 30
Facilities: Hiking Trails, Playing Fields, Tents (#19878)

Camp Fiver   △ 🚐

Earlville, NY; (315) 691-6770
James Flint, Director

Camp comments: To provide a camp experience for economically disadvantaged youth that fosters the development of self-esteem.
Activities: Academics, Aquatic Activities, Camping Skills/Outdoor Living, Canoeing, Computer, Drama, Horseback — Western, Leadership Development, Music, Nature/Environment Studies
Session lengths & capacity: June-August; 2 week sessions; 80 campers
Clientele & fees: coed 8-12; Fees: A △ 🐷
Contact: Jim Flint, Executive Director at (212) 971-9562; fax: (212) 971-9564
e-mail: jim@fiver.org
Web site: www.fiver.org
Operated by: The Fiver Foundation, 481 Eigth Ave Ste 826, New York, NY 10001 at (212) 971-9562 (#36900)

Camp Gan Israel of Rockland   ☀

New City, NY; (845) 634-0951
Activities: Ceramics/Pottery, Field Trips, Gymnastics, Religious Study, Sports — Field & Team, Swimming — Instructional, Swimming — Recreational, Tennis
Contact: Web site: www.chabadofrockland.org
Operated by: Camp Gan Israel of Rockland, 315 N Main St, New City, NY 10956 at (845) 634-0951 (#10335)

Camp Good Days Special Times

(est 1980)   △ 🚐

Branchport, NY (Yates Co.); (315) 595-2779
Wendy Bleier-Mervis, Director

Camp comments: A camp for children and their families whose lives have been touched by cancer, AIDS, violence, or sickle cell anemia.
Activities: Aquatic Activities, Arts/Crafts, Boating, Challenge/Rope Courses, Computer, Music, Nature/Environment Studies
Session lengths & capacity: June-October; 1 week sessions; 75 campers
Clientele & fees: coed 7-17; families; single adults; Fees: A △ 🐷
Contact: Wendy Bleier-Mervis, Camp Director at (716) 624-5555; fax: (716) 624-5799
e-mail: mervis@campgooddays.org
Web site: www.campgooddays.org
Operated by: Camp Good Days Special Times, 58 West Lake Rd, Branchport, NY 14418 at (585) 624-5555 (#2953)

Camp Henry   ☀

New York, NY; (212) 254-3100
Danielle Algranti, Director
Activities: Academics, Aquatic Activities, Baseball/Softball, Basketball, Counselor Training (CIT), Dance, Drama, Field Trips, Swimming — Recreational, Team Building
Operated by: Henry Street Settlement, 301 Henry Street, New York, NY 10002 at (212) 254-3100 (#33585)

Camp Henry Kaufmann

(est 1953)   🏠

Holmes, NY; (845) 878-6846
Operated by: GSC Of Greater New York, 43 West 23rd Street, New York, NY 10010 at (212) 645-4000

Group Rental Information
Site comments: Located in the scenic mountains of upstate NY. Girl Scouts enjoy a full range of traditional & educational activities.
Seasons & Capacity: Spring 200, Summer 200, Fall 200, Winter 84
Facilities: Cabins, Dorm-Style, Double Occupancy, Food Service, Hiking Trails, Kitchen Facilities, Lake, Meeting Rooms, Playing Fields, Pool
Programs: Boating, Environmental Education, Swimming (#3360)

Camp Hi Hello (est 1968)   ☀

Freeport, NY (Nassau Co.)
Joann Bousquet, Director

Camp comments: Camp Hi-Hello offers a multicultural suburban day camp experience in our quiet waterfront community. 'Beginnings that last a lifetime.'
Activities: Arts/Crafts, Baseball/Softball, Basketball, Counselor Training (CIT), Drama, Field Trips, Soccer, Swimming — Instructional, Swimming — Recreational, Team Building
Session lengths & capacity: July-August; 8 week sessions; 200 campers
Clientele & fees: coed 5-13; Fees: B ☀ 🐷
Contact: Joann Bousquet, Executive Director at (516) 379-1825; fax: (516) 379-1880
e-mail: hihellochildcare@aol.com
Web site: www.hihellochildcare.org

Operated by: Hi Hello Child Care Center Inc, 212 S Ocean Ave, Freeport, NY 11520 at (516) 379-1825 (#26601)

Camp Hillard (est 1929)

Scarsdale, NY (Westchester Co.); (914) 949-8857
Jon & Jim Libman, Director

Camp comments: 74th yr. of 1 family ownership.Facility incl. 6 heated pools/large fields/indoor buildings.Serving NYC/ Westchester CT.
Activities: Arts/Crafts, Baseball/Softball, Basketball, Drama, Gymnastics, Horseback — Western, Soccer, Sports — Field & Team, Swimming — Instructional, Tennis
Session lengths & capacity: June-August; 5 & 8 week sessions; 800 campers
Clientele & fees: coed 3-13; Fees: F
Contact: Jim Libman, Director at (914) 949-8857; fax: (914) 949-5843
e-mail: jim@camphillard.com
Web site: www.camphillard.com
Operated by: Camp Hillard Inc, 26 Elizabeth St, Scarsdale, NY 10583 at (914) 949-8857 (#3132)

Camp Hilltop (est 1924)

Hancock, NY (Delaware Co.); (607) 637-5201
Bill Young, Director

Camp comments: Beautiful Mtn setting, supportive atmosphere, family values, 4:1 ratio. 1st time campers & self-esteem our speciality
Activities: Aquatic Activities, Archery, Arts/Crafts, Bicycling/Biking, Challenge/Rope Courses, Dance, Horseback — English, Soccer, Tennis, Waterskiing
Session lengths & capacity: June-August; 2, 4, 6 & 8 week sessions; 250 campers
Clientele & fees: coed 7-15; Fees: E
Contact: Kathy ,Bill or Scott Young, Owners/Directors at (607) 637-5201; fax: (607) 637-2389
e-mail: hilltop@hancock.net
Web site: www.camphilltop.com
Operated by: Camp Hilltop, 7825 County Hwy 67, Hancock, NY 13783 at (607) 637-5201

Group Rental Information
Seasons & Capacity: Spring 325, Summer 325, Fall 325
Facilities: A/V Equipment, Cabins, Food Service, Hiking Trails, Lake, Meeting Rooms, Playing Fields, Pool
Programs: Boating, Challenge/Ropes Course, Environmental Education, Horseback Riding, Swimming (#2074)

Camp Homeward Bound

(est 1984)

Beat Mountain, NY; (914) 351-2650
David Morgan, Director

Camp comments: Where good times are forever.
Activities: Academics, Aquatic Activities, Arts/Crafts, Camping Skills/Outdoor Living, Counselor Training (CIT), Drama, Gymnastics, Leadership Development, Nature/Environment Studies, Sports — Field & Team
Session lengths & capacity: June-September; 3 week sessions; 200 campers
Clientele & fees: coed 6-17; Fees: A
Contact: David Morgan, Director of Youth Services at (212) 964-5900 ext. 180; fax: (212) 964-1303
e-mail: david@camphomewardbound.org
Web site: w.coalition for homeless.org
Operated by: Coalition for the Homeless, 89 Chamber St, New York, NY 10007 at (212) 964-5900 (#39563)

Camp Jened (est 1979)

Rock Hill, NY (Sullivan Co.); (845) 434-2220
Stuart Mace, Director

Camp comments: Resident camp for adults, 18+, with severe physical & developmental disabilities. Travel camp. In the Catskill Mtns.
Activities: Arts/Crafts, Boating, Camping Skills/Outdoor Living, Dance, Drama, Field Trips, Music, Sports — Field & Team, Swimming — Recreational, Travel/Tour
Session lengths & capacity: May-August; 1 & 2 week sessions; 125 campers
Clientele & fees: coed 18-99; seniors; single adults; Fees: F
Contact: Stuart Mace, Administrator at (845) 434-2220; fax: (845) 434-2253
e-mail: jened@catskill.net
Operated by: United Cerebral Palsy Assn NY, 330 W 34th St 13th Floor, New York, NY 10001 at (212) 947-5770 (#18896)

Camp Kaufmann (est 2002)

Holmes, NY (Dutchess Co.); (845) 878-3351
Jeanne Scigliano, Director

Camp comments: Community living on over 400 acres in the southeastern corner of Dutchess County through which girls develop skills, build new friendships, and contribute.
Activities: Arts/Crafts, Boating, Camping Skills/Outdoor Living, Canoeing, Challenge/Rope Courses, Climbing/Rappelling, Hiking, Leadership Development, Nature/Environment Studies, Swimming — Recreational
Session lengths & capacity: July-August; 1, 2, 3, 4 & 5 week sessions; 200 campers
Clientele & fees: girls 6-17; Fees: C
Fees: C
Contact: Jeanne Scigliano, Director of Outdoor Program at (845) 452-1810 ext. 21; fax: (845) 452-1878
e-mail: gsdcsciggy@cs.com
Operated by: Girl Scouts of Dutchess County, 41 Page Park Dr, Poughkeepsie, NY 12603-2534 at (845) 452-1810 (#12448)

Camp Lakeland (est 1910)

Franklinville, NY (Cattaragus Co.); (716) 676-9942
David Miller, Director

Camp comments: Foothills Allegheny Mts. Emphasis on living Jewish experiences, learning new skills & making friends. Kosher.
Activities: Arts/Crafts, Bicycling/Biking, Ceramics/Pottery, Challenge/Rope Courses, Drama, Horseback — Western, Leadership Development, Model Rocketry, Sailing, Waterskiing
Session lengths & capacity: June-August; 1, 3 & 7 week sessions; 225 campers
Clientele & fees: coed 8-16; Fees: D
Contact: David Miller, Director at (716) 688-4033; fax: (716) 688-3572
e-mail: summer@camplakeland.com
Web site: www.camplakeland.com
Operated by: JCC of Greater Buffalo Inc, 2640 North Forest Rd, Getzville, NY 14068 at (716) 688-4033

Group Rental Information
Site comments: Located in foothills of Allgeny Mtns.,733 acres;warm Jewish atmosphere;full range of activities & programs. Kosher
Seasons & Capacity: Spring 250, Summer 250, Fall 75, Winter 75
Facilities: A/V Equipment, Cabins, Double Occupancy, Food Service, Hiking Trails, Kitchen Facilities, Lake, Lodges, Meeting Rooms, Ocean, Playing Fields, Pool
Programs: Boating, Challenge/Ropes Course, Environmental Education, Horseback Riding, Swimming (#1861)

Camp Li-Lo-Li (est 1953)

Randolph, NY (Cattaraugus Co.); (716) 945-4900
Allan R McIntee, Director

Camp comments: Nestled on 450 acres of mountain beauty with a lake. Bubbling brooks in a rural setting/friendships are made here.
Activities: Aquatic Activities, Archery, Boating, Challenge/Rope Courses, Counselor Training (CIT), Horseback — Western, Leadership Development, Nature/Environment Studies, Riflery, Swimming — Instructional
Session lengths & capacity: July-August; 1/2, 1 & 2 week sessions; 240 campers
Clientele & fees: coed 8-25; families; seniors; single adults; Fees: A, B
Contact: Allan R Mc Intee, Administrator at (905) 687-9814; fax: (905) 687-9851
e-mail: administrator@campli-lo-li.com
Web site: www.campli-lo-li.com
Operated by: Camp Li-Lo-Li, 197 Russell Avenue, Saint Catherines, ON L2R 1W9, CANADA at (905) 687-9814

Group Rental Information
Facilities: A/V Equipment, Cabins, Dorm-Style, Double Occupancy, Food Service, Hiking Trails, Kitchen Facilities, Lake, Lodges, Meeting Rooms, Playing Fields, Pool
Programs: Boating, Challenge/Ropes Course, Environmental Education, Horseback Riding, Swimming, Winter Sports (#1588)

Camp Little Notch

(est 1939)

Fort Ann, NY (Albany Co.); (518) 793-0223
Brenda Silkman, Director

Camp comments: Traditional outdoor program. Exciting camp trips into surrounding Adirondacks. Emphasis on group decision-making.
Activities: Bicycling/Biking, Boating, Camping Skills/Outdoor Living, Challenge/Rope Courses, Counselor Training (CIT), Hiking, Horseback — Western, Leadership Development, Nature/Environment Studies, Sailing
Session lengths & capacity: July-August; 7 week sessions; 160 campers
Clientele & fees: girls 8-18; Fees: C, D
Contact: Ann Aronson, Outdoor Specialist at (518) 489-8110; fax: (518) 489-8065
e-mail: aaronson@girlscoutshugsc.org
Web site: www.girlscoutshvgsc.org
Operated by: Girl Scouts, Hudson Valley Cou, 8 Mountain View Ave, Albany, NY 12205 at (518) 489-8110 (#1810)

Camp Lokanda (est 1937)

Glen Spey, NY (Sullivan Co.); (914) 557-6686
Ray & Linda Diamond, Director

Camp comments: Balanced program, excellent staff, state of the art equipment, Kosher food,structured, lighted fields, pool & lake swim.
Activities: Arts/Crafts, Baseball/Softball, Basketball, Challenge/Rope Courses, Dance, Golf, SCUBA, Soccer, Swimming — Recreational, Tennis
Session lengths & capacity: 8 week sessions; 400 campers
Clientele & fees: coed 6-16; Fees: F
Contact: Lois Seinfeld, Admin Asst at (516) 791-4548;
e-mail: Lokanda1@aol.com
Operated by: Camp Lokanda, 1401 Park Street, Atlantic Beach, NY 11509 at (516) 239-8235 (#16446)

Camp Mark Seven (est 1981) ⛺ 🚐

Old Forge, NY; (315) 357-6089
Dave Staehle, Director

Camp comments: Lakefront recreational,educational&leadership camp in the Adirondack Mountains,diverse summer prgrms are for deaf, hard-of-hearing, & hearing inds of all ages.
Activities: Aquatic Activities, Arts/Crafts, Backpacking, Basketball, Camping Skills/Outdoor Living, Canoeing, Field Trips, Hiking, Sailing, Team Building
Session lengths & capacity: June-September; 1, 2 & 3 week sessions; 65 campers
Clientele & fees: coed 1-99; families; seniors; single adults; Fees: **C, D** ⛺ 🏕
Contact: Dave Staehle, Executive Director at (315) 357-6089; fax: (315) 357-6403
e-mail: execdur@campmark7.org
Web site: www.campmark7.org
Operated by: Mark Seven Deaf Foundation, 144 Mohawk Hotel Rd, Old Forge, NY 13420 at (315) 357-6089 (#19416)

Camp Moed (est 2000) ☀ ⛺ 🚐

Ft Schuylen, NY; (212) 627-8442
Elisa Lunzer, Director

Camp comments: Whether for day camp or overnight-camp, Moed is for you. Find out about our new camp and unique blend of Jewish day and overnight options.
Activities: Arts/Crafts, Basketball, Music, Nature/Environment Studies, Religious Study, Sports — Field & Team, Swimming — Instructional
Session lengths & capacity: June-August; 4, 6 & 8 week sessions; 200 campers
Clientele & fees: boys 7-14; girls 7-14; coed 7-14; Fees: **D** ☀
Contact: Elisa Lunzer, Administrator at (212) 627-8442; fax: (212) 691-0573
e-mail: campmoed@aol.com
Operated by: Moish Wein, 1123 Broadway, New York, NY 10010 at (212) 627-8442 (#11981)

Camp Na-Sho-Pa (est 1937) ⛺ 🚐

Bloomingburg, NY (Sullivan Co.); (845) 733-2000
Charlotte Kroll, Director

Camp comments: A beautiful campus, an experienced staff, and diverse activities will produce an extraordinary experience for your child.
Activities: Baseball/Softball, Basketball, Camping Skills/Outdoor Living, Drama, Hockey, Horseback — English, Horseback — Western, SCUBA, Soccer, Tennis
Session lengths & capacity: June-August; 2, 3, 4, 5, 6, 7 & 8 week sessions; 300 campers

ICON LEGEND

☀ Day Camp
⛺ Resident Camp
🏠 Facilities Available To Rent
🚐 Transportation Available
🏕 Financial Aid Available

FEE RANGES PER WEEK

A	$0-75
B	$75-200
C	$201-350
D	$351-500
E	$501-650
F	over $650

Clientele & fees: coed 5-16; Fees: **E** ⛺
Contact: Charlotte, Erik or Annette Kroll, Directors at (516) 466-8014; fax: (516) 487-4727
e-mail: info@campnashopa.com
Operated by: Camp Na-Sho-Pa, 9 Pond Park Rd, Great Neck, NY 11023 at (516) 466-8014 (#2115)

Camp Northwood (est 1976) ⛺ 🚐

Remsen, NY; (315) 831-3621
Gordon W. Felt, Director

Camp comments: Specializing in socially immature campers with minimal learning challenges. Formal social skills training, academic support and over 40 traditional activites.
Activities: Academics, Aquatic Activities, Arts/Crafts, Basketball, Drama, Model Rocketry, Sailing, Tennis, Waterskiing
Session lengths & capacity: July-August; 7 week sessions; 170 campers
Clientele & fees: coed 8-18; Fees: **F** ⛺
Contact: Gordon Felt, Director at (315) 831-3621; fax: (315) 831-5867
e-mail: gfelt@nwood.com
Web site: www.nwood.com
Operated by: Camp Northwood, 132 State Route 365, Remsen, NY 13438 at (315) 831-3621 (#3224)

Camp Pontiac (est 1922) ⛺ 🏠 🚐

Copake, NY (Columbia Co.); (518) 329-6555
Rich Kandel and Marc Sklar, Director

Camp comments: Located in the Berkshires, 100 miles north of NYC. Emphasizes top quality sports instruction, crafts, water and outdoor adventure, self-esteem & friendships.
Activities: Arts/Crafts, Baseball/Softball, Basketball, Challenge/Rope Courses, Gymnastics, Soccer, Sports — Field & Team, Swimming — Instructional, Tennis
Session lengths & capacity: June-August; 7 week sessions; 450 campers
Clientele & fees: coed 6-16; Fees: **F** ⛺
Contact: Ken, Karen, or Rick Etra, Owner at (516) 626-8943; fax: (516) 626-7668
e-mail: camppontiac@hotmail.com
Web site: www.camppontiac.com
Operated by: Camp Pontiac, 10 Brook Lane, Brookville, NY 11545 at (516) 626-7668

Group Rental Information
Site comments: Outstanding Attention to detail to serve organizations planning retreats, conferences, outings and sports training camps for high schools and colleges.
Seasons & Capacity: Spring 400, Fall 400
Facilities: A/V Equipment, Cabins, Food Service, Lake, Linens, Meeting Rooms, Playing Fields, Pool
Programs: Boating, Challenge/Ropes Course, Swimming (#18249)

Camp Ralph and Rose Hittman (est 1949) ⛺ 🚐

Southfields, NY (Orange Co.); (845) 351-2285
Richard J Ravinsky, Director

Camp comments: A chance for never-to-be-forgotten outdoors adventure where values are ingrained & prejudices abandoned, for a lifetime
Activities: Academics, Arts/Crafts, Baseball/Softball, Basketball, Boating, Camping Skills/Outdoor Living, Leadership Development, Nature/Environment Studies, Swimming — Recreational
Session lengths & capacity: June-August; 2 & 3 week sessions; 125 campers
Clientele & fees: coed 7-13; Fees: **C** ⛺ 🏕
Contact: Richard J Ravinsky, Asst Director, Boys and Girls Republic at (212) 686-8888; fax: (212) 477-3400
Operated by: Henry Street Settlement, Boys and Girls Republic, 888 East Sixth St, New York, NY 10009 at (212) 686-8888 (#2080)

Camp Ramah In The Berkshires (est 1964) ⛺ 🏠 🚐

Wingdale, NY; (845) 832-6622
Rabbi Paul Resnick, Director

Camp comments: Jewish educational, cultural & recreational prog; activities in various arts, sports, water front & outdoor education.
Activities: Aquatic Activities, Camping Skills/Outdoor Living, Challenge/Rope Courses, Counselor Training (CIT), Drama, Leadership Development, Sports — Field & Team, Swimming — Recreational
Session lengths & capacity: June-August; 4 & 8 week sessions; 550 campers
Clientele & fees: boys 9-15; girls 9-15; coed 9-15; Fees: **E** ⛺ 🏕
Contact: Rabbi Amy Roth, Assistant Director at (212) 749-0754; fax: (212) 749-2643
e-mail: aroth@ramahberkshires.org
Web site: www.ramahberkshires.org
Operated by: Camp Ramah in the Berkshires, 25 Rockwood Place, Englewood, NJ 07631 at (201) 871-7262

Group Rental Information
Facilities: Cabins, Dorm-Style, Food Service, Hiking Trails, Lake, Linens, Playing Fields
Programs: Boating, Challenge/Ropes Course, Swimming (#2141)

Camp Ramaquois (est 1922) ☀ 🚐

Pomona, NY (Rockland Co.); (845) 354-1600
Bonny Weiss, Director

Camp comments: Day camp the same as sleep-a-way, private lake, 45 indoor buildings, 7 pools, water skiing, hot lunches, transportation.
Activities: Basketball, Boating, Challenge/Rope Courses, Computer, Drama, Field Trips, Gymnastics, Tennis
Session lengths & capacity: 4 & 8 week sessions; 800 campers
Clientele & fees: coed 4-15; Fees: **E** ☀
Contact: Bonny Weiss, Director at (914) 354-1600; fax: (914) 354-0764
e-mail: bonny@ramaquois.com
Web site: www.campgrp.com
Operated by: CampGroup, LLC, 3 New King St, White Plains, NY 10604 at (914) 997-2177 (#2198)

Camp Schodack (est 1957) ⛺ 🏠

Nassau, NY (Rensselaer Co.); (518) 766-3100
Dr Paul Krouner, Director

Camp comments: Warm, nurturing camp in the beautiful Berkshires. Loads of tradition, spirit & fun. Structured & elective program.
Activities: Basketball, Challenge/Rope Courses, Drama, Golf, Gymnastics, Horseback — Western, Sports — Field & Team, Tennis, Waterskiing, Wilderness Trips
Session lengths & capacity: June-August; 4 & 8 week sessions; 250 campers
Clientele & fees: coed 7-16; families; seniors; single adults; Fees: **F** ⛺
Contact: Paul Krouner, Director at (800) 851-1164; fax: (617) 964-8144
e-mail: camp@schodack.com
Web site: www.schodack.com
Operated by: Camp Schodack, 54 Sheffield Rd, Newtonville, MA 02460-2119 at (800) 851-1164

Group Rental Information
Site comments: All types of events -daily/overnight, pool, tennis, golf, softball, etc. Food service, great BBQs! Challenge course training w/ zip line available onsite.
Seasons & Capacity: Spring 300, Fall 300, Winter 40
Facilities: A/V Equipment, Cabins, Dorm-Style, Double Occupancy, Food Service, Hiking Trails, Lake, Lodges, Meeting Rooms, Playing Fields, Pool
Programs: Challenge/Ropes Course, Environmental Education, Swimming, Winter Sports (#3041)

Camp Scully (est 1920)

Wynantskill, NY; (518) 283-1617
Scott Mac Kellar, Director

Camp comments: Serving children from the Capital District for the past 80 years.
Activities: Archery, Arts/Crafts, Basketball, Boating, Camping Skills/Outdoor Living, Canoeing, Challenge/Rope Courses, Hiking, Sports — Field & Team, Swimming — Instructional
Session lengths & capacity: June-August; 1 week sessions; 100 campers
Clientele & fees: coed 7-14; Fees: C ⛺ 🚌
Contact: Angela Keller, Administrator at (518) 283-1617; fax: (518) 286-1943
e-mail: campscully@ccalbany.org
Web site: www.campscully.bunk1.com
Operated by: Catholic Charitie Albany & Ren, 100 Slingerland St, Albany, NY 12202 at (518) 426-3511 (#13935)

Camp Seneca Lake (est 1928)

Penn Yan, NY (Yates Co.); (315) 536-9981
Michael Miller, Director

Camp comments: Warm,nurturing staff. Celebrate Jewish identity. Beautiful lake front setting with ski & sailing programs. Group and individual activities
Activities: Archery, Arts/Crafts, Challenge/Rope Courses, Counselor Training (CIT), Drama, Hiking, Leadership Development, Sailing, Tennis, Waterskiing
Session lengths & capacity: June-August; 2, 3, 4 & 7 week sessions; 250 campers
Clientele & fees: coed 8-16; Fees: E ⛺
Contact: John M Golden, Director at (716) 461-2000 ext. 263; fax: (716) 461-0805
e-mail: campsenecalake@aol.com
Web site: www.jccrochester.org/campsisol

Operated by: Jewish Community Center, Accounts Payable Dept, 1200 Edgewood Ave, Rochester, NY 14618 at (716) 461-2000 (#8323)

Camp Seven Hills (est 1930)

Holland, NY (Erie Co.); (716) 537-9421
Jennifer Collins, Director

Camp comments: Over 600 acres of meadows, woodlands & ponds. New & spacious sports complex. Rustic tent & cabin units. Many intl staff.
Activities: Backpacking, Canoeing, Challenge/Rope Courses, Climbing/Rappelling, Counselor Training (CIT), Horseback — English, Horseback — Western, Rafting, Wilderness Trips
Session lengths & capacity: July-August; 1/2, 1, 2 & 4 week sessions; 170 campers
Clientele & fees: girls 6-17; families; Fees: C, D ⛺
Contact: Janet DePetrillo, Director of Outdoor Programs at (716) 837-6400 ext. 255;
fax: (716) 837-6407
e-mail: jdepetrillo@bflogirlscouts.org
Web site: www.bflogirlscouts.org
Operated by: GSC of Buffalo and Erie County, 70 Jewett Pkwy, Buffalo, NY 14214 at (716) 837-6400

Group Rental Information

Site comments: Camp Seven Hills offers attractive, comfortable, easy-to-access vacation and meeting faciltes. We will provide you with the best value for your money.
Seasons & Capacity: Spring 600, Summer 300, Fall 600, Winter 112
Facilities: Cabins, Hiking Trails, Kitchen Facilities, Lake, Lodges, Meeting Rooms, Playing Fields, Tents
Programs: Boating, Challenge/Ropes Course (#13771)

Camp Shane (Weight Loss) (est 1968)

Ferndale, NY; (845) 292-4644
David Ettenberg & Simon Greenwood, Director

Camp comments: Weight reducing camp: Beautiful & extensive facilities. Nutrition & cooking classes, portion controlled meals. Featured ABC's 20/20, MTV & NY Times.
Activities: Aerobics/Exercise, Arts/Crafts, Computer, Drama, Horseback — Western, Performing Arts, Sports — Field & Team, Swimming — Recreational, Waterskiing
Session lengths & capacity: June-August; 3, 6 & 9 week sessions; 450 campers
Clientele & fees: girls 17-25; coed 7-17; Fees: F ⛺
Contact: David Ettenberg, CCD, Director at (914) 271-4141; fax: (914) 271-2103
e-mail: office@campshane.com
Web site: www.campshane.com
Operated by: Camp Shane, 134 Teatown Rd, Croton On The Hudson, NY 10520 at (914) 271-4141

Group Rental Information

Facilities: A/V Equipment, Cabins, Dorm-Style, Double Occupancy, Food Service, Hiking Trails, Playing Fields, Pool, Tents
Programs: Challenge/Ropes Course, Swimming (#2156)

Camp Sisol - JCC (est 1938)

Honeoye Falls, NY (Monroe Co.); (716) 624-3668
Rachel Rosner, Director

Camp comments: Camp Sisol offers a wide variety of experiences in a noncompetitive, yet challenging environment.

Activities: Arts/Crafts, Camping Skills/Outdoor Living, Counselor Training (CIT), Field Trips, International Culture, Leadership Development, Music, Nature/Environment Studies, Sports — Field & Team, Swimming — Instructional
Session lengths & capacity: June-August; 2, 4 & 8 week sessions; 300 campers
Clientele & fees: coed 5-16; Fees: B ☀ 🐖
Contact: Rachel Rosner, Camp Director at (716) 461-2000; fax: (716) 461-0805
e-mail: jcc@eznet.net
Web site: www.jccrochester.org/campsisol
Operated by: Jewish Community Center, Accounts Payable Dept, 1200 Edgewood Ave, Rochester, NY 14618 at (716) 461-2000 (#7021)

Camp Sobaco (est 1948) ☀

Yaphank, NY (Suffolk Co.); (516) 924-6433
Margaret McCue, Director

Camp comments: Girl Scout coed day camp. Beautiful wooded location.
Activities: Arts/Crafts, Basketball, Camping Skills/Outdoor Living, Dance, Drama, Horseback — English, Nature/Environment Studies, Swimming — Recreational, Team Building
Session lengths & capacity: 1 week sessions; 80 campers
Clientele & fees: boys 6-11; girls 6-11; Fees: B ☀
Contact: Claudia Bowers, Camp Directo at (516) 543-6622; fax: (516) 543-9005
Operated by: Suffolk County GSC, 1500 Lakeview Ave, Bayport, NY 11725 at (516) 472-1625 (#2237)

Camp Stella Maris Inc

(est 1926) ☀ ⚠ 🏠

Livonia, NY (Livingston Co.); (716) 346-2243
Heather Jones, Director

Camp comments: Beautiful Consus Lake. Extraordinary waterfront program. Leadership & counselor training for teens. Christian emphasis.
Activities: Aquatic Activities, Archery, Arts/Crafts, Challenge/Rope Courses, Counselor Training (CIT), Leadership Development, Sailing, Swimming — Instructional, Waterskiing, Windsurfing
Session lengths & capacity: 8 week sessions; 258 campers
Clientele & fees: coed 5-16; Fees: B ☀
Fees: D ⚠ 🐖
Contact: Karen Bell, Registrar at (716) 346-2243; fax: (716) 346-6921
e-mail: starotsea@aol.com
Operated by: Camp Stella Maris Inc, 4395 East Lake Road, Livonia, NY 14487 at (716) 346-2243
Group Rental Information
Site comments: Lg meeting area, fully equipped kitchen

ICON LEGEND

☀   Day Camp
⚠   Resident Camp
🏠   Facilities Available To Rent
🚐   Transportation Available
🐖   Financial Aid Available

FEE RANGES PER WEEK

A $0-75
B $75-200
C $201-350
D $351-500
E $501-650
F   over $650

Seasons & Capacity: Spring 140, Winter 140
Facilities: Cabins, Dorm-Style, Double Occupancy, Food Service, Lake, Lodges (#3437)

Camp Summit (est 1961) ⚠ 🏠 🚐

Wurtsboro, NY (Sullivan Co.); (845) 888-5000
David Stern, Director

Camp comments: Traditional camp emphasis on individual attention & staffing. Superior facilities.
Activities: Aquatic Activities, Arts/Crafts, Baseball/Softball, Basketball, Challenge/Rope Courses, Golf, Horseback — English, Performing Arts, Tennis
Session lengths & capacity: June-August; 8 week sessions; 365 campers
Clientele & fees: coed 6-16; Fees: F ⚠
Contact: David Elichman, Assistant Director at (201) 560-9870; fax: (212) 214-0871
e-mail: info@campsummit.com
Web site: www.campsummit.com
Operated by: Camp Summit, 120 Route 17 North Ste 120, Paramus, NJ 07652 at (201) 967-1600
Group Rental Information
Site comments: Camp Summit is a traditional eight-week overnight summer camp, with a four-week option for first time campers.
Seasons & Capacity: Spring 500, Fall 500
Facilities: Cabins, Double Occupancy, Food Service, Lake, Meeting Rooms, Playing Fields
Programs: Boating, Swimming (#3330)

Camp Te Ata (est 1993) ⚠

Central Valley, NY (Orange Co.); (845) 928-9460
Kim Tram, Director

Camp comments: Contemporary program in an historic setting, focuses on weekly themes and trips, fitness, leadership and all traditional camp activities.
Activities: Archery, Arts/Crafts, Bicycling/Biking, Boating, Canoeing, Counselor Training (CIT), Horseback — English, Kayaking, Swimming — Instructional, Swimming — Recreational
Session lengths & capacity: June-August; 1, 2 & 4 week sessions; 90 campers
Clientele & fees: girls 8-17; Fees: C ⚠
Contact: Kim Tram, Outdoor Program/Property Manager at (973) 248-8200; fax: (973) 248-8050
e-mail: info@llgsc.org
Web site: www.gsllc.org
Operated by: Lenni Lenape GSC, 95 Newark Pompton Tpk, Riverdale, NJ 07457 at (973) 248-8200 (#2277)

Camp Tel Yehudah (est 1948) ⚠ 🚐

Barryville, NY (Sullivan & Orange Co.); (914) 557-8311
Jonah Geller, Director

Camp comments: Jewish & Israeli culture on the Delaware, peer leadership skills. Team sports, rafting, social action, hiking, Kosher.
Activities: Arts/Crafts, Camping Skills/Outdoor Living, Challenge/Rope Courses, Dance, Language Studies, Leadership Development, Rafting, Sports — Field & Team, Swimming — Recreational, Travel/Tour
Session lengths & capacity: June-August; 1/2, 3 & 7 week sessions; 350 campers
Clientele & fees: coed 14-18; Fees: D, E ⚠ 🐖
Contact: (212) 303-8293; fax: (212) 303-4572
Operated by: Hadassah Womens Zionist Org, 50 West 58th St, New York, NY 10019 at (212) 303-4591 (#1957)

Camp Timbercrest (est 1965) ⚠ 🏠

Randolph, NY (Cattaraugus Co.); (716) 358-3593
Jennifer Coe, Director

Camp comments: Beautiful 900 acre camp with private lake. Self-esteem building programs for girls in an outdoor setting.

Activities: Aquatic Activities, Backpacking, Boating, Camping Skills/Outdoor Living, Canoeing, Counselor Training (CIT), Drama, Field Trips, Horseback — Western, Leadership Development
Session lengths & capacity: June-August; 1/2, 1 & 2 week sessions; 128 campers
Clientele & fees: girls 6-17; families; Fees: B ⚠ 🐖
Contact: Jennifer Coe, Camping Services Director at (716) 665-2225; fax: (716) 661-9704
e-mail: gsswny@yahoo.com
Web site: www.gsswny.org
Operated by: Girl Scouts of SW New York, 2661 Horton Rd, Jamestown, NY 14701 at (716) 665-2225
Group Rental Information
Facilities: Cabins, Hiking Trails, Lake, Lodges, Meeting Rooms, Tents
Programs: Boating, Horseback Riding, Swimming (#1814)

Camp Top of the Pines

(est 1983) ☀ ⚠ 🚐

Bear Mountain, NY (Rockland Co.); (845) 351-5787
Sandi Friedman, Director

Camp comments: Small group. Cooperative activities. Emphasis on personal development.
Activities: Academics, Arts/Crafts, Backpacking, Challenge/Rope Courses, Computer, Drama, Hiking
Session lengths & capacity: 1, 2 & 3 week sessions
Clientele & fees: coed 7-14; Fees: D ⚠ 🐖
Contact: Sandi Friedman, Director of Camp Operations at (212) 765-4420; fax: (973) 838-7534
e-mail: vacprogram@aol.com
Web site: www.vacamas.org
Operated by: Camp Vacamas Assn Inc, 256 Macopin Rd, West Milford, NJ 07480-9971 at (973) 838-1394 (#2804)

Camp Victory Lake (est 1950) ⚠ 🚐

Hyde Park, NY (Dutchess Co.); (914) 229-8851
Garnet M Morris, Director

Camp comments: It's more than a vacation it's an investment in a child's future. We maintain an open-door policy for children age 8-15.
Activities: Academics, Aquatic Activities, Arts/Crafts, Ceramics/Pottery, Computer, Field Trips, Music, Nature/Environment Studies, Sports — Field & Team, Swimming — Instructional
Session lengths & capacity: June-August; 2, 3 & 5 week sessions; 300 campers
Clientele & fees: coed 8-15; Fees: B ⚠
Contact: Garnet M Morris, Camp Director at (718) 291-8006 ext. 246; fax: (718) 739-5133
e-mail: gmorris@northeastern.org
Web site: www.campvictorylake.org
Operated by: Northeastern Conference of SDA, 115-50 Merrick Blvd, Jamaica, NY 11434 at (718) 291-8006 (#27854)

Camp Wakoda (est 1924) ☀ ⚠ 🚐

Central Valley, NY (Orange Co.); (914) 928-6729

Camp comments: Beautiful setting on lake in state park. Outstanding staff, friendly, caring environment. Unique program opportunities.
Activities: Aquatic Activities, Archery, Camping Skills/Outdoor Living, Canoeing, Hiking, Leadership Development, Nature/Environment Studies, Sports — Field & Team, Swimming — Instructional, Swimming — Recreational
Session lengths & capacity: July-August; 1/2 & 1 week sessions; 80 campers
Clientele & fees: girls 5-17; Fees: C ⚠ 🐖
Contact: (845) 361-2898; fax: (845) 361-2915
e-mail: swgsc@citlink.net
Operated by: Sarah Wells GSC, 162 Bloomingburg Rd, Middletown, NY 10940 at (845) 361-2898 (#2243)

Camp Walden (est 1935)

Diamond Point, NY (Warren Co.); (407) 523-1917
Larry & Renee Pitt, Robyn Spector, Director

Camp comments: Idyllic lakefront setting, warm caring experienced staff. Full range of land & water sports, crafts, drama, trips & great fun!
Activities: Arts/Crafts, Challenge/Rope Courses, Drama, Field Trips, Gymnastics, Horseback — Western, Soccer, Tennis, Waterskiing
Session lengths & capacity: June-August; 2, 4 & 8 week sessions; 200 campers
Clientele & fees: coed 6-16; Fees: F
Contact: Larry & Renee Pitt, Owners/Directors at (407) 523-1917; fax: (775) 535-6627
e-mail: waldenmail@yahoo.com
Web site: www.campwalden.org
Operated by: Camp Walden LLC, PO Box 2640, Windermere, FL 34786 at (407) 523-1917 (#19159)

Camp Welmet (est 1998)

Putnam Valley, NY (Putnam Co.)
Rita Santelia, Director

Camp comments: Camp Welmet is a co-ed multicultural sleep away camp with strong emphasis on performing and cultural arts as well as sports and teamwork.
Activities: Aquatic Activities, Archery, Arts/Crafts, Boating, Nature/Environment Studies, Performing Arts, Radio/TV/Video, Sports — Field & Team, Team Building
Session lengths & capacity: June-August; 2, 4 & 6 week sessions; 200 campers
Clientele & fees: coed 8-15; Fees: D
Contact: Rita Santelia, Director at (718) 882-4000; fax: (718) 882-6369
e-mail: campwelmet@aol.com
Web site: www.campwelmet.org
Operated by: Mosholu Montefiore Comm Ctr, 3450 DeKalb Ave, Bronx, NY 10467 at (718) 944-3283

Group Rental Information
Site comments: Camp Welmet offers 250 acres nestled in Fahnestock State Park. It offers great accomodations for overnights or day retreats. Lake, pool, trails available.
Seasons & Capacity: Spring 200, Fall 200
Facilities: Cabins, Food Service, Hiking Trails, Lake, Meeting Rooms, Playing Fields, Pool
Programs: Boating, Swimming (#27634)

Camp Whitman on Seneca Lake
(est 1952)

Dresden, NY (Yates Co.)
Thomas D Montgomery, Director

Camp comments: Camp Whitman offers varieties of non-sectarian experiences that provide personal growth through Christian fellowship.
Activities: Bicycling/Biking, Canoeing, Counselor Training (CIT), Hiking, Music, Sailing, Swimming — Recreational
Session lengths & capacity: July-August; 1 week sessions; 120 campers
Clientele & fees: coed 8-18; families; Fees: C
Contact: Samuel Edwards, Executive Presbyter at (315) 536-7753; fax: (315) 536-2128
Web site: www.campwhitman.org
Operated by: Camp Whitman on Seneca Lake, PO Box 278, Dresden, NY 14441 at (315) 536-7753

Group Rental Information
Facilities: Cabins, Kitchen Facilities, Lake, Meeting Rooms, Pool (#26894)

Campus Kids - Minisink
(est 2001)

Port Jervis, NY (Orange Co.); (845) 856-6433
Jani Brokaw Williams, CCD, Director

Camp comments: Monday through Friday, home with the family on the weekend. Camper choice program. Friendly, fun, positive camp community. Transportation provided.
Activities: Aquatic Activities, Archery, Arts/Crafts, Boating, Challenge/Rope Courses, Gymnastics, Horseback — English, Nature/Environment Studies, Performing Arts, Sports — Field & Team
Session lengths & capacity: June-August; 2, 4, 6 & 8 week sessions; 230 campers
Clientele & fees: coed 7-15; Fees: E
Contact: Jani Brokaw Williams, Director at (845) 621-2193; fax: (845) 621-2383
e-mail: ckminisink@aol.com
Web site: www.campuskids.com
Operated by: Campus Kids Summer Camps, PO Box 422, Mahopac, NY 10541 at (845) 621-2193 (#45205)

Candy Mountain Day Camp
(est 1942)

New City, NY (Rockland Co.); (845) 638-0700
Ruth & Herbert Levitsky, Director

Camp comments: 50 Acres-Go-Karts-Biking-Driving Range-Mini Golf-Bumper Boats-Fishing-Froghunting-Horses-Hot Lunches-Teen/CIT Programs.
Activities: Aquatic Activities, Archery, Arts/Crafts, Baseball/Softball, Basketball, Bicycling/Biking, Boating, Challenge/Rope Courses, Horseback — Western, Swimming — Instructional
Session lengths & capacity: June-August; 4, 6, 7 & 8 week sessions; 800 campers
Clientele & fees: coed 3-15; Fees: D
Contact: Ruth & Herbert Levitsky, Directors/Owners at (845) 638-0700; fax: (845) 634-7198
e-mail: herblevitsky@yahoo.com
Operated by: Candy Mountain Day Camp, 420 Phillips Hill Rd, New City, NY 10956 at (845) 638-0700 (#2143)

Casowasco Camp, Conf & Rtr Ctr (est 1946)

Moravia, NY (Cayuga Co.); (315) 364-8756
Michael D Huber, Director

Camp comments: Christian community set in the heart of the Finger Lakes. A place where lives are changed. Fun, friends, & fellowship.
Activities: Aquatic Activities, Archery, Arts/Crafts, Boating, Challenge/Rope Courses, Horseback — English, Music, Religious Study, Sailing, Sports — Field & Team
Session lengths & capacity: June-August; 1/2, 1 & 2 week sessions; 80 campers
Clientele & fees: coed 6-18; families; Fees: B, C, D
Contact: (315) 364-8756; fax: (315) 364-7636
e-mail: casconfctr@aol.com
Web site: www.ncnyumc.org
Operated by: North Central NY Conf UMC, PO Box 1515, 8422 N Main, Cicero, NY 13039 at (800) 699-8715

Group Rental Information
Site comments: Beautiful setting on the shore of one of NY's Finger Lakes.
Seasons & Capacity: Spring 200, Winter 100
Facilities: A/V Equipment, Cabins, Dorm-Style, Double Occupancy, Food Service, Hiking Trails, Kitchen Facilities, Lake, Linens, Lodges, Meeting Rooms, Playing Fields, Tents
Programs: Boating, Challenge/Ropes Course, Environmental Education, Horseback Riding, Swimming, Winter Sports (#11900)

Catalpa Ave YMCA

Ridgewood, NY (Queens Co.); (718) 821-6271
Lester J Bates, Director

Camp comments: YMCA day camp offering swimming, arts/crafts, nature, sports instruction, focusing on character development and values.
Activities: Arts/Crafts, Counselor Training (CIT), Field Trips, Leadership Development, Sports — Field & Team
Session lengths & capacity: June-August; 9 week sessions; 200 campers
Clientele & fees: coed 5-14; Fees: B
Contact: Lester J Bates, Center Director at (718) 821-6271; fax: (718) 417-3427
e-mail: lbates@ymcanyc.org
Operated by: Catalpa YMCA Day Camps, 69-02 64th St, Ridgewood, NY 11385 at (718) 821-6271 (#6696)

Challenge 2002 (est 1981)

New Rochelle, NY; (914) 633-7744
Carole B Berman, Director

Camp comments: Challenge, a unique program to enrich your child. Education and athletics combine for a summer of fun and enlightenment.
Activities: Academics, Arts/Crafts, Baseball/Softball, Clowning, Computer, Dance, Model Rocketry, Music, Performing Arts, Radio/TV/Video
Session lengths & capacity: June-August; 3 & 4 week sessions; 350 campers
Clientele & fees: coed 4-14; Fees: D
Contact: Carole B Berman, Director/Founder at (914) 779-6024; fax: (914) 793-2685
e-mail: cbberman@aol.com
Web site: www.challengecamps.com
Operated by: The Gifted & Talented Develmnt, PO Box 586, Bronxville, NY 10708 at (914) 779-6024 (#3242)

Champion Day Camp (est 1979)

New City, NY (Rockland Co.); (845) 356-5005
Ian-Matthew Cutler, Director

Camp comments: All activity traditional day camp. Baseball camp. Baseball all day. All sports camp just sports. Swim all programs.
Activities: Arts/Crafts, Baseball/Softball, Basketball, Challenge/Rope Courses, Climbing/Rappelling, Gymnastics, Sports — Field & Team, Swimming — Instructional, Tennis
Session lengths & capacity: July-August; 2, 4, 6 & 8 week sessions; 500 campers
Clientele & fees: coed 3-16; Fees: D
Contact: Judy Bunchuk & Rita Saladucha, Director/Owner at (845) 356-5005; fax: (845) 356-5009
e-mail: sash11@aol.com
Operated by: Champion Day Camp, 175 W Clarkstown Rd, New City, NY 10956 at (845) 356-5005 (#3002)

Chelsea Piers Summer Sports Ca (est 1996)

New York, NY (Kings Co.); (212) 336-6800
Stacey Demar, Director

Camp comments: Chelsea Piers offers 9 diff. sports camps. Through spirited play, children develop competence and discover a love for sports.
Activities: Baseball/Softball, Basketball, Golf, Gymnastics, Hockey, Skating, Soccer, Sports — Field & Team, Tennis
Session lengths & capacity: June-September; 1 week sessions; 4000 campers
Clientele & fees: coed 3-17; Fees: C
Contact: Stacey Demar, Camp Director at (212) 336-6846; fax: (212) 336-6725
e-mail: camps@chelseapiers.com
Web site: www.chelseapiers.com
Operated by: Chelsea Piers LP, Pier 62 Ste 300, New York, NY 10011 at (212) 336-6800 (#4013)

Cherith In The Adirondacks Inc

(est 1966) ⚠ 🚐

Corinth, NY (Saratoga Co.); (518) 654-6262
Nancy Halliday, Director

Camp comments: A Christian camp for girls 7-17.
Quality experience in guided Christian living
outdoors. Wide variety of activities.
Activities: Archery, Arts/Crafts, Backpacking,
Camping Skills/Outdoor Living, Canoeing,
Challenge/Rope Courses, Horseback — English,
Sailing, Swimming — Instructional
Session lengths & capacity: June-August; 1 week
sessions; 160 campers
Clientele & fees: girls 7-17; Fees: **C** ⚠
Contact: Mrs Lisa Wagner, Registrar at
(908) 813-1316;
e-mail: camp_cherith@juno.com
Web site: www.cherith.com
Operated by: Cherith In The Adirondacks Inc, 55
Greenmeadow Court, Deer Park, NY 11729-5619 at
(516) 595-2033 (#1977)

Cherith Of Western New York

(est 1946) ☀ ⚠ 🏠

Hunt, NY (Livingston Co.); (716) 468-3850
Nancy Hanson, Director

Camp comments: Christian, nonprofit camp
ministering to children and youth in the out of
doors.
Activities: Aquatic Activities, Archery, Arts/Crafts,
Camping Skills/Outdoor Living, Canoeing,
Counselor Training (CIT), Horseback — Western,
Leadership Development, Nature/Environment
Studies, Riflery
Session lengths & capacity: June-August; 1, 2, 3,
4, 5, 6 & 7 week sessions; 95 campers
Clientele & fees: boys 8-10; girls 7-18; Fees: **A** ☀
Fees: **B** ⚠
Contact: Donna Schmid, PR at (716) 836-7066;
e-mail: ccwny@juno.com
Web site: www.campcherithwny.org
Operated by: Camp Cherith Western New York,
PO Box 324, Williamsville, NY 14231-0324 at
(716) 836-7066

Group Rental Information

Seasons & Capacity: Spring 30, Summer 95, Fall
95, Winter 30
Facilities: Cabins, Food Service, Hiking Trails,
Kitchen Facilities, Lake, Lodges, Pool, Tents
Programs: Horseback Riding, Swimming (#1811)

ICON LEGEND

☀ Day Camp

⚠ Resident Camp

🏠 Facilities Available To Rent

🚐 Transportation Available

🖐 Financial Aid Available

FEE RANGES PER WEEK

A	$0-75
B	$75-200
C	$201-350
D	$351-500
E	$501-650
F	over $650

Chinatown YMCA (est 1974) ☀

New York, NY (Manhattan Co.); (212) 219-8393
Nilka Yau, Director

Camp comments: Quality staff & programs that
challenge skills, nurture strengths & provide the
values necessary for self respect.
Activities: Academics, Arts/Crafts, Basketball,
Computer, Dance, Photography
Session lengths & capacity: June-September; 1, 2
& 3 week sessions; 200 campers
Clientele & fees: boys 4-11; girls 4-11; coed 4-11;
families; Fees: **A, B** ☀ 🖐
Contact: Anna Eng, Day Camp Director at
(212) 219-8393; fax: (212) 941-9046
e-mail: annaeng1@aol.com
Web site: www.ymcanyc.org
Operated by: Chinatown YMCA, 100 Hester Street,
New York, NY 10002 at (212) 219-8393 (#569)

Chingachgook on Lake George

(est 1913) ☀ ⚠ 🏠

Kattskill Bay, NY (Washington Co.); (518) 656-9462
PJ Motsiff, Director

Camp comments: Adirondacks Moutains! YMCA
character development since 1913.
Sailing,canoeing,hiking,sports,arts,extensive high
ropes course,Teen Adventure Trips,families.
Activities: Aquatic Activities, Arts/Crafts, Canoeing,
Challenge/Rope Courses, Hiking, Photography,
Sailing, Sports — Field & Team, Waterskiing,
Wilderness Trips
Session lengths & capacity: 1 & 2 week sessions;
240 campers
Clientele & fees: coed 7-16; families; seniors;
single adults; Fees: **D** ⚠ 🖐
Contact: George W Painter,CCD, Executive Director
at (518) 656-9462; fax: (518) 656-9362
e-mail: gpainter@cdymca.org
Web site: www.chingachgook.org
Operated by: Capital District YMCA, 1872 Pilot
Knob Rd, Kattskill Bay, NY 12844 at (518) 656-9462

Group Rental Information

Seasons & Capacity: Spring 200, Summer 200,
Fall 200, Winter 100
Facilities: A/V Equipment, Cabins, Dorm-Style,
Double Occupancy, Food Service, Hiking Trails,
Kitchen Facilities, Lake, Lodges, Meeting Rooms,
Ocean, Playing Fields, River, Tents
Programs: Boating, Challenge/Ropes Course,
Environmental Education, Swimming, Winter Sports
(#1856)

Chipinaw (est 1926) ⚠ 🏠 🚐

Swan Lake, NY (Sullivan Co.); (845) 583-5600
Michael Baer, Director

Camp comments: Tradition and innovation
combine for an unforgettable summer experience.
Activities: Aquatic Activities, Archery, Arts/Crafts,
Bicycling/Biking, Challenge/Rope Courses,
Computer, Gymnastics, Horseback — English,
Performing Arts, Sports — Field & Team
Session lengths & capacity: June-August; 4, 6 &
8 week sessions; 300 campers
Clientele & fees: coed 7-17; Fees: **E** ⚠
Contact: Camp Chipinaw Winter Office at
(800) 244-7462; fax: (954) 227-0481
e-mail: info@chipinaw.com
Operated by: UCA, PO Box 770096, Coral Springs,
FL 33077 at (954) 422-7700

Group Rental Information

Seasons & Capacity: Spring 400, Fall 400
Facilities: A/V Equipment, Cabins, Dorm-Style,
Double Occupancy, Food Service, Lake, Linens,
Meeting Rooms, Playing Fields, Pool
Programs: Boating, Challenge/Ropes Course,
Horseback Riding, Swimming (#18756)

Clover Patch Camp (est 1965) ☀ ⚠ 🏠

Scotia, NY (Saratoga Co.); (518) 384-3080
Christopher K Schelin, Director

Camp comments: Accessible camp for children &
adults with disabilities. 1:2 camper/staff ratio. 24 hr.
nursing. Highly qualified staff.
Activities: Aquatic Activities, Arts/Crafts, Camping
Skills/Outdoor Living, Drama, Drawing/Painting,
Music, Nature/Environment Studies, Swimming —
Recreational
Session lengths & capacity: June-August; 1 &
2 week sessions; 24 campers
Clientele & fees: coed 6-99; Fees: **F** ⚠ 🖐
Contact: Christopher K Schelin at (518) 384-3081;
fax: (518) 384-3001
e-mail: schelin@cftd.org
Operated by: Clover Patch Camp, 55 Helping
Hand Lane, Glenville, NY 12302 at (518) 384-3081

Group Rental Information

Facilities: A/V Equipment, Cabins, Food Service,
Hiking Trails, Kitchen Facilities, Playing Fields, Pool
Programs: Environmental Education, Swimming
(#1872)

Coleman Country Day Camp

(est 1982) ☀ 🚐

Merrick, NY (Nassau Co.); (516) 223-2267
Marla & George Coleman, Director

Camp comments: Discover the spirit: Build
courage, self-esteem, cooperation & responsibility
while having fun & making new friends!
Activities: Baseball/Softball, Basketball, Computer,
Gymnastics, Horseback — Western, Soccer, Sports
— Field & Team, Swimming — Instructional, Tennis,
Travel/Tour
Session lengths & capacity: June-August; 4, 6 &
8 week sessions; 1000 campers
Clientele & fees: coed 3-15; Fees: **D** ☀
Contact: Marla or George Coleman,
Owner/Directors at (516) 223-2267;
fax: (516) 868-7449
e-mail: mailbox@colemancountry.com
Web site: www.colemancountry.com
Operated by: Coleman Family Camps, PO Box 34,
Merrick, NY 11566 at (516) 223-2267 (#5650)

Cross Island YMCA Day Camp

(est 1966) ☀ 🚐

Bellerose, NY (Queens Co.); (718) 479-0505
Michele Wright, Director

Camp comments: Day camp offers opportunity to
improve self esteem through age appropriate,
structured activities and trips.
Activities: Arts/Crafts, Baseball/Softball, Basketball,
Counselor Training (CIT), Field Trips, Swimming —
Instructional, Swimming — Recreational, Tennis
Session lengths & capacity: 2 week sessions;
320 campers
Clientele & fees: coed 5-13; Fees: **B, C** ☀ 🖐
Contact: Michele Wright, Camp Director at
(718) 479-0505; fax: (718) 468-9568
Operated by: YMCA of Greater New York, 238 10
Hillside Ave, Bellerose, NY 11426 at (718) 479-0505
(#6276)

Day Camp In The Park

(est 1979) ☀ 🚐

Stony Point, NY (Rockland Co.); (845) 351-4781
Ken Glotzer, Director

Camp comments: 500 Acres, 3 mile pristine lake,
pools, waterpark, tennis, ball fields, karate,
computer, climbingwall. Complete sports prog. arts,
nature, boating & swimming.
Activities: Academics, Boating, Computer, Drama,
Gymnastics, Kayaking, Martial Arts, Sports — Field
& Team, Swimming — Instructional, Swimming —
Recreational
Session lengths & capacity: July-August; 4, 6 &
8 week sessions; 420 campers

Clientele & fees: coed 4-15; Fees: C ☀
Contact: Ken Glotzer, Director at (845) 638-2515;
fax: (845) 638-2515
e-mail: dcitp@aol.com
Web site: www.daycampinthepark.com
Operated by: Day Camp in the Park, 6 Kendall
Drive, New City, NY 10956 at (845) 638-2515
(#12452)

Deer Mountain Day Camp

(est 1956)

Pomona, NY (Rockland Co.); (914) 354-2727
Roberta Katz, Director

Camp comments: 45 yr trad. 3:1 camper to staff.
25 acs, 6 pools, 7 tennis courts, athletics, crafts &
drama. Rockland & Bergen Cos.
Activities: Arts/Crafts, Baseball/Softball, Boating,
Challenge/Rope Courses, Computer,
Nature/Environment Studies, Performing Arts,
Sports — Field & Team, Swimming — Instructional,
Travel/Tour
Session lengths & capacity: July-August; 4, 6 &
8 week sessions; 800 campers
Clientele & fees: coed 3-15; Fees: E ☀
Contact: Roberta, Rita, or Mel Katz, Owers &
Directors at (845) 354-2727; fax: (845) 354-5248
e-mail: deermtn1@aol.com
Operated by: Deer Mountain Day Camp, 63 Call
Hollow Rd, Pomona, NY 10970 at (845) 354-2727
(#3049)

Deerfoot Lodge (est 1930)

Speculator, NY (Hamilton Co.); (518) 548-5277
Chuck Gieser, Director

Camp comments: Seeking to build godly young
men in a Christ-centered environment of wilderness
camping.
Activities: Aquatic Activities, Archery, Arts/Crafts,
Camping Skills/Outdoor Living, Challenge/Rope
Courses, Leadership Development,
Nature/Environment Studies, Riflery, Sports — Field
& Team, Wilderness Trips
Session lengths & capacity: June-August; 2 week
sessions; 165 campers
Clientele & fees: boys 8-16; Fees: D, E ⚠ 🚐
Contact: Chuck & SallyJo Gieser, Director/Office
Manager at (518) 966-4115; fax: (518) 966-4605
e-mail: DL12164@juno.com
Web site: www.deerfoot.org
Operated by: Christian Camps Inc, 205 Highland
Rd, Greenville, NY 12083 at (518) 966-4115
(#13604)

Deerkill Day Camp (est 1958)

Suffern, NY (Rockland Co.); (845) 354-1466
Robert & Karen Rhodes, Director

Camp comments: A balanced, noncompetitive
program with an exceptionally mature staff.
Instruction in 14 areas.
Activities: Arts/Crafts, Baseball/Softball, Boating,
Computer, Drama, Gymnastics, Martial Arts,
Swimming — Instructional, Swimming —
Recreational, Tennis
Session lengths & capacity: June-August; 4, 6, 7
& 8 week sessions; 450 campers
Clientele & fees: coed 3-14; Fees: D, E ☀
Contact: Karen & Robert Rhodes, Director at
(845) 354-1466; fax: (845) 362-4597
e-mail: deerkill@worldnet.att.net
Web site: www.deerkilldaycamp.com
Operated by: Deerkill Day Camp, 54 Wilder Rd,
Suffern, NY 10901 at (845) 354-1466 (#2038)

Double H Hole in the Woods Rch

(est 1992)

Lake Luzerne, NY (Warren Co.); (518) 696-5676
Peter J. Carner, Director

Camp comments: Located in the Adirondack Mtns.
Offering hope & adventure to 1000 critically ill

children, 500 children in our adaptive ski program &
800 for specialty fmy cmps
Activities: Arts/Crafts, Challenge/Rope Courses,
Drama, Nature/Environment Studies, Performing
Arts, Team Building
Session lengths & capacity: June-August; 1 week
sessions; 129 campers
Clientele & fees: boys 6-16; girls 6-16; Fees: A ⚠
Contact: Peter J Carner, Director of Operations at
(518) 696-5676; fax: (518) 696-4528
e-mail: petercarner@doublehranch.org
Web site: www.doublehranch.org
Operated by: Double H Hole in the Woods Rch, 97
Hidden Valley Road, Lake Luzerne, NY 12846 at
(518) 696-5676 (#10377)

DP Flint NASSAU Cty 4H Camp

(est 1924)

Riverhead, NY (Suffolk Co.); (516) 454-0900
Maria T. Devlin, Director

Camp comments: 159 acres + 48 acre working
farm on L.I. Sound. A living lab in leadership
development. Open to all children 8-18 years.
Activities: Archery, Arts/Crafts, Camping
Skills/Outdoor Living, Canoeing, Challenge/Rope
Courses, Farming/Ranching/Gardening, Horseback
— Western, Model Rocketry, Nature/Environment
Studies, Swimming — Instructional
Session lengths & capacity: June-August; 1, 2 &
8 week sessions; 350 campers
Clientele & fees: coed 8-18; Fees: C ⚠
Contact: Harold A Ifft, Camp Facility Coordinator at
(516) 454-0900 ext. 245; fax: (516) 454-0365
e-mail: hifft@cce.cornell.edu
Operated by: Cornell Coop Ext of Nassau Co, 1425
Old country Rd Bldg J, Plainview, NY 11803 at
(516) 454-0900

Group Rental Information
Facilities: Cabins, Food Service, Hiking Trails,
Lodges, Meeting Rooms, Ocean
Programs: Horseback Riding (#1996)

Eastern District YMCA Day Camp

Brooklyn, NY (Kings Co.); (718) 782-8300
Ida Perez, Director
Activities: Arts/Crafts, Dance, Drawing/Painting,
Farming/Ranching/Gardening, Field Trips, Music,
Nature/Environment Studies, Sports — Field &
Team, Swimming — Recreational
Session lengths & capacity: 8 week sessions;
120 campers
Clientele & fees: boys 5-12; girls 5-12;
Fees: A ☀ 🚐
Contact: Ida Perez, Day Camp Director at
(718) 782-8300; fax: (718) 782-1474
Operated by: Eastern District YMCA, 125
Humboldt St, Brooklyn, NY 11206 at
(718) 782-8300 (#541)

Echo Lake (est 1945)

Warrensburg, NY (Warren Co.); (518) 623-9635
Amy, George, Mary, and Tony Stein, Director

Camp comments: Echo Lake is committed to
empowering children. Confidence built via cutting
edge program implemented by exemplary staff.
Activities: Arts/Crafts, Challenge/Rope Courses,
Community Service, Leadership Development,
Skating, Sports — Field & Team, Tennis, Wilderness
Trips
Session lengths & capacity: 8 week sessions;
450 campers
Clientele & fees: coed 7-17; Fees: F ⚠
Contact: George Stein, Directors at
(914) 345-9099; fax: (914) 345-2120
Web site: www.campecholake.com
Operated by: Echo Lake Camp Inc, 3 West Main
St, Elmsford, NY 10523 at (914) 345-9099 (#1929)

Echo Lake Southwoods

(est 1998)

Paradox, NY; (518) 532-7717
Scott & Andrea Ralls, Director

Camp comments: A 4-Week values based
experience including the best in crafts, watersports,
landsports, theater & outdoor tripping.
Activities: Aquatic Activities, Arts/Crafts, Camping
Skills/Outdoor Living, Challenge/Rope Courses,
Horseback — English, Sports — Field & Team,
Tennis, Waterskiing
Session lengths & capacity: June-October;
4 week sessions; 300 campers
Clientele & fees: coed 6-15; families; single adults;
Fees: F ⚠
Contact: Scott Ralls, Owner/Director at
(914) 345-2444; fax: (914) 345-2107
e-mail: info@southwoods.com
Web site: www.southwoods.com
Operated by: Southwoods Recreation Inc,
PO Box 459, North White Plains, NY 10603-0459 at
(914) 345-2444

Group Rental Information
Seasons & Capacity: Fall 300
Facilities: Cabins, Dorm-Style, Food Service,
Hiking Trails, Lake, Linens, Meeting Rooms, Playing
Fields
Programs: Boating, Challenge/Ropes Course,
Horseback Riding, Swimming (#2391)

Edward Isaacs (est 1966)

Holmes, NY (Dutchess Co.); (914) 878-6885
Bill Frankel, Director

Camp comments: Full athletic programs,heated
pool, private lake, dance, crafts, computers, drama,
nature & much more. Kosher kitchen.
Activities: Archery, Arts/Crafts, Basketball,
Canoeing, Computer, Dance, Drama,
Nature/Environment Studies, Soccer
Session lengths & capacity: June-August; 4, 6 &
8 week sessions; 200 campers
Clientele & fees: coed 8-15; Fees: D ⚠
Contact: Bill Frankel, Director at (718) 268-5011
ext. 207; fax: (718) 793-0515
e-mail: campedi@aol.com
Operated by: Central Queens YM and YWHA,
67-09 108th St, Forest Hills, NY 11375 at
(718) 268-5011 (#1940)

Elmwood Country Day

(est 1957)

White Plains, NY (Westchester Co.); (914) 592-6121
Jeff Ackerman, Director

Camp comments: Safe, caring, nurturing
environment where children grow through exciting
programs & friendly staff. Individual attn.
Activities: Arts/Crafts, Baseball/Softball, Basketball,
Drama, Field Trips, Hockey, Music, Performing Arts,
Soccer, Swimming — Instructional
Session lengths & capacity: July-August; 4, 6 &
8 week sessions; 400 campers
Clientele & fees: coed 3-11; Fees: E ☀
Contact: Jeff Ackerman & Bobbi Wittenberg,
Directors at (914) 592-6121; fax: (914) 592-2195
e-mail: Jeff@Elmwooddaycamp.com
Web site: www.elmwooddaycamp.com
Operated by: Elmwood Country Day, 900 Dobbs
Ferry Rd, White Plains, NY 10607 at (914) 592-6121
(#3000)

Epworth (est 1959)

High Falls, NY (Ulster Co.); (845) 687-0215
Melinda Trotti, Director

Camp comments: 150 acres in the mountains.
Hiking, biking, swimming, animals, crafts,
environmental activities & more. Mature,
experienced, caring staff at a year round site.

Activities: Arts/Crafts, Backpacking, Bicycling/Biking, Canoeing, Caving, Challenge/Rope Courses, Hiking, Religious Study, Sports — Field & Team, Swimming — Recreational
Session lengths & capacity: June-August; 1 & 2 week sessions; 120 campers
Clientele & fees: coed 5-18; Fees: B ☀
Fees: C △ 🚐
Contact: Melinda Trotti, Director at (845) 687-0215; fax: (845) 687-0502
e-mail: melindatrotti@hotmail.com
Web site: www.umcamps.org
Operated by: NY Conf United Methodist, PO Box 549, Shelter Island Hts, NY 11965 at (631) 749-0430

Group Rental Information
Site comments: 150 acres 90 miles north of NYC. Open to religious & not-for-profit groups. Heated lodges available for school year. Plentiful home-cooked meals served.
Seasons & Capacity: Spring 112, Fall 112, Winter 112
Facilities: Cabins, Dorm-Style, Food Service, Hiking Trails, Kitchen Facilities, Lodges, Playing Fields
Programs: Environmental Education (#2047)

Father Drumgoole CYO Camp
(est 1996) ☀ 🚐

Staten Island, NY; (718) 317-2754
Julia Larsen, Director

Camp comments: The CYO helps children reach their full potential as loving human being through many fun activities.
Activities: Arts/Crafts, Basketball, Counselor Training (CIT), Drama, Hiking, Nature/Environment Studies, Sports — Field & Team, Swimming — Recreational
Session lengths & capacity: July-August; 2 week sessions; 350 campers
Clientele & fees: coed 5-13; Fees: B ☀ 🚐
Contact: Julia Larsen, S1 CYO Community Center Director at (718) 420-1010; fax: (718) 273-8361
Operated by: Catholic Youth Organization, 6451 Hylan Blvd, Staten Island, NY 10309 at (718) 317-2754 (#18889)

Flatbush YMCA Day Camp
(est 1980) ☀

Brooklyn, NY (Brooklyn Co.); (718) 469-8100
Derrick Dawson, Director

Camp comments: Day camp with a sleep-away location & we have day trips all week long. We accept ACD referrals.

ICON LEGEND

☀ Day Camp
△ Resident Camp
🏠 Facilities Available To Rent
🚐 Transportation Available
🐷 Financial Aid Available

FEE RANGES PER WEEK

A	$0-75
B	$75-200
C	$201-350
D	$351-500
E	$501-650
F	over $650

Activities: Aerobics/Exercise, Arts/Crafts, Basketball, Counselor Training (CIT), Dance, Drawing/Painting, Field Trips, Leadership Development, Soccer
Session lengths & capacity: 9 week sessions
Clientele & fees: boys 6-17; girls 6-17; coed 6-17; single adults; Fees: B ☀ 🚐
Contact: Ismael Lallave, Program Director at (718) 469-8100; fax: (718) 284-5537
Operated by: Flatbush YMCA Day Camp, 1401 Flatbush Ave, Brooklyn, NY 11210 at (718) 469-8100 (#6408)

Flushing YMCA Sports Camp
(est 1939) ☀ 🚐

Flushing, NY (Queens Co.); (718) 961-6880
Sylvia Sanchez, Director

Camp comments: Flushing Y Summer Camp program through a variety of recreational, educational, social & cultural activities, strives to give children an opportunity to grow.
Activities: Academics, Arts/Crafts, Baseball/Softball, Basketball, Dance, Drama, Field Trips, Gymnastics, Sports — Field & Team
Session lengths & capacity: 8 week sessions; 300 campers
Clientele & fees: coed 5-16; Fees: B ☀ 🚐
Contact: Sylvia Sanchez, School Age Child Care Director at (718) 961-6880 ext. 145; fax: (718) 445-8392
e-mail: ssanchez@ymcanyc.org
Operated by: Flushing YMCA, 138-46 Northern Blvd, Flushing, NY 11354 (#4360)

Forest Lake Camp Inc (est 1926) △

Warrensburg, NY (Warren Co.); (518) 623-4771
Gary Confer, Director

Camp comments: Cabins with 400 acres & private lake. Full program of sports, arts, riding, aquatics & trips. Choices made daily.
Activities: Arts/Crafts, Bicycling/Biking, Drama, Horseback — English, Kayaking, Nature/Environment Studies, Soccer, Sports — Field & Team, Tennis, Wilderness Trips
Session lengths & capacity: June-August; 4 & 8 week sessions; 200 campers
Clientele & fees: boys 8-16; girls 8-16; Fees: E △
Contact: Gary Confer, Director at (908) 534-9809; fax: (908) 534-8474
Web site: www.forestlakecammp.com
Operated by: Forest Lake Camp Inc, Box 648, Oldwick, NJ 08858 at (908) 534-9809 (#12860)

French Woods Festival
(est 1970) △ 🏠

Hancock, NY (Delaware Co.); (914) 887-5600
Ronald Schaefer, Director

Camp comments: Individualized prog in performing & visual arts. Campers choose from these & sports, waterfront, horsemanship.
Activities: Clowning, Computer, Dance, Drama, Gymnastics, Horseback — English, Music, Performing Arts, Radio/TV/Video, Tennis
Session lengths & capacity: 3, 6 & 9 week sessions; 400 campers
Clientele & fees: coed 7-17; Fees: F △
Contact: Ron Schaefer, Director at (800) 634-1703; fax: (954) 346-7564
e-mail: admin@frenchwoods.com
Operated by: UCA, PO Box 770096, Coral Springs, FL 33077 at (954) 422-7700

Group Rental Information
Site comments: Picturesque setting with meeting facilities for up to 800.
Seasons & Capacity: Spring 800, Summer 800, Fall 800
Facilities: Cabins, Food Service, Lake, Meeting Rooms
Programs: Boating, Horseback Riding (#2055)

Fresh Air Fund Camp
(est 1948) △ 🏠 🚐

Fishkill, NY (Dutchess Co.); (914) 897-4320
Thomas Karger, Director

Camp comments: Free camp for NYC disadvantaged children. Special career awareness program.
Activities: Arts/Crafts, Camping Skills/Outdoor Living, Challenge/Rope Courses, Dance, Farming/Ranching/Gardening, Hiking, Nature/Environment Studies, Photography, Radio/TV/Video, Swimming — Instructional
Session lengths & capacity: June-August; 2 week sessions; 828 campers
Clientele & fees: boys 8-15; girls 8-13; coed 8-15; Fees: A △
Contact: Thomas Karger, Deputy Exec Director at (212) 897-8900; fax: (212) 681-0147
e-mail: freshair@freshair.org
Web site: www.freshair.org
Operated by: The Fresh Air Fund, 633 Third Avenue 14th Fl, New York, NY 10018 at (212) 897-8900

Group Rental Information
Site comments: Two fully winterized retreat centers, 65 miles from NYC.
Seasons & Capacity: Spring 0, Fall 0, Winter 0
Facilities: Cabins, Food Service, Hiking Trails, Lake, Linens, Meeting Rooms, Pool
Programs: Challenge/Ropes Course, Environmental Education (#2042)

Friends Academy Summer Camps (est 1969) ☀ 🚐

Locust Valley, NY (Nassau Co.); (516) 393-4207
Richard Mack, Director

Camp comments: Inst. program designed to develop self confidence. Emphasis on sportsmanship/respect for every person. Family atmosphere
Activities: Arts/Crafts, Community Service, Golf, Hockey, Horseback — English, Sailing, Swimming — Instructional
Session lengths & capacity: June-August; 2, 4 & 8 week sessions; 550 campers
Clientele & fees: coed 3-14; families; Fees: D ☀
Contact: Matthew Bradley, Director at (516) 393-4207; fax: (516) 465-1720
e-mail: camp@fa.org
Web site: www.fa.org
Operated by: Friends Academy, Duck Pond Rd, Locust Valley, NY 11560 at (516) 676-0393 (#2135)

Frost Valley YMCA Camps
(est 1901) ☀ △ 🏠 🚐

Claryville, NY (Ulster Co.); (845) 985-2291
Elizabeth Horne, Director

Camp comments: Traditional programs plus focus on well-ness lifestyles. Located on 6000 acres in Catskill Mts.
Activities: Boating, Challenge/Rope Courses, Climbing/Rappelling, Drama, Hiking, Horseback — Western, Nature/Environment Studies, Sports — Field & Team, Travel/Tour, Wilderness Trips
Session lengths & capacity: June-August; 2 week sessions; 500 campers
Clientele & fees: coed 7-16; families; Fees: D △ 🚐
Contact: Elizabeth Horne, Director of Camping at (845) 985-2291; fax: (845) 985-0056
e-mail: lhorne@frostvalley.org
Operated by: Frost Valley YMCA, 2000 Frost Valley Rd, Claryville, NY 12725 at (845) 985-2291

Group Rental Information
Site comments: Frost Valley YMCA celebrates diversity in camping - mainstreaming the different populations served while focusing on sharing, caring, respect & responsibility.
Facilities: Food Service, Hiking Trails, Lake, Lodges, Meeting Rooms

Programs: Boating, Environmental Education (#2254)

Gate Hill Day Camp (est 1951)

Stony Point, NY (Rockland Co.); (845) 947-3223
Jennifer & Bob Male, Director

Camp comments: Situated on 33 wooded acres. Campers experience an 'I can do it' sense of achievement. Specialty & traditional programs.
Activities: Academics, Arts/Crafts, Boating, Camping Skills/Outdoor Living, Challenge/Rope Courses, Performing Arts, Sports — Field & Team, Swimming — Instructional, Tennis, Travel/Tour
Session lengths & capacity: 4, 5, 6, 7 & 8 week sessions; 400 campers
Clientele & fees: coed 3-15; Fees: C, D
Contact: Jennifer & Bob Male, Director/Owner at (845) 947-3223; fax: (845) 942-0958
Web site: www.gatehilldaycamp.com
Operated by: Gate Hill Day Camp, PO Box 592, Stony Point, NY 10980 at (845) 947-3223 (#1976)

Girls Vacation Fund Inc

(est 1935)

East Windham, NY (Greene Co.); (518) 734-3850
Eva Lewandowski, Director

Camp comments: Rustic Catskill Mountain camp. Traditional program providing a caring place to build self-esteem for inner city girls.
Activities: Archery, Arts/Crafts, Backpacking, Boating, Camping Skills/Outdoor Living, Ceramics/Pottery, Challenge/Rope Courses, Nature/Environment Studies, Swimming — Instructional, Team Building
Session lengths & capacity: July-August; 2 week sessions; 110 campers
Clientele & fees: girls 7-14; Fees: B
Contact: Elizabeth Morales, Registrar at (212) 532-7050; fax: (212) 532-7061
Web site: www.girlsvacationfund.com
Operated by: Girls Vacation Fund, 370 Lexington Ave, New York, NY 10017 at (212) 532-7050 (#2062)

Glen Spey (est 1966)

Glen Spey, NY (Sullivan Co.); (845) 856-6521
Arliss Perfetti, Director

Camp comments: Accept the challenge to explore, learn, and develop self confidence in a safe and caring environment girl scouts-where girls grow strong.
Activities: Arts/Crafts, Boating, Camping Skills/Outdoor Living, Canoeing, Hiking, Horseback — English, Leadership Development, Nature/Environment Studies, Sailing, Swimming — Recreational
Session lengths & capacity: July-July; 1/2 & 1 week sessions; 100 campers
Clientele & fees: girls 5-17; Fees: C, D
Contact: Arliss Perfetti, Director of Resident Camp at (201) 967-8100; fax: (201) 967-7175
e-mail: gscobc@bergen.org
Operated by: GSC of Bergen County, 300 Forest Ave, Paramus, NJ 07652 at (201) 967-8100

Group Rental Information
Site comments: Come and enjoy our secluded paradise of 600 acres of plush woodlands and crystal clear 70 acre heart-shaped spring fed lake.
Seasons & Capacity: Spring 270, Summer 270, Fall 270, Winter 86
Facilities: Cabins, Food Service, Hiking Trails, Kitchen Facilities, Lake, Playing Fields, Tents
Programs: Boating, Environmental Education, Swimming, Winter Sports (#3392)

Glengarra (est 1965)

Camden, NY (Oswego Co.); (315) 964-2889
Judith H. Reilly, Director

Camp comments: Day and Resident Girl Scout camp focusing on traditional outdoor living skills and high-adventure trips.
Activities: Arts/Crafts, Backpacking, Bicycling/Biking, Boating, Camping Skills/Outdoor Living, Canoeing, Challenge/Rope Courses, Nature/Environment Studies, Sailing, Swimming — Recreational
Session lengths & capacity: July-August; 1/2, 1 & 2 week sessions; 100 campers
Clientele & fees: girls 6-17; Fees: B
Fees: B, C, D
Contact: Judith H Reilly, Program Manager at (315) 733-2391; fax: (315) 733-1909
Operated by: Foothills GSC, 33 Jewett Place, Utica, NY 13501 at (315) 733-2391

Group Rental Information
Facilities: Food Service, Hiking Trails, Kitchen Facilities, Lake, Meeting Rooms, Tents
Programs: Boating (#1885)

Great South Bay YMCA Day Camp (est 1980)

Bay Shore, NY (Suffolk Co.); (631) 665-4255
Bob Pettersen, Director

Camp comments: Day camp with a wide variety of activities, events, and trips. Dynamic staff, great facility, warm caring atmosphere!
Activities: Arts/Crafts, Basketball, Dance, Drama, Leadership Development, Nature/Environment Studies, Soccer, Swimming — Recreational
Session lengths & capacity: 2, 4 & 8 week sessions; 500 campers
Clientele & fees: boys 3-15; girls 3-15; coed 3-15; Fees: B
Contact: Bob Pettersen, Associate Executive Director at (631) 665-4255; fax: (631) 665-4261
Operated by: YMCA Long Island, 155 Buckley Road, Holtsville, NY 11742 at (631) 289-4440 (#3082)

Greenpoint YMCA Summer Camp (est 1980)

Bilyn, NY (Brooklyn Co.)
Denise Ross, Director

Camp comments: Safe, adult supervised programs promotes creativity, social skills, cooperation & enrichment.
Activities: Arts/Crafts, Basketball, Field Trips, Music, Swimming — Recreational
Session lengths & capacity: 2, 4 & 8 week sessions
Clientele & fees: boys 5-12; girls 5-12; coed 5-12; Fees: B
Contact: Denise L Ross, Childcare Director at (718) 389-3700; fax: (718) 349-2146
Operated by: Greenpoint YMCA, 99 Meserole Ave, Brooklyn, NY 11222 at (718) 389-3700 (#677)

GSC Camp Pinewood

Arkport, NY; (607) 295-7036
Bernadette Bowie, Director

Camp comments: 40 miles south of Dansville NY. In caring & naturing environment, girls learn to challenge themselves participating in activities like swimming and canoeing.
Activities: Aquatic Activities, Backpacking, Boating, Camping Skills/Outdoor Living, Canoeing, Challenge/Rope Courses, Drama, Hiking, Leadership Development
Session lengths & capacity: June-August; 1/2 & 1 week sessions; 80 campers
Clientele & fees: girls 5-18; Fees: B
Fees: B, C, D
Contact: Web site: www.gsgv.org

Operated by: GSC of Genesee Valley Inc, 1020 John Street, West Henrietta, NY 14586 at (585) 239-7915

Group Rental Information
Facilities: Cabins, Hiking Trails, Lake, Lodges, Meeting Rooms, Ocean, Playing Fields, Pool, Tents
Programs: Boating, Challenge/Ropes Course, Swimming (#34835)

Harlem YMCA Jackie Robinson

New York, NY (Manhattan Co.); (212) 283-8543
Adrian Harris/Antoinette Burrows, Director

Camp comments: Harlem Y day camp is the place to be. There's fun, there's games & activities, So, 'Come on down so you can see.'
Activities: Arts/Crafts, Basketball, Computer, Dance, Drawing/Painting, Field Trips, Martial Arts, Sports — Field & Team, Swimming — Recreational
Session lengths & capacity: 5 week sessions
Clientele & fees: boys 5-13; girls 5-13; Fees: B
Contact: A. D. Harris, Youth Program Director at (212) 281-4100; fax: (212) 491-3178
Operated by: Harlem YMCA, 181 W 135th St, New York, NY 10030 at (212) 281-4100 (#522)

Hidden Pond Park Day Camp

(est 1993)

Hauppauge, NY (Suffolk Co.); (631) 232-3222
Richard Haggerty, Director

Camp comments: A camp where every child feels welcome to have fun, learn and make new friends while having a summer to remember.
Activities: Arts/Crafts, Baseball/Softball, Bicycling/Biking, Climbing/Rappelling, Computer, Performing Arts, Soccer, Swimming — Instructional, Tennis
Session lengths & capacity: June-August; 3, 4, 5, 6, 7, 8 week sessions; 500 campers
Clientele & fees: coed 3-15; Fees: B, C
Contact: Pamela Pavone, Administrative Asst at (631) 232-3222 ext. 201; fax: (631) 232-3228
Web site: www.hiddenponddaycamp.com
Operated by: Hidden Pond Park Sports Camp, 660 Terry Rd, Hauppauge, NY 11788 at (631) 232-3222 (#2233)

Hillcroft Day Camp

(est 1950)

Billings, NY (Dutchess Co.); (845) 223-5826
Dennis, Judy, Greg & Sally Buttinger, Director

Camp comments: Long recognized as a camp where campers come & feel special. Offers friendship, fun & excellent program, mature staff.
Activities: Archery, Arts/Crafts, Ceramics/Pottery, Dance, Drama, Farming/Ranching/Gardening, Fencing, Gymnastics, Sports — Field & Team, Swimming — Instructional
Session lengths & capacity: June-August; 4 & 8 week sessions; 400 campers
Clientele & fees: coed 4-14; Fees: C
Contact: Dennis Buttinger, Director/Owner at (845) 223-5826; fax: (845) 677-5562
e-mail: dennis@camphillcroft.com
Web site: www.camphillcroft.com
Operated by: The Buttinger Family, Camp Hillcroft, Box 5, Billings, NY 12510 at (845) 223-5826

Group Rental Information
Seasons & Capacity: Spring 12, Fall 12
Facilities: Cabins, Food Service, Hiking Trails, Lake, Playing Fields, Pool
Programs: Challenge/Ropes Course, Swimming (#2227)

Hillside Day and Tripping Camp

(est 1971) ☀

Brewster, NY (Putnam Co.); (914) 279-2996
Marty Newell, Director

Camp comments: Day camp offers diverse program with exceptional staff. Special limited enrollment day, horse and trip camp.
Activities: Archery, Arts/Crafts, Camping Skills/Outdoor Living, Canoeing, Challenge/Rope Courses, Farming/Ranching/Gardening, Leadership Development, Nature/Environment Studies, Swimming — Recreational
Session lengths & capacity: 3 week sessions; 300 campers
Clientele & fees: coed 3-14; Fees: **B, C** ☀ Fees: **C** ▲ 🐷
Contact: Marty Newell, Public Program Office at (914) 279-2996 ext. 104; fax: (914) 279-3077
e-mail: hillside@bestweb.net
Web site: www.greenchimneys.org
Operated by: Green Chimneys School, 400 Doawnburg Rd Box 719, Brewster, NY 10509-0719 at (845) 279-2996 (#11995)

Hofstra University Summer Camp (est 1984) ☀ 🚗

Hempstead, NY; (516) 463-5018
Terence Ryan, Director

Camp comments: Hofstra University is unique with a broad spectrum of summer day camp programs a coed camp; ranging from 5 years of age by September to 14 years of age.
Activities: Academics, Baseball/Softball, Basketball, Computer, Dance, Soccer, Sports — Field & Team, Swimming — Instructional, Tennis
Session lengths & capacity: July-August; 2, 4, 6 & 7 week sessions; 800 campers
Clientele & fees: coed 5-14; Fees: **E** ☀
Contact: (516) 463-5018; fax: (516) 463-6114
Web site: www.hofstra.edu/uccesummercamps
Operated by: Hofstra University Summer Camp, 250 Hofstra Univ, Hempstead, NY 11549 at (516) 463-5018 (#6236)

Holiday Hills YMCA Day Camp

(est 1988) ☀

Pawling, NY (Dutchess Co.); (914) 855-0204
Bob Lassonde, Director

Camp comments: A safe, secure growth-oriented environment. Warm & supportive staff offering a variety of fun, choice & theme programs.

ICON LEGEND

☀ Day Camp
▲ Resident Camp
🏠 Facilities Available To Rent
🚗 Transportation Available
🐷 Financial Aid Available

FEE RANGES PER WEEK

A	$0-75
B	$75-200
C	$201-350
D	$351-500
E	$501-650
F	over $650

Activities: Arts/Crafts, Camping Skills/Outdoor Living, Hiking, Leadership Development, Nature/Environment Studies, Soccer, Sports — Field & Team, Swimming — Instructional, Swimming — Recreational, Tennis
Session lengths & capacity: June-August; 1, 2, 4, 6 & 8 week sessions; 99 campers
Clientele & fees: boys 3-16; girls 3-16; coed 3-16; Fees: **B** ☀
Contact: Bob Lassonde, Day Camp & Associate Program Director at (914) 855-0204; fax: (914) 855-9535
Web site: www.ymcanyc.org
Operated by: YMCA Of Greater New York, 333 Seventh Avenue, New York, NY 10011 at (212) 630-9600 (#543)

Holy Family Summer Camp

(est 1993) ☀ 🚗

Hicksville, NY (Nassau Co.); (516) 937-0636
Gary R Turnier, Director

Camp comments: Campers thrive in non-competitive, caring atmosphere with opportunities to belong, learn, contribute. Bussing available.
Activities: Aerobics/Exercise, Arts/Crafts, Baseball/Softball, Basketball, Dance, Field Trips, Soccer, Swimming — Recreational, Travel/Tour
Session lengths & capacity: 4, 6 & 8 week sessions; 250 campers
Clientele & fees: coed 4-15; families; Fees: **B** ☀ 🚗
Contact: Gary R Turnier, Director/Coordinator at (516) 937-0636; fax: (516) 937-1058
Operated by: Holy Family Roman Catholic, 25 Fordham Ave, Hicksville, NY 11801 at (516) 937-0636 (#1679)

Huntington (est 1961) ▲ 🏠 🚗

High Falls, NY (Ulster Co.); (914) 687-7840
Dr Bruria K Falik, Director

Camp comments: Special needs camp, learning/developmental disabled & ADD campers. Traditional prog of excellence. 2:1 cmpr:staff ratio.
Activities: Academics, Arts/Crafts, Basketball, Drama, Drawing/Painting, Farming/Ranching/Gardening, Horseback — Western, Music, Performing Arts, Swimming — Recreational
Session lengths & capacity: June-August; 1, 3, 4, 7 & 8 week sessions; 200 campers
Clientele & fees: boys 6-21; coed 6-21; Fees: **F** ▲
Contact: Bruria K Falik, Phd, Director at (845) 679-4903; fax: (845) 679-4903
e-mail: camphtgtn@aol.com
Web site: www.camphuntington.com
Operated by: Bururia Bodek Falik PhD, PO Box 368, Woodstock, NY 12498 at (845) 679-4903

Group Rental Information

Facilities: Cabins, Dorm-Style, Food Service, Hiking Trails, Linens, Meeting Rooms, Playing Fields, Pool, River
Programs: Swimming (#2126)

Huntington Township YMCA Camp (est 1953) ☀

Huntington, NY (Suffolk Co.); (631) 421-4242
Karen Blackburn, Director
Activities: Arts/Crafts, Basketball, Counselor Training (CIT), Dance, Nature/Environment Studies, Soccer, Sports — Field & Team, Swimming — Instructional, Swimming — Recreational, Team Building
Contact: Karen Blackburn, Youth Development Director at (631) 421-4242; fax: (631) 421-5807
Operated by: YMCA Long Island, 155 Buckley Road, Holtsville, NY 11742 at (631) 289-4440 (#4012)

International Riding Camp

(est 1978) ▲

Greenfield Park, NY (Vister Co.); (845) 647-3240
Arno Mares, Director

Camp comments: The ultimate experience for developing riders.Fulfill your riding dreams,from polo/foxhunting/horseshows to galloping on the beach.
Activities: Arts/Crafts, Drawing/Painting, Golf, Horseback — English, Swimming — Recreational, Tennis
Session lengths & capacity: 1, 2, 3, 4, 5, 6, 7, 8 & 9 week sessions; 60 campers
Clientele & fees: girls 6-18; Fees: **F** ▲
Contact: Arno Mares, Director at (845) 647-3240; fax: (845) 647-3286
Web site: www.horseridingcamp.com
Operated by: International Riding Camp, Birchal Road, Greenfield Park, NY 12435 at (845) 647-3240 (#3105)

Iroquois Springs Camp Sequois ▲ 🏠

Rock Hill, NY; (845) 434-6500
Activities: Boating, Challenge/Rope Courses, Horseback — Western, Swimming — Instructional, Swimming — Recreational
Contact: Web site: www.campecholake.com
Operated by: Echo Lake Camp Inc, 3 West Main St, Elmsford, NY 10523 at (914) 345-9099 (#48145)

Ivy League Day Camp Inc

(est 1961) ☀ 🚗

Smithtown, NY (Suffolk Co.); (631) 265-4177
Linda Kaplan/Noah Cooper/Mandy Goldberg, Director

Camp comments: Let us provide your child with a summer of fun, friends & fabulous memories.
Activities: Arts/Crafts, Challenge/Rope Courses, Computer, Field Trips, Performing Arts, Sports — Field & Team, Swimming — Instructional, Swimming — Recreational, Travel/Tour
Session lengths & capacity: June-August; 4, 6 & 8 week sessions; 450 campers
Clientele & fees: coed 2-15; Fees: **D** ☀
Contact: Linda Kaplan, Director at (631) 265-4177; fax: (631) 265-4698
e-mail: linda@ivyleaguekids.com
Web site: www.ivyleaguekids.com
Operated by: Cooper Camps LLC, 211 Brooksite Dr, Smithtown, NY 11787 at (631) 265-4177 (#7607)

Jamaica YMCA Day Camp

(est 1927) ☀ 🚗

Jamaica, NY (Queens Co.); (718) 739-6600

Camp comments: The Jamaica Y's Day Camp/Sports Camp offers a warm and friendly atmosphere with caring, certified staff. For ages 5-15.
Activities: Arts/Crafts, Basketball, Field Trips, Leadership Development, Sports — Field & Team, Swimming — Recreational
Session lengths & capacity: 1 & 8 week sessions; 300 campers
Clientele & fees: coed 5-15; Fees: **B** ☀ 🐷
Contact: Nyam Smith, Associate Executive Director at (718) 739-6600 ext. 131; fax: (718) 658-7233
Operated by: Jamaica YMCA, 89 25 Parsons Blvd, Jamaica, NY 11432 at (718) 739-6600 (#519)

JCC Midwestchester Camps ☀ 🚗

Scarsdale, NY (Westchester Co.); (914) 472-3300
Allison Horn, Director

Camp comments: Offering 4 camp programs. Camp Gadol - a general day camp, summer arts center, and two travel programs for grades 5-9.

Activities: Arts/Crafts, Field Trips, Gymnastics, Performing Arts, Sports — Field & Team, Swimming — Instructional, Swimming — Recreational, Travel/Tour
Session lengths & capacity: June-August; 4, 6 & 8 week sessions
Clientele & fees: coed 2-14; Fees: C ☀
Contact: Allison Horn, Director at (914) 472-3300 ext. 336; fax: (914) 472-9270
e-mail: horna@jcca.org
Web site: www.Jccmidwestchester.org
Operated by: JCC Mid-Westchester, 999 Wilmot Road, Scarsdale, NY 10583 at (914) 472-3300 (#45046)

Jeanne d'Arc Camp (est 1922) ⚠ 🚗

Merrill, NY (Clinton Co.); (518) 425-3311
Frances D. McIntyre, Director

Camp comments: Fun-filled, friendly camp. Beautiful Adirondack Lake. Individual activities, choice prog develop confidence & self-esteem
Activities: Archery, Arts/Crafts, Canoeing, Drama, Horseback — English, Sailing, Tennis, Waterskiing
Session lengths & capacity: 3 & 7 week sessions; 120 campers
Clientele & fees: girls 6-17; Fees: E ⚠
Contact: Fran McIntyre (Mrs. J.C., Owner/Director at (518) 425-3311;
e-mail: FUNATCJDA@aol.com
Web site: www.campjeannedarc.com
Operated by: Jeanne d'Arc Inc, 154 Gadway Rd, Merrill, NY 12955 at (518) 425-3311 (#19711)

Kamp Kiwanis (est 1930) ⚠ 🚗

Taberg, NY (Onedia Co.); (315) 336-4568
Nancy Ann Nowak, Director

Camp comments: A mainstream camp for all children including special needs. Program is non-competitive w/ an emphasis on team building.
Activities: Arts/Crafts, Basketball, Camping Skills/Outdoor Living, Canoeing, Hiking, International Culture, Swimming — Recreational
Session lengths & capacity: 1 week sessions; 120 campers
Clientele & fees: boys 8-14; girls 8-14; coed 8-14; seniors; single adults; Fees: C ⚠ 🚢
Contact: Nancy Ann Nowak, Executive Director at (315) 336-4568; fax: (315) 336-3845
e-mail: kampkiwanis@mybizz.net
Web site: www.kiwanis-ny.org/kamp/
Operated by: Kamp Kiwanis, 9020 Kiwanis Rd, Taberg, NY 13471 at (315) 336-4568 (#4139)

Kennybrook (est 1941) ⚠ 🏠 🚗

Monticello, NY (Sullivan Co.); (914) 794-5320
Peter & Howard Landman, Director

Camp comments: A place to have fun and grow in a caring structured environment. Many activities, excellent instruction. Continued outstanding leadership for 40 years.
Activities: Aquatic Activities, Arts/Crafts, Baseball/Softball, Basketball, Challenge/Rope Courses, Gymnastics, Hockey, Horseback — Western, Tennis, Waterskiing
Session lengths & capacity: June-September; 4 & 8 week sessions; 300 campers
Clientele & fees: coed 6-16; Fees: F ⚠
Contact: Peter Landman, Owner/Director at (914) 693-3037; fax: (914) 693-7678
e-mail: kennybrook@aol.com
Web site: www.kennybrook.com
Operated by: Camp Kennybrook Inc, 633 Saw Mill River Road, Ardsley, NY 10502 at (914) 693-3037 (#7227)

Kingswood (est 1958) ⚠

Hancock, NY (Delaware Co.); (607) 637-5401
Rev Donna Schmid, Director

Camp comments: Unique family vacation. Camp safely in a Christian community. 720 Catskill mountain acres. 22 sites. All gear provided.
Activities: Arts/Crafts, Camping Skills/Outdoor Living, Hiking, Nature/Environment Studies, Religious Study, Swimming — Recreational
Session lengths & capacity: July-August; 1 & 2 week sessions; 30 campers
Clientele & fees: families; Fees: C ⚠ 🚢
Contact: D Taylor, Site Chairperson at (914) 234-3157; fax: (914) 234-2182
Web site: www.umcamps.org
Operated by: NY Conf United Methodist, PO Box 549, Shelter Island Hts, NY 11965 at (631) 749-0430 (#1964)

Kiwi Inc (est 1952) ☀

Mahopac, NY (Putnam Co.); (914) 277-3876
Louis F. Bellotto, Director

Camp comments: Since 1952, day camp with overnight atmosphere. Outstanding staff. Total elective system.
Activities: Aquatic Activities, Arts/Crafts, Canoeing, Dance, Farming/Ranching/Gardening, Leadership Development, Nature/Environment Studies, Sports — Field & Team, Swimming — Recreational, Tennis
Session lengths & capacity: 4, 6 & 8 week sessions; 600 campers
Clientele & fees: boys 3-15; girls 3-15; families; Fees: C ☀
Contact: Lou,Hildy,Ivan Bellotto/Karla,Brad, Owners/Directors at (845) 277-3876;
fax: (845) 277-0875
e-mail: campkiwi1@aol.com
Web site: www.campkiwi.com
Operated by: The Bellotto-Brown Family, PO Box 435, Mahopac, NY 10541 at (845) 277-3876 (#7422)

Koinonia Community (est 1963) ⚠ 🏠

Highland Lake, NY (Sullivan Co.); (800) 980-2267
Steve Lee, Director

Camp comments: 1200 ac. of beautiful wilderness with mountain lakes. Great activities with a focus on community building. Faith-centered program and quality staff.
Activities: Arts/Crafts, Camping Skills/Outdoor Living, Canoeing, Hiking, Nature/Environment Studies, Rafting, Religious Study, Swimming — Recreational
Session lengths & capacity: June-August; 1/2, 1 & 2 week sessions; 120 campers
Clientele & fees: coed 8-18; families; seniors; single adults; Fees: C ⚠ 🚢
Contact: (800) 980-2267; fax: (914) 557-8335
e-mail: koinoniany@yahoo.com
Web site: www.koinoniany.org
Operated by: Martin Luther Camp Corp, 165 Lakeview Dr, Highland Lake, NY 12743 at (845) 557-8335

Group Rental Information
Site comments: Enjoy warm hospitality and experience spiritual renewal in the 1200 ac. wilderness of Koinonia. Many options to meet the needs of all ages and varied groups.
Seasons & Capacity: Spring 120, Summer 120, Fall 120, Winter 120
Facilities: A/V Equipment, Cabins, Dorm-Style, Double Occupancy, Food Service, Hiking Trails, Kitchen Facilities, Lake, Linens, Meeting Rooms, Playing Fields
Programs: Boating, Challenge/Ropes Course, Environmental Education, Swimming, Winter Sports (#7007)

Kutshers Sports Academy

(est 1968) ⚠ 🚗

Monticello, NY (Sullivan Co.); (914) 794-5400
Marc White, Director

Camp comments: Elective instructional progs taught by quality coaches, top facilities, individual attention, supportive,fun atmosphere.
Activities: Arts/Crafts, Baseball/Softball, Basketball, Golf, Gymnastics, Soccer, Sports — Field & Team, Tennis
Session lengths & capacity: June-August; 3, 4 & 7 week sessions; 450 campers
Clientele & fees: coed 7-17; families; Fees: F ⚠
Contact: Jodi Raffa, Office Manager at (888) 874-5400; fax: (845) 794-0157
e-mail: kutsport@warwick.net
Web site: www.ksacad.com
Operated by: Kutsher's Sports Academy, Anawana Lake Rd, Monticello, NY 12701 at (914) 794-5400 (#7486)

Lake Chautauqua Lutheran Ctr

(est 1937) ☀ ⚠ 🏠

Bemus Point, NY (Chautauqua Co.); (716) 386-4125
Glenn C Oswald, Director

Camp comments: Christian youth camp open to all. Camp activities, services, nature, sailing, performing arts. Lake, sports fields, forest. Between Buffalo & Cleveland.
Activities: Arts/Crafts, Canoeing, Challenge/Rope Courses, Community Service, Leadership Development, Nature/Environment Studies, Religious Study, Sailing, Swimming — Recreational
Session lengths & capacity: June-August; 1/2, 1 & 2 week sessions; 160 campers
Clientele & fees: boys 7-19; girls 7-19; coed 7-19; families; seniors; single adults; Fees: A ☀
Fees: C ⚠
Contact: Linda Andrews, Registrar at (716) 386-4125; fax: (716) 386-5714
e-mail: lclc-elca@juno.com
Operated by: Lake Chautauqua Lutheran Ctr, 5013 Rout 430, Bemus Point, NY 14712 at (716) 386-4125

Group Rental Information
Site comments: Year-round adult center. Cabins, Lake, trails, snow sports, challenge course, leadership available. 1.5-2.5 hrs. to Buffalo-Cleveland. Near I-90, airport.
Seasons & Capacity: Spring 96, Summer 160, Fall 96, Winter 96
Facilities: A/V Equipment, Cabins, Dorm-Style, Double Occupancy, Food Service, Hiking Trails, Kitchen Facilities, Lake, Linens, Lodges, Meeting Rooms, Playing Fields, Tents
Programs: Boating, Challenge/Ropes Course, Environmental Education, Swimming, Winter Sports (#1804)

Lake Placid Soccer Camp

(est 1976) ☀ ⚠ 🚗

Lake Placid, NY (Essex Co.); (800) 845-9959
Michael McGlynn, Director

Camp comments: North America's premier youth soccer educational program, Coerver coaching top international staff teams advanced skill sessions.
Activities: Aquatic Activities, International Culture, Soccer, Sports — Field & Team, Swimming — Recreational
Session lengths & capacity: June-August; 1 week sessions; 300 campers
Clientele & fees: coed 5-18; Fees: C ☀
Fees: D ⚠
Contact: Jean Kendrick, Manager at (800) 845-9959; fax: (518) 523-9476
e-mail: lpsoccer@capital.net
Web site: www.lakeplacidsoccer.com
Operated by: Lake Placid Soccer Centre Inc, PO Box 847, Lake Placid, NY 12946 at (800) 845-9959 (#3160)

Lakota (est 1930) ▲

Wurtsboro, NY; (845) 888-5611
Gil Hollander, Director

Camp comments: Traditional structure, high variety of activities, top facilities, caring environment 'We love it so much we bought it.'
Activities: Aquatic Activities, Basketball, Bicycling/Biking, Climbing/Rappelling, Computer, Leadership Development, SCUBA, Soccer, Tennis, Waterskiing
Session lengths & capacity: June-August; 4 & 8 week sessions; 425 campers
Clientele & fees: coed 6-16; families; Fees: **E** ▲
Contact: Gil Hollander, Director at (800) 252-5682; fax: (732) 548-2469
e-mail: camplakota@aol.com
Operated by: Kota Kamp Inc, 200 Route 17 North, Paramus, NJ 07652 at (800) 252-5682 (#10703)

Le Club Des Enfants/Los Ninos

(est 1986) ☀

New York, NY (Manhattan Co.); (212) 396-1369
Francois Thibaut, Director

Camp comments: French & Spanish day camps. Explore language & culture through songs, games, arts & crafts, baking, field trips & summer fun.
Activities: Academics, Arts/Crafts, Field Trips, Language Studies, Music, Sports — Field & Team
Session lengths & capacity: June-August; 2, 3, 4, 5, 6, 7, 8 & 9 week sessions; 75 campers
Clientele & fees: boys 3-10; girls 3-10; Fees: **C** ☀
Contact: Francois Thibaut, Director at (212) 396-1369;
Operated by: Language Workshop For Children, 888 Lexington Ave, New York, NY 10021 at (212) 396-1369 (#6260)

Lenoloc ▲ 🚐

Bear Mountain, NY (Orange Co.); (845) 351-4410
Lonzella Brize, Director

Camp comments: Camp Lenoloc is fun! fun! fun! Trad. program on Lake Cohasset, Bear Mtn.,NY. Beautiful, rustic environment. Campers' self-confidence soars from the love & care.
Activities: Archery, Baseball/Softball, Boating, Canoeing, Drama, Hiking, Nature/Environment Studies, Sports — Field & Team, Swimming — Instructional, Swimming — Recreational
Session lengths & capacity: July-August; 1 & 2 week sessions; 80 campers
Clientele & fees: boys 6-10; girls 6-13; Fees: **D** ▲
Contact: Daphne Brown, Adm. Asst. at (973) 672-9500; fax: (973) 672-6266
Operated by: YWCA Of Essex and West Hudson, 395 Main St, Orange, NJ 07050 at (973) 672-9500 (#2248)

ICON LEGEND

☀	Day Camp
▲	Resident Camp
🏠	Facilities Available To Rent
🚐	Transportation Available
🐷	Financial Aid Available

FEE RANGES PER WEEK

A	$0-75
B	$75-200
C	$201-350
D	$351-500
E	$501-650
F	over $650

Long Island City YMCA (est 1987) ☀

Long Island City, NY; (718) 392-7932
Activities: Academics, Aerobics/Exercise, Arts/Crafts, Community Service, Counselor Training (CIT), Field Trips, Nature/Environment Studies, Sports — Field & Team, Team Building
Session lengths & capacity: July-August; 2 week sessions; 200 campers
Clientele & fees: boys 3-16; girls 3-16; coed 3-16; Fees: **B** ☀ 🚐
Contact: Web site: www.ymcanyc.org
Operated by: Long Island City YMCA, 32-23 Queens Blvd, Long Island City, NY 11101 at (718) 392-7932 (#16283)

Long Point Camp (est 1953) ▲ 🏠

Penn Yan, NY (Yates Co.); (315) 536-6301
Captain Terry Wood, Director

Camp comments: Resident camp, rustic setting. Emphasizes self-worth & character building. Christian emphasis with outdoor specialization, econ. disadvantaged.
Activities: Arts/Crafts, Baseball/Softball, Basketball, Camping Skills/Outdoor Living, Canoeing, Drama, Hiking, Music, Nature/Environment Studies, Swimming — Instructional
Session lengths & capacity: 1 week sessions; 192 campers
Clientele & fees: coed 6-12; Fees: **C** ▲ 🐷
Contact: Terry Wood, Camp Director at (315) 434-1325; fax: (315) 434-1399
Operated by: The Salvation Army, 200 Twin Oaks Dr, Syracuse, NY 13206 at (315) 434-1325

Group Rental Information
Facilities: A/V Equipment, Cabins, Dorm-Style, Double Occupancy, Food Service, Hiking Trails, Kitchen Facilities, Lake, Linens, Lodges, Meeting Rooms, Playing Fields, Pool
Programs: Boating, Swimming (#1841)

Lourdes Camp (est 1943) ▲ 🏠

Skaneateles, NY (Onondaga Co.); (315) 673-2888
Michael A Preston, Director

Camp comments: A nice place to make friends and memories that will last a lifetime.
Activities: Arts/Crafts, Basketball, Canoeing, Challenge/Rope Courses, Horseback — English, Sailing, Swimming — Instructional, Tennis
Session lengths & capacity: July-August; 1 week sessions; 240 campers
Clientele & fees: coed 7-14; Fees: **C** ▲
Contact: Michael Preston, Director at (315) 424-1812;
e-mail: Lourdes4me@aol.com
Web site: www.lourdescamp.com
Operated by: Lourdes Camp Inc, 1654 West Onondaga St, Syracuse, NY 13204 at (315) 424-1812

Group Rental Information
Facilities: Cabins, Kitchen Facilities, Lake, Lodges
Programs: Challenge/Ropes Course (#1833)

Ma-He-Tu (est 1937) ▲ 🏠

Bear Mountain, NY (Rockland Co.); (845) 351-4508
Janet Igoe Paddack, Director

Camp comments: All Girls' camp-ages 7-15. Beautiful lakeside setting, activities include athletics, arts & crafts, drama, boating.
Activities: Arts/Crafts, Camping Skills/Outdoor Living, Canoeing, Drama, Drawing/Painting, Hiking, Leadership Development, Music, Swimming — Instructional, Swimming — Recreational
Session lengths & capacity: 2, 4 & 6 week sessions; 90 campers
Clientele & fees: girls 7-15; Fees: **C** ▲
Contact: Marion Schumacher, Registrar at (888) 262-4388; fax: (631) 351-1657
Operated by: Lutheran Girls Camp Assn Inc, 6 Soundview Dr N, Huntington, NY 11746 at (888) 262-4388

Group Rental Information
Facilities: Cabins, Food Service, Hiking Trails, Kitchen Facilities, Lake, Playing Fields, Tents
Programs: Boating, Swimming (#2170)

Ma-Kee-Ya (est 1989) ☀ ▲ 🏠 🚐

Bear Mountain, NY (Orange Co.); (914) 351-2460
Christine Phillips, Director

Camp comments: Rustic noncompetitive back to nature weekly resident prog available, professional staff, caring, safe & fun.
Activities: Archery, Arts/Crafts, Canoeing, Counselor Training (CIT), Nature/Environment Studies, Sports — Field & Team, Swimming — Instructional, Swimming — Recreational
Session lengths & capacity: June-August; 2, 4 & 8 week sessions; 200 campers
Clientele & fees: boys 7-15; girls 7-15; coed 7-15; Fees: **D** ☀ Fees: **A** ▲
Contact: Christine Phillips, Director at (201) 444-0291; fax: (201) 670-4548
e-mail: cmakeeya@juno.com
Operated by: YWCA of Bergen County, 112 Oak Street, Ridgewood, NJ 07450 at (201) 444-5600 (#6378)

Madison (est 1984) ▲

Kingston, NY (Ulster Co.); (914) 336-7124
Jack Thomas, Director

Camp comments: Agency camp serving the youth of New York City. Members of Madison Square Boys & Girls Club.
Activities: Academics, Arts/Crafts, Camping Skills/Outdoor Living, Computer, Dance, Drawing/Painting, Hiking, Nature/Environment Studies, Swimming — Recreational
Session lengths & capacity: 3 week sessions; 160 campers
Clientele & fees: coed 7-12; Fees: **A, C** ▲
Contact: Jack Thomas, Camp Director at (845) 336-7124; fax: (845) 336-7126
e-mail: campmad84@aol.com
Web site: www.madisonsquare.org
Operated by: Madison, 201 Powder Mill Bridge Rd, Kingston, NY 12401 at (845) 336-7124 (#18733)

Maplewood School (est 1949) ☀

Wantagh, NY; (516) 221-2121
Joseph Holden, Director
Activities: Aquatic Activities, Arts/Crafts, Baseball/Softball, Basketball, Computer, Dance, Soccer, Sports — Field & Team, Swimming — Instructional, Tennis
Contact: Joe Holden, Director at (516) 221-2121; fax: (516) 221-9309
e-mail: hldnj@aol.com
Operated by: Maplewood, 2166 Wantagh, Wantagh, NY 11793 at (516) 221-2121 (#10775)

Mark Country Day School

(est 1962) ☀

Bay Shore, NY (Suffolk Co.); (516) 665-1935
Jan Finkelstein, Director
Activities: Aquatic Activities, Arts/Crafts, Baseball/Softball, Basketball, Computer, Counselor Training (CIT), Dance, Music, Nature/Environment Studies, Soccer
Session lengths & capacity: 8 week sessions
Clientele & fees: coed 3-15
Contact: Jan Finkelstein, Owner/Director at (516) 665-1935; fax: (516) 666-2544
Operated by: Mark Country Day School, 67 Greenwood Rd, Bay Shore, NY 11706 at (516) 665-1935 (#12353)

Maximum Teen Travel Camp

(est 1990)

Oceanside, NY (Nassau Co.); (516) 594-2000
Marje Fraser, Director

Camp comments: Creative travel program of day & overnight trips; small groups, nurturing environment; fantastic staff, great campers.
Activities: Aquatic Activities, Boating, Canoeing, Climbing/Rappelling, Field Trips, Kayaking, Skating, Swimming — Recreational, Travel/Tour, Waterskiing
Session lengths & capacity: July-August; 4, 5, 6, 7 & 8 week sessions; 150 campers
Clientele & fees: coed 10-14; Fees: **E**
Contact: Marje Fraser, Camp Director at (516) 594-2000; fax: (516) 594-2105
e-mail: marje@maximumtours.com
Web site: www.maximumtours.com
Operated by: Maximum Teen Travel Camp, 3132 Long Beach Rd, Oceanside, NY 11572 at (516) 594-2000 (#738)

Mc Burney YMCA Day Camps

New York, NY (Manhattan Co.); (212) 741-8729
Osama Hassan, Director

Camp comments: Our quality program combines sports, trips, swim, arts & crafts & fun for a memorable experience. Value based.
Activities: Arts/Crafts, Basketball, Community Service, Field Trips, Leadership Development, Nature/Environment Studies, Performing Arts, Swimming — Recreational
Session lengths & capacity: July-August; 2 week sessions; 200 campers
Clientele & fees: coed 3-12; Fees: **B**
Contact: (212) 741-9272; fax: (212) 741-9216
Web site: www.ymca.org
Operated by: Mc Burney YMCA Day Camps, 122 West 17th St, New York, NY 10011 at (212) 741-8715 (#6355)

Merrick Woods Cntry Day School (est 1956)

Merrick, NY; (516) 483-7272
Jack Langbart, Director

Camp comments: Est.1956. Family operated. Mature, supportive staff. Strong Instructional programs in swim, sports, crafts. Teen travel.
Activities: Arts/Crafts, Challenge/Rope Courses, Climbing/Rappelling, Drama, Golf, Gymnastics, Sports — Field & Team, Tennis, Travel/Tour
Session lengths & capacity: June-August; 4, 6 & 8 week sessions; 500 campers
Clientele & fees: coed 2-15; Fees: **D**
Contact: Adam Langbart, Director at (516) 483-7272; fax: (516) 483-3950
e-mail: info@merrickwoods.com
Web site: www.merrickwoods.com
Operated by: Merrick Woods Country Day Sch, 26 Catalpa Lane, Valley Stream, NY 11581 at (516) 483-7272 (#15503)

Mid Island Y JCC (est 1963)

Wheattey Heights, NY (Nassau Co.); (516) 822-3535

Camp comments: Camp fosters a social & recreational camp experience. Small groups. 1:4 counselor:camper ratio. All sports.
Activities: Aquatic Activities, Arts/Crafts, Baseball/Softball, Camping Skills/Outdoor Living, Computer, Counselor Training (CIT), Dance, Field Trips, Music, Sports — Field & Team
Session lengths & capacity: 3 & 7 week sessions; 1000 campers
Clientele & fees: boys 4-16; girls 4-16; coed 4-16; Fees: **C**
Contact: Sheryl Kirschenbaum, Director of Camping Services at (516) 822-3535; fax: (516) 822-3288

e-mail: miyjcc.org@aol.com
Web site: www.miyjcc.org
Operated by: Mid Island Y JCC, 45 Manetto Hill Road, Plainview, NY 11803 at (516) 822-3535 (#6682)

Miss Sues Summer Fun

(est 1963)

Plainview, NY (Nassak Co.); (516) 938-0894
Ron Kuznetz, Director

Camp comments: We specialize in children ages 3-6.
Activities: Arts/Crafts, Field Trips, Gymnastics, Martial Arts, Music, Performing Arts, Soccer, Sports — Field & Team, Swimming — Instructional, Team Building
Session lengths & capacity: 4, 6 & 8 week sessions; 200 campers
Clientele & fees: coed 3-6; Fees: **D**
Contact: Ron Kuznetz, Director at (516) 938-0894; fax: (516) 938-3184
e-mail: scubaron@aol.com
Operated by: Miss Sues Summer Fun, 1191 Old Country Road, Plainview, NY 11803 at (516) 938-0894 (#17936)

Mohawk Day Camp (est 1930)

White Plains, NY (Westchester Co.); (914) 949-2635
Barbara & Steve Schainman, Director

Camp comments: 80+ teachers form core of supportive staff. Instruction in broad sports & cultural program on unique, 40 acre site.
Activities: Arts/Crafts, Baseball/Softball, Basketball, Ceramics/Pottery, Dance, Nature/Environment Studies, Soccer, Sports — Field & Team, Swimming — Instructional, Tennis
Session lengths & capacity: June-August; 5, 6 & 8 week sessions
Clientele & fees: boys 5-12; girls 5-12; coed 3-4; Fees: **E**
Contact: Barbara & Steve Schainman, Directors at (914) 949-2635; fax: (914) 949-7345
e-mail: campmohawk@aol.com
Web site: www.campmohawk.com
Operated by: Mohawk Day Camp, Old Tarrytown Rd, White Plains, NY 10603 at (914) 949-2635 (#1892)

Monroe (est 1941)

Monroe, NY (Orange Co.); (845) 782-8695
Stanley Felsinger, Director

Camp comments: Great facilities, mature staff, lasting friendships, Fun structured Jewish camp. Strictly Kosher. Always open for visit.
Activities: Arts/Crafts, Basketball, Computer, Drama, Gymnastics, Horseback — Western, Nature/Environment Studies, Soccer, Tennis
Session lengths & capacity: June-August; 4 & 8 week sessions; 350 campers
Clientele & fees: coed 6-16; Fees: **E A**
Contact: Stanley Felsinger, Director at (845) 782-8695; fax: (845) 782-2247
Operated by: Camp Stan Jack Inc, PO Box 475, Monroe, NY 10950 at (845) 782-8695 (#2022)

Morrys Camp Inc (est 1996)

White Plains, NY (Westchester Co.); (914) 592-3055
Teresa Younger & Dawn Ewing, Director

Camp comments: A very special camp and a caring environment, a dream for Morry. A dream come true for children.
Activities: Academics, Aquatic Activities, Arts/Crafts, Baseball/Softball, Basketball, Camping Skills/Outdoor Living, Leadership Development, Music, Nature/Environment Studies
Session lengths & capacity: June-August; 4 week sessions; 100 campers
Clientele & fees: coed 10-14; Fees: **A A**

Contact: Teresa Younger and Dawn Ewing, Co-Executive Directors at (914) 592-3055; fax: (914) 592-2195
e-mail: dream@morryscamp.org
Web site: www.morryscamp.org
Operated by: Morrys Camp Inc, 900 Dobbs Ferry Rd, White Plains, NY 10607 at (914) 592-3055 (#4465)

Mount Tom Country Day Camp

(est 1955)

New Rochelle, NY (Westchester Co.); (914) 636-8130
Doug Volan, Director

Camp comments: Magnificent facilities, close to Manhattan & Westchester. Small groups, 1:4 Ratios. Parents asked to visit & compare.
Activities: Aquatic Activities, Arts/Crafts, Baseball/Softball, Dance, Drama, Nature/Environment Studies, Performing Arts, Soccer, Swimming — Instructional, Tennis
Session lengths & capacity: July-August; 4, 5, 6, 7 & 8 week sessions; 400 campers
Clientele & fees: boys 3-13; girls 3-13; coed 3-13; Fees: **D, E**
Contact: Doug Volan, Directors at (914) 636-8130; fax: (914) 576-3270
e-mail: mttomcamp@aol.com
Web site: www.mounttomdaycamp.com
Operated by: Mount Tom Country Day Camp, 48 Mount Tom Road, New Rochelle, NY 10805 at (914) 636-8130 (#4407)

Nabby Day Camp (est 1940)

Mohegan Lake, NY (Westchester Co.); (914) 528-7796
Joe Bertino, Director

Camp comments: 55 year. 3 tennis courts, 3 swimming pools, nature, crafts, music. Excellent facilities, program & staff.
Activities: Archery, Arts/Crafts, Baseball/Softball, Basketball, Gymnastics, Music, Nature/Environment Studies, Soccer, Swimming — Instructional, Tennis
Session lengths & capacity: 4, 6 & 8 week sessions; 400 campers
Clientele & fees: boys 4-12; girls 4-12; Fees: **C**
Contact: Joe Bertino, Director at (914) 944-3049;
Operated by: Nabby Day Camp, 1 Nabby Hill, Mohegan Lake, NY 10547 at (914) 528-7796 (#16689)

Normandie (est 1966)

Westport, NY (Essex Co.); (800) 206-8333
Waldemar Kasriels, Director

Camp comments: Water sports concentration. Campers create their own program daily, on Lake Champ lain! In the Adirondacks.
Activities: Boating, Canoeing, Counselor Training (CIT), Sailing, SCUBA, Soccer, Tennis, Waterskiing, Windsurfing
Session lengths & capacity: 2, 4 & 8 week sessions; 150 campers
Clientele & fees: coed 9-17; Fees: **E A**
Contact: Waldemar Kasriels, Director at (800) 206-8333; fax: (518) 962-2050
e-mail: normandie@aol.com
Web site: www.normandie-watersports.com
Operated by: Camp Normandie, Furnace Point Rd, Westport, NY 12993 at (518) 962-4750 (#7107)

North Country Camps

(est 1920)

Keeseville, NY; (518) 834-5152
Nancy Birdsall and Bruce Hennessey, Director

Camp comments: Program emphasizes adventurous hiking, canoe, mountain, bicycle trips; strong sense of community; learning at own pace.

Activities: Aquatic Activities, Arts/Crafts, Bicycling/Biking, Camping Skills/Outdoor Living, Horseback — English, Sailing, Sports — Field & Team, Swimming — Instructional, Tennis, Wilderness Trips
Session lengths & capacity: June-August; 5 & 7 week sessions; 160 campers
Clientele & fees: boys 8-15; girls 8-15; Fees: E △ 🚐
Contact: Nancy Birdsall and Bruce Hennessey, Directors at (802) 235-2908; fax: (802) 235-2908
e-mail: nancy@nccamps.com
Web site: www.nccamps.com
Operated by: North Country Camps Inc, 395 Frontage Rd, Keeseville, NY 12944 at (518) 834-5527 (#2188)

North Shore Day Camp

(est 1943)   ☀ 🚐

Glen Cove, NY (Nassau Co.); (516) 676-0904
Paula Rothman & Andy Pritikin, Director
Camp comments: Warm nurturing atmosphere. Creative & innovative program. Mature, caring staff. Small groups. Specialty camps available.
Activities: Arts/Crafts, Baseball/Softball, Basketball, Climbing/Rappelling, Drama, Field Trips, Horseback — English, Soccer, Swimming — Instructional, Tennis
Session lengths & capacity: June-August; 4, 6 & 8 week sessions; 450 campers
Clientele & fees: coed 2-15; Fees: D, E ☀
Contact: Paula Rothman & Andy Pritikin, Directors at (516) 676-0904; fax: (516) 676-0965
e-mail: Fun@northshoredaycamp.com
Web site: www.camptlc.com
Operated by: Timber Lake, 85 Crescent Beach Rd, Glen Cove, NY 11542 at (516) 656-4227 (#3881)

North Shore Holiday House Camp

                                          △

Huntington, NY; (516) 427-7630
Debra Deal, Director
Activities: Arts/Crafts, Computer, Dance, Drama, Field Trips, Sports — Field & Team, Swimming — Recreational
Operated by: North Shore Holiday House Inc, 74 Huntington Road, Huntington, NY 11743 at (631) 427-7630 (#32512)

Northern Frontier (est 1946)   △ 🚐

North River, NY (Hamilton Co.); (518) 251-2322
Ralph Essery, Director
Camp comments: Rustic setting in the beautiful Adirondack Mountains. Counselor: camper ratio 1:4. Christian service brigade camp.

ICON LEGEND

☀	Day Camp
△	Resident Camp
🏠	Facilities Available To Rent
🚐	Transportation Available
🐷	Financial Aid Available

FEE RANGES PER WEEK

A	$0-75
B	$75-200
C	$201-350
D	$351-500
E	$501-650
F	over $650

Activities: Archery, Aviation, Boating, Camping Skills/Outdoor Living, Climbing/Rappelling, Hiking, Leadership Development, Religious Study, Riflery, Sailing
Session lengths & capacity: June-August; 1/2, 1 & 2 week sessions; 140 campers
Clientele & fees: boys 8-18; families; Fees: C △ 🚐
Contact: Ralph Essery, Director at (845) 876-8009; fax: (845) 876-6075
e-mail: nfrontier@aol.com
Operated by: Northern Frontier, 3298 State Route 9G, Rhinebeck, NY 12572 at (845) 876-8009 (#1979)

Northwest YMCA Day Camp

(est 1972)   ☀

Rochester, NY (Monroe Co.); (716) 227-3900
Christina Vito, Director
Camp comments: The Northwest YMCA Day Camp offers a variety of activities that include fun, friends, and adventure all summer long.
Activities: Arts/Crafts, Basketball, Canoeing, Counselor Training (CIT), Drama, Field Trips, Hiking, Sports — Field & Team, Swimming — Recreational, Team Building
Session lengths & capacity: June-September; 1 week sessions; 240 campers
Clientele & fees: coed 6-16; Fees: B ☀ 🚐
Contact: Christina Vito, Senior Program Director at (716) 227-3900; fax: (716) 227-4829
e-mail: chrisv@rochesterymca.org
Web site: www.rochesterymca.org
Operated by: YMCA of Greater Rochester, 444 E Main St, Rochester, NY 14604 at (716) 546-5500 (#4176)

Oasis Brooklyn

                                          ☀

Brownsville & Central, NY; (000) 000-0718
Jennifer Zanger, Justin Weiss, Director
Camp comments: Oasis runs on-site summer programs for organizations such as schools, agencies, corporations and local communities.
Activities: Academics, Arts/Crafts, Basketball, Drawing/Painting, Leadership Development, Nature/Environment Studies, Sports — Field & Team, Swimming — Recreational, Team Building
Session lengths & capacity: July-August; 3, 5 & 8 week sessions; 300 campers
Clientele & fees: coed 7-13; Fees: C ☀
Contact: Shora Perloron, Program Coordinator at (718) 595-4900; fax: (718) 855-2435
e-mail: info@oasischildren.com
Operated by: Oasis Children Services LLC, 100 Water St Ste 411, Brooklyn, NY 11201 at (718) 596-4900 (#44922)

Oasis Central Park   ☀

Brooklyn, NY; (718) 596-4900
Activities: Academics, Arts/Crafts, Basketball, Drawing/Painting, Leadership Development, Nature/Environment Studies, Sports — Field & Team, Swimming — Recreational, Team Building
Operated by: Oasis Children Services LLC, 100 Water St Ste 411, Brooklyn, NY 11201 at (718) 596-4900 (#49057)

Olmsted (est 1901)   △ 🏠 🚐

Cornwall on Hudson, NY (Orange Co.); (845) 534-7900
April Callender, Director
Camp comments: Located at foot of Storm King Mt in beautiful Hudson Valley, small camp for inner city children with spiritual emphasis.
Activities: Arts/Crafts, Challenge/Rope Courses, Computer, Drama, Hiking, Performing Arts, Sports — Field & Team, Swimming — Recreational, Tennis
Session lengths & capacity: June-August; 2 week sessions; 81 campers

Clientele & fees: boys 6-12; girls 6-12; coed 6-12; Fees: B △ 🚐
Contact: April Callender, Associate Exec Director at (212) 870-3084; fax: (212) 870-3091
e-mail: acumcs@att.net
Operated by: Five Points Mission, 475 Riverside Dr Rm 1922, New York, NY 10115 at (212) 870-3084

Group Rental Information
Site comments: The rental facilities at Olmsted offer three types of accomodations for your agency, group, family or personal needs.
Seasons & Capacity: Spring 119, Summer 20, Fall 119, Winter 119
Facilities: A/V Equipment, Cabins, Dorm-Style, Double Occupancy, Food Service, Hiking Trails, Meeting Rooms, Playing Fields, Pool
Programs: Challenge/Ropes Course, Swimming (#2222)

Our Kids Day Camp II Inc   ☀ 🚐

Woodbourne, NY; (914) 434-3788
Camp comments: We are a traditional camp with all sports, swimming, arts & crafts, drama, canoeing & swim instruction. We promise to send our campers home with smiles.
Activities: Arts/Crafts, Baseball/Softball, Basketball, Dance, Drama, Football, Sports — Field & Team, Swimming — Instructional
Session lengths & capacity: July-August; 1, 2, 3, 4, 5, 6, 7, 8 & 9 week sessions; 350 campers
Clientele & fees: coed 3-14; Fees: B ☀
Operated by: Our Kids Day Camp II Inc, 661 Budd Rd, Woodbourne, NY 12788 at (718) 349-9678 (#39542)

Park Shore Country Day Camp

(est 1959)   ☀ 🚐

Dix Hills, NY (Suffolk Co.); (516) 499-8580
Bob Budah, Director
Camp comments: Our 44th yr. 15 wooded acres, 7 tennis cts, 3 heated pools & 3 slides; comp athletic, cultural arts & performing arts prog; new skate park & inline instruction.
Activities: Arts/Crafts, Dance, Hockey, Music, Performing Arts, Skating, Soccer, Sports — Field & Team, Swimming — Instructional, Tennis
Session lengths & capacity: June-August; 4, 6 & 8 week sessions; 500 campers
Clientele & fees: coed 3-14; Fees: D ☀
Contact: Bob or Chuck Budah, Owners/Directors at (631) 499-8580; fax: (996) 917-0000
e-mail: info@ParkShoreDayCamp.com
Web site: www.parkshoredaycamp.com
Operated by: Park Shore Country Day Camp, 450 Deer Park Rd, Dix Hills, NY 11746-5298 at (516) 499-8580 (#3878)

Pathfinder Country Day Camp

(est 1965)   ☀ 🚐

Montauk, NY (Suffolk Co.); (631) 668-2080
Leon Lefkowitz, Director
Camp comments: Designed by educ. specialists. Camp provides each child with opportunities to develop socially creatively & athletically
Activities: Arts/Crafts, Baseball/Softball, Basketball, Boating, Ceramics/Pottery, Drama, Field Trips, Sailing, Swimming — Instructional
Session lengths & capacity: July-August; 2, 3, 4, 5, 6, 7 & 8 week sessions; 200 campers
Clientele & fees: boys 4-12; girls 4-12; coed 4-12; Fees: C, D ☀ 🚐
Contact: Dr. Leon Lefkowitz or Nancy Burns, Director/Owner at (516) 668-2080;
Operated by: Pathfinder Country Day Camp, Box 807, Montauk, NY 11954 at (516) 668-2080 (#2123)

Pierce Country Day Camp

(est 1918) ☀ 🚗

Roslyn, NY (Nassau Co.); (516) 621-2211
Doug Pierce, Director

Camp comments: Outstanding staff, exceptional facilities, famous programs, spirit soars,laughter roars, est. 1918 an oasis of fun!!
Activities: Arts/Crafts, Baseball/Softball, Basketball, Dance, Field Trips, Music, Soccer, Sports — Field & Team, Swimming — Instructional, Tennis
Session lengths & capacity: 8 week sessions; 1000 campers
Clientele & fees: boys 3-13; girls 3-13; coed 3-13; Fees: D ☀
Contact: Doug Pierce, Owner/Director at (516) 621-2211; fax: (516) 621-5765
e-mail: camp1918@aol.com
Operated by: Pierce Country Day Camp, Villa Marina, Roslyn, NY 11576 at (516) 621-2211 (#13271)

Point O' Pines Camp for Girls

(est 1957) ⛺ 🚗

Brant Lake, NY (Warren Co.); (518) 494-3213
Jim & Sue Himoff, Director

Camp comments: Summer camping, facility, setting at it's very best. Friendships and strong self-image for a lifetime.
Activities: Aquatic Activities, Arts/Crafts, Basketball, Camping Skills/Outdoor Living, Drama, Gymnastics, Horseback — English, Soccer, Tennis, Waterskiing
Session lengths & capacity: June-August; 8 week sessions; 300 campers
Clientele & fees: girls 7-15; Fees: F ⛺
Contact: Sue & Jim Himoff, Directors/Owners at (518) 494-3213; fax: (518) 494-3489
e-mail: info@pointopines.com
Web site: www.pointopines.com
Operated by: Point O Pines Corporation, 7201 State Route 8, Brant Lake, NY 12815-2236 at (518) 494-3213 (#2048)

Pok-O-Mac Cready

(est 1905) ⛺ 🏠 🚗

Willsboro, NY (Essex Co.); (518) 963-7656
Margaret Swan Reinckens, Director

Camp comments: Pok-O-Mac Cready located in beautiful Adirondacks is known for its friendliness, fun & adventure. Family owned since 1905.
Activities: Archery, Backpacking, Ceramics/Pottery, Climbing/Rappelling, Horseback — English, Nature/Environment Studies, Sailing, Soccer, Sports — Field & Team, Wilderness Trips
Session lengths & capacity: 3, 4 & 6 week sessions; 250 campers
Clientele & fees: boys 7-16; girls 7-16; Fees: E ⛺
Contact: Jack Swan, Director/Owner at (518) 963-7656; fax: (518) 963-4165
e-mail: pokomac@aol.com
Operated by: Camp Pok O Mac Cready, PO Box 397, Willsboro, NY 12996 at (518) 963-7656

Group Rental Information
Site comments: Adirondack mts,lakes,8 streams are our learning lab.Earth studies,rockclimbing,biking,team building,winter camping,wilderness trips become adventure challenges.
Seasons & Capacity: Spring 150, Fall 150, Winter 90
Facilities: A/V Equipment, Dorm-Style, Double Occupancy, Food Service, Hiking Trails, Lake, Lodges, Meeting Rooms, Playing Fields, River
Programs: Boating, Challenge/Ropes Course, Environmental Education, Winter Sports (#1937)

Presbyterian Center At Holmes

(est 1946) ⛺ 🏠 🚗

Holmes, NY (Putnam/Dutchess Co.); (845) 878-6383
William A Key, Director

Camp comments: Christian camping experiences in the Presbyterian tradition for youth, adults and families of the greater New York City area.
Activities: Arts/Crafts, Camping Skills/Outdoor Living, Challenge/Rope Courses, Hiking, Leadership Development, Nature/Environment Studies, Religious Study, Swimming — Instructional, Swimming — Recreational
Session lengths & capacity: June-September; 1/2, 1 & 2 week sessions; 155 campers
Clientele & fees: coed 8-18; families; seniors; single adults; Fees: D ⛺
Contact: Diane Ball, Administrative Assistant at (845) 878-6383; fax: (845) 878-7824
e-mail: holmespca@aol.com
Web site: www.presbyteriancenter.org
Operated by: Presbyterian Conference Assn, 60 Denton Lake Rd, Holmes, NY 12531-9706 at (845) 878-6383

Group Rental Information
Facilities: Cabins, Dorm-Style, Double Occupancy, Food Service, Meeting Rooms, Tents
Programs: Boating (#2083)

Prospect Park YMCA Summer Camp (est 1900) ☀

Brooklyn, NY (Kings Co.); (718) 768-7100
Ed Michel, Director

Camp comments: Our objectives focus on helping young people develop self respect, self-confidence & self-sufficiency.
Activities: Arts/Crafts, Basketball, Community Service, Drama, Drawing/Painting, Field Trips, Leadership Development, Nature/Environment Studies, Soccer
Session lengths & capacity: 9 week sessions
Clientele & fees: coed 5-15; Fees: B ☀ 🐷
Contact: Ed Michel, Youth Director at (718) 768-7100; fax: (718) 499-0425
Operated by: Prospect Park YMCA Summer Camp, 984 E 54th St, Brooklyn, NY 11234 at (718) 768-7100 (#6410)

Quinipet (est 1947) ☀ ⛺ 🏠 🚗

Shelter Island Height, NY (Suffolk Co.); (516) 749-0430
Roy W Quist, Director

Camp comments: Small group overnight camping. Located on Peconic Bay. Caring, Christian staff. Open to all faiths.
Activities: Arts/Crafts, Counselor Training (CIT), Field Trips, Kayaking, Music, Nature/Environment Studies, Religious Study, Sailing, Swimming — Instructional, Swimming — Recreational
Session lengths & capacity: July-August; 1 & 2 week sessions; 110 campers
Clientele & fees: coed 7-18; families; Fees: B ☀ Fees: C ⛺
Contact: Roy Krauss, Director at (631) 749-0430; fax: (631) 749-3403
e-mail: umcamps@peconic.net
Web site: www.umcamps.org
Operated by: NY Conf United Methodist, PO Box 549, Shelter Island Hts, NY 11965 at (631) 749-0430

Group Rental Information
Seasons & Capacity: Spring 145, Summer 55, Fall 145, Winter 145
Facilities: A/V Equipment, Cabins, Dorm-Style, Double Occupancy, Food Service, Kitchen Facilities, Linens, Lodges, Meeting Rooms, Playing Fields
Programs: Environmental Education (#2087)

Ramah Day Camp in Nyack

☀ 🏠 🚗

Nyack, NY (Rockland Co.); (845) 358-6240
Amy Skopp Cooper, Director

Camp comments: The Ramah Day Camp is a unique summer experience of fun learning and growth. We offer a full gamut of camp activities all with a Jewish dimension! Conservative
Activities: Arts/Crafts, Challenge/Rope Courses, Drama, Field Trips, Music, Nature/Environment Studies, Religious Study, Sports — Field & Team, Swimming — Instructional, Team Building
Session lengths & capacity: June-August; 4, 5, 6, 7 & 8 week sessions
Clientele & fees: boys 5-13; girls 5-13; coed 5-13; Fees: D ☀
Contact: Amy Skopp Cooper, Director at (212) 678-8884; fax: (212) 749-8251
e-mail: amcooper@jtsa.edu
Web site: www.ramahberkshires.org
Operated by: Camp Ramah in the Berkshires, 25 Rockwood Place, Englewood, NJ 07631 at (201) 871-7262 (#11784)

Ramapo Anchorage Camp

(est 1923) ⛺ 🚗

Rhinebeck, NY (Dutchess Co.); (845) 876-8403
Bernard Kosberg, Director

Camp comments: Ramapo is an exciting and challenging program designed to build self-confidence, trust, discipline & motivation. Our focus is on teaching these & other skills.
Activities: Arts/Crafts, Boating, Camping Skills/Outdoor Living, Ceramics/Pottery, Challenge/Rope Courses, Computer, Leadership Development, Nature/Environment Studies, Swimming — Instructional
Session lengths & capacity: 3, 6 & 9 week sessions; 200 campers
Clientele & fees: coed 4-16; Fees: E ⛺ 🐷
Contact: Michael Kunin, Associate Director at (914) 876-8403; fax: (914) 876-8414
e-mail: mike@ramapoanchorage.org
Web site: www.ramapoanchorage.org
Operated by: Ramapo Anchorage Camp Inc, PO Box 266, Rhinebeck, NY 12572 at (914) 876-8403 (#1942)

Ramapo Country Day Camp

(est 1960) ☀ 🚗

Monsey, NY (Rockland Co.); (845) 356-6440
Mike Kulchin, Director
Activities: Archery, Arts/Crafts, Challenge/Rope Courses, Gymnastics, Horseback — English, Performing Arts, Sports — Field & Team, Swimming — Instructional, Tennis, Travel/Tour
Session lengths & capacity: 4, 6 & 8 week sessions
Clientele & fees: coed 3-14; Fees: E ☀
Contact: Mike Kulchin, Director at (845) 356-6440; fax: (845) 356-0317
Operated by: Ramapo Country Day Camp, 600 Saddle River Rd, Monsey, NY 10952 at (845) 356-6440 (#6308)

Raquette Lake Camps (est 1916) ⛺

Raquette Lake, NY (Hamilton Co.); (315) 354-4382
Ed & Kathi Lapidus & Steve Norman & (CRC)Tim Cox, Director

Camp comments: Camping at its best! Top facilities in incomparable Adirondack setting. Excellent instruction by caring, professional staff. A summer that is beyond fun!
Activities: Aquatic Activities, Arts/Crafts, Camping Skills/Outdoor Living, Challenge/Rope Courses, Horseback — English, Performing Arts, Sailing, Sports — Field & Team, Tennis, Waterskiing
Session lengths & capacity: June-August; 7 week sessions
Clientele & fees: boys 6-16; girls 6-15

Contact: Ed & Kathi Lapidus & Steve Norman, Directors at (914) 633-9525; fax: (914) 633-5666
e-mail: director@raqittelake.com
Web site: www.raqittelake.com
Operated by: Raquette Lake Camps, Inc, 629 5th Ave, Pelham, NY 10803 at (914) 633-9525 (#2176)

Redwood (est 1961)
Walden, NY (Orange Co.); (914) 564-1180
Jon & Steve Estis, Director

Camp comments: Personal & close supervision. Excel facilities. We build social, emotional, phys

ICON LEGEND
☀ Day Camp
▲ Resident Camp
🏠 Facilities Available To Rent
🚐 Transportation Available
🚌 Financial Aid Available

FEE RANGES PER WEEK
A $0-75
B $75-200
C $201-350
D $351-500
E $501-650
F over $650

skills, confidence & self-esteem. Olympic pool, spring-fed lake, FAA flight tng
Activities: Academics, Aquatic Activities, Archery, Arts/Crafts, Aviation, Basketball, Hockey, Soccer, Tennis, Waterskiing
Session lengths & capacity: 2, 3, 4, 5, 6, 7 & 8 week sessions; 150 campers
Clientele & fees: coed 5-16; Fees: C ☀ Fees: F ▲
Contact: Jon & Steve Estis, Directors at (888) 600-6655; fax: (845) 564-1128
Web site: www.campredwood.net
Operated by: Redwood, 576 Rock Cut Rd, Walden, NY 12586 at (888) 600-6655 (#2155)

Regis-Applejack (est 1946)
Paul Smiths, NY (Franklin Co.); (518) 327-3117
Michael Humes, Director
Camp comments: MultiCultural. Spec attn & prog for 1st time camper. Teen prog w/travel. Cabins have living room w/fireplace & bathroom
Activities: Aquatic Activities, Arts/Crafts, Camping Skills/Outdoor Living, Drama, Nature/Environment Studies, Performing Arts, Sailing, Soccer, Tennis, Waterskiing
Session lengths & capacity: June-August; 4 & 8 week sessions; 220 campers
Clientele & fees: coed 6-16; Fees: E ▲
Contact: Michael E Humes, Director at (609) 688-0368; fax: (609) 688-0369
e-mail: campregis@aol.com
Web site: www.campregis-applejack.com
Operated by: Camp Regis Inc, 60 Lafayette Road West, Princeton, NJ 08540 at (609) 688-0368 (#2086)

Rising Sun at Clinton Corners ▲
Rhinebeck, NY; (914) 266-4561
Activities: Aquatic Activities, Arts/Crafts, Camping Skills/Outdoor Living, Community Service, Drama, Hiking, International Culture, Leadership Development, Music, Team Building
Operated by: Louis August Jonas Foundation, 9 W Market St A, Rhinebeck, NY 12572 at (914) 876-4331 (#6536)

Rising Sun at Redhook
(est 1930) ▲ 🚐
Rhinebeck, NY (Dutchess Co.); (914) 758-3501
Camp comments: Dedicated to developing lifelong commitments to sensitive & responsible leadership for the betterment of the world.
Activities: Backpacking, Basketball, Community Service, Drama, Field Trips, International Culture, Leadership Development, Music
Session lengths & capacity: 8 week sessions; 60 campers
Clientele & fees: boys 15-15; 🚌
Contact: David T. Ives, Executive Director at (914) 876-4331; fax: (914) 876-4278
e-mail: papabear@risingsun.org
Operated by: Louis August Jonas Foundation, 9 W Market St A, Rhinebeck, NY 12572 at (914) 876-4331 (#2095)

Robin Hood Country Day School

(est 1957)

Brookville Long Islan, NY (Nassau Co.);
(516) 626-1094
Glenn Roberts, Director

Camp comments: Outstanding staff. Excellent swim & sports program. Beautiful facility on 15 acres.
Activities: Arts/Crafts, Baseball/Softball, Challenge/Rope Courses, Computer, Gymnastics, Music, Nature/Environment Studies, Soccer, Swimming — Instructional, Tennis
Session lengths & capacity: June-August; 4, 6 & 8 week sessions
Clientele & fees: coed 3-13; Fees: D ☀
Contact: Glenn Roberts, Co-Director at (516) 626-1094; fax: (516) 626-4677
Web site: www.robinhoodcountryday.com
Operated by: Robin Hood Country Day School, PO Box 257, Greenvale, NY 11548 at (516) 626-1094 (#19807)

Rochester Rotary Sunshine Camp (est 1922)

Rush, NY (Monroe Co.); (716) 533-2080
Sheila Knipper, Director

Camp comments: A camp serving Greater Rochesters children with physical disabilities. Sponsored by the Rochester Rotary club.
Activities: Aquatic Activities, Archery, Arts/Crafts, Boating, Climbing/Rappelling, Fishing, Nature/Environment Studies
Session lengths & capacity: 1 week sessions; 100 campers
Clientele & fees: boys 7-21; girls 7-21; Fees: A ⚠
Contact: Sheila Knipper, Sunshine Camp Director at (716) 546-7435 ext. 204; fax: (716) 546-8675
e-mail: sknipper@rochesterrotary.org
Operated by: Rochester Rotary Charity Trst, 125 East Main, Rochester, NY 14604 at (716) 546-7435 (#15222)

Rock Hill Camps (est 1922)

Mahopac, NY (Putnam Co.); (914) 628-6611
Gail McBride, Director

Camp comments: Day Camp-overnights, special events. Resident tent & cabin living, caring staff,self-esteem & girl planning emphasized.
Activities: Aquatic Activities, Arts/Crafts, Backpacking, Bicycling/Biking, Boating, Camping Skills/Outdoor Living, Canoeing, Drama, Leadership Development, Swimming — Recreational
Session lengths & capacity: 1, 2 & 3 week sessions; 200 campers
Clientele & fees: girls 6-14; Fees: C ⚠ 🚍
Contact: Gail McBride, Camp Director at (914) 747-3080 ext. 236; fax: (914) 747-4263
e-mail: pmakin@girlscoutswp.org
Web site: www.girlscoutswp.org
Operated by: Westchester Putnam GSC, 2 Great Oak Lane, Pleasantville, NY 10570 at (914) 747-3080

Group Rental Information
Facilities: Cabins, Dorm-Style, Hiking Trails, Lake, Meeting Rooms, Tents
Programs: Boating (#1985)

Rocky Brook Day Camp (est 1956) ☀

Eastchester, NY (Westchester Co.); (914) 961-4301
Joyce M Malone, Director

Camp comments: Beautiful setting.Girl input to program.Theme weeks & days.Girl Scout emphasis.Non Girl Scouts welcome.Camper:staff 6:1.
Activities: Arts/Crafts, Dance, Drama, Field Trips, Horseback — English, Music, Nature/Environment Studies, Swimming — Recreational

Session lengths & capacity: 2 week sessions; 90 campers
Clientele & fees: girls 5-13; Fees: B ☀ 🚍
Contact: Joyce Malone, Camp Director at (914) 747-3080; fax: (914) 747-4263
e-mail: jmalone@girlscoutswp.org
Web site: www.girlscoutswp.org
Operated by: Westchester Putnam GSC, 2 Great Oak Lane, Pleasantville, NY 10570 at (914) 747-3080 (#2136)

Rolling Hills Country Day Camp

(est 1995)

Coram, NY; (631) 736-3696
Amy Engelberg, Director

Camp comments: Rolling Hills Country Day Camp - where every child is important.
Activities: Arts/Crafts, Baseball/Softball, Basketball, Challenge/Rope Courses, Sports — Field & Team, Swimming — Instructional, Swimming — Recreational
Session lengths & capacity: July-August; 4, 5, 6, 7 & 8 week sessions; 250 campers
Clientele & fees: coed 3-12; Fees: C, D ☀
Contact: Amy Engelberg, Director at (631) 736-3696; fax: (631) 736-7316
e-mail: rhdcamy@unix.asb.com
Operated by: Rolling Hills Country Day Camp, PO Box 837, Coram, NY 11727 at (631) 736-3696 (#39963)

Rolling River Day Camp

(est 1992)

East Rockaway, NY (Nassau Co.); (516) 593-2267
Mark & Rhonda Goodman, Director

Camp comments: Catch the wave of excitement at day camp that offers campers, ages 3-15yrs old,a diversified program & warm environment.
Activities: Aquatic Activities, Arts/Crafts, Baseball/Softball, Basketball, Boating, Computer, Drama, Field Trips, Gymnastics, Sports — Field & Team
Session lengths & capacity: June-August; 4 & 8 week sessions; 600 campers
Clientele & fees: coed 2-15; Fees: D ☀
Contact: Rhonda Goodman or Marjorie Sherer, Director/Assoc Director at (516) 593-2267; fax: (516) 593-5796
e-mail: rollingriv@aol.com
Web site: www.RollingRiver.com
Operated by: Rolling River Day Camp, 477 Ocean Ave, East Rockaway, NY 11518 at (516) 593-2267 (#2112)

Rosmarins Day Camp

(est 1949)

Monroe, NY (Orange Co.); (845) 783-7222
Michelle & Berry Goodman, Director

Camp comments: Well-established family run day camp. Extensive, expanding summer program. Warm experienced staff, limited enrollment.
Activities: Arts/Crafts, Basketball, Camping Skills/Outdoor Living, Computer, Counselor Training (CIT), Music, Nature/Environment Studies, Sports — Field & Team, Swimming — Instructional, Tennis
Session lengths & capacity: 4, 6 & 8 week sessions; 300 campers
Clientele & fees: coed 3-15; Fees: D ☀
Contact: M Rosmarin, Owner at (914) 783-7222; fax: (914) 782-7038
Operated by: Camp Rosmarin Inc, 12 School Road, Monroe, NY 10950 at (845) 783-7222 (#7015)

RYE YMCA (est 1950)

Rye, NY (Westchester Co.); (914) 967-6363
Scott S Reynolds, Director

Camp comments: A summer camp with caring & qualified staff. Fun atmosphere and new adventures that kids love and parents trust.
Activities: Arts/Crafts, Basketball, Counselor Training (CIT), Field Trips, Nature/Environment Studies, Swimming — Instructional, Swimming — Recreational
Session lengths & capacity: 2 week sessions; 200 campers
Clientele & fees: coed 4-10; Fees: C ☀ 🚍
Contact: Scott Reynolds, Program Director at (914) 967-6363 ext. 220; fax: (914) 967-0644
Operated by: Rye YMCA, 21 Locust Ave, Rye, NY 10580 at (914) 967-6363 (#1473)

Saddle River Valley Day Camp

(est 1999)

Tallman, NY (Bergen County Co.); (845) 368-2015
Joanne Trizano, Director

Camp comments: Our counselors and specialists provide a spirit that encourages campers to get along, to feel part of our camp community.
Activities: Aquatic Activities, Archery, Baseball/Softball, Boating, Challenge/Rope Courses, Counselor Training (CIT), Drama, Horseback — English, Horseback — Western, Swimming — Instructional
Session lengths & capacity: July-August; 4, 6 & 8 week sessions; 400 campers
Clientele & fees: coed 4-14; Fees: D, E ☀
Contact: Loretta Scafuro, Owner/Operator at (877) 760-6444; fax: (845) 368-2015
e-mail: info@srvdc.com
Operated by: Saddle River Valley Day Camp, PO Box 226, Saddle River, NJ 07458 at (201) 825-7314

Group Rental Information
Facilities: Lake, Playing Fields, Pool
Programs: Boating, Swimming (#46803)

Samuel Field Bay Terrace YMHA

(est 1958)

Wheatley Heights, NY; (516) 643-9696
David Slotnick, Director

Camp comments: Day, sleepaway, travel, sport & special needs camps serving ages 3-16, based on developmentally appropriate activities
Activities: Archery, Arts/Crafts, Counselor Training (CIT), Hiking, Nature/Environment Studies, Soccer, Sports — Field & Team, Swimming — Instructional, Swimming — Recreational, Travel/Tour
Session lengths & capacity: 4 & 8 week sessions
Clientele & fees: coed 3-16; Fees: C ☀ 🚍
Contact: Marisa Plotkin David Slotnick, Camp Directors at (718) 225-6750 ext. 2611; fax: (718) 423-8276
e-mail: samfieldy@aol.com
Web site: www.samuelfieldy.org
Operated by: Samuel Field YM&YWCA, Inc., 58 20 Little Neck Parkway, Little Neck, NY 11362 at (718) 225-6750 (#29974)

Scatico (est 1921)

Elizaville, NY (Columbia Co.); (845) 756-2444
David Fleischner, Director

Camp comments: The skills, values, friendships & memories that make traditional camping a special experience.
Activities: Aquatic Activities, Baseball/Softball, Basketball, Camping Skills/Outdoor Living, Drama, Golf, Nature/Environment Studies, Photography, Sports — Field & Team, Tennis
Session lengths & capacity: June-August; 7 week sessions; 250 campers
Clientele & fees: boys 7-15; girls 7-15; Fees: F ⚠
Contact: David Fleischner, Director at (914) 632-7791; fax: (212) 362-2440
e-mail: info@scatico.com
Web site: www.scatico.com
Operated by: Camp Scatico Inc, 25 Fenimore Rd, New Rochelle, NY 10804 at (914) 632-7791

Group Rental Information
Facilities: Cabins, Food Service, Kitchen Facilities, Lake, Playing Fields
Programs: Swimming (#6131)

Shibley Summer Day Camp

(est 1930)

Roslyn, NY (Nassau Co.); (516) 621-8777
Harvey Kulchin, Director

Camp comments: The Day Camping leader in sports education. 40 wooded acres, 5 heated pools.
Activities: Arts/Crafts, Baseball/Softball, Basketball, Drama, Skating, Soccer, Sports — Field & Team, Swimming — Instructional, Tennis
Session lengths & capacity: June-August; 4, 6, 7 & 8 week sessions; 500 campers
Clientele & fees: coed 3-14; Fees: **E**
Contact: Harvey Kulchin, Director at (516) 621-8777; fax: (516) 625-2975
Web site: www.kidscamps.com/daycamps/shibley
Operated by: Shibley Summer Day Camp, Box 333, Roslyn, NY 11576 at (516) 621-8777 (#2202)

Sky Lake Of Wyoming Conference (est 1947)

Windsor, NY (Broome Co.); (800) 577-9508
James Krager, Director
Activities: Aquatic Activities, Arts/Crafts, Camping Skills/Outdoor Living, Hiking, Music, Religious Study
Session lengths & capacity: June-August; 1 week sessions; 130 campers
Clientele & fees: coed 8-17; Fees: **B**
Contact: (607) 467-2750; fax: (607) 467-4612
e-mail: skylake@pronetisp.net
Operated by: Sky Lake of Wyoming Conference, 501 William Law Rd, Windsor, NY 13865 at (607) 467-2750

Group Rental Information
Seasons & Capacity: Spring 75, Winter 75
Facilities: Dorm-Style, Double Occupancy, Food Service, Hiking Trails, Lake, Linens, Meeting Rooms, Playing Fields
Programs: Boating (#12213)

South Shore Day Camp

(est 1958)

North Bellmore, NY (Nassau Co.); (516) 785-3311
Christine Vicedomini, Director

Camp comments: Each camper receives personalized attention in a fun filled supportive environment that enhances self-esteem.

ICON LEGEND

☀　Day Camp
▲　Resident Camp
⌂　Facilities Available To Rent
🚐　Transportation Available
🐷　Financial Aid Available

FEE RANGES PER WEEK

A	$0-75
B	$75-200
C	$201-350
D	$351-500
E	$501-650
F	over $650

Activities: Arts/Crafts, Baseball/Softball, Basketball, Computer, Dance, Nature/Environment Studies, Soccer, Sports — Field & Team, Swimming — Instructional, Travel/Tour
Session lengths & capacity: 4, 6 & 8 week sessions; 250 campers
Clientele & fees: boys 3-15; girls 3-15; coed 3-15; Fees: **C**
Contact: Christine Vicedomini, Director at (516) 785-3311; fax: (516) 785-3311
e-mail: sshoredaycamp@aol.com
Operated by: South Shore Day Camp, 1149 Newbridge Rd, North Bellmore, NY 11710 at (516) 785-3311 (#10352)

St Aidan's Summer Camp

Williston Park, NY; (516) 827-5673
Gary R Turnier, Director

Camp comments: Campers thrive in noncompetitive, caring atmosphere with opportunities to belong, learn and contribute,caring staff
Activities: Arts/Crafts, Counselor Training (CIT), Dance, Field Trips, Leadership Development, Performing Arts, Sports — Field & Team, Swimming — Recreational, Team Building
Session lengths & capacity: June-August; 4, 6 & 8 week sessions; 250 campers
Clientele & fees: coed 3-15; families; Fees: **B**
Contact: Gary R Turnier, Director/Coordinator at (516) 827-5673; fax: (516) 937-1058
Operated by: Holy Family Roman Catholic, 25 Fordham Ave, Hicksville, NY 11801 at (516) 937-0636 (#16837)

St Barnabas Summer Camp

(est 1995)

Bellmore, NY (Nassau Co.); (516) 781-2933
Gary R Turnier, Director

Camp comments: Day Camp offers warm supportive atmosphere. Caring staff. Campers thrive in noncompetitive activities for exciting fun.
Activities: Arts/Crafts, Baseball/Softball, Basketball, Counselor Training (CIT), Dance, Field Trips, Fishing, Hockey, Sports — Field & Team, Swimming — Recreational
Session lengths & capacity: 4, 6 & 8 week sessions
Clientele & fees: coed 3-15; families; Fees: **B**
Contact: Gary R Turnier, Director/Coordinator at (516) 827-5810; fax: (516) 937-1058
Operated by: Holy Family Roman Catholic, 25 Fordham Ave, Hicksville, NY 11801 at (516) 937-0636 (#3947)

Staten Island Day Camp Inc

(est 1979)

Staten Island, NY (Staten Island Co.); (800) 301-2267
Michael Halpern, Director

Camp comments: To provide our children a safe & happy recreational experience.
Activities: Arts/Crafts, Baseball/Softball, Basketball, Community Service, Dance, Drama, Football, Soccer, Swimming — Instructional, Swimming — Recreational
Session lengths & capacity: 8 week sessions; 400 campers
Clientele & fees: boys 7-14; girls 7-14; coed 4-6; Fees: **B**
Contact: Michael Halpern, Director at (800) 301-2267; fax: (800) 301-2267
Operated by: Staten Island Day Camp Inc, PO Box 70159, Staten Island, NY 10307 at (800) 301-2267 (#3220)

Staten Island YMCA Day Camp

(est 1980)

Staten Island, NY (Richmond Co.); (718) 667-5210
John J. Semerad, Director

Camp comments: 50 beautiful acres. Lake for swimming & boating. Plays & field trips each session. Outstanding staff. Transportation.
Activities: Archery, Arts/Crafts, Basketball, Boating, Counselor Training (CIT), Drama, Leadership Development, Nature/Environment Studies, Soccer, Swimming — Recreational
Session lengths & capacity: 2, 4 & 8 week sessions; 450 campers
Clientele & fees: boys 5-13; girls 5-13; Fees: **B**
Contact: John J. Semerad, Camp Director at (718) 981-1493; fax: (718) 720-4365
Operated by: Staten Island YMCA Day Camp, 651 Broadway, Staten Island, NY 10310 at (718) 981-4933 (#19020)

Summer Trails Day Camp

(est 1974)

Granite Springs, NY (Westchester Co.); (914) 245-1776
David Silverstein, Director

Camp comments: Flexible scheduling, part-time & extended hours available. Regular day camp plus baseball sports camp.
Activities: Arts/Crafts, Baseball/Softball, Dance, Drama, Music, Nature/Environment Studies, Sports — Field & Team, Swimming — Instructional, Swimming — Recreational
Session lengths & capacity: July-August; 4, 6 & 8 week sessions; 500 campers
Clientele & fees: coed 3-15; Fees: **C**
Contact: Dave Silverstein, Director at (914) 245-1776; fax: (201) 573-0350
e-mail: davestdc@aol.com
Operated by: Summer Trails Day Camp Inc, 10 Pine Knoll Court, Monsey, NY 10952 at (845) 352-3718 (#645)

Surprise Lake Camp

(est 1902)

Cold Spring, NY (Putnam Co.); (845) 265-3616
Jordan Dale, Director

Camp comments: Jewish/Kosher/self-esteem building/5 day introductory program for 6-10 yr olds/2 week program/work program for 15 yr olds.
Activities: Aquatic Activities, Arts/Crafts, Boating, Camping Skills/Outdoor Living, Challenge/Rope Courses, Drama, Music, Nature/Environment Studies, Performing Arts, Sports — Field & Team
Session lengths & capacity: June-August; 2, 4 & 8 week sessions; 480 campers
Clientele & fees: coed 7-15; Fees: **E**
Contact: Sylvie Erlich, Registrar at (212) 924-3131; fax: (212) 924-5112
e-mail: info@surpriselake.org
Web site: www.surpriselake.org
Operated by: Surprise Lake Camp, 307 7th Ave Ste 900, New York, NY 10001-6007 at (212) 924-3131

Group Rental Information
Site comments: Located in Cold Spring, NY, 60 min from NYC. Private lake. Situated on 750 acres, no showers in winter, kosher kitchen.
Seasons & Capacity: Spring 450, Summer 100, Fall 450
Facilities: Cabins, Food Service, Hiking Trails, Lake, Meeting Rooms
Programs: Boating, Environmental Education (#1993)

Talooli (est 1945)

Pennellville, NY (Oswego Co.); (315) 695-5932
Jan Peneston, Director

Camp comments: Each small group is led by well trained staff, which fosters a supportive environment for both camper & parent.
Activities: Archery, Arts/Crafts, Canoeing, Challenge/Rope Courses, Counselor Training (CIT), Kayaking, Nature/Environment Studies, Swimming — Instructional, Swimming — Recreational, Team Building
Session lengths & capacity: June-August; 1 week sessions; 160 campers
Clientele & fees: boys 5-15; girls 5-15; coed 5-15; Fees: **B** ☀ Fees: **C** ⚠ 🚐
Contact: Jan Peneston, Camp Director at (315) 463-8799; fax: (315) 463-8739
e-mail: jan@campfireusacny.org
Web site: www.campfireusacny.org
Operated by: Camp Fire Boys and Girls, 7 Adler Dr, East Syracuse, NY 13057 at (315) 463-8799

Group Rental Information
Site comments: Rustic wooded site with private lake. Sites range from lodges with modern facilities to tenting. Interstates convenient.
Facilities: Cabins, Food Service, Hiking Trails, Lake, Lodges
Programs: Boating, Challenge/Ropes Course (#948)

Tapawingo (est 1959) ⚠

Speculator, NY (Hamilton Co.); (518) 548-4311
Kim Winters, Director

Camp comments: Our staff loves campers & will role model a walk w/Christ while seeking fun & adventure in safe & friendly environment.
Activities: Archery, Arts/Crafts, Camping Skills/Outdoor Living, Canoeing, Climbing/Rappelling, Hiking, Horseback — Western, Sailing, Swimming — Instructional, Waterskiing
Session lengths & capacity: 1 week sessions; 72 campers
Clientele & fees: girls 9-17; Fees: **D** ⚠ 🚐
Contact: Kim Winters, Director at (518) 548-4311; fax: (518) 548-4324
e-mail: tapawingo@camp-of-the-woods.org
Operated by: Gospel Volunteers Inc, PO Box 250, Speculator, NY 12164-0250 at (518) 548-4311 (#16335)

The Nature Place Day Camp
(est 1986) ☀ 🚐

Chestnut Ridge, NY (Rockland Co.); (914) 356-1234
Ed Bieber, Director

Camp comments: A full program day camp based on a noncompetitive, nature-oriented & philosophy. Superb staff.
Activities: Archery, Arts/Crafts, Backpacking, Camping Skills/Outdoor Living, Canoeing, Farming/Ranching/Gardening, Hiking, Nature/Environment Studies, Swimming — Instructional, Wilderness Trips
Session lengths & capacity: July-August; 2, 4 & 6 week sessions; 250 campers
Clientele & fees: coed 4-15; Fees: **D** ☀ 🐷
Contact: Ed Bieber/ Maureen Regan, Owner-Director/Asst. Director at (914) 356-6477;
Web site: www.thenatureplace.com
Operated by: The Nature Place, 22 Snake Path Lane, Chester, NY 10918 at (914) 356-6477 (#1682)

The Ranch Camp - Lake Placid
(est 1989) ⚠ 🚐

Lake Clear, NY (Franklin Co.); (518) 891-5684
Harvey Goodman, Director

Camp comments: Horses, Horses, Horses! Ranch Camp a horse to care for during your stay. Jumping, trails, shows, over-night pack trips. Lake Placid-lets horses around!
Activities: Archery, Arts/Crafts, Dance, Drama, Farming/Ranching/Gardening, Field Trips, Hiking, Horseback — English, Horseback — Western, Travel/Tour

Session lengths & capacity: June-September; 2, 3, 4, 5, 6, 7 & 8 week sessions; 55 campers
Clientele & fees: girls 7-17; families; Fees: **E** ⚠
Contact: Marleen Goodman, Assistant Director at (518) 891-5684; fax: (518) 891-6350
Web site: www.childrenscamps.com
Operated by: The Ranch Camp, 4 Yankee Glen, Madison, CT 06443 at (518) 891-5684 (#3243)

Thomas School Of
Horsemanship (est 1943) ☀ 🚗

Melville, NY (Suffolk Co.); (631) 692-6840
Nancy Thomas & Dee Jacobitti, Director

Camp comments: Horses bring out best in everyone. Full day camp. Specializing in English horseback. Outstanding staff & environment.
Activities: Arts/Crafts, Computer, Counselor Training (CIT), Dance, Gymnastics, Horseback — English, Soccer, Sports — Field & Team, Swimming — Instructional, Tennis
Session lengths & capacity: June-August; 3, 4 & 7 week sessions; 400 campers
Clientele & fees: coed 3-15; Fees: **E** ☀
Contact: Nancy Thomas at (631) 692-6840; fax: (631) 692-9536
e-mail: tshcamp@optonline.net
Web site: www.tshcamp.com
Operated by: Thomas School of Horsemanship, 772 N Cedar Brook Rd, Boulder, CO 80304 at (631) 692-6840 (#3378)

Timber Lake (est 1962) ⚠ 🏠 🚐

Shandaken, NY (Green Co.); (845) 688-2266
Jay S. Jacobs, Director

Camp comments: We teach self confidence
Activities: Baseball/Softball, Basketball, Challenge/Rope Courses, Drama, Golf, Hockey, Horseback — English, Sports — Field & Team, Tennis, Waterskiing
Session lengths & capacity: June-August; 8 week sessions; 450 campers
Clientele & fees: coed 7-16; Fees: **F** ⚠
Contact: Mindy Jacobs, Registrar at (516) 656-4200; fax: (516) 656-4206
e-mail: mindy@camptlc.com
Web site: www.camptlc.com
Operated by: Timber Lake, 85 Crescent Beach Rd, Glen Cove, NY 11542 at (516) 656-4227 (#3889)

Timber Lake West (est 1987) ⚠ 🚐

Roscoe, NY (Sullivan Co.); (845) 439-4440
Bob & Alice Rosenberg, Director

Camp comments: 4 week traditional program, each session has a beginning, middle & end.
Activities: Arts/Crafts, Bicycling/Biking, Challenge/Rope Courses, Drama, Field Trips, Hockey, Tennis, Waterskiing
Session lengths & capacity: June-September; 4 week sessions; 350 campers
Clientele & fees: coed 8-16; Fees: **F** ⚠
Contact: Jennifer Quinn, Assistant Director at (516) 656-4210; fax: (516) 656-4215
e-mail: west@camptlc.com
Web site: www.camptlc.com
Operated by: Timber Lake, 85 Crescent Beach Rd, Glen Cove, NY 11542 at (516) 656-4227 (#2134)

Town N Country Day
Camp ☀ ⚠ 🚐

Camden, NY (Oswego Co.); (315) 964-2889
Judith H Reilly/ Karen Lubecki, Director

Camp comments: A well-rounded traditional day camp program. Overnights; skilled, trained, caring staff. A summer to remember.
Activities: Arts/Crafts, Boating, Camping Skills/Outdoor Living, Challenge/Rope Courses, Hiking, Leadership Development, Nature/Environment Studies, Sports — Field & Team, Swimming — Recreational, Team Building

Session lengths & capacity: July-August; 1/2, 1 & 2 week sessions; 120 campers
Clientele & fees: girls 5-17; Fees: **B** ☀ Fees: **B, C** ⚠ 🚐
Contact: Judith H Reilly, Program Manager at (315) 733-2391; fax: (315) 733-1909
e-mail: jreilly@borg.com
Operated by: Foothills GSC, 33 Jewett Place, Utica, NY 13501 at (315) 733-2391 (#44592)

Trade Winds Lake Camp Inc
(est 1988) ⚠ 🚐

Windsor, NY (Broome Co.); (607) 467-3356
Linda Fishelman, Director

Camp comments: 253 acre Majestic Mountain top estate. Beautiful private lake, woodlands, modern cabins, academically enriched traditional programs/inner city.
Activities: Academics, Arts/Crafts, Basketball, Drama, Farming/Ranching/Gardening, Gymnastics, Nature/Environment Studies, Photography, Swimming — Instructional, Tennis
Session lengths & capacity: June-August; 4 week sessions; 160 campers
Clientele & fees: coed 8-15; Fees: **D** ⚠ 🚐
Contact: Linda Fishelman, Camp Director at (732) 446-9150; fax: (732) 446-9150
e-mail: twlc@msn.com
Operated by: Trade Winds Lake Camp Inc, 21 Old Queens Blvd, Englishtown, NJ 07726 at (732) 446-9150 (#5425)

Treetops (est 1921) ⚠ 🚐

Lake Placid, NY (Essex Co.); (518) 523-9329
Brad Konkler, Director

Camp comments: Traditional Adirondack camp. Organic farm & garden. Family atmosphere. Mountain hiking, watersports. 1:3 staff ratio.
Activities: Backpacking, Camping Skills/Outdoor Living, Canoeing, Ceramics/Pottery, Farming/Ranching/Gardening, Horseback — English, Nature/Environment Studies, Performing Arts, Swimming — Instructional, Wilderness Trips
Session lengths & capacity: June-August; 7 week sessions; 160 campers
Clientele & fees: coed 8-14; Fees: **F** ⚠ 🚐
Contact: Brad Konkler, Director at (518) 523-9329 ext. 112; fax: (518) 523-4858
e-mail: bradk@nct.org
Web site: www.nct.org
Operated by: North Country School, Box 187, Lake Placid, NY 12946-0187 at (518) 523-9329 (#1965)

Twelve Towns YMCA Day ☀

Brooklyn, NY; (718) 277-1600
Activities: Academics, Aquatic Activities, Arts/Crafts, Basketball, Dance, Music
Operated by: Twelve Towns YMCA, 570 Jamaica Ave, Brooklyn, NY 11208 at (718) 277-1600 (#552)

Twin Oaks Day Camp
(est 1957) ☀ 🚐

Freeport, NY (Nassau Co.); (516) 623-4550
Hal Elman, Director

Camp comments: Campers thrive in warm loving accepting atmosphere, skill building in all sports dynamic arts & crafts programs.
Activities: Arts/Crafts, Dance, Drama, Leadership Development, Music, Swimming — Instructional, Tennis
Session lengths & capacity: June-August; 4, 5, 6, 7 & 8 week sessions; 350 campers
Clientele & fees: coed 2-12; Fees: **D** ☀
Contact: Hal Elman, Owner/Director at (516) 623-4550; fax: (516) 223-1568
Web site: www.twinoaksdaycamp.com
Operated by: Twin Oaks Day Camp, PO Box 750, Freeport, NY 11520 at (516) 623-4550 (#2129)

UAHC Camp Shalom Day Camp

Warwick, NY; (845) 987-6300
Contact: Web site: www.kutzcamp.org
Operated by: Union American Hebrew Congreg, PO Box 443, Warwick, NY 10990 at (845) 987-6300

UAHC Kutz Camp (est 1965)

Warwick, NY (Orange Co.); (845) 987-6300
Rabbi Glynis Conyer, Director

Camp comments: Leadership training for Jewish teenagers from around the world. Have fun, learn, make lasting friends, change your life
Activities: Ceramics/Pottery, Challenge/Rope Courses, Drama, Drawing/Painting, Leadership Development, Performing Arts, Photography, Religious Study, Team Building, Tennis
Session lengths & capacity: 3 week sessions; 175 campers
Clientele & fees: coed 13-17; Fees: E
Contact: Rabbi Glynis Conyer, Director at (845) 987-6300; fax: (845) 986-7185
e-mail: kutzcamp@warwick.net
Web site: www.kutzcamp.org
Operated by: Union American Hebrew Congreg, PO Box 443, Warwick, NY 10990 at (845) 987-6300

Group Rental Information
Facilities: Dorm-Style, Food Service, Lodges, Meeting Rooms (#17276)

University Settlement Beacon

(est 1910)

Beacon, NY (Dutchess Co.); (845) 831-6950
Patrick Freeman, Director

Camp comments: The teen work camp provides unique leadership training. The camp emphasizes cooperative activities in sports & arts.
Activities: Academics, Arts/Crafts, Community Service, Leadership Development, Nature/Environment Studies, Performing Arts, Sports — Field & Team, Swimming — Instructional, Swimming — Recreational, Team Building
Session lengths & capacity: 3 week sessions
Clientele & fees: coed 6-15; families; seniors; single adults; Fees: D
Contact: Michael Zisser, Executive Director at (212) 674-9120 ext. 4559; fax: (212) 475-3278
e-mail: mzisser@universitysettlement.org
Web site: www.universitysettlement.org
Operated by: University Settlement, 184 Eldridge St, New York, NY 10002 at (212) 674-9120

Group Rental Information
Site comments: The Beacon campus is only one hour from NYC and offers unique facilities in a beautiful setting.

ICON LEGEND

☀ Day Camp
▲ Resident Camp
⌂ Facilities Available To Rent
🚐 Transportation Available
🐷 Financial Aid Available

FEE RANGES PER WEEK

A	$0-75
B	$75-200
C	$201-350
D	$351-500
E	$501-650
F	over $650

Seasons & Capacity: Spring 60, Summer 200, Fall 60
Facilities: Cabins, Dorm-Style, Food Service, Pool (#27319)

Vanderbilt YMCA Summer Camp

(est 1978)

New York, NY (Manhattan Co.); (212) 756-9600
Kim Waldon, Director

Camp comments: Day camp offers varied activities that are progressive with trained staff in a warm environment.
Activities: Academics, Aquatic Activities, Baseball/Softball, Basketball, Field Trips, Performing Arts, Sports — Field & Team
Session lengths & capacity: June-August; 2 week sessions; 250 campers
Clientele & fees: boys 5-16; girls 5-16; coed 5-16; Fees: B
Contact: Kim Waldon, Youth & Teen Director at (212) 756-9600; fax: (212) 756-9901
e-mail: kwaldon@ymcanyc.org
Operated by: Vanderbilt YMCA, 224 E 47th St, New York, NY 10017 at (212) 756-9650 (#5535)

Wagon Road Camp

(est 1956)

Chappaqua, NY (Westchester Co.); (914) 238-4761
Lukas Weinstein, Director

Camp comments: Dedicated to serving youth coming from a wide range of cultural, ethnic & social economic backgrounds. Meeting the needs of todays youth.
Activities: Aquatic Activities, Arts/Crafts, Challenge/Rope Courses, Horseback — English, Nature/Environment Studies, Sports — Field & Team, Swimming — Instructional, Team Building
Session lengths & capacity: 3, 4 & 7 week sessions
Clientele & fees: coed 6-17; Fees: C
Fees: A ▲
Contact: Lukas Weinstein, Director at (914) 238-4761; fax: (914) 238-0714
e-mail: caswrc@aol.com
Web site: www.childrensaidsociety.org
Operated by: The Childrens Aid Society, Wagon Road Camp, PO Box 47, Chappaqua, NY 10514 at (914) 238-4761

Group Rental Information
Facilities: Food Service, Hiking Trails, Meeting Rooms
Programs: Environmental Education, Horseback Riding (#33821)

Wendy (est 1931)

Wallkill, NY (Ulster Co.); (845) 895-3004
Rena Hill, Director

Camp comments: Non-competitive, focusing on self-esteem, outdoor skills, appreciation of other cultures, new skills, in all girl camp.
Activities: Aquatic Activities, Bicycling/Biking, Camping Skills/Outdoor Living, Canoeing, Challenge/Rope Courses, Counselor Training (CIT), Hiking, Horseback — Western, Nature/Environment Studies, Swimming — Instructional
Session lengths & capacity: July-August; 1/2 & 1 week sessions; 100 campers
Clientele & fees: girls 7-16; Fees: B
Fees: B ▲
Contact: Rean Hill, Camp Director at (845) 338-5367; fax: (845) 338-6802
Operated by: Girl Scouts of Ulster County, 65 St James St, Kingston, NY 12402 at (845) 338-5367

Group Rental Information
Facilities: Cabins, Hiking Trails, Kitchen Facilities, Lake, Meeting Rooms, Tents
Programs: Boating (#1816)

West Hills Day Camp

(est 1954)

Huntington, NY (Suffolk Co.); (631) 427-6700
Mike Moore & Bob Minott, Director

Camp comments: Mature group & special staff provide support & leadership. Teen & preteen travel,6 heated pools in a sleep-a-way setting
Activities: Arts/Crafts, Basketball, Challenge/Rope Courses, Climbing/Rappelling, Dance, Drama, Field Trips, Sports — Field & Team, Swimming — Instructional, Travel/Tour
Session lengths & capacity: 4, 6 & 8 week sessions
Clientele & fees: boys 3-16; girls 3-16; coed 14-16; Fees: D
Contact: Michael Moore & Robert Minott, Directors at (631) 427-6700; fax: (631) 427-6504
e-mail: mike@westhillscamp.com
Operated by: West Hills Day Camp, 21 Sweet Hollow Rd, Huntington, NY 11743 at (631) 427-6700 (#2171)

West Side YMCA (est 1926)

New York, NY (Manhattan Co.); (212) 875-4138
Toni Turnbull, Director

Camp comments: Preschool thru young teen participate in developmentally appropriate program with opportunity for choice of specialties.
Activities: Arts/Crafts, Basketball, Dance, Drawing/Painting, Field Trips, Leadership Development, Sports — Field & Team, Swimming — Instructional, Swimming — Recreational, Team Building
Session lengths & capacity: 1 & 2 week sessions; 350 campers
Clientele & fees: boys 4-14; girls 4-14; coed 4-14; Fees: B
Contact: (212) 875-4138; fax: (212) 580-0441
e-mail: tturnbull@ymcanyc.org
Operated by: YMCA of Greater NY, 5 West 63rd St, New York, NY 10023 at (212) 875-4138 (#6538)

Wilbur Herrlich (est 1922)

Patterson, NY (Putnam Co.); (914) 878-6662
Bob & Wendy Gentile, Director

Camp comments: Opportunities for education, inspiration & recreation. The treasure of a life time! A little piece of heaven on earth!
Activities: Arts/Crafts, Basketball, Drama, Hiking, Horseback — English, Horseback — Western, Leadership Development, Nature/Environment Studies, Sports — Field & Team, Swimming — Recreational
Session lengths & capacity: June-August; 1 & 2 week sessions; 160 campers
Clientele & fees: boys 7-15; girls 7-15; coed 7-15; families; Fees: C ▲ 🐷
Contact: Bob Gentile, Exec Director at (914) 878-6620; fax: (914) 878-2030
e-mail: cherrlich@aol.com
Web site: www.campherrlich.org
Operated by: Mt Tremper Outdoor Ministries, 101 Deacon Smith Hill Rd, Patterson, NY 12563-9555 at (914) 878-6662

Group Rental Information
Seasons & Capacity: Spring 80, Fall 80, Winter 80
Facilities: Cabins, Dorm-Style, Food Service, Hiking Trails, Kitchen Facilities, Lake, Playing Fields
Programs: Boating, Challenge/Ropes Course, Environmental Education, Swimming (#6134)

Willow Hill Farm Camp (est 1985)

Keeseville, NY (Essex Co.); (518) 834-9746
Julie Edwards Jr., Director

Camp comments: Especially for horse lovers. Riding 2X daily. One horse/child. Jumping, Cross country, Farm animals. 36 campers. Horse care. Indoor Arena. Mountain trail games.
Activities: Hiking, Horseback — English, Swimming — Recreational

Session lengths & capacity: June-August; 2, 4, 6 & 8 week sessions; 40 campers
Clientele & fees: coed 8-16; Fees: B ☀ Fees: F ⚠
Contact: (518) 834-9746; fax: (518) 834-9746
e-mail: julie@willowhillfarm.com
Web site: www.willowhillfarm.com
Operated by: Willow Hill Farm Camp, 75 Cassidy Rd, Keeseville, NY 12944 at (518) 834-9746 (#46024)

Woodsmoke (est 1964) ⚠

Lake Placid, NY (Essex Co.); (518) 523-3868
Kris Hansen, Director

Camp comments: Sports oriented camp in a wilderness setting: emphasizing social skills, safety, responsibility & concern for others.
Activities: Archery, Arts/Crafts, Camping Skills/Outdoor Living, Canoeing, Hiking, Sailing, Swimming — Instructional, Tennis, Waterskiing, Wilderness Trips
Session lengths & capacity: 2, 3, 4 & 5 week sessions; 65 campers
Clientele & fees: boys 7-13; girls 7-13; coed 7-13; Fees: E ⚠
Contact: Kris Hansen, Owner/Director at (518) 523-9344; fax: (518) 523-3868
e-mail: wdsmoke@northnet.org
Web site: www.campwoodsmoke.com
Operated by: Woodsmoke, PO Box 628, Lake Placid, NY 12946 at (518) 523-9344 (#2063)

Yaiewano Program Center ⚠ ⌂

Auburn, NY (Cayuga Co.); (315) 784-5906
Amy George, Director

Camp comments: New facilities on Owasco Lake. Great program for younger girls & first time campers. Specialized older girl programs.
Activities: Aquatic Activities, Archery, Arts/Crafts, Boating, Camping Skills/Outdoor Living, Hiking, Leadership Development, Nature/Environment Studies, Sailing, Swimming — Recreational
Session lengths & capacity: July-August; 1/2, 1 & 2 weeks; 116 campers
Clientele & fees: girls 6-17; families; Fees: B ⚠ 🚐
Contact: Amy George, Program Specialist at (315) 539-5085 ext. 728; fax: (315) 539-8783
Operated by: Girl Scouts Seven Lakes Cncl, 300 Route 318, Phelps, NY 14532 at (315) 539-5085

Group Rental Information
Site comments: Modern cabin units, winterized lodges, waterfront on east shore of Owasco Lake near Auburn. A place where girls grow strong through Girl Scout programming!
Facilities: Cabins, Double Occupancy, Kitchen Facilities, Lake, Lodges, Meeting Rooms, Playing Fields, Tents
Programs: Boating, Swimming, Winter Sports (#6646)

YMCA at Glen Cove Day Camp ☀ ⌂

(est 1958)

Glen Cove, NY (Nassau Co.); (516) 671-8270
Billy Arasa, Director
Activities: Aquatic Activities, Arts/Crafts, Baseball/Softball, Challenge/Rope Courses, Field Trips, Horseback — English, Leadership Development, Martial Arts, Soccer, Swimming — Recreational
Session lengths & capacity: June-August; 3 week sessions; 500 campers
Clientele & fees: coed 3-15; Fees: B ☀ 🚐
Contact: Billy Arasa, Camp Youth Director at (516) 671-8270; fax: (516) 671-8275
e-mail: billya@flashcom.net
Operated by: YMCA Long Island, 155 Buckley Road, Holtsville, NY 11742 at (631) 289-4440 (#6681)

YMCA Camp Arrowhead ☀ ⌂ ⌂

(est 1954)

Pittsford, NY (Monroe Co.); (716) 383-4590
Jay Polston, Director

Camp comments: Traditional Day Camp in a 55 acre setting. Emphasis on character development, group work, friendship, and outdoor fun.
Activities: Archery, Arts/Crafts, Challenge/Rope Courses, Climbing/Rappelling, Drama, Hiking, Nature/Environment Studies, Sports — Field & Team, Swimming — Recreational
Session lengths & capacity: June-August; 1 & 2 week sessions; 400 campers
Clientele & fees: coed 4-15; families; Fees: B ☀ 🚐
Contact: Mike Reed, Program Director at (716) 383-4593; fax: (716) 383-4598
e-mail: mikere@rochesterymca.org
Web site: www.rochesterymca.org
Operated by: YMCA of Greater Rochester, 444 E Main St, Rochester, NY 14604 at (716) 546-5500 (#7665)

YMCA Camp Cory (est 1921) ⚠ ⌂ ⌂

Penn Yan, NY (Yates Co.); (315) 536-3840
Rick Coyle, Director

Camp comments: Outstanding staff, beautiful facility in Finger Lakes-Upstate NY. Traditional program plus sailing & waterskiing emphasis.
Activities: Aquatic Activities, Archery, Arts/Crafts, Canoeing, Counselor Training (CIT), Leadership Development, Sailing, Waterskiing
Session lengths & capacity: June-August; 1 & 2 week sessions; 214 campers
Clientele & fees: coed 7-16; Fees: D ⚠ 🚐
Contact: Rick Coyle, Executive Director at (716) 325-2889; fax: (716) 325-1602
e-mail: rickc@rochesterymca.org
Web site: www.rochesterymca.org
Operated by: YMCA of Greater Rochester, 444 E Main St, Rochester, NY 14604 at (716) 546-5500

Group Rental Information
Seasons & Capacity: Spring 180, Fall 180
Facilities: Cabins, Food Service, Lake, Lodges, Meeting Rooms, Playing Fields
Programs: Environmental Education (#7663)

YMCA Camp Gorham ⚠ ⌂ ⌂

(est 1961)

Eagle Bay, NY (Herkimer Co.); (315) 357-6401

Camp comments: Outstanding staff,beautiful facility in Adirondack Mtns,Upstate NY.Traditional program plus exciting speciality emphasis
Activities: Archery, Arts/Crafts, Boating, Climbing/Rappelling, Horseback — Western, Kayaking, Leadership Development, Sailing, Waterskiing, Wilderness Trips
Session lengths & capacity: June-August; 2 week sessions; 184 campers
Clientele & fees: coed 8-17; families; seniors; Fees: C, D ⚠ 🚐
Contact: Kurt Sample, Camp Gorham Director at (315) 357-6401; fax: (315) 357-3103
e-mail: corygorh@aol.com
Web site: www.rochesterymca.org
Operated by: YMCA of Greater Rochester, 444 E Main St, Rochester, NY 14604 at (716) 546-5500

Group Rental Information
Facilities: Cabins, Dorm-Style, Food Service, Hiking Trails, Kitchen Facilities, Lake, Lodges, Playing Fields
Programs: Boating, Challenge/Ropes Course, Environmental Education, Swimming (#7664)

YMCA Camp Kenan (est 1924) ☀ ⚠ ⌂

Barker, NY (Niagara Co.)
Mike Stevens, Director

Camp comments: YMCA Camp Kenan Residence camp, Day camp & Adventure center provides the

picturesque setting for all individuals to grow personally and professionally.
Activities: Archery, Arts/Crafts, Camping Skills/Outdoor Living, Canoeing, Challenge/Rope Courses, Fishing, Leadership Development, Sports — Field & Team, Swimming — Instructional, Team Building
Session lengths & capacity: 1 week sessions; 160 campers
Clientele & fees: boys 7-16; girls 7-16; coed 7-16; Fees: B ☀ Fees: B ⚠ 🚐
Contact: Bethann Kibby, Camping Secretary at (716) 434-8887; fax: (716) 434-0227
Operated by: Lockport Family YMCA, 19 East Avenue, Lockport, NY 14094 at (716) 434-8887

Group Rental Information
Seasons & Capacity: Spring 250, Summer 250, Fall 250, Winter 200
Facilities: A/V Equipment, Cabins, Food Service, Hiking Trails, Lake, Meeting Rooms, Playing Fields, Pool
Programs: Challenge/Ropes Course, Environmental Education, Swimming (#33567)

YMCA Camp Onyahsa ⚠ 🚐

(est 1898)

Dewittville, NY (Chautauqua Co.); (716) 753-5244
Jonathan O'Brian, Director

Camp comments: YMCA Camp Onyahsa over 100 years of individual growth and community building within a nurturing outdoor environment.
Activities: Aquatic Activities, Arts/Crafts, Challenge/Rope Courses, Counselor Training (CIT), International Culture, Nature/Environment Studies, Sailing, Swimming — Instructional, Waterskiing
Session lengths & capacity: June-September; 1/2, 1, 2, 3, 4, 5, 6, 7 & 8 week sessions; 120 campers
Clientele & fees: coed 7-16; families; Fees: B ⚠
Contact: Jonathan O'Brian, Camp Director at (716) 664-2802 ext. 223; fax: (716) 487-1174
e-mail: onyahsa@cecomet.net
Web site: www.onyahsa.org
Operated by: Jamestown NY YMCA, 101 E Fourth Street, Jamestown, NY 14701 at (716) 664-2802 (#3452)

YMCA Camp Pioneer ☀ 🚐

(est 1964)

Smithtown, NY (Suffolk Co.); (631) 265-6344
Denise Merdon, Director
Activities: Aquatic Activities, Arts/Crafts, Basketball, Field Trips, Nature/Environment Studies, Performing Arts, Soccer, Sports — Field & Team, Swimming — Instructional, Swimming — Recreational
Session lengths & capacity: June-September; 9 week sessions; 260 campers
Clientele & fees: coed 3-14; Fees: B ☀ 🚐
Contact: Denise Merdon, Program Director at (631) 265-6344; fax: (631) 366-1231
Operated by: YMCA Long Island, 155 Buckley Road, Holtsville, NY 11742 at (631) 289-4440 (#7717)

YMCA of Greater Buffalo ⚠ ⌂

(est 1897)

Gainesville, NY (Wyoming Co.); (515) 786-2940
Robert W Walker, Director

Camp comments: 1000 acre setting. Trails, brooks, heated pool, world class adventure ropes course. Small groups. Intensely trained staff team.
Activities: Archery, Canoeing, Challenge/Rope Courses, Counselor Training (CIT), Horseback — Western, Leadership Development, Nature/Environment Studies, Sailing, Travel/Tour, Wilderness Trips
Session lengths & capacity: 1 & 2 week sessions; 175 campers
Clientele & fees: coed 7-16; families; single adults; Fees: D ⚠ 🚐

Contact: Robert W Walker, Executive Director at (716) 565-6008; fax: (716) 565-6007
Web site: www.wnybiz.com/campweona
Operated by: YMCA of Greater Buffalo, 280 Cayuga Rd, Buffalo, NY 14225 at (716) 565-6008

Group Rental Information
Seasons & Capacity: Spring 3000, Summer 850, Fall 1000, Winter 350
Facilities: A/V Equipment, Cabins, Dorm-Style, Double Occupancy, Food Service, Hiking Trails, Lake, Meeting Rooms, Playing Fields, Pool, Tents
Programs: Boating, Challenge/Ropes Course, Environmental Education, Horseback Riding, Swimming, Winter Sports (#1832)

YMCA Of Greater NY
(est 1924)

Huguenot, NY (Orange Co.); (845) 858-2200
Chris Scheuer, Director

Camp comments: Each of our 3 camps is a safe, caring, community. Dedicated to developing strong values, self-esteem & skills.
Activities: Archery, Arts/Crafts, Camping Skills/Outdoor Living, Challenge/Rope Courses, Gymnastics, Horseback — Western, International Culture, Nature/Environment Studies, Sailing, Swimming — Instructional
Session lengths & capacity: June-September; 1 & 2 week sessions; 600 campers
Clientele & fees: coed 6-18; families; seniors; single adults; Fees: B ☀ Fees: D ⚠ 🐖
Contact: Chris Scheuer, Director of Camping at (845) 858-2200; fax: (845) 858-7823
e-mail: camps@ymcanyc.org
Web site: www.ymcanyc.org
Operated by: YMCA Camping Services, YMCA of Greater New York, 300 Big Pond Rd Box B, Huguenot, NY 12746 at (845) 858-2200

Group Rental Information
Site comments: Greenkil Outdoor Environmental Education & Conference Ctr provides residential instructional programs for schools using 1000 acre classroom & weekend retreats.
Seasons & Capacity: Spring 220, Fall 220, Winter 220
Facilities: A/V Equipment, Dorm-Style, Double Occupancy, Food Service, Hiking Trails, Lake, Linens, Lodges, Meeting Rooms, Playing Fields
Programs: Boating, Challenge/Ropes Course, Environmental Education (#2026)

ICON LEGEND
☀ Day Camp
⚠ Resident Camp
🏠 Facilities Available To Rent
🚗 Transportation Available
🐖 Financial Aid Available

FEE RANGES PER WEEK
A $0-75
B $75-200
C $201-350
D $351-500
E $501-650
F over $650

Young Judaea Sprout Lake
(est 1976)

Verbank, NY; (845) 677-3411
Helene Drobenare, Director

Camp comments: Jewish Zionist camp. Excellent well rounded program of sports & arts. Fully Kosher. A taste of Israel in Hudson Valley.
Activities: Archery, Arts/Crafts, Ceramics/Pottery, Challenge/Rope Courses, Hiking, Nature/Environment Studies, Radio/TV/Video, Sports — Field & Team, Swimming — Instructional, Swimming — Recreational
Session lengths & capacity: June-August; 2 & 4 week sessions; 200 campers
Clientele & fees: coed 7-14; Fees: D ⚠ 🐖
Contact: (201) 487-2448;
e-mail: cyjsl@aol.com
Operated by: Hadassah Womens Zionist Org, 50 West 58th St, New York, NY 10019 at (212) 303-4591

Group Rental Information
Site comments: Fully kosher, beautiful setting. 2 hrs from NYC.
Seasons & Capacity: Spring 300, Fall 300, Winter 300
Facilities: A/V Equipment, Cabins, Dorm-Style, Double Occupancy, Food Service, Hiking Trails, Linens, Meeting Rooms, Playing Fields, Pool
Programs: Boating, Challenge/Ropes Course, Environmental Education, Swimming (#3203)

Young Peop Day Camp-Queens
(est 1972)

Plainview, NY (Queens Co.); (800) 856-1043
Mr Steven Vessallo, Director

Camp comments: The very best in day camping. Free transportation.
Activities: Arts/Crafts, Baseball/Softball, Basketball, Camping Skills/Outdoor Living, Ceramics/Pottery, Soccer, Sports — Field & Team, Swimming — Instructional, Swimming — Recreational
Session lengths & capacity: June-August; 2, 4, 6 & 8 week sessions; 250 campers
Clientele & fees: coed 5-14; Fees: C ☀
Contact: Vincent Ferrante, Director at (516) 349-0296; fax: (516) 349-7167
e-mail: youngpeoples@aol.com
Web site: www.ypdc.com
Operated by: Young Peoples Day Camps, 20 Highland Court, Freehold, NJ 07728 at (800) 933-9732 (#1109)

Young Peop Day Camp-Staten Isl (est 1972)

Staten Island, NY (Staten Island Co.); (718) 984-0807
Larry Marantz, Director

Camp comments: Non-traditional day camp combines sports, swimming, karate, music w/daily trips, special events. Transportation included
Activities: Arts/Crafts, Baseball/Softball, Dance, Field Trips, Football, Skating, Sports — Field & Team, Swimming — Recreational
Session lengths & capacity: July-August; 2, 4, 6 & 8 week sessions; 250 campers
Clientele & fees: coed 5-14; Fees: B, C ☀
Contact: Larry Marantz, Director at (718) 984-0807; fax: (732) 761-9323
e-mail: youngpeoples@aol.com
Web site: www.ypdc.com
Operated by: Young Peoples Day Camps, 20 Highland Court, Freehold, NJ 07728 at (800) 933-9732 (#1346)

Young Peop Day Camp-Suffolk Co (est 1974)

Smithtown, NY (Suffolk Co.); (631) 476-3330
Mike Davidson, Director

Camp comments: We are good at giving your children a great summer.
Activities: Arts/Crafts, Baseball/Softball, Basketball, Dance, Field Trips, Golf, Leadership Development, Nature/Environment Studies, Swimming — Recreational
Session lengths & capacity: June-August; 2, 4, 6 & 8 week sessions; 200 campers
Clientele & fees: coed 5-14; Fees: B, C ☀
Contact: Mike Davidson, Director at (631) 476-3330; fax: (631) 265-1869
e-mail: youngpeoples@aol.com
Web site: www.ypdc.com
Operated by: Young Peoples Day Camps, 20 Highland Court, Freehold, NJ 07728 at (800) 933-9732 (#3065)

Young Peop Day Camp-Westchestr (est 1973)

Yonkers, NY (Westchester Co.); (800) 329-2267
Brian Lipchik, Director

Camp comments: Beautiful Westchester setting. Superb pool. Serving Bronx, Lower Westchester and Manhattan. Includes transportation.
Activities: Arts/Crafts, Baseball/Softball, Basketball, Football, Golf, Nature/Environment Studies, Soccer, Swimming — Recreational, Tennis
Session lengths & capacity: July-August; 2, 4, 6 & 8 week sessions; 300 campers
Clientele & fees: coed 5-14; Fees: B, C ☀
Contact: Brian Lipchick, Director at (914) 792-6555; fax: (516) 486-5280
e-mail: youngpeoples@aol.com
Web site: www.ypdc.com
Operated by: Young Peoples Day Camps, 20 Highland Court, Freehold, NJ 07728 at (800) 933-9732 (#7608)

Young Peop Day Camps-Nassau
(est 1972)

Plainview, NY (Nassau Co.); (516) 349-0296
Vincent Ferrante, Director

Camp comments: Nurturing environment, exciting activities. Adult staff. Affordable & safe trips & travel.
Activities: Arts/Crafts, Baseball/Softball, Basketball, Dance, Drama, Drawing/Painting, Leadership Development, Nature/Environment Studies, Swimming — Instructional, Swimming — Recreational
Session lengths & capacity: June-August; 2, 4, 6 & 8 week sessions; 250 campers
Clientele & fees: coed 5-14; Fees: C ☀
Contact: Vincent Ferrante, Director at (516) 349-0296; fax: (516) 349-7167
e-mail: youngpeoples@aol.com
Web site: www.ypdc.com
Operated by: Young Peoples Day Camps, 20 Highland Court, Freehold, NJ 07728 at (800) 933-9732 (#3069)

Young Peoples Day of Brooklyn
(est 1973)

Brooklyn, NY (Brooklyn Co.); (718) 451-9700
John Digennaro, Director

Camp comments: Young People's Day Camps Fun Educational Diversified Convenient We've kept children smiling & parents at ease since 1972
Activities: Arts/Crafts, Baseball/Softball, Basketball, Drawing/Painting, Football, Soccer, Swimming — Recreational
Session lengths & capacity: July-August; 2, 4, 6 & 8 week sessions; 250 campers
Clientele & fees: coed 5-14; Fees: C ☀
Contact: John Digennaro, Director at (718) 451-9700; fax: (718) 531-2688
e-mail: youngpeoples@aol.com
Web site: www.ypdc.com
Operated by: Young Peoples Day Camps, 20 Highland Court, Freehold, NJ 07728 at (800) 933-9732 (#1077)

YWCA Camp Cedarcliff (est 1934) ☀

Poughkeepsie, NY (Dutchess Co.); (914) 454-6770
Rupert Cort, Director

Camp comments: Youth sharing and growing in a safe, loving, respectful environment. Noncompetitive team-building activities. Great staff.
Activities: Arts/Crafts, Counselor Training (CIT), Field Trips, Leadership Development, Nature/Environment Studies, Sports — Field & Team, Swimming — Instructional, Tennis
Session lengths & capacity: 2 week sessions; 150 campers
Clientele & fees: coed 6-15; Fees: B ☀ 🐖
Contact: Rupert Cort, Camp Director at (914) 454-6770; fax: (914) 454-6373
Operated by: YWCA of Dutchess CO, 18 Bancroft Rd Eastman Park, Poughkeepsie, NY 12601 at (914) 454-6770 (#10904)

North Carolina

4H Rural Life Center (est 1984) ☀ 🏠

Halifax, NC (Halifax Co.); (252) 583-1821
Joe Long, Director

Camp comments: A fun day camp with a great staff and delicious food, open to everyone. Full of many exciting adventures.
Activities: Academics, Arts/Crafts, Canoeing, Challenge/Rope Courses, Drama, Farming/Ranching/Gardening, Hiking, Music, Nature/Environment Studies, Sports — Field & Team
Session lengths & capacity: May-September; 1 week sessions; 125 campers
Clientele & fees: coed 6-19; Fees: A ☀
Contact: Joe Long, 4-H Rural Life Center Director at (252) 583-1821; fax: (252) 583-1683
e-mail: jlong@schoollink.net
Operated by: Halifax County Coop Ext Srv, PO Box 37, Halifax, NC 27839 at (252) 583-5161

Group Rental Information
Site comments: A great facility capable of adapting to group needs.
Seasons & Capacity: Spring 50, Fall 50, Winter 50
Facilities: Dorm-Style (#3117)

Ashe County 4H Blue Ridge Advn (est 1977) ▲

Jefferson, NC (Ashe Co.); (336) 219-2650
Walker Massey, Director

Camp comments: Wilderness trips for at-risk or court involvede youth to improve self-esteem, problem solving, and social responsibility
Activities: Backpacking, Camping Skills/Outdoor Living, Canoeing, Caving, Challenge/Rope Courses, Climbing/Rappelling, Hiking, Wilderness Trips
Session lengths & capacity: June-August; 1 week sessions; 10 campers
Clientele & fees: boys 9-17; girls 9-17; Fees: C ▲
Contact: Wilderness Experience, 4-H Program Associate at (336) 219-2650; fax: (336) 246-4466
e-mail: walker_massey@ncsu.edu
Web site: ashe.ces.state.nc.us
Operated by: Ashe County 4H, 134 Government Circle Ste 202, Jefferson, NC 28640 at (336) 219-2650 (#3893)

Autism Society of NC (est 1972) ▲ 🏠

Moncure, NC (Chatham Co.); (919) 542-1033
David Yell, Director

Camp comments: ASNC Camp gives campers a structured day of typical camp activities, with emphasis on the campers' enjoyment.
Activities: Aerobics/Exercise, Arts/Crafts, Baseball/Softball, Basketball, Boating, Dance, Drawing/Painting, Hiking, Music, Swimming — Recreational
Session lengths & capacity: May-August; 1 week sessions; 36 campers
Clientele & fees: coed 4-99; Fees: C ▲ 🐖
Contact: David Yell, Camp Royall Director at (919) 542-1033; fax: (919) 542-1033
e-mail: dyell@autismsociety-nc.org
Web site: www.autismsociety-nc.org
Operated by: Camp Royall, 250 Bill Ash Road, Moncure, NC 27569 at (919) 542-1033

Group Rental Information
Seasons & Capacity: Spring 120, Fall 120, Winter 120
Facilities: A/V Equipment, Cabins, Dorm-Style, Double Occupancy, Hiking Trails, Kitchen Facilities, Lake, Lodges, Meeting Rooms, Playing Fields, Pool, Tents
Programs: Boating, Swimming (#5627)

Betsy Jeff Penn 4H Camp (est 1964) ☀ ▲ 🏠 🚗

Reidsville, NC (Rockingham Co.); (919) 349-9445
Emily Fisher, Director

Camp comments: Strong focus on building diversity. Serves a broad audience with strong science & social values focus.
Activities: Archery, Camping Skills/Outdoor Living, Canoeing, Challenge/Rope Courses, Climbing/Rappelling, Horseback — Western, Nature/Environment Studies, Swimming — Instructional, Team Building, Wilderness Trips
Session lengths & capacity: 1 & 2 week sessions; 168 campers
Clientele & fees: coed 6-17; seniors; Fees: B ☀ Fees: C ▲
Contact: Jeffery North, 4-H Center Director at (336) 349-9445; fax: (336) 634-0110
e-mail: jeff_north@ncsu.edu
Web site: www.nc4-H.com
Operated by: Betsy Jeff Penn 4H Camp, 804 Cedar Lane, Reidsville, NC 27320 at (336) 349-9445

Group Rental Information
Site comments: Environmental & adventure programs available year round.
Facilities: Cabins, Double Occupancy, Food Service, Kitchen Facilities, Lake, Linens, Meeting Rooms, Playing Fields
Programs: Boating, Challenge/Ropes Course, Environmental Education (#7102)

Blue Star Camps (est 1948) ▲ 🏠

Hendersonville, NC (Henderson Co.); (828) 692-3591
Rodger and Candy Popkin, Director

Camp comments: Blue Star is a sanctuary from stresses of real world and a thread woven into tapestry of Jewish American experiences.
Activities: Arts/Crafts, Bicycling/Biking, Camping Skills/Outdoor Living, Challenge/Rope Courses, Climbing/Rappelling, Drama, Horseback — English, Kayaking, Riflery, Tennis
Session lengths & capacity: June-August; 4 & 8 week sessions; 750 campers
Clientele & fees: coed 7-17; Fees: F ▲
Contact: Lita Robbins, Office Manager at (954) 963-4494; fax: (954) 963-2145
e-mail: lita@bluestarcamps.com
Web site: www.bluestarcamps.com
Operated by: Blue Star Camps, 3595 Sheridan St Ste 107, Hollywood, FL 33021-3649 at (954) 963-4494

Group Rental Information
Site comments: 125 cabins,Mts near 2 airpts. 2 lakes & pool.Kosher kitchen.Bike trails,climbing tower,12 tennis cts,high ropes,bask cts
Seasons & Capacity: Spring 1000, Summer 1000, Fall 1000
Facilities: Cabins, Double Occupancy, Food Service, Kitchen Facilities, Lake, Playing Fields
Programs: Boating (#742)

Broadstone (est 1952) ▲ 🏠

Banner Elk, NC (Watauga Co.); (828) 963-4640
Judith Bevan, Director

Camp comments: Enrichment program for gifted & talented. Noncompetitive, caring atmosphere. Blend of academic & adventure programs.
Activities: Academics, Arts/Crafts, Canoeing, Challenge/Rope Courses, Climbing/Rappelling, Counselor Training (CIT), Field Trips, Nature/Environment Studies, Rafting, Team Building
Session lengths & capacity: June-July; 2 week sessions; 72 campers
Clientele & fees: coed 10-15; Fees: D ▲
Contact: Judith Bevan, Camp Director at (828) 963-4640; fax: (828) 963-6588
e-mail: bevanjk@appstate.edu
Web site: www.conferences-camps.appstate.edu
Operated by: Appalachian State University, Office of Conferences and Inst, University Hall ASU, Boone, NC 28608 at (828) 262-3045

Group Rental Information
Site comments: Lodge and cabins available Fall, Winter and Spring for retreats, conferences, workshops, meetings, private parties, and reunions.
Seasons & Capacity: Spring 88, Fall 88, Winter 88
Facilities: Cabins, Food Service, Lodges, Playing Fields
Programs: Challenge/Ropes Course (#727)

Camp Arrowhead (est 1937) ▲ 🏠

Tuxedo, NC (Henderson Co.); (828) 692-1123
Stephen C Reynolds, Director

Camp comments: In the heart of the Blue Ridge Mountains Camp Arrowhead is fun, adventure - the ultimate summer experience!
Activities: Archery, Camping Skills/Outdoor Living, Climbing/Rappelling, Fishing, Horseback — English, Horseback — Western, Kayaking, Riflery, Sailing
Session lengths & capacity: June-August; 2, 3 & 4 week sessions; 128 campers
Clientele & fees: boys 7-15; Fees: D ▲
Contact: Steve C Reynolds, Owner at (828) 692-1123; fax: (828) 692-3789
e-mail: arrowarden@aol.com
Web site: www.camparrowheadforboys.com
Operated by: Camp Arrowhead, PO Box 248, Tuxedo, NC 28784 at (828) 692-1123

Group Rental Information
Seasons & Capacity: Spring 160, Fall 160
Facilities: Cabins, Food Service, Hiking Trails, Lake, Meeting Rooms, Playing Fields
Programs: Challenge/Ropes Course, Environmental Education (#29215)

Camp Carolina (est 1924) ▲ 🏠

Brevard, NC (Transylvania Co.); (828) 884-2414
Cha Cha Thompson & Alfred Thompson, Director

Camp comments: Our philosophy centers around simplicity of life, self-reliance, human relations, wonders of nature, & high adventure.
Activities: Bicycling/Biking, Caving, Climbing/Rappelling, Counselor Training (CIT), Horseback — Western, Kayaking, Riflery, SCUBA, Skating, Travel/Tour
Session lengths & capacity: June-August; 2, 3 & 4 week sessions; 250 campers
Clientele & fees: boys 7-17; Fees: F ▲
Contact: Charles Thompson & Alfred Thompson, Directors at (828) 884-2414; fax: (828) 884-2454
e-mail: chacha@campcarolina.com
Web site: www.campcarolina.com
Operated by: The Thompson Family, Camp Carolina, PO Box 919, Brevard, NC 28712 at (828) 884-2414

Group Rental Information
Seasons & Capacity: Spring 100, Fall 100

Facilities: A/V Equipment, Cabins, Food Service, Hiking Trails, Lake, Lodges, Meeting Rooms, Playing Fields
Programs: Boating, Environmental Education (#2440)

Camp Carolina Trails for Child

(est 1982) ▲

Clemmons, NC; (910) 766-7436
Rick Bridges, Director
Activities: Aerobics/Exercise, Aquatic Activities, Archery, Camping Skills/Outdoor Living, Canoeing, Challenge/Rope Courses, Counselor Training (CIT), Dance, Leadership Development, Swimming — Recreational
Session lengths & capacity: July-August; 1 week sessions
Clientele & fees: Fees: D ▲ 🐷
Contact: American Diabetic Association at (704) 373-9111; fax: (704) 373-9113
Operated by: American Diabetes Assn South, 1820 E Seventh St, Charlotte, NC 28204 at (336) 766-7436 (#5666)

Camp Ginger Cascades

(est 1963) ▲ 🏠

Lenoir, NC (Caldwell Co.); (828) 758-5321
Deb Dowling, Director

Camp comments: Challenging high adventure programs in a scenic mountain setting. Varied programs to meet the interests of all girls.
Activities: Arts/Crafts, Backpacking, Bicycling/Biking, Camping Skills/Outdoor Living, Canoeing, Challenge/Rope Courses, Climbing/Rappelling, Horseback — English, Nature/Environment Studies, Swimming — Instructional
Session lengths & capacity: June-July; 1/2 & 1 week sessions; 100 campers
Clientele & fees: girls 6-16; Fees: B, C ▲
Contact: Deb Dowling, Camp Director at (828) 328-2444; fax: (828) 328-6870
e-mail: dowling@cvgirlscouts.org
Web site: www.cvgirlscouts.org
Operated by: Catawba Valley Area GSC, 530 Fourth St S W, Hickory, NC 28602 at (828) 328-2444

Group Rental Information
Site comments: Great weekend retreat facility. Beautiful mountain setting.
Seasons & Capacity: Spring 120, Winter 120
Facilities: Cabins, Hiking Trails, Kitchen Facilities, Lake, Lodges, Meeting Rooms, Pool, Tents
Programs: Boating, Challenge/Ropes Course (#11356)

ICON LEGEND

☀ Day Camp
▲ Resident Camp
🏠 Facilities Available To Rent
🚐 Transportation Available
🐷 Financial Aid Available

FEE RANGES PER WEEK

A	$0-75
B	$75-200
C	$201-350
D	$351-500
E	$501-650
F	over $650

Camp Golden Valley

(est 1971) ☀ ▲ 🏠

Bostic, NC (Rutherford Co.); (828) 245-1946
Karen Prine, Director

Camp comments: Challenging programs designed to meet the needs of every girl.Horses,travel,adventure & arts all in a mountain setting.
Activities: Arts/Crafts, Bicycling/Biking, Camping Skills/Outdoor Living, Drama, Field Trips, Hiking, Horseback — Western, Leadership Development, Nature/Environment Studies, Swimming — Instructional
Session lengths & capacity: June-July; 1 week sessions; 160 campers
Clientele & fees: girls 6-17; Fees: B ▲ 🐷
Contact: Karen Prine, Outdoor Program Specialist at (828) 245-1946; fax: (828) 245-2424
Operated by: Girl Scouts Pioneer Cncl, 250 S New Hope Rd, Gastonia, NC 28054 at (704) 864-3245

Group Rental Information
Facilities: Cabins, Hiking Trails, Kitchen Facilities, Lake, Meeting Rooms, Playing Fields, Pool
Programs: Boating, Swimming (#7312)

Camp Greystone

▲ 🏠

Tuxedo, NC (Henderson Co.)
James F Miller IV, Director

Camp comments: Greystone strives to facilitate growth in the physical, social, mental, and spiritual dimensions of each camper's life.
Session lengths & capacity: May-August; 2, 3 & 5 week sessions; 450 campers
Clientele & fees: girls 7-17; families; Fees: F ▲
Contact: Katie Warrington, Assistant Director at (828) 693-3182; fax: (828) 693-1562
e-mail: office@campgreystone.com
Web site: www.campgreystone.com
Operated by: Camp Greystone, South Lake Summit Road, Tuxedo, NC 28784 at (828) 693-3182 (#38174)

Camp Hanes YMCA (est 1927) ▲ 🏠

King, NC (Stokes Co.); (336) 983-3131
Bob Kahle, Director

Camp comments: Dynamic staff. Beautiful mountainside facility. Exciting program taught in a positive Christian value environment.
Activities: Archery, Camping Skills/Outdoor Living, Challenge/Rope Courses, Climbing/Rappelling, Horseback — Western, Leadership Development, Model Rocketry, Nature/Environment Studies, Riflery
Session lengths & capacity: June-August; 1 & 2 week sessions; 300 campers
Clientele & fees: coed 6-16; families; seniors; single adults; Fees: C ▲ 🐷
Contact: Patrick Kelly, Program Director at (336) 983-3131; fax: (336) 983-4624
e-mail: fun@camphanes.org
Web site: www.camphanes.org
Operated by: Winston Salem YMCA, 1144 W Fourth St, Winston Salem, NC 27101 at (336) 777-8055

Group Rental Information
Site comments: Beautiful mountainside location. Great food, helpful staff.
Seasons & Capacity: Spring 300, Fall 300, Winter 300
Facilities: Cabins, Food Service, Hiking Trails, Lake, Lodges, Meeting Rooms, Playing Fields, Pool
Programs: Boating, Challenge/Ropes Course, Environmental Education (#3314)

Camp Hollymont for Girls

(est 1983) ▲

Asheville, NC (Buncombe Co.); (828) 252-2123
Loren M McKibbens, Director

Camp comments: Christian Camp in NC Mountains. Excellent facilities and beautiful setting for a variety of traditional camp activities and high adventures.
Activities: Arts/Crafts, Challenge/Rope Courses, Dance, Gymnastics, Horseback — English, Photography, Swimming — Instructional, Tennis, Waterskiing
Session lengths & capacity: June-August; 2, 3 & 4 week sessions; 200 campers
Clientele & fees: girls 6-15; Fees: F ▲
Contact: Gail Mashburn or Loren McKibbens, Administrative Dir./Camp Dir. at (828) 686-5343; fax: (828) 686-7206
e-mail: info@hollymont.com
Operated by: Hollymont Inc, 475 Lake Eden Rd, Black Mountain, NC 28711 at (828) 686-5343 (#3747)

Camp Judaea (est 1960) ▲ 🏠

Hendersonville, NC (Henderson Co.); (828) 685-8841
Marc Howard, Director

Camp comments: Overnight Zionist camp in beautiful Blue Ridge Mtns. Offering a caring atmosphere with opportunity to belong & learn.
Activities: Aquatic Activities, Camping Skills/Outdoor Living, Challenge/Rope Courses, Field Trips, Hockey, Horseback — Western, Music, Sports — Field & Team, Travel/Tour
Session lengths & capacity: June-August; 2 & 4 week sessions; 250 campers
Clientele & fees: coed 7-15; Fees: D, E ▲
Contact: Phyllis Major, Office Manager at (404) 634-7883; fax: (404) 325-2743
e-mail: info@campjudaea.org
Web site: www.campjudaea.org
Operated by: Hadassah/Camp Judaea, 1996 Cliff Valley Way Ste 104, Atlanta, GA 30329 at (404) 634-7883

Group Rental Information
Site comments: Blue Ridge Mountain hideaway. Kosher kitchen, rustic setting.
Seasons & Capacity: Spring 200, Fall 200
Facilities: Cabins, Double Occupancy, Food Service, Kitchen Facilities, Meeting Rooms, Pool (#3152)

Camp Kanuga For Boys And Girls (est 1931) ▲ 🚐

Hendersonville, NC (Henderson Co.); (828) 692-9136
Alyson Thorn, Director

Camp comments: Young people 7-16 have enjoyable, stimulating experiences in a Christian outdoor setting. Recreational/Personal Growth.
Activities: Aquatic Activities, Archery, Arts/Crafts, Backpacking, Canoeing, Challenge/Rope Courses, Nature/Environment Studies, Performing Arts, Sports — Field & Team, Wilderness Trips
Session lengths & capacity: June-August; 2 week sessions; 120 campers
Clientele & fees: coed 7-16; Fees: D ▲ 🐷
Contact: Betty Barnett, Camp Kanuga Registrar at (828) 692-9136; fax: (828) 696-3589
e-mail: info@kanuga.org
Web site: www.kanuga.org/camp
Operated by: Kanuga Conferences Inc, Kanuga Conference Drive, PO Box 250, Hendersonville, NC 28793-0250 at (828) 692-9136 (#3)

Camp Merri Mac (est 1950) ⛰ 🏠

Black Mountain, NC (Buncomb Co.);
(828) 669-8766
Adam Boyd, Director

Camp comments: A fun-filled growing experience. Outstanding staff. Christian camp setting, sister camp to Timberlake for Boys.
Activities: Archery, Backpacking, Climbing/Rappelling, Dance, Drama, Gymnastics, Horseback — English, Performing Arts, Riflery, Tennis
Session lengths & capacity: June-August; 2, 3 & 4 week sessions; 190 campers
Clientele & fees: girls 6-16; Fees: **E, F** ⛰
Contact: Adam Boyd, Owners/Director at (828) 669-8766; fax: (828) 669-6822
e-mail: adam@merri-mac.com
Web site: www.merri-mac.com
Operated by: Merri-Mac/Timberlake LLC, 1123 Montreat Road, Black Mountain, NC 28711 at (828) 669-8766

Group Rental Information
Facilities: Cabins, Hiking Trails, Lake, Meeting Rooms, Playing Fields, Tents (#796)

Camp Merrie Woode

(est 1919) ⛰ 🚗

Sapphire, NC (Jackson Co.); (828) 743-3300
Gordon and Laurie Strayhorn, Director

Camp comments: A traditional camp program providing high adventure activities in an unsurpassed wilderness setting for girls 7 - 17.
Activities: Canoeing, Climbing/Rappelling, Drama, Horseback — English, Nature/Environment Studies, Sailing, Wilderness Trips
Session lengths & capacity: June-August; 2, 3 & 5 week sessions; 200 campers
Clientele & fees: girls 7-17; Fees: **E** ⛰ 🐖
Contact: Laurie and Gordon Strayhorn, Directors at (828) 743-3300; fax: (828) 743-5846
e-mail: gordon@merriewoode.com
Operated by: Merrie Woode Inc, 100 Merrie Woode Road, Sapphire, NC 28774 at (828) 743-3300 (#739)

Camp Monroe (est 1954) ☀ ⛰ 🏠

Laurel Hill, NC; (910) 276-1654
Jon Stricklin, Director

Camp comments: Relate to God, others, world, and self in the outdoor setting!
Activities: Archery, Arts/Crafts, Canoeing, Challenge/Rope Courses, Field Trips, Horseback — Western, Religious Study, Swimming — Recreational, Team Building
Session lengths & capacity: June-July; 1/2 & 1 week sessions; 95 campers
Clientele & fees: coed 6-16; families; Fees: **B** ☀
Fees: **C** ⛰
Contact: Jonathan Sherrod, Associate for Outdoor Ministries at (910) 862-8300; fax: (910) 862-3524
e-mail: cjsherrod@presbycc.org
Web site: www.presbycc.org
Operated by: Presbytery of Coastal Carolina, 807 West King Street, Elizabethtown, NC 28337 at (910) 862-8300

Group Rental Information
Site comments: Our challenge course/ropes course is available year round!
Seasons & Capacity: Spring 150, Fall 94, Winter 94
Facilities: A/V Equipment, Cabins, Food Service, Hiking Trails, Kitchen Facilities, Lake, Lodges, Meeting Rooms, Playing Fields, Pool
Programs: Boating, Challenge/Ropes Course, Swimming (#41494)

Camp Sea Gull (est 1948) ☀ ⛰ 🏠 🚗

Arapahoe, NC; (252) 249-1111
Lloyd Griffith, Director

Camp comments: Coastal camp featuring seamanship, sailing, motor boating and golf.
Activities: Aquatic Activities, Archery, Basketball, Boating, Challenge/Rope Courses, Golf, Leadership Development, Sailing, Waterskiing, Windsurfing
Session lengths & capacity: 1 & 4 week sessions; 760 campers
Clientele & fees: boys 7-16; Fees: **D, E** ⛰ 🐖
Contact: Lloyd Griffith, Director at (252) 249-1111; fax: (252) 249-1266
e-mail: webmaster@seagull-seafarer.org
Web site: www.seagull-seafarer.org
Operated by: Capital Area YMCA, 1601 Hillsborough St, Raleigh, NC 27605 at (919) 832-6602

Group Rental Information
Facilities: A/V Equipment, Cabins, Double Occupancy, Food Service, Lake, Linens, Meeting Rooms, Playing Fields, River
Programs: Boating, Challenge/Ropes Course, Environmental Education, Swimming (#759)

Camp Seafarer (est 1961) ☀ ⛰ 🏠 🚗

Arapahoe, NC (Pamlico Co.); (252) 249-1212
Cille Griffith, Director

Camp comments: YMCA resident camp with unique seamanship programs in sailing, motorboating + popular land, climbing, camping activities
Activities: Aquatic Activities, Arts/Crafts, Boating, Canoeing, Challenge/Rope Courses, Golf, Horseback — English, Nature/Environment Studies, Riflery, Sailing
Session lengths & capacity: 1 & 4 week sessions; 580 campers
Clientele & fees: girls 7-16; families; single adults; Fees: **D, E** ⛰ 🐖
Contact: Cille Griffith, Director at (252) 249-1212; fax: (252) 249-2259
e-mail: webmaster@seagull-seafarer.org
Web site: www.seagull-seafarer.org
Operated by: Capital Area YMCA, 1601 Hillsborough St, Raleigh, NC 27605 at (919) 832-6602

Group Rental Information
Facilities: A/V Equipment, Cabins, Dorm-Style, Double Occupancy, Food Service, Hiking Trails, Lake, Linens, Lodges, Meeting Rooms, Playing Fields, River
Programs: Boating, Challenge/Ropes Course, Environmental Education, Swimming (#757)

Camp Tekoa UMC (est 1949) ☀ ⛰ 🏠

Hendersonville, NC (Hendersonville Co.); (828) 692-6516
James S Johnson, Director

Camp comments: Camp Tekoa engaged in ministry to touch hearts,change lives,share Christ's light.Fun/learning in beautiful NC mountains.
Activities: Backpacking, Bicycling/Biking, Camping Skills/Outdoor Living, Canoeing, Challenge/Rope Courses, Climbing/Rappelling, Leadership Development, Nature/Environment Studies, Religious Study, Swimming — Recreational
Session lengths & capacity: 1/2 & 1 week sessions; 200 campers
Clientele & fees: coed 6-17; Fees: **A** ☀
Fees: **B, D** ⛰ 🐖
Contact: James S Johnson, Director at (828) 692-6516; fax: (828) 697-3288
e-mail: director@camptekoa.org
Web site: www.camptekoa.org
Operated by: United Methodist Camp Tekoa, PO Box 160, Hendersonville, NC 28793-0160 at (828) 692-6516

Group Rental Information
Seasons & Capacity: Spring 185, Fall 185, Winter 185
Facilities: Cabins, Food Service, Hiking Trails, Kitchen Facilities, Lake, Lodges, Playing Fields
Programs: Boating (#3956)

Camp Timberlake (est 1983) ⛰ 🏠

Black Mountain, NC; (828) 669-8766
Adam Boyd, Director

Camp comments: Outstanding staff & traditional Christian camp setting, brother camp to Merri Mac for girls.
Activities: Archery, Backpacking, Challenge/Rope Courses, Climbing/Rappelling, Fencing, Horseback — English, Soccer, Tennis
Session lengths & capacity: 2 & 4 week sessions; 90 campers
Clientele & fees: boys 7-16; Fees: **D, E** ⛰
Contact: Adam Boyd, Director at (828) 669-8766; fax: (828) 669-6822
e-mail: adam@camptimberlake.com
Web site: www.merri-mac.com
Operated by: Merri-Mac/Timberlake LLC, 1123 Montreat Road, Black Mountain, NC 28711 at (828) 669-8766

Group Rental Information
Facilities: Cabins, Hiking Trails, Lake, Meeting Rooms, Playing Fields, Tents (#6227)

Camp Ton-A-Wandah

(est 1933) ⛰ 🏠 🚗

Hendersonville, NC (Henderson Co.); (828) 692-4251
William B Haynes, Director

Camp comments: Traditional camp emphasizing teamwork, independence, self confidence and traditional values in a natural setting in mtns
Activities: Archery, Arts/Crafts, Backpacking, Baseball/Softball, Basketball, Camping Skills/Outdoor Living, Counselor Training (CIT), Horseback — English, Rafting, Swimming — Instructional
Session lengths & capacity: Year-round; 2 & 3 week sessions; 220 campers
Clientele & fees: girls 6-15; Fees: **E** ⛰
Contact: Judy Haynes, Owner at (828) 692-4251; fax: (828) 692-9780
e-mail: tonawandah@cytechcis.net
Web site: www.camptonawandah.com
Operated by: Camp Ton-A-Wandah, Rt 13 Box 75, Hendersonville, NC 28739 at (828) 692-4251

Group Rental Information
Facilities: Cabins, Food Service, Hiking Trails, Lake, Meeting Rooms (#12338)

Camp Trinity (est 1986) ⛰

Salter Path, NC (Carteret Co.); (252) 247-5354
Penn Perry, Director

Camp comments: Christian based program, Atlantic Ocean Island. Beautiful setting. Offering community for spiritual growth, affirmation.
Activities: Arts/Crafts, Basketball, Challenge/Rope Courses, Counselor Training (CIT), Leadership Development, Music, Nature/Environment Studies, Sailing, Swimming — Instructional, Team Building
Session lengths & capacity: May-August; 1 week sessions; 80 campers
Clientele & fees: coed 9-18; Fees: **C** ⛰ 🐖
Contact: Penn Perry, Director of Camp Trinity at (252) 247-5354; fax: (252) 247-3290
e-mail: camptrinity@trinityctr.com
Web site: www.trinityctr.com
Operated by: Trinity Center Camp & Conf, Episcopal Diocese of East CA, PO Box 380, Salter Path, NC 28575 at (252) 247-5600 (#6304)

Camp Willow Run (est 1968) ⛰ 🏠

Littleton, NC (Warren Co.); (252) 586-4665
Robbie Harris & Kevin Adams, Director

Camp comments: Year-round Christian youth camp on Lake Gaston. Built on a unique railroad theme with HTD/AC Boxcars as dormitories.

Activities: Archery, Arts/Crafts, Basketball, Canoeing, Challenge/Rope Courses, Climbing/Rappelling, Model Rocketry, Sailing, Swimming — Instructional, Waterskiing
Session lengths & capacity: June-August; 1 week sessions; 190 campers
Clientele & fees: coed 8-17; Fees: C ▲ �" title
Contact: Robbie Harris, Summer Camp Director at (252) 586-4665; fax: (252) 586-4909
e-mail: info@campwillowrun.org
Web site: www.campwillowrun.org
Operated by: Youth Camps For Christ Inc, 1 Mangum Lane, Littleton, NC 27850 at (252) 586-4665

Group Rental Information
Seasons & Capacity: Spring 220, Fall 220, Winter 220
Facilities: A/V Equipment, Cabins, Dorm-Style, Double Occupancy, Food Service, Lake, Meeting Rooms, Playing Fields
Programs: Boating, Challenge/Ropes Course, Swimming (#2103)

Camp Winding Gap (est 1979) ▲ 🏠

Lake Toxaway, NC (Transylvannia Co.); (828) 966-4520
Ann Hertzberg, Director

Camp comments: Focus on camper choice, building self esteem, and giving children experiences that will last a lifetime.
Activities: Archery, Backpacking, Bicycling/Biking, Camping Skills/Outdoor Living, Canoeing, Hiking, Horseback — Western, Martial Arts, Riflery
Session lengths & capacity: June-August; 1, 2 & 3 week sessions; 85 campers
Clientele & fees: coed 6-14; Fees: E ▲
Contact: Ann S Hertzberg, Director at (828) 966-4520; fax: (828) 883-8720
e-mail: campwgap@citcom.net
Web site: www.campwindinggap.com
Operated by: Gaylord O & Marjorie Shepherd, Rt 1 Box 56, Lake Toxaway, NC 28747 at (828) 862-4896

Group Rental Information
Seasons & Capacity: Spring 100, Fall 100
Facilities: Cabins, Food Service, Hiking Trails, Linens, Lodges, River
Programs: Horseback Riding, Swimming (#3864)

Cheerio (est 1960) ▲ 🏠

Glade Valley, NC (Alleghany Co.); (336) 363-2604
Michaux Crocker, Director

Camp comments: Traditional YMCA camp located in Blue Ridge Mtns of NC. Coed wilderness tripping program offered. Christian emphasis.

ICON LEGEND

☀   Day Camp

▲   Resident Camp

🏠   Facilities Available To Rent

🚐   Transportation Available

🚌   Financial Aid Available

FEE RANGES PER WEEK

A	$0-75
B	$75-200
C	$201-350
D	$351-500
E	$501-650
F	over $650

Activities: Aquatic Activities, Archery, Arts/Crafts, Backpacking, Canoeing, Climbing/Rappelling, Horseback — English, Horseback — Western, Riflery, Tennis
Session lengths & capacity: March-November; 1 & 2 week sessions; 200 campers
Clientele & fees: boys 7-15; girls 7-15; coed 7-15; families; seniors; Fees: D ▲
Contact: Lynda Norris, Administrative Assistant at (800) 226-7496; fax: (910) 869-0118
e-mail: director@campcheerio.org
Web site: www.cheerioadventures.com
Operated by: YMCA of Greater High Point, PO Box 6258, High Point, NC 27262-6258 at (336) 869-0151

Group Rental Information
Seasons & Capacity: Spring 230, Summer 192, Fall 230
Facilities: Cabins, Hiking Trails, Lake, Lodges, Meeting Rooms
Programs: Boating (#805)

Chestnut Ridge (est 1959) ☀ ▲ 🏠

Efland, NC (Orange Co.); (919) 304-3900
Allen & Rhonda Parker, Director

Camp comments: Christian, rustic, small group camping. Limited enrollment for adults & children with mild mental retardation.
Activities: Arts/Crafts, Camping Skills/Outdoor Living, Canoeing, Challenge/Rope Courses, Counselor Training (CIT), Horseback — English, Nature/Environment Studies, Swimming — Recreational, Team Building
Session lengths & capacity: June-August; 1/2, 1 & 2 week sessions; 180 campers
Clientele & fees: coed 6-17; Fees: B ☀
Fees: C ▲ 🚌
Contact: David Wheeler, Facility Manager at (919) 304-3900; fax: (919) 563-3559
e-mail: info@campchestnutridge.org
Web site: www.ncumcamps.org
Operated by: NC United Methodist Commission, PO Box 726, Fuquay Varina, NC 27526-0726 at (919) 552-4673 (#7271)

Don Lee Center (est 1950) ▲ 🏠

Arapahoe, NC (Pamlico Co.); (800) 535-5475
John A Farmer, CCD, Director

Camp comments: Small group camping, open to all.Building strong communities in the UMC tradition in a coastal camping setting.Specialties in sailing, trip adventures & ecology
Activities: Arts/Crafts, Camping Skills/Outdoor Living, Canoeing, Challenge/Rope Courses, Leadership Development, Nature/Environment Studies, Sailing, Swimming — Recreational, Team Building, Travel/Tour
Session lengths & capacity: May-August; 1/2, 1, 2, 3 & 4 week sessions; 176 campers
Clientele & fees: coed 7-17; families; Fees: D ▲ 🚌
Contact: Rev John A Farmer CCD, Director at (800) 535-5475; fax: (919) 249-0497
e-mail: john@donleecenter.org
Web site: www.ncumcamps.org
Operated by: NC United Methodist Commission, PO Box 726, Fuquay Varina, NC 27526-0726 at (919) 552-4673

Group Rental Information
Site comments: Retreats for family, youth, and church groups. Fantastic coastal environmental deucation for school groups too. 150 students. Great food service & programs.
Seasons & Capacity: Spring 250, Fall 250, Winter 250
Facilities: A/V Equipment, Cabins, Food Service, Meeting Rooms, Pool, River, Tents
Programs: Boating, Challenge/Ropes Course, Environmental Education, Swimming (#7052)

Eagles Nest Camp (est 1922) ▲

Pisgah Forest, NC (Transylvania Co.); (828) 877-4349
Noni Waite-Kucera, Director

Camp comments: Experiential education for young people promoting the natural world and the betterment of human character.
Activities: Arts/Crafts, Backpacking, Camping Skills/Outdoor Living, Canoeing, Climbing/Rappelling, Drama, Horseback — English, Nature/Environment Studies, Soccer, Wilderness Trips
Session lengths & capacity: June-August; 3 & 6 week sessions; 190 campers
Clientele & fees: coed 6-17; Fees: E ▲ 🚌
Contact: Emmylou Ferris, Asst Director at (336) 761-1040; fax: (336) 727-0030
e-mail: promotions@enf.org
Web site: www.enf.org
Operated by: Eagles Nest Foundation, 633 Summit St, Winston Salem, NC 27101-1116 at (336) 761-1040 (#767)

Falling Creek Camp for Boys
(est 1969) ▲ 🏠

Tuxedo, NC (Henderson Co.); (704) 692-0262
Donnie Bain & Chuck Mc Grady, Director

Camp comments: Falling Creek seeks to provide a max. opportunity for growth & development in a mountain setting. Low camper/staff ratio
Activities: Backpacking, Bicycling/Biking, Camping Skills/Outdoor Living, Canoeing, Climbing/Rappelling, Horseback — English, Kayaking, Nature/Environment Studies, Soccer, Tennis
Session lengths & capacity: June-August; 2, 3 & 4 week sessions; 224 campers
Clientele & fees: boys 7-16; Fees: F ▲
Contact: Donnie Bain, Director at (828) 692-0262; fax: (828) 696-1616
e-mail: djbain@ioa.com
Web site: www.fallingcreek.com
Operated by: Falling Creek Camp for Boys, Box 98, Tuxedo, NC 28784 at (828) 692-0262 (#11385)

Graham (est 1956) ▲ 🏠

Henderson, NC (Vance Co.); (252) 492-4109
Alicia Garcia, Director

Camp comments: Specializing in swimming, canoeing, sailing & kayaking. The Kerr Lake Cove is the place to be. Ask about group camp!
Activities: Arts/Crafts, Canoeing, Counselor Training (CIT), Fishing, Kayaking, Nature/Environment Studies, Sailing, Swimming — Recreational

Session lengths & capacity: June-August; 1 & 2 week sessions; 120 campers
Clientele & fees: girls 8-17; Fees: **B, C** ⬛
Contact: Kate Hoppe, Director of Outdoor Programs at (919) 782-3021; fax: (919) 782-2083
e-mail: khoppe@pinesofcarolina.org
Web site: www.pinesofcarolina.org
Operated by: Pines of Carolina GSC, PO Box 52294, Raleigh, NC 27612 at (919) 782-3021 (#775)

Green River Preserve (est 1988) ⬛ 🏠

Cedar Mountain, NC (Transylvania Co.); (828) 885-2250
Sandy Schenck, Director

Camp comments: Non-profit natural science camp for gifted and motivated learners ages 9 to 13, nurturing, hands on learning, fun.
Activities: Archery, Arts/Crafts, Backpacking, Camping Skills/Outdoor Living, Canoeing, Ceramics/Pottery, Climbing/Rappelling, Fencing, Hiking, Nature/Environment Studies
Session lengths & capacity: May-October; 1, 2 & 3 week sessions; 98 campers
Clientele & fees: coed 9-13; Fees: **E** ☀
Fees: **F** ⬛ 🚌
Contact: Sandy & Missy Schenck, Owners/Directors at (828) 885-2250; fax: (828) 885-2210
e-mail: grpreserve@citcom.net
Web site: www.greenriverpreserve.com
Operated by: Green River Preserve, 301 Green River Road, Cedar Mountain, NC 28718 at (828) 885-2250

Group Rental Information
Site comments: 3 & 4 day programs, based on the book The Education of Little Tree, with themes of ecological respect, cultural heritage, & interconnectioness.
Seasons & Capacity: Spring 98, Winter 98 (#884)

Greenville YMCA (est 1912) ⬛ 🏠 🚗

Cedar Mountain, NC (Transylvania Co.); (864) 836-3291
Gregory T McKee, Jr, Director

Camp comments: Trad adventure & travel programs: 1600 acre mtn top setting, Blue Ridge Mtns, Western Carolinas. Int'l staff & campers.
Activities: Archery, Backpacking, Challenge/Rope Courses, Climbing/Rappelling, Horseback — Western, International Culture, Leadership Development, Riflery, Travel/Tour, Wilderness Trips
Session lengths & capacity: 1, 2 & 4 week sessions; 275 campers
Clientele & fees: coed 7-17; Fees: **C, D, E** ⬛ 🐟
Contact: Greg McKee, Exec Director at (864) 836-3291; fax: (864) 836-3140
e-mail: gtmckee@campgreenville.org
Web site: www.campgreenville.org
Operated by: YMCA of Greenville SC, 601 E McBee St, Greenville, SC 29601 at (864) 242-1111

Group Rental Information
Facilities: A/V Equipment, Cabins, Food Service, Hiking Trails, Lake, Lodges, Meeting Rooms, Playing Fields
Programs: Boating, Challenge/Ropes Course, Environmental Education, Horseback Riding, Swimming (#732)

Gwynn Valley (est 1935) ☀ ⬛

Brevard, NC (Transylvania Co.); (828) 885-2900
Grant & Anne Bullard, Director

Camp comments: A farm wilderness and traditional camp program which nurtures the child while fostering a connection with the land and the simple joys of childhood.
Activities: Archery, Arts/Crafts, Camping Skills/Outdoor Living, Canoeing, Climbing/Rappelling, Drama, Farming/Ranching/Gardening, Horseback — English, Nature/Environment Studies, Soccer

Session lengths & capacity: June-August; 1, 2 & 3 week sessions; 220 campers
Clientele & fees: coed 5-12; Fees: **C** ☀
Fees: **E** ⬛ 🚌
Contact: Anne and Grant Bullard, Director at (828) 885-2900; fax: (828) 885-2413
e-mail: mail@gwynnvalley.com
Web site: www.gwynnvalley.com
Operated by: Gwynn Valley, 1080 Island Ford Rd, Brevard, NC 28712 at (828) 885-2900 (#780)

Hardee ⬛ 🏠

Blounts Creek, NC (Wayne Co.); (252) 946-8214
Lynn Sebring, Director

Camp comments: Join us for a summer of fun and adventure! Make new friends,learn new skills and have a great time in the out-of-doors.
Activities: Aquatic Activities, Archery, Arts/Crafts, Canoeing, Drama, Field Trips, Horseback — Western, Sailing, Swimming — Recreational
Session lengths & capacity: July-August; 72 campers
Clientele & fees: girls 6-17; Fees: **A, B** ⬛
Contact: Beth Casey, Director of Program Services at (919) 734-6231 ext. 113; fax: (919) 734-9038
e-mail: bethscout@hotmail.com
Web site: www.gscoastalnc.org
Operated by: Girl Scout Coastal Carolina, PO Box 1735, Goldsboro, NC 27533-1735 at (919) 734-6231 (#46281)

Harris YMCA Camps (est 1980) ☀

Charlotte, NC (Mecklenburg Co.); (704) 716-6866
Laurel M Zitney, Director

Camp comments: Building character in a positive, fun & safe environment. Come join the summer adventure at the Harris YMCA!
Activities: Caving, Climbing/Rappelling, Counselor Training (CIT), Field Trips, Gymnastics, Nature/Environment Studies, Soccer, Sports — Field & Team, Swimming — Recreational
Session lengths & capacity: June-August; 1 week sessions; 500 campers
Clientele & fees: coed 3-15; Fees: **B** ☀ 🐟
Contact: Mary Michael, Sr. Family Services Director at (704) 716-6866; fax: (704) 716-6801
e-mail: mary.michael@ymcacharlotte.org
Operated by: James J Harris YMCA, 5900 Quail Hollow Road, Charlotte, NC 28210 at (704) 716-6869 (#5415)

Highlander (est 1964) ⬛ 🚗

Horse Shoe, NC; (866) 891-7721
Gaynell Tinsley, Jr., Director

Camp comments: Beautiful Blue Ridge Mountain setting. 40 on-camp activities, 15 off-camp trips. Outstanding staff, caring atmosphere.
Activities: Archery, Arts/Crafts, Backpacking, Basketball, Camping Skills/Outdoor Living, Ceramics/Pottery, Climbing/Rappelling, Horseback — English, Riflery, Waterskiing
Session lengths & capacity: June-August; 3, 6 & 9 week sessions; 320 campers
Clientele & fees: coed 7-16; Fees: **F** ⬛
Contact: Gaynell Tinsley, Jr., Director at (866) 891-7721; fax: (828) 891-1960
Web site: www.camphighlander.com
Operated by: Camp Highlander, 42 Dalton Road, Horse Shoe, NC 28742 at (866) 891-7721 (#881)

Holston Presbytery Camp & Retr (est 1955) ⬛ 🏠

Banner Elk, NC (Avery Co.); (828) 898-6611
Craig Bell, Director

Camp comments: Resident camp in mountains. Small group camping. Great staff. Cabins & rustic sites. Bonfires & lake, canoe.

Activities: Arts/Crafts, Backpacking, Bicycling/Biking, Camping Skills/Outdoor Living, Canoeing, Caving, Climbing/Rappelling, Hiking, Rafting, Religious Study
Session lengths & capacity: June-July; 1 week sessions; 100 campers
Clientele & fees: boys 7-19; girls 7-19; coed 7-19; families; Fees: **C** ⬛
Contact: Patsy Laster-Ford, Office Manager at (828) 898-6611; fax: (828) 898-6603
Web site: www.holstoncamp.org
Operated by: Holston Presbytery Inc, 6993 Hickory Nut Gap Rd, Banner Elk, NC 28604-0428 at (828) 898-6611

Group Rental Information
Seasons & Capacity: Spring 132, Winter 132
Facilities: A/V Equipment, Cabins, Dorm-Style, Double Occupancy, Food Service, Hiking Trails, Lake, Linens, Lodges, Meeting Rooms, Playing Fields
Programs: Boating, Challenge/Ropes Course, Environmental Education, Swimming, Winter Sports (#14494)

ID Tech Camps - Nor Cal ☀ ⬛

Campbell, CA; (408) 626-9500
Activities: Academics, Basketball, Computer, Photography, Radio/TV/Video, Soccer, Sports — Field & Team, Swimming — Recreational, Team Building
Contact: Web site: www.internaldrive.com
Operated by: InternalDrive, 2103 S Bascom Ave, Campbell, CA 95008 at (408) 626-9500 (#8141)

Illahee (est 1921) ⬛

Brevard, NC (Transylvania Co.); (828) 883-2181
Frank & Elizabeth Tindall, Director

Camp comments: Founded in 1921, Illahee's caring community is an ideal setting for building children's self-esteem.
Activities: Arts/Crafts, Canoeing, Ceramics/Pottery, Climbing/Rappelling, Horseback — English, Kayaking, Riflery, Soccer, Swimming — Instructional, Tennis
Session lengths & capacity: June-August; 2, 3 & 4 week sessions; 230 campers
Clientele & fees: girls 7-16; Fees: **E, F** ⬛
Contact: Frank & Elizabeth Tindall, Directors at (828) 883-2181; fax: (828) 883-8738
e-mail: frank@campillahee.com
Web site: www.campillahee.com
Operated by: Illahee, PO Box 272, Brevard, NC 28712-0272 at (828) 883-2181 (#14495)

Johns River Valley Camp (est 1936) ⬛ 🏠

Collettsville, NC (Caldwell Co.); (828) 754-7067
C.L. 'Curly' Stumb, Director

Camp comments: Foothills of Blue Ridge. Program offers traditional or 'wilderness' living in Christian community.
Activities: Archery, Arts/Crafts, Bicycling/Biking, Camping Skills/Outdoor Living, Canoeing, Hiking, Nature/Environment Studies, Religious Study, Swimming — Recreational
Session lengths & capacity: June-August; 1 week sessions; 64 campers
Clientele & fees: coed 8-18; Fees: **C** ⬛
Contact: Rev C.L. 'Curly' Stumb, Exec Director at (828) 264-1516; fax: (828) 262-0701
e-mail: stumb@boone.net
Web site: www.jrvc.org
Operated by: United Church of Christ, 1055 Niley Cook Rd, Blowing Rock, NC 28605 at (828) 264-1516

Group Rental Information
Facilities: Cabins, Kitchen Facilities, Lodges, Meeting Rooms, River (#19308)

Johnston YMCA Camp Rainbow ☀

Charlotte, NC (Meeklenburg Co.); (704) 716-6323
Ken Leak, Director

Camp comments: High quality day camp offers a variety of activities that support Christian values and most of all fun.
Activities: Arts/Crafts, Basketball, Community Service, Computer, Drawing/Painting, Field Trips, Leadership Development, Sports — Field & Team, Swimming — Recreational, Team Building
Session lengths & capacity: June-August; 1 week sessions
Clientele & fees: coed 5-11; Fees: A ☀ 🐘
Contact: Ken Leak, Daycamp Director at (704) 716-6332; fax: (704) 716-6303
e-mail: ken.leak@ymcacharlotte.org
Web site: www.ymcacharlotte.org
Operated by: Johnston YMCA Camp Rainbow, 3025 N Davidson St, Charlotte, NC 28205 at (704) 716-6300 (#26497)

Keyauwee Program Center TT GSC (est 1945) ▲ 🏠

Sophia, NC (Randolph Co.); (336) 861-1198
Gayle Taylor, Director

Camp comments: To provide girls opportunities for learning skills, enhancing personal development, gaining leadership and having FUN!
Activities: Aquatic Activities, Archery, Arts/Crafts, Camping Skills/Outdoor Living, Challenge/Rope Courses, Counselor Training (CIT), Field Trips, Horseback — Western, Photography, Sports — Field & Team
Session lengths & capacity: 1/2, 1 & 2 week sessions; 175 campers
Clientele & fees: girls 7-17; families; Fees: B ▲ 🐘
Contact: Gayle Taylor, KPC Director at (336) 861-1198; fax: (336) 861-1188
e-mail: keyauwee@aol.com
Web site: www.tarheeltriad.org
Operated by: Girl Scouts Tarheel Triad Cncl, 8432 Norcross Rd, Colfax, NC 27235 at (336) 274-8491

Group Rental Information
Site comments: Year-round facility available to community groups.
Facilities: Cabins, Hiking Trails, Lake, Pool, Tents
Programs: Boating, Challenge/Ropes Course, Horseback Riding, Swimming (#7651)

ICON LEGEND
☀ Day Camp
▲ Resident Camp
🏠 Facilities Available To Rent
🚐 Transportation Available
🐘 Financial Aid Available

FEE RANGES PER WEEK
A $0-75
B $75-200
C $201-350
D $351-500
E $501-650
F over $650

Kirkwood Camp & Retreat Center (est 1961) ☀ ▲ 🏠

Watha, NC; (910) 259-4791
Ralph Evans, Director

Camp comments: We specialize in Service Camp opportunities!
Activities: Aquatic Activities, Canoeing, Community Service, Fishing, Hiking, Religious Study, Swimming — Recreational, Team Building
Session lengths & capacity: June-July; 1/2 & 1 week sessions; 96 campers
Clientele & fees: coed 5-16; Fees: B, C 🐘 🚐
Contact: Jonathan Sherrod, Associate for Outdoor Ministries at (910) 862-8300; fax: (910) 862-3524
e-mail: cjsherrod@presbycc.org
Web site: www.presbycc.org
Operated by: Presbytery of Coastal Carolina, 807 West King Street, Elizabethtown, NC 28337 at (910) 862-8300

Group Rental Information
Site comments: Call us to plan your customized service camp experience!
Seasons & Capacity: Spring 96, Summer 96, Fall 96, Winter 96
Facilities: Cabins, Food Service, Hiking Trails, Kitchen Facilities, Meeting Rooms, Pool
Programs: Boating (#41490)

Lutherock (est 1963) ▲ 🏠

Newland, NC; (828) 733-5868
Jim Polanzke, Director

Camp comments: Beautiful, pristine, mile-high mountain setting. Specializing in high adventure & Christian emphasis. Outstanding staff.
Activities: Backpacking, Camping Skills/Outdoor Living, Caving, Challenge/Rope Courses, Climbing/Rappelling, Hiking, Leadership Development, Nature/Environment Studies, Rafting, Wilderness Trips
Session lengths & capacity: June-August; 1 week sessions; 120 campers
Clientele & fees: coed 11-18; Fees: C ▲ 🐘
Contact: Jim Polanzke, Director at (828) 733-5868; fax: (828) 733-5868
e-mail: camplutherock@juno.com
Web site: www.lutherock.com
Operated by: Lutheridge Lutherock Ministry, 84 Camp Luther Rd, Newland, NC 28657 at (828) 733-5868

Group Rental Information
Facilities: A/V Equipment, Cabins, Dorm-Style, Hiking Trails, Kitchen Facilities, Meeting Rooms
Programs: Challenge/Ropes Course (#14512)

Mary Atkinson (est 1958) ▲

Selma, NC (Johnston Co.); (919) 965-8985
Anna Ruggiero, Director

Camp comments: Located in the heart of North Carolina Camp offers a variety of programs for girls.
Activities: Arts/Crafts, Camping Skills/Outdoor Living, Canoeing, Ceramics/Pottery, Challenge/Rope Courses, Counselor Training (CIT), Drama, Horseback — Western, Nature/Environment Studies, Swimming — Recreational
Session lengths & capacity: June-August; 1/2 & 1 week sessions; 114 campers
Clientele & fees: girls 6-17; Fees: B, C ▲
Contact: Kate Hoppe, Director of Outdoor Progams at (919) 782-3021; fax: (919) 782-2083
e-mail: khoppe@pinesofcarolina.org
Web site: www.pinesofcarolina.org
Operated by: Pines of Carolina GSC, PO Box 52294, Raleigh, NC 27612 at (919) 782-3021 (#786)

McCrorey Family YMCA Camp ☀

Charlotte, NC; (704) 716-6500
Activities: Aquatic Activities, Arts/Crafts, Basketball, Dance, Nature/Environment Studies, Religious Study, Tennis
Contact: Babette Alston, Family Services Director at (704) 716-6512; fax: (704) 716-6501
e-mail: babette.alston@ymcacharlotte.org
Operated by: McCrorey Family YMCA, 3801 Beatties Ford Road, Charlotte, NC 28216 at (704) 716-6500 (#41456)

Millstone 4H Center (est 1939) ▲ 🏠

Ellerbe, NC; (910) 652-5905
Activities: Archery, Arts/Crafts, Canoeing, Horseback — Western, Nature/Environment Studies, Riflery, Sports — Field & Team, Swimming — Instructional, Swimming — Recreational
Session lengths & capacity: June-August; 1 week sessions
Clientele & fees: Fees: B, C ▲
Contact: Gene Shutt, Director at (910) 652-5905; fax: (910) 652-5905
e-mail: rshutt@etinternet.net
Operated by: NC State 4H Department, NC State University, PO Box 7606, Raleigh, NC 27695-7606 at (919) 515-3242

Group Rental Information
Facilities: Cabins, Hiking Trails
Programs: Environmental Education (#3535)

Occoneechee (est 1956) ▲ 🏠 🚐

Mill Spring, NC (Polk Co.); (828) 625-9062
Christy Pieper, Director

Camp comments: Mountains of Western North Carolina. Traditional adventure programs for all girls. Housing includes cabins and adirondacks.
Activities: Aquatic Activities, Archery, Bicycling/Biking, Canoeing, Challenge/Rope Courses, Counselor Training (CIT), Horseback — English, Nature/Environment Studies, Rafting, Swimming — Recreational
Session lengths & capacity: June-August; 1/2, 1 & 2 week sessions; 140 campers
Clientele & fees: girls 7-17; families; Fees: C, D ▲
Contact: Christy Pieper, Camp Director at (704) 537-7974; fax: (704) 567-0598
e-mail: Occoneechee@hngirlscouts.org
Operated by: Girl Scouts Hornets' Nest Cncl, 7007 Idlewild Road, Charlotte, NC 28212 at (704) 537-7974

Group Rental Information
Seasons & Capacity: Spring 200, Fall 200, Winter 20
Facilities: Cabins, Hiking Trails, Kitchen Facilities, Lake, Playing Fields
Programs: Boating, Challenge/Ropes Course, Swimming (#756)

Pisgah Girl Scout Camp (est 1966) ▲ 🏠 🚐

Brevard, NC (Transylvania Co.); (828) 862-4435
Michele Hathcock, Director

Camp comments: Mountain setting. Girl Scout program + trips, challenge course, adventure program, horseback. Non Girl Scouts welcome.
Activities: Arts/Crafts, Backpacking, Bicycling/Biking, Camping Skills/Outdoor Living, Challenge/Rope Courses, Climbing/Rappelling, Counselor Training (CIT), Field Trips, Horseback — English, Swimming — Instructional
Session lengths & capacity: June-August; 1/2, 1 & 2 week sessions; 120 campers
Clientele & fees: girls 6-17; Fees: B, C ▲
Contact: Michele Hathcock, Camp Director at (828) 252-4442; fax: (828) 255-8306
e-mail: camppisgah@citcom.net
Web site: www.girlscoutswnc.org

Operated by: GS of Western NC Pisgah Cncl, PO Box 8249, Asheville, NC 28814 at (828) 252-4442

Group Rental Information
Facilities: Cabins, Hiking Trails, Kitchen Facilities, Pool, Tents (#803)

Pretty Pond (est 1951)

Winnabow, NC; (910) 845-2482
Lynn Sebring, Director
Activities: Archery, Arts/Crafts, Camping Skills/Outdoor Living, Canoeing, Counselor Training (CIT), Horseback — English, Nature/Environment Studies, Swimming — Instructional, Swimming — Recreational
Session lengths & capacity: June-July; 1/2 & 1 week sessions; 72 campers
Clientele & fees: girls 6-18; Fees: B
Contact: Beth Casey, Director of Program Services at (919) 734-6231 ext. 113; fax: (919) 734-9038
e-mail: bethscout@hotmail.com
Web site: www.gscoastalnc.org
Operated by: Girl Scout Coastal Carolina, PO Box 1735, Goldsboro, NC 27533-1735 at (919) 734-6231

Group Rental Information
Facilities: Cabins, Kitchen Facilities, Lake, Pool, Tents
Programs: Boating (#41624)

Quaker Lake Camp (est 1949)

Climax, NC (Guilford Co.); (910) 674-2321

Camp comments: Resident camp with emphasis on Christian faith as experienced by Quakers through worship, study, work, play, swimming, boating, team sports, climbing tower.
Activities: Aquatic Activities, Arts/Crafts, Camping Skills/Outdoor Living, Challenge/Rope Courses, Climbing/Rappelling, Model Rocketry, Nature/Environment Studies, Religious Study, Sports — Field & Team, Swimming — Recreational
Session lengths & capacity: June-July; 1/2 & 1 week sessions; 90 campers
Clientele & fees: coed 7-17; Fees: B
Contact: Ann Parks, Director at (910) 674-2321; fax: (910) 674-8656
e-mail: quakerlakecamp@juno.com
Operated by: NC Yearly Meeting of Friends Q, 1503 NC Hwy 62 East, Climax, NC 27233 at (336) 674-2321 (#3111)

Ridgecrest Summer Camps

(est 1929)

Ridgecrest, NC (Buncombe Co.); (800) 968-1630
Ron Springs, Director

Camp comments: Christian camping at its finest. Outstanding Christian staff. 5:1 camper/counselor ratio. 3:1 camper/staff ratio.
Activities: Archery, Arts/Crafts, Horseback — Western, Model Rocketry, Music, Riflery, Soccer, Swimming — Recreational, Tennis, Wilderness Trips
Session lengths & capacity: June-August; 2, 4, 6 & 8 week sessions; 200 campers
Clientele & fees: boys 7-16; girls 7-16; Fees: D
Contact: Ron Springs, Camp Director at (800) 968-1630; fax: (828) 669-5512
e-mail: uncron@aol.com
Web site: www.ridgecrestcamps.com
Operated by: Ridgecrest Summer Camps, Box 279, Ridgecrest, NC 28770 at (828) 669-8051

Group Rental Information
Facilities: Cabins, Hiking Trails, Lake
Programs: Boating (#776)

Riverlea (est 1971)

Bahama, NC (Durham Co.); (919) 477-8739
Joe Harris, Director

Camp comments: Traditional program, excellent facilities, individual skill development emphasized, noncompetitive. Mature staff.
Activities: Archery, Arts/Crafts, Camping Skills/Outdoor Living, Canoeing, Drama, Kayaking, Music, Nature/Environment Studies, Swimming — Instructional, Tennis
Session lengths & capacity: June-August; 2 & 3 week sessions; 125 campers
Clientele & fees: coed 5-12; Fees: C
Contact: Joe Harris, Owner/Director at (919) 477-8739; fax: (919) 477-8739
Operated by: Riverlea, 8302 S Lowell Rd, Bahama, NC 27503 (#2959)

Rockbrook Camp For Girls

(est 1921)

Brevard, NC (Transylvania Co.); (828) 884-6151
Jerry Stone, Director

Camp comments: Traditional program in noncompetitive environment. Outdoor adventure in Blue Ridge Mountains. 1:3 staff to camper ratio.
Activities: Arts/Crafts, Backpacking, Canoeing, Ceramics/Pottery, Challenge/Rope Courses, Climbing/Rappelling, Drama, Gymnastics, Horseback — English, Kayaking
Session lengths & capacity: June-August; 2, 3 & 4 week sessions; 200 campers
Clientele & fees: girls 6-15; Fees: F
Contact: Brenda Ivers, Office Manager at (828) 884-6151; fax: (828) 884-6459
e-mail: office@rockbrookcamp.com
Web site: www.rockbrockcamp.com
Operated by: Rockbrook Camp for Girls, PO Box 792, Brevard, NC 28712-0792 at (828) 884-6151 (#14531)

Rockfish Outdoor Center

(est 1965)

Parleton, NC; (910) 425-3529
Dennis D Tawney, Director

Camp comments: Christian prog. Nondenominational, strong noncompetitive atmosphere. Cabins, treehouses, yurts, 3:1 camper:staff. Adult retreat center.
Activities: Archery, Arts/Crafts, Camping Skills/Outdoor Living, Canoeing, Challenge/Rope Courses, Field Trips, Hiking, Nature/Environment Studies, Religious Study, Swimming — Recreational
Session lengths & capacity: June-August; 1/2, 1 & 2 week sessions; 60 campers
Clientele & fees: coed 6-16; families; Fees: B, C
Contact: Dennis D Tawney, Director at (910) 425-3529; fax: (910) 425-8665
e-mail: info@rockfishoutdoorcenter.org
Web site: www.ncumcamps.org
Operated by: NC United Methodist Commission, PO Box 726, Fuquay Varina, NC 27526-0726 at (919) 552-4673

Group Rental Information
Facilities: Cabins, Dorm-Style, Double Occupancy, Food Service, Hiking Trails, Kitchen Facilities, Meeting Rooms (#19287)

Rockmont For Boys (est 1956)

Black Mountain, NC (Buncombe Co.); (704) 686-3885
R. David Bruce, Director

Camp comments: Prestigious Christian camp for boys in the mountains of N. Carolina near Asheville.
Activities: Aquatic Activities, Camping Skills/Outdoor Living, Horseback — English, Kayaking, Model Rocketry, Nature/Environment Studies, Riflery, Soccer, Sports — Field & Team, Swimming — Recreational
Session lengths & capacity: 2, 3 & 4 week sessions; 400 campers
Clientele & fees: boys 7-16; Fees: E
Contact: R David Bruce, President/Director at (828) 686-3885; fax: (828) 686-7332
e-mail: david@rockmont.com
Operated by: Camp Rockmont, 375 Lake Eaden, Black Mountain, NC 28711 at (828) 686-3885 (#799)

Swannanoa 4H Camp (est 1933)

Swannanoa, NC; (704) 686-3196
Activities: Archery, Arts/Crafts, Backpacking, Camping Skills/Outdoor Living, Challenge/Rope Courses, Hiking, Nature/Environment Studies, Sports — Field & Team, Swimming — Recreational
Session lengths & capacity: 1 week sessions
Clientele & fees: Fees: B, C
Contact: Chris Weaver, Director at (828) 686-3196; fax: (828) 686-7072
e-mail: chris@springbranch.net
Operated by: NC State 4H Department, NC State University, PO Box 7606, Raleigh, NC 27695-7606 at (919) 515-3242 (#3547)

The Salvation Army Camp Walter

Denton, NC; (336) 859-2105
Capt Kent Davis, Director
Activities: Aquatic Activities, Archery, Arts/Crafts, Basketball, Fishing, Music, Performing Arts, Religious Study
Operated by: The Salvation Army, 501 Archdale Dr, Charlotte, NC 28217 at (704) 972-3490 (#25925)

The Vineyard Camp & Conference (est 1983)

Westfield, NC (Stokes Co.); (336) 351-2070
Dean Barley, Director

Camp comments: Premier Christian camping 3:2 ratio of campers to staff 40 skills & sports 180 campers with 120 staff located in NC Mts.
Activities: Arts/Crafts, Challenge/Rope Courses, Climbing/Rappelling, Football, Horseback — English, International Culture, Riflery, Tennis, Wilderness Trips
Session lengths & capacity: 1, 2 & 3 week sessions; 300 campers
Clientele & fees: boys 6-17; girls 6-17; coed 6-17; Fees: F
Contact: Dean Barley, Executive Director at (336) 351-2070; fax: (336) 351-2902
e-mail: letters@vineyardcamp.com
Operated by: The Vineyard, 1945 Vineyard Road, Westfield, NC 27053 at (336) 351-2070

Group Rental Information
Facilities: Cabins, Double Occupancy, Food Service, Hiking Trails, Meeting Rooms
Programs: Horseback Riding (#5767)

University Y Day Camp

(est 1992)

Charlotte, NC (Mecklenburg Co.); (704) 716-6700
Karie Barbieri, Director

Camp comments: Christian emphasis in a rustic outdoor camp full of fresh air, nature & the beauty of outdoors.
Activities: Archery, Arts/Crafts, Basketball, Camping Skills/Outdoor Living, Dance, Leadership Development, Nature/Environment Studies, Swimming — Recreational
Session lengths & capacity: June-August; 1 week sessions; 450 campers
Clientele & fees: coed 3-12; Fees: B

Contact: Karie Barbieri, Director of Camping & Youth Services at (704) 716-6738; fax: (704) 716-6701 e-mail: karie.barbieri@ymcacharlotte.org Web site: www.ymcacharlotte.org **Operated by:** University City YMCA, 8100 Old Mallard Creek Road, Charlotte, NC 28262 at (704) 716-6700 (#1094)

Uptown YMCA Day Camp

(est 1994) ☀

Charlotte, NC; (704) 716-6400 Maurice Hikes & Tonya Anderson, Director

Camp comments: A great summer camp with a wide variety of activities in a Christian setting! **Activities:** Aquatic Activities, Bicycling/Biking, Field Trips, Kayaking, Rafting, Soccer, Sports — Field & Team, Swimming — Instructional, Swimming — Recreational, Wilderness Trips **Session lengths & capacity:** June-August; 1/2, 1, 2, 3, 4, 5, 6, 7, 8 & 9 week sessions; 350 campers **Clientele & fees:** coed 5-15; Fees: B ☀ 🚐 **Contact:** Maurice Hikes, District Family Services Director at (704) 716-6460; fax: (704) 716-6401 e-mail: maurice.hikes@ymcacharlotte.org Web site: www.ymcacharlotte.org **Operated by:** YMCA of Greater Charlotte, 500 E Morehead St Ste 300, Charlotte, NC 28202 at (704) 716-6200 (#38634)

WOW ENC Woodmen Youth Camp
▲ 🏠

Dover, NC (Craven Co.); (919) 523-1642 Larry Brice, Director **Activities:** Aquatic Activities, Archery, Arts/Crafts, Challenge/Rope Courses, Golf, Swimming — Recreational, Team Building **Session lengths & capacity:** 1/2 & 1 week sessions **Clientele & fees:** boys 8-15; girls 8-15; seniors **Contact:** Larry R Brice, Fraternal Coordinator at (252) 527-6027; **Operated by:** WOW Life Insurance (SE), 1700 Farnam, Omaha, NE 68120 at (402) 271-7258 **Group Rental Information** **Seasons & Capacity:** Spring 200, Summer 200, Fall 200, Winter 200 **Facilities:** Cabins, Food Service, Kitchen Facilities, Lake, Lodges, Pool **Programs:** Boating (#6247)

WOW RC Cliff Payne Youth Camp (est 1954) ▲ 🏠

Randleman, NC (Randolph Co.); (336) 498-7750 Mark Case, Director

ICON LEGEND

☀ Day Camp
▲ Resident Camp
🏠 Facilities Available To Rent
🚐 Transportation Available
🐷 Financial Aid Available

FEE RANGES PER WEEK

A	$0-75
B	$75-200
C	$201-350
D	$351-500
E	$501-650
F	over $650

Camp comments: Open to Woodmen members, site approved for other nonprofit groups at great rates. **Activities:** Archery, Arts/Crafts, Canoeing, Challenge/Rope Courses, Nature/Environment Studies, Riflery, Swimming — Recreational **Session lengths & capacity:** June-August; 1 week sessions; 120 campers **Clientele & fees:** coed 8-15; seniors; Fees: A ▲ **Contact:** Mark Case, Camp Director at (336) 275-5949; fax: (336) 271-2036 e-mail: mcase@woodmen.com **Operated by:** WOW Life Insurance (SE), 1700 Farnam, Omaha, NE 68120 at (402) 271-7258 **Group Rental Information** **Site comments:** Fun and educational programs that focus on campers making choices and taking responsibility. **Seasons & Capacity:** Spring 139, Summer 139, Fall 139, Winter 100 **Facilities:** Dorm-Style, Hiking Trails, Meeting Rooms, Playing Fields, Pool **Programs:** Boating, Environmental Education, Swimming (#6250)

YMCA Camp Pioneer ☀

High Point, NC (Guilford Co.); (336) 869-0151 Jeanine Martin, Director

Camp comments: Climbing tower, fishing, canoeing, crafts, hiking, devotions, field trips, movies, sports, character development, archery, CPR & 1st aid trained staff. **Activities:** Archery, Arts/Crafts, Canoeing, Challenge/Rope Courses, Climbing/Rappelling, Counselor Training (CIT), Field Trips, Fishing, Sports — Field & Team, Swimming — Recreational **Session lengths & capacity:** June-August; 1 week sessions; 200 campers **Clientele & fees:** boys 4-15; girls 4-15; coed 4-15; Fees: B ☀ 🐷 **Contact:** Jeanine Martin, Senior Program Director at (336) 869-0151; fax: (336) 869-0118 e-mail: jdmartin@hpymca.org Web site: www.cheerioadventures.com **Operated by:** YMCA of Greater High Point, PO Box 6258, High Point, NC 27262-6258 at (336) 869-0151 (#10214)

YMCA Camp Regatta (est 1980) ☀

Cornelius, NC (Mecklenburg Co.); (704) 716-4442 Karen Wheeler, Director

Camp comments: Our goal is to provide a safe wholesome Christian environment for campers where they can experience adventures and grow physically, mentally and spiritually. **Activities:** Arts/Crafts, Basketball, Canoeing, Field Trips, Fishing, Gymnastics, Sailing, Soccer, Swimming — Recreational, Waterskiing **Session lengths & capacity:** June-August; 1 week sessions; 3500 campers **Clientele & fees:** boys 2-15; coed 2-15; Fees: B ☀ 🐷 **Contact:** Karen Wheeler, Family Services Director at (704) 716-4442; fax: (704) 716-4401 e-mail: karen.wheeler@ymcacharlotte.org **Operated by:** Lake Norman YMCA, 21300 Davidson St, Cornelius, NC 28031-8553 at (704) 716-4400 (#1035)

YMCA Eagle Rock Day Camp

(est 1987) ☀ 🚐

Charlotte, NC (Mecklenberg Co.); (704) 716-4300 Chris Winkler, Director

Camp comments: Dedicated Christian staff, 1:12 staff/camper ratio. Archery, riflery, climbing towers, outdoor pool, low ropes, fishing & more. **Activities:** Archery, Arts/Crafts, Challenge/Rope Courses, Fishing, Horseback — English, Nature/Environment Studies, Riflery, Sports — Field & Team, Swimming — Instructional, Swimming — Recreational

Session lengths & capacity: June-August; 1 & 2 week sessions; 350 campers **Clientele & fees:** boys 4-16; girls 4-16; coed 4-16; Fees: B ☀ 🐷 **Contact:** Business Office at (704) 716-4300; fax: (704) 716-4301 **Operated by:** YMCA of Gtr Charlotte Metro, 500 East Morehead St Ste 300, Charlotte, NC 28202 at (704) 716-6200 (#4302)

YMCA Kanata (est 1954) ▲ 🏠

Wake Forest, NC; (919) 556-2661 Richard R. Hamilton, Director

Camp comments: Kanata offers a value-centered fun and friendly atomsphere and the opportunity to make lasting friendships in the outdoors. **Activities:** Archery, Arts/Crafts, Canoeing, Challenge/Rope Courses, Drama, Leadership Development, Nature/Environment Studies, Riflery, Sailing, Sports — Field & Team **Session lengths & capacity:** June-August; 1 week sessions; 200 campers **Clientele & fees:** coed 6-15; families; Fees: D ▲ 🐷 **Contact:** Tammy Pullin, Secretary at (919) 556-2661; fax: (919) 556-9459 e-mail: campkanata@earthlink.net Web site: www.camp kanata.org **Operated by:** YMCA of Greater Durham, 2119 Chapel Hill Road, Durham, NC 27707 at (919) 493-4502 **Group Rental Information** **Site comments:** A rustic cozy atmosphere for your group's next get-a-way retreat. a wonderful place to develop teamwork and hone leadership skills. **Seasons & Capacity:** Spring 200, Fall 200, Winter 90 **Facilities:** Cabins, Food Service, Hiking Trails, Kitchen Facilities, Lake **Programs:** Boating, Challenge/Ropes Course, Environmental Education (#777)

North Dakota

Camp Sioux (est 1952) ▲

Binford, ND (Grand Forks Co.); (701) 676-2681 Lynette Dicksen, Director

Camp comments: Free summer camp for children with diabetes ages 8-14. **Activities:** Aquatic Activities, Arts/Crafts, Boating, Canoeing, Counselor Training (CIT), Dance, Horseback — Western, Skating, Swimming — Recreational, Team Building **Session lengths & capacity:** July-August; 1 week sessions; 45 campers **Clientele & fees:** coed 8-14; Fees: A ▲ **Contact:** Lynette Dickson, Camp Director at (701) 746-4427; fax: (701) 746-9337 e-mail: ldickson@diabetes.org **Operated by:** American Diabetes Association, 314 N 4th Street, Grand Forks, ND 58203 at (701) 746-4427 (#1518)

Metigoshe Ministries

(est 1963) ▲ 🏠

Bottineau, ND (Bottineau Co.); (701) 263-4788 Rev. Marsh Drege, Director

Camp comments: Adventure anchored in Christ in the beautiful Turtle Mountains of North Dakota. Serving Lutherans & other Christians. **Activities:** Academics, Arts/Crafts, Boating, Challenge/Rope Courses, Counselor Training (CIT), Music, Nature/Environment Studies, Religious Study, Swimming — Recreational **Session lengths & capacity:** June-August; 1 week sessions; 170 campers **Clientele & fees:** coed 9-18; families; Fees: B ▲ 🐷

Contact: Katherine Pattee, Office Manager at (701) 263-4788; fax: (701) 263-4250
Web site: www.campmetigoshe.tripod.com
Operated by: Metigoshe Ministries, 10605 Lake Loop Rd E, Bottineau, ND 58318-8055 at (701) 263-4788

Group Rental Information
Facilities: Cabins, Food Service, Hiking Trails, Lake, Lodges, Meeting Rooms, Playing Fields, Tents
Programs: Boating, Challenge/Ropes Course, Swimming (#1139)

Red Willow Bible Camp

Binford, ND; (701) 676-2681
Ron Abrahamson, Director
Activities: Aquatic Activities, Camping Skills/Outdoor Living, Horseback — Western, Leadership Development, Nature/Environment Studies, Religious Study, Swimming — Recreational, Team Building
Operated by: Red Willow Bible Camp, 1561 Jacob Dr, Binford, ND 58416 at (701) 676-2681

Group Rental Information
Seasons & Capacity: Spring 100, Summer 100, Fall 100, Winter 100
Facilities: Cabins, Dorm-Style, Food Service, Hiking Trails, Lake, Linens, Lodges, Meeting Rooms, Playing Fields, Pool, Tents
Programs: Boating, Challenge/Ropes Course, Environmental Education, Horseback Riding, Swimming (#6737)

Ohio

4-H Camp Palmer Inc (est 1947)

Fayette, OH (Fulton Co.); (419) 237-2247
Contact: Web site: www.ag.ohio-state.edu/~camppalm
Operated by: 4H Camp Palmer Inc, 26450 County Rd MN, Fayette, OH 43521 at (419) 237-2247

Group Rental Information
Site comments: The new Woodland Lodge holds 60 people and has a meeting room, commons, private bed/bathrooms, and dorm rooms. Perfect for retreat all under one roof.
Seasons & Capacity: Spring 250, Summer 250, Fall 250
Facilities: Cabins, Dorm-Style, Food Service, Hiking Trails, Lodges, Meeting Rooms, Playing Fields, Pool
Programs: Boating, Challenge/Ropes Course, Environmental Education, Swimming (#6320)

4H Camp Graham (est 1953)

Clarksville, OH (Clinton Co.); (937) 289-2085
Deborah Showalter, Camp Manager, Director
Contact: Elizabeth Wingerter, Ext. Agent 4-H Youth Development at (937) 224-9654; fax: (937) 224-5110
e-mail: bwingerter@osu.edu
Operated by: Southwestern Ohio 4H Camps Inc, 1001 S Main St, Dayton, OH 45409 at (937) 224-9654

Group Rental Information
Site comments: 70 wooded acres for hiking, group activities, fossil search, surround open fields, pool, 14 cabins, rec & dining halls. Rental groups welcome. Food service.
Seasons & Capacity: Spring 150, Summer 150, Fall 150
Facilities: Cabins, Food Service, Hiking Trails, Kitchen Facilities, Lodges, Playing Fields, Pool, River
Programs: Environmental Education, Swimming (#27161)

4H Camp Ohio (est 1928)

St Louisville, OH (Licking Co.); (740) 745-2194
Gerald Duffie, Director

Camp comments: Camp leases site to groups who do own registration of campers. No registration possible through Camp Ohio.
Activities: Archery, Arts/Crafts, Canoeing, Challenge/Rope Courses, Climbing/Rappelling, Nature/Environment Studies, Riflery, Swimming — Recreational
Session lengths & capacity: 1/2 week sessions; 250 campers
Clientele & fees: coed 9-14; Fees: B ▲
Contact: Gerald C Duffie CCD, Exec Director at (740) 745-2194; fax: (740) 745-3327
Web site: www.4hcampohio.com
Operated by: Agricultural Extension Camps, 11461 Camp Ohio Rd, St Louisville, OH 43071 at (740) 745-2194

Group Rental Information
Site comments: Site available to outside groups other than June 1 to Aug 15.
Seasons & Capacity: Spring 200, Summer 250, Fall 200, Winter 200
Facilities: Cabins, Dorm-Style, Food Service, Hiking Trails, Lodges, Meeting Rooms, Pool
Programs: Environmental Education (#3264)

Agape Resident Camp (est 1966) ▲

Cleveland, OH (Cuyahoga Co.); (216) 696-6525
Molly Worthington, Director

Camp comments: Camp Agape offers social skills development and recreation to adults with various disabilities.
Activities: Aerobics/Exercise, Arts/Crafts, Computer, Counselor Training (CIT), Drawing/Painting, Field Trips, Music, Nature/Environment Studies
Session lengths & capacity: July-July; 4 week sessions; 20 campers
Clientele & fees: coed 21-75; Fees: C ▲ 🐖
Contact: James Gepperth, Camp Administrator at (216) 696-6525 ext. 2700; fax: (216) 344-9962
e-mail: jimg@ccd.cle.dioc.org
Operated by: Catholic Charities Services, 1111 Superior Avenue, Cleveland, OH 44114 at (216) 696-6525 (#6430)

Akron Rotary Camp (est 1924) ▲ 🏠

Akron, OH (Summit Co.); (330) 644-4512
Dan Reynolds CTRS, Director

Camp comments: The Akron Rotary Camp for Children with Special Needs provides programs to build character and foster independence.
Activities: Aquatic Activities, Archery, Arts/Crafts, Boating, Camping Skills/Outdoor Living, Ceramics/Pottery, Leadership Development, Nature/Environment Studies, Performing Arts
Session lengths & capacity: June-August; 1 week sessions; 56 campers
Clientele & fees: coed 6-17; Fees: A ▲ 🐖
Contact: Dan Reynolds, Program Director at (330) 644-4512; fax: (330) 644-1013
e-mail: danr@akronymca.org
Web site: www.akronymca.org
Operated by: Akron Rotary Camp, 4460 Rex Lake Dr, Akron, OH 44319 at (330) 644-4512

Group Rental Information
Seasons & Capacity: Spring 90, Fall 90, Winter 90
Facilities: A/V Equipment, Cabins, Food Service, Kitchen Facilities, Lake, Meeting Rooms, Playing Fields
Programs: Boating, Swimming (#3745)

Aldersgate (est 1948) ▲ 🏠

Carrollton, OH (Carroll Co.); (800) 831-3972
Eric Dingler, Director

Camp comments: We are here to serve your needs. Specializing in small group retreats and program development assistance. Meal service and audio/video equipment available.
Activities: Aquatic Activities, Boating, Camping Skills/Outdoor Living, Fishing, Hiking, Horseback — Western, Music, Performing Arts, Religious Study
Session lengths & capacity: June-August; 1/2 & 1 week sessions; 180 campers
Clientele & fees: coed 6-20; Fees: B ☀
Fees: C ▲
Contact: Eric Dingler, Interim Director at (330) 627-4369; fax: (330) 627-6368
e-mail: alders@raex.com
Operated by: E Ohio Conf United Methodist, 8800 Cleveland Ave NW, North Canton, OH 44720 at (800) 831-3972

Group Rental Information
Site comments: You're guaranteed to love this place. Sailing, canoeing, and our own waterpark all on scenic Leesville Lake. And for the thrill seekers-ROLLER COASTER CAMP.
Seasons & Capacity: Spring 120, Summer 180, Fall 120, Winter 54
Facilities: A/V Equipment, Cabins, Double Occupancy, Food Service, Hiking Trails, Kitchen Facilities, Lake, Lodges, Meeting Rooms, Playing Fields, Tents
Programs: Boating, Environmental Education, Swimming (#3134)

Anisfield Day Camp (est 1966) ☀

Beachwood, OH (Cuyahoga Co.); (216) 831-0700
Joel Gulko, Director

Camp comments: Country & city sites offer tremendous range of activities. JCC membership is required.
Activities: Archery, Arts/Crafts, Challenge/Rope Courses, Drama, Horseback — Western, Photography, Radio/TV/Video, Soccer, Sports — Field & Team
Session lengths & capacity: June-August; 2, 6 & 8 week sessions; 360 campers
Clientele & fees: coed 5-12; Fees: B ☀ 🐖
Contact: Joel Gulko, Director at (216) 831-0700 ext. 351; fax: (216) 831-7796
e-mail: jgulko@clevejcc.org
Operated by: JCC of Cleveland, 26001 South Woodland Road, Beachwood, OH 44122 at (216) 831-0700 (#7571)

Asbury (est 1948) ☀ ▲ 🏠

Hiram, OH (Portage Co.); (330) 569-3171
William Graham, Director

Camp comments: Co-ed, small group camping. Curriculum teaches Christian values & builds community. Celebrating diversity & tolerance.
Activities: Backpacking, Bicycling/Biking, Camping Skills/Outdoor Living, Canoeing, Challenge/Rope Courses, Horseback — Western, Nature/Environment Studies, Religious Study, Swimming — Recreational, Travel/Tour
Session lengths & capacity: 1/2 & 1 week sessions; 250 campers
Clientele & fees: coed 6-20; families; Fees: B ☀
Fees: C ▲ 🐖
Contact: William Graham, Director Camp Asbury at (330) 569-3171; fax: (330) 569-3148
e-mail: casbury@aol.com
Operated by: E Ohio Conf United Methodist, 8800 Cleveland Ave NW, North Canton, OH 44720 at (800) 831-3972

Group Rental Information
Site comments: Located in NE Ohio, within one hour drive of greater Cleveland, Akron and Youngstown. A sanctuary of spiritual and natural beauty. Gracious hospitality.
Seasons & Capacity: Spring 142, Summer 250, Fall 142, Winter 142
Facilities: Cabins, Dorm-Style, Food Service, Kitchen Facilities, Lake, Lodges, Meeting Rooms (#3138)

Augustine Rainbow Camp

(est 1972) ☀ 🚗

Cleveland, OH (Cuyahoga Co.); (216) 621-3460
Gerry Kasper, Director

Camp comments: Day camp for all children, disabled and non-disabled working together.
Activities: Academics, Arts/Crafts, Community Service, Computer, Drawing/Painting, Field Trips, Leadership Development, Nature/Environment Studies, Swimming — Recreational
Session lengths & capacity: June-August; 5 week sessions; 150 campers
Clientele & fees: coed 5-13; 🐷
Contact: Gerry Kasper, Summer Program Director at (216) 781-5530;
Operated by: St Augustine, 2486 W 14th St, Cleveland, OH 44113 at (216) 781-5530 (#1825)

Butterworth (est 1930) ☀ ⚠ 🏠

Maineville, OH (Warren Co.); (513) 683-2892
Mary Beth King, Director

Camp comments: Girls thrive in a caring atmosphere where they can participate in traditional camp program as well as adventure programs
Activities: Camping Skills/Outdoor Living, Canoeing, Wilderness Trips
Session lengths & capacity: June-August; 1/2 & 1 week sessions; 200 campers
Clientele & fees: girls 7-17; Fees: B ☀
Fees: B, C, D ⚠ 🐷
Contact: Cyndy Self, Property Manager at (513) 489-1025; fax: (513) 489-1417
e-mail: cself@grgsc.org
Web site: www.grgsc.org
Operated by: Great Rivers GSC Inc, 4930 Cornell Rd, Cincinnati, OH 45242 at (513) 489-1025
Group Rental Information
Facilities: Pool, Tents (#1982)

Camp Allyn (est 1921) ⚠ 🏠

Batavia, OH (Clemont Co.); (513) 732-0240
Chris Brockman, Director

Camp comments: Creative staff encourage development of independence, recreation & group living skills. Special need diets accommodated.
Activities: Arts/Crafts, Basketball, Camping Skills/Outdoor Living, Drama, Fishing, Hiking, Nature/Environment Studies, Swimming — Recreational
Session lengths & capacity: June-August; 1 & 2 week sessions; 69 campers
Clientele & fees: coed 7-60; Fees: C ⚠ 🐷
Contact: Jenny Epaves, Client Services Coordinator at (513) 831-4660;
Web site: www.steppingstonescenter.org

ICON LEGEND

☀	Day Camp
⚠	Resident Camp
🏠	Facilities Available To Rent
🚗	Transportation Available
🐷	Financial Aid Available

FEE RANGES PER WEEK

A	$0-75
B	$75-200
C	$201-350
D	$351-500
E	$501-650
F	over $650

Operated by: Stepping Stones Center, 5650 Given Road, Cincinnati, OH 45243 at (513) 831-4660
Group Rental Information
Site comments: Close to Cincinnati, modern facility, special diets, easily accessed.
Seasons & Capacity: Spring 60, Fall 60, Winter 60
Facilities: Dorm-Style, Food Service, Hiking Trails, Pool
Programs: Swimming (#957)

Camp Burton (est 1955) ⚠ 🏠

Burton, OH (Geauga Co.); (440) 834-8984
Roger Kerry, Director

Camp comments: Focusing on Christ in a fun outdoor setting. Camp Burton is a place where it is fun to grow.
Activities: Aquatic Activities, Archery, Camping Skills/Outdoor Living, Challenge/Rope Courses, Climbing/Rappelling, Leadership Development, Nature/Environment Studies, Riflery, Wilderness Trips
Session lengths & capacity: 1/2 & 1 week sessions; 150 campers
Clientele & fees: coed 6-18; families;
Fees: A, B, D ⚠
Contact: Roger Kerry, Director at (440) 834-8984; fax: (440) 834-0525
e-mail: campburton@yahoo.com
Web site: www.campburton.org
Operated by: Camp Burton, 14282 Butternut Rd, Burton, OH 44021 at (440) 834-8984
Group Rental Information
Facilities: Cabins, Food Service, Hiking Trails, Meeting Rooms, Pool (#18871)

Camp Chabad ☀

Cincinnati, OH; (513) 731-5111
Activities: Aerobics/Exercise, Martial Arts, Swimming — Instructional
Operated by: Chabad of Southern Ohio, 1863 Section Rd, Cincinnati, OH 45237-2006 at (513) 821-5100 (#265)

Camp Cheerful (est 1940) ☀ ⚠

Strongsville, OH (Cuyahoga Co.); (440) 238-6200
Tim Fox, Director

Camp comments: First camp in Ohio designed to serve physically challenged. Northeast Ohio. Cabins, dining hall, horses, pool, 42 acres.
Activities: Archery, Arts/Crafts, Basketball, Ceramics/Pottery, Challenge/Rope Courses, Hiking, Horseback — Western, Nature/Environment Studies, Swimming — Instructional, Swimming — Recreational
Session lengths & capacity: 1 week sessions; 60 campers
Clientele & fees: coed 7-99; Fees: B ☀
Fees: C, D ⚠ 🐷
Contact: Timothy Fox, Director at (440) 238-6200; fax: (440) 238-1858
Web site: www.achievementcentersforchildren.org
Operated by: Achievement Ctr for Children, 15000 Cheerful Ln, Strongsville, OH 44136 at (440) 238-6200 (#1403)

Camp Courageous Inc

(est 1963) ☀ ⚠

Whitehouse, OH (Lucas Co.); (419) 875-6828
Cheryl Tresnan, Director

Camp comments: Residential and Day camp services for children and adults with mental retardation and developmental disabilities.
Activities: Aerobics/Exercise, Arts/Crafts, Baseball/Softball, Basketball, Camping Skills/Outdoor Living, Dance, Farming/Ranching/Gardening, Hiking, Music, Sports — Field & Team
Session lengths & capacity: June-October; 1 & 2 week sessions; 35 campers

Clientele & fees: coed 7-75; Fees: B ☀
Fees: D, F ⚠ 🐷
Contact: Cheryl Tresnan, Camp Director at (419) 242-9587 ext. 117; fax: (419) 242-6316
e-mail: cherylt@uhs-toledo.org
Web site: www.campcourageous.com
Operated by: Camp Courageous Inc, 1 Stranahan Square 540, Toledo, OH 43604 at (419) 242-9587 (#1277)

Camp Crowell/Hilaka (est 1937) 🏠

Richfield, OH (Summitt Co.); (300) 659-9494
Michell Bellomo, Director
Contact: Michelle Bellomo, Outdoor Program Specialist at (216) 481-1313 ext. 246;
fax: (216) 692-4060
e-mail: bellomm@gslec.org
Web site: www.girlscouts.org/gslec
Operated by: GS of Lake Erie Council, 19201 Villaview Rd, Cleveland, OH 44119 at (300) 481-1313
Group Rental Information
Facilities: Cabins, Lake, Pool, Tents
Programs: Boating, Environmental Education, Horseback Riding (#1423)

Camp Francis Asbury ⚠ 🏠

Thurman, OH (Gallia Co.); (740) 245-5254

Camp comments: 'Serving all people for Christian birth, growth, and renewal'
Activities: Academics, Aquatic Activities, Archery, Canoeing, Climbing/Rappelling, Horseback — Western, Nature/Environment Studies, Rafting, Religious Study, Team Building
Session lengths & capacity: June-August; 1/2 & 1 week sessions; 100 campers
Clientele & fees: coed 6-18; Fees: B, C ⚠
Contact: Chris & Sue Lewis, Directors/Managers at (740) 245-5254; fax: (740) 245-5254
e-mail: info@camp-asbury.org
Web site: www.westohiocamps.com
Operated by: W Ohio Conf United Methodist, 32 Wesley Blvd, Worthington, OH 43085-3585 at (614) 781-2630 (#3764)

Camp Frederick Ctr Spiritual

(est 1966) ⚠ 🏠

Rogers, OH (Columbiana Co.); (330) 227-3633
Marie Steven, Director

Camp comments: Beautiful facilities & life changing programs for Christian & non-Christian groups.
Activities: Arts/Crafts, Camping Skills/Outdoor Living, Challenge/Rope Courses, Community Service, Horseback — Western, Leadership Development, Nature/Environment Studies, Rafting, Team Building, Wilderness Trips
Session lengths & capacity: 1/2, 1 & 2 week sessions; 100 campers
Clientele & fees: boys 5-99; girls 5-99; coed 5-99; families; seniors; single adults; Fees: C ⚠ 🐷
Contact: Marie Skweir and Andrew Molnar, Co-Directors at (330) 227-3633; fax: (330) 227-9005
e-mail: campfred@reax.com
Web site: www.lomocamps.org
Operated by: Lutheran Outdoor Ministries OH, 863 Eastwind Dr, Westerville, OH 43081 at (614) 890-2267
Group Rental Information
Site comments: Spiritual camp with team-building, adventure, and service emphasis. Intense focus on individual growth and care.
Seasons & Capacity: Spring 100, Winter 100
Facilities: A/V Equipment, Cabins, Dorm-Style, Food Service, Hiking Trails, Lodges, Meeting Rooms, Playing Fields, Pool, Tents
Programs: Challenge/Ropes Course, Environmental Education, Horseback Riding, Swimming (#3756)

Camp Hamwi (est 1968) ▲

Danville, OH (Knox Co.); (800) 422-7946
Darlene Honigford, Director

Camp comments: A special camp for kids with diabetes. All staff are trained in the special needs of youth with diabetes.
Activities: Archery, Arts/Crafts, Canoeing, Dance, Drama, Hiking, Horseback — Western, Leadership Development, Soccer, Swimming — Recreational
Session lengths & capacity: August-August; 1 week sessions; 80 campers
Clientele & fees: coed 7-17; Fees: C ▲ 🚌
Contact: Darlene Harnigford, Social Services Director at (614) 486-7124; fax: (614) 486-1005
e-mail: coda@diabetesohio.org
Web site: www.diabetesohio.org
Operated by: Central Ohio Diabetes Assn, 1580 King Ave, Columbus, OH 43212 at (614) 486-7124 (#1641)

Camp J B Mac ☀

Mason, OH; (513) 459-9500
Amanda D Siderits, Director

Camp comments: Day camp offered to children ages K-12 yrs. Outdoor activities to keep your child happy and healthy.
Activities: Aquatic Activities, Arts/Crafts, Baseball/Softball, Basketball, Counselor Training (CIT), Dance, Drama, Drawing/Painting, Nature/Environment Studies, Swimming — Recreational
Session lengths & capacity: June-August; 2 week sessions; 150 campers
Clientele & fees: coed 6-12; Fees: A ☀
Contact: Amanda Siderits, Admissions at (513) 772-5888; fax: (513) 672-3387
e-mail: siderits@netzero.net
Web site: www.youthlandacademy.com
Operated by: Camp J B Mac, 110 Merchant St, Cincinnati, OH 45246-3731 at (513) 772-5888 (#2458)

Camp Libbey (est 1936) ▲ 🏠

Defiance, OH (Defiance Co.); (419) 784-5888
Christy Gustin, Director

Camp comments: State-of-the-art facility, noncompetitive, traditional programs incl Env Ed, horses, theater. We build self-esteem!
Activities: Arts/Crafts, Camping Skills/Outdoor Living, Ceramics/Pottery, Counselor Training (CIT), Horseback — Western, Nature/Environment Studies, Performing Arts, Photography
Session lengths & capacity: 1 & 2 week sessions; 150 campers
Clientele & fees: girls 7-18; Fees: A ☀
Fees: B, C ▲ 🚌
Contact: Christy Gustin, Camp Manager at (419) 784-5888; fax: (419) 782-9408
e-mail: clibbey@defnet.com
Web site: www.mvgsc.org
Operated by: Maumee Valley GSC, 2244 Collingwood Blvd, Toledo, OH 43620 at (800) 860-4516

Group Rental Information

Site comments: First class, world class and full conf facilities!Lodges,cabins,platform tents,dining lodge,pool,horses&miles of trails.
Facilities: Dorm-Style, Food Service, Hiking Trails, Meeting Rooms, River
Programs: Environmental Education (#1248)

Camp Luther (est 1940) ▲ 🏠

Conneaut, OH (Ashiabula Co.); (440) 224-2196
Jeffrey D Burkett, Director

Camp comments: We create places apart where lives are changed through spiritual growth, through the love and joy of Jesus Christ.

Activities: Aerobics/Exercise, Arts/Crafts, Baseball/Softball, Challenge/Rope Courses, Leadership Development, Music, Religious Study, Swimming — Instructional, Swimming — Recreational, Team Building
Session lengths & capacity: May-October; 1 week sessions; 150 campers
Clientele & fees: families; Fees: C ▲
Contact: Mary Marvin, Office Manager at (440) 224-2196; fax: (440) 224-2267
e-mail: luther@lomocamps.org
Web site: www.lomocamps.org
Operated by: Lutheran Outdoor Ministries OH, 863 Eastwind Dr, Westerville, OH 43081 at (614) 890-2267

Group Rental Information

Seasons & Capacity: Spring 150, Summer 150, Fall 150
Facilities: A/V Equipment, Cabins, Dorm-Style, Food Service, Hiking Trails, Lodges, Meeting Rooms, Playing Fields, Pool, Tents
Programs: Challenge/Ropes Course, Swimming (#31249)

Camp Myeerah (est 1952) ▲ 🏠

Bellefontaine, OH (Logan Co.); (937) 593-5106
Dennis R. Rose, Director

Camp comments: Resident camp and rental usage keep Camp Myeerah busy year round. Owned/Operated by the Girl Scouts of Appleseed Ridge
Activities: Archery, Backpacking, Camping Skills/Outdoor Living, Canoeing, Counselor Training (CIT), Hiking, Nature/Environment Studies
Session lengths & capacity: 1/2 & 1 week sessions; 48 campers
Clientele & fees: girls 5-17; Fees: B ☀
Contact: Maggie Slovik, Development Registrar at (419) 225-4085; fax: (419) 229-7570
Web site: www.gsar.org
Operated by: Appleseed Ridge GSC, 1870 W Robb Ave, PO Box 956, Lima, OH 45802 at (419) 225-4085

Group Rental Information

Facilities: Dorm-Style, Hiking Trails, Kitchen Facilities, Playing Fields, Tents (#46733)

Camp Neosa The Salvation Army

(est 1975) ▲

Carrollton, OH (Carrol Co.); (216) 735-2671
Captain James W Betts, Director

Camp comments: Christian emphasis with caring staff serving NE Ohio. Children register through local Salvation Army. Nominal fee.
Activities: Aquatic Activities, Arts/Crafts, Baseball/Softball, Basketball, Challenge/Rope Courses, Hiking, Nature/Environment Studies, Performing Arts, Soccer, Swimming — Recreational
Session lengths & capacity: June-August; 1 week sessions; 220 campers
Clientele & fees: boys 6-12; girls 6-12; families; Fees: B ▲ 🚌
Contact: James Betts, Captain at (216) 623-7454; fax: (216) 861-0737
e-mail: james_betts@use.salvationarmy.org
Operated by: The Salvation Army, 2507 East 22nd St, Cleveland, OH 44115 at (216) 861-8185 (#2933)

Camp O'Bannon (est 1922) ▲ 🏠 🚗

Newark, OH; (740) 345-8295
Ted Cobb, Director

Camp comments: Serves only referred youth from local area. Emphasis on fostering self-esteem.
Activities: Arts/Crafts, Camping Skills/Outdoor Living, Drawing/Painting, Field Trips, Leadership Development, Nature/Environment Studies, Swimming — Recreational
Session lengths & capacity: 1 & 2 week sessions; 67 campers
Clientele & fees: coed 9-14; Fees: A ▲

Contact: Ted Cobb, Executive Director at (740) 345-8295; fax: (740) 349-5093
Operated by: Camp O'Bannon of Licking Co, 9688 Butler Rd NE, Newark, OH 43055 at (740) 345-8295

Group Rental Information

Facilities: Cabins, Food Service, Kitchen Facilities, Lodges, Meeting Rooms, Pool (#1003)

Camp Oty Okwa (est 1942) ▲ 🏠 🚗

South Bloomingville, OH (Hocking Co.); (740) 385-5279
Paul Holcomb, Director

Camp comments: Campers thrive in noncompetitive, caring atmosphere with opportunities to belong, learn, contribute.
Activities: Backpacking, Camping Skills/Outdoor Living, Challenge/Rope Courses, Climbing/Rappelling, Counselor Training (CIT), Hiking, Leadership Development, Nature/Environment Studies, Swimming — Recreational, Team Building
Session lengths & capacity: Year-round; 1, 2 & 3 week sessions; 125 campers
Clientele & fees: coed 6-16; Fees: B ▲
Contact: Michael A Jolley, Marketing Director at (614) 839-2447; fax: (614) 839-5437
Operated by: Big Brother Big Sister Assoc, 1855 E Dublin Granville Rd, Columbus, OH 43229 at (614) 839-2447

Group Rental Information

Site comments: 617 acres in Hocking Hills.
Facilities: Cabins, Dorm-Style, Food Service, Hiking Trails, Lodges, Meeting Rooms (#1002)

Camp Stepping Stone

(est 1963) ☀ 🚗

Cincinnati, OH (Hamilton Co.); (513) 831-4660
Sara Jacobs, Director

Camp comments: Day camp specializing in services for persons with disabilities promoting involvement with typical peers
Activities: Arts/Crafts, Boating, Drama, Fishing, Nature/Environment Studies, Sports — Field & Team, Swimming — Instructional, Swimming — Recreational
Session lengths & capacity: June-August; 1, 2, 3, 4, 5, 6, 7, 8 & 9 week sessions; 180 campers
Clientele & fees: coed 5-21; Fees: B ☀
Contact: Barb Sorrell, Client Services Coordinator at (513) 831-4660; fax: (513) 831-5918
e-mail: ssc@one.net
Web site: www.steppingstonescenter.org
Operated by: Stepping Stones Center, 5650 Given Road, Cincinnati, OH 45243 at (513) 831-4660 (#8300)

Camp Wildbrook, LTD

(est 1952) ☀ 🚗

Cincinnati, OH (Hamilton Co.); (513) 931-2196
Gayle Lucas, Director

Camp comments: Active outdoor oriented programs. Camp offers creative arts, nature & athletic activities to develop individual self-esteem along with team building skills.
Activities: Archery, Arts/Crafts, Camping Skills/Outdoor Living, Drama, Field Trips, Riflery, Soccer, Sports — Field & Team, Swimming — Instructional, Tennis
Session lengths & capacity: June-July; 6 week sessions; 264 campers
Clientele & fees: coed 5-12; Fees: B ☀
Contact: Gayle Lucas, Director at (513) 931-2196;
e-mail: Campwildbrook@cinci.rr.com
Operated by: Camp Wildbrook, LTD, 9664 Daly Rd, Cincinnati, OH 45231 at (513) 931-2196 (#990)

Camp Wise (est 1907)

Chardon, OH (Geauga Co.); (440) 635-5444
Brian Lefkoff, Director

Camp comments: Camp Wise creates a friendly and cooperative atmosphere which encourages campers individual growth at their own pace.
Activities: Archery, Arts/Crafts, Bicycling/Biking, Challenge/Rope Courses, Drama, Horseback — Western, Nature/Environment Studies, Photography, Radio/TV/Video, Tennis
Session lengths & capacity: June-August; 2, 3, 4 & 7 week sessions; 200 campers
Clientele & fees: coed 8-15; Fees: E ▲ 🐟
Contact: Brian Lefkoff, Director at (216) 831-0700 ext. 350; fax: (216) 831-0966
e-mail: blefkoff@clevejcc.org
Operated by: JCC of Cleveland, 26001 South Woodland Road, Beachwood, OH 44122 at (216) 831-0700

Group Rental Information
Facilities: A/V Equipment, Cabins, Food Service, Hiking Trails, Kitchen Facilities, Lake, Playing Fields, Pool, Tents
Programs: Boating, Challenge/Ropes Course, Environmental Education, Horseback Riding, Swimming (#1420)

Campbell Gard YMCA Outdoor Ctr (est 1926)

Hamilton, OH (Butler Co.); (513) 867-0600
Rick Taylor, Director

Camp comments: Traditional YMCA camp. Outstanding staff, beautiful facility. Caring atmosphere with opportunities to grow & have fun.
Activities: Aquatic Activities, Archery, Bicycling/Biking, Canoeing, Challenge/Rope Courses, Climbing/Rappelling, Horseback — English, Horseback — Western, Leadership Development, Swimming — Recreational
Session lengths & capacity: 1 & 2 week sessions; 200 campers
Clientele & fees: coed 6-17; families; Fees: B ☀ Fees: C, D ▲ 🐟
Contact: Donna Danekind, Office Manager at (513) 867-0600; fax: (513) 867-0127
e-mail: campstaff@ccgymca.org
Web site: www.ccgymca.org
Operated by: Campbell Gard YMCA Outdoor Ctr, PO Box 122, Overpeck, OH 45011 at (513) 867-0600

Group Rental Information
Site comments: Beautiful facility 45 minutes from Cincinnati & Dayton.
Seasons & Capacity: Spring 240, Summer 240, Fall 240, Winter 240

ICON LEGEND

☀ Day Camp
▲ Resident Camp
🏠 Facilities Available To Rent
🚐 Transportation Available
🐟 Financial Aid Available

FEE RANGES PER WEEK

A $0-75
B $75-200
C $201-350
D $351-500
E $501-650
F over $650

Facilities: A/V Equipment, Cabins, Food Service, Hiking Trails, Lake, Lodges, Meeting Rooms, Playing Fields, Pool, River
Programs: Boating, Challenge/Ropes Course, Environmental Education, Horseback Riding, Swimming (#978)

Canters Cave 4H Camp Inc
(est 1949)

Jackson, OH (Jackson Co.); (614) 286-4058
Anita G. Harris, Director

Camp comments: Nestled in a scenic valley in southern Ohio. Modern, year round facilities. Ideal for retreats/seminars. Available to groups.
Activities: Archery, Canoeing, Challenge/Rope Courses, Climbing/Rappelling, Leadership Development, Nature/Environment Studies, Radio/TV/Video, Riflery, Swimming — Recreational, Team Building
Session lengths & capacity: 1/2 & 1 week sessions; 200 campers
Clientele & fees: boys 8-18; girls 8-18; coed 8-18; families; Fees: B ▲
Contact: Anita G Harris, Executive Director at (740) 286-4058; fax: (614) 280-8622
e-mail: eleoec4h@bright.net
Operated by: Canters Cave 4H Camp Inc, 1362 Caves Rd, Jackson, OH 45640 at (614) 286-4058

Group Rental Information
Seasons & Capacity: Spring 120, Summer 225, Fall 120, Winter 120
Facilities: Cabins, Dorm-Style, Food Service, Hiking Trails, Lake, Meeting Rooms, Playing Fields, Pool
Programs: Boating, Challenge/Ropes Course, Environmental Education, Swimming (#2362)

Centerville Mills YMCA
(est 1902)

Chagrin Falls, OH (Geauga Co.); (440) 543-8184
Terry Wiles, Director

Camp comments: 150 acre camp. Waterfall, lake, horseback riding, sports. Resident and day camp as well as year round rental available.
Activities: Archery, Arts/Crafts, Camping Skills/Outdoor Living, Challenge/Rope Courses, Hiking, Horseback — Western, Model Rocketry, Nature/Environment Studies
Session lengths & capacity: 1 & 2 week sessions; 256 campers
Clientele & fees: coed 3-16; families; seniors; single adults; Fees: B ☀ Fees: C ▲ 🐟
Contact: Terry Wiles, Executive Director at (440) 543-8184; fax: (440) 543-7290
Operated by: YMCA of Cleveland, 2200 Prospect Ave 9th Fl, Cleveland, OH 44115 at (216) 344-0095

Group Rental Information
Facilities: Cabins, Food Service, Hiking Trails, Lake, Playing Fields, Pool
Programs: Boating, Challenge/Ropes Course, Environmental Education, Horseback Riding, Swimming (#3599)

CHAMP Camp (est 1986)

Cleveland, OH; (216) 795-7100
Nicole Bilkins, Director
Activities: Arts/Crafts, Basketball, Drawing/Painting, Music, Nature/Environment Studies, Sports — Field & Team
Contact: Web site:
www.achievementcentersforchildren.org
Operated by: Achievement Ctr for Children, 15000 Cheerful Ln, Strongsville, OH 44136 at (440) 238-6200 (#1323)

Champ Camp (est 1990)

Ashley, OH (Delaware Co.); (614) 548-7006
Nancy McCurdy; David Carter, Director

Camp comments: A special camp for children with Tracheotomies and those that need ventilator assistance.
Activities: Arts/Crafts, Camping Skills/Outdoor Living, Canoeing, Climbing/Rappelling, Horseback — Western, Nature/Environment Studies, Swimming — Recreational
Session lengths & capacity: 1 week sessions; 24 campers
Clientele & fees: coed 6-18; Fees: B ▲
Contact: Nancy McCurdy, Program Coordinator at (317) 415-5530; fax: (317) 415-5595
e-mail: nmccurdy@champcamp.org
Web site: www.champcamp.org
Operated by: Board of Directors, PO Box 40407, Indianapolis, IN 46240 at (317) 415-5530 (#1352)

Chincapin (est 1957)

Kirtland, OH (Lake Co.); (216) 256-0716
Ken Roskos, Director

Camp comments: Girls day camp, 8 to 12. They play tennis, swim, canoe, fish, hike, archery, horse back lessons, and crafts.
Activities: Archery, Arts/Crafts, Backpacking, Canoeing, Challenge/Rope Courses, Hiking, Horseback — English, Nature/Environment Studies, Swimming — Instructional, Tennis
Session lengths & capacity: June-July; 1 & 7 week sessions; 42 campers
Clientele & fees: girls 8-12; Fees: C ☀
Contact: Gerry Roskos, Receptionist at (216) 256-0716; fax: (216) 256-3093
e-mail: redoakcamp@lightstream.net
Web site: www.redoakcamp.com
Operated by: Red Oaks/Red Barn/Chincapin, 9057 Kirtland Chardon Rd, Kirtland, OH 44094 at (440) 256-0716 (#3966)

Clifton 4H Camp (est 1937)

Yellow Springs, OH (Greene Co.); (937) 767-7552
Activities: Aquatic Activities, Archery, Baseball/Softball, Basketball, Challenge/Rope Courses, Dance, Farming/Ranching/Gardening, Fishing, Soccer, Swimming — Recreational
Session lengths & capacity: June-August; 1 week sessions; 250 campers
Clientele & fees: Fees: B ☀
Operated by: Clifton 4H Camp, 2256 Clifton, Yellow Springs, OH 45387 at (937) 767-7552

Group Rental Information
Seasons & Capacity: Spring 250, Summer 250, Fall 250
Facilities: Cabins, Food Service, Hiking Trails, Kitchen Facilities, Meeting Rooms, Playing Fields, Pool, River
Programs: Boating, Challenge/Ropes Course, Environmental Education, Swimming (#5418)

Countryside YMCA Day Camp (est 1979)

Lebanon, OH (Warren Co.); (513) 932-1424
Shane Riffle, Director

Camp comments: Traditional day camp with activities including climbing, archery, sports, leave no trace and nature, and adventure games. Located in YMCA wooded facility.
Activities: Archery, Arts/Crafts, Camping Skills/Outdoor Living, Challenge/Rope Courses, Climbing/Rappelling, Hiking, International Culture, Leadership Development, Nature/Environment Studies, Swimming — Recreational
Session lengths & capacity: 1 week sessions
Clientele & fees: coed 3-12; Fees: A, B ☀ 🐟
Contact: Shane Riffle, Program Director at (513) 932-1424; fax: (513) 933-9390
e-mail: shanerif@countrysideymca.org
Web site: www.countrysideymca.org
Operated by: Countryside YMCA, 1699 Deerfield Rd, Lebanon, OH 45036 at (513) 932-1424 (#348)

CYO Camp Christopher

(est 1924) ☀ ▲ ⌂

Bath, OH (Summit Co.); (330) 376-2267
Richard G. Garbinsky, Director

Camp comments: 160 acres including four lakes, cliffs & thousands of trees. CYO Camp Christopher... 'camping at its finest.'
Activities: Archery, Arts/Crafts, Canoeing, Challenge/Rope Courses, Climbing/Rappelling, Hiking, Horseback — Western, Nature/Environment Studies, Swimming — Instructional, Swimming — Recreational
Session lengths & capacity: 1 week sessions; 235 campers
Clientele & fees: coed 6-16; families; seniors; Fees: B ☀ Fees: C ▲ 🐷
Contact: Richard G. Garbinsky, Director at (330) 376-2267; fax: (330) 762-2001
e-mail: campregistrar@akroncyo.org
Web site: www.campchris.org
Operated by: CYO and Community Services Inc, 812 Biruta St, Akron, OH 44307 at (330) 376-2267

Group Rental Information
Facilities: Cabins, Dorm-Style, Food Service, Hiking Trails, Kitchen Facilities, Lodges, Meeting Rooms, Playing Fields
Programs: Challenge/Ropes Course, Environmental Education (#1399)

CYO Camp Corde (est 1950) ☀

Parma, OH (Cuyahoga Co.); (216) 884-3950
Kim Brosnan, Director

Camp comments: Celebrate summer with CYO! Wonderful programming, super staff, beautiful site.
Activities: Archery, Arts/Crafts, Community Service, Field Trips, Nature/Environment Studies, Sports — Field & Team, Swimming — Recreational, Team Building
Session lengths & capacity: June-August; 1 week sessions; 100 campers
Clientele & fees: coed 6-15; Fees: B ☀
Contact: Kim Brosnan, Camp Director at (440) 585-7736; fax: (440) 585-7747
e-mail: cyoeast@dioceseofcleveland.org
Operated by: Youth and Young Adult Ministry, 28706 Euclid Ave, Wickliffe, OH 44092 at (440) 585-7736 (#1426)

CYO Day Camp Amherst

(est 1995) ☀

Amherst, OH (Lorain Co.); (440) 585-7736
Kim Brosnan, Director

Camp comments: Celebrate summer with CYO! Traditional Program, Beautiful site, fantastic staff.
Activities: Archery, Arts/Crafts, Community Service, Nature/Environment Studies, Sports — Field & Team, Swimming — Recreational, Team Building
Session lengths & capacity: June-August; 1 week sessions; 100 campers
Clientele & fees: coed 5-12; Fees: B ☀
Contact: Kim Brosnan, Camp Director at (440) 585-7736; fax: (440) 585-7747
e-mail: cyoeast@dioceseofcleveland.org
Operated by: Youth and Young Adult Ministry, 28706 Euclid Ave, Wickliffe, OH 44092 at (440) 585-7736 (#4146)

CYO Day Camp Wickliffe

(est 1975) ☀

Wickliffe, OH (Lake Co.); (440) 585-7736
Kim Brosnan, Director

Camp comments: Celebrate summer with CYO! Traditional programming, beautiful site, superior staff.
Activities: Archery, Arts/Crafts, Community Service, Nature/Environment Studies, Sports — Field & Team, Swimming — Recreational, Team Building
Session lengths & capacity: June-August; 1 week sessions; 100 campers

Clientele & fees: coed 6-15; Fees: B ☀
Contact: Kim Brosnan, Camp Director at (440) 585-7736; fax: (440) 585-7747
e-mail: cyoeast@dioceseofcleveland.org
Operated by: Youth and Young Adult Ministry, 28706 Euclid Ave, Wickliffe, OH 44092 at (440) 585-7736 (#1868)

Earth Arts Camp (est 1995) ▲

Peninsula, OH (Summit Co.); (330) 657-2796
Joni Starr, Director

Camp comments: Cayahoga Valley Earth Arts Camp fully integrates arts & environmental studies in a National Park setting.
Activities: Arts/Crafts, Bicycling/Biking, Dance, Drama, Drawing/Painting, Field Trips, Hiking, Music, Nature/Environment Studies, Performing Arts
Session lengths & capacity: June-August; 1/2 & 1 week sessions; 100 campers
Clientele & fees: coed 8-16; Fees: D ▲ 🐷
Contact: Joni Starr, Camp Director at (330) 657-2796 ext. 114; fax: (330) 657-2058
e-mail: jstarr@cvnpa.org
Web site: www.cvnpa.org
Operated by: Cuyahoga Valley Natl Prk Assoc, 3675 Oak Hill Rd, Peninsula, OH 44264 at (330) 657-2796 (#26723)

Echoing Hills (est 1966) ▲ ⌂

Warsaw, OH (Coshocton Co.); (740) 327-2311
Shaker Samuel, Director

Camp comments: We serve people with developmental disabilities of all ages, adapting a variety of activities to suit campers needs.
Activities: Archery, Arts/Crafts, Basketball, Camping Skills/Outdoor Living, Counselor Training (CIT), Music, Nature/Environment Studies, Religious Study, Swimming — Recreational, Travel/Tour
Session lengths & capacity: June-August; 1 & 2 weeks sessions; 60 campers
Clientele & fees: coed 7-70; Fees: D ▲
Contact: Shaker Samuel, Camp Administrator at (740) 327-2311 ext. 228; fax: (740) 327-6371
Operated by: Echoing Hills Village Inc, 36272 C R 79, Warsaw, OH 43844 at (740) 327-2311

Group Rental Information
Facilities: A/V Equipment, Cabins, Dorm-Style, Double Occupancy, Food Service, Meeting Rooms, Playing Fields, Pool
Programs: Swimming (#3205)

Emanuel Resident (est 1974) ▲

Bellefontaine, OH; (937) 278-2928
Nan Crawford, Director

Camp comments: Provides a quality educational & recreational program. A unique camping experience for all.
Activities: Arts/Crafts, Boating, Climbing/Rappelling, Fishing, Horseback — Western, Nature/Environment Studies
Session lengths & capacity: 1 week sessions; 30 campers
Clientele & fees: boys 9-17; girls 9-17; coed 9-17; Fees: B ▲ 🐷
Contact: Nan Crawford, Administrative Director at (937) 278-2928; fax: (937) 228-7466
Operated by: Camp Emanuel Board Directors, PO Box 2146, Dayton, OH 45401 at (937) 312-1012 (#212)

FFA Camp Muskingum

(est 1944) ▲ ⌂

Carrollton, OH (Carroll Co.)
Todd Davis, Director
Activities: Academics, Boating, Canoeing, Challenge/Rope Courses, Farming/Ranching/Gardening, Fishing, Kayaking, Leadership Development, Nature/Environment Studies, Swimming — Recreational

Session lengths & capacity: June-July; 1/2 & 1 week sessions; 320 campers
Clientele & fees: coed 10-18; Fees: B ▲
Contact: Todd Davis, Director at (330) 627-2208; fax: (330) 627-4485
e-mail: ffacm@roex.com
Web site: www.ffacamp.com
Operated by: Ohio FFA Camps Inc, 3266 Dyewood Rd S W, Carrollton, OH 44615 at (330) 627-2208

Group Rental Information
Site comments: Available for group camping. We can provide the facilities as well as many program options call us today!
Seasons & Capacity: Spring 320, Summer 320, Fall 320, Winter 320
Facilities: A/V Equipment, Dorm-Style, Food Service, Hiking Trails, Lake, Meeting Rooms, Playing Fields
Programs: Boating, Challenge/Ropes Course, Environmental Education, Swimming, Winter Sports (#6243)

Fort Hill Christian Youth Camp

(est 1948) ▲ ⌂

Hillsboro, OH (Highland Co.); (513) 466-2489
Activities: Basketball, Hiking, Nature/Environment Studies, Sports — Field & Team, Swimming — Recreational
Operated by: Fort Hill Christian Youth Camp, 13500 Fort Hill Rd, Hillsboro, OH 45133 at (937) 588-2026

Group Rental Information
Facilities: Cabins, Dorm-Style, Food Service, Hiking Trails, Lodges, Meeting Rooms, Pool (#993)

Friendship Camping Programs ▲

Clarksville, OH (Warren Co.); (614) 718-4484
Angela Woody, Director
Activities: Aquatic Activities, Archery, Arts/Crafts, Canoeing, Challenge/Rope Courses, Climbing/Rappelling, Fishing, Hiking, Music, Swimming — Recreational
Session lengths & capacity: 1 week sessions
Clientele & fees: boys 7-15; girls 7-15
Contact: Web site: www.cancer.org
Operated by: American Cancer Society, 5555 Frantz Road, Dublin, OH 43017 at (614) 718-4484 (#44051)

Geneva Hills Center

(est 1959) ☀ ▲ ⌂

Lancaster, OH (Fairfield Co.); (740) 746-8439

Camp comments: Children provided supervision, opportunity for growth, development, programs designed for age groups. Positive and strong leadership development for campers.
Activities: Aquatic Activities, Arts/Crafts, Backpacking, Camping Skills/Outdoor Living, Canoeing, Challenge/Rope Courses, Counselor Training (CIT), Hiking, Nature/Environment Studies, Performing Arts
Session lengths & capacity: June-August; 1/2 & 1 week sessions; 108 campers
Clientele & fees: coed 5-19; families; Fees: B ☀ Fees: B, C ▲ 🐷
Contact: Angie Hill, Office Manager at (740) 746-8439; fax: (740) 746-7955
e-mail: genevahills@ameritech.net
Operated by: Presbytery of Scioto Valley, 6172 Busch Blvd Ste 3000, Columbus, OH 43229-2564 at (740) 746-8439

Group Rental Information
Site comments: Beautiful environment provides respite, team building, leadership development opportunities. Accomodation for small and large groups.
Facilities: Dorm-Style, Food Service, Hiking Trails, Lodges, Meeting Rooms, Playing Fields, Pool
Programs: Boating, Challenge/Ropes Course, Environmental Education, Swimming (#13181)

George L Forbes (est 1933)   ▲ 🚗

Highland Hills, OH (Cuyahoga Co.); (216) 831-5910
Dwight N. Brown, Director

Camp comments: Fun-filled week of group activities. Children learn socialization skills. Must be city of Cleveland residents.
Activities: Archery, Arts/Crafts, Baseball/Softball, Camping Skills/Outdoor Living, Canoeing, Dance, Hiking, Swimming — Recreational
Session lengths & capacity: 1 week sessions; 100 campers
Clientele & fees: coed 9-13; Fees: A ▲
Contact: Dwight N Brown, Camp Director at (216) 831-5910; fax: (216) 765-6993
Operated by: Div Of Rec City Of Cleveland, 601 Lakeside Ave, Cleveland, OH 44114 at (216) 831-5910 (#1408)

Girl Scout Camp Ledgewood

(est 1932)   ☀ ▲ 🏠

Peninsula, OH (Northern Summit Co.); (330) 650-4743
Susana Barba, Director

Camp comments: All girls grades 1-12 welcome! Enjoy a noncompetitive place, new friends, swim, hike, bike or ride! Ledgewood is for you
Activities: Aquatic Activities, Arts/Crafts, Backpacking, Camping Skills/Outdoor Living, Canoeing, Climbing/Rappelling, Counselor Training (CIT), Horseback — Western, Sports — Field & Team
Session lengths & capacity: June-August; 1/2, 1 & 2 week sessions; 150 campers
Clientele & fees: girls 7-17; Fees: B, C ▲
Contact: Miriam Somero, Outdoor Program Manager at (330) 864-9933; fax: (330) 864-5720
e-mail: msomero@girlscoutswr.org
Web site: www.girlscoutswr.org
Operated by: Girl Scouts Western Reserve, 345 White Pond Dr, Akron, OH 44320-1155 at (330) 864-9933

Group Rental Information
Facilities: Cabins, Hiking Trails, Kitchen Facilities, Lake, Lodges, Playing Fields, Pool, Tents (#1431)

Great Trail Girl Scout Camp

(est 1951)   ☀ ▲ 🏠

Malvern, OH (Carroll Co.); (330) 868-6065
Jean Emerick, Director

Camp comments: Emphasis on camping skills & group living provide well rounded programs; swimming, canoeing, archery, & more.

ICON LEGEND

☀	Day Camp
▲	Resident Camp
🏠	Facilities Available To Rent
🚗	Transportation Available
🐷	Financial Aid Available

FEE RANGES PER WEEK

A	$0-75
B	$75-200
C	$201-350
D	$351-500
E	$501-650
F	over $650

Activities: Aquatic Activities, Archery, Arts/Crafts, Backpacking, Camping Skills/Outdoor Living, Counselor Training (CIT), Hiking, Leadership Development, Music, Nature/Environment Studies
Session lengths & capacity: June-August; 1/2, 1 & 2 week sessions; 200 campers
Clientele & fees: girls 7-17; Fees: A, B ▲
Contact: Jean Emerick, Outdoor Program Director at (330) 455-9485; fax: (330) 455-2204
e-mail: gtprogram@ezo.net
Operated by: Great Trail GSC, 1010 Applegrove St NW, North Canton, OH 44720-1630 at (330) 455-9485

Group Rental Information
Facilities: Cabins, Lake, Lodges, Tents (#1392)

Happiness at OLA/St Joe

(est 1966)   ☀

Cleveland, OH (Cuyahoga Co.); (216) 696-6525
Molly Worthington, Director

Camp comments: Camp Happiness offers prog designed for persons who are developmentally disabled in a camping enviro for 6 wks.
Activities: Academics, Arts/Crafts, Computer, Counselor Training (CIT), Field Trips, Leadership Development, Music, Nature/Environment Studies, Swimming — Recreational
Session lengths & capacity: June-July; 6 week sessions; 24 campers
Clientele & fees: coed 6-21; Fees: B ☀
Contact: Molly Worthinton, Camp Administrator at (216) 696-6525 ext. 2700; fax: (216) 861-9795
e-mail: maworthington@dioceseofcleveland.org
Operated by: Catholic Charities Services, 1111 Superior Avenue, Cleveland, OH 44114 at (216) 696-6525 (#6200)

Happiness Day at Ctr for Pastoral (est 1966)   ☀ 🚗

Wickliffe, OH (lake Co.); (216) 696-6525
Molly Worthington, Director

Camp comments: Camp Happiness offers prog for persons who are developmentally disabled in a healthy/rec setting for 6 wks.
Activities: Academics, Arts/Crafts, Computer, Counselor Training (CIT), Field Trips, Leadership Development, Music, Nature/Environment Studies, Swimming — Recreational
Session lengths & capacity: June-July; 6 week sessions; 24 campers
Clientele & fees: coed 6-21; Fees: B ☀ 🐷
Contact: Molly Worthington, Camp Admin. at (216) 696-6525 ext. 2700; fax: (216) 861-9795
e-mail: maworthington@dioceseofcleveland.org
Operated by: Catholic Charities Services, 1111 Superior Avenue, Cleveland, OH 44114 at (216) 696-6525 (#2973)

Happiness Day at Parmadale

(est 1966)   ☀ 🚗

Parma, OH (Cuyahoga Co.); (216) 696-6525
Molly Worthington, Director

Camp comments: Camp Happiness offers programs for persons who are developmentally disabled in a camping & recreational setting.
Activities: Academics, Arts/Crafts, Computer, Counselor Training (CIT), Field Trips, Leadership Development, Music, Nature/Environment Studies, Swimming — Recreational
Session lengths & capacity: June-July; 6 week sessions; 22 campers
Clientele & fees: coed 6-21; Fees: B ☀ 🐷
Contact: Molly Worthington, Camp Administration at (216) 696-6525 ext. 2700; fax: (216) 344-9962
e-mail: maworthington@dioceseofcleveland.org
Operated by: Catholic Charities Services, 1111 Superior Avenue, Cleveland, OH 44114 at (216) 696-6525 (#6201)

Happiness Day at St Augustine

(est 1966)   ☀ 🚗

Lakewood, OH (Cuyahoga Co.); (216) 696-6525
Molly Worthington, Director

Camp comments: Camp Happiness offers programs for persons who are developmentally disabled in a camping/rec setting for 6 wks.
Activities: Academics, Arts/Crafts, Computer, Counselor Training (CIT), Field Trips, Leadership Development, Music, Nature/Environment Studies, Swimming — Recreational
Session lengths & capacity: June-July; 6 week sessions; 24 campers
Clientele & fees: coed 6-21; Fees: B ☀ 🐷
Contact: Molly Worthington, Camp Admin at (216) 696-6525 ext. 2700; fax: (216) 861-9795
e-mail: maworthington@dioceseofcleveland.org
Operated by: Catholic Charities Services, 1111 Superior Avenue, Cleveland, OH 44114 at (216) 696-6525 (#5389)

Hidden Hollow Camp (est 1940)   ▲ 🏠

Bellville, OH (Richland Co.); (419) 892-2007
Thelda Dillon, Director

Camp comments: Trad. camp-no specialty other than a place to have fun & make friends. A well rounded program permits all campers a chance to experience all phases of camp life
Activities: Aquatic Activities, Archery, Arts/Crafts, Baseball/Softball, Canoeing, Drama, Horseback — Western, Leadership Development, Nature/Environment Studies, Tennis
Session lengths & capacity: July-August; 1 week sessions; 180 campers
Clientele & fees: boys 8-15; girls 8-15; coed 8-15; Fees: B ▲
Contact: Terry Conard, Assistant Director at (419) 522-0521; fax: (419) 522-2166
Operated by: Friendly House Assoc, 380 N Mulberry St, Mansfield, OH 44902 at (419) 522-0521

Group Rental Information
Site comments: 551 acres, main lodge accommodates 230, heated dorms,kitchen facilities,meeting rooms,cabins,well rounded programs,coed.
Seasons & Capacity: Spring 80, Summer 180, Fall 80
Facilities: Cabins, Food Service, Hiking Trails, Lodges (#1418)

Highbrook Lodge (est 1928)   ▲ 🚗

Chardon, OH (Geauga Co.); (216) 286-3121

Camp comments: Highly caring camp for blind, disabled infants, children, adults and families. Beautiful ambiance & independent living.
Activities: Aquatic Activities, Arts/Crafts, Baseball/Softball, Camping Skills/Outdoor Living, Dance, Hiking, Leadership Development, Music, Nature/Environment Studies, Swimming — Recreational
Session lengths & capacity: 1 & 7 week sessions; 50 campers
Clientele & fees: boys 6-21; girls 6-21; coed 6-21; families; Fees: B, D ▲ 🐷
Contact: Jacqueline Crayton, Camp Director at (216) 791-8118; fax: (216) 791-1101
Web site: www.clevelandsightcenter.org
Operated by: Cleveland Sight Center, 1909 E 101st St, Cleveland, OH 44106-8696 at (216) 791-8118 (#1414)

Hillcrest Meadow Rdg Day Camp   ☀

Lyndhurst, OH; (216) 382-4300
Steve Hare, Director
Operated by: YMCA of Cleveland, 2200 Prospect Ave 9th Fl, Cleveland, OH 44115 at (216) 344-0095 (#13472)

Hiram House Camp

(est 1896) ☀ ⛺ 🏠

Chagrin Falls, OH (Cuyahoga Co.); (216) 831-5045
Russell R Grundke, Director

Camp comments: Self-esteem specialty. Campers thrive in noncompetitive, caring atmosphere, opportunities to belong, learn, contribute.
Activities: Archery, Arts/Crafts, Boating, Camping Skills/Outdoor Living, Hiking, Nature/Environment Studies, Swimming — Recreational
Session lengths & capacity: June-August; 1 & 2 week sessions; 125 campers
Clientele & fees: coed 6-13; Fees: D ⛺
Contact: Russell R Grundke, Director at (216) 831-5045; fax: (216) 831-2477
Web site: www.hiramhousecamp.org
Operated by: The Hiram House, 33775 Hiram Trail, Chagrin Falls, OH 44022 at (216) 831-5045
Group Rental Information
Site comments: Hiram House Camp aims to give children a healthy, wholesome, stimulating experience in the out-of-doors.
Seasons & Capacity: Spring 150, Summer 300, Fall 150, Winter 150
Facilities: Cabins, Dorm-Style, Food Service, Kitchen Facilities, Lake, Meeting Rooms (#1409)

Ho Mita Koda (est 1929) ⛺ 🏠

Newbury, OH (Geauga Co.); (216) 564-5125
Sally Burton-Szabo, Director

Camp comments: Camp for diabetic children offers full recreational experience in medically safe environment.
Activities: Aquatic Activities, Archery, Arts/Crafts, Boating, Challenge/Rope Courses, Field Trips, Hiking, Horseback — Western, Nature/Environment Studies, Tennis
Session lengths & capacity: June-August; 1 & 2 week sessions; 60 campers
Clientele & fees: boys 6-15; girls 6-15; coed 6-15; Fees: C ⛺ 🚐
Contact: Hallee O'Brien, Administrator at (216) 594-0800; fax: (216) 591-0320
e-mail: hobrien@dagc.org
Web site: www.camphomitakoda.org
Operated by: Ho Mita Koda, 3601 S Green Rd Suite 100, Cleveland, OH 44122 at (216) 591-0800 (#1410)

Jeffrey Summer Camp (est 1997) ☀

Bexley, OH (Franklin Co.); (614) 258-5755
Mike Price, Director

Camp comments: The Bexley Rec. Dept. summer camp provides a superb seasoned staff & enriching experience. Our goal is to provide a family atmosphere conductive to selfgrowth.
Activities: Aquatic Activities, Arts/Crafts, Field Trips, Nature/Environment Studies, Sports — Field & Team, Swimming — Instructional, Swimming — Recreational
Session lengths & capacity: June-August; 1 week sessions; 100 campers
Clientele & fees: coed 6-12; Fees: B ☀
Contact: Doug Jackson, Recreation Supervisor at (614) 258-5755; fax: (614) 258-9709
e-mail: Doug@Bexley.org
Web site: www.bexley.org
Operated by: City of Bexley Recreation Dept, 165 N Parkview, Bexley, OH 43209 at (614) 258-5755 (#25451)

Joy Outdoor Education Center

(est 1938) ☀ ⛺ 🏠 🚐

Clarksville, OH (Warren Co.); (800) 300-7094
Mike McGinty, Director

Camp comments: Joy OEC runs an overnight summer camp for low income youth in Gr Cinci,summer day camp,speciality camps,retreats,outdoor ED,& corp Teambldg.

Activities: Archery, Arts/Crafts, Bicycling/Biking, Canoeing, Challenge/Rope Courses, Counselor Training (CIT), Leadership Development, Nature/Environment Studies, Sports — Field & Team, Swimming — Recreational
Session lengths & capacity: June-August; 1 week sessions; 140 campers
Clientele & fees: coed 6-15; Fees: B ☀
Fees: A ⛺ 🚐
Contact: Mike McGinty, Executive Director at (800) 300-7094; fax: (937) 289-3179
e-mail: campjoy@hotmail.com
Web site: www.joec.org
Operated by: Joy Outdoor Education Center, Box 157, Clarksville, OH 45113 at (800) 300-7094
Group Rental Information
Seasons & Capacity: Spring 160, Summer 160, Fall 160, Winter 160
Facilities: A/V Equipment, Cabins, Dorm-Style, Food Service, Hiking Trails, Linens, Lodges, Meeting Rooms, Playing Fields, Pool, River
Programs: Boating, Challenge/Ropes Course, Environmental Education, Swimming (#1014)

Ken Jockety (est 1929) ☀

Galloway, OH (Franklin Co.); (614) 878-5203
Aileen L. Blyth, Director

Camp comments: Traditional Girl Scout day camp program in friendly, supportive rustic setting.
Activities: Arts/Crafts, Camping Skills/Outdoor Living, Nature/Environment Studies
Session lengths & capacity: 1 week sessions
Clientele & fees: girls 7-17; Fees: B ☀
Operated by: GS Seal Of Ohio Council, 1700 Water Mark Dr, Columbus, OH 43215-1097 at (614) 487-8101 (#986)

Ko-Man-She (est 1963) ⛺

Hamilton, OH (Greene Co.); (513) 867-0600
Geri Lester, Director

Camp comments: Camp Ko-Man-She is a camp for youth with diabetes, program for uses on diabetes education and outdoor adventure.
Activities: Aquatic Activities, Arts/Crafts, Basketball, Canoeing, Hiking, Horseback — Western, Nature/Environment Studies, Sports — Field & Team, Swimming — Recreational
Session lengths & capacity: June-July; 1 week sessions; 65 campers
Clientele & fees: boys 8-17; girls 8-17; coed 8-17; Fees: C ⛺
Contact: Geri Lester, Camp Coordinator at (937) 220-6611; fax: (937) 220-6609
e-mail: glester@core.com
Operated by: Diabetes Assn Dayton Area, 120 Zeigler St, Dayton, OH 45402 at (937) 220-6611 (#3439)

Leo Yassenoff JCC Day Camps

(est 1913) ☀ 🚐

Columbus, OH (Franklin Co.); (614) 231-2731
Martha Goldberg, Director

Camp comments: Traditional day camp with broad range of activities and electives. Strong Jewish environment. Warm caring FUN!!
Activities: Aquatic Activities, Arts/Crafts, Canoeing, Challenge/Rope Courses, Nature/Environment Studies, Rafting, Sailing, Sports — Field & Team, Swimming — Instructional
Session lengths & capacity: June-August; 2, 4, 6 & 8 week sessions; 700 campers
Clientele & fees: coed 3-15; Fees: A, B, C ☀ 🚐
Contact: Martha Goldberg, Director of Camping Services at (614) 559-6253; fax: (614) 231-8222
e-mail: mgoldberg@columbusjcc.org
Web site: www.columbusjcc.org
Operated by: Leo Yassenoff JCC, 1125 College Avenue, Columbus, OH 43209 at (614) 231-2731 (#30768)

Licking Co Family YMCA Camp

☀ 🚐

Newark, OH (Licking Co.); (740) 345-9622
Nancy Davenport, Director
Activities: Baseball/Softball, Bicycling/Biking, Clowning, Counselor Training (CIT), Dance, Drama, Gymnastics, Soccer, Sports — Field & Team, Swimming — Recreational
Session lengths & capacity: June-August; 350 campers
Clientele & fees: coed 5-15; Fees: A ☀
Contact: Nancy Davenport, Senior Program at (740) 345-9622; fax: (740) 349-8535
e-mail: nancydav@yahoo.com
Operated by: Licking County Family YMCA, 470 W Church St, Newark, OH 43055 at (740) 345-9622 (#46604)

Lutheran Memorial Camp

(est 1948) ⛺ 🏠

Fulton, OH (Morrow Co.); (419) 864-8030
Rebecca Stabler, Director

Camp comments: A 400 acre site of beautiful forest and meadows. Program is Christ-centered and small-group oriented. Exceptional staff.
Activities: Aquatic Activities, Arts/Crafts, Camping Skills/Outdoor Living, Challenge/Rope Courses, Climbing/Rappelling, Farming/Ranching/Gardening, Hiking, Leadership Development, Nature/Environment Studies, Religious Study
Session lengths & capacity: 1/2 & 1 week sessions; 200 campers
Clientele & fees: coed 5-18; families; Fees: C ⛺ 🚐
Contact: Reservationist at (419) 864-8030; fax: (419) 864-1582
e-mail: luthmem@bright.net
Web site: www.lomocamps.org
Operated by: Lutheran Outdoor Ministries OH, 863 Eastwind Dr, Westerville, OH 43081 at (614) 890-2267
Group Rental Information
Site comments: Exceptional hospitality, first-rate food, programs provided.
Facilities: Cabins, Double Occupancy, Food Service, Hiking Trails, Meeting Rooms, Pool
Programs: Environmental Education (#977)

Marmon Valley Farm (est 1963) ⛺ 🏠

Zanesfield, OH (Logan Co.); (937) 593-6900
Matthew Wiley, Director

Camp comments: We provide a wholesome Christian environment with a quality horsemanship program located on a 450 acre farm, 120 horses.
Activities: Aquatic Activities, Archery, Arts/Crafts, Camping Skills/Outdoor Living, Challenge/Rope Courses, Horseback — English, Horseback — Western, Nature/Environment Studies, Swimming — Recreational
Session lengths & capacity: 1/2 & 1 week sessions; 89 campers
Clientele & fees: coed 7-17; Fees: D ⛺ 🚐
Contact: Matthew Wiley, Director at (937) 593-8000; fax: (937) 593-6900
e-mail: info@marmonvalley.com
Web site: www.marmonvalley.com
Operated by: Marmon Valley Farm, 7754 State Route 292 South, Zanesfield, OH 43360 at (937) 593-6900
Group Rental Information
Facilities: Cabins, Food Service, Lake
Programs: Challenge/Ropes Course, Horseback Riding (#1019)

Miami County YMCA Summer Camp (est 1910) ☀

Piqua, OH (Miami Co.); (937) 773-9622
Donn Craig, Director

Camp comments: The Miami Co. YMCA builds strong families, strong communities and strong kids.
Activities: Aquatic Activities, Arts/Crafts, Baseball/Softball, Basketball, Community Service, Field Trips, Leadership Development, Nature/Environment Studies, Sports — Field & Team, Swimming — Recreational
Session lengths & capacity: June-August; 9 week sessions; 75 campers
Clientele & fees: coed 6-12; Fees: B ☀
Contact: Donn Craig, Program Director at (937) 773-9622; fax: (937) 440-9243
e-mail: d.craig@miamicountyymca.com
Web site: www.miamicountyymca.com
Operated by: Miami County YMCA, 223 W High Street, Piqua, OH 45356 at (973) 773-9622 (#1853)

Molly Lauman (est 1929) ⚊ 🚍

Lucasville, OH (Scioto Co.); (740) 259-4287
Becky Foreman, Director

Camp comments: Traditional, noncompetitive camp program in friendly, supportive rustic setting.
Activities: Arts/Crafts, Backpacking, Camping Skills/Outdoor Living, Counselor Training (CIT), Hiking, Horseback — Western, Leadership Development, Nature/Environment Studies, Swimming — Recreational
Session lengths & capacity: June-August; 1/2, 1 & 2 week sessions; 120 campers
Clientele & fees: girls 7-17; Fees: B ⚊
Contact: Becky Foreman, Resident Camp Director at (614) 487-8101; fax: (614) 487-8189
e-mail: becky@sealofohio.org
Operated by: GS Seal Of Ohio Council, 1700 Water Mark Dr, Columbus, OH 43215-1097 at (614) 487-8101 (#967)

Mowana (est 1941) ⚊ 🏠

Mansfield, OH (Richland Co.); (419) 589-7406
Eric Kretzmann, Director

Camp comments: Camp Mowana is a 'place apart' where lives are changed as people of all ages experience God's love and joy within a Christ-centered community.
Activities: Arts/Crafts, Camping Skills/Outdoor Living, Canoeing, Challenge/Rope Courses, Counselor Training (CIT), Farming/Ranching/Gardening, Nature/Environment Studies, Religious Study, Sports — Field & Team, Swimming — Recreational
Session lengths & capacity: 1/2 & 1 week sessions; 200 campers
Clientele & fees: coed 5-18; families; seniors; single adults; Fees: C ⚊ 💰
Contact: Eric Kretzmann, Director at (419) 589-7406; fax: (419) 589-3096

ICON LEGEND

☀ Day Camp
⚊ Resident Camp
🏠 Facilities Available To Rent
🚍 Transportation Available
💰 Financial Aid Available

FEE RANGES PER WEEK

A $0-75
B $75-200
C $201-350
D $351-500
E $501-650
F over $650

e-mail: mowana@lomocamps.org
Web site: www.lomocamps.org
Operated by: Lutheran Outdoor Ministries OH, 863 Eastwind Dr, Westerville, OH 43081 at (614) 890-2267

Group Rental Information
Site comments: Beautiful wooded site, rugged terrain. Easy access from I71. Diverse summer camps. Year round retreat facilities.
Seasons & Capacity: Spring 90, Summer 250, Fall 90, Winter 90
Facilities: A/V Equipment, Cabins, Double Occupancy, Food Service, Hiking Trails, Kitchen Facilities, Lodges, Meeting Rooms, Playing Fields, Pool, River
Programs: Challenge/Ropes Course, Swimming (#991)

Muskingum Family Y ☀

Zanesville, OH; (740) 453-0335
Activities: Academics, Aquatic Activities, Camping Skills/Outdoor Living, Computer, Drama, Drawing/Painting, Football, Music, Sports — Field & Team, Swimming — Recreational
Operated by: YMCA of Zanesville, 700 McIntire Avenue, Zanesville, OH 43701 at (740) 453-9622 (#33549)

Ohio Camp Cherith (est 1949) ⚊

Madison, OH (Lake Co.); (440) 298-3938

Camp comments: Nondenominational Christian camp, East of Cleveland. Affil. w/ Pioneer Clubs. Emphasis 'Christ in every phase of life.'
Activities: Archery, Arts/Crafts, Camping Skills/Outdoor Living, Canoeing, Counselor Training (CIT), Fishing, Hiking, Horseback — Western, Riflery, Swimming — Instructional
Session lengths & capacity: July-August; 4 week sessions; 100 campers
Clientele & fees: boys 8-18; girls 8-18; families; Fees: B ⚊
Contact: Gretta Weaver, Registrar at (304) 272-6525;
e-mail: ohio.cherith@juno.com
Operated by: Ohio Camp Cherith, 3854 Remsen Rd, Medina, OH 44256 at (330) 725-4202 (#1389)

Otterbein (est 1943) ⚊ 🏠

Logan, OH (Hocking Co.); (740) 385-5712

Camp comments: Serving all people for Christian birth, growth, and renewal.
Activities: Archery, Camping Skills/Outdoor Living, Canoeing, Challenge/Rope Courses, Climbing/Rappelling, Hiking, Religious Study, Swimming — Recreational, Team Building
Session lengths & capacity: June-August; 1/2 & 1 week sessions; 180 campers
Clientele & fees: coed 7-18; families; Fees: C ⚊
Contact: (740) 385-5712; fax: (740) 385-5712
Web site: www.westohiocamps.com
Operated by: W Ohio Conf United Methodist, 32 Wesley Blvd, Worthington, OH 43085-3585 at (614) 781-2630

Group Rental Information
Site comments: Serving all people for Christian birth, growth, and renewal.
Seasons & Capacity: Spring 102, Summer 143, Fall 102, Winter 102
Facilities: Cabins, Dorm-Style, Food Service, Hiking Trails, Lake, Meeting Rooms, Playing Fields, Tents
Programs: Boating, Challenge/Ropes Course, Swimming (#1011)

Pilgrim Hills Conference Ctr
(est 1956) 🏠 🚍

Brinkhaven, OH (Coshocton Co.); (740) 599-6314
Jeff Thompson, Director
Contact: Helen Schultz, Registrar at (800) 282-0740 ext. 207; fax: (614) 885-8824

e-mail: campregistrar@ocucc.org
Web site: www.ocucc.org
Operated by: Ohio Conf Untd Church Christ, 6161 Busch Blvd 95, Columbus, OH 43229-2547 at (800) 282-0740

Group Rental Information
Site comments: A place for personal spiritual growth and connections. Located in scenic Ohio Amish country.
Facilities: Dorm-Style, Double Occupancy, Food Service, Hiking Trails, Lake, Meeting Rooms, Pool
Programs: Boating, Challenge/Ropes Course, Swimming (#4102)

Recreation Unlimited
(est 1960) ☀ ⚊ 🏠

Ashley, OH (Delaware Co.); (740) 548-7006
Laura Smith and Paul Huttlin, Director

Camp comments: 165 acres, accessible campus serving individuals with disabilities. Ohio offers sports recreation & education.
Activities: Aquatic Activities, Archery, Arts/Crafts, Camping Skills/Outdoor Living, Canoeing, Challenge/Rope Courses, Fishing, Golf, Nature/Environment Studies, Team Building
Session lengths & capacity: 7 week sessions; 70 campers
Clientele & fees: coed 5-99; families; seniors; single adults; Fees: B ☀ Fees: D ⚊ 💰
Contact: John Loree, Sales Director at (740) 548-7006; fax: (740) 747-4037
e-mail: recunl@midohio.net
Web site: www.recreationunlimited.org
Operated by: Recreation Unlimited, 7700 Piper Road, Ashley, OH 43003 at (740) 548-7006

Group Rental Information
Seasons & Capacity: Spring 300, Summer 200, Fall 200, Winter 300
Facilities: A/V Equipment, Dorm-Style, Food Service, Lake, Linens, Lodges, Meeting Rooms, Pool
Programs: Boating, Challenge/Ropes Course, Environmental Education, Swimming (#6674)

Red Barn (est 1947) ☀ 🚍

Kirtland, OH (Lake Co.); (216) 256-0716
Ken Roskos, Director

Camp comments: Day camp, boys 7-11. Spend time at nature study center, play tennis, softball, swim, fish, hike, shoot archery, crafts.
Activities: Archery, Baseball/Softball, Canoeing, Challenge/Rope Courses, Field Trips, Fishing, Hiking, Model Rocketry, Music, Swimming — Instructional
Session lengths & capacity: June-July; 7 week sessions; 80 campers
Clientele & fees: boys 7-11; Fees: B ☀
Contact: Gerry Roskos, Receptionist at (216) 256-0716; fax: (216) 256-3093
e-mail: redoakcamp@lightstream.net
Web site: www.redoakcamp.com
Operated by: Red Oaks/Red Barn/Chincapin, 9057 Kirtland Chardon Rd, Kirtland, OH 44094 at (440) 256-0716 (#3965)

Red Oak Camp (est 1947) ⚊

Kirtland, OH (Lake Co.); (440) 256-0716
Ken Roskos, Director

Camp comments: Small camp with personal instruction, learning wilderness skills for backpack-canoe trip.
Activities: Archery, Backpacking, Camping Skills/Outdoor Living, Challenge/Rope Courses, Climbing/Rappelling, Hiking, Nature/Environment Studies, Swimming — Instructional
Session lengths & capacity: 1 & 8 week sessions; 30 campers
Clientele & fees: boys 11-14; Fees: C ⚊
Contact: Gerry Roskos, Receptionist at (440) 256-0716; fax: (440) 256-3093
e-mail: redoakcamp@redoakcamp.com

Web site: www.redoakcamp.com
Operated by: Red Oaks/Red Barn/Chincapin, 9057 Kirtland Chardon Rd, Kirtland, OH 44094 at (440) 256-0716 (#1393)

Roosevelt Firebird (est 1918)

Bowerston, OH (Carroll Co.); (740) 269-7891
Robyn Lorimer, Director

Camp comments: Safety Fun Growth
Activities: Aquatic Activities, Archery, Arts/Crafts, Drama, Horseback — English, Riflery, Sailing, Sports — Field & Team, Tennis, Waterskiing
Session lengths & capacity: June-August; 2, 4 & 6 week sessions; 200 campers
Clientele & fees: boys 7-15; girls 7-15; families; single adults; Fees: D ▲
Contact: WV Lorimer-R. Lorimer, Directors at (440) 259-2901; fax: (440) 259-2901
e-mail: roosevelt-firebird@coolmail.net
Web site: www.roosevelt-firebird.com
Operated by: Roosevelt Firebird, 2814 Perry Road, Perry, OH 44081 at (440) 259-2901 (#1432)

Salvation Army Camp Swoneky
(est 1958)

Oregonia, OH (Warren Co.); (513) 932-1794
David Childs, Director

Camp comments: Salvation Army camp. Christian emphasis. Serving children in SW OH & NE KY. Register through local Salvation Army.
Activities: Academics, Camping Skills/Outdoor Living, Canoeing, Challenge/Rope Courses, Climbing/Rappelling, Hiking, Horseback — Western, Music, Religious Study, Swimming — Recreational
Session lengths & capacity: June-August; 1 week sessions; 270 campers
Clientele & fees: coed 6-17; families;
Fees: A, B ▲ 🐖
Contact: Dave Childs, Assistant Camp Director at (513) 762-5631; fax: (513) 762-5679
e-mail: dchilds1@juno.com
Operated by: The Salvation Army, Box 596, Cincinnati, OH 45201 at (513) 762-5600 (#969)

Sheldon Calvary Camp
(est 1936)

Conneaut, OH (Ashtabula Co.); (440) 593-4381
Anne M Muhl, Director

Camp comments: Recreational camp which nurtures friendship, models the acceptance of individuals & values all of God's creation.
Activities: Aquatic Activities, Archery, Arts/Crafts, Canoeing, Challenge/Rope Courses, Horseback — Western, Leadership Development, Sailing, Tennis
Session lengths & capacity: June-August; 1 & 2 week sessions; 180 campers
Clientele & fees: coed 8-17; families;
Fees: C, E ▲ 🐖
Contact: Anne M Muhl, Administrative Director at (412) 343-0224; fax: (412) 343-0224
e-mail: ammuhl@aol.com
Operated by: Sheldon Calvary Camp, 315 Shady Ave, Pittsburgh, PA 15206 at (412) 343-0224

Group Rental Information
Seasons & Capacity: Spring 100, Fall 100
Facilities: Cabins, Dorm-Style, Hiking Trails, Kitchen Facilities, Meeting Rooms, Playing Fields
Programs: Challenge/Ropes Course (#13291)

Stonybrook (est 1953)

Waynesville, OH (Warren Co.); (513) 897-1078
Judy Turley, Director
Contact: Cyndy Self, Property Manager at (513) 489-1025; fax: (513) 489-1417
e-mail: cself@grgsc.org
Web site: www.grgsc.org
Operated by: Great Rivers GSC Inc, 4930 Cornell Rd, Cincinnati, OH 45242 at (513) 489-1025

Group Rental Information
Facilities: Pool, Tents (#1966)

Sugarbush

Kinsman, OH (Trumbull Co.); (330) 772-4200
Donna DeFiore, Director
Activities: Arts/Crafts, Camping Skills/Outdoor Living, Canoeing, Climbing/Rappelling, Clowning, Nature/Environment Studies, Swimming — Instructional, Swimming — Recreational, Wilderness Trips
Session lengths & capacity: June-August; 1/2 & 1 week sessions; 100 campers
Clientele & fees: girls 6-16; Fees: B ▲
Contact: Donna DeFiore, Director Camps/Properties/Program at (330) 652-5877; fax: (330) 544-7959
e-mail: dmdefiore@hotmail.com
Operated by: Lake To River GSC, 980 Warren Ave, Niles, OH 44446 at (330) 652-5877

Group Rental Information
Facilities: Cabins, Hiking Trails, Kitchen Facilities, Lodges, Meeting Rooms, Playing Fields, Pool, Tents
Programs: Boating, Swimming (#1394)

Tall Pines Day Camp @ YMCA Cmp (est 1982)

Clinton, OH (Summit Co.); (330) 896-1964
Mike McElhinney, Director

Camp comments: 250 acres with private lake diverse. Day camp program. Perfect for the first time camper or campers on the move.
Activities: Aquatic Activities, Archery, Arts/Crafts, Boating, Counselor Training (CIT), Field Trips, Horseback — Western, Nature/Environment Studies, Sports — Field & Team, Swimming — Recreational
Session lengths & capacity: June-September; 1/2, 1 & 2 week sessions; 100 campers
Clientele & fees: coed 6-15; Fees: B ☀ 🐖
Contact: Dennis Van Kampen, Executive Director at (330) 896-1964; fax: (330) 896-2956
e-mail: ycamp@akronymca.org
Web site: www.akronymca.org
Operated by: Akron YMCA, 209 S Main St, Akron, OH 44308 at (330) 376-1335 (#1812)

Templed Hills Camp (est 1957)

Bellville, OH (Richland Co.); (419) 886-2380
Don Harding, Director
Contact: Web site: www.ocucc.org
Operated by: Ohio Conf Untd Church Christ, 6161 Busch Blvd 95, Columbus, OH 43229-2547 at (800) 282-0740

Group Rental Information
Site comments: A place for personal spiritual growth and connections.
Seasons & Capacity: Spring 145, Summer 262, Fall 145, Winter 145
Facilities: A/V Equipment, Cabins, Dorm-Style, Double Occupancy, Food Service, Hiking Trails, Linens, Lodges, Meeting Rooms, Pool
Programs: Challenge/Ropes Course, Environmental Education, Swimming, Winter Sports (#4101)

The Salvation Army Greenwood
(est 1932)

Delaware, OH (Delaware Co.); (740) 369-4821
Major Henrietta Klemanski, David Klemanski, Director

Camp comments: Christian resident camping program.
Activities: Arts/Crafts, Baseball/Softball, Basketball, Boating, Camping Skills/Outdoor Living, Music, Nature/Environment Studies, Swimming — Recreational

Session lengths & capacity: 1 week sessions; 192 campers
Clientele & fees: coed 6-11; Fees: A ☀
Fees: B ▲ 🐖
Contact: Major Henrietta Klemanski, Camp Director at (614) 221-6561 ext. 104; fax: (614) 221-1896
e-mail: henriklem@hotmail.com
Operated by: The Salvation Army, 340 E Fulton St, Columbus, OH 43215 at (614) 221-6561

Group Rental Information
Facilities: Cabins, Food Service (#983)

Timberlane GS Camp (est 1959)

Wakeman, OH (Erie Co.); (440) 965-7234
Michele Freeman, Director

Camp comments: Beautiful woods, outstanding staff. Challenging, noncompetitive, traditional program. Leadership training.
Activities: Archery, Arts/Crafts, Boating, Camping Skills/Outdoor Living, Counselor Training (CIT), Hiking, Horseback — Western, Nature/Environment Studies, Swimming — Instructional, Swimming — Recreational
Session lengths & capacity: June-August; 1/2 & 1 week sessions; 115 campers
Clientele & fees: girls 6-17; families;
Fees: B, C ▲ 🐖
Contact: Brenda Warren, Program Director at (440) 233-6112; fax: (440) 233-7393
Operated by: GS of Erie Shores, 6111 S Broadway, Lorain, OH 44053 at (440) 233-6112 (#1405)

Triple S Camp (est 1947)

Sugar Grove, OH (Fairfield Co.); (614) 746-8556
Thomas G. Ferguson, Director

Camp comments: Provides value based program with excellent staff in a rustic setting.
Activities: Academics, Arts/Crafts, Community Service, Counselor Training (CIT), Field Trips, Leadership Development, Nature/Environment Studies, Swimming — Recreational
Session lengths & capacity: 1, 2 & 6 week sessions; 110 campers
Clientele & fees: coed 5-17; families;
Fees: B ▲ 🐖
Contact: Thomas G. Ferguson, Camp Direcor at (614) 746-8556; fax: (614) 444-7776
Web site: www.southsidesettlement.com
Operated by: South Side Settlement, 310 Innis Ave, Columbus, OH 43207 at (614) 444-9868 (#1022)

Wakatomika (est 1942)

Utica, OH (Licking Co.); (740) 745-5911
Amy Clendenen, Director

Camp comments: Develop self-esteem, values, friendships and confidence. Enjoy a low-cost, high-impact Girl Scout Adventure.
Activities: Arts/Crafts, Camping Skills/Outdoor Living, Climbing/Rappelling, Field Trips, Hiking, Horseback — Western, Leadership Development, Nature/Environment Studies, Swimming — Recreational, Team Building
Session lengths & capacity: June-August; 1/2 & 1 week sessions; 120 campers
Clientele & fees: girls 5-17; families;
Fees: B, C ▲ 🐖
Contact: Amy Clendenen, Camp Director at (740) 454-8563; fax: (740) 454-8111
Web site: www.gsheart.org
Operated by: Girl Scouts-Heart of Ohio Inc, 3230 Bowers Lane, Zanesville, OH 43701 at (740) 454-8563

Group Rental Information
Seasons & Capacity: Spring 214, Fall 214, Winter 214
Facilities: Cabins, Hiking Trails, Lodges, Tents (#965)

Wanake (est 1946)

Beach City, OH (Stark Co.); (330) 833-9924
John Erdman, Director

Camp comments: Christian camping with a wide variety of programs including performing arts, sport, high adventure and special needs.
Activities: Backpacking, Camping Skills/Outdoor Living, Challenge/Rope Courses, Climbing/Rappelling, Clowning, Counselor Training (CIT), Hiking, Religious Study, Swimming — Recreational
Session lengths & capacity: June-August; 1/2 & 1 week sessions; 210 campers
Clientele & fees: coed 8-20; families; Fees: B ☀ Fees: C ⚠ 🐷
Contact: John Erdman, Director Camp Wanake at (330) 756-2333; fax: (330) 833-9924
e-mail: campwanake@juno.com
Operated by: E Ohio Conf United Methodist, 8800 Cleveland Ave NW, North Canton, OH 44720 at (800) 831-3972

Group Rental Information
Site comments: Near Amish country. Excellent food service. Well maintained.
Seasons & Capacity: Spring 158, Summer 228, Fall 158, Winter 158
Facilities: A/V Equipment, Cabins, Dorm-Style, Food Service, Hiking Trails, Lake, Lodges, Meeting Rooms
Programs: Boating, Challenge/Ropes Course, Environmental Education, Swimming (#7095)

Whip Poor Will (est 1936)

Morrow, OH (Warren Co.); (513) 899-2751

Camp comments: Beautiful, wooded camp. Success oriented programs with self-esteem building. Diverse staff promotes acceptance.
Activities: Backpacking, Camping Skills/Outdoor Living, Challenge/Rope Courses, Field Trips, Horseback — Western, Nature/Environment Studies, Rafting, Swimming — Recreational, Travel/Tour, Wilderness Trips
Session lengths & capacity: June-August; 1/2, 1 & 3 week sessions; 130 campers
Clientele & fees: girls 6-17; Fees: C ⚠ 🐷
Contact: Patti Davy, Director of Facilities & Camp Services at (937) 279-6521; fax: (937) 279-6521
e-mail: Patti_Davy@btgirlscouts.org
Web site: www.btgirlscouts.org
Operated by: Buckeye Trails GSC, 450 Shoup Mill Rd, Dayton, OH 45415-3518 at (937) 279-6521

Group Rental Information
Site comments: Wooded camp with creek. Trim orienteering course/map.

ICON LEGEND

☀ Day Camp
⚠ Resident Camp
🏠 Facilities Available To Rent
🚗 Transportation Available
🐷 Financial Aid Available

FEE RANGES PER WEEK

A $0-75
B $75-200
C $201-350
D $351-500
E $501-650
F over $650

Facilities: Cabins, Double Occupancy, Kitchen Facilities, Lake, Lodges, Meeting Rooms, Pool, Tents
Programs: Boating (#987)

Whitewood 4H Camp (est 1940)

Windsor, OH (Ashtabula Co.); (440) 272-5275
Lena Detweiler, Director

Camp comments: Site of Erie Indians. 226 ac land on historic registry. Glacier cut gorge, live stream, lake, meadows. Access off US 322
Activities: Aquatic Activities, Archery, Arts/Crafts, Boating, Challenge/Rope Courses, Hiking, Leadership Development, Nature/Environment Studies, Riflery, Swimming — Recreational
Session lengths & capacity: 1 & 7 week sessions; 180 campers
Clientele & fees: coed 8-13; families; seniors; single adults; Fees: A ☀ Fees: B ⚠
Contact: Lena Detweiler, Exec Director at (440) 272-5276; fax: (440) 272-5275
e-mail: ldetweiler@agvax2.ag.ohio-state.edu
Web site: www.og.ohio-state.edu/~wwood4-h
Operated by: Northeast Ohio 4H Camps Inc, 7983 Wiswell Road, Windsor, OH 44099 at (440) 272-5275

Group Rental Information
Site comments: 226 acres on historical registry site of Erie Indians.
Seasons & Capacity: Summer 180
Facilities: Cabins, Dorm-Style, Food Service, Hiking Trails, Lake, Meeting Rooms, Playing Fields
Programs: Boating, Challenge/Ropes Course, Environmental Education, Swimming (#3281)

Widewater Retreat Center

(est 1992)

Liberty Center, OH (Henry Co.)
Eric Witte, Director

Camp comments: Serving all people for Christian birth, growth, and renewal.
Activities: Aquatic Activities, Archery, Canoeing, Drawing/Painting, Fishing, Leadership Development, Religious Study, Swimming — Recreational, Team Building
Session lengths & capacity: June-August; 1/2 & 1 week sessions; 80 campers
Clientele & fees: coed 8-90; families; seniors; Fees: C, D ☀
Contact: Eric Witte, Director at (419) 533-5900; fax: (419) 533-5900
e-mail: wwretreat@aol.com
Web site: www.westohiocamps.com
Operated by: W Ohio Conf United Methodist, 32 Wesley Blvd, Worthington, OH 43085-3585 at (614) 781-2630

Group Rental Information
Site comments: Serving all people for Christian birth, growth, and renewal.
Facilities: A/V Equipment, Dorm-Style, Food Service, Lodges, Meeting Rooms, Playing Fields, Pool, River
Programs: Boating, Challenge/Ropes Course, Swimming (#44936)

Wildwood Camp & Conference Ctr (est 1960)

Milford, OH (Clermont Co.); (513) 831-3242
Scott Henderson, Director

Camp comments: Christian resident & day camp programs; spiritual, emotional, intellectual & physical development. Low camper/counselor ratio. International counselor on staff.
Activities: Archery, Arts/Crafts, Canoeing, Challenge/Rope Courses, Community Service, Leadership Development, Performing Arts, Sports — Field & Team, Swimming — Recreational, Team Building
Session lengths & capacity: June-August; 1/2, 1 & 2 week sessions; 136 campers

Clientele & fees: boys 6-18; girls 6-18; coed 6-18; families; Fees: C ⚠ 🐷
Contact: Scott Henderson, Executive Director at (513) 831-3242; fax: (513) 831-8348
e-mail: wildwoodctr@pcusa.org
Web site: www.wildwoodcenter.org
Operated by: Wildwood Camp and Conf Ctr, 941 Barg Salt Run Rd, Milford, OH 45150 at (513) 831-3242

Group Rental Information
Site comments: 235 acres of rolling hills & woods for groups seeking spiritual development in a natural setting for all generations. Retreat, meeting & conference services.
Seasons & Capacity: Spring 80, Summer 80, Fall 80, Winter 80
Facilities: Cabins, Dorm-Style, Double Occupancy, Food Service, Hiking Trails, Kitchen Facilities, Lodges, Playing Fields, Pool, Tents
Programs: Challenge/Ropes Course (#960)

Woodhaven Program Center

(est 1946)

Lima, OH (Allen Co.); (419) 225-4085
Valarie Crabb, Director

Camp comments: Girl Scout Environmental center, team building & leadership opportunities. Appreciation of nature & outdoors for all.
Activities: Archery, Arts/Crafts, Camping Skills/Outdoor Living, Ceramics/Pottery, Challenge/Rope Courses, Hiking, Leadership Development, Nature/Environment Studies, Photography, Team Building
Session lengths & capacity: June-August; 1 week sessions; 100 campers
Clientele & fees: boys 5-18; girls 5-18; coed 5-18; families; Fees: A ☀
Contact: Donna Dickman, Director of Program Services at (419) 225-4085; fax: (419) 229-7570
e-mail: ddickman@gsar.org
Web site: www.gsar.org
Operated by: Appleseed Ridge GSC, 1870 W Robb Ave, PO Box 956, Lima, OH 45802 at (419) 225-4085

Group Rental Information
Site comments: Team building adventure course and environmental programs available in a retreat setting.
Facilities: Dorm-Style, Food Service, Hiking Trails, Kitchen Facilities, Meeting Rooms
Programs: Challenge/Ropes Course (#3676)

Woodland Altars (est 1960)

Peebles, OH (Adams Co.); (937) 588-4411

Camp comments: Family oriented that emphasizes Christian values. Strong high adventure utilizing very experienced leadership.
Activities: Aquatic Activities, Camping Skills/Outdoor Living, Caving, Challenge/Rope Courses, Climbing/Rappelling, Drama, Horseback — Western, Leadership Development, Performing Arts, Travel/Tour
Session lengths & capacity: June-August; 1/2, 1 & 2 week sessions; 200 campers
Clientele & fees: coed 8-80; families; seniors; single adults; Fees: B, C ⚠ 🐷
Contact: Bruce E Rosenberger, Interim Director at (800) 213-1161; fax: (937) 588-4431
e-mail: altars@bright.net
Web site: www.woodlandaltars.org
Operated by: S OH Dist Church of Brethren, 1001 Mill Ridge Circle, Union, OH 45322 at (937) 831-6399

Group Rental Information
Site comments: Services for groups from 10 to 200. Private rooms and baths to dorms. Full line food service & a variety of recreational activities.
Seasons & Capacity: Spring 125, Summer 200, Fall 125, Winter 125

Facilities: A/V Equipment, Cabins, Dorm-Style, Double Occupancy, Food Service, Hiking Trails, Kitchen Facilities, Lake, Linens, Lodges, Meeting Rooms, Playing Fields, Pool
Programs: Challenge/Ropes Course, Environmental Education, Horseback Riding, Swimming (#962)

Wooster YMCA Day Camp Spirit

(est 1987)

Wooster, OH (Wayne Co.); (330) 264-3131
Tricia Huffman, Director

Camp comments: Camp Spirit offers a caring environment that grows healthy bodies, minds, and spirits.
Activities: Arts/Crafts, Drawing/Painting, Field Trips, Hiking, International Culture, Leadership Development, Nature/Environment Studies, Swimming — Recreational
Session lengths & capacity: June-August; 1 week sessions; 100 campers
Clientele & fees: coed 6-13; Fees: A ☀ 🐖
Contact: Tricia Huffman, Program Director at (330) 264-3131; fax: (330) 262-7227
Operated by: YMCA of Wooster, 680 Woodland Ave, Wooster, OH 44691 at (330) 264-3131 (#159)

YMCA Camp Kern (est 1910)

Oregonia, OH (Warren Co.); (513) 932-3756
Jeff Merhige, Director

Camp comments: Traditional YMCA Resident Camp focusing on character development through creative programs with excellent role models.
Activities: Arts/Crafts, Canoeing, Challenge/Rope Courses, Horseback — English, International Culture, Nature/Environment Studies, Sports — Field & Team, Travel/Tour, Wilderness Trips
Session lengths & capacity: 1/2, 1 & 2 week sessions; 380 campers
Clientele & fees: boys 7-17; girls 7-17; coed 7-17; families; Fees: D △ 🐖
Contact: Jeff Merhige, Executive Director at (513) 932-3756; fax: (513) 932-8607
Web site: www.campkern.org
Operated by: YMCA of Metropolitan Dayton, 5291 St Rt 350, Oregonia, OH 45054 at (513) 932-3756

Group Rental Information
Site comments: YMCA Camp Kern is located on 420 wooded acres adjacent to the Little Miami National Scenic River. A year round outdoor center serving school,groups and families
Seasons & Capacity: Spring 348, Summer 440, Fall 348, Winter 348
Facilities: Double Occupancy, Food Service, Hiking Trails, Lake, Meeting Rooms, Pool
Programs: Boating, Challenge/Ropes Course, Environmental Education, Horseback Riding, Swimming (#1010)

YMCA Camp Tippecanoe

(est 1958)

Tippecanoe, OH (Harrison Co.); (800) 922-0679
Brian Seagraves, Director

Camp comments: Fun and adventure in traditional camping programs develop spirit, mind, body thru values-caring, honesty, responsibility
Activities: Archery, Boating, Camping Skills/Outdoor Living, Canoeing, Counselor Training (CIT), Horseback — Western, Leadership Development, Team Building
Session lengths & capacity: 1 & 2 week sessions
Contact: Connie Clark, Camp Director at (800) 922-0679; fax: (740) 922-1152
e-mail: ycamptippe@aol.com
Web site: www.YMCAStark.org
Operated by: YMCA of Central Stark County, 405 Second St NW, Canton, OH 44702-1705 at (330) 580-4162

Group Rental Information
Facilities: Cabins, Food Service, Hiking Trails, Lake, Lodges
Programs: Boating, Horseback Riding (#1421)

YMCA Camp Y-Noah

(est 1929)

Clinton, OH (Summit Co.); (800) 944-9705
Jeanne Armbruster, Director

Camp comments: 250 acres w/private lake. Diverse res. & day camp programs. Specialties in equestrian & teen programs. Focus on character development in traditional setting.
Activities: Aquatic Activities, Archery, Arts/Crafts, Camping Skills/Outdoor Living, Challenge/Rope Courses, Climbing/Rappelling, Counselor Training (CIT), Horseback — Western, Leadership Development, Sailing
Session lengths & capacity: June-September; 1/2, 1, 2 & 3 week sessions; 300 campers
Clientele & fees: girls 6-17; Fees: B ☀
Fees: C, D △
Contact: Dennis Van Kampen, Executive Director at (330) 896-1964; fax: (330) 896-2956
e-mail: ycamp@akronymca.org
Web site: www.akronymca.org
Operated by: Akron YMCA, 209 S Main St, Akron, OH 44308 at (330) 376-1335

Group Rental Information
Site comments: Wonderful setting for any retreat or training. Private lake, great food, variety of facilities and opportunities.
Seasons & Capacity: Spring 300, Summer 300, Fall 300, Winter 300
Facilities: A/V Equipment, Cabins, Dorm-Style, Double Occupancy, Food Service, Hiking Trails, Lake, Lodges, Meeting Rooms, Playing Fields
Programs: Boating, Challenge/Ropes Course, Environmental Education, Horseback Riding, Swimming, Winter Sports (#3736)

YMCA Gtr Toledo Teen Camp

(est 2000)

Oregon, OH; (419) 531-2612
Vickie Bauman, Director

Camp comments: We Build strong kids, strong families, and strong communities.
Activities: Aquatic Activities, Arts/Crafts, Baseball/Softball, Camping Skills/Outdoor Living, Community Service, Field Trips, Leadership Development, Nature/Environment Studies, Swimming — Recreational, Team Building
Session lengths & capacity: June-August; 9 week sessions; 80 campers
Clientele & fees: coed 11-14; Fees: B ☀ 🐖
Contact: Vickie E Bauman, Branch Director at (419) 531-2612; fax: (419) 531-7722
Web site: www.ymcatoledo.org
Operated by: YMCA of Greater Toledo, Riverside Mercy Health Mark, 1500 N Superior St 2nd Fl, Toledo, OH 43604 at (419) 729-8135 (#41114)

YMCA Hilliard Adventure Camp

(est 1998)

Amlin, OH (Franklin Co.); (614) 276-8224
Stephanie Reese, Director

Camp comments: To serve the whole community through programs expressing Judeo-Christian principles that build a healthy spirit, mind, and body.
Activities: Baseball/Softball, Basketball, Counselor Training (CIT), Field Trips, Hiking, Nature/Environment Studies, Soccer, Sports — Field & Team, Swimming — Recreational, Team Building
Session lengths & capacity: June-August; 1 week sessions; 50 campers
Clientele & fees: coed 6-12; Fees: B ☀ 🐖
Contact: Stephanie Reese, Program Director at (614) 276-8224; fax: (614) 276-5579

Web site: www.ymcawillson.com
Operated by: YMCA Willson Outdoor Center, 2732 County Rd 11, Bellefontaine, OH 43311 at (937) 593-9001 (#45883)

YMCA Hoover Y Park Day Camp

(est 1983)

Lockbourne, OH (Franklin Co.); (614) 491-0980
Linda S Gaietto, Director

Camp comments: Program located on a beautiful 65 acre site with plenty of fun for all ages and a focus on the YMCA core values!
Activities: Aquatic Activities, Arts/Crafts, Challenge/Rope Courses, Climbing/Rappelling, Field Trips, Leadership Development, Nature/Environment Studies, SCUBA, Swimming — Recreational, Team Building
Session lengths & capacity: June-August; 1 week sessions; 100 campers
Clientele & fees: coed 6-14; Fees: B ☀ 🐖
Contact: Linda S Gaietto, Day Camp Director at (614) 491-0980; fax: (614) 491-1024
Web site: www.ymcawillson.com
Operated by: YMCA Willson Outdoor Center, 2732 County Rd 11, Bellefontaine, OH 43311 at (937) 593-9001

Group Rental Information
Facilities: Cabins, Hiking Trails, Meeting Rooms, Playing Fields
Programs: Challenge/Ropes Course, Environmental Education (#6709)

YMCA Jerry L Garver Day Camp

(est 1967)

Canal Winchester, OH (Franklin Co.);
(614) 834-9622
April Bush, Director

Camp comments: Day camp metro park location. Hiking, arts, crafts, sports, swimming, outdoor education.
Activities: Aquatic Activities, Arts/Crafts, Camping Skills/Outdoor Living, Counselor Training (CIT), Drawing/Painting, Hiking, Leadership Development, Nature/Environment Studies, Sports — Field & Team, Swimming — Recreational
Session lengths & capacity: June-August; 1 week sessions; 100 campers
Clientele & fees: coed 6-14; Fees: B ☀ 🐖
Contact: April Garrabrant, Program Director at (614) 834-9622; fax: (614) 834-9625
Web site: www.ymcawillson.com
Operated by: YMCA Willson Outdoor Center, 2732 County Rd 11, Bellefontaine, OH 43311 at (937) 593-9001 (#6761)

YMCA North Day Camps

(est 1974)

Columbus, OH (Franklin Co.); (614) 885-4252
Nancy Hoffman, Director

Camp comments: Day camp providing challenging activities in a natural setting to help children grow mentally, physically, and socially.
Activities: Arts/Crafts, Counselor Training (CIT), Dance, Drama, Drawing/Painting, Hiking, Nature/Environment Studies, Sports — Field & Team, Swimming — Recreational
Session lengths & capacity: June-August; 1 week sessions; 350 campers
Clientele & fees: coed 6-16; Fees: B ☀ 🐖
Contact: Nancy Hoffman, Program Director at (614) 885-4252; fax: (614) 885-6244
Web site: www.ymcawillson.com
Operated by: YMCA Willson Outdoor Center, 2732 County Rd 11, Bellefontaine, OH 43311 at (937) 593-9001 (#656)

YMCA of Gtr Toledo Day Camp
(est 1999)

Perrysburg, OH; (419) 251-9622
Mark Brunsman, Director

Camp comments: We build strong kids, strong families, strong communities.
Activities: Aquatic Activities, Archery, Arts/Crafts, Camping Skills/Outdoor Living, Fishing, Hiking, Nature/Environment Studies, Soccer, Swimming — Recreational, Team Building
Session lengths & capacity: June-August; 9 week sessions; 80 campers
Clientele & fees: coed 6-12; Fees: B ☀ 🐃
Contact: Mark Brunsman, Associate Executive Director at (419) 251-9622; fax: (419) 251-0970
Web site: www.ymcatoledo.org
Operated by: YMCA of Greater Toledo, Riverside Mercy Health Mark, 1500 N Superior St 2nd Fl, Toledo, OH 43604 at (419) 729-8135 (#33420)

YMCA Summer Down South Day Cmp (est 1958)

Canton, OH (Stark Co.); (330) 484-3909
Mickie Richards, Director

Camp comments: Summer Down South is a series of one week theme camps. Programming is built upon age appropriate activities and skills, and character values.
Activities: Arts/Crafts, Camping Skills/Outdoor Living, Counselor Training (CIT), Field Trips, Hiking, Horseback — Western, Nature/Environment Studies, Sports — Field & Team, Swimming — Recreational
Session lengths & capacity: June-August; 1 week sessions; 40 campers
Clientele & fees: coed 6-12; Fees: B ☀ 🐃
Contact: Web site: www.YMCAStark.org
Operated by: YMCA of Central Stark County, 405 Second St NW, Canton, OH 44702-1705 at (330) 580-4162 (#117)

YMCA Willson Outdoor Center
(est 1918)

Bellefontaine, OH (Logan Co.); (800) 423-0427
Anne Brienza, Director

Camp comments: Traditional year-round YMCA program. 1 hour NW of Columbus. Specialty camps: fishing, sports, horseback riding, golf, arts, wilderness, teens.
Activities: Aquatic Activities, Archery, Challenge/Rope Courses, Counselor Training (CIT), Golf, Horseback — Western, Leadership Development, Nature/Environment Studies, Swimming — Recreational, Team Building

ICON LEGEND
☀ Day Camp
🔺 Resident Camp
🏠 Facilities Available To Rent
�car Transportation Available
🐃 Financial Aid Available

FEE RANGES PER WEEK
A	$0-75
B	$75-200
C	$201-350
D	$351-500
E	$501-650
F	over $650

Session lengths & capacity: June-August; 1 & 2 week sessions; 200 campers
Clientele & fees: coed 7-17; families; Fees: A ☀ Fees: C 🔺 🐃
Contact: Anne Brienza, Executive Director at (937) 593-9001; fax: (937) 593-6194
e-mail: ywillson@bright.net
Web site: www.ymcawillson.com
Operated by: YMCA Willson Outdoor Center, 2732 County Rd 11, Bellefontaine, OH 43311 at (937) 593-9001

Group Rental Information
Site comments: Church retreats, family camps, meetings, beautiful lake, full meal service, great recreational activities.
Seasons & Capacity: Spring 200, Summer 386, Fall 200, Winter 200
Facilities: A/V Equipment, Cabins, Food Service, Hiking Trails, Lake, Meeting Rooms, Playing Fields
Programs: Boating, Challenge/Ropes Course, Environmental Education, Horseback Riding, Swimming, Winter Sports (#8368)

Oklahoma

Camp Arrowhead (est 1989)
Choctaw, OK; (405) 733-9622
Tammy Bratcher, Director

Camp comments: To put Christian principles into practice through programs that build a healthy spirit, mind and body.
Activities: Archery, Arts/Crafts, Camping Skills/Outdoor Living, Counselor Training (CIT), Drama, Field Trips, Fishing, Hiking, Sports — Field & Team, Swimming — Recreational
Session lengths & capacity: June-August; 1 week sessions; 75 campers
Clientele & fees: coed 6-12; Fees: A, B ☀
Contact: (405) 733-9622; fax: (405) 733-9626
Operated by: YMCA of Greater Oklahoma City, 500 N Broadway Ste 150, Oklahoma City, OK 73102 at (405) 297-7740 (#33771)

Camp Classen YMCA (est 1941)
Davis, OK (Murray Co.); (580) 369-2272
Albert P McWhorter, Director

Camp comments: Traditional program + teen adventure programs, specialty horse camp (live on the ranch), leadership training. School year environ. & conference programs avail
Activities: Archery, Backpacking, Camping Skills/Outdoor Living, Counselor Training (CIT), Horseback — Western, Leadership Development, Nature/Environment Studies, Riflery, Sailing, Wilderness Trips
Session lengths & capacity: February-December; 1, 2 & 7 week sessions; 225 campers
Clientele & fees: coed 8-17; families; seniors; single adults; Fees: C 🔺 🐃
Contact: Albert P McWhorter, Exec Director at (405) 297-7740; fax: (405) 297-7745
e-mail: amcwhort@ymcaokc.org
Operated by: YMCA of Greater Oklahoma City, 500 N Broadway Ste 150, Oklahoma City, OK 73102 at (405) 297-7740

Group Rental Information
Site comments: Coed summer camp ages 8-17. 2400 acres in Arbuckle Mts OK.
Seasons & Capacity: Spring 300, Summer 225, Fall 300
Facilities: A/V Equipment, Cabins, Double Occupancy, Food Service, Hiking Trails, Lake, Lodges, Playing Fields
Programs: Boating, Challenge/Ropes Course, Environmental Education, Horseback Riding, Swimming (#672)

Camp Fire USA Camp Happy Lake (est 1985)
Claremore, OK; (918) 341-1468
Vicki Proctor, Director

Camp comments: Happy Lake offers fun & adventure, located in a treed area on 25 acres along shore, campers are in small groups by age.
Activities: Archery, Arts/Crafts, Camping Skills/Outdoor Living, Canoeing, Hiking, Horseback — Western, Leadership Development, Nature/Environment Studies, Swimming — Recreational
Session lengths & capacity: 1 & 2 week sessions; 80 campers
Clientele & fees: coed 6-13; Fees: A ☀
Contact: Sharon Smith, Camping Service Director at (918) 592-2267; fax: (918) 592-3473
e-mail: campdirector33@hotmail.com
Operated by: Camp Fire USA Green Country, 706 S Boston, Tulsa, OK 74119 at (918) 592-2267 (#6357)

Camp Fire USA Camp Okiwanee
(est 1951)
Sapulpa, OK (Creek Co.); (918) 224-0216
Vicki Proctor, Director

Camp comments: Fun, safe traditional camp programs with emphasis on camper growth & development. Non Camp Fire members welcome
Activities: Arts/Crafts, Camping Skills/Outdoor Living, Drawing/Painting, Fishing, Hiking, Music, Nature/Environment Studies
Session lengths & capacity: June-June; 1 week sessions; 100 campers
Clientele & fees: coed 5-12; Fees: A ☀
Contact: Sharon Smith, Director at (918) 592-2267; fax: (918) 592-3473
Operated by: Camp Fire USA Green Country, 706 S Boston, Tulsa, OK 74119 at (918) 592-2267 (#667)

Camp Fire USA Camp Waluhili
(est 1949)
Chouteau, OK (Wagoner Co.); (918) 476-5482
Denny Winters, Director

Camp comments: Camper safety, growth & development are top priorities. Noncompetitive, esteem-building programs that are age-tailored.
Activities: Archery, Basketball, Bicycling/Biking, Canoeing, Climbing/Rappelling, Hiking, Horseback — Western, Leadership Development, Nature/Environment Studies, Sailing
Session lengths & capacity: June-July; 1 week sessions; 120 campers
Clientele & fees: coed 8-15; Fees: A ☀ Fees: B 🔺 🐃
Contact: Sharon Smith, Camp Director at (918) 592-2267; fax: (918) 592-3473
e-mail: campdirector33@hotmail.com
Operated by: Camp Fire USA Green Country, 706 S Boston, Tulsa, OK 74119 at (918) 592-2267

Group Rental Information
Seasons & Capacity: Spring 120, Summer 120, Fall 120
Facilities: Cabins, Dorm-Style, Food Service, Hiking Trails, Kitchen Facilities, Lake, Lodges, Meeting Rooms, Playing Fields
Programs: Environmental Education, Horseback Riding, Swimming (#669)

Camp Fire USA Shek-Ki-Ta-Wa
Cleveland, OK; (918) 592-2267
Vicki Proctor, Director

Camp comments: Traditional camp programs with camper safety, growth, and development top priority. Non camp fire members welcome.

Activities: Archery, Arts/Crafts, Camping Skills/Outdoor Living, Canoeing, Fishing, Hiking, Leadership Development, Nature/Environment Studies, Swimming — Recreational
Session lengths & capacity: July-July; 1 week sessions; 120 campers
Clientele & fees: coed 5-12; Fees: **A** ☀
Contact: Sharon Smith, Camping Services Director at (918) 592-2267; fax: (918) 592-3473
e-mail: campdirector33@hotmail.com
Operated by: Camp Fire USA Green Country, 706 S Boston, Tulsa, OK 74119 at (918) 592-2267 (#2264)

Camp Fire USA Took-A-Boo-Chee (est 1957) ☀

Catoosa, OK
Vicki Proctor, Director
Camp comments: Camper growth and development are top priorities. Noncompetitive esteem-building programs that are age-tailered.
Activities: Aquatic Activities, Archery, Arts/Crafts, Camping Skills/Outdoor Living, Fishing, Hiking, Nature/Environment Studies, Team Building
Session lengths & capacity: June-June; 150 campers
Clientele & fees: coed 5-12; 🐷
Operated by: Camp Fire USA Green Country, 706 S Boston, Tulsa, OK 74119 at (918) 592-2267 (#657)

Camp Greenbriar ☀

Oklahoma City, OK
Joey Capps, Director
Activities: Aquatic Activities, Archery, Arts/Crafts, Camping Skills/Outdoor Living, Field Trips, Swimming — Recreational
Session lengths & capacity: 1 week sessions
Clientele & fees: coed 6-12; Fees: **B** ☀ 🐷
Operated by: YMCA of Greater Oklahoma City, 500 N Broadway Ste 150, Oklahoma City, OK 73102 at (405) 297-7740 (#33802)

Camp Harrison ☀

Oklahoma City, OK
Kathryn Moore, Director
Activities: Aerobics/Exercise, Aquatic Activities, Archery, Arts/Crafts, Camping Skills/Outdoor Living, Counselor Training (CIT), Field Trips, Hiking, Nature/Environment Studies, Sports — Field & Team
Operated by: YMCA of Greater Oklahoma City, 500 N Broadway Ste 150, Oklahoma City, OK 73102 at (405) 297-7740 (#14533)

Camp Heart O'Hills ▲ ⌂

Welling, OK (Cherokee Co.); (918) 456-9882
Dan Beard, Director
Activities: Arts/Crafts, Canoeing, Challenge/Rope Courses, Fishing, Music, Performing Arts, Religious Study, Sports — Field & Team, Swimming — Recreational
Session lengths & capacity: May-October; 1/2, 1 & 4 week sessions; 450 campers
Clientele & fees: boys 7-18; girls 7-18; coed 7-18; families; seniors; single adults; Fees: **B** ▲ 🐷
Contact: Wendy Cochran, Guest Services Director at (918) 456-9882; fax: (918) 453-2400
Operated by: The Salvation Army A OK, PO Box 68, Welling, OK 74471 at (918) 456-9882
Group Rental Information
Seasons & Capacity: Spring 600, Winter 600
Facilities: A/V Equipment, Cabins, Dorm-Style, Double Occupancy, Food Service, Hiking Trails, Lake, Linens, Lodges, Meeting Rooms, Playing Fields, Pool, River, Tents
Programs: Boating, Challenge/Ropes Course, Swimming (#5786)

Camp Loughridge (est 1959) ☀ ⌂

Tulsa, OK (Creek Co.); (918) 446-4194
Mark Ewing, Director
Camp comments: A classic tradition in Christian camping. Located just 15 minutes from central Tulsa. Summer day camp programs for kids ages 6-13.
Activities: Aquatic Activities, Archery, Arts/Crafts, Basketball, Camping Skills/Outdoor Living, Canoeing, Challenge/Rope Courses, Counselor Training (CIT), Nature/Environment Studies, Swimming — Recreational
Session lengths & capacity: June-August; 1 week sessions; 160 campers
Clientele & fees: coed 6-13; Fees: **B** ☀
Contact: Lori Combs, Office Manager at (918) 446-4194; fax: (918) 446-3535
e-mail: lcombs@camploughridge.org
Web site: www.camploughridge.org
Operated by: Camp Loughridge, 4900 W 71st St, Tulsa, OK 74131 at (918) 446-4194
Group Rental Information
Site comments: 140 acres of beautiful wooded country with meeting, dining, lodging, and activity facilities. Available for rental by churches, individuals, and business groups
Seasons & Capacity: Spring 48, Summer 1608, Fall 48, Winter 48
Facilities: A/V Equipment, Dorm-Style, Food Service, Hiking Trails, Kitchen Facilities, Lake, Lodges, Meeting Rooms, Playing Fields, Pool, Tents
Programs: Boating, Challenge/Ropes Course (#3465)

Camp Peck ☀

Guthrie, OK
Erin Sweet, Director
Activities: Aerobics/Exercise, Aquatic Activities, Archery, Arts/Crafts, Camping Skills/Outdoor Living, Community Service, Field Trips, Hiking, Nature/Environment Studies, Sports — Field & Team
Clientele & fees: 🐷
Operated by: YMCA of Greater Oklahoma City, 500 N Broadway Ste 150, Oklahoma City, OK 73102 at (405) 297-7740 (#673)

Camp Woodmen ▲

Wewoka, OK; (405) 382-5469
Tommy G Azlin, Director
Activities: Archery, Backpacking, Boating, Canoeing, Counselor Training (CIT), Dance, Fishing, Leadership Development, Riflery, Swimming — Instructional
Session lengths & capacity: 1 week sessions
Clientele & fees: coed 8-15; Fees: **A** ▲
Contact: Tommy G Azlin, Fraternal Coord/Camp Director at (405) 948-8440; fax: (405) 948-8441
Operated by: WOW Life Insurance (TO), 1700 Farnam, Omaha, NE 68120 at (402) 271-7258 (#41027)

Cleveland County Family YMCA ☀

(est 1985)
Norman, OK; (405) 364-9200
Camp comments: We have over 15 activities on site, daily field trips & the greatest campers & staff in Oklahoma.
Activities: Arts/Crafts, Basketball, Field Trips, Leadership Development, Sports — Field & Team, Swimming — Recreational, Team Building
Session lengths & capacity: 1 week sessions; 180 campers
Clientele & fees: coed 6-16; Fees: **B** ☀ 🐷
Contact: Matt Eads, Youth & Teen Director at (405) 364-9200 ext. 25; fax: (405) 364-9799
Web site: www.ymcanorman.org

Operated by: Cleveland County Family YMCA, 1801 Halley Ave, Norman, OK 73069 at (405) 364-9200 (#26930)

E-Ko-Wah (est 1962) ▲

Marlow, OK (Stephens Co.); (405) 444-2519
Robyn Hazlett, Director
Camp comments: Girl Scout program in camp. Non-scouts welcome!
Activities: Archery, Arts/Crafts, Backpacking, Basketball, Camping Skills/Outdoor Living, Canoeing, Counselor Training (CIT), Leadership Development, Swimming — Recreational
Session lengths & capacity: June-August; 1/2 & 1 week sessions; 120 campers
Clientele & fees: girls 6-17; Fees: **B** ▲
Contact: Robyn Hazlett, Camp Director at (405) 224-5455; fax: (405) 222-2502
e-mail: soonergs@swbell.net
Operated by: Girl Scouts Sooner Council, 224 South 14th St Box 1466, Chickasha, OK 73023 at (405) 224-5455 (#7627)

Hudgens (est 1960) ▲

Mc Alester, OK (Pittsburg Co.); (918) 423-0031
Mark Long, Director
Camp comments: Beautiful setting. Waterfront, hiking, outdoor living, cabins, summer resident camps available for retreats year-round.
Activities: Archery, Backpacking, Boating, Camping Skills/Outdoor Living, Canoeing, Challenge/Rope Courses, Computer, Hiking, Riflery, Sailing
Session lengths & capacity: 1/2 & 1 week sessions; 167 campers
Clientele & fees: boys 6-17; families; Fees: **B** ▲
Contact: Sam Porter, Camp Director at (405) 942-3000 ext. 337; fax: (405) 942-5839
e-mail: sporter@bgco.org
Web site: www.bgco.org
Operated by: Baptist General Convention, 3800 N May, Oklahoma City, OK 73112-6506 at (405) 942-3800 (#653)

Kate Portwood Camp (est 1975) ▲ ⌂

Granite, OK (Greer Co.); (405) 535-4423
Robyn Hazlett, Director
Camp comments: Girl Scout program in camp. Non scouts welcome!
Activities: Archery, Arts/Crafts, Bicycling/Biking, Camping Skills/Outdoor Living, Climbing/Rappelling, Hiking, Horseback — Western, Nature/Environment Studies, Photography, Swimming — Recreational
Session lengths & capacity: June-August; 1/2 & 1 week sessions; 104 campers
Clientele & fees: girls 6-17; Fees: **B** ▲
Contact: Barbara Thompson, Director of Camping Services at (405) 224-5455; fax: (405) 222-2502
e-mail: soonergs@swbell.net
Operated by: Girl Scouts Sooner Council, 224 South 14th St Box 1466, Chickasha, OK 73023 at (405) 224-5455 (#3575)

Magic Empire Day Camps ☀ 🚗

(est 1927)
Tulsa, OK (Tulsa Co.); (918) 749-2551
Volunteers X 12, Director
Camp comments: 1 week session in various areas of the council. Outdoor education, badge work, affordable. Non-scouts welcome.
Activities: Archery, Arts/Crafts, Camping Skills/Outdoor Living, Canoeing, Counselor Training (CIT), Hiking, Leadership Development, Music, Nature/Environment Studies, Swimming — Recreational
Session lengths & capacity: May-June; 1 week sessions; 150 campers
Clientele & fees: girls 5-17; Fees: **A** ☀ 🐷

Contact: Pam Edge, Outdoor Program Manager at (918) 745-5220; fax: (918) 749-2556
e-mail: pam@mecgs.org
Web site: www.girlscouts.org/mecgs
Operated by: GSC of Magic Empire, 2432 E 51st St, Tulsa, OK 74105-6002 at (918) 749-2551 (#652)

New Life Ranch (est 1958)   ☀ ⚠ ⌂

Colcord, OK (Delaware Co.); (918) 422-5506
David Jaquess, Director

Camp comments: Focus is on Christian growth in relationships.40 years of outstanding camps for kids & families in the beautiful Ozarks.
Activities: Archery, Bicycling/Biking, Canoeing, Challenge/Rope Courses, Climbing/Rappelling, Counselor Training (CIT), Horseback — Western, Riflery, Swimming — Instructional, Tennis
Session lengths & capacity: June-August; 1/2 & 1 week sessions; 1920 campers
Clientele & fees: coed 8-18; families;
Fees: C ⚠ 🐖
Contact: Berry Enloe, Administrative Coordinator at (918) 422-5506; fax: (918) 422-5644
e-mail: berry@newliferanch.com
Operated by: New Life Ranch, RR 5 Box 306, Colcord, OK 74338 at (918) 422-5506
Group Rental Information
Facilities: Cabins, Food Service, Hiking Trails, Kitchen Facilities, Lake, Meeting Rooms, Playing Fields, Pool, River
Programs: Challenge/Ropes Course, Environmental Education, Horseback Riding, Swimming (#5719)

Northwest Optimist   ☀

Oklahoma City, OK
Toby Tobin, Director
Activities: Dance, Drama, Music, Performing Arts
Operated by: City of Oklahoma, Parks & Recreation Dept, 420 W Main Ste 310, Oklahoma City, OK 73102 at (405) 297-2386 (#49248)

Nunny-Cha-Ha (est 1956)   ⚠

Davis, OK (Murray Co.); (405) 369-3219
Lawana Roberts, Director

Camp comments: Outstanding Christian staff. Christian emphasis. Hiking, cookouts and leadership training.
Activities: Arts/Crafts, Clowning, Drama, Hiking, Leadership Development, Music, Nature/Environment Studies, Religious Study, Swimming — Recreational, Team Building
Session lengths & capacity: June-July; 1/2 & 1 week sessions; 160 campers
Clientele & fees: girls 10-18; Fees: B ⚠

ICON LEGEND

☀	Day Camp
⚠	Resident Camp
⌂	Facilities Available To Rent
🚐	Transportation Available
🐖	Financial Aid Available

FEE RANGES PER WEEK

A	$0-75
B	$75-200
C	$201-350
D	$351-500
E	$501-650
F	over $650

Contact: Lawana Roberts, Camp Director at (405) 942-3800; fax: (405) 942-5839
e-mail: lroberts@bgco.org
Web site: www.bgco.org
Operated by: Baptist General Convention, 3800 N May, Oklahoma City, OK 73112-6506 at (405) 942-3800 (#662)

Sellers Camp   ☀

Oklahoma, OK; (405) 685-3311
Operated by: City of Oklahoma, Parks & Recreation Dept, 420 W Main Ste 310, Oklahoma City, OK 73102 at (405) 297-2386 (#40840)

Southern Oaks   ☀

Oklahoma City, OK; (405) 631-5441
Teresa Hoddy, Director
Activities: Arts/Crafts, Ceramics/Pottery, Drama, Field Trips, Golf, Nature/Environment Studies, Sports — Field & Team
Operated by: City of Oklahoma, Parks & Recreation Dept, 420 W Main Ste 310, Oklahoma City, OK 73102 at (405) 297-2386 (#49247)

Tallchief Girl Scout Camp

(est 1981)   ⚠

Tulsa, OK (Tulsa Co.); (918) 749-2551
Sherri Burks, Director

Camp comments: Provide a traditional summer resident camp experience. Specialize in meeting the unique needs of girls. Lake setting.
Activities: Archery, Arts/Crafts, Bicycling/Biking, Camping Skills/Outdoor Living, Canoeing, Horseback — Western, Photography, Sailing, Waterskiing, Windsurfing
Session lengths & capacity: June-July; 1/2, 1 & 2 weeks sessions; 120 campers
Clientele & fees: girls 8-17; Fees: B ⚠ 🐖
Contact: Sherri Burks, Camp Director at (918) 745-5213; fax: (918) 749-2556
e-mail: sherri@mecgs.org
Web site: www.girlscouts.org/mecgs
Operated by: GSC of Magic Empire, 2432 E 51st St, Tulsa, OK 74105-6002 at (918) 749-2551 (#4093)

Tulsa County Park Dept   ☀

Tulsa, OK; (918) 596-5982
Session lengths & capacity: 1 week sessions
Clientele & fees: Fees: A ☀
Contact: Mike Woody, Park Services Superintendent at (918) 596-5982; fax: (918) 596-5997
e-mail: mwoody@tulsacounty.org
Operated by: Board of Tulsa County Comm, 500 S Denver Ave, Tulsa, OK 74127 at (918) 596-5000 (#41758)

Tulsa Park and Recreation Dept

(est 1977)   ☀

Tulsa, OK (Tulsa Co.); (918) 596-2490
Hugh McKnight, Director

Camp comments: Fun, safe summertime activities. Play Tulsa!
Activities: Aquatic Activities, Arts/Crafts, Ceramics/Pottery, Dance, Drama, Field Trips, Nature/Environment Studies, Skating, Sports — Field & Team, Swimming — Recreational
Session lengths & capacity: May-August; 2 week sessions; 50 campers
Clientele & fees: coed 6-12; Fees: A ☀
Contact: Lucy Dolman at (918) 596-7275; fax: (918) 596-2530
e-mail: ldolman@ci.tulsa.ok.us
Operated by: City of Tulsa Parks and Rec, 1710 W Charles Page Blvd, Tulsa, OK 74127 at (918) 596-7877 (#2210)

Wah-Shah-She (est 1961)   ⚠ ⌂

Bartlesville, OK (Osage Co.); (918) 336-8666
Becky Simpson, Director

Camp comments: Traditional camp program, emphasis on outdoor skills, recreation & water activities. Non girl scouts welcome.
Activities: Aquatic Activities, Archery, Arts/Crafts, Boating, Caving, Challenge/Rope Courses, SCUBA
Session lengths & capacity: June-July; 1/2 & 1 week sessions; 120 campers
Clientele & fees: girls 6-17; families;
Fees: B, C ⚠ 🐖
Contact: Becky Simpson, Assistant Executive Director at (918) 336-3378; fax: (918) 336-3377
e-mail: bluestemgs@aol.com
Operated by: Girl Scouts - Bluestem Council, 511 E 11th St, Bartlesville, OK 74003 at (918) 336-3378
Group Rental Information
Site Information: Food service available
Seasons & Capacity: Spring 210, Summer 210, Fall 210, Winter 120
Facilities: A/V Equipment, Dorm-Style, Double Occupancy, Food Service, Hiking Trails, Kitchen Facilities, Lake, Meeting Rooms, Playing Fields, Pool, Tents
Programs: Boating, Challenge/Ropes Course, Swimming (#654)

YMCA Camp Takatoka

(est 1913)   ⚠ ⌂ 🚐

Chouteau, OK; (918) 476-5191
Peter Cristnact, Director

Camp comments: Located in the heart of Green Country. On Lake Ft. Gibson. Offering a variety o f programs for 8-15 yr olds. Fun for all.
Activities: Archery, Canoeing, Challenge/Rope Courses, Climbing/Rappelling, Counselor Training (CIT), Horseback — Western, Sailing, Swimming — Recreational, Team Building, Waterskiing
Session lengths & capacity: May-August; 1/2, 1, 2 & 3 week sessions; 150 campers
Clientele & fees: boys 8-15; girls 8-15; coed 8-15; families; seniors; single adults; Fees: B, C, D ⚠ 🐖
Contact: Peter Cristnact, Camp Director at (918) 446-1424; fax: (918) 446-9879
Web site: www.camptak.com
Operated by: YMCA Camp Takatoka, 5400 S Olympia, Tulsa, OK 74107 at (918) 446-1424
Group Rental Information
Seasons & Capacity: Spring 200, Summer 200, Fall 200, Winter 200
Facilities: Cabins, Double Occupancy, Food Service, Hiking Trails, Lake, Meeting Rooms, Playing Fields, Pool
Programs: Boating, Challenge/Ropes Course, Horseback Riding (#312)

Oregon

B'Nai B'Rith Camp (est 1921)   ⚠ ⌂ 🚐

Otis, OR (Lincoln Co.); (541) 994-2218
Michelle Koplan, Director

Camp comments: B'nai B'rith Camp, located on a lakeside campus of the scenic Oregon coast, is the premier Jewish resident camp in the Pacific Northwest with varied activities.
Activities: Aquatic Activities, Arts/Crafts, Boating, Challenge/Rope Courses, Leadership Development, Performing Arts, Sailing, Swimming — Recreational, Tennis, Waterskiing
Session lengths & capacity: June-August; 1 & 3 week sessions; 175 campers
Clientele & fees: coed 8-16; families; seniors; Fees: D, E ⚠ 🐖
Contact: Michelle Koplan, Director at (503) 452-3444; fax: (503) 245-4233
e-mail: mkoplan@oregonjcc.org
Web site: www.bbcamp.org

Operated by: Mittleman JCC/B'nai B'rith Cmp, 6651 SW Capitol Hwy, Portland, OR 97219 at (503) 244-0111

Group Rental Information
Site comments: Sparkly water, shady trees, cozy cabins. The perfect spot to gather with friendsand family, or for your organization's event. Rent B'nai B'rith Camp.
Seasons & Capacity: Spring 250, Fall 250, Winter 250
Facilities: Cabins, Double Occupancy, Food Service, Kitchen Facilities, Lake, Lodges, Meeting Rooms, Ocean, Playing Fields, Pool, River
Programs: Boating, Challenge/Ropes Course, Swimming (#229)

Big Lake Youth Camp

(est 1962)

Sisters, OR
Rob Lang, Director

Camp comments: Big Lake values incl character dev., awesome campfire programs & exciting activities in God's great outdoors. Our caring staff tradition is celebrating 40 yrs!
Activities: Archery, Canoeing, Horseback — Western, Radio/TV/Video, Sailing, Sports — Field & Team, Swimming — Recreational, Waterskiing, Windsurfing
Session lengths & capacity: June-August; 1 week sessions; 260 campers
Clientele & fees: coed 7-17; families; Fees: **C** ▲
Contact: Donna Johnson, Secretary at (503) 652-2225; fax: (503) 654-5657
e-mail: biglake@biglake.org
Web site: www.biglake.org
Operated by: Big Lake Youth Camp, 13455 SE 97th Avenue, Clarkamas, OR 97015 at (503) 652-2225

Group Rental Information
Facilities: Cabins, Dorm-Style, Double Occupancy, Food Service, Hiking Trails, Kitchen Facilities, Lake, Lodges, Meeting Rooms, Playing Fields, River
Programs: Boating, Horseback Riding, Winter Sports (#269)

Camp Angelos

Corbett, OR; (503) 695-5267
Greg Malby, Director
Contact: Web site: www.campangelos.org
Operated by: Hellenic Educational Center, 32149 S E Stevens Road, Corbett, OR 97019 at (503) 695-5267

Group Rental Information
Facilities: Cabins, Dorm-Style, Kitchen Facilities, Lodges, Meeting Rooms (#34958)

Camp Christmas Seal (est 1975) ▲

Sistersood, OR (Clackamas Co.); (541) 595-6663
Dave Grieshammer, Director

Camp comments: The American Lung Association's residential summer camp for children with asthma. We provide an outdoor experience in a secure and controlled environment.
Activities: Aquatic Activities, Archery, Arts/Crafts, Bicycling/Biking, Canoeing, Challenge/Rope Courses, Fishing, Hiking, Swimming — Recreational, Team Building
Session lengths & capacity: 50 campers
Clientele & fees: coed 8-15; 🐷
Contact: Gail Murray, Asthma Program Coordinator at (503) 246-1997 ext. 20; fax: (503) 246-1924
e-mail: gail@lungoregon.org
Web site: www.lungoregon.org
Operated by: American Lung Assn of Oregon, 7420 SW Bridgeport Rd 200, Tualatin, OR 97224 at (503) 924-4094 (#40117)

Camp Cleawox (est 1929) ▲ ⋔ 🚌

Florence, OR (Lane Co.); (541) 997-5386
Don Truex CCD, Director

Camp comments: Beautiful setting on fresh water lake 1 mile from Pacific Ocean. Girl Scouts & non-members are welcome!
Activities: Aquatic Activities, Archery, Arts/Crafts, Boating, Camping Skills/Outdoor Living, Canoeing, Horseback — Western, Leadership Development, Nature/Environment Studies, Swimming — Recreational
Session lengths & capacity: June-August; 1/2, 1 & 2 week sessions; 100 campers
Clientele & fees: girls 6-17; families; Fees: **B, C, D** ▲ 🐷
Contact: Liz Vollmer-Buhl, Outdoor Program Executive at (541) 485-5911 ext. 116; fax: (541) 485-5913
e-mail: lvollmer-buhl@wrgirlscouts.org
Web site: www.wrgirlscouts.org
Operated by: Girl Scouts Western Rivers Cnl, 2292 Oakmont Way, Eugene, OR 97401 at (541) 485-5911

Group Rental Information
Facilities: Cabins, Hiking Trails, Kitchen Facilities, Lake, Lodges
Programs: Boating (#249)

Camp Howard (est 1953) ▲ ⋔ 🚌

Corbett, OR (Clackamas Co.); (503) 695-2972
Mike Raffaele, Director

Camp comments: Over 50 years of excellence in providing a well rounded program emphasizing living skills, values, and self-esteem building.
Activities: Archery, Arts/Crafts, Camping Skills/Outdoor Living, Canoeing, Counselor Training (CIT), Hiking, Nature/Environment Studies, Radio/TV/Video, Riflery, Swimming — Recreational
Session lengths & capacity: June-August; 1/2 & 1 week sessions; 152 campers
Clientele & fees: coed 7-14; Fees: **C** ▲ 🐷 🦌
Contact: Krista Von Borstel, Executive Director at (503) 231-9484; fax: (503) 231-9531
e-mail: cyopdx@aol.com
Operated by: Catholic Youth Organization, 825 NE 20th Ave 320, Portland, OR 97232 at (503) 231-9484

Group Rental Information
Site comments: Over 50 years of camping excellence in providing a well rounded program emphasizing living skills, values, and self esteem building.
Facilities: Cabins, Dorm-Style, Food Service, Hiking Trails, Kitchen Facilities, Meeting Rooms, Playing Fields, Pool
Programs: Environmental Education, Swimming (#247)

Camp Latgawa (est 1954) ▲ ⋔

Eagle Point, OR (Jackson Co.); (541) 826-9699
Eva LaBonty, Director

Camp comments: A small intimate camp in the Rogue Valley.Waterfalls, soda springs & creeks to explore. Experience Christian community.
Activities: Aquatic Activities, Archery, Arts/Crafts, Camping Skills/Outdoor Living, Counselor Training (CIT), Drama, Hiking, Nature/Environment Studies, Rafting, Team Building
Session lengths & capacity: 1/2 & 1 week sessions; 48 campers
Clientele & fees: coed 8-18; families; seniors; single adults; Fees: **A, B, C** ▲ 🐷
Contact: Eva LaBonty, Director at (541) 826-9699; e-mail: camplatgawa@grrtech.com
Web site: www.gocamping.org
Operated by: UM Camps of OR-ID Conference, 1505 SW 18th Ave, Portland, OR 97201 at (503) 226-7931

Group Rental Information
Seasons & Capacity: Spring 90, Summer 90, Fall 90, Winter 90 (#31917)

Camp Low Echo (est 1945) ▲ ⋔

Klamath Falls, OR; (541) 773-8423

Camp comments: Waterfront prop. Lake of the Woods, view of Mt.McLoughlin, emphasis on safe quality programs. Wkly theme sessions.
Activities: Aquatic Activities, Arts/Crafts, Boating, Camping Skills/Outdoor Living, Canoeing, Counselor Training (CIT), Hiking, Swimming — Recreational
Session lengths & capacity: July-August; 5 week sessions; 100 campers
Clientele & fees: girls 5-17; families; Fees: **B** ▲
Contact: Cindy Bright, Director of Program Services at (541) 773-8423; fax: (541) 857-8525
e-mail: WinemaGS@aol.com
Operated by: Winema GSC Inc, 2001 N Keeneway Dr, Medford, OR 97504 at (541) 773-8423

Group Rental Information
Seasons & Capacity: Spring 100, Summer 100, Fall 100
Facilities: Cabins, Kitchen Facilities, Lake
Programs: Boating, Swimming (#243)

Camp Lutherwood ▲ ⋔

Cheshire, OR
Activities: Climbing/Rappelling, Fishing, Horseback — English, Model Rocketry, Rafting, Religious Study
Contact: Web site: www.lutherwood.org
Operated by: Camp Lutherwood Association, 22960 Hwy 36, Cheshire, OR 97419 at (541) 998-6444

Group Rental Information
Facilities: Cabins, Dorm-Style, Food Service, Kitchen Facilities, Lodges, Pool, Tents
Programs: Horseback Riding, Swimming (#15394)

Camp Magruder (est 1945) ▲ ⋔

Rockaway Beach, OR (Tillamook Co.); (503) 355-2310
Ted Hulbert, Director

Camp comments: Enjoy Christian hospitality, outdoor recreation and nature discovery on the North Oregon coast.
Activities: Aquatic Activities, Archery, Arts/Crafts, Boating, Ceramics/Pottery, Challenge/Rope Courses, Counselor Training (CIT), Music, Nature/Environment Studies, Team Building
Session lengths & capacity: June-August; 1/2 & 1 week sessions; 150 campers
Clientele & fees: coed 8-18; families; seniors; single adults; Fees: **B, C** ▲ 🦌
Contact: Ted Hulbert, Director at (503) 355-2310; fax: (503) 355-8701
e-mail: director@campmagruder.org
Web site: www.gocamping.org
Operated by: UM Camps of OR-ID Conference, 1505 SW 18th Ave, Portland, OR 97201 at (503) 226-7931

Group Rental Information
Site comments: Ocean beach and freshwater lake offer recreation and ecology learning for youth and adults.
Seasons & Capacity: Spring 250, Summer 250, Fall 250, Winter 250
Facilities: A/V Equipment, Cabins, Dorm-Style, Double Occupancy, Food Service, Hiking Trails, Kitchen Facilities, Lake, Lodges, Meeting Rooms, Ocean, Playing Fields
Programs: Boating, Challenge/Ropes Course, Environmental Education, Swimming (#6612)

Camp Taloali Inc (est 1973) ▲ ⋔

Stayton, OR (Marion Co.)
Ken Irving, Director

Camp comments: A camp for children & youth who are deaf, hard of hearing and hearing children of deaf adults. Nestled in the foothills 111 acres of the Cascade Mountains.

Activities: Arts/Crafts, Basketball, Drama, Field Trips, Horseback — Western, Leadership Development, Nature/Environment Studies, Sports — Field & Team, Swimming — Recreational
Session lengths & capacity: July-August; 1 & 2 week sessions; 100 campers
Clientele & fees: coed 9-17; Fees: C △ 🐷
Contact: Ken Irving, Camp Director at (503) 769-6415;
e-mail: camptaloali@aol.com
Web site: www.taloali.us
Operated by: Camp Taloali Inc, PO Box 4658, Salem, OR 97302
Group Rental Information
Facilities: Cabins, Kitchen Facilities, Playing Fields, Pool (#12735)

Camp UKANDU △

Portland, OR; (503) 295-6422
Activities: Boating, Challenge/Rope Courses, Field Trips, Horseback — Western, Swimming — Recreational
Operated by: American Cancer Society NW, 2120 First Ave N Box 19140, Seattle, WA 98109 at (206) 283-1152 (#12847)

Easter Seals Oregon Camp Prgm △

(est 1952)

Corbett, OR (Maltnomah Co.); (503) 695-5388
Diane Mathews, Director

Camp comments: Quality camping opportunity for children and adults with disabilities. 2 to 1 camper/staff ratio.24 hour nursing staff.
Activities: Archery, Arts/Crafts, Fishing, Hiking, Nature/Environment Studies
Session lengths & capacity: July-August; 1 week sessions; 48 campers
Clientele & fees: coed 6-90; Fees: E △ 🐷
Contact: Diane Mathews, Camp Director at (541) 552-1199; fax: (541) 552-1199
e-mail: camp@oregonseals.org
Web site: www.or.easter-seals.org
Operated by: Easter Seals Oregon, 5757 SW Macadam Ave, Portland, OR 97201 at (503) 228-5108 (#245)

Gales Creek Diabetes Camp

(est 1952) △

Forest Grove, OR (Washington Co.); (503) 357-1793
Barbara Edwards/Brian Bolstad, Director

Camp comments: Helping children with diabetes since 1952. Emphasis on fun, friends & improvement of diabetes self-care skills.

ICON LEGEND

☀ Day Camp
△ Resident Camp
🏠 Facilities Available To Rent
🚐 Transportation Available
🐷 Financial Aid Available

FEE RANGES PER WEEK

A	$0-75
B	$75-200
C	$201-350
D	$351-500
E	$501-650
F	over $650

Activities: Arts/Crafts, Baseball/Softball, Basketball, Counselor Training (CIT), Hiking, Leadership Development, Soccer, Swimming — Recreational
Session lengths & capacity: June-August; 1 & 2 week sessions; 64 campers
Clientele & fees: coed 6-16; families;
Fees: C △ 🐷
Contact: Patti Sadowski, Executive Director at (503) 699-8433; fax: (503) 699-8457
e-mail: diabchld@aracnet.com
Web site: www.childrenwithdiabetes.com
Operated by: Gales Creek Camp Foundation, 415 N State Street #120, Lake Oswego, OR 97034 at (503) 699-8433 (#1234)

High Cascade Snowboard Camp

(est 1989) △ 🚐

Government Camp, OR (Clackamas Co.); (800) 334-4272
Victoria Malendoski/Sherrie Soumie, Director

Camp comments: Ultimate summer experience on beautiful Mt. Hood, OR. Ages 11 and up. Snowboard, skateboard, BMX/mountain bike, wakeboard & raft.
Activities: Aquatic Activities, Arts/Crafts, Bicycling/Biking, Golf, Hiking, Rafting, Skating, Snow Sports, Soccer, Waterskiing
Session lengths & capacity: June-August; 1 & 8 week sessions; 150 campers
Clientele & fees: coed 11-18; Fees: F △
Contact: Sherrie Soumie, Camp Director at (800) 334-4272; fax: (541) 389-6371
e-mail: highcascade@empnet.com
Web site: www.highcascade.com
Operated by: High Cascade Snowboard Camp, PO Box 6622, Bend, OR 97708 at (541) 389-7404 (#665)

Kilowan (est 1933) △ 🏠

Dallas, OR (Polk Co.); (503) 787-3605

Camp comments: Beautiful creeks, forest, 400+ acres. Other specialty & traditional Camp Fire program. Open to all youth.
Activities: Archery, Arts/Crafts, Camping Skills/Outdoor Living, Canoeing, Counselor Training (CIT), Hiking, Swimming — Recreational
Session lengths & capacity: June-August; 1, 2 & 3 week sessions; 80 campers
Clientele & fees: coed 5-18; Fees: B ☀
Fees: B, C △
Contact: Melissa Thiel, Director of Camping Services at (503) 581-0477; fax: (503) 581-0022
e-mail: melisaathiel@willamettecouncil.org
Web site: www.willamettecouncil.org
Operated by: Willamette Council Camp Fire, PO Box 6138, Salem, OR 97304 at (503) 581-0477
Group Rental Information
Facilities: Cabins, Dorm-Style, Double Occupancy, Kitchen Facilities, Lodges, Meeting Rooms, Pool
Programs: Environmental Education, Swimming (#255)

Mount Hood Snowboard Camp

(est 1991) ☀ △ 🏠

Rhododendron, OR; (503) 622-3044
Mary LaCesa, Director

Camp comments: Summer Snowboarding! Winter and Spring camps too! We offer all inclusinve snowboard camps for all ability levels. Visit www.snowboardcamp.com for details.
Activities: Snow Sports
Session lengths & capacity: June-August; 1 week sessions; 80 campers
Clientele & fees: boys 11-99; girls 11-99; coed 11-99; families; seniors; single adults;
Fees: F △
Contact: (800) 247-5552; fax: (503) 622-3553
e-mail: info@snowboardcamp.com
Web site: www.snowboardcamp.com

Operated by: Mount Hood Snowboard Camp, PO Box 140, Rhododendron, OR 97049 at (503) 622-3044
Group Rental Information
Site comments: Our facilities are available for groups. Custom camps can be quoted by request. Email info@snowboardcamp.com for information.
Seasons & Capacity: Spring 80, Summer 120, Winter 80
Facilities: Cabins, Dorm-Style, Double Occupancy, Food Service
Programs: Winter Sports (#11355)

Mt Hood Kiwanis Camp

(est 1933) △ 🏠

Government Camp, OR (Clackamas Co.); (503) 272-3288
Ev Coffey, Leann Horrocks, and Denise Wright, Director

Camp comments: For children & adults with disabilities. 1:1 counselor/camper ratio. Counselors are PSU students. Supervised by SpEd professionals. National Forest setting.
Activities: Aquatic Activities, Arts/Crafts, Canoeing, Challenge/Rope Courses, Fishing, Hiking, Horseback — Western, Nature/Environment Studies, Swimming — Recreational
Session lengths & capacity: June-August; 1 week sessions; 40 campers
Clientele & fees: coed 9-35; Fees: D △ 🐷
Contact: Jennifer Li, Programs Coordinator at (503) 452-7416; fax: (503) 452-0062
e-mail: mhkc@hevanet.com
Operated by: Mt Hood Kiwanis Camp, 9320 SW Barbur Blvd Ste 165, Portland, OR 97219-5430 at (503) 452-7416
Group Rental Information
Site comments: The camp exists to provide excellence in outdoor experiences to people with disabilities in order to enhance their personal growth and quality of life.
Seasons & Capacity: Spring 110, Fall 110, Winter 110
Facilities: A/V Equipment, Dorm-Style, Food Service, Hiking Trails, Kitchen Facilities, Lodges, River
Programs: Challenge/Ropes Course, Environmental Education, Winter Sports (#6296)

Namanu (est 1924) △ 🏠 🚐

Sandy, OR (Clackamas Co.); (503) 224-7800
Brian Hayes, Director

Camp comments: Over 600 acres of natural beauty in the foothills of the Cascade Mountains. A traditional camp experience for all ages.
Activities: Aquatic Activities, Archery, Arts/Crafts, Backpacking, Camping Skills/Outdoor Living, Hiking, Horseback — Western, Leadership Development, Nature/Environment Studies
Session lengths & capacity: July-September; 1/2, 1, 2 & 3 week sessions; 290 campers
Clientele & fees: coed 6-17; families;
Fees: C, D △ 🐷
Contact: Brian Hayes, Resident Camp Director at (503) 224-7800; fax: (503) 223-3916
e-mail: bhayes@portlandcampfire.org
Web site: www.portlandcampfire.org
Operated by: CF USA Portland Metro Council, 619 SW 11th Ave Suite 200, Portland, OR 97205-2694 at (503) 224-7800
Group Rental Information
Seasons & Capacity: Spring 300, Summer 300, Fall 300
Facilities: Cabins, Hiking Trails, Kitchen Facilities, Lodges, Meeting Rooms
Programs: Boating, Challenge/Ropes Course, Environmental Education, Swimming (#262)

Oregon 4H Center (est 1970)

Salem, OR (Polk Co.); (503) 371-7920

Camp comments: Center is capable of hosting a wide variety of outings: EE visits, conferences, retreats, family reunions, specialty camps and special events.
Session lengths & capacity: 1/2 & 1 week sessions
Clientele & fees: Fees: A ☀ Fees: B △
Contact: Connie Reid, Interim Manager at (503) 371-7920; fax: (503) 581-6696
e-mail: oregon4hcenter@proaxis.com
Operated by: Oregon 4H Foundation, Oregon State University, Ballard Extension Hall Rm 119, Corvallis, OR 97331-3608 at (541) 737-2602

Group Rental Information
Site comments: Centrally located outside Salem. Natural setting with modern facilities for camps, workshops, meetings and conferences.
Seasons & Capacity: Spring 180, Summer 234, Fall 180, Winter 60
Facilities: Cabins, Double Occupancy, Food Service, Hiking Trails, Kitchen Facilities, Meeting Rooms, Playing Fields, Pool, River
Programs: Boating, Environmental Education, Swimming (#12766)

Oregon Camp Cherith (est 1969)

Wamic, OR

Camp comments: Creative Christ-centered personal growth/skill building focus. Mature volunteer staff. Scenic rented Cascade site.
Activities: Archery, Arts/Crafts, Backpacking, Camping Skills/Outdoor Living, Canoeing, Climbing/Rappelling, Counselor Training (CIT), Religious Study, Swimming — Recreational
Session lengths & capacity: June-July; 1 week sessions; 80 campers
Clientele & fees: boys 8-18; girls 8-18; Fees: C △
Contact: Linda Plant, Camp Administrator at (541) 747-7798;
e-mail: 4a3147f49r@vyanet.com
Web site: www.cherith.com/oregon
Operated by: Oregon Camp Cherith Inc, 3467 Sue Ann Ct, Springfield, OR 97477 at (541) 747-7798 (#3192)

Suttle Lake United Methodist

(est 1918)

Sisters, OR; (541) 595-6663
Jane Petke, Director

Camp comments: Year-round recreation & Christian hospitality in Central OR. For all ages; facilities available for nonprofit groups
Activities: Aquatic Activities, Arts/Crafts, Bicycling/Biking, Camping Skills/Outdoor Living, Challenge/Rope Courses, Climbing/Rappelling, Rafting, Snow Sports, Team Building, Wilderness Trips
Session lengths & capacity: 1/2 & 1 week sessions; 250 campers
Clientele & fees: boys 6-18; girls 6-18; coed 6-18; families; seniors; single adults; Fees: B, C △ ➡
Contact: Jane Petke, Director at (541) 595-6663; fax: (541) 595-2818
e-mail: suttle@outlawnet.com
Web site: www.gocamping.org
Operated by: UM Camps of OR-ID Conference, 1505 SW 18th Ave, Portland, OR 97201 at (503) 226-7931

Group Rental Information
Site comments: A place apart to be together in beautiful central Oregon.
Seasons & Capacity: Spring 150, Summer 150, Fall 150, Winter 150
Facilities: A/V Equipment, Cabins, Double Occupancy, Food Service, Hiking Trails, Kitchen Facilities, Lake, Linens, Lodges, Playing Fields, River
Programs: Boating, Challenge/Ropes Course, Environmental Education, Swimming (#3558)

Tamarack (est 1935)

Sisters, OR (Jefferson Co.); (541) 595-6665
Matt Garcia, Director

Camp comments: Pristine mtn lake. Equestrian training wilderness camping. Develop skills/self-esteem.International staff fun & friends.
Activities: Aquatic Activities, Backpacking, Boating, Canoeing, Drama, Hiking, Horseback — English, Horseback — Western, Swimming — Instructional, Swimming — Recreational
Session lengths & capacity: June-August; 2, 3 & 4 week sessions; 90 campers
Clientele & fees: boys 8-12; girls 8-17; coed 12-17; families; Fees: D, E △
Contact: Tyler Silver, Camp Director/Owner at (541) 595-6665; fax: (541) 317-5904
e-mail: tamarack@empnet.com
Web site: www.camptamarack.com
Operated by: Tamarack, PO Box 97, Sisters, OR 97759 at (541) 595-6665

Group Rental Information
Site comments: Rustic lodge & cozy cabins on pristine mountain lake,delicious meals,ski & bike trails tranquil ambiance.
Seasons & Capacity: Spring 120, Fall 120, Winter 80
Facilities: A/V Equipment, Cabins, Dorm-Style, Double Occupancy, Food Service, Hiking Trails, Kitchen Facilities, Lake, Linens, Lodges, Meeting Rooms, Ocean, Playing Fields, Pool, River, Tents
Programs: Boating, Challenge/Ropes Course, Environmental Education, Horseback Riding, Swimming, Winter Sports (#256)

Triangle Lake Camp & Conf Ctr

Blachly, OR; (541) 927-6132
Dina Mikesell, Director

Camp comments: A Christian camp and year-round conference center for relaxation and renewal. Great food and peaceful setting.
Activities: Aquatic Activities, Arts/Crafts, Boating, Canoeing, Ceramics/Pottery, Counselor Training (CIT), Music, Swimming — Recreational
Session lengths & capacity: 1/2 & 1 week sessions; 65 campers
Clientele & fees: coed 5-17; families; Fees: C △
Contact: Dina Mikesell, Executive Director at (541) 927-6132; fax: (541) 927-3203
e-mail: service@trianglelake.com
Web site: www.trianglelake.com
Operated by: Episcopal Diocese of Oregon, 19291 Highway 36, Blachly, OR 97412 at (541) 927-6132

Group Rental Information
Seasons & Capacity: Spring 75, Winter 50
Facilities: Cabins, Double Occupancy, Food Service, Hiking Trails, Lake, Linens, Lodges, Meeting Rooms, Playing Fields
Programs: Boating, Environmental Education, Swimming (#4333)

Twin Rocks Friends Camp

(est 1918)

Rockaway Beach, OR; (503) 355-2284
Ken Beebe, Director

Camp comments: Christian camping programs for all ages. Located on 118 acres incl mountain trails, lakefront property, & modern accommodations. Just one block from the beach!
Activities: Aquatic Activities, Arts/Crafts, Camping Skills/Outdoor Living, Canoeing, Hiking, Leadership Development, Music, Religious Study, Team Building, Waterskiing
Session lengths & capacity: 1/2 & 1 week sessions; 325 campers
Clientele & fees: boys 9-11; girls 9-11; coed 12-18; families; seniors; single adults; Fees: B △
Contact: Dennis Littlefield, Associate Director at (503) 355-2284; fax: (503) 355-8341
e-mail: dennis@twinrocks.com
Web site: www.twinrocks.org

Operated by: Twin Rocks Friends Camp, PO Box 6, Rockaway, OR 97136 at (503) 355-2284

Group Rental Information
Site comments: Rental groups from 10 to 300. Located on 118 acres including mountain trails, lakefront property, & modern accommodations. Just one block from the beach!
Facilities: A/V Equipment, Cabins, Dorm-Style, Double Occupancy, Food Service, Hiking Trails, Kitchen Facilities, Lake, Linens, Lodges, Meeting Rooms, Ocean, Playing Fields, River
Programs: Boating, Environmental Education, Swimming (#36385)

Upward Bound Camp/Evans Creek (est 1978)

Lyons, OR (Marion Co.); (503) 897-2447
Jerry & Laura Pierce, Director

Camp comments: Highly trained committed staff serve persons w/disabilities. Forest/river recreation for individual choice & fun.
Activities: Aquatic Activities, Archery, Arts/Crafts, Basketball, Camping Skills/Outdoor Living, Drama, Fishing, Hiking, Music, Nature/Environment Studies
Session lengths & capacity: 1/2, 1, 2, 3, 4, 5 & 6 week sessions; 35 campers
Clientele & fees: boys 12-99; girls 12-99; coed 12-99; seniors; single adults; Fees: C △ 🐷
Contact: Jerry or Laura Pierce, Directors at (503) 897-2447; fax: (503) 897-4116
Web site: www.upwardboundcamp.org
Operated by: Upwardbound Camp Inc, 36155 North Fork Rd, Lyons, OR 97358 at (503) 897-2447

Group Rental Information
Site comments: Peaceful forest,clear rivers,great food,spirit of hospitality. Specializing in small groups & persons w/disabilities.
Seasons & Capacity: Spring 40, Fall 40, Winter 40
Facilities: Dorm-Style, Food Service, Hiking Trails, Meeting Rooms, River, Tents
Programs: Environmental Education (#6026)

Whispering Winds (est 1969)

Philomath, OR (Benton Co.); (503) 929-2342
Kelly Ronning, Director

Camp comments: Outdoor fun in an all girl, supportive environment.
Activities: Arts/Crafts, Backpacking, Camping Skills/Outdoor Living, Canoeing, Counselor Training (CIT), Field Trips, Horseback — Western, Leadership Development, Performing Arts, Swimming — Recreational
Session lengths & capacity: June-August; 1/2, 1 & 2 week sessions; 300 campers
Clientele & fees: girls 7-17; Fees: B △
Contact: Kelly Ronning, Director of Camping at (503) 581-2451; fax: (503) 581-7629
e-mail: glscouts@open.org
Operated by: Santiam GSC, 1922 McGilchrist SE, Salem, OR 97302 at (503) 581-2451 (#252)

Windells Snowboard Camp

(est 1988)

Sandy, OR; (800) 765-7669
Kim Larecy, Director

Camp comments: Windell's offers a fun,safe environment to learn to snowboard. It's the most complete camp experience!
Activities: Basketball, Bicycling/Biking, Boating, Radio/TV/Video, Skating, Snow Sports, Sports — Field & Team, Waterskiing
Session lengths & capacity: 1 week sessions; 200 campers
Clientele & fees: coed 10-99; families; seniors; single adults; Fees: F △
Contact: Kim Larecy, Reservations & Information at (800) 765-7669; fax: (503) 622-4582
e-mail: info@windells.com
Web site: www.windells.com

Operated by: Windells Snowboard Camp, PO Box 628, Welches, OR 97067 at (503) 970-9331 (#3842)

YMCA Camp Collins

(est 1926)   ☀ ▲ ⌂

Gresham, OR (Multnomah Co.); (503) 663-5813
Dimitri Stankevich, Director

Camp comments: Program designed to emphasize lifetime skills: Cooperation, acceptance of others, problem solving and decision making.
Activities: Aquatic Activities, Archery, Arts/Crafts, Challenge/Rope Courses, Climbing/Rappelling, Horseback — Western, Leadership Development, Nature/Environment Studies, Travel/Tour, Wilderness Trips
Session lengths & capacity: June-September; 1/2, 1 & 2 week sessions; 180 campers
Clientele & fees: coed 6-17; families; Fees: **B** ☀
Fees: **C** ▲ 🐖
Contact: Chris Glaser, Registrar at (503) 663-5813; fax: (503) 663-2323
e-mail: campcollins@ymca-portland.org
Web site: www.ymca-portland.org
Operated by: YMCA Of Columbia Willamette, 9500 SW Barbur Blvd #200, Portland, OR, 97219 at (503) 223-9622

Group Rental Information
Site comments: Rustic retreat center nestled on the Sandy River, 45 minutes east of Portland. High & low ropes course, large climbing tower. Groups of all sizes welcome.
Seasons & Capacity: Spring 250, Summer 250, Fall 250, Winter 250
Facilities: Cabins, Double Occupancy, Food Service, Hiking Trails, Kitchen Facilities, Lodges, Meeting Rooms, Playing Fields, Pool, River
Programs: Challenge/Ropes Course, Environmental Education, Horseback Riding, Swimming (#7395)

YMCA Camp Silver Creek

(est 1938)   ▲

Sublimity, OR (Marion Co.); (503) 873-7749
Matt Sampson, Director

Camp comments: Traditional resident camp located in beautiful surroundings of Silver Falls St Pk - an experience that lasts a lifetime.
Activities: Aquatic Activities, Archery, Arts/Crafts, Bicycling/Biking, Camping Skills/Outdoor Living, Canoeing, Hiking, Horseback — Western, International Culture, Leadership Development
Session lengths & capacity: June-August; 1 week sessions; 164 campers

---

ICON LEGEND

☀	Day Camp
▲	Resident Camp
⌂	Facilities Available To Rent
🚗	Transportation Available
🐖	Financial Aid Available

FEE RANGES PER WEEK

A	$0-75
B	$75-200
C	$201-350
D	$351-500
E	$501-650
F	over $650

Clientele & fees: boys 6-17; girls 6-17; coed 6-17; families; Fees: **C** ▲ 🐖
Contact: Matthew Sampson, Camp Director at (503) 399-2761; fax: (503) 581-9626
e-mail: sorymca@open.org
Operated by: Family YMCA Marion & Polk Co, 685 Court St NE, Salem, OR 97301 at (503) 399-2762 (#264)

YWCA Camp Westwind

(est 1936)   ▲ ⌂ 🚗

Neotsu, OR (Lincoln Co.); (541) 994-2393
Kim Wilson, Director

Camp comments: Traditional program on Oregon coast with horses, nature study, ropes course. Staff encourage adventure and personal growth.
Activities: Archery, Arts/Crafts, Camping Skills/Outdoor Living, Canoeing, Challenge/Rope Courses, Hiking, Horseback — Western, Leadership Development, Nature/Environment Studies, Team Building
Session lengths & capacity: 1 week sessions; 150 campers
Clientele & fees: coed 7-17; families; Fees: **C** ▲ 🐖
Contact: Kim Wilson, Camp Director at (503) 294-7472; fax: (503) 721-1751
e-mail: kimw@ywca-pdx.org
Web site: www.campwestwind.org
Operated by: YWCA of Greater Portland, 1111 SW Tenth Avenue, Portland, OR, 97205 at (503) 294-7472

Group Rental Information
Facilities: Cabins, Dorm-Style, Hiking Trails, Kitchen Facilities, Lodges, Meeting Rooms, Ocean, River (#267)

Pennsylvania

4H Camp Shehaqua (est 1970)   ▲

White Haven, PA (Carbon Co.); (570) 443-0678
Helaine Brown, Director

Camp comments: Resident camp for 4-H member in a 20 county region of PA. 4-H camp builds self-esteem & independent living skills.
Activities: Archery, Arts/Crafts, Camping Skills/Outdoor Living, Challenge/Rope Courses, Counselor Training (CIT), Hiking, Leadership Development, Nature/Environment Studies, Riflery, Swimming — Recreational
Session lengths & capacity: 1 week sessions; 149 campers
Clientele & fees: coed 8-13; Fees: **A** ▲ 🐖
Contact: Helaine Brown at (610) 489-4315; fax: (610) 489-9277
e-mail: hxbl@psu.edu
Operated by: Montgomery Co 4H, 1015 Bridge Rd Ste H, Collegeville, PA 19426 at (610) 489-4315 (#1482)

Agape Bible Camp (est 1963)   ▲ ⌂

Hickory, PA (Washington Co.); (724) 356-2268
Tom Reddinger, Director

Camp comments: Campers participate in a great variety of activities that teach problem solving,develop creativity, build relationships and nurture faith.
Activities: Arts/Crafts, Camping Skills/Outdoor Living, Canoeing, Fishing, Religious Study, Sports — Field & Team, Swimming — Recreational, Team Building
Session lengths & capacity: June-September; 1 week sessions; 50 campers
Clientele & fees: coed 5-15; Fees: **B** ▲ 🐖
Contact: Deb Jandt, Registrar at (412) 885-3371; fax: (412) 884-2211
e-mail: webmaster@campage.org
Web site: www.campagape.org

Operated by: Agape Bible Camp, 420 Nike Dr, Pittsburgh, PA 15235 at (412) 824-5945

Group Rental Information
Site comments: Beautiful rustic site available for week or weekend rental.
Seasons & Capacity: Spring 26, Summer 76, Fall 26
Facilities: Cabins, Double Occupancy, Food Service, Hiking Trails, Kitchen Facilities, Lodges, Meeting Rooms, Playing Fields, Pool, Tents
Programs: Swimming (#1723)

Allegheny Camp   ▲

Tyrone, PA (Huntington Co.); (814) 684-3000
Katherine Adame, Director

Camp comments: Safe, friendly, and creative environment which nurtures respect for nature, each other and for themselves.
Activities: Arts/Crafts, Canoeing, Challenge/Rope Courses, Dance, Drama, Drawing/Painting, Horseback — English, Horseback — Western, Performing Arts, Swimming — Recreational
Session lengths & capacity: June-August; 2, 3, 4 & 6 week sessions; 100 campers
Clientele & fees: girls 7-15; Fees: **F** ▲
Contact: Katherine Adame, Director at (814) 684-3000; fax: (814) 684-2177
e-mail: bestcamp@grier.org
Web site: www.bestcamp.org
Operated by: The Grier School, PO Box 308, Tyrone, PA 16686 at (814) 684-3000 (#13967)

Ambler YMCA Camp Fantastic

(est 1979)   ☀

Ambler, PA (Montgomery Co.)
Jo Ann Putney, Director

Camp comments: Summer, friends, and fun at YMCA Camp Fantastic! We build strong kids, strong families, strong communities.
Activities: Arts/Crafts, Baseball/Softball, Basketball, Drawing/Painting, Field Trips, Hockey, Performing Arts, Soccer, Swimming — Instructional
Session lengths & capacity: June-August; 1 week sessions; 120 campers
Clientele & fees: coed 6-12; Fees: **B** ☀ 🐖
Contact: Lindy Rote, Assoc Exec Director at (215) 628-9950; fax: (215) 628-4747
e-mail: lrote@philaymca.org
Web site: www.amblerymca.org
Operated by: Ambler Area YMCA, 400 N Bethlehem Pike, Ambler, PA 19002 at (215) 628-9950 (#44118)

Antiochian Village

(est 1978)   ▲ ⌂ 🚗

Bolivar, PA (Westmoreland Co.); (724) 238-9565
Rev Michael Nasser, Director

Camp comments: Promotes growth & awareness of the Orthodox Christian faith.
Activities: Arts/Crafts, Basketball, Canoeing, Challenge/Rope Courses, Hiking, Horseback — Western, Nature/Environment Studies, Religious Study, Soccer, Swimming — Recreational
Session lengths & capacity: June-August; 1 & 2 week sessions; 245 campers
Clientele & fees: coed 9-17; Fees: **C** ▲ 🐖
Contact: Rev. Michael Nasser, Camp Director at (724) 238-9565; fax: (724) 238-2102
e-mail: avcamp@antiochian.org
Web site: www.antiochian.org/antiochianvillage/camp
Operated by: Antiochian Orthodox Christian, 358 Mountain Rd, Englewood, NJ 07631 at (724) 238-9565

Group Rental Information
Seasons & Capacity: Spring 310, Fall 310
Facilities: A/V Equipment, Cabins, Double Occupancy, Hiking Trails, Lodges, Meeting Rooms, Playing Fields, Pool, Tents
Programs: Environmental Education (#4276)

Archbald (est 1920)

Kingsley, PA (Susquehanna Co.); (570) 289-4331
Shirley Kelly, Director

Camp comments: Celebrating over 80 years. All girls 6-17. Gen prog + specialty sessions - canoe trip, leadership, bicycling & back riding.
Activities: Archery, Arts/Crafts, Camping Skills/Outdoor Living, Canoeing, Challenge/Rope Courses, Hiking, Horseback — Western, Leadership Development, Nature/Environment Studies, Swimming — Recreational
Session lengths & capacity: July-August; 1 & 2 week sessions; 150 campers
Clientele & fees: girls 6-17; families; Fees: B
Contact: Shirley Kelly, Outdoor Program Specialist at (570) 344-1224; fax: (570) 346-7259
e-mail: spgsc@epix.net
Operated by: Scranton Pocono GSC, 333 Madison Ave, Scranton, PA 18510 at (570) 344-1224 (#2951)

Arrowhead Day Camp

(est 1956)

W Chester, PA (Chester Co.); (610) 353-5437
Howie or Ellen Gilbert, Director

Camp comments: Traditional & comprehensive day camp serving the main line area under same family since 1956 all inclusive tuition.
Activities: Aquatic Activities, Archery, Arts/Crafts, Challenge/Rope Courses, Computer, Gymnastics, Horseback — English, Nature/Environment Studies, Sports — Field & Team, Tennis
Session lengths & capacity: June-August; 4, 6 & 8 week sessions; 300 campers
Clientele & fees: coed 4-14; Fees: C
Contact: Howie or Ellen Gilbert, Owners/Directors at (610) 353-5437; fax: (610) 695-8118
e-mail: cheifarrowhead@arrowheaddaycamp.com

Web site: www.arrrowheaddaycamp.com
Operated by: Arrowhead Day Camp, 240 Dutton Mill Rd, West Chester, PA 19380 at (610) 644-1435 (#2459)

Ballibay Camps Inc (est 1964)

Camptown, PA (Bradford Co.); (570) 746-3223
Gerard, Dorothy & John Jannone, Director

Camp comments: Noncompetitive. Individual choice: theater, art, music, dance, video, radio, riding, swimming, tennis.
Activities: Arts/Crafts, Ceramics/Pottery, Dance, Drama, Drawing/Painting, Horseback — English, Music, Performing Arts, Radio/TV/Video, Tennis
Session lengths & capacity: June-August; 3, 4 & 7 week sessions; 150 campers
Clientele & fees: coed 6-16; Fees: E
Contact: Gerard or Dorothy Jannone, Owner/Director at (570) 746-3223;
fax: (570) 746-3691
e-mail: jannone@ballibay.com
Web site: www.ballibay.com
Operated by: Ballibay Camps Inc, 1 Ballibay Rd, Camptown, PA 18815 at (570) 746-3223 (#2278)

Bear Creek Camp (est 1974)

Bear Creek, PA (Luzerne Co.); (570) 472-3741

Camp comments: Pristine mtn top site. 3000 acres, environmental focus, noncompetitive, religious camp focusing on self-esteem.
Activities: Backpacking, Bicycling/Biking, Camping Skills/Outdoor Living, Challenge/Rope Courses, Climbing/Rappelling, Counselor Training (CIT), Hiking, Leadership Development, Nature/Environment Studies, Wilderness Trips
Session lengths & capacity: June-August; 1/2, 1 & 2 week sessions; 160 campers

Clientele & fees: coed 7-17; Fees: C
Contact: Bear Creek Camp at (570) 472-3741; fax: (570) 472-3742
e-mail: campinfo@bearcreekcamp.org
Operated by: E PA Lutheran Camp Corporation, PO Box 278, Bear Creek, PA 18602 at (570) 472-3741

Group Rental Information
Facilities: Cabins, Food Service, Hiking Trails, Kitchen Facilities, Lake
Programs: Boating, Environmental Education (#3447)

Breezy Point Day Camp Inc

(est 1955)

Upper Holland, PA (Bucks Co.); (215) 750-9786
Doug Wiik, Director

Camp comments: Our professionally run camp on 85 acres offers parents peace of mind. Kids love our waterslide!
Activities: Arts/Crafts, Challenge/Rope Courses, Computer, Drama, Golf, Horseback — English, Nature/Environment Studies, Soccer, Tennis
Session lengths & capacity: 4 & 8 week sessions; 600 campers
Clientele & fees: coed 3-14; Fees: C
Contact: Nina Gorsky, Administrative Director at (215) 752-1987;
Operated by: Breezy Point Day Camp, 1759 Musket Circle, Upper Holland, PA 19053 at (215) 750-9786 (#4644)

Briarwood Day Camp

(est 1985)

Furlong, PA; (215) 757-0888
Ted Levin, Director

Camp comments: Mature staff, beautiful setting, 40 plus acres of fun & excitement from ages 3-14, indoor facilities available.
Activities: Aquatic Activities, Archery, Arts/Crafts, Boating, Challenge/Rope Courses, Counselor Training (CIT), Drama, Gymnastics, Tennis
Session lengths & capacity: 4, 6 & 8 week sessions; 500 campers
Clientele & fees: coed 3-14; Fees: C ☀
Contact: Ted Levin, Director at (215) 757-0888; fax: (215) 702-1060
e-mail: brubabe13@aol.com
Operated by: Briarwood Day Camp, 10 Nikol Dr, Richboro, PA 18954 at (215) 757-0888 (#4651)

Bryn Mawr Camp (est 1921) ⛺ 🏠 🚙

Honesdale, PA (Wayne Co.); (570) 253-2488
Jane & Dan Kagan, Director

Camp comments: Traditional, spirited & highly structured environment. Special attention given to first time campers.
Activities: Arts/Crafts, Challenge/Rope Courses, Drama, Gymnastics, Horseback — English, Nature/Environment Studies, Soccer, Sports — Field & Team, Swimming — Recreational, Tennis
Session lengths & capacity: 8 week sessions; 340 campers
Clientele & fees: girls 5-15; Fees: F ⛺
Contact: Jane&Dan Kagan, Owners& Head Counselors at (717) 253-2488; fax: (717) 253-1342
e-mail: jane@campbrynmawr.com
Web site: www.campbrynmawr.com
Operated by: Bryn Mawr Camp, PO Box 612, Short Hills, NJ 07078-0612 at (973) 467-3518 (#5647)

Camp America Day Camp Inc

(est 1967) ☀ 🚙

Chalfont, PA; (215) 822-6313
Norma Levin, Director

Camp comments: Country setting. Warm, caring staff provide supportive atmosphere for your child to learn, laugh & grow. Join our family
Activities: Arts/Crafts, Baseball/Softball, Ceramics/Pottery, Challenge/Rope Courses, Computer, Counselor Training (CIT), Drama, Gymnastics, Soccer, Swimming — Instructional
Session lengths & capacity: June-August; 4, 6 & 8 week sessions; 425 campers
Clientele & fees: boys 6-14; girls 6-14; coed 2-14; Fees: C
Contact: Norma Levin, Director at (215) 822-6313; fax: (215) 822-3444
Operated by: Camp America Day Camp Inc, PO Box 737, Warrington, PA 18976 at (215) 822-6313 (#3222)

ICON LEGEND

☀ Day Camp

⛺ Resident Camp

🏠 Facilities Available To Rent

🚙 Transportation Available

🐷 Financial Aid Available

FEE RANGES PER WEEK

A	$0-75
B	$75-200
C	$201-350
D	$351-500
E	$501-650
F	over $650

Camp Arc Spencer (est 1974) ⛺ 🚙

Fombell, PA (Venango Co.); (724) 758-2260
Marc Grivna, Director

Camp comments: Rustic & scenic program for campers with mental retardation. Caring staff. Special activities geared toward individual.
Activities: Arts/Crafts, Camping Skills/Outdoor Living, Field Trips, Hiking, Music, Nature/Environment Studies, Swimming — Recreational
Session lengths & capacity: June-July; 1 week sessions; 55 campers
Clientele & fees: coed 5-99; Fees: C ⛺
Contact: Drew Grivna, Executive Director at (724) 775-1602; fax: (724) 775-2905
e-mail: arcbvr@cobweb.net
Operated by: ARC Beaver County Inc, 3582 Broadhead Rd Ste 202, Monaca, PA 15061 at (724) 775-1602 (#3414)

Camp ArthuReeta (est 1928) ⛺ 🚙

Schwenksville, PA; (610) 287-6299
Mike Sam, Kevin Ochs, Lew Horvitz, Director

Camp comments: Combining tradition and sports in a family environment.
Activities: Arts/Crafts, Challenge/Rope Courses, Drama, Golf, Gymnastics, Hockey, Sports — Field & Team, Swimming — Recreational, Tennis
Session lengths & capacity: June-August; 8 week sessions; 300 campers
Clientele & fees: coed 7-16; Fees: E ⛺
Contact: Lew Horvitz, Director at (215) 658-1225; fax: (215) 658-1277
e-mail: Lew@camparthureeta.com
Web site: www.camparthureeta.com
Operated by: Moonlight Mile Limited, 1630 Old York Rd, Abington, PA 19001 at (215) 658-1225 (#27233)

Camp Blue Diamond (est 1963) ⛺ 🏠

Petersburg, PA (Huntingdon Co.); (814) 667-2355
Dean & Jerri Heiser Wenger, Director

Camp comments: Mountain & lake setting near State College. Sandy beach, swimming, canoeing & surfbikes. Christian, ecumenical, non-copetitive, caring. Cave, river, bike camps.
Activities: Arts/Crafts, Canoeing, Climbing/Rappelling, Counselor Training (CIT), Hiking, Nature/Environment Studies, Performing Arts, Rafting, Religious Study, Swimming — Recreational
Session lengths & capacity: June-August; 1/2 & 1 week sessions; 80 campers
Clientele & fees: coed 7-18; Fees: B, C ⛺
Contact: Dean or Jerri Heiser Wenger, Executive Co-Directors at (814) 667-2355; fax: (814) 667-2152
e-mail: bludia@penn.com
Web site: www.campbluediamond.org
Operated by: Middle PA Dist Church Brethern, PO Box 240, Diamond Valley Road, Petersburg, PA 16669 at (814) 667-2355

Group Rental Information
Site comments: Well maintained modern retreat center & cabins. Located between State College & Altoona. Reasonable rates, spectacular woodland setting with recreational lake.
Seasons & Capacity: Spring 200, Summer 200, Fall 200, Winter 100
Facilities: A/V Equipment, Cabins, Dorm-Style, Double Occupancy, Food Service, Hiking Trails, Kitchen Facilities, Lake, Lodges, Meeting Rooms, Playing Fields
Programs: Boating, Challenge/Ropes Course, Swimming (#2538)

Camp Can Do ⛺

Lebanon, PA; (717) 273-6525
Sheryl Johnson, Director

Activities: Aquatic Activities, Archery, Camping Skills/Outdoor Living, Canoeing, Challenge/Rope Courses, Drawing/Painting, Fishing, Leadership Development, Model Rocketry, Swimming — Recreational
Contact: Web site: www.cancer.org
Operated by: American Cancer Society, PO Box 897, Hershey, PA 17033 at (717) 533-6144 (#4942)

Camp Can Do (est 1959) ☀ 🚙

Kulpsville, PA (Montgomery Co.); (215) 368-7000
Katherine Tobias, Director

Camp comments: Specialized Day Camp serving children from Montgomery County. Transportation available.
Activities: Arts/Crafts, Field Trips, Music, Sports — Field & Team, Swimming — Recreational
Session lengths & capacity: July-August; 6 week sessions; 45 campers
Clientele & fees: coed 5-21; Fees: B ☀ 🐷
Contact: (215) 368-7000; fax: (215) 368-1199
Web site: www.easterseals-sepa.org
Operated by: Easter Seals Southeastern PA, 468 N Middletown Road, Media, PA 19063 at (610) 565-2353 (#7020)

Camp Carefree (est 1976) ☀ 🚙

Coatesville, PA (Chester Co.); (610) 486-6220
Andrew Serdich, Director

Camp comments: Day camp serving children who are disabled. Transportation available for Chester County residents.
Activities: Arts/Crafts, Field Trips, Music, Nature/Environment Studies, Swimming — Recreational
Session lengths & capacity: July-August; 5 week sessions; 80 campers
Clientele & fees: coed 5-21; Fees: B ☀ 🐷
Contact: Marie Walker, Administrative Assistant at (610) 873-3990; fax: (610) 873-3992
Web site: www.easterseals-sepa.org
Operated by: Easter Seals Southeastern PA, 468 N Middletown Road, Media, PA 19063 at (610) 565-2353 (#154)

Camp Cayuga (est 1957) ⛺ 🏠 🚙

Honesdale, PA (Wayne Co.); (570) 253-3133
Brian Buynak, Director

Camp comments: Comprehensive facilities, great staff, fun trips, noncompetitive, over 60 activities:horses, trapeze, all sports. Specializeing in first-time campers since 1957
Activities: Aquatic Activities, Ceramics/Pottery, Challenge/Rope Courses, Gymnastics, Horseback — English, Performing Arts, Radio/TV/Video, Sailing, Sports — Field & Team, Tennis
Session lengths & capacity: June-August; 4 & 8 week sessions; 390 campers
Clientele & fees: coed 5-15; Fees: E ⛺
Contact: Lee White, Assistnat Director at (908) 470-1224; fax: (908) 470-1228
e-mail: info@campcayuga.com
Web site: www.campcayuga.com
Operated by: Camp Cayuga LLC, PO Box 151 Ste ACA, Peapack, NJ 07977 at (800) 422-9842

Group Rental Information
Site comments: Catering to groups since 1957. modern cabins, practice fields, indoor rehearsal buildings, large meeting rooms. Friendly staff. 3 hours from NYC/Ohiladelphia
Seasons & Capacity: Summer 390, Fall 390
Facilities: Cabins, Food Service, Hiking Trails, Lake, Meeting Rooms, Playing Fields, Pool
Programs: Boating, Swimming (#2089)

Camp Cherith In Pennsylvania

(est 1984) ⛺

Honey Brook, PA (Chester Co.)
Paula Worden/Jeff Sherwood, Director

Camp comments: Christ-centered, Bible-based program. Focus on individual uniqueness, appreciation of God's creation.
Activities: Archery, Arts/Crafts, Camping Skills/Outdoor Living, Canoeing, Counselor Training (CIT), Drama, Horseback — Western, Nature/Environment Studies, Riflery, Swimming — Instructional
Session lengths & capacity: July-July; 1 week sessions; 125 campers
Clientele & fees: boys 6-18; girls 6-18; Fees: C ⚠ 🐎
Contact: Paula Worden, Camp Director at (302) 738-8186; fax: (302) 738-8186
e-mail: quail_ccpa@msn.com
Web site: www.cherith.com
Operated by: Camp Cherith in Pennsylvania, 26 Broadfield Drive, Newark, DE 19713 at (302) 738-8186 (#3405)

Camp Conrad Weiser Bynden Wood (est 1948)

Wernersville, PA (Berks Co.); (610) 670-2267
Janet Marquis, Director
Camp comments: Exceptional 500 acre mountain top facility, qualified trained staff, over 50 yrs in operation. Large program selection
Activities: Archery, Challenge/Rope Courses, Hockey, Horseback — English, Riflery, Sailing, Sports — Field & Team, Swimming — Recreational, Tennis, Travel/Tour
Session lengths & capacity: June-August; 2 week sessions; 185 campers
Clientele & fees: coed 6-16; families; Fees: B ☀ Fees: D ⚠ 🐎
Contact: Thomas L McGrath, Executive Director at (610) 670-2267; fax: (610) 670-5010
e-mail: tmcgrath@smymca.org
Web site: www.smymca.org
Operated by: South Mountain YMCA, PO Box 147, Wernersville, PA 19565 at (610) 670-2267
Group Rental Information
Facilities: A/V Equipment, Cabins, Food Service, Lodges, Meeting Rooms, Playing Fields, Pool, Tents
Programs: Challenge/Ropes Course, Environmental Education, Horseback Riding, Swimming (#2537)

Camp Curiosity (est 1986)

Doylestown, PA; (215) 348-7221
Eugene G Leffever, Director
Camp comments: Where the curious come to learn and plan.
Activities: Bicycling/Biking, Challenge/Rope Courses, Fishing, Horseback — English, International Culture, Leadership Development, Soccer, Swimming — Instructional, Wilderness Trips
Session lengths & capacity: June-August; 1 week sessions; 600 campers
Clientele & fees: coed 3-16; Fees: C ☀ 🐎
Contact: Tom Hawxwell at (215) 348-7221; fax: (215) 348-0834
e-mail: gleft@aol.com
Web site: www.campcuriosity.com
Operated by: Curiosity Camp, 4425 Landisville Road, Doylestown, PA 18901 at (215) 348-7221 (#19809)

Camp Deer Valley YMCA

Fort Hill, PA; (814) 662-4005
Richard Deer, Director
Contact: Web site: www.ycamps.org
Operated by: YMCA Of Pittsburgh, 126 Nagel Rd, Fombell, PA 16123 at (412) 758-6238
Group Rental Information
Facilities: A/V Equipment, Cabins, Dorm-Style, Food Service, Linens, Meeting Rooms
Programs: Challenge/Ropes Course, Environmental Education, Winter Sports (#48437)

Camp Dumore (est 1957)

Media, PA (Delaware Co.); (610) 565-2353
Frances Carmen, Director
Camp comments: Day camp for children with physical disabilities and developmental disabilities.
Activities: Arts/Crafts, Drawing/Painting, Field Trips, Music, Nature/Environment Studies, Sports — Field & Team, Swimming — Recreational
Session lengths & capacity: July-August; 5 week sessions; 50 campers
Clientele & fees: coed 5-21; Fees: B ☀
Contact: (610) 565-2353; fax: (610) 565-5256
Web site: www.easterseals-sepa.org
Operated by: Easter Seals Southeastern PA, 468 N Middletown Road, Media, PA 19063 at (610) 565-2353 (#2392)

Camp Eder (est 1957)

Fairfield, PA (Adams Co.); (717) 642-8256
Mr. Mel Fleming, Director
Camp comments: Quality Christian programming in small group units. Noncompetitive. Leadership training. Mountain stream setting.
Activities: Arts/Crafts, Backpacking, Bicycling/Biking, Caving, Challenge/Rope Courses, Climbing/Rappelling, Counselor Training (CIT), Nature/Environment Studies, Photography, Swimming — Recreational
Session lengths & capacity: June-August; 1/2 & 1 week sessions; 96 campers
Clientele & fees: coed 6-17; families; Fees: C ⚠ 🐎
Contact: Christopher Fitz, Program Director at (717) 642-8256; fax: (717) 642-9797
e-mail: chris@campeder.org
Web site: www.campeder.org
Operated by: So PA Church of The Brethren, 914 Mount Hope Road, Fairfield, PA 17320 at (717) 642-8256
Group Rental Information
Site comments: 400 acres along peaceful stream in Blue Ridge Mts. Year-round well equiped lodges, cabins & recreational facilities. Programming & food service available.
Seasons & Capacity: Spring 125, Fall 125, Winter 125
Facilities: A/V Equipment, Cabins, Dorm-Style, Food Service, Hiking Trails, Kitchen Facilities, Lodges, Meeting Rooms, Playing Fields, Pool
Programs: Challenge/Ropes Course, Environmental Education, Swimming (#2549)

Camp Green Lane (est 1946)

Green Lane, PA; (215) 234-8666
Mel Brodsky, Director
Camp comments: A nurturing, structured camp where the uniqueness of every camper is treasured & fun & growth are daily companions.
Activities: Arts/Crafts, Baseball/Softball, Basketball, Bicycling/Biking, Challenge/Rope Courses, Drama, Gymnastics, Horseback — Western, Soccer
Session lengths & capacity: June-September; 4 & 8 week sessions; 320 campers
Clientele & fees: coed 6-16; Fees: D ⚠
Contact: Mel Brodsky, Owner/Director at (610) 834-3866; fax: (610) 834-4392
e-mail: melcgl@greenlane.com
Web site: www.greenlane.com
Operated by: Camp Green Lane, 1000 Germantown Pike F3, Plymouth Meeting, PA 19462 at (610) 270-1700
Group Rental Information
Facilities: Cabins, Food Service, Hiking Trails, Kitchen Facilities, Lake, Meeting Rooms, Playing Fields, Pool
Programs: Boating, Challenge/Ropes Course, Swimming (#2358)

Camp Henry Kaufmann (est 1957)

Bolivar, PA (Westermoreland Co.); (724) 235-2680
Juliene Grocham, Director
Camp comments: Girl Scout camp w/ a variety of traditional activities. Tents, tree houses, Adirondack shelters. Burro rides, fishing, kayaks & row boating. Girl/adult weekends
Activities: Archery, Arts/Crafts, Boating, Camping Skills/Outdoor Living, Challenge/Rope Courses, Climbing/Rappelling, Counselor Training (CIT), Rafting, Swimming — Recreational
Session lengths & capacity: June-August; 1/2 & 1 week sessions; 150 campers
Clientele & fees: girls 6-17; Fees: A, B ⚠ 🐎
Contact: (412) 594-2229; fax: (412) 391-4413
Web site: www.girlscouts-wpa.org
Operated by: Southwestern Pennsylvania GSC, 606 Liberty Ave, Pittsburgh, PA 15222-2721 at (412) 594-2218
Group Rental Information
Site comments: 1/2 camp available in summer. 5 tent units, dining hall & access to all other program facilities.
Seasons & Capacity: Spring 320, Summer 160, Fall 320, Winter 120
Facilities: Hiking Trails, Kitchen Facilities, Lodges, Meeting Rooms, Pool, Tents
Programs: Boating, Swimming (#1729)

Camp Joseph and Betty Harlam (est 1958)

Kunkletown, PA (Monroe Co.); (570) 629-1390
Arie Gluck, Director
Camp comments: Poconos. Arts, athletic program & swimming instruction. Jewish program with excellent staff and beautiful facility.

Activities: Aquatic Activities, Arts/Crafts, Basketball, Climbing/Rappelling, Drama, Radio/TV/Video, Soccer, Swimming — Instructional, Tennis
Session lengths & capacity: June-August; 4 week sessions; 500 campers
Clientele & fees: boys 8-17; girls 8-17; coed 8-17; Fees: **E ▲**
Contact: Rabbi Frank DeWoskin, Associate Director at (215) 563-8184; fax: (215) 563-1549
e-mail: camphariam@aol.com
Operated by: Union Amer Hebrew Congregation, 1511 Walnut Suite 401, Philadelphia, PA 19102 at (215) 563-8183 (#2428)

Camp Lambec (est 1947)   ▲ 🏠

N Springfield, PA (Erie Co.); (814) 922-7370
Mrs. Debra Moseley, Director

Camp comments: 1500' Lake Erie beach. Special sports & music camps. Extensive family camp programs serving newborns thru senior citizens.
Activities: Aquatic Activities, Archery, Arts/Crafts, Basketball, Boating, Music, Religious Study, Sailing, Sports — Field & Team, Tennis
Session lengths & capacity: June-August; 1 week sessions; 200 campers
Clientele & fees: coed 8-18; families; Fees: **B ▲ 🐷**
Contact: Lisa Miller, Camp Registrar at (724) 662-4481; fax: (724) 662-1080
e-mail: capnwp@shenango.org
Web site: www.capnwp.org
Operated by: Camping of the Presbyterian, 114 W Venango St, Mercer, PA 16137 at (724) 662-4481

ICON LEGEND

☀	Day Camp
▲	Resident Camp
🏠	Facilities Available To Rent
🚗	Transportation Available
🐷	Financial Aid Available

FEE RANGES PER WEEK

A	$0-75
B	$75-200
C	$201-350
D	$351-500
E	$501-650
F	over $650

Group Rental Information
Site comments: 1500' Lake Erie beach; 12 cabins (16 persons in 4-person rooms); 20-person lodge; adjacent bathhouses; dining hall; rec hall; church; play courts; boating pond.
Seasons & Capacity: Spring 200, Summer 200, Fall 200, Winter 30
Facilities: Dorm-Style, Kitchen Facilities, Lake, Playing Fields
Programs: Boating (#7452)

Camp Lee Mar (est 1953)   ▲ 🚗

Lackawaxen, PA (Pike Co.); (570) 685-7188
Ariel J. Segal, Director

Camp comments: Highly acclaimed program for children with mild to moderate developmental challenges. All camp activities & academics, speech & language therapy. Mature staff.
Activities: Academics, Arts/Crafts, Basketball, Computer, Drama, Drawing/Painting, Music, Soccer, Swimming — Instructional, Tennis
Session lengths & capacity: June-August; 7 week sessions; 160 campers
Clientele & fees: coed 5-21; Fees: **E ▲**
Contact: Ariel J Segal, Exec. Director at (215) 658-1708; fax: (215) 658-1710
e-mail: gtour400@aol.com
Web site: www.leemar.com
Operated by: Camp Lee Mar, 805 Redgate Rd, Dresher, PA 19025 at (215) 658-1708 (#12512)

Camp Lindenmere (est 1998)   ▲ 🚗

Henryville, PA; (570) 629-0240
Enid & Jerry Marcus, Director

Camp comments: Individualized programming for all campers with special consideration given to our youngest and first time campers.
Activities: Challenge/Rope Courses, Clowning, Computer, Counselor Training (CIT), Drama, Hockey, Horseback — English, Performing Arts, Skating, Tennis
Session lengths & capacity: 3, 6 & 9 week sessions; 250 campers
Clientele & fees: coed 7-17; Fees: **E, F ▲**
Contact: Enid & Jerry Marcus, Owner/Director at (888) 220-4773; fax: (208) 723-3288
e-mail: admin@camplindenmere.com
Operated by: UCA, PO Box 770096, Coral Springs, FL 33077 at (954) 422-7700 (#1907)

Camp Lohikan in the Pocono Mts (est 1957)   ▲ 🏠 🚗

Lake Como, PA (Wayne Co.); (570) 798-2707
Mark Buynak, Director

Camp comments: Superb staff, 1st time camper specialty, noncompetitive, 65 activities! All sports, arts, circus, horses, jet ski & fun!

Activities: Arts/Crafts, Camping Skills/Outdoor Living, Gymnastics, Horseback — English, Performing Arts, Radio/TV/Video, Sports — Field & Team, Swimming — Recreational, Tennis, Waterskiing
Session lengths & capacity: June-August; 4 & 8 week sessions; 400 campers
Clientele & fees: coed 6-15; Fees: **E ▲**
Contact: Kathy Wentworth, Administrator at (908) 470-9317; fax: (908) 470-9319
e-mail: mail@lohikan.com
Web site: www.lohikan.com
Operated by: Camp Lohikan LLC, PO Box 189A, Gladstone, NJ 07934 at (908) 470-9317

Group Rental Information
Seasons & Capacity: Spring 600, Summer 600, Fall 600, Winter 600
Facilities: A/V Equipment, Cabins, Dorm-Style, Double Occupancy, Food Service, Hiking Trails, Kitchen Facilities, Lake, Linens, Lodges, Meeting Rooms, Ocean, Playing Fields, Pool
Programs: Boating, Challenge/Ropes Course, Swimming (#4472)

Camp Louise (est 1969)   ▲ 🏠

Shickshinny, PA (Columbia Co.); (570) 759-8236
Jamie P Kozemko, Director

Camp comments: Traditional Girl Scout program. Campers enjoy a wide variety of activities in a noncompetitive, fun & caring environment
Activities: Aquatic Activities, Archery, Arts/Crafts, Boating, Camping Skills/Outdoor Living, Field Trips, Hiking, Nature/Environment Studies, Performing Arts
Session lengths & capacity: 1/2 & 1 week sessions; 120 campers
Clientele & fees: girls 6-17; Fees: **A, B, C ▲**
Contact: Jamie P Kozemko, Program Specialist, Property Manager at (570) 759-8236; fax: (570) 759-8254
e-mail: jkozemko@yahoo.com
Web site: www.pennswoodgirlscouts.org
Operated by: Penns Woods GSC, The Cross Valley Ctr Ste 206, 667 North River St, Plains, PA 18705-1024 at (717) 829-2631

Group Rental Information
Seasons & Capacity: Spring 120, Fall 120, Winter 52
Facilities: Cabins, Hiking Trails, Kitchen Facilities, Lake, Lodges, Meeting Rooms, Ocean, Pool, River, Tents
Programs: Boating, Environmental Education, Swimming (#7196)

Camp Nazarene (est 1958)   ▲ 🏠 🚗

Lahaska, PA (Bucks Co.); (215) 794-7284
James E Scott, Director

Camp comments: We are located in the beautiful Buckingham Mountains. A dynamite Christian camping program in God's great outdoors.
Activities: Aquatic Activities, Arts/Crafts, Baseball/Softball, Basketball, Camping Skills/Outdoor Living, Drama, Farming/Ranching/Gardening, Hiking, Nature/Environment Studies, Sports — Field & Team
Session lengths & capacity: June-August; 2, 4, 6 & 8 week sessions; 70 campers
Clientele & fees: coed 8-16; Fees: **B ▲ 🐷**
Contact: Debra Deshields, Board Director at (215) 223-9821; fax: (215) 223-9861
Operated by: Nazarene Baptist Church, 3975 Germantown Ave, Philadelphia, PA 19140 at (215) 223-9821

Group Rental Information
Site comments: The natural place to grow in christ, camp nazarene rests on 93 acres of land in the beautiful mountains of Bucks County, once a stop on the underground railroad
Seasons & Capacity: Spring 65, Fall 65

Facilities: Cabins, Dorm-Style, Food Service, Hiking Trails, Meeting Rooms, Playing Fields, Pool (#3930)

Camp Nazareth (est 1977) ⚠ 🏠

Mercer, PA (Mercer Co.); (724) 662-4840
David Zuder, Director

Camp comments: Scenic Christian Camp/Retreat/Conference Ctr, rolling hills of NW PA. Centralized location, easy access, PA Rts 80 & 79.
Activities: Arts/Crafts, Baseball/Softball, Basketball, Football, Hiking, Religious Study, Sports — Field & Team, Swimming — Recreational
Session lengths & capacity: June-August; 1, 2 & 3 week sessions; 176 campers
Clientele & fees: boys 8-18; girls 8-18; coed 8-18; Fees: B ⚠ 🐾
Contact: David Zuder, Director at (724) 662-4840; fax: (724) 662-4840
e-mail: nazareth@infonline.net
Web site: www.acrod.org
Operated by: Am Carpatho Russian Orthodox, 312 Garfield Street, Johnstown, PA 15906 at (814) 539-8086

Group Rental Information
Site comments: Scenic Christian Camp/Retreat/Conference Ctr, rolling hills of NW PA. Centralized location, easy access, PA Rts 80 & 79.
Seasons & Capacity: Spring 176, Fall 176
Facilities: Cabins, Dorm-Style, Double Occupancy, Food Service, Hiking Trails, Lodges, Meeting Rooms, Playing Fields, Pool
Programs: Environmental Education, Swimming (#3819)

Camp Netimus for Girls

(est 1930) ⚠ 🏠 🚗

Milford, PA (Pike Co.); (717) 296-6131
Donna A Kistler, Director

Camp comments: Community living, 40 activities offers warm, supportive, safe caring atmosphere. Have fun, belong, learn and contribute.
Activities: Aquatic Activities, Arts/Crafts, Camping Skills/Outdoor Living, Challenge/Rope Courses, Field Trips, Horseback — English, Leadership Development, Performing Arts, Sports — Field & Team, Waterskiing
Session lengths & capacity: June-August; 2, 4 & 8 week sessions; 145 campers
Clientele & fees: girls 7-16; Fees: E, F ⚠ 🐾
Contact: Widge & Adrian Hazell, Assist. Directors at (800) 225-0604; fax: (717) 296-6128
e-mail: netimus@warwick.net
Web site: www.netimus.com
Operated by: Camp Netimus Inc, 708 Raymondskill Rd, Milford, PA 18337 at (570) 296-6131

Group Rental Information
Site comments: Outdoor center fall and spring. Ideal for retreats, seminars, specialty camps. Food service available. Accomodate groups of 20 to 200. Cabins w/ half baths.
Seasons & Capacity: Spring 200, Fall 200
Facilities: A/V Equipment, Cabins, Dorm-Style, Double Occupancy, Food Service, Hiking Trails, Kitchen Facilities, Lake, Lodges, Playing Fields
Programs: Boating, Challenge/Ropes Course, Environmental Education, Swimming (#2371)

Camp Pennbrook (est 1993) ⚠ 🚗

Pennsburg, PA; (215) 679-1169
Flip Shulman, Director

Camp comments: Girls! Lose weight, feel great, have fun! We're not just a weight loss camp. Most land & water sports. Trips to Bdwy shows/concerts. 1:1 nutritional counseling.
Activities: Aerobics/Exercise, Aquatic Activities, Arts/Crafts, Basketball, Dance, Drama, Field Trips, Tennis

Session lengths & capacity: June-August; 2, 3, 4, 6, 7, 8 week sessions; 200 campers
Clientele & fees: girls 8-21; Fees: F ⚠
Contact: Flip Shulman, Owner/Director at (800) 442-7366; fax: (212) 254-6258
e-mail: camppennbrook@worldnet.att.net
Web site: www.camppennbrook.com
Operated by: Camp Pennbrook, 71 Eagle Notch Dr, Englewood, NJ 07631 at (212) 354-2267 (#2346)

Camp Poyntelle Lewis Village

(est 1949) ⚠ 🏠 🚗

Poyntelle, PA; (570) 448-2161
Deborah Shriber, Director

Camp comments: Caring, environment with diverse athletics, aquatics, and crafts. Incorporates Jewish culture and community service.
Activities: Arts/Crafts, Canoeing, Climbing/Rappelling, Drama, Horseback — English, Sailing, Sports — Field & Team, Swimming — Instructional, Tennis, Waterskiing
Session lengths & capacity: June-August; 4, 6 & 8 week sessions; 300 campers
Clientele & fees: coed 7-16; Fees: D ⚠ 🐾
Contact: Deborah Shriber, Executive Director at (718) 279-8690; fax: (718) 224-4676
e-mail: summers@poyntelle.com
Web site: www.poyntelle.com
Operated by: Samuel Field YM & YWHA Inc, 212 00 23rd Ave, Bayside, NY 11360 at (718) 279-0690

Group Rental Information
Facilities: Cabins, Dorm-Style, Double Occupancy, Food Service, Lake, Pool
Programs: Boating (#2190)

Camp R (est 1940) ⚠ 🚗

Rockwood, PA (Somerset Co.); (814) 352-9920
Gretchen Fay, Director

Camp comments: Co-ed residential camp located in Laurel Highlands. Rustic cabins & beautiful setting. Outstanding college age staff.
Activities: Archery, Basketball, Boating, Football, Hiking, Horseback — Western, Leadership Development, Nature/Environment Studies, Soccer, Sports — Field & Team
Session lengths & capacity: July-September; 8 week sessions; 72 campers
Clientele & fees: coed 7-14; Fees: B ⚠
Contact: Gretchen Fay, Executive Director at (412) 621-3342; fax: (412) 682-2428
Operated by: Catholic Youth Association, 286 Main St, Pittsburgh, PA 15201 at (412) 621-3342 (#1704)

Camp Redwing (est 1923) ⚠ 🏠

Renfrew, PA (Butler Co.); (412) 789-9401
Erika Metting, Director

Camp comments: Heated pool & water slide. Girl Scout camp with a variety of traditional camp activities. Non-Scouts are welcome.
Activities: Aquatic Activities, Bicycling/Biking, Camping Skills/Outdoor Living, Canoeing, Challenge/Rope Courses, Climbing/Rappelling, Counselor Training (CIT), Drama, Horseback — Western, Swimming — Recreational
Session lengths & capacity: June-August; 1/2, 1 & 2 week sessions; 120 campers
Clientele & fees: girls 6-17; families; Fees: B, C ⚠ 🐾
Contact: (412) 594-2229; fax: (412) 391-4413
Web site: www.girlscouts-wpa.org
Operated by: Southwestern Pennsylvania GSC, 606 Liberty Ave, Pittsburgh, PA 15222-2721 at (412) 594-2218

Group Rental Information
Site comments: Lodges & tent units available for lease - fall, spring, winter.
Seasons & Capacity: Spring 120, Fall 120, Winter 56
Facilities: Hiking Trails, Kitchen Facilities, Lodges, Pool, Tents

Programs: Boating, Swimming (#1717)

Camp Sandy Cove (est 1950) ⚠

White Haven, PA (Carbon Co.); (410) 287-5433
Tim Nielsen, Director

Camp comments: Nondenominational Christian camp in the Pocono Mountains of PA. Choose from 20 activities taught by trained staff.
Activities: Archery, Arts/Crafts, Camping Skills/Outdoor Living, Climbing/Rappelling, Counselor Training (CIT), Leadership Development, Martial Arts, Radio/TV/Video, Wilderness Trips
Session lengths & capacity: June-August; 1 week sessions; 124 campers
Clientele & fees: boys 7-15; girls 7-15; coed 7-15; Fees: C ⚠ 🐾
Contact: Tim Nielsen, Director at (410) 287-5433 ext. 454; fax: (410) 287-3196
e-mail: chieftimn@aol.com
Web site: ww.sandycove.org/camp.htm
Operated by: Morning Cheer Inc, 60 Sandy Cove Road, North East, MD 21901 at (410) 287-5433 (#3234)

Camp Setebaid (est 1978) ⚠

Winfield, PA; (570) 524-9090
Mark Moyer, Director

Camp comments: Setebiad services programs specialize in diabetes education. We offer a normal camping exp. for children with diabetes.
Activities: Archery, Arts/Crafts, Boating, Camping Skills/Outdoor Living, Counselor Training (CIT), Drama, Hiking, Nature/Environment Studies
Session lengths & capacity: August-August; 1 week sessions; 84 campers
Clientele & fees: coed 8-12; Fees: C ⚠ 🐾
Contact: Mark Moyer, Camp Administrator at (570) 524-9090; fax: (570) 523-0769
e-mail: info@setebaidservices.org
Web site: www.setebaidservices.org
Operated by: Setebaid Services Inc, PO Box 196, Winfield, PA 17889-0196 at (570) 524-9090 (#542)

Camp Shohola (est 1943) ⚠ 🏠 🚗

Greeley, PA (Pike Co.); (570) 685-7186
Frank Barger, Director

Camp comments: Strong staff and programming. Experienced leadership. Over 40 activity choices. Exceptional trips. High rate of return. Cabins with screens. Located on lake.
Activities: Basketball, Bicycling/Biking, Camping Skills/Outdoor Living, Challenge/Rope Courses, Horseback — English, Radio/TV/Video, Sailing, Sports — Field & Team, Tennis, Windsurfing
Session lengths & capacity: June-August; 4 & 8 week sessions; 155 campers
Clientele & fees: boys 8-16; Fees: E, F ⚠
Contact: Frank Barger, Director at (570) 226-4270; fax: (570) 685-4563
e-mail: shohola@ptd.net
Web site: www.netimus.com
Operated by: Camp Netimus Inc, 708 Raymondskill Rd, Milford, PA 18337 at (570) 296-6131

Group Rental Information
Site comments: Ideal for band camps, soccer clinics, church groups, family reunions.
Seasons & Capacity: Spring 200, Fall 200
Facilities: Cabins, Dorm-Style, Food Service, Hiking Trails, Lake, Lodges, Meeting Rooms, Playing Fields
Programs: Swimming (#2386)

Camp Speers Eljabar YMCA

(est 1948) ☀ ⚠ 🏠

Dingmans Ferry, PA (Pike Co.); (570) 828-2329
Lynette K Boheman, Director

Camp comments: 1100 scenic acres Pocono Mts YMCA camp teaches caring, respect, honesty, responsibility thru fun program. Experienced

Activities: Aquatic Activities, Arts/Crafts, Camping Skills/Outdoor Living, Challenge/Rope Courses, Counselor Training (CIT), Horseback — English, Kayaking, Leadership Development, Photography, Sailing
Session lengths & capacity: June-August; 2 week sessions; 310 campers
Clientele & fees: coed 8-16; families; seniors; Fees: B ☀ Fees: D ▲ 🐷
Contact: Susanne K Edmonds, Executive Director at (570) 828-2329; fax: (570) 828-2984
e-mail: speersy@ptdprolog.net
Web site: www.campspeersymca.org
Operated by: Camp Speers Eljabar YMCA, RR1 Box 89, Dingmans Ferry, PA 18328 at (570) 828-2329

Group Rental Information
Seasons & Capacity: Spring 400, Fall 400, Winter 400
Facilities: A/V Equipment, Cabins, Dorm-Style, Food Service, Hiking Trails, Lake, Linens, Meeting Rooms, Playing Fields, River
Programs: Boating, Challenge/Ropes Course, Environmental Education, Horseback Riding, Swimming, Winter Sports (#2283)

Camp Starlight (est 1947) ▲ 🚐

Starlight, PA; (570) 798-2525
David & Allison Miller, Director

Camp comments: Traditional full program including lacrosse. Many electives. Extensive indoor and outdoor facilities. Outstanding staff.
Activities: Arts/Crafts, Baseball/Softball, Basketball, Drama, Golf, Gymnastics, Hockey, Soccer, Tennis, Waterskiing
Session lengths & capacity: June-August; 7 week sessions; 400 campers
Clientele & fees: coed 7-16; Fees: F ▲
Contact: David & Allison Miller, Owners/Directors at (212) 644-4789; fax: (212) 644-4214
e-mail: info@campstarlight.com
Web site: www.campstarlight.com
Operated by: Camp Starlight, PO Box 288, Old Westbury, NY 11568 at (212) 644-4789 (#2977)

Camp Sunshine (est 1934) ▲ 🏠

Thornton, PA (Delaware Co.); (610) 459-5284

Camp comments: Camp Sunshine is a non-profit residential camp for youth "at-risk" and children that in most circumstances would not have the opportunity to attend camp.
Activities: Aquatic Activities, Challenge/Rope Courses, Fishing, Hiking, Nature/Environment Studies, Swimming — Instructional, Swimming — Recreational, Team Building
Session lengths & capacity: June-August; 6 week sessions; 110 campers

---

ICON LEGEND
☀   Day Camp
▲   Resident Camp
🏠   Facilities Available To Rent
🚐   Transportation Available
🐷   Financial Aid Available

FEE RANGES PER WEEK
A	$0-75
B	$75-200
C	$201-350
D	$351-500
E	$501-650
F	over $650

Clientele & fees: coed 7-12; 🐷
Contact: Richard T Garrett, Executive Director at (610) 459-5284; fax: (610) 558-2034
Operated by: Delaware Co Children's Camp As, PO Box 444, Media, PA 19063 at (610) 459-5284
Group Rental Information
Facilities: A/V Equipment, Cabins, Double Occupancy, Hiking Trails, Kitchen Facilities, Lake
Programs: Boating, Challenge/Ropes Course, Environmental Education, Swimming (#3735)

Camp Surefoot (est 1956) ☀ 🚐

Levittown, PA (Bucks Co.); (215) 945-7200
Bill Barnes, Director

Camp comments: Specialized day camp; community involvement with special activities. Overnight camping experience.
Activities: Arts/Crafts, Nature/Environment Studies, Sports — Field & Team, Swimming — Recreational
Session lengths & capacity: 5 week sessions; 50 campers
Clientele & fees: coed 5-21; Fees: B ☀
Contact: Patricia Van Artschlen, Admin Asst at (215) 945-7200; fax: (215) 945-4073
Web site: www.easterseals-sepa.org
Operated by: Easter Seals Southeastern PA, 468 N Middletown Road, Media, PA 19063 at (610) 565-2353 (#2436)

Camp Susquehannock For Boys (est 1905) ☀ ▲ 🏠 🚐

Brackney, PA (Susquehannock Co.); (570) 967-2323
Edwin H Shafer Jr, Director

Camp comments: Traditional camp that offers a variety of outdoor activities, including individual and team sports, challenge course and lake activities for each camper.
Activities: Arts/Crafts, Basketball, Challenge/Rope Courses, Climbing/Rappelling, Horseback — English, Nature/Environment Studies, Sailing, Soccer, Tennis
Session lengths & capacity: June-August; 2, 3, 4, 5 & 7 week sessions; 150 campers
Clientele & fees: boys 7-16; Fees: B ☀ Fees: F ▲ 🐷
Contact: Robert Slagle, Director at (866) 482-2677; fax: (410) 515-4316
e-mail: coachslagle@aol.com
Web site: www.susquehannock.com
Operated by: Camp Susquehannock Inc, RR1 Box 1375, Brackney, PA 18812 at (866) 482-2677
Group Rental Information
Seasons & Capacity: Spring 150, Summer 150, Fall 150
Facilities: Cabins, Dorm-Style, Food Service, Hiking Trails, Lake, Lodges
Programs: Boating, Challenge/Ropes Course, Swimming (#2349)

Camp Susquehannock For Girls (est 1986) ☀ ▲ 🚐

Friendsville, PA (Susquehannock Co.); (717) 553-2343
Holly and Dave Brown, Director

Camp comments: Traditional prog team & individual sports, crafts, outdoor pursuits & fun led by excellent staff. 750 acre private lake.
Activities: Aquatic Activities, Archery, Arts/Crafts, Camping Skills/Outdoor Living, Challenge/Rope Courses, Climbing/Rappelling, Hockey, Horseback — English, Soccer, Tennis
Session lengths & capacity: June-August; 2, 3, 4, 5 & 7 week sessions; 85 campers
Clientele & fees: girls 7-17; Fees: B ☀ Fees: F ▲ 🐷
Contact: Robert Slagle, Director at (866) 482-2677; fax: (410) 515-4316
e-mail: coachslagle@aol.com
Web site: www.susquehannock.com

Operated by: Camp Susquehannock Inc, RR1 Box 1375, Brackney, PA 18812 at (866) 482-2677 (#6310)

Camp Tioga (est 1997) ▲ 🚐

Thompson, PA; (570) 756-2660
Mike Wagenberg & Mike Kuznetz, Director

Camp comments: Our campers have the time of their lives. We focus on fun, friendships, and fantastic lifelong memories. COME JOIN US!
Activities: Arts/Crafts, Baseball/Softball, Basketball, Challenge/Rope Courses, Hiking, Nature/Environment Studies, Performing Arts, Soccer, Swimming — Instructional, Tennis
Session lengths & capacity: June-August; 4 & 8 week sessions; 200 campers
Clientele & fees: coed 8-14; Fees: F ▲
Contact: Ron or Mike Kuznetz & Mike Wagenberg, Directors at (516) 938-0894; fax: (516) 938-3184
e-mail: info@camptioga.com
Operated by: Camp Tioga, 1191 Old Country Road, Plainview, NY 11803 at (516) 938-0894 (#40070)

Camp Wayne for Boys and Girls (est 1921) ▲ 🚐

Preston Park, PA (Wayne Co.); (570) 798-2591
Noel & Georgeann Corpuel and Peter Corpuel, Director

Camp comments: Family owned since 1921. We provide a caring environment with outstanding staff. All sports, water, fine arts, cultural activities.
Activities: Arts/Crafts, Baseball/Softball, Basketball, Camping Skills/Outdoor Living, Golf, Gymnastics, Soccer, Sports — Field & Team, Tennis, Waterskiing
Session lengths & capacity: 8 week sessions
Clientele & fees: boys 6-16; girls 6-16; Fees: F ▲
Contact: Noel Corpuel, Owner/Director at (516) 889-3217; fax: (516) 897-7339
e-mail: Campwayneg@aol.com
Web site: www.campwaynegirls.com
Operated by: Camp Wayne for Boys & Girls, 12 Allevard St, Lido Beach, NY 11561 at (516) 889-3217 (#3487)

Camp Weequahic Inc (est 1953) ▲ 🚐

Lakewood, PA (Wayne Co.); (570) 798-2716
Gail Lustig, Director

Camp comments: Caring, traditional family. Creative programs, mature staff, specialties include canoe, land trips & ice skating. Outstanding waterfront, olympic pool,lit.
Activities: Aquatic Activities, Arts/Crafts, Baseball/Softball, Basketball, Gymnastics, Sailing, SCUBA, Soccer, Tennis, Waterskiing
Session lengths & capacity: 7 week sessions; 300 campers
Clientele & fees: coed 6-16; Fees: F ▲
Contact: Buddy Seffer, Director at (973) 736-5587; fax: (973) 736-2226
Operated by: Camp Weequahic Inc, 42 Underwood Dr, West Orange, NJ 07052 at (973) 736-5587 (#4788)

Camp William Penn (est 1953) ▲ 🚐

East Stroudsburg, PA (Pike/Monroe Co.); (570) 223-8458
Roland Chandler, Jr, Director

Camp comments: Pocono Mountain setting. Nature and outdoor based activities.
Activities: Arts/Crafts, Boating, Camping Skills/Outdoor Living, Canoeing, Hiking, International Culture, Nature/Environment Studies, Swimming — Recreational
Session lengths & capacity: July-August; 1 week sessions; 250 campers
Clientele & fees: boys 8-12; girls 8-12; Fees: A ▲
Contact: Rosemary Parrott, Secretary at (215) 683-3695;

Operated by: City of Philadelphia Rec Dept, 1515 Arch St 10th Flr, Philadelphia, PA 19102 at (215) 683-3694 (#3844)

Camps Equinunk & Blue Ridge

(est 1920)

Equinunk, PA; (570) 224-4121
Richard Kamen, Director

Camp comments: Traditional values. Modern environment. Diverse programs. Aquatics/sports/hobbies. High return of staff & campers.
Activities: Arts/Crafts, Baseball/Softball, Basketball, Climbing/Rappelling, Drama, Hockey, Soccer, Swimming — Instructional, Tennis, Waterskiing
Session lengths & capacity: June-August; 8 week sessions; 220 campers
Clientele & fees: boys 7-16; girls 7-16; Fees: F △
Contact: Sheryl Baker or Carolyn Cranham, Director at (631) 329-3239; fax: (631) 329-3023
Web site: www.campblueridge.com
Operated by: Camp Equinunk Blue Ridge, PO Box 808, East Hampton, NY 11937 at (631) 329-3239 (#2124)

Canadensis (est 1941)

Canadensis, PA (Monroe Co.); (570) 595-7461
Terri Saltzman, Steven Smilk, Toby Cohen, Director

Camp comments: An amazing camp with caring staff, varied programs. Over 60 activities.
Activities: Arts/Crafts, Baseball/Softball, Basketball, Bicycling/Biking, Boating, Ceramics/Pottery, Challenge/Rope Courses, Performing Arts, Sports — Field & Team, Tennis
Session lengths & capacity: June-August; 7 & 8 week sessions; 450 campers
Clientele & fees: coed 7-16; Fees: E △
Contact: Steven Smilk, Director at (215) 572-8222; fax: (215) 572-8298
e-mail: camp4you@aol.com
Web site: www.canadensis.com
Operated by: Camp Canadensis, Box 182, Wyncote, PA 19095 at (215) 572-8222

Group Rental Information
Seasons & Capacity: Spring 500
Facilities: Cabins, Dorm-Style, Food Service, Hiking Trails, Lake, Meeting Rooms, Playing Fields, Pool
Programs: Boating, Swimming (#3554)

Chen-A-Wanda (est 1939)

Thompson, PA (Susquehanna Co.); (570) 756-2016
Morey Baldwin, Director

Camp comments: Coed sleepaway camp w/great facilities, heated pool, beautiful lake, structured & elective program, land & water sports, musical theatre, go-carts, ATVs, ropes
Activities: Baseball/Softball, Basketball, Challenge/Rope Courses, Climbing/Rappelling, Golf, Hockey, Sailing, Soccer, Tennis, Waterskiing
Session lengths & capacity: June-August; 7 week sessions; 400 campers
Clientele & fees: coed 6-16; Fees: F △
Contact: Morey Baldwin, Director at (631) 643-5878; fax: (631) 643-0920
e-mail: cneier@aol.com
Web site: www.campchen-a-wanda.com
Operated by: Chen-A-Wonda, 8 Claverton Court, Dix Hills, NY 11747 at (631) 643-5878 (#3695)

Collegiate YMCA

Pittsburgh, PA; (412) 648-7960
Maria Conrad & Lila deKlaver, Director
Activities: Arts/Crafts, Field Trips, Sports — Field & Team, Swimming — Recreational
Contact: Web site: www.ycamps.org
Operated by: YMCA Of Pittsburgh, 126 Nagel Rd, Fombell, PA 16123 at (412) 758-6238 (#48438)

Conshatawba (est 1962)

Summerhill, PA (Cambria Co.); (814) 495-9300
Paula Peters, Director

Camp comments: Rustic setting Girl Scout camp focusing on Girl Scout Program in the outdoors. Tents, cabins and lodges.
Activities: Archery, Arts/Crafts, Camping Skills/Outdoor Living, Challenge/Rope Courses, Hiking, Horseback — Western, Nature/Environment Studies, Sports — Field & Team
Session lengths & capacity: June-August; 1/2 & 1 week sessions; 60 campers
Clientele & fees: girls 7-17; Fees: B △ 🚌
Contact: Frankie Graham, Program Director at (814) 536-5371; fax: (814) 536-5373
e-mail: fgrahamgstrg@netscape.net
Operated by: Girl Scouts of Talus Rock Cncl, 612 Locust St, Johnstown, PA 15901 at (814) 536-5371

Group Rental Information
Site comments: Rustic girl scout camp with winterized lodges.
Seasons & Capacity: Spring 100, Fall 100, Winter 64
Facilities: Cabins, Hiking Trails, Kitchen Facilities, Lodges, Playing Fields (#1707)

Crestfield (est 1948)

Slippery Rock, PA (Butler Co.); (412) 794-4022
Carolyn S Diercksen, Director

Camp comments: Crestfield uses small camper groups to develop Christian living skills and personal mastery.
Activities: Aquatic Activities, Arts/Crafts, Bicycling/Biking, Canoeing, Challenge/Rope Courses, Counselor Training (CIT), Leadership Development, Nature/Environment Studies, Sailing, Swimming — Recreational
Session lengths & capacity: June-August; 1/2 & 1 week sessions; 100 campers
Clientele & fees: coed 9-18; families; Fees: C △ 🚌
Contact: Peter Surgenor, CCD, Director at (724) 794-4022; fax: (724) 794-1665
e-mail: psurgen@nauticom.net
Web site: www.pgnpresbytery.org
Operated by: Pittsburgh Presbytery, 801 Union Place, Pittsburgh, PA 15212 at (412) 323-1400

Group Rental Information
Facilities: Cabins, Food Service, Hiking Trails, Lodges, Meeting Rooms, Pool (#1712)

Crystal Lake Camps (est 1949)

Hughesville, PA (Lycoming Co.); (717) 584-5608
Jessica Henderson, Director

Camp comments: Summer camp program for Christian Scientists only.
Activities: Archery, Bicycling/Biking, Canoeing, Challenge/Rope Courses, Counselor Training (CIT), Horseback — English, Leadership Development, Model Rocketry, Religious Study, Swimming — Instructional
Session lengths & capacity: 1 & 2 week sessions
Clientele & fees: coed 6-17; families; Fees: E △
Contact: Jessica Henderson, Director at (877) 252-5437; fax: (570) 584-0169
e-mail: camp@crystallakecamps.org
Web site: www.crystallakecamps.org
Operated by: Crystal Lake Camps Inc, 1676 Crystal Lake Rd, Hughesville, PA 17737-9797 at (570) 584-5608 (#2532)

Eagle Springs Programs

Pine Grove, PA; (570) 345-8705
Activities: Swimming — Recreational
Operated by: Eagle Springs Programs, 58 Eagle Springs Ln, Pine Grove, PA 17963 at (570) 345-8705 (#11257)

Echo Trail (est 1953)

Felton, PA (York Co.); (717) 927-6143

Camp comments: Camp serves all girls ages 5-17. Diverse, exciting program. Non-scouts are welcome.
Activities: Archery, Camping Skills/Outdoor Living, Canoeing, Challenge/Rope Courses, Field Trips, International Culture, Nature/Environment Studies, Swimming — Instructional, Swimming — Recreational
Session lengths & capacity: June-August; 1/2, 1 & 2 week sessions; 120 campers
Clientele & fees: girls 5-17; families;
Fees: A, B, C, D △ 🚌
Contact: Vicky Miley, Outdoor Program Administrator at (717) 757-3561; fax: (717) 755-1550
e-mail: vmiley@plgsc.org
Web site: wwwpennlaurel.org
Operated by: Penn Laurel GSC, 1600 Mt Zion Rd, PO Box 20159, York, PA 17402-0140 at (717) 757-3561

Group Rental Information
Facilities: Double Occupancy, Lodges, Meeting Rooms, River, Tents (#2552)

Elliott (est 1960)

Volant, PA (Lawrence Co.); (724) 533-3824
Linda Sue Wilson, Director

Camp comments: Exciting specialty sessions centered around traditional program. Mature staff promote an atmosphere of fun & friendship.
Activities: Archery, Arts/Crafts, Camping Skills/Outdoor Living, Gymnastics, Horseback — English, Horseback — Western, Leadership Development, Nature/Environment Studies, Swimming — Recreational
Session lengths & capacity: June-August; 1/2 & 1 week sessions; 60 campers
Clientele & fees: girls 5-17; Fees: A ☀
Fees: A, B, C △ 🚌
Contact: Betty Jeleniowski, Camp Director at (724) 774-3553 ext. 11-Jan; fax: (724) 728-0775
e-mail: bcgsc@brads.net
Web site: www.girlscouts-wpa.org
Operated by: GS of Beaver & Lawrence Co.Inc, 443 3rd Street, Beaver, PA 15009 at (724) 774-3553

Group Rental Information
Site comments: Situated along the Neshannock Creek near historic Volant, 100 acres provides two fully equipped lodges, platform tents, outdoor pool, and hiking trails.
Seasons & Capacity: Spring 40, Summer 40, Fall 40, Winter 40
Facilities: Dorm-Style, Hiking Trails, Kitchen Facilities, Lodges, Meeting Rooms, Playing Fields, Pool, Tents
Programs: Swimming (#1728)

Family YMCA Camp Skycrest

(est 1945)

Hawley, PA (Wayne Co.); (570) 253-1350
Lori L. Metz, Director

Camp comments: A growth oriented camp environment structured by traditional YMCA values of caring, respect, responsibility and honesty
Activities: Arts/Crafts, Boating, Camping Skills/Outdoor Living, Canoeing, Leadership Development, Sports — Field & Team, Swimming — Instructional, Team Building
Session lengths & capacity: June-August; 1, 2, 3, 4, 5, 6 week sessions; 120 campers
Clientele & fees: coed 7-14; families; Fees: C △
Contact: Tammy Korosec, Administrative Assistant at (610) 258-6158 ext. 14; fax: (610) 258-8903
e-mail: campskycrest@familyymca.org
Web site: www.familyymca.org
Operated by: Family YMCA Easton Phillipsbrg, 1225 W Lafayette St, Easton, PA 18042 at (610) 258-6158 (#2384)

Furnace Hills (est 1948) ⛰ 🏠

Denver, PA (Lancaster Co.); (717) 733-8515

Camp comments: Camp serves all girls ages 5-17. Diverse, exciting program. Penn. historical program. Non-scouts are welcome.
Activities: Arts/Crafts, Backpacking, Bicycling/Biking, Camping Skills/Outdoor Living, Canoeing, Field Trips, Horseback — English, Nature/Environment Studies, Swimming — Instructional, Swimming — Recreational
Session lengths & capacity: June-August; 1/2, 1 & 2 week sessions; 120 campers
Clientele & fees: girls 5-17; families; Fees: A, B, C, D ⛰ �🐷
Contact: Vicky Miley, Outdoor Progam Administrator at (717) 757-3561; fax: (717) 755-1550
e-mail: vmiley@plgsc.org
Web site: wwwpennlaurel.org
Operated by: Penn Laurel GSC, 1600 Mt Zion Rd, PO Box 20159, York, PA 17402-0140 at (717) 757-3561

Group Rental Information
Facilities: Lodges, Tents (#2541)

Gan Israel Country Day Camp

(est 1990) ☀ 🚐

Collegeville, PA; (610) 831-9700

Camp comments: Fun,safe,Jewish,place to be with Red Cross Swim,sports,nature,canoeing,arts & trips. Friendships, learning & fun!
Activities: Arts/Crafts, Camping Skills/Outdoor Living, Canoeing, Ceramics/Pottery, Community Service, Field Trips, Performing Arts, Religious Study, Sports — Field & Team, Swimming — Instructional
Session lengths & capacity: June-August; 4 week sessions; 200 campers
Clientele & fees: coed 5-13; Fees: C ☀ 🚐 🐷
Contact: Zalman Gerber, Rabbi/Director of Camp at (610) 896-9967; fax: (610) 896-9968
e-mail: cgiphila@ix.netcom.com
Operated by: Camp Gan Israel, Guideline Services, Inc, 7708 City Ave Ste 205, Philadelphia, PA 19147 at (215) 871-7600 (#3183)

Golden Slipper Camp (est 1948) ⛰

Stroudsburg, PA (Monroe Co.); (570) 629-1654
Steven Alper, Director

Camp comments: Our camp program rewards children with valuable new skills and self confidence for lifetime growth. A unique experience.

ICON LEGEND

☀ Day Camp
⛰ Resident Camp
🏠 Facilities Available To Rent
🚐 Transportation Available
🐷 Financial Aid Available

FEE RANGES PER WEEK

A $0-75
B $75-200
C $201-350
D $351-500
E $501-650
F   over $650

Activities: Aquatic Activities, Arts/Crafts, Baseball/Softball, Bicycling/Biking, Boating, Challenge/Rope Courses, Computer, Gymnastics, Waterskiing
Session lengths & capacity: June-August; 4 week sessions; 320 campers
Clientele & fees: coed 7-15; Fees: B ⛰ 🚐
Contact: Jennifer Wolov, Camp Administrator at (610) 660-0520; fax: (610) 660-0515
e-mail: jwolov@goldenslipper.org
Web site: www.goldenslippercamp.org
Operated by: Golden Slipper Club & Charity, 215 N Presidential Blvd 1st FL, Bala Cynwyd, PA 19004 at (610) 660-0520 (#2376)

Gretna Glen Camp (est 1948) ☀ ⛰ 🏠

Lebanon, PA (Lebanon Co.); (717) 273-6525

Camp comments: Christian program in small groups. Beautiful woodland setting with cabin living or rustic outpost area.
Activities: Aquatic Activities, Archery, Arts/Crafts, Boating, Challenge/Rope Courses, Drama, Music, Nature/Environment Studies, Religious Study, Travel/Tour
Session lengths & capacity: 1/2 & 1 week sessions; 85 campers
Clientele & fees: coed 4-18; Fees: B ☀ Fees: B, C ⛰
Contact: Paul Douglas, Manager/Director at (717) 273-6525; fax: (717) 273-6525
e-mail: gretglen@ptd.net
Web site: www.epaumc.org/camping
Operated by: E PA United Methodist Church, PO Box 820, Valley Forge, PA 19482 at (610) 666-9090

Group Rental Information
Facilities: A/V Equipment, Cabins, Food Service, Hiking Trails, Kitchen Facilities, Lake, Meeting Rooms, Pool
Programs: Boating, Challenge/Ropes Course, Swimming (#6597)

Habonim Dror Camp Galil

(est 1946) ⛰

Ottsville, PA; (610) 847-2505
Sharon Waimberg, Director

Camp comments: Jewish Israel cultural activities, simulates Kibbutz life, community-centered work groups, sharing, trips, Hebrew speaking.
Activities: Baseball/Softball, Challenge/Rope Courses, Community Service, Counselor Training (CIT), Farming/Ranching/Gardening, Field Trips, Leadership Development, Team Building
Session lengths & capacity: June-August; 3, 4 & 7 week sessions; 180 campers
Clientele & fees: coed 9-16; Fees: D ⛰ 🐷
Contact: Sharon Waimberg, Camp Administrator at (215) 968-2013; fax: (215) 968-2013
e-mail: campgalil@aol.com
Web site: www.campgalil.org
Operated by: Midstates Habonim Camping Assn, PO Box 1245, Newtown, PA 18940 at (215) 968-2013 (#19792)

Harrisburg Diabetic Youth Camp

(est 1977) ⛰

Millville, PA (Columbia Co.); (570) 524-9090
Mark Moyer, Director

Camp comments: The HDYC specializes in diabetes education. The camp offers a normal camping experience for children who happen to have diabetes.
Session lengths & capacity: June-June; 1 week sessions; 72 campers
Clientele & fees: boys 8-15; girls 8-15; coed 8-15; Fees: D ⛰
Contact: Mark Moyer, Director at (570) 524-9090; fax: (570) 523-0769
e-mail: info@setebaidservices.org
Web site: www.setebaidservices.org

Operated by: Setebaid Services Inc, PO Box 196, Winfield, PA 17889-0196 at (570) 524-9090 (#11412)

Heinz House Camp (est 1926) ⛰

Ellwood City, PA (Lawrence Co.); (724) 924-2174
Jennifer Roberts/Bob Bechtold, Director

Camp comments: We provide children with a variety of programs and activities. Every day is active and fun. The children participate in camping activities as well.
Activities: Aquatic Activities, Archery, Arts/Crafts, Boating, Camping Skills/Outdoor Living, Challenge/Rope Courses, Fishing, Sports — Field & Team, Swimming — Instructional, Swimming — Recreational
Session lengths & capacity: June-August; 2 week sessions; 79 campers
Clientele & fees: boys 7-14; girls 7-14; Fees: B ⛰
Contact: Jennifer Roberts, Camp Director at (412) 231-2377; fax: (412) 231-2428
e-mail: roberts@sarahheinzhouse.com
Web site: www.sarahheinzhouse.org
Operated by: Sarah Heinz House, One Heinz St, Pittsburgh, PA 15212 at (412) 231-2377 (#1732)

Henry J and Willemina B Kuhn D

(est 1950) ☀ 🚐

Horsham, PA (Montgomery Co.); (215) 542-7974
Frank R Gerome, Director

Camp comments: Serves economically needy children from targeted Philadelphia area schools.
Activities: Archery, Camping Skills/Outdoor Living, Nature/Environment Studies, Sports — Field & Team, Swimming — Instructional, Swimming — Recreational
Session lengths & capacity: June-August; 4 week sessions; 140 campers
Clientele & fees: coed 7-12; Fees: A ☀
Contact: Frank R Gerome, Executive Director at (215) 542-7974; fax: (215) 542-7457
e-mail: camps@i-bob.com
Web site: www.collegesettlement.org
Operated by: Kuhn Day Camp, 600 Witmer Rd, Horsham, PA 19044 at (215) 542-7974 (#6779)

Hidden Falls (est 1958) ⛰ 🏠 🚐

Dingmans Ferry, PA; (570) 828-2813
Ann Gillard, Director

Camp comments: Join the fun at Girl Scout camp! Horseback riding, aquatic activities, adventure programs, and more for all girls.
Activities: Aquatic Activities, Arts/Crafts, Backpacking, Boating, Canoeing, Climbing/Rappelling, Counselor Training (CIT), Horseback — English, Horseback — Western, Swimming — Recreational
Session lengths & capacity: June-August; 1, 2 & 3 week sessions; 200 campers
Clientele & fees: girls 9-17; Fees: B, C, D ⛰ 🚐 🐷
Contact: Dotti Martin, Volunteer Services Coordinator at (888) 564-4657 ext. 226; fax: (215) 564-6953
e-mail: dmartin@gssp.org
Web site: www.gssp.org
Operated by: GSC Southeastern Pennsylvania, PO Box 27540, Philadelphia, PA 19118-0540 at (215) 564-4657

Group Rental Information
Facilities: Cabins, Hiking Trails, Playing Fields, Tents
Programs: Environmental Education (#2412)

Holland Day Camp (est 1978) ☀ 🚐

Richboro, PA (Bucks Co.); (215) 598-3958
Nancy Sosnow, Director

Camp comments: Since 1978, we have provided children with a safe & fun-filled summer in a beautiful country setting. Our goal is to continue our 'tradition of excellence'.

Activities: Archery, Arts/Crafts, Baseball/Softball, Basketball, Boating, Challenge/Rope Courses, Hockey, Nature/Environment Studies, Tennis
Session lengths & capacity: June-August; 4, 6 & 8 week sessions; 350 campers
Clientele & fees: coed 3-14; Fees: C ☀
Contact: Nancy Sosnow, Owner/Director at (215) 598-3958; fax: (215) 322-7630
e-mail: nsosnow@aol.com
Operated by: Holland Day Camp, 167 W Lynford Rd, Richboro, PA 18954-1362 at (215) 598-3958 (#3026)

Indian Head Camp

(est 1940)   ▲ 🏠 🚗

Honesdale, PA (Wayne Co.); (570) 224-4111
Shelley & David Tager, Director

Camp comments: 8 week resident camp, outstanding facilities, broad based creative program which is differentiated by age & experience.
Activities: Arts/Crafts, Baseball/Softball, Basketball, Challenge/Rope Courses, Drama, Gymnastics, Sports — Field & Team, Swimming — Recreational, Tennis, Waterskiing
Session lengths & capacity: June-August; 8 week sessions; 475 campers
Clientele & fees: coed 7-17; Fees: F ▲
Contact: David & Shelley Tager, Directors at (914) 345-2155; fax: (914) 345-2479
e-mail: ihcisfun@indianhead.com
Web site: www.indianhead.com
Operated by: Indian Head Camp, PO Box 1199, Scarsdale, NY 10583 at (914) 345-2155

Group Rental Information
Site comments: Can accomodate groups up to 600 in May, Sept., & Oct. Programs developed to meet the group needs.
Seasons & Capacity: Spring 600, Fall 600
Facilities: A/V Equipment, Cabins, Food Service, Hiking Trails, Lake, Meeting Rooms, Playing Fields, Pool
Programs: Boating, Challenge/Ropes Course, Swimming (#2157)

Innabah Program Center

(est 1929)   ☀ ▲ 🏠

Spring City, PA (Chester Co.); (610) 469-6111
Christy Heflin, Director
Activities: Arts/Crafts, Camping Skills/Outdoor Living, Challenge/Rope Courses, Counselor Training (CIT), Hiking, Horseback — English, Music, Nature/Environment Studies, Religious Study, Swimming — Recreational
Session lengths & capacity: 1/2 & 1 week sessions; 160 campers
Clientele & fees: boys 4-18; girls 4-18; coed 4-18; families; seniors; Fees: B ☀ Fees: C ▲
Contact: Christy Heflin, Manager/Director at (610) 469-6111; fax: (610) 469-0330
e-mail: innabah@juno.com
Web site: www.epaumc.org/camping
Operated by: E PA United Methodist Church, PO Box 820, Valley Forge, PA 19482 at (610) 666-9090

Group Rental Information
Facilities: A/V Equipment, Cabins, Food Service, Hiking Trails, Linens, Lodges, Meeting Rooms, Playing Fields, Pool
Programs: Boating, Challenge/Ropes Course, Swimming (#2020)

International Sports Training

(est 1991)   ▲ 🏠

Stroudsburg, PA; (570) 620-2267
Mark Major, Director

Camp comments: ISTC's dedicated to providing a complete and comprehensive training to our campers in a safe and fun environment condusive to learning!

Activities: Baseball/Softball, Basketball, Challenge/Rope Courses, Gymnastics, Horseback — Western, Kayaking, Soccer, Sports — Field & Team
Session lengths & capacity: June-August; 1 week sessions; 200 campers
Clientele & fees: coed 8-18; Fees: D, E ▲
Contact: Mark Major, Camp Director at (570) 620-2267; fax: (570) 620-1692
e-mail: mark@international-sports.com
Web site: www.international-sports.com
Operated by: International Sports Training, 1100 Twin Lake Road, Stroudsburg, PA 18360-8143 at (570) 620-2267

Group Rental Information
Facilities: Double Occupancy, Food Service, Hiking Trails, Kitchen Facilities, Lake, Lodges, Ocean, Playing Fields
Programs: Boating, Challenge/Ropes Course, Horseback Riding, Swimming (#27903)

Judson Baptist Camp & Retreat

(est 1949)   ☀ ▲ 🏠

N Springfield, PA (Erie Co.); (814) 922-3834
Activities: Archery, Arts/Crafts, Bicycling/Biking, Canoeing, Horseback — Western, Nature/Environment Studies, Sailing, Sports — Field & Team, Swimming — Instructional, Swimming — Recreational
Contact: Web site: www.campjudson.com
Operated by: American Baptist Churches NWPA, 398 Holliday Road, N Springfield, PA 16430 at (814) 922-3834

Group Rental Information
Facilities: A/V Equipment, Cabins, Food Service, Hiking Trails, Kitchen Facilities, Lake, Linens, Meeting Rooms, Playing Fields, Pool
Programs: Boating, Horseback Riding, Swimming (#7652)

Keystone Pocono Residence/ Camp (est 1964)

☀ ▲ 🚗

Gouldsboro, PA (Lackawanna Co.); (570) 270-3210
Gloria J Lance M.S., Director

Camp comments: Outstanding camp for youth and adults with mental retardation. Experienced staff creative program w/modern facilities.
Activities: Arts/Crafts, Camping Skills/Outdoor Living, Clowning, Dance, Field Trips, International Culture, Music, Nature/Environment Studies, Sports — Field & Team, Swimming — Recreational
Session lengths & capacity: Year-round; 2, 8 & 9 week sessions; 100 campers
Clientele & fees: boys 6-66; girls 6-66; coed 6-66; seniors; single adults; Fees: C ☀ Fees: E ▲
Contact: Gloria Lance M.S., Camp Director at (570) 207-3210; fax: (570) 842-2158
e-mail: campkey4u@aol.com
Web site: www.campkey.com
Operated by: Keystone Community Resrcs Inc, PO Box 711, Scranton, PA 18501-0711 at (717) 346-7561 (#2414)

Kirchenwald (est 1969)

☀ ▲ 🏠

Colebrook, PA (Lebanon Co.); (717) 964-3121
Michael Youse, Director

Camp comments: Provides children a unique place to grow. Bible study, nature activities and adventure camps are led by trained staff.
Activities: Aquatic Activities, Arts/Crafts, Backpacking, Bicycling/Biking, Camping Skills/Outdoor Living, Climbing/Rappelling, Kayaking, Nature/Environment Studies, Religious Study, Wilderness Trips
Session lengths & capacity: June-August; 1/2 & 1 week sessions; 80 campers
Clientele & fees: coed 6-17; Fees: C ▲
Contact: Michael Youse, Director at (717) 964-3121;
e-mail: kirchenwald@lutherancamping.org
Web site: www.lutherancamping.org

Operated by: Lutheran Camping Ctrl Penn, Box 459, Arendtsville, PA 17303 at (717) 677-8211

Group Rental Information
Seasons & Capacity: Spring 32, Fall 32, Winter 32
Facilities: Cabins, Dorm-Style, Hiking Trails, Kitchen Facilities, Lodges, Meeting Rooms, River
Programs: Challenge/Ropes Course, Environmental Education, Winter Sports (#19853)

Kirkwood Camp (est 1960)

▲ 🏠

Stroudsburg, PA; (570) 421-2269
Bruce Shelton, Director

Camp comments: Magnificent mtn setting fast water stream for tubing, emphasis on teaching Biblical principles, athletics, art, music.
Activities: Archery, Arts/Crafts, Camping Skills/Outdoor Living, Drama, Hiking, Leadership Development, Music, Nature/Environment Studies, Sports — Field & Team, Wilderness Trips
Session lengths & capacity: June-August; 1/2, 1 & 3 week sessions; 100 campers
Clientele & fees: coed 7-18; families;
Fees: B, C, E, F ▲ 🚌
Contact: Bruce Shelton, Director at (215) 546-7878; fax: (215) 546-7800
e-mail: kirector@kirkwoodcamp.org
Web site: www.kirkwoodcamp.org
Operated by: Kirkwood Camp and Conf Ctr, Presbytery of Philadelphia, 2200 Locust St, Philadelphia, PA 19103 at (215) 732-1842

Group Rental Information
Site comments: Magnificent mountain setting. Fast water stream for tubing. Appalachian trail. Delaware water gap & ski resorts nearby
Seasons & Capacity: Spring 106, Fall 106, Winter 106
Facilities: Cabins, Dorm-Style, Food Service, Hiking Trails, Kitchen Facilities, Lake, Lodges, Meeting Rooms, Playing Fields
Programs: Winter Sports (#2365)

Kon-O-Kwee YMCA (est 1925)

▲ 🏠

Fombell, PA (Beaver Co.); (412) 758-6238
Harry Kramer, Director

Camp comments: Traditional overnight camp located in W PA. Diverse activities and lots of fun! Also weekend retreats Sept. through May
Activities: Aquatic Activities, Archery, Backpacking, Camping Skills/Outdoor Living, Canoeing, Climbing/Rappelling, International Culture, Nature/Environment Studies, Swimming — Instructional, Team Building
Session lengths & capacity: 1 & 2 week sessions
Clientele & fees: coed 7-15; Fees: D ▲
Contact: Harry C Kramer, Exec Director at (724) 758-6238;
Web site: www.ycamps.org
Operated by: YMCA Of Pittsburgh, 126 Nagel Rd, Fombell, PA 16123 at (412) 758-6238

Group Rental Information
Facilities: Cabins, Dorm-Style, Food Service, Hiking Trails, Lake, Playing Fields, Pool
Programs: Boating, Challenge/Ropes Course, Environmental Education, Horseback Riding, Swimming (#1711)

Krislund Camp (est 1963)

▲ 🏠

Madisonburg, PA (Centre Co.); (814) 422-8878
Steve Cort, Director

Camp comments: Intergenerational, wilderness programming stressing Christian living & education in supportive community experiences.
Activities: Arts/Crafts, Backpacking, Camping Skills/Outdoor Living, Canoeing, Caving, Challenge/Rope Courses, Climbing/Rappelling, Swimming — Recreational, Team Building, Wilderness Trips
Session lengths & capacity: Year-round; 1/2 & 1 week sessions; 120 campers

Clientele & fees: coed 7-18; families; seniors; single adults; Fees: **B, C** △
Contact: Steve Cort, Administrator at (814) 422-8878; fax: (814) 422-8774
e-mail: krislnd@juno.com
Operated by: Krislund Camp, PO Box 116, Madisonburg, PA 16852 at (814) 684-2803
Group Rental Information
Facilities: Cabins, Dorm-Style, Double Occupancy, Food Service, Kitchen Facilities, Lodges, Meeting Rooms (#2540)

Kweebec (est 1935) △ ⌂

Schwenksville, PA (Montgomery Co.); (610) 287-8117
Les & Maddy Weiser, Director·

Camp comments: Professional athletes & coaches teaching superb athletic program. Family atmosphere. 64th Yr. Fun & friendship.
Activities: Arts/Crafts, Baseball/Softball, Basketball, Challenge/Rope Courses, Dance, Golf, Hockey, Radio/TV/Video, Soccer, Tennis
Session lengths & capacity: April-November; 3, 4 & 8 week sessions; 300 campers
Clientele & fees: coed 6-16; families; seniors; single adults; Fees: **E** △
Contact: Les Weiser, Director at (800) 543-9830; fax: (610) 667-6376
e-mail: ckweebec@aol.com
Web site: www.kweebec.com
Operated by: Camp Kweebec Inc, PO Box 511, Narberth, PA 19072-0511 at (800) 543-9830
Group Rental Information
Facilities: Cabins, Food Service, Lake, Meeting Rooms, Pool
Programs: Boating, Environmental Education (#2375)

Ladore (est 1967) △ ⌂

Waymart, PA (Wayne Co.); (570) 488-6121
Maj. Jeffrey Bassett, Director

Camp comments: Christian camp. Pocono Mts, great opportunity to meet wonderful staff & campers .Seeking committed young people.
Activities: Arts/Crafts, Boating, Camping Skills/Outdoor Living, Challenge/Rope Courses, Hiking, Music, Nature/Environment Studies
Session lengths & capacity: 1 week sessions; 450 campers
Clientele & fees: boys 7-12; girls 7-12; Fees: **C** △ 🐷
Contact: Ray Purvis, Camp Director at (570) 488-6129; fax: (570) 488-5168
e-mail: ladore@socantel.net
Web site: www.ladore.org

ICON LEGEND

☼	Day Camp
△	Resident Camp
⌂	Facilities Available To Rent
🚐	Transportation Available
🐷	Financial Aid Available

FEE RANGES PER WEEK

A	$0-75
B	$75-200
C	$201-350
D	$351-500
E	$501-650
F	over $650

Operated by: The Salvation Army, 701 N Broad, Philadelphia, PA 18472 at (570) 488-6129
Group Rental Information
Seasons & Capacity: Spring 500, Summer 500, Fall 300, Winter 200
Facilities: A/V Equipment, Cabins, Dorm-Style, Double Occupancy, Food Service, Hiking Trails, Lake, Linens, Lodges, Meeting Rooms, Playing Fields, Pool, Tents
Programs: Boating, Challenge/Ropes Course, Environmental Education, Swimming, Winter Sports (#2326)

Lake Greeley Camp

(est 1957) △ ⌂ 🚐

Greeley, PA (Pike Co.); (717) 685-7196
Matt Buynak, Director

Camp comments: We specialize in first-time campers, 50+ different activities. Fun, caring, nurturing environment. 90 miles from NYC!
Activities: Arts/Crafts, Baseball/Softball, Basketball, Dance, Gymnastics, Horseback — English, Horseback — Western, Radio/TV/Video, Swimming — Instructional, Tennis
Session lengths & capacity: June-August; 4 & 8 week sessions; 350 campers
Clientele & fees: boys 6-15; girls 6-15; coed 6-15; Fees: **E** △
Contact: Matt Buynak, Director at (800) 743-6754; fax: (908) 276-8778
e-mail: info@lakegreeley.com
Web site: www.lakegreeley.com
Operated by: Lake Greeley Camp, PO Box 219, Moscow, PA 18444 at (570) 842-3739
Group Rental Information
Seasons & Capacity: Spring 450, Fall 450
Facilities: A/V Equipment, Cabins, Dorm-Style, Double Occupancy, Food Service, Hiking Trails, Kitchen Facilities, Linens, Lodges, Meeting Rooms, Playing Fields, Pool
Programs: Challenge/Ropes Course, Swimming (#4794)

Lake Owego Camp (est 1961) △ 🚐

Greeley, PA (Pike Co.); (717) 226-3636
Shelly Silver, Director

Camp comments: All boys camp with a complete program & top instructors. Timber Tops is sister camp 1/2 mile away.
Activities: Archery, Arts/Crafts, Backpacking, Baseball/Softball, Basketball, Canoeing, Climbing/Rappelling, Model Rocketry, Swimming — Recreational, Tennis
Session lengths & capacity: 4, 6 & 8 week sessions; 180 campers
Clientele & fees: boys 7-16; Fees: **E** △
Contact: Shelly Silver, Director at (215) 887-9700; fax: (215) 887-3901
e-mail: pinetree@pond.com

Operated by: The Black Family, 151 Washington Lane, Jenkintown, PA 19046 at (215) 887-9700 (#2448)

Laurel Mountain Camp

(est 1978) ☼ △ ⌂

Rector, PA (Westmoreland Co.); (724) 593-7362
Paula Newman, Director

Camp comments: Non-scouts encouraged to attend. Noncompetitive, caring atmosphere. Mountain setting with tents, cabins, and lodges.
Activities: Archery, Arts/Crafts, Basketball, Camping Skills/Outdoor Living, Ceramics/Pottery, Challenge/Rope Courses, Hiking, Swimming — Recreational
Session lengths & capacity: 1/2 & 1 week sessions; 110 campers
Clientele & fees: girls 5-17; Fees: **B** △
Contact: Paula Newman, Site Manager at (724) 238-4822; fax: (724) 238-8052
e-mail: campbutterfly@aol.com
Operated by: GSC of Westmoreland, 126 East Otterman St, Greensburg, PA 15601 at (724) 834-9450
Group Rental Information
Facilities: Cabins, Hiking Trails, Kitchen Facilities, Lodges, Playing Fields, Tents
Programs: Challenge/Ropes Course (#3651)

Lend A Hand Camp △ ⌂

Edinboro, PA (Crawford Co.); (814) 734-3793
Activities: Aquatic Activities, Archery, Arts/Crafts, Canoeing, Ceramics/Pottery, Leadership Development, Music
Operated by: Penn Lakes GSC, 5681 Route 6 N, Edinboro, PA 16412 at (814) 234-3793 (#2902)

Ligonier Camp & Conference Ctr (est 1914) △ ⌂

Ligonier, PA (Westmoreland Co.); (724) 238-6428
Patrick G Myers, Director

Camp comments: Christian camping since 1914! Excellent staff; build character and cooperation through emphasis in adventure education.
Activities: Archery, Arts/Crafts, Caving, Challenge/Rope Courses, Climbing/Rappelling, Riflery, Soccer, Swimming — Recreational, Team Building, Tennis
Session lengths & capacity: June-August; 1 & 2 week sessions; 215 campers
Clientele & fees: coed 8-17; Fees: **C** △ 🐷
Contact: Patrick G Myers, Summer Camp Director at (724) 238-6428; fax: (724) 238-6971
e-mail: P.Myers@ligoniercamp.org
Web site: www.ligoniercamp.org
Operated by: Ligonier Camp & Conference Ctr, RD1 Box 16, Ligonier, PA 15658 at (724) 238-6428

Group Rental Information
Facilities: Cabins, Dorm-Style, Food Service, Hiking Trails, Lodges, Meeting Rooms, Pool (#1718)

Lillian Taylor Camp

(est 1903)

Valencia, PA (Butler Co.)
Carl Redwood, Director

Camp comments: Lillian Taylor Day Camp - where the fun and learning never stops.
Activities: Arts/Crafts, Drama, Fishing, Hiking, Swimming — Instructional, Swimming — Recreational
Session lengths & capacity: June-August; 1 week sessions; 60 campers
Clientele & fees: coed 6-12; Fees: B
Contact: Carl Redwood, Director of Program Services at (412) 661-8751; fax: (412) 661-1063
e-mail: redwood@hillhouse.ckp.edu
Web site: www.kingsley.pittsburgh.pa.us
Operated by: Kingsley Association, 6118 Penn Circle South, Pittsburgh, PA 15206 at (412) 661-8751

Group Rental Information
Seasons & Capacity: Spring 100, Summer 100, Fall 100, Winter 100
Facilities: A/V Equipment, Dorm-Style, Kitchen Facilities, Meeting Rooms, Playing Fields, Pool
Programs: Swimming (#1703)

Living Waters (est 1965)

Schellsburg, PA (Bedford Co.); (814) 733-4212
Activities: Archery, Arts/Crafts, Canoeing, Community Service, Nature/Environment Studies, Religious Study, Soccer, Sports — Field & Team, Swimming — Recreational
Session lengths & capacity: 1/2 & 1 week sessions; 150 campers
Clientele & fees: boys 6-96; girls 6-96; coed 6-96; families; Fees: B, C
Contact: Beverly Answine, Secretary at (724) 834-0344; fax: (724) 834-0324
e-mail: pennwest@westol.com
Web site: www.westel.com/~pennwest/
Operated by: Penn West Conference UCC, 320 South Maple Ave, Greensburg, PA 15601 at (724) 834-0344

Group Rental Information
Facilities: Cabins, Food Service, Hiking Trails, Kitchen Facilities, Linens, Lodges, Meeting Rooms, Playing Fields (#2944)

Lutherlyn (est 1948)

Prospect, PA (Butler Co.); (412) 865-2161
Rev Randal Gullickson, Director

Camp comments: Christian emphasis, small group,camper-centered, diverse prog. opportunities provides life-changing adventures in faith.
Activities: Challenge/Rope Courses, Climbing/Rappelling, Farming/Ranching/Gardening, Hiking, Horseback — English, Horseback — Western, Model Rocketry, Music, Nature/Environment Studies, Team Building
Session lengths & capacity: 1/2 & 1 week sessions; 350 campers
Clientele & fees: coed 6-18; families; Fees: A Fees: C
Contact: Lee Lindeman, Assistant Director at (724) 865-2161; fax: (724) 865-9794
e-mail: lee@lutherlyn.com
Web site: www.lutherlyn.com
Operated by: Lutherlyn, Box 355, Prospect, PA 16052 at (724) 865-2161

Group Rental Information
Site comments: Service oriented, centralized site, one hour from Pittsburgh International Airport.
Seasons & Capacity: Spring 440, Summer 375, Fall 440, Winter 200

Facilities: A/V Equipment, Cabins, Dorm-Style, Double Occupancy, Food Service, Hiking Trails, Kitchen Facilities, Lake, Meeting Rooms, Playing Fields, Pool
Programs: Boating, Challenge/Ropes Course, Environmental Education, Horseback Riding, Swimming (#1716)

Miquon Day Camp (est 1942)

Conshohocken, PA (Montgomery Co.); (610) 825-7767
Activities: Arts/Crafts, Basketball, Ceramics/Pottery, Drama, Field Trips, Music, Nature/Environment Studies, Swimming — Instructional, Swimming — Recreational
Session lengths & capacity: June-August; 4, 6 & 8 week sessions; 240 campers
Clientele & fees: coed 4-10; Fees: B
Contact: Chuck Connor or Cindy Fleming-Powell, Director/Asst Director at (215) 757-2368; fax: (215) 281-5803
e-mail: cconnor@phila.k12.pa.us
Web site: www.miquon.org
Operated by: Miquon School, 2025 Harts Lane, Conshohocken, PA 19428 at (610) 825-7767 (#3503)

Mont Lawn Camp (est 1894)

Bushkill, PA (Pike Co.); (570) 588-6618
Michael O'Neill, Director

Camp comments: Christian camp providing an environment where children are challenged to dream and equipped to achieve those dreams.
Activities: Arts/Crafts, Boating, Camping Skills/Outdoor Living, Canoeing, Counselor Training (CIT), Drama, Music, Nature/Environment Studies, Swimming — Instructional, Swimming — Recreational
Session lengths & capacity: June-August; 2 week sessions; 200 campers
Clientele & fees: boys 6-12; girls 6-12; coed 6-12; Fees: B
Contact: Johannes Arias, Camp Registrar at (212) 684-2800 ext. 158; fax: (212) 684-3396
Web site: www.nyc.kids.org
Operated by: Kids with a Promise, 132 Madison Ave, New York, NY 10016 at (212) 684-2800

Group Rental Information
Facilities: Dorm-Style, Food Service, Hiking Trails, Lake, Linens, Lodges, Meeting Rooms, Playing Fields
Programs: Boating (#2173)

Mosey Wood (est 1939)

White Haven, PA (Carbon Co.); (570) 722-9284
Kathryn Anthony, Director

Camp comments: Girl Scout resident camp in Pocono Mtns. Adventure, trip and travel, and traditional programs for girls.
Activities: Archery, Arts/Crafts, Backpacking, Boating, Camping Skills/Outdoor Living, Challenge/Rope Courses, Climbing/Rappelling, Sailing, Swimming — Instructional, Travel/Tour
Session lengths & capacity: 1, 2, 3 & 4 week sessions; 180 campers
Clientele & fees: girls 6-17; Fees: B
Contact: Judy Arendt, Outdoor Program Adminstrator at (610) 791-2411; fax: (610) 791-4401
Web site: www.girlscouts-greatvalley.org
Operated by: Girl Scouts Great Valley Cncl, 2633 Moravian Ave, Allentown, PA 18103 at (610) 791-2411 (#2450)

Moshava (est 1945)

Honesdale, PA (Wayne Co.); (570) 253-4271
Alan Silverman, Director

Camp comments: Religious Zionist camp. All activities, emphasis on educ prog, hiking, religious studies, Israel. Complete sports facilities. Heated pool, ropes crse, biking pr

Activities: Arts/Crafts, Baseball/Softball, Basketball, Boating, Challenge/Rope Courses, Drama, Field Trips, Nature/Environment Studies, Swimming — Instructional, Tennis
Session lengths & capacity: June-August; 4 & 8 week sessions; 550 campers
Clientele & fees: coed 8-14; Fees: E
Contact: Alan Silverman, Director at (212) 683-4484; fax: (212) 213-3053
e-mail: cmosh@atdial.net
Web site: www.moshava.org
Operated by: Camp Moshava, 7 Penn Plaza Ste 205, New York, NY 10001 at (212) 465-9021

Group Rental Information
Site comments: Available May 15 until June 15 and August 28 until September 15. Moshava must supply food (Kosher).
Seasons & Capacity: Spring 600, Fall 600
Facilities: Cabins, Dorm-Style, Food Service, Lake, Meeting Rooms, Playing Fields, Pool
Programs: Boating (#2179)

Mount Luther (est 1963)

Mifflinburg, PA (Union Co.); (570) 922-1587
Chad Hershberger, Director

Camp comments: Intentional Christian community, 385 acres mountain setting. Place for spiritual growth, life skill enhancement and fun.
Activities: Archery, Arts/Crafts, Bicycling/Biking, Camping Skills/Outdoor Living, Challenge/Rope Courses, Leadership Development, Nature/Environment Studies, Religious Study, Team Building, Wilderness Trips
Session lengths & capacity: June-August; 1/2 & 1 week sessions; 96 campers
Clientele & fees: coed 8-18; families; Fees: A Fees: C
Contact: (570) 922-1587; fax: (570) 922-1118
e-mail: cml@sunlink.net
Web site: www.campmountluther.org
Operated by: Camp Mount Luther Corporation, RR 1 Box 347, Mifflinburg, PA 17844 at (570) 922-1587

Group Rental Information
Facilities: A/V Equipment, Cabins, Food Service, Hiking Trails, Lake, Lodges, Playing Fields, Pool (#6380)

Nawakwa (est 1929)

Arendtsville, PA (Adams Co.); (717) 677-8211
Marianne Brock, Director

Camp comments: Caring staff guide children as they explore God's creation, their relation to it, through Bible study, craft, recreation
Activities: Aquatic Activities, Arts/Crafts, Bicycling/Biking, Camping Skills/Outdoor Living, Hiking, Horseback — Western, Nature/Environment Studies, Religious Study, Sports — Field & Team, Swimming — Recreational
Session lengths & capacity: June-August; 1 week sessions; 175 campers
Clientele & fees: coed 6-18; families; Fees: C
Contact: Marianne Brock, Associate Executive Director at (717) 677-8211; fax: (717) 677-7597
e-mail: mbrock@lutherancamping.org
Web site: www.lutherancamping.org
Operated by: Lutheran Camping Ctrl Penn, Box 459, Arendtsville, PA 17303 at (717) 677-8211

Group Rental Information
Seasons & Capacity: Spring 200, Fall 200, Winter 100
Facilities: A/V Equipment, Cabins, Dorm-Style, Double Occupancy, Food Service, Hiking Trails, Kitchen Facilities, Lodges, Meeting Rooms, Playing Fields, Pool
Programs: Challenge/Ropes Course, Swimming (#12538)

Neumann (est 1965)

Jamison, PA (Bucks Co.); (215) 343-6552
Stephen M Taylor, Director

Camp comments: Christian camp, campers thrive in traditional caring program with opportunities to belong, learn & live together.
Activities: Archery, Arts/Crafts, Basketball, Boating, Challenge/Rope Courses, Nature/Environment Studies, Religious Study, Soccer, Swimming — Instructional, Swimming — Recreational
Session lengths & capacity: June-August; 1 week sessions; 220 campers
Clientele & fees: coed 7-15; Fees: **B** ☀
Fees: **C** ⚠ 🚐
Contact: Stephen M Taylor, Director at (215) 343-8840; fax: (215) 343-8849
Web site: www.campneumann.com
Operated by: Roman Catholic Archdiocese, PO Box 297, Jamison, PA 18929 at (215) 343-6552
Group Rental Information
Seasons & Capacity: Spring 250, Fall 250, Winter 250
Facilities: Cabins, Dorm-Style, Food Service, Hiking Trails, Kitchen Facilities, Lake, Lodges, Meeting Rooms, Playing Fields
Programs: Challenge/Ropes Course (#2416)

New Image Camp at Pocono Trail (est 1991) ⚠ 🚐

Reeders, PA; (800) 365-0556
Tony Sparber, Director

Camp comments: Weight loss & fitness combined with traditional camp activities. Upscale, modern facilities. Low stress environment.
Activities: Aerobics/Exercise, Aquatic Activities, Arts/Crafts, Basketball, Boating, Challenge/Rope Courses, Drama, Soccer, Tennis
Session lengths & capacity: June-August; 2, 4 & 8 week sessions; 350 campers
Clientele & fees: coed 8-18; Fees: **F** ⚠
Contact: Tony Sparber, Owner/Director at (800) 365-0556; fax: (201) 750-1558
e-mail: sparber@newimagecamp.com
Operated by: Tony Sparbers New Image Camps, PO Box 417, Norwood, NJ 07648 at (800) 365-0556 (#1549)

New Jersey Camp Jaycee

(est 1974) ⚠ 🏠
Effort, PA (Monroe Co.); (570) 629-3291
Jim Worrall, Director

Camp comments: Residential camp for children & adults with developmental disabilities. Located in the beautiful Pocono Mountains of PA.
Activities: Arts/Crafts, Basketball, Boating, Dance, Drama, Drawing/Painting, Horseback — Western, Music, Nature/Environment Studies, Swimming — Recreational

ICON LEGEND

☀ Day Camp
⚠ Resident Camp
🏠 Facilities Available To Rent
🚐 Transportation Available
🐷 Financial Aid Available

FEE RANGES PER WEEK

A	$0-75
B	$75-200
C	$201-350
D	$351-500
E	$501-650
F	over $650

Session lengths & capacity: June-August; 1, 2 & 8 week sessions; 180 campers
Clientele & fees: coed 7-85; seniors; single adults; Fees: **D** ⚠
Contact: Jim Worrall, Executive Director at (609) 443-1200; fax: (609) 443-1202
Web site: www.campjaycee.org
Operated by: New Jersey Camp Jaycee, 33 Lake Drive, Hightstown, NJ 08520 at (609) 443-1200
Group Rental Information
Facilities: Cabins, Double Occupancy, Food Service, Kitchen Facilities, Meeting Rooms
Programs: Boating (#1912)

New Jersey YMHA YWHA Camps

(est 1920) ⚠ 🚐
Milford, PA (Pike Co.); (570) 296-8596
Leonard M Robinson, Director

Camp comments: 3 coed age-appropriate camps. Quality instruction. Full athletic pool & lake program. High quality arts. Variety-specialties. Caring staff. Adult supervision.
Activities: Aquatic Activities, Arts/Crafts, Basketball, Boating, Challenge/Rope Courses, Drama, Nature/Environment Studies, Soccer, Sports — Field & Team, Tennis
Session lengths & capacity: June-August; 4 & 8 week sessions
Clientele & fees: coed 6-17; families; Fees: **E** ⚠ 🚐
Contact: Leonard M Robinson, Exec Director at (973) 575-3333; fax: (973) 575-4188
e-mail: info@njycamps.org
Web site: www.njycamps.org
Operated by: NJ of YMHA and YWHA Camps, 21 Plymouth St, Fairfield, NJ 07004 at (973) 575-3333 (#8296)

New Jersey YMHA-YWHA Camps

(est 1920) ⚠ 🏠 🚐
Milford, PA (Pike Co.); (570) 798-2551
Leonard M Robinson, Director

Camp comments: Quality programming, exceptional staff, making life-long friends are all evident at the NJ "Y" Camps.
Activities: Academics, Arts/Crafts, Boating, Camping Skills/Outdoor Living, Challenge/Rope Courses, Computer, Sports — Field & Team, Swimming — Instructional, Swimming — Recreational, Team Building
Session lengths & capacity: June-August; 4 & 8 week sessions; 1500 campers
Clientele & fees: boys 6-17; families; single adults; Fees: **F** ⚠ 🚐
Contact: Amy Schwartz at (973) 575-3333; fax: (973) 575-4188
e-mail: info@njycamps.org
Web site: www.njycamps.org
Operated by: NJ of YMHA and YWHA Camps, 21 Plymouth St, Fairfield, NJ 07004 at (973) 575-3333
Group Rental Information
Seasons & Capacity: Summer 1500
Facilities: Cabins, Food Service, Lake, Playing Fields, Pool
Programs: Boating, Challenge/Ropes Course, Swimming (#8291)

Newtown Day Camp (est 1995) ☀

Newtown, PA (Bucks Co.); (215) 860-6537
Patrice Agger, Director

Camp comments: Day camp w/fun & caring counselors. Many hands on activities in a warm environment. Socialization & teamwork encouraged.
Activities: Arts/Crafts, Computer, Counselor Training (CIT), Golf, Nature/Environment Studies, Performing Arts, Sports — Field & Team, Swimming — Instructional, Team Building, Tennis
Session lengths & capacity: June-August; 4, 6 & 8 week sessions; 180 campers

Clientele & fees: boys 6-12; girls 6-12; coed 2-5; Fees: **A, B, C** ☀
Contact: Patrice Agger, Director at (215) 860-6537;
Operated by: Newtown Day Camp, 761 Newtown Yardley Rd, Newtown, PA 18940 at (215) 860-6537 (#4989)

Nock-A-Mixon (est 1938) ⚠ 🏠 🚐

Kintnersville, PA (Bucks Co.); (610) 847-5963
Mark & Bernice Glaser, Director

Camp comments: Private camp with family atmosphere. Aquatics, sports, and arts activities to meet the interests of all campers. 2 pools, golf range, lakes, 10 tennis cts., etc
Activities: Arts/Crafts, Baseball/Softball, Basketball, Challenge/Rope Courses, Golf, Hockey, Model Rocketry, Swimming — Instructional, Tennis
Session lengths & capacity: June-August; 7 week sessions; 390 campers
Clientele & fees: coed 7-15; Fees: **F** ⚠
Contact: Mark & Bernice Glaser, Directors at (610) 941-0128; fax: (610) 941-1307
e-mail: mglaser851@aol.com
Web site: www.campnockamixon.com
Operated by: Camp Nock A Mixon, 16 Gum Tree Lane, Lafayette Hill, PA 19444 at (610) 941-0128
Group Rental Information
Seasons & Capacity: Spring 600, Fall 600
Facilities: Cabins, Double Occupancy, Food Service, Kitchen Facilities, Lake, Meeting Rooms, Pool
Programs: Boating, Challenge/Ropes Course, Swimming (#2333)

Northeast Family YMCA ☀

Philadelphia, PA; (215) 632-0100
Sue Swanson, Director

Camp comments: We build strong kids, strong families, and strong communities.
Activities: Arts/Crafts, Basketball, Community Service, Field Trips, Nature/Environment Studies, Sports — Field & Team, Swimming — Instructional, Swimming — Recreational, Team Building
Session lengths & capacity: June-August; 2 week sessions; 230 campers
Clientele & fees: coed 5-15; Fees: **B** ☀ 🐷 🚐
Contact: Sue Swanson, Senior Program Director at (215) 632-0100; fax: (215) 632-1484
Operated by: YMCA Philadelphia & Vicinity, Ste 1202 2000 Market Street, Philadelphia, PA 19103 at (215) 963-3700 (#41090)

Onas (est 1922) ⚠ 🏠

Ottsville, PA (Bucks Co.); (610) 847-5858
Suzan Neiger Gould, Director

Camp comments: Onas is designed to let kids be kids. Rich & varied program stresses sharing, cooperation, simple living & fun!
Activities: Archery, Arts/Crafts, Backpacking, Camping Skills/Outdoor Living, Canoeing, Challenge/Rope Courses, Drama, Music, Team Building
Session lengths & capacity: June-August; 2 & 4 week sessions; 130 campers
Clientele & fees: coed 8-13; Fees: **C** ⚠ 🐷
Contact: Suzan Neiger Gould, Camp Director at (610) 847-5858;
e-mail: friends@camponas.org
Web site: www.campones.org
Operated by: Friends Camp Assn, 609 Geigel Hill Rd, Ottsville, PA 18942 at (610) 847-5858
Group Rental Information
Seasons & Capacity: Spring 100, Fall 100, Winter 42
Facilities: Dorm-Style, Food Service, Hiking Trails, Kitchen Facilities, Meeting Rooms, Tents
Programs: Environmental Education (#19938)

Oneka (est 1908) ▲

Tafton, PA (Pike Co.); (717) 226-4049
Dale & Barbara Dohner, Director

Camp comments: Clean mountain lake; comprehensive program; skill instruction; small; quality interaction, caring well-trained staff.
Activities: Aquatic Activities, Archery, Arts/Crafts, Camping Skills/Outdoor Living, Drama, Hiking, Horseback — English, Nature/Environment Studies, Sports — Field & Team, Tennis
Session lengths & capacity: June-August; 4 & 7 week sessions; 112 campers
Clientele & fees: girls 7-16; Fees: D, E, F ▲
Contact: Dale or Barbara Dohner, Owners/Directors at (610) 687-6260; fax: (610) 687-6260
Operated by: Camp Oneka, 10 Oakford Rd, Wayne, PA 19087 at (610) 687-6260 (#2413)

Outside In School Inc

(est 1990) ▲ 🚐

Bolivar, PA (Westmoreland Co.); (724) 837-1518
Michael C Henkel, Director

Camp comments: Year-round residential and weekend programs for youth at risk. We specialize in substance abuse treatment and behavior problems. Individualized service plans.
Activities: Academics, Aerobics/Exercise, Aquatic Activities, Backpacking, Caving, Climbing/Rappelling, Community Service, Kayaking, Leadership Development, Wilderness Trips
Session lengths & capacity: 32 campers
Clientele & fees: boys 11-18; girls 13-18; Fees: F ▲
Contact: Michael C Henkel, Director at (724) 837-1518; fax: (724) 837-0801
e-mail: outside@icubed.com
Web site: www.outsideinschool.com
Operated by: Outside In School Inc, 303 Center Ave, Greensburg, PA 15601 at (724) 837-1518 (#6345)

Paradise Farm Camps

(est 1875) ▲ 🏠 🚐

Downingtown, PA (Chester Co.); (610) 269-9111
Greg Thornton, Director

Camp comments: Resident camp serving children from low income families in the Delaware Valley. 500 acres of rolling countryside.
Activities: Archery, Arts/Crafts, Baseball/Softball, Basketball, Camping Skills/Outdoor Living, Canoeing, Challenge/Rope Courses, Hiking, Nature/Environment Studies
Session lengths & capacity: June-August; 1 & 2 week sessions; 125 campers
Clientele & fees: coed 7-12; Fees: A, B ▲ 🐎
Contact: Adina Laver, Executive Director at (610) 269-9111; fax: (610) 269-3646
e-mail: ccwapfc@paradisefarmcamps.org
Web site: www.paradisefarmcamps.org
Operated by: Childrens Country Week Assn, 1300 Valley Creek Road, Downington, PA 19335 at (610) 269-9111

Group Rental Information
Site comments: 500 acres of rolling country-side.
Seasons & Capacity: Spring 125
Facilities: Cabins, Double Occupancy, Food Service, Hiking Trails, Kitchen Facilities, Lake, Lodges, Meeting Rooms, Playing Fields, Pool
Programs: Boating, Challenge/Ropes Course, Swimming (#2460)

Penn Lakes Day Camps ☀

Edinboro, PA (Crawford Co.)
Leisa Ulasz, Director

Camp comments: Girl Scout programming combined with each camps unique quality. Located in beautiful Crawford & Mercer counties.

Activities: Arts/Crafts, Camping Skills/Outdoor Living, Drama, Drawing/Painting, Music, Nature/Environment Studies
Session lengths & capacity: 1 week sessions; 150 campers
Clientele & fees: girls 6-14; Fees: A ☀
Contact: Penn Lakes GSC, Program Director at (814) 734-3793; fax: (814) 734-7701
e-mail: pennlake@erie.net
Operated by: Penn Lakes GSC, 5681 Route 6 N, Edinboro, PA 16412 at (814) 234-3793 (#7363)

Pine Forest Camp (est 1931) ▲ 🏠 🚐

Greeley, PA (Pike Co.); (717) 685-7141
Mickey Black, Director

Camp comments: Award-Winning. 73nd summer same family ownership. Fun with great staff. All-around program.
Activities: Arts/Crafts, Baseball/Softball, Basketball, Camping Skills/Outdoor Living, Challenge/Rope Courses, Climbing/Rappelling, Drama, Soccer, Sports — Field & Team, Tennis
Session lengths & capacity: 8 week sessions; 300 campers
Clientele & fees: coed 7-16; Fees: F ▲
Contact: Mickey Black, Owner/Director at (215) 887-9700; fax: (215) 887-3901
e-mail: pinetree@pond.com
Operated by: The Black Family, 151 Washington Lane, Jenkintown, PA 19046 at (215) 887-9700

Group Rental Information
Facilities: A/V Equipment, Cabins, Food Service, Lake, Meeting Rooms, Playing Fields, Pool
Programs: Boating, Challenge/Ropes Course, Swimming (#2390)

Pinemere Camp (est 1942) ▲ 🏠

Stroudsburg, PA; (570) 629-0266
Aaron Selkow, Director

Camp comments: Mnt setting. Kosher kitchen. Warm, caring atmosphere. Fine supervision. Mini sports camps. Bunk & free choice activities
Activities: Basketball, Camping Skills/Outdoor Living, Canoeing, Challenge/Rope Courses, Climbing/Rappelling, Soccer, Sports — Field & Team, Tennis
Session lengths & capacity: 4 & 8 week sessions; 200 campers
Clientele & fees: coed 6-14; Fees: C ▲
Contact: Aaron Selkow, Executive Director at (215) 925-8000; fax: (215) 925-3941
e-mail: aaron@pinemere.com
Web site: www.pinemere.com
Operated by: Pinemere Camp Association, 222 Race Street #B, Philadelphia, PA 19106-1925 at (215) 925-8000

Group Rental Information
Site comments: 10 min to Camelback ski area. Lighted bsktbal & tennis cts, fieldhouse, rec hall & other indoor areas. Mini golf & sand volleyball.Kosher
Seasons & Capacity: Spring 250, Fall 250, Winter 88
Facilities: Cabins, Dorm-Style, Food Service, Hiking Trails, Meeting Rooms, Pool
Programs: Boating (#2322)

Pocono Plateau Camp & Retreat

(est 1946) ▲ 🏠

Cresco, PA (Monroe Co.); (717) 676-3665
Mr Glenn Oswald, Director

Camp comments: Beautiful Pocono Mts. 750 acres, Christian focus, dorms or tents. Day resident or trips. High/low ropes climbing tower.
Activities: Aquatic Activities, Archery, Camping Skills/Outdoor Living, Challenge/Rope Courses, Climbing/Rappelling, Hiking, Nature/Environment Studies, Team Building, Wilderness Trips
Session lengths & capacity: 1/2 & 1 week sessions; 150 campers

Clientele & fees: boys 5-18; girls 5-18; coed 5-18; Fees: C ▲
Contact: Glenn Oswald, Manager Director at (570) 676-3665; fax: (570) 676-9388
e-mail: poconoplateau@noln.com
Web site: www.epaumc.org/camping
Operated by: E PA United Methodist Church, PO Box 820, Valley Forge, PA 19482 at (610) 666-9090 (#4742)

Pocono Ridge (est 1957) ▲ 🏠 🚐

South Sterling, PA; (570) 676-3478
Tom Santay/Michelle Santay Visinski, Director

Camp comments: Established 1958, located 90 miles from Phila/NYC, takes pride in providing a safe, warm, friendly, and fun place for children to develop as individuals.
Activities: Arts/Crafts, Challenge/Rope Courses, Counselor Training (CIT), Horseback — English, Nature/Environment Studies, Performing Arts, SCUBA, Soccer, Sports — Field & Team, Waterskiing
Session lengths & capacity: June-August; 1, 3, 4 & 7 week sessions; 250 campers
Clientele & fees: coed 8-15; Fees: F ▲
Contact: Michelle Santay Visinski, Director at (732) 521-3211; fax: (732) 521-8250
e-mail: poconoridg@aol.com
Web site: www.poconoridge.com
Operated by: Pocono Ridge, 49 North State Home Rd, Monroe Township, NJ 08831 at (732) 521-3211

Group Rental Information
Facilities: Cabins, Dorm-Style, Double Occupancy, Food Service, Meeting Rooms, Playing Fields
Programs: Environmental Education (#4756)

Ramah In The Poconos

(est 1950) ▲ 🏠

Lake Como, PA (Wayne Co.); (570) 798-2504
Cheryl Magen, Director

Camp comments: Conservative, Jewish, educatnl, Kosher camp. Sports, music, dance, drama. Emphasis on Hebrew & warm family atmosphere.
Activities: Arts/Crafts, Baseball/Softball, Basketball, Camping Skills/Outdoor Living, Community Service, Language Studies, Leadership Development, Music, Sailing, Swimming — Instructional
Session lengths & capacity: June-August; 4 & 8 week sessions; 380 campers
Clientele & fees: coed 10-16; families; seniors; Fees: D ▲ 🗣
Contact: Cheryl Magen, Director at (215) 885-8556; fax: (215) 885-8905
e-mail: magen18@aol.com
Web site: www.RamahPoconos.org
Operated by: Ramah In The Poconos, The Pavilion, 261 Old York Road Ste 734, Jenkintown, PA 19046 at (215) 885-8556 (#2393)

Saginaw (est 1930) ▲ 🏠

Oxford, PA (Chester Co.); (610) 932-8467
Jay Petkov, Director

Camp comments: For 'The Summer of Your Life.' Spectacular setting providing every aspect of camping,fun & companionship. Join us!
Activities: Archery, Arts/Crafts, Challenge/Rope Courses, Drama, Gymnastics, Hockey, Horseback — English, Riflery, Tennis, Waterskiing
Session lengths & capacity: June-August; 4 & 8 week sessions; 400 campers
Clientele & fees: boys 6-16; girls 6-16; Fees: F ▲
Contact: Roberta Frankel & Jay Petkov, Director/Owner at (856) 782-9080; fax: (856) 782-2750
Web site: www.campsaginaw.com
Operated by: Saginaw, 1010 Old Egg Harbor Rd Ste 200, Voorhees, NJ 08043 at (856) 782-9080

Group Rental Information
Seasons & Capacity: Spring 500, Winter 500

Facilities: A/V Equipment, Cabins, Double Occupancy, Food Service, Kitchen Facilities, Lake, Meeting Rooms, Ocean, Playing Fields, Pool, River
Programs: Challenge/Ropes Course, Environmental Education, Swimming (#2463)

Seneca Hills Bible Conference

(est 1936)

Franklin, PA (Venango Co.); (814) 432-3026
James Cossin, Director

Camp comments: Christian camp emphasizing Bible study, missions and chapel with a focus on evangelism and discipleship.
Activities: Archery, Basketball, Boating, Challenge/Rope Courses, Climbing/Rappelling, Hiking, Nature/Environment Studies, Sports — Field & Team, Swimming — Recreational, Team Building
Session lengths & capacity: June-August; 1/2 & 1 week sessions; 100 campers
Clientele & fees: coed 6-18; Fees: C A
Contact: Rev. James A Cossin, Executive Director at (814) 432-3026; fax: (814) 437-5442
e-mail: info@senecahills.org
Web site: www.senecahills.org
Operated by: Seneca Hills Bible Conf, Board of Trustees, PO Box 288, Franklin, PA 16323 at (814) 432-3026

Group Rental Information

Facilities: A/V Equipment, Cabins, Dorm-Style, Hiking Trails, Meeting Rooms, Playing Fields (#12587)

Sequanota (est 1947)

Jennerstown, PA (Somerset Co.); (814) 629-6627
Rev. F. Wayne Williams, Director

Camp comments: Mature staff assist campers in changing lives & strengthening faith. Conference Center for adults.
Activities: Arts/Crafts, Backpacking, Challenge/Rope Courses, Climbing/Rappelling, Horseback — Western, Nature/Environment Studies, Rafting, Religious Study, Wilderness Trips
Session lengths & capacity: June-August; 1/2 & 1 week sessions; 125 campers
Clientele & fees: boys 6-18; girls 6-18; coed 6-18; families; seniors; Fees: A Fees: B, C A
Contact: F Wayne Williams at (814) 629-6627; fax: (814) 629-0128
e-mail: sequanota1@aol.com
Web site: www.sequanota.net
Operated by: Lutheran Camp Association, Box 245, Jennerstown, PA 15547 at (814) 629-6627

ICON LEGEND

☀ Day Camp

⛺ Resident Camp

🏠 Facilities Available To Rent

🚐 Transportation Available

🐷 Financial Aid Available

FEE RANGES PER WEEK

A	$0-75
B	$75-200
C	$201-350
D	$351-500
E	$501-650
F	over $650

Group Rental Information

Site comments: Conference Center for up to 48 people. Linens, food service provided, cabins available for up to 125 people. AV & recreational equipment provided.
Seasons & Capacity: Spring 150, Summer 150, Fall 150, Winter 138
Facilities: A/V Equipment, Cabins, Double Occupancy, Food Service, Hiking Trails, Kitchen Facilities, Linens, Meeting Rooms, Playing Fields, Pool
Programs: Challenge/Ropes Course, Environmental Education, Swimming, Winter Sports (#1697)

Sesame Rockwood Camps

(est 1954)

Blue Bell, PA (Montgomery Co.); (610) 275-2267
Howard & Dale Batterman, Director

Camp comments: One fun year after another fun year. Traditional camp programs, caring staff, instruction at all activities.
Activities: Arts/Crafts, Ceramics/Pottery, Challenge/Rope Courses, Computer, Nature/Environment Studies, Sports — Field & Team, Swimming — Instructional, Swimming — Recreational, Tennis
Session lengths & capacity: 4, 5, 6, 7 & 8 week sessions; 650 campers
Clientele & fees: coed 3-14; Fees: D ☀
Contact: Howard and Dale Batterman, Owners/Directors at (610) 275-2267; fax: (610) 279-4463
e-mail: srdaycamps@aol.com
Operated by: Recreational Development Corp, PO Box 385, Blue Bell, PA 19422-0385 at (610) 275-2267 (#2446)

Shelly Ridge Day Camp

(est 1960)

Miquon, PA (Montgomery Co.); (215) 487-0452
Sede Saunders, Director

Camp comments: Diverse population. Girl planning for many activities, nature program, crafts, hiking trails. Transportation provided. Early and after camp care.
Activities: Arts/Crafts, Camping Skills/Outdoor Living, Dance, Drama, Hiking, Leadership Development, Nature/Environment Studies, Performing Arts, Swimming — Instructional, Swimming — Recreational
Session lengths & capacity: 1 & 2 week sessions; 225 campers
Clientele & fees: girls 5-14; Fees: B, C 🚐 🐷
Contact: Dotti Martin, Volunteer Services Coordinator at (215) 564-4657 ext. 226; fax: (215) 564-6953
e-mail: dmartin@gssp.org
Web site: www.gssp.org
Operated by: GSC Southeastern Pennsylvania, PO Box 27540, Philadelphia, PA 19118-0540 at (215) 564-4657 (#1324)

Southampton Summer Day Camp (est 1973)

Southampton, PA (Bucks Co.); (215) 355-4567
Richard Blum, Director
Activities: Basketball, Boating, Challenge/Rope Courses, Dance, Hockey, Performing Arts, Soccer, Sports — Field & Team, Swimming — Instructional, Swimming — Recreational
Session lengths & capacity: 8 week sessions; 650 campers
Clientele & fees: coed 3-14; Fees: C ☀
Contact: Jacquelyn A Blum, Director at (215) 355-4567; fax: (215) 355-5641
Operated by: Southampton Summer Day Camp, 1459 Second Street PK, Southampton, PA 18966 at (215) 355-4567 (#32576)

Sports & Arts Ctr at Islnd Lke

(est 1985)

Starrucca, PA (Wayne Co.); (570) 798-2550
Stoltz Family, Director

Camp comments: Individualized program in family-oriented setting, all sports, circus, theater, science, magic, dance, music, horseback, art, pioneering, mtn. bike, waterfront.
Activities: Camping Skills/Outdoor Living, Golf, Gymnastics, Horseback — English, Horseback — Western, Music, Performing Arts, Skating, Tennis, Waterskiing
Session lengths & capacity: June-August; 2, 3, 5, 6 & 8 week sessions; 500 campers
Clientele & fees: coed 7-17; Fees: F A
Contact: Bev & Mike Stoltz, Directors at (212) 753-7777; fax: (212) 753-7761
e-mail: islndlake@aol.com
Operated by: Sports & Arts Ctr at Islnd Lke, 136 E 57 St Ste 1001, New York, NY 10022 at (212) 753-7777

Group Rental Information

Site comments: Excellent facilities for meetings and recreation. Fields for all sports. Theatre holds 900. Large gym. Great food.
Facilities: Food Service, Lake, Lodges, Meeting Rooms, Playing Fields, Pool
Programs: Boating, Challenge/Ropes Course, Environmental Education, Horseback Riding, Swimming (#5433)

Spruce Lake Wilderness Camp

(est 1963)

Canadensis, PA (Monroe Co.); (570) 595-7505
Daniel A Ziegler, Director

Camp comments: Adventure camping in a rustic Pocono Mtn setting! Carefully chosen staff model Christian integrity and individual value
Activities: Archery, Arts/Crafts, Backpacking, Camping Skills/Outdoor Living, Climbing/Rappelling, Hiking, Model Rocketry, Nature/Environment Studies, Swimming — Recreational, Wilderness Trips
Session lengths & capacity: June-August; 1/2, 1 & 2 week sessions; 150 campers
Clientele & fees: coed 8-18; Fees: B A 🐷
Contact: Kent Kauffman, Wilderness Camp Director at (570) 595-7505; fax: (570) 595-0328
e-mail: wilderness.camp@juno.com
Web site: www.sprucelake.org
Operated by: Franconia Mennonite Camp Assn, RR 1 Box 605, Canadensis, PA 18325-9749 at (570) 595-7505 (#5988)

Summit Camp Inc (est 1969)

Honesdale, PA (Wayne Co.); (570) 253-4381
Mayer A Stiskin, Director

Camp comments: Summit offers a program of therapeutic recreation to boys and girls classified as having ADD, ADHD, LD, Asperger's, Tourettes and/or OCD.
Activities: Aquatic Activities, Arts/Crafts, Baseball/Softball, Basketball, Challenge/Rope Courses, Computer, Nature/Environment Studies, Radio/TV/Video, Soccer, Tennis
Session lengths & capacity: June-August; 1, 4 & 8 week sessions; 300 campers
Clientele & fees: coed 8-17; Fees: F A
Contact: Regina Skyer, Director at (718) 268-0020; fax: (718) 268-0671
e-mail: summitinst@aol.com
Web site: www.summitcamp.com
Operated by: Summit Camp, 110-45 71 Rd, Forest Hills, NY 11375 at (718) 268-0020 (#4783)

Swatara (est 1943)   △ ⌂

Bethel, PA (Berks Co.); (717) 933-8510
Marlin D Houff, Director

Camp comments: Christian church camp located adjacent to Appalachian Trail on Blue Mt. in Berks County Pennsylvania.
Activities: Camping Skills/Outdoor Living, Canoeing, Challenge/Rope Courses, Climbing/Rappelling, Counselor Training (CIT), Hiking, Leadership Development, Music, Nature/Environment Studies, Wilderness Trips
Session lengths & capacity: June-August; 1/2 & 1 week sessions; 80 campers
Clientele & fees: coed 7-17; Fees: B △ 🚌
Contact: Marlin D Houff, Administrator at (717) 933-8510; fax: (717) 469-7825
e-mail: swatara@redrose.net
Web site: www.campswatara.org
Operated by: Camp Swatara, 2905 Camp Swatara Road, Bethel, PA 19507-9554 at (717) 933-8510 (#2544)

The College Settlement Camps

(est 1922)   △ ⌂ 🚗

Horsham, PA (Montgomery Co.); (215) 542-7974
Frank R Gerome, Director

Camp comments: Serves economically needy children from five county Philadelphia area.
Activities: Archery, Arts/Crafts, Boating, Camping Skills/Outdoor Living, Challenge/Rope Courses, Field Trips, Nature/Environment Studies, Sports — Field & Team, Travel/Tour
Session lengths & capacity: June-August; 2 week sessions; 140 campers
Clientele & fees: coed 7-14; Fees: B △ 🚌
Contact: Frank R Gerome, Executive Director at (215) 542-7974; fax: (215) 542-7457
e-mail: camps@i-bob.com
Web site: www.collegesettlement.org
Operated by: Kuhn Day Camp, 600 Witmer Rd, Horsham, PA 19044 at (215) 542-7974 (#2420)

The Salvation Army Camp Alleghany (est 1945)   △ ⌂ 🚗

Ellwood City, PA (Lawrence Co.); (724) 758-5546
Captain Kevin Stoops, Director

Camp comments: Residential camp for Underprivileged children serving all of W. Pennsylvania, fees based on sliding scale.
Activities: Archery, Arts/Crafts, Camping Skills/Outdoor Living, Music, Nature/Environment Studies, Sports — Field & Team
Session lengths & capacity: June-August; 1 week sessions; 250 campers
Clientele & fees: coed 6-18; seniors; Fees: A △ 🚌
Contact: Cpt Kevin Stoops, Camp Director at (412) 394-4840; fax: (412) 261-4076
e-mail: dys@wepasa.org
Web site: www.camppage.com/alleghny
Operated by: The Salavation Army, 424 Third Ave, Pittsburgh, PA 15219 at (412) 394-4800

Group Rental Information
Facilities: A/V Equipment, Cabins, Double Occupancy, Hiking Trails, Kitchen Facilities, Linens, Meeting Rooms, Playing Fields, River (#1726)

The Woodlands   ☀ △ ⌂

Wexford, PA; (724) 935-6533
Leslie Heck, Director

Camp comments: The Woodlands is committed to extending the use of facility to all children who have disability or chronic illness.Through programs,services,education, culture.
Activities: Aquatic Activities, Arts/Crafts, Music, Performing Arts, Sports — Field & Team
Session lengths & capacity: June-August; 1 & 2 week sessions; 48 campers
Clientele & fees: coed 7-21; Fees: C ☀ Fees: F △

Contact: Peter Clakeley, Executive Director at (724) 935-6533; fax: (724) 934-9610
e-mail: pclakeley@woodlandsfoundation.org
Operated by: The Woodlands Foundation Inc, 134 Shenot Road, Wexford, PA 15090 at (724) 935-6533

Group Rental Information
Site comments: A year round facility, fully accessible. Includes 54 bed lodge, indoor pool, food service, health center, amphitheater, multipurpose center, and beautiful woods
Seasons & Capacity: Spring 48, Summer 48, Fall 48, Winter 48
Facilities: Dorm-Style, Food Service, Meeting Rooms, Pool
Programs: Swimming (#33111)

Timber Tops (est 1963)   △ ⌂ 🚗

Greeley, PA (Pike Co.); (717) 226-1955
Ted Weinstein, Director

Camp comments: All girls. Great specialty staff in a nurturing environment. Brother camp, Lake Owego 1/2 mile away.
Activities: Arts/Crafts, Camping Skills/Outdoor Living, Challenge/Rope Courses, Climbing/Rappelling, Dance, Drama, Gymnastics, Soccer, Swimming — Recreational, Tennis
Session lengths & capacity: 4 & 8 week sessions; 200 campers
Clientele & fees: girls 7-16; Fees: F △
Contact: Ted Weinstein, Director at (215) 887-9700; fax: (215) 887-3901
e-mail: timbertops@pond.com
Operated by: The Black Family, 151 Washington Lane, Jenkintown, PA 19046 at (215) 887-9700

Group Rental Information
Facilities: Cabins, Double Occupancy, Kitchen Facilities
Programs: Boating, Challenge/Ropes Course, Environmental Education, Swimming (#2395)

Tohikanee (est 1953)   △

Quakertown, PA (Montgomery Co.); (610) 536-6270
Emma Newnham, Director

Camp comments: Age appropriate programs. Open to non-scouts. Also horsemanship, theater, arts, nature, and other specialty programs.
Activities: Arts/Crafts, Backpacking, Camping Skills/Outdoor Living, Challenge/Rope Courses, Counselor Training (CIT), Drama, Horseback — English, Leadership Development, Photography
Session lengths & capacity: June-August; 1/2, 1 & 2 week sessions; 150 campers
Clientele & fees: girls 6-17; Fees: B, C, D △ 🚌
Contact: Rhonda Morris, Camp Administrator at (610) 933-7555 ext. 238; fax: (610) 933-2714
e-mail: rescamp@aol.com
Web site: www.gsfvc.org
Operated by: Girl Scouts of Freedom Valley, 100 Juliette Low Way, Valley Forge, PA 19482 at (610) 933-7555 (#2396)

Towanda (est 1923)   △ ⌂ 🚗

Honesdale, PA (Wayne Co.); (570) 253-3266
Mitch & Stephanie Reiter, Director

Camp comments: Well-rounded, all land/water activities, highly personalized, owners very involved. High quality, not high gloss!
Activities: Arts/Crafts, Baseball/Softball, Bicycling/Biking, Challenge/Rope Courses, Drama, Hockey, Soccer, Swimming — Instructional, Tennis, Waterskiing
Session lengths & capacity: June-August; 7 week sessions; 400 campers
Clientele & fees: coed 6-17; Fees: F △
Contact: Mitch & Stephanie Reiter, Owner & Director at (845) 639-4582; fax: (845) 638-2194
e-mail: info@camptowanda.com
Web site: www.camptowanda.com
Operated by: Camp Towanda Inc, RR1 Box 1585, Honesdale, PA 18431-9798 at (570) 253-3266

Group Rental Information
Site comments: Please call us for specific rental information.
Seasons & Capacity: Spring 500, Fall 500
Facilities: A/V Equipment, Cabins, Dorm-Style, Double Occupancy, Food Service, Hiking Trails, Kitchen Facilities, Lake, Linens, Meeting Rooms, Playing Fields, Pool, Tents
Programs: Boating, Challenge/Ropes Course, Environmental Education, Swimming (#4296)

Trail's End Camp (est 1947)   △ ⌂ 🚗

Beach Lake, PA (Wayne Co.); (570) 729-7111
Starr & Stan Goldberg, Rona & Marc Honigfeld, Director

Camp comments: A warm family atmosphere w/individual attention, programs in all sports/crafts/swimming/golf/tennis;Kosher style food
Activities: Arts/Crafts, Challenge/Rope Courses, Drama, Golf, Leadership Development, Sports — Field & Team, Tennis
Session lengths & capacity: June-August; 8 week sessions; 450 campers
Clientele & fees: coed 7-17; Fees: F △
Contact: Starr/Stan Goldberg or Rona/Marc Honigfe, Directors at (516) 781-5200; fax: (516) 781-5021
e-mail: contact@trailsendcamp.com
Web site: www.trailsendcamp.com
Operated by: Trail's End Camp, 1714 Wantagh Ave, Wantagh, NY 11793 at (516) 781-5200

Group Rental Information
Site comments: More than a summer camp it is an 'experience of a lifetime'. Top facilities, top staff. Success in our community is based on attitude not aptitude.
Seasons & Capacity: Spring 600, Winter 600
Facilities: Cabins, Double Occupancy, Food Service, Lake, Linens, Meeting Rooms, Playing Fields, Pool
Programs: Boating, Challenge/Ropes Course, Environmental Education, Swimming (#2118)

Tweedale (est 1930)   ☀ △ ⌂

Oxford, PA (Chester Co.); (717) 529-2594
Kathie Cronk or Marybeth King, Director

Camp comments: Various program sessions for girls of all ages including non-scouts. Specialties include canoeing, sports, high ropes.
Activities: Arts/Crafts, Backpacking, Bicycling/Biking, Camping Skills/Outdoor Living, Canoeing, Counselor Training (CIT), Leadership Development, Nature/Environment Studies
Session lengths & capacity: June-August; 1/2, 1 & 2 week sessions; 130 campers
Clientele & fees: girls 6-17; Fees: B, C, D △ 🚌
Contact: (610) 933-7555 ext. 228; fax: (610) 935-2714
e-mail: rescamp@aol.com
Web site: www.gsfvc.org
Operated by: Girl Scouts of Freedom Valley, 100 Juliette Low Way, Valley Forge, PA 19482 at (610) 933-7555 (#2310)

Tyler Hill Camp (est 1955)   △ 🚗

Tyler Hill, PA (Wayne Co.); (570) 224-4131
Allen & Arlene Leibowitz, Director
Activities: Challenge/Rope Courses, Golf, Gymnastics, Horseback — English, Performing Arts, Sailing, Sports — Field & Team, Swimming — Instructional, Swimming — Recreational, Waterskiing
Session lengths & capacity: June-August; 8 week sessions; 400 campers
Clientele & fees: coed 8-16; Fees: F △
Contact: Andy Siegel, Asst Director at (516) 656-4220; fax: (516) 656-4215
e-mail: andy@camptlc.com
Web site: www.camptlc.com
Operated by: Timber Lake, 85 Crescent Beach Rd, Glen Cove, NY 11542 at (516) 656-4227 (#2205)

Variety Club Camp &Development (est 1949)

Worcester, PA (Montgomery Co.); (610) 584-4366
Daniel Findley, Director

Camp comments: Over 50 years experience in camping, offering residential camp for children with physical disabilities & day camp for children with developmental disabilities
Activities: Archery, Arts/Crafts, Baseball/Softball, Computer, Counselor Training (CIT), Field Trips, Music, Nature/Environment Studies, Swimming — Instructional, Swimming — Recreational
Session lengths & capacity: 2 & 3 week sessions; 92 campers
Clientele & fees: coed 7-17; Fees: A ☀
Fees: B ⚑ 🚌
Contact: Daniel Findley, Executive Director at (610) 584-4366; fax: (610) 584-5586
e-mail: djfindley@msn.com
Operated by: Variety Club Camp & Devel Ctr, Valley Forge and Potshop Rds, Box 609, Worcester, PA 19490 at (610) 584-4366

Group Rental Information
Site comments: A great retreat location for small groups! Reserve early!
Seasons & Capacity: Spring 88, Fall 88, Winter 88
Facilities: Cabins, Double Occupancy, Food Service, Kitchen Facilities, Playing Fields, Pool, Tents
Programs: Environmental Education, Swimming (#2426)

Watonka (est 1963) ⚑

Hawley, PA (Wayne Co.); (570) 226-4779
Donald Wacker, Director

Camp comments: A camper selected program combining hands on experiences in the sciences along with the traditional camp activities.
Activities: Academics, Archery, Challenge/Rope Courses, Climbing/Rappelling, Computer, Model Rocketry, Nature/Environment Studies, Photography, Radio/TV/Video, Riflery
Session lengths & capacity: June-August; 4 & 8 week sessions; 120 campers
Clientele & fees: boys 7-15; Fees: E ⚑
Contact: Donald Wacker, Director at (570) 857-1401; fax: (570) 857-9653
e-mail: wacd1@voicenet.com
Web site: www.watonka.com
Operated by: Camp Watonka, PO Box 356, Paupack, PA 18451 at (570) 857-1401 (#2304)

Westminster Highlands Camp

(est 1957) ⚑ 🏠

Emlenton, PA (Venango Co.); (724) 867-6271
Todd Eckstein, Director

Camp comments: 640 rustic acres. Strong basic Christian programs for all ages. High adventure & tripping sessions for teens.
Activities: Aquatic Activities, Archery, Arts/Crafts, Canoeing, Challenge/Rope Courses, Climbing/Rappelling, Counselor Training (CIT), Hiking, Leadership Development, Wilderness Trips
Session lengths & capacity: June-August; 1/2 & 1 week sessions; 124 campers
Clientele & fees: coed 8-18; seniors;
Fees: B, C ⚑ 🚌
Contact: Lisa Miller, Camp Registrar at (724) 662-4481; fax: (724) 662-1080
e-mail: capnwp@shenango.org
Web site: www.capnwp.org
Operated by: Camping of the Presbyterian, 114 W Venango St, Mercer, PA 16137 at (724) 662-4481

Group Rental Information
Seasons & Capacity: Spring 90, Summer 120, Fall 90, Winter 90
Facilities: Cabins, Hiking Trails, Kitchen Facilities, Pool
Programs: Challenge/Ropes Course (#7025)

Westmont (est 1980) ⚑ 🏠 🚐

Poyntelle, PA (Wayne Co.); (570) 448-2500
Jack Pinsky & Fred Moskowitz, Director

Camp comments: Spirit! Tradition! Instruction! Fun & tournament play! Structured & choice program! Compu-nature! Trapeze & trips & TLC! Pool & all lake sports! All land sports
Activities: Archery, Baseball/Softball, Basketball, Boating, Canoeing, Horseback — Western, Sports — Field & Team, Swimming — Instructional, Tennis, Waterskiing
Session lengths & capacity: 8 week sessions; 375 campers
Clientele & fees: coed 6-16; Fees: E ⚑
Contact: Jack Pinsky or Fred Moskowitz, Owner/Directors at (516) 599-2963;
fax: (516) 599-1979
e-mail: westmont4u@aol.com
Operated by: UCA, PO Box 770096, Coral Springs, FL 33077 at (954) 422-7700

Group Rental Information
Facilities: Cabins, Dorm-Style, Double Occupancy, Food Service, Hiking Trails, Kitchen Facilities, Lake, Meeting Rooms, Playing Fields, Pool
Programs: Boating, Challenge/Ropes Course, Swimming (#6653)

Willow Grove Day Camp

(est 1955) ☀ 🚐

Willow Grove, PA (East Montgomery Co.);
(215) 659-4393
Larry ZeitZ, Director

Camp comments: 44 yrs exceptional counseling & specialist staff All sports Creative and Performing Arts Lunch Transportation Pools Lake
Activities: Arts/Crafts, Challenge/Rope Courses, Computer, Dance, Drama, Golf, Horseback — English, Sports — Field & Team, Swimming — Instructional, Tennis
Session lengths & capacity: June-August; 4, 6 & 8 week sessions; 500 campers
Clientele & fees: coed 4-14; Fees: D ☀
Contact: Larry Zeitz, Director at (215) 659-4393;
fax: (215) 659-5187
e-mail: willowgrovecamp@cs.com
Operated by: Willow Grove Day Camp, 3400 Davisville Rd POB 398, Willow Grove, PA 19090-0398 at (215) 659-4393 (#2379)

Windmill Day Camp (est 1985) ☀

Doylestown, PA (Bucks Co.); (215) 348-2660
Lisa Allyn Silverstein, Director

Camp comments: 25 acre farm setting: craziness is what we're all about! Your child will be guaranteed a safe, fun and wacky summer!
Activities: Aquatic Activities, Bicycling/Biking, Boating, Challenge/Rope Courses, Counselor Training (CIT), Drama, Field Trips, Football, Horseback — English, Soccer
Session lengths & capacity: June-August; 6, 7, 8 & 9 week sessions; 200 campers
Clientele & fees: coed 3-13; Fees: B, C ☀ 🚌
Contact: Lisa Allyn Silverstein, Director/Administrator at (215) 348-2660;
fax: (215) 348-5363
e-mail: wdcamp@hotmail.com
Web site: www.wimdmilldaycamp.com
Operated by: Windmill Day Camp, 36 Chapman Rd, Doylestown, PA 18901 at (215) 348-2660 (#460)

Wood Haven (est 1954) ☀ ⚑ 🏠

Pine Grove, PA (Schuylkill Co.); (570) 345-4288
Michele Bement, Director

Camp comments: Girl Scout Resident camp in Eastern PA, close to the Appalachian Trail. Horseback riding, trip & travel programs.
Activities: Archery, Backpacking, Bicycling/Biking, Camping Skills/Outdoor Living, Challenge/Rope Courses, Hiking, Horseback — English, Leadership Development, Swimming — Instructional, Swimming — Recreational
Session lengths & capacity: June-August; 1, 2 & 4 week sessions; 160 campers
Clientele & fees: girls 6-17; Fees: B ⚑

Contact: Judy Arendt, Outdoor Program Administrator at (610) 791-2411; fax: (610) 791-4401
Web site: www.girlscouts-greatvalley.org
Operated by: Girl Scouts Great Valley Cncl, 2633 Moravian Ave, Allentown, PA 18103 at (610) 791-2411 (#2332)

Woodrock   △ ⌂

Pottstown, PA; (215) 231-9810
Reginald E Dickson, Director
Activities: Camping Skills/Outdoor Living, Ceramics/Pottery, Challenge/Rope Courses, Hiking, Nature/Environment Studies, Performing Arts, Team Building
Operated by: Woodrock Inc, PO Box 2510, Sanatoga, PA 19464 at (610) 323-9045
Group Rental Information
Facilities: Cabins, Dorm-Style, Food Service, Hiking Trails, Kitchen Facilities, Lodges, Tents (#4699)

WOW Keystone Youth Camp Inc

(est 1986)   △

Lemoyne, PA (Mifflin Co.); (717) 770-0225
Roger Mervine, Director
Activities: Archery, Arts/Crafts, Basketball, Climbing/Rappelling, Community Service, Riflery, Swimming — Recreational
Session lengths & capacity: 1 week sessions; 150 campers
Clientele & fees: boys 8-15; girls 8-15; families; seniors; Fees: A △
Contact: Roger Mervine, Fraternal Coordinator-Director at (717) 770-0225; fax: (717) 770-0236
Operated by: WOW Life Insurance (KR), 1700 Farnam, Omaha, NE 68120 at (402) 271-7258 (#6552)

YMCA Camp Fitch (est 1914)   △ ⌂

North Springfield, PA (Erie Co.); (814) 922-3219
William L. Lyder, Director
Camp comments: Lake front setting. Traditional programs with outstanding staff offers a wide variety of programs, leadership training.
Activities: Archery, Arts/Crafts, Climbing/Rappelling, Computer, Counselor Training (CIT), Horseback — Western, Riflery, Sailing, Waterskiing, Wilderness Trips
Session lengths & capacity: 1, 2, 3, 4, 5, 6, 7 & 8 week sessions; 240 campers
Clientele & fees: boys 8-16; girls 8-16; coed 8-16; families; seniors; Fees: C, D △
Contact: William L Lyder, Executive Director at (330) 744-8411; fax: (330) 744-8416
Web site: www.campfitch.com
Operated by: Youngstown YMCA, 17 N Champion St, Youngstown, OH 44501-1287 at (330) 744-8411
Group Rental Information
Site comments: Four conference centers available with full food service and program staff to meet group needs.
Seasons & Capacity: Spring 300, Fall 300, Winter 300
Facilities: Cabins, Food Service, Hiking Trails, Kitchen Facilities, Lake, Lodges, Meeting Rooms, Ocean, Playing Fields, Pool, River
Programs: Boating, Environmental Education, Horseback Riding, Swimming, Winter Sports (#1434)

YMCA Camp Kresge (est 1953)   ☀

White Haven, PA (Luzerne Co.); (717) 443-8870
Nicky Pachucki, Director
Camp comments: Mountain setting. Traditional camping programs with free choice given to campers . Family camping. Both pre & post season group rentals.

Activities: Archery, Arts/Crafts, Boating, Swimming — Recreational
Session lengths & capacity: 1 week sessions; 125 campers
Clientele & fees: coed 7-14; 🐖
Contact: Nicky Pachucki, Camp Director at (717) 823-2191; fax: (717) 443-8870
Operated by: Wilkes Barre Family YMCA, 40 W Northampton St, Wilkes Barre, PA 18702 at (570) 823-2191 (#3988)

YMCA Camp Shand

(est 1894)   ☀ △ ⌂ 🚌

Cornwall, PA; (717) 397-7474
Todd Brinkman, Director

Camp comments: Set your compass for Adventure! We build strong kids, strong families, and strong communities.
Activities: Archery, Boating, Camping Skills/Outdoor Living, Canoeing, Challenge/Rope Courses, Climbing/Rappelling, Counselor Training (CIT), Horseback — Western, Nature/Environment Studies, Rafting
Session lengths & capacity: June-August; 1/2, 1 & 2 week sessions; 180 campers
Clientele & fees: boys 5-16; girls 5-16; coed 5-16; Fees: C △ 🐖
Contact: Todd Brinkman, Director at (717) 272-8001; fax: (717) 397-7815
e-mail: TJBrinkman@prodigy.net
Web site: www.LancasterYMCA.org
Operated by: Lancaster YMCA, 572 N Queen St, Lancaster, PA 17603 at (717) 397-7474
Group Rental Information
Site comments: We build strong kids, strong families, and strong communities. High and low ropes course, pool, lake, archery, and more.
Seasons & Capacity: Spring 110, Fall 110
Facilities: A/V Equipment, Cabins, Hiking Trails, Kitchen Facilities, Lake, Meeting Rooms, Playing Fields
Programs: Boating, Challenge/Ropes Course, Environmental Education (#9171)

YMCA of Pittsb N Boroughs Camp (est 1978)   ☀

Pittsburgh, PA (Allegheny Co.); (412) 761-1227
Janet Ambrass, Director

Camp comments: YMCA we build strong kids, strong families, and strong communities.
Activities: Aquatic Activities, Arts/Crafts, Counselor Training (CIT), Drama, Football, Hiking, Leadership Development, Nature/Environment Studies, Swimming — Recreational, Team Building
Session lengths & capacity: June-August; 4 week sessions; 150 campers
Clientele & fees: coed 5-16; Fees: B ☀ 🐖
Contact: Janet Ambrass, Child Care Director at (412) 761-1227; fax: (412) 766-9408
e-mail: yellowdog9622@aol.com
Web site: www.ycamps.org
Operated by: YMCA Of Pittsburgh, 126 Nagel Rd, Fombell, PA 16123 at (412) 758-6238 (#2700)

YMCA of Pittsburgh North Hills

(est 1990)   ☀

Pittsburgh, PA (Allegheny Co.); (412) 364-3404
Deborah Heal, Director

Camp comments: YMCA we build strong kids, strong families, and strong coummunities.
Activities: Arts/Crafts, Counselor Training (CIT), Swimming — Recreational
Session lengths & capacity: June-August; 8 week sessions; 100 campers
Clientele & fees: coed 3-16; Fees: B ☀ 🐖
Contact: Deborah A Heal, Senior Program Director at (412) 761-1227; fax: (412) 766-9408

e-mail: yellowdog9622@aol.com
Web site: www.ycamps.org
Operated by: YMCA Of Pittsburgh, 126 Nagel Rd, Fombell, PA 16123 at (412) 758-6238 (#19258)

Puerto Rico

Camp Antilles   ☀

Trujillo Alto, PR; (809) 761-1710
Activities: Archery, Arts/Crafts, Camping Skills/Outdoor Living, Dance, Martial Arts, Sports — Field & Team, Swimming — Instructional, Swimming — Recreational, Tennis
Operated by: Antilles Military Academy, Bo Las Cuevas Car 850, GPO Box 1919, Trujillo Alto, PR 00977 at (809) 761-1710 (#4475)

Camp Radians (est 1979)   ☀ 🚗

Cayey, PR
Luis A Medona, Director
Activities: Aquatic Activities, Archery, Arts/Crafts, Canoeing, Field Trips, Swimming — Recreational, Tennis
Session lengths & capacity: June-July; 4, 5 & 6 week sessions; 700 campers
Clientele & fees: coed 4-15; Fees: A ☀
Contact: Luis A Medina, Camp Director at (787) 738-4822; fax: (787) 728-2700
e-mail: gaston@prtc.net
Operated by: Colegio Radians Inc, PO Box 371298, Cayey, PR 00727-1298 at (787) 738-4822 (#41447)

Mabo Day Camp (est 1963)   ☀ 🚗

Guaynabo, PR; (787) 720-6801
Lilliam B Consuegra, Director

Camp comments: Happiness with safety.
Activities: Arts/Crafts, Canoeing, Dance, Field Trips, Horseback — Western, Martial Arts, Snow Sports, Soccer, Swimming — Recreational, Tennis
Session lengths & capacity: June-July; 4 week sessions; 500 campers
Clientele & fees: boys 3-13; Fees: B ☀
Contact: Lilliam Consuegra, Camp Director at (787) 720-6801; fax: (787) 720-6841
e-mail: ama@coqui.net
Operated by: American Military Academy, Box 7884, Guaynabo, PR 00970-7884 at (787) 720-6801 (#3390)

Sound Of Music Girls Camp

(est 1970)   ☀ 🚗

Guaynabo, PR; (787) 720-6801
Lilliam B. Consuegra, Director

Camp comments: Happiness with safety.
Activities: Arts/Crafts, Canoeing, Dance, Field Trips, Martial Arts, Music, Swimming — Recreational
Session lengths & capacity: June-July; 4 week sessions; 500 campers
Clientele & fees: girls 3-13; Fees: B ☀
Contact: Lilliam B Consuegra, Director at (787) 720-6801; fax: (787) 720-6841
e-mail: ama@coqui.net
Operated by: American Military Academy, Box 7884, Guaynabo, PR 00970-7884 at (787) 720-6801 (#3706)

Wonderland Camp (est 1976)   ☀

Guaynabo, PR; (787) 720-3634
Ana Christina Sanchez, Director

Camp comments: A camp specialized in baby campers (3-5 years), outstanding staff, working in a noncompetitive and caring atmosphere.

Activities: Aerobics/Exercise, Aquatic Activities, Arts/Crafts, Basketball, Computer, Counselor Training (CIT), Dance, Field Trips, Sports — Field & Team, Swimming — Recreational
Session lengths & capacity: June-July; 1, 2, 3 & 4 week sessions; 500 campers
Clientele & fees: coed 3-12; Fees: **B** ☀
Contact: Ana Christina Sanchez, Camp Director at (787) 720-3634; fax: (787) 789-6665
Operated by: Colegio Adianez, Box 2210, Guaynabo, PR 00970 at (787) 720-2998 (#1917)

Rhode Island

Aldersgate (est 1945)   ☀ ▲ ⌂

North Scituate, RI (Providence Co.); (401) 568-4350
Jeffrey Thomas, Director

Camp comments: 50 years of Christian camping. All are welcome. Make friends that last forever. Traditional camp fun. A people place.
Activities: Arts/Crafts, Bicycling/Biking, Camping Skills/Outdoor Living, Canoeing, Challenge/Rope Courses, Counselor Training (CIT), Horseback — English, Nature/Environment Studies, Swimming — Recreational
Session lengths & capacity: June-August; 1 week sessions; 90 campers
Clientele & fees: coed 7-99; families; Fees: **B** ☀
Fees: **B, C** ▲ 🐷
Contact: Jeffrey C Thomas, Director at (401) 568-4350; fax: (401) 568-1840
e-mail: Aldersgate@juno.com
Web site: www.campaldersgate.com
Operated by: United Methodist Church, 1043 Snake Hill Rd, North Scituate, RI 02857 at (401) 568-4350
Group Rental Information
Seasons & Capacity: Spring 100, Summer 100, Fall 100, Winter 50
Facilities: A/V Equipment, Cabins, Dorm-Style, Food Service, Hiking Trails, Kitchen Facilities, Lake, Lodges, Meeting Rooms, Playing Fields
Programs: Boating (#7351)

Alton Jones Camp (est 1966)   ☀ ▲ ⌂

West Greenwich, RI (Kent Co.); (401) 397-3304
John Jacques, Director

Camp comments: 2300 acres. Private lakefront, historic working farm, hands-on approach to learning. An ideal place to explore nature.

ICON LEGEND

☀   Day Camp
▲   Resident Camp
⌂   Facilities Available To Rent
🚐   Transportation Available
🐷   Financial Aid Available

FEE RANGES PER WEEK

A	$0-75
B	$75-200
C	$201-350
D	$351-500
E	$501-650
F	over $650

Activities: Aquatic Activities, Backpacking, Camping Skills/Outdoor Living, Canoeing, Climbing/Rappelling, Farming/Ranching/Gardening, Hiking, Nature/Environment Studies, Team Building, Wilderness Trips
Session lengths & capacity: June-August; 1 week sessions; 200 campers
Clientele & fees: coed 5-17; Fees: **B** ☀
Fees: **D** ▲
Contact: Cheryl Conti, Office Manager at (401) 397-3304 ext. 6043; fax: (401) 397-3293
e-mail: uriecc@etal.uri.edu
Web site: www.uri.edu/ajc/eec
Operated by: University of Rhode Island, Alton Jones Campus, 401 Victory Highway, West Greenwich, RI 02817-2158 at (401) 397-3304
Group Rental Information
Site comments: 2300 acre pristine setting for a retreat, conference, family reunion or company picnic. Includes dining hall, meeting rooms, sleeping cabins, trails & lake.
Seasons & Capacity: Spring 100, Fall 100, Winter 100
Facilities: A/V Equipment, Cabins, Double Occupancy, Food Service, Kitchen Facilities, Lake, Meeting Rooms, Playing Fields
Programs: Boating, Challenge/Ropes Course, Environmental Education, Swimming (#12631)

Camp Jori   ☀ ▲

Narragansett, RI
Activities: Arts/Crafts, Canoeing, Ceramics/Pottery, Hockey, Soccer, Swimming — Instructional, Tennis
Contact: Web site: www.jori.com
Operated by: Camp Jori, 22 Harding Ave, Cranston, RI 02905 at (401) 781-3016 (#901470)

Camp Ok-Wa-Nessett   ☀

Warwick, RI (Nessett Co.); (401) 828-0130
Steven Nadeau, Director

Camp comments: YMCA day camp located at the Kent County YMCA. Dynamic programs & staff provide a safe, fun, and nurturing environment.
Activities: Archery, Arts/Crafts, Canoeing, Gymnastics, Leadership Development, Nature/Environment Studies, Performing Arts, Sports — Field & Team, Swimming — Recreational, Tennis
Session lengths & capacity: June-August; 2 week sessions; 800 campers
Clientele & fees: coed 3-17; Fees: **B** ☀ 🐷
Contact: Steven J Nadeau, Executive Director at (401) 828-0130; fax: (401) 821-8480
e-mail: sjnado@ids.net
Operated by: YMCA Gtr Providence Camping, 70 Ship St, Providence, RI 02903 at (401) 521-9622 (#1048)

Camp Ruggles (est 1965)   ☀ 🚐

Glocester, RI (Providence Co.); (401) 568-6525
George M Jacques, Director

Camp comments: Day camp for emotionally handicapped children. Campers must be referred by special education coordinator or psychologist
Activities: Aquatic Activities, Arts/Crafts, Basketball, Boating, Canoeing, Drawing/Painting, Fishing, Kayaking, Nature/Environment Studies, Swimming — Instructional
Session lengths & capacity: June-August; 1 & 6 week sessions; 60 campers
Clientele & fees: coed 6-12; Fees: **D** ☀ 🐷
Contact: George M Jacques, Director at (401) 647-5508;
Operated by: Camp Ruggles Inc, 133 Stone Dam Road, North Scituate, RI 02857 at (401) 647-5508 (#3527)

Camp Shepard   ☀

Greenville, RI; (401) 949-4543
Sennia Rogers, Director
Activities: Archery, Arts/Crafts, Boating, Challenge/Rope Courses, Fishing, Swimming — Recreational, Team Building
Contact: Sennia A Rogers, Camp Director at (401) 456-0100 ext. 165; fax: (401) 274-0828
Operated by: YMCA Gtr Providence Camping, 70 Ship St, Providence, RI 02903 at (401) 521-9622 (#40862)

Camp Watchaug (est 1948)   ☀ ⌂ 🚐

Charlestown, RI (Washington Co.); (401) 364-6535
D. Scott McLeod, Director

Camp comments: Serving the Westerly & Chariho towns in RI to the Mystic, Stonington & North STonington towns in CT since 1948.
Activities: Archery, Arts/Crafts, Boating, Canoeing, Counselor Training (CIT), Kayaking, Leadership Development, Sailing, Sports — Field & Team, Swimming — Instructional
Session lengths & capacity: June-August; 1, 2 & 4 week sessions; 320 campers
Clientele & fees: coed 4-15; families; Fees: **B, C** ☀ 🚐
Contact: D Scott McLeod, Program & Camp Director at (401) 596-2894; fax: (401) 596-8675
Web site: www.wpymca.org
Operated by: Westerly Pawcatuck YMCA, 95 High Street, Westerly, RI 02891 at (401) 596-2894
Group Rental Information
Facilities: Kitchen Facilities, Lake, Lodges, Playing Fields
Programs: Swimming (#44839)

Canonicus Camp And Conference (est 1948)   ☀ ▲ ⌂ 🚐

Exeter, RI (Washington Co.); (800) 294-6318
Mark Bates, Director

Camp comments: Quality Christian camp located on 308 acres of field, woodland and lake. Established in 1948 we serve boys & girls in a general camping program.
Activities: Archery, Aviation, Camping Skills/Outdoor Living, Challenge/Rope Courses, Horseback — English, Leadership Development, Music, Religious Study, Soccer, Swimming — Recreational
Session lengths & capacity: June-August; 1/2 & 1 week sessions; 180 campers
Clientele & fees: coed 4-18; Fees: **B** ☀
Fees: **C** ▲ 🐷
Contact: Colleen Tolhurst, Registrar at (800) 294-6318 ext. 106;
e-mail: camp@canonicus.org
Web site: www.canonicus.org
Operated by: American Baptist Churches RI, PO Box 330, Exeter, RI 02822 at (401) 294-6318
Group Rental Information
Site comments: Facilities to accomodate 10-150 people day or overnight. Beautiful setting and excellent food.
Facilities: A/V Equipment, Double Occupancy, Food Service, Lake, Lodges, Meeting Rooms, Playing Fields, Tents
Programs: Boating, Challenge/Ropes Course (#2868)

Fuller (est 1887)   ▲ ⌂ 🚐

Wakefield, RI (Washington Co.); (401) 783-5359
Peter Swain, Director

Camp comments: Salt water sailing & aquatics. Strong emphasis in noncompetitive activities, strong camp traditions, register early.
Activities: Archery, Arts/Crafts, Canoeing, Leadership Development, Radio/TV/Video, Sailing, Skating, Swimming — Recreational, Waterskiing, Windsurfing

Session lengths & capacity: June-August; 1, 2 &
4 week sessions; 275 campers
Clientele & fees: coed 7-16; Fees: D ◬ 🚐
Contact: Patricia Driscoll, Associate Director at
(800) 521-1470; fax: (401) 782-6083
e-mail: ymcafuller@aol.com
Operated by: YMCA Gtr Providence Camping, 70
Ship St, Providence, RI 02903 at (401) 521-9622
Group Rental Information
Site comments: Fuller provides the perfect setting
for youth retreats or church groups.
Seasons & Capacity: Spring 125, Fall 125
Facilities: Dorm-Style, Food Service, Kitchen
Facilities, Ocean, Playing Fields
Programs: Challenge/Ropes Course (#2662)

YMCA Camp Massasoit

(est 1946)   ☼ ⌂ 🚐

Cronstor, RI; (401) 943-0444
Jean Colaneri, Director

Camp comments: Program is designed to build
self-confidence, encourage group participation and
create opportunities for self discovery.
Activities: Aquatic Activities, Arts/Crafts,
Baseball/Softball, Basketball, Canoeing, Hiking,
Performing Arts, Soccer, Sports — Field & Team,
Swimming — Instructional
Session lengths & capacity: June-September;
2 week sessions; 300 campers
Clientele & fees: coed 6-12; Fees: B ☼ 🐷
Contact: Jean Colaneri, Youth and Family Services
Director at (401) 943-0444; fax: (404) 946-7589
Operated by: YMCA Gtr Providence Camping, 70
Ship St, Providence, RI 02903 at (401) 521-9622
(#33660)

YMCA Camp Waseca

                                        ☼ 🚐

Barrington, RI; (401) 245-2444
Julie Fontaine, Director
Activities: Arts/Crafts, Community Service, Drama,
Field Trips, Leadership Development,
Nature/Environment Studies, Swimming —
Instructional, Swimming — Recreational
Session lengths & capacity: 2 week sessions;
350 campers
Clientele & fees: coed 3-15; Fees: B ☼
Contact: Julie Fontaine, Child Care Director at
(401) 245-2444; fax: (401) 245-6584
Operated by: YMCA Gtr Providence Camping, 70
Ship St, Providence, RI 02903 at (401) 521-9622
(#40801)

YMCA of South County Day Camp

                                        ☼

Peacedale, RI; (401) 783-3900
Activities: Archery, Arts/Crafts, Challenge/Rope
Courses, Dance, Leadership Development,
Nature/Environment Studies, Performing Arts,
Soccer, Sports — Field & Team, Swimming —
Recreational
Operated by: YMCA Gtr Providence Camping, 70
Ship St, Providence, RI 02903 at (401) 521-9622
(#42553)

South Carolina

Asbury Hills Camp & Retrt Ctr

(est 1961)   ◬ ⌂

Cleveland, SC (Greenville Co.); (864) 836-3711
C Russell Davis, Director

Camp comments: Our vision statement: People
experiencing God's transforming love through
communion with God's people and creation.

Activities: Aquatic Activities, Archery, Backpacking,
Camping Skills/Outdoor Living, Canoeing,
Challenge/Rope Courses, Hiking,
Nature/Environment Studies, Religious Study,
Swimming — Recreational
Session lengths & capacity: June-August; 1/2, 1 &
2 week sessions; 150 campers
Clientele & fees: coed 7-18; families;
Fees: A, B, C ◬
Contact: C Russell Davis, Director at
(864) 836-3711; fax: (864) 836-5522
e-mail: contact@asburyhills.org
Web site: www.asburyhills.org
Operated by: South Carolina Brd Camps & Ret,
150 Asbury Dr, Cleveland, SC 29635-9748 at
(864) 836-3711
Group Rental Information
Site comments: Our vision Statement: People
experiencing God's transforming ove through
communion with God's people and creation.
Seasons & Capacity: Spring 206, Summer 206,
Fall 206, Winter 106
Facilities: A/V Equipment, Cabins, Dorm-Style,
Food Service, Hiking Trails, Lake, Lodges, Meeting
Rooms, Ocean, Pool, River
Programs: Boating, Challenge/Ropes Course,
Environmental Education, Swimming (#766)

Burnt Gin Camp (est 1945)   ◬ ⌂

Wedgefield, SC (Sumter Co.); (803) 494-3145
Marie Aimone, Director

Camp comments: A camp for children with special
health care needs. 2:1 camper/staff ratio.
Activities: Arts/Crafts, Basketball, Canoeing,
Drama, Music, Nature/Environment Studies,
Swimming — Instructional
Session lengths & capacity: June-August; 1 week
sessions; 80 campers
Clientele & fees: coed 7-19; Fees: A ◬
Contact: Marie I Aimone, Camp Director at
(803) 898-0455; fax: (803) 898-0613
e-mail: aimonemi@columb60.dhec.state.sc.us
Web site: www.scdhec.net/hs/mch/burntgin/
hsbgin1.htm
Operated by: Children with Spec Health Care,
DHEC CSHCN, Box 101106, Columbia, SC 29211
at (803) 898-0455 (#3379)

Camp Chatuga (est 1956)   ◬ ⌂ 🚐

Mountain Rest, SC (Oconee Co.); (864) 638-3728
Kelly Moxley, Director

Camp comments: Fun, adventure, relaxation.
Family-run camp. All-inclusive reasonable fee. Over
30 activity choices.
Activities: Archery, Arts/Crafts, Camping
Skills/Outdoor Living, Field Trips, Horseback —
Western, Riflery, Sports — Field & Team, Swimming
— Recreational, Waterskiing
Session lengths & capacity: June-August; 1, 2 &
3 week sessions; 165 campers
Clientele & fees: coed 6-16; Fees: D ◬
Contact: Kelly Gordon Moxley, Director at
(864) 638-3728; fax: (864) 638-0898
e-mail: mail@campchatuga.com
Web site: www.campchatuga.com
Operated by: R&K Moxley LBarnett ASullivan, 291
Camp Chatuga Rd, Mountain Rest, SC 29664 at
(864) 638-3728
Group Rental Information
Facilities: Cabins, Food Service, Hiking Trails,
Lake, Lodges, Meeting Rooms, Playing Fields
Programs: Boating, Swimming (#737)

Camp Cherith In The Carolinas

(est 1984)   ◬

Clemson, SC (Pickens Co.); (864) 646-7502
Cindy Hunnicutt, Brenda Lain, Lori Pierce, Director

Camp comments: Camping ministry of Pioneer
Clubs in middle southeast. All campers welcome.
Low camper to staff ratio. Adult staff.

Activities: Archery, Arts/Crafts, Ceramics/Pottery,
Challenge/Rope Courses, Drama, Horseback —
Western, Riflery, Sailing, Swimming — Instructional,
Waterskiing
Session lengths & capacity: July-August; 1 week
sessions; 140 campers
Clientele & fees: boys 7-17; girls 7-17; Fees: C ◬
Contact: Karen Simons, Administrative Advisor at
(919) 489-9300; fax: (919) 493-8428
e-mail: klsimons@ipass.net
Operated by: Camp Cherith in the Carolinas, 2937
Welcome Dr, Durham, NC 27705 at (919) 489-9300
(#75)

Camp Cherokee (est 1946)   ◬

Blacksburg, SC; (803) 517-1740
Jay Thompson, Director

Camp comments: Camp Cherokee provides
individuals the opportunities to reach their potential
by building self-esteem, friendships and character
in a safe positive environment.
Activities: Aquatic Activities, Archery, Arts/Crafts,
Canoeing, Climbing/Rappelling, Counselor Training
(CIT), Sailing
Session lengths & capacity: June-August; 1/2, 1 &
2 week sessions; 100 campers
Clientele & fees: boys 6-14; girls 6-14; coed 6-14;
Fees: C ◬ 🐷
Contact: Jay Thompson, Camp Director at
(803) 329-9622; fax: (803) 327-9622
e-mail: jaythompson@rhareaymca.org
Web site: www.campcherokee.org
Operated by: Rock Hill Area YMCA, PO Box 2955,
Rock Hill, SC 29732 at (803) 329-9622 (#6038)

Camp Gravatt (est 1947)   ◬ ⌂

Aiken, SC (Aiken Co.); (803) 642-3264
The Rev'd L. Sue vonRautenkranz, Director

Camp comments: Christian camp with a focus on
friendship, self-esteem, and fun in a community that
cares. Carefully screened and trained staff.
Activities: Aquatic Activities, Archery, Arts/Crafts,
Bicycling/Biking, Canoeing, Challenge/Rope
Courses, Leadership Development, Music,
Nature/Environment Studies, Team Building
Session lengths & capacity: 1 week sessions;
120 campers
Clientele & fees: coed 7-15; Fees: C ◬ 🐷
Contact: Dr. Paul M Price, Executive Director at
(800) 597-1764; fax: (803) 648-7453
e-mail: bgravatt@mindspring.com
Web site: www.bishopgravatt.org
Operated by: The Bishop Gravatt Center Inc, 1006
Camp Gravatt Road, Aiken, SC 29805 at
(803) 648-1817
Group Rental Information
Site comments: Retreat conference, and meeting
facilities for small or large groups. Overnight
lodging and challenge courses available.
Seasons & Capacity: Spring 65, Summer 65, Fall
65, Winter 65
Facilities: A/V Equipment, Cabins, Double
Occupancy, Food Service, Hiking Trails, Lake,
Linens, Lodges, Meeting Rooms, Playing Fields
Programs: Boating, Challenge/Ropes Course
(#15271)

Camp La Vida (est 1983)   ◬ ⌂

Winnsboro, SC; (803) 635-6608
Cindy Chandler Skelton, Director

Camp comments: Program enables campers to
learn and participate in Southern Baptist mission
efforts in an outdoor setting.
Activities: Archery, Camping Skills/Outdoor Living,
Canoeing, Challenge/Rope Courses, Drama,
Riflery, Swimming — Recreational
Session lengths & capacity: June-August; 1/2 &
1 week sessions; 200 campers
Clientele & fees: girls 8-17; coed 8-17; Fees: B ◬
Contact: Cindy Chandler, Camp Director at
(803) 765-0030; fax: (803) 799-1044

e-mail: cindyskelton@scbaptist.org
Operated by: Womans Missionary Union Aux, South Carolina Baptist Convent, 190 Stoneridge Dr, Columbia, SC 29210 at (803) 765-0030
Group Rental Information
Facilities: A/V Equipment, Cabins, Dorm-Style, Double Occupancy, Food Service, Linens, Meeting Rooms, Playing Fields, Pool
Programs: Boating, Swimming (#6627)

Camp Low Country (est 1963) △

Cordesville, SC (Berkeley Co.); (843) 336-3251
Tiffany Hesting, Director

Camp comments: Girl Scout program, non scouts welcome. Tents, cabins, trad prog + adventure challenge, swim, canoe, nature & crafts.
Activities: Aquatic Activities, Archery, Arts/Crafts, Counselor Training (CIT), Field Trips, Horseback — English, Horseback — Western, Leadership Development, Nature/Environment Studies
Session lengths & capacity: June-August; 1, 2 & 3 week sessions; 120 campers
Clientele & fees: girls 7-17; Fees: B, C △
Contact: Tiffany Hesting, Camp Director at (843) 552-9910; fax: (843) 552-6221
e-mail: clcgs@ix.netcom.com
Web site: www.girlscoutsclc.org
Operated by: GS of Carolina Low Country, 7257 Cross County Road, Charleston, SC 29418 at (843) 552-9910 (#750)

Clemson Univ Outdoor Lab

(est 1971) △ ⌂

Clemson, SC (Pickens County Co.); (864) 646-7502

Camp comments: Several different programs serving special populations. Available throughout year for conference center use, including retreats, receptions, training, workshops
Activities: Aquatic Activities, Archery, Boating, Camping Skills/Outdoor Living, Canoeing, Challenge/Rope Courses, Drama, Hiking, Sailing, Swimming — Instructional
Session lengths & capacity: June-August; 1 & 2 week sessions; 150 campers
Clientele & fees: coed 5-99; Fees: C △ 🚐
Contact: Charlie R White, Director at (864) 646-7502; fax: (864) 646-3620
e-mail: cuolcamps-l@clemson.edu
Operated by: Clemson University/PRTM, PO Box 340735, Clemson, SC 29634-0735 at (864) 656-3401

Group Rental Information
Site comments: Winterized facilities open year round. Connection with Clemson University affords opportunity for student leadership in all programs. Five miles from campus.

ICON LEGEND

☀ Day Camp
△ Resident Camp
⌂ Facilities Available To Rent
🚐 Transportation Available
🐷 Financial Aid Available

FEE RANGES PER WEEK

A	$0-75
B	$75-200
C	$201-350
D	$351-500
E	$501-650
F	over $650

Seasons & Capacity: Spring 200, Fall 200, Winter 200
Facilities: A/V Equipment, Cabins, Double Occupancy, Food Service, Hiking Trails, Lake, Linens, Meeting Rooms, Playing Fields, Pool
Programs: Boating, Challenge/Ropes Course, Environmental Education, Swimming (#3186)

Congaree Program Center

(est 1949) ☀ △

Lexington, SC (Lexington Co.); (803) 894-4169
Jennifer Bollo, Director

Camp comments: Girl Scout camp offers exciting opportunities to allow girls to have fun while learning more about themselves and nature
Activities: Archery, Arts/Crafts, Camping Skills/Outdoor Living, Canoeing, Challenge/Rope Courses, Horseback — Western, Leadership Development, Nature/Environment Studies, Swimming — Recreational
Session lengths & capacity: June-August; 1/2, 1 & 2 week sessions; 150 campers
Clientele & fees: girls 6-17; Fees: A ☀ Fees: B, C △ 🐷
Contact: Jennifer M Bollo, Program Director at (803) 782-5133 ext. 3039; fax: (803) 782-0410
e-mail: bolloj@congaree.org
Operated by: Girl Scouts Congaree Area, PO Box 7637, Columbia, SC 29202-7637 at (803) 782-5133 (#792)

Mc Call Royal Ambassador Camp (est 1960) △

Sunset, SC (Pickens Co.); (864) 878-6025
N Clifton Satterwhite, Director

Camp comments: Mtn setting, boys grades 1-12. Southern Baptist Camp with missions, education, hiking, swimming, adventure, recreation.
Activities: Archery, Backpacking, Basketball, Challenge/Rope Courses, Climbing/Rappelling, Hiking, Kayaking, Leadership Development, Riflery, Team Building
Session lengths & capacity: 1/2 & 1 week sessions; 220 campers
Clientele & fees: boys 6-18; Fees: B △
Contact: N Clifton Satterwhite, Administrative Director at (803) 765-0030; fax: (803) 799-1044
e-mail: cliffsatterwhite@scbaptist.org
Operated by: So Carolina Baptist Convention, 190 Stoneridge Dr, Columbia, SC 29210 at (803) 765-0030 (#2956)

Robert M Cooper 4H Leadership

(est 1935) △ ⌂

Summerton, SC (Clarendon Co.); (803) 478-2105
DuValle Elliott, Jr., Director

Camp comments: Residential 4-H camp located on the shores of beautiful Lake Marion. Summer camp, outdoor education, and year round groups. We operate 365 days a year.
Activities: Archery, Arts/Crafts, Baseball/Softball, Basketball, Canoeing, Challenge/Rope Courses, Climbing/Rappelling, Kayaking, Riflery, Team Building
Session lengths & capacity: 1/2, 1 & 2 week sessions; 480 campers
Clientele & fees: boys 8-16; girls 8-16; coed 8-16; Fees: B △
Contact: Lori Frager, Summer Camp Registrar at (864) 656-3145; fax: (864) 656-5723
e-mail: lfrager@clemson.edu
Operated by: Clemson University, Youth Learning Institute, 230 Poole Agricultural Center, Clemson, SC 29634-0133 at (864) 656-1659

Group Rental Information
Site comments: Located on the beautiful shores of Lake Marion. Our exciting active camping experience is open to youth, adult, and family groups using our modern facilities.
Seasons & Capacity: Spring 550, Summer 550, Fall 550, Winter 550
Facilities: A/V Equipment, Dorm-Style, Double Occupancy, Food Service, Hiking Trails, Lake, Linens, Lodges, Meeting Rooms, Playing Fields
Programs: Boating, Challenge/Ropes Course, Environmental Education, Horseback Riding, Swimming (#3719)

St Christopher Camp & Conf Ctr

(est 1938) △ ⌂

Johns Island, SC (Charleston Co.); (843) 768-4035
Norman Ross, Director

Camp comments: Christian focus, Barrior Island. Professional and caring staff.
Activities: Aquatic Activities, Arts/Crafts, Community Service, Counselor Training (CIT), Dance, Fishing, Leadership Development, Nature/Environment Studies, Religious Study, Sailing
Session lengths & capacity: 1/2, 1 & 2 week sessions; 130 campers
Clientele & fees: boys 7-17; girls 7-17; coed 7-17; families; seniors; Fees: C △
Contact: Anna Sims, Conference Coordinator at (843) 768-0429; fax: (843) 768-0918
e-mail: stchris@dycon.com
Web site: www.stchristopher.org
Operated by: St Christopher Camp & Conf Ctr, 2810 Seabrook Island Rd, Johns Island, SC 29455-6219 at (843) 768-0429

Group Rental Information
Site comments: Inviting, ocean front setting conducive to successful prgms.
Facilities: Cabins, Double Occupancy, Food Service, Meeting Rooms, Ocean, River
Programs: Boating (#3051)

Thunderbird (est 1936) ☀ △ ⌂

Lake Wylie, SC (York Co.); (704) 716-4100
Dave Purcell, Director

Camp comments: Located just south of Charlotte, Camp Thunderbird celebrates 68 years of excellence. One and two week sessions ages 7-16. Nationally recognized water programs.
Activities: Challenge/Rope Courses, Gymnastics, Horseback — English, Sailing, Soccer, Tennis, Waterskiing
Session lengths & capacity: 1 & 2 week sessions; 462 campers
Clientele & fees: boys 7-16; girls 7-16; Fees: B ☀ Fees: E △ 🐷
Contact: Dave Purcell, Executive Director of Operations at (704) 716-4129; fax: (704) 716-4101
e-mail: staff@campthunderbird.org
Web site: www.campthunderbird.org
Operated by: YMCA Of Greater Charlotte, One Thunderbird Lane, Lake Wylie, SC 29710-8811 at (704) 716-4100

Group Rental Information
Site comments: Located just 17 miles from Charlotte NC.
Seasons & Capacity: Spring 450, Fall 450, Winter 300
Facilities: A/V Equipment, Cabins, Food Service, Hiking Trails, Lake, Lodges, Meeting Rooms, Playing Fields
Programs: Boating, Challenge/Ropes Course, Environmental Education, Swimming (#788)

W W Long 4H Leadership Center

(est 1933) ▲ ⌂

Aiken, SC (Aiken Co.); (803) 649-9512
Jarrod Dubose-Schmitt, Director

Camp comments: Beautiful rustic camp located on over 400 acres in Central South Carolina. South Carolina 4-H Camp is open to everyone.
Activities: Aquatic Activities, Archery, Bicycling/Biking, Boating, Canoeing, Challenge/Rope Courses, Climbing/Rappelling, Counselor Training (CIT), Fishing, Kayaking
Session lengths & capacity: 1/2, 1 & 2 week sessions; 418 campers
Clientele & fees: boys 8-16; girls 8-16; coed 8-16; Fees: B ▲
Contact: Lori Frager, Summer Camp Registrar at (864) 656-3145; fax: (864) 656-5723
e-mail: lfrager@clemson.edu
Operated by: Clemson University, Youth Learning Institute, 230 Poole Agricultural Center, Clemson, SC 29634-0133 at (864) 656-1659

Group Rental Information

Site comments: Cabins, food services, adventure courses, meeting rooms, hiking trails, and boating are available for year round use for groups.
Seasons & Capacity: Spring 250, Summer 480, Fall 480, Winter 250
Facilities: A/V Equipment, Cabins, Dorm-Style, Food Service, Hiking Trails, Lake, Lodges, Meeting Rooms, Playing Fields
Programs: Boating, Challenge/Ropes Course, Environmental Education, Horseback Riding, Swimming (#3715)

Wabak (est 1948) ▲ ⌂

Marietta, SC (Greenville Co.); (864) 297-5890
Lynn Arve, Director

Camp comments: Beautiful mountain setting. Non Girl Scouts welcomed. Traditional outdoor program.
Activities: Archery, Arts/Crafts, Camping Skills/Outdoor Living, Canoeing, Ceramics/Pottery, Counselor Training (CIT), Hiking, Horseback — English, Swimming — Recreational
Session lengths & capacity: June-August; 1/2, 1 & 2 week sessions; 90 campers
Clientele & fees: girls 7-16; Fees: B ▲
Contact: Lynn Arve, Camp Director at (864) 675-1605; fax: (864) 675-1616
e-mail: larve@old96girlscouts.org
Web site: www.old96girlscouts.org
Operated by: Old Ninety Six GSC Inc, 412 E Butler Rd, Mauldin, SC 29662-1227 at (864) 297-5890

Group Rental Information

Facilities: Cabins, Hiking Trails, Kitchen Facilities, Lodges, Meeting Rooms, Playing Fields, Pool, Tents (#791)

WOW South Carolina Youth Camp

▲ ⌂

Patrick, SC (Chesterfield Co.); (843) 498-6577
Christopher Henson, Director

Camp comments: Woodmen camp strives to provide an enriching experience for young people physically, mentally and emotionally.
Activities: Archery, Arts/Crafts, Basketball, Canoeing, Challenge/Rope Courses, Nature/Environment Studies, Riflery, Soccer, Swimming — Recreational, Team Building
Session lengths & capacity: May-August; 1/2 & 1 week sessions; 180 campers
Clientele & fees: coed 8-15; families; seniors; Fees: A ▲
Contact: Christopher Henson, Director at (803) 788-6912; fax: (803) 736-5099
Operated by: WOW Life Insurance (SE), 1700 Farnam, Omaha, NE 68120 at (402) 271-7258

Group Rental Information

Seasons & Capacity: Summer 169
Facilities: Cabins, Food Service, Kitchen Facilities, Lake, Playing Fields, Pool, Tents
Programs: Challenge/Ropes Course, Swimming (#6561)

South Dakota

NeSoDak Bible Camp/Klein Ranch (est 1942) ▲ ⌂

Waubay, SD; (605) 947-4440
Tricia Larson, Director

Camp comments: We provide you experiences to discover and reflect God's love in Christ through worship,study,music,& play in our rugged yet unique South Dakota setting.
Activities: Aquatic Activities, Bicycling/Biking, Canoeing, Hiking, Horseback — Western, Leadership Development, Music, Nature/Environment Studies, Performing Arts, Religious Study
Session lengths & capacity: 1/2 & 1 week sessions; 120 campers
Clientele & fees: coed 8-18; Fees: A, B, C ▲ 🐷
Contact: Neil Sorensen, Director Lutheran Outdoors in S. Dakota at (605) 947-4440; fax: (605) 947-4379
e-mail: nsdlo@itctel.com
Web site: www.lutheransoutdoors.org
Operated by: Lutherans Outdoors So Dakota, Augustana College, 2001 S Summit Ave, Sioux Falls, SD 57197-0001 at (605) 274-5326

Group Rental Information

Facilities: Cabins, Double Occupancy, Food Service, Hiking Trails, Lake, Linens, Lodges, Meeting Rooms
Programs: Environmental Education (#15311)

Outlaw & Atlantic Mtn Ranches

(est 1958) ☀ ▲ ⌂

Custer, SD (Custer Co.); (605) 673-4040
Jeff Rohr, Director

Camp comments: Mtn. Western ranch setting. Comfortable for families/primitive for older youth. Backpacking, horses. Christian emphasis.
Activities: Arts/Crafts, Backpacking, Camping Skills/Outdoor Living, Canoeing, Community Service, Hiking, Horseback — Western, Leadership Development, Nature/Environment Studies, Religious Study
Session lengths & capacity: June-August; 1 week sessions; 220 campers
Clientele & fees: coed 9-18; families; seniors; Fees: B, C ▲ 🐷
Contact: Jeff Rohr, Director at (605) 673-4040; fax: (605) 673-3044
e-mail: outlaw@gwtc.net
Web site: www.lutheransoutdoors.org
Operated by: Lutherans Outdoors So Dakota, Augustana College, 2001 S Summit Ave, Sioux Falls, SD 57197-0001 at (605) 274-5326

Group Rental Information

Site comments: Beautiful retreat facility in the southern Black Hills of SD. Lodge with 10 rooms, each with semi-private baths. Cabins and meeting rooms. Horses, canoeing.
Seasons & Capacity: Spring 100, Fall 100, Winter 80
Facilities: Cabins, Double Occupancy, Food Service, Hiking Trails, Linens, Lodges, Meeting Rooms
Programs: Challenge/Ropes Course, Environmental Education, Horseback Riding (#6397)

Tennessee

AJCC Milton Collins Day Camp

(est 1929) ☀

Knoxville, TN; (865) 690-6343
Ashlie Kunkel, Director

Camp comments: Campers grow as individuals, form long lasting friendships. Emerge as leaders, value team work. A fun & safe environment
Activities: Arts/Crafts, Counselor Training (CIT), Field Trips, Leadership Development, Performing Arts, Sports — Field & Team, Swimming — Instructional
Session lengths & capacity: June-August; 2 week sessions; 100 campers
Clientele & fees: coed 1-13; Fees: B ☀
Contact: Ashlie Kunkel, Camp Director at (865) 690-6343; fax: (865) 694-4861
e-mail: ajcckjf@aol.com
Operated by: Arnstein JCC, 6800 Deane Hill, Knoxville, TN 37919 at (865) 690-6343 (#3711)

Bethany Hills Camp (est 1945) ⌂

Kingston Springs, TN (Cheatham Co.); (615) 952-9184
Each rental provides own director & counselors, Director
Contact: David Johnson, Camp Manager at (615) 952-9184;
Web site: www.ccdctn.org
Operated by: Christian Church in Tennessee, 50 Vantage Way Ste 251, Nashville, TN 37228 at (615) 251-3400

Group Rental Information

Site comments: Bethany Hills provides lodging, meals & meeting space for groups, 96 in winter, 140 in summer. Bunk beds in lodge or cabins, rec hall, outdoor pool, 300 acre wd
Seasons & Capacity: Spring 100, Summer 130, Fall 100, Winter 96
Facilities: A/V Equipment, Cabins, Dorm-Style, Food Service, Hiking Trails, Lodges, Meeting Rooms, Playing Fields, Pool
Programs: Swimming (#11976)

Buffalo Mtn Camp & Retreat Ctr (est 1949) ☀ ▲ ⌂

Jonesborough, TN; (423) 753-6678
Christina DowlingSoka, Director

Camp comments: Small group Christian living, adventure, personal growth, noncompetitive. In E.Tennessee mountains. United Methodist
Activities: Aquatic Activities, Arts/Crafts, Camping Skills/Outdoor Living, Climbing/Rappelling, Kayaking, Music, Nature/Environment Studies, Religious Study, Swimming — Recreational
Session lengths & capacity: June-August; 1/2 & 1 week sessions; 110 campers
Clientele & fees: coed 6-18; families; seniors; single adults; Fees: B ☀ Fees: B ▲
Contact: Christina DowlingSoka, Camp Director at (423) 753-6678; fax: (423) 753-5380
e-mail: buffalomountain@hotmail.com
Operated by: Holston Conference Camping, PO Box 1178, Johnson City, TN 37605-1178 at (423) 928-2156

Group Rental Information

Site comments: Retreat center and rustic lodge in beautiful mountain setting. Ideal for family reunions, church and community retreats. Lovely waterfall and creek.
Seasons & Capacity: Spring 160, Winter 75
Facilities: A/V Equipment, Cabins, Dorm-Style, Double Occupancy, Food Service, Hiking Trails, Kitchen Facilities, Lake, Linens, Lodges, Meeting Rooms, Playing Fields, Pool
Programs: Boating, Environmental Education, Swimming (#13642)

Buford-Ellington 4H Center ▲ 🏠

Milan, TN; (731) 686-8111
Activities: Aquatic Activities, Archery, Arts/Crafts, Riflery, Swimming — Instructional, Swimming — Recreational
Operated by: University of Tennessee, Agricultural Extension Service, PO Box 1071, Knoxville, TN 37901 at (865) 974-7108 (#48690)

Camp Discovery (est 1982) ▲

Gainesboro, TN (Jackson Co.); (931) 268-0239
Dawn Hickman, Director

Camp comments: Lake front setting, log dorms, special design for mental & physical handicapped.
Activities: Academics, Aquatic Activities, Arts/Crafts, Hiking, Nature/Environment Studies
Session lengths & capacity: 1 & 2 week sessions; 90 campers
Clientele & fees: boys 7-65; girls 7-65; coed 7-65; Fees: C ▲ 🐷
Contact: Adam and Shanna Howell, Directors at (615) 360-3678;
e-mail: campdirector2000@aol.com
Operated by: Tennessee Jaycee Fnd Inc, 651 E 4th St Ste 600, Chattanooga, TN 37403 at (423) 267-9718 (#5383)

Camp Horizon (est 1983) ▲

Kingston Springs, TN (Cheatham Co.)
Susanne Manning, Director

Camp comments: A camping program held each summer just outside Nashville for cancer survivors & siblings at no charge. Staffed by doctors, nurses & other dedicated volunteers.
Activities: Aquatic Activities, Camping Skills/Outdoor Living, Canoeing, Counselor Training (CIT), Field Trips, Leadership Development, Music, Nature/Environment Studies, Sports — Field & Team, Swimming — Instructional
Session lengths & capacity: 2 week sessions
Contact: Suzanne Manning at (615) 341-7313;
e-mail: suzanne.manning@cancer.org
Web site: www.cancer.org
Operated by: American Cancer Society, 1100 Ireland Way Ste 300, Birmingham, AL 37203 at (205) 930-3360 (#11220)

Camp Marymount (est 1939) ▲ 🏠

Fairview, TN (Williamson Co.); (615) 799-0410
Tommy Hagey, Director

Camp comments: Individual care and personal interest in every child.

ICON LEGEND

☀ Day Camp
▲ Resident Camp
🏠 Facilities Available To Rent
🚐 Transportation Available
🐷 Financial Aid Available

FEE RANGES PER WEEK

A $0-75
B $75-200
C $201-350
D $351-500
E $501-650
F over $650

Activities: Archery, Arts/Crafts, Camping Skills/Outdoor Living, Canoeing, Counselor Training (CIT), Farming/Ranching/Gardening, Horseback — Western, Nature/Environment Studies, Riflery, Swimming — Instructional
Session lengths & capacity: June-August; 2, 3 & 5 week sessions; 200 campers
Clientele & fees: boys 6-16; girls 6-16; Fees: C ▲ 🐷
Contact: Tommy Hagey, Director at (615) 799-0410; fax: (615) 799-2261
e-mail: info@campmarymount.com
Operated by: Catholic Dioceses of Nashville, Camp Marymount, 1318 Fairview Blvd, Fairview, TN 37062 at (615) 799-0410

Group Rental Information
Seasons & Capacity: Spring 250, Fall 250
Facilities: Cabins, Hiking Trails, Kitchen Facilities, Lake, Lodges, Playing Fields (#7308)

Camp Sky-Wa-Mo (est 1947) ▲ 🏠

BLUFF CITY, TN; (423) 538-6741
Angela Claxton-Freeman, Director

Camp comments: Sky, Water, Mountains! Decentralized Girl Scout prog, troop-sized groups, democratic planning & decision making. Where Girls Grow Strong
Activities: Arts/Crafts, Camping Skills/Outdoor Living, Canoeing, Counselor Training (CIT), Hiking, Nature/Environment Studies, Swimming — Recreational, Team Building
Session lengths & capacity: June-July; 1 & 2 week sessions; 80 campers
Clientele & fees: girls 6-18; families; Fees: B, C ▲ 🐷
Contact: Angela Claxton-Freeman, Camp Director at (423) 929-8185; fax: (423) 929-8117
e-mail: agsc@naxs.com
Operated by: Appalachian GSC Inc, PO Box 3100, Johnson City, TN 37602 at (423) 929-8185

Group Rental Information
Facilities: Pool, Tents (#700)

Camp Sycamore Hills ▲ 🏠

Ashland City, TN (Davidson Co.)
Activities: Aquatic Activities, Archery, Arts/Crafts, Canoeing, Challenge/Rope Courses, Climbing/Rappelling, Counselor Training (CIT), Horseback — Western, Nature/Environment Studies, Swimming — Recreational
Contact: Web site: www.girlscoutsofcv.org
Operated by: GSC of Cumberland Valley, PO Box 40466, Nashville, TN 37204 at (615) 383-0490

Group Rental Information
Facilities: Cabins, Dorm-Style, Food Service, Hiking Trails, Lodges, Playing Fields, Pool, Tents
Programs: Boating, Challenge/Ropes Course, Environmental Education, Horseback Riding, Swimming (#44444)

Camp Thunderbird (est 1950) ▲

Chattanooga, TN (Daividson Co.); (423) 892-2129

Camp comments: Camp Thunderbird is a Christian Youth Camp for all races we emphasize Christian values, nature, fun and fellowship
Activities: Aquatic Activities, Arts/Crafts, Baseball/Softball, Basketball, Drama, Football, Gymnastics, Hiking, Skating, Swimming — Recreational
Session lengths & capacity: June-August; 110 campers
Clientele & fees: coed 6-12; Fees: B ▲
Contact: Lorenzo B Shepherd, Associate Youth Ministries Director at (615) 226-6500 ext. 141; fax: (615) 262-9141
Operated by: South Central Conference, 715 Youngs Lane, Nashville, TN 37207 at (615) 262-9141 (#3198)

Circle Yi Ranch (est 1945) ▲ 🏠

La Vergne, TN (Rutherford Co.); (615) 459-3971
Charlie Tygard, Director

Camp comments: Located on beautiful Percy Priest Lake, Youth Inc. proudly offers an unexcelled camping experience at a moderate cost.
Activities: Arts/Crafts, Challenge/Rope Courses, Horseback — Western
Session lengths & capacity: June-August; 2 week sessions; 125 campers
Clientele & fees: coed 7-14; Fees: B, C ▲
Contact: Sue Ownby, Camp Director at (615) 865-0003; fax: (615) 865-0094
e-mail: camp@youthincorporated.org
Web site: www.youthincorporated.org
Operated by: Youth Incorporated, 209 Plaza Prof Bldg, Madison, TN 37115 at (615) 865-0003

Group Rental Information
Seasons & Capacity: Spring 150, Fall 150, Winter 40
Facilities: Cabins, Dorm-Style, Kitchen Facilities, Lake, Lodges, Playing Fields, Pool
Programs: Boating, Challenge/Ropes Course, Horseback Riding, Swimming (#5422)

Clyde Austin 4H Center

(est 1949) ▲ 🏠

Greeneville, TN (Greene Co.); (423) 639-3811
Andy J Seals, Director

Camp comments: Conveniently located in the mountains of East Tennessee. Modern facilities, private setting. Friendly staff & environment
Activities: Archery, Arts/Crafts, Canoeing, Challenge/Rope Courses, Fishing, Nature/Environment Studies, Riflery, Swimming — Recreational
Session lengths & capacity: 1 week sessions; 336 campers
Clientele & fees: coed 8-18; Fees: B ▲
Contact: Andy Seals, Center Manager at (423) 639-3811; fax: (423) 639-4911
e-mail: aseals@utk.edu
Operated by: University of Tennessee, Agricultural Extension Service, PO Box 1071, Knoxville, TN 37901 at (865) 974-7108

Group Rental Information
Site comments: Mountains east TN setting dedicated staff fully accessible modern dorms traditional pro facilities rentaltonon4-hgroups
Facilities: Dorm-Style, Food Service, Lake, Meeting Rooms, Pool
Programs: Boating, Environmental Education (#19249)

Clyde M York 4H Center

(est 1949) ▲ 🏠

Crossville, TN (Cumberland Co.); (931) 788-2288
Mr. Scottie Fillers, Director

Camp comments: Spacious camp, wooded area, ropes course. Traditional programs. Challenging activities. Friendly staff & environment.
Activities: Aquatic Activities, Arts/Crafts, Camping Skills/Outdoor Living, Ceramics/Pottery, Challenge/Rope Courses, Farming/Ranching/Gardening, Nature/Environment Studies, Riflery, Team Building
Session lengths & capacity: 1 week sessions; 400 campers
Clientele & fees: boys 9-19; girls 9-19; coed 9-19; Fees: B ▲ 🐷
Contact: Scottie Fillers, Manager at (931) 788-2288; fax: (931) 788-6003
e-mail: camp4h@usit.net
Operated by: University of Tennessee, Agricultural Extension Service, PO Box 1071, Knoxville, TN 37901 at (865) 974-7108

Group Rental Information
Facilities: Dorm-Style, Food Service, Kitchen Facilities, Lake, Linens, Lodges, Meeting Rooms, Playing Fields, Pool
Programs: Swimming (#15990)

Confrontation Point Ministries

(est 1980)

Crossville, TN (Cumberland Co.); (800) 884-8483
Randy Velker, Director
Contact: Randy Velker, Executive Director at (800) 884-8483; fax: (931) 484-7819
e-mail: cp@ConfrontationPoint.org
Web site: www.confrontationpoint.org
Operated by: Confrontation Point Ministries, PO Box 572, Crossville, TN 38557 at (800) 884-8483
Group Rental Information
Facilities: Kitchen Facilities, Tents (#4021)

Crystal Springs Camp Inc

Kelso, TN (Lincoln Co.); (931) 937-8621
Contact: Carol Medley, Director at (931) 937-8621; fax: (931) 937-8621
e-mail: medley@cafes.net
Operated by: Crystal Springs Camp Inc, 566 Country Club Ln, Winchester, TN 37398 at (931) 967-8585
Group Rental Information
Facilities: A/V Equipment, Cabins, Dorm-Style, Food Service, Hiking Trails, Lake, Playing Fields, Pool
Programs: Boating, Swimming (#44121)

Easter Seals Camp Lindahl

(est 1959)

Mt Juliet, TN; (615) 444-2829
Rob Ogden, Director

Camp comments: Beautiful lake setting. Dedicated, warm, caring staff. Safe & challenging programs. Fully accessible.
Activities: Aquatic Activities, Arts/Crafts, Boating, Canoeing, Fishing, Nature/Environment Studies, Swimming — Recreational
Session lengths & capacity: June-August; 1/2 & 1 week sessions; 75 campers
Clientele & fees: boys 6-99; girls 6-99; coed 6-99; Fees: C ⚠ 🐖
Contact: Michael Currence, Director of Recreation/Camping at (615) 444-2829; fax: (615) 444-8576
e-mail: escamp@bellsouth.net
Operated by: Easter Seals Camp Lindahl, 6300 Benders Ferry Rd, Mt Juliet, TN 37122 at (615) 444-2829
Group Rental Information
Facilities: Cabins, Food Service, Kitchen Facilities, Lodges, Meeting Rooms
Programs: Boating (#7695)

Girl Scout Kamp Kiwani

(est 1965)

Middleton, TN (Hardeman Co.); (901) 376-8281
Kim Jones, Director

Camp comments: Girl Scout fun & activities presented in general & specific programs. Inexperienced & experienced campers welcomed.
Activities: Archery, Arts/Crafts, Camping Skills/Outdoor Living, Canoeing, Counselor Training (CIT), Hiking, Horseback — Western, Leadership Development, Nature/Environment Studies, Swimming — Recreational
Session lengths & capacity: June-August; 1/2, 1 & 2 week sessions; 150 campers
Clientele & fees: girls 7-17; Fees: B, C ⚠ 🐖
Contact: Mary McHugh, Property Manager at (701) 767-1440; fax: (901) 797-2183

Operated by: Girl Scout Council Mid-South, PO Box 240246, Memphis, TN 38124 at (901) 767-1440
Group Rental Information
Facilities: Cabins, Hiking Trails, Kitchen Facilities, Lake, Playing Fields
Programs: Boating, Swimming (#719)

Indian Creek Camp (est 1992)

Liberty, TN; (615) 548-4411
Jerry Mahn, Director

Camp comments: A Christian camp on a beautiful lake. The program features great recreation & Christian values.
Activities: Aquatic Activities, Archery, Arts/Crafts, Bicycling/Biking, Canoeing, Ceramics/Pottery, Horseback — Western, Nature/Environment Studies, Swimming — Instructional, Waterskiing
Session lengths & capacity: June-August; 1 week sessions; 200 campers
Clientele & fees: coed 7-17; families; seniors; Fees: B ⚠
Contact: Debbie Hilliard, Youth Department Secretary at (615) 859-1391 ext. 243; fax: (615) 859-2120
e-mail: darlenebee@aol.com
Operated by: Kentucky Tennessee Conference, PO Box 1088, Goodlettsville, TN 37070 at (615) 859-1391
Group Rental Information
Site comments: Indian Creek is a beautiful camp on Center Hill Lake. We offer a variety of recreation options, plus meeting space.
Seasons & Capacity: Spring 200, Fall 200, Winter 200
Facilities: A/V Equipment, Cabins, Double Occupancy, Food Service, Hiking Trails, Kitchen Facilities, Lake, Linens, Meeting Rooms, Playing Fields, Pool
Programs: Boating, Environmental Education, Horseback Riding, Swimming (#13434)

John Knox Center

Ten Mile, TN; (865) 376-2236

Camp comments: On the shores of beautiful Walls Bar Lake
Activities: Aquatic Activities, Arts/Crafts, Camping Skills/Outdoor Living, Challenge/Rope Courses, Leadership Development, Religious Study, Team Building
Session lengths & capacity: 1/2, 1 & 2 week sessions; 144 campers
Clientele & fees: families; seniors; single adults; Fees: B ☀ Fees: B ⚠
Contact: Barbara Flowers, Administrative Assistant at (865) 376-2236; fax: (865) 376-1719
Operated by: John Knox Center, 591 W Rockwood Ferry Rd, Ten Mile, TN 37880 at (865) 376-2236
Group Rental Information
Seasons & Capacity: Spring 144, Summer 144, Fall 144, Winter 120
Facilities: Cabins, Dorm-Style, Food Service, Hiking Trails, Lake, Meeting Rooms
Programs: Environmental Education (#13566)

NaCoMe (est 1939)

Pleasantville, TN (Hickman Co.); (931) 729-9723
Rev Steve Thomas, Director

Camp comments: Largest Christian conference center in mid-south, one hour west of Nashville. For pictures see Web site www.nacome.org
Activities: Archery, Arts/Crafts, Camping Skills/Outdoor Living, Canoeing, Counselor Training (CIT), Drama, Kayaking, Music, Religious Study, Soccer
Session lengths & capacity: 1 week sessions; 390 campers
Clientele & fees: coed 5-18; families; seniors; Fees: C ⚠
Contact: Aaron Horn, Assistant Director at (931) 729-9723; fax: (931) 729-9723

e-mail: aaron@nacome.org
Operated by: NaCoMe, 3232 Sulphur Creek Rd, Pleasantville, TN 37147 at (913) 729-9723
Group Rental Information
Seasons & Capacity: Spring 390, Summer 390, Fall 390, Winter 210
Facilities: A/V Equipment, Cabins, Double Occupancy, Food Service, Hiking Trails, Kitchen Facilities, Lake, Linens, Meeting Rooms, Playing Fields, River, Tents
Programs: Boating, Swimming (#16763)

Oak Hill Day Camp (est 1952)

Nashville, TN (Davidson Co.); (615) 298-9527
Rev Ted Martin, Director

Camp comments: A christian daycamp that encourages campers in a variety of activities. Year round programs: sports, enrichment, after care.
Activities: Archery, Arts/Crafts, Camping Skills/Outdoor Living, Drama, Horseback — English, Religious Study, Soccer
Session lengths & capacity: June-August; 1 & 2 week sessions; 232 campers
Clientele & fees: coed 4-12; Fees: B 🐖 🕊
Contact: Ted Martin, Director at (615) 298-9527; fax: (615) 298-9552
e-mail: recdept@nashville.com
Web site: www.fpcnashville.org
Operated by: First Presbyterian Church, 4815 Franklin Road, Nashville, TN 37220 at (615) 383-1815 (#1079)

Tanasi (est 1954)

Andersonville, TN (Union Co.); (423) 494-7470
Brooke Bradley, Director

Camp comments: Beautiful lake & mtns. Modern lodge for younger girls. Fun & friendly camp open to all girls.
Activities: Arts/Crafts, Camping Skills/Outdoor Living, Challenge/Rope Courses, Climbing/Rappelling, Horseback — English, Leadership Development, Nature/Environment Studies, Swimming — Instructional, Waterskiing
Session lengths & capacity: June-July; 1/2, 1 & 2 week sessions; 140 campers
Clientele & fees: girls 7-15; Fees: B ☀ Fees: C ⚠
Contact: Brooke Bradley, Camp Director at (423) 494-7470; fax: (423) 689-9835
e-mail: Bbradley@tanasi.org
Web site: www.tanasi.org
Operated by: Tanasi GSC Inc, 1600 Breda Dr, Knoxville, TN 37918 at (865) 688-9440 (#689)

Tates Day Camp (est 1982)

Knoxville, TN (Knox Co.); (865) 690-9208
Chris Strevel, Director

Camp comments: Inspired staff creates totally safe and caring environment. Beautiful 50 acre landscape, 3 pools, exciting activities!
Activities: Archery, Arts/Crafts, Camping Skills/Outdoor Living, Challenge/Rope Courses, Climbing/Rappelling, Counselor Training (CIT), Nature/Environment Studies, Sports — Field & Team, Swimming — Instructional, Swimming — Recreatio
Session lengths & capacity: May-August; 1 week sessions; 300 campers
Clientele & fees: coed 3-15; Fees: B ☀
Contact: Chris Strevel, Camp Director at (865) 690-9208; fax: (865) 670-9229
e-mail: tatescamp@aol.com
Operated by: Tates Day Camp, 1031 Cedar Bluff Road, Knoxville, TN 37923 at (865) 693-3021 (#6234)

Wesley Woods UM Camp

(est 1959) ☀ ⚠ ⌂

Townsend, TN (Blount Co.); (865) 448-2246
David Leach, Director
Camp comments: Small group Christian living in the Smoky Mountains. Noncompetitive, caring atmosphere. Many specialty camps for youth.
Activities: Arts/Crafts, Camping Skills/Outdoor Living, Challenge/Rope Courses, Climbing/Rappelling, Hiking, Horseback — Western, Kayaking, Nature/Environment Studies, Wilderness Trips
Session lengths & capacity: 1/2 & 1 week sessions; 120 campers
Clientele & fees: coed 7-18; Fees: **B, C** ⚠ ➹
Contact: David Leach, Director/Manager at (865) 448-6556; fax: (865) 448-3904
e-mail: dleach@campwesleywoods.com
Operated by: Holston Conference Camping, PO Box 1178, Johnson City, TN 37605-1178 at (423) 928-2156

Group Rental Information
Facilities: Cabins, Lodges (#7314)

Whippoorwill Farm Day Camp

(est 1972) ☀ 🚗

Fairview, TN (Williamson Co.); (615) 799-8244
Laurie Rosa, Director
Camp comments: Day campers explore creeks, wooded hills, fields & the diverse wild & farm life while having fun at Whippoorwill Farm.
Activities: Arts/Crafts, Bicycling/Biking, Camping Skills/Outdoor Living, Climbing/Rappelling, Farming/Ranching/Gardening, Horseback — English, Kayaking, Leadership Development, Nature/Environment Studies, Swimming — Recreational
Session lengths & capacity: June-August; 1 & 2 week sessions; 200 campers
Clientele & fees: boys 6-15; girls 6-15; coed 6-15; Fees: **B** ☀
Contact: Sidney Wooten, Director at (615) 799-8244;
e-mail: wiporwil@edge.net
Web site: www.whippoorwill.com
Operated by: Whippoorwill Farm Day Camp, 7840 Whippoorwill Ln, Fairview, TN 37062 at (615) 799-9925 (#7703)

ICON LEGEND

☀	Day Camp
⚠	Resident Camp
⌂	Facilities Available To Rent
🚗	Transportation Available
➹	Financial Aid Available

FEE RANGES PER WEEK

A	$0-75
B	$75-200
C	$201-350
D	$351-500
E	$501-650
F	over $650

William P Ridley 4H Center

☀ ⚠ ⌂

Columbia, TN (Maury Co.); (931) 388-4011
William 'Boone' Morrow, Director
Activities: Academics, Archery, Baseball/Softball, Camping Skills/Outdoor Living, Football, Nature/Environment Studies, Riflery, Sports — Field & Team, Swimming — Recreational, Team Building
Contact: Boone Morrow, 4H Center Manager at (931) 388-4011; fax: (931) 381-8765
e-mail: boone@utk.edu
Operated by: University of Tennessee, Agricultural Extension Service, PO Box 1071, Knoxville, TN 37901 at (865) 974-7108

Group Rental Information
Facilities: Cabins, Dorm-Style, Food Service, Meeting Rooms, Pool
Programs: Environmental Education (#12257)

WOW Camp Ta-Ni-Si (est 1994) ⚠ ⌂

Westmoreland, TN (Sumner Co.); (615) 644-2726
Linda Dowdell, Director
Activities: Archery, Arts/Crafts, Challenge/Rope Courses, Climbing/Rappelling, Counselor Training (CIT), Fishing, Riflery, Sports — Field & Team, Swimming — Recreational
Session lengths & capacity: May-October; 3 week sessions; 75 campers
Clientele & fees: coed 8-15; families; seniors; Fees: **F** ⚠
Contact: Linda Dowdell, Fraternal Coordinator at (615) 859-1161; fax: (615) 859-1640
e-mail: ldowdell@woodmen.com
Web site: www.woodmen.com
Operated by: WOW Life Insurance (HS), 1700 Farnam, Omaha, NE 68120 at (402) 271-7258

Group Rental Information
Seasons & Capacity: Spring 75, Summer 75, Fall 75
Facilities: Cabins, Hiking Trails, Kitchen Facilities, Meeting Rooms, Pool (#46136)

YMCA Camp Montvale

(est 1949) ☀ ⚠ ⌂ 🚗

Maryville, TN (Blount Co.); (865) 983-9622
Markham Peykoff, Director
Camp comments: YMCA Camp Montvale builds strong kids families & communities! YMCA Camp Montvale -- a real Smoky Mountain adventure.
Activities: Archery, Arts/Crafts, Canoeing, Challenge/Rope Courses, Hiking, Horseback — Western, International Culture, Model Rocketry, Swimming — Recreational
Session lengths & capacity: May-August; 1 & 2 week sessions; 180 campers
Clientele & fees: coed 7-16; families; Fees: **B** ☀ Fees: **C** ⚠ ➹
Contact: Markham Peykoff, Executive Director at (865) 983-9622; fax: (865) 982-1380
e-mail: havefun@campmontvale.org
Web site: www.ymcaknoxville.org
Operated by: Knoxville YMCA, PO Box 2776, Knoxville, TN 37901 at (865) 522-9625

Group Rental Information
Seasons & Capacity: Spring 100, Winter 100
Facilities: Cabins, Dorm-Style, Food Service, Meeting Rooms, Pool
Programs: Boating, Horseback Riding (#24932)

YMCA Camp Ocoee (est 1923) ⚠

Ocoee, TN (Polk Co.); (423) 338-5588
Latta C Johnston, Director
Camp comments: Traditional & adventure prog. 5 day, 1 & 2 wk sessions. Focus on individual. Christian emphasis. 1:4 staff-camper ratio
Activities: Aquatic Activities, Archery, Backpacking, Canoeing, Challenge/Rope Courses, Climbing/Rappelling, Counselor Training (CIT), Kayaking, Team Building, Waterskiing

Session lengths & capacity: June-August; 1 & 2 week sessions; 170 campers
Clientele & fees: coed 6-17; families; Fees: **D** ⚠
Contact: Rachael Roy, Admin Assistant at (423) 265-0455; fax: (423) 265-2430
e-mail: ocoee@ix.netcom.com
Web site: www.campocoee.com
Operated by: YMCA Camp Ocoee, 301 W 6th St, Chattanooga, TN 37402 at (423) 265-0455 (#697)

YMCA Camp Widjiwagan ☀ ⌂

Antioch, TN (Davidson Co.); (615) 360-2267
April Keyser, Director
Activities: Aquatic Activities, Archery, Boating, Challenge/Rope Courses, Climbing/Rappelling, Horseback — Western, Kayaking, Swimming — Instructional, Swimming — Recreational
Session lengths & capacity: May-August; 400 campers
Contact: Web site: www.ymcamidtn.org/joecdavis
Operated by: Joe C Davis YMCA Outdoor Ctr, 3088 Smith Spring Rd, Antioch, TN 37013 at (615) 360-2267

Group Rental Information
Facilities: A/V Equipment, Double Occupancy, Lake, Linens, Lodges, Meeting Rooms, Playing Fields, Pool
Programs: Boating, Challenge/Ropes Course, Horseback Riding, Swimming (#46221)

Texas

ADA Texas Youth Camps

(est 1985) ☀

New Bloomfield, PA; (717) 582-3802
Michelle Knight, Director
Camp comments: Day camp for children with diabetes & their siblings. Emphasis on diabetes management & education. Activities vary.
Activities: Aerobics/Exercise, Arts/Crafts, Counselor Training (CIT), Drawing/Painting, Leadership Development, Nature/Environment Studies, Sports — Field & Team, Swimming — Recreational, Team Building, Tennis
Session lengths & capacity: June-July; 1 week sessions; 100 campers
Clientele & fees: coed 4-18; Fees: **A** ☀ ➹
Contact: Michelle Knight, National Director at (717) 582-3802; fax: (717) 582-3402
e-mail: mknight@diabetes.org
Operated by: ADA Texas Youth Camps, 62 Silver Crown Dr, Mechanicsburg, PA 17050-1637 at (717) 852-3802 (#6230)

Agnes Arnold (est 1944) ⚠ ⌂

Conroe, TX (Montgomery Co.)
Shelley "Roxy" Curiel, Director
Camp comments: GS Scout camp - rustic setting, focus is environment & outdoor skills. Tents & cabins. 1 week & 2 week sessions.
Activities: Archery, Bicycling/Biking, Camping Skills/Outdoor Living, Canoeing, Challenge/Rope Courses, Counselor Training (CIT), Hiking, Nature/Environment Studies, Photography, Sports — Field & Team
Session lengths & capacity: June-July; 1 & 2 week sessions; 200 campers
Clientele & fees: girls 6-17; Fees: **C** ⚠ ➹
Contact: Nicole McInnes, Program Manager at (713) 292-0353; fax: (713) 292-0330
e-mail: nmcinnes@sjgs.org
Web site: www.gssjc.org
Operated by: Girl Scouts of San Jacinto Cnl, 3110 Southwest Freeway, Houston, TX 77098 at (713) 292-0300

Group Rental Information
Facilities: Cabins, Hiking Trails, Kitchen Facilities, Lake, Meeting Rooms, Pool, Tents
Programs: Boating, Challenge/Ropes Course, Swimming (#514)

Airport YMCA

Bedford, TX; (817) 571-3371
Rachel Poling, Director
Activities: Academics, Aerobics/Exercise, Arts/Crafts, Ceramics/Pottery, Drama, Field Trips, Sports — Field & Team, Swimming — Recreational
Operated by: YMCA of Metropolitan Ft Worth, 540 Lamar St, Fort Worth, TX 76102 at (817) 335-6147 (#13410)

Benbrook Communtiy Center YMCA

Benbrook, TX; (817) 249-0500
Pam Bumpas, Director
Activities: Archery, Arts/Crafts, Climbing/Rappelling, Counselor Training (CIT), Field Trips, Fishing, Swimming — Recreational
Operated by: YMCA of Metropolitan Ft Worth, 540 Lamar St, Fort Worth, TX 76102 at (817) 335-6147 (#13429)

Boothe Oaks (est 1952)

Sweetwater, TX (Nolan Co.); (915) 235-3840
Shirley I. Olson, Director
Camp comments: Rustic setting in a grove of live oak trees. Tents & cabins. Traditional program with a noncompetitive atmosphere.
Activities: Archery, Arts/Crafts, Basketball, Camping Skills/Outdoor Living, Canoeing, Drama, Hiking, Soccer, Swimming — Recreational, Team Building
Session lengths & capacity: June-July; 1/2, 1, 2 & 3 week sessions; 200 campers
Clientele & fees: girls 7-17; Fees: A
Fees: B, C
Contact: West Texas GSC at (915) 670-0432; fax: (915) 670-0981
e-mail: gscookie@camalott.com
Web site: www.camalott.com/~gscookie
Operated by: West Texas GSC, PO Box 5586, Abilene, TX 79608 at (915) 698-1738
Group Rental Information
Site comments: Oak trees, wildlife, a creek & canyon describes Camp Boothe Oaks. Near Sweetwater, TX. Camp offers a pool, canoes, archery & more to delight any girl.
Seasons & Capacity: Spring 200, Summer 200, Fall 200, Winter 200
Facilities: A/V Equipment, Cabins, Dorm-Style, Hiking Trails, Kitchen Facilities, Playing Fields, Tents
Programs: Swimming (#592)

Briarwood Retreat Center

(est 1959)
Argyle, TX (Denton Co.); (940) 455-7002
Rev Bill Irons, Director
Camp comments: Briarwood focuses on building Christian community through noncompetitive activities and camper-directed programming.
Activities: Archery, Arts/Crafts, Challenge/Rope Courses, Counselor Training (CIT), Hiking, Leadership Development, Music, Nature/Environment Studies, Religious Study, Swimming — Recreational
Session lengths & capacity: June-July; 1/2 & 1 week sessions; 70 campers
Clientele & fees: coed 7-17; families; seniors; Fees: C
Contact: Kathy Naish, Registar at (800) 441-0016; fax: (940) 455-2157
e-mail: kathy@briarwoodretreat.org
Web site: www.briarwoodretreat.org

Operated by: Briarwood Lutheran Ministries, 670 Copper Canyon Rd, Argyle, TX 76226-9716 at (940) 455-7002
Group Rental Information
Seasons & Capacity: Spring 175, Summer 70, Fall 175, Winter 175
Facilities: A/V Equipment, Cabins, Dorm-Style, Double Occupancy, Food Service, Hiking Trails, Kitchen Facilities, Linens, Lodges, Meeting Rooms, Playing Fields, Pool, Tents
Programs: Challenge/Ropes Course, Environmental Education, Swimming (#604)

Camp Balcones Springs

Marble Falls, TX (Burnet Co.); (830) 598-7699
Marietta Johnson & Jeff Bice, Director
Camp comments: A Christian youth camp for children ages 8-16. We offer 2,3,5 & 6 week terms packed full of fun, challenge and growth!
Activities: Aquatic Activities, Camping Skills/Outdoor Living, Challenge/Rope Courses, Counselor Training (CIT), Horseback — Western, Sailing, Sports — Field & Team, Tennis, Waterskiing, Wilderness Trips
Session lengths & capacity: June-August; 2, 3 & 5 week sessions; 270 campers
Clientele & fees: coed 8-16; Fees: F
Contact: Elissa Janney, Registrar at (800) 485-5151; fax: (830) 598-1095
e-mail: ejanney@campbalconessprings.com
Operated by: Camp Champions, 775 Camp Rd, Marble Falls, TX 78654 at (830) 598-2571 (#520)

Camp Buckner (est 1987)

Burnet, TX (Burnet Co.); (512) 756-7540
David English, Director
Camp comments: A high energy, Christian recreational camp located in the heart of Texas hill country.
Activities: Archery, Bicycling/Biking, Camping Skills/Outdoor Living, Challenge/Rope Courses, Drama, Hiking, Horseback — Western, Leadership Development, Music
Session lengths & capacity: June-July; 1 & 2 week sessions; 140 campers
Clientele & fees: boys 6-15; girls 6-15; coed 6-15; Fees: B Fees: D
Contact: David English, Administrator at (512) 756-7540; fax: (512) 756-6121
e-mail: denglish@buckner.org
Web site: www.campbuckner.org
Operated by: Buckner Children Family Servs, 3835 FM2342, Burnet, TX 78611 at (512) 756-7540
Group Rental Information
Seasons & Capacity: Spring 225, Winter 225
Facilities: A/V Equipment, Cabins, Dorm-Style, Double Occupancy, Food Service, Hiking Trails, Lake, Linens, Lodges, Meeting Rooms, Playing Fields, Pool
Programs: Challenge/Ropes Course, Environmental Education, Horseback Riding, Swimming (#3165)

Camp C.A.M.P. (est 1979)

Center Point, TX (Kerr Co.); (830) 634-2267
Brad Gilbert, Director
Camp comments: Primarily serves severe & profound special needs/disabled population not otherwise served & their siblings.
Activities: Archery, Arts/Crafts, Canoeing, Horseback — Western, Riflery, Swimming — Recreational
Session lengths & capacity: 1 week sessions; 300 campers
Clientele & fees: coed 5-21; Fees: D
Contact: Brad Gilbert, Director at (210) 292-3574; fax: (210) 292-3577
e-mail: campmail@sprynet.com
Operated by: Childrens Assn Max Potential, PO Box 27086, San Antonio, TX 78227 at (210) 292-3566

Group Rental Information
Site comments: Special rate for nonprofit organizations serving those with special needs/developmental disabilities.
Facilities: Cabins, Dorm-Style, Food Service, Meeting Rooms, Pool, River (#1461)

Camp Carter YMCA

(est 1948)
Fort Worth, TX (Tarrant Co.); (817) 738-9241
Holly Craddock, Director
Camp comments: Beauiful YMCA Camp in Ft.Worth, TX. Outstanding staff, quality program including skeet, horsemanship & challenge course
Activities: Archery, Arts/Crafts, Bicycling/Biking, Canoeing, Challenge/Rope Courses, Horseback — Western, Riflery, Sailing, Sports — Field & Team, Swimming — Recreational
Session lengths & capacity: 1 & 2 week sessions; 150 campers
Clientele & fees: coed 8-14; Fees: B
Fees: C
Contact: Lisa Cook, Program Director at (817) 738-9241; fax: (817) 731-1673
Operated by: YMCA of Metropolitan Ft Worth, 540 Lamar St, Fort Worth, TX 76102 at (817) 335-6147 (#517)

Camp Chai (est 1950)

Dallas, TX (Dallas Co.); (214) 739-2737
Laura Seymour, Director
Camp comments: Jewish day camp with emphasis on community & individual growth. Full range of activities plus trips & overnights.
Activities: Arts/Crafts, Counselor Training (CIT), Drama, Field Trips, Music, Sports — Field & Team, Swimming — Instructional, Swimming — Recreational, Team Building
Session lengths & capacity: June-July; 3 & 6 week sessions; 450 campers
Clientele & fees: boys 6-12; girls 6-12; coed 6-12; Fees: B
Contact: Laura Seymour, Camp Director at (214) 739-2737; fax: (214) 368-4709
e-mail: lseymour@jccdallas.com
Operated by: JCC, 7900 Northaven Rd, Dallas, TX 75230 at (214) 739-2737 (#564)

Camp Coyote (est 1990)

Huntsville, TX; (936) 295-8702
Sidney Grisham, Director
Camp comments: Now a Texas tradition, let us show your kids our beautiful 2000 acre working ranch and fun-filled family environment!
Activities: Archery, Arts/Crafts, Challenge/Rope Courses, Climbing/Rappelling, Horseback — Western, SCUBA, Swimming — Recreational, Waterskiing
Session lengths & capacity: June-August; 1, 2 & 3 week sessions; 125 campers
Clientele & fees: coed 7-17; families; seniors; single adults; Fees: D
Contact: Kay King at (800) 677-2267; fax: (936) 295-9303
e-mail: campc@lcc.net
Web site: www.campcoyote.com
Operated by: Camp Coyote, PO Box 276, Huntsville, TX 77342 at (936) 294-9338
Group Rental Information
Site comments: Annual Ladies Only Retreats as well as Mother/Daughter and Father/Son Retreats. Annually in the Fall and the Spring
Seasons & Capacity: Spring 125, Fall 125, Winter 125
Facilities: Dorm-Style, Food Service, Lake, Meeting Rooms, Playing Fields, Pool
Programs: Boating, Challenge/Ropes Course, Horseback Riding, Swimming (#1170)

Camp Crabgrass (est 1980) ☀

Deer Park, TX (Harris Co.); (281) 478-2049
Jazmin Hernandez, Director
Activities: Archery, Arts/Crafts, Drawing/Painting,
Field Trips, Riflery, Sports — Field & Team,
Swimming — Recreational
Session lengths & capacity: 1 & 2 week sessions;
60 campers
Clientele & fees: coed 7-12; Fees: **B** ☀
Contact: City of Deer Park Parks &, Assistant
Recreation Supervisor at (713) 478-2050;
fax: (281) 479-8091
Web site: www.ci.deer-park.tx.us
Operated by: Camp Crabgrass, PO Box 700, Deer
Park, TX 77536 at (281) 478-2050 (#1739)

Camp Discovery ▲

Austin, TX; (830) 896-8500
Activities: Aquatic Activities, Archery, Arts/Crafts,
Baseball/Softball, Basketball, Challenge/Rope
Courses, Golf, Horseback — Western, Swimming
— Recreational, Tennis
Operated by: American Cancer Society, 2433
Ridgepoint Dr, Austin, TX 78754 at (512) 919-1800
(#13709)

Camp Echo ☀

North Richland Hills, TX (Tarrant Co.);
(817) 281-7676
Brent Weaver, Director
Activities: Arts/Crafts, Basketball, Camping
Skills/Outdoor Living, Drawing/Painting, Field Trips,
Leadership Development, Sports — Field & Team,
Swimming — Recreational, Team Building
Session lengths & capacity: 130 campers
Operated by: YMCA of Metropolitan Ft Worth, 540
Lamar St, Fort Worth, TX 76102 at (817) 335-6147
(#47983)

Camp El Har (est 1937) ☀ ▲ 🏠 🚐

Dallas, TX (Dallas Co.); (972) 298-3873
David Nelson, Director

Camp comments: Christian camping 15 minutes
from Dallas. Day & overnight camps, outdoor ed.,
equestrian & Wilderness tripping programs.
Activities: Archery, Challenge/Rope Courses,
Horseback — Western, Nature/Environment
Studies, Riflery, Sailing, SCUBA, Swimming —
Recreational, Waterskiing, Wilderness Trips
Session lengths & capacity: June-August; 1 &
2 week sessions; 240 campers
Clientele & fees: coed 5-14; seniors; single adults;
Fees: **B** 🌑 Fees: **D ▲** 🚐
Contact: (972) 298-3873; fax: (972) 296-9129
e-mail: Campelhar@hotmail.com
Web site: www.campelhar.org

ICON LEGEND

☀   Day Camp

▲   Resident Camp

🏠   Facilities Available To Rent

🚐   Transportation Available

🌑   Financial Aid Available

FEE RANGES PER WEEK

A $0-75

B $75-200

C $201-350

D $351-500

E $501-650

F   over $650

Operated by: Camp El Har, 5218 Kiwanis Rd,
Dallas, TX 75236 at (972) 298-3873
Group Rental Information
Seasons & Capacity: Spring 120, Fall 120, Winter
120
Facilities: A/V Equipment, Cabins, Dorm-Style,
Food Service, Hiking Trails, Kitchen Facilities,
Lodges, Meeting Rooms, Playing Fields, Pool
Programs: Challenge/Ropes Course,
Environmental Education, Horseback Riding,
Swimming (#14795)

Camp For All (est 1993) ▲ 🏠

Burton, TX (Harris Co.); (979) 289-3752
Janet Johnson, Director

Camp comments: Camp For All is a year-round
facility specially designed to serve the needs of
people with chronic illnesses or disabilities.
Activities: Aquatic Activities, Archery, Arts/Crafts,
Bicycling/Biking, Canoeing, Challenge/Rope
Courses, Fishing, Horseback — Western,
Nature/Environment Studies, Sports — Field &
Team
Session lengths & capacity: May-August; 1/2 &
1 week sessions; 250 campers
Clientele & fees: coed 5-35; families; Fees: **C ▲**
Contact: (979) 289-3752; fax: (979) 289-5046
Operated by: Camp For All Foundation, 10500 NW
Freeway 145, Houston, TX 77092 at (713) 686-5666
Group Rental Information
Seasons & Capacity: Spring 250, Summer 250,
Fall 250, Winter 250
Facilities: A/V Equipment, Cabins, Dorm-Style,
Double Occupancy, Food Service, Hiking Trails,
Lake, Linens, Meeting Rooms, Playing Fields
Programs: Challenge/Ropes Course, Horseback
Riding, Swimming (#46289)

Camp Gilmont (est 1940) 🏠

Gilmer, TX; (903) 797-6400
Thomas Truitt, Director
Contact: Web site: www.campgilmont.org
Operated by: Presbyterian Camps at Gilmont, 6075
SH 155 N, Gilmer, TX 75644 at (903) 797-6400
Group Rental Information
Site comments: Established in 1940, Camp
Gilmont has been a place where the young and old
can come and relax and enjoy a natural setting in
Northeast Texas.
Facilities: Cabins, Double Occupancy, Food
Service, Hiking Trails, Lodges, Meeting Rooms,
Ocean, Pool, Tents
Programs: Boating, Challenge/Ropes Course,
Environmental Education, Swimming (#3754)

Camp Good News (est 1965) ▲

Huntsville, TX (Walker Co.); (800) 395-4536
Eric Albert, Director

Camp comments: Christian camp in the east Texas
woods with awesome activities, Christian
counselors & great food for a memorable time.
Where Christ is life and life is fun!
Activities: Archery, Arts/Crafts, Canoeing,
Challenge/Rope Courses, Climbing/Rappelling,
Drama, Fishing, Model Rocketry, Riflery, Soccer
Session lengths & capacity: 1 week sessions;
150 campers
Clientele & fees: coed 8-13; Fees: **C ▲**
Contact: e-mail: goodnews@forestglen.org
Operated by: Child Evangelism Fellowship, 34
Forest Glen, Huntsville, TX 77340 at (936) 295-7641
(#18172)

Camp Grady Spruce YMCA

(est 1949)   ☀ ▲ 🏠 🚐

Graford, TX; (940) 779-3411
Mike Roberts, Director

Camp comments: Traditional camp. Excellent,
caring staff. Accent on water sports, Christian
emphasis. Trip camping available.
Activities: Archery, Arts/Crafts, Challenge/Rope
Courses, Counselor Training (CIT), Horseback —
Western, Leadership Development, Riflery, Sailing,
Swimming — Recreational, Waterskiing
Session lengths & capacity: June-August; 1 &
2 week sessions; 400 campers
Clientele & fees: boys 8-12; girls 8-12; coed 13-16;
families; Fees: **D ▲**
Contact: Joan Peoples, Registrar at
(214) 319-9944; fax: (214) 382-9977
Operated by: YMCA of Metropolitan Dallas, 601 N
Akard, Dallas, TX 75201 at (214) 880-9622
Group Rental Information
Site comments: Yr round Y-camp summer
specialties waterskiing, sailing, challenge course &
leadership dev. OE & conf/retreat opportunity.
Seasons & Capacity: Spring 900, Summer 400,
Fall 900, Winter 500
Facilities: Double Occupancy, Food Service,
Hiking Trails, Kitchen Facilities, Lodges, Playing
Fields, Tents
Programs: Boating, Challenge/Ropes Course,
Environmental Education, Horseback Riding,
Swimming (#554)

Camp John Marc (est 1991) ▲ 🏠

Meridian, TX (Bosque Co.); (254) 635-8811
Vance Gilmore, Director

Camp comments: Camp John Marc exists to
provide a renewed quality of life for children with
chronic illnesses or major physical disabilities.
Activities: Arts/Crafts, Boating, Camping
Skills/Outdoor Living, Canoeing, Challenge/Rope
Courses, Horseback — Western,
Nature/Environment Studies, Photography, Sports
— Field & Team, Swimming — Recreational
Session lengths & capacity: 1 week sessions;
150 campers
Clientele & fees: coed 6-16; families;
Fees: **B ▲** 🌑
Contact: Karen Campbell, Office Manager at
(214) 360-0056; fax: (214) 368-2003
e-mail: mail@campjohnmarc.org
Operated by: Special Camps for Special Kids,
8111 Preston Rd Suite 807, Dallas, TX 75225 at
(214) 360-0056
Group Rental Information
Site comments: Camp John Marc serves children
w/chronic illness & major physical disabilities in a
setting of rolling hills & beauty.
Facilities: Cabins, Dorm-Style, Food Service,
Hiking Trails, Lake, Meeting Rooms, Pool (#2383)

Camp Stewart for Boys Inc

(est 1924)   ▲ 🚐

Hunt, TX (Kerr Co.); (830) 238-4670
Si Ragsdale III, Director

Camp comments: Exciting 79th summer.
Multi-skills, personal development. Excellent staff &
facilities. Texas Hill country. Top USA Camp
Activities: Archery, Basketball, Ceramics/Pottery,
Challenge/Rope Courses, Golf, Horseback —
English, Horseback — Western, Riflery, Sports —
Field & Team, Waterskiing
Session lengths & capacity: June-August; 2, 4 &
8 week sessions; 275 campers
Clientele & fees: boys 6-16; Fees: **E ▲**
Contact: Si Ragsdale Jr & Kathy Ragsdale,
Owners/Directors at (830) 238-4670;
fax: (830) 238-4737
e-mail: si@campstewart.com
Web site: www.campstewart.com
Operated by: Camp Stewart for Boys Inc, HC 1
Box 110, Hunt, TX 78024-9714 at (210) 238-4670
(#12866)

Camp Summit (est 1993)   ▲ ⌂ 🚌

Argyle, TX (Denton Co.); (940) 241-2809
Lura J. Hammond, Director

Camp comments: The mission of Camp Summit is to provide a residential camping experience for children, youth & adults with disabilities
Activities: Arts/Crafts, Camping Skills/Outdoor Living, Challenge/Rope Courses, Counselor Training (CIT), Dance, Horseback — Western, Music, Nature/Environment Studies, Performing Arts, Swimming — Recreational
Session lengths & capacity: 1 week sessions; 80 campers
Clientele & fees: coed 6-99; Fees: D ▲ 🚌

Contact: Lisa J Braziel, Camp Director at (972) 484-8900; fax: (972) 620-1945
e-mail: L.BRAZIEL@campsummittx.org
Web site: wwwcampsummittx.org
Operated by: Camp Summit Inc, 2915 LBJ Freeway Ste 185, Dallas, TX 75234-7607 at (972) 484-8900

Group Rental Information
Site comments: Rustic setting nestled among oak trees 23 miles north of Dallas,meeting space,ropes course,10 cabins sleep 12,A/C-heated
Seasons & Capacity: Spring 140, Fall 140, Winter 140
Facilities: Double Occupancy, Food Service, Meeting Rooms, River
Programs: Challenge/Ropes Course (#560)

Camp Val Verde (est 1948)   ▲ ⌂ 🚌

Mc Gregor, TX (McClennan Co.); (254) 848-4281
Cynthia Davis, Director

Camp comments: 400 acres of rolling hills and forest located along the Middle Bosque River. Western Horseback Riding, Challenge Course, Canoeing, Environmental Ed.
Activities: Archery, Challenge/Rope Courses, Horseback — Western
Session lengths & capacity: June-August; 1/2, 1, 2, 3 & 4 week sessions; 150 campers
Clientele & fees: coed 6-18; Fees: B, C, D ▲
Contact: Cynthia L Davis, Executive Director at (254) 752-5515; fax: (254) 752-0088
e-mail: info@campvalverde.com
Operated by: Camp Fire USA Tejas Council, 1826 Morrow, Waco, TX 76707 at (817) 752-5515

Group Rental Information
Site comments: Excellent facilities for up to 200, wild turkey, deer, air conditioned facilities just 10 minutes from downtown Waco, TX
Facilities: Cabins, Dorm-Style, Food Service, Hiking Trails, Kitchen Facilities, Lake, Meeting Rooms, Pool, River
Programs: Boating, Challenge/Ropes Course, Environmental Education, Horseback Riding, Swimming (#531)

Camp Whata Chawannabe   ☀

Fort Worth, TX; (817) 237-7237
Barbara Cooper, Director
Activities: Aquatic Activities, Arts/Crafts, Camping Skills/Outdoor Living, Field Trips, Hiking, Horseback — Western, Nature/Environment Studies, Religious Study, Sports — Field & Team
Operated by: YMCA of Metropolitan Ft Worth, 540 Lamar St, Fort Worth, TX 76102 at (817) 335-6147 (#13422)

Camp Wind-A-Mere (est 1986)   ⌂

Alvin, TX (Galveston Co.); (281) 337-6738
Contact: Web site: www.gsst.org
Operated by: Girl Scouts of South Texas Cou, 231 W Highway 332, Lake Jackson, TX 77566 at (979) 297-5556

Group Rental Information
Site comments: Available for registered Girl Scout troops only.
Facilities: Hiking Trails, Lodges, Meeting Rooms, Tents (#168)

Camp Young Judaea (est 1953)   ▲ ⌂

Wimberley, TX (Hays Co.); (512) 847-9564
Frank Silberlicht, Director
Activities: Aquatic Activities, Arts/Crafts, Basketball, Challenge/Rope Courses, Leadership Development, Nature/Environment Studies, Performing Arts, Religious Study, Sports — Field & Team, Travel/Tour
Session lengths & capacity: June-August; 3 week sessions; 175 campers
Clientele & fees: coed 8-14; Fees: D ▲ 🚌

Contact: Frank Silberlicht, Director at (713) 723-8354; fax: (713) 728-5061
e-mail: info@cyjtexas.org
Web site: www.cyjtexas.org
Operated by: Southwest Zionist Youth Comm, 9647 Hillcroft, Houston, TX 77096 at (713) 723-8354

Group Rental Information
Facilities: Cabins, Double Occupancy, Food Service, Hiking Trails, Lake, Linens, Lodges, Meeting Rooms, Playing Fields, Pool
Programs: Boating, Swimming (#597)

Casa Mare (est 1958)   ▲ ⌂

Seabrook, TX (Harris Co.); (281) 474-2181
Nicole "Bart" McInnes, Director

Camp comments: GS Camp-Focus is on sailing (11 & older), swimming & arts. Dorm facilities. Located on Galveston Bay. 4 day; 1-2 week cmps.
Activities: Aquatic Activities, Archery, Arts/Crafts, Dance, Drama, Drawing/Painting, Field Trips, Sailing, SCUBA, Swimming — Instructional
Session lengths & capacity: June-July; 1 & 2 week sessions; 150 campers
Clientele & fees: girls 8-17; Fees: C ▲
Contact: Nicole McInnes, Program Manager at (713) 292-0353; fax: (713) 292-0330
e-mail: nmcinnes@sjgs.org
Web site: www.gssjc.org
Operated by: Girl Scouts of San Jacinto Cnl, 3110 Southwest Freeway, Houston, TX 77098 at (713) 292-0300

Group Rental Information
Facilities: Cabins, Dorm-Style, Kitchen Facilities, Meeting Rooms, Ocean, Playing Fields, Pool
Programs: Boating (#556)

Cho-Yeh Camp & Conference Ctr (est 1947)   ▲ ⌂

Livingston, TX (Polk Co.); (936) 328-3200
Jason D Brown, Director

Camp comments: Committed staff dedicated to sharing the unconditional love of Christ with campers in a fun and safe environment.
Activities: Archery, Challenge/Rope Courses, Football, Golf, Horseback — Western, Leadership Development, Martial Arts, Riflery, Soccer, Swimming — Recreational
Session lengths & capacity: 1 & 2 week sessions; 248 campers
Clientele & fees: boys 6-17; girls 6-17; coed 6-17; Fees: B ☼ Fees: D ▲ 🚌
Contact: Jason D Brown, Executive Director at (936) 328-3200; fax: (936) 328-3231
Web site: www.cho.yeh.org
Operated by: Presbytery of New Convenant, 2200 S Washington St, Livingston, TX 77351 at (936) 328-3200

Group Rental Information
Site comments: Operating year-round, we provide excellent food, outstanding service, hotel & cabin accommodations and adequate meeting space. Located 1 1/2 hrs N of Houston.
Facilities: A/V Equipment, Cabins, Double Occupancy, Food Service, Hiking Trails, Lake, Linens, Meeting Rooms, Playing Fields, Pool
Programs: Boating, Challenge/Ropes Course, Environmental Education, Horseback Riding, Swimming (#13553)

City of Bellaire Day Camp
(est 1988)   ☀

Bellaire, TX (Harris Co.); (713) 662-8285
Buster Adams, Director

Camp comments: Bellaire Day Camps provide quality opportunities and experiences not found at school, church, or home.
Activities: Arts/Crafts, Baseball/Softball, Basketball, Counselor Training (CIT), Field Trips, Nature/Environment Studies, Soccer, Swimming — Instructional

Session lengths & capacity: 3 week sessions; 200 campers
Clientele & fees: coed 5-12; Fees: B ☀ 🚐
Contact: Buster Adams, Youth Program Supervisor at (713) 662-8285; fax: (713) 662-8295
e-mail: badams@campassnet.com
Operated by: City of Bellaire, 7008 S Rice, Bellaire, TX 77401 at (713) 662-8285 (#6584)

Eastside Branch YMCA ☀

Fort Worth, TX; (817) 451-8276
Shari Gordon, Director
Activities: Aquatic Activities, Arts/Crafts, Camping Skills/Outdoor Living, Counselor Training (CIT), Drama, Field Trips, Leadership Development, Nature/Environment Studies, Swimming — Recreational, Team Building
Operated by: YMCA of Metropolitan Ft Worth, 540 Lamar St, Fort Worth, TX 76102 at (817) 335-6147 (#13419)

Ebert Ranch Camp (est 1983) ▲ 🏠

Harper, TX (Gillespie Co.); (830) 864-4669

Camp comments: Ebert Ranch focuses on building Christian community through camper directed programming and experiencing the ranch lifestyle in the Texas Hill Country.
Activities: Archery, Arts/Crafts, Camping Skills/Outdoor Living, Challenge/Rope Courses, Farming/Ranching/Gardening, Horseback — Western, Nature/Environment Studies, Religious Study, Swimming — Recreational, Team Building
Session lengths & capacity: 1 week sessions
Clientele & fees: coed 10-99; families; seniors; single adults; Fees: C ▲
Contact: Web site: www.crosstrails.org
Operated by: Cross Trails Ministry, 760 Upper Turtle Creek Road, Kerrville, TX 78028 at (830) 257-6340

Group Rental Information
Site comments: Animal care, archery, arts & crafts, high & low ropes courses, gardening, hiking, horseback riding (Western), nature/environmental studies, outdoor cooking.
Seasons & Capacity: Spring 50, Fall 50, Winter 50
Facilities: A/V Equipment, Dorm-Style, Food Service, Hiking Trails, Meeting Rooms, Playing Fields, Pool
Programs: Challenge/Ropes Course, Environmental Education, Horseback Riding, Swimming (#8731)

El Tesoro (est 1934) ▲ 🏠

Granbury, TX (Hood Co.); (817) 443-6064

ICON LEGEND

☀	Day Camp
▲	Resident Camp
🏠	Facilities Available To Rent
🚐	Transportation Available
🐖	Financial Aid Available

FEE RANGES PER WEEK

A	$0-75
B	$75-200
C	$201-350
D	$351-500
E	$501-650
F	over $650

Toni Hooten, Director

Camp comments: 45 min. SW of Ft Worth, several activities to choose from. Warm supportive staff; outstanding camper/staff ratio.
Activities: Aquatic Activities, Archery, Arts/Crafts, Camping Skills/Outdoor Living, Canoeing, Challenge/Rope Courses, Counselor Training (CIT), Hiking, Horseback — Western, Leadership Development
Session lengths & capacity: 1/2, 1 & 2 week sessions; 250 campers
Clientele & fees: coed 6-16; Fees: C, D ▲ 🐖
Contact: Amy Boyd, Assistant Executive Director at (817) 831-2111; fax: (817) 831-5070
e-mail: amy@firsttexascampfire.org
Web site: www.firsttexascampfire.org
Operated by: Camp Fire USA First Texas Cnl, 2700 Meacham Blvd, Fort Worth, TX 76137 at (817) 831-2111

Group Rental Information
Site comments: A variety of cabins & lodges to rent. Excellent food, beautiful scenery, great rates. Two pools & hiking trails.
Seasons & Capacity: Spring 350, Summer 250, Fall 350, Winter 350
Facilities: Double Occupancy, Kitchen Facilities, Lodges, Meeting Rooms, River
Programs: Challenge/Ropes Course, Swimming (#579)

ER Van Zandt Southwest YMCA ☀

Fort Worth, TX (Tarrant Co.); (817) 292-8694
Myke Shuman, Director
Activities: Aerobics/Exercise, Arts/Crafts, Dance, Field Trips, Music, Nature/Environment Studies, Radio/TV/Video, Soccer, Swimming — Recreational
Session lengths & capacity: 1, 2, 3, 4, 5, 6, 7, 8 & 9 week sessions
Clientele & fees: Fees: A, B ☀
Contact: Myke Shuman, Child Care Coordinator at (817) 292-9612 ext. 236;
Operated by: YMCA of Metropolitan Ft Worth, 540 Lamar St, Fort Worth, TX 76102 at (817) 335-6147 (#47979)

Frontier Camp (est 1969) ▲ 🏠

Grapeland, TX (Houston Co.); (936) 544-3206
Wesley Woodard, Jr., Director

Camp comments: An exciting, quality, Christian camp in beautiful East Texas where your child is more than a number.
Activities: Aquatic Activities, Archery, Arts/Crafts, Horseback — Western, Kayaking, Riflery, Sailing, Sports — Field & Team, Swimming — Recreational, Waterskiing
Session lengths & capacity: May-August; 1 week sessions; 156 campers
Clientele & fees: coed 8-17; Fees: D ▲
Contact: Matt Raines, Assistant Director at (936) 544-3206; fax: (936) 546-0341
e-mail: fcinfo@frontiercamp.org
Web site: www.frontiercamp.org
Operated by: Frontier Camp, Route 1 Box 138, Grapeland, TX 75844 at (936) 544-3206

Group Rental Information
Site comments: We host only one group at a time to give you maximum service and the facilities you need when you need them.
Seasons & Capacity: Spring 175, Fall 175, Winter 175
Facilities: A/V Equipment, Cabins, Dorm-Style, Food Service, Hiking Trails, Lake, Meeting Rooms, Playing Fields
Programs: Boating, Challenge/Ropes Course, Horseback Riding, Swimming (#3974)

Girl Scout Camp Kiwanis

(est 1928) ▲ 🏠

Amarillo, TX (Potter Co.); (806) 352-7121
Natalie Stephenson, Director

Camp comments: Semi-rustic camp for Girl Scouts & non-Girl Scouts. Campers learn cooperation, sharing, teamwork & friendship. Fun activities include: swimming, horses, tennis.
Activities: Bicycling/Biking, Camping Skills/Outdoor Living, Canoeing, Drama, Golf, Horseback — Western, Nature/Environment Studies, Swimming — Instructional, Swimming — Recreational, Tennis
Session lengths & capacity: June-July; 1/2, 1 & 2 week sessions; 85 campers
Clientele & fees: girls 6-16; Fees: B ▲ 🐖
Contact: Natalie Stephenson, Director of Program & Property at (806) 356-0096; fax: (806) 356-0099
e-mail: nstephenson@gs-tpc.org
Operated by: Girl Scouts Texas Plains Cncl, 6011 W 45th, Amarillo, TX 79109 at (806) 356-0096 (#583)

Girl Scout Camp Texlake

(est 1949) ▲ 🏠

Spicewood, TX (Travis Co.); (512) 264-1044
Jayne Van Osten, Director

Camp comments: 480 acre site on beautiful Lake Travis offering Girl Scout program, water & horseback riding certification.
Activities: Archery, Arts/Crafts, Bicycling/Biking, Camping Skills/Outdoor Living, Canoeing, Challenge/Rope Courses, Horseback — Western, Sailing, SCUBA, Waterskiing
Session lengths & capacity: May-July; 1/2 & 1 week sessions; 180 campers
Clientele & fees: girls 6-17; Fees: B ▲
Contact: Jayne Van Osten, Director of Program at (512) 453-7391 ext. 123; fax: (512) 458-2390
e-mail: jaynev@girlscouts-lonestar.org
Operated by: Lone Star GSC, PO Box 15385, Austin, TX 78761 at (512) 453-7391

Group Rental Information
Facilities: Cabins, Dorm-Style, Kitchen Facilities, Lake, Lodges, Meeting Rooms, Pool, Tents
Programs: Boating, Challenge/Ropes Course, Environmental Education, Swimming (#524)

Girlstart ☀

Austin, TX (Travis Co.); (512) 916-4775
Sharon Lozano, Director

Camp comments: Empowering and encouraging girls in math,science,engineering, and technology in a fun and energetic environment.
Activities: Academics, Computer, Team Building
Session lengths & capacity: June-August; 1 week sessions; 20 campers
Clientele & fees: girls 9-14; Fees: D ☀ 🐖
Contact: Sharon Lozano, Program Coordinator at (512) 916-4775; fax: (512) 916-4776
e-mail: sharon@girlstart.org
Web site: www.girlstart.org
Operated by: Girlstart, 608 W 22nd Street, Austin, TX 78705 at (512) 916-4775 (#40723)

Greene Family Camp

(est 1976) ▲ 🏠 🚐

Bruceville, TX (Mc Lennan Co.); (254) 859-5411
Louis J Dobin, Director

Camp comments: Reform Jewish (UAHC) Full-range prog. Modern, barrier-free facilities with AC, lake, pools, sports, alpine tower, more.
Activities: Archery, Arts/Crafts, Bicycling/Biking, Challenge/Rope Courses, Gymnastics, Religious Study, Sailing, Skating, Sports — Field & Team, Swimming — Recreational
Session lengths & capacity: June-August; 2, 4 & 8 week sessions; 425 campers
Clientele & fees: coed 7-16; Fees: D ▲ 🐖
Contact: Louis J Dobin, Camp Director at (254) 859-5411; fax: (254) 859-5225
e-mail: gfc@greene.org
Web site: www.greene.org

Operated by: Greene Family Camp, 1192 Smith Lane, Bruceville, TX 76630 at (254) 859-5411

Group Rental Information

Site comments: Modern air-conditioned, barrier-free, full mtg rec, AV, great food, central location.
Seasons & Capacity: Spring 550, Summer 550, Fall 550, Winter 550
Facilities: A/V Equipment, Dorm-Style, Double Occupancy, Food Service, Hiking Trails, Lake, Linens, Meeting Rooms, Playing Fields, Pool
Programs: Challenge/Ropes Course, Swimming (#3825)

Growing Together Diabetes Camp (est 1993)

Tyler, TX; (800) 232-8318
Marie Taylor, Director

Camp comments: A day camp with an emphasis on the diabetic child. Medical staff on site. Children sharing their life experiences.
Activities: Archery, Arts/Crafts, Fishing, Hiking, Horseback — English, Horseback — Western, Swimming — Recreational
Session lengths & capacity: 1 week sessions; 30 campers
Clientele & fees: coed 6-14; Fees: **A**
Contact: Marie Taylor, Diabetes Educator at (800) 232-8318; fax: (903) 535-6783
Operated by: E Texas Medical Ctr Rose City, PO Box 6400, Tyler, TX 75711 at (903) 535-6354 (#740)

Heart O' the Hills Camp

(est 1953)

Hunt, TX (Kerr Co.); (830) 238-4650
C Jane Ragsdale, Director

Camp comments: Beautiful Guadalupe River. Air-conditioned. Christian atmosphere, myriad skills & fun family-style dining, etiquette.
Activities: Archery, Arts/Crafts, Camping Skills/Outdoor Living, Dance, Gymnastics, Horseback — English, Horseback — Western, Music, Riflery, Swimming — Instructional
Session lengths & capacity: June-August; 2, 4, 6 & 8 week sessions; 180 campers
Clientele & fees: girls 6-16; Fees: **E A**
Contact: Jane Ragsdale, Director at (830) 238-4650; fax: (830) 238-4067
e-mail: info@hohcamp.com
Web site: www.hohcamp.com
Operated by: Heart O'The Hills Camp, HCR 2 Box 250, Hunt, TX 78024-9702 at (830) 238-4650

Group Rental Information

Site comments: All facilites central air. Five star chef. Fireplaces. Rustic yet comfortable retreat.
Seasons & Capacity: Spring 100, Fall 100, Winter 100
Facilities: A/V Equipment, Dorm-Style, Double Occupancy, Food Service, Hiking Trails, Linens, Meeting Rooms, Playing Fields, River
Programs: Horseback Riding, Swimming (#10761)

Hermann Sons Youth Camp

(est 1954)

Comfort, TX; (830) 995-3223
Buddy Preuss, Director

Camp comments: Scenic hill country. Hilltop for boys, Riverside for girls. Membership only.
Activities: Archery, Arts/Crafts, Camping Skills/Outdoor Living, Canoeing, Counselor Training (CIT), Model Rocketry, Nature/Environment Studies, Riflery, Swimming — Instructional, Tennis
Session lengths & capacity: June-August; 1 week sessions; 410 campers
Clientele & fees: boys 9-13; girls 9-13
Contact: Buddy Preuss, Executive Director at (830) 995-3223; fax: (830) 995-2394
e-mail: hsyc@hctc.net

Operated by: Order of the Sons of Hermann, PO Box 1941, San Antonio, TX 78297 at (210) 226-9261 (#11836)

Jo Jan Van (est 1960)

Barksdale, TX (Real Co.); (210) 234-3273
Linda M Hubbard, Director

Camp comments: Explore scenic Texas hill country, learn new skills, songs, & self-confidence, while creating memories with new friends.
Activities: Archery, Arts/Crafts, Camping Skills/Outdoor Living, Canoeing, Challenge/Rope Courses, Drama, Hiking, Nature/Environment Studies, Photography, Swimming — Recreational
Session lengths & capacity: 1/2, 1 & 2 week sessions; 64 campers
Clientele & fees: girls 7-18; Fees: **B, C A**
Contact: Nancy Henderson, Executive Director at (800) 688-2845; fax: (915) 658-7253
e-mail: elcaminogsc@aol.com
Web site: www.elcaminogsc.com
Operated by: El Camino GSC, 304 W Avenue A, San Angelo, TX 76903 at (800) 688-2845

Group Rental Information

Facilities: Cabins, Hiking Trails, Kitchen Facilities, Lodges, River (#3485)

John Knox Ranch (est 1962)

Fischer, TX (Hays/Comal Co.); (830) 935-4568
Beth Watson, Director

Camp comments: Presbyterian, Hill Country camp on the Blanco River. Camps focus on relationships and Christian community. Many water and adventure activities.
Activities: Archery, Camping Skills/Outdoor Living, Challenge/Rope Courses, Climbing/Rappelling, Leadership Development, Music, Nature/Environment Studies, Sports — Field & Team, Swimming — Recreational, Team Building
Session lengths & capacity: June-August; 1 & 2 week sessions; 100 campers
Clientele & fees: coed 8-18; Fees: **B**
Fees: **C A**
Contact: Beth Watson, Director at (830) 935-4568; fax: (830) 935-2102
e-mail: johnknox@gvtc.com
Web site: www.johnknoxcamp.org
Operated by: Mission Presbytery Outdoor Min, 1661 John Knox Rd, Fischer, TX 78623-9720 at (830) 935-4568

Group Rental Information

Seasons & Capacity: Spring 200, Fall 200, Winter 200
Facilities: Cabins, Dorm-Style, Food Service, Hiking Trails, Kitchen Facilities, Linens, Lodges, Playing Fields, Pool, River
Programs: Challenge/Ropes Course, Environmental Education, Swimming (#18494)

Kachina (est 1960)

Belton, TX (Bell Co.); (254) 780-1851
Donna Henderson, Director

Camp comments: Camp Kachina gives girls the opportunity to work with others, discover their independence & develop their self-esteem.
Activities: Aquatic Activities, Archery, Arts/Crafts, Boating, Camping Skills/Outdoor Living, Canoeing, Hiking, Horseback — Western, Sailing, Swimming — Recreational
Session lengths & capacity: 1/2 & 1 week sessions; 150 campers
Clientele & fees: girls 6-17; Fees: **B A**
Contact: Donna Henderson, Camp Director at (254) 756-4497; fax: (254) 756-3237
Operated by: Bluebonnet GSC, 3700 West Waco Drive, Waco, TX 76710 at (254) 756-4497

Group Rental Information

Facilities: Cabins, Double Occupancy, Food Service, Hiking Trails, Lake, Lodges, Meeting Rooms, Pool, Tents

Programs: Boating, Horseback Riding, Swimming (#7172)

Kamp Kwantas

Fort Worth, TX; (871) 531-2738
Activities: Aquatic Activities, Arts/Crafts, Basketball, Team Building
Operated by: YMCA of Metropolitan Ft Worth, 540 Lamar St, Fort Worth, TX 76102 at (817) 335-6147 (#15293)

La Jita (est 1948)

Utopia, TX (Uvalde Co.); (210) 966-3526
Becky Jennings, Director

Camp comments: Hill country, river camp. Horseback riding. Camping skills. Aquatic and nature activities. Non girl scouts are welcome.
Activities: Aquatic Activities, Arts/Crafts, Camping Skills/Outdoor Living, Hiking, Horseback — Western, Leadership Development, Nature/Environment Studies, Swimming — Recreational
Session lengths & capacity: June-August; 1 & 2 week sessions; 160 campers
Clientele & fees: girls 7-17; Fees: **B, C, D A**
Contact: Becky Jennings, Camp Director at (210) 349-2404; fax: (210) 349-2666
e-mail: bjennings@sagirlscouts.org
Operated by: Girl Scouts San Antonio Area, 10443 Gulfdale, San Antonio, TX 78216 at (210) 349-2404 (#567)

Lutheran Camp Chrysalis

(est 1949)

Kerrville, TX; (830) 257-6340
Erick & Deanna Christensen, Director

Camp comments: Chrysalis focuses on building Christian community through noncompetitive activities and camper-directed programming.
Activities: Archery, Arts/Crafts, Canoeing, Challenge/Rope Courses, Hiking, Leadership Development, Music, Nature/Environment Studies, Sports — Field & Team, Team Building
Session lengths & capacity: 1/2, 1, 2 & 3 week sessions; 180 campers
Clientele & fees: coed 7-18; families; Fees: **C A**
Contact: Erick and Deanna Christensen, Co-Executive Directors at (830) 257-6340; fax: (830) 257-3060
e-mail: info@crosstrails.org
Web site: www.crosstrails.org
Operated by: Cross Trails Ministry, 760 Upper Turtle Creek Road, Kerrville, TX 78028 at (830) 257-6340

Group Rental Information

Site comments: Beautiful Texas hill country location.
Seasons & Capacity: Spring 185, Winter 125
Facilities: A/V Equipment, Cabins, Dorm-Style, Food Service, Hiking Trails, Kitchen Facilities, Meeting Rooms, Playing Fields, Pool, River
Programs: Challenge/Ropes Course, Environmental Education, Swimming (#568)

Lutherhill Camp & Retreat Ctr

(est 1954)

La Grange, TX (Fayette Co.); (979) 249-3232
Rev Kathy Haueisen, Director

Camp comments: Lutherhill focuses on building Christian community through noncompetitive events & camper-directed programming.
Activities: Archery, Arts/Crafts, Camping Skills/Outdoor Living, Canoeing, Challenge/Rope Courses, Hiking, Leadership Development, Music, Nature/Environment Studies, Religious Study
Session lengths & capacity: June-August; 1/2, 1 & 2 week sessions; 100 campers
Clientele & fees: boys 7-18; girls 7-18; coed 7-18; families; seniors; single adults; Fees: **C A**

Contact: Nora Otto, Registrar at (888) 266-4613; fax: (979) 249-4032
e-mail: cwoffice@cvtv.net
Web site: www.crosswiseluth.org
Operated by: CrossWise Lutheran Ministries, PO Box 99, LaGrange, TX 78945 at (979) 249-3232

Group Rental Information
Site comments: Small group based for maximum growth & supervision great view & lots of shade, air conditioned facilities, good rates.
Seasons & Capacity: Spring 125, Winter 125
Facilities: A/V Equipment, Cabins, Double Occupancy, Food Service, Hiking Trails, Kitchen Facilities, Lodges, Pool
Programs: Challenge/Ropes Course, Swimming (#527)

Midsouth Covenant Camp

(est 1988)

San Antonio, TX; (210) 543-9903
Dale Lusk, Director
Activities: Archery, Arts/Crafts, Challenge/Rope Courses, Drama, Horseback — Western, Riflery, Sports — Field & Team
Session lengths & capacity: 2 week sessions; 130 campers
Clientele & fees: coed 8-18; Fees: **C**
Contact: Nancy Dieckow, Camp Board Chairman at (210) 543-9903;
e-mail: ndieckow@aol.com
Operated by: Midsouth Region of Evangalical, 9614 Fern Crest, San Antonio, TX 78250 at (210) 543-9903 (#3087)

Misty Meadows (est 1990)

Conroe, TX (Montgomery Co.)
Ann "Ms. P" Plattsmier, Director
Camp comments: Girl Scout camp focus on riding, arts & crafts, swimming. Cabins & dorm facilities. 1 & 2 week sessions.
Activities: Archery, Drama, Hiking, Horseback — Western, Sports — Field & Team
Session lengths & capacity: 1 week sessions; 160 campers
Clientele & fees: girls 6-17; Fees: **C**
Contact: Nicole McInnes, Program Manager at (713) 292-0353; fax: (713) 292-0330
e-mail: nmcinnes@sjgs.org
Web site: www.gssjc.org
Operated by: Girl Scouts of San Jacinto Cnl, 3110 Southwest Freeway, Houston, TX 77098 at (713) 292-0300 (#6622)

ICON LEGEND
☀ Day Camp
▲ Resident Camp
🏠 Facilities Available To Rent
🚐 Transportation Available
🐷 Financial Aid Available

FEE RANGES PER WEEK
A $0-75
B $75-200
C $201-350
D $351-500
E $501-650
F over $650

MO Ranch Camps & Outdoor Educ (est 1977)

Hunt, TX (Kerr Co.); (800) 460-4401
Grant Irons, Director

Camp comments: Beautiful Texas hill country. Caring Christian environment. Enhances development of self-esteem and leadership.
Activities: Aquatic Activities, Archery, Arts/Crafts, Canoeing, Challenge/Rope Courses, Climbing/Rappelling, Field Trips, Horseback — Western, Religious Study, Swimming — Instructional
Session lengths & capacity: May-August; 1, 2 & 3 week sessions; 100 campers
Clientele & fees: boys 10-15; girls 8-15; coed 8-16; Fees: **B** ☀ Fees: **D** ▲ 🚐
Contact: Patrick Fitzgerald, Director Environmental Leadership Progra at (800) 460-4401 ext. 148; fax: (830) 238-4202
e-mail: patrickf@moranch.com
Web site: www.moranch.com
Operated by: Presbyterian Mo Ranch Assembly, HC 1 Box 158, Hunt, TX 78024 at (830) 238-4455

Group Rental Information
Site comments: Christian conference center along Guadalupe River in the Texas Hill Country. Superb meeting and dining facilities.
Seasons & Capacity: Spring 500, Summer 500, Fall 500, Winter 500
Facilities: A/V Equipment, Cabins, Dorm-Style, Double Occupancy, Food Service, Hiking Trails, Kitchen Facilities, Linens, Lodges, Meeting Rooms, Playing Fields, Pool, River, Tents
Programs: Boating, Challenge/Ropes Course, Environmental Education, Horseback Riding, Swimming (#13551)

Olympia (est 1968)

Trinity, TX (Trinity Co.); (936) 594-2541
Tommy Ferguson, Director

Camp comments: Camp Olympia is dedicated to having fun together, helping people grow in body, spirit, & mind.
Activities: Archery, Arts/Crafts, Basketball, Bicycling/Biking, Challenge/Rope Courses, Football, Golf, Horseback — Western, Sailing, Waterskiing
Session lengths & capacity: Year-round; 2 & 3 week sessions; 296 campers
Clientele & fees: coed 7-16; Fees: **F** ▲
Contact: Tommy Ferguson, Director at (936) 594-2541; fax: (936) 594-8143
e-mail: tferguson@campolympia.com
Operated by: Olympia, 723 Olympia Dr, Trinity, TX 75862 at (936) 594-2541

Group Rental Information
Site comments: Camp Olympia is dedicated to having fun together, helping people grow in body, spirit and mind.
Seasons & Capacity: Spring 336, Fall 336, Winter 336
Facilities: Cabins, Food Service, Lake, Meeting Rooms, Pool
Programs: Environmental Education, Horseback Riding (#525)

Pantego Camp Thurman Inc

(est 1969)

Arlington, TX (Tarrant Co.); (817) 274-8441
Jim Rose, Director

Camp comments: Since 1969 Camp Thurman has been providing a fun in-the woods Christian day-camp experience for kids 4-12.
Activities: Archery, Arts/Crafts, Challenge/Rope Courses, Climbing/Rappelling, Counselor Training (CIT), Religious Study, Riflery, Swimming — Recreational, Team Building
Session lengths & capacity: May-August; 1 week sessions; 400 campers
Clientele & fees: coed 4-12; Fees: **B** ☀

Contact: Jim Rose, Camp Director at (817) 274-8441; fax: (817) 274-2316
e-mail: cthurman@flash.net
Web site: www.campthurman.org
Operated by: Pantego Camp Thurman Inc, 1918 Valley Lane, Arlington, TX 76013 at (817) 274-8441 (#14115)

Pine Cove Inc (est 1967)

Tyler, TX (Smith Co.); (903) 561-0231
Mario Zandstra, Director

Camp comments: Year round interdenominational camp in East Texas meeting the spiritual and recreational needs of families and youth.
Activities: Aquatic Activities, Archery, Arts/Crafts, Basketball, Challenge/Rope Courses, Horseback — Western, Religious Study, Riflery, Swimming — Recreational, Waterskiing
Session lengths & capacity: 1 week sessions; 800 campers
Clientele & fees: coed 6-18; families; seniors; Fees: **E** ▲
Contact: Registration Department at (800) 225-9069; fax: (903) 561-7257
e-mail: info@pinecove.com
Web site: www.pinecove.com
Operated by: Pine Cove, PO Box 9055, Tyler, TX 75711 at (903) 561-0231

Group Rental Information
Site comments: Year round interdenominational camp in East Texas meeting the spiritual and recreational needs of families and youth.
Seasons & Capacity: Fall 200, Winter 200
Facilities: A/V Equipment, Cabins, Dorm-Style, Double Occupancy, Food Service, Hiking Trails, Lake, Linens, Lodges, Meeting Rooms, Playing Fields, Pool
Programs: Boating, Challenge/Ropes Course, Environmental Education, Horseback Riding, Swimming (#12840)

Pinebrook Farms Hrsemanshp Cmp (est 1975)

Magnolia, TX (Montgomery Co.); (281) 356-3441
Jorine Seale, Director

Camp comments: Since 1975, safe, fun, family oriented atmosphere, riding & horsemanship skills are taught by a CHA Master Instructor.
Activities: Archery, Arts/Crafts, Baseball/Softball, Basketball, Drawing/Painting, Farming/Ranching/Gardening, Horseback — English, Horseback — Western, Nature/Environment Studies, Swimming — Recreational
Session lengths & capacity: June-August; 1 & 2 week sessions; 35 campers
Clientele & fees: coed 7-15; Fees: **C** ☀ Fees: **D**, **E** ▲
Contact: Jorine Seale, Owner/Camp Director at (281) 356-3441; fax: (281) 356-7018
e-mail: jorine@pinebrook-farms.com
Web site: www.pinebrook-farms.com
Operated by: Pinebrook Farms, 611 Virgie Community, Magnolia, TX 77354-3932 at (281) 356-3441 (#26834)

Piney Woods Camp Cherith

(est 1961)

Rosebud, TX (Falls Co.); (254) 583-2020
Shirley Jamieson, Director

Camp comments: Christ-centered camping. Skill building opportunities. Beautiful 450 acre wooded facility. Separate weeks girls - boys.
Activities: Archery, Camping Skills/Outdoor Living, Canoeing, Challenge/Rope Courses, Horseback — Western, Kayaking, Nature/Environment Studies, Riflery, Sailing, Team Building
Session lengths & capacity: June-August; 1 & 2 week sessions; 110 campers

Clientele & fees: boys 7-18; girls 7-18;
Fees: **C** ▲ 🚌
Contact: Susan Mitchell, Executive Administrator at (713) 937-9717;
e-mail: scooter@texascherith.com
Operated by: Piney Woods Camp Cherith, 391 CR 333, Rosebud, TX 76570 at (254) 583-0230 (#8384)

Prude Ranch Summer Camp

(est 1951) ▲ ⌂ 🚌

Fort Davis, TX; (915) 426-3202
Kelly Prude Boultinghouse, Director

Camp comments: Prude Ranch has offered a true Southwest camping exp. since 1951. Wide open spaces, mile high air and real ranch life.
Activities: Archery, Camping Skills/Outdoor Living, Challenge/Rope Courses, Climbing/Rappelling, Dance, Horseback — Western, Nature/Environment Studies, Team Building
Session lengths & capacity: June-August; 1, 2 & 3 week sessions; 150 campers
Clientele & fees: coed 7-15; Fees: **D, E** ▲
Contact: Betty or John Robert Prude, Owner/Director at (915) 426-3202;
fax: (915) 426-3502
e-mail: prude@overland.net
Web site: www.prude-ranch.com
Operated by: Prude Ranch, Box 1431, Fort Davis, TX 79734 at (915) 426-3202

Group Rental Information

Facilities: Cabins, Double Occupancy, Food Service, Hiking Trails, Linens, Lodges, Meeting Rooms, Playing Fields, Pool
Programs: Challenge/Ropes Course, Environmental Education, Horseback Riding, Swimming (#6108)

Quillian Memorial Center Inc

(est 1984) ☼

Houston, TX (Harris Co.); (713) 781-9195
Tom Gaden, Director

Camp comments: Our Day Camp has morning specialty camps, field trips, daily swims&special events.Traditional camp has sports programs while Enrichment camp has arts&education.
Activities: Baseball/Softball, Basketball, Drama, Field Trips, Golf, Gymnastics, Soccer, Sports — Field & Team, Swimming — Instructional, Swimming — Recreational
Session lengths & capacity: June-August; 2 week sessions; 350 campers
Clientele & fees: coed 6-14; Fees: **B** ☼
Contact: Jack Long, Program Director at (713) 781-9195 ext. 5; fax: (713) 789-6580
e-mail: jlong@quilliancenter.org
Web site: www.firstmethodist.houston.org
Operated by: First United Methodist Church, 1320 Main, Houston, TX 77002 at (713) 652-2999 (#36716)

Rocky River Ranch Inc

(est 1951) ▲ ⌂ 🚌

Wimberley, TX (Hays Co.); (512) 847-2513
Rue Hatfield, Director

Camp comments: Central Texas Hill Country Camp. Quality horse program. Girls: 1-2-3 wks, June & July; Boys: 1-2 wks, Aug.
Activities: Archery, Arts/Crafts, Canoeing, Climbing/Rappelling, Counselor Training (CIT), Drama, Horseback — Western, Riflery, Swimming — Recreational, Team Building
Session lengths & capacity: 1, 2 & 3 week sessions; 120 campers
Clientele & fees: girls 7-15; Fees: **D** ▲
Contact: Rue Hatfield, Camp Director at (800) 863-2267; fax: (512) 847-9067
e-mail: rrrcamp@aol.com
Web site: www.rockyriverranch.com
Operated by: Rocky River Ranch Inc, Box 109, Wimberley, TX 78676-0109 at (800) 863-2267

Group Rental Information

Facilities: A/V Equipment, Cabins, Dorm-Style, Food Service, Kitchen Facilities, Meeting Rooms, Pool, River
Programs: Horseback Riding (#550)

Ryan Family YMCA Day Camps

☼

Fort Worth, TX (Tarrant Co.); (817) 551-9325
Activities: Aerobics/Exercise, Arts/Crafts, Field Trips, Nature/Environment Studies, Performing Arts, Sports — Field & Team, Swimming — Recreational
Operated by: YMCA of Metropolitan Ft Worth, 540 Lamar St, Fort Worth, TX 76102 at (817) 335-6147 (#47974)

SeaWorld Adventure Camps

(est 1992) ☼ ▲ 🚌

San Antonio, TX (Bexar Co.); (800) 700-7786
Ann Quinn, Director

Camp comments: Discover ocean animals, take excursions, explore marine careers, and enjoy Sea World of Texas, 280 acre theme park.
Activities: Academics, Aquatic Activities, Arts/Crafts, Field Trips, Hiking, Nature/Environment Studies, Team Building
Session lengths & capacity: 1/2, 1 & 2 week sessions; 60 campers
Clientele & fees: coed 3-18; families; single adults; Fees: **B, C** ☼ Fees: **E** ▲
Contact: Ann Quinn, Director at (210) 523-3608; fax: (210) 523-3898
e-mail: ann.quinn@anheuser-busch.com
Web site: www.seaworld.org
Operated by: Sea World of San Antonio, 10500 Sea World Dr, San Antonio, TX 78251-3002 at (800) 700-7786 (#2895)

Southeast YMCA

☼

Fort Worth, TX; (817) 534-1591
Activities: Arts/Crafts, Drawing/Painting, Field Trips, Nature/Environment Studies, Swimming — Recreational
Operated by: YMCA of Metropolitan Ft Worth, 540 Lamar St, Fort Worth, TX 76102 at (817) 335-6147 (#13402)

Stevens Ranch On The Brazos

(est 1969) ▲ ⌂

Nemo, TX (Somerville Co.); (254) 897-2515
Neina Chapman, Director

Camp comments: Rustic setting with western pleasure horseback riding,photographer,woodworking,hiking,cabins,tents,cookouts,primitive camping and more. Girl Scout emphasis.
Activities: Archery, Arts/Crafts, Camping Skills/Outdoor Living, Counselor Training (CIT), Hiking, Horseback — Western, Nature/Environment Studies, Photography, Swimming — Instructional, Swimming — Recreational
Session lengths & capacity: June-July; 1 & 2 week sessions; 120 campers
Clientele & fees: girls 9-17; Fees: **C** ▲ 🚌
Contact: Kim Hutchison, Camping Administrator at (817) 737-7272 ext. 209; fax: (817) 732-1261
e-mail: khutchison@circletgsc.org
Web site: www.circletgsc.org
Operated by: Girl Scouts Circle T Council, 4901 Briarhaven, Fort Worth, TX 76109-4499 at (817) 737-7272 (#7040)

Sweeney (est 1947)

▲ ⌂

Gainesville, TX (Cooke Co.); (817) 665-2011
Dr Ernie Fernandez MD, Director

Camp comments: Teaches diabetic kids how to live with their disorder while having summer camping fun too.
Activities: Aerobics/Exercise, Archery, Arts/Crafts, Basketball, Challenge/Rope Courses, Riflery, Soccer, Sports — Field & Team, Tennis
Session lengths & capacity: 1 & 3 week sessions; 190 campers
Clientele & fees: boys 6-18; girls 6-18; coed 6-18; families; Fees: **D** ▲ 🚌
Contact: Karen Talley, Registrar at (940) 665-2011; fax: (940) 665-7467
e-mail: info@campsweeney.org
Web site: www.campsweeney.org
Operated by: Southwestern Diabetic Fnd, PO Box 918, Gainesville, TX 76241 at (940) 665-2011 (#1243)

Texas 4H Center (est 1975)

▲ ⌂

Brownwood, TX; (915) 784-5482
Kenneth Scott Cross, Director

Camp comments: Conf. & Retrt facility offering youth camping programs family reunions shcool activities corp. functions & corp. & youth trainging on teamwork & communication
Activities: Aquatic Activities, Archery, Arts/Crafts, Canoeing, Challenge/Rope Courses, Sailing, Swimming — Recreational
Session lengths & capacity: May-August; 1/2 & 1 week sessions; 308 campers
Clientele & fees: boys 9-19; girls 9-19; coed 9-19; families; seniors; single adults; Fees: **A, B** ☼ Fees: **A, B, C** ▲
Contact: Scott Cross, Director at (915) 784-5482; fax: (915) 784-6486
e-mail: s-cross@tamu.edu
Operated by: Texas 4H Center, RR 1 Box 527, Brownwood, TX 76801 at (915) 784-5482

Group Rental Information

Site comments: Texas 4-H Center - Get away, learn to play at our beautiful lakeside retreat.
Seasons & Capacity: Spring 300, Summer 80, Fall 300, Winter 300
Facilities: A/V Equipment, Dorm-Style, Double Occupancy, Food Service, Hiking Trails, Kitchen Facilities, Lake, Linens, Meeting Rooms, Playing Fields, Pool
Programs: Boating, Challenge/Ropes Course, Environmental Education, Swimming (#3943)

Texas Elks Camp (est 1987)

▲

Gonzales, TX (Gonzales Co.); (830) 672-7561
Chance A Freeman, Director

Camp comments: Safe, fun, free camp serving only-Texas children with special needs-in a therapeutic recreation setting.
Activities: Arts/Crafts, Baseball/Softball, Basketball, Camping Skills/Outdoor Living, Drawing/Painting, Hiking, Horseback — Western, Nature/Environment Studies, Soccer, Swimming — Recreational
Session lengths & capacity: June-August; 1 week sessions; 50 campers
Clientele & fees: boys 7-17; girls 7-17; coed 7-17; Fees: **A** ▲ 🚌
Contact: Chance A Freeman, Director at (830) 875-2425; fax: (830) 672-7563
e-mail: txelks@gvec.net
Operated by: Texas Elks Camp, 1963 FM 1586, Gonzales, TX 78629-9613 at (830) 672-7561 (#6411)

Texas Lions Camp (est 1949)

▲ ⌂ 🚌

Kerrville, TX (Kerr Co.); (830) 896-8500
Stephen S Mabry, Director

Camp comments: TLC offers camping experience to children w/ phys. handicaps & type I diabetes at no cost to participant. The Camp's goal is to increase children's self-esteem.
Activities: Aquatic Activities, Archery, Arts/Crafts, Camping Skills/Outdoor Living, Challenge/Rope Courses, Drama, Horseback — Western, Music, Nature/Environment Studies
Session lengths & capacity: June-August; 1 week sessions; 240 campers

Clientele & fees: boys 7-16; girls 7-16;
Fees: A Δ 🐖
Contact: Stephen S Mabry, Executive Director at
(830) 896-8500; fax: (830) 896-3666
e-mail: tlc@ktc.com
Web site: www.lionscamp.com
Operated by: Lions Clubs of Texas,
PO Box 290247, Kerrville, TX 78029-0247 at
(830) 896-8500

Group Rental Information
Site comments: TLC offers camping experience to
children w/ phys. handicaps & type I diabetes at no
cost to participant. The Camp's goal is to increase
children's self-esteem.
Facilities: A/V Equipment, Cabins, Dorm-Style,
Food Service, Hiking Trails, Meeting Rooms,
Playing Fields, Pool, River
Programs: Challenge/Ropes Course, Horseback
Riding, Swimming (#19957)

The Equestrian Ranch Camp LLC (est 1998)   Δ

Leonard, TX (Fannin Co.); (214) 891-0501
Jackie Kollins, Director
Activities: Aquatic Activities, Archery, Arts/Crafts,
Boating, Canoeing, Ceramics/Pottery, Fishing,
Horseback — English, Horseback — Western,
Swimming — Recreational
Session lengths & capacity: May-August; 1/2, 2 &
3 week sessions; 25 campers
Clientele & fees: girls 7-12; families; Fees: F Δ
Contact: Neal L Fisher, Owner at (214) 987-4109;
fax: (214) 987-0897
e-mail: nfisher@gte.net
Operated by: The Equestrian Ranch Camp LLC,
7232 Glendora Avenue, Dallas, TX 75230 at
(214) 987-4109 (#32835)

The Pines Catholic Camp

(est 1988)   Δ 🏠

Big Sandy, TX; (903) 845-5834
Hank Lanik, Director

Camp comments: Outstanding staff. Rustic setting
in tall pines of East Texas. Noncompetitive, friendly.
Catholic program emphasis.
Activities: Archery, Arts/Crafts, Basketball,
Challenge/Rope Courses, Counselor Training (CIT),
Nature/Environment Studies, Riflery, Sports — Field
& Team, Swimming — Recreational
Session lengths & capacity: 1 week sessions;
175 campers
Clientele & fees: boys 7-16; girls 7-16; coed 7-16;
families; seniors; single adults; Fees: D Δ
Contact: Fran Lobpries, Marketing Coordinator at
(214) 522-6533; fax: (214) 522-2600
e-mail: thepines@flash.net

ICON LEGEND

☀ Day Camp

Δ Resident Camp

🏠 Facilities Available To Rent

🚐 Transportation Available

🐖 Financial Aid Available

FEE RANGES PER WEEK

A	$0-75
B	$75-200
C	$201-350
D	$351-500
E	$501-650
F	over $650

Web site: www.thepines.org
Operated by: The Pines Education Group Inc, 3519
Cedar Springs A, Dallas, TX 75219 at
(214) 522-6533 (#2880)

Timberlake (est 1946)   Δ 🏠

Azle, TX (Tarrant Co.); (817) 444-3590
Misty Baptiste, Director

Camp comments: Sailing, canoeing, covered
wagons. Girl Scout program.
Activities: Archery, Arts/Crafts, Camping
Skills/Outdoor Living, Canoeing, Hiking,
Nature/Environment Studies, Sailing, Swimming —
Recreational
Session lengths & capacity: June-July; 1/2, 1 &
2 week sessions; 104 campers
Clientele & fees: girls 7-17; Fees: B Δ 🐖
Contact: Kim Hutchison, Camp Administrator at
(817) 737-7272 ext. 209; fax: (817) 732-1261
e-mail: khutchison@circletgsc.org
Web site: www.circletgsc.org
Operated by: Girl Scouts Circle T Council, 4901
Briarhaven, Fort Worth, TX 76109-4499 at
(817) 737-7272

Group Rental Information
Facilities: Cabins, Food Service, Lake, Pool, Tents
Programs: Boating (#557)

Victory Camp (est 1992)   Δ 🏠

Alvin, TX (Brazoria Co.); (281) 388-2267
Kevin Kinchen, Director

Camp comments: Come to Victory Camp for a
whole new camp experience. Great staff, best camp
food in the world, go-karts, waterslide, zipline, train
rides, and more.
Activities: Aquatic Activities, Arts/Crafts,
Basketball, Challenge/Rope Courses,
Climbing/Rappelling, Soccer, Swimming —
Recreational, Team Building
Session lengths & capacity: June-July; 1 week
sessions; 325 campers
Clientele & fees: coed 8-19; Fees: B Δ
Contact: Kevin Kinchen, Director at (281) 388-2267;
fax: (281) 388-2365
e-mail: info@victorycamp.com
Operated by: Living Stones Church, 1407 Victory
Ln, Alvin, TX 77511 at (281) 388-2267

Group Rental Information
Seasons & Capacity: Spring 350, Fall 350,
Winter 350
Facilities: Dorm-Style, Food Service, Meeting
Rooms, Playing Fields, Pool
Programs: Challenge/Ropes Course, Swimming
(#3195)

Westside YMCA of Metropolitan   ☀

Fort Worth, TX; (817) 244-4544
Activities: Aquatic Activities, Arts/Crafts, Counselor
Training (CIT), Field Trips, Hiking, Music,
Nature/Environment Studies, Skating, Swimming —
Recreational, Team Building
Operated by: YMCA of Metropolitan Ft Worth, 540
Lamar St, Fort Worth, TX 76102 at (817) 335-6147
(#47670)

WOW Northeast Texas Youth Camp   Δ 🏠

Quitman, TX (Wood Co.); (903) 878-2265
Scott Melson, Director
Activities: Archery, Arts/Crafts, Camping
Skills/Outdoor Living, Canoeing, Challenge/Rope
Courses, Counselor Training (CIT), Fishing,
Nature/Environment Studies, Riflery, Swimming —
Recreational
Session lengths & capacity: May-August; 1 week
sessions; 80 campers
Clientele & fees: coed 8-15; seniors; Fees: A Δ
Contact: Scott Melson, Fraternal Coordinator at
(903) 534-0141; fax: (903) 534-5187

Operated by: WOW Life Insurance (TO), 1700
Farnam, Omaha, NE 68120 at (402) 271-7258
(#6253)

WOW SE Texas Youth Camp   Δ 🏠

Bellville, TX; (979) 865-5420
Stewart H Roberts, Director
Activities: Aquatic Activities, Archery, Arts/Crafts,
Basketball, Canoeing, Counselor Training (CIT),
Riflery, Swimming — Recreational
Session lengths & capacity: 1 week sessions
Clientele & fees: Fees: A Δ
Contact: William R Dees, State Mgr - President
SETYA at (281) 364-0764; fax: (281) 298-8722
Operated by: WOW Life Insurance (TO), 1700
Farnam, Omaha, NE 68120 at (402) 271-7258

Group Rental Information
Facilities: Dorm-Style, Hiking Trails, Meeting
Rooms, Pool
Programs: Boating, Swimming (#6707)

YMCA Camp Cullen

(est 1974)   Δ 🏠 🚐

Trinity, TX; (713) 659-2733
Willard Burks, Director

Camp comments: Resident summer camp.
Beautiful lake and tall pines. Strong values
emphasis. Nondenominational. Wonderful
counselors.
Activities: Aquatic Activities, Archery, Arts/Crafts,
Canoeing, Challenge/Rope Courses, Hiking,
Horseback — Western, Riflery, Sailing, Waterskiing
Session lengths & capacity: June-August; 1 & 2
week sessions; 220 campers
Clientele & fees: coed 6-16; families; Fees: C Δ
Contact: Lou Ann Ward, Registration Secretary at
(713) 659-2733; fax: (409) 594-3237
Operated by: YMCA of Greater Houston, 2122 E
Governors Circle, Houston, TX 77092 at
(713) 353-5214

Group Rental Information
Site comments: YMCA Christian camp emphasizes
value of responsibility caring honesty
&respect.Beautiful setting on lake in Piney Woods.
Seasons & Capacity: Spring 350, Fall 350,
Winter 350
Facilities: Cabins, Food Service, Hiking Trails,
Lake, Meeting Rooms
Programs: Boating, Horseback Riding (#3602)

YMCA Camp Flaming Arrow

(est 1927)   Δ 🏠 🚐

Hunt, TX (Kerr Co.); (800) 765-9622
Shanna King, Director

Camp comments: Texas Hill country camp. Great
1st camp experience. Caring counselors, leadrship
& character development, friends & fun.
Activities: Aquatic Activities, Archery, Arts/Crafts,
Canoeing, Challenge/Rope Courses,
Climbing/Rappelling, Horseback — Western,
Nature/Environment Studies
Session lengths & capacity: 1 & 2 week sessions;
120 campers
Clientele & fees: coed 6-15; Fees: D Δ 🐖
Contact: Rita Fisher, Office Manager at
(800) 765-9622; fax: (210) 238-4280
Operated by: YMCA San Antonio & Hill Cntry,
PO Box 770, Hunt, TX 78024 at (830) 238-4631

Group Rental Information
Site comments: Texas Hill Country Camp for
Boys&Girls. Great 1st camp experience. Caring
counselors,ldrshp&character dev,friends & fun.
Seasons & Capacity: Summer 150
Facilities: A/V Equipment, Cabins, Hiking Trails,
Kitchen Facilities, Lake, Lodges, Meeting Rooms,
Playing Fields, Pool, River
Programs: Boating, Challenge/Ropes Course,
Environmental Education, Horseback Riding,
Swimming (#528)

YMCA Camp Pine Tree ⚠ 🏠

Spring, TX (Harris Co.); (281) 353-6229
Paula D. Criel, Director

Camp comments: A special camp for younger children. A special camp for younger children. Serves the Houston area.
Activities: Aquatic Activities, Archery, Canoeing, Challenge/Rope Courses, Drama, Fishing, Hiking, Horseback — Western, Nature/Environment Studies, Swimming — Recreational
Session lengths & capacity: June-August; 1 week sessions; 100 campers
Clientele & fees: coed 6-10; Fees: **C** ⚠ 🐷
Contact: DeAnne Pickett, Director at (281) 353-6229; fax: (281) 288-4212
Operated by: YMCA of Greater Houston, 2122 E Governors Circle, Houston, TX 77092 at (713) 353-5214

Group Rental Information
Facilities: Cabins, Food Service, Hiking Trails, Playing Fields, Pool
Programs: Challenge/Ropes Course, Environmental Education, Horseback Riding, Swimming (#4057)

YMCA Hamman Ranch

(est 1988) ⚠ 🏠 🚗

Bandera, TX (Bandera Co.); (830) 796-7449
Kori Parker, Director

Camp comments: Program geared toward teens. Character development in a fun and exciting environment. Located in Texas hill country.
Activities: Backpacking, Camping Skills/Outdoor Living, Canoeing, Challenge/Rope Courses, Climbing/Rappelling, Horseback — Western, Nature/Environment Studies, Riflery, Swimming — Recreational, Team Building
Session lengths & capacity: 1 & 2 week sessions; 65 campers
Clientele & fees: boys 12-16; girls 12-16; coed 12-16; families; Fees: **C, D** ⚠
Contact: Len Masengale, Ranch Director at (830) 796-7449; fax: (830) 796-8308
e-mail: ymca@indian-creek.net
Operated by: YMCA of Greater Houston, 2122 E Governors Circle, Houston, TX 77092 at (713) 353-5214

Group Rental Information
Facilities: Food Service, Hiking Trails
Programs: Horseback Riding (#2723)

Utah

Camp Cloud Rim (est 1936) ⚠

Park City, UT; (435) 649-8641
Amy Hugh, Director

Camp comments: Camp Cloud Rim offers girls a place where they can develop their skills, make new friends & strengthen their self esteem.
Activities: Aquatic Activities, Arts/Crafts, Camping Skills/Outdoor Living, Canoeing, Ceramics/Pottery, Climbing/Rappelling, Hiking, Sailing, Swimming — Recreational, Team Building
Contact: Amy Hugh, Program Spec/Camp Director at (801) 265-8472 ext. 21; fax: (801) 261-1213
e-mail: ahugh@gsutah.org
Web site: www.gsutah.org
Operated by: Utah GSC, PO Box 57280, Salt Lake City, UT 84157 at (801) 265-8472 (#39270)

Camp Hobe (est 1985) ⚠

Salt Lake City, UT (Salt Lake Co.); (801) 483-1500
Christina Beckwith, Director

Camp comments: A camping experience for children with cancer and their siblings that allows them to run, swim, hike & just be kids

Activities: Archery, Arts/Crafts, Basketball, Counselor Training (CIT), Drama, Hiking, Nature/Environment Studies, Swimming — Recreational
Session lengths & capacity: 1 week sessions; 140 campers
Clientele & fees: boys 4-19; girls 4-19; coed 4-19; Fees: **A** ⚠ 🐷
Contact: Christina Beckwith, Camp Director at (801) 483-1500; fax: (801) 483-1558
e-mail: christina.beckwith@hsc.utah.edu
Web site: www.camphobe.com
Operated by: American Cancer Society, 941 East 3300 South, Salt Lake City, UT 84106 at (801) 483-1500 (#6546)

Camp Kostopulos (est 1967) ⚠ 🏠

Salt Lake City, UT (Salt Lake Co.); (801) 582-0700
Gary Ethington, Director

Camp comments: Long tradition of serving special needs campers. Nondisabled campers may also attend. Variety of activities on site. Close to town and airport. 1 to 4 ratio.
Activities: Arts/Crafts, Camping Skills/Outdoor Living, Challenge/Rope Courses, Field Trips, Hiking, Horseback — English, Horseback — Western, Nature/Environment Studies, Swimming — Recreational, Travel/Tour
Session lengths & capacity: June-August; 1 week sessions; 40 campers
Clientele & fees: boys 7-65; girls 7-65; coed 7-65; Fees: **C** ⚠
Contact: Gary Ethington, Executive Director at (801) 582-0700; fax: (801) 583-5176
e-mail: gethington@campk.org
Web site: www.campk.org
Operated by: Camp Kostopulos, 2500 Emigration Canyon, Salt Lake City, UT 84108 at (801) 582-0700

Group Rental Information
Site comments: Weekend rentals from Friday night through Sunday afternoon. Sleeps 40 during summer, 75 during off summer, heated cabins and lodge. winter sports equip. on site
Facilities: Cabins, Dorm-Style, Food Service, Hiking Trails, Kitchen Facilities, Lodges, Playing Fields, Pool
Programs: Challenge/Ropes Course, Horseback Riding, Swimming, Winter Sports (#3771)

Camp Trefoil Ranch (est 1946) ⚠ 🏠

Provo, UT (Utah City Co.); (801) 225-7274
Peggy Murphy, Director

Camp comments: Trefoil Ranch offers girls a place where they can develop their skills, make new friends & strengthen their self esteem
Activities: Archery, Arts/Crafts, Backpacking, Camping Skills/Outdoor Living, Challenge/Rope Courses, Climbing/Rappelling, Counselor Training (CIT), Horseback — Western, Leadership Development, Nature/Environment Studies
Session lengths & capacity: June-August; 1/2, 1 & 2 week sessions; 150 campers
Clientele & fees: girls 7-17; Fees: **B, C** ⚠ 🐷
Contact: Peggy Murphy, Outdoor Program Specialist/Camp Director at (801) 265-8472 ext. 27; fax: (801) 261-1213
e-mail: pmurphy@gsutah.org
Web site: www.gsutah.org
Operated by: Utah GSC, PO Box 57280, Salt Lake City, UT 84157 at (801) 265-8472

Group Rental Information
Facilities: Dorm-Style, Food Service, Kitchen Facilities, Lodges, Meeting Rooms, Tents
Programs: Environmental Education (#497)

FCYD Camp/aka Camp UTADA

(est 1962) ⚠

West Jordan, UT; (801) 566-6913
David Okubo, MD, Director

Camp comments: Established by leaders in diabetes and camping in 1962. 4 weeks, 3 family

weekends, and 5 winter weekends. Activites, education, and medical supervision.
Activities: Archery, Arts/Crafts, Basketball, Counselor Training (CIT), Hiking, Leadership Development, Snow Sports, Sports — Field & Team, Swimming — Recreational, Waterskiing
Session lengths & capacity: January-December; 1/2 & 1 week sessions; 150 campers
Clientele & fees: boys 1-18; girls 1-18; coed 1-18; families; Fees: **B** ⚠ 🐷
Contact: David Okubo, MD, Camp Director at (801) 566-6913; fax: (801) 566-9899
Web site: www.FCYD-inc.org
Operated by: Foundation for Chldren & Yth, with Diabetes, Inc., 1995 West 9000 South #ACA, West Jordan, UT 84088 at (801) 566-6913 (#42232)

Navajo Trails Adventure Camp

(est 1965) ⚠

Bicknell, UT; (435) 425-3469
Dan and Jen Sampson, Director

Camp comments: Weekly adventure trips. Explore Utah horseback riding, backpacking, kayaking, waterskiing, rock-climbing, or mtn biking.
Activities: Backpacking, Bicycling/Biking, Camping Skills/Outdoor Living, Climbing/Rappelling, Counselor Training (CIT), Horseback — Western, Kayaking, Waterskiing, Wilderness Trips, Windsurfing
Session lengths & capacity: June-August; 2, 3 & 4 week sessions; 60 campers
Clientele & fees: coed 9-17; Fees: **F** ⚠ 🐷
Contact: Dan Sampson, Director at (801) 571-0804; fax: (801) 576-0759
e-mail: ddsampson@earthlink.net
Web site: www.navajotrails.com
Operated by: Navajo Trails Adventure Camp, PO Box 55, Draper, UT 84020 at (801) 571-0804 (#466)

Vermont

4H Camp Waubanong (est 1924) ⚠ 🏠

Brattleboro, VT (Windham Co.); (802) 254-8026
Jennifer Jacobs, Director

Camp comments: Community centered camp on wooded mountain side in beautiful southern Vermont. Rooted in 4-H tradtion with outstanding staff and creative programming.
Activities: Archery, Arts/Crafts, Camping Skills/Outdoor Living, Challenge/Rope Courses, Hiking, Horseback — English, Leadership Development, Nature/Environment Studies, Swimming — Recreational, Team Building
Session lengths & capacity: June-August; 1 & 2 week sessions; 60 campers
Clientele & fees: coed 8-14; Fees: **C** ⚠ 🐷
Contact: Janet O'Keefe, Registrar at (802) 257-7967; fax: (802) 257-0112
e-mail: jokeefe@clover.urm.edu
Web site: www.campwaubanong.org
Operated by: 4H Camp Waubanong, 157 Old Guilford Rd 4, Brattleboro, VT 05301 at (802) 257-7967

Group Rental Information
Site comments: Unique and invinting wilderness gathering center. Camp available to rent late summer thru fall. A delightful time at the wooded mountainside location.
Facilities: Cabins, Hiking Trails, Kitchen Facilities, Lodges, Meeting Rooms, Playing Fields, Pool
Programs: Challenge/Ropes Course (#6642)

Abnaki (est 1901) ⚠ 🏠 🚗

North Hero, VT (Grand Isle Co.); (802) 372-8275
Adam C Brooks, Director

Camp comments: Camp Abnaki for boys on Lake Camp Champlain. Traditional camp program with

emphasis on character development. Established in 1901.
Activities: Archery, Camping Skills/Outdoor Living, Climbing/Rappelling, Counselor Training (CIT), Hiking, Kayaking, Sailing, Sports — Field & Team, Swimming — Instructional, Windsurfing
Session lengths & capacity: June-August; 1, 2 & 4 week sessions; 160 campers
Clientele & fees: boys 6-16; families; Fees: **D** △ 🐖
Contact: Adam Brooks, Director of Camping Services at (802) 862-9622; fax: (802) 862-9984
e-mail: abrooks@gbymca.org
Web site: www.campabnaki.org
Operated by: Greater Burlington YMCA, 266 College Street, Burlington, VT 05401 at (802) 862-9622

Group Rental Information
Facilities: Cabins, Food Service, Hiking Trails, Kitchen Facilities, Lake, Meeting Rooms, Playing Fields, Tents
Programs: Boating, Swimming (#2590)

Aloha (est 1905) △ 🚐

Fairlee, VT (Orange Co.); (802) 333-3410
Nancy L Pennell, Director

Camp comments: For 90 yrs we've been building community with a 2:1 cmpr/counselor ratio & a non-competitive pgm. Indiv attn a reality!
Activities: Aquatic Activities, Backpacking, Counselor Training (CIT), Drama, Horseback — English, Leadership Development, Sailing, Soccer, Swimming — Instructional, Tennis
Session lengths & capacity: June-August; 3 & 7 week sessions; 140 campers
Clientele & fees: girls 12-17; Fees: **F** △ 🐖
Contact: Ellen Bagley, Administrative Assistant at (802) 333-3400; fax: (802) 333-3404
e-mail: ellen_bagley@alohafoundation.org
Web site: www.alohafoundation.org
Operated by: The Aloha Foundation Inc, 2968 Lake Morey Rd, Fairlee, VT 05045 at (802) 333-3400 (#2819)

Aloha Hive (est 1915) △ 🚐

Fairlee, VT (Orange Co.); (802) 333-3420
Helen R Butler, Director

Camp comments: For 90 yrs we've been building community with a 2:1 camper:counselor ratio & a noncompetitive pgm. Individual attention a reality!
Activities: Arts/Crafts, Camping Skills/Outdoor Living, Canoeing, Challenge/Rope Courses, Drama, Gymnastics, Music, Sailing, Swimming — Instructional, Tennis
Session lengths & capacity: June-August; 3 & 7 week sessions; 155 campers

ICON LEGEND

☀	Day Camp
△	Resident Camp
🏠	Facilities Available To Rent
🚐	Transportation Available
🐖	Financial Aid Available

FEE RANGES PER WEEK

A	$0-75
B	$75-200
C	$201-350
D	$351-500
E	$501-650
F	over $650

Clientele & fees: girls 7-12; Fees: **F** △ 🐖
Contact: Ellen Bagley, Administrative Assistant at (802) 333-3400; fax: (802) 333-3404
e-mail: ellen_bagley@alohafoundation.org
Web site: www.alohafoundation.org
Operated by: The Aloha Foundation Inc, 2968 Lake Morey Rd, Fairlee, VT 05045 at (802) 333-3400 (#2794)

Betsey Cox (est 1952) △ 🏠

Pittsford, VT; (802) 483-6611
Lorrie Byrom, Director

Camp comments: The program is all elective campers choose daily. Progressive philosophy with global view. Rustic farm with cabins.
Activities: Archery, Arts/Crafts, Backpacking, Boating, Ceramics/Pottery, Farming/Ranching/Gardening, Hiking, Horseback — English, Leadership Development
Session lengths & capacity: June-August; 2, 3, 5 & 8 week sessions; 85 campers
Clientele & fees: girls 9-15; Fees: **E** △
Contact: Mike Byrom, Associate Director at (888) 345-9193;
e-mail: betcoxvt@aol.com
Web site: www.campbetseycox.com
Operated by: Camp Betsey Cox Inc, 349 South Mountain Rd, Northfield, MA 01360 at (888) 345-9193

Group Rental Information
Facilities: Cabins, Kitchen Facilities, Lake, Lodges, Playing Fields (#2802)

Brown Ledge Camp (est 1926) △

Colchester, VT (Chattenden Co.); (800) 246-1958
Bill & Kathy Neilsen, Director

Camp comments: Noncompetitive, elective program. Giving campers responsibility & choice. Superior instruction. Beautiful location
Activities: Archery, Arts/Crafts, Canoeing, Drama, Horseback — English, Sailing, Swimming — Instructional, Tennis, Waterskiing
Session lengths & capacity: June-August; 4 & 8 week sessions; 180 campers
Clientele & fees: girls 10-18; Fees: **E** △
Contact: Bill & Kathy Neilsen, Directors at (800) 246-1958; fax: (802) 658-1614
e-mail: blc@brownledge.org
Web site: www.brownledge.org
Operated by: The Brown Ledge Foundation Inc, 25 Wilson Street, Burlington, VT 05401 at (800) 882-2442 (#2609)

Camp Billings (est 1906) △

Fairlee, VT; (802) 333-4317
Bob Green, Director

Camp comments: One of Americas oldest camps located in the camping center of NE Traditional camping featuring athletics, water sports.
Activities: Aquatic Activities, Arts/Crafts, Backpacking, Basketball, Canoeing, Drama, Sailing, Tennis, Waterskiing, Windsurfing
Session lengths & capacity: June-August; 2, 4 & 8 week sessions; 170 campers
Clientele & fees: coed 7-16; Fees: **C** △ 🐖
Contact: Bob Green, Director at (954) 345-7290;
e-mail: campbillings@juno.com
Operated by: Billings Camp Board Directors, PO Box 379, Moscow, VT 05662 at (802) 476-7341 (#2701)

Camp Catherine Capers

(est 1952) ☀ △

Wells, VT (Rutland Co.); (802) 645-0216

Camp comments: Daily horse or animal care, riding, swimming, & elective sports. Campers help build program of fun, caring & respect.

Activities: Backpacking, Camping Skills/Outdoor Living, Counselor Training (CIT), Horseback — English, Photography, Sailing, Swimming — Instructional, Swimming — Recreational, Tennis, Waterskiing
Session lengths & capacity: June-August; 1, 2, 3, 4, 5, 6, 7 & 8 week sessions; 60 campers
Clientele & fees: girls 9-15; coed 8-15; Fees: **C, F** ☀ Fees: **F** △
Contact: Audrey Nelson & Liz Ambuhl, Directors at (802) 645-0216; fax: (802) 645-9818
e-mail: info@campcatherinecapers.com
Web site: www.campcatherinecapers.com
Operated by: Camp Catherine Capers Inc, PO Box 68, W Pawlet, VT 05775 at (802) 645-0216 (#2738)

Camp Hochelaga (est 1919) ☀ △ 🏠

South Hero, VT (Grand Isle Co.); (802) 372-4510
Sandy Valine, Director

Camp comments: Lake Champlain; perfect setting for waterfront activities, arts/crafts drama more-82= years of empowering girls YWCA VT!
Activities: Aquatic Activities, Archery, Arts/Crafts, Canoeing, Counselor Training (CIT), Drama, Nature/Environment Studies, Sailing, Sports — Field & Team
Session lengths & capacity: June-August; 1/2, 1 & 2 week sessions; 100 campers
Clientele & fees: girls 6-16; Fees: **B** ☀ Fees: **D** △
Contact: (802) 862-7520; fax: (802) 862-0926
Operated by: YWCA of Vermont, 278 Main St, Burlington, VT 05401 at (802) 862-7520

Group Rental Information
Facilities: Cabins, Kitchen Facilities, Lake, Lodges, Playing Fields (#11837)

Camp Sangamon (est 1922) △

Pittsford, VT (Rutland Co.); (802) 483-2862
Mike Byrom, Director

Camp comments: Free choice! Daily self-scheduled program emphasizes crafts/art in 5 studios. Life-long outdoor sports & skills.
Activities: Archery, Arts/Crafts, Camping Skills/Outdoor Living, Ceramics/Pottery, Challenge/Rope Courses, Horseback — English, Model Rocketry, Sailing
Session lengths & capacity: 2, 3, 5 & 8 week sessions; 80 campers
Clientele & fees: boys 9-15; Fees: **E** △
Contact: Mike Byrom, Director at (888) 345-9193;
e-mail: sangamonvt@aol.com
Web site: www.campsangamon.com
Operated by: Camp Sangamon For Boys Inc, 382 Camp Lane, Pittsford, VT 05763 at (888) 345-9193 (#2675)

Camp Thoreau In Vermont

(est 1962) △ 🚐

Thetford Center, VT (Orange Co.); (802) 333-9106
Gregory H Finger, Director

Camp comments: Inter-racial, democratic community living where campers choose their activities & enjoy them in a non-competitive, caring, child-centered envirnment.
Activities: Challenge/Rope Courses, Climbing/Rappelling, Community Service, Hiking, Horseback — English, Kayaking, Music, Photography, Radio/TV/Video, Sports — Field & Team
Session lengths & capacity: June-August; 4 & 8 week sessions; 145 campers
Clientele & fees: coed 8-15; Fees: **F** △
Contact: Gregory H Finger, Director at (845) 895-2974; fax: (845) 895-1281
e-mail: gfinger@frontiernet.net
Web site: www.campthoreau-in-vermont.org
Operated by: An Experience in People Inc, 157 Tillson Lake Rd, Wallkill, NY 12589-3265 at (845) 895-2974 (#2041)

Challenge Wilderness Camp

(est 1965)

Bradford, VT (Orange Co.); (802) 222-5702
Drs Thayer & Candice Raines, Director

Camp comments: Outdoor challenge adventure: survival, orienteering, fitness, fishing, blacksmith, woodwork, canoe trip, rock climbing!
Activities: Archery, Arts/Crafts, Backpacking, Camping Skills/Outdoor Living, Canoeing, Challenge/Rope Courses, Climbing/Rappelling, Kayaking, Nature/Environment Studies, Riflery
Session lengths & capacity: June-August; 4 week sessions; 46 campers
Clientele & fees: boys 9-16; Fees: E ▲
Contact: Drs J Thayer & Candice Raines, Owners/Directors at (800) 832-4295;
fax: (802) 786-0653
e-mail: rainest@sover.net
Web site: www.challengewilderness.com
Operated by: Challenge Wilderness Camp, 300 Grove St Country Grove 4, Rutland, VT 05701 at (800) 832-4295 (#4480)

Downer 4H Camp Inc (est 1945)

Sharon, VT (Windsor Co.); (802) 763-7007
Harold Mitchell, Director

Activities: Archery, Arts/Crafts, Baseball/Softball, Canoeing, Drama, Nature/Environment Studies, Photography, Riflery, Soccer, Swimming — Instructional
Session lengths & capacity: June-August; 1 & 2 week sessions; 140 campers
Clientele & fees: boys 8-16; girls 8-16; coed 8-16; Fees: B ▲
Contact: Harold Mitchell, Director at (802) 796-3636; fax: (802) 933-2812
e-mail: hkenmitchell@hotmail.com
Operated by: Vermont Extension Service 4H, University Of Vermont, Burlington, VT 05405 at (802) 656-2990 (#2727)

Farnsworth (est 1909)

Thetford, VT (Orange Co.); (802) 785-2171
Nancy Frankel, Director

Camp comments: Creative program planned by campers and staff in small groups to build self esteem & community. Swimming, boating, arts, riding, campcraft, tripping, & CIT.
Activities: Aquatic Activities, Arts/Crafts, Backpacking, Camping Skills/Outdoor Living, Challenge/Rope Courses, Counselor Training (CIT), Drama, Horseback — English, Wilderness Trips
Session lengths & capacity: June-August; 1/2, 1 & 2 week sessions; 260 campers
Clientele & fees: girls 7-17; Fees: C ▲
Contact: Nancy Frankel, Camp Director at (603) 627-4158 ext. 124; fax: (603) 627-4169
e-mail: camping@swgirlscouts.org
Web site: www.swgirlscouts.org
Operated by: Girl Scouts Swift Water Cncl, 8 Perimeter Road, Manchester, NH 03103-3307 at (603) 627-4158

Group Rental Information
Facilities: Cabins, Hiking Trails, Lake, Tents (#2629)

Farwell for Girls (est 1906)

Newbury, VT (Orange Co.); (802) 429-2244
Charyl & Bob Hanson, Director

Camp comments: Warm, nurturing environment. Lakeside setting. Outstanding riding program for all abilities. Cabins, trips, great food.
Activities: Aquatic Activities, Archery, Arts/Crafts, Drama, Horseback — English, Performing Arts, Sports — Field & Team, Tennis
Session lengths & capacity: June-August; 3, 4 & 7 week sessions; 125 campers
Clientele & fees: girls 6-16; Fees: F ▲
Contact: Charyl & Bob Hanson, Directors at (610) 793-9303; fax: (610) 793-9304

e-mail: chanson@farwell.com
Web site: www.farwell.com
Operated by: Camp Farwell Ltd, PO Box 1479, Chadds Ford, PA 19317 at (610) 793-9303 (#8258)

Flying Cloud (est 1965)

Plymouth, VT (Windsor Co.); (802) 422-3761
Sunshine Mathon, Director

Camp comments: Remote simple-living camp surrounded by 2500 acres of woods & mountains honoring rustic living skills, community, respect for each other & the land we live on.
Activities: Arts/Crafts, Backpacking, Camping Skills/Outdoor Living, Canoeing, Hiking, Leadership Development, Nature/Environment Studies, Wilderness Trips
Session lengths & capacity: June-August; 4 & 8 week sessions; 40 campers
Clientele & fees: boys 11-14; Fees: F ▲ 🐷
Contact: (802) 422-3761; fax: (802) 422-8660
e-mail: fandw@fandw.org
Web site: www.fandw.org
Operated by: Farm and Wilderness Foundation, 263 Farm and Wilderness Road, Plymouth, VT 05056 at (802) 422-3761 (#7372)

Horizons Summer Day Camp

(est 1997)

Fairlee, VT (Orange Co.); (802) 333-3450
Daniel R Kerr, Director

Camp comments: The Aloha Foundation's day camp for K-6th graders. Two-week sessions, transportation, great food and fun!
Activities: Aquatic Activities, Archery, Arts/Crafts, Boating, Drama, Gymnastics, Hiking, Nature/Environment Studies, Sports — Field & Team, Tennis
Session lengths & capacity: July-August; 2 week sessions; 125 campers
Clientele & fees: coed 5-12; Fees: B, C ☀
Contact: Ellen Bagley, Administrative Assistnat at (802) 333-3400; fax: (802) 333-3404
e-mail: ellen_bagley@alohafoundation.org
Web site: www.alohafoundation.org
Operated by: The Aloha Foundation Inc, 2968 Lake Morey Rd, Fairlee, VT 05045 at (802) 333-3400 (#42238)

Indian Brook (est 1940)

Plymouth, VT (Windsor Co.); (802) 422-3761
Laura Fitch, Director

Camp comments: Nurtured by supportive staff, girls are inspired to develop confidence, new skills & abiding joy. Organic farming/cooperative work projects/outdoor living/arts.
Activities: Backpacking, Camping Skills/Outdoor Living, Canoeing, Ceramics/Pottery, Challenge/Rope Courses, Climbing/Rappelling, Farming/Ranching/Gardening, Hiking, Swimming — Instructional, Wilderness Trips
Session lengths & capacity: June-August; 4 & 8 week sessions; 120 campers
Clientele & fees: girls 9-14; Fees: F ▲ 🐷
Contact: (802) 422-3761; fax: (802) 422-8660
e-mail: fandw@fandw.org
Web site: www.fandw.org
Operated by: Farm and Wilderness Foundation, 263 Farm and Wilderness Road, Plymouth, VT 05056 at (802) 422-3761

Group Rental Information
Site comments: Outdoor education. Rustic rental facilities.
Seasons & Capacity: Spring 0, Fall 0
Facilities: Cabins, Double Occupancy, Hiking Trails, Lake, Lodges, Meeting Rooms, River
Programs: Boating, Challenge/Ropes Course, Environmental Education, Swimming (#2839)

Keewaydin Dunmore (est 1894)

Salisbury, VT (Addison Co.); (802) 352-4770
Peter Hare, Director

Camp comments: Traditional camp famous for canoe & hiking trips. Rich in-camp program. Character building experiences in safe, fun environment. Experienced, caring staff.
Activities: Aquatic Activities, Archery, Camping Skills/Outdoor Living, Canoeing, Climbing/Rappelling, Kayaking, Riflery, Sailing, Tennis, Wilderness Trips
Session lengths & capacity: June-August; 2, 4 & 8 week sessions; 215 campers
Clientele & fees: boys 8-16; Fees: E, F ▲ 🐷
Contact: Peter Hare, Direcor at (802) 352-4770; fax: (802) 388-4772
e-mail: peter@keewaydincamps.org
Web site: www.keewaydincamps.org
Operated by: The Keewaydin Foundation, 10 Keewaydin Road, Salisbury, VT 05769 at (802) 352-4247 (#2840)

Killooleet (est 1927)

Hancock, VT (Addison Co.); (802) 767-3152
Kate Spencer Seeger, Director

Camp comments: Specialization in a wide variety of sports and arts activities. Hikes and trips. Supportive cabin groups. Full season promotes social and emotional growth.
Activities: Arts/Crafts, Baseball/Softball, Bicycling/Biking, Boating, Hiking, Horseback — English, Music, Performing Arts, Sports — Field & Team, Swimming — Instructional
Session lengths & capacity: June-August; 8 week sessions; 100 campers
Clientele & fees: coed 9-14; Fees: E ▲ 🐷
Contact: Kate Spencer Seeger, Director at (617) 666-1484; fax: (617) 666-0378
e-mail: camp05748@aol.com
Web site: www.killooleet
Operated by: Killooleet, 70 Trull Street, Somerville, MA 02145 at (617) 666-1484 (#1902)

Kiniya (est 1919)

Colchester, VT (Chittenden Co.); (802) 893-2785
Mr and Mrs J H Williams, Director

Camp comments: On Lake Champlain 150 acres of pine forests and meadows. Quality summer camp for 130 girls ages 6-17. Founded in 1919.
Activities: Aquatic Activities, Arts/Crafts, Boating, Camping Skills/Outdoor Living, Dance, Drama, Gymnastics, Horseback — English, Tennis, Waterskiing
Session lengths & capacity: June-August; 1, 3, 4 & 7 week sessions; 130 campers
Clientele & fees: girls 6-17; Fees: F ▲
Contact: Marilyn and Jack Williams, Directors/Owner at (802) 893-2785; fax: (802) 893-7849
e-mail: kiniya@webtv.net
Operated by: Kiniya, 1281 Camp Kiniya Rd, Colchester, VT 05446 at (802) 893-7849 (#3788)

Lanakila (est 1922)

Fairlee, VT (Orange Co.); (802) 333-3430
D Barnes Boffey, Director

Camp comments: 90 years of building community with 2:1 camper/counselor ratio & a noncompetitive prog. Individual attention a reality!
Activities: Archery, Arts/Crafts, Camping Skills/Outdoor Living, Canoeing, Challenge/Rope Courses, Drama, Photography, Riflery, Sports — Field & Team, Wilderness Trips
Session lengths & capacity: June-August; 3 & 7 week sessions; 155 campers
Clientele & fees: boys 8-14; Fees: F ▲ 🐷
Contact: Ellen Bagley, Administrative Assistant at (802) 333-3400; fax: (802) 333-3404
e-mail: ellen_bagley@alohafoundation.org
Web site: www.alohafoundation.org

Operated by: The Aloha Foundation Inc, 2968 Lake Morey Rd, Fairlee, VT 05045 at (802) 333-3400 (#4180)

Lochearn Camp for Girls

(est 1916)   ☀ ⚠ 🏠 🚐

Post Mills, VT (Orange Co.); (802) 333-4211
Rich and Ginny Maxson, Director

Camp comments: Magnificent lakeside setting, first-rate facilities, mature loving staff, committed to values of kindness, cooperation.
Activities: Arts/Crafts, Gymnastics, Hiking, Horseback — English, Performing Arts, Sailing, Sports — Field & Team, Swimming — Instructional, Tennis, Waterskiing
Session lengths & capacity: June-August; 1, 4 & 8 week sessions; 180 campers
Clientele & fees: girls 8-16; Fees: F ⚠
Contact: Rich and Ginny Maxson, Owners & Directors at (877) 649-4151; fax: (802) 333-4856
e-mail: lochearn@together.net
Web site: www.camppage.com/lochearn
Operated by: Lochearn Camp for Girls, PO Box 44, Post Mills, VT 05058 at (802) 333-4211
Group Rental Information
Facilities: Cabins, Lake, Meeting Rooms, Playing Fields (#3426)

Lotus Lake Camp (est 1952)   ☀ 🚐

Williamstown, VT (Orange Co.); (802) 433-5451
John or Dorothy Milne, Director

Camp comments: Day camp offers outdoor activities, rural setting on private lake. Emphasis on making choices & working in small groups w/caring staff
Activities: Aquatic Activities, Bicycling/Biking, Horseback — English, Leadership Development, Nature/Environment Studies, Sailing, Soccer, Swimming — Instructional, Tennis
Session lengths & capacity: June-August; 1, 2 & 8 week sessions; 150 campers
Clientele & fees: coed 6-14; Fees: B ☀
Contact: John or Dorothy Milne, Co-Directors at (413) 773-7205;
Operated by: Lotus Lake Corp, 4785 VT Rte 14, Williamstown, VT 05679 at (802) 433-5451 (#2729)

Night Eagle Wilderness   ⚠

E Wallingford, VT; (802) 773-7866
Bruce T Moreton, Director

Camp comments: Through earth based activities boys learn to live and play in a spirit of cooperation rather than competition

ICON LEGEND

☀	Day Camp
⚠	Resident Camp
🏠	Facilities Available To Rent
🚐	Transportation Available
🐷	Financial Aid Available

FEE RANGES PER WEEK

A	$0-75
B	$75-200
C	$201-350
D	$351-500
E	$501-650
F	over $650

Activities: Archery, Arts/Crafts, Backpacking, Camping Skills/Outdoor Living, Canoeing, Community Service, Hiking, Music, Nature/Environment Studies, Swimming — Recreational
Session lengths & capacity: June-August; 2, 4 & 8 week sessions; 40 campers
Clientele & fees: boys 10-14; Fees: D ⚠ 🐷
Contact: Bruce or Kelly Moreton, Owners at (802) 773-7866; fax: (802) 773-7866
e-mail: nightegl@sover.net
Web site: www.nighteaglewilderness.com
Operated by: Night Eagle Wilderness Avdvent, PO Box 374, Cuttingsville, VT 05738 at (802) 773-7866 (#40725)

Saltash Mountain Camp

(est 1962)   ⚠ 🚐

Plymouth, VT (Windsor Co.); (802) 422-3761
Joanna Morse, Director

Camp comments: Wilderness tripping camp using hiking, canoeing, climbing, and service to build community. In-camp activities; gardening, theatre, music, crafts, swim & sail.
Activities: Arts/Crafts, Backpacking, Camping Skills/Outdoor Living, Challenge/Rope Courses, Climbing/Rappelling, Drama, Farming/Ranching/Gardening, Hiking, Swimming — Recreational, Wilderness Trips
Session lengths & capacity: June-August; 4 & 8 week sessions; 48 campers
Clientele & fees: coed 11-14; Fees: F ⚠ 🐷
Contact: (802) 422-3761; fax: (802) 422-8660
e-mail: fandw@fandw.org
Web site: www.fandw.org
Operated by: Farm and Wilderness Foundation, 263 Farm and Wilderness Road, Plymouth, VT 05056 at (802) 422-3761 (#4370)

Songadeewin of Keewaydin   ⚠

Salisbury, VT (Addison Co.); (802) 352-9860
Ellen M Flight, Director

Camp comments: Canoeing and Hiking trips w/full in-camp program. Character-building experiences in friendly, informal, unpressured atmosphere. Experienced staff, (3.5:1)
Activities: Aquatic Activities, Archery, Camping Skills/Outdoor Living, Canoeing, Climbing/Rappelling, Drama, Kayaking, Riflery, Sailing, Wilderness Trips
Session lengths & capacity: June-August; 4 & 8 week sessions
Clientele & fees: girls 8-15; Fees: E, F ⚠
Contact: Ellen Flight, Camp Director at (802) 352-9860; fax: (802) 352-4772
e-mail: ellen@keewaydincamps.com
Web site: www.keewaydincamps.org
Operated by: The Keewaydin Foundation, 10 Keewaydin Road, Salisbury, VT 05769 at (802) 352-4247 (#47879)

Tamarack Farm (est 1951)   ⚠ 🚐

Plymouth, VT (Windsor Co.); (802) 422-3761
Tina Tannen & Tom Barrup, Director

Camp comments: Teens grow in a safe, open, nurturing, and diverse community centered on simple living, community building, cooperative work projects, and service.
Activities: Arts/Crafts, Camping Skills/Outdoor Living, Ceramics/Pottery, Community Service, Farming/Ranching/Gardening, Leadership Development, Performing Arts, Photography, Swimming — Recreational, Wilderness Trips
Session lengths & capacity: June-August; 8 week sessions; 72 campers
Clientele & fees: coed 15-17; Fees: E ⚠ 🐷
Contact: (802) 422-3761; fax: (802) 422-8660
e-mail: fandw@fandw.org
Web site: www.fandw.org

Operated by: Farm and Wilderness Foundation, 263 Farm and Wilderness Road, Plymouth, VT 05056 at (802) 422-3761 (#2779)

The Barn Day Camp

(est 1984)   ☀ 🏠 🚐

Plymouth, VT (Windsor Co.); (802) 422-3761
Helen Richards-Peelle, Director

Camp comments: Campers explore and learn new skills: swimming/creative arts/farm & gardens/campcraft/rock climbing/nature/canoeing/work projects/Quaker values/fun/friendship.
Activities: Arts/Crafts, Backpacking, Camping Skills/Outdoor Living, Challenge/Rope Courses, Farming/Ranching/Gardening, Hiking, Nature/Environment Studies, Swimming — Instructional, Swimming — Recreational
Session lengths & capacity: June-August; 2 week sessions; 80 campers
Clientele & fees: coed 3-11; Fees: D ☀ 🐷
Contact: (802) 422-3761; fax: (802) 422-8660
e-mail: fandw@fandw.org
Web site: www.fandw.org
Operated by: Farm and Wilderness Foundation, 263 Farm and Wilderness Road, Plymouth, VT 05056 at (802) 422-3761
Group Rental Information
Seasons & Capacity: Spring 25, Fall 25
Facilities: Dorm-Style, Hiking Trails, Kitchen Facilities, Lake, Lodges, Meeting Rooms, Playing Fields
Programs: Boating, Challenge/Ropes Course, Environmental Education, Swimming (#5471)

The Hulbert Outdoor Center

(est 1995)   🏠

Fairlee, VT (Orange Co.); (802) 333-3450
Greg Auch, Director
Contact: Ellen Bagley, Administrative Assistant at (802) 333-3400; fax: (802) 333-3404
e-mail: ellen_bagley@alohafoundation.org
Web site: www.alohafoundation.org
Operated by: The Aloha Foundation Inc, 2968 Lake Morey Rd, Fairlee, VT 05045 at (802) 333-3400 (#33667)

Timberlake (est 1939)   ⚠ 🏠

Plymouth, VT (Windsor Co.); (802) 422-3761
Mike Vecchiarelli, Director

Camp comments: With wilderness adventure, organic farming/gardening, supportive community, and Quaker values, Timberlake boys have fun & discover new parts of themselves.
Activities: Backpacking, Camping Skills/Outdoor Living, Canoeing, Challenge/Rope Courses, Climbing/Rappelling, Farming/Ranching/Gardening, Hiking, Leadership Development, Swimming — Instructional, Wilderness Trips
Session lengths & capacity: June-August; 4 & 8 week sessions; 120 campers
Clientele & fees: boys 9-14; Fees: F ⚠ 🐷
Contact: (802) 422-3761; fax: (802) 422-8660
e-mail: fandw@fandw.org
Web site: www.fandw.org
Operated by: Farm and Wilderness Foundation, 263 Farm and Wilderness Road, Plymouth, VT 05056 at (802) 422-3761
Group Rental Information
Facilities: Cabins, Food Service, Hiking Trails, Kitchen Facilities, Lake, Lodges
Programs: Boating, Challenge/Ropes Course, Environmental Education, Swimming (#2674)

Voyageurs Wilderness Trips   ▲

Fairlee, VT; (802) 333-3405
Greg Auch, Director
Activities: Wilderness Trips
Contact: Web site: www.alohafoundation.org
Operated by: The Aloha Foundation Inc, 2968 Lake Morey Rd, Fairlee, VT 05045 at (802) 333-3400 (#12106)

Wapanacki (est 1938)   ▲

Hardwick, VT (Lamoille Co.); (802) 472-8227
Wendy Shea, Director

Camp comments: Girls learn to develop values & increase their self-esteem in outdoor setting in beautiful Vermont.
Activities: Aquatic Activities, Arts/Crafts, Backpacking, Canoeing, Drama, Horseback — Western, Leadership Development, Sailing, Skating, Team Building
Session lengths & capacity: June-August; 1/2, 1, 2, 3 & 4 week sessions; 120 campers
Clientele & fees: girls 6-17; Fees: B, C ▲
Contact: Wendy Shea, Camp Director at (802) 878-7131; fax: (802) 878-3943
Web site: www.girlscoutsvt.org
Operated by: Vermont GSC, 79 Allen Martin Dr, Essex Junction, VT 05452-3400 at (802) 878-7131 (#12280)

Windridge at Teela Wooket   ▲ ⌂

(est 1986)
Roxbury, VT (Washington Co.); (802) 485-5400
Deb Fenell, Director

Camp comments: Tennis, soccer, and horseback riding in Vermont's green mountains. Strong electives too! Fun and sportsmanship, 4:1 camper to counselor ratio.
Activities: Aerobics/Exercise, Archery, Arts/Crafts, Basketball, Bicycling/Biking, Hockey, Horseback — English, Soccer, Swimming — Recreational, Tennis
Session lengths & capacity: June-August; 2, 3 & 4 week sessions; 180 campers
Clientele & fees: coed 9-15; Fees: F ▲
Contact: Deb Fenell, Camp Director at (888) 386-7859; fax: (802) 644-6300
e-mail: windridgetenniscamps@pshift.com
Web site: www.windridgetenniscamps.com
Operated by: Windridge Tennis Camps, PO Box 1298, Jeffersonville, VT 05464 at (888) 386-7859

Group Rental Information

Site comments: Located in the heart of Vermont's green mountains! Rustic cabins house 200+, meeting space for 200+, smaller breakout areas, tennis, hiking, & more; Call us!
Seasons & Capacity: Spring 180, Fall 180
Facilities: Cabins, Kitchen Facilities, Lodges, Meeting Rooms, Playing Fields (#4081)

Windridge Tennis At Craftsbury   ▲ ⌂ 🚗

(est 1973)
Craftsbury Common, VT (Orleans Co.); (802) 586-9646
Charles Witherell, Director

Camp comments: Chosen by Tennis Magazine as 'one of the top ten tennis camps in America.' A superb staff & unique lakeside setting in VT's mountains insure kids a special time
Activities: Aquatic Activities, Archery, Arts/Crafts, Bicycling/Biking, Fishing, Photography, Sailing, Soccer, Swimming — Recreational, Tennis
Session lengths & capacity: June-August; 3 & 4 week sessions; 110 campers
Clientele & fees: coed 9-15; Fees: F ▲
Contact: Pam Witherell, Office Manager at (802) 644-6500; fax: (802) 644-6300
e-mail: windridgetenniscamps@pshift.com
Web site: www.windridgetenniscamps.com

Operated by: Windridge Tennis Camps, PO Box 1298, Jeffersonville, VT 05464 at (888) 386-7859

Group Rental Information

Site comments: Privacy, open fields, woods and lake side cabins. Ideal for family reunions or wedding parties.
Seasons & Capacity: Fall 150
Facilities: Cabins, Kitchen Facilities, Lake, Lodges, Meeting Rooms
Programs: Boating (#6496)

Virginia

Adventure Day Camp   ☀

Manassas, VA (Prince Williams Co.); (703) 590-3659

Camp comments: Children forge through the summer w/new & exciting themes every 2 wks. They will experience each topic through demonstrations,crafts,stories,songs,games,trips.
Activities: Academics, Aquatic Activities, Arts/Crafts, Baseball/Softball, Field Trips, Nature/Environment Studies, Soccer, Sports — Field & Team, Swimming — Instructional
Session lengths & capacity: 1, 2, 3, 4, 5, 6, 7, 8 & 9 week sessions
Clientele & fees: coed 2-13; Fees: B ☀
Operated by: Early Years Academy Inc, 13817 Spriggs Rd, Manassas, VA 20112 at (703) 590-3659 (#4026)

Adventure Links (est 1994)   ☀ ▲ 🚗

Paris, VA; (540) 592-3682
Anna Birch, Director
Activities: Backpacking, Boating, Canoeing, Caving, Challenge/Rope Courses, Climbing/Rappelling, Kayaking, Rafting, Swimming — Recreational, Wilderness Trips
Session lengths & capacity: June-August; 1 & 2 week sessions; 100 campers
Clientele & fees: coed 8-17; families; single adults; Fees: C ☀ Fees: D ▲
Contact: (540) 592-3682; fax: (540) 592-3316
e-mail: programs@adventurelinks.net
Web site: www.adventurelinks.net
Operated by: Adventure Links, 21498 Blue Ridge Mtn Rd, Paris, VA 20130 at (540) 592-3682 (#7368)

Airfield 4H Center (est 1981)   ▲ ⌂

Wakefield, VA (Sussex Co.); (757) 899-4901
Marvin Heimbach, Director

Camp comments: Secluded in a natural wooded setting. Nestled beside beautiful Airfield Lake. Where youth experience the joys of nature.
Activities: Archery, Arts/Crafts, Canoeing, Challenge/Rope Courses, Fishing, Nature/Environment Studies, Performing Arts, Riflery, Sports — Field & Team, Swimming — Recreational
Session lengths & capacity: June-August; 1 week sessions; 200 campers
Clientele & fees: coed 9-19; Fees: B ▲
Contact: Marvin Heimbach, Program Director at (757) 899-4901; fax: (757) 899-6611
e-mail: mheimbac@vt.edu
Web site: www.ext.vt.edu/resources/4h/camping.htm
Operated by: State 4H Office Virginia Tech, 107 Hutcheson Hall (0419), Blacksburg, VA 24061 at (540) 231-9414

Group Rental Information

Site comments: Secluded in a natural wooded setting. Nestled beside beautiful Airfield Lake. Where adults experience the joys of nature.
Seasons & Capacity: Spring 250, Fall 250, Winter 250

Facilities: A/V Equipment, Cabins, Dorm-Style, Double Occupancy, Food Service, Hiking Trails, Lake, Linens, Lodges, Meeting Rooms, Playing Fields, Pool, Tents
Programs: Boating, Challenge/Ropes Course, Environmental Education, Swimming (#98)

Alkulana (est 1915)   ▲ ⌂ 🚗

Millboro Springs, VA (Rockbridge Co.)
Grace Kirkpatrick, Director

Camp comments: Camp for inner city children from Richmond Virginia.
Activities: Caving, Challenge/Rope Courses, Climbing/Rappelling
Session lengths & capacity: June-August; 2 week sessions; 50 campers
Clientele & fees: boys 9-15; girls 9-15; Fees: A ▲ 🐷
Contact: Grace Kirkpatrick, Director at (804) 329-1701;
e-mail: alkulana@juno.com
Operated by: Richmond Baptist Association, 3111 Moss Side Avenue, Richmond, VA 23222 at (804) 329-1701

Group Rental Information

Seasons & Capacity: Spring 50, Summer 22, Fall 50, Winter 22
Facilities: A/V Equipment, Cabins, Dorm-Style, Kitchen Facilities, Lodges, Meeting Rooms
Programs: Challenge/Ropes Course (#1751)

Baker (est 1957)   ☀ ▲ ⌂

Chesterfield, VA (Chesterfield Co.); (804) 748-4789
Melissa Walters, Director

Camp comments: Residential camp offering activities and supports to persons with disabilities 3:1 camper staff ratio.
Activities: Aerobics/Exercise, Arts/Crafts, Camping Skills/Outdoor Living, Canoeing, Horseback — Western, Music, Swimming — Recreational
Session lengths & capacity: June-August; 1 week sessions; 46 campers
Clientele & fees: coed 5-99; seniors; single adults; Fees: C ☀ Fees: D ▲ 🐷
Contact: Melissa Walters, Director of Camp Baker Services at (804) 748-4789; fax: (804) 796-6880
e-mail: camp.baker.arc@erols.com
Operated by: Richmond Assn Retarded Citizen, 1901 Westwood Ave, Richmond, VA 23227 at (804) 748-4789

Group Rental Information

Facilities: Cabins, Food Service, Meeting Rooms, Pool (#1749)

Bethel (est 1927)   ☀ ▲ ⌂

Fincastle, VA (Botetourt Co.); (540) 992-2940
Wayne Garst, Director

Camp comments: Christian camp, great staff, mountain setting aura is non-competitive encourages responsibility, coop group building.
Activities: Arts/Crafts, Backpacking, Camping Skills/Outdoor Living, Challenge/Rope Courses, Hiking, Leadership Development, Music, Nature/Environment Studies, Religious Study, Team Building
Session lengths & capacity: June-August; 1 week sessions; 150 campers
Clientele & fees: coed 5-18; families; Fees: A ☀ Fees: B ▲ 🐷
Contact: Glenn D. Stevens, Camp Manager at (540) 992-2940; fax: (540) 992-6498
e-mail: camp.bethel@juno.com
Web site: www.campbethelvirginia.org
Operated by: Church of the Brethren, 330 Hershberger Rd NW, Roanoke, VA 24012 at (540) 362-1816

Group Rental Information

Site comments: Comfortable modern facilities for year-round use, spacious conf. rooms, winterized lodges, food serv, challenge course, large sports complex, outdoor activities

Seasons & Capacity: Spring 187, Fall 187, Winter 187
Facilities: A/V Equipment, Cabins, Dorm-Style, Double Occupancy, Food Service, Hiking Trails, Kitchen Facilities, Linens, Lodges, Meeting Rooms, Playing Fields, Pool, Tents
Programs: Challenge/Ropes Course, Environmental Education, Swimming (#1764)

Brethren Woods Camp & Retreat (est 1958)

Keezletown, VA (Rockingham Co.); (540) 269-2741
Doug Phillips, Director

Camp comments: Mountain setting Christian emphasis. Traditional & adventure programs. Something for everyone.
Activities: Arts/Crafts, Backpacking, Camping Skills/Outdoor Living, Challenge/Rope Courses, Climbing/Rappelling, Hiking, Nature/Environment Studies, Religious Study, Swimming — Recreational
Session lengths & capacity: June-August; 1/2 & 1 week sessions; 100 campers
Clientele & fees: coed 6-17; families; seniors; Fees: B ☀ Fees: B ⚠
Contact: Doug Phillips or Andy Wells, Director/Program Director at (540) 269-2741; fax: (540) 269-2741
e-mail: dphillip@bridgewater.edu
Operated by: Brethren Woods, 4896 Armentrout Path, Keezletown, VA 28832 at (540) 269-2741

Group Rental Information
Facilities: Cabins, Double Occupancy, Food Service, Hiking Trails, Kitchen Facilities, Lake, Lodges, Meeting Rooms, Ocean, Playing Fields, Pool, Tents
Programs: Boating, Challenge/Ropes Course, Environmental Education, Swimming (#14556)

Browne Summer Day Camp

(est 1975)
Alexandria, VA (Fairfax Co.); (703) 960-3000
Raquel Boucher & Andrew Taylor, Director

Camp comments: Exciting day camp program. Wonderful 11 acre campus for campers. Specialty camps for CIT programs offered. Click on our website for more information.
Activities: Academics, Arts/Crafts, Camping Skills/Outdoor Living, Counselor Training (CIT), Field Trips, Leadership Development, Music, Nature/Environment Studies, Swimming — Instructional
Session lengths & capacity: June-August; 1 week sessions; 360 campers
Clientele & fees: boys 3-14; girls 3-14; coed 3-14; Fees: C ☀

ICON LEGEND

☀ Day Camp
⚠ Resident Camp
🏠 Facilities Available To Rent
🚐 Transportation Available
🐷 Financial Aid Available

FEE RANGES PER WEEK

A $0-75
B $75-200
C $201-350
D $351-500
E $501-650
F over $650

Contact: Main Office, Receptionist at (703) 960-3000; fax: (703) 960-7325
Web site: www.browneacademy.org
Operated by: Browne Academy, 5917 Telegraph Road, Alexandria, VA 22310 at (703) 960-3000 (#13616)

Burgundy Farm Summer Day Camp (est 1952)

Alexandria, VA (Fairfax Co.); (703) 329-9495
Travis Hudson, Director

Camp comments: Trad day camp on 22 acres w/pond & barnyard. 7-12 yr olds choose interest area. Science, visual arts, theater or sports.
Activities: Arts/Crafts, Ceramics/Pottery, Computer, Counselor Training (CIT), Drama, Drawing/Painting, Nature/Environment Studies, Sports — Field & Team, Swimming — Recreational
Session lengths & capacity: June-August; 2 & 3 week sessions; 300 campers
Clientele & fees: coed 3-14; Fees: B ☀
Contact: Lynne Farmer, Director at (703) 329-9495; fax: (703) 960-5056
e-mail: bfsdcamp@aol.com
Web site: camppage.com/bcws
Operated by: Burgundy Farm Country Day Sch, 3700 Burgundy Rd, Alexandria, VA 22303 at (703) 960-3431 (#2492)

Camp Chaverim

Newport News, VA; (757) 930-1422
Carmella Malkin-Kuhn, Director
Activities: Aquatic Activities, Arts/Crafts, Counselor Training (CIT), Dance, Drama, Religious Study, Sports — Field & Team, Swimming — Instructional, Swimming — Recreational, Tennis
Contact: Web site: www.ujcvp.org
Operated by: United Jewish Communities, 2700 Spring Rd, Newport News, VA 23606 at (757) 930-1422 (#7485)

Camp Dickenson

(est 1970)
Fries, VA (Grayson Co.); (276) 744-7241
John W Ousley, Director
Activities: Backpacking, Bicycling/Biking, Boating, Camping Skills/Outdoor Living, Fishing, Horseback — Western, Kayaking, Music, Religious Study, Team Building
Session lengths & capacity: 1/2 & 1 week sessions; 170 campers
Clientele & fees: coed 5-18; families; seniors; single adults; Fees: B ☀ Fees: B, C ⚠
Contact: John W Ousley, Director at (540) 744-7241; fax: (540) 744-7241
e-mail: ousley@tcia.net
Operated by: Holston Conference Camping, PO Box 1178, Johnson City, TN 37605-1178 at (423) 928-2156

Group Rental Information
Seasons & Capacity: Spring 148, Summer 168, Fall 148, Winter 148
Facilities: Cabins, Dorm-Style, Food Service, Hiking Trails, Kitchen Facilities, Meeting Rooms, Pool, River
Programs: Swimming (#31633)

Camp Dogwood Summer Academy (est 1996)

Wolftown, VA (Madison Co.); (540) 948-5703
Beatrice W Welters, Director

Camp comments: Exposure to positive influences make a positive impact on a child's future development & stimulate thirst for learning.
Activities: Academics, Arts/Crafts, Counselor Training (CIT), Farming/Ranching/Gardening, Field Trips, Hiking, Nature/Environment Studies, Swimming — Recreational, Tennis
Session lengths & capacity: June-July; 2 week sessions; 20 campers

Clientele & fees: coed 6-10; Fees: A ⚠ 🐷
Contact: Beatrice W Welters, Founder at (703) 506-3507; fax: (703) 506-3556
e-mail: dogwood@erols.com
Operated by: Camp Dogwood Summer Academy, PO Box 1819, Vienna, VA 22182 (#4363)

Camp Easter Seal East

(est 1984)
Milford, VA (Caroline Co.); (804) 633-9855
Devin Brown, Director

Camp comments: For children and adults with disabilities. Modern facility, friendly staff. Staff to camper ratio 1:2 Come join the fun.
Activities: Arts/Crafts, Camping Skills/Outdoor Living, Canoeing, Climbing/Rappelling, Computer, Hiking, Horseback — Western, Music, Swimming — Recreational
Session lengths & capacity: June-August; 1 & 2 week sessions; 45 campers
Clientele & fees: coed 5-99; Fees: F ⚠ 🐷
Contact: Devin Brown, Camp Director at (804) 633-9855; fax: (804) 633-6203
e-mail: dbrown@va.easter-seals.org
Web site: www.vaseals.org
Operated by: Easter Seals-Virginia, 201 E Main St, Salem, VA 24153 at (540) 777-7325

Group Rental Information
Site comments: Modern facility, great food. Contact us for more rental information.
Seasons & Capacity: Spring 100, Fall 100, Winter 100
Facilities: Dorm-Style, Food Service, Linens, Lodges, Meeting Rooms, Playing Fields, Pool (#5463)

Camp Easter Seal West

(est 1957)
New Castle, VA (Craig Co.); (540) 864-5750
Deborah Duerk, Director

Camp comments: Located in Blue Ridge Mtns. Non-competitive, traditional program for children and adults with disabilities. Speech and occupational therapy sessions offered.
Activities: Arts/Crafts, Camping Skills/Outdoor Living, Canoeing, Drama, Hiking, Horseback — English, Music, Nature/Environment Studies, Swimming — Recreational, Team Building
Session lengths & capacity: June-August; 1, 2 & 4 week sessions; 75 campers
Clientele & fees: coed 5-99; families; Fees: F ⚠ 🐷
Contact: Deborah Duerk, Camp Director at (540) 864-5750; fax: (540) 864-6797
e-mail: dduerk@va.easter-seals.com
Web site: www.vaseals.org
Operated by: Easter Seals-Virginia, 201 E Main St, Salem, VA 24153 at (540) 777-7325

Group Rental Information
Seasons & Capacity: Spring 120, Fall 120, Winter 40
Facilities: Cabins, Dorm-Style, Double Occupancy, Food Service, Hiking Trails, Kitchen Facilities, Linens, Meeting Rooms, Playing Fields, River
Programs: Environmental Education (#1767)

Camp Friendship (est 1966)

Palmyra, VA (Fluvanna Co.); (800) 873-3223
Diane Tyrrell CCD and Ray Ackenbom CCD, Director

Camp comments: General program, over 30 elective activities. Also, challenge adventure trips, equestrian, golf, tennis, gymnastics programs.
Activities: Archery, Bicycling/Biking, Canoeing, Ceramics/Pottery, Golf, Gymnastics, Horseback — English, Swimming — Recreational, Tennis, Wilderness Trips
Session lengths & capacity: June-August; 1, 2, 3, 4, 5, 6, 7, 8 & 9 week sessions; 400 campers

Clientele & fees: coed 6-16; families;
Fees: **F ⚠ 🚌**
Contact: Diane Tyrrell,CCD or Ray Ackenbom,
CCD at (800) 873-3223; fax: (804) 589-5880
e-mail: info@campfriendship.com
Operated by: Camp Friendship, PO Box 145,
Palmyra, VA 22963 at (800) 873-3223
Group Rental Information
Site comments: Recreation, ropes & iitiatives,
environmental education programming. Lodges,
meeting rooms, pool, lake and river.
Seasons & Capacity: Spring 400, Fall 400,
Winter 100
Facilities: Cabins, Food Service, Hiking Trails,
Kitchen Facilities, Lake, Linens, Lodges, Meeting
Rooms, Playing Fields, Pool, River
Programs: Boating, Challenge/Ropes Course,
Environmental Education, Horseback Riding,
Swimming (#1741)

Camp Hanover (est 1957)   ☼ ⚠ ⌂
Mechanicsville, VA (Hanover Co.); (804) 779-2811
Bob Pryor, Director

Camp comments: Building Christ-centered
community through challenging small group rustic
living. Traditional; high adventure; Service.
Activities: Backpacking, Camping Skills/Outdoor
Living, Canoeing, Challenge/Rope Courses,
Climbing/Rappelling, Community Service,
Nature/Environment Studies, Religious Study, Team
Building, Wilderness Trips
Session lengths & capacity: June-August; 1/2, 1,
2 & 4 week sessions; 164 campers
Clientele & fees: coed 7-17; Fees: **A ☼**
Fees: **C, D ⚠ 🚌**
Contact: Kay Shelton, Registrar at (877) 687-2267;
fax: (804) 779-3056
e-mail: chanover@erols.com
Operated by: Presbytery of the James, 1251
Presbytery Court, Glen Allen, VA 23060 at
(804) 262-2074
Group Rental Information
Site comments: "The rustic atmosphere of
Hanover helps people to come back to the
basics:Life, Nature, God". Join us for a time apart, a
time to grow. 30 min. from Richmond, VA
Seasons & Capacity: Spring 135, Fall 135,
Winter 135
Facilities: A/V Equipment, Cabins, Dorm-Style,
Double Occupancy, Food Service, Hiking Trails,
Kitchen Facilities, Lake, Linens, Lodges, Meeting
Rooms, Playing Fields, Pool, River
Programs: Boating, Challenge/Ropes Course,
Environmental Education, Swimming (#1754)

Camp Happyland (est 1946)   ⚠
Richardsville, VA (Culpeper Co.); (540) 399-1031
Captin Kelly Igleheart, Director

Camp comments: Christian camp serving youth
and adults. Near Fredericksburg. Swimming,
boating, ropes, music, Bible classes.
Activities: Archery, Boating, Challenge/Rope
Courses, Hiking, Music, Nature/Environment
Studies, Religious Study, Sports — Field & Team,
Swimming — Instructional, Swimming —
Recreational
Session lengths & capacity: June-August; 1/2, 1 &
4 week sessions; 192 campers
Clientele & fees: coed 6-17; Fees: **B ⚠**
Contact: Captain Kelly Igleheart, Camp Director at
(202) 756-2600; fax: (202) 756-2665
Web site: www.salvationarmydcmetro.org
Operated by: The Salvation Army, 2626
Pennsylvania Ave NW, Washington, DC 20036 at
(202) 756-2600 (#2466)

Camp Holiday Trails (est 1972)   ⚠ ⌂
Charlottesville, VA (Albemarle Co.); (804) 977-3781

Camp comments: Residential camp for children
with chronic health problems.

Activities: Canoeing, Challenge/Rope Courses,
Climbing/Rappelling, Drama, Field Trips,
Horseback — English, Nature/Environment Studies,
Sports — Field & Team, Swimming — Recreational,
Team Building
Session lengths & capacity: June-August; 2 week
sessions; 70 campers
Clientele & fees: coed 7-17; Fees: **D ⚠ 🚌**
Contact: Mark Andersen, Executive Director at
(804) 977-3781; fax: (804) 977-8814
e-mail: cht@firstva.com
Operated by: Camp Holiday Trails, PO Box 5806,
Charlottesville, VA 22905 at (434) 977-3781
Group Rental Information
Facilities: Cabins, Dorm-Style, Kitchen Facilities,
Lake, Lodges, Meeting Rooms, Pool (#1771)

Camp Horizons (est 1982)   ⚠ ⌂ 🚗
Harrisonburg, VA (Rockingham Co.);
(540) 896-7600
Ben and Jean Swartz, Director

Camp comments: International camp for 7-15 yr
olds and exciting teen adventures! 2 hrs. from
Washington DC in the Shenandoah Valley!
Activities: Archery, Canoeing, Challenge/Rope
Courses, Climbing/Rappelling, Horseback —
Western, Nature/Environment Studies, Rafting,
Soccer, Swimming — Recreational, Wilderness
Trips
Session lengths & capacity: June-August; 2, 4 &
6 week sessions; 250 campers
Clientele & fees: coed 7-16; Fees: **D, E ⚠**
Contact: Ben and Jean Swartz, Director at
(800) 729-9230; fax: (540) 896-5455
e-mail: camp@horizonsva.com
Web site: www.camphorizonsva.com
Operated by: Camp Horizons LC, 3586 Horizons
Way, Harrisonburg, VA 22802 at (540) 896-7600
Group Rental Information
Facilities: A/V Equipment, Cabins, Dorm-Style,
Double Occupancy, Food Service, Hiking Trails,
Lake, Meeting Rooms, Playing Fields, Pool, Tents
Programs: Challenge/Ropes Course,
Environmental Education, Horseback Riding,
Swimming (#12436)

Camp Kum-Ba-Yah (est 1950)   ☼ 🚗
Lynchburg, VA (Lynchburg Co.); (804) 384-1755
Jean F Clements, Director

Camp comments: Outdoor nature and adventure
program children and counselors of all
backgrounds learning and growing together
Activities: Arts/Crafts, Camping Skills/Outdoor
Living, Ceramics/Pottery, Challenge/Rope Courses,
Counselor Training (CIT), Leadership Development,
Nature/Environment Studies, Swimming —
Instructional, Team Building
Session lengths & capacity: 1, 2 & 7 week
sessions; 100 campers
Clientele & fees: coed 5-15; Fees: **B ☼ 🚌**
Contact: Joan Lucy, Director at (804) 384-1755;
fax: (804) 384-1755
Operated by: Camp Kum-Ba-Yah Board, 4415
Boonsboro Rd, Lynchburg, VA 24503 at
(804) 384-1755 (#1748)

Camp McLean (est 1980)   ☼
Mclean, VA (Fairfax Co.); (703) 790-0123
Martha Coester, Director

Camp comments: Traditional day camp,
experienced staff involve campers in many
recreational activities in fun & supervised
environment.
Activities: Arts/Crafts, Dance, Drama, Field Trips,
Music, Sports — Field & Team, Swimming —
Recreational
Session lengths & capacity: June-August; 2 week
sessions; 155 campers
Clientele & fees: coed 3-12; Fees: **B ☼**
Contact: Martha Coester, Youth Director at
(703) 790-0123; fax: (703) 556-0547

e-mail: marther.coester@co.fairfax.va.us
Web site: www.mcleancenter.org
Operated by: Mc Lean Community Center, 1234
Ingleside Ave, Mc Lean, VA 22101 at
(703) 790-0123 (#13262)

Camp Mont Shenandoah   ⚠ ⌂ 🚗
(est 1927)
Millboro Springs, VA (Bath Co.); (540) 997-5994
Jay Batley & Ann Batley, Director

Camp comments: Traditional girls camp w/ a wide
variety of activities, incl. a strong equest. program.
Exceptional rate of return. Loc. in VA mtns. 75 yrs of
excellent camping
Activities: Archery, Arts/Crafts, Camping
Skills/Outdoor Living, Canoeing, Drama, Hiking,
Horseback — English, Sports — Field & Team,
Swimming — Instructional, Tennis
Session lengths & capacity: June-August; 1, 3 &
6 week sessions; 120 campers
Clientele & fees: girls 7-15; Fees: **E ⚠**
Contact: Jay & Ann Batley, Directors at
(540) 997-5994; fax: (540) 997-0678
e-mail: cms1927@aol.com
Operated by: Camp Mont Shenandoah, HCR 04
Box 19, Millboro Springs, VA 24460 at
(540) 997-5994
Group Rental Information
Seasons & Capacity: Spring 150
Facilities: Cabins, Dorm-Style, Double Occupancy,
Food Service, Hiking Trails, Lodges, Meeting
Rooms, Playing Fields, River
Programs: Boating, Swimming (#1745)

Camp Skimino (est 1955)   ☼ ⚠ ⌂
Williamsburg, VA (York & James Cy Co.);
(804) 565-2303
Liz Hobson, Director

Camp comments: Traditional girl scout camp
prgrm. Girls can select individual interest programs.
Tents, modern bathrooms, pool, good food!
Activities: Aquatic Activities, Arts/Crafts, Camping
Skills/Outdoor Living, Canoeing, Challenge/Rope
Courses, Drama, Kayaking, Sports — Field & Team,
Swimming — Instructional
Session lengths & capacity: June-August; 1/2, 1 &
2 week sessions; 130 campers
Clientele & fees: girls 6-17; families; Fees: **B ☼**
Fees: **C ⚠ 🚌**
Contact: Liz Hobson, Director at (757) 547-4405
ext. 227; fax: (757) 547-1872
e-mail: lizh@gsccc.com
Web site: www.gsccc.com
Operated by: GSC of Colonial Coast, 912 Cedar
Road, Chesapeake, VA 23322-7002 at
(757) 547-4405 (#1777)

Camp Virginia Incorporated   ⚠
(est 1928)
Goshen, VA; (540) 997-5977
Malcolm Pitt, Director
Activities: Archery, Arts/Crafts, Basketball, Hiking,
Horseback — English, Nature/Environment Studies,
Riflery, Soccer, Swimming — Instructional, Tennis
Clientele & fees: Fees: **D ⚠**
Contact: Mac Pitt, Director at (804) 282-2339;
e-mail: pittmill@aol.com
Operated by: Camp Virginia Inc, 8122 Greystone
Circle East, Richmond, VA 23229 at (804) 282-2339
(#14608)

Camp Virginia Jaycee   ☼ ⚠ ⌂
(est 1971)
Blue Ridge, VA (Bedford Co.); (540) 947-2972
Everett M Werness, Director

Camp comments: Serves campers with mental
retardation. Caring staff. Other program: fishing,
boating, sports. Fall and spring respites.

Activities: Arts/Crafts, Drawing/Painting, Fishing, Horseback — English, Horseback — Western, Music, Swimming — Recreational
Session lengths & capacity: June-August; 1, 8 & 9 week sessions; 100 campers
Clientele & fees: coed 7-70; seniors; Fees: D ▲ ⚫
Contact: Everett Werness, President at (540) 947-2972; fax: (540) 947-2043
e-mail: campvajc@roanoke.infi.net
Web site: www.campvirginiajaycee.com
Operated by: Camp Virginia Jaycee Inc, 2494 Camp Jaycee Rd, Blue Ridge, VA 24064 at (540) 947-2972

Group Rental Information
Facilities: Cabins, Dorm-Style, Double Occupancy, Food Service, Kitchen Facilities, Meeting Rooms, Pool, Tents
Programs: Swimming (#3698)

Carysbrook (est 1923)   ▲ 🚐

Riner, VA (Montgomery Co.); (540) 382-1670
Toni M Baughman,CCD, Director

Camp comments: Experience a summer to remember at Virginia's oldest camp for girls. Traditional program, instruction in 18 activities.
Activities: Archery, Arts/Crafts, Camping Skills/Outdoor Living, Climbing/Rappelling, Dance, Drama, Fencing, Horseback — English, Nature/Environment Studies, Tennis
Session lengths & capacity: June-August; 1, 2, 4, 6 & 8 week sessions; 100 campers
Clientele & fees: girls 6-16; Fees: B ☀ Fees: D ▲
Contact: Toni M Baughman, CCD, Owner/Director at (703) 836-7548; fax: (703) 751-2974
e-mail: Tmoose@aol.com
Web site: www.campcarysbrook.com
Operated by: Carysbrook, 4421 Seminary Rd, Alexandria, VA 22304 at (703) 836-7548 (#8326)

Chanco on the James (est 1968) ▲ 🏠

Surry, VA (Surry Co.); (757) 294-0915
Rev William B Taylor Jr, Director

Camp comments: Traditional program plus exciting trips. Emphasis on values and living in a Christian community. Self-esteem specialty.
Activities: Aquatic Activities, Archery, Arts/Crafts, Canoeing, Challenge/Rope Courses, Climbing/Rappelling, Nature/Environment Studies, Sailing, Swimming — Recreational, Team Building
Session lengths & capacity: June-August; 1 & 2 week sessions; 120 campers
Clientele & fees: coed 9-18; Fees: C, D ▲
Contact: Louise Yasaitis, Registrar at (757) 423-8287; fax: (757) 440-5354
e-mail: chancol@aol.com
Web site: www.chanco.org

ICON LEGEND

☀ Day Camp

▲ Resident Camp

🏠 Facilities Available To Rent

🚐 Transportation Available

🐷 Financial Aid Available

FEE RANGES PER WEEK

A	$0-75
B	$75-200
C	$201-350
D	$351-500
E	$501-650
F	over $650

Operated by: Chanco on the James, PO Box 378, Surry, VA 23883 at (757) 423-8287

Group Rental Information
Seasons & Capacity: Spring 272, Summer 272, Fall 272, Winter 80
Facilities: Cabins, Double Occupancy, Food Service, Meeting Rooms, Pool, River
Programs: Boating (#1762)

Cheerio Adventures

(est 1982)   ▲ 🏠 🚐

Mouth of Wilson, VA (Grayson Co.); (540) 579-6731
Keith Russell, Director

Camp comments: Our mission is to provide participants a quality adventure experience in a Christian atmosphere. Trips in mountains of SW Virginia, NW North Carolina & beyond.
Activities: Backpacking, Bicycling/Biking, Canoeing, Caving, Climbing/Rappelling, Hiking, Kayaking, Rafting, Sailing, Wilderness Trips
Session lengths & capacity: June-August; 1 & 2 week sessions; 60 campers
Clientele & fees: coed 10-16; Fees: F ▲
Contact: Keith Russell, Director at (336) 363-2604; fax: (336) 363-3671
e-mail: krussell@campcheerio.org
Web site: www.cheerioadventures.com
Operated by: YMCA of Greater High Point, PO Box 6258, High Point, NC 27262-6258 at (336) 869-0151

Group Rental Information
Seasons & Capacity: Spring 60, Summer 60, Fall 60
Facilities: Hiking Trails, Playing Fields, River, Tents
Programs: Boating, Environmental Education (#32943)

Civitan Acres for the Disabled

(est 1960)   ▲ 🚐

Chesapeake, VA; (757) 487-6062
Marie Dugan, Director

Camp comments: Day & residential camp for persons with various disabilities, ages 5 & up.
Activities: Arts/Crafts, Field Trips, Swimming — Recreational
Session lengths & capacity: June-August; 1 week sessions; 50 campers
Clientele & fees: coed 5-99; Fees: B ☀ Fees: C ▲
Contact: Marie Dugan, General Manager at (757) 487-6062; fax: (757) 487-4143
e-mail: maried@egglestonservices.org
Web site: www.egglestonservices.org
Operated by: Eggleston Services, 2210 Cedar Road, Chesapeake, VA 23323 at (757) 487-6062 (#5557)

Congressional Day Camp

(est 1940)   ☀ 🚐

Falls Church, VA (Falls Church Co.); (703) 533-9711
Greg Cronin, Director

Camp comments: 40 Acres of fun. This beautiful setting is ideal for camp. Special events, overnights, travel programs, lunch, and transportation provided. Specialty Camps
Activities: Archery, Arts/Crafts, Basketball, Challenge/Rope Courses, Counselor Training (CIT), Drama, Horseback — English, Leadership Development, Swimming — Instructional, Travel/Tour
Session lengths & capacity: June-August; 1 & 2 week sessions; 400 campers
Clientele & fees: coed 6-14; Fees: C ☀
Contact: Greg Cronin CCD, Camp Director at (703) 533-9711; fax: (703) 533-8231
e-mail: campdir@congressionalschools.org
Web site: www.congocamp.org
Operated by: Congressional Schools of VA, 3229 Sleepy Hollow Rd, Falls Church, VA 22042 at (703) 533-9711 (#3021)

Eagle Eyrie Baptist Conference

(est 1956)   🏠

Lynchburg, VA (Lynchburg Co.); (434) 384-2211
Contact: W Wesley Huff, Director at (434) 384-2211; fax: (434) 384-1891
e-mail: eagleyrie1@aol.com
Web site: www.vbnb.org
Operated by: Eagle Eyrie Baptist Conference, Virginia Baptist Mission Board, 1 Eagle Eyrie Drive, Lynchburg, VA 24503 at (434) 384-2211

Group Rental Information
Seasons & Capacity: Spring 1000, Summer 1000, Fall 1000, Winter 1000
Facilities: A/V Equipment, Cabins, Dorm-Style, Double Occupancy, Food Service, Hiking Trails, Kitchen Facilities, Linens, Lodges, Meeting Rooms, Playing Fields, Pool
Programs: Swimming (#220)

FONZ Nature Camp (est 1995)   ▲

Front Royal, VA (Warren Co.); (540) 635-6540
Elena Lomicky, Director

Camp comments: Discover wildlife nature & outdoor science at the national zoo's private 3100 acre property; includes fun camping trip.
Activities: Arts/Crafts, Camping Skills/Outdoor Living, Drawing/Painting, Field Trips, Hiking, Nature/Environment Studies, Swimming — Recreational, Team Building
Session lengths & capacity: July-August; 1 & 2 week sessions; 60 campers
Clientele & fees: coed 9-12; Fees: E ▲ 🐷
Contact: Elena Lomicky, Program Coordinator at (202) 673-4637; fax: (202) 673-4738
e-mail: efaber@nzp.si.org
Operated by: Friends of the National Zoo, National Zoological Park, 3001 Connecticut Ave, Washington, DC 20008 at (202) 673-4637 (#3537)

Global Youth Village (est 1979)   ▲

Bedford, VA (Bedford Co.); (540) 297-5982
Mary Helmig, Director

Camp comments: 3 week workshops, youth from 20 countries. Leadership, dialogue, environment, global issues, arts, esl.
Activities: Arts/Crafts, Community Service, Field Trips, International Culture, Language Studies, Leadership Development, Nature/Environment Studies, Performing Arts, Soccer
Session lengths & capacity: July-August; 3 week sessions; 60 campers
Clientele & fees: coed 13-18; Fees: E ▲
Contact: Mary Helmig, Director at (540) 297-5982; fax: (540) 297-1860
e-mail: inquiries@globalyouthvillage.org
Web site: www.globalyouthvillage.org
Operated by: Legacy International, 1020 Legacy Dr, Bedford, VA 24523 at (540) 297-5982 (#12576)

Hemlock Overlook   ☀ ▲ 🏠

Clifton, VA (Fairfax Co.); (703) 993-4354
Martha Slover, Director

Camp comments: The mission of Hemlock Overlook Center for Outdoor Education is to facilitate, educate and involve indiv and orgs in experiential, outdoor and envir education.
Activities: Camping Skills/Outdoor Living, Canoeing, Challenge/Rope Courses, Climbing/Rappelling, Community Service, Counselor Training (CIT), Leadership Development, Nature/Environment Studies, Team Building, Wilderness Trips
Session lengths & capacity: June-August; 1 & 2 week sessions; 150 campers
Clientele & fees: coed 7-17; families; Fees: C ☀ Fees: D ▲
Contact: Camp Registrar at (703) 993-4354; fax: (703) 266-7781
e-mail: hmovcamp@gmu.edu
Web site: hemlock.gmu.edu

Operated by: George Mason University, Hemlock Overlook MS 5B9, 4400 University Dr, Fairfax, VA 22030-4444 at (703) 993-4354

Group Rental Information
Seasons & Capacity: Spring 96, Summer 96, Fall 96, Winter 96
Facilities: Cabins, Dorm-Style, Food Service, Hiking Trails, River
Programs: Boating, Challenge/Ropes Course, Environmental Education (#41593)

Highroad Program Center

(est 1949)   ▲ 🏠

Middleburg, VA; (540) 687-6262
Jim Rowe, Director

Camp comments: Small group camping with Christian emphasis, 657 acres with outstanding view of Blue Ridge Mountains.
Activities: Arts/Crafts, Camping Skills/Outdoor Living, Canoeing, Challenge/Rope Courses, Hiking, Horseback — Western, Nature/Environment Studies, Swimming — Recreational
Session lengths & capacity: 1/2, 1 & 2 week sessions; 110 campers
Clientele & fees: coed 8-18; families; Fees: C ▲
Contact: (540) 687-6262; fax: (540) 687-6959
Web site: www.camphighroad.org
Operated by: United Methodist Church, 21164 Steptoe Hill Rd, Middleburg, VA 22117-3136 at (540) 687-6262

Group Rental Information
Facilities: Cabins, Food Service, Hiking Trails, Lodges, Pool, Tents
Programs: Environmental Education (#2476)

Holiday Lake 4H Educ Center

(est 1941)   ▲ 🏠

Appomattox, VA (Appomattox Co.); (804) 248-5444
Richard Pulliam, CCD, Director

Camp comments: Special 1 week shooting sport camp. Rental available to outside groups. Year round.
Activities: Aquatic Activities, Archery, Camping Skills/Outdoor Living, Challenge/Rope Courses, Fishing, Hiking, Nature/Environment Studies, Performing Arts, Riflery, Team Building
Session lengths & capacity: 1 week sessions; 260 campers
Clientele & fees: coed 9-19; families; Fees: B ▲
Contact: Richard Pulliam, Center Director at (804) 248-5444; fax: (804) 248-6749
e-mail: rpulliam@vt.edu
Web site: www.ext.vt.edu/resources/4h/camping.htm
Operated by: State 4H Office Virginia Tech, 107 Hutcheson Hall (0419), Blacksburg, VA 24061 at (540) 231-9414

Group Rental Information
Seasons & Capacity: Spring 125, Summer 272, Fall 125, Winter 125
Facilities: A/V Equipment, Cabins, Dorm-Style, Food Service, Hiking Trails, Lake, Meeting Rooms, Pool (#3814)

Jamestown 4H Center

(est 1928)   ▲ 🏠

Williamsburg, VA (James City Co.); (757) 253-4931
Terry Patterson, Director

Camp comments: In historic Williamsburg area youth have a traditional camp experience, explore nature with wilderness trips for teens.
Activities: Aquatic Activities, Archery, Arts/Crafts, Camping Skills/Outdoor Living, Canoeing, Challenge/Rope Courses, Kayaking, Nature/Environment Studies, Performing Arts, Wilderness Trips
Session lengths & capacity: June-August; 1 week sessions; 212 campers
Clientele & fees: coed 5-19; seniors; Fees: B ▲

Contact: Cindi Eicher, Program Director at (757) 253-4931; fax: (757) 253-7231
Web site: www.ext.vt.edu/resources/4h/camping.htm
Operated by: State 4H Office Virginia Tech, 107 Hutcheson Hall (0419), Blacksburg, VA 24061 at (540) 231-9414

Group Rental Information
Facilities: Dorm-Style, Double Occupancy, Food Service, Meeting Rooms, Pool, River
Programs: Environmental Education (#3777)

Kittamaqund (est 1968)   ▲ 🏠

Burgess, VA (Northumberland Co.); (804) 580-8112

Camp comments: Building skills for the future in a secure outdoor setting, surrounded by adults who care about girls' successes.
Activities: Aquatic Activities, Arts/Crafts, Backpacking, Camping Skills/Outdoor Living, Canoeing, Drama, Nature/Environment Studies, Sailing, Swimming — Instructional
Session lengths & capacity: June-August; 1/2, 1 & 2 week sessions; 128 campers
Clientele & fees: girls 6-17; Fees: B ▲ 🐷
Contact: Outdoor Program Specialist at (800) 472-6884; fax: (804) 746-3127
Web site: www.comgirlscouts.org
Operated by: Commonwealth GSC, PO Box 548, Mechanicsville, VA 23111 at (800) 472-6884 (#7220)

Ma Wa Va Camp Cherith

(est 1959)   ▲

Madison, VA (Culpeper Co.); (540) 923-4300
Diane Ogden, Director

Activities: Archery, Clowning, Counselor Training (CIT), Hiking, Horseback — English, Leadership Development, Nature/Environment Studies, Riflery, Sports — Field & Team, Swimming — Recreational
Session lengths & capacity: July-August; 1 week sessions; 90 campers
Clientele & fees: coed 7-17; Fees: C ▲
Contact: Melissa Liberatore, Vice President at (343) 985-7628;
e-mail: mawavacc@baxnets.com
Operated by: Ma Wa Va Camp Cherith, 605 S Gerald Dr, Newark, DE 19713 at (302) 731-5754 (#3428)

Makemie Woods (est 1964)   ▲ 🏠

Barhamsville, VA (New Kent Co.); (800) 566-1496
Rev Michelle 'Mike' Burcher, Director

Camp comments: Have fun, make friends, build self esteem in a caring noncompetitive Christian setting. Beginners programs, adventure. Drama, drums.
Activities: Arts/Crafts, Canoeing, Community Service, Drama, Hiking, Nature/Environment Studies, Religious Study, Sailing, Swimming — Recreational
Session lengths & capacity: June-August; 1/2, 1 & 2 week sessions; 85 campers
Clientele & fees: coed 6-18; Fees: B, C ▲ 🐷
Contact: Rev Michelle 'Mike' Burcher, Director at (800) 566-1496; fax: (757) 566-8803
e-mail: burcherm@makwoods.org
Web site: www.pcusa-peva.org
Operated by: Presbytery of Eastern Virginia, PO Box 39, Barhamsville, VA 23011 at (800) 989-2193

Group Rental Information
Site comments: Attractive retreat facilities near Williamsburg. Discounts for large groups, youth, seniors, mid-week use.
Seasons & Capacity: Spring 120, Fall 120, Winter 120

Facilities: A/V Equipment, Cabins, Dorm-Style, Double Occupancy, Food Service, Hiking Trails, Kitchen Facilities, Lake, Meeting Rooms, Playing Fields
Programs: Boating, Environmental Education (#3530)

Northern Virginia 4H Ed Center

(est 1980)   ▲ 🏠

Front Royal, VA (Warren Co.); (540) 635-7171
Lance E Johnson, Director

Camp comments: Residential camp in mountain setting. Traditional programs plus exciting outdoor adventures and ropes challenge course.
Activities: Aquatic Activities, Archery, Backpacking, Camping Skills/Outdoor Living, Canoeing, Caving, Challenge/Rope Courses, Horseback — English, Riflery, Wilderness Trips
Session lengths & capacity: May-August; 1 week sessions; 300 campers
Clientele & fees: coed 5-19; Fees: B ▲
Contact: Lance E Johnson, Program Director at (540) 635-7171; fax: (540) 635-6876
e-mail: lajohns4@vt.edu
Web site: www.ext.vt.edu/resources/4h/camping.htm
Operated by: State 4H Office Virginia Tech, 107 Hutcheson Hall (0419), Blacksburg, VA 24061 at (540) 231-9414

Group Rental Information
Seasons & Capacity: Spring 300, Summer 300, Fall 300, Winter 300
Facilities: A/V Equipment, Double Occupancy, Food Service, Hiking Trails, Linens, Lodges, Meeting Rooms, Playing Fields, Pool
Programs: Challenge/Ropes Course, Environmental Education, Swimming (#2423)

Rising Star Sports & Adventure

(est 1998)   ☀

Roanoke, VA; (540) 774-7725
Chris Pollock, Director

Camp comments: To offer the finest year round sports camp experience for children and adults.
Activities: Baseball/Softball, Basketball, Hiking, Hockey, Snow Sports, Soccer, Sports — Field & Team, Team Building
Clientele & fees: coed 3-99; Fees: B ☀
Contact: Chris Pollock, Camp Director/Owner at (540) 774-7725; fax: (540) 774-6612
e-mail: risingstarsports@netzero.net
Operated by: Rising Star Sports & Adventure, 5488 Yellow Mountain Rd, Roanoke, VA 24015 at (540) 774-7725 (#41134)

Smith Mountain Lake 4H Educ

(est 1966)   ▲ 🏠

Wirtz, VA (Franklin Co.); (540) 721-2759
Becky Gilles, Director

Camp comments: The 4H center offers a wide variety of educational and recreational programs, emphasizing technology and adventure ed.
Activities: Archery, Canoeing, Challenge/Rope Courses, Climbing/Rappelling, Computer, Leadership Development, Nature/Environment Studies, Performing Arts, Riflery
Session lengths & capacity: 1 week sessions; 296 campers
Clientele & fees: coed 9-19; Fees: B ▲
Contact: Becky Gilles, Program Director at (540) 721-2759; fax: (540) 721-2766
e-mail: bgilles@vt.edu
Web site: www.ext.vt.edu/resources/4h/camping.htm
Operated by: State 4H Office Virginia Tech, 107 Hutcheson Hall (0419), Blacksburg, VA 24061 at (540) 231-9414

Group Rental Information

Facilities: A/V Equipment, Food Service, Hiking Trails, Lake, Linens, Lodges, Meeting Rooms, Playing Fields, Pool
Programs: Boating, Challenge/Ropes Course, Environmental Education, Swimming (#4366)

Southwest VA 4H Ed Center Inc

(est 1958)   ⚠ 🏠

Abingdon, VA (Washington Co.); (540) 676-6180
Sandra Fisher, Director

Camp comments: Contact your local cooperative extension office for a 4-H center near you!
Activities: Baseball/Softball, Basketball, Challenge/Rope Courses, Climbing/Rappelling, Horseback — Western, Leadership Development, Nature/Environment Studies, Riflery, Swimming — Recreational, Team Building
Session lengths & capacity: June-August; 1 week sessions; 230 campers
Clientele & fees: coed 9-13; Fees: B ⚠ �"
Contact: Sandra Fisher, Center Director at (540) 676-6180; fax: (540) 676-6188
e-mail: safishe3@vt.edu
Web site:
www.ext.vt.edu/resources/4h/camping.htm
Operated by: State 4H Office Virginia Tech, 107 Hutcheson Hall (0419), Blacksburg, VA 24061 at (540) 231-9414

Group Rental Information

Site comments: Come to the center of it all! Year-round converence and rental facilities located in historic Abingdon, Virginia.
Facilities: A/V Equipment, Double Occupancy, Food Service, Kitchen Facilities, Meeting Rooms, Pool
Programs: Challenge/Ropes Course, Environmental Education (#821)

Virginia Elks Youth Camp Inc

(est 1949)   ⚠ 🏠

Millboro, VA (Bath Co.); (540) 862-9489
George M Wood, Director

Camp comments: Resident camp in the Alleghany Mts. of western VA. Deserving youth sponsored by Elks lodges.
Activities: Archery, Arts/Crafts, Basketball, Hiking, Nature/Environment Studies, Riflery, Team Building
Session lengths & capacity: June-August; 1 week sessions; 104 campers
Clientele & fees: boys 9-13; girls 8-13; �",
Contact: George M Wood, Camp Director at (540) 862-7981;
e-mail: vaelkscamp@aol.com
Operated by: VA Elks Youth Camp Inc, HCR 04 Box 69, Millboro, VA 24460 at (540) 862-7981

ICON LEGEND

☀	Day Camp
⚠	Resident Camp
🏠	Facilities Available To Rent
�",	Transportation Available
🐷	Financial Aid Available

FEE RANGES PER WEEK

A	$0-75
B	$75-200
C	$201-350
D	$351-500
E	$501-650
F	over $650

Group Rental Information

Facilities: Cabins, Food Service, Linens, Lodges, Playing Fields, River
Programs: Challenge/Ropes Course, Environmental Education, Swimming (#2187)

Westview On The James Camp/Ret (est 1966)   ⚠ 🏠

Goochland, VA (Goochland Co.); (804) 457-4210
John Edwards, Director

Camp comments: Fun & friendships in atmosphere of Christian love. Campers bunk in cabins with caring counselors. Choice of activities.
Activities: Archery, Bicycling/Biking, Canoeing, Climbing/Rappelling, Kayaking, Model Rocketry, Nature/Environment Studies, Photography, Religious Study, Wilderness Trips
Session lengths & capacity: June-August; 1/2 & 1 week sessions; 110 campers
Clientele & fees: coed 7-16; families; seniors; Fees: C ⚠
Contact: Sharon Edwards, Business Manager at (804) 457-4210; fax: (804) 457-2178
e-mail: westvu@juno.com
Operated by: United Methodist Church, 1231 West View Rd, Goochland, VA 23063 at (804) 457-4210

Group Rental Information

Site comments: Westview is dedicated to providing a quality environment of Christian hospitality and learning.
Facilities: Cabins, Dorm-Style, Food Service, Kitchen Facilities, Lake, Lodges, Meeting Rooms, Pool, River
Programs: Boating, Challenge/Ropes Course, Environmental Education, Swimming (#3633)

Wilderness Adventure at Eagle

(est 1990)   ⚠ 🏠 �",

New Castle, VA (Craig Co.); (800) 782-0779
Gene Nervo, Director

Camp comments: Develops teamwork, leadership & confidence through adventure & challenge. No experience needed. All equipment provided.
Activities: Backpacking, Bicycling/Biking, Camping Skills/Outdoor Living, Canoeing, Caving, Challenge/Rope Courses, Climbing/Rappelling, Hiking, Kayaking, Wilderness Trips
Session lengths & capacity: June-September; 1, 2, 3 & 4 week sessions; 120 campers
Clientele & fees: coed 9-17; families; single adults; Fees: E, F ⚠
Contact: Dave Cohan, Dir. of Administration at (800) 782-0779; fax: (540) 864-6800
e-mail: wildadel@swva.net
Web site: www.eagle-landing.com
Operated by: Wilderness Adventure Eagle Lnd, PO Box 760, New Castle, VA 24127 at (800) 782-0779

Group Rental Information

Site comments: Conference and Retreat Center, corporate team building. High & low ropes, climbing wall, & much more. Great food, expert instruction. Expert care.
Seasons & Capacity: Spring 48, Summer 48, Fall 48, Winter 48
Facilities: Cabins, Food Service, Hiking Trails, Kitchen Facilities, Linens, Lodges, Meeting Rooms, River, Tents
Programs: Boating, Challenge/Ropes Course, Environmental Education (#6604)

WOW SW Virginia Youth Camp

(est 1989)   ⚠ 🏠 �",

Thaxton, VA (Craig Co.); (540) 798-6968
Thomas Ross, Director

Camp comments: The SW VA WOW Family Activity Center opeined in 2001 for Woodmen members & user groups. Great facility - good rates - asl about Woodmen membership.

Activities: Archery, Arts/Crafts, Canoeing, Counselor Training (CIT), Fishing, Golf, Hiking, Performing Arts, Riflery, Sports — Field & Team
Session lengths & capacity: June-August; 1 week sessions; 100 campers
Clientele & fees: coed 8-15; seniors; Fees: A ⚠
Contact: Thomas M Ross, Fraternal Coordinator at (540) 989-6109; fax: (540) 989-6103
e-mail: tross@woodmen.com
Web site: www.woodmen.com
Operated by: WOW Life Insurance (VA), 1700 Farnam, Omaha, NE 68120 at (402) 271-7258

Group Rental Information

Seasons & Capacity: Spring 50, Summer 50, Fall 50, Winter 50
Facilities: Dorm-Style, Food Service, Hiking Trails, Kitchen Facilities, Lake, Meeting Rooms, Playing Fields
Programs: Boating, Swimming (#3131)

YMCA Camp Silver Beach

(est 2000)   ⚠ 🏠 🚗

Jamesville, VA; (757) 442-4634
Dan Credle, Director

Camp comments: To put Judeo/Christian principles into practice through programs that build healthy spirit, mind, and body for all
Activities: Boating, Challenge/Rope Courses, Kayaking, Leadership Development, Nature/Environment Studies, Riflery, Sailing, Swimming — Recreational
Session lengths & capacity: 1, 2 & 3 week sessions; 320 campers
Clientele & fees: coed 8-16; families; seniors; single adults; Fees: E ⚠
Contact: Rhonda Marsh, Office Administrator at (757) 442-4634; fax: (757) 442-4786
e-mail: info@campsilverbeach.org
Web site: www.campsilverbeach.org
Operated by: YMCA Camp Silver Beach, PO Box 69, Jamesville, VA 23398 at (757) 442-4634

Group Rental Information

Seasons & Capacity: Spring 400, Summer 320, Fall 400, Winter 400
Facilities: A/V Equipment, Cabins, Dorm-Style, Double Occupancy, Food Service, Hiking Trails, Linens, Lodges, Meeting Rooms, Playing Fields, Pool
Programs: Challenge/Ropes Course, Swimming (#38160)

Washington

Auburn YMCA Summer Day Camp   ☀

Auburn, WA (King Co.); (253) 833-2770
Kaja Olsson, Director

Camp comments: Supportive atmosphere of a Day Camp setting. Encourages participates to develop fullest potential in spirit, mind & body.
Activities: Archery, Arts/Crafts, Camping Skills/Outdoor Living, Climbing/Rappelling, Counselor Training (CIT), Field Trips, Hiking, Leadership Development
Session lengths & capacity: June-August; 1 week sessions; 225 campers
Clientele & fees: coed 5-17; Fees: B ☀ 🐷
Contact: Kaja Olsson, Program Director at (253) 833-2770; fax: (206) 852-8469
Operated by: YMCA of Greater Seattle, 909 4th Ave, Seattle, WA 98104 at (206) 382-5003 (#2308)

Brinkley (est 1967)   ⚠

Snohomish, WA; (360) 568-6295
Steven Dazey, Director

Camp comments: Traditional Boy Scout Camp located near mountains & horse trails. Has 2 lakes for aquatic activities.
Activities: Aquatic Activities, Archery, Bicycling/Biking, Camping Skills/Outdoor Living, Challenge/Rope Courses, Hiking, Leadership Development, Nature/Environment Studies, Riflery, Waterskiing
Session lengths & capacity: 1 week sessions; 300 campers
Clientele & fees: boys 8-18; Fees: B ⛺ 🚌
Contact: Steven Dazey, Camp Director at (360) 568-6295; fax: (360) 568-5044
Operated by: Chief Seattle Council BSA, PO Box 440408, Seattle, WA 98114 at (206) 725-0361 (#3438)

Buck Creek Center (est 1961) ⛺ 🏠

Greenwater, WA (Pierce Co.); (360) 663-2201
Karen Puckett, Director

Camp comments: A-frames, cabins, lodge deep in the Snoqualmie Natl Forest, only three miles from Mt Rainier. Year round alpine fun!
Activities: Archery, Arts/Crafts, Backpacking, Bicycling/Biking, Camping Skills/Outdoor Living, Leadership Development, Religious Study, Wilderness Trips
Session lengths & capacity: July-August; 1/2, 1, 2 & 3 week sessions; 235 campers
Clientele & fees: coed 7-77; families; Fees: C ⛺ 🚌
Contact: Karen Puckett, Center Director at (206) 767-6368; fax: (206) 763-9521
e-mail: karenpuckett@buckcreek.org
Operated by: Presbytery of Seattle, 1625 S Columbian Way, Seattle, WA 98108 at (206) 767-6368

Group Rental Information
Seasons & Capacity: Spring 240, Fall 240, Winter 240
Facilities: A/V Equipment, Cabins, Dorm-Style, Double Occupancy, Food Service, Hiking Trails, Kitchen Facilities, Lodges, Meeting Rooms, Playing Fields, Pool, River
Programs: Challenge/Ropes Course, Swimming (#7436)

Burton (est 1909) ⛺ 🏠 🚗

Vashon, WA (King Co.); (206) 463-2512
Rev Randolph Farrar, Director

Camp comments: Resident camp with waterfront on Puget Sound, specializing in religious education, music & camps for special populations
Activities: Aquatic Activities, Archery, Arts/Crafts, Bicycling/Biking, Challenge/Rope Courses, Counselor Training (CIT), Leadership Development, Music, Photography
Session lengths & capacity: 1 week sessions; 140 campers
Clientele & fees: coed 6-18; families; Fees: B, C ⛺
Contact: Kathleen Hendrickson, Camp Manager at (206) 463-2512; fax: (206) 463-6738
e-mail: cburtonwa@aol.com
Operated by: Washington Baptist Convention, 409 3rd Ave S Ste A, Kent, WA 98032-5843 at (253) 859-2226

Group Rental Information
Seasons & Capacity: Spring 175, Summer 200, Fall 175, Winter 175
Facilities: A/V Equipment, Cabins, Dorm-Style, Food Service, Hiking Trails, Kitchen Facilities, Linens, Lodges, Meeting Rooms, Ocean, Playing Fields
Programs: Boating, Challenge/Ropes Course, Swimming (#7187)

Camp Arnold at Timberlake

(est 1965) ⛺ 🏠 🚗

Eatonville, WA (Pierce Co.); (253) 847-2511
Ed Covert, Administrator, Director

Camp comments: Over 600 acres pristine land and forests, natural lake, spectacular view Mt Ranier-watersports, hiking ages 8-12, wilderness ed 13-16, low camper/staff ratio
Activities: Archery, Arts/Crafts, Camping Skills/Outdoor Living, Canoeing, Challenge/Rope Courses, Hiking, Music, Nature/Environment Studies, Swimming — Recreational, Wilderness Trips
Session lengths & capacity: June-August; 1 week sessions; 220 campers
Clientele & fees: coed 8-16; Fees: B ⛺ 🚌
Contact: Pene Mathison, Business Manager at (253) 847-2511; fax: (253) 847-2910
e-mail: cmparnold@aol.com
Web site: www.camparnold.org
Operated by: Camp Arnold at Timberlake, 33712 Webster Road East, Eatonville, WA 98328-9662 at (253) 847-2511

Group Rental Information
Site comments: Over 600 acres pristine land and untouched forests, natural lake, spectacular view of Mt Ranier, ropes course, pool, outdoor ed, groups from 35 to 350.
Seasons & Capacity: Spring 320, Fall 320, Winter 320
Facilities: A/V Equipment, Cabins, Double Occupancy, Food Service, Hiking Trails, Lake, Lodges, Meeting Rooms, Playing Fields, Pool
Programs: Boating, Challenge/Ropes Course, Environmental Education, Swimming (#426)

Camp Dart-Lo (est 1945) ☀ 🏠 🚐

Spokane, WA (Spokane Co.); (509) 747-6191
Tracy Taitch, Director

Camp comments: Something for everyone. Leadership training for teens. Come 2 weeks or all summer. State-of-the-art pool complex nestled in forest provides unique experience.
Activities: Archery, Arts/Crafts, Camping Skills/Outdoor Living, Challenge/Rope Courses, Counselor Training (CIT), Hiking, Leadership Development, Nature/Environment Studies, Swimming — Instructional, Swimming — Recreational
Session lengths & capacity: June-August; 1 & 2 week sessions; 140 campers
Clientele & fees: coed 3-15; families; Fees: B ☀ 🚌
Contact: Tracy Taitch, Camp Director at (509) 327-1558; fax: (509) 327-1558
e-mail: campfireiec@msn.com
Web site: www.campfireiec.org
Operated by: Camp Fire USA Inland Northwest, 524 N Mullan Road, Spokane, WA 99206-3864 at (509) 747-6191

Group Rental Information
Site comments: Beautiful, rustic site is great for picnics, retreats,and other day events. Optional programs and activities provide ease in planning, stay overnight, it's fun!
Seasons & Capacity: Spring 150, Fall 150, Winter 50
Facilities: Hiking Trails, Kitchen Facilities, Lodges, Meeting Rooms, Pool, River
Programs: Challenge/Ropes Course, Environmental Education, Swimming (#833)

Camp Easter Seal Washington

(est 1975) ⛺ 🏠

Vaughn, WA (Pierce Co.); (253) 884-2722
Mike Mooney, Director

Camp comments: Accessible program on Puget Sound. Outstanding camper-staff ratio. Experience of lifetime for people with disabilities.
Activities: Archery, Basketball, Boating, Camping Skills/Outdoor Living, Drawing/Painting, Hiking, Horseback — Western, Nature/Environment Studies, Swimming — Recreational
Session lengths & capacity: June-August; 1/2 & 1 week sessions; 36 campers
Clientele & fees: coed 7-65; seniors; Fees: E ⛺

Contact: Mary McIntyre, Office Manager at (253) 884-2722; fax: (253) 884-0200
e-mail: mary@seals.org
Web site: www.seals.org
Operated by: Easter Seal Society of WA, 521 2nd Ave W, Seattle, WA 98119 at (206) 281-5700

Group Rental Information
Site comments: Facility available late August thru May for groups up to 60 for conferences, retreats, camping, or eductional classes.
Seasons & Capacity: Spring 60, Fall 60, Winter 60
Facilities: Cabins, Dorm-Style, Food Service, Hiking Trails, Lake, Lodges, Meeting Rooms, Playing Fields, Pool
Programs: Boating, Swimming (#8388)

Camp Fire USA Day Camps

(est 1940) ☀

Seattle, WA (King Co.)
Karen Aoyama, Director

Camp comments: Week long day camps in outdoor settings. Small groups, trained volunteer staff, nature, crafts, camp skills, games.
Activities: Archery, Arts/Crafts, Camping Skills/Outdoor Living, Community Service, Drama, Hiking, Leadership Development, Nature/Environment Studies, Sports — Field & Team, Swimming — Recreational
Session lengths & capacity: 1 week sessions; 150 campers
Clientele & fees: coed 5-13; Fees: A ☀ 🚌
Contact: Karen Aoyama, Council Day Camp Coordinator at (206) 461-8550; fax: (206) 525-3351
Web site: www.campfirecpsc.org
Operated by: Camp Fire USA Central Snd Cnl, 14500 SW Camp Sealth Rd, Vashon, WA 98070 at (206) 463-3174 (#6666)

Camp Firwood (est 1954) ⛺ 🏠

Bellingham, WA (Whatcom Co.); (360) 733-6840

Camp comments: Firwood is a counelor-centered, high-energy, activity-oriented, summer camp.
Activities: Aquatic Activities, Arts/Crafts, Camping Skills/Outdoor Living, Challenge/Rope Courses, Climbing/Rappelling, Counselor Training (CIT), Horseback — Western, Kayaking, Sailing, Waterskiing
Session lengths & capacity: May-September; 1 & 2 week sessions; 240 campers
Clientele & fees: coed 8-18; Fees: C ⛺
Contact: Darell Smith or Craig Timmer, Director/Assistant Director at (360) 733-6840; fax: (360) 733-6926
e-mail: firwood@thefirs.org
Web site: www.thefirs.org
Operated by: The Firs Bible and Missionary, 4605 Cable Street, Bellingham, WA 98226 at (360) 733-6840

Group Rental Information
Seasons & Capacity: Spring 200, Summer 240, Fall 200
Facilities: Cabins, Food Service, Hiking Trails, Lake, Meeting Rooms, Playing Fields
Programs: Boating, Challenge/Ropes Course, Environmental Education (#27042)

Camp Fun in the Sun (est 1980) ⛺

Spokane, WA; (509) 473-6960
Dee Jameson, Director

Camp comments: Dedicated to children w/diabetes, A unique opportunity to share experiences and learn more about managing their disease
Activities: Arts/Crafts, Bicycling/Biking, Boating, Challenge/Rope Courses, Swimming — Recreational
Session lengths & capacity: July-August; 1 week sessions; 96 campers
Clientele & fees: coed 6-18; Fees: C ⛺
Contact: Dee Jameson, Camp Director at (509) 473-6960; fax: (509) 473-6961

e-mail: jamesod@cherspokane.org
Operated by: Inland Northwest Health Serv, 715 S Cowley Ste 324, Spokane, WA 99202 at (509) 232-8138 (#41106)

Camp Good Times   △

Seattle, WA; (206) 283-1152
Tom Nielsen, Director

Camp comments: Resident camp for children with cancer and their siblings. All fees are covered.
Activities: Aquatic Activities, Archery, Arts/Crafts, Canoeing, Fishing, Kayaking, Swimming — Recreational
Session lengths & capacity: June-June; 1 week sessions; 125 campers
Clientele & fees: coed 7-17; 🚐
Operated by: American Cancer Society NW, 2120 First Ave N Box 19140, Seattle, WA 98109 at (206) 283-1152 (#11762)

Camp Highline   ☀

Seattle, WA; (206) 244-5880
Megan Dehan, Director
Activities: Aquatic Activities, Archery, Arts/Crafts, Camping Skills/Outdoor Living, Climbing/Rappelling, Field Trips, Nature/Environment Studies, Sports — Field & Team, Swimming — Recreational
Session lengths & capacity: June-September; 1 week sessions; 150 campers
Clientele & fees: coed 6-12; Fees: B ☀ 🚐
Operated by: YMCA of Greater Seattle, 909 4th Ave, Seattle, WA 98104 at (206) 382-5003 (#41319)

Camp Huston (est 1928)   △ 🏠 🚐

Gold Bar, WA (Snohomish Co.); (360) 793-0441
Bill Tubbs, Director

Camp comments: Episcopal camp in foot hills of Cascade Mtns. Small group experience in a Christian community. Adventure trips.
Activities: Archery, Arts/Crafts, Backpacking, Camping Skills/Outdoor Living, Challenge/Rope Courses, Counselor Training (CIT), Leadership Development, Nature/Environment Studies, Rafting, Swimming — Recreational
Session lengths & capacity: June-August; 1/2 & 1 week sessions; 95 campers
Clientele & fees: coed 6-15; Fees: B, C △ 🚐
Contact: Bill Tubbs, Director at (360) 793-0441; fax: (360) 793-3822
e-mail: info@huston.org
Operated by: Huston Camp & Conference Ctr, PO Box 140, Gold Bar, WA 98251 at (360) 793-0441

ICON LEGEND

☀ Day Camp
△ Resident Camp
🏠 Facilities Available To Rent
🚐 Transportation Available
🚐 Financial Aid Available

FEE RANGES PER WEEK

A	$0-75
B	$75-200
C	$201-350
D	$351-500
E	$501-650
F	over $650

Group Rental Information
Facilities: Cabins, Dorm-Style, Double Occupancy, Food Service, Kitchen Facilities, Meeting Rooms, River
Programs: Challenge/Ropes Course (#3257)

Camp Kirby (est 1923)   △ 🏠

Bow, WA (Skagit Co.); (360) 733-5710
Jennifer Brown, Director

Camp comments: Rustic facility w/ forest & tidal beaches. Campers w/ special needs can call Camp Fire to make appropriate arrangements.
Activities: Archery, Arts/Crafts, Backpacking, Camping Skills/Outdoor Living, Counselor Training (CIT), Hiking, Leadership Development, Nature/Environment Studies, Rafting, Sailing
Session lengths & capacity: 1/2 & 1 week sessions
Clientele & fees: coed 6-17; Fees: A ☀ Fees: B △ 🚐
Contact: (360) 733-5710; fax: (360) 733-5711
Web site: www.campkirby.org
Operated by: Camp Fire USA Samish Council, 2217 Woburn St, Bellingham, WA 98226-6264 at (360) 733-5710

Group Rental Information
Site comments: Non-competitive prog, leadership opportunities for teens.
Seasons & Capacity: Summer 100
Facilities: Cabins, Food Service, Hiking Trails, Kitchen Facilities, Lodges, Meeting Rooms, Ocean, Playing Fields
Programs: Boating, Challenge/Ropes Course, Environmental Education (#454)

Camp Sealth (est 1920)   △ 🏠 🚐

Vashon Is., WA (King Co.); (206) 463-3174
Jan L. Milligan, Director

Camp comments: Woodlands and beach on Puget Sound. Emphasis on teamwork, group living and camper involvement in planning activities. Outstanding and extensive teen programs.
Activities: Archery, Arts/Crafts, Boating, Camping Skills/Outdoor Living, Challenge/Rope Courses, Hiking, Horseback — Western, Leadership Development, Nature/Environment Studies, Wilderness Trips
Session lengths & capacity: April-October; 1/2, 1 & 2 week sessions; 380 campers
Clientele & fees: coed 6-17; families; Fees: D △ 🚐
Contact: Kathy Wiren, Camp Registrar at (206) 461-8550; fax: (206) 525-3351
e-mail: sealthinfo@campfire-usa.org
Web site: www.campfirecpsc.org
Operated by: Camp Fire USA Central Snd Cnl, 14500 SW Camp Sealth Rd, Vashon, WA 98070 at (206) 463-3174

Group Rental Information
Site comments: Rustic, comfortable cabins; many lodges and meeting rooms; optional food service, challenge activities, environmental education. Waterfront/boating.
Seasons & Capacity: Spring 500, Fall 500, Winter 300
Facilities: A/V Equipment, Cabins, Dorm-Style, Food Service, Hiking Trails, Kitchen Facilities, Lodges, Meeting Rooms, Ocean, Playing Fields, Tents
Programs: Boating, Challenge/Ropes Course, Environmental Education, Swimming (#431)

Canoe Island French Camp

(est 1969)   △ 🏠

Orcas, WA (San Juan Co.); (360) 468-2329
Richard Carter, Director

Camp comments: Private isl. WA's lovely San Juans. French language/culture. International staff 3:1 Camper/staff ratio. Fun & Learning

Activities: Archery, Arts/Crafts, Drama, Fencing, International Culture, Kayaking, Language Studies, Photography, Sailing, Swimming — Recreational
Session lengths & capacity: June-August; 2 & 3 week sessions; 40 campers
Clientele & fees: coed 9-15; Fees: F △
Contact: Richard Carter, Camp Director at (360) 468-2329; fax: (360) 468-3027
e-mail: canoe@rockisland.com
Operated by: Canoe Island French Camp, 1731 Center Rd, Lopez, WA 98261 at (360) 468-2329 (#7750)

Cascade Camp Cherith (est 1947) △

Belfair, WA (Thurston Co.); (425) 337-1678
Steve Duke, Judy Elbert, Director

Camp comments: Campers learn new skills & enjoy each other while practicing Christian living. Separate programs for girls & boys.
Activities: Aquatic Activities, Archery, Canoeing, Clowning, Horseback — Western, Leadership Development, Model Rocketry, Religious Study, Riflery, Swimming — Instructional
Session lengths & capacity: June-July; 1/2 & 1 week sessions; 120 campers
Clientele & fees: boys 8-18; girls 8-18; Fees: B △
Contact: Elaine Barr, Registrar at (425) 337-1678; e-mail: teamelbert@juno.com
Operated by: Cascade Camp Cherith, 21918 107th Ave SE, Kent, WA 98031 at (253) 856-2211 (#7379)

Cascade Meadows Bapt Camp

(est 1965)   △ 🏠

Leavenworth, WA (Chelan Co.); (206) 463-2512
Rev Randolph Farrar, Director

Camp comments: Cascade Meadows Camp is available for use by churches and other non profit groups. Housing and u-cook for up to 65
Activities: Archery, Arts/Crafts, Camping Skills/Outdoor Living, Hiking, Leadership Development, Nature/Environment Studies, Religious Study, Sports — Field & Team, Swimming — Recreational
Session lengths & capacity: 1/2 & 1 week sessions; 119 campers
Clientele & fees: coed 10-18; families; Fees: B △
Contact: Rev Randolph Farrar, Executive Director at (206) 463-2512; fax: (206) 463-6738
e-mail: cburtonwa@aol.com
Operated by: Washington Baptist Convention, 409 3rd Ave S Ste A, Kent, WA 98032-5843 at (253) 859-2226

Group Rental Information
Seasons & Capacity: Spring 70, Summer 70, Fall 70, Winter 50
Facilities: Cabins, Dorm-Style, Hiking Trails, Kitchen Facilities, Lodges, Meeting Rooms, Playing Fields, River
Programs: Environmental Education (#14043)

Don Bosco (est 1950)   △ 🏠 🚐

Carnation, WA; (425) 869-1787
Michael Heinrich, Director

Camp comments: Children discover a sense of self, and appreciation of others & nature. See all these wonders as a reflection of God.
Activities: Archery, Arts/Crafts, Camping Skills/Outdoor Living, Challenge/Rope Courses, Drama, Horseback — Western, Nature/Environment Studies, Soccer, Sports — Field & Team, Swimming — Recreational
Session lengths & capacity: 1 week sessions; 190 campers
Clientele & fees: boys 7-12; girls 7-12; coed 7-12; families; Fees: C, D △
Contact: Michael Heinrich, Director at (206) 903-4625; fax: (206) 903-4627
e-mail: mikeh@seattlearch.org
Web site: www.seattlearch.org/cyo
Operated by: Catholic Youth Organization, 814 NE 85th St, Seattle, WA 98115 at (206) 903-4625

Group Rental Information
Seasons & Capacity: Spring 80, Fall 80
Facilities: Cabins, Dorm-Style, Hiking Trails, Kitchen Facilities, Meeting Rooms (#7008)

Federal Way Norman Center YMCA (est 1998)

Federal Way, WA; (253) 838-4708

Camp comments: Combine healthy portions of the great outdoors & skill building sprinkled with cultural expeniences all wrapped up in fun & you've got YMCA Outdoor Day Camp.
Activities: Aerobics/Exercise, Archery, Arts/Crafts, Camping Skills/Outdoor Living, Field Trips, Hiking, Kayaking, Nature/Environment Studies, Swimming — Recreational, Team Building
Session lengths & capacity: June-August; 1, 2, 3, 4, 5, 6, 7, 8 & 9 week sessions; 100 campers
Clientele & fees: coed 6-13; Fees: B ☀ 🚐
Contact: (253) 838-4708; fax: (253) 838-9490
e-mail: kwagner@fw.seattleymca.org
Operated by: YMCA of Greater Seattle, 909 4th Ave, Seattle, WA 98104 at (206) 382-5003 (#32844)

Four Winds and Westward Ho

(est 1927)

Deer Harbor, WA (San Juan Co.); (360) 376-2277
Adam Kaplan, Director

Camp comments: Washington's San Juan Islands. Long standing coed prog, individual choice 20 activities, sailing, sports, arts, riding, & garden
Activities: Arts/Crafts, Ceramics/Pottery, Counselor Training (CIT), Horseback — English, Horseback — Western, Sailing, Soccer, Tennis, Wilderness Trips
Session lengths & capacity: June-August; 1 & 4 week sessions; 170 campers
Clientele & fees: coed 6-16; Fees: E, F 🔺 🐷
Contact: Adam Kaplan, Director at (360) 376-2277; fax: (360) 376-5741
e-mail: jobs@fourwindscamp.org
Web site: www.fourwindscamp.org
Operated by: Four Winds Inc, PO Box 140, Deer Harbor, WA 98243 at (360) 376-2277

Group Rental Information
Facilities: Cabins, Dorm-Style, Double Occupancy, Food Service, Hiking Trails, Kitchen Facilities, Lodges, Meeting Rooms, Ocean, Playing Fields, Tents
Programs: Boating (#422)

Gallagher (est 1961)

Lake Bay, WA; (206) 903-4625
Michael Heinrich, Director

Camp comments: Teens discover a sense of self & appreciation of others, nature & see all these wonders as a reflection of God.
Activities: Aquatic Activities, Arts/Crafts, Boating, Camping Skills/Outdoor Living, Canoeing, Kayaking, Sailing, Swimming — Recreational, Wilderness Trips, Windsurfing
Session lengths & capacity: 1 week sessions; 70 campers
Clientele & fees: boys 13-18; girls 13-18; coed 13-18; families; Fees: C, D 🔺
Contact: Michael Heinrich at (206) 903-4625; fax: (206) 903-4627
e-mail: mikeh@seattlearch.org
Web site: www.seattlearch.org/cyo
Operated by: Catholic Youth Organization, 814 NE 85th St, Seattle, WA 98115 at (206) 903-4625 (#3854)

Hamilton (est 1990)

Monroe, WA (Snohomish Co.); (206) 903-4625
Michael Heinrich, Director

Camp comments: Children discover a sense of self, an appreciation of others & nature. See all these as a reflection of God.

Activities: Archery, Arts/Crafts, Backpacking, Camping Skills/Outdoor Living, Challenge/Rope Courses, Hiking, Horseback — Western, Nature/Environment Studies
Session lengths & capacity: 1 week sessions; 120 campers
Clientele & fees: boys 9-15; girls 9-15; coed 9-15; Fees: C, D 🔺 🐷
Contact: Noreen Elbert, Director of Outdoor Ministries at (206) 382-4562; fax: (206) 382-2071
e-mail: cyo@seattlearch.org
Web site: www.seattlearch.org/cyo
Operated by: Catholic Youth Organization, 814 NE 85th St, Seattle, WA 98115 at (206) 903-4625

Group Rental Information
Facilities: Cabins, Hiking Trails, Kitchen Facilities, Lodges (#6661)

Hidden Valley Camp (est 1947)

Granite Falls, WA (Snohomish Co.); (425) 334-1040
Todd McKinlay, Director

Camp comments: Small group program emphasis. Carefully selected & trained staff. Rustic experience in caring & supportive atmosphere. A very special place for kids since 1947.
Activities: Archery, Arts/Crafts, Backpacking, Camping Skills/Outdoor Living, Canoeing, Drama, Horseback — Western, Leadership Development, Sailing, Swimming — Recreational
Session lengths & capacity: June-September; 2, 3 & 4 week sessions; 120 campers
Clientele & fees: boys 7-17; girls 7-17; coed 7-17; Fees: D, E 🔺
Contact: Todd McKinlay, Camp Director at (425) 844-8896; fax: (425) 844-8302
e-mail: hvc-wa@ix.netcom.com
Web site: www.hvc-wa.com
Operated by: Hidden Valley Camp, 24314 Hidden Valley Rd, Granite Falls, WA 98252-9314 at (425) 334-1040 (#420)

Indianola Camp & Retreat Ctr

(est 1958)

Indianola, WA (Kitsap Co.); (360) 297-2223
Pete Simpson, Director
Activities: Aquatic Activities, Arts/Crafts, Camping Skills/Outdoor Living, Field Trips, Hiking, Kayaking, Leadership Development, Nature/Environment Studies, Religious Study, Swimming — Recreational
Contact: Web site: www.pnwumc.org
Operated by: United Methodist Conference, 2112 Third Ave, Seattle, WA 98121-2333 at (800) 755-7710

Group Rental Information
Site comments: Year-round on Puget Sound, one hour west of Seattle.
Facilities: A/V Equipment, Cabins, Dorm-Style, Double Occupancy, Food Service, Hiking Trails, Kitchen Facilities, Lodges, Meeting Rooms, Ocean, Playing Fields
Programs: Boating, Environmental Education, Swimming (#3513)

Island Lake Camp (est 1974)

Poulsbo, WA (Kitsap Co.); (360) 697-1212
Paul Hill, Director

Camp comments: Motorbikes, water sports, trails, court sports, high-ropes course & skateboards. 130 acres of fun for kids 8-18
Activities: Basketball, Boating, Challenge/Rope Courses, Counselor Training (CIT), Leadership Development, Model Rocketry, Riflery, Swimming — Recreational
Session lengths & capacity: June-August; 1 week sessions; 194 campers
Clientele & fees: coed 8-18; Fees: C 🔺 🐷
Contact: (360) 697-1212; fax: (360) 697-1709
e-mail: information@cristacamps.com
Web site: www.cristacamps.com

Operated by: CRISTA Ministries, 19303 Fremont Ave N, Seattle, WA 98133 at (206) 622-8583
Group Rental Information
Site comments: 130 wooded acres of waterfront, trails, & ropes course. Nearby golf, shopping. Mtg rooms hold 15-275.
Seasons & Capacity: Spring 275, Fall 275, Winter 275
Facilities: Cabins, Food Service, Hiking Trails, Lake, Lodges, Meeting Rooms
Programs: Boating (#2614)

Killoqua (est 1941)

Stanwood, WA (Snohomish Co.); (360) 652-6250
Carol Johnson, Director

Camp comments: Small group emphasis and camper planned program on lake.
Activities: Archery, Arts/Crafts, Bicycling/Biking, Boating, Challenge/Rope Courses, Horseback — Western, Sailing, Windsurfing
Session lengths & capacity: 1/2 & 1 week sessions; 150 campers
Clientele & fees: coed 6-17; Fees: C 🔺 🐷
Contact: Carol Johnson, Assistant Executive Director at (425) 258-5437; fax: (425) 252-2267
e-mail: info@snohomishcampfire.org
Web site: www.snohomishcampfire.org
Operated by: Camp Fire USA, 4312 Rucker Ave, Everett, WA 98203-2233 at (425) 258-5437

Group Rental Information
Site comments: Forested lake site, one hour North of Seattle.
Seasons & Capacity: Spring 200, Summer 200, Fall 200, Winter 120
Facilities: Cabins, Food Service, Hiking Trails, Lake, Meeting Rooms, Playing Fields
Programs: Boating, Challenge/Ropes Course, Environmental Education (#421)

Koinonia (est 1958)

Cle Elum, WA (Kittitas Co.); (509) 674-5767
Activities: Aquatic Activities, Baseball/Softball, Fishing, Snow Sports
Contact: Michael O'Cain, Director at (509) 674-5767;
e-mail: campman@inlandnet.com
Operated by: Church of the Brethren Oregon, 850 Camp Koinonia Lane, Cle Elum, WA 98922 at (509) 674-5767

Group Rental Information
Facilities: Cabins, Food Service, Hiking Trails, Lake, Lodges, Meeting Rooms, Playing Fields, Tents (#3949)

Lake Heights YMCA Day Camp

Bellevue, WA; (425) 644-8417
Tim Barr, Director

Camp comments: We build strong kids, strong families, strong communities.
Activities: Aquatic Activities, Archery, Arts/Crafts, Climbing/Rappelling, Drama, Field Trips, Leadership Development, Performing Arts, Team Building
Session lengths & capacity: June-August; 1 week sessions; 130 campers
Clientele & fees: coed 6-12; Fees: B ☀ 🐷
Contact: Tina Holmberg at (425) 644-8417; fax: (425) 746-1830
e-mail: tbarr@seatleymca.org
Operated by: YMCA of Greater Seattle, 909 4th Ave, Seattle, WA 98104 at (206) 382-5003 (#4387)

Lake Wenatchee YMCA Camp

(est 1928)

Leavenworth, WA; (509) 763-9622
Tim McElravy, Director

Camp comments: Focus is on building character based on caring, honesty, respect, and responsibility through quality leadership.
Activities: Archery, Arts/Crafts, Camping Skills/Outdoor Living, Canoeing, Challenge/Rope Courses, Counselor Training (CIT), Horseback — Western, Kayaking, Leadership Development, Rafting
Session lengths & capacity: 1/2 & 1 week sessions; 140 campers
Clientele & fees: coed 5-18; families; Fees: **B, C** ⚠ 🐷
Contact: Deanna Hubele, Camp Director at (509) 763-9622; fax: (509) 763-5200
e-mail: wenycamp@aol.com
Web site: www.lwycamp.org
Operated by: Wenatchee Valley YMCA, PO Box 1974, Wenatchee, WA 98807-1974 at (509) 763-9622

Group Rental Information
Site comments: 26 acres, 1/2 mile of waterfront, 1 hr from Wenatchee, WA. 2 1/2 hrs from Seattle WA on Stevens Pass (Hwy 2).Nice 2 story lodge, 17 cabins, rental packet avail.
Seasons & Capacity: Spring 140, Summer 140, Fall 140, Winter 120
Facilities: Cabins, Double Occupancy, Food Service, Hiking Trails, Lake, Lodges, Playing Fields, River
Programs: Boating, Challenge/Ropes Course, Environmental Education, Winter Sports (#3125)

Lazy F Camp and Retreat Center
(est 1954)   ⚠ 🏠

Ellensburg, WA (Kihitas Co.); (509) 962-2780
Dave Burfeind, Director

Camp comments: Lazy F Camp provides summer camp in a Christian environment in a convenient location. Also open for non-profit guest groups year round.
Activities: Archery, Arts/Crafts, Challenge/Rope Courses, Climbing/Rappelling, Fishing, Horseback — Western, Religious Study
Session lengths & capacity: 1 week sessions
Clientele & fees: boys 9-11; girls 9-11; coed 6-18; Fees: **B** ⚠
Contact: Dave Burfeind, Director at (509) 962-2780; fax: (509) 962-2781
e-mail: lazy-f@ebrg.com
Web site: www.pnwumc.org
Operated by: United Methodist Conference, 2112 Third Ave, Seattle, WA 98121-2333 at (800) 755-7710

Group Rental Information
Site comments: Conveniently located in Central Washington on 110 acres. Clean,comfortable facilities with delicious home-cooked meals.

ICON LEGEND
☀   Day Camp
⚠   Resident Camp
🏠   Facilities Available To Rent
🚐   Transportation Available
🐷   Financial Aid Available

FEE RANGES PER WEEK
A	$0-75
B	$75-200
C	$201-350
D	$351-500
E	$501-650
F	over $650

Seasons & Capacity: Spring 150, Summer 120, Fall 150, Winter 150
Facilities: Cabins, Dorm-Style, Food Service, Hiking Trails, Lodges, Meeting Rooms, River (#3505)

Melacoma (est 1949)   🏠

Washougal, WA (Skamania Co.); (360) 837-3943
Mary Baddgor, Director
Contact: Michele Jones, Administrative Assistant at (360) 693-1419 ext. 201; fax: (360) 696-2751
Web site: www.camp-fire-mthood.org
Operated by: Mt Hood Council Camp Fire, 2004 Broadway, Vancouver, WA 98663 at (360) 693-1419

Group Rental Information
Seasons & Capacity: Spring 150, Summer 150, Fall 150, Winter 150
Facilities: Cabins, Hiking Trails, Lodges, Meeting Rooms, Pool
Programs: Boating (#258)

Miracle Ranch (est 1960)   ☀ ⚠ 🏠 🚐

Port Orchard, WA (Kitsap Co.); (253) 851-4410
Phil Peterson, Director

Camp comments: Ranch camp, staff encourage positive character, teamwork, achievement. Wooded lakefront. Summer fun for all ages.
Activities: Archery, Arts/Crafts, Boating, Golf, Horseback — English, Horseback — Western, Model Rocketry, Riflery, Swimming — Recreational
Session lengths & capacity: June-August; 1 week sessions; 181 campers
Clientele & fees: coed 6-18; Fees: **B** ☀ Fees: **C** ⚠ 🐷
Contact: Ronda Caddell, Registrar at (360) 697-1212; fax: (360) 697-1709
e-mail: information@cristacamps.com
Web site: www.cristacamps.com
Operated by: CRISTA Ministries, 19303 Fremont Ave N, Seattle, WA 98133 at (206) 622-8583

Group Rental Information
Site comments: Wooded lakefront on Horseshoe Lake 15 miles N of Tacoma. Heated cabins and conference rooms. Full service dining room.
Facilities: A/V Equipment, Cabins, Food Service, Hiking Trails, Lake, Meeting Rooms, Playing Fields
Programs: Boating, Environmental Education, Horseback Riding, Swimming (#7404)

Museum of Flight (ACE)   ☀ 🏠

Seattle, WA; (206) 768-7141

Camp comments: The Museum of Flight takes summer camp to the air with it's popular Aerospace Camp Experience (ACE).
Activities: Academics, Aviation, Leadership Development, Model Rocketry, Swimming — Recreational, Team Building
Session lengths & capacity: July-August; 1 week sessions
Clientele & fees: coed 6-15; Fees: **C, D** ☀
Contact: Chris Peguero, ACE Manager at (206) 768-7141; fax: (206) 764-5707
e-mail: acemanager@museumofflight.org
Web site: www.museumofflight.org
Operated by: Museum of Flight, 9404 E Marginal Way South, Seattle, WA 98108-4097 at (206) 764-5700 (#39075)

Northshore YMCA Day Camp
(est 1977)   ☀ 🚐

Bothell, WA (King Co.); (425) 485-9797
Kyla Smith, Director

Camp comments: Full day camp program focused on teaching values to children using outdoor programs with a family emphasis.
Activities: Aquatic Activities, Arts/Crafts, Baseball/Softball, Basketball, Camping Skills/Outdoor Living, Field Trips, Hiking, Nature/Environment Studies, Soccer, Swimming — Recreational

Session lengths & capacity: June-August; 1 week sessions; 240 campers
Clientele & fees: coed 5-12; Fees: **B** ☀ 🐷
Contact: Kyla Smith, Associate Executive at (425) 485-9797; fax: (425) 486-7757
e-mail: ksmith@ns.seattleymca.org
Operated by: YMCA of Greater Seattle, 909 4th Ave, Seattle, WA 98104 at (206) 382-5003 (#3791)

Ocean Park Retreat Center
(est 1940)   ⚠ 🏠

Ocean Park, WA (Pacific Co.); (360) 665-4367
Cindy Heckman, Director
Activities: Aquatic Activities, Archery, Arts/Crafts, Hiking, Kayaking, Religious Study
Session lengths & capacity: June-August; 1 week sessions
Clientele & fees: coed 5-19; families; Fees: **B** ⚠
Contact: Darcy Lee, Secretary at (360) 665-4367; fax: (360) 665-6579
e-mail: opretreat@willapabay.org
Web site: www.pnwumc.org
Operated by: United Methodist Conference, 2112 Third Ave, Seattle, WA 98121-2333 at (800) 755-7710

Group Rental Information
Site comments: 80 acres of beach, dunes & forest. Year round facilities.
Seasons & Capacity: Spring 225, Summer 225, Fall 225, Winter 225
Facilities: A/V Equipment, Cabins, Dorm-Style, Double Occupancy, Food Service, Kitchen Facilities, Linens, Lodges, Meeting Rooms, Ocean, Playing Fields, Tents
Programs: Boating, Challenge/Ropes Course (#3509)

Parsons (est 1918)   ⚠ 🏠

Brinnon, WA (Jefferson Co.); (206) 796-4427
Ken McEdwards, Director

Camp comments: Waterfront setting. Close to the mountains. Program offered to registered Boy Scouts.
Activities: Archery, Arts/Crafts, Camping Skills/Outdoor Living, Climbing/Rappelling, Hiking, Nature/Environment Studies, Riflery
Session lengths & capacity: 1/2 & 1 week sessions; 300 campers
Clientele & fees: boys 11-18; Fees: **B** ⚠
Contact: Ken McEdwards, Camp Director at (360) 796-4427; fax: (360) 796-2039
Operated by: Chief Seattle Council BSA, PO Box 440408, Seattle, WA 98114 at (206) 725-0361

Group Rental Information
Seasons & Capacity: Spring 300, Summer 300, Fall 300
Facilities: Cabins, Food Service, Hiking Trails, Kitchen Facilities, Lodges, Meeting Rooms, Ocean, Tents
Programs: Boating, Swimming (#3334)

Renton Family YMCA (est 2000)   ☀

Maple Valley, WA; (423) 430-8850
Mark Johnson, Director

Camp comments: Building a community where all people, especially the young, are encouraged to develop to their fullest potential is spirit, mind & body.
Activities: Arts/Crafts, Camping Skills/Outdoor Living, Climbing/Rappelling, Field Trips, Hiking, Swimming — Recreational, Team Building
Session lengths & capacity: June-August; 1 week sessions; 150 campers
Clientele & fees: coed 5-16; Fees: **B, C** ☀ 🐷
Contact: Mark Johnson or Roxanne Rose, Day Camp Director / Admin Supervisor at (423) 430-8850; fax: (423) 430-8610
e-mail: mjohnson@rn.seattleymca.org
Operated by: YMCA of Greater Seattle, 909 4th Ave, Seattle, WA 98104 at (206) 382-5003 (#40939)

River Ranch (est 1952) ⛺ 🏠

Carnation, WA (King Co.); (425) 333-4553
Margie Culbertson, Director

Camp comments: Girl Scout camp serving all girls. Horseback riding, swimming, arts & crafts, nature activities & leadership development
Activities: Backpacking, Camping Skills/Outdoor Living, Challenge/Rope Courses, Climbing/Rappelling, Hiking, Horseback — Western, Leadership Development, Nature/Environment Studies, Wilderness Trips
Session lengths & capacity: 1/2, 1 & 2 week sessions; 190 campers
Clientele & fees: girls 7-17; families; Fees: C ⛺ 🐷
Contact: Jan Viney, Director at (800) 878-4682; fax: (425) 333-6236
e-mail: jancv@girlscoutstotem.org
Web site: www.girlscoutstotem.org
Operated by: Totem GSC, 3611 Woodland Park Ave N, Seattle, WA 98103 at (206) 633-5600

Group Rental Information
Site comments: Beautiful camp near Seattle available for non-member rental.
Seasons & Capacity: Spring 320, Fall 320, Winter 96
Facilities: Cabins, Double Occupancy, Lake, Lodges, Meeting Rooms, River
Programs: Boating, Challenge/Ropes Course, Swimming (#405)

Robbinswold (est 1928) ⛺ 🏠 🚐

Lilliwaup, WA; (360) 877-5455
Julie Russell, Director

Camp comments: Girl Scout camp, on Hood Canal serving all girls. Boating, ocean beach, nature activities,leadership development & more
Activities: Aquatic Activities, Backpacking, Camping Skills/Outdoor Living, Canoeing, Counselor Training (CIT), Hiking, Kayaking, Leadership Development, Nature/Environment Studies, Sailing
Session lengths & capacity: June-August; 1/2, 1 & 2 week sessions; 100 campers
Clientele & fees: girls 7-17; Fees: C ⛺ 🐷
Contact: Jan Viney, Director Outdoor Program Services at (800) 878-4682; fax: (425) 333-6236
e-mail: jancv@girlscoutstotem.org
Web site: www.girlscoutstotem.org
Operated by: Totem GSC, 3611 Woodland Park Ave N, Seattle, WA 98103 at (206) 633-5600

Group Rental Information
Site comments: Camp on the Hood Canal, available for non-member rental.
Seasons & Capacity: Spring 140, Summer 100, Fall 140, Winter 140
Facilities: A/V Equipment, Cabins, Dorm-Style, Hiking Trails, Kitchen Facilities, Lake, Lodges, Meeting Rooms, Ocean (#410)

Roganunda (est 1923) ⛺ 🏠

Naches, WA (Yakima Co.); (509) 658-2647
Ellen Mallonee, Director

Camp comments: Sunshine & mountain breezes, child centered programming, respecting diversity, accepting responsibility, caring staff
Activities: Archery, Arts/Crafts, Camping Skills/Outdoor Living, Challenge/Rope Courses, Counselor Training (CIT), Hiking, Horseback — Western, Nature/Environment Studies, Swimming — Recreational, Team Building
Session lengths & capacity: April-November; 1/2, 1 & 2 week sessions; 95 campers
Clientele & fees: girls 7-17; coed 7-17; families; Fees: C ⛺ 🐷
Contact: Ellen Mallonee, Camp Director at (509) 453-9151; fax: (509) 452-6021
e-mail: campfire@televar.com
Web site: www.yakima-campfire.com

Operated by: Camp Fire USA-Roganunda Cncl, 1001 South 3rd St, Yakima, WA 98901 at (800) 281-9151

Group Rental Information
Site comments: Sunshine and mountain breezes,scenic hikes,challenge course,small group focus building self esteem,mature caring staff.
Seasons & Capacity: Spring 125, Fall 125, Winter 50
Facilities: Cabins, Food Service, Hiking Trails, Kitchen Facilities, Pool, Tents
Programs: Challenge/Ropes Course, Horseback Riding, Swimming (#434)

Ross Point Baptist Camp

(est 1948) ⛺ 🏠

Post Falls, ID (Kootenai Co.); (208) 773-1655

Camp comments: To provide a glimpse of God's universe through hearing the gospel and experiencing Christian Community.
Activities: Aquatic Activities, Canoeing, Challenge/Rope Courses, Counselor Training (CIT), Music, Religious Study, Swimming — Recreational
Session lengths & capacity: 1 week sessions; 100 campers
Clientele & fees: coed 6-18; families; seniors; Fees: C ⛺ 🐷
Operated by: Washington Baptist Convention, 409 3rd Ave S Ste A, Kent, WA 98032-5843 at (253) 859-2226

Group Rental Information
Site comments: Private rooms with linens for 70 & cabin space for 140. 5 meeting rooms, gym, minigolf, bouldering wall, game field, RVs & tents. (#18895)

Sammamish YMCA Camp Terry ☀

Preston, WA

Camp comments: YMCA Terry is a day camp for children ages 6-12. It is located on the raging river in Preston, WA. Camping skills are a major component of our camp.
Activities: Archery, Arts/Crafts, Baseball/Softball, Bicycling/Biking, Canoeing, Challenge/Rope Courses, Climbing/Rappelling, Field Trips, Sports — Field & Team, Swimming — Recreational
Session lengths & capacity: June-August; 1 week sessions; 200 campers
Clientele & fees: coed 6-14; Fees: B ☀ 🐷
Contact: Kimm Klassen, Director, Child & Family Development at (425) 391-4840; fax: (425) 391-4815
e-mail: kkirschner@sam.seattleymca.org
Operated by: YMCA of Greater Seattle, 909 4th Ave, Seattle, WA 98104 at (206) 382-5003 (#4390)

Shoreline Family YMCA ☀

Shoreline, WA (King Co.); (206) 364-1700
Bryan O'Donnell, Director

Camp comments: We strive to put camp into day camp. Go on field trip, swimming, make new friends in a safe, supportive atmosphere.
Activities: Arts/Crafts, Camping Skills/Outdoor Living, Climbing/Rappelling, Field Trips, Hiking, Leadership Development, Nature/Environment Studies, Rafting, Sports — Field & Team, Swimming — Recreational
Session lengths & capacity: June-August; 1 week sessions
Clientele & fees: coed 5-14; Fees: B ☀ 🐷
Contact: YMCA Office at (206) 364-1700; fax: (206) 363-3142
Operated by: YMCA of Greater Seattle, 909 4th Ave, Seattle, WA 98104 at (206) 382-5003 (#3746)

Singing Wind (est 1958) ⛺ 🏠

Toledo, WA (Lewis Co.); (360) 864-4259
Patricia Watson, Director

Camp comments: Trained staff live with campers who choose activities. Camper council & newsletter highlight individuals.
Activities: Aquatic Activities, Archery, Arts/Crafts, Camping Skills/Outdoor Living, Counselor Training (CIT), Hiking, Leadership Development, Nature/Environment Studies, Swimming — Instructional, Swimming — Recreational
Session lengths & capacity: July-July; 1/2 & 1 week sessions; 85 campers
Clientele & fees: boys 5-15; girls 5-15; Fees: B ⛺ 🐷
Contact: Brian McCrady, Executive Director at (360) 425-3891; fax: (360) 425-3891
e-mail: campfire@tdn.com
Web site: www.lower.qpg.com
Operated by: Lower Columbia Cncl Camp Fire, 1407 Commerce Suite 106, Longview, WA 98632 at (360) 425-3890

Group Rental Information
Site comments: Mile long creek, heated pool, large craft house with fireplace, great lodge on 184 acres.
Seasons & Capacity: Spring 150, Summer 150, Fall 150
Facilities: Cabins, Dorm-Style, Hiking Trails, Kitchen Facilities, Lodges, Meeting Rooms, Playing Fields, Pool, River (#7241)

Sound View Camp (est 1987) ⛺ 🏠 🚐

Long Branch, WA (Pierce Co.); (253) 884-9202
Don McIntyre, Director

Camp comments: Beautiful ocean front in Puget Sound. Faith based programs with the NW's largest challenge course! Leadership training.
Activities: Aquatic Activities, Archery, Arts/Crafts, Canoeing, Challenge/Rope Courses, Horseback — Western, Leadership Development, Music, Sports — Field & Team, Wilderness Trips
Session lengths & capacity: 1 & 2 week sessions; 95 campers
Clientele & fees: coed 8-18; families; Fees: B, C, ⛺ 🐷
Contact: Don McIntyre, Director at (253) 884-9202; fax: (253) 884-9137
e-mail: don_at_soundview@compuserve.com
Web site: www.soundviewcamp.com
Operated by: Presbytery of Olympia, PO Box 5560, Lacey, WA 98509-5560 at (253) 884-9202

Group Rental Information
Facilities: A/V Equipment, Cabins, Dorm-Style, Double Occupancy, Food Service, Hiking Trails, Kitchen Facilities, Lodges, Meeting Rooms, Ocean, Tents
Programs: Boating, Challenge/Ropes Course, Swimming (#6344)

St Albans (est 1935) ⛺ 🏠 🚐

Belfair, WA (Mason Co.); (360) 275-1040
Michelle Van Alstine, Director

Camp comments: Freshwater lake, Viking boats, waterfront, horses, trip programs, care for earthskills, camper planning, FUN!
Activities: Archery, Arts/Crafts, Boating, Camping Skills/Outdoor Living, Canoeing, Counselor Training (CIT), Horseback — Western, Nature/Environment Studies, Swimming — Recreational, Wilderness Trips
Session lengths & capacity: June-August; 1/2, 1 & 2 week sessions; 160 campers
Clientele & fees: girls 7-17; Fees: B, C, D ⛺ 🐷
Contact: Stephanie Winters, Resident Camp Administration at (360) 943-0490; fax: (360) 943-8653
e-mail: swinters@gsppc.org
Web site: www.gsppc.org
Operated by: Girl Scouts Pacific Peaks Cncl, 5326 Littlerock Rd SW, Tumwater, WA 98512-7394 at (360) 943-0490

Group Rental Information
Facilities: Cabins, Double Occupancy, Kitchen Facilities, Lake, Lodges, Playing Fields, Tents
Programs: Boating, Swimming (#448)

Sunset Lake (est 1957)

Wilkeson, WA (Pierce Co.); (360) 829-0311
Craig Heinrich, Director

Camp comments: Noncompetitive program focuses on group cooperation & encouragement, affirming Christian values & healthful lifestyle.
Activities: Aquatic Activities, Archery, Bicycling/Biking, Camping Skills/Outdoor Living, Ceramics/Pottery, Computer, Drama, Fishing, Horseback — Western, Waterskiing
Session lengths & capacity: June-August; 1 week sessions; 100 campers
Clientele & fees: coed 8-16; families; Fees: **B A**
Contact: Ask for Camp Registrar, Camp Registrar at (360) 829-0311; fax: (360) 829-0558
e-mail: pc7@tx3.com
Web site: www.sunsetlake.org
Operated by: Sunset Lake Camp, PO Box 90, Wilkeson, WA 98396 at (360) 829-0311
Group Rental Information
Facilities: A/V Equipment, Cabins, Hiking Trails, Kitchen Facilities, Lake, Meeting Rooms, Playing Fields
Programs: Challenge/Ropes Course, Environmental Education, Swimming (#3572)

The Firs Chalet (est 1958)

Mt Baker, WA (Whatcom Co.); (360) 733-6840
Bob Anderson, Director
Contact: e-mail: info@thefirs.org
Web site: www.thefirs.org
Operated by: The Firs Bible and Missionary, 4605 Cable Street, Bellingham, WA 98226 at (360) 733-6840
Group Rental Information
Site comments: Located in a Nat'l recreation area with view of N Cascades Nat'l Park,hiking,sight seeing,adjacent to downhill ski area.
Facilities: Dorm-Style, Food Service, Hiking Trails, Kitchen Facilities, Meeting Rooms
Programs: Winter Sports (#2640)

Twinlow (est 1928)

Rathdrum, ID (Kootenai Co.); (208) 687-1146
Ben & Claudia Moore, Director

Camp comments: Lake frontage with many water activities, challenge course, large activity field, basketball, variety of lodging facilities.
Activities: Aquatic Activities, Arts/Crafts, Basketball, Boating, Canoeing, Challenge/Rope Courses, Fishing, Kayaking, Sports — Field & Team, Swimming — Recreational
Session lengths & capacity: January-December; 1/2 & 1 week sessions

---

ICON LEGEND

☀ Day Camp

A Resident Camp

⌂ Facilities Available To Rent

🚐 Transportation Available

🐷 Financial Aid Available

FEE RANGES PER WEEK

A $0-75

B $75-200

C $201-350

D $351-500

E $501-650

F   over $650

Clientele & fees: families; seniors; single adults; Fees: **B A**
Contact: Ben & Claudia Moore, Directors at (208) 687-1146; fax: (208) 687-2768
e-mail: twinlowcamp@integrityonline4.com
Web site: www.pnwumc.org
Operated by: United Methodist Conference, 2112 Third Ave, Seattle, WA 98121-2333 at (800) 755-7710
Group Rental Information
Site comments: Lake frontage with many water activities.
Seasons & Capacity: Spring 140, Summer 150, Fall 140, Winter 100
Facilities: Cabins, Dorm-Style, Double Occupancy, Food Service, Kitchen Facilities, Lake, Linens, Lodges, Meeting Rooms, Playing Fields
Programs: Boating, Challenge/Ropes Course, Environmental Education, Swimming, Winter Sports (#3501)

University Family YMCA Day Cmp

Seattle, WA (King Co.); (206) 985-0075
Jen Sawyer, Director

Camp comments: North Seattle family YMCA provides 'camp' experience in day camp setting.Emphasis on nature, self-confidence and fun!
Activities: Archery, Arts/Crafts, Camping Skills/Outdoor Living, Canoeing, Field Trips, Hiking, Nature/Environment Studies, Swimming — Recreational
Session lengths & capacity: June-August; 1 week sessions; 120 campers
Clientele & fees: coed 5-12; Fees: **B ☀ 🐷**
Contact: Jen Sawyer, Camp Director at (206) 524-1400; fax: (206) 524-8613
e-mail: jsawyer@univ.seattleymca.org
Operated by: YMCA of Greater Seattle, 909 4th Ave, Seattle, WA 98104 at (206) 382-5003 (#441)

Volasuca Volunteers Of America (est 1941)

Sultan, WA (Snohomish Co.); (360) 793-0646
Chris Shroy, Director

Camp comments: A camp for every child, nurturing self-esteem, leadership and social development. Financial assistance available.
Activities: Aquatic Activities, Arts/Crafts, Baseball/Softball, Basketball, Camping Skills/Outdoor Living, Counselor Training (CIT), Hiking, Leadership Development, Nature/Environment Studies, Swimming — Recreational
Session lengths & capacity: June-August; 1 week sessions; 95 campers
Clientele & fees: coed 6-13; families; single adults; Fees: **A, B, C A 🐷**
Contact: Chris Shroy, Director at (360) 793-0646; fax: (360) 793-8919
e-mail: camp@voaww.org
Web site: www.voaww.org
Operated by: Volunteers of America, 2802 Broadway, Everett, WA 98201-0839 at (425) 259-3191
Group Rental Information
Site comments: A great place for your youth group activities.
Seasons & Capacity: Spring 80, Winter 40
Facilities: Dorm-Style, Double Occupancy, Food Service, Hiking Trails, Kitchen Facilities, Meeting Rooms, Playing Fields, Pool, River
Programs: Challenge/Ropes Course, Environmental Education, Swimming (#429)

West Seattle YMCA Day Camp (est 1920)

Seattle, WA (King Co.); (206) 935-6000

Camp comments: Traditional outdoor day camp in natural setting with emphasis on outdoor recreation and education. Convenient drop off locations and hours.
Activities: Arts/Crafts, Backpacking, Camping Skills/Outdoor Living, Drama, Field Trips, Leadership Development, Nature/Environment Studies, Performing Arts, Swimming — Recreational
Session lengths & capacity: June-August; 1 week sessions; 250 campers
Clientele & fees: coed 6-12; Fees: **B ☀ 🐷**
Contact: Robin Reynolds, Family Programs Director at (206) 935-6000; fax: (206) 938-1676
Operated by: YMCA of Greater Seattle, 909 4th Ave, Seattle, WA 98104 at (206) 382-5003 (#392)

YMCA Camp Colman (est 1912)

Longbranch, WA (Pierce Co.); (253) 884-3844
Koffi Kpachavi, Director

Camp comments: On 1/2 mile of beach-front facing west. Swimming & boating in salt water lagoon. Environmental ed prog year round.
Activities: Aquatic Activities, Archery, Arts/Crafts, Backpacking, Canoeing, Challenge/Rope Courses, International Culture, Leadership Development, Nature/Environment Studies
Session lengths & capacity: June-August; 1/2 & 1 week sessions; 120 campers
Clientele & fees: boys 6-18; girls 6-18; coed 6-18; families; seniors; Fees: **C A 🐷**
Contact: Koffi Kpachavi, Director at (253) 884-3844; fax: (253) 884-5757
e-mail: kkpachavi@cs.seattleymca.org
Operated by: YMCA of Greater Seattle, 909 4th Ave, Seattle, WA 98104 at (206) 382-5003
Group Rental Information
Site comments: Kids come first at YMCA Camp Colman
Seasons & Capacity: Spring 120, Summer 120, Fall 120, Winter 70
Facilities: Cabins, Food Service, Hiking Trails, Lake, Meeting Rooms
Programs: Boating, Environmental Education (#446)

YMCA Camp Dudley (est 1938)

Naches, WA; (509) 672-2480
Dustin Yeager, Director

Camp comments: Located in the beautiful Cascade Mountains. We focus on developing self-esteem, leadership, social skills and FUN!
Activities: Archery, Bicycling/Biking, Canoeing, Challenge/Rope Courses, Counselor Training (CIT), Hiking, Leadership Development
Session lengths & capacity: June-August; 1/2, 1 & 2 week sessions; 80 campers
Clientele & fees: coed 5-16; families; Fees: **C A 🐷**
Contact: Dustin Yeager, Camp Director at (509) 248-1202; fax: (509) 248-0125
e-mail: rpcyeag@yahoo.com
Operated by: Yakima Family YMCA, 5 N Naches Ave, Yakima, WA 98901 at (509) 248-1202
Group Rental Information
Seasons & Capacity: Spring 144, Summer 144, Fall 144, Winter 137
Facilities: Cabins, Dorm-Style, Food Service, Hiking Trails, Kitchen Facilities, Lake, Lodges, Meeting Rooms, Playing Fields, Pool
Programs: Boating, Challenge/Ropes Course, Environmental Education, Swimming (#2999)

YMCA Camp Orkila

(est 1906)

Seattle, WA (King Co.); (206) 382-5009
David Hembree, Director

Camp comments: Breathtaking setting in Washington's San Juan Islands. Emphasis on out-of-camp trips. Diverse program and caring staff.
Activities: Archery, Arts/Crafts, Camping Skills/Outdoor Living, Challenge/Rope Courses, Climbing/Rappelling, Counselor Training (CIT), Horseback — Western, Leadership Development, Riflery, Sailing
Session lengths & capacity: 2 & 3 week sessions; 450 campers
Clientele & fees: boys 8-18; girls 8-18; coed 8-18; families; Fees: C △ 🐷
Contact: Geoff Ball, Director at (360) 376-2478; fax: (360) 376-2267
Operated by: YMCA of Greater Seattle, 909 4th Ave, Seattle, WA 98104 at (206) 382-5003

Group Rental Information
Facilities: A/V Equipment, Cabins, Food Service, Hiking Trails, Linens, Lodges, Meeting Rooms, Ocean, Playing Fields
Programs: Boating, Challenge/Ropes Course, Environmental Education (#425)

YMCA Camp Reed (est 1915)

Deer Park, WA (Spokane Co.); (509) 276-5262
Dan Crosbie, Director

Camp comments: Breathtaking setting in Eastern Washington. Traditional camp; out of camp trip; caring staff.
Activities: Archery, Arts/Crafts, Camping Skills/Outdoor Living, Ceramics/Pottery, Challenge/Rope Courses, Climbing/Rappelling, Horseback — Western, Leadership Development, Riflery, Wilderness Trips
Session lengths & capacity: 8 week sessions; 205 campers
Clientele & fees: boys 8-14; girls 8-14; Fees: C △ 🐷
Contact: Brad Rupp, Camp Service Director at (509) 838-3577; fax: (509) 625-1424
Web site: www.ymcaspokane.org
Operated by: YMCA of the Inland Empire, North 507 Howard, Spokane, WA 99201-0898 at (509) 838-3577

Group Rental Information
Seasons & Capacity: Spring 200, Summer 200, Fall 200
Facilities: A/V Equipment, Cabins, Food Service, Hiking Trails, Kitchen Facilities, Lake, Meeting Rooms, Playing Fields
Programs: Boating, Challenge/Ropes Course, Swimming (#6302)

YMCA Camp Seymour (est 1905)

Gig Harbor, WA (Pierce Co.); (253) 884-3392
Aaron Keating, Director

Camp comments: Progressive, values-oriented, camper-centered programs combining adventure, friendship, and growth. The days we create are as unique as each of our campers.
Activities: Archery, Arts/Crafts, Boating, Camping Skills/Outdoor Living, Challenge/Rope Courses, Leadership Development, Riflery, Swimming — Recreational, Travel/Tour, Wilderness Trips
Session lengths & capacity: June-August; 1/2, 1 & 2 week sessions; 168 campers
Clientele & fees: coed 6-18; families; Fees: C △ 🐷
Contact: Claire Bowen, Camp Registrar at (253) 884-3392; fax: (253) 460-8897
e-mail: campseymour@ymcatacoma.org
Web site: www.ymcatacoma.org
Operated by: YMCA of Tacoma Pierce County, 1002 S Pearl St, Tacoma, WA 98465 at (253) 564-9622

Group Rental Information
Site comments: Offers amenities of home in a beautiful environment. A perfect setting for those who appreciate a relaxed outdoor atmoshpere. Available September-June.
Facilities: A/V Equipment, Cabins, Double Occupancy, Food Service, Hiking Trails, Kitchen Facilities, Lodges, Meeting Rooms, Playing Fields, Tents
Programs: Boating, Challenge/Ropes Course, Environmental Education, Swimming (#387)

YMCA Day Camp Bellevue

Bellevue, WA; (425) 746-9900
Apryl Brinkley, Director

Camp comments: YMCA fun on several sites. Values-based program in outdoor setting for youth. Specialty and adventure programs offered.
Activities: Arts/Crafts, Bicycling/Biking, Camping Skills/Outdoor Living, Field Trips, Hiking, Skating, Soccer, Swimming — Recreational, Team Building
Session lengths & capacity: 1 week sessions
Clientele & fees: coed 5-14; Fees: B 🌞 🐷
Contact: Heidi Fray, Senior Program Director at (425) 746-9900; fax: (425) 746-6265
Operated by: YMCA of Greater Seattle, 909 4th Ave, Seattle, WA 98104 at (206) 382-5003 (#6218)

YMCA Day Camp Puyallup

(est 1989)

Puyallup, WA (Pierce Co.); (253) 841-9622
Elizabeth Curtain, Director

Camp comments: Exciting theme-based activities in 4 locations. Special programming, age 10-12. Separate teen camp has an overnight trips.
Activities: Archery, Arts/Crafts, Camping Skills/Outdoor Living, Community Service, Field Trips, Hiking, Music, Nature/Environment Studies, Swimming — Recreational, Team Building
Session lengths & capacity: June-August; 1 & 2 week sessions; 165 campers
Clientele & fees: coed 4-15; Fees: B 🌞 🐷
Contact: Elizabeth Curtain, Program Director at (253) 460-8960; fax: (253) 770-8993
e-mail: ecurtin@ymcatacoma.org
Web site: www.ymcatacoma.org
Operated by: YMCA of Tacoma Pierce County, 1002 S Pearl St, Tacoma, WA 98465 at (253) 564-9622 (#2034)

YMCA Lakewood Day Camp

(est 1991)

Tacoma, WA (Pierce Co.); (253) 584-9622
Allison Ramsey, Director

Camp comments: Day camps for ages 3-4, 5-8, 9-12 & 12-15! Lots of fun activities and field trips at several locations!
Activities: Aquatic Activities, Arts/Crafts, Camping Skills/Outdoor Living, Community Service, Field Trips, Nature/Environment Studies, Swimming — Recreational
Session lengths & capacity: 1 week sessions; 166 campers
Clientele & fees: coed 3-15; Fees: B 🌞 🐷
Contact: Allison Ramsey, Program Coordinator at (206) 584-9622; fax: (206) 589-1240
e-mail: aramsey@ymcatacoma.org
Web site: www.ymcatacoma.org
Operated by: YMCA of Tacoma Pierce County, 1002 S Pearl St, Tacoma, WA 98465 at (253) 564-9622 (#3208)

YMCA Tacoma Day Camp

(est 1977)

Tacoma, WA (Pierce Co.); (253) 564-9622
Jessica Smeall, Director

Camp comments: Traditional day camp emphasizes fun, noncompetitive activities. Child-focused staff. Camper to staff ratio is 6:1.

Activities: Arts/Crafts, Camping Skills/Outdoor Living, Counselor Training (CIT), Dance, Drama, Field Trips, Leadership Development, Swimming — Recreational, Team Building
Session lengths & capacity: June-August; 1/2, 1 & 2 week sessions; 100 campers
Clientele & fees: coed 4-14; Fees: B, C 🌞 🐷
Contact: Jaclyn Vargo, Program Director at (253) 564-9622; fax: (253) 460-8854
Web site: www.ymcatacoma.org
Operated by: YMCA of Tacoma Pierce County, 1002 S Pearl St, Tacoma, WA 98465 at (253) 564-9622 (#4038)

Zanika Lache (est 1932)

Leavenworth, WA (Chelan Co.); (509) 663-1609
Wendy Borden, Director

Camp comments: Mountain setting on Lake Wenatchee, caring camp, traditional Camp Fire program, mature staff.
Activities: Aquatic Activities, Archery, Arts/Crafts, Backpacking, Camping Skills/Outdoor Living, Challenge/Rope Courses, Counselor Training (CIT), Hiking, Leadership Development, Nature/Environment Studies
Session lengths & capacity: June-August; 1/2 & 1 week sessions; 85 campers
Clientele & fees: coed 6-17; Fees: B, C △ 🐷
Contact: Wendy Borden & Tracy Bowlware, Outdoor Programs Director at (509) 663-1609; fax: (509) 664-3038
e-mail: camp4@crcwnet.com
Web site: www.ncwcampfire.org
Operated by: Camp Fire USA NCW Council, PO Box 1734, Wenatchee, WA 98807 at (509) 663-1609

Group Rental Information
Site comments: Camp Zanika Lache, located on a beautiful lake, surrounded by the Wenatchee National Forest. Facilities offer secluded, rustic environment perfect for rentals.
Seasons & Capacity: Spring 125, Fall 125
Facilities: Cabins, Food Service, Hiking Trails, Kitchen Facilities, Lake, Lodges, Meeting Rooms, Tents
Programs: Boating, Challenge/Ropes Course, Environmental Education, Swimming (#416)

West Virginia

Bluestone Conference Center

(est 1953)

Hinton, WV (Summers Co.); (304) 466-0660
Mark Miller, Director

Camp comments: Space is available for retreats and conferences, spring and fall. A relaxed mountain setting with quality food service.
Activities: Arts/Crafts, Backpacking, Camping Skills/Outdoor Living, Drama, Hiking, Leadership Development, Religious Study, Swimming — Recreational, Travel/Tour
Session lengths & capacity: 1/2 & 1 week sessions; 200 campers
Clientele & fees: coed 7-18; families; Fees: B △
Contact: Mark Miller, Director at (304) 466-0660;
Web site: www.bluestonepwv.com
Operated by: Presbytery of West Virginia, 520 Second Ave, So Charleston, WV 25951 at (304) 744-7634

Group Rental Information
Facilities: A/V Equipment, Cabins, Food Service, Hiking Trails, Lodges, Meeting Rooms, Playing Fields, Pool
Programs: Swimming (#3900)

Burgundy Wildlife Center

(est 1962) △

Capon Bridge, WV (Hampshire Co.);
(304) 856-3758
Lavinia Schoene, Director

Camp comments: Explore nature in a remote valley with dynamic, knowledgeable staff. High staff:camper ratio builds strong community, indiv. projects, variety and laughter.
Activities: Arts/Crafts, Backpacking, Camping Skills/Outdoor Living, Drawing/Painting, Hiking, Leadership Development, Nature/Environment Studies, Photography, Swimming — Recreational, Team Building
Session lengths & capacity: June-August; 1 & 2 week sessions; 32 campers
Clientele & fees: coed 8-15; seniors; single adults; Fees: E △ ⬤
Contact: Lavinia Schoene, Director at (703) 960-3431; fax: (703) 960-5056
e-mail: bcws2@earthlink.net
Web site: camppage.com/bcws
Operated by: Burgundy Farm Country Day Sch, 3700 Burgundy Rd, Alexandria, VA 22303 at (703) 960-3431 (#26923)

Camp Alleghany (est 1922) △ 🚐

Lewisburg, WV (Greenbrier Co.); (304) 645-1316
Samuel C Dawson, III, CCD, Director

Camp comments: Magical place to make new friends. Structured program. Great staff, high return rate. Camper-counselor ratio 4:1.
Activities: Archery, Arts/Crafts, Canoeing, Challenge/Rope Courses, Dance, Drama, Nature/Environment Studies, Riflery, Swimming — Instructional, Tennis
Session lengths & capacity: June-August; 3 week sessions; 220 campers
Clientele & fees: girls 8-16; families; Fees: E △
Contact: Samuel C Dawson, III, CCD, Associate Director at (540) 898-4782; fax: (540) 898-5475
e-mail: campghany@aol.com
Web site: www.campalleghany.com
Operated by: Camp Alleghany, PO Box 664, Fredricksburg, VA 22404 at (540) 898-4782 (#1786)

Camp Greenbrier For Boys

(est 1898) ☀ △ 🚐

Alderson, WV (Greenbrier Co.); (304) 445-7168
William J. Harvie, Director

Camp comments: Individualized prog, mountain setting. 3:1 camper/staff ratio. Boys have fun in safe & supportive atmosphere. Great food

---

ICON LEGEND

☀ Day Camp

△ Resident Camp

🏠 Facilities Available To Rent

🚐 Transportation Available

🐷 Financial Aid Available

FEE RANGES PER WEEK

A $0-75

B $75-200

C $201-350

D $351-500

E $501-650

F over $650

Activities: Archery, Arts/Crafts, Baseball/Softball, Basketball, Camping Skills/Outdoor Living, Canoeing, Climbing/Rappelling, Riflery, Soccer, Tennis
Session lengths & capacity: June-August; 3 & 7 week sessions; 150 campers
Clientele & fees: boys 7-15; Fees: E ☀ Fees: E △
Contact: William J Harvie, Director at (757) 789-3477; fax: (757) 789-3477
e-mail: woofus@juno.com
Web site: www.campgreenbrier.com
Operated by: Camp Greenbrier for Boys, Box 585, Exmore, VA 23350 at (757) 789-3477 (#1791)

Camp Rim Rock (est 1952) △ 🚐

Yellow Spring, WV (Hampshire Co.); (800) 662-4650
Jim Matheson & Deborah Matheson, Director

Camp comments: All girls. Supportive, noncompetitive atmosphere in beautiful mountain setting. Excellent traditional camp with strong riding & performing arts programs.
Activities: Aquatic Activities, Archery, Arts/Crafts, Dance, Drama, Horseback — English, Performing Arts, Soccer, Swimming — Instructional, Tennis
Session lengths & capacity: June-August; 1, 2, 3, 4, 5, 6 week sessions; 280 campers
Clientele & fees: girls 6-17; families; Fees: F △
Contact: Jim or Deborah Matheson, Executive Director/Director at (800) 662-4650;
fax: (304) 856-3201
e-mail: office@camprimrock.com
Web site: www.camprimrock.com
Operated by: Camp Rim Rock, Box 69, Yellow Spring, WV 26865-0069 at (800) 662-4650 (#2503)

Camp Tall Timbers (est 1970) △ 🚐

High View, WV (Hampshire Co.); (800) 862-2678
Glenn Smith, Director

Camp comments: Mountain setting on 120 acre campus. 90 miles from Washington DC. 35 activities. Warm, caring staff and directors.
Activities: Arts/Crafts, Baseball/Softball, Basketball, Dance, Drama, Horseback — English, Horseback — Western, Sports — Field & Team, Tennis, Waterskiing
Session lengths & capacity: June-August; 2 & 4 week sessions; 175 campers
Clientele & fees: boys 7-15; girls 7-15; coed 7-15; Fees: F △
Contact: Glenn Smith, Director at (800) 862-2678; fax: (301) 681-6662
e-mail: funcamp@aol.com
Web site: www.camptalltimbers.com
Operated by: Camp Tall Timbers, 11615 Fulham St, Silver Spring, MD 20902 at (301) 649-5577 (#1843)

Camp Twin Creeks (est 1944) △ 🚐

Marlinton, WV; (304) 799-6156
Gordon and Fran Josey, Director

Camp comments: We offer chidren a wonderful opportunity to spend their summer in a place of spectacular beauty, adventure & fun, set in the Allegheny Mountains of W. Virginia
Activities: Archery, Arts/Crafts, Boating, Canoeing, Golf, Horseback — English, Model Rocketry, Sailing, Swimming — Instructional, Swimming — Recreational, Tennis
Session lengths & capacity: June-August; 2 week sessions; 220 campers
Clientele & fees: boys 7-16; Fees: F △
Contact: Gordon & Fran Josey, Owner/Directors at (800) 451-8806; fax: (914) 345-2120
Web site: www.camptwincreeks.com
Operated by: Twin Creeks LLC, PO Box 219, Elmsford, NY 10523 at (914) 345-0707 (#770)

Emma Kaufmann Camp △ 🏠

Morgantown, WV (Monogalia Co.); (304) 599-4435
Activities: Aquatic Activities, Camping Skills/Outdoor Living, Challenge/Rope Courses, Horseback — English, Horseback — Western, Swimming — Instructional, Swimming — Recreational
Contact: Web site: www.emmakaufmanncamp.com
Operated by: Emma Kaufmann Camp, 297 Emma Kaufmann Camp Rd, Morgantown, WV 26508 at (412) 521-8010

Group Rental Information
Facilities: Cabins, Dorm-Style, Food Service, Kitchen Facilities, Lake, Meeting Rooms, Playing Fields, Pool
Programs: Boating, Challenge/Ropes Course, Swimming (#33102)

Salvation Army-Camp Tomahawk △ 🏠

Hedgesville, WV
Major Art Denhale, Director

Camp comments: The Salvation Army's Camp Tomahawk provides a Christian-based environment where character-building & socialization skills are taught in the great out-of-doors.
Activities: Archery, Arts/Crafts, Boating, Challenge/Rope Courses, Music, Religious Study, Swimming — Recreational
Operated by: The Salvation Army, 814 Light St, Baltimore, MD 21230 at (410) 347-9944

Group Rental Information
Facilities: A/V Equipment, Cabins, Dorm-Style, Double Occupancy, Hiking Trails, Kitchen Facilities, Lodges, Meeting Rooms, Playing Fields, Pool
Programs: Challenge/Ropes Course (#42334)

The Salvation Army-Camp Happy △ 🏠

Scott Depot, WV
Capt Roy Williams, Director

Camp comments: CHV offers rich & varied programs which bring out the best in children by embracing new ideas, values & lasting friendships.
Activities: Archery, Bicycling/Biking, Challenge/Rope Courses, Fishing, Hiking, Religious Study, Swimming — Recreational
Contact: Capt Kathy Williams, Director of Women's Services at (304) 343-4548; fax: (304) 343-6701
Operated by: The Salvation Army, 814 Light St, Baltimore, MD 21230 at (410) 347-9944

Group Rental Information
Site comments: Picturesque WV mountains, clean air & varied camp amenities provide the perfect backdrop for retreats, reunions, meetings, picnics, etc.
Seasons & Capacity: Spring 160, Summer 160, Fall 160
Facilities: Cabins, Hiking Trails, Kitchen Facilities, Lake, Pool
Programs: Challenge/Ropes Course, Swimming (#33649)

White Rock (est 1945) △

High View, WV (Hampshire Co.); (304) 856-2854
Bonnie J DeBoard, Director

Camp comments: Wooden terrain along river. Platform tents/cabins/lodge/traditional program; Exciting field trips, leadership training.
Activities: Arts/Crafts, Camping Skills/Outdoor Living, Canoeing, Counselor Training (CIT), Dance, Field Trips, Hiking, Horseback — Western, Nature/Environment Studies, Swimming — Recreational
Session lengths & capacity: 1 week sessions; 144 campers
Clientele & fees: girls 6-18; Fees: B, C △

Contact: Bonnie J DeBoard, Director at
(304) 263-8833; fax: (304) 263-8836
Web site: www.intrepid.net/~shawnee
Operated by: Girl Scouts of Shawnee Council, 153
McMillan Court, Martinsburg, WV 25401 at
(304) 263-8833 (#2489)

YMCA Camp Horseshoe

(est 1940)

St George, WV (Tucker Co.); (304) 478-2481
David King, Director

Camp comments: Teen leadership-service our
specialty. General recreation for 7-12 yrs old.
Excellent staff. Mountain location.
Activities: Archery, Arts/Crafts, Challenge/Rope
Courses, Community Service, Hiking, Leadership
Development, Music, Riflery, Team Building
Session lengths & capacity: June-August; 1 week
sessions; 150 campers
Clientele & fees: boys 7-18; girls 7-18; coed 7-18;
Fees: B △
Contact: David King, Director at (304) 478-2481;
fax: (304) 478-4446
e-mail: david@hi-y.org
Web site: www.hi-y.org
Operated by: Ohio West Virginia YMCA, Rt 2 Box
138, St George, WV 26287 at (304) 478-2481

Group Rental Information

Site comments: Beautiful quiet mountain location
for your group. Delicious home cooking.
Seasons & Capacity: Spring 150, Fall 150, Winter
150
Facilities: Cabins, Dorm-Style, Double Occupancy,
Food Service, Hiking Trails, Lodges, Meeting
Rooms, Playing Fields, River
Programs: Challenge/Ropes Course,
Environmental Education (#1795)

Wisconsin

American Collegiate Adventures

Madison, WI; (800) 509-7867
Jason Lubar, Director
Activities: Academics, Aerobics/Exercise,
Computer, Drama, Field Trips, Golf, Language
Studies, Team Building, Tennis
Contact: Jason Lubar, Director of Summer
Programs at (800) 509-7867; fax: (847) 509-9908
e-mail: acasumr@aol.com
Web site: www.acasumr.com
Operated by: American Collegiate Adv, 666
Dundee Road Suite 803, Northbrook, IL 60062 at
(847) 509-9900 (#28954)

Amnicon (est 1966)

South Range, WI (Douglas Co.); (715) 364-2602
Alana Butler, Director

Camp comments: Trip Camp. High Adventure.
Serving the Lutheran Church & greater community
with canoe & backpack trips in the western Lake
Superior area.
Activities: Backpacking, Camping Skills/Outdoor
Living, Canoeing, Challenge/Rope Courses,
Counselor Training (CIT), Kayaking, Religious
Study, Team Building, Tennis, Wilderness Trips
Session lengths & capacity: 1/2, 1 & 2 week
sessions; 75 campers
Clientele & fees: boys 12-18; girls 12-18;
coed 12-18; families; single adults;
Fees: B, C △ 🛥
Contact: Simon Gretton/ Steve Lindstrom, Director
at (715) 364-2602; fax: (715) 364-2652
e-mail: amnicon@usa.net
Operated by: Central Lutheran Church, 333 12th
Street South, Minneapolis, MN 55404 at
(612) 870-4416

Group Rental Information

Seasons & Capacity: Spring 35, Summer 75, Fall
35, Winter 35
Facilities: Cabins, Dorm-Style, Food Service,
Hiking Trails, Lake, Lodges, Meeting Rooms, River,
Tents
Programs: Challenge/Ropes Course, Swimming,
Winter Sports (#8356)

B'nai B'rith Beber Camp

(est 1976)

Mukwonago, WI (Walworth Co.); (262) 363-6800
Danielle Litt, Director

Camp comments: Camper chosen specialty prog.
in water sports, land sports, creative arts. All in a
supportive, fun, family atmosphere.
Activities: Arts/Crafts, Baseball/Softball, Basketball,
Bicycling/Biking, Climbing/Rappelling, Horseback
— Western, Radio/TV/Video, Sailing, Tennis,
Waterskiing
Session lengths & capacity: June-August; 2, 4 &
8 week sessions; 200 campers
Clientele & fees: coed 7-17; Fees: E △
Contact: Danielle Litt, Director at (847) 498-1441;
fax: (847) 564-8285
e-mail: bebercamp@aol.com
Web site: www.bebercamp.com
Operated by: Bnai Brith Henry Monsky Found,
1901 Raymond Drive Suite 15, Northbrook, IL
60062 at (847) 498-1441

Group Rental Information

Facilities: Double Occupancy, Food Service,
Hiking Trails, Lake, Lodges, Meeting Rooms
Programs: Environmental Education (#1558)

Bethel Horizons (est 1969)

Dodgeville, WI (Iowa Co.); (608) 935-5885
Pastor Duane E Hanson, Director

Camp comments: Year round, all education &
adventure programs. Excellent nature center.
Diverse summer prog. Adult pottery workshop.
Activities: Bicycling/Biking, Camping
Skills/Outdoor Living, Canoeing, Caving,
Ceramics/Pottery, Challenge/Rope Courses,
Climbing/Rappelling, Hiking, Nature/Environment
Studies, Team Building
Session lengths & capacity: June-August; 1 week
sessions; 70 campers
Clientele & fees: boys 8-16; girls 8-16; coed 8-16;
families; Fees: C △
Contact: Pastor Duane E Hanson, Executive
Director at (608) 257-3577; fax: (608) 257-4044
e-mail: bhorizons@bethel-madison.org
Web site: www.bethel-madison.org
Operated by: Bethel Horizons, 312 Wisconsin Ave,
Madison, WI 53703-2108 at (608) 257-3577

Group Rental Information

Site comments: Three retreat centers, 473 acres
adjacent to state park. Specialized adventure &
environmental education programs.
Seasons & Capacity: Spring 110, Summer 150,
Fall 110, Winter 110
Facilities: Food Service, Hiking Trails, Linens,
Lodges, Meeting Rooms
Programs: Challenge/Ropes Course,
Environmental Education (#3805)

Bright Horizons Summer Camp

(est 1980)

Williams Bay, WI (Walworth Co.); (414) 245-5531
Valerie C. Beckley, Director
Activities: Aquatic Activities, Arts/Crafts, Camping
Skills/Outdoor Living, Counselor Training (CIT),
Nature/Environment Studies, Swimming —
Recreational, Team Building
Session lengths & capacity: July-July; 1 week
sessions; 60 campers
Clientele & fees: boys 7-13; girls 7-13; coed 7-13
Contact: Howard D Anderson, President at
(312) 345-1100; fax: (312) 345-1103

Web site: www.sicklecelldisease-il.org
Operated by: Sickle Cell Disease Assn of IL, 200 N
Michigan Ave Ste 605, Chicago, IL 60601 at
(312) 345-1100 (#5644)

Camp Alice Chester

(est 1924)

East Troy, WI; (262) 642-5845
Adrea Yanacheck, Director

Camp comments: Outdoor action, fun & friends in
a all girl environment that builds courage,
confidence, independence & skills for life.
Activities: Aquatic Activities, Archery, Arts/Crafts,
Boating, Camping Skills/Outdoor Living, Counselor
Training (CIT), Horseback — Western,
Nature/Environment Studies, Sports — Field &
Team, Wilderness Trips
Session lengths & capacity: June-August; 1/2, 1 &
2 week sessions; 150 campers
Clientele & fees: girls 8-17; Fees: B, C △ 🛥
Contact: Jenny Sliker, Outdoor Program Manager
at (414) 476-1050; fax: (414) 476-5958
e-mail: jsliker@girlscoutsmilwaukee.org
Web site: www.girlscoutsmilwaukee.org
Operated by: GS of Milwaukee Area Inc, 131 S
69th St, Milwaukee, WI 53214 at (414) 476-1050

Group Rental Information

Site comments: Limited outside rental use for Girl
Scouts and other youth groups. Contact the Girl
Scouts of Milwaukee Area at 414-476-1050 ext 153
for further information.
Seasons & Capacity: Spring 60, Fall 60, Winter 50
Facilities: Cabins, Hiking Trails, Lake, Playing
Fields, Tents
Programs: Boating, Swimming (#25100)

Camp Birch Trails

Irma, WI (Lincoln Co.); (920) 734-4559
Carrie Schroyer, Director

Camp comments: Camp Birch Trails offers a day to
3 week programming for girls ages 6-17. Come
enjoy fun and adventure in the sun in beautiful
northern Wisconsin.
Activities: Archery, Arts/Crafts, Backpacking,
Bicycling/Biking, Boating, Camping Skills/Outdoor
Living, Canoeing, Counselor Training (CIT),
Horseback — Western, Wilderness Trips
Session lengths & capacity: June-August; 1/2, 1,
2 & 3 week sessions; 120 campers
Clientele & fees: girls 6-17; families; Fees: B △
Contact: Carrie Schroyer, Camp Director at
(800) 924-1211; fax: (920) 734-1304
e-mail: cschroyer@girlscoutsfoxriverarea.org
Web site: www.girlscoutsfoxriverarea.org
Operated by: Girl Scouts Fox River Area, 4693 N
Lynndale Dr, Appleton, WI 54913-9614 at
(920) 734-4559 (#8358)

Camp Birchrock (est 1947)

Rhinelander, WI (Oneida Co.); (715) 282-5547
Traci Wehrman, Director

Camp comments: Rustic camp specializing in fun,
self-esteem building & development of self-reliance
skills in a noncompetitive setting.
Activities: Aquatic Activities, Arts/Crafts, Camping
Skills/Outdoor Living, Canoeing, Fishing, Hiking,
Leadership Development, Nature/Environment
Studies, Sports — Field & Team, Swimming —
Recreational
Session lengths & capacity: June-July; 1/2 &
1 week sessions; 40 campers
Clientele & fees: coed 4-14; Fees: B ☀ Fees: B △
Contact: Traci Wehrman, Executive Director at
(715) 362-3513;
Operated by: Camp Fire USA Oneida Cnl Inc,
PO Box 658, Rhinelander, WI 54501 at
(715) 362-3513

Group Rental Information

Facilities: Cabins, Dorm-Style, Hiking Trails, Kitchen Facilities, Lake, Lodges, Playing Fields, Tents
Programs: Boating, Swimming (#873)

Camp Black Hawk (est 1956) ▲ ⌂ 🚗

Elton, WI (Langlade Co.); (715) 882-2641
Kim Shafer, Director

Camp comments: CBH provides a safe setting for girls to explore, take risks, have fun, and learn about themselves, others, and the outdoors.
Activities: Arts/Crafts, Backpacking, Boating, Camping Skills/Outdoor Living, Climbing/Rappelling, Counselor Training (CIT), Horseback — Western, Leadership Development, Travel/Tour, Wilderness Trips
Session lengths & capacity: June-September; 1, 2, 3, 4 & 8 week sessions; 150 campers
Clientele & fees: girls 8-17; families;
Fees: **B, C, D, E** ▲ 🐷
Contact: Kim Shafer, Camp Director at (608) 276-8500 ext. 3005; fax: (608) 276-9160
e-mail: kims@girlscoutsofblackhawk.org
Operated by: Girl Scouts of Black Hawk Cncl, 2710 Ski Lane, Madison, WI 53713-3267 at (608) 276-8500

Group Rental Information

Seasons & Capacity: Spring 48, Winter 48
Facilities: Dorm-Style, Hiking Trails (#924)

Camp Chi (est 1921) ▲ 🚗

Lake Delton, WI (Sauk Co.); (608) 253-1681
Ron Levin, Director

Camp comments: Promote indiv. growth, self esteem, skill building Jewish values. 30 specialities. Pool. A/C, gyms/rollerblade court, high ropes program. Adult supervision.
Activities: Arts/Crafts, Baseball/Softball, Climbing/Rappelling, Horseback — Western, Radio/TV/Video, Sailing, SCUBA, Sports — Field & Team, Tennis, Waterskiing
Session lengths & capacity: 2, 4 & 8 week sessions; 500 campers
Clientele & fees: coed 8-16; families; seniors;
Fees: **E** ▲
Contact: Ron Levin, Camp Director at (847) 272-2301; fax: (847) 272-5357
e-mail: info@campchi.com
Operated by: JCC of Chicago, 3050 Woodridge Rd, Northbrook, IL 60062 at (847) 272-7050 (#1601)

ICON LEGEND

☀	Day Camp
▲	Resident Camp
⌂	Facilities Available To Rent
🚗	Transportation Available
🐷	Financial Aid Available

FEE RANGES PER WEEK

A	$0-75
B	$75-200
C	$201-350
D	$351-500
E	$501-650
F	over $650

Camp Eagle Ridge (est 1994) ▲ 🚗

Mellen, WI (Ashland Co.); (715) 274-4204
Kelly and Eddie Byrnes, Director

Camp comments: We combine a traditional camp experience with a focus on leadership, teamwork and achieving your personal best! Lots of individual attention.
Activities: Canoeing, Challenge/Rope Courses, Climbing/Rappelling, Leadership Development, Martial Arts, Sailing, Soccer, Sports — Field & Team, Team Building, Tennis
Session lengths & capacity: June-August; 1, 2, 3, 4, 5, 6 & 7 week sessions; 90 campers
Clientele & fees: coed 7-17; Fees: **D, E** ▲
Contact: Kelly Byrnes, Director at (414) 774-2621; fax: (414) 774-2634
e-mail: eglridge@wi.rr.com
Operated by: Camp Eagle Ridge, 1225 S 109th St, West Allis, WI 53214 at (414) 774-2621 (#27584)

Camp Evelyn (est 1948) ▲ ⌂

Plymouth, WI (Sheboygan Co.); (920) 892-4945
Cathy Palmer, Director

Camp comments: Beautiful camp environment that focuses on personal growth, self-esteem, responsibility, courage and cooperation.
Activities: Arts/Crafts, Bicycling/Biking, Caving, Counselor Training (CIT), Horseback — Western, Leadership Development, Nature/Environment Studies, Sailing, Swimming — Recreational, Windsurfing
Session lengths & capacity: June-August; 1/2, 1 & 2 week sessions; 150 campers
Clientele & fees: girls 7-18; families; Fees: **B, C** ▲
Contact: Cathy Palmer, Camp Director at (920) 565-4575; fax: (920) 565-4583
Operated by: Girl Scouts of Manitou Council, 5212 Windward Ct, Sheboygan, WI 53083 at (920) 565-4575

Group Rental Information

Site comments: Beautiful facility for youth groups or business meetings. Heated swimming pool available in season. 240 acres of woodland, peaceful and serene.
Seasons & Capacity: Spring 100, Fall 100, Winter 100
Facilities: Kitchen Facilities, Lake, Lodges, Meeting Rooms, Playing Fields, Pool, River, Tents
Programs: Boating, Swimming (#923)

Camp Gan Israel (est 1971) ☀ 🚗

Mequon, WI (Ozaukee Co.); (414) 961-6100
Devorah Shmotkin, Director

Camp comments: Warm, devoted counselors provide children a comprehensive program, fostering growth individually, socially & Jewishly.
Activities: Arts/Crafts, Baseball/Softball, Basketball, Challenge/Rope Courses, Field Trips, Hockey, Skating, Soccer, Sports — Field & Team, Swimming — Instructional
Session lengths & capacity: June-August; 1, 2 & 3 week sessions; 120 campers
Clientele & fees: coed 6-11; Fees: **B** ☀ 🐷
Contact: Devorah L Shmotkin, Camp Director at (414) 961-6100 ext. 6; fax: (414) 961-1920
e-mail: cgi@naspa.net
Operated by: The Lubavitch House, 3109 N Lake Dr, Milwaukee, WI 53211 at (414) 961-6100 (#2926)

Camp Gray (est 1953) ▲ ⌂

Reedsburg, WI (Sauk Co.); (608) 356-8200
Phil DeLong, Director

Camp comments: Fun, caring Christian community. Ages 6-18. Programs include swimming, horses, leadership training, rock climbing. Located near the Wisconsin Dells.
Activities: Archery, Camping Skills/Outdoor Living, Canoeing, Climbing/Rappelling, Fishing, Horseback — Western, Religious Study, Swimming — Recreational, Team Building, Wilderness Trips

Session lengths & capacity: 1/2, 1 & 2 week sessions; 135 campers
Clientele & fees: coed 6-18; families;
Fees: **B, C** ▲ 🐷
Contact: Chris Baumgart, Registrar at (800) 711-4729; fax: (608) 356-5855
e-mail: chris@campgray.com
Web site: www.campgray.com
Operated by: Camp Gray Inc, E10213 Shady Lane Rd, Reedsburg, WI 53959 at (608) 356-8200

Group Rental Information

Site comments: Beautiful 225 acre site near Wis Dells. Only 45 miles from Madison. Close to Devil's Lake & 3 ski areas. Rock climbing.
Seasons & Capacity: Spring 128, Summer 168, Fall 128, Winter 128
Facilities: A/V Equipment, Cabins, Dorm-Style, Food Service, Hiking Trails, Kitchen Facilities, Linens, Lodges, Meeting Rooms, Playing Fields, Pool, River, Tents
Programs: Boating, Challenge/Ropes Course, Environmental Education, Horseback Riding, Swimming, Winter Sports (#2975)

Camp Jorn YMCA

(est 1953) ☀ ▲ ⌂ 🚗

Manitowish Waters, WI; (715) 543-8808
Dennis Lipp, Director

Camp comments: Traditional YMCA resident camp on famous Manitowish Chain of Lakes in N. Wisconsin. Canoeing, sailing, horses, waterskiing, overnight trips, campfires & more.
Activities: Archery, Arts/Crafts, Camping Skills/Outdoor Living, Canoeing, Fishing, Horseback — Western, Nature/Environment Studies, Sailing, Swimming — Recreational, Waterskiing
Session lengths & capacity: June-August; 1 & 2 week sessions; 120 campers
Clientele & fees: coed 8-15; families; Fees: **B** ☀
Fees: **D** ▲ 🐷
Contact: Rhonda Haymaker, Director of Camping Services at (847) 360-9622; fax: (847) 623-2386
e-mail: administrator@campjorn.org
Web site: www.campjorn.org
Operated by: Lake County Family YMCA, 2000 Western Ave, Waukegan, IL 60087 at (847) 360-9622

Group Rental Information

Site comments: Beautiful facility on Rest Lake Manitowish Waters, Wisc. Accomodations, dining hall and program areas to meet the needs of youth groups, families & businesses.
Seasons & Capacity: Spring 100, Fall 100, Winter 50
Facilities: A/V Equipment, Cabins, Dorm-Style, Food Service, Hiking Trails, Kitchen Facilities, Lake, Lodges, Meeting Rooms, Playing Fields, Tents
Programs: Boating, Environmental Education, Horseback Riding, Swimming, Winter Sports (#3541)

Camp Manito-wish YMCA

(est 1919) ▲ ⌂ 🚗

Boulder Junction, WI; (715) 385-2312
Anne S Derber, Director

Camp comments: Wilderness tripping is core of program. A number of traditional camp activities are blended. Northwoods setting.
Activities: Archery, Arts/Crafts, Backpacking, Canoeing, Challenge/Rope Courses, Horseback — Western, Nature/Environment Studies, Sailing, Tennis, Wilderness Trips
Session lengths & capacity: Year-round; 2 & 3 week sessions; 220 campers
Clientele & fees: boys 10-18; girls 11-18; families;
Fees: **D** ▲ 🐷
Contact: Anne Derber, Executive Director at (715) 385-2312; fax: (715) 385-2461
e-mail: camp@manito-wish.org
Web site: www.manito-wish.org

CAMP ST. JOHN'S NORTHWESTERN

Our one- and two-week boarding and day camps for boys combine military and adventure skills training with fun activities to promote
Leadership Development, Physical Training, and **Team Building**.

Boarding camp for boys ages 12-16 years old
June 22-28 or July 6-19, 2003

Day camp for boys entering 6th-8th grades
July 6-12 or July 6-19, 2003

Paintball
Rappelling
Archery
Obstacle Courses
Self-Defense
Sailing
Marksmanship
Hiking
Orienteering
Swimming
Off-Campus Field Trips
Fishing
New Friends

An Experience of a Lifetime!

For more information, call *1-800-SJ-CADET*

website: www.sjnma.org • e-mail: admissions@sjnma.org
1101 North Genesee Street • Delafield, Wisconsin 53018

PAID ADVERTISEMENT

Operated by: Camp Manito-wish YMCA, PO Box 246, Boulder Junction, WI 54512 at (715) 385-2312

Group Rental Information
Facilities: Cabins, Dorm-Style, Food Service, Kitchen Facilities, Lake, Lodges
Programs: Boating (#883)

Camp Nawakwa (est 1926)　　　　Λ ⌂

Cornell, WI (Chippewa Co.); (715) 239-6775
Dave Salling, Director

Camp comments: Classic north woods wilderness setting. 'Challenging today's girls, creating tomorrow's leaders!'

Activities: Aquatic Activities, Arts/Crafts, Camping Skills/Outdoor Living, Challenge/Rope Courses, Counselor Training (CIT), Hiking, Horseback — Western, Leadership Development, Nature/Environment Studies
Session lengths & capacity: June-August; 1/2, 1 & 2 week sessions; 100 campers
Clientele & fees: girls 6-18; Fees: **B, C** Λ
Contact: Charity L Hovre, Director of Program & Camping Services at (715) 835-5331; fax: (715) 835-2768
Operated by: Girl Scouts of Indian Waters, 4222 Oakwood Hills Pkwy, Eau Claire, WI 54701 at (715) 835-5331

Group Rental Information
Seasons & Capacity: Spring 106, Summer 630, Fall 106, Winter 106

Facilities: Cabins, Dorm-Style, Food Service, Hiking Trails, Kitchen Facilities, Lake, Lodges, Meeting Rooms, Playing Fields, Tents
Programs: Boating, Swimming (#11093)

Camp Ojibwa (est 1928)　　　　Λ 🚗

Eagle River, WI (Vilas Co.); (715) 479-8611
Dennis Rosen, Director

Camp comments: THE GAME-to play is great, to win is greater, but to love the game is the greatest of them all. Counselors are heroes.
Activities: Baseball/Softball, Basketball, Drama, Football, Sailing, Soccer, Sports — Field & Team, Swimming — Instructional, Tennis, Waterskiing
Session lengths & capacity: June-August; 4 & 8 week sessions; 225 campers
Clientele & fees: boys 8-16; Fees: **E** Λ
Contact: Dennis Rosen, Director at (847) 831-5374; fax: (847) 831-2445
e-mail: campojibwa@aol.com
Operated by: Camp Ojibwa, 1549 Arbor, Highland Park, IL 60035 at (847) 831-5374 (#1572)

Camp Ramah in Wisconsin

(est 1947)　　　　　　　　　　　　Λ

Conover, WI (Vilas Co.); (715) 479-4400
Rabbi David Soloff, Director

Camp comments: Kosher kitchen, Hebrew language, full recreational & Jewish educational program. Teenage L.D. program available.
Activities: Arts/Crafts, Basketball, Camping Skills/Outdoor Living, Dance, Drama, Language Studies, Sailing, Sports — Field & Team, Swimming — Instructional, Tennis
Session lengths & capacity: June-August; 8 week sessions; 400 campers
Clientele & fees: coed 10-16; families
Contact: Camp Ramah in Wisconsin at (312) 606-9316; fax: (312) 606-7136
Web site: www.ramahwisconsin.com
Operated by: Ramah In Wisconsin, 65 East Wacker Pl Rm 1200, Chicago, IL 60601-7297 at (312) 606-9316 (#1676)

Camp Singing Hills (est 1953)　　Λ ⌂

Elkhorn, WI (Walworth Co.); (262) 495-8821
Sue Hink, Director

Camp comments: Camp Singing Hills provides girls with a fun group living experience that links G.S. programs with the natural environment to help girls grow strong.
Activities: Archery, Arts/Crafts, Bicycling/Biking, Camping Skills/Outdoor Living, Canoeing, Counselor Training (CIT), Horseback — Western, Nature/Environment Studies, Sailing, Swimming — Recreational
Session lengths & capacity: June-August; 1/2 & 1 week sessions; 120 campers
Clientele & fees: girls 7-17; families; Fees: **B, C** Λ
Contact: Theresa Brady, Camp Administrator at (414) 598-0909; fax: (414) 598-0898
e-mail: tbrady@girlscoutsracineco.org
Web site: www.girlscoutsracineco.org
Operated by: Girl Scouts of Racine County, 6240 Bankers Rd, Racine, WI 53403-9785 at (262) 598-0909

Group Rental Information
Seasons & Capacity: Spring 100, Fall 100, Winter 30
Facilities: Lake, Lodges, Playing Fields, Tents
Programs: Boating, Swimming (#907)

Camp St Johns Northwestern

(est 1995)　　　　　　　　　　　　Λ 🚗

Delafield, WI; (262) 646-7228
LTC James Kebisek, Director

Camp comments: We offer an exciting adventure camp for boys 12-16 years old. Fun military

activities promote personal growth, confidence & self-esteem.
Activities: Aquatic Activities, Archery, Canoeing, Challenge/Rope Courses, Hiking, Leadership Development, Sailing, SCUBA, Team Building
Session lengths & capacity: June-July; 2 week sessions; 86 campers
Clientele & fees: boys 12-16; Fees: F △
Contact: (262) 646-7115; fax: (262) 646-7128
e-mail: admissions@sjnma.org
Web site: www.sjnma.org
Operated by: St Johns Northwestern Military, 1101 N Genesee Street, Delafield, WI 53018 at (262) 646-7115 (#40782)

Camp St Mary and St George
(est 1930)

Eagle River, WI (Oneida Co.); (715) 479-8905
Stephen Samuelson, Director
Contact: Stephen Samuelson & Ed Strabel, Directors at (847) 824-6126; fax: (847) 824-7190
Operated by: Maryville Academy Archdiocese, 1150 N River Road, Des Plaines, IL 60016 at (847) 824-6126
Group Rental Information
Facilities: Cabins, Food Service, Hiking Trails, Kitchen Facilities, Lake, Lodges, Playing Fields, Tents
Programs: Boating, Horseback Riding, Swimming (#6499)

Camp Timberlane For Boys
(est 1960)

Woodruff, WI (Vilas Co.); (715) 356-6022
Leslie & Mike Cohen, Director
Camp comments: Warm family setting. Emphasis on fun/friendship. Genuinely noncompetitive. Huge choice of activities & wilderness trips
Activities: Arts/Crafts, Camping Skills/Outdoor Living, Climbing/Rappelling, Gymnastics, Horseback — English, Sailing, SCUBA, Sports — Field & Team, Waterskiing, Wilderness Trips
Session lengths & capacity: June-August; 4 & 8 week sessions; 150 campers
Clientele & fees: boys 8-15; Fees: E △
Contact: Mike Cohen, Directors at (800) 480-1188; fax: (520) 615-7771
e-mail: mike@camptimberlane.com
Web site: www.camptimberlane.com
Operated by: Camp Timberlane, 6202 N Camino Almonte, Tucson, AZ 85718 at (520) 615-7770 (#942)

ICON LEGEND
☀ Day Camp
△ Resident Camp
🏠 Facilities Available To Rent
🚗 Transportation Available
🐷 Financial Aid Available

FEE RANGES PER WEEK
A $0-75
B $75-200
C $201-350
D $351-500
E $501-650
F over $650

Camp Webb (est 1961)
Wautoma, WI; (920) 787-3812
Michele Drake, Director
Camp comments: A traditional camp experience within a fun and supportive Chirstian community! Celebrating 40 years of outdoor ministry.
Activities: Archery, Arts/Crafts, Canoeing, Challenge/Rope Courses, Horseback — Western, Leadership Development, Music, Nature/Environment Studies, Religious Study, Sailing
Session lengths & capacity: 1/2, 1 & 2 week sessions; 170 campers
Clientele & fees: coed 4-17; families; seniors; single adults; Fees: C △ 🚗
Contact: Michele R Drake, Camp Director at (920) 787-3812; fax: (920) 787-1385
e-mail: campwebb@hotmail.com
Web site: www.campwebb.org
Operated by: Episcopal Diocese of Milwaukee, 804 E Juneau Ave, Milwaukee, WI 53202 at (414) 291-2895
Group Rental Information
Site comments: New dining hall, conference rooms in resort area on quiet lake. Area boasts golf, downhill skiing, fishing, hunting, antiques. 3 winterized cabins with kitchens
Seasons & Capacity: Spring 40, Summer 170, Fall 40, Winter 40
Facilities: Cabins, Food Service, Hiking Trails, Lake, Lodges, Meeting Rooms, Tents
Programs: Boating, Swimming (#908)

Camp Whitcomb/Mason
(est 1887)
Hartland, WI; (262) 538-1190
Gail Tumidajewicz, Director
Activities: Aquatic Activities, Boating, Camping Skills/Outdoor Living, Challenge/Rope Courses, Counselor Training (CIT), Nature/Environment Studies, Sports — Field & Team, Swimming — Recreational, Waterskiing
Session lengths & capacity: June-August; 1 week sessions; 132 campers
Clientele & fees: coed 6-17; Fees: B ☀ Fees: B △
Contact: Gail Tumidajewicz, Camp Director at (262) 538-1190; fax: (262) 538-1904
e-mail: whitcomb@boysgirlsclub.org
Web site: www.campwhitcomb/mason.com
Operated by: Boys & Girls Clb Gtr Milwaukee, PO Box 12486, Milwaukee, WI 53203-0486 at (262) 267-8100
Group Rental Information
Seasons & Capacity: Spring 200, Summer 100, Fall 200, Winter 200
Facilities: Cabins, Dorm-Style, Food Service, Hiking Trails, Lake, Lodges, Meeting Rooms
Programs: Boating, Challenge/Ropes Course, Environmental Education (#886)

Camp Winnecomac
(est 1954)
Kaukauna, WI (Outagamie Co.); (920) 766-9880
Annie Fahrenkrug, Director
Camp comments: We are committed to providing girls with opportunities to develop life skills in a positive and caring environment.
Activities: Archery, Arts/Crafts, Camping Skills/Outdoor Living, Field Trips, Horseback — Western, Soccer, Sports — Field & Team, Swimming — Recreational, Team Building
Session lengths & capacity: June-August; 1 week sessions; 130 campers
Clientele & fees: girls 6-11; Fees: B ☀ 🐷
Contact: Annie Fahrenkrug, Camp Director at (920) 734-4559; fax: (920) 734-1304
Web site: www.girlscoutsfoxriverarea.org
Operated by: Girl Scouts Fox River Area, 4693 N Lynndale Dr, Appleton, WI 54913-9614 at (920) 734-4559 (#38427)

Camp Woodbrooke (est 1979)
Richland Center, WI (Richland Co.); (608) 647-8703
Jenny Lang, Director
Camp comments: Enhance self-esteem, experience caring, noncompetitive community, increase knowledge/appreciation of the environment.
Activities: Archery, Arts/Crafts, Camping Skills/Outdoor Living, Canoeing, Ceramics/Pottery, Drama, Farming/Ranching/Gardening, Hiking, Nature/Environment Studies, Swimming — Instructional
Session lengths & capacity: June-August; 2 & 3 week sessions; 35 campers
Clientele & fees: coed 7-12; Fees: D △ 🚗
Contact: Jenny Lang, Director at (608) 647-8703; fax: (608) 647-5923
e-mail: ajlang@mhtc.net
Web site: www.campwoodbrooke.com
Operated by: Camp Woodbrooke, 30002 Shedivy Lane, Richland Center, WI 53581 at (608) 647-8703 (#3970)

Camp Woodland For Girls
(est 1940)
Eagle River, WI (Oneida Co.); (715) 479-8287
JoAnne Jordan Trimpe & Anne Jordan, Director
Camp comments: Traditional program with emphasis on individual achievement & happy group relationships. Brother Camp Towering Pines.
Activities: Archery, Arts/Crafts, Gymnastics, Horseback — English, Riflery, Sailing, Swimming — Instructional, Tennis, Waterskiing
Session lengths & capacity: June-August; 4 & 6 week sessions; 75 campers
Clientele & fees: girls 7-16; Fees: E △
Contact: Anne G Jordan, Director at (847) 446-7311; fax: (847) 446-7710
e-mail: info@campwoodland.com
Web site: www.toweringpinescamp.com
Operated by: Towering Pines Inc, 242 Bristol St, Northfield, IL 60093 at (847) 446-7311 (#1625)

Camp Young Judaea
(est 1969)
Waupaca, WI; (715) 258-2288
Ben Sadek, Director
Camp comments: Camp with staff:camper ratio of 1:3. Program varied with sports & culture. Emphasis on Judaism & Zionism.
Activities: Aquatic Activities, Archery, Arts/Crafts, Basketball, Dance, Drama, Leadership Development, Religious Study, Tennis, Waterskiing
Session lengths & capacity: June-August; 4 & 8 week sessions; 140 campers
Clientele & fees: coed 8-14; Fees: E △ 🐷
Contact: Ben Sadek, Director at (419) 537-7171; fax: (419) 537-7177
e-mail: cyjmid@aol.com
Web site: www.cyjmid.org
Operated by: Camp Young Judaea, 6600 N Lincoln Ave Ste 304, Lincolnwood, IL 60712 at (847) 568-0255
Group Rental Information
Facilities: Cabins, Food Service, Kitchen Facilities, Lake, Playing Fields
Programs: Boating, Swimming (#7604)

Chippewa Ranch Camp Inc
(est 1946)
Eagle River, WI; (715) 479-8277
Thomas & Pamela Adler, Director
Camp comments: Pretty setting, family atmosphere, English riding, climbing, aquatics, theater, trips. Many returning campers & staff.
Activities: Aquatic Activities, Arts/Crafts, Climbing/Rappelling, Dance, Horseback — English, Performing Arts, Soccer, Tennis, Waterskiing

Session lengths & capacity: June-August; 4 & 6 week sessions; 110 campers
Clientele & fees: girls 8-15; Fees: **E** △
Contact: Tom & Pamela Adler, Owner-Director at (866) 209-9322; fax: (520) 721-6809
e-mail: tca1218@aol.com
Web site: www.chippewaranchcamp.com
Operated by: Chippewa Ranch Camp Inc, 3822 N Calle Hondonada, Tucson, AZ 85750 at (866) 209-9322 (#1695)

Clearwater Camp (est 1933) △ 🚐

Minocqua, WI (Oneida Co.); (715) 356-5030
Sunny Moore, Director

Camp comments: Exquisite setting on 3600 acre lake. Cabins on mainland & 5 acre island. Traditional, noncompetitive, character stressed. Caring staff. Be yourself. HAVE FUN!
Activities: Archery, Arts/Crafts, Canoeing, Horseback — English, Kayaking, Sailing, Swimming — Instructional, Tennis, Waterskiing, Wilderness Trips
Session lengths & capacity: June-August; 3 & 7 week sessions; 120 campers
Clientele & fees: girls 8-16; families; Fees: **F** △
Contact: Sunny Moore, Director at (800) 399-5030; fax: (715) 356-3124
e-mail: clearwatercamp@newnorth.net
Web site: www.clearwatercamp.com
Operated by: Clearwater Camp, 7490 Clearwater Rd, Minocqua, WI 54548 at (715) 356-5762 (#899)

Covenant Harbor Bible Camp

(est 1947) ☀ △ ⌂

Lake Geneva, WI (Walworth Co.); (262) 248-3600
Dale Holte, Director

Camp comments: Covenant Harbor draws people from their routines into opportunities to enjoy. Creation and relationships, so that all experience God through Jesus Christ.
Activities: Aerobics/Exercise, Aquatic Activities, Archery, Arts/Crafts, Challenge/Rope Courses, Leadership Development, Nature/Environment Studies, Sailing, Team Building
Session lengths & capacity: 1/2 & 1 week sessions; 200 campers
Clientele & fees: coed 7-18; families; seniors; Fees: **B** ☀ Fees: **C, D** △ 🚐
Contact: Sue Walter, Registrar at (262) 248-2600; fax: (262) 248-6814
e-mail: registrar@covenantharbor.org
Web site: www.covenantharbor.org
Operated by: Harbor Point Ministries, 3311 W Foster Ave, Chicago, IL 60625 at (773) 583-0220

Group Rental Information
Site comments: Sumemr camps, youth and family retreats and conferences, a variety of adventure programs and Elderhostel events make Covenant Harbor a favorite place for many.
Seasons & Capacity: Summer 200, Fall 150, Winter 150
Facilities: A/V Equipment, Cabins, Dorm-Style, Double Occupancy, Food Service, Hiking Trails, Kitchen Facilities, Lake, Linens, Lodges, Meeting Rooms, Playing Fields
Programs: Boating, Challenge/Ropes Course, Environmental Education, Swimming, Winter Sports (#2759)

Downtown YMCA Day Camp ☀

Milwaukee, WI; (414) 274-0834
Activities: Aquatic Activities, Arts/Crafts, Field Trips, Hiking, Team Building
Session lengths & capacity: June-August; 100 campers
Clientele & fees: boys 5-12; girls 5-12; coed 5-12; Fees: **B** ☀
Operated by: Triangle Y Ranch YMCA, 5535 S Church Road, West Bend, WI 53095 at (262) 255-9622 (#9700)

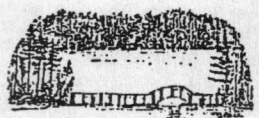

EAA Air Academy (est 1984) △

Oshkosh, WI (Winnebago Co.); (920) 426-4815
Chuck Larsen, Director

Camp comments: The Premier Youth Aviation Camp. Since 1984 EAA has hosted thousands of students on voyages of self-discovery and aviation adventure.
Activities: Academics, Aviation, Bicycling/Biking, Challenge/Rope Courses, Computer, Model Rocketry
Session lengths & capacity: June-August; 1/2 & 1 week sessions; 48 campers
Clientele & fees: coed 12-18; families; seniors; single adults; Fees: **F** △
Contact: (920) 426-6820; fax: (920) 426-6865
e-mail: education@eaa.org
Web site: www.eaa.org

Operated by: EAA Aviation Foundation Inc, PO Box 3065, Oshkosh, WI 54903-3065 at (920) 426-4815 (#44293)

Easter Seal Camp Wawbeek

(est 1938) ☀ △ ⌂

Wisconsin Dells, WI (Columbia Co.); (608) 254-8319
Chris Hollar, Director

Camp comments: Camp for people with physical disabilities 6&12 day sessions. Dedicated staff, tradtional activitites, safe yet challenging programs youth & adults.
Activities: Arts/Crafts, Boating, Camping Skills/Outdoor Living, Canoeing, Challenge/Rope Courses, Riflery, Swimming — Recreational

Session lengths & capacity: June-August; 1/2, 1 & 2 week sessions; 85 campers
Clientele & fees: coed 8-99; families; Fees: D ▲ 🐷
Contact: Ken Saville, Vice Pres Camping Services at (608) 277-8288; fax: (608) 277-8333
e-mail: ksaville@wi-easterseals.org
Web site: www.wi-easterseals.org
Operated by: Easter Seals Wisconsin, 101 Nob Hill Rd 301, Madison, WI 53713-2149 at (608) 277-8288
Group Rental Information
Facilities: Cabins, Dorm-Style, Food Service, Hiking Trails, Kitchen Facilities, Meeting Rooms (#906)

Edwards YMCA CAMP (est 1929) ▲ ⌂

East Troy, WI (Walworth Co.); (262) 642-7466
Craig Steward, Director

Camp comments: Trad prog, rustic cabins 90 min from Chicago, aquatics, wilderness trips, teens, family camps, youth ldrship, kayaks and theater programs.
Activities: Aquatic Activities, Archery, Arts/Crafts, Camping Skills/Outdoor Living, Canoeing, Counselor Training (CIT), Kayaking, SCUBA, Swimming — Recreational, Windsurfing
Session lengths & capacity: 1 & 2 week sessions; 188 campers
Clientele & fees: coed 9-14; families; seniors; single adults; Fees: C, E ▲ 🐷
Contact: Mary Jo Swayze, Administrative Assistant at (262) 642-7466; fax: (262) 642-5108
e-mail: camped@netwurx.net
Operated by: Edwards YMCA Camp, N8901 Army Lake, East Troy, WI 53120 at (847) 888-7400
Group Rental Information
Site comments: 90 mins from Chicago.Cabins & platform tents. Coed yr-round.Canoes,archery,sailing,kayaking,mtn bikes,theater trips, family camp.Staff dedicated to campers.
Facilities: Cabins, Food Service, Lake, Lodges, Meeting Rooms, Playing Fields
Programs: Boating, Challenge/Ropes Course, Environmental Education, Winter Sports (#946)

Ehawee (est 1951) ▲ ⌂

Mindoro, WI (La Crosse Co.); (608) 784-2614
Sarah Resch, Director

Camp comments: Beautiful pine forest. High camper staff ratio. Non-scouts welcome. Caring environment teaching independence.
Activities: Backpacking, Canoeing, Counselor Training (CIT), Horseback — Western, Nature/Environment Studies, Swimming — Recreational, Wilderness Trips

ICON LEGEND

☀ Day Camp
▲ Resident Camp
⌂ Facilities Available To Rent
🚐 Transportation Available
🐷 Financial Aid Available

FEE RANGES PER WEEK

A	$0-75
B	$75-200
C	$201-350
D	$351-500
E	$501-650
F	over $650

Session lengths & capacity: June-August; 1/2, 1, 2 & 3 week sessions; 160 campers
Clientele & fees: girls 5-17; Fees: B ▲ 🚐
Contact: Sarah Resch, Camp Director at (608) 784-2614; fax: (608) 857-3707
e-mail: campehawee@yahoo.com
Web site: www.wi.centurytel.net/gscouts
Operated by: Riverland GSC, 2710 Quarry Rd, La Crosse, WI 54601 at (608) 784-3693
Group Rental Information
Facilities: Dorm-Style, Kitchen Facilities, Meeting Rooms, Pool, Tents
Programs: Boating (#955)

Family Service-On Belay TCP

(est 1982) ⌂

Madison, WI (Dane Co.); (608) 241-1214
Kirsten Noislien, Director
Contact: Kirsten Norslien, Coordinator at (608) 252-1325 ext. 1176; fax: (608) 252-1333
e-mail: kirstenn@fsmad.org
Operated by: Family Service, 128 E Olin Ave, Madison, WI 53713 at (608) 255-1325 (#6376)

Happy Hollow Girl Scouts III

(est 1959) ⌂

Elkhorn, WI (Lake County Co.); (262) 642-3424
Anna Robertson, Director
Contact: Anna Robertson, Program Specialist at (414) 642-3424; fax: (414) 642-5487
e-mail: annar1@netwurx.net
Web site: www.ilcrossroads.org
Operated by: Illinois Crossroads Girl Scout, PO Box 8116, Vernon Hills, IL 60061-8116 at (847) 573-0500
Group Rental Information
Facilities: Hiking Trails, Kitchen Facilities, Lodges, Tents
Programs: Horseback Riding (#3951)

Harand Camp Of The Theatre Art (est 1955) ▲ 🚐

Beaver Dam, WI (Dodge Co.); (414) 885-4517
Sulie Harand, Director

Camp comments: Through a unique combination of theater & sports, each child is given opportunities to grow to his/her potential.
Activities: Arts/Crafts, Basketball, Dance, Drama, Music, Photography, Radio/TV/Video, Soccer, Swimming — Instructional, Tennis
Session lengths & capacity: June-August; 3 & 6 week sessions; 200 campers
Clientele & fees: coed 8-18; Fees: F ▲
Contact: Sulie Harand, Director at (847) 864-1500; fax: (847) 864-1588
e-mail: harandcamp@aol.com
Web site: www.harandcamp.com
Operated by: Harand Camp of the Theatre Art, 708 Church Street, Evanston, IL 60201 at (847) 864-1500 (#1693)

Helen Brachman (est 1906) ▲ ⌂ 🚐

Almond, WI (Portage Co.); (715) 366-2234
Jake Czarnik Neimeyer, Director

Camp comments: Multicultural programs, beautiful lake and forest offer children opportunities for fun, learning and adventure.
Activities: Arts/Crafts, Bicycling/Biking, Boating, Camping Skills/Outdoor Living, Challenge/Rope Courses, Nature/Environment Studies, Sports — Field & Team, Swimming — Instructional, Swimming — Recreational, Team Building
Session lengths & capacity: June-August; 1, 2 & 3 week sessions; 110 campers
Clientele & fees: coed 8-15; families; Fees: B ▲ 🐷
Contact: James Bertrand, Camp Registrar at (414) 263-8383; fax: (414) 263-8386
e-mail: coa@execpc.com

Web site: www.wctc.net/~chb
Operated by: COA, 909 E North Ave, Milwaukee, WI 53212 at (414) 263-8383
Group Rental Information
Site comments: Year-round facilities, food service, lake swimming, 200 acres, ropes course, retreat team, trainings.
Seasons & Capacity: Spring 74, Fall 74, Winter 74
Facilities: Cabins, Dorm-Style, Food Service, Kitchen Facilities, Lake, Lodges, Meeting Rooms (#915)

Herzl Camp (est 1946) ▲ ⌂ 🚐

Webster, WI (Burnett Co.); (715) 866-8177
Steve Mintz, Director

Camp comments: Fun, safe & exciting Jewish camping. Tradition of identity & confidence building. 20+ activities daily. Kosher kitchen.
Activities: Arts/Crafts, Baseball/Softball, Canoeing, Climbing/Rappelling, Drama, Music, Sailing, Sports — Field & Team, Swimming — Recreational, Tennis
Session lengths & capacity: June-August; 1, 2, 3 & 4 week sessions; 300 campers
Clientele & fees: coed 8-15; seniors; Fees: D ▲ 🐷
Contact: Steve Mintz, Executive Director at (952) 927-4002; fax: (952) 927-0949
e-mail: HerzlCamp@aol.com
Operated by: Herzl Camp Association, 4517 Minnetonka Blvd 206, St Louis Park, MN 55416 at (952) 927-4002
Group Rental Information
Facilities: Cabins, Food Service, Hiking Trails, Lake, Meeting Rooms (#1115)

Holiday Home Camp (est 1887) ▲ 🚐

Williams Bay, WI (Walworth Co.); (262) 245-5161
Carl Hobbs, Director

Camp comments: HHC is an independent not for profit camp serving at risk children and youth since 1887. We focus on team building and cooperative living skills.
Activities: Aquatic Activities, Arts/Crafts, Boating, Counselor Training (CIT), Drama, Drawing/Painting, Hiking, Leadership Development, Nature/Environment Studies, Team Building
Session lengths & capacity: May-September; 1 & 2 week sessions; 100 campers
Clientele & fees: coed 7-18; Fees: B ▲ 🐷
Contact: Carol Hobbs, Director at (262) 245-5161; fax: (262) 245-6518
e-mail: hhomecamp@elknet.net
Web site: www.holidayhomecamp.org
Operated by: Lake Geneva Fresh Air Assn, 361 N Lake Shore Dr PO Box 10, Williams Bay, WI 53191 at (262) 245-5161 (#4162)

Honey Rock Camp (est 1951) ☀ ▲ 🚐

Three Lakes, WI (Oneida Co.); (715) 479-7474
Rob Ribbe, Director

Camp comments: Northwoods campus of Wheaton College. Focus on Christian character & leadership development. Wilderness trips for teens.
Activities: Backpacking, Camping Skills/Outdoor Living, Canoeing, Climbing/Rappelling, Counselor Training (CIT), Horseback — Western, Kayaking, Leadership Development, Waterskiing, Wilderness Trips
Session lengths & capacity: June-August; 2, 6 & 8 week sessions; 160 campers
Clientele & fees: boys 10-18; girls 10-18; coed 10-18; Fees: B ☀ Fees: D ▲ 🐷
Contact: Registrar at (715) 479-7474 ext. 301; e-mail: info@honeyrockcamp.org
Web site: www.honeyrockcamp.org
Operated by: Honey Rock Camp, Wheaton College, 8660 Honey Rock Rd, Three Lakes, WI 54562 at (715) 479-7474 (#928)

Hoofbeat Ridge Resident Camp

(est 1962)

Mazomanie, WI; (608) 767-2593
Ted Marthe CCD, Director

Camp comments: Family operated girls camp. Specializing in English & Western horsemanship. Indoor riding. Complete horse care.
Activities: Arts/Crafts, Drama, Farming/Ranching/Gardening, Hiking, Horseback — English, Horseback — Western, Nature/Environment Studies
Session lengths & capacity: June-August; 1, 2 & 3 week sessions; 65 campers
Clientele & fees: girls 7-16; Fees: D ▲
Contact: Ted Marthe, Owner/Director at (608) 767-2593; fax: (608) 767-2590
Web site: www.hoofbeat.org
Operated by: Hoofbeat Ridge, 5304 Reeve Rd, Mazomanie, WI 53560 at (608) 767-2593

Group Rental Information

Facilities: A/V Equipment, Dorm-Style, Food Service, Hiking Trails, Lodges, Meeting Rooms, Playing Fields
Programs: Environmental Education, Horseback Riding, Winter Sports (#914)

House In The Wood (est 1910)

Delavan, WI (Walworth Co.); (262) 728-2752
Valerie Wright, Director

Camp comments: Serving disadvantaged children, teens, families, seniors from Chicago. Emphasizes small group interaction.
Activities: Arts/Crafts, Boating, Camping Skills/Outdoor Living, Canoeing, Field Trips, Leadership Development, Nature/Environment Studies, Sailing, Swimming — Recreational
Session lengths & capacity: 1, 2 & 4 week sessions; 80 campers
Clientele & fees: coed 7-16; families; seniors; Fees: A, B ▲ 🚌
Contact: For Camper Registrat Pat Jaszka Emergenc, Services Director at (773) 278-7471; Web site: www.houseinthewood.org
Operated by: Northwestern University Settle, 1400 Augusta Blvd, Chicago, IL 60622 at (773) 278-7471

Group Rental Information

Facilities: Cabins, Food Service, Kitchen Facilities, Lake, Meeting Rooms (#1559)

Interlaken Jcc (est 1966)

Eagle River, WI (Vilas Co.); (715) 479-8030
Howard Wagan, Director

Camp comments: Judaic program, Kosher kitchen. Individual attention & scheduling. Pristine northwoods lakefront. Outstanding facilities
Activities: Aquatic Activities, Arts/Crafts, Camping Skills/Outdoor Living, Challenge/Rope Courses, Music, Photography, Rafting, Swimming — Instructional, Waterskiing, Wilderness Trips
Session lengths & capacity: June-August; 2, 4 & 8 week sessions; 250 campers
Clientele & fees: coed 8-15; families; Fees: E ▲ 🚌
Contact: Howard Wagan, Camp Director at (414) 967-8249; fax: (414) 964-0922
e-mail: ciljcc@execpc.com
Web site: www.campinterlaken.org
Operated by: JCC of Milwaukee, 6255 N Santa Monica, Milwaukee, WI 53217 at (414) 964-4444 (#902)

Kawaga For Boys (est 1915)

Minocqua, WI (Oneida Co.); (715) 356-6262
David Tasner, Director

Camp comments: For more than 85 years Kawaga has offered a fun, safe & rewarding experience in the beautiful Northwoods.

Activities: Baseball/Softball, Basketball, Camping Skills/Outdoor Living, Football, Golf, Hockey, Sailing, Soccer, Tennis, Waterskiing
Session lengths & capacity: June-August; 4 & 8 week sessions; 190 campers
Clientele & fees: boys 8-16; Fees: E ▲
Contact: David Tasner, Director at (773) 929-7611; fax: (312) 663-0420
e-mail: braves@kawaga.com
Web site: www.kawaga.com
Operated by: Kawaga for Boys, 2828 Highland Ave, Cincinnati, OH 45212 at (513) 731-3400 (#1576)

Lake Lucerne Camp and Retreat

(est 1947)

Neshkoro, WI (Waushara Co.); (920) 293-4488
Brad Sherman, Director

Camp comments: Traditional and specialty programs. Clear 50 acre lake. Christian emphasis. Ideal facilities and caring staff. Join us!
Activities: Archery, Boating, Canoeing, Golf, Hiking, Skating, Snow Sports, Sports — Field & Team, Swimming — Recreational, Tennis
Session lengths & capacity: 1/2 & 1 week sessions; 200 campers
Clientele & fees: boys 6-18; girls 6-18; coed 6-18; families; seniors; Fees: A, C ▲
Contact: Brad Sherman, Site Director at (920) 293-4488; fax: (920) 293-4361
e-mail: lucerne@vbe.com
Web site: www.wisconsinumc.org/lakelucerne
Operated by: Wisconsin United Methodist Chu, W6460 County YY, Neshkoro, WI 54960 at (920) 293-4488

Group Rental Information

Site comments: Clear lake. Many recreational opportunities. 2 golf courses.
Seasons & Capacity: Spring 100, Summer 200, Fall 100, Winter 100
Facilities: A/V Equipment, Cabins, Dorm-Style, Double Occupancy, Food Service, Hiking Trails, Kitchen Facilities, Lake, Linens, Lodges, Meeting Rooms, Playing Fields
Programs: Boating, Environmental Education, Swimming, Winter Sports (#14932)

Lake Wapogasset Lutheran Bible (est 1948)

Amery, WI (Polk Co.); (715) 268-8434
Loren S Teig, Director

Camp comments: Beautiful lake setting. All ages in all seasons. Cultural, leadership, family, youth camping in a Christian environment.
Activities: Aquatic Activities, Canoeing, Challenge/Rope Courses, Horseback — Western, Kayaking, Leadership Development, Religious Study, Sailing, Sports — Field & Team, Swimming — Recreational
Session lengths & capacity: 1 week sessions; 310 campers
Clientele & fees: boys 8-18; girls 8-18; coed 8-18; families; seniors; Fees: B ▲ 🚌
Contact: Loren Teig, Exec Director at (715) 268-8434; fax: (715) 268-4451
e-mail: camp.wapo@spacestar.net
Web site: www.spacestar.net/~campwapo
Operated by: Lake Wapogasset Lutheran Bible, 738 Hickory Point Lane, Amery, WI 54001-5129 at (715) 268-8434 (#14979)

Luther Dell Lutheran Bible Cmp

(est 1951)

Remer, MN; (218) 556-2329
Al Johnson, Director

Camp comments: Welcome to (A Place of Growth). Luther Dell offers a great opportunity to spiritually grow through our rustic setting, beautiful wildlife & Boy Lake sunsets.

Activities: Aquatic Activities, Arts/Crafts, Canoeing, Leadership Development, Music, Religious Study, Swimming — Recreational, Team Building
Session lengths & capacity: June-August; 1/2 & 1 week sessions; 80 campers
Clientele & fees: coed 9-16; families; seniors; Fees: C ▲ 🚌
Contact: Dixie Teig, Registrar at (715) 268-8434; fax: (715) 268-4451
e-mail: campwapo@spacestar.net
Web site: www.spacestar.net/~campwapo
Operated by: Lake Wapogasset Lutheran Bible, 738 Hickory Point Lane, Amery, WI 54001-5129 at (715) 268-8434

Group Rental Information

Seasons & Capacity: Spring 110, Fall 110
Facilities: Cabins, Dorm-Style, Food Service, Hiking Trails, Lake, Lodges, Meeting Rooms, Playing Fields
Programs: Swimming (#47805)

Luther Park Inc

(est 1958)

Danbury, WI (Burnett Co.); (715) 656-7244
Joel Legred, Director

Camp comments: Nestled by a beautiful spring-fed lake in the Northwoods, Luther Park offers Christ-centered, Bible-based programs hosted by caring, Christian role models.
Activities: Aquatic Activities, Bicycling/Biking, Camping Skills/Outdoor Living, Canoeing, Challenge/Rope Courses, Counselor Training (CIT), Leadership Development, Nature/Environment Studies, Religious Study, Team Building
Session lengths & capacity: June-August; 1/2, 1 & 2 week sessions; 100 campers
Clientele & fees: coed 7-18; families; seniors; single adults; Fees: C ☀ 🚌
Contact: Kay Bartzyk, Office Manager/Registrar at (715) 656-7244; fax: (715) 656-3013
e-mail: kay@lutherpark.com
Web site: www.lutherpark.com
Operated by: Luther Park Inc, 30376 Lakes Dr, Danbury, WI 54830 at (715) 656-7244

Group Rental Information

Site comments: Experience treehouse village, canoe trips, pedal and paddle; cabin camping and day camp for grades 1-12; international mission trips and family camps.
Seasons & Capacity: Spring 116, Summer 121, Fall 116, Winter 116
Facilities: A/V Equipment, Cabins, Food Service, Hiking Trails, Lake, Meeting Rooms, Playing Fields, Tents
Programs: Boating, Challenge/Ropes Course, Environmental Education, Swimming, Winter Sports (#9562)

Luther Point Bible Camp

(est 1946)

Grantsburg, WI (Burnett Co.); (715) 689-2347
Rev Craig M Corbin, Director

Camp comments: Bible Camp in beautiful lakeside setting. Excellent college age staff. Outpost /canoeing program.
Activities: Aquatic Activities, Camping Skills/Outdoor Living, Canoeing, Counselor Training (CIT), Field Trips, Fishing, Leadership Development, Music, Religious Study, Swimming — Recreational
Session lengths & capacity: June-August; 1/2 & 1 week sessions; 145 campers
Clientele & fees: coed 6-18; families; Fees: C ▲ 🚌
Contact: Marcel Snow, Office Manager at (715) 689-2347; fax: (715) 689-2348
e-mail: lutherpt@grantsburgtelcom.net
Web site: www.lutherpoint.org
Operated by: Lutheran Bible Camp Assn, 11525 Luther Point Rd, Grantsburg, WI 54840 at (715) 689-2347

Group Rental Information

Site comments: We offer new and newly remodeled retreat facilities. Great location from the twin cities. We encourage retreating emphasizing Christian spiritual significance.
Seasons & Capacity: Spring 80, Summer 80, Fall 80, Winter 80
Facilities: Cabins, Dorm-Style, Double Occupancy, Food Service, Lake, Lodges, Meeting Rooms, Playing Fields, River
Programs: Boating, Environmental Education, Swimming (#3155)

Lutherdale Bible Camp Inc

(est 1944) ▲ ⌂

Elkhorn, WI (Walworth Co.); (262) 742-2352
Jeffrey A Bluhm, Director

Camp comments: Christian ministry to build positive relationships through worship, and study. Group dynamics, lakeside, wooded setting.
Activities: Arts/Crafts, Camping Skills/Outdoor Living, Challenge/Rope Courses, Counselor Training (CIT), Farming/Ranching/Gardening, Leadership Development, Music, Nature/Environment Studies, Sailing, Team Building
Session lengths & capacity: June-August; 1 week sessions; 202 campers
Clientele & fees: coed 9-18; families; seniors; Fees: B ☀ Fees: B, C ▲
Contact: Carol K, Registrar/Receptionist at (262) 742-2352; fax: (262) 742-3169
Web site: www.lutherdale.org
Operated by: Lutherdale Bible Camp Inc, N7891 US Hwy 12, Elkhorn, WI 53121 at (262) 742-2352

Group Rental Information

Seasons & Capacity: Spring 250, Fall 250, Winter 250
Facilities: Cabins, Dorm-Style, Food Service, Lake, Meeting Rooms
Programs: Boating, Environmental Education (#3237)

Marimeta For Girls (est 1947) ▲ 🚐

Eagle River, WI (Vilas Co.); (715) 479-9990
Sandy Cohen & Jody Bradley-Ruby, Director

Camp comments: Land and water sports are included in a Marimeta summer. Individual attention makes us more than a camp. It's a feeling.
Activities: Archery, Baseball/Softball, Basketball, Canoeing, Golf, Gymnastics, Sailing, Swimming — Instructional, Tennis, Waterskiing
Session lengths & capacity: June-August; 4 & 8 week sessions; 130 campers
Clientele & fees: girls 7-16; Fees: E ▲
Contact: Sandy Cohen, Director at (847) 970-4386; fax: (847) 970-9766

ICON LEGEND

☀	Day Camp
▲	Resident Camp
⌂	Facilities Available To Rent
🚐	Transportation Available
🐷	Financial Aid Available

FEE RANGES PER WEEK

A	$0-75
B	$75-200
C	$201-350
D	$351-500
E	$501-650
F	over $650

e-mail: sandy@marimeta.com
Web site: www.marimeta.com
Operated by: Marimeta for Girls, 3782 Gaffney Drive, Eagle River, WI 54521 at (715) 479-9990 (#1595)

Menominee for Boys (est 1928) ▲ 🚐

Eagle River, WI; (715) 479-2267
Steve Kanefsky, Director

Camp comments: Unconditionally accepted boys are loved in strong, family setting. Sports & traditional fun. 800-236-CAMP, free video.
Activities: Archery, Basketball, Boating, Climbing/Rappelling, Golf, Riflery, Soccer, Swimming — Recreational, Tennis, Waterskiing
Session lengths & capacity: June-August; 4 & 8 week sessions; 180 campers
Clientele & fees: boys 7-15; Fees: E ▲ 🚐
Contact: Steve Kanefsky, Owner/Director at (480) 515-5474; fax: (480) 515-5475
e-mail: fun@campmenominee.com
Web site: www.campmenominee.com
Operated by: Menominee for Boys, 15253 N 104th Way, Scottsdale, AZ 85259 at (480) 515-5474 (#1594)

Natures Edge (est 1966) ☀ ▲ ⌂

Waupaca, WI; (715) 258-2286
Rod Chapman, Director

Camp comments: We provide a safe and fun atmosphere as we work to link education and recreation with the environment in the heart of Wisconsin.
Activities: Arts/Crafts, Boating, Canoeing, Challenge/Rope Courses, Fishing, Nature/Environment Studies, Photography
Session lengths & capacity: July-August; 1 week sessions; 96 campers
Clientele & fees: coed 6-15; families; seniors; Fees: A ☀ Fees: C ▲ 🐷
Contact: Rod or Joyce Chapman, Administrator/Program Director at (715) 258-2286; fax: (715) 258-2439
e-mail: info@naturesedge.org
Operated by: Odd Fellow Rebekah Home Assn, 1229 S Jackson St, Green Bay, WI 54301 at (920) 437-6523

Group Rental Information

Site comments: Nature's edge is a great place to get away from it all, to plan, to meet, to reflect. Nature's Edge's expereince is one which ill have a lasting effect on you.
Seasons & Capacity: Spring 108, Summer 108, Fall 108, Winter 108
Facilities: A/V Equipment, Cabins, Dorm-Style, Food Service, Hiking Trails, Lake, Meeting Rooms, Pool
Programs: Boating, Challenge/Ropes Course, Swimming, Winter Sports (#35418)

Nebagamon (est 1929) ▲

Lake Nebagamon, WI (Douglas Co.); (715) 374-2275
Roger & Judy Wallenstein, Director

Camp comments: Individualized balanced program. Expert instruction. Exciting wilderness trips. 120 staff. Diversity welcomed.
Activities: Arts/Crafts, Backpacking, Basketball, Camping Skills/Outdoor Living, Nature/Environment Studies, Sailing, Soccer, Swimming — Instructional, Tennis, Wilderness Trips
Session lengths & capacity: June-August; 4 & 8 week sessions; 240 campers
Clientele & fees: boys 8-15; Fees: F ▲ 🚐
Contact: Roger & Judy Wallenstein, Owners/Directors at (773) 271-9500; fax: (773) 271-9816
e-mail: cnebagamon@aol.com
Web site: www.campnebagamon.com
Operated by: Nebagamon, 5237 N Lakewood Ave, Chicago, IL 60640 at (773) 271-9500 (#1044)

Needlepoint Daypoint

(est 1957) ☀ ▲ 🚐

Hudson, WI (St Croix Co.); (715) 386-4380
Becky Martin, Director

Camp comments: For children with type 1 diabetes. Programs tailored to specific age levels. Experienced counseling & medical staff.
Activities: Archery, Arts/Crafts, Camping Skills/Outdoor Living, Counselor Training (CIT), Horseback — English, Horseback — Western, Nature/Environment Studies, Sailing, Wilderness Trips
Session lengths & capacity: 1 & 2 week sessions
Clientele & fees: coed 5-16; Fees: B ☀ Fees: D, E ▲ 🐷
Contact: Tracy Haglund, Program Assistant at (763) 593-5333 ext. 6611; fax: (763) 593-1520
e-mail: thaglund@diabetes.org
Web site: www.diabetes.org
Operated by: American Diabetes Association, 715 Florida Ave S Ste 307, Minneapolis, MN 55426-1759 at (763) 593-5333 (#1169)

Nicolet For Girls (est 1944) ▲ ⌂ 🚐

Eagle River, WI (Forest Co.); (715) 545-2522
Georgianna Starz, Director

Camp comments: Beautiful northwoods setting. International camp family. A summer home where memories & friendships last a life time!
Activities: Arts/Crafts, Bicycling/Biking, Camping Skills/Outdoor Living, Drama, Horseback — English, Sailing, Soccer, Swimming — Instructional, Tennis, Waterskiing
Session lengths & capacity: June-August; 3, 4 & 7 week sessions; 115 campers
Clientele & fees: girls 8-15; Fees: E ▲
Contact: Georgianna S Starz, Director at (715) 545-2522; fax: (715) 545-3737
e-mail: campnico@newnorth.net
Web site: www.campnicolet.com
Operated by: Camp Nicolet Inc, Box 1359, Eagle River, WI 54521 at (715) 545-2522

Group Rental Information

Site comments: A summer residential camp in the beautiful Northwoods of Wisconsi. International camp family. Quality instruction in numerous activities and trip adventures.
Facilities: A/V Equipment, Cabins, Dorm-Style, Hiking Trails, Lake, Meeting Rooms
Programs: Boating, Swimming (#889)

North Star Camp For Boys

(est 1945) ▲

Hayward, WI (Sawyer Co.); (715) 462-3254
Robert & Sue Lebby, Director

Camp comments: Fun, caring counselors, doctor on residence, noncompetitive atmosphere, overnight camping program, 57 super summers.
Activities: Bicycling/Biking, Challenge/Rope Courses, Horseback — Western, Model Rocketry, Riflery, Sailing, Sports — Field & Team, Tennis, Waterskiing, Wilderness Trips
Session lengths & capacity: June-August; 4 & 8 week sessions; 160 campers
Clientele & fees: boys 9-15; families; Fees: E ▲
Contact: Robert Lebby, Director at (520) 577-7925; fax: (520) 529-2140
e-mail: leb@northstarcamp.com
Web site: www.northstarcamp.com
Operated by: North Star Camp for Boys, 6101 Paseo Cimarron, Tucson, AZ 85750 at (520) 577-7925 (#887)

Olin Sang Ruby Union Institute

(est 1951) ▲ ⌂ 🚐

Oconomowoc, WI (Waukesha Co.); (262) 567-6277
Susan Alexander, Director

Camp comments: Residential, reform VANC camp. Arts, sports and wilderness trips.

Activities: Basketball, Camping Skills/Outdoor Living, Challenge/Rope Courses, Dance, Drama, Horseback — Western, Photography, Soccer, Swimming — Recreational
Session lengths & capacity: June-August; 2, 3, 4 & 7 week sessions
Clientele & fees: coed 8-17; Fees: D ▲ 🚐
Contact: Irene Bennett, Registrar at (847) 509-0990 ext. 25; fax: (847) 509-0970
e-mail: osrinfo@aol.com
Operated by: Union Of American Hebrew Cong, 555 Skokie Blvd Suite 225, Northbrook, IL 60062 at (847) 509-0990

Group Rental Information
Facilities: Cabins, Dorm-Style, Double Occupancy, Food Service, Hiking Trails, Linens, Lodges, Meeting Rooms
Programs: Challenge/Ropes Course (#1627)

Ox Lake Lutheran Bible Camp ▲ ⌂

Amery, WI
Char Sunde, Director

Camp comments: International Village campers welcomed to a multi-cultural learning experience in God's family without leaving the United States.
Activities: Aquatic Activities, Bicycling/Biking, Camping Skills/Outdoor Living, Canoeing, Ceramics/Pottery, Horseback — Western, International Culture, Nature/Environment Studies, Religious Study, Team Building
Session lengths & capacity: 1 week sessions; 84 campers
Clientele & fees: coed 9-16; families; Fees: C ▲ 🚐
Contact: Char Sunde, Site Coordinator at (715) 268-8434; fax: (715) 268-4451
Web site: www.spacestar.net/~campwapo
Operated by: Lake Wapogasset Lutheran Bible, 738 Hickory Point Lane, Amery, WI 54001-5129 at (715) 268-8434

Group Rental Information
Seasons & Capacity: Spring 80, Fall 80
Facilities: Cabins, Food Service, Hiking Trails, Lake, Playing Fields, River
Programs: Boating, Challenge/Ropes Course, Swimming (#47804)

Ozaukee YMCA Day Camp ☀

Port Washington, WI (Ozaukee Co.)
Jennifer Sutherland, Director

Camp comments: Our 3 year old facility includes adventure pool, rock climbing wall and youth fun room. Choose from regular, sport, 1/2 day camp.
Activities: Aquatic Activities, Arts/Crafts, Climbing/Rappelling, Field Trips, Nature/Environment Studies, Sports — Field & Team
Session lengths & capacity: June-August; 100 campers
Clientele & fees: coed 5-11; Fees: B ☀ 🚐
Contact: Jennifer Sutherland, Youth & Family Director at (262) 268-9622; fax: (262) 268-1724
e-mail: jsutherland.oz@ymcamke.org
Operated by: Triangle Y Ranch YMCA, 5535 S Church Road, West Bend, WI 53095 at (262) 255-9622 (#9701)

Phantom Lake YMCA Camp

(est 1896) ☀ ▲ ⌂
Mukwonago, WI (Waukesha Co.); (262) 363-4386
Dave Lee, Director

Camp comments: Beautiful Kettle Moraine. Self-esteem, social & personal values stressed. Traditional program & adventure trips.
Activities: Archery, Arts/Crafts, Bicycling/Biking, Camping Skills/Outdoor Living, Climbing/Rappelling, Gymnastics, Leadership Development, Riflery, Sailing, Wilderness Trips

Session lengths & capacity: June-September; 1 week sessions; 175 campers
Clientele & fees: boys 7-15; girls 7-15; coed 7-15; families; Fees: B ☀ Fees: C ▲ 🚐
Contact: Cynthia Holt, Camp Director at (262) 363-4386; fax: (262) 363-4351
e-mail: office@phantomlakeymca.com
Web site: www.phantomlakeymca.com
Operated by: Phantom Lake YMCA Camp Inc, PO Box 228, Mukwonago, WI 53186 at (262) 363-4386

Group Rental Information
Seasons & Capacity: Spring 175, Fall 175, Winter 100
Facilities: Dorm-Style, Food Service, Hiking Trails, Lake, Meeting Rooms, Tents
Programs: Boating (#925)

Pokonokah Hills (est 1966) ▲ 🚐

New Auburn, WI (Chippewa Co.); (715) 967-2146
Diane Lancour, Director

Camp comments: Camp is a lively & energetic place. We want girls to pursue new adventures & action, & enjoy camp to laugh & sing.
Activities: Archery, Arts/Crafts, Backpacking, Camping Skills/Outdoor Living, Canoeing, Hiking, Horseback — Western, Leadership Development, Swimming — Recreational
Session lengths & capacity: 1, 2 & 3 week sessions; 80 campers
Clientele & fees: girls 9-17; Fees: C ▲ 🚐
Contact: Diane Lancour, Camp Director at (847) 741-5521 ext. 129; fax: (847) 741-5667
e-mail: pokie@gs-sybaquay.org
Operated by: Girl Scouts Sybaquay Council, 12N124 Coombs Rd, Elgin, IL 60123 at (847) 741-5521 (#1905)

Pottawatomie Hills GS

(est 1927) ▲ ⌂
East Troy, WI (Walworth Co.); (262) 642-9512
Tamera Steele, Director

Camp comments: Serene lake setting. Traditional program + in an environment that builds confidence & self-esteem. Leadership training.
Activities: Canoeing, Counselor Training (CIT), Drama, Horseback — Western, Leadership Development, Sailing, SCUBA, Swimming — Recreational, Team Building
Session lengths & capacity: June-July; 1/2, 1 & 2 week sessions; 130 campers
Clientele & fees: girls 7-18; Fees: A, B, C ▲ 🚐
Contact: Claire Hiller, Executive Director at (262) 657-7102; fax: (262) 657-7104
e-mail: gscout@execpc.com
Operated by: GS of Kenosha Cty, 2303 37th St, Kenosha, WI 53140 at (262) 657-7102

Group Rental Information
Seasons & Capacity: Spring 200, Fall 200, Winter 200
Facilities: Cabins, Dorm-Style, Hiking Trails, Kitchen Facilities, Lake, Lodges, Meeting Rooms, Playing Fields, Tents
Programs: Boating, Swimming, Winter Sports (#919)

Red Pine Camp For Girls Inc

(est 1937) ▲ 🚐
Minocqua, WI (Oneida Co.); (715) 356-6231
Sarah Wittenkamp Rolley, Director

Camp comments: Individual attention professional staff excellent maintenance, wide geographic representation. Full program 65th Season.
Activities: Canoeing, Drama, Gymnastics, Horseback — English, Sailing, Soccer, Swimming — Instructional, Tennis, Waterskiing, Windsurfing
Session lengths & capacity: 2, 4 & 8 week sessions; 130 campers
Clientele & fees: girls 6-16; Fees: E ▲

Contact: Sarah Wittenkamp Rolley, Director at (715) 356-6231; fax: (715) 356-1077
Web site: www.redpinecamp.com
Operated by: Red Pine Camp for Girls Inc, Box 69, Minocqua, WI 54548 at (715) 356-6231 (#909)

Roundelay (est 1963) ▲ ⌂

Minong, WI (Douglas Co.); (715) 376-4476
Karen Kjolhaug, Director

Camp comments: Beautiful northern Wisconsin site with canoe, kayak, trips, folk, and leadership programs. Non-scout campers and staff welcome. Call for current session info.
Activities: Arts/Crafts, Camping Skills/Outdoor Living, Canoeing, Hiking, Horseback — Western, Leadership Development, Nature/Environment Studies, Swimming — Recreational, Wilderness Trips
Session lengths & capacity: 1/2, 1 & 2 week sessions; 96 campers
Clientele & fees: girls 6-17; Fees: B, C ▲ 🚐
Contact: Karen Kjolhaug, Camp Director at (218) 726-4710; fax: (218) 726-4715
Operated by: Northern Pine GSC, Ordean Bldg Ste G3, Duluth, MN 55802 at (218) 726-4710

Group Rental Information
Facilities: Cabins, Food Service, Hiking Trails, Lake, Lodges, Playing Fields, Tents
Programs: Boating, Challenge/Ropes Course, Environmental Education, Horseback Riding, Swimming, Winter Sports (#8355)

Schroeder Day Camp (est 1987) ☀

Brown Deer, WI; (414) 354-9622
Jennifer Lawton, Director

Camp comments: For kids, every day is an adventure. At YMCA Day Camp, a lifetime of rewarding memories awaits.
Activities: Aquatic Activities, Arts/Crafts, Boating, Climbing/Rappelling, Counselor Training (CIT), Field Trips, International Culture, Nature/Environment Studies, Swimming — Instructional
Session lengths & capacity: June-August; 1 week sessions; 400 campers
Clientele & fees: coed 5-16; Fees: B ☀ 🚐
Operated by: Triangle Y Ranch YMCA, 5535 S Church Road, West Bend, WI 53095 at (262) 255-9622 (#19147)

South Shore YMCA Day Camp

(est 1974) ☀
Cudahy, WI (Milwaukee Co.); (414) 764-6400
Jeff Skoug, Director

Camp comments: At YDay Camp we pack alot into a child's day.Learn new skills,meet new friends and have lots of fun at South Shore YDay Camp.
Activities: Aquatic Activities, Arts/Crafts, Baseball/Softball, Counselor Training (CIT), Drawing/Painting, Field Trips, Leadership Development, Nature/Environment Studies, Sports — Field & Team, Team Building
Session lengths & capacity: June-August; 1 week sessions; 100 campers
Clientele & fees: coed 5-12; Fees: B 🚐 🚐
Contact: Jeff Skoug, Youth & Sports Director at (414) 764-6400; fax: (414) 764-4144
e-mail: ymcassjrs@aol.com
Operated by: Triangle Y Ranch YMCA, 5535 S Church Road, West Bend, WI 53095 at (262) 255-9622 (#46251)

Southwest YMCA Day Camp ☀

Greenfield, WI (Milwaukee Co.); (414) 546-9622
Eric La Pointe, Director

Camp comments: The YMCA builds strong kids, strong families, and strong communities.
Activities: Aquatic Activities, Archery, Arts/Crafts, Field Trips, Nature/Environment Studies, Swimming — Recreational, Team Building

Session lengths & capacity: June-August; 1 week sessions; 200 campers
Clientele & fees: coed 5-18; Fees: B ☀ 🚐
Contact: Eric La Pointe, Program Operations Director at (414) 546-9622; fax: (414) 546-9630
Operated by: Triangle Y Ranch YMCA, 5535 S Church Road, West Bend, WI 53095 at (262) 255-9622 (#46247)

Sugar Creek Bible Camp Retreat (est 1966)

Ferryville, WI; (608) 734-3113

Camp comments: A year round ministry for people of all ages. A christian ministry but open to all. We provide great memories and personal growth experiences.
Activities: Boating, Canoeing, Challenge/Rope Courses, Community Service, Hiking, Horseback — Western, International Culture, Nature/Environment Studies, Wilderness Trips
Session lengths & capacity: 1 & 9 week sessions; 150 campers
Clientele & fees: coed 8-18; Fees: B ▲
Contact: Dick Iverson, Executive Director at (608) 734-3113;
Operated by: Sugar Creek Bible Camp, 13141 Sugar Creek Rd, Ferryville, WI 54628 at (608) 734-3113

Group Rental Information
Facilities: Cabins, Dorm-Style, Food Service, Hiking Trails, Kitchen Facilities, Lodges, Meeting Rooms (#13035)

The Salvation Army Wonderland (est 1903)

Camp Lake, WI (Kenosha Co.); (262) 889-4305
Richard S Horen, Director

Camp comments: Multicultural Christ centered environment. 1.5 hrs N. of Chicago in SE Wisconsin. Wooded property on lake.
Activities: Aquatic Activities, Boating, Camping Skills/Outdoor Living, Canoeing, Counselor Training (CIT), Leadership Development, Music, Nature/Environment Studies, Religious Study, Swimming — Recreational
Session lengths & capacity: June-August; 1/2, 1 & 2 week sessions; 800 campers
Clientele & fees: boys 8-12; girls 8-12; coed 8-12; families; seniors; single adults; Fees: C ▲ 🐷
Contact: Trisha Buster, Outreach Coordinator at (414) 889-4305 ext. 305; fax: (414) 889-4307
e-mail: wonderland@westoshaonline.com
Operated by: The Salvation Army, 9241 Camp Lake Rd, Camp Lake, WI 53109 at (262) 889-4305

ICON LEGEND

☀ Day Camp
▲ Resident Camp
🏠 Facilities Available To Rent
🚐 Transportation Available
🐷 Financial Aid Available

FEE RANGES PER WEEK

A	$0-75
B	$75-200
C	$201-350
D	$351-500
E	$501-650
F	over $650

Group Rental Information
Facilities: A/V Equipment, Cabins, Dorm-Style, Double Occupancy, Food Service, Hiking Trails, Lake, Linens, Lodges, Meeting Rooms, Playing Fields, Pool
Programs: Boating, Challenge/Ropes Course, Environmental Education, Swimming, Winter Sports (#1654)

Timber-lee Christian Center (est 1972)

East Troy, WI (Walworth Co.); (262) 642-7345
John Welch, Director

Camp comments: This ministry is year-round and includes eight weeks of summer youth camps for grade three through junior high school, with 426 campers per week.
Activities: Academics, Archery, Challenge/Rope Courses, Drama, Horseback — Western, Nature/Environment Studies, Religious Study, Soccer, Sports — Field & Team, Wilderness Trips
Session lengths & capacity: 1/2, 1 & 2 week sessions; 420 campers
Clientele & fees: coed 8-18; families; seniors; single adults; Fees: A, B ☀ Fees: C ▲ 🐷
Contact: Carol Andreoni, Director of Registration at (262) 642-7345; fax: (262) 642-7517
e-mail: timber-lee@timber-lee.com
Web site: www.timber-lee.com
Operated by: Timber-lee Christian Center, N8705 Scout Rd, East Troy, WI 53120 at (262) 642-7341

Group Rental Information
Site comments: In obiedience to the Word of God our mission is to present Jesus Christ as Savior and Lord and to reveal His embracing love, ministering to the needs of groups.
Facilities: A/V Equipment, Cabins, Dorm-Style, Food Service, Hiking Trails, Lake, Linens, Lodges, Meeting Rooms, Playing Fields
Programs: Boating, Challenge/Ropes Course, Environmental Education, Horseback Riding, Swimming, Winter Sports (#10366)

Towering Pines Camp (est 1945)

Eagle River, WI (Oneida Co.); (715) 479-4540
John M Jordan & Jeff Jordan, Director

Camp comments: Traditional program with emphasis on individual achievement. Large private site. Sister Camp Woodland.
Activities: Archery, Arts/Crafts, Canoeing, Horseback — Western, Nature/Environment Studies, Riflery, Sailing, Swimming — Instructional, Tennis, Waterskiing
Session lengths & capacity: June-August; 4 & 6 week sessions; 110 campers
Clientele & fees: boys 7-16; Fees: E ▲
Contact: John M Jordan, Director at (847) 446-7311; fax: (847) 446-7710
e-mail: Towpines@aol.com
Web site: www.toweringbingocamp.com
Operated by: Towering Pines Inc, 242 Bristol St, Northfield, IL 60093 at (847) 446-7311 (#1624)

Tri-County YMCA Day Camp ☀

Menomonee Falls, WI; (262) 255-9622

Camp comments: YMCA Daycamp includes organized games, sports, hiking, arts and crafts, values education and special activities built around exciting weekly themes.
Activities: Arts/Crafts, Community Service, Drama, Field Trips, Nature/Environment Studies, Sports — Field & Team, Swimming — Recreational
Session lengths & capacity: 1, 2, 3, 4, 5, 6, 7, 8 & 9 week sessions
Clientele & fees: Fees: B ☀ 🐷
Contact: Mary Kay Murray, Program Operation Director at (262) 255-9622; fax: (262) 255-8549

Operated by: Triangle Y Ranch YMCA, 5535 S Church Road, West Bend, WI 53095 at (262) 255-9622 (#46249)

Triangle Y Ranch YMCA (est 1971) ☀ 🏠 🚐

West Bend, WI; (262) 675-9622
Rob Tegtmeier, Director

Camp comments: Unique day camp on 160 acres. Riding programs, sport camps,(incl. skateboarding), ropes course, ADHD camp are but a few of out offerings. One night sleep over.
Activities: Aquatic Activities, Archery, Arts/Crafts, Canoeing, Challenge/Rope Courses, Drama, Hockey, Horseback — English, Horseback — Western, Skating
Session lengths & capacity: June-August; 1 & 2 week sessions; 220 campers
Clientele & fees: coed 5-14; Fees: B ☀ 🚐
Contact: Rob Tegtmeier, Executive Director at (262) 675-9622; fax: (262) 675-4982
e-mail: rtegtmeier@ymcamke.org
Operated by: Triangle Y Ranch YMCA, 5535 S Church Road, West Bend, WI 53095 at (262) 255-9622

Group Rental Information
Site comments: School, church, organization outings and picnics with unique activities. Including: pony rides, rock climbing, hayrides, swimming, boating, hiking, archery.
Facilities: Hiking Trails, Lake, Meeting Rooms
Programs: Boating, Challenge/Ropes Course, Horseback Riding, Swimming (#7066)

U-Nah-Li-Ya (est 1937) ▲ 🏠 🚐

Suring, WI (Oconto Co.); (715) 276-7116
Ken Losinski, Director

Camp comments: Beautiful coed resident camp located in Nicolet National Forest of Wisconsin. Quality camp with full tripping program.
Activities: Archery, Arts/Crafts, Backpacking, Bicycling/Biking, Boating, Camping Skills/Outdoor Living, Nature/Environment Studies, Riflery, Sports — Field & Team, Wilderness Trips
Session lengths & capacity: 1/2, 1 & 2 week sessions; 175 campers
Clientele & fees: coed 7-17; families; Fees: C ▲ 🐷
Contact: Ken Losinski, Camp Director at (715) 276-7116; fax: (715) 276-1701
e-mail: campuni@greenbayymca.org
Web site: www.greenbayymca.org
Operated by: Green Bay YMCA, 235 N Jefferson, Green Bay, WI 54301 at (920) 436-9613

Group Rental Information
Facilities: Cabins, Dorm-Style, Food Service, Lake, Meeting Rooms
Programs: Boating, Environmental Education (#7700)

Union League Boys & Girls Club (est 1924) ▲ 🚐

Salem, WI (Kenosha Co.); (262) 537-2510
Kenneth Soohov, Director

Camp comments: Residential camp serving the communities of Pilsen, Humboldt Park and West Town in Chicago. Great staff, beautiful site.
Activities: Archery, Arts/Crafts, Baseball/Softball, Camping Skills/Outdoor Living, Challenge/Rope Courses, Leadership Development, Nature/Environment Studies, Swimming — Instructional, Tennis
Session lengths & capacity: June-August; 2 week sessions; 136 campers
Clientele & fees: coed 6-12; Fees: C ▲
Contact: Kenneth Soohov, Camp Director at (773) 235-0870; fax: (773) 235-8244
Operated by: Union League Boys & Girls Club, 65 W Jackson Blvd, Chicago, IL 60604 at (312) 435-4574 (#1565)

Wander Wisconsin △

Madison, WI (Dane Co.); (608) 276-9782
David Curtiss, Director

Camp comments: Fostering personal growth through adventure travel & camping experiences for youth. Based in Madison WI & traveling the USA! Trips for various ages and skills.
Activities: Backpacking, Bicycling/Biking, Camping Skills/Outdoor Living, Canoeing, Fishing, Hiking, Kayaking, Photography, Travel/Tour, Wilderness Trips
Session lengths & capacity: 1/2, 1 & 2 week sessions
Clientele & fees: Fees: C, D △
Contact: David Curtiss, Director at (608) 276-9782; fax: (608) 276-4050
e-mail: wander@wanderwisconsin.org
Web site: www.afterschoolwi.org
Operated by: Wisconsin Youth Company, 1201 Mckenna Blvd., Madison, WI 53719 at (800) 238-1174 (#44332)

We-Ha-Kee (est 1923) △ 🚐

Winter, WI (Sawyer Co.); (715) 266-3263
Arturo Cranston, CCD, Director

Camp comments: A multi-national, long-standing camp for girls ages 7-17. Operated since 1923 by Catholic Sisters. Cabins, 40 activity area. Carefully selected counselors, 3:1
Activities: Backpacking, Camping Skills/Outdoor Living, Gymnastics, Horseback — Western, Sailing, Soccer, Swimming — Instructional, Tennis, Waterskiing
Session lengths & capacity: June-August; 2, 4 & 6 week sessions; 100 campers
Clientele & fees: girls 7-17; Fees: F △
Contact: Arturo Cranston, O.P., Director at (800) 582-2267; fax: (715) 266-2267
e-mail: wehakee@pctcnet.net
Web site: www.campwehakee.com
Operated by: Sinsinawa Dominicans, N8104 Barker Lake Rd, Winter, WI 54896-7804 at (715) 266-3263 (#892)

Wesley Woods Conference Center (est 1955) △ 🏠

Williams Bay, WI (Walworth Co.); (262) 245-6631
Jeffrey E. Fry, Director

Camp comments: Wesley Woods provides a beautiful setting in which resident campers and retreat groups can pursue group goals with the support of our hospitality staff.
Activities: Aquatic Activities, Archery, Boating, Canoeing, Counselor Training (CIT), Fishing, Horseback — Western, Sailing, Swimming — Recreational, Wilderness Trips
Session lengths & capacity: June-August; 1/2 & 1 week sessions; 100 campers
Clientele & fees: coed 6-18; Fees: C △
Contact: (800) 642-2267; fax: (262) 245-1446
e-mail: niccamp@aol.com
Operated by: Outdoor and Retreat Ministries, 200 Stam Street, Williams Bay, WI 53191 at (262) 245-6706

Group Rental Information
Site comments: The goal of our support staff is to provide a safe, clean and friendly setting for groups to pursue their goals.
Seasons & Capacity: Spring 250, Summer 225, Fall 180, Winter 150
Facilities: Cabins, Dorm-Style, Food Service, Hiking Trails, Kitchen Facilities, Lake, Linens, Lodges, Meeting Rooms, Playing Fields
Programs: Boating, Challenge/Ropes Course, Horseback Riding, Swimming, Winter Sports (#10473)

Wisconsin Badger Camp

(est 1966) △ 🏠

Prairie Du Chien, WI (Grant Co.); (608) 988-4558
Steven Tatlow, Director

Camp comments: Serve children and adults with developmental disabilities. Programs adapted to all abilities. Outdoor and travel programs.
Activities: Arts/Crafts, Camping Skills/Outdoor Living, Canoeing, Hiking, Horseback — Western, Music, Nature/Environment Studies, Performing Arts, Swimming — Recreational, Travel/Tour
Session lengths & capacity: June-August; 1 & 2 week sessions; 90 campers
Clientele & fees: coed 4-99; Fees: C △ 🐖
Contact: Steven Tatlow, Executive Director at (608) 348-9689; fax: (608) 348-9737
e-mail: wbc@pcii.net
Operated by: Wisconsin Badger Camp, Box 723, Platteville, WI 53818 at (608) 348-9689

Group Rental Information
Seasons & Capacity: Spring 120, Fall 120, Winter 40
Facilities: Cabins, Dorm-Style, Hiking Trails, Kitchen Facilities, Meeting Rooms, Playing Fields (#3847)

Wisconsin Lions Camp

(est 1956) △ 🏠

Rosholt, WI (Portage Co.); (715) 677-4761
Russell Link, Director

Camp comments: Serves visually & hearing impaired & mild cognitive disabled children only.Family camp wkends & facility rental Sept-May
Activities: Aquatic Activities, Archery, Arts/Crafts, Boating, Camping Skills/Outdoor Living, Canoeing, Challenge/Rope Courses, Nature/Environment Studies, Sailing, Swimming — Recreational
Session lengths & capacity: 1 & 2 week sessions; 150 campers
Clientele & fees: coed 6-17; families; seniors; Fees: A △ 🐖
Contact: Russell Link, Camp Director at (715) 677-4761; fax: (715) 677-4527
e-mail: lioncamp@wi-net.com
Operated by: Wisconsin Lions Foundation, 3834 County Rd A, Rosholt, WI 54473 at (715) 677-4761

Group Rental Information
Site comments: Year-round camp/conference center designed for special population groups. Private lake,wheelchair accessible,challenge course,nature center.
Seasons & Capacity: Spring 200, Fall 200, Winter 200
Facilities: Dorm-Style, Food Service, Hiking Trails, Lake, Linens, Lodges, Meeting Rooms
Programs: Boating, Challenge/Ropes Course, Environmental Education (#927)

YMCA Camp Anokijig

(est 1926) △ 🏠 🚐

Plymouth, WI
Jim Scherer, Director

Camp comments: 'Anokijig' means 'we serve', but it is also synonymous with positive values, personal growth, and outrageous fun.
Activities: Archery, Arts/Crafts, Canoeing, Challenge/Rope Courses, Fishing, Horseback — Western, Leadership Development, Sailing, Swimming — Instructional, Wilderness Trips
Session lengths & capacity: 1/2, 1 & 2 week sessions; 250 campers
Clientele & fees: coed 7-16; families; seniors; single adults; Fees: C △
Contact: Jim Scherer, Director at (920) 893-0782; fax: (920) 893-0873
e-mail: anokijig@excel.net
Operated by: YMCA Camp Anokijig, W 5639 Anokijig Lane, Plymouth, WI 53073-2868 at (920) 893-0782

Group Rental Information
Site comments: Anokijig is the perfect place for a group outing.Available for retreats,conferences,recreation,& outdoor education. Come join us, you will be glad you did!
Seasons & Capacity: Spring 300, Summer 250, Fall 300, Winter 100
Facilities: Cabins, Food Service, Hiking Trails, Lake, Lodges, Meeting Rooms, Playing Fields, Tents
Programs: Boating, Challenge/Ropes Course, Environmental Education, Horseback Riding, Swimming, Winter Sports (#18753)

YMCA Camp Mac Lean

(est 1941) ☀ △ 🏠 🚐

Burlington, WI (Racine Co.); (262) 763-7742
Jeff Tremmel & Julie-Ann Niziolek, Director

Camp comments: Increase self-esteem, learn new skills, have fun, cabin group emphasis. High return rate of campers & staff.
Activities: Archery, Arts/Crafts, Canoeing, Challenge/Rope Courses, Kayaking, Leadership Development, Sailing, Soccer, Swimming — Recreational, Windsurfing
Session lengths & capacity: 1 & 2 week sessions; 200 campers
Clientele & fees: coed 7-17; families; Fees: C, D △
Contact: Brian Ensberg, Executive Director at (262) 763-7742; fax: (262) 763-9944
Operated by: YMCA Of Metropolitan Chicago, 801 N Dearborn St, Chicago, IL 60610 at (312) 932-1200

Group Rental Information
Facilities: Cabins, Food Service, Hiking Trails, Lake, Lodges, Meeting Rooms
Programs: Boating (#1569)

YMCA Camp Matawa (est 1996) △ 🏠

Campbellsport, WI (Fond du Lac Co.); (262) 626-2149
Bruce Greer, Director

Camp comments: Located in Kettle Morain State Forest Equestrian Mountain. Bike adventure rope & climbing.
Activities: Archery, Arts/Crafts, Bicycling/Biking, Canoeing, Challenge/Rope Courses, Climbing/Rappelling, Horseback — English, Horseback — Western, Leadership Development, Nature/Environment Studies
Session lengths & capacity: 1 & 2 week sessions
Clientele & fees: Fees: C, D △
Contact: Craig Dawson, Program Director at (262) 626-2149; fax: (262) 626-8189
e-mail: CDawson.ma@ymcamke.org
Operated by: Triangle Y Ranch YMCA, 5535 S Church Road, West Bend, WI 53095 at (262) 255-9622 (#25739)

YMCA Camp Minikani

(est 1919) ☀ △ 🏠

Hubertus, WI (Washington Co.); (414) 251-9080
Cliff Clauer, Director

Camp comments: Traditional camp program allowing campers to grow as individuals and as a community while working as a team.
Activities: Aquatic Activities, Camping Skills/Outdoor Living, Challenge/Rope Courses, Horseback — Western, Leadership Development, Nature/Environment Studies, Riflery, Sailing, Team Building, Wilderness Trips
Session lengths & capacity: June-August; 1/2, 1 & 2 week sessions; 236 campers
Clientele & fees: coed 8-18; families; seniors; single adults; Fees: A ☀ Fees: D △ 🐖
Contact: John Emling, Senior Program Director at (262) 251-9080; fax: (262) 628-4051
e-mail: ymcaminije@aol.com

Operated by: Triangle Y Ranch YMCA, 5535 S Church Road, West Bend, WI 53095 at (262) 255-9622

Group Rental Information
Site comments: Educational retreat facilities for all ages. Conveniently located 30 miles from Milwaukee. Come and relax and reflect in nature.
Seasons & Capacity: Spring 250, Fall 250, Winter 250
Facilities: A/V Equipment, Cabins, Double Occupancy, Food Service, Hiking Trails, Lake, Lodges, Meeting Rooms, Playing Fields, Pool
Programs: Boating, Challenge/Ropes Course, Environmental Education, Horseback Riding, Swimming, Winter Sports (#880)

YMCA Camp Nan A Bo Sho

(est 1964)

Lakewood, WI (Oconto Co.); (715) 276-6084
Rob Rathsack, Director

Camp comments: Explore Camp Nan A Bo Sho in the majestic Nicolet National Forest. Christian emphasis, values based traditional program.
Activities: Aquatic Activities, Archery, Challenge/Rope Courses, Climbing/Rappelling, Leadership Development, Nature/Environment Studies, Riflery, Sailing, Wilderness Trips, Windsurfing
Session lengths & capacity: June-August; 1/2, 1 & 2 week sessions; 120 campers
Clientele & fees: coed 6-16; families; seniors; single adults; Fees: C A
Contact: Rob Rathsack, Camp Director at (920) 954-7630; fax: (920) 734-2000
e-mail: rrathsac@ymcafoxcities.org
Web site: www.ymcafoxcities.org/campnabs
Operated by: YMCA of the Fox Cities, 218 E Lawrence St, Appleton, WI 54911 at (920) 954-7630

Group Rental Information
Facilities: Cabins, Dorm-Style, Food Service, Hiking Trails, Lake, Playing Fields, Tents
Programs: Boating, Challenge/Ropes Course, Environmental Education, Swimming (#910)

YMCA Day Camp Wabansi

(est 1952)

Brussels, WI; (920) 680-5938
Cassandra Poquette, Director

Camp comments: YMCA Day Camp Wabansi is located in beautiful Door on the waters of Green Bay. Full service day camp-coed-ages 7-10.
Activities: Archery, Arts/Crafts, Boating, Camping Skills/Outdoor Living, Field Trips, Fishing, Horseback — Western, Nature/Environment Studies, Soccer, Swimming — Recreational
Session lengths & capacity: May-September; 1 week sessions; 100 campers
Clientele & fees: coed 7-10; Fees: B
Contact: Cassandra Poquette at (920) 436-9693; fax: (920) 436-9699
e-mail: poquetca@greenbayymca.org
Web site: www.greenbayymca.org
Operated by: Green Bay YMCA, 235 N Jefferson, Green Bay, WI 54301 at (920) 436-9613 (#12983)

YMCA Icaghowan (est 1909)

Amery, WI (Polk Co.); (715) 268-8377
Peter Wieczorek, Director

Camp comments: Values-based traditional camping program. Beautiful island peninsula. Excellent staff. Challenging, positive program.
Activities: Archery, Arts/Crafts, Backpacking, Camping Skills/Outdoor Living, Challenge/Rope Courses, Climbing/Rappelling, Horseback — Western, Leadership Development, Nature/Environment Studies, Sailing
Session lengths & capacity: June-August; 1/2, 1 & 2 week sessions; 125 campers
Clientele & fees: coed 7-16; families; Fees: B
Fees: D A
Contact: (612) 822-2267;
e-mail: info@campicaghowan.org
Web site: www.ymcacamping.org
Operated by: Minneapolis YMCA Camping Serv, 4 W Rustic Lodge, Minneapolis, MN 55409 at (612) 822-2267

Group Rental Information
Site comments: Peaceful island setting in beautiful Amery, WI. Progs avail.
Seasons & Capacity: Spring 102, Fall 102, Winter 102
Facilities: Cabins, Food Service, Hiking Trails, Lake, Meeting Rooms
Programs: Boating, Challenge/Ropes Course, Environmental Education, Winter Sports (#1130)

Wyoming

Trails Wilderness School

(est 1994)

Jackson Hole-Kelly, WY (Teton Co.); (307) 733-0124
Whigger and Mary Jo Mullins, Director

Camp comments: Wilderness adventure programs in WY, AK, MO, Mexico, Canada and Europe. Join us to rock climb, surf, backpack, canoe, raft, kayak, ski, snowboard & lots of fun!
Activities: Backpacking, Camping Skills/Outdoor Living, Canoeing, Challenge/Rope Courses, Climbing/Rappelling, Hiking, Kayaking, Leadership Development, Travel/Tour, Wilderness Trips
Session lengths & capacity: June-September; 1, 2, 3, 4 & 6 week sessions; 250 campers
Clientele & fees: coed 12-18; families; Fees: D, E, F
Contact: Whigger Mullins, Director at (800) 869-8228; fax: (314) 994-9307
e-mail: info@trailsws.com
Web site: www.trailsws.com
Operated by: Trails Wilderness School, 5 Whitegate Ln, St Louis, MO 63124 at (800) 869-8228 (#3009)

ICON LEGEND
☀ Day Camp
⛰ Resident Camp
🏠 Facilities Available To Rent
🚐 Transportation Available
🐷 Financial Aid Available

FEE RANGES PER WEEK
A $0-75
B $75-200
C $201-350
D $351-500
E $501-650
F over $650

Alphabetical Index of All Camps

ACCREDITED CAMP ACA® American Camping Association

To find the camp you are looking for, you may need to check in more than one place in the index. The camp might be alphabetized by the first word "camp" as in Camp Cherrio and be located in the Cs. It might be alphabetized by the first word after "camp" as in Hantesa and be located in the Hs. Or, it might be alphabetized by the name of the organization as in YMCA Camp Crosley and be located in the Ys.